"I have always told students that one cannot understand modern theology, including Barthian theology, without a firm grasp of Kant. Dorrien's work substantiates this claim with an attention to detail that is nothing short of breathtaking. This book is a brilliant and much needed account of the influence of Immanuel Kant and the tradition of post-Kantian idealism on modern theology."

William Stacy Johnson, Princeton Theological Seminary

"This is a brilliant and much needed book. Dorrien's magisterial achievements to date lend his voice a special authority, but in this book, the reader is simply compelled by the deft interplay of nuance and overview to trust his mentorship. Dorrien has masterfully approached this most intimidating and yet indispensable corpus of texts with depth and breadth of analysis, and with an extraordinarily fresh perspective."

Catherine Keller, Drew University

"Gary Dorrien is a superstar as an interpreter of modern religious thought. This unique, fascinating, aggressively revisionary book will have no competition until books appear to argue against it."

Frederick Ferré, University of Georgia

"This is an extraordinarily fine book, a delight to read, a real page-turner, and a brilliant interpretation, all of which one expects of such an accomplished scholar and author as Dorrien. As a theologian and historian, Dorrien is in top form. As a theologian and philosopher, he writes with precise, analytical control over the ideas involved, offering, among other things, the best treatment I know of the evolving relations among Fichte, Schelling, and Hegel. No one else I know could have written this book, which will be the dominant treatment of its subject. *Kantian Reason and Hegelian Spirit* is a magisterial interpretive history of one of the most important theological deltas of our time."

Robert C. Neville, Boston University

Books by Gary Dorrien

Logic and Consciousness
The Democratic Socialist Vision,
Reconstructing the Common Good
The Neoconservative Mind: Politics, Culture, and the War of Ideology
Soul in Society: The Making and Renewal of Social Christianity
The Word as True Myth: Interpreting Modern Theology
The Remaking of Evangelical Theology
The Barthian Revolt in Modern Theology
The Making of American Liberal Theology: Imagining Progressive Religion, 1805–1900
The Making of American Liberal Theology: Idealism, Realism and Modernity, 1900–1950
Imperial Designs: Neoconservatism and the New Pax Americana
The Making of American Liberal Theology: Crisis, Irony and Postmodernity, 1950–2005
Social Ethics in the Making: Interpreting an American Tradition
Economy, Difference, Empire: Social Ethics for Social Justice
Obama in Question: A Progressive Critique and Defense
Kantian Reason and Hegelian Spirit: The Idealistic Logic of Modern Theology

Kantian Reason and Hegelian Spirit

The Idealistic Logic of Modern Theology

Gary Dorrien

Reinhold Niebuhr Professor of Social Ethics,
Union Theological Seminary Professor of Religion,
Columbia University

WILEY Blackwell

This paperback edition first published 2015
© 2012 John Wiley & Sons, Ltd.

Edition history: John Wiley & Sons, Ltd (hardback, 2012)

Registered Office
John Wiley & Sons Ltd, The Atrium, Southern Gate,
Chichester, West Sussex, PO19 8SQ, UK

Editorial Offices
350 Main Street, Malden, MA 02148-5020, USA
9600 Garsington Road, Oxford, OX4 2DQ, UK
The Atrium, Southern Gate, Chichester, West Sussex, PO19 8SQ, UK

For details of our global editorial offices, for customer services, and for information
about how to apply for permission to reuse the copyright material in this book
please see our website at www.wiley.com/wiley-blackwell.

The right of Gary Dorrien to be identified as the author of this work has been
asserted in accordance with the UK Copyright, Designs and Patents Act 1988.

Library of Congress Cataloging-in-Publication Data

Dorrien, Gary J.Kantian reason and Hegelian spirit : the idealistic logic of modern theology /
    Gary Dorrien.
        p. cm.
    Includes bibliographical references and index.
    ISBN 978-0-470-67331-7 (hardcover : alk. paper)
    ISBN 978-1-119-01654-0 (paperback)
  1. Philosophical theology.   2. Kant, Immanuel, 1724-1804–Influence.   3. Hegel, Georg
    Wilhelm Friedrich, 1770-1831–Influence. I. Title. BT40.D67 2012
    230.09′034–dc23

                                        2011045996

A catalogue record for this book is available from the British Library.

Cover images: Interior of Köln Cathedral, Germany
© Florian Monheim / Arcaid / Corbis Portrait of George Hegel © World History Archive / Alamy
Portrait of Friedrich Schleiermacher and Portrait of Immanuel Kant, both © Interfoto / Alamy.

Set in 10/12.5pt Galliard by Thomson Digital, Noida, India

Printed in Singapore by C.O.S. Printers Pte Ltd

1   2015

For Cindy, Nelleke, Mike, Xan, Kevin, and Hannah, with affection and treasured memories.

Contents

Preface and Acknowledgments

Until now, I lacked an answer for one of the nicest questions: "Which book of yours means the most to you?" Usually I stammered the truth – "I have no idea." Otherwise I settled for an evasion – "The next one." At last I have a real answer, because this book makes an argument about the thinkers and ideas that underlie modern religious thought as a whole.

My work ranges across social ethics and politics, on the one hand, and modern religious philosophy and theology, on the other. I am equally committed to these subject areas, having never tried to settle on one of them or even ranked one higher than the other. There is a disciplinary link between the fields of ethics and theology – theological ethics – but that is not where most of my work takes place. On the ethical side, I work mostly at the intersections of social ethics, social theory, and politics, and on the theological side, I work mostly in the branch of historical theology that deals with modern religious and philosophical thought.

I started this book with the idea of something analogous to my three volumes on *The Making of American Liberal Theology,* but soon I realized that I had too much at stake in this project to give it the encyclopedic treatment. Instead of tracking, in a multi-volume format, the history and variations of modern German and British theology, I went straight for an argument about the importance of Kantian and post-Kantian idealism in the founding of modern theology.

This decision reflects something about how I learned modern religious and philosophical thought, something about how I teach it, and something about my constructive perspective. In college, I cut my teeth intellectually on G. W. F. Hegel and Paul Tillich. Long before I had an inkling of a future in the academy or anything pertaining to religion, I was drawn to Hegel's theory of self-knowing Spirit arising through the realization of consciousness, an idea that, importantly to me, held a similar lure for Martin Luther King, Jr. But one day I realized that it was pointless to grapple any further with modern philosophers and theologians until I took on Immanuel Kant's critiques of reason. Kant is the single unavoidable thinker in modern philosophy, and one of the founders of modern religious thought along with Hegel and Friedrich Schleiermacher. Today, in the classroom, I find it impossible to teach almost any subject in religious thought or social ethics without spending at least two weeks on what the subject in question owes to Kant and Hegel. This interpretive and pedagogical standpoint underlies the normative argument that I make in this book – that progressive theology at its best is always buoyed with idealistic conviction and armed with a realistic brake on it.

Karl Barth enjoyed regaling his students with the story of how Hegel and Schleiermacher came up at the same time, Hegel eclipsed Schleiermacher when they lived, and Schleiermacher overtook Hegel, at least in theology, after they were gone. Usually Barth cautioned his students about their acquired liberalism, telling them that they lived in Schleiermacher's age and under his influence, whether or not they realized it. Sometimes he urged them to imagine what theology might have been like had Schleiermacher never existed. But I will argue that even Barthian theology is unimaginable without Kant, Hegel, and Schleiermacher.

This book is like my previous one for Wiley-Blackwell, *Social Ethics in the Making*, in that I held my students at Union Theological Seminary and Columbia University chiefly in mind as I wrote it, especially my doctoral students. For me, it is always a high priority to help students grasp the story of the field they are entering. My understanding of it has been greatly enriched by working with three recently graduated doctoral students (Ian Doescher, Eboni Marshall Turman, and Christine Pae), and a special group of graduate students with whom I have worked closely (Nixon Cleophat, Preston Davis, Peter Herman, Dwayne Meadows, and Elijah Prewitt-Davis), and my current group of doctoral students: Lisa Anderson, Nkosi Anderson, Malinda Berry, Chloe Breyer, Babydoll Kennedy, Jeremy Kirk, David Orr, Tracy Riggle, Dan Rohrer, Gabriel Salguero, Charlene Sinclair, Joe Strife, Rima Vesely-Flad, Colleen Wessel-McCoy, Demian Wheeler, and Todd Willison. Blessings and thanks to all.

All my colleagues at Union and Columbia are superb colleagues and some are special friends; in the latter category I am especially grateful to James Cone, Roger Haight, Esther Hamori, Kelby Harrison, Obery M. Hendricks, Jr., Brigitte Kahl, Paul Knitter, Serene Jones, Barbara Lundblad, Daisy Machado, John McGuckin, Christopher Morse, Aliou Niang, Su Yon Pak, Jan Rehmann, Mark C. Taylor, John Thatamanil, and Janet Walton. Many thanks to my editors at Blackwell for their skillful work, especially project manager and copy-editor Graeme Leonard and publisher Rebecca Harkin. And thanks to Diana Witt for another superb index.

1

Introduction

Kantian Concepts, Liberal Theology, and Post-Kantian Idealism

This is a book about the role of Kantian and post-Kantian idealism in founding modern theology. More specifically, it is a book about the impact of Kantian and post-Kantian idealism in creating what came to be called "liberal" theology in Germany and "modernist" theology in Great Britain. My descriptive argument is implied in this description, which folds together with my normative argument: Modern religious thought originated with idealistic convictions about the spiritual ground and unifying reality of freedom, and there is no vital progressive theology that does not speak with idealistic conviction, notwithstanding the ironies and problems of doing so.

Liberal theology was born in largely illiberal contexts in eighteenth-century Germany and England, a fact that helps to explain why much of it was far from liberal. Most of the great thinkers in this story were Germans, the key founding thinkers were Germans, and there was a vital intellectual movement of liberal theology in Germany for a century before a similar movement existed in Britain. Thus, the German story dominates this book. British theology comes into the picture mostly as it engages German idealism, as do the book's principal other non-German thinkers, Søren Kierkegaard and Karl Barth, although the British story begins with a figure that preceded Kant by a century, John Locke. For better and for worse, German thinkers dominated modern theology right up to the point that liberal theology in Germany crashed and burned, after which the field was still dominated by the intellectual legacies of Immanuel Kant, G. W. F. Hegel, Friedrich Schleiermacher, and the Ritschlian School.

The idea of a distinctly modern approach to Christian theology built upon early Enlightenment attempts in Britain and Germany to blend Enlightenment reason with a Christian worldview. I will argue, however, that early Enlightenment rationalism and empiricism did not privilege the questions of subjectivity, historical relativity, and freedom, and thus did not develop a liberal approach to theology. It took Kant's three critiques of reason and his writings on religion and ethics to launch a fully modern

Kantian Reason and Hegelian Spirit: The Idealistic Logic of Modern Theology, First Edition. Gary Dorrien.
© 2012 John Wiley & Sons, Ltd. Published 2015 by John Wiley & Sons, Ltd.

departure in religious thought, through which Kant became the quintessential modern philosopher and inspired rival streams of theology and idealism.

I will argue that Kant's influence in modern religious thought is unsurpassed by any thinker, that his use of metaphysical reason is usually misconstrued, that he was a subjective idealist who mediated between extreme subjective idealism and objective idealism, that his recognition of universal forms of experience paved the way to post-Kantian objective idealism, that his moral faith mattered more to him than anything except his idea of freedom to which it was linked, and that the key to his system – terrible ironies notwithstanding – was the emancipating and unifying reality of freedom. I will argue that Kant's transcendental idealism laid the groundwork for all post-Kantian versions and that the post-Kantian idealisms of Hegel, Schleiermacher, Friedrich W. J. Schelling, and, very differently, Kierkegaard, surpassed Kant in creatively construing religious experience and the divine. I will argue that the dominant forms of liberal theology flowed out of German idealism and tried to calibrate the right kind of idealism to distinct positions about the way that any religion is true. And I will argue that even the important critiques of religious idealism proffered by Kierkegaard, William James, G. E. Moore, Paul Tillich, and Karl Barth demonstrated its adaptability and continued importance.

Philosophers loom large in this story. Kant defined himself against René Descartes, the founder of modern philosophy, G. W. Leibniz and Christian Wolff, the leaders of the German Enlightenment, and John Locke, George Berkeley, and David Hume, the luminaries of British empiricism. By the late 1780s, everyone had to deal with Kant and the beginnings of post-Kantian idealism. Samuel Taylor Coleridge plays a major role in this book for doing so, as Coleridge brought post-Kantian idealism to England. Kierkegaard plays a similar role in the book's scheme by prefiguring the twentieth-century reaction against religious idealism from a standpoint that assumed it. Alfred North Whitehead plays a key role in this book's account of the beginning of process theology in England. None of these thinkers was a theologian.

One should not make too much of the lack of theologians. Schleiermacher and Barth, the major Protestant theologians of the modern era, are central figures in this book's narrative. The book also features theologians Albrecht Ritschl, Adolf von Harnack, Wilhelm Herrmann, Ernst Troeltsch, Hastings Rashdall, William Temple, and Paul Tillich. But it matters that non-theologians played such important roles in founding and shaping modern theology.

Until the eighteenth century, Christian theology operated exclusively within houses of biblical and ecclesiastical authority. External authorities established and compelled what had to be believed on specific points of doctrine if one was to claim the Christian name. In theory, the Anglican tradition cracked open the rule of external authority by making reason an authority second to scripture and (in Richard Hooker's formulation) ahead of church tradition. But Anglican theology up to and through the Enlightenment was cautious about what it meant to recognize the authority of reason. The English tradition, though producing a major forerunner of modern theology, John Locke, did not produce any important founders. An ethos of provincialism and the oppressive weight of the state church slowed the development of liberalizing trends in British theology. Plus, the greatest British philosopher, David Hume, was someone that religious thinkers had to get around, not someone who helped them get somewhere. The modern departure in religious thought had to wait for the later Enlightenment, biblical criticism, the liberalizing of German universities, Kant, an upsurge of Romantic and Absolute idealism, and Schleiermacher's determination to liberalize Christian theology within the context of the Christian church and tradition.

The founding and early development of liberal theology was sufficiently rich in Germany and Britain that this book restricts itself to accounting for it, always in a manner that focuses on the importance of German idealism. I do not pursue the founding of liberal religious thought in other national contexts, aside from occasional references that illuminate what happened in Germany and Britain. I do not take the story of liberal theology beyond the responses of Barth and Tillich to it; otherwise I would have another multi-volume project on my hands. For the same reason, plus two more, I do not describe the attempts to develop a Roman Catholic version of liberal theology that occurred during the historical frame of this account. Roman Catholic Modernism was mostly a French phenomenon, and the Vatican crushed it in the early twentieth century. The development of a Catholic tradition of liberal theology had to wait until Vatican Council II.

For over a century the only distinctly modern approach to theology was the liberal one; thus, when analyzing trends in eighteenth- and nineteenth-century theology, I shall use these terms interchangeably, always with the caveat that neither term had a stable meaning until the twentieth century. "Liberal theology" is more complex and slippery than most of the literature about it, and the same thing is true of German idealism. In the former case, an over-identification of liberal theology with late nineteenth-century Progressivist idealism, or a too-simple rendering of a Kant-to-Harnack tradition, made liberal theology too easily debunked by its neo-orthodox detractors, who convinced the rest of the field to define liberalism as they did. In the case of German idealism, complexity was undeniable, but much of the literature gets around it by treating idealism as only one thing or by simplistically rendering Kant as a subjective idealist.

For historical understanding and constructive purposes, it is better not to evade the historical and theoretical complexities. Liberal theology cannot be understood without coming to grips with post-Kantian idealism and its influence in the Kierkegaardian and Barthian reactions to it. More importantly, it cannot be revitalized lacking a robust sense of the divine presence in movements that lift up the poor and oppressed and that contribute to the flourishing of all people and creation.

Imagining Modern Theology

Modern theology began when theologians looked beyond the Bible and Christian tradition for answers to their questions and acknowledged that the mythical aspects of Christian scripture and tradition are mythical. How should theology deal with modern challenges to belief that overthrow the external authority of Christian scripture and tradition? What kind of Christian belief is possible after modern science and Enlightenment criticism desacralized the world? How should Christian theology deal with the mythical aspects of Christianity and the results of biblical criticism? These questions were peculiar to religious thinkers of the modern era; Thomas

Aquinas and John Calvin did not ask themselves how to do theology without an infallible external authority or whether Christian myth should be demythologized.[1]

Eventually there were distinctly modern theologies that were not liberal; Kierke-gaard was the key precursor of that possibility. The founding of modern theology, however, was a decidedly liberal enterprise. The roots of liberalism lie deep in the history of Western thought, especially in the Pauline theme of spiritual freedom, the fifth-century Pelagian emphasis on free will, the limitations on sovereign authority in the Magna Carta Libertatum of 1215, and the Renaissance humanist stress on free expression, all of which resonate in the modern Western appeal to the rights of freedom. As a political philosophy, liberalism originated in the seventeenth century, asserting that individuals have natural rights to freedom that are universal. As an economic theory it originated in the eighteenth century, asserting the priority of free trade and self-regulating markets. As a cultural/philosophical movement it arose in the eighteenth century as a rationalist critique of tradition and authority-based belief. As a theological tradition it originated in the eighteenth century in tandem with modern humanism, biblical criticism, and Enlightenment philosophy.

Historically and theoretically, the cornerstone of liberalism is the assertion of the supreme value and universal rights of the individual. The liberal tradition of Benedict de Spinoza, John Locke, Charles Louis de Secondat Montesquieu, Immanuel Kant and Thomas Jefferson taught that the universal goal of human beings is to realize their freedom and that state power is justified only to the extent that it enables and protects individual liberty. From the beginning this tradition had an ambiguous, often tortured relationship to its own rhetoric of freedom, for liberalism arose as an ideological justification of capitalism *and* as the recognition that tolerance was the only humane alternative to the religious wars of the seventeenth century. In both cases liberal ideology deemed that vast categories of human beings were disqualified from basic human rights. Liberalism valorized the rights-bearing individual to underwrite the transition to a political economy based on self-interested market exchanges, which benefited the capitalist bourgeoisie. The liberal state tolerated plural religious tradi-tions, which led to the separation of church and state, which led, eventually, to the principle of tolerance for other kinds of beliefs and practices. The state, under liberalism, became an ostensibly neutral guarantor of the rights of individuals and communities to pursue diverse conceptions of the good life, which did not stop liberals from denying the rights of human beings who were not white, male, and owners of property like themselves.

The founding of modern theology is an aspect of this story. Liberal theology, in my definition, was and is a three-layered phenomenon. Firstly it is the idea that all claims to truth, in theology and other disciplines, must be made on the basis of reason and experience, not by appeal to external authority. From a liberal standpoint, Christian scripture or ecclesiastical doctrine may still be authoritative for theology and faith, but its authority operates within Christian experience, not as an outside word that establishes or compels truth claims about particular matters of fact.[2]

Secondly, liberal theology argues for the viability and necessity of an alternative to orthodox over-belief and secular disbelief. In Germany, the liberal movement called itself "mediating theology" because it took so seriously the challenge of a rising culture of aggressive deism and atheism. Liberal religious thinkers, unavoidably, had to battle with conservatives for the right to liberalize Christian doctrine. But usually they worried more about the critical challenges to belief from outsiders. The agenda of modern theology was to develop a credible form of Christianity before the "cultured despisers of religion" routed Christian faith from intellectual and cultural respectability. This agenda was expressed in the title of the founding work of modern theology, Schleiermacher's *Über die Religion: Reden an die Gebildeten unter ihren Verächtern (On Religion: Speeches to its Cultured Despisers)*. Here, Britain was ahead of the curve, as there was an ample tradition of aggressive British deism and skepticism by the time that Schleiermacher wrote. British critics ransacked the Bible for unbelievable things; in Germany, a deceased anonymous deist (Hermann Samuel Reimarus) caused a stir in the mid-1770s by portraying Jesus as a misguided political messiah lacking any idea of being divine; Schleiermacher, surrounded by cultured scoffers in Berlin, contended that true religion and the divinity of Jesus were fully credible on modern terms.[3]

The third layer consists of specific things that go with overthrowing the principle of external authority and adopting a mediating perspective between authority religion and disbelief. The liberal tradition reconceptualizes the meaning of Christianity in the light of modern knowledge and values. It is reformist in spirit and substance, not revolutionary. It is open to the verdicts of modern intellectual inquiry, especially historical criticism and the natural sciences. It conceives Christianity as an ethical way of life, it advocates moral concepts of atonement or reconciliation, and it is committed to making progressive religion credible and socially relevant.

This definition is calibrated to describe the entire tradition of liberal theology from Kant and Schleiermacher to the present day. A great deal of the literature in this field defines liberal theology by features that were distinctive to its heyday in the late nineteenth and early twentieth centuries, when Ritschlian School theology ruled the field and powerful movements for social Christianity existed in England, Germany, Switzerland, and the United States. For most of the twentieth century, the standard definition of liberal theology equated it with Albrecht Ritschl, Adolf von Harnack, and Social Gospel progressivism. Some critics, following Karl Barth, treated Schleiermacher and Hegel as founders of a bad tradition of theology that led straight to Ritschl and Harnack. Other critics, following Paul Tillich and an older usage, identified liberal theology wholly with the bourgeois culture-religion of the Ritschlian School. In both cases, liberal theology was defined, polemically, as Christ-of-culture optimism and modernism – a usage that was adopted by all manner of dialectical, neo-orthodox, Niebuhrian, Anglo-Catholic, Roman Catholic, and conservative evangelical critics. It became so pervasive that even liberal theologians who rejected Progressive era liberalism swallowed the regnant definition. For example, Daniel Day Williams, an American process theologian, offered this definition of liberal theology in 1949: "By 'liberal theology' I mean the movement in modern Protestantism which during the nineteenth century tried to bring Christian thought into organic unity with the evolutionary world view, the movements for social reconstruction, and the expectations of 'a better world' which dominated the general mind. It is that form of Christian faith in which a prophetic-progressive philosophy of history culminates in the expectation of the coming of the Kingdom of God on earth."[4]

Here, as was typical by 1949, liberal theology was equated with the evolutionary ideology, cultural optimism, and social idealism of its Social Gospel heyday. It was identified with factors that were peculiar to its dominant moment, 1890 to 1914. A century of pre-Ritschlian liberal theology centered on Kant, Schleiermacher, and Hegel fell out of this definition; more importantly for twentieth-century critics of liberalism, liberal theology only existed after World War I among tiny bands of ideal- istic progressives and Christ-of-culture modernists who refused to get their clocks fixed. That did not describe Williams or any of the liberals that influenced him, notably Alfred North Whitehead and Henry Nelson Wieman, yet Williams recycled the very definition of his tradition that marginalized him and it.

The standard definition was wrong at both ends. It ignored that the liberal tradition had its richest intellectual flowering before Ritschlian theology existed and it denigrated an ongoing tradition that is still creatively refashioning itself a century after World War I. Moreover, the fact that British liberal theology was called "Modernism" is a tribute to the fateful, soon crushed, but creative attempts by Alfred F. Loisy, Maurice Blondel, Lucien Laberthonniere, Friedrich von Hügel, and George Tyrell to imagine a Roman Catholic form of modern theology. The party vehicle of Anglican liberal theology, the Modern Churchmen's Union, embraced the term "Modernism" during the very period that the Vatican abolished liberal wellsprings in the Catholic Church. Although Anglican liberals tended to come from the church's liberal Protestant wing, they respected what their Roman Catholic counterparts had tried to do.[5]

The father of liberal theology, Schleiermacher, did not call himself a liberal, and the icons of liberal theology stood for various things that were far from liberal. These facts considerably complicate the idea, which I endorse, of a liberal tradition that began in the eighteenth century and that remains an important approach today. The key to the ascendancy of liberal theology in the nineteenth century is that it outgrew its origins as an ideology of freethinking criticism to become a theology grounded in, and at home with, the Christian church.

Kantian Liberalism and Mediating Theology

Johann S. Semler, a biblical scholar at the University of Halle, was the first person to embrace the name "*liberalis theologia*," in the late 1760s. Semler was a "neologian," the name by which the founders of German historical criticism identified themselves. They included Johann Gottfried Eichhorn, Johann Jakob Griesbach, J. G. Herder, Johann David Michaelis, F. V. Reinhard, and J. J. Spalding. Before liberal theology existed, there was a basis for it in the work of these pioneering biblical and historical scholars.[6]

The neologians claimed to study the Bible from a scientific standpoint stripped of dogmatic presuppositions. They revolutionized biblical scholarship by deciphering the historical development of the biblical text, rejecting the taxonomical and naturalistic interpretations of rationalist criticism. They took a third way between orthodox supernaturalism and deist criticism, charging that both were ideological, superficial, and lacking in critical rigor. Revelation confirms the truths of reason, they argued. The Old Testament contains myths like other scriptures, not all parts of the Bible are equally inspired, and the gospels were written out of distinct historical contexts that shaped what Christianity became. Semler, responding to a public outcry over Reimarus' interpretation of the gospels (which was published by G. E. Lessing), charged that

Reimarus offered sloppy scholarship and warmed-over deist tropes. There is such a thing as a rational Christianity that sticks to facts and does not indulge in special pleading of any kind, Semler urged. This was the kind of Christianity that suited the modern age. Under Semler's leadership, Halle became the center of critical theology in the 1750s and sustained this leadership position into the 1780s, when a declining Semler backed away from defending academic freedom. By the 1780s, the neologians had embraced *liberalis theologia* as the best name for their party, now under the intellectual leadership of a commanding thinker, Immanuel Kant.[7]

The expressed aim of the original liberal theologians was to win doctrinal freedom in the church by diminishing the power of the regnant Lutheran orthodoxy. "Liberal theology" was the moniker of an agenda, achieving doctrinal freedom, and a group, the Kantian theologians. Before 1789 it was possible to fight for intellectual freedom in the German church without getting political. Kant was cagey in dealing with the politics, as were the neologians. All had to deal with the tyranny of the princes, and most were grateful to King Friedrich II (Frederick the Great) for tolerating, to a point, opinionated intellectuals. But Friedrich II died in 1786, and three years later the French Revolution broke out. Keeping religion and politics separate became impossible, especially for republican types like Kant, especially under a king, Friedrich Wilhelm II, that Kant loathed. In 1792 Kant published a book about religion, *Religion Within the Boundaries of Mere Reason;* two years later the king censored Kant for disseminating wrong views about religion.

Kant submitted to silencing, waited for Friedrich Wilhelm II to die in 1797, and resumed writing about religion. *Liberalis theologia* became known, above all, for the belief that religious and political freedom go together, though Kant's first three biographers, all theologians that knew him personally, played down his republican radicalism. The public identity of liberal theology was solidified in Germany during the fall of the French Revolution, the Napoleonic invasions, an upsurge of German nationalism, and the rise of a so-called "Restorationist" government, which in fact established a new political order under the trappings of the old one. The "Restoration" of 1815 had little to do with the absolutism of eighteenth-century princes and everything to do with the rise of state absolutism.

In this historical and political context, cautious reformers like Schleiermacher and Hegel were sometimes called liberals, but ownership of the term was usually reserved for pushy types like biblical scholar Wilhelm Martin Leberecht de Wette and philosopher Jakob Friedrich Fries. Old-style rationalists such as Carl Gottlieb Bretschneider, Wilhelm Traugott Krug and H. G. Tzschirner also held out for freethinking religious liberalism. Hans-Joachim Birkner and Friedrich Wilhelm Graf, countering the myth of a homogeneous German liberal tradition, rightly stress that the self-identifying liberals of Hegel's time fought as hard for human rights, freedom of opinion, and freedom of the press as they fought for their right to academic freedom in interpreting Christianity. The willingness of liberals to cause trouble on these topics was a cautionary specter to Schleiermacher, and, to Hegel in his later life, an odious one.[8]

Formally, Schleiermacher and Hegel were both liberals in religion and politics. But Schleiermacher was a moderate reformer in politics, Hegel grew cynical and conservative about politics in his later life, and in their time, "liberal theology" meant freethinking religious thought removed from the ongoing life of the Christian church.

This radical idea of liberal theology, a Kantian notion, was a non-starter for Schleiermacher. He was an every-week preacher who sharply separated his philosophy from his
theology. Though Schleiermacher was a Romantic and a post-Kantian, his crowning
work was a liberal dogmatics – an oxymoron to freethinking liberals. Schleiermacher
saw no reason to renounce the church's tradition of dogmatic theology; what was
needed was a thoroughly modern refashioning of it. Good theology held no bias
against the church or its dogmatic tradition. It was completely at home in Christian
communities that broke free from the old houses of authority, as long as they held out
for the right to do so.

The association of liberal theology with freethinking Kantianism was sufficiently
strong that even most of Schleiermacher's disciples did not call themselves liberal
theologians after Schleiermacher was gone. "Mediating theology," a form of church
theology holding a secure place in the academy, suited them perfectly. Only as the
legacy of Schleiermacher expanded through his disciples (Carl Ullmann, C. I. Nitzsch,
August Twesten, Willibald Beyschlag), and a leading Pietist (Friedrich August Tholuck),
and two blenders of Schleiermacher and Hegel (Richard Rothe and Isaak August
Dorner) did "liberal theology" begin to be used in a broader sense than the usual one
of freethinking or scientific criticism, and even then, the name belonged mostly to
freethinkers and culture-religionists.[9]

Advocates of freethinking liberal theology did not surrender the category without a
fight. In the 1840s they called themselves "friends of light," espousing a radical
democratic ideology often linked with democratic nationalism. Mediating theologians like Rothe and Dorner replied that they, too, believed in intellectual freedom,
human rights, and liberal theology. They opposed the mid-century alliance between
confessional orthodoxy and the German police state. They wanted a liberalized,
united state church that held together Germany's disparate populations in a common
religious culture. Germany could not be a successful empire if it lacked a unifying
religion, they warned. Liberal theology as represented by later mediating theology
and the movement that overtook it, Ritschlian theology, underwrote the civil religion
of an expanding German empire – culture Protestantism. In that form it achieved its
greatest influence and power, on degraded terms.[10]

The Ritschlian movement led by Ritschl, Harnack, Wilhelm Herrmann, and (before
and after he morphed away) Ernst Troeltsch got some important things right;
otherwise it would have lacked the power to overtake a distinguished intellectual
tradition. It made an advance in modern theology by accentuating the social and
historical character of religion. It was the vehicle that lifted Kant to a prominent place in
church-based modern theology. It produced unsurpassed historical scholarship on
Christianity, in the works of Harnack. Its Troeltschian offshoot established the history
of religions approach to religion, a major achievement. But the Ritschlian School also
set up German liberal theology for a mighty fall, at the very moment when Britain
belatedly acquired a liberal movement.

Ironically, even the Ritschlians usually did not call themselves liberals, although they
were eventually blamed for ruining liberal theology. In Ritschl's time, bourgeois
optimists like Otto Pfleiderer claimed the liberal name, asserting their belief in the
progress of modern culture. Pfleiderer, a religious philosopher and professor of
theology at the University of Berlin, wrote influential works on the philosophy and

history of religion, conceiving his perspective as a straightforward outgrowth of Kantian, Schleiermacherian, and Hegelian idealism. At Berlin, he was the only member of the theological faculty to vote against Harnack's invitation to teach there. German theology had no need of a Ritschlian corrective, Pfleiderer believed; thus, Berlin had no need of Harnack, no matter how many shelves of books he had already written.[11]

To Pfleiderer, the line of Enlightened progress in theology ran from Kant to Fichte to Schleiermacher to Hegel to himself. He lauded Kant for overthrowing the principle of external authority in religion and for deriving the content of religious consciousness – the moral faith of practical reason – directly from the individual's inner moral experience. Kant showed that believing in God is a necessary demand of one's moral self-consciousness, which belongs to practical reason, not to the sensibility of theoretical reason. Pfleiderer lauded Fichte for replacing Kant's postulated distant God with the active presence of the divine spirit in the heart – the spiritual ground of ethical idealism. He lauded Schleiermacher for correcting Kant's excessive individualism and for introducing into theology "the fundamental thought of idealism, that the mind is able to recognize as truth only that in which it finds its own nature again."[12]

Schleiermacher, Pfleiderer explained, reunited the bond between the knowing subject and historical Christianity that Kant severed. On the other hand, Schleiermacher reopened the door to supernaturalism by lifting Jesus above the plane of ordinary human existence. Schleiermacher had the right idea – historical development – but he did not carry it out. Pfleiderer lauded Hegel as the genius that carried it out. In Hegelian idealism, Kant's subjective idealism was applied to the historical life of humanity. Hegel brilliantly conceived history as a developmental process of divine unfolding in which no point was entirely without truth and no point was the whole truth. To Pfleiderer, that was the high point of religious thought thus far, but Hegel was too one-sidedly intellectualist in conceiving religion as a thing of the thinking spirit. A thought obtains religious significance only by exciting feeling and will, Pfleiderer urged. The ideal was to combine Hegel's religion of reason with the religion of the heart as expounded by Fichte and Schleiermacher.

Pfleiderer agreed with Hume that the old rationalist idea of "natural religion" was a fantasy of rationalists – an idea about an essence of religion that never existed. The old rationalists imagined that historical religions were deformations of the original "natural" religion, which espoused rational universal truths unfettered by provincial myths, superstitions, and dogmas. But even if the old rationalists were wrong about natural religion, Pfleiderer urged, that did not mean that their latter-day successors were right in claiming that the essence of religion is irrational. This was where historical consciousness made a huge advance on the Enlightenment. The crucial difference between eighteenth-century rationalism and nineteenth-century historical consciousness was that nineteenth- century liberals understood that every living thing unfolds its essential nature "only in the whole course of its life." To understand an oak, Pfleiderer explained, one studies full-grown trees as well as acorns. To understand the essence of human beings, one does not focus solely on infants, "nor will he choose as his models the savages who are to be found in the crude state of nature."[13]

What mattered about any subject or thing was its development. German idealism and historical criticism had an evolutionary mindset before anyone heard of Charles Darwin. After Darwin, Pfleiderer's generation made evolution the master category of thought. Pfleiderer urged that everything depended on giving priority to "what the human race has developed itself into in the course of thousands of years." Religious life and thought are not different than other fields; what matters is to advance to the highest attainable forms of moral and intellectual culture. Christianity, Pfleiderer assured, is the most developed religion. To keep development going, however, modern Christianity as a whole needed to take instruction from German religious philosophy, and to win the cultured despisers back to Christianity, German Christianity needed to become more German. Pfleiderer was nearly as popular in England as in Germany, because he wrote winsomely in both languages, but his English audience had to swallow a good deal of Teutonic-centrism.[14]

The Ritschlians agreed with Pfleiderer-style liberals about development and German intellectual superiority, but their historicism was more thoroughgoing, their theology was more deeply rooted in gospel Christianity, and they were more critical of bourgeois progressivism. They believed that these differences shielded them from going overboard with cultural conceits and German nationalism. If cultural Protestants like Pfleiderer and Arthur Bonus were liberals, the Ritschlians were inclined to let them have the term. Ritschlians prized their differences with the Pfleiderer liberals, a point of pride that seemed ridiculous to a succeeding generation after Barth's Ritschlian teachers enlisted Christianity in the cause of German militarism. Birkner and Graf, explaining the upshot a bit too sharply, contend that "German liberal theology" was a construction of the Barthian anti-liberals of the 1920s; the Barthian reaction lumped Schleiermacher and Hegel with Ritschl and Harnack to put an end to a century of heresies.[15]

That, indeed, is how the idea of a homogenous liberal tradition was constructed, but homogeneity always falls apart whenever one looks closely at things assembled under a category such as "liberal," "rationalist," "Enlightenment," or "Barthian." There never was a homogeneous tradition of liberal theology in Germany. Nonetheless, there were core affinities that passed from Kant and Schleiermacher to Ritschl and Harnack. All theologians in this stream sought to make Christianity modern by accepting biblical criticism and the modern scientific worldview, and by fitting Christian theology to the right kind of idealism. And the liberal tradition in Germany, by whatever name, never recovered from its complicity in the Ritschlian disaster of 1914.

Meanwhile British theology took a slower and less dramatic road to making Christianity modern. Here the Anglican difference played a key role, as the Church of England, despite allowing greater doctrinal latitude than the Lutheran and Reformed traditions, proved to be more repressive over time. More important was the dramatic difference in academic institutions. By the mid-nineteenth century Germany had twenty-one universities, while England had four (Oxford, Cambridge, Durham, and London). In Germany, princes took for granted that they needed their own universities to produce clerics and administrators that managed their domains. German university instruction featured lectures; the professors that delivered them were expected to be published experts in their fields; and they were usually not required to subscribe to doctrinal standards.

In England none of these scholarship-enhancing conditions existed. Britain had a Broad Church tradition in the mid-nineteenth century that claimed the spirit of Coleridge, but it was a modest affair, and in 1860 a group of Broad Church liberals led by Henry Bristow Wilson and Benjamin Jowett published a movement manifesto, *Essays and Reviews,* that backfired spectacularly, setting off a national furor that killed the question of liberalization for another generation. Britain had no liberalizing movement until Hastings Rashdall and a handful of Ritschlians launched parallel movements in the Anglican and non-conforming Protestant churches at the end of the nineteenth century.[16]

By then the Victorian era was ending, the British empire was fading, and the British and German empires were on a collision course. After the war, there was no reaction against British modernism for enabling the nation's fall into disaster, so the liberalizing movement carried on as before – revising Christian doctrines in the face of modern criticism, seeking to reconcile religion and science, and appropriating post-Kantian idealism. British theology refashioned mid-nineteenth-century German debates over the Christian basis of Hegel's system and the compatibility of Hegelian idealism with personal Christian theism. The British tradition modernized sufficiently that its greatest figure, William Temple, opposed the existence of an organized liberal faction; Temple wanted modernization to proceed without having to fight about it.

This was a plausible strategy for as long as post-Kantian idealism and historicism remained on the upswing in British thought. It took the Great Depression and World War II for British theology to join the reaction against the nineteenth century. Temple and Charles E. Raven, the leading British religious thinkers of the 1940s, watched the field turn against their concerns with religious philosophy, consciousness, science, and theories of emergence. Britain opted for home-brewed forms of neo-orthodoxy. A half-century later, British theology picked up where Temple and Raven had left off, rethinking the relationships between religion and science and theorizing the implications of historical and cultural relativism for disestablished Christianities.

Kantian and Hegelian Ordering

This book emphasizes the Kantian basis of modern theology, showing that every major option from Schleiermacher and Hegel, to Kierkegaard and David Friedrich Strauss, to Ritschl and Troeltsch, to Rashdall and Temple, to Tillich and Barth got its bearings by figuring its relationship to Kantian and post-Kantian ideas. It explains the origin and theoretical basis of Whitehead's process-relational thought, but not the development of the Whiteheadian school, which was a US American phenomenon.

There is a certain asymmetry between the discussions of German and British theology that reflects what happened. All the German thinkers discussed in this book are major figures in modern philosophy or theology, while several of the British thinkers are little known outside England. Had I restricted this book to the German story, there would have been room for longer accounts of mid-nineteenth-century Mediating Theology than I provide in chapters 3 and 5. But the Mediating theologians are secondary figures in the history of theology, and here they are crowded out by my discussions of Kierkegaard, how post-Kantian idealism played out in Britain, and the Barthian revolt against liberal theology.

My argument ties Hegel and the other post-Kantians to Kant, stressing the Kantian basis of Hegel's theory of the categories and the transcendental aspects of Kant's idealism that undergird all post-Kantian idealisms, including Kierkgaard's. Equally important, I make a case for the stronger role of Hegelian idealism in founding schools of German and British religious thought, evoking the Kierkegaardian and Marxist reactions, and helping modern theology cope with Darwinian evolution and the Nietzschean critique of theology.

The latter issue, in particular, raises contested topics in contemporary philosophy and theology. Against much of the recent scholarship on Hegel that tries to rehabilitate Hegel for philosophy departments by lopping off his metaphysical and religious commitments, I feature these aspects of Hegel's thought. But I do not do so by adopting the "system" view of Hegel's philosophy or the "right-Hegelian" tradition usually assigned to theological interpreters of Hegel. I argue for the primacy of negation in Hegel's dialectic, a dynamic panentheist reading of his religious thought, and an integral, religion-friendly view of the *Phenomenology of Spirit*. Schelling and Hegel, by privileging becoming over being, broke open the deadliest assumption of Western thought about the nature of (divine) reality.

Similar issues are at play in interpreting Kierkegaard, where too many academics have tried to strip their ostensible subject of the religious passions that fueled his life and thought. Postmodern renderings of Kierkegaard have rightly played up the instability, indirect communication, and heterogeneity of Kierkegaard's pseudonyms, helping to deliver Kierkegaard scholarship from the blunt readings of theological types that preferred Kierkegaard's edifying mode. However, Kierkegaard was obsessed with Christianity, he certainly believed that he was stating truths amid his ironic spinning, and he also wrote works of very direct communication featuring religious beliefs. Here, as with Hegel, my aim is to hold in view a complex thinker in his wholeness, which cannot be done without taking seriously the integral role of religion in his thought.

I have a special interest in getting Hegel right because I believe that his idea of God as relational Spirit was an important anticipatory response to the critiques of onto-theology that fuel postmodern criticism. Friedrich Nietzsche rejected the God of Christian theism as an enemy of freedom and subjectivity. Martin Heidegger, contending that Western theism wrongly took being for God, sought to liberate being from the metaphysical God. Emanuel Levinas, contending that Western onto-theology wrongly took God for being, sought to dissociate God from being, conceiving God as the "other" of being. Hegel brilliantly prefigured and undercut these critiques, offering a concept of God as spiraling relationality that embraces all otherness and difference. My discussion of Tillich in chapter 8 highlights the ways in which his debts to Hegel and Schelling allowed him to take Nietzschean/Marxist/Freudian criticism seriously without losing his religious wellspring.[17]

God's infinite subjectivity, in Hegel's idea, was an infinite inter-subjectivity of holding differences together in a play of creative relationships not dissolving into sameness. Before Hegel and Schleiermacher, any theology that smacked of Spinoza was condemned as pantheistic atheism. Schelling and Hegel, reworking Spinoza's concept of substance, theorized absolute idealism as a theory of the dynamic inter-subjective in itself. Hegel, more than Schelling and Schleiermacher, put panentheism into play in modern theology by conceiving it as irreducibly dynamic and relational. God is the inter-subjective whole of wholes, not the Wholly Other. In my view, Hegel's logical mill wrongly left no room for apophatic theology, the intuition of God as the holy unknowable mystery of the world. But Hegel's fluid, spiraling, relational panentheism changed the debate in theology about how God might relate to the world. Hegel paved the way for Troeltsch, Temple, Whitehead, Tillich, and numerous Hegelians by offering an alternative to pantheism *and* the static being-God rejected by Nietzsche, Heidegger, and Levinas.[18]

The influence of Kant and Hegel in religious thought shows through not only in the schools of theology that explicitly claimed Kant, Hegel, and Schleiermacher, but in the field-upending reaction against all of them, the Barthian revolt. In his early career Barth drew deeply on Kierkegaard. Throughout his career Barth took fundamental aspects of Kant's dualism so much for granted that he rarely bothered to discuss them. He gave greater attention to Hegel, with whom he had fundamental disagreements, except for the large matters of doctrinal ambition and logic on which he closely resembled Hegel. He took core aspects of his theology from his teacher, Herrmann, and refashioned them. And he kept returning to Schleiermacher because Schleiermacher was his great foil, the one who defined Barth negatively by approaching dogmatics in exactly the wrong way – unless, perhaps, Schleiermacher was best understood as a theologian of the Holy Spirit. The liberal tradition lost its ownership of modern theology after Barth turned against his teachers, and modern theology immediately became more interesting and profound.

I shall emphasize the implication of liberal theology in nationalism, imperialism, and white supremacism, but not because I am out to discredit liberal theology or its appeal to ideals. Liberal theology, by virtue of being liberal and Christian, might have been expected not to denigrate the humanity of non-Caucasian human beings or to rationalize imperialism. Both practices violated the Christian norm that all people are children of God bearing God's image and spirit, and the Enlightenment norm that all people must be treated as ends-in-themselves, not as means to an end. But Christianity had a thin history of advocating social justice of any kind, and liberalism had no history that was not infected with the personal and social inheritance of slavery, nationalism, white supremacism, empire, misogyny, and class oppression. To believe in progress required overlooking a great many exceptions. For beneficiaries of the expanding English and German empires, the facile solution to the contradiction was that the world would improve with the cultural and commercial advance of one's nation, in which a strong military had a vital role to play. This was a sustaining faith, long on pretensions paralleled in every empire, until both nations were pulled down by war and imperial debacles.

Religious idealism was not much of a brake on all that. But we tend to hold idealists to a higher standard than self-professed realists, skeptics, conservatives, materialists, and nihilists because the idealists stubbornly insist on the necessity of holding an ideal, even if it is unattainable. We expect philosophical idealism to lead to social idealism, even after we understand that often it does not. In the Kantian revolution that launched modern theology, powers of mind were said to be fundamental to human life and experience. The seemingly unstoppable march of materialistic empiricism was stopped in its tracks. Enlightenment, at least as conceived by Kant and the post-Kantians, dethroned the things of sense, offering a new way to color the world religiously without bowing to antiquated dogmas. And it did so while taking seriously the reality of radical evil. Enlightenment reason, seemingly no friend to religion, inspired a modern departure in religious thought by mapping the epistemological and spiritual ground of freedom and imagining a cosmopolitan commonwealth of freedom.

Ideal and Normative, Subjective and Objective

Any attempt to show the impact of German and British idealism on theology must take up notoriously complex and disputed questions about how to interpret German idealism. Much of the complexity and disagreement owes much to the fact that philosophical "idealism" has two significantly different meanings that German and British idealists often mixed together. In philosophy, the "ideal" can refer to spiritual or mental ideality as contrasted with the material or physical, or it can refer to a normative ideal as contrasted with the substantive. Idealism in the first sense, subjective idealism, is the idea that there is no reality without self-conscious subjectivity. The classic form is Berkeley's doctrine that only the ideas of individual minds are real. Idealism in the second sense, objective idealism, is the idea that everything is a manifestation of the ideal, an unfolding of reason. Plato and Leibniz taught that all reality conforms to the archetypes of some intelligible structure. One can easily affirm the equal and independent reality of the spiritual and material on objective idealistic grounds, but strongly subjective forms of idealism are more expansive and exclusive. As Frederick Beiser observes, subjective idealism stretches the concept of the mental to do the work of the ideal or the rational, making it the world's entire reality. The logic of subjective idealism, left unchecked, drives toward the triumph of subjectivism.[19]

This issue permeates the questions of how Kant's system and the legacy of post-Kantian idealism should be understood. Transcendental realism is the idea that truth consists in the conformity of concepts to objects. Kant's transcendental idealism, though not lacking realistic aspects, rested on the opposite idea, that truth consists in the conformity of objects to concepts. The field of Kant studies is a battleground over the nature and extent of Kant's conceptualism, which plays out as a debate over subjective versus objective idealism. Subjective and objective idealisms are both idealistic in claiming that reality depends upon the ideal or the rational. Subjective idealism, however, binds the forms of experience to the transcendental subject. In subjective idealism, the transcendental subject is the precondition of the forms of experience, and the ideal or the rational is subjective or spiritual. Objective idealism, on the contrary, detaches the forms of experience from the transcendental subject. Here the forms of experience apply to the realm of being as such, and the ideal or the rational is archetypal and structural.

This distinction correlates with the two chief traditions of interpreting Kant. Many leading scholars, notably H. A. Prichard, P. F. Strawson, Jonathan Bennett, and Robert Paul Wolff contend that Kant was a subjective idealist. Advocates of this view emphasize Kant's affinities with Descartes, Hume, and, especially, Berkeley, arguing that Kant's transcendental idealism was the key to his system: We have no direct knowledge of reality; immediate objects of perception are the ideas of a perceiving subject; all that we know are our own representations, the appearances of things; the reality of an independent world must be inferred from our representations. This school of interpretation maintains that Kantianism is coherent only as a thoroughgoing form of subjective idealism contending that we cannot know anything beyond experience. On this reading, which dates back to the earliest reviews of the *Critique of Pure Reason*, Kant's transcendental idealism was a rationalistic refashioning of Berkeley's idealism that lopped off Berkeley's empiricism and misguidedly appealed to the thing-in-itself.[20]

The rival tradition of interpretation contends that Kant was insistently anti-subjective and that the key to his system was his determination to overcome the skepticism of Descartes, Hume, and Berkeley. Even if the thing-in-itself was a mistake, the objectivist aspects of Kant's thought must be taken seriously. Kant's "subjectivism" was actually a form of objective idealism in which the ideas of the knowing subject were *determined* by the intersubjective world of the concepts of the understanding. In this reading, the ideas of the individual mind are not primary in Kant's system; rather, as Kant argued in the Transcendental Deduction of the first *Critique,* the *a priori* concepts of the understanding constitute an intersubjective order that is the necessary condition of any ideas that the individual mind may have. Contrary to the subjectivist interpretation, Kant's doctrine of the categories of understanding is epistemological, not psychological. The forms of understanding are conditions of the possibility of experience, not objects within experience. As the conditions by which something might be identified as subjective or objective, the forms of understanding are not subjective or objective. Leading exponents of this interpretation include the neo-Kantian Marburg School (Hermann Cohen, Paul Natorp, Ernst Cassirer) and, more recently, Karl Ameriks, Graham Bird, Henry Allison, and Arthur Collins. In this reading, Kant's transcendental idealism was much closer to Schelling and Hegel than to Berkeley and Hume.[21]

Both of these interpretive traditions have impressive prooftexts from the first *Critique* and other works of Kant. Both are predisposed to make Kant's position logically consistent, even if that requires playing down or eliminating some aspect of Kant's thought that he emphasized. A third major tradition of interpretation, taking hold of the contradictions between the subjectivist and anti-subjectivist readings, has long maintained that Kant mixed these two doctrines. In some cases, scholars have espoused "patchwork" theories, claiming that the first *Critique* incoherently patched together conflicting doctrines from different stages of Kant's development. Hans Vaihinger and Norman Kemp Smith wrote the classic works of patchwork theory.[22] More recently, Ralph Walker, Sebastian Gardner, and Frederick Beiser have argued that the mixture view is right, but not as a patchwork. Persistently, from the first *Critique* onward, Kant sought to steer a middle path between subjective and objective idealism, which left him with somewhat ambiguous doctrines about ideas and transcendental idealism. In this reading, Kant's critical idealism is best understood as a form of subjective idealism that struggled against subjectivist captivity.[23]

My reading of Kant is closest to Beiser's mixed-theory interpretation, although I have differences with Beiser on related issues, and I will argue that Kant never straightened out key sections of the first *Critique*. The patchwork theory, though wrong about Kant's essential coherence, rightly stressed that Kant assembled much of the first *Critique* by collecting it. Moreover, in the first edition of the first *Critique*, Kant expounded a problematic doctrine of the transcendental object, which he eliminated in the most relevant sections of the second editions, but not elsewhere – probably because he couldn't face up to rewriting certain sections.

The basis of Kant's position was subjective idealism, since Kant contended that the forms of experience derive from the transcendental subject. But Kant warded off extreme subjectivism by insisting that the matter of experience is given, and he provided the starting point of post-Kantian objective idealism by contending that the very possibility of self-consciousness depends on universal forms of experience. To render Kant as a thoroughgoing subjective or objective idealist is to misconstrue his position and the mediating spirit behind it.

Kant's discussions of transcendental idealism in the first *Critique* expounded his subjective idealist starting point, but he also made statements in the first and third *Critiques* about the universal forms of experience that qualified his subjectivism. The latter forms became the basis of post-Kantian objective idealism, though in a tangled process. The differences between subjective and objective idealism were not elaborated until Hegel tried to explain them in 1801, and even Hegel did not straighten out the matter, as his rendering was peculiar to his emerging position. By then, "absolute idealism" was in play as a name for the view that everything is ideal as an aspect or appearance of the absolute idea. Friedrich Hölderlin and Friedrich Schlegel, in the late 1790s, described their idealism as "absolute," a name that Schelling and Hegel took up in the journal they co-edited for two years (1802–1803), *Kritisches Journal der Philosophie*.[24]

There was no bright-line difference between objective and absolute idealism, but for those that preferred the latter name, it signified that good idealism transcended subjectivity versus objectivity. Absolute idealism was about the "unconditioned" or the "in-itself." Here again, "idealism" could mean two different things. Everything is a manifestation of the idea or reason, such that ideal status refers to that which is inside the absolute. Or, all oppositions between the subjective and objective, or the ideal and the real, have an ideal existence, not a real one, in which case ideal status refers to that which is outside the absolute. The point of absolute idealism was to overcome Kantian dualism, yet even here, "idealism" was never just one thing. The fact that idealism is never just one thing compounds its complexity and elusiveness. Sometimes German and British idealists stressed this point, often they ignored it, sometimes they straddled it confusedly, and the most noted critics of idealism, such as F. H. Jacobi and G. E. Moore, tended to purchase intelligibility and polemical advantage by treating their subject as just one thing.[25]

Kant revolutionized philosophy by asking two questions: How should one explain the possibility of knowledge? And how should one account for the reality of the external world? His dilemma, which has perplexed philosophers ever since, was that solving either of these problems undermines the answer that one needs to solve the other one. To solve the first question, one has to demonstrate some kind of identity between subject and object, for if the subject and object are completely distinct from each other, they cannot interact to produce knowledge. But to explain the reality of the external world, one has to establish some kind of dualism between subject and object; otherwise objects are not really independent of our subjectivity. Kant's rich, twisting, turgid, and conflicted wrestling with this problem yielded what Beiser aptly calls "a synthesis of subjectivism and objectivism in transcendental idealism" and a wide array of competing interpretations of what he said, yielding similar readings about the post-Kantian alternatives that succeeded him.[26]

For two centuries, Hegelian interpretations dominated scholarly discussion of the meaning of German idealism. In this rendering, Kant took up the Cartesian notions that only self-knowledge is certain and that the immediate objects of knowledge are ideas, which raised the question of radical subjectivism: Does the knowing subject have immediate knowledge only of its own ideas? Kant, in this account, set German idealism on the path of saying "yes," but balked at going through with it. Fichte and Schelling made creative attempts to push farther, conceptualizing Kant's transcendental self as the source of experience in form and content, but they got only so far. Hegel saw the matter through by expanding the unbroken circle of consciousness to embrace everyone, construing the absolute as an infinite mind. Hegelianism solved the clash of idealisms by taking absolute idealism as far as possible: Everything is an appearance of the idea, the structure of reality in general. Josiah Royce, the greatest Anglo-American interpreter of German idealism, taught that this was the meaning of German idealism. For better or worse, Hegel's absolute idealism culminated the tradition launched by Kant.[27]

Royce was emphatically an advocate of "better." His Hegelian understanding of history led straight to his lucid rendering of the Hegelian meaning of German idealism. Other leading interpreters of the "Kant to Hegel" story took a similar line, whether or not they were Hegelians. Karl Rosenkranz, a theologian of the original Hegelian school, interpreted German idealism from this standpoint, as did Richard Kroner and Nicolai Hartmann, though Kroner and Hartmann were sympathetic to Hegel only in a broad fashion, not as school Hegelians.[28]

More importantly, the Royce/Kroner version of what happened and what it meant was taken for granted by all manner of idealists, realists, pragmatists, phenomenologists, existentialists, Marxists, positivists, and analytic philosophers. William James assumed Royce's account of German idealism when James famously described idealism as a doctrine of "absolute all-withness" that related all things to each other "by throwing 'categories' over them like a net." Philosophical idealism was a rescue operation for an idealist problem, James contended. It detached experience from reason and truth in order to make a case for a "unifying higher agency" that united the world. James, at least, sympathized with ethical idealism; outright anti-idealists liked Royce's account because it gave ballast to their dismissal of idealism as subjectivism run wild, the swallowing of everything by ego. For many critics, taking Hegelianism seriously absolved them from having to bother any further with idealist philosophy.[29]

Recent interpreters of German idealism, including some who have influenced me, have sought to renew interest in their subject by diminishing Hegel's place within it. I am more sympathetic with the Hegelian reading of the idealist tradition. In my view, Kant's critical idealism led to post-Kantian objective idealism, the conversion of Kant's transcendental self into a metaphysical principle, which led to Hegel's idea of a universal self or Spirit. I do not share Beiser's interest in "exorcising the spirit" from philosophical idealism or his related tendency to downgrade Hegel's importance. But I share Beiser's view that the German idealist story is not about the triumph of subjectivism. Kant, Schelling, Schleiermacher, Hegel, and even the later Fichte resisted the aggressive logic of subjective idealism. German idealism, by taking so seriously the problems of subjectivity and freedom, could not avoid the problem of subjectivism. But it would not have been such a rich, powerful, complex, conflicted, and even tortured tradition had it simply opted for an ego trapped inside the circle of consciousness, and its rhetoric of freedom would have been meaningless had it done so.

Kant's transcendental idealism was subjectivist in attaching all appearances to a transcendental subject. But Kant's idealism was objectivist in conceiving the intersubjective forms of experience as *necessary conditions* of ideas, not as ideas. Moreover, post-Kantian idealists construed the absolute in transcendental terms as the condition of the possibility of experience. It was not subjective or objective, because subjectivity and objectivity fall within experience. The logic of the absolute, as a concept, militates against rendering it as either subjective or objective; otherwise it cannot be unlimited.[30]

On the mediating ambiguity of Kant's transcendentalism and the German idealist struggle against subjectivism, I am indebted to Beiser. On the primacy of freedom in Kant's thought and the primacy of negation in Hegel's dialectic, I am indebted to Dieter Henrich, under whom I studied Kant and Hegel at Harvard in the mid-1970s. Henrich launched the revisionist wave of scholarship in this area, stressing the "keystone of freedom" in Kant's thought, the importance of Schelling and Hölderlin in the development of German idealism, and the role of negation in Hegel's thought. Beiser and others build on Henrich's pathbreaking scholarship, and that of Manfred Frank, when they emphasize the importance of the Romantics to German idealism and resist the theory of Hegelian culmination. To some extent this book takes a similar tack by treating Schelling as an important religious thinker on his own, explaining Hölderlin's role in the early development of absolute idealism, and stressing Fichte's role in launching post-Kantian criticism. I will argue that Schelling was, for a time, the most brilliant and original of the post-Kantian idealists, however much he truncated his own legacy by radically changing course three times, lapsing into silence in the middle, and allowing Hegel to overtake him.[31]

I have much at stake in my arguments about how German and British idealism should be understood. But my overriding concern is the importance of German and British idealism in modern theology and the Barthian reaction against it. If I were not principally concerned with theology, I would have given greater attention to Friedrich Schlegel and F. H. Bradley. But Schlegel had little impact on religious thought, and British theologians viewed Bradley's impersonal idealism as something to overcome. Moreover, the dominant story about Hegel's culminating importance had a large impact.

Whether or not Hegel culminated German idealism, a great many religious thinkers in Germany and Britain were quite sure that he did. In his lifetime, Hegel had a strong following of theologians and religious philosophers. After he died it acquired cultic overtones. Hegelians of that generation had read Fichte and Schelling; most of them knew Schelling personally. They knew that Hegel had not originated some of the Hegelian ideas for which he was famous – dialectic, self-positing spirit, the absolute as the identity of identity and nonidentity, alienation. That didn't matter. Hegel was the genius that synthesized the riches of German idealism. More importantly, for religious thinkers who lived intellectually in the modern world but for whom giving up on metaphysical reason was unacceptable, no one came close to Hegel as an intellectual guide and savior. Above all, I will argue, Hegel's brilliant obsession with the emergence of social subjectivity – the collective self-transformations of Spirit – yielded the richest intellectual legacy of any modern Western thinker.

Scottish Hegelian Edward Caird caught some of it. A half-century after Hegel's death, Caird was willing to let Hegelianism die so that the brilliance of Hegel's achievement might be grasped by the next generation. The period of discipleship had passed, Caird advised. Hegel no longer needed Hegelians. Hegel belonged to the top rank of philosophers, along with Plato, Aristotle, Spinoza, and Kant. Thus, he belonged already to the ages, on a scale that was impossible to measure. Caird observed that Hegel's thought overpowered all rivals in metaphysics, ethics, philosophy of religion, and religion. But that was just the beginning of what had to be measured. Hegel was like Dante and Shakespeare, so entangled with the "whole culture" of his time, especially its movement of thought, that it was hard to say what was distinctly Hegelian. Caird did not claim to know what was distinctly Hegelian. He added that it didn't matter. All that mattered was to recognize "the existence of a living develop-ment of philosophy, and especially of that spiritual or idealistic view of things in which philosophy culminates – a development which begins in the earliest dawn of speculation, and in which Kant and Hegel are, not indeed the last names, but the last names in the highest order of speculative genius."[32]

Thus did the highest flying form of German idealism find a surprising home in the land of common sense empiricism, a nation that for decades had dismissed German idealism as impossibly obscure, ridiculous, and abstract.

Notes

1. For an interpretation of modern theology that, working with this definition, revolves around various strategies to solve the myth problem, see Gary Dorrien, *The Word as True Myth: Interpreting Modern Theology* (Louisville: Westminster John Knox Press, 1997). For an interpretation that similarly emphasizes the criterion of looking beyond the answers of the Christian tradition, see Gareth Jones, ed., *The Blackwell Companion to Modern Theology* (Oxford: Blackwell, 2004).
2. This is the same definition that I employed in my three-volume work, *The Making of American Liberal Theology: Imagining Progressive Religion; The Making of American Liberal Theology: Idealism, Realism, and Modernity;* and *The Making of American Liberal Theology: Crisis, Irony, and Postmodernity* (Louisville: Westminster John Knox Press, 2001, 2003, 2006).
3. See Friedrich D. E. Schleiermacher, *Über die Religion: Reden an die Gebildeten unter ihren Verächtern* (Hamburg: Verlag von Felix Meiner, 1958); English editions, *On Religion: Speeches to Its Cultured Despisers,* trans. Richard Crouter (Cambridge: Cambridge University Press, 1988); *On Religion: Addresses in Response to its Cultured Critics,* trans. Terrence N. Tice (Richmond: John Knox Press, 1969); *Reimarus: Fragments,* ed. Charles H. Talbert, trans. Ralph S. Fraser (Philadelphia: Fortress Press, 1970); Hermann Samuel, Reimarus, *Apologie oder Schutzschrift für die vernünftigen Verehrer Gottes,* 2 vols. (Frankfurt: Suhrkamp Verlag, 1972).
4. Daniel Day Williams, *God's Grace and Man's Hope* (New York: Harper & Brothers, 1949), 22.
5. On Roman Catholic Modernism, see Dorrien, *The Making of American Liberal Theology: Imagining Progressive Religion,* 394–396; Alfred F. Loisy, *The Gospel and the Church,* trans. Christopher Home (New York: Charles Scribner's Sons, 1903); Loisy, *The Birth of the Christian Religion* and *The Origins of the New Testament,* single-volume edition,

trans. L. P. Jacks (New Hyde Park: University Books, 1962); Maurice Blondel. *L'Action: Essai d'une critique de la vie et d' une science de la pratique* (Paris: Alcan, 1893); Friedrich von Hügel, *The Mystical Element in Religion* (New York: J. M. Dent, 1923); George Tyrell, *Tradition and the Critical Spirit: Catholic Modernist Writings*, ed. James C. Livingston (Minneapolis: Fortress Press, 1991); *Roman Catholic Modernism*, ed. Bernard M. G. Reardon (Stanford: Stanford University Press, 1970).

6.   Johann S. Semler, *Institutio Brevio ad Liberalem Eruditionem Theologicam*, 2 vols. (Halle: Trampe, 1765–1766); Johann Gottfried Eichhorn, *Einleitung in das Neue Testament*, 2nd edn., 3 vols. (Leipzig: Weidmannischen Buchhandlung, 1810–1820); Johann Jacob Griesbach, *Vorlesungen über Hermeneutik des Neuen Testaments, mit Anwendung auf die Leidens und Auferstehungsgeschichte Christi*, ed. J. C. S. Steiner (Nuremberg: In der Zeh'schen Buchhandlung, 1815); Johann David Michaelis, *Einleitung in die göttlichen Schriften des Neuen Bundes*, 2 vols. (Göttingen: Jandenhoeck, 1777).

7.   Johann S. Semler, *Beantwortung der Fragmente eines Ungenannten insbesondere vom Zweck Jesu und seiner Jünger* (Halle: Erziehungsinstitut, 1779); Semler, *Hallische Samlungen zur Beförderung theologischer Gelehrsamkeit* (Halle: Trampe, 1767–1770); Werner Georg Kümmel, *The New Testament: The History of the Investigation of its Problems*, trans. S. McLean Gilmour and Howard C. Kee (New York: Abingdon Press, 1972), 62–73.

8.   Hans-Joachim Birkner, "Liberale Theologie," in Martin Schmidt und Georg Schwaiger, eds., *Kirchen und Liberalismus im 19. Jahrhundert* (Göttingen: Vandenhoeck und Ruprecht, 1976), 33–42; Friedrich Wilhelm Graf, "Liberale Theologie," in *Evangelisches Kirchenlexikon* (Göttingen: Vandenhoeck und Ruprecht, 1992), 3: 86–98; Graf, "What Has London (or Oxford or Cambridge) to Do with Augsburg?" in *The Future of Liberal Theology*, ed. Mark D. Chapman (Aldershot, England: Ashgate, 2002), 23–24.

9.   See Carl Ullmann, *Das Wesen des Christentums* (Hamburg: Perthes, 1845); C. I. Nitzsch, *System der christlichen Lehre* (Bonn: Adolph Marcus, 1829); August Twesten, *Vorlesungen über die Dogmatik* (Hamburg: Perthes, 1838); Willibald Beyschlag, *Die Christologie des Neuen Testaments* (Berlin: Rauh, 1866); Richard Rothe, *Theologische Ethik*, 3 vols. (Wittenberg: Zimmermann, 1845–1848); I. A. Dorner, *A System of Christian Doctrine*, 4 vols., trans. Alfred Cave and J. S. Banks (Edinburgh: T. & T. Clark, 1888).

10.   See Birkner, "Liberale Theologie," 35–39; Graf, "Liberale Theologie," 88–92.

11.   See George Rupp, *Culture-Protestantism: German Liberal Theology at the Turn of the Twentieth Century* (Atlanta: Scholars Press, 1986), 18; Graf, "What Has London (or Oxford or Cambridge) to Do with Augsburg?" 28.

12.   Otto Pfleiderer, *Philosophy and Development of Religion*, 2 vols. (Edinburgh: William Blackwood and Sons, 1894), quote 1: 21; see Pfleiderer, *Religion and Historic Faiths*, trans. Daniel A. Huebsch (New York: B. W. Huebsch, 1907).

13.   Pfleiderer, *Philosophy and Development of Religion*, quotes 1: 29.

14.   Ibid., quote 1: 29; see Otto Pfleiderer, *Evolution and Theology and Other Essays*, trans. Orello Cone (London: A. & C. Black, 1900); Pfleiderer, *Die Entwicklung der protestantischen Theologie in Deutschland seit Kant und in Grossbritannien seit 1825* (Freiberg: J. C. B. Mohr, 1891); Pfleiderer, *The Philosophy of Religion on the Basis of its History* (London: Williams and Norgate, 1886); Pfleiderer, *The Influence of the Apostle Paul on the Development of Christianity*, trans. John F. Smith (New York: Charles Scribner's Sons, 1885).

15.   Birkner, "Liberale Theologie," 35–42; Graf, "Liberale Theologie," 90–98; Graf, "What Has London (or Oxford or Cambridge) to Do with Augsburg?" 28–29.

16.   See M. S. Crowther, *Church Embattled: Religious Controversy in Mid-Victorian England* (London: Archon Books, 1970), 40–41; *Essays and Reviews: The 1860 Text and Its Reading*, ed. Victor Shea and William Whitla (Charlottesville: University Press of Virginia, 2000), 55–56.

17. See Friedrich Nietzsche, *Thus Spoke Zarathustra,* trans. R. J. Hollingdale (Harmondsworth: Penguin, 1973); Martin Heidegger, *The End of Philosophy,* trans. Joan Stambaugh (London: Souvenir Press, 1975); Heidegger, *Identity and Difference,* trans. Joan Stambaugh (New York: Harper & Row, 1969); Emmanuel Levinas, *Totality and Infinity: An Essay on Exteriority,* trans. Alphonso Lingis (The Hague: Martinus Nijhoff, 1979); Levinas, *Otherwise than Being or Beyond Essence,* trans. Alphonso Lingis (The Hague: Martinus Nijhoff, 1981).

18. For significant recent works taking this line of Hegelian theology, see Peter C. Hodgson, *God in History: Shapes of Freedom* (Nashville: Abingdon Press, 1989); Hodgson, *Liberal Theology: A Radical Vision* (Minneapolis: Fortress Press, 2007); and Hodgson, *Hegel and Christian Theology: A Reading of the Lectures on the Philosophy of Religion* (Oxford: Oxford University Press, 2005).

19. Frederick C. Beiser, *German Idealism: The Struggle Against Subjectivism, 1781–1801* (Cambridge: Harvard University Press, 2002), 6.

20. H. A. Prichard, *Kant's Theory of Knowledge* (Oxford: Clarendon Press, 1909); P. F. Strawson, *The Bounds of Sense* (London: Methuen, 1966); Jonathan Bennett, *Kant's Analytic* (Cambridge: Cambridge University Press, 1966); Robert Paul Wolff, *Kant's Theory of Mental Activity* (Cambridge: Harvard University Press, 1963).

21. Hermann Cohen, *Kants Theorie der Erfahrung* (Berlin: Ferdinand Dümmler, 1885); Paul Natorp, *Philosophie, ihr Problem und ihre Probleme; einführung in den kritischen Idealismus* (Gottingen: Vandenhoeck & Ruprecht, 1911); Ernst Cassirer, *Kant's Life and Thought* (New Haven: Yale University Press, 1981); Karl Ameriks, *Kant and the Fate of Autonomy* (Cambridge: Cambridge University Press, 2000); Graham Bird, *Kant's Theory of Knowledge* (New York: Humanities Press, 1962); Henry Allison, *Kant's Transcendental Idealism* (New Haven: Yale University Press, 1983); Allison, "Transcendental Idealism: The Two Aspect View," in *New Essays on Kant,* ed. Bernard den Ouden and Marcia Moen (New York: Lang, 1987), 155–178; Arthur Collins, *Possible Experience* (Berkeley: University of California Press, 1999).

22. Hans Vaihinger, "Die transcendentale Deduktion der Kategorien in der Erste Ausgabe der Kritik der reinen Vernunft," in *Philosophische Abhandlungen* (Halle: Niemeyer, 1902), 24–98; Norman Kemp Smith, *A Commentary to Kant's Critique of Pure Reason,* 2nd edn. (New York: Macmillan, 1923).

23. Ralph Walker, *Kant* (London: Routledge, 1978); Sebastian Gardner, *Kant and the Critique of Pure Reason* (London: Routledge, 1999); Beiser, *German Idealism: The Struggle Against Subjectivism, 1781–1801.*

24. See G. W. F. Hegel, *The Difference Between Fichte's and Schelling's System of Philosophy,* trans. H. S. Harris and Walter Cerf (Albany: State University of New York Press, 1977); Hegel, *Faith and Knowledge or the Reflective Philosophy of Subjectivity in the Complete Range of Its Forms as Kantian, Jacobian, and Fichtean Philosophy,* trans. Walter Cerf and H. S. Harris (Albany: State University of New York Press, 1977); Ernst Behler, "Friedrich Schlegel und Hegel," Hegel-Studien 2 (1963), 203–250; Walter Benjamin, *Der Begriff der Kunstkritik in der deutschen Romantik* (Bern: Francke, 1920).

25. See Beiser, *German Idealism: The Struggle Against Subjectivism, 1781–1801,* 148–179, 465–482; F. H. Jacobi, *David Hume on Faith, or Idealism and Realism: A Dialogue by Friedrich Heinrich Jacobi* (1787), in Jacobi, *The Main Philosophical Writings and the Novel Allwill,* trans. George Di Giovanni (Montreal: McGill-Queen's University Press, 1994), 255–338; G. E. Moore, "The Refutation of Idealism," *Mind* 12 (October 1903), 341–370, reprinted in Moore, *Philosophical Studies* (1922; reprint, London: Routledge & Kegan Paul, 1965), 1–30.

26. Beiser, *German Idealism: The Struggle Against Subjectivism, 1781–1801,* quote 25.

27. Josiah Royce, *The Spirit of Modern Philosophy* (Boston: Houghton Mifflin, 1892); Royce, *Lectures on Modern Idealism,* ed. J. Loewenberg (New Haven: Yale University Press, 1919); Royce, *The World and the Individual,* 2 vols. (New York: Macmillan, 1899, 1901).

28. Karl Rosenkranz, *Geschichte der kantische Philosophie* (Leipzig: Voss, 1840); Richard Kroner, *Von Kant bis Hegel* (Tübingen: Mohrn, 1921); Nicolai Hartmann, *Die Philosophie des deutschen Idealismus* (Berlin: de Gruyter, 1954).

29. William James, *Pragmatism* (New York: Longmans, 1907); James, *The Meaning of Truth: A Sequel to Pragmatism,* in James, *Pragmatism* and *The Meaning of Truth: A Sequel to Pragmatism* (Cambridge: Harvard University Press, 1975), quotes 173.

30. See Beiser, *German Idealism: The Struggle Against Subjectivism, 1781–1801,* 20–21, 132–162.

31. Dieter Henrich, *Konstellationen: Probleme und Debatten am Ursprung der idealistischen Philosophie (1789–1795)* (Stuttgart: Klett-Cotta, 1991); Henrich, *Bewusstes Leben: Untersuchungen zum Verhältnis von Subjektivität und Metaphysik* (Stuttgart: Philipp Reclam, 1999); Henrich, *Between Kant and Hegel: Lectures on German Idealism,* ed. David S. Pacini (Cambridge: Harvard University Press, 2003); Henrich, "Formen der Negation in Hegels Logik," in *Seminar: Dialektik in der Philosophie Hegels,* ed. Rolf-Peter Horstmann (Frankfurt: Suhrkamp Verlag), 1978; Manfred Frank, *Eine Einführung in Schellings Philosophie* (Frankfurt: Suhrkamp Verlag, 1985); Frank, *Einführung in die frühromantische Aesthetik* (Frankfurt: Suhrkamp Verlag, 1989).

32. Edward Caird, *Hegel* (Edinburgh: Wm. Blackwood and Sons, 1883), 223–224.

2

Subjectivity in Question
Immanuel Kant, Johann G. Fichte, and Critical Idealism

The modern departure in religious thought begins with the unavoidable figure in modern philosophy, Immanuel Kant. Modern philosophy began with Descartes, who introduced the problem of subjectivity that Kant took on, but in religious thought, Kant has the Descartes role. Enlightenment rationalism had a critique of authority religion before Kant came along, and it advocated using reason to its utmost. But it had no theory of the creative power of subjectivity or the grounding of religion and freedom in moral experience. Kant became the towering figure of modern philosophy and the first modern religious thinker by providing both.

Kant had barely published his three critiques of reason when post-Kantian alternatives to his metaphysics, theology, and ethics began to appear, launching modern theology. Johann G. Fichte heightened Kant's subjectivism in the name of taking it to its logical conclusion. Friedrich Schleiermacher accepted most of Kant's system except most of what he said about religion. Every post-Kantian began with Kant's transcendental idealism, which attached all appearances to a transcendental subject, but every post-Kantian rejected or refashioned the thing-in-itself. Modern theology was born in the attempts by Schleiermacher, F.W. J. Schelling, G. W. F. Hegel and others to construe Christianity from the standpoint of a transcendental post-Kantian subject that was inconceivable without Kant.

To understand Kant, it is better to know nothing about him than to know the usual stereotypes. He was not a thought machine lacking in personality or an interesting life. He did not float above the politics of his time, but was radical enough to require sanitizing by his friends. He was not opposed to metaphysics, although he importantly changed his mind, in mid-career, about the limits of metaphysics. His moral argument for God's existence was not a stopgap or a sop to religious types; it was his own second-deepest conviction, which was tied to his deeper one about the reality of freedom. Though Kant is famous for discrediting metaphysical reason, he spent most of his career trying to refashion the rationalist metaphysics of Gottfried W. Leibniz and Christian

Kantian Reason and Hegelian Spirit: The Idealistic Logic of Modern Theology, First Edition. Gary Dorrien.
© 2012 John Wiley & Sons, Ltd. Published 2015 by John Wiley & Sons, Ltd.

Wolff. Afterwards he pulled Germany to the front rank of philosophy and launched the modern departure in religious thought by fixing on the creativity and limits of reason.

Refashioning Enlightenment Metaphysics: Immanuel Kant

One measure of Kant's impact on modern thought is that when he first proposed the nebular hypothesis of the origin of the solar system in 1755, it was ignored. German universities, and the German language, were just beginning to acquire respect when Kant began his career. There was no "Germany" at the time; there was only a grab bag of principalities more or less held together by the so-called Holy Roman Empire. A century had passed since the Peace of Westphalia (1648), which ended the Thirty Years' War, which was fought mostly on German lands. Very little intellectual or cultural life had arisen in the German principalities in the meantime. England was the world's dominant power, which exercised direct influence on the German lands through its possession of Hanover. France was on the way to becoming the continent's strongest nation. In England, Scotland, and France, powerful movements for "Enlightenment" existed; the early German version was very modest by comparison. Had Kant been English or French, his idea that the solar system formed from a spinning cloud of gas might have lifted him to Newton-like fame. As it was, the nebular theory had to wait for Pierre Simon Laplace in 1796. By then the German Enlightenment was the crucial one for theology and philosophy, chiefly because of Kant.[1]

The standard rendering of Kant describes a life of all thought and no life. This account, which is a caricature, was established by three foundational biographies that strove to make Kant as lifeless as possible and by German Romantics who had different reasons for perpetuating the caricature. In 1804, the year of Kant's death, three theologians – Ludwig Ernst Borowski, Reinhold Bernhard Jachmann, and Ehregott A. Christian Wasianski – sought to defend Kant from recent aspersions on his character. In their telling, Kant was a morally earnest academic who was habituated to a rigidly ordered regime of quiet and reflective dignity. Contrary to recent allegations, he was not petty, selfish, egotistical, subversive, or zealously devoted to the French Revolution. Kant, they insisted, was a dutiful Prussian citizen, albeit with eccentricity issues. He was not harmful to public morals or to the role of religion in modern society; in fact, he was quite the opposite. The biographers that knew Kant personally fixated on his later life and warded off any suggestion that he was a dangerous character.[2]

German Romantics seized on this picture in opposing German rationalism, which reinforced the impression that Kant's biographers got him right. According to the Romantics, Königsberg was a provincial backwater, from which Kant never roamed because he had no life and didn't want one. Heinrich Heine, in the classic version of the Romantic account, immortalized by citation, claimed that Kant "neither had a life nor a history." The cathedral clock in Königsberg had no less passion or regularity than Kant, and neighbors were able to set their clocks by Kant's daily constitutional, which consisted of eight trips up and down a quiet, tree-lined alley. Everything had its precisely scheduled time and nothing was allowed to interfere with the production of thought.[3]

But this picture of Kant as an obsessive thought machine cut off from the real world and any inner world of feeling was based on Kant's later life, not his early career or his harvest years in which he wrote his major works. For the Königsberg biographers, the mechanical picture of Kant was calculated to defend a local hero, who had to be thoroughly Prussian, non-republican, and no threat to religion. Subsequently, the Romantics liked it because it lampooned the Rationalist devotion to logical order and abstraction.[4]

Kant had a life, one that was shaped by and that reacted to the tumultuous political, social, and intellectual events of his time. He was an epochal thinker, a fervent advocate of the French Revolution, a sharp critic of traditional religion, and a dreamer of cosmopolitan global peace, albeit a world order reflecting his white supremacist prejudices. Otherwise he would not have become the epitome of the German Enlightenment.

He was born in 1724, a year after Prussian King Friedrich Wilhelm I inadvertently gave ballast to Enlightenment rationalism by expelling Christian Wolff from Prussia. Wolff was a mathematician and scientist at Halle who gravitated to philosophy in 1709 and sustained a close intellectual collaboration with Leibniz until the latter's death in 1716. Leibniz, an objective idealist in the Platonic mold, was the preeminent philosopher of the German Enlightenment before Kant. He opposed Descartes' skeptical idealism on rationalist grounds, formulating a picture of a perfectly rational and harmonious world ordained by God. Ultimately the universe consists only of God and of non-composite, immaterial "monads," Leibniz argued. Space, time, material things, and causality appear to exist only because God ordained a pre-established harmony among all that does exist. The idea of space is a concept or ideal, not a specific thing or intuition. We attain this idea by abstraction from particular distances that make the idea possible. Bodies in space are not mere illusions – contrary to many readings of Leibniz – but rather, necessary sensible manifestations of monads. Leibniz had a good word for scholastic masters like Thomas Aquinas, admonishing that they were far smarter than "our moderns" acknowledged. In Leibniz's time, and for 65 years after he was gone, his deterministic and optimistic system ruled philosophy in Germany, where Wolff put enough of his personal stamp upon it that it was usually called Wolffian philosophy.[5]

Wolff was more than a popularizer of Leibniz's ideas. He ranged widely, prolifically, and somewhat eclectically, blending Leibniz with Descartes, arguing for the existence of immaterial souls (not Leibnizian monads) that related to bodies through a pre-established harmony. At Halle, a stronghold of Pietism, Wolff sparred uneasily during his early career with colleagues who distrusted his deductive, mathematical rationalism. The Pietist movement supplemented Protestant dogma with a strong emphasis on the necessity of inward spiritual experience and commitment. In 1721 Wolff put himself in danger by arguing that one did not have to believe in God to arrive at sound principles of moral and political reasoning. Morality requires respect for God, Wolff assured, but it does not depend on divine commands; rather it depends on an antecedent comprehension of moral truth. Even ethical atheists respect God without realizing it.[6]

Wolff's colleagues, appealing to the king, warned that Wolff's theory of rational harmony was fatalistic, which offered an excuse to army deserters. This was alarming to Friedrich Wilhelm I, who had organized Prussia strictly around the needs of the army.

The king responded by banishing Wolff, making him famous. Wolff fled to Marburg as a symbol of intellectual freedom, where he became a popular lecturer. Verbose as well as prolific, Wolff virtually invented German as a scholarly language, wrote in Latin to gain an international audience, and ranged over philosophy, science, mathematics, economics, public administration, and other subjects. In 1740 Friedrich II (Frederick the Great), a more reflective type than his father, devoted to philosophy, ascended to the throne and called Wolff to come home. By then Wolff was wealthy from his lecture fees and royalties.

Wolff returned triumphantly to a hero's welcome in Halle, where he taught for the rest of his career. He was the first German philosopher to found a school of thought and the first scholar to be made a hereditary Baron of the Holy Roman Empire on the basis of academic work. His philosophy dominated German universities for decades under the reign of Frederick, who, for all his philosophizing, maintained the pro-military policies of his father. In Germany, enlightenment went hand in hand with the rise of state absolutism.

When Kant reflected on the influences on his thought he usually mentioned Leibniz, Wolff, Locke, Hume, and Jean Jacques Rousseau. Sometimes he gave a grudging acknowledgment to Descartes. He did not credit George Berkeley, the Anglo-Irish Bishop of Cloyne and theorist of extreme subjective idealism, though many critics of his time found that incredible. And he rarely had even a grudging word of gratitude for Pietist moralism, though in that case, the influence was too obvious to need mentioning. Kant spent half his career trying to solve Wolffian problems; then he became Immanuel Kant.

Kant's father, Johann Georg Kant, a master harness maker in Königsberg, and his mother, Anna Regina Kant, were devout Lutheran Pietists, especially his mother. The Pietist reaction against orthodox formalism was strong among the trade guildsmen and less educated townspeople of Königsberg. During Kant's youth, local theology professors derided Pietism as a poor-people's movement specializing in simple-minded moralism and street preaching. More importantly, nobles, orthodox clergy, and government officials held the same view, citing theologians for support. Kant's parents replied by welcoming the arrival, in 1731, of Pietist leader Franz Albert Schulz, who lifted the movement to respectable status in Königsberg, partly by playing down its enthusiastic tendencies. Kant's family practiced independent Bible study and family devotions, and embraced the Pietist emphasis on the priesthood of the laity; religion centered on personal faith and morality. With appreciation, Kant later recalled that his parents were religiously sincere, but not enthusiasts. He was grateful to have had "perfectly honest, morally decent, and orderly" parents. But he grieved for years at his mother's tragic early death, and he shuddered at the memory of his formal schooling in Pietist institutions.[7]

When Kant was thirteen his mother, caring for a friend afflicted with smallpox, accidently used the same spoon as her friend, became infected, and died quickly. Kant's later idea that morality is essentially freedom from affection and desire may have been rooted in his guilt over blaming his mother for dying. His education was another source of psychic pain. Kant acknowledged that his parents were motivated by moral sincerity in sending him to Pietist schools affiliated with Königsberg's *Collegium Fridericianum;* they wanted him to be good and to have a good life. But Kant shuddered with revulsion at the memory of his schooling, even though he would not have qualified for university without it. Religiously, the *Collegium Fridericianum* sought to save students from spiritual corruption and to implant righteous Christianity in their hearts. Academically, it drilled them in Latin, Greek, Hebrew, classical authors, the Bible, and Martin Luther's small and large catechisms. Classes met six days per week, Latin was the backbone of the curriculum, pedagogy rested on rote memorization and repetition, and the only teacher that Kant liked taught Latin. He later recalled that his teachers had no talent for lighting a spark of intellectual interest, but plenty for blowing one out.

Even worse, for Kant, he was required to write reports on the state of his soul. Any inclination to introspection that Kant may have had was erased by this experience. His teachers, determined to break "the natural willfulness of the child," routinely administered beatings to willful and low-achieving students. Kant probably got few beatings, but he hated the school's punitive atmosphere. For the rest of his life he expressed incredulity that the Pietists thought they could punish children into being saved. How could they know which students were really converted and which ones were just trying to avoid another beating? Kant's best biographer, Manfred Kuehn, argues persuasively that Kant's melding of true morality to autonomy had its genesis in his repugnance at Pietist education.[8]

In 1740, the same year that Friedrich II allowed Wolff to return triumphantly to Halle, Kant entered the University of Königsberg, at the age of sixteen. Contrary to convention, his hometown, though somewhat insular and outside the domains of the Holy Roman Empire, was no backwater. Königsberg was an important city in the northeastern corner of Prussia, near Poland and the Russian border. Until 1701 it was the capital of Prussia, and it remained the capital of East Prussia during Kant's youth. The Prussian state was weak during Kant's youth and most Prussians called themselves "Berliners," "Westphalians," and the like, not Prussians. Königsbergians were different; they called themselves Prussians, and their number included sizable populations of Poles, Russians, Lithuanians, and Huguenots, plus Mennonites, a Jewish community, and numerous Dutch and English merchants. The last group proved to be significant for modern philosophy, as the British Navy, needing Baltic timber for its masts, was deeply invested in Königsberg, which brought the Scottish Enlightenment to Kant's university and to him.[9]

Some of Kant's teachers at the university, hearing of Wolff's return to Halle, hoped that it augured a defeat for Pietism. But Frederick II was more interested in expanding Prussia's territory than in changing its universities. Thus he left the universities more or less as he found them, and Kant cut his teeth intellectually on the struggle between Pietists and Wolffians. Königsberg had faculties in philosophy, theology, law, and medicine. Pietists dominated the theological faculty, which also included a few orthodox Lutherans. In philosophy, most of Kant's teachers were Pietists, with a smattering of Wolffians and a remnant of diehard Aristotelians. For decades, Pietism versus Wolffianism was a bitter affair in German universities, pitting empiricism and induction against rationalist deduction and the appearance of impiety. Pietist philosophers J. F. Budde, J. Lange, A. F. Hoffmann, and Christian August Crusius urged that philosophy should analyze concepts given in experience. Often they charged that their opponents were infidels. At Königsberg, however, the bitter feeling was somewhat alleviated by the mediating spirit of Schulz and Kant's favorite teacher,

Martin Knutzen, who acknowledged that Wolffian philosophy was compatible with Christian belief.[10]

This battle between Pietists and Wolffians played out the dethronement of Aristotelian physics and metaphysics by the geometrical method of René Descartes (1596–1650) and the inductive-mathematical method of Isaac Newton (1642–1727). Aristotle taught that objects acquire impetus, but Newtonian physics taught that the universe is a closed system with universal physical laws. Newton discovered the generalized binomial theorem, the law of gravitation, and the principle of the composition of light. He also invented calculus, although he did not publish until after Leibniz, decades later. Newton's *Philosophiae Naturalis Principia Mathematica* (1687) was modeled on Euclidean geometry, demonstrating its propositions mathematically from definitions and mathematical axioms. He taught that the world consists of material bodies that interact according to three laws of motion concerning the uniformity of motion, change of motion, and mutuality of action. In Newton's conception, the ultimate conditions of reality – absolute time, space, place, and motion – were absolute quantities constituting an absolute framework for measure.[11]

Newtonian physics devastated metaphysical systems based on Aristotle; the question for Kant's teachers was whether it devastated any possible metaphysics. The symbols of Enlightenment rationality in Kant's time – Leibniz and Wolff – held out for a new form of metaphysical reason, as did Kant, who equated the search for a new metaphysical foundation with the Enlightenment project of establishing the authority of reason in all spheres of life. From 1744 to 1759 Kant sought to provide a new foundation for metaphysical claims about God, immortality, and the first causes of nature. From 1760 to 1766 he took a skeptical turn, developing arguments about the sense-bound limitations of scientific knowledge that he later made famous in the *Critique of Pure Reason* (1781). From 1766 to 1772 he went back to metaphysics, fashioning a modest ontology. In 1772 he turned away from full-orbed metaphysics again, setting on a course that produced the *Critique of Pure Reason* (1781). In each phase Kant grappled with the attempts of Leibniz and Wolff to provide a mathematical foundation for metaphysics in the light of Newtonian physics. When he finally made up his mind, at least about metaphysics, he developed an elaborate metaphysical foundation for natural science, the *Critique of Pure Reason*.[12]

He began with a book that aggressively corrected Leibniz and Newton, *Thoughts on the True Estimation of Living Forces* (1746). Normally, this book would have been written in Latin and offered as a university dissertation, but Kant spurned normal proceeding that might have launched an academic career. At the age of twenty, he was already aiming over the heads of his professors. Kant assured that he respected the "great masters" of knowledge, referring to Leibniz and Newton; on the other hand, "I have already prescribed the route I want to take. I will begin my course and nothing shall prevent me from continuing it." If that smacked of overweening presumption, "at times it is not without benefit to have a certain noble trust in one's ability."[13]

From the beginning Kant was determined to be an independent thinker who trusted his ample ability. Leibniz, blasting the mechanical physics of Descartes, contended that the essence of matter is inner living force, not mere extension. Speed and force are not the same thing, and matter is not completely inert; rather, some principle of living force is indispensable for understanding motion and the nature of bodies. Kant sought to provide a foundation for Leibniz's metaphysics of nature. Defending Leibniz's doctrine of living force, but also the validity of Cartesian mechanics, Kant distinguished between two kinds of motion – the impressed motion of a body that continues only as long as it is acted upon by an external force and the free motion of a body that continues to infinity as long as something doesn't stop it. Cartesian measurement worked for impressed motions, Kant reasoned, where the power of a body is proportionate to the cause of motion, but Leibniz had a better measure for free motions, where the inner force of bodies multiplies the power they receive from the cause of motion. The Cartesian mathematical and Leibnizian metaphysical approaches to nature were complementary, not in opposition, Kant argued. They only appeared to conflict because Cartesians and Leibnizians both assumed that only mathematics grasped the living forces of nature. Young Kant confidently judged that mathematics worked only for forces arising from external causes.[14]

Momentum was the right measure for all motions except free motions; living force was possible only if free motions existed; Kant, while admitting that he could not prove the existence of free motions, reasoned that assuming it as a hypothesis made sense of an otherwise impossible tangle. In his telling, this was all that Leibniz had argued, or at least had meant to say, in his *Theodicy*, where the doctrine of living forces was crucial to Leibniz's theory of monads.

Leibniz described monads, the fundamental elements of life, as immaterial entities lacking spatial parts. The basic properties of monads are functions of their perceptions and appetites, he argued. Each monad perceives other monads more or less clearly, and God perceives all monads perfectly. Each monad is different from every other, "for there are never in nature two beings which are exactly alike, and in which it is not possible to find a difference either internal or based on an intrinsic property." Leibniz did not conceive the monads as interacting or as having external relations with each other. Kant, however, by distinguishing between mathematical bodies and natural bodies, gave up Leibniz's doctrine that monads do not act on each other in order to save Leibniz's doctrine that nature cannot be explained by dead force alone.[15]

Moreover, Kant began his intellectual career as an advocate of Leibniz's theory of pre-established harmony. Leibniz taught that the internal states of substances and the order of the world are pre-established, and the internal principles of substances harmonize with their external relations. Kant accepted Leibnizian harmony as the metaphysical upshot of Newtonian physics, though in Kant's case, there were further consequences to draw from the distinction between mathematical and natural bodies. If Leibniz's monads interacted, Kant reasoned, the internal states of substances and their interactions must have been pre-established too. The world was established precisely by interactions between the world's pre-established fundamental elements.

To defend Leibnizian pre-established harmony at Königsberg was, for Kant, an act of defiance that limited his career options. Kant's Pietist teachers, especially Knutzen, loathed anything that smacked of determinism. Pietism prized the freedom of the will, which bought it into conflict with Lutheran and Calvinist orthodoxies. To Kant's teachers, Leibnizian harmony was a baleful refashioning of a bad idea, fatalism. On that account Kant's first book probably had no chance of being accepted as a doctoral thesis. As it was, he did not offer it as one, and his father died shortly afterward, which turned Kant's life into a web of obligations (shared with an older sister) to his younger brother and two younger sisters. For six years he worked as a private teacher to provide for his siblings, studying independently and polishing his social skills in polite society. In 1854 Kant returned to Königsberg to write two dissertations, qualifying him for an academic career; by then, Knutzen was dead and the university was more hospitable to Enlightenment rationalism. Kant's dissertations (on fire and metaphysical first principles) did not test the university's tolerance, but he risked public censure with a book on the natural history of the universe, *Universal Natural History and Theory of the Heavens.*[16]

Newton taught that the order of the solar system shows the hand of God at work, because the empty spaces between the planets could not have had a material cause. Kant allowed that Newton's supernaturalism was convincing if one assumed that the present order of the universe is eternal – something that no material cause could have produced. However, if one assumed that space was originally filled with a primal mass, it was possible to explain the order of the solar system as arising from mechanical forces of attraction and repulsion. The created order did not happen in an instant, and it is destined to continue forever, Kant argued. Though the cosmos gives the appearance of eternity, in fact the order of the solar system is the product of a very long natural history. The universe is infinite in space and time, its order arises from laws governing matter, and matter contains a striving to create order. The force of attraction causes matter to contract into a central body, while the force of repulsion causes collisions that produce other bodies. In effect, Kant argued that if one combined a mechanical concept of nature with a dynamic view of matter, no resort to a supernatural hypothesis was needed. Matter and force are enough to explain everything.[17]

This theory, after Laplace made it famous in 1796, was eventually called the "Kant-Laplace Theory" of the origin of the solar system. But Kant had to become famous before he received credit for a theory that he proposed four decades before Laplace. In his early career Kant's theory was ignored, his publisher went bankrupt, and he had to scratch out a living by collecting fees from students who attended his lectures. As a lecturer at Königsberg, Kant made no salary; his income, when he did not take private students, depended entirely on the students he attracted. Like other lecturers and associate professors, he had to offer his courses at times that did not conflict with the public lectures given by full professors.[18]

From the beginning Kant was a popular lecturer. All professors and lecturers were required to base their lectures on a textbook, but Kant freely departed from the text, tossing off witticisms, admonishing students against taking too many notes, and flashing his dry humor, although he almost never laughed. He told students to think for themselves; Kant didn't want followers. Lecturing at a brisk pace, he made no effort to help slower students comprehend the material, yet his lecture hall was nearly always filled to capacity.

In his early career Kant taught metaphysics, logic, mathematics, physics, and ethics; later he added geography to boost his income. In metaphysics and ethics he used Alexander G. Baumgarten's *Metaphysica,* a staple of the most rationalistic wing of the Leibnizian/Wolffian school, and Baumgarten's *Ethica philosophica.* Hume's first *Enquiry Concerning Human Understanding* (1748), which was published in a German edition in 1755, had a featured role in Kant's teaching. Kant respected Hume enormously, wrestling with Hume's skeptical treatment of causality, although he probably never read Hume's *Treatise on Human Nature* (1739), which was not translated into German until 1793. Kant wrongly considered Hume to be a transcendental realist, and he restricted Hume's skepticism to the issue of causality. Had he known Hume's *Treatise,* he would not have lingered in either misconception. As it was, he debated only Hume's summary version of the *Treatise* (which is what the *Enquiry* was), which was enough to propel him to transcendental idealism. In ethics Kant favored Scottish moralist Francis Hutcheson's *System of Moral Philosophy,* which taught that rational agents possess an objective moral sense that perceives the moral right, as feeling, just as agents perceive a physical object. The German edition of Hutcheson that Kant used was translated by G. E. Lessing and published in 1756. In mathematics he used Wolff's textbook, *Anfangsgründe aller mathematischen Wissenschaften.* Most professors supplemented their meager lecture incomes with night jobs or private instruction, but Kant relied on his lecture income, teaching for 16 to 24 hours per week each semester.[19]

In the late 1750s Kant worked hard at providing better foundations for Wolffian rationalism. Leibniz founded all knowledge on a few self-evident first principles. Wolff argued that all knowledge reduces to a single first principle. Kant reasoned that there are two: "Everything that is, is" (for true affirmative propositions) and "Everything that is not, is not" (for true negative propositions). Following Wolff, Kant derived the principle of sufficient reason from the principle of identity: Nothing is true without a sufficient reason. Any subject, by virtue of being a subject, must have something in it that excludes the opposite predicate from being true of it. It followed for Kant that there must be a reason for everything that exists; reason justifies the principle underlying all knowledge of matters of fact, the principle of causality. This was the cornerstone of Kant's early rationalism. In his later language, by which time he had taken the opposite view, the principle of causality is analytical, not synthetic *a priori*.[20]

A bit to his surprise, Kant worked hard at securing a place in polite society, at which he succeeded. In 1758 Königsberg fell to Russia, without a fight, as a casualty of the Russian-Prussian Seven Year War. Kant soon judged that being occupied by a wealthier and more cosmopolitan nation had its advantages. Russian money, culture, and officers poured into the city, the Russians stayed for five years, and they brought a freer way of life, one featuring a taste for beautiful things. Russian worldliness eroded Prussian customs; at the same time, Russian officers crowded into university classrooms, especially Kant's, who boosted his income by giving private instruction to officers. Local bankers, merchants, and nobles, noting Kant's suave intelligence, invited him to dinner parties, where Kant sparkled, which evoked more invitations. Kant found himself becoming something of a dandy. He cultivated the social graces of his new friends, and became a family favorite of Count and Countess Keyserlingk, especially the countess, whom he rated, for the rest of his bachelor life, far above other women.[21]

Kant's exemplars of ruminating opinion were Hume and Jean Jacques Rousseau. Inspired by his intellectual heroes, and his successful banter at dinner parties, Kant published some ruminating banter of his own in 1764 on matters aesthetic, *Observations on the Feeling of the Beautiful and Sublime.* In Kant's telling, women had a "strong inborn feeling for all that is beautiful, elegant, and decorated," while men came naturally to reason and achievement. Women had no use for geometry or the principle of sufficient reason, he explained: "Her philosophy is not to reason, but to sense."

When men turned away from wickedness, they did so because wickedness is morally wrong, though Kant allowed that, in fact, very few men lived by rational and moral principles. In any case, women as a class turned away from wickedness only because it is ugly: "Nothing of duty, nothing of compulsion, nothing of obligation! Woman is intolerant of all commands and all morose constraint. They do something only because it pleases them." Kant didn't blame women for being that way, for "I hardly believe that the fair sex is capable of principles." A woman that tried to understand intellectual things was a violation of nature, Kant opined; she might as well grow a beard. For a man, the worst insult was to be judged a fool; in morals, the worst thing was to be found a liar. For women, however, vanity was excusable, even charming, although Kant noted that women were often severe critics of each other's vanity. For a woman the worst insult was to be called disgusting, and the worst moral failing was to be unchaste.[22]

These opinions were apparently well received by the women that Kant met at dinner parties; he had very little engagement with any others. In his early career he took for granted that beauty is objective, existing in objects outside the mind, although he allowed that taste is subjective, varying among individuals. Beauty was not yet a point of dispute between rationalists and empiricists; both defined it as an objective, orderly, harmonious, and attractive unity of things, emphasizing unity. Kant added an emphasis on the multiplicity of beauty, and, venturing comparative judgments, opined on places he had never visited and ethnic groups that he knew mostly from books. In his rendering, the scale of pleasures ranged in quality from coarse sensual pleasures at the low end to "finer" feelings at the high end requiring cultivation and talent. At the extreme ends of the scale the differences between the sublime and the beautiful did not apply, but Kant labored this distinction in the middle of the scale, which helped him sort out defining national characteristics.

The sublime evokes awe, while the beautiful evokes joy, Kant explained. There are three kinds of sublimity (terrifying, noble, and splendid) and two kinds of beauty (outward attractiveness and a combination of outward and inward attractiveness mixed with elements of the sublime), and in all five cases, beauty and virtue go together to some degree. Kant's examples of the sublime included snow-capped mountains, nighttime, courage, honesty, unselfish zeal, and understanding, while the beautiful included flowerbeds, daytime, artfulness, pleasant flattery, refinement, and courtesy. By these standards he rated the Italians and French as epitomizing the feeling of beauty and the Germans, English, and Spanish as keepers of the sublime. The Dutch had no taste for either and the Russians he tactfully did not mention.[23]

Overall the English came off second best, next to the Germans, though Kant had a few reservations about his group. The Englishman, in Kant's telling, was temperamentally cool, which was mostly a good thing, and he had a strong sense of the sublime: "He takes little trouble to be witty in society, or to display a polite demeanor; but rather, he is reasonable and steady. He is a bad imitator, cares very little about what others judge, and follows solely his own taste. In relation to woman he is not of French politeness, but displays toward her far more respect, and perhaps carries this too far, as in marriage he generally grants to his wife an unlimited esteem." Kant admired the steadfast and determined qualities of the English, although he noted that they often lapsed into outright obstinacy. Despite their obvious eccentricities, the English were not vain, unlike the French, and they seldom charmed like the French, but usually deserved higher esteem.[24]

Kant's fellow Germans, in his view, were lower on sublimity than the English and lower on beauty than the French, but surpassed both in combining the two feelings. Moreover, German cultivation was growing on both counts. Kant judged that Germans were "reasonably methodical" in all forms of taste, including marital love. They were more affable than the English in social relations and more reasonable than the French, although less witty. Their sublimity was decidedly of the noble type, which caused Germans to prize "demeanor, splendor, and appearances." The latter character trait, in Kant's view, led to a mostly admirable preoccupation with family, title, and rank, although it had a down side, that Germans cared too much about what others thought of them. Kant wanted his fellow Germans to unleash their talents, fretting less about the opinions of others.[25]

As for the rest of the world, Kant was not lacking in putatively enlightened opinions. In his view, Arab hospitality and truthfulness made the Arabs the noblest race in the Orient, though Kant shook his head at the Arab weakness for adventure and "inflamed imagination," which turned even the propagation of Islam into a "great adventure." The Persians were "the French of Asia," excelling at poetry, courtesy, and pretty things. Since the Persians loved pleasure, Kant explained, they devised a mild version of Islam. The Japanese resembled the English in one respect, resoluteness, although this quality degenerated into a stubborn disdain of death. Otherwise the Orient was virtually devoid of finer feeling, Kant contended. Indian religion and culture were "grotesque" through and through, featuring idols, atonements, adventure, and the sacrifice of widows, and the Chinese were equally repugnant in their own way, producing the most grotesque painting and literature in the world.[26]

Kant realized that he was pedaling stereotypes. He claimed only a "passing justice" for his generalizations, admitted that no nation completely lacked finer feeling, and took no position on whether national differences were contingent or necessary, dependent on types of government or climate, or the like. The exception was the entire race of blacks living in or descending from Africa, where Kant was emphatically categorical. "The Negroes of Africa have by nature no feeling that rises above the trifling," he pronounced. Hume was Kant's authority on the humanity of blacks. Hume claimed in his essay, "National Characters" (1748), that black Africa never produced a single significant thinker or person of accomplishment: "No ingenious manufactures amongst them, no arts, no sciences." Though Negro slaves were "dispersed all over Europe," Hume observed, none had ever shown the slightest ability, in contrast even to the lowest of white populations: "Such a uniform and constant difference could not happen, in so many countries and ages, if nature had not made an original distinction between these breeds of men." Hume heard of a black Jamaican who was said to be learned, "but it is likely he is admired for slender accomplishments, like a parrot who speaks a few words plainly."[27]

Kant cited Hume and topped him, stressing that even though many black slaves had been set free, "still not a single one was ever found who presented anything great in art or science or any other praiseworthy quality, even though among the whites some continually arise aloft from the lowest rabble, and through superior gifts earn respect in the world." In this case, Kant judged, the contrast was too great not to take a position on the question of nature versus circumstance: "So fundamental is the difference between these two races of man, and it appears to be as great in regard to mental capacities as in color." Since blacks were dramatically inferior to whites in mental ability, the religion of blacks was hopelessly riddled with superstition and idolatry, "a sort of idolatry that sinks as deeply into the trifling as appears to be possible to human nature." Kant doubted that human nature could sink any lower than the existing backwardness of blacks, and he had a word about the necessity of forcing them to behave: "The blacks are very vain but in the Negro's way, and so talkative that they must be driven apart from each other with thrashings."[28]

These prejudices were popular well beyond the dinner parties at which Kant moved up in society. He embraced the standard bigotries of his time and context with no acknowledgment that anything in them might contradict his claim to enlightened cosmopolitanism. Kant never ventured outside his province, but that did not restrain him. In his middle career he was best known for his book on aesthetics, which earned him a nickname, "the beautiful Magister." *Observations on the Beautiful and Sublime* was published when Kant turned forty, the time of life when, he believed, individuals reach maturity and thus acquire a character. Individual character is an individual's creation, Kant believed. It does not happen to anyone, and no one is born with it. The crucial issue for every individual is whether one will be governed by instinct or reason.

For Kant, the choice between instinct and reason was never in question; enlightenment was about using the power of one's reason to the utmost. In his fortieth year, however, he resolved that to strengthen his rational moral character, he needed to adopt certain principles on which he acted all the time. He needed a set of maxims – basic principles of conduct and thinking by which he lived everyday without exceptions. A good maxim, such as "Take an evening constitutional" was a rule that one could practice on a daily basis and which, once accepted, one never revoked. Kant was a worrier, frail in health, and plagued by nervous anxiety and constipation, all of which militated against any urge he may have felt to venture outside Königsberg. In 1764 he became friends with Joseph Green, a maxim-following, bachelor, English merchant who had moved to Königsberg in his youth. Green looked down on theater and music, shunned parties, admired Hume and Rousseau intellectually, and prided himself on his extreme punctuality. Gradually, Kant became Green's closest friend and adopted his way of life. Kant's regime of maxims helped him cope with his neuroses, even as they created some new ones, and sharply reduced his enthusiasm for social diversions. For Kant, living by maxims and fulfilling his intellectual potential became synonymous.[29]

Though he desperately wanted a professorship at Königsberg, Kant did not get one until 1770. Though he kept trying to find a new foundation for metaphysics, in the 1760s he began to doubt that it was possible. His doubts yielded early versions of arguments that later made him famous. In 1762 Kant charged that scholastic logicians specialized in producing pointless subtleties. The purpose of logic, he admonished, is to simplify the first principles of knowledge, not to underwrite impossibly complicated systems. Scholastic logicians, by identifying four forms of syllogism, purveyed a false subtlety. There is only one pure type of syllogism; the others were hybrid variations.[30]

This was a rationalist argument, rehearsing Wolff's critique of scholasticism, but later the same year Kant published an attack on the ontological proof of God's existence that struck at the core of rationalist theology. In 1762, Kant still believed in the necessity of rational theology, as he explained in *The One Possible Basis for a Demonstration of the Existence of God*. He opposed the Augustinian/Anselmian tradition, however, which proved God's existence by definition, and he believed that Descartes and Leibniz had steered modern philosophy in the wrong direction by deducing the existence of a perfect being from the concept of a perfect being. These arguments became famous after Kant recycled them, two decades later, in the *Critique of Pure Reason*. In *The One Possible Basis,* he offered a full-orbed attack on the ontological proof and other proofs, except one, of God's existence.[31]

The classic form of the ontological argument, developed by Anselm, defines God as "that which nothing greater can be conceived." Anselm reasoned that that which exists in reality is greater than that which exists only in the mind. Since we have a concept of perfect being, it is undeniable that God exists in our minds as an object of the understanding. The question is whether God also exists as an extra-mental reality. If God existed in the mind alone, we could conceive of a being greater than that which nothing greater can be conceived. But that is absurd, Anselm argued; one cannot conceive of something greater than that which nothing greater can be conceived. Thus, God cannot exist in the mind alone, but must exist also as an extra-mental reality. God's nonexistence is not conceivable, for God is that which cannot be conceived not to exist.[32]

Descartes and Leibniz similarly espoused definitional proofs of God's existence, contending that God's existence is a necessary deduction from the concept of a perfect being. Descartes reasoned that just as geometry is not possible if one does not accept its axioms and postulates, metaphysics requires the concept of a being in which all perfections are united. If such a definition for God is accepted, the necessity of God's existence follows immediately as an implication of the logic of perfection. The non-existence of God the perfect being is as inconceivable as a four-sided triangle, Descartes argued. The reality of the unity of perfections bears the same degree of necessity and certainty as that of a triangle possessing three sides. Put differently, the concept of God necessarily involves God's existence. Leibniz took this argument a step further, arguing that God's perfect being is not only the source of all that exists but also of all possibility insofar as anything is real in possibility: "In God is found not only the source of existences, but also that of essences, in so far as they are real. In other words, he is the source of whatever there is real in the possible."[33]

Kant replied that all such ontological reasoning misuses the concept of existence. Rightly understood, he argued, existence is the absolute position of a thing, not a predicate or determination of something. A predicate is always posited with respect to some other thing, but "existence" and "being" are not concepts of things that can be added to the concept of a thing. Adding existence to a thing does not give it any additional properties; a real something contains no more than a merely possible something. In the *Critique of Pure Reason,* Kant explained that a hundred real thalers contained no more coin than a hundred possible thalers; to say that something exists does not add any value to it. *The One Possible Basis* lacked an equally homely example, though Kant urged readers to consider that Julius Caesar and sea unicorns had all the same properties whether or not they existed. From a common sense standpoint, Kant conceded, this argument seemed "strange and absurd"; nonetheless, he had logic on his side. Kant had nothing against common sense on everyday matters. He assured that there is no real harm, in everyday speech, in employing existence as a predicate, "so long as it is not proposed to deduce being from merely possible concepts as one is wont to do in proving absolutely necessary existence." Unfortunately that was exactly how Descartes and Leibniz provided a rational foundation for belief in God.[34]

The One Possible Basis gave equally short shrift to the traditional cosmological and teleological proofs of God's existence. Kant allowed that the order, beauty, and harmony of nature offer impressive evidence for a divine craftsman who shaped nature, "a creator of the conjunction and artificial coordination of the world." But this is far from proving an omnipotent God that created matter itself, he cautioned. The cosmological and teleological proofs actually prove nothing; at most, they buttress the inference of a divine Shaper. Everything that does not depend on the direct will of God derives from inner forces within matter, Kant argued. Since the order, beauty, and harmony of nature derive from the inherent laws of matter, they do not constitute proof of direct creation by God. The only basis for demonstrating God's existence is that the internal possibility of things presupposes an existence of some kind. There must be something that, if it did not exist, all internal possibility would be cancelled out. Kant reasoned that this necessary thing is God, who includes all that is possible and real. God is the ground of all possibility and as such is a necessarily existent being.[35]

Kant's single credible proof was a novel blend of the ontological and cosmological arguments, but he did not rest in believing that he had found a rational basis for theology. He had barely finished *The One Possible Basis,* a work on which he stewed for years, when he wrote a book on the principles of natural theology (a prize essay for the Berlin Academy) that renounced his faith in mathematics as the proper method for metaphysics. Kant still wanted to formulate a metaphysical system based on mathematical deduction, but by the end of 1762 he no longer believed it was possible. Now he argued that metaphysics needed to follow the inductive empirical method of the natural sciences. The prize essay introduced his subsequently famous distinction between the *synthetic* method of mathematics and the *analytic* method of metaphysics. Synthetic method begins with universal concepts formed according to definitions and it deduces conclusions from the concepts, Kant explained. Analytic method, by contrast, begins with concepts given in ordinary language, breaks them into analyzable components, and forms conclusions about them through empirical tests. Only with great reluctance did Kant conclude that metaphysics could not attain mathematical certainty; merely scientific certainty would have to suffice. Then he decided that scientific certainty was out of reach too.[36]

In the late 1760s Kant concluded that he had the wrong project. By his account, Rousseau's *Discourses* convinced him that the arts and sciences were corrupting morality, not providing a better foundation for it. Kant resolved that if Rousseau was right, he (Kant) needed to give up his contempt for common people. High culture was part of the problem, including his idea of metaphysics as speculation about things transcending sense experience. Taking seriously Rousseau's critique of the modern academy, Kant overhauled his idea of the aim and value of metaphysics, vowing to do something useful for humanity as a whole.[37]

Instead of trying to provide a rational foundation for religion and morality, which made both dependent on a speculative worldview, Kant reconceived metaphysics as the science of the *limits* of reason. The fundamental source of morality is freedom, not a speculative worldview, he reasoned. Morality is founded on the power of the free will to prescribe laws. If metaphysics started there, with philosophical modesty and the power of freedom, it could do something enormously useful, establishing the universal rights of humanity. Scholastic and rationalist metaphysics both projected the source of morality into a world transcending human powers, which alienated human beings from their freedom. Both metaphysical traditions, like the rest of the academy skewered by Rousseau, ignored the true source of virtue, which is human freedom. Rousseau famously protested, "Man is born free, and everywhere he is in chains." In his book *Dreams of a Spirit-Seer Illustrated by Dreams of Metaphysics* (1766), Kant put it derisively, likening metaphysicians to spirit-seeing shamans and charlatans. He was finished with metaphysical speculation about things transcending sense experience; at least he claimed to be.[38]

Kant turned out to be less ready than he claimed to live without old-style metaphysical certainty. For two years after finally winning a professorship in logic and metaphysics at Königsberg he went back to assuring that reason provides knowledge of things as they are in themselves, though he held firm that metaphysics knows nothing of spiritual substances. This was the period that he later described as a dogmatic slumber. Kant still believed that some concepts are independent of space and time and that he could make justified knowledge claims about things in themselves that are not objects of sense. For ten years he labored in silence, wrestling with Hume's contention that there are no links between facts in the world of experience. No one ever saw causality; all that we know are ideas and impressions. Kant, resolving to "deal with nothing save reason itself and its pure thinking," puzzled over the possibility of cognition, wrote lengthy scraps, and finally, in a four month frenzy of writing and assembling, produced the *Critique of Pure Reason,* which pursued a single question: How does a mental representation relate to its object? Or more broadly, how does the mind intuit objects of sense data?[39]

In addition to not wanting to give up full-orbed metaphysics, Kant had not wanted to be an idealist of any kind. He did not want to end up with Leibniz's Platonic idealism or the skeptical idealism of Descartes or Berkeley's empirical idealism. But thinking about thinking – the point of the first *Critique* – drove him to some kind of idealism that he torturously struggled to work out. Kant reasoned that the hard problem has to do with the *a priori* concepts of the understanding. Empirical representations are effects corresponding to the objects given to a subject, and in the case of mathematical concepts, the mind creates its objects in the act of knowing them. There is nothing in a mathematical object that is not in its concept. *A priori* concepts, however, are not the effects of objects given in experience, nor do they create their objects. So how do they correspond to objects? What can be known on an *a priori* basis apart from experience?

Kant focused his tremendous powers of intellection on these questions, disciplining himself to his maxims, ignoring his students, publishing nothing, and developing his theory. Very few students got a moment with him, and he lectured only to those who understood him, whoever they were. Kant wasn't sure they existed: "I have almost no private acquaintance with my listeners, and it is difficult for me even to find out which ones might have accomplished something useful." When his severely intellectualistic first *Critique* was finally published in 1781, local readers were disappointed. *Critique of Pure Reason* had none of the juicy flair of *Observations on the Feeling of the Beautiful and Sublime.* Kant's method was analytical; he focused relentlessly on the faculties of knowledge, which he disclosed by transcendental logic; the book was extremely long, sprawling, and at times structurally disjointed; and the age of bad writing in philosophy began with the first *Critique*, the greatest work of modern Western philosophy.[40]

Pure Reason and the Bounds of Sense

One of Kant's major achievements in the first *Critique* was to convince philosophers and the public that the history of philosophy led to him. In his telling, there were two kinds of philosophy worth considering, both were partly justified and partly wrong, and his critical idealism was the solution. Rationalists taught that we cannot know anything about things-in-themselves except through pure reason and logic; thus they made substantive knowledge claims apart from experience. Empiricists taught that we cannot know anything about things-in-themselves except that which we glean from our experience of them; thus they contended that all knowledge derives from sensation and reflection.

Kant rejected and fused aspects of both traditions. He hammered against metaphysical presumption, but he also urged that knowledge has an *a priori* component that allows rational subjects to make synthetic *a priori* judgments about the world. Synthetic *a priori* claims are not about reality per se, Kant argued. They are about reality only as it is experienced by subjects possessing certain *a priori* principles. Metaphysics, in Kant's conception, was about the requisite conditions of experience, which he called transcendental. There are three forms of such conditions, he asserted: the forms of sensibility, understanding, and reason.

The forms of sensibility are space and time, which are subjective conditions of knowledge. We view the world as spatial and temporal, Kant argued, not because space and time are out there as objects of perception, but because they are necessary conditions of all experience. Human subjects, being finite, cannot see things as they are in themselves. We can only experience in and through the pure forms of sensibility, which are space and time. Kant explained: "Objects are *given* to us by means of sensibility, and it alone yields us *intuitions;* they are *thought* through the understanding, and from the understanding arise *concepts.* But all thought must, directly or indirectly, by way of certain characters, relate ultimately to intuitions, and therefore, with us, to sensibility, because in no other way can an object be given to use."[41]

Intuition apprehends objects of sense through the forms of space and time. These representations are unified by the understanding, which contains pure forms or concepts that Kant, following Aristotle, called categories. To explain how such diverse entities as the particulars of the external world and the pure concepts of mind can be related, Kant pointed to the universal applicability of time, for both the particulars of the external world and the pure concepts of the mind exist in time. Time and space, besides not being realities that reason apprehends in the world, are not ideas innate in the mind either, Kant insisted. They are essential preconditions of thought through which the mind receives representations of objects, "and which therefore must also always affect the concept of these objects." Human reason makes sense of the world by applying its *a priori* categories of understanding to phenomena perceived by the senses.[42]

Kant postulated twelve categories under four headings, insisting that there had to be exactly twelve such categories. The four headings were quantity, quality, relation, and modality. Unity, plurality, and totality are categories of quantity; reality, negation, and limitation belong to quality; subsistence, causality, and social reciprocity are relational; and possibility/impossibility, existence/nonexistence, and necessity/contingency are categories of modality. These categories, he argued, make knowledge of phenomena possible by unifying the manifold of intuition (the plurality of representations or sensations given by the object through intuition) into a thought for consciousness. There are three steps to knowing something. The manifold of pure intuition is given, it is synthesized by the imagination, and the concepts unify the synthesis.[43]

Does that mean that the categories have a wider application than the concepts of space and time? If the categories enable knowledge claims about things not belonging to the world of spatio-temporal experience, how far can one take them? Theologians invoked the concept of causality in proving God's existence, yet they also claimed that God is beyond space and time. Was that legitimate? Kant agreed with Hume that invoking causality to prove God's existence is not legitimate. However, Kant rejected Hume's contention that the concept of causality, being derived from experience, is meaningful only within experience. In Kant's telling, Hume failed to grasp that the understanding might, through its concepts, create the very experience in which its concepts are found. Thus Hume fell back on a weak resort to subjective necessity, confining causality to experience. Hume tried to explain too much by appealing to mere custom, which, as Kant explained, "arises from repeated association in experience, and which comes mistakenly to be regarded as objective."[44]

That failed to account for the scientific *a priori* knowledge that we do possess, Kant admonished, namely, pure mathematics and the science of nature. Since the categories are *a priori* concepts, they are independent of experience. The tricky question is whether the categories, which make experiential knowledge possible through their independence from experience, also make other kinds of knowledge possible. In 1770, in his Inaugural Dissertation, Kant made a case for saying yes. Now he made a convoluted, messy case for the view that the categories, though necessary for experiential knowledge, do not provide substantive knowledge of objects independent of space and time.[45]

This analysis, the key to the first *Critique,* he called the Transcendental Deduction of the categories. Kant's first edition of the first *Critique* struggled for 21 pages with it, but failed to demonstrate the unity of what he called pure apperception (the original consciousness that is the necessary condition of experience), objective consciousness, and judgment. Thus he substantially rewrote this section in the second edition of 1787, pressing hard on the functional unity of the categories. In both editions Kant twisted and turned, piling up arguments that didn't always prove his points or even stay on the subject. Eminent Kant scholar H. J. Paton, summarizing his painstaking interpretive efforts, remarked in 1936: "The crossing of the Great Arabian Desert can scarcely be a more exhausting task than is the attempt to master the windings and twistings of the Transcendental Deduction."[46]

But Kant's central contention in both versions of his Transcendental Deduction can be stated plainly: The categories are possible concepts to the extent that they make experience possible and *only* to that extent. They are empty when applied to anything beyond experience. The version of the Transcendental Deduction on which Kant rested, in the second edition, began with the manifold of pure intuition and a spontaneous act of combination performed by the understanding. This act of combination, which he called synthesis, is the source of all combination. In addition to the manifold and its synthetic acts, the concept of combination requires a representation of the unity of the manifold, for in Kant's theory, a combination is precisely a representation of the *synthetic unity* of the manifold. The representation of unity cannot arise out of the combination, Kant reasoned; it is that which, by adding itself to the representation of the manifold, "first makes possible the concept of the combination." This unity precedes all concepts of combination and is not the category of unity itself, "for all categories are grounded in logical functions of judgment, and in these functions combination, and therefore unity of given concepts, is already thought." The category of unity presupposes combination.[47]

The manifold of intuition, although given, is not represented, Kant argued; otherwise the "I think" of self-consciousness would not be able to accompany every representation that I may have. In Kant's words, "for otherwise something would be represented in me which could not be thought at all, and that is equivalent to saying that the representation would be impossible, or at least nothing to me." The kind of representation that is given prior to all thought is intuition. The manifold of intuition has a necessary relationship to the "I think" of self-consciousness as an act of spontaneity. Only that which can be combined in a unified consciousness can be related to the "I think." Kant called this act of spontaneity "pure apperception," distinguished from empirical apperception, because the pure form generates the representation "I think" and cannot be accompanied by other representations. The unity of pure apperception he called the "transcendental unity of self-consciousness" to designate that *a priori* knowledge can arise from it. This unity is necessary and self-identical, Kant stressed. My representations are mine only to the extent that I grasp the manifold of representations in one consciousness. The unity of apperception is expressed, most purely, in the statement, "I am I." Kant explained, "For through the 'I,' as simple representation, nothing manifold is given; only in intuition, which is distinct from the "I," can a manifold be given; and only through *combination* in one consciousness can it be thought." The understanding can only think, and every self is a necessary synthesis of representations.[48]

For Kant, the principle of apperception was "the highest principle in the whole sphere of human knowledge," and the transcendental unity of apperception – the unity of the manifold given in intuition with a concept of the object – was both subjective and objective. The subjective unity of consciousness is a "determination of inner sense," he observed. But the conditions of the transcendental unity of apperception are the very conditions under which consciousness of objects occurs. An object is that in which the manifold of given intuitions is combined, which requires a unity of consciousness. Oddly, Kant made a stronger defense of the objective unity of self-consciousness in the first edition; in the second, he covered too much ground with a bad sentence: "The pure form of intuition in time, merely as intuition in general, which contains a given manifold, is subject to the original unity of consciousness, simply through the necessary relation of the manifold of the intuition to the one "*I think*," and so through the pure synthesis of understanding which is the *a priori* underlying ground of the empirical synthesis. Only the original unity is objectively valid." In other words, the unity of pure apperception is objective for two reasons: It apprehends its unity by discovering unity in the given, and the process of unifying the manifold is the same one by which representations acquire reference to objects.[49]

On the other hand, Kant's second edition significantly strengthened his concept of the Transcendental Deduction by adding an analysis of judgment that sought to unify his theory of the categories. Contrary to logic textbooks, Kant argued, judgment is not the representation of a relation between two concepts, since that could refer to any ideas connected by association. The textbook definition wrongly failed to determine in what the relation consists. Kant contended that judgment is about relations of a particular kind, namely, "the manner in which given modes of knowledge are brought to the objective unity of apperception." Judgments distinguish the *objective* unity of representations from the subjective unity, indicating the relation of objectively unified representations to pure apperception. Even empirical judgments, despite being contingent, have this quality, Kant argued. To judge that a given body is heavy, for example, is to imply that the two representations are conjoined subjectively in one's perception, but judgment is about something else – representations connecting in the object. No matter how often the perception occurs or what the state of the perceiver may be, a judgment such as "the body is heavy" refers to two representations that are conjoined in the object. The "is" is a relational term through which the subjective meaning, whatever it may be, is distinguished from the objective unity of given representations.[50]

A judgment is a mode of connecting cognitions to the objective unity of apperception, and the categories are the conditions through which pure apperception occurs. These were the essential planks of Kant's Transcendental Deduction, which yielded the verdict that the categories have no wider application than to objects of experience, though Kant piled on supplementary arguments. Thinking and knowing an object are decidedly different things, he stressed. All knowing involves a concept through which an object in general is thought (the category) and an intuition through which an object is given. Without an intuition corresponding to the concept, the concept remains merely a thought lacking an object, and no knowledge comes of it. In that case, there is simply nothing, as far as one can tell, to which one's thought applies. Under the conditions of sensibility (space and time), things are given to reason only as perceptions (representations accompanied by a sensation). Thus the pure concepts of understanding, even when they are applied to *a priori* intuitions such as mathematical concepts, yield knowledge only to the extent that they apply to empirical intuitions. The categories do not provide any knowledge of things, Kant contended. They serve only to make empirical knowledge possible: "The categories, as yielding knowledge of *things,* have no kind of application, save only in regard to things which may be objects of possible experience."[51]

Critique of Pure Reason, though steeped in transcendental analysis, fiercely resisted applying it to subjects transcending the bounds of sense. In Kantian theory, form was abstracted from content with a logical zeal that prized the purity of pure concepts. Kant described some concepts as empirical, possessing a sensible content actualized in thought or reality, but the transcendental concepts that made knowledge possible were purely formal, lacking any content. Purely formal entities controlled the structure of all human knowledge of phenomena.

But that raised the question of how purely formal categories apply to phenomena. How can pure forms impinge on sensuous particularity? Kant realized that he had a problem bridging from the purity of his categories to anything in the real world. He allowed that no category, such as causality, can be intuited through sense or observed. No one ever saw or felt causality: "How, then, is the *subsumption* of intuitions under pure concepts, the *application* of a category to appearances, possible?"[52]

His solution introduced "a third thing," the transcendental schema, which mediated between the categories and appearances through the pure form of time. Since time is the pure form of inner sense, Kant reasoned (just as space is the pure form of outer sense), all representations and thoughts occur in time. The categories are actualized through time and applied to sensuous appearances, and the schema must be applied as a rule. In itself, Kant argued, the schema is always a product of imagination. But the imaginative synthesis aims only at unifying the determination of the sensibility, not at any particular intuition or image. Thus the schema is always distinct from the image. Kant wrote: "This representation of a universal procedure of imagination in providing an image for a concept, I entitle the schema of this concept."[53]

The schema, not images of objects, underlies all pure concepts. Consciousness becomes aware of an entity as a member of a class subsumed by a given category. To apply a concept, Kant argued, the mind must know the rule from which an image of the entity can be correlated with an image of the category, which is the schema, the category in time. The schema of a triangle, for example, exists only in thought. No image of a right-angled or obtuse-angled triangle is as valid for all triangles as the schema underlying the pure concept of a triangle. The schema is a rule of synthesis of the imagination through which the categories and intuition come together to create the possibility of experience. To apply a concept, one must know how to make images.[54]

The first edition of the first *Critique* took two passes at defining Kant's transcendental idealism. Both definitions straightforwardly identified appearances with representations, not with an object in itself or a perspective on objects in themselves: "By *transcendental idealism* I mean the doctrine that appearances are to be regarded as being, one and all, representations only, not things in themselves, and that time and space are therefore only sensible forms of our intuition, not determinations given as existing by themselves, nor conditions of objects viewed as things in themselves." Immediately upon defining his position for the first time, Kant contrasted it to transcendental realism, the doctrine that time and space are given in themselves independently of sensibility: "The transcendental realist thus interprets outer appearances (their reality being taken as granted) as things-in-themselves, which exist independently of us and of our sensibility, and which are therefore outside us – the phrase 'outside us' being interpreted in conformity with pure concepts of understanding."[55]

Transcendental realists wrongly supposed that objects of the senses, to be external, must exist by themselves. Kant countered that transcendental idealism, correctly understood, does not deny or doubt the existence of matter. Transcendental idealism is perfectly compatible with empirical realism, because matter, for the transcendental idealist, is a species of representation. As long as one bears in mind that space is a representation within knowing subjects, there is no contradiction in describing matter as an external representation relating perceptions to things that appear in space. Matter is a species of representation that relates perceptions "to the space in which all things are external to one another, while yet the space itself is in us."[56]

Kant began with Descartes in order to get somewhere else: I am conscious of my representations. Therefore, these representations and I exist. External objects, however, being mere appearances, are "nothing but a species of my representations." External objects are something only through somebody's representations – "apart from them they are nothing." Kant stressed that the existence of external things and the existence of myself both depend on the "immediate witness of my self-consciousness." The only difference between them is that the representation of myself belongs entirely to inner sense, while the representations marking external things belong also to outer sense. In both cases the objects in question are "nothing but representations." Transcendental idealism is a type of empirical realism because it acknowledges the reality of matter as an appearance that is immediately perceived, not something inferred. Thus it differs from what Kant, in the second edition of the first *Critique,* called "the usual type of idealism" which doubts or denies the existence of external things.[57]

This definition is the goldmine of interpretations of Kant as a subjectivist. Kant reinforced it on the only other occasion that he defined transcendental idealism in the first *Critique:* "Everything intuited in space and time, and therefore all objects of any experience possible to us, are nothing but appearances, that is, mere representations, which, in the manner in which they are represented, as extended beings, or as series of alterations, have no independent existence outside our thoughts." Here again, Kant described appearances as representations detached from objects in themselves. Appearances are distinct entities identified with representations, not aspects of an object in itself or a perspective on objects in themselves. That is, Kant did not refer to appearances *of* things-in-themselves, a realistic turn that would have rendered appearances as the way by which an independent reality manifests itself in human knowing. Representations, Kant argued, do not detach from objects in themselves. Appearances are representations, without qualification, and representations depend entirely on the perceiving subject.[58]

Kant believed that his combination of transcendental idealism and empirical realism saved his position from subjectivism. He was against transcendental realism because it claimed too much – that the way objects appear to us is how they are in themselves. He was against empirical idealism because it led to skepticism (Descartes) or denial (Leibniz and Berkeley) about the existence of an external world. Kant never seriously doubted the existence of the empirical world. The objects of consciousness, he believed, whatever they are, are real. We cannot claim to know what things are in themselves, or even that things-in-themselves definitely exist. We can only hypothesize that they exist, and we must accept that we do not necessarily know them through appearances. The crucial choice is between the empirical realism of transcendental idealism and the skeptical or dogmatic denial of empirical idealism. If Kant was going to be an idealist, he had to be the kind that affirmed the existence of external objects in the empirical sense. Even if we realize that we know things only as appearances, there is no reason to opt for the view that we do not see things in space.

Our representations of objects in space are reliable, except when they are not. Kant's second edition of the first *Critique* was stronger on the caveat, inspiring a torturous addition on the refutation of idealism, but the first edition wrestled with the problem that our representations are sometimes deceptive. Sometimes a deception is caused by a sensory illusion or a false judgment of another kind, he acknowledged. Sometimes it is caused by a delusion. To avoid being deceived, we must determine whether the representation is consistent with empirical laws: "Whatever is connected with a perception according to empirical laws, is actual." Thus, the perception of external objects is not immediate, a point that Kant tacitly conceded to skeptical idealists even as he implored against skeptical idealism; the validity of perceptions must be determined by empirical tests. Empirical idealism, Kant insisted, although clever, is "sufficiently refuted" by the proof of outer perception that something actual exists in space, notwithstanding that this space is in itself a mere form of representations and that all outer appearances are also mere representations.[59]

That was paradoxical enough. Kant heightened the paradox by taking on the problem of spatial perception. Unless one argues that spatial objects are illusory, Kant acknowledged, it is undeniable that they are three-dimensional. However, ideas have no length, breadth, or depth. Ideas – representations – belong to inner sense, and the objects of inner sense cannot be in space, a point that Kant established in the opening section (the Transcendental Aesthetic) of the first *Critique*. So how should one account for spatiality? If our ideas do not represent three-dimensionality, how does it happen that things-in-themselves are represented as spatial? How is the outer intuition of space, "with its filling-in of shape and motion," a possibility for a thinking subject? How does a thinking subject interact with things-in-themselves to yield spatial perception? What kind of ontological status does the object of representation possess? If the object is only mental, it cannot be three-dimensional, but if it is the actual thing represented – something more than mental – that would be a transcendental realist answer.[60]

Kant never solved this problem on his terms. We cannot understand how outer intuition is possible in a thinking subject, he concluded. The question exceeds the limits of experience, for we know nothing about the transcendental object that causes this type of representation: "This is a question which no man can possibly answer. This gap in our knowledge can never be filled; all that can be done is to indicate it through the ascription of outer appearances to that transcendental object which is the cause of this species of representations, but of which we can have no knowledge whatsoever and of which we shall never acquire any concept." It is legitimate, Kant contended, even necessary, to treat such appearances as objects in themselves without claiming to understand the ground of their possibility as appearances.[61]

In the course of wrestling with this problem, however, Kant invoked a distinction about appearances that complicated his subjectivism. Basically, he applied the distinction between the transcendental and empirical levels to the language of appearance. The question of how an appearance can be a three-dimensional spatial object is a problem at the empirical level, Kant suggested. Here, an appearance is a specific kind of thing in experience, an object of outer sense. As a representation, however, an appearance is transcendental, something set against the thing-in-itself that lies beyond all experience. In this transcendental sense of the term, an appearance involves a relation between perceiving subjects and independent objects. It is how a thing-in-itself appears to a perceiving subject. Empirical idealism reduced appearances to entities; transcendental realism reduced appearances to monadic properties or things-in-themselves; Kant contended that both terms of this relation are necessary for there to be an appearance. Frederick Beiser explains, "According to this sense of appearance, it is simply a false dilemma to say that spatial objects must be material or mental, because this would be to treat appearances as if they were some kind of entity or monadic property. What is spatial, then, are the appearances *of* things-in-themselves, their manner of appearing to a human sensibility, or how they are perceived by it."[62]

This idea of appearances as aspects of things made only furtive appearances in the first *Critique*. In the Transcendental Aesthetic Kant vaguely described spatial appearances as being *of* things-in-themselves, having two sides. One side is the object viewed in and by itself; the other is through the form of the intuition of an object. The form appears in the subject to which the object appears, not in the object in itself. In his section on Phenomena and Noumena, Kant contended that the idea of an appearance implies that it is the appearance of some reality. This was the verdict of his Transcendental Aesthetic, he declared: Sensibility deals with the *mode* in which things-in-themselves appear. Moreover, this verdict follows from the concept of an appearance in general, "Namely, that something which is not in itself appearance must correspond to it." In the Paralogisms of Pure Reason, Kant argued that the unknown substratum of matter produces in our senses the intuition of something extended: "Matter is mere outer appearance, the substratum of which cannot be known through any predicate that we can assign to it. I can therefore very well admit the possibility that it is in itself simple, although owing to the manner in which it affects our senses it produces in us the intuition of the extended and so of the composite."[63]

This idea of appearances as "aspects of things" *(rerum species)* grew stronger in Kant's work after the first *Critique* evoked reviews condemning him as a skeptical subjective idealist. Risking ambiguity of another sort, Kant contended that appearances are representations in us *and* they are representations of things-in-themselves. In his view, this ambiguity was not incoherent as long as one stuck to a Kantian view of the limits of knowledge, something that post-Kantians refused to do. We can think of appearances as aspects of things-in-themselves, Kant argued, but we cannot claim to know that they are. Epistemology is more modest than metaphysics. All that we can do is make the best possible account on the basis of what we know, without claiming to know ontologically that appearances are aspects of things-in-themselves. In the Transcendental Aesthetic, Kant contended that space and time are merely the conditions under which objects are given to us, they are valid only for objects of the senses, and beyond these limits they represent nothing. In the second edition of the first *Critique* he stressed that the categories are similarly limited. The categories do not provide any knowledge of things, even with the aid of pure intuition; they provide knowledge only as they are applied to *empirical* intuition toward the possibility of attaining *empirical* knowledge. All that we can do is rest content with empirical knowledge, "what we entitle experience."[64]

Kant's favorite image for the domain of understanding was an island, "enclosed by nature itself within unalterable limits." With unusual drama he asserted that this island is the land of truth "surrounded by a wide and stormy ocean, the native home of illusion, where many a fog bank and many a swiftly melting iceberg give the deceptive appearance of farther shores, deluding the adventurous seafarer ever anew with empty hopes, and engaging him in enterprises which he can never abandon and yet is unable to carry to completion." On Kant's telling, all proofs of God's existence fall into this category, along with all claims to know things as they are in themselves. The first *Critique* had sections on the "impossibility" of the ontological, cosmological, and teleological proofs and the "illusion" of a transcendental proof. Kant recycled his negative arguments from *The One Possible Basis* and dropped his transcendental proof, although he urged that it was still a good argument, just not a proof. To claim that one has proved God's existence is to show that one has not understood the problem. On things in themselves, he famously distinguished between the appearances of things (phenomena) and the unknowable reality of things as they are in themselves (noumena), and developed a doctrine of the transcendental object, but dropped the latter in the second edition.[65]

Kant's exceedingly difficult attempt to distinguish between phenomena and noumena began with a summary of the Transcendental Analytic: Apart from the manifold of sensibility, the categories are merely logical functions lacking any content. Though the categories are *a priori*, they have to be supplemented through empirical intuition. The pure concepts of understanding admit only of empirical use, just as the principles of pure understanding apply only to objects experienced by the senses. The categories yield only "rules for the exposition of appearances" and cannot be extended beyond possible experience.[66]

The concept of a noumenon, however, being unknowable, negative, and yet the true real, was hard to explain. Kant struggled with it in both editions, rewriting this section extensively in the second edition. In the first edition he developed a doctrine of the transcendental object, a positive sense of the noumenon that opened a Pandora's box of possibilities about special modes of intuition. In the second edition he slammed the box shut, eliminating the transcendental object from his sections on Phenomena and Noumena, the Transcendental Deduction, and the Paralogisms of Pure Reason, although he let it stand in his sections on the Antinomies of Pure Reason and the Second Analogy of Experience, apparently because tearing it out of the latter sections would have required more extensive rewriting than he could bear.[67]

In both editions Kant described the noumenon as the idea of a thing-in-itself that is not an object of the senses and is not positive in any way. Essentially it signified the thought of something in general, in which one abstracts from everything belonging to sensible intuition. A noumenon is a thing so far as it is not an object of sensible intuition. But what kind of thing is that? How can it signify a true object by Kant's principles? In the first edition, Kant reasoned that for a noumenon to signify a true object distinct from all phenomena, it is not enough to free one's thought of all conditions of sensible intuition: "I must likewise have ground for *assuming* another kind of intuition, different from the sensible, in which such an object may be given. For otherwise my thought, while indeed without contradictions, is none the less empty." Kant admitted that he could not prove that sensible intuition is the only possible kind of intuition. On the other hand, he also could not prove that another kind of intuition is possible: "Consequently, although our thought can abstract from all sensibility, it is still an open question whether the notion of a noumenon be not a mere form of a concept, and whether, when this separation has been made, any object whatsoever is left."[68]

In the second edition he wrested more control over his most elusive concept by eliminating the transcendental object, at least in the most relevant sections. Any suggestion that the noumenon has a positive content or sense must be eliminated, he urged. To apply the categories to objects that are not appearances is to assume that some type of intellectual intuition exists. But sensible intuition is the only type that we know, and the Transcendental Analytic made no sense if the categories extended beyond objects of experience. Kant allowed that perhaps there are intelligible entities to which human sensible intuition has no relation. But since the concepts of understanding are forms corresponding to our sensible intuition, it is pointless to speculate on the subject; there is no knowledge. Kant realized that his critics would say the same thing about the thing-in-itself, but he needed the idea of the noumenon to account for the given manifold and the ground of moral freedom. The idea of a thing-in-itself that is not a thing of the senses is not contradictory, he assured. It is crucially important, wholly negative, and a thing of pure understanding.[69]

This idea cast a long, ironic shadow over modern theology. Kant conceived his unknowable *Ding an sich* as a brake on metaphysical speculation in philosophy and theology, which it did for Kantians. Yet his dualism of known and unknown worlds also sparked an explosion of high-flying metaphysical systems claiming that the world exists as the externalization of consciousness. His metaphysical and religious views, though enormously influential, yielded offshoots that turned his dualistic agnosticism on its head. For much of modern theology, the deficiencies of Kant's truncated metaphysics and his moral rendering of religion were more important and fecund than the things he got right.

For Kant, metaphysics had a very limited role and so did religion. Traditional metaphysicians sought to prove that the world has a beginning, there is something simple, freedom exists, and there is a necessary Supreme Being. Kant countered that theoretical reason proves nothing either way concerning such matters. The arguments for and against such claims are equally strong, as both the thesis and its denial follow logically from principles of reason; Kant called this impasse the antinomy of reason. Though Enlightenment was all about using reason to its utmost capacities, Kant cautioned that theoretical reason is not reliable for the things that matter most. To get as much out of reason as possible, and to give morality the exalted status it deserves, and to keep religion in its place as a servant of morality, philosophy must distinguish strongly between pure theoretical reason and pure practical reason.

Moral Religion Within the Bounds of Reason

Critique of Pure Reason famously explained that the theoretical knowledge of pure reason is knowledge of "what is," while the practical knowledge of pure practical reason is knowledge of "what ought to be." Traditional metaphysics, whether Platonist, Aristotelian, Thomist, or Enlightenment rationalist, sought to prove the existence of the soul, immortality, and God. Kant countered that unaided theoretical reason cannot establish the existence of transcendent realities such as God or immortality. The theoretical proofs of God's existence do not prove anything, for scientific reason is limited, conditioned, and sense-bound, restricted to the web of sense experience within the space/time continuum. Thus it cannot know of spiritual realities transcending space and time. The place for religion is in practical reason, where the necessity of moral laws, to Kant, was unquestionable. He put it with typical laboriousness: "Now since there are practical laws which are absolutely necessary, that is, the moral laws, it must follow that if these necessarily presuppose the existence of any being as the condition of the possibility of their *obligatory* power, this existence must be *postulated;* and this for the sufficient reason that the conditioned, from which the inference is drawn to this determinate condition, is itself known *a priori* to be absolutely necessary."[70]

Kant's metaphysic revolved around two conceptual pivots, the idea of the ideality of space and time, and the idea of a cognizable and yet supersensible freedom. The latter belongs to practical reason and is the basis of morality, which is the basis of religion. To Kant it was transcendently important to say that religion has a secure home and that it rests entirely in the moral concerns of practical reason. In *Foundations of the Metaphysics of Morals* (1785), *Critique of Practical Reason* (1788) and *Religion Within the Boundaries of Mere Reason* (1793), he explained that human beings are moral agents as well as creatures of sense experience. Human experience includes a sense of moral obligation not subsumed under or explained by sense-bound theoretical reason. Freedom is a basic idea to which theoretical reason leads us, but we cannot prove its existence on theoretical grounds. Rather, our moral experience, or more precisely, the experience of our morality, impels us to believe in the reality of freedom, which gives us the right to postulate the reality of God and immortality as the ground of moral faith.[71]

Kant did not believe that metaphysics is useless or that pure reason is not practical. His ethical theory of freedom and the moral law – which he prized above everything – would have made no sense had he believed either of these things. For Kant, two kinds of metaphysics were still imperative after he destroyed the old metaphysics in the *Critique of Pure Reason:* the metaphysics of nature expounded the *a priori* principles of what is, and the metaphysics of morals expounded the *a priori* principles of what ought to be. *Critique of Pure Reason* modeled the new, restrained, critical metaphysics of nature, taking an inventory of scientific rationality by expounding a system of *a priori* knowledge from pure concepts. *Foundations of the Metaphysics of Morals* expounded Kant's Enlightenment individualistic ethic of the categorical imperative, in which autonomous rational beings provided their own moral laws by universalizing situations of apparent norm conflict. *Critique of Practical Reason* expounded the *a priori* laws of conduct, conceiving the metaphysics of morals as the rational understanding of the moral law and its ramifications. *Religion Within the Boundaries of Mere Religion* explained what kind of religion came from taking Enlightenment rationality and moral duty with utter seriousness.

Emphatically Kant based religion on morality, not the other way around, because religion is essentially moral and it has no warranted claim to knowledge except by its connection to morals, where the mode of knowing is strictly practical. In the preface to the second edition of the *Critique of Pure Reason* he put it boldly, declaring that he had found it "necessary to deny *knowledge,* in order to make room for *faith.*" However, the closing section of Kant's first *Critique* and his subsequent writings on practical reason and religion made moral arguments for God's existence that seemed, to many interpreters, to erase Kant's distinction between knowledge and faith. Did he not make a knowledge claim for religion through its connection to morality? More precisely, did Kant's moral arguments for God's existence not amount to a substitute natural theology?[72]

Here Kant's interpreters have quarreled for centuries. Some hold fast to the dichotomy between faith and knowledge, others claim that Kant (wisely or not) crafted his own form of natural theology after destroying the traditional types, some contend that he failed to sustain a consistent position, and others contend for a mixture of these views, for example, that he ultimately rejected his own misguided argument. Critics that see little difference between Kant's moral arguments for God's existence and the traditional speculative proofs usually contend that he undermined or contradicted his own argument. In my view, Kant generally held to his distinction between knowledge and faith, which corresponded to his distinction between theoretical reason and practical reason, but these distinctions broke down at the point of intersection between the two *Critiques* – Kant's grounding of freedom in moral experience, which yielded his arguments for God and immortality.[73]

Kant regarded his moral arguments defending God's existence as justifications of faith or belief, not as claims to knowledge. For him, as for the German language, faith and belief were the same thing, *Glaube*. Faith and knowledge are valid, justified, and "sufficient" (*zureichendes*) ways of holding judgments, Kant argued. Both are forms of conviction (*Überzeugung*) as distinguished from opinion (*Meinung*), which is a judgment lacking sufficiency. But faith and knowledge are sufficient in different ways, he reasoned. There are three degrees of sufficiency in holding a judgment: Mere opinion has no sufficiency, faith has subjective sufficiency alone, and knowledge (*Wissen*) has subjective and objective sufficiency. On matters of pure mathematics, Kant noted, one does not hold opinions; in this area, either we have knowledge or we have no business holding a judgment. But belief is a slippery area, because terribly important issues are at stake, yet knowledge is lacking. Kant defined belief as the "theoretically insufficient holding of a thing to be true" from the standpoint of practical reason. Believing refers either to a skill, which is concerned with contingent ends, or to morality, where the ends are absolutely necessary and religion is grounded.[74]

Kant stressed that theoretical knowledge is universal, being valid for everyone. But moral faith, he argued, is no less universal, however lacking in objective sufficiency. There is such a thing as a justified, even necessary, conviction that is subjective in character. Faith, being essentially different from knowledge, cannot be built up or strengthened by appeals to proofs, theoretical claims, or evidence. Faith is personal and subjective, holding to crucially important convictions in full awareness that objective sufficiency does not apply to them. In the realm of faith, which Kant called "moral faith" when describing the ideal, something has to happen: The believer is compelled to conform to the moral law. Kant moved straight to the upshot: "The end is here irrefragably established, and according to such insight as I can have, there is only one possible condition under which this end can connect with all other ends, and thereby have practical validity, namely, that there be a God and a future world."[75]

Without a divine Moral Guarantor there can be no moral unity of ends. Kant insisted that we cannot pursue the good if we do not believe it is real and attainable. To act as moral beings, we must postulate the idea of God as a condition for the possibility of the highest good, believing as we must in order to live as we ought. Speaking of his belief in God and a future world, Kant put it personally: "I am certain that nothing can shake this belief, since my moral principles would thereby be themselves overthrown, and I cannot disclaim them without becoming abhorrent in my own eyes." He could not imagine living with himself if he did not live in a moral universe. The alternative was moral nihilism and despair. Life had no meaning on these terms, and his passionate intellectual and moral endeavors would have been pointless.[76]

On the one hand, Kant cautioned that no one *knows* if there is a God and a future life; on the other hand, he called his conviction of God's existence a "moral certainty," because he never really doubted the existence of moral truth. Every day he pursued the truth and struggled to obey the moral law; he would not pretend to believe that life might really be meaningless. To say, "It is morally certain that there is a God," is not quite correct, Kant admonished; that smacks too much of an unwarranted theoretical claim. Moral certainty is personal and practical, taking the form, "I am certain that there is a God," which Kant affirmed. Since he knew himself to be in "little danger" of losing his moral convictions, and since believing in God and a future world was so deeply interwoven with these moral convictions, there was "equally little cause for fear" that he would ever lose his faith in God: "I am certain that there is a God" was no exaggeration.[77]

Does that mean that everyone who wants to be good has to believe in God? Kant replied that dogmatic atheism is definitely out of bounds; one cannot be faithful to the moral law and negate its ground simultaneously. At a minimum, one must say that God might exist. Kant called this minimum a "negative belief." He doubted that negative believing gives rise to moral sentiments, yet at least it serves as a check on nihilistic evil sentiments. Outright atheism is intolerable; religious skepticism, though tolerable, is far from the ideal; at the other end of the scale, all forms of religious authoritarianism were repugnant to him, plus religious ceremonies, ecclesiastical organizations, and all forms of mysticism. Kant was contemptuous of ceremonial worship, which struck him as self-degrading. He loathed petitionary prayer, which struck him as pathetic whee-dling. He refused to attend religious observances, even when his responsibilities as university rector required him to participate. *Religion Within the Boundaries of Mere Reason* abounded with sneering put-downs of "priestcraft," religious dogma, super-stition, "religious acts of cult," and anything else that detracted from the one true religion of Enlightened moral faith.[78]

Everything that human beings do to please God, except for conducting themselves morally, is a stupid waste of time and energy. *Religion Within the Boundaries of Mere Reason* said it repeatedly: "The one and true religion contains nothing but laws, i.e., practical principles ... Apart from a good life-conduct, anything which the human being supposes that he can do to become well-pleasing to God is mere religious delusion and counterfeit service of God ... It is superstitious delusion to want to become well-pleasing to God through actions that any human being can do without even needing to be a good human being." Kant was incredulous that anyone could believe that salvation has anything to do with going to church, accepting biblical myths as historical, or holding a particular theory of justification. Morality, too, as Kant explained in *Foundations of the Metaphysics of Morals,* is not really moral if it is handed down or compelled by authority. For Kant, autonomy was the supreme principle of morality. A moral belief accepted on the basis of authority is no more legitimate than any other kind of belief accepted on the basis of authority. In situations of moral perplexity, one should ask, "What should everyone do in this situation?" Kant put it formally: "Act only according to that maxim by which you can at the same time will that it should become a universal law." True morality, Kant taught, is action in accordance with self-given maxims that deserve to be universal laws for all rational beings, and true religion, subjectively considered, is the acceptance of one's self-given moral duties as divine commands and nothing else.[79]

Kant had a version of the doctrine of original sin and even the rudiments of a Christology, but to him, sadly, historic Christianity was about the wrong things. Instead of expounding its sacred narrative exclusively in the interests of morality, historic Christianity compelled people to believe propositions about matters of history and dogma. Instead of focusing on what human beings must do to become worthy of salvation, historic Christianity, especially Lutheranism, focused on dogmas about things that God supposedly did to win our salvation. *Religion Within the Boundaries of Mere Reason* distinguished between the parts of Christianity that reflected its basis in "pure rational faith" and the parts that degenerated, however inevitably, into sectarian dogmas that distracted from pure moral faith. One needs no appeal to revelation or miracles to see that human beings have a propensity or disposition *(Gesinnung)* to evil, Kant argued. From a purely rational perspective, it is terribly obvious that there is a "radical evil" in the human heart from which nobody is free and against which true religion must devote itself.[80]

Kant cautioned that we cannot say where, exactly, this radical evil, which is inherent in human rationality, came from. It is inscrutable, yet certain things about it can be read off from the universal human condition. It cannot be known in itself, it is characteristic of every human being, and it is something that human beings freely adopt. Kant identified three grades of this natural propensity to evil. Everywhere, he observed, human beings show the frailty of human nature by failing to comply with moral norms against lying, cheating, murder, and the like. Secondly, human beings everywhere show the impurity of human nature by adulterating moral incentives with immoral ones. Thirdly, human beings everywhere show the depravity of human nature by adopting outright evil maxims. On frailty, even the morally earnest Apostle Paul was an example, lamenting his inability to follow the moral law that he preached. On impurity, Kant noted that people rarely if ever act out of a pure motive of moral duty, even when they act according to the moral law. On depravity, every page of history testifies to the corruption and perversion of the human heart, which uses the power of free moral choice to do evil, reversing the ethical order of things.[81]

This is what religion should be about and against, Kant contended. The very propensity to evil in human beings is evil itself, even if it did not originate in any free act in time; Kant took the Adam and Eve story of Genesis to be an illustration of the problem, not an explanation. As for how this propensity could be morally evil if it did not originate in a free act in time, Kant reasoned that it originated in a free act that was not in time. Every propensity is either physical or moral, but there cannot be a physical propensity to moral evil, because moral evil is necessarily a byproduct of freedom. Nothing is morally evil that is not the consequence of a freely chosen deed, and every moral propensity includes a subjective determining ground of the power of free will that precedes every deed.

This idea of a subjective determining power – the noumenal ground of moral freedom – provided the basis for Kant's distinction between two kinds of deeds at issue in the problem of moral evil. The determining noumenal ground of freedom yields acts of free will that transcend time, while the second kind of deed is empirical, applying to acts in time. Original sin (*peccatum originarium*) is grounded in noumenal reality, which is inscrutable, not phenomenal, and derivative sins (*peccatum derivativum*) are empirical transgressions of the moral law in time. Original sin remains in the human heart even if one resists committing derivative sins: "The former is an intelligible deed, cognizable through reason alone apart from any temporal condition; the latter is sensible, empirical, given in time [*factum phenomenon*]."[82]

Kant's religion, like the ethic of which it was part, was centered on the moral aspiration of being worthy of happiness. In religious form it asked the question, "How can I be well-pleasing to God?" This question is not about escaping divine punishment, he stressed – an egocentric, amoral question that misses the point of religion. The object of moral aspiration is a pure heart, not a utilitarian outcome such as avoiding hellfire or attaining the greatest good for the greatest number, degraded schemes for which the moral good is merely instrumental. Kant urged that morality is an intrinsic good and that only the truly good will is good without qualification. All morally reflective people know that they are not as good as they ought to be. The moral ideal is to be so pure in one's willing that one would be pleased with oneself even if one knew one's heart as fully as God knows it. Toward this end Kant had a place for the Christ figure, which he called the "personified idea of the good principle."[83]

Kant explained, "Now it is our universal human duty to *elevate* ourselves to this ideal of moral perfection, i.e., to the prototype of moral disposition in its entire purity, and for this the very idea, which is presented to us by reason for emulation, can give us force." But we are not the authors of this idea, Kant observed; moreover, as sinful beings we lack the moral power to attain a perfectly good will by our powers alone. Thus it is helpful to have a God-like human prototype of moral perfection that came down from heaven to take up our humanity. Kant cautioned that it is very hard to imagine how human beings, being "evil by nature," might renounce evil on their own and raise themselves up to the ideal of holiness. The Christian idea is more plausible – that a God-like human prototype might lift human beings to holiness by descending into their life and providing a perfect moral example: "This union with us may therefore be regarded as a state of *abasement* of the Son of God if we represent to ourselves this God-like human being, our prototype, in such a way that, though himself holy and hence not bound to submit to sufferings, he nonetheless takes these upon himself in the fullest measure for the sake of promoting the world's greatest good." For Kant the figure of Christ was the exemplary idea of a human being perfectly fulfilling his moral duties, spreading goodness as far as possible through teaching and example, and taking on suffering for the good of the world and even his enemies. Here, Kant followed the lead of G. E. Lessing's "The Education of the Human Race," where Lessing attributed a very large, but strictly moral, importance to Jesus and the Bible. A great deal of liberal Protestantism took exactly that tack in rendering the meaning of Jesus and the Bible.[84]

Religion Within the Boundaries of Mere Reason ended with a scornful assault on "priestcraft," public prayer ("a superstitious delusion"), and "all such artificially induced self-deceptions." Kant shook his head at the spectacle of rational beings presenting petitions to an all-knowing God. If God already knows what we want, what is the point of slathering him with pathetic ritual petitions? Kant warned sternly that such "fetish-making" is not harmless to society. Wherever it took hold, it had a tendency to take over, corrupting true religion. Clerical religion, instead of promoting moral faith, personal integrity, and the loyalty of subjects, led straight to hypocrisy and sham. Kant believed that his beloved Prussia had fallen deeply into religious corruption with the ascension of Friedrich Wilhelm II to the Prussian throne in 1786. The golden age of Frederick the Great had ended, giving way to Frederick's self-indulgent, adulterous, mystical, Rosicrucian brother, who appointed a slick Rosicrucian and Freemason operator, Johann Wöllner, as his minister of ecclesiastical affairs. Kant despised Friedrich Wilhelm II and his all-but-official prime minister, Wöllner. He blasted the unnamed leaders of Prussian religion and society for being more interested in ritual, theology, and preserving their privileges than in being good. Imagining themselves the favorites of heaven, they buttressed these imaginings with theological arguments and shows of piety. In his closing sentence, Kant declared that Prussia's supposed elect could "hardly withstand comparison" to humble ordinary people who concentrated on their duties, "which proves that the right way to advance is not from grace to virtue but rather from virtue to grace."[85]

That was a frontal challenge, virtually defying the king to respond, which occurred ten months after the book was published in January 1794. Friedrich Wilhelm II compelled Kant to stop writing about religion, yet even the king had to be tactful in approaching Kant, for by 1794 Kant was famous as the symbol of German Enlightenment. The first *Critique*, after being ignored for years, dominated philosophy. Kant's succeeding works lifted him to singular preeminence. By the time that Kant disclosed his views on religion, he was too big not to be treated gingerly, despite offending the king.

The Kantian Legacy

When the first *Critique* was published in 1781, Kant counted on three philosophers, besides his Königsberg colleague Kraus, to understand it and commend its importance: Johann Nicolaus Tetens, Moses Mendelssohn, and Christian Garve. But Tetens, having retired four years earlier, kept quiet. Mendelssohn, a revered Enlightenment figure, pushed the weighty book aside, pleading that his frailty and nervous disability made him unable to understand it. For eight months nobody reviewed it, and Kant feared that the book would be ignored. Like Hume's *Treatise*, the first *Critique* was too large and forbidding to find an audience. Johann Schultz, the book's first expositor, later recalled that German readers perceived it as a "sealed book" containing nothing but "hieroglyphics." Finally Garve, a prominent figure in the *Popularphilosophie* movement, published a somewhat off-kilter review that sullied the book's reputation for over a decade and enraged Kant, but which at least got a controversy going.[86]

Popularphilosophie was a popular version of the German Enlightenment. Essentially it was a German counterpart to French *philosophe*, led by intellectuals – Garve, Johann G. H. Feder, J. A. Eberhard, J. Engel, and G. A. Tittel – who were as well known in their time as Voltaire, Diderot, and D'Alembert were known in France. The popular philosophers disseminated a variable blend of Leibniz and Wolff that incorporated strands of Lockean empiricism, Scottish commonsense realism, and French *philosophe*. Most were admirers of Scottish philosopher Thomas Reid (1710–1796), who taught that sensation automatically causes belief in external objects. To go against common sense is a kind of madness or perversity, they argued, often citing Reid. The popular philosophers, though generally liberal, reformist, and in favor of intellectual freedom and religious tolerance, were stoutly against democracy and radicalism. They took for granted the need for elite rule, which included a strong state, and their own privileges, which included royal patronage. They were committed to enlightening the public and to defeating Pietist opposition to the Enlightenment. On both counts they lauded Frederick the Great for supporting intellectual freedom. Before Kant published the first *Critique,* the popular philosophers generally admired him. Afterward, following Garve and Feder, they adamantly opposed him, forging an unlikely alliance with Pietist critics.[87]

Kant's first reviewer was anonymous and heavily edited. Garve, the foremost popular philosopher of his time, submitted an overlong review of the first *Critique* to Feder, who cut and compressed it, summarizing parts of it with a polemical tone that Garve had lacked, and adding that Kant failed to acknowledge his obvious dependence on Berkeley's pure idealism. Garve was subsequently embarrassed by the tone after Kant demanded to know the author's identity. Though Garve played up Kant's debt to Hume, he did not say that the *Critique of Pure Reason* was a belabored scholastic version of Berkeley's idealism; Feder added that opinion. The review that Feder published, however, preserved Garve's essential argument, that Kant wrongly reduced matter and spirit to mere representations by contending that perception consists of nothing but representations. Garve urged that the criterion of reality must be found in some aspect of sensation, not merely in the rules of understanding. Otherwise we cannot distinguish reality from illusion. Garve and Feder, like most of the popular philosophers, admired Reid's critique of Berkeley – that Berkeley confused the object of perception with the act of perception. Feder claimed that Kant similarly reduced experience to an illusion.[88]

Kant was infuriated by the review's suggestion that he was unoriginal and, even worse, a more confused version of the thinker that he imitated but never mentioned, Berkeley. It galled him that the anonymous reviewer never mentioned the Transcendental Deduction, which was the core of the book, and that his transcendental idealism was treated as a metaphysical system, which ignored his central argument about the limits of metaphysics. He fought back with a feisty reply, *Prolegomena to Any Future Metaphysic, which May Be Called a Science* (1783), all the while hoping to see better reviews before his reply was published, which did not appear. Kant endured two more years of silence after the Garve review. It was as though no one in Germany could be bothered to read such a difficult work. Unknown to Kant, even his single reviewer had not meant to read the first *Critique.* Garve, repaying a favor, had accepted Feder's request to review Kant's latest work, assuming it would be something like *Observations on the Feeling of the Beautiful and Sublime.* The tome that Feder handed to him became a torment to Garve. Kant, in a despairing letter to his disciple, Johann Schultz, reported that nobody understood his masterwork. He fretted that all his work had been in vain.[89]

Kant's reply-book broke the silence. He was angry at his only reviewer, and at others who should have reviewed the book but didn't, and at colleagues who told him that the book defeated them. He reported that he didn't mind being compared to Hume, because he admired Hume immensely. But he and Hume disagreed about metaphysics, he deeply resented being compared to Berkeley, and he wearied of complaints that the *Critique of Pure Reason* was too hard to understand. Kant chided that many would-be readers tried "to skim through the book, and not to *think* through it." On the one hand, he sympathized, to some extent, because the book was undeniably "dry, obscure, opposed to all ordinary notions, and moreover voluminous." On the other hand, he was appalled: "I did not expect to hear from philosophers complaints of want of popularity, entertainment, and facility." Moving back to the first hand, Kant stooped to win a larger audience for his masterwork before it was too late, by writing the *Prolegomena*. On the other hand, if any reader found the *Prolegomena* to be too hard or abstract too, "let him consider that every one is not bound to study Metaphysic."[90]

In a soon-famous recollection that took him back to the early 1770s, Kant confessed that it was Hume who shook him from his "dogmatic slumber" by interrogating the connection between cause and effect. Hume never doubted that the concept of causality is correct and indispensable, Kant observed, yet he showed that reason does not establish the necessary conjunction between cause and effect that is inherent in the concept of causality. Kant's rendering of Hume's argument, though tortuously composed, was foundational for modern philosophy: If the causal relation is rational, it can be thought *a priori* and on the basis of concepts. If objects are causally related, they must be necessarily related. But reason alone does not establish how the existence of one object necessitates the existence of another object. Thus, the conjunction between cause and effect is not something that can be thought *a priori* and out of concepts. Kant put the upshot colorfully: "Hence he inferred, that reason was altogether deluded by this concept, which it considered erroneously as one of its children, whereas in reality the concept was nothing but the bastard offspring of the imagination, impregnated by experience, and so bringing certain representations under the Law of Association."[91]

Kant went that far with Hume. What he rejected was Hume's conclusion that because the causal relation is not rational, metaphysics is impossible – all that we have are imagination and custom, which produce merely subjective necessities. Hume was wrong about the impossibility of metaphysics, Kant argued. To show why Hume was wrong, however, Kant had to drag beleaguered readers through hundreds of pages of dense transcendental argument; thus the *Critique of Pure Reason* was admittedly as forbidding and abstract as defeated readers claimed. The *a priori* connections that Hume did not find, Kant deduced from the pure understanding.[92]

Kant despaired that his only reviewer judged the first *Critique* by the standards of his own commonsense metaphysical beliefs and ignored that the book was mainly about the possibility of synthetic *a priori* judgments. Then the reviewer ridiculed the book for drawing conclusions that he didn't like. Kant countered that transcendental idealism was not the book's first principle; it was the consequence of the book's solution to the question of how synthetic *a priori* judgments are possible. As for Kant's supposed Berkeleyianism, Kant noted that Berkeley denied the existence of things-in-themselves and he taught that *esse est percipi* – experience consists only of perceptions or ideas, or literally, to be is to be perceived. Kant, by contrast, stoutly defended things-in-themselves and taught that experience consists of appearances of things-in-themselves. He did not believe that the objects of perception are only ideas. He believed that objects of perception are appearances of things-in-themselves:

"All cognition of things from mere pure Understanding and Reason is nothing but mere illusion and only in experience is there truth."[93]

As for originality, Kant set the record straight: "I was the first to show that space (and time, which Berkeley overlooked) with all its determinations is known by us *a priori,* because it and time are in us as pure forms of sensibility before all perception or experience, and make all intuition and consequently all phenomena possible." This difference yielded Kant's clincher, the crucial difference between him and Berkeley: On the terms of his transcendental idealism, experience was real, but for Berkeley, experience was illusory. Kant explained that truth rests on "universal and necessary laws as its criteria." But Berkeley had no synthetic *a priori* principles; thus, in his system, experience had no criteria of truth. In fact, Berkeley rendered all experience as illusion, "whereas with me space and time (in connection with the Categories) prescribe *a priori* the law of all possible experience, and this law gives us the sure criterion for distinguishing truth from illusion."[94]

Kant's claims about Berkeley and Hume were dubious on several points. It was Berkeley's empiricism, not his idealism as Kant claimed, that committed him to denying the existence of synthetic *a priori* principles. Had Berkeley opted for rationalistic idealism, like Kant, instead of empiricist idealism, he would not have been driven logically to claim that all experience is an illusion. As for Hume, Kant underestimated his skepticism and simply didn't read enough of Hume's work. Kant overlooked that Hume exaggerated the implications of one problem, causality; he failed to challenge Hume's mistaken assertion that the causal relation is the only way to establish the concept of a connection *a priori*. In addition, Kant believed that Hume did not deny the existence of necessary synthetic judgments, which was probably mistaken.

But Kant's self-defense got the biggest thing right. The historic significance of the *Critique of Pure Reason* lay in its transcendental argument that the mind is active in producing experience out of its *a priori* categories. The mind is not passive in taking in whatever is out there, Kant insisted; at the same time, it "never came into my head" to cast doubt on the existence of external things. His transcendental idealism, for which he also liked the name "critical idealism," was about the sensuous representation of things "to which space and time especially belong," not about doubting that things exist. Kant's vigorous self-defense on this point helped him find an audience, most of which charged either that Kant wrongly exalted reason as the highest authority or that he dangerously undermined reason in the name of defending it.[95]

The popular philosophers championed the latter view, that Kant undermined the authority of reason and common sense. A mostly rival group of critics led by Friedrich Heinrich Jacobi and Kant's friend Johann G. Hamann countered that Kant wrongly lifted reason above faith and common sense. These groups tended to loath each other, yet they were indebted to the same philosophy, Scottish commonsense realism, and they both considered themselves to be defenders of reason correctly understood, which was something very different from Kant's strangely abstract combination of skepticism and dogmatism.

The leading thinkers in both groups usually espoused Reid's commonsense contention that sensations automatically cause belief in external objects. Sensations, Reid argued, despite being mental acts that give rise to knowledge, are not the direct objects of knowledge. The objects are the things of the external world towards which the acts of sense are directed. We do not acquire our beliefs about external objects by comparing ideas. Such beliefs are caused by the occurrence of a sensation and are included in the very nature of a sensation. Believing anything else is to defy the facts of experience. The Jacobi-style religious types and the popular philosophers both shook their heads that Kant defied the facts of experience by blending skepticism and dogmatism. He skewered religion and common sense, yet revived dogmatic metaphysics with a pre-Lockean belief in *a priori* ideas. His idealism contradicted common sense; his technical vocabulary and dogmatic method smacked of a new scholasticism; and he harmed either Christian faith, or natural religion, or both. Both groups charged that Kant distorted reason in the name of defending it, which confused the public about the real thing. Both attacked his doctrine about the ideality of space and time, countering that space and time are *a posteriori* concepts abstracted from particular distances and intervals, not *a priori* intuitions. The popular philosophers became so ardent about refuting Kant that they launched two anti-Kantian journals, Feder's *Philosophische Bibliothek* and Eberhard's *Philosophisches Magazin,* both of which made a creed of Feder's thesis that Kantianism was Berkeleyian solipsism wrapped in obscurantist scholasticism.[96]

Kant hated having to defend himself, so he pressed his friends and allies to do it for him. Schultz, K. C. Schmid, and Karl Leonhard Reinhold came to his defense, which relieved and gratified him. Schultz published a helpful exposition of the first *Critique* in 1784; Reinhold became prominent in the field, teaching at Jena, where he espoused a warm-hearted version of Kant's approach. Kant crossed a line with Christian Jacob Kraus, however, his closest friend after Green died. Kraus taught moral philosophy, economics, law, and other fields of practical philosophy at Königsberg. He chafed at having to defend Kant with logic-chopping abstractions that were foreign to his practical sensibility. Shortly after Kant rewarded Kraus with a diamond ring, Kraus cut off relations with him, which cut Kant deeply.[97]

Ironically, Kant's critics were more effective than his defenders in lifting him to prominence. 'The popular philosophers, and, notably, three others, helped to make him famous by blasting him. Kant's former student Johann Gottfried Herder, a Lutheran pastor and church official, blasted the so-called Enlightenment as a disastrous conceit and criticized Kant's abstract separation of thought from language. Herder's close friend, Hamann, similarly objected that Kant's mistaken purism of reason stripped philosophy of its vital basis in sensation and ordinary language. Jacobi became prominent by poking holes in Kant's faith in abstract reason. Jacobi warned that Kant did not really believe in real objects, notwithstanding his misleading statements to this effect. Kant's idealism turned real objects into subjective determinations of the soul devoid of real objectivity, Jacobi protested. For Kant, empirical objects were mere appearances, the laws of reason were prized above sensation, and the Enlightenment prejudice against sensation was left in place.[98]

Hamann was a minor civil servant in Frederick the Great's widely loathed tax office who got his job through Kant's help. Hamann's lowly station helped him see the despotic side of a regime that its privileged intellectuals tried to overlook; he had to defer to tax experts that Frederick imported from France. Embittered, but also liberated by his humiliation, Hamann developed a personal, enigmatic writing style specializing in parody. Theologically he was a Lutheran believer in the self-emptying of God and the divine power of powerlessness. Hamann loved the kenotic hymn of Philippians 2 that Christ willingly gave up equality with God to take the form of a slave. With a sharp edge he applied the spirit of kenosis theology to Enlightenment presumptions about the objectivity of reason. To Hamann, Kant's belief in the abstract purity of philosophy was ludicrous. In 1782 he began to labor on a meta-critique of Kant's first *Critique*. Herder nagged Hamann to finish the work, which took him two years to complete. Hamann's meta-critique totaled only ten pages, but in it, he anticipated the post-Kantian protest against Kant's dualism and the post-modern critique of hypostatized reason.

Hamann argued that Kant's entire project labored under a mistaken abstraction, a vain attempt to liberate reason from history, experience, and language. Kant postulated a self-sufficient noumenal realm set apart from everything belonging to the phenom-enal realm; one concept generated another, creating arbitrary dualisms: "Receptivity of language and spontaneity of concepts! From this double source of ambiguity, pure reason draws all the elements of its doctrinairism, doubt, and connoisseurship." Hamann was sarcastic, but also penetrating. He protested that when Kant was finished abstracting, he was actually proud to have nothing but a purely formal transcendental subject=X, which Hamann called "a windy sough, a magic shadow play, at most." Hamann countered that Kant's object, a special faculty called reason, does not exist. What exists are rational ways of thinking and acting in specific languages and cultural contexts. Kant's Platonism, however, stood in the way of dealing with anything real. This critique was not published until 1800, after Hamann had died; he was sensitive about offending Kant in public. But it had a significant subterranean influence, as Jacobi and Herder mined it for insights.[99]

In 1784 the *Berlinische Monatsschrift* sponsored a series of articles on the question, "What is Enlightenment?" Kant's answer was aggressive, triumphal, self-congratulatory, a bit preachy, and more than a bit snobbish: *"Enlightenment is mankind's exit from its self-incurred immaturity."* Immaturity is the inability to reason without depending on someone or something else, he declared. It is self-incurred if it is caused not by a lack of rational capacity but rather by a lack in courage and resolve. The Enlightenment was rightly named, in his view, because its motto was: "Have the courage to use your *own* understanding!" In Kant's telling, enlightenment needed nothing but freedom; moreover, the kind on which it depended was "the most harmless" of all freedoms, "the freedom to make a *public use* of one's reason in all matters."[100]

Kant cautioned that the enemies of such freedom were many and pervasive. The military officer commanded good Germans to march and not argue; the tax collector commanded them to pay and not argue; the clergyman commanded them to believe and not argue. In Kant's telling, only one ruler in the world allowed people to argue as much as they wanted, although he required obedience. This, of course, was Frederick the Great, who, being enlightened, did not fear shadows; plus, the king had "a large, well-disciplined army as a guarantee of public peace."[101]

It was too soon to speak of an enlightened age, Kant judged, because darkness still prevailed over too much of modern life, especially in religious matters, where "immaturity is the most harmful as well as the most dishonorable." But the present age was, indeed, "the age of enlightenment," or what was the same thing, "the century of *Frederick*," because the King of Prussia allowed his subjects to argue freely, making public use of their reason, even on matters of government. Kant enthused that Frederick was the "shining example" of enlightened rule, one who understood the paradoxical necessity of restraining civic freedom in order to allow the full flourishing of spiritual freedom. It was a very good thing that Prussia had a large army and a firm hand at the top, Kant assured. The seed of German freedom was blossoming under the "hard shell" of an enlightened ruler, improving the character of the people, who thereby became "more and more and more capable of *acting freely,*" which created the preconditions for a more liberalized government.[102]

Hamann and Herder, like Lessing before them, took a much dimmer view of their age, stressing that German freedom did not extend much beyond the privileges of intellectuals like Kant. In a letter to Kraus, Hamann remarked tartly on the limitations of Enlightenment freedom. Every line of Kant's apologia reeked of snobbery and sneering, Hamann protested. What kind of "conscience" was it that accused humble religious people of immaturity and cowardice "when their blind guardian has a large, well-disciplined army to guarantee his infallibility and orthodoxy?" How could Kant mock their supposed laziness in contrast to a king who "sees them not even as machines but as mere shadows of his grandeur"? Kant's pride and joy, the public use of reason and freedom, was "nothing but a dessert, a sumptuous dessert," Hamann judged. What mattered was the "daily bread" of a life of dignity, on which Kant gave the king a pass. Hamann gagged on his friend's presumption, suggesting that all women should gag on it too: "The *self-incurred immaturity* is just such a sneer as he makes at the whole fair sex."[103]

Hamann had his friend's number on presumption and self-congratulation, never mind that the first *Critique* had one review at the time, a scornful one. Kant had no feminist impulse either. But Kant realized that Hamann was at least half-right about the limits of German enlightenment. Until the French Revolution, Kant harbored deeper republican convictions than his writings showed. Keeping his privileges required a certain amount of brown-nosing of local potentates, or so he told himself. But when the French Revolution broke out in July 1789, Kant was ecstatic. He told his students and friends that the revolution represented the first real-world triumph of philosophy, in which a government would be constructed on the basis of rational principles. This was a cause on which old-style rationalists, new-style rationalists like him, and the young generation headed toward Romanticism could agree.

Upon learning that France had formed a republic, Kant exclaimed, "Now let your servant go in peace to his grave, for I have seen the glory of the world." Staunchly he defended the storming of the Bastille, the National Assembly's abolition of feudal privileges, and the building of a new order. After the Terror began and "Jacobin" became a fearsome epithet in Prussia, Kant still defended the revolution, though he played a careful hand in print, defending a constructionist version of social contract theory while denying that citizens had a right to rebellion. In Kant's telling, the French Revolution was not a rebellion, because Louis XVI had in effect abdicated when he called the National Assembly. An acquaintance later recalled that in the early 1790s Kant "lived and moved" in the revolution, speaking of it constantly with friends and students; others added that he lectured polite society friends about it at dinner parties too, including nobles.[104]

By then Kant was too much an object of Prussian pride to be endangered socially or professionally by his politics, as long as he did not overreach, which he was careful not to do. Even some of his friends, blushing at his open republicanism, brushed it off as a personal quirk not to be counted against his towering stature. Kant had a keen understanding of where the line of danger was in politics, and he played the game adroitly. Meanwhile he completed his trilogy of critiques with a book on aesthetics, *Critique of Judgment* (1790) that played up the creative role of mind in aesthetic experience.

The *Critique of Judgment* contended that our descriptions of the world and judgments about what is beautiful do not simply mirror the world. We do not simply take in raw data that the world offers us, nor do we simply impose our forms on the world, Kant argued. In aesthetic experience we are always doing both, imaginatively creating modes of judgment that take their bearings from experiences of the world. Always there is an interplay of creative freedom and responsiveness to the world as it is. Kant stressed the creative reciprocity of nature and freedom in aesthetic experience, but he asserted, briefly, that the deepest wellspring of aesthetic experience is "the super-sensible," the basis of freedom, not freedom itself or nature. The understanding, by supplying *a priori* laws for nature, shows that we cognize nature only as phenomenal, "and in so doing points to its having a supersensible substrate," which it leaves undetermined. Kant explained: "Judgment by the *a priori* principle of its estimation of nature according to its possible particular laws provides this supersensible substrate (within as well as without us) with *determinability through the intellectual faculty*. But reason gives *determination* to the same *a priori* by its practical law." Thus it is *judgment* that makes it possible to move from the sphere of the concept of nature to that of freedom.[105]

For two kinds of judgments, Kant argued, we must hold some concept of a purposive whole, even if we can never prove that a purposive whole actually exists. Judgments concerning organisms are of this type; the parts of an organism can only be understood by the function that they serve in the whole that is the organism. Beauty is the second type. In both cases we cannot dispense with the concept of purpose, even though we cannot say that the world is actually purposive; thus Kant proposed, as a *regulative* idea, the idea of an intuitive intellect, "a complete spontaneity of intuition." This cognitive power must be independent of sensibility, he reasoned, proceeding from the intuition of the whole as a whole (which Kant called the "synthetic universal") to the particular. The intuitive understanding moves from the whole to the parts. The mind takes up a teleological whole and selects from it the parts that must be. At least, as a regulative understanding, something like this must be what happens, even though the existence of an intuitive intellect cannot be demonstrated.[106]

Kant did not shrink from referring to the supersensible substrate as a thing-in-itself, thus expanding on his most controversial idea. Understanding and the "hand of nature" do not yield what we need in this area, he argued, a "synthesis displaying finality." Since it is possible to regard the material world as a mere appearance, and to think of something – a thing-in-itself – as its substrate, we are justified in regarding this thing-in-itself as something based on a corresponding intellectual intuition. Although the supersensible substrate of nature lies in nature, "all possible insight" into it is beyond our reach: "So by the constitution of our human faculty of knowledge it becomes necessary to look for the supreme source of this finality in an original understanding as the cause of the world." When we judge that something is beautiful, we do not base this judgment on mere experience, for the point is to justify judgments containing an *ought*. We do not say that everyone will agree with my judgment, but it belongs to the nature of judgment to say that they ought to. In teleological judgments, Kant explained, which are objective, one judges that an object is as it ought to be in fulfilling its purpose; in aesthetic judgments, which are subjective, one judges that an object ought to be judged in a certain way.[107]

Post-Kantian idealists and Romantics took note: there was a Kantian basis for playing up the reality of a pre-conceptual understanding of nature as a whole. If one was predisposed to lift imagination and feeling above theoretical and practical reason, or to play up the objective idealist aspect of Kant's thought, one could find a foothold for doing so in Kant's third *Critique*. At the same time, all post-Kantians agreed that something was wrong with Kant's thing-in-itself, though they didn't agree on what it was or what he said about it.

Somehow Kant had to be wrong about being completely cut off from the super-sensible substrate of nature. Kant was ambiguous about how the categories of appearances were supposed to apply to things-in-themselves, and his reference to a "ground" *(Grund)* of appearances in things-in-themselves was equally ambiguous, inviting creative appropriations. Did it mean that things-in-themselves cause sensations? Or that things-in-themselves provide reasons to believe anything? Schelling answered "no" to both questions, but in Romantic thought, the thing-in-itself was often transformed into being-in-itself or a functional equivalent. Kant's leading protégé, Johann Gottlieb Fichte, started German idealism down this path, followed quickly by Schleiermacher, Schelling and Hegel. They broke down the Kantian dualisms of subject and object, and intuition and concept, sometimes noting, pointedly, that Kant himself had not actually held them apart.

In October 1794 Wöllner informed Kant that tolerating *Religion within the Boundaries of Mere Reason* was out of the question for Friedrich Wilhelm II. The book distorted and maligned Christianity, Wöllner charged, Kant failed to uphold his duty as a teacher of youth, and his "continued obstinancy" would not be tolerated. Kant, stewing over the parallel with Christian Wolff, fixed on a key difference, that he was 70 years old. Though wealthy by this point, he was very concerned not to be fired, forced into retirement without pension, or, especially, banished. So he capitulated, despite denying that he had done anything wrong. In Kant's telling, he had never disparaged religion in his lectures, neglected his duty as a teacher, or denigrated Christianity. He had always modeled tolerance to his lecture audiences and readers. But to show his sincerity in being "Your Majesty's loyal subject," he vowed to stop writing about religion, which was enough for the king, who prevailed without causing an explosion. Kant kept silent about religion for three years, until the king died, whereupon Kant returned to making the case for rationalistic moral religion and intellectual freedom. Frederick William II had made the issue personal, Kant reasoned; thus the promise ended with the end of him.[108]

In between the promise and the king's death Kant wrote a classic specimen of idealistic ordering that put his cosmopolitan cards on the table, "Perpetual Peace: A Philosophical Sketch" (1795) and a case for the autonomy of philosophy that he later published as the first part of his last book, *The Conflict of the Faculties* (1798). "Perpetual Peace" offered Kant's vision of a peaceful global order based on cosmopolitan law. Though he hedged with a "saving clause" that he was a mere theorist, not a "practical politician," Kant observed sharply that heads of state "can never have enough of war." Thus it fell to philosophers to imagine how states might be thwarted from starting wars.[109]

His solution replaced the classical law of nations (*Völkerrecht*) with cosmopolitan law (*Weltbürgerrecht*) stating the rights of human beings as citizens of the world. The first section of Kant's charter, containing preliminary articles for a perpetual peace among states, forbade peace treaties that secretly reserved war material for a future war and the acquisition of one state by another by any means. It called for the gradual abolition of all standing armies and forbade national debts connected to the external affairs of states. It forbade forcible interference between states and employing assassins or instigating treason. The second section contained definitive articles: Every state shall have a republican constitution founded on the principles of freedom for all members of a society, the dependence of all members on a single common legislative structure, and legal equality for all citizens. Kant stressed that he was a republican, not a democrat, yet his cosmopolitan republic had a good deal of democracy. His second definitive article secured the rights of nations through a federation of free states (a type of world federalism) and his third article limited the cosmopolitan rights of immigrants and visitors to the conditions of universal hospitality, stating that all strangers had a right not to be treated with hostility.[110]

Obviously, Kant observed, there was a huge gap between politics and morality. Even to imagine a political order that conformed to what is morally right ran the risk of seeming foolish. But that did not diminish the necessity of establishing what a morally just international order would look like: "For we cannot simply conclude by a reverse process that all maxims which can be made public are therefore also just, because the person who has decisive supremacy has no need to conceal his maxims." To the contrary, this was the kind of politics that had to be overcome; reducing morality to it was no advance: "A federative association of states whose sole intention is to eliminate war is the only *lawful* arrangement which can be reconciled with their *freedom*. Thus politics and morality can only be in agreement within a federal union, which is therefore necessary and given *a priori* through the principles of right." First and foremost, Kant considered himself a cosmopolitan citizen of the world, not a Prussian. The hope of the world, politically, lay in founding a federative global union that took a maximal view of comprehensiveness and moral legitimacy. Religiously, the hope of the world was to build a cosmopolitan civil religion that took the same view of comprehensiveness and moral rightness.[111]

This vision was linked to Kant's belief that philosophy should be the central and leading discipline of the modern university. In the context of his battle with the government censors he put it narrowly, contending that philosophers should not have to submit their work for approval to a theological faculty and that philosophers should be free of government censorship. The Prussian state, being Christian, had a legitimate interest in censoring what theologians could say, Kant allowed. But philosophy had matured sufficiently to be independent of other faculties, especially theology. In the summer of 1794 Kant wrote an essay on this topic, put it aside, and published it after Friedrich Wilhelm II was gone, now as the first part of a book on the ascension of philosophy in the modern university. *The Conflict of the Faculties* argued that philosophy alone was an autonomous discipline not dependent on any other faculty for its core doctrines. Unlike law, philosophy was not beholden to whatever laws that legislators enacted; unlike theology, philosophy was not the guardian of an ecclesiastical tradition, though Kant held out for his version of what religion should be. Philosophy needed to be free if modern universities were to become truly modern and enlightened.[112]

Here again, in the 1790s Fichte took a Kantian theme and radicalized it. Fichte wanted universities to be zones of intellectual freedom and cultivation, centers for building modern civilization. They were the best places to acquire *Bildung* – an educated, self-directed, cultivated grasp of things. At least, universities had a chance to become such places if they saw the Enlightenment through, fending off the nepotistic corruption and conformism of traditional society and education. On this theme, Fichte was a good Kantian, though a bit too pushy for Kant's taste. On other issues Kant soon wished that he had inspired someone else to be his leading disciple.

Kant, Jacobi, Fichte, and Post-Kantianism

Two contrary figures, Jacobi and Fichte, had the greatest impact on the trajectory of Kantian thought in the 1790s. Jacobi was privy counselor to the Bavarian court, the son of a wealthy sugar manufacturer, a novelist and critic, and a sharp critic of Kant's assurance that reason provides its own justification. In his early career, Jacobi and his wife Betty von Clermont ran a celebrated literary salon in Pempelfort near Düsseldorf, at his father's country estate. In his later career he served as the first president of the Academy of the Sciences in Munich. In 1785, already known to intellectuals for his salon, Jacobi made a spectacular splash as a thinker by claiming that G. E. Lessing told him, shortly before his death, that he was secretly a Spinozist. Jacobi's charge about Lessing ignited "the Pantheism Controversy," which tarred an iconic figure in German letters, Lessing, and dredged up the dreaded, secular, Jewish, pantheist, seventeenth-century philosopher, Benedict de Spinoza.[113]

According to Jacobi, he had visited Lessing in July 1780 and shared Goethe's then-unpublished poem *Prometheus* with Lessing, who liked it very much. In fact, Lessing told Jacobi that he agreed with Goethe's pantheistic viewpoint: "The orthodox concepts of the Divinity are no longer for me; I cannot stomach them. *Hen kai pan!* [One and All!] I know of nothing else." Jacobi asked Lessing if he went all the way with Spinoza; Lessing said yes, there was no philosopher greater than Spinoza. If he were to name himself after any thinker, it would surely be Spinoza. The following day, Jacobi pressed harder about going all the way: Did Lessing really embrace Spinoza's pantheism, fatalism, and determinism? Lessing said yes again: Pantheism was exactly right; free will meant nothing to him; final causes and free will were anthropomorphic ideas, just as Spinoza said: "There is no other philosophy than the philosophy of Spinoza."[114]

For five years Jacobi wrangled privately with Lessing's ally and closest friend, Moses Mendelssohn, over the meaning of this shocking exchange. Then Jacobi went public with it, racing to beat Mendelssohn's whitewashed version into print. To Jacobi, the moral of the story was that German Enlightenment, as symbolized by Goethe and Lessing, was heading straight for atheistic pantheism and fatalism, sometimes openly and sometimes not.

An uproarious debate over pantheism ensued. Many critics blasted Jacobi for smearing a great man, though hardly anyone questioned his account of what Lessing said. Others contended that Spinoza was overdue to be culturally rehabilitated. Mendelssohn claimed that Jacobi was out of his depth with a master ironist; Lessing evidently had fun playing with Jacobi's pious sincerity, which Jacobi misconstrued as a serious intellectual exchange. Jacobi replied that Lessing had not been spoofing and the issues in play were deadly serious. Pantheism was atheism by another name; speculative philosophy led to fatalism and atheism; Enlightenment types were becoming pantheistic atheists.[115]

Jacobi implored that faith is the key to human knowing. Any rational demonstration requires a fundamental principle or set of principles that cannot be proved. All knowledge rests on some kind of faith, for all epistemic dependence is inferential. If one believes something, one must be able to justify that belief by showing that it follows logically from another true belief, which must be justified by another true belief, and so on, to some stopping point. There must be some stopping point to the regress of justifications, Jacobi contended – *something* that one knows without having to deduce it from something else. Reason cannot provide it, since reason sets the regress into motion. Only faith – something given by feeling, or reasons of the heart – can provide it: "Through faith we know that we have a body, and that there are other bodies and other thinking beings outside of us. A veritable and wondrous revelation!" In truth, Jacobi allowed, one merely senses one's body as constituted one way or another, but in thus feeling it, one becomes aware of its alterations *and* of something else that is neither mere sensation or thought. One becomes aware of other things with the "very same certainty" that one becomes aware of one's self, "for without the *Thou*, the *I* is impossible." The revelation of nature impels every person to believe through faith, and without it, nobody knows anything.[116]

Ironically, Jacobi's intervention elevated Spinoza to new respectability, which did not bother him, as Jacobi judged that German idealism was heading in that direction anyway without admitting it. It was better to name the disease and fight it openly. Two years after making a splash he followed up with an oddly titled book, *David Hume on Faith; or Idealism and Realism* (1787) that had almost nothing to do with Hume aside from a strange attempt to enlist Hume on his side against Kant. Despite the oddities, Jacobi aimed shrewdly at a contradiction in Kant's system. Kant taught that things-in-themselves cause our sensations, which are synthesized into intuitions. But Kant also taught that causality is a transcendental condition of experience, not a property of things-in-themselves. Both things cannot be true, Jacobi admonished. Things-in-themselves cannot cause our sensations if causality is not a property of things-in-themselves. Instead of struggling with Kant's impossible maze of abstractions, it was better to stick with common sense realism coupled with faith in the way that the world reveals itself to us. Jacobi sealed his point by enlisting Hume on his side, never mind that Hume was not a common sense realist or a proponent of religious faith. Hume taught, Jacobi noted, that a belief is something felt by the mind that separates imaginative fictions from the ideas of rational judgment. Jacobi urged that we cannot get farther or deeper than this feeling; certainly Kant had not done so. Though Kant never said that objects make impressions on the senses and thus bring about representations, he had to assume it; otherwise he would have gotten nowhere: "For even the word 'sensibility' is without any meaning, unless we understand by it a distinct real intermediary between one real thing and another, an actual means *from* something *to* something else."[117]

The concept of existence is simple, Jacobi reasoned. It cannot be inferred from a collection of properties and it is not a special kind of property, as Kant showed in refuting the ontological proof. A thing has all the same properties whether it exists or not. Existence is also immediate, because we cannot establish it or refute it through reasoning. It must be given to us in experience. And existence is fundamental because it is the basis of identity and thought. Who we are and what we think depends on existence, which does not depend on us. Since we cannot demonstrate or refute our belief in the reality of external things, Jacobi urged, we must accept on faith what is given to us in experience. Existence precedes thought. Every researcher knows from experience that building up knowledge depends on the power of one's sense: "The purest and richest reason is what follows from the purest and richest sensation."[118]

The latter statement electrified Hölderlin, Schelling, and other Romantics, who cheered Jacobi as an ally against sterile rationalism. In his time, Jacobi was respected as a powerful critic of idealism, rationalism, and atheism who helped post-Kantians find a way beyond Kant. He had good relationships with Fichte and most post-Kantians up to 1799, when he published a strange attack on Fichte that mixed high compliments – "I consider you the true Messiah of speculative reason" – and expressions of tender affection with a slew of accusations that introduced the word nihilism (*Nihilismus*) into modern philosophy. Nihilism, in Jacobi's usage, was a compound of egoism and atheism, the triumph of nothingness. For the nihilist, nothing existed except one's own momentary conscious states. Jacobi declared, "I feel a terrible horror before the *nothing, the absolutely indeterminate, the utterly void.*" Fichte, Jacobi charged, despite enthusing about freedom constantly, did not believe in freedom any more than Kant or Leibniz believed in it. Fichte was against freedom because, like other philosophers of his ilk, his idea of freedom was a "materialistic principle of mechanics, an original, *purely indeterminate activity as such,* an actuosity or agility." After Jacobi accused Fichte of atheistic nihilism, in a time of danger for Fichte, the post-Kantians treated Jacobi warily, but with no lack of respect for his intellectual acumen.[119]

Later Jacobi became an object of ridicule for his purported irrationalism, which carried on for over a century. Heinrich Heine skewered Jacobi as "nothing but a quarrelsome sneak, who disguised himself in the cloak of philosophy and insinuated himself among the philosophers, first whimpering to them ever so much about his affection and softheartedness, then letting loose a tirade against reason." Many intellectual historians piled on, describing Jacobi as a raving irrationalist who opposed the noble and high-minded Enlightenment. Isaiah Berlin was still recycling this rendering in the 1970s. But Jacobi, though definitely a sentimentalist, was not contemptuous of reason, and he kept in play the idea of faith – existential daring and commitment – as an alternative to speculative rationalism. Kant was still writing books when the post-Kantian movement began, a movement that took off partly in response to Jacobi's critiques. To a considerable extent, Jacobi played on Kant's ground. He agreed with Kant that the field of knowledge is limited to sense experience; moreover, Jacobi treated existence and sensation as abstractions that could be separated from thought – the very procedure that Hamann rejected.[120]

Post-Kantians debated whether Jacobi's critique of the thing-in-itself confused the empirical and transcendental levels of analysis. Did Jacobi wrongly suppose that Kant used the term in a transcendental sense? But that question, regardless of the answer, opened up the possibility of post-Kantian absolute idealism. Hamann, Herder, Fichte, Schelling, Hölderlin, and Hegel took Jacobi very seriously, even cheering him on as he cut Kant down to size. They would not have done so had they shared Heine's view of his intellect. All had to deal with the vast influence of Jacobi's thought, especially his insistence that there is no knowing without faith.

The major post-Kantian in Kant's lifetime was Fichte, whom Kant boosted to prominence. Fichte was the son of a ribbon weaver in Rammenau, Saxony, an only recently emancipated serf. A *Gymnasium* education would have been out of reach for him, but at the age of nine he impressed a local noble by his ability to recite sermons in detail. Fichte was sent to a boarding school and later a *Gymnasium,* where his social inferiority made him ripe for denigration, which helped to make him contentious with an overbearing streak for the rest of his life. He studied theology and jurisprudence in Jena, Leipzig, and Wittenberg between 1780 and 1784, always lacking funds; for six years he scratched out a living as a private tutor; in 1790 he returned to Leipzig as a tutor, where he pored over Kant's first two *Critiques* and embraced Kant's system. Fichte journeyed to Königsberg to meet Kant, who gave him a brusque welcome; Kant as a lecturer was not much better, appearing sleepy and bored to Fichte.[121]

But Fichte persisted in wanting a serious exchange with Kant. He took a private tutorial post in Warsaw, wrote a Kantian-like book in six weeks, and returned to Königsberg with it, asking Kant to read his *Attempt at a Critique of All Revelation* (1792). Kant was impressed by Fichte's mastery of Kant's concepts. He told Borowski that he liked Fichte because of his modesty, urging Borowski to find a publisher for this "young destitute man." Fichte stayed in Königsberg for four months, hoping for greater illumination from Kant's lectures, which didn't happen. He judged sadly that Kant's weak body had become too frail "to house such a great mind." The book was soon finished, but the censorship process took several months, partly because Fichte's rendering of Kant's divine moral guarantor pressed a sensitive point. Fichte contended that the idea of God as moral guarantor is founded on a human projection of something subjective within human beings to an external being. Revelation is possible only on two conditions, he contended: that one wants to be good, and that one needs the representation of a revelation having occurred "as a means for producing the good in himself."[122]

That was, indeed, a Kantian argument; Kant taught that each person must make a God for one's self in order to worship in one's self the One who made all things. But Fichte put the projection argument more aggressively, suggesting that he dropped Kant's postulation of an actual outside God, which anticipated Ludwig Feuerbach's projection argument by more than a half-century. In the spring of 1792 Kant's book on religion was published at the same time as Fichte's book. Since Fichte's book had no name or preface, and it sounded like Kant, readers assumed that Kant wrote it. *Allgemeine Literaturzeitung* editorialized that the author was obviously the great philosopher from Königsberg to whom all humankind owed "eternal gratitude."[123]

Fichte became an instant celebrity when Kant set the public straight about the book's author. In 1794 Fichte succeeded Reinhold as professor of philosophy at Jena, soaring straight to a high-prestige position, where he attracted overflow audiences with strident lectures on the truth-finding vocation of scholars. From the beginning he was prone to spark controversy and make enemies, even among people who wanted to admire him. Fichte's full-throated defense of the French Revolution made enemies, as did his attacks on student fraternities, which were filled with carousing, frivolous, highborn types that Fichte despised.

At Jena Fichte quickly disposed of the thing-in-itself, or at least Kant's version of it, calling it "a piece of whimsy, a pipe-dream, a non-thought." Kant had the right project, Fichte assured, and Kant towered above all others. His project was the Enlightenment's at its best, conceiving rational and moral agents as subject only to norms for which such agents are the authors. Kant showed that rational agents encounter themselves as subjects making judgments about objects and that these judgments, if true, answer to the objects that make them true. But the Kantian dichotomy between subjects and objects is subjectively established, Fichte argued. Kant showed that everything we encounter is either a subject or an object, but he failed to acknowledge the thoroughgoing subjectivism of his idealism. His very distinction between subject and object was subjective without remainder.[124]

Fichte later told his students that his fundamental corrective to Kant's idealism came to him in a flash of insight that "truth consists in the unity of thought and object." Since Kant had a notion of intellectual intuition, Fichte believed that his flash of insight was perfectly Kantian – the mind must be capable of grasping certain *a priori* features of reality through intuition. The closest that Kant came to saying that was in the *Critique of Judgment,* but he hedged even there, describing intellectual intuition as a regulative idea. That was too modest for Fichte. If we are given two sides of a triangle, he reasoned, we immediately see that only one side can complete it. We do not make a judgment about our mode of apprehending triangles or about how we use words; we immediately intuit a necessary truth about triangles themselves. In intellectual intuition we grasp the necessary structure of reality itself.[125]

Fichte spelled out what that meant in the book that launched post-Kantian idealism, *Wissenschaftslehre* (*Science of Knowledge,* 1894). At least, he took his first shot at doing so upon arriving at Jena. Later he revised the book fifteen times, twice in major new editions, and always with what his English translators called "bad punctuation, idiosyncratic sentence structure, and a dismaying overabundance of nonfunctional expletives." Even the title is impossible to translate, as *Wissenschaftslehre* was, in Fichte's usage, a *sui generis* term referring to the doctrine of all forms of knowledge. Fichte sealed his truncated legacy by rewriting the book constantly, changing many of his positions, never producing a polished text, and displaying his penchant for polemic. His translators added, "His literary *persona,* alternating between arrogance and mock humility, and always ready for vitriolic personal attacks, is thoroughly unbearable."[126]

Certainly many of Fichte's contemporaries agreed on both points. Rudolf Steiner observed that there was "something violent" about Fichte's personality and behavior. When something stood in his way, "his inflexibility turned into rudeness, and his energy into recklessness. He was never able to understand that old habits are stronger than new ideas; thus he was continually coming into conflict with the persons with whom he had to deal . . . Fichte lacked the ability to put up with everyday life." For five years, however, students and lecture-grazers flocked to Jena to hear Fichte. His first version of the

Wissenschaftshlehre was produced to relieve students of having to take lecture notes, so they could concentrate on his freewheeling performances; also, Jena had denied him the initial sabbatical that he requested to write a system, so he composed it on a week-by-week basis before class. Rejecting Kant's agnosticism about the thing-in-itself and Kant's distinction between the transcendental aesthetic and analytic, Fichte unified Kant's theoretical and practical forms of reason by fashioning a transcendental dialectic claiming primacy for intuition: "Our task is to *discover* the primordial, absolutely unconditioned first principle of all human knowledge. This can be neither *proved* nor *defined,* if it is to be an absolutely primary principle."[127]

Fichte found this first principle in the pure "I," the willful ego of "I think," from which he derived the categories of space, time, being, sensation, causality, and everything else. The pure "I" is purely activity, not a thing or substance, he argued. It is the activity of positing itself, which exists only through its awareness of itself. We say with perfect certainty that A equals A, Fichte observed. This proposition requires a connection (Fichte called it X) between A as subject and A as predicate, which must exist in the judging self, along with the A that constitutes the subject and predicate of the judgment. This X between the two sides of the judgment also requires a unified self to make the judgment, just as Kant contended that understanding requires the unity of the "I think" of consciousness.

From this principle, I *am* I, or I=I, Fichte moved to the equally certain proposition, "not-A is not equal to A." This positing of not-A requires the original positing of A and is conditioned by it, but it rests on a second principle of knowledge, that a not-self must be opposed to the self that it is not. This counterpositing of the not-self by the self leads to a contradiction, Fichte argued. The self is negated if the not-self is posited, but the not-self can only come to be by being posited by the self. Being and non-being, or reality and negation, would negate each other in a dance of mutual necessity and destruction if not for the third principle of knowledge: "In the self I oppose a divisible not-self to the divisible self." In the synthesis a finite I is limited by a finite not-I. The absolute I, an infinite sphere including all reality, becomes restricted through the process of negation.[128]

Fichte put the dialectic concisely: "*I am absolutely, i.e., I am absolutely BECAUSE I am; and am absolutely WHAT I am; both FOR THE SELF.*" The absolute I begins by positing its existence, which is the thesis. This self-positing of the I must limit itself to be aware of itself, which gives rise to a contradiction (antithesis) causing the I to posit *and* negate itself, which gives rise to a synthesis of the posited, limited, and negated I and not-I. Fichte boasted that this was the "universal and satisfactory" answer to Kant's question about how synthetic judgments are *a priori* possible: "We have established a synthesis between the two opposites, self and not-self, by postulating them each to be divisible; there can be no further question as to the possibility of this, nor can any ground for it be given." In essence, Fichte replaced Kant's thing-in-itself with an unconsciously self-limiting I that constructed the world through its dialectical experience of its posited and negated self. Fichte originated thesis-antithesis-synthesis dialectic, which he fashioned in Kant-like sentences: "Just as there can be no antithesis without synthesis, no synthesis without antithesis, so there can be neither without a thesis – an absolute positing, whereby an A (the self) is neither equated nor opposed to any other, but is just absolutely posited. This, as applied to our system, is what gives strength and completeness to the whole; it must be a system, and it must be *one;* the opposites must be united, as long as opposition remains, until absolute unity is effected; a thing, indeed – as will appear in due course – which could be brought about only by a completed approximation to infinity, which in itself is impossible."[129]

Unequivocally, Fichte belonged to the Cartesian tradition. Philosophy must begin with self-consciousness, he insisted. We must explain nature by referring to our consciousness of it instead of accounting for consciousness by some impossible reference to nature. But Fichte realized that he had special problems with intelligibility. Did he really believe that the "I" *creates* the empirical world by positing it? Did he believe that all *a priori* concepts about knowledge, action and objects of experience could be deduced from the concepts of identity and negation? Kant, interpreting Fichte as making the latter claim, protested that he violated the basic principles of the first *Critique*. Fichte, claiming to straighten out Kant's idealism, responded to Kant in his next edition by playing down the language of assertion and negation, emphasizing that the transcendental "I" is a normative status that makes experience possible, not a datum within experience. But that did not settle the question of how Fichte interpreted the thing-in-itself or the given manifold. Fichte could be quoted as seeming to deny that things-in-themselves exist *and* as claiming that we grasp things-in-themselves through intellectual intuition.[130]

In 1801 he tried to be more intelligible in a book titled *A Crystal Clear Report to the General Public Concerning the Actual Essence of the Newest Philosophy: An Attempt to Force the Reader to Understand*. This book, despite its over-the-top title, did not settle the question of what Fichte really thought. It did, however, clarify that he did not identify the transcendental "I" with the "I" of everyday experience; moreover, Fichte stressed that one's knowledge of a first principle can occur only in a flash of insight. When the flash occurs, it does not require further proof, nor can it be further proven. It is immediately evident as the "absolute intuition of reason through itself."[131]

Fichte was still writing books when the two main traditions about how his early idealism should be understood took shape. In one view, Fichte eliminated the thing-in-itself and the given manifold, adopting a form of absolute idealism in which an absolute ego posited itself as all reality. In essence, Fichte radicalized Kant's transcendental idealism by universalizing the transcendental subject: There is only one infinite subject, not one subject per person. The absolute ego creates the form *and the content* of experience. In the rival interpretation, which Jacobi pioneered, and which Schelling and Hegel adopted, Fichte's early idealism was a form of radical subjectivism that limited knowledge to the representations of finite subjects. Kant bordered on solipsism, and Fichte plunged into it, denying the reality of anything beyond one's representations. In this view, Fichte took subjective idealism almost as far as it could go, trapping the ego in a circle of its own consciousness, save for his Kantian qualification that there is a *practical* necessity to believing in an external world.[132]

These contradictory readings of Fichte correspond to similar disagreements about Kant, though on a smaller scale, since less is at stake. As in the case with Kant, both of the dominant traditions of interpretation are loaded with variant readings. One can get a radical subjectivist Fichte out of the view that he "rejected" the thing-in-itself, which can mean different things, but the abolition view is usually the basis for construing

Fichte as an absolute idealist. The intuitionist reading plays up the Platonic aspects of Fichte's thought and the Kantian basis of intuitionism, but here again, one can get different Fichtes out of it. The two dominant readings of Fichte feature a transcendental subject holding a cognitive status versus a transcendental subject holding a regulative status. The absolute idealist reading usually gets rid of the thing-in-itself and the empirical manifold, while the radical subjectivist reading usually retains both. The former reading has an unlimited transcendental subject and the latter reading has a limited one.

Attempts to mediate these contradictory readings usually play up Fichte's practical or pragmatic commitments, interpreting Fichte's system as a defense of the primacy of practical reason. Beiser and A. J. Mandt are leading advocates of this view, contending that even Fichte struggled against subjectivist captivity, albeit in a way that rivaled Kant for ambiguity and torturous exegesis. In my view, Fichte was a strong intuitionist, not a radical subjectivist, for whom practical-ethical commitments prevailed, but not consistently. The view that Fichte got rid of things-in-themselves tends to overlook Kant's third *Critique* and Fichte's radicalization of it. In some senses, Fichte did get rid of Kant's thing-in-itself, describing it as absurd, a self-refuting impossibility. If the thing-in-itself is independent of the forms of sensibility, it is imperceptible, and if it is independent of the categories of understanding, it is inconceivable. Yet Kant wrote page after page about it.

Fichte urged that when Kant postulated the existence of an unthinkable something, he thought it, and thus destroyed its existence as something unthinkable. Yet Fichte also had an intuitionist idea of the thing-in-itself as the idea of something that is the product of pure thinking alone. The thing-in-itself is the *noumenon,* an object created by the necessary laws of reason. This idea was fundamental to Fichte's system. He insisted, not implausibly, that his rendering of it was Kantian. Even Fichte postulated an unknowable entity as a check on the expansive, creative activity of the ego. But Fichte's intelligibility problem was partly a consistency problem, which provided prooftexts for wildly disparate renderings of him as the ultimate subjective idealist or the first absolute idealist.[133]

Fichte's overriding commitments to practical-ethical causes came through to audiences that could not follow his I=I dialectics. His combative personality made him irresistible to students and lecture-grazers. His lecture hall was always packed; latecomers stood on ladders outside the window to hear him speak; streams of culture-yearning visitors came to Jena to hear him. He roared for the French Revolution, declaring that universities were overdue to graduate from the Middle Ages. On the other hand, Fichte's radical ethical idealism did not extend to equal rights for women – an idiotic idea, he insisted. Women existed to provide nurturing homes for husbands and children. Only degenerate women sought to be authors, painters, or voters – one of Fichte's few opinions that endeared him to local faculty. His older colleagues found their staid university becoming a different kind of place as a consequence of his celebrity and the company it attracted. Many of them resented the difference. Fichte's penchant for accusatory polemic did not wear well, either; he was quick to say that people who disagreed with him were bad people. Reinhold, a genial type, gently told Fichte that he wounded people unnecessarily, making it hard to consider his ideas. Fichte replied that he sincerely regretted having offended so many people; nonetheless, in his experience, most of them were averse to being told "honestly what terrible errors they usually embrace."[134]

One of Fichte's stock opinions was that good Kantian religion did not need a personal deity; all that it needed was a divine world-governance, a moral world order through which righteous action achieved a morally just end. He recognized that publishing on this theme was more hazardous than lecturing about it. Nonetheless, in 1798 Fichte ventured publication in the journal that he co-edited with Friedrich I. Niethammer, *Philosophisches Journal einer Gesellschaft Teutscher Gelehrten*. Explaining that he felt duty-bound to explain his position, Fichte assured that he respected "the holiness that the subject has for so many venerable minds." Much of his audience, he acknowledged, assumed that believing in God had to do with believing in a separate being who created the moral world-order. This being was supposedly distinct from individual selves and the world, it was active in the world by means of concepts, and it possessed concepts such as personality and consciousness. But Fichte admonished his readers that they didn't really believe it. Personality and consciousness are things that human subjects find within themselves, which cannot be conceived without limitation and finitude. To attribute these predicates to God is to render God as something finite, something that ordinary believers surely didn't intend: "You have not thought of God, as you wished, but rather you have only multiplied yourselves in your thinking."[135]

Fichte countered that the world is nothing but the appearance of our inner activity as it is manifested sensibly in accordance with the laws of reason: "Our world is the sensibly manifested material of our duty. This is what is actually real in things, the true basic element of all appearance." To believe in the reality of the world is to be driven to a moral compulsion, "the only compulsion that is possible for a free being." Revelation, Fichte urged, is precisely the revelation of our duty as free subjects in a moral world-order: "This is the true faith. This moral order is what we are assuming to be *divine*. It is constituted by right action." In his telling, the only confession of faith that passed the tests of enlightened reason and morality was the one that Kant described: Joyfully fulfilling the demands of moral duty without "quibbling about the consequences" or doubting that only moral faith deserves to be called faith. Atheism, actual disbelief, is quibbling and doubt of that kind, Fichte admonished. Atheism is the refusal or failure to obey the voice of one's conscience to the end. If one believes in a moral world-governance, it is impossible to think that good ever results from evil: "In this way the divine becomes living and real to us. Each of our actions is performed in the presupposition of the divine, and only in it are all of the consequences of those actions kept in store."[136]

In a closing flourish that proved ironic, Fichte contended that God's existence is not debatable. Those who said that they doubted God's existence simply misunderstood the question: "It is not doubtful at all but rather the most certain thing that there is. Indeed, it is the ground of all other certainty, the single absolutely valid objective fact: that there is a moral world-order, that a determinate place in this order is assigned to every rational individual and his work is taken into account; that the destiny of each individual, in so far as it is not caused, so to speak, by his own conduct, is a result of this plan; that without this plan no hair falls from his head and within his sphere of activity no sparrow falls from a roof; that each truly good action succeeds and each truly evil one fails; and that for those who rightly love only the good, all things must conduce to the best." That was almost poetic, but Fichte, going for broke, ended with two stirring pieces of poetic ethical idealism. The first was from Goethe:

> Fill your heart with it, as great as it is
> And when you, wholly in this feeling, are blessed,
> Then call it what you will,
> Call it Fortune! Heart! Love! God!
> I have no name
> For it. Feeling is all,
> Names but noise and smoke
> Clouding over celestial ardor.

The second was from Friedrich von Schiller:

> … a holy *will* lives,
> As the human one wavers.
> High above time and space there stirs,
> Alive, the highest *thought*.
> And although everything whirls round in eternal change,
> It endures through change as a tranquil spirit.[137]

This article set off an explosion about Fichte's purported atheism. The controversy began with an anonymous maudlin tract, styled as a concerned father's letter to his son, that circulated throughout Saxony. Pietistic intellectuals joined in, alarmed by the contagion of pantheistic atheism. A pamphlet war ensued. Jacobi, never one to miss a good fight, weighed in with a rambling, dramatic public letter in March 1799 that "squeezed" Fichte in tender friendship while blasting him for purveying a nihilistic stew of egoism and atheism: "Truly, my dear Fichte, I would not be vexed if you, or anyone else, were to call *Chimerism* the view I oppose to the Idealism that I chide for *Nihilism*."[138]

At first Fichte had plenty of defenders, but he alienated them by haughtily dismissing the controversy as something beneath him. Though he and Niethammer presented a juridical defense to the local Ernestine Dukes, led by Karl August, Fichte told August's privy-councilor that he would not promise to speak more carefully in the future and he would resign if they required him to do anything of the kind. That alienated even Goethe, who had made Jena a center of intellectual freedom through his influence as Minister at the court in Weimar. In April 1799, with the University of Jena's approval, August treated Fichte's threat to resign as a resignation, informing him in a postscript to a letter of reprimand. A petition signed by 280 students demanded Fichte's reinstatement, but August rebuffed it. The meteoric phase of Fichte's career was over; Goethe lamented that his out-of-control contentiousness cost him the career that he should have had.[139]

By then Kant was disgusted with his prize protégé. To defend his own legacy, Kant was reduced to assuring that he was not an atheist and neither was Fichte. But the controversy raged on, and in August 1799 Kant threw Fichte overboard in a public forum, the *Allgemeine Literaturzeitung:* "I herewith declare that I consider Fichte's *Wissenschaftslehre* a wholly untenable system." On the record, Kant's reason was that

Fichte treated Kant's philosophy as a *propaedeutic* for transcendental philosophy, not the system itself. Kant countered that that was ridiculous, "since I myself have praised the completed whole of pure philosophy in the *Critique of Pure Reason* as the best mark of the truth of it." The Kantian system was the gold standard, Kant assured; he would not allow it to be besmirched by "fraudulent, crafty ones who plot our destruction while yet employing the language of benevolence of whom and whose traps one cannot sufficiently beware."[140]

With this announcement, Kant's public view of Fichte caught up to his private one. When Kant died in 1804, Fichte was making his living as a writer in Berlin, having authored a popular book, *The Vocation of Man,* that settled a few scores with his detractors. In 1807, while French troops occupied Berlin, Fichte gave rousing speeches on the native superiority of German culture, imploring Germans to redeem the hope of a rational social order, which the French had betrayed by opting for Napoleonic tyranny. The German spirit was inherently intuitive, creative, and vital, he urged. It contrasted with the imitative backwardness of other peoples, especially the Latin peoples. The vision of freedom, equality, fraternity, and modernity now rested on the rise of the German nation: "If you sink, all humanity sinks with you, without hope of future restoration."[141]

In 1809 the founding of the University of Berlin gave Fichte a second chance at an academic career, where he had Friedrich Schleiermacher for a colleague. Briefly Fichte served as university rector, but his social skills had not improved, the faculty turned against him, and he resigned in a huff. The last versions of his *Wissenschaftslehre* were more complex and reflective than the one that launched post-Kantian idealism, and more religious. Fichte's early versions insisted that the science of knowledge is scientific, not something that improves one's moral character or religious life. In his last years he took it back, contending that *Wissenschaftslehre* is also a doctrine of wisdom. The science of knowledge gives itself to actual life, Fichte asserted, "not to that life exhibited in its nothingness of blind and intelligible impulses, but rather to the visibly obligating divine life that is coming-to-be." The way to the "blessed life," he wrote elsewhere, is the way of fulfilling the good; Fichte argued that human consciousness develops through five levels of awareness: sensibility, legality, morality, religiosity, and philosophy. Had he talked that way in his early career, Fichte might have cast a longer shadow over religious thought.[142]

As it was he made his mark as the first post-Kantian idealist and an apostle of German nationalism. In his lifetime Fichte found notable admirers in the latter cause such as Wilhelm von Humboldt and Carl von Clausewitz, though nothing like the mass following that he sought. Because of his radicalism, Fichte's status as a hero of German nationalism was not established until the 1860s. Afterward he found right-wing admirers whom he would have despised, who reveled in his nationalistic sneers against the purported inferiority of foreigners. Fichte, though hard to take, and cursed with a very ambiguous legacy, had immense moral courage, practicing what he preached. In 1814 he died of typhoid, as Germany's most famous living philosopher served as a chaplain to troops in the anti-Napoleonic wars.[143]

By the time that Fichte took a religious turn, Schelling was famous, Hegel was getting started, and Schleiermacher was hitting his stride as an academic theologian. All got their bearings by interrogating Kant's critiques. All made contributions to religious thought, a field accustomed to dealing with an unavailable object, by seizing on the ostensible unknowability of things-in-themselves.

Despite Kant's emphasis on the limits of theoretical, practical, and aesthetic reason, he appeared to authorize an understanding of appearances, sensibility, things-in-themselves, understanding, nature, and freedom as aspects of a single underlying reality. There was a Kantian basis for apophatic monism. Kant said it explicitly in the third *Critique,* a treasure box for imaginative-aesthetic types like Schleiermacher, Schelling, and Samuel Taylor Coleridge. Moreover, Kant opened the door to it in the second edition of the *Critique of Pure Reason*: "But if our Critique is not in error in teaching that the object is to be taken *in a twofold sense,* namely as appearance and as thing in itself; if the deduction of the concepts of understanding is valid, and the principle of causality therefore applies only to things taken in the former sense, namely, in so far as they are objects of experience – these same objects, taken in the other sense, not being subject to the principle – then there is no contradiction in supposing that one and the same will is, in the appearance, that is, in its visible acts, necessarily subject to the law of nature, and so far *not free,* while yet, as belonging to a thing in itself, it is not subject to that law, and is therefore *free.*"[144]

There is no contradiction in saying that "one and the same will" is both not free and free. Though Kant dramatically shredded the monist/Spinozist "illusion" that the one reality underlying all things can be known by pure thought, he cracked open the door to saying that there is such an underlying reality consisting of appearances, sensibility, things-in-themselves, and other aspects. Schelling and Hegel, taking 80 percent of Kant for granted, threw the door wide open. Schleiermacher, taking 80 percent of Kant for granted, seized on something different that Kant, from his perspective, got wrong.

Schleiermacher urged that religion is rooted in something deeper than the ordering impulse, even idealistic ordering. The wellspring of religion is spiritual feeling or intuition, the pre-cognitive sense of one's relationship to all that is. Religion is not fundamentally about morality, which is grasping and utilitarian. Kant made religion essentially a matter of control. Schleiermacher made a more creative move, contending that religion consists of an immediate relation to the source of life, the Spirit of the Whole.

Notes

1. See Immanuel Kant, *Universal Natural History and the Theory of the Heavens* (1855), trans. W. Hastie (Ann Arbor: University of Michigan Press, 1969); Pierre Simon Laplace, *Celestial Mechanics,* 5 vols., trans. Nathaniel Bowditch (Bronx: Chelsea, 1825–1839).

2. See Ludwig Ernst Borowski, *Darstellung des Leben und Charakters Immanuel Kants* (Königsberg, 1804; reprint, Brussels: Culture et civilization, 1968); Reinhold Bernhard Jachmann, *Immanuel Kant geschildert in Briefen an einen Freund* (Königsberg: F. Nicolovius, 1804); Ehregott A. Christian Wasianski, *Immanuel Kant in seinen letzten Lebensjahren* (Königsberg: Nicolovius, 1804).

3. Heinrich Heine, *Zur Geschichte der Religion und Philosophie in Deutschland* (Hamburg: Hoffmann und Campe, 1868), reprinted in Heine, *Lyrik und Prosa,* 2 vols., ed. Martin Greiner (Frankfurt: Büchergilde Gutenberg, 1962), II: 461.

4. Two major biographical works on Kant superseded the literature in this field, providing a richer account of Kant's life and character: Karl Vorländer, *Immanuel Kant: Der Mann und das Werk,* 2 vols. (Leipzig: Felix Meiner, 1924); and Manfred Kuehn, *Kant: A Biography* (Cambridge: Cambridge University Press, 2001).

5. G. W. Leibniz, *Discourse on Metaphysics; Correspondence with Arnauld; Monadology,* trans. George Montgomery (La Salle: Open Court, 1902), 5–7, 14–15, 18–19, quote 18; Leibniz to Arnauld, October 6, 1687, 211–235; Leibniz, *New Essays on Human Understanding,* trans. Peter Remnant and Jonathan Bennett (Cambridge: Cambridge University Press, 1982).

6. Gottfried W. Leibniz and Christian Wolff, *Briefwechsel zwischen Leibniz und Christian Wolff* (Hildesheim: G. Olms, 1860); Christian Wolff, *Gesammelte Werke* (Hildesheim: G. Olms, 1962); see Johann D. Walch, *Kontroversstücke gegen die Wolffsche Metaphysik* (Hildesheim: G. Olms, 1724); Ulrich Ricken, *Leibniz, Wolff und einige sprachtheoretische Entwicklungen in der deutschen Aufklärung* (Berlin: Akademie-Verlag, 1989); Joachim Birke, *Christian Wolffs Metaphysik und die zeitgenössische Literatur-und Musiktheorie* (Berlin: de Gruyter, 1966); Erich Riedesel, *Pietismus und Orthodoxie in Ostpreußen* (Königsberg: Ost-Europa Verlag, 1937), 39; Peter C. Erb, ed., *Pietists: Selected Writings* (New York: Paulist Press, 1983); Richard Benz, *Die Zeit der Deutschen Klassik, 1750–1800* (Stuttgart: Reclam, 1953); Hajo Holborn, *A History of Modern Germany, 1648–1840* (New York: Knopf, 1968). For a modern edition of Wolff's famous speech at Halle on Chinese philosophy that got him in trouble, see Wolff, *Oratio de Sinarum philosophia practica / Rede über praktische Philosophie der Chinesen,* ed. Michael Albrecht (Hamburg: Meiner, 1985). On the Pietist battle against Wolff, see Max Wundt, *Die deutsche Schulphilosophie im Zeitalter der Aufklärung* (Hildesheim: G. Olds, 1964), 230–264.

7. Kuehn, *Kant: A Biography,* 26–39, quote 31.

8. Hartmut Böhme and Gernot Böhme, *Das Andere der Vernunft: Zur Entwicklung von Rationalitätsstrukturen am Beispiel Kant* (Frankfurt: Suhrkamp Verlag, 1983), 484–485; Kuehn, *Kant: A Biography,* 45–55, "natural" quote, citing Pietist leader August H. Franke, 53.

9. See Kuehn, *Kant: A Biography,* 56–60; Riedesel, *Pietismus und Orthodoxie in Ostpreufsen,* 138–139; Vorländer, *Immanuel Kant: Der Mann und das Werk,* I: 5–9.

10. See Benno Erdmann, *Martin Knutzen und seine Zeit: Ein Beitrag zur Geschichte der Wolfischen Schule und Insbesondere zur Entwicklungsgeschichte Kants* (Leipzig: L. Voss, 1876); Christian August Crusius, *Kleinere philosophische Schriften* (1737; Hildesheim: G. Olms, 1987); Crusius, *Weg zur gewissheit und Zuverlässigkeit der menschlichen Erkenntnis* (1744; Hildesheim: G. Olms, 1969); Pietists: Selected Writings, 97–215; Erich Beyreuther, *Geschichte des Pietismus* (Stuttgart: Steinkopf, 1978).

11. See Isaac Newton, *Philosophiae Naturalis Principia Mathematica* (1689) (*Sir Isaac Newton's Mathematical Principles of Natural Philosophy and his System of the World,* trans. Florian Cajori [Berkeley: University of California Press, 1934]); H. S. Thayer, "Sir Isaac Newton," *Cambridge Dictionary of Philosophy* (Cambridge: Cambridge University Press, 1995), 529–530.

12. See Frederick C. Beiser, "Kant's Intellectual Development: 1746–1781," in *The Cambridge Companion to Kant,* ed. Paul Guyer (Cambridge: Cambridge University Press, 1992), 26–27; Ernst Cassirer, *Kants Leben und Lehre* (Berlin: B. Cassirer, 1921), 22–58; A. Drews, *Kants Naturphilosophie als Grundlage seines Systems* (Berlin: Mitscher and Röstell, 1894).

13. Immanuel Kant, *Gesammelte Schriften,* 29 vols., ed. Königlich PreuBischen Akademie der Wissenschaften und Deutsche Akademie der Wissenschaften (Berlin: Gerg Reimer und Walter de Gruyter, 1900–1995), quotes I: 10; cited in Kuehn, *Kant: A Biography,* 86–87.

14. Kant, *Gesammelte Schriften,* I:10; Kuehn, *Kant: A Biography,* 87–90; Beiser, "Kant's Intellectual Development, 1746–1781," 31–32; see G. W. Leibniz, *Discourse on Metaphysics; Correspondence with Arnauld; Monadology,* trans. George Montgomery (La Salle: Open Court, 1902).

15. Leibniz, *Discourse on Metaphysics; Correspondence with Arnauld; Monadology,* quote 252; G. W. Leibniz, *Theodicy,* trans E. M. Huggard (La Salle: Open Court, 1985); Kuehn, *Kant: A Biography,* 91–92.

16. Kuehn, *Kant: A Biography,* 95–98.

17. See Kant, *Universal Natural History and Theory of the Heavens;* Beiser, "Kant's Intellectual Development: 1746–1781," 32–33.

18. Kuehn, *Kant: A Biography,* 107–109; Borowski, *Darstellung des Leben und Charakters Immanuel Kants,* 94–97.

19. Alexander G. Baumgarten, *Metaphysica* (Hildesheim: G. Olms, 1982); Baumgarten, *Ethica philosophica* (Hildesheim: G. Olms, 1969); David Hume, *Enquiry Concerning Human Understanding* (1748) and *Enquiry Concerning the Principles of Morals* (1751), one-volume edn., eds. L. A. Selby-Bigge and P. H. Nidditch (Oxford: Clarendon Press, 1975); Hume, *A Treatise of Human Nature* (1739, 1740), eds. L. A. Selby-Bigge and P. H. Nidditch (Oxford: Clarendon Press, 1978); Francis Hutcheson, *A System of Moral Philosophy in Three Books,* 2 vols. (Glasgow: R. & A. Foulis, 1755); Christian Wolff, *Anfangsgründe aller mathematischen Wissenschaften* (Hildesheim: G. Olms, 1973); Frederick C. Beiser, *German Idealism: The Struggle Against Subjectivism, 1781–1801* (Cambridge: Harvard University Press, 2002), 44–47.

20. See Immanuel Kant, *Novo dilucidatio,* in Kant, *Gesammelte Schriften,* I: 460–510; Beiser, "Kant's Intellectual Development: 1746–1781," 34–35.

21. Kuehn, *Kant: A Biography,* 112–116.

22. Immanuel Kant, *Observations on the Feeling of the Beautiful and Sublime,* trans. John T. Goldthwait (1764; reprint, Berkeley: University of California Press, 1991), quotes 77, 79, 81.

23. Ibid., 45–75.

24. Ibid., quotes 103–104.

25. Ibid., quotes 104.

26. Ibid., 109–110.

27. Ibid., quotes 97, 110; David Hume, "Of National Characters," 1748, reprinted in Hume, *Essays and Treatises on Several Subjects,* 2 vols. (Edinburgh: Bell and Pradfute, 1825), I: 521–522.

28. Kant, *Observations on the Feeling of the Beautiful and Sublime,* quote 111.

29. See Kuehn, *Kant: A Biography,* 144–158; Jachmann, *Immanuel Kant geschildert in Briefen an einen Freund,* 152–155, 185.

30. Immanuel Kant, *Die falsche Spitzfindigkeit der vier syllogistischen Figuren,* in Kant, *Gesammelte Schriften,* II: 42–59.

31. Immanuel Kant, *The One Possible Basis for a Demonstration of the Existence of God,* trans. Gordon Treash (New York: Abaris Books, 1979).

32. Anselm, *Basic Writings: Proslogium, Monologium, Gaunilon's Reply on behalf of the Fool, Cur Deus Homo,* 2nd edn., trans. S. W. Deane (La Salle: Open Court, 1962), 53–55.

33. Descartes, third and fifth *Meditations;* Leibniz, *Monadology,* quote 260.

34. Kant, *The One Possible Demonstration for the Existence of God,* 57–61, quote 57; Immanuel Kant, *Critique of Pure Reason,* trans. Norman Kemp Smith (New York: Macmillan Press, 1973), 505, A599/B627. In citations of Kant's first Critique, "A" refers to the first edition (1781), "B" refers to the second edition (1787). Smith's text is

based on the second edition, but Smith also folded into the text passages and sections that Kant omitted from the second edition.

35. Kant, *The One Possible Basis for the Existence of God*, quote 157.

36. Immanuel Kant, *Untersuchhung über die Deutlichkeit der Grundsätze der natürlichen Theologie und der Moral*, Prize Essay for Berlin Academy, 1764, Kant, *Gesammelte Schriften*, II: 276–286; see Beiser, "Kant's Intellectual Development: 1746–1781," 40-41.

37. Kant, "*Bemerkungen zu den Beobachtungen über das Gefühl des Schönen und Erhabenen*," (1764), in Kant, *Gesammelte Schriften*, 20: 44; see Jean Jacques Rousseau, *The Discourses and other early political writings*, ed. and trans., Victor Gourevitch (Cambridge: Cambridge University Press, 1997), 3–28, 113–188.

38. Immanuel Kant, *Dreams of a Spirit-Seer Illustrated by Dreams of Metaphysics*, trans. E. F. Goerwitz (New York: Macmillan, 1900); Kant, *Theoretical Philosophy, 1755–1770*, trans. David Walford and Ralf Meerbote (Cambridge: Cambridge University Press, 1992), 299–311; Jean Jacques Rousseau, *The Social Contract and Other Later Political Writings*, ed. and trans. Victor Gourevitch (Cambridge: Cambridge University Press, 1997), quote 41; Beiser, "Kant's Intellectual Development: 1746–1781," 43–44.

39. Immanuel Kant, *De mundi sensibilis atque intelligibilis forma et principiis*," in Kant, *Theoretical Philosophy*, 1755–1770, 405–415; Kant, *Critique of Pure Reason*, quote, 10, Axiv.

40. Kuehn, *Kant: A Biography*, quote 212; see Kant, *Theoretical Philosophy, 1755–1770*, 388–416.

41. Kant, *Critique of Pure Reason*, 65, A19.

42. Ibid., 111, B102/A77.

43. Ibid., 113–114, A80/B106.

44. Ibid., 120–128, quote 127, A84–95/B117–129.

45. See Kant, *De mundi sensibilis atque intelligibilis forma et principiis*," in Kant, *Theoretical Philosophy, 1755–1770*, 405–415; Kuehn, *Kant: A Biography*, 243–244.

46. H. J. Paton, *Kant's Metaphysic of Experience*, 2 vols. (1936; reprint, London: George Allen & Unwin, 1970), II: 547. On the differences between Kant's rendering of the Transcendental Deduction in the first and second editions of the *Critique of Pure Reason*, see Norman Kemp Smith, *A Commentary to Kant's Critique of Pure Reason* (Atlantic Highlands: Humanities Press, 1962), 284–291.

47. Kant, *Critique of Pure Reason*, 151–152, quotes 152, B130–131.

48. Ibid., 152–155, quotes 152, 153, B131–135.

49. Ibid., 157–158, quotes 154, 158, B139–140; see Smith, *A Commentary to Kant's Critique of Pure Reason*, 285–286.

50. Kant, *Critique of Pure Reason*, 158–159, quote 159, B141–142.

51. Ibid., 161–162, quote 162, B147–148.

52. Ibid., 180, B177/A138.

53. Ibid., 180–182, quotes 181, 182, B177/A138-B179-A140, B180.

54. Ibid., 182–183, A141-B181/A142.

55. Ibid., 345–346, A369.

56. Ibid., 346, A370.

57. Ibid., 346–347, A370–371, "usual type," 439, B519.

58. Ibid., 439, A491/B519; see P. F. Strawson, *The Bounds of Sense: An Essay on Kant's Critique of Pure Reason* (London: Methuen, 1966), 235–263; Karl Ameriks, *Kant's Theory of Mind: An Analysis of the Paralogisms of Pure Reason* (Oxford: Clarendon Press, 1982), 255–294.

59. Kant, *Critique of Pure Reason*, 349–350, A376–377; see Beiser, *German Idealism: The Struggle Against Subjectivity, 1781–1801*, 66.

60. Kant, *Critique of Pure Reason*, quote 359, A393; 67–70, B37/A23-A25/B40; see Beiser, *German Idealism: The Struggle Against Subjectivity, 1781–1801*, 69.

61. Kant, *Critique of Pure Reason*, 359–360, A393.

62. Beiser, *German Idealism: The Struggle Against Subjectivity, 1781–1801*, 70.

63. Kant, *Critique of Pure Reason*, 79–80, A38/B55; 268–269, A251–252, "namely," 269, A252; 339–340, A359, "Matter is"; see Beiser, *German Idealism: The Struggle Against Subjectivity, 1781–1801*, 71.

64. Kant, *Critique of Pure Reason*, 161–164, B146–149, quote 162, B147.

65. Ibid., 257–275, B295/A236-B315/A260, 500–524, A592/B620-A630/B658, quotes 257, B295/A236.

66. Ibid., 257–264, B295/A236-A247/B304, quote 264, A247.

67. See Smith, *A Commentary on Kant's Critique of Pure Reason*, 406–407; J. N. Findlay, *Kant and the Transcendental Object: A Hermeneutic Study* (Oxford: Clarendon Press, 1981), 195–225.

68. Kant, *Critique of Pure Reason*, quotes, 270–271, A253.

69. Ibid., 270–272, B309/A255-B311.

70. Ibid., 525–527, A631/B659-A635/B663, quotes 526, 526–7; see Immanuel Kant, *Lectures on Philosophical Theology*, trans. Allen W. Wood and Gertrude M. Clark (Ithaca: Cornell University Press, 1978), 28–31.

71. Immanuel Kant, *Foundations of the Metaphysics of Morals*, trans. Lewis White Beck, with critical essays ed. Robert Paul Wolff (1785; reprint, Indianapolis: Bobbs-Merrill, 1969); Kant, *Critique of Practical Reason*, trans. Lewis White Beck (1788; Indianapolis: Bobbs-Merrill, 1956); Kant, *Religion Within the Limits of Reason Alone*, trans. Theodore M. Greene and Hoyt H. Hudson (1793; reprint, Chicago: Open Court, 1934), or Kant, *Religion Within the Boundaries of Mere Reason and Other Writings*, ed. and trans. Allen Wood and George De Giovanni (Cambridge: Cambridge University Press, 1998).

72. Kant, *Critique of Pure Reason*, 29, BXXX.

73. For the view that Kant more or less successfully held knowledge and faith separately, see Allen W. Wood, *Kant's Moral Religion* (Ithaca: Cornell University Press, 1970); for the view that he offered a moral proof that was illegitimate on Kant's grounds, see Norman Kemp Smith, *A Commentary to Kant's Critique of Pure Reason*, 637–641, and Lewis White Beck, *A Commentary on Kant's Critique of Practical Reason* (Chicago: University of Chicago Press, 1960); for the view that he formulated a moral proof in the 1790s and later repudiated it, see Erich Adickes, *Kants Opus Postumum, dargestellt und beurteilt* (Berlin: Reuther & Reichard, 1920), 769–785.

74. Kant, *Critique of Pure Reason*, 646–647, A822/B850-A823/B851, quote 646, A823/B851; Kant, *Critique of Practical Reason*, 4–7.

75. Kant, *Critique of Pure Reason*, 650, A828/B856.

76. Ibid.

77. Ibid.; Kant, *Lectures on Philosophical Theology*, 121–131.

78. Kant, *Critique of Pure Reason*, 651, A830/B858; Kant, *Religion within the Boundaries of Mere Reason*, 169–170, 6:174–6:176; see Allen W. Wood, "Rational Theology, Moral Faith, and Religion," in *The Cambridge Companion to Kant*, 396–397.

79. Kant, *Religion within the Boundaries of Mere Reason*, quotes, 164, 6:168; 166, 6:171; 170, 6:174; Kant, *Foundations of the Metaphysics of Morals*, 19–25, 44, quote 44.

80. Kant, *Religion within the Boundaries of Mere Reason*, 160–161, 6:163–6:164.

81. Ibid., 52–73, 6:29–6:53.

82. Ibid., 52–55, 6:29–6:32.

83. Ibid., quote 79, 6:60.

84. Ibid., quote 80, 6:61; G. E. Lessing, "The Education of the Human Race," in Lessing, *Lessing's Theological Writings,* trans. Henry Chadwick (London: Adam & Charles Black, 1956), 82–98.

85. Kant, *Religion within the Boundaries of Mere Reason,* 190–191, 6:200–202.

86. Frederick C. Beiser, *The Fate of Reason: German Philosophy from Kant to Fichte* (Cambridge: Harvard University Press, 1987), 165–172, quote 172; Kuehn, *Kant: A Biography,* 250–254; Johann Schulz, *Exposition of Kant's Critique,* trans. James C. Morrison (Ottowa: University of Ottowa Press, 1995).

87. See Christian Garve, *Abhandlung über die Verbindung der Moral mit der Politik* (Breslau: Korn, 1788); J. A. Eberhard, *Neue Apologie des Sokrates* (Berlin: Voss, 1772); J. G. H. Feder, *Ueber Raum und Causalität* (Frankfurt: Dietrich, 1788); Thomas Reid, *An Inquiry into the Human Mind, on the principles of Common Sense,* 3rd edn. (Dublin: R. Marchbank, 1779); Reid, *Essays on the Intellectual Powers of Man* (1785), in *The Works of Thomas Reid,* ed. Sir William Hamilton (Edinburgh: MacLachlan and Stewart, 1872), I: 255–259; Beiser, *The Fate of Reason: German Philosophy from Kant to Fichte,* 165–167; S. A. Grave, *The Scottish Philosophy of Common Sense* (Oxford: Oxford University Press, 1960).

88. (Christian Garve), "Kritik der reinen Vernunft von Immanuel Kant," *Zugaben zu den Göttinger gelehrte Anzeigen* 3 (January 19, 1782), 40–48; see Garve, "Kritik der reinen Vernunft von Immanuel Kant," *Allgemeine deutsche Bibliothik* (1783), 838–862; A. Stern, *Ueber die Beziehung Garves zu Kant* (Leipzig: Denicke, 1884); Beiser, *The Fate of Reason: German Philosophy from Kant to Fichte,* 172–175; Thomas Reid, *An Inquiry into the Human Mind, on the Principles of Common Sense,* 3rd edn. (Dublin: R. Marchbank, 1779); Frances Hutcheson, *An Inquiry into the Original of ur Ideas of Beauty and Virtue,* 2nd edn. (London: J. Darby and others, 1726).

89. Immanuel Kant to Johann Schultz, August 26, 1783, in Kant, *Briefe, Akademie Ausgabe,* ed. R. Reicke (Berlin: Reimer, 1912), X: 350–351; Beiser, *The Fate of Reason: German Philosophy from Kant to Fichte,* 177.

90. Immanuel Kant, *Kant's Critical Philosophy,* II: *Prolegomena to Any Future Metaphysic,* trans. John P. Mahaffy and John H. Bernard (1783; London: Macmillan, 1889), quotes 8, 11.

91. Ibid., quotes 7, 4.

92. Ibid., 7–12.

93. Kant, appendix to ibid., "Specimen of a Judgment on the *Kritik* Prior to Its Examination," 145–151; Beiser, *The Fate of Reason: German Philosophy from Kant to Fichte,* 174.

94. Kant, "Specimen of a Judgment on the *Kritik* Prior to Its Examination," 147–148.

95. Kant, *Prolegomena to Any Future Metaphysic,* quotes 48.

96. See Reid, *Essays on the Intellectual Powers of Man,* I: 255–259; G. A. Tittel, *Ueber Herr Kants Moralreform* (Frankfurt: Pfahler, 1786); Tittel, *Kantische Denkformen oder Kategorien* (Frankfurt: Gebhardt, 1787); Heinrich Weber, *Hamann und Kant: ein Beitrag zur Geschichte der Philosophie im Zeitalter der Aufklärung* (Munich: C. H. Beck, 1904); Beiser, *The Fate of Reason: German Philosophy from Kant to Fichte,* 167–172; Manfred Kuehn, *Scottish Common Sense in Germany, 1768–1800: A Contribution to the History of Critical Philosophy* (Montreal: McGill-Queens, 1987);

97. See Johann Schultz, *Erläuterungen über des Herrn Prof. Kants Kritik der reinen Vernunft* (Königsberg: Dengel, 1784); Karl Leonhard Reinhold, *Brife über die kantische Philosophie*

(Leipzig: G. J. Göshen, 1790); Reinhold, *Über das Fundament des Philosophischen Wissens* (1791; reprint, Hamburg: Felix Meiner, 1978); Reinhold, *Über die Möglichkeit der Philosophie als strenge Wissenschaft* (1790; reprint, Hamburg: Felix Meiner, 1978); Kuehn, Kant: A Biography, 329–334.

98. Johann Gottfried Herder, *Against Pure Reason: Writings on Religion, Language, and History,* ed. and trans. Marcia Bung (Minneapolis: Fortress Press, 1993); Herder, *Metacritique* (1799) and *Calligone* (1800), in Herder, *Werke,* 3 vols., ed. Wolfgang Pross and Pierre Penisson (Munich: Carl Hanser, 1984–1985); Herder, *Outlines of a Philosophy of the History of Man,* trans. T. O. Churchill (London: J. Johnson, 1880); Friedrich Heinrich Jacobi, *Werke,* 2 vols., ed. Friedrich Roth and Friedrich Köppen (Darmstadt: Wissenschaftliche Buchgesellschaft, 1976), II: 299–308; Jacobi, *Wider Mendelssohns Beschuldigungen* (Leipzig: Goschen, 1786).

99. J. G. Hamann, "Metakritik über den Purismum der reinen Vernunft," in Hamann, *Sämtliche Werke, Historisch-Kritische Ausgabe,* ed. J. Nadler (Vienna: Herder, 1949–1957), 277–287; English edition in Hamann, *Writings on Philosophy and Language,* trans. Kenneth Haynes (Cambridge: Cambridge University Press, 2007), 205–218, quotes, 208, 210; see Hamann, *Schriften zur Sprache,* ed. J. Simon (Frankfurt: Suhrkamp, 1967); Beiser, *The Fate of Reason: German Philosophy from Kant to Fichte,* 38–43.

100. Immanuel Kant, "Beantwortung der Frage: Was ist Aufklärung?" *Berlinische Monatsschrift* 4 (1784), 481–494; Kant, "An Answer to the Question: What Is Enlightenment?," trans. James Schmidt, in *What Is Enlightenment? Eighteenth-Century Answers and Twentieth-Century Questions,* ed. James Schmidt (Berkeley: University of California Press, 1996), 58–64, quotes 58, 59.

101. Ibid., quote 63.

102. Ibid., quotes 62, 63.

103. Johann Georg Hamann, "Letter to Christian Jacob Kraus," December 18, 1784, trans. Garrett Green, reprinted in *What Is Enlightenment? Eighteenth-Century Answers and Twentieth-Century Questions,* 145–148, quotes 147, 148.

104. Kuehn, *Kant: A Biography,* quotes 340, 341; Immanuel Kant, "On the Common Saying: 'This May be True in Theory, But It Does Not Apply in Practice'" (1793), in Kant, *Kant's Political Writings,* ed. Hans Reiss, trans. H. B. Nisbet (Cambridge: Cambridge University Press, 1970), 61–92.

105. Immanuel Kant, *Critique of Judgment* trans. James Creed Meredith (1790; Oxford: Oxford University Press, 1952), quote 38.

106. Ibid., 55–67, quotes 62, 63.

107. Ibid., 65–68, 84–88, quotes 67.

108. Kuehn, *Kant: A Biography,* 378–380, quote 379.

109. Immanuel Kant, "Perpetual Peace: A Philosophical Sketch," in *Kant's Political Writings,* 93–108.

110. Ibid., quote 93.

111. Ibid., quote 129.

112. Immanuel Kant, *The Conflict of the Faculties,* trans. Mary J. Gregor (New York: Abaris Books, 1979).

113. Benedict de Spinoza, *Works of Spinoza,* 2 vols, *Theologico-Political Treatise and Political Treatise,* and *On the Improvement of the Understanding; The Ethics; Correspondence,* trans. R. H. M. Elwes (London: George Bell and Sons, Bohn Library Edition, 1883).

114. Friedrich Heinrich Jacobi, *Ueber die Lehre des Spinoza in Briefen an Herrn Moses Mendelssohn* (Breslau: G. Lowe, 1785); in Jacobi, *Werke,* 6 vols., ed. F. H. Jacobi and F. Köppen (Leipzig: Fleischer, 1812), IV: 1–47; and Jacobi, *Concerning the Doctrine of*

Spinoza in Letters to Herr Moses Mendelssohn, in *F. H. Jacobi: The Main Philosophical Writings and the Novel "Allwill,"* ed. and trans. George di Giovanni (Montreal: McGill-Queen's University Press, 1994), 181–251, quote 187.

115. F. H. Jacobi, *wider Mendelssohns Beschuldigungen betreffend die Briefe über die Lehre des Spinoza* (Leipzig: Bey Georg Joachim Goeschen, 1786), 215–225; Jacobi, Werke, IV: 1, 210–227; Jacobi, *Concerning the Doctrine of Spinoza in Letters to Moses Mendelssohn,* 2nd edn., 1789, in *F. H. Jacobi: The Main Philosophical Writings and the Novel "Allwill,"* 341–386; Moses Mendelssohn, "Erinnerungen an Herrn Jacobi," in Mendelssohn, *Gesammelte Schriften,* ed. A. Altmann, et al. (Stuttgart: Holzborg, 1971), III: 2, 200–207; Beiser, *The Fate of Reason: German Philosophy from Kant to Fichte,* 44–91.

116. Jacobi, *Concerning the Doctrine of Spinoza in Letters to Herr Moses Mendelssohn,* quotes 231.

117. Friedrich Heinrich Jacobi, *David Hume über den Glauben, oder, Idealismus und Realismus* (1787; reprint, New York: Garland, 1983); and Jacobi, *David Hume on Faith, or Idealism and Realism, A Dialogue,* in *F. H. Jacobi: The Main Philosophical Writings and the Novel "Allwill,"* 253–338, quote 336.

118. Jacobi, *David Hume on Faith, or Idealism and Realism, A Dialogue,* quote 321; see Beisner, *German Idealism: The Struggle Against Subjectivism, 1781–1801,* 384–385.

119. F. H. Jacobi, *Jacobi an Fichte* (Hamburg: Perthes, 1799); Jacobi, *Jacobi to Fichte,* in *F. H. Jacobi: The Main Philosophical Writings and the Novel "Allwill,"* 501–533, quotes 501, 519, 531.

120. Jacobi, *wider Mendelssohns Beschuldigungen betreffend die Briefe über die Lehre des Spinoza,* 228; Heinrich Heine, *The Romantic School and Other Essays,* ed. Jost Hermand and Robert C. Holub (New York: Continuum Books, 1985), 181; Isaiah Berlin, *Against the Current: Essays in the History of Ideas* (New York: Viking Press, 1979), 162–187; see Terry Pinkard, *German Philosophy, 1760–1860: The Legacy of Idealism* (Cambridge: Cambridge University Press, 2002), 90–96; George di Giovanni, "Introduction: The Unfinished Philosophy of Friedrich Heinrich Jacobi," in *F. H. Jacobi: The Main Philosophical Writings and the Novel "Allwill,"* 152–167.

121. Pinkard, *German Philosophy, 1760–1860: The Legacy of Idealism,* 106–107; Kuehn, *Kant: A Biography,* 355–356; Rudolf Malter, *Immanuel Kant in Rede und Gespräch* (Hamburg: Felix Meiner Verlag, 1990), 371–376.

122. Johann G. Fichte, *Attempt at a Critique of All Revelation,* trans. Garrett Green (Cambridge: Cambridge University Press, 2010), quote 129; Kuehn, *Kant: A Biography,* "young" and "to house," 356; Malter, *Immanuel Kant in Rede und Gespräch,* 371, 375.

123. Kuehn, *Kant: A Biography,* quote 363; Malter, *Immanuel Kant in Rede und Gespräch,* 375; see Ludwig Feuerbach, *The Essence of Christianity* (1841), trans. George Eliot (New York: Harper & Row, 1957).

124. J. G. Fichte, "Review of *Aenesidemus,*" in Fichte, *Fichte: Early Philosophical Writings,* ed. and trans. Daniel Breazeale (Ithaca: Cornell University Press, 1988), "piece of," 71.

125. Breazeale, "Fichte in Jena," ibid., "truth consists," 13; Pinkard, *German Philosophy, 1760–1860: The Legacy of Idealism,* 106–111.

126. Translators' Preface to J. G. Fichte, *Science of Knowledge,* trans. Peter Heath and John Lachs (Cambridge: Cambridge University Press, 1982), quotes vii.

127. Rudolf Steiner, "Sieben Briefe von Fichte an Goethe – zwei von Fichte an Schiller," *Goethe-Jahrbuch* 15 (1894), 49, cited in Breazeals, editor's introduction, *Fichte: Early Philosophical Writings,* 22; Fichte, *Science of Knowledge,* 93.

128. Fichte, *Science of Knowledge,* 93–110, quote 110.

129. Ibid., quotes 99, 112, 113–114; see Tom Rockmore and Daniel Breazeale, *New Perspectives on Fichte* (Atlantic Highlands: Humanities Press, 1996); Frederick Neuhouser, *Fichte's Theory of Subjectivity* (Cambridge: Cambridge University Press, 1990); Robert Pippin, *Hegel's Idealism* (Cambridge: Cambridge University Press, 1989), 42–59.

130. Pinkard, *German Philosophy, 1760–1860: The Legacy of Idealism*, 110–119; Wayne M. Martin, *Idealism and Objectivity: Understanding Fichte's Jena Project* (Palo Alto: Stanford University Press, 1997), 75. Pinkard defends the intuitionist construal of things-in-themselves and Martin defends the view that Fichte eliminated things-in-themselves.

131. J. G. Fichte, *A Crystal Clear Report to the General Public Concerning the Actual Essence of the Newest Philosophy: An Attempt to Force the Reader to Understand*, trans. John Botterman and William Rasch, in *Philosophy of German Idealism*, ed. Ernst Behler (New York: Continuum, 1987), quote 80; see *Johann Gottlieb Fichtes nachgelassene Werke*, 3 vols., ed. Immanuel H. Fichte (Bonn: Adolph-Marcus, 1834–1835).

132. The classic rendering of Fichte as absolute idealist is Josiah Royce, *The Spirit of Modern Philosophy* (Cambridge: Houghton Mifflin, 1892), 158–165. For similar readings, see Frederick Copleston, *History of Philosophy* (New York: Doubleday, 1965), VII: 72, 79; John Lachs, "Fichte's Idealism," *American Philosophical Quarterly* 9 (1972), 311–318; Robert C. Solomon, *In the Spirit of Hegel* (Oxford: Oxford University Press, 1983), 85–96; Heath and Lachs, preface to Fichte, *The Science of Knowledge*, vii–xviii; Manfred Frank, *Unendliche Annäherung: die Anfänge der philosophischen Frühromantk* (Frankfurt: Suhrkamp, 1997), 133–151. For Fichte as subjective idealist, see Jacobi, *Jacobi to Fichte*, in *Friedrich Heinrich Jacobi: The Main Philosophical Writings and the Novel Allwill*, 503–526; Manfred Buhr, *Revolution und Philosophie: Die Ursprüngliche Philosophie Johann Gottlieb Fichte und die französische Revolution* (Berlin: Akademie, 1965), 106–111, 126; Georg Lukács, *Der junge Hegel* (Frankfurt: Suhrkamp, 1969), II: 409–445. For discussion of these interpretive traditions, see Beiser, *German Idealism: The Struggle Against Subjectivism, 1781–1801*, 217–239.

133. Beiser, *German Idealism: The Struggle Against Subjectivism, 1781–1801*, 223–345; A. J. Mandt, "Fichte's Idealism in Theory and Practice," *Idealistic Studies* 14 (1984), 127–147. For critiques of pragmatic interpretations of Fichte, see John Lachs, "Is There an Absolute Self?" *Philosophical Forum* 19 (1987–1988), 169–182; Daniel Breazeale, "The Theory of Practice and the Practice of Theory: Fichte and 'the Primacy of Practical Reason,'" *International Philosophical Quarterly* 36 (1996), 47–64.

134. J. G. Fichte, *Grundlage des Naturrechts nach Prinzipien der Wissenschaftslehre* (1796), in Fichte. *Sämmtliche Werke*, 8 vols., ed. Immanuel H. Fichte (Berlin: Veit, 1845–1846), III: 343–350; *Fichte's Early Philosophical Writings*, quote 417; see Pinkard, *German Philosophy, 1760–1860: The Legacy of Idealism*, 124–126.

135. J. G. Fichte, "On the Ground of Our Belief in a Divine World-Governance," *Philosophisches Journal einer Gesellschaft Teutscher Gelehrten* (Fall 1798), in *J. G. Fichte and the Atheism Dispute (1798–1800)*, ed. Yolanda Estes and Curtis Bowman (Aldershot: Ashgate, 2010), 21–28, quotes 21, 26.

136. Ibid., quote 25.

137. Ibid., quote 27; Johann Wolfgang von Goethe, *Faust: Ein Trauerspiel* (Leipzig: 1790), 137–139, and Friedrich von Schiller, "Words of Faith," in *Musen-Almanach für das Jahr 1798* (Tübingen: 1798), cited in ibid., 28.

138. Jacobi, *Jacobi to Fichte*, quote 519.

139. J. G. Fichte, "Appeal to the Public," *J. G. Fichte and the Atheism Dispute (1798–1800)*, 85–126; Fichte, "Juridical Defense," ibid., 145–204; G., "A Father's Letter to His Student Son about Fichte's and Forberg's Atheism," ibid., 49–76; Yolanda Estes,

"Commentator's Introduction," ibid., 4–9; Students of the University of Jena, "First Petition to Karl August of Saxony-Weimar-Eisenach," ibid., 220–226; F. H. Jacobi, *Jacobi to Fichte,* 503–526.

140. Immanuel Kant, open letter, August 7, 1799, *Allgemeine Literaturzeitung,* 109 (1799), reprinted in *Fichte's Leben und literarischer Briefwechsel,* ed. I. H. Fichte (1862), II: 161–162; cited in Walter Kaufman, *Hegel: Reinterpretation, Texts, and Commentary* (Garden City: Doubleday, 1965), 122–123; see Students of the University of Jena, "Second Petition to Karl August of Saxony-Weimar-Eisenach," January 10, 1800, in *J. G. Fichte and the Atheism Dispute (1798–1800),* 227–231.

141. J. G. Fichte, *The Vocation of Man* (1800), ed. and trans. Peter Preuss (Indianapolis: Hackett, 1987); Fichte, *Addresses to the German Nation,* ed. and trans. Gregory Moore (Cambridge: Cambridge University Press, 2008), "if you sink," 196; *Fichte's Early Philosophical Writings,* 44–45; Kuehn, *Kant: A Biography,* 390–391, 412–413.

142. J. G. Fichte, *Die Wissenschaftslehre in ihrem allgemeinen Umrisse, in Sämmtliche Werke,* II: 708–709; Pinkard, *German Philosophy, 1760–1860: The Legacy of Idealism,* 127–128; *New Essays on Fichte's later Wissenschaftslehre,* ed. Daniel Breazeale and Tom Rockmore (Evanston: Northwestern University Press, 2002); Estes, "Commentator's Introduction," *J. G. Fichte and the Atheism Dispute (1798–1800),* 14–15.

143. Gregory Moore, editor's introduction to Fichte, *Addresses to the German Nation,* xxxii–xxxiv; see C. Jeffrey Kinlaw, "The Being of Appearance: Absolute, Image, and the Trinitarian Structure of the 1813 *Wissenschaftslehre,*" in *New Perspectives on Fichte,* 127–142.

144. Kant, *Critique of Pure Reason,* Bxxviii, 28.

3

Making Sense of Religion

Friedrich Schleiermacher, John Locke, Samuel Taylor Coleridge, and Liberal Theology

Immanuel Kant, despite his towering stature in modern philosophy, had barely a moment in the sun by himself. He never commanded the field by himself. The thinkers that boosted him to prominence were adamant critics of his idealism and scholasticism. He had not even finished his third *Critique* when post-Kantian idealism began to be conjured. From the beginning of Kant's ascension it was open season on his dualism, the thing-in-itself, and his rendering of religion. Romantic idealists in Jena, Berlin, Frankfurt, and Homburg, though disagreeing about what Kant said, agreed that his dualism was unacceptable and he didn't understand what religion was about.

Two absolute idealists, F. W. J. Schelling and G. W. F. Hegel, took post-Kantian idealism as far as it could go. But they were not theologians, and both were too intellectualist to convey recognizably Christian piety to ordinary church-goers. The theologian of the post-Kantian reaction was Friedrich Schleiermacher, a product of the same Romantic generation and atmosphere that shaped Schelling, Hegel, and Samuel Taylor Coleridge. Schleiermacher was just beginning to make a name for himself when Coleridge traveled to Germany to study Kantian idealism. Coleridge got his idealism from Kant and Schelling, not Schleiermacher, and afterward he thought with Kant and Schelling, not Schleiermacher, whose system came too late for Coleridge to assimilate to his already fully formed thought.

But Coleridge had the Schleiermacher role in British theology, founding a modern approach to religion by fashioning post-Kantian idealism to the language and lifeworld of the existing Christian Church. For Schleiermacher, Leibniz-style rationalism had made a good start in some respects, but it was dreadfully deficient in what really mattered. Coleridge had similar feelings about John Locke, the luminary of British empiricism, whose standing in British thought and culture had to be deflated if British religion was to reach for the higher things.

Kantian Reason and Hegelian Spirit: The Idealistic Logic of Modern Theology, First Edition. Gary Dorrien.
© 2012 John Wiley & Sons, Ltd. Published 2015 by John Wiley & Sons, Ltd.

Sense for the Infinite: Friedrich Schleiermacher

Wilhelm Dilthey, in his unfinished life and letters of Schleiermacher, declared that Schleiermacher, unlike Kant, could not be understood without understanding his life and character. Dilthey was wrong about Kant, but right about Schleiermacher, whose life and character pervaded his work distinctly. Schleiermacher taught that religion draws its life from feeling, not from doctrine or morality. Besides teaching it, Schleiermacher lived this belief, preached it, and theorized about it, drawing on his background in Moravian piety.[1]

Friedrich Daniel Ernst Schleiermacher was born in 1768 in Breslau (today's Wroclaw in southern Poland) and named, like a great many Germanic males of his generation, after King Friedrich II, in whose army his father Gottlieb Schleiermacher served as a chaplain. Gottlieb, a Reformed cleric and studious type, had been forced as a youth to testify in his father's criminal trial for witchcraft. In his early career Gottlieb struggled with Reformed theology, drifted through a rationalist phase, and periodically instructed his three children in religion on his occasional stopovers at home. Friedrich Schleiermacher later recalled that because his father traveled extensively with the army, his mother assumed the major burden of religious instruction: "My mother, who, though she was fondly attached to me, was by no means blind to my faults, endeavored, by acting upon my religious feelings, to change my pride into gratitude toward God."[2]

In 1778, Gottlieb experienced a Pietistic awakening upon encountering the Moravian community at Gnadenfrei in Upper Silesia and becoming acquainted with the Moravian school at Niesky in Upper Lusatia, both in Prussia. The Moravian Brethren practiced a devotional, communal, warm-hearted personal religion centered on Christ's expiatory sacrifice on the cross. Being a Reformed army chaplain, Gottlieb could not join the Moravians without losing his position, but he converted his family to Moravian pietism, stressing to his children that moral depravity prevailed in the non-Moravian schools. Gottlieb was grateful to have thrown off rationalistic disbelief and was anxious to protect his children from it. Thus he placed his sons Friedrich and Carl in the boarding school at Niesky and eventually placed his daughter Charlotte in the school at Gnadenfrei. Friedrich was 14 years old when he left home, by his account happily anticipating the "innocent piety" of the Moravians. He never saw either of his parents again, as his mother died shortly afterward, and his father traveled approximately two thousand miles per year with the army. Schleiermacher, however, exchanged letters with his father until Gottlieb's death in 1794, and for the rest of his life his intimate personal relationships, nearly all with women, were the mainstays of his existence.[3]

The Moravians were devoted to Jesus and taught that religion can only be awakened, not really taught – two predispositions that stuck with Schleiermacher long after he threw off Moravian theology. The boarding school at Niesky was monastic in ethos and pietistic academically. It was strict in the area of personal life, seeking to protect students from the evils of the world, but fairly lax academically, allowing time for independent study. Schleiermacher later recalled that "every discourse and every lesson" stressed the depravity of human nature and the supernatural means of grace; communion with Jesus was the goal, which depended on a breakthrough of grace by the Holy Spirit. To be saved was to gratefully accept Christ's atoning sacrifice for sin. The Moravians were serious about wanting their students to experience the joy of salvation; thus they avoided the penitential severities of other Pietist groups, which Schleiermacher appreciated. Twenty years later, after visiting Gnadenfrei, he recalled gratefully that it was among the Moravians that he first awoke to his sense of being related to a higher world: "Here it was that that mystic tendency developed itself, which has been of so much importance to me, and has supported and carried me through all the storms of skepticism. Then it was only germinating, now it has attained its full development, and I may say, that after all I have passed through, I have become a Herrnhuter again, only of a higher order." (Herrnhut was an estate of Nicolas von Zinzendorf's that became a central outpost of the Moravian community.)[4]

At the Moravian seminary at Barby, however, Schleiermacher rebelled against monastic seclusion, censorship, and orthodox theology. Barby students were forbidden to read many modern writers, notably Goethe, which goaded Schleiermacher and his friends to read Goethe. Schleiermacher's teachers railed against J. S. Semler and the school of biblical criticism that he established at Halle, which made Schleiermacher yearn to study at Halle. School administrators cracked down on Schleiermacher's group, prohibiting independent studies and expelling an English student. Schleiermacher later recalled, "The investigations of modern theologians into the Christian system, and the inquiries of modern philosophers regarding the soul of man, were of no avail to us, for although we heard occasionally that something of the kind was going on in the world, we could only guess at the results from what we discovered ourselves." Feeling alienated from the Moravian Brethren, Schleiermacher told his father in a letter that things were going badly for him, mainly because he didn't believe in traditional atonement theory.[5]

How could a loving God subject human beings to everlasting punishment for their sins? But if that was unbelievable, Christ's expiatory sacrifice was unnecessary, in addition to making no sense. Schleiermacher explained: "I cannot believe that He, who called Himself the Son of Man, was the true, eternal God; I cannot believe that His death was a vicarious atonement, because He never expressly said so Himself; and I cannot believe it to have been necessary, because God, who evidently did not create men for perfection, but for the pursuit of it, cannot possibly intend to punish them eternally, because they have not attained it." Asking his father for permission to enroll at Halle, Schleiermacher signed off, "Your distressed and most dutiful Son."[6]

Gottlieb's reply was anguished and furious: "Oh, thou insensate son! Who has deluded thee, that thou no longer obeyest the truth, thou, before whose eyes Christ was pictured, and who now crucifiest him? You were so well started, who has held you back from obeying the truth?" Had Friedrich really become so degenerate in merely a few months? Or were his early letters filled with hypocrisy and deception? Had he never tasted "one little drop of balsam" from the wounds of Jesus? It seemed to Gottlieb that his son had chosen a different god; thus he bade farewell to Friedrich: "With heart-rending grief I discard thee, for discard thee I must, as thou no longer worshippest the God of thy fathers, as thou no longer kneelest at the same altar with him – yet, once more, my son, before we part – oh! tell me, what has the poor, meek, and humble-hearted Jesus done to thee, that thou renouncest his strength and his divine peace? Did you find no consolation when you laid before Him your need, the anguish of your heart? And now, in return for the divine long-suffering and patience with which He listened to you, you deny Him?" As for Halle, where Friedrich's (maternal) uncle Samuel Stubenrauch taught theology, Gottlieb was willing to pay for three semesters, as a farewell gift. Since Friedrich longed for the world's approval, he might as well find out if his soul could feed on the world's husks.[7]

Friedrich's reply was sensitive but unyielding. His feeling of "wretchedness" was unbearable, especially at grieving his father. He had never been a hypocrite – "I did really feel it," but he could not continue to feel devoted to doctrines that he no longer believed. He implored his father to stop overreacting, for their views were not as different as Gottlieb claimed: "You say that the glorification of God is the end of our being, and I say the glorification of the creature; is not this in the end the same thing? Is not the Creator more and more glorified the happier and the more perfect his creatures are?" Schleiermacher protested that he felt "the most sincere love and filial gratitude towards the all-good God, who, even in the midst of the painful circumstances that are now besetting me, lets me experience such far preponderating good." How could that count for nothing to his father? Why did Gottlieb insist that mere doubts about atonement theory and Christology made his son an enemy of God? "Why do you say, dearest father, that I no longer worship your God, but that I desire to serve stranger gods? Is it not one and the same God who has created you and me, and whom we both reverence?" Since he was still a believing Christian, Schleiermacher asked his father to reconsider casting him aside.[8]

Gottlieb Schleiermacher half-relented, sustaining a relationship with his son, though he grieved that "pride, egotism, and intolerance have taken possession of you," which made it repugnant for Friedrich to claim that he was inspired by the love of Christ. At Halle, the leading university of the German Enlightenment, Schleiermacher lived with his uncle Samuel Stubenrauch, a moderate supernaturalist with rationalist leanings. The university's golden age had faded before Schleiermacher arrived there. Leading German enlighteners had taught at Halle – Christian Wolff, Alexander G. Baumgarten, J. S. Semler, and briefly, Johann David Michaelis – but Schleiermacher had no teachers of that order. Under Johann August Eberhard he studied philosophy, notably Kant, whose *Critique of Practical Reason* was published shortly after Schleiermacher matriculated. Schleiermacher consumed Kant's philosophy, judging that Kant got the balance exactly right between upholding and limiting metaphysical reason, though Eberhard criticized Kant's skepticism. Otherwise Schleiermacher got little from his academic training, later recalling that he might have learned more had be been less obstinate and possessed "more outward culture." After two years at Halle, he followed his uncle Samuel to a semi-retirement country pastorate in Drossen, where Schleiermacher floundered, doubting that he believed in anything besides Kantian ethics.[9]

Schleiermacher was lonely, depressed, and physically ill in Drossen. Instead of studying for his theology examination for the Reformed Church, he brooded that theology was pointlessly complex and scholastic, fixated on conceptual subtleties that proved nothing. For that matter, he thought, Christianity probably should be tossed aside and replaced with Kantian ethics, except that Schleiermacher rejected Kant's moral argument for God too. To regain his theological vocation, Schleiermacher had to feel religious, which could not happen in lonely Drossen, though he passed his theology exam in 1790. His life turned a corner that year upon taking a private tutorial position with the family of a nobleman, Count Wilhelm Dohna, at Schlobitten in East Prussia. Count Dohna and his wife, a born countess, were conservative monarchists, friendly, refined, and skilled conversationalists, with twelve children. Schleiermacher adored one of the teen-aged countesses, awakened emotionally, and stayed with the Dohna family for three years, preaching philosophical sermons at a local church. Later he recalled that he first awakened to "the beauty of human fellowship" in the Dohna home: "I saw that it requires freedom to ennoble and give right expression to the delicate intimacies of human nature."[10]

In 1794 Schleiermacher belatedly took his second theology exam, and two years later he was appointed as a Reformed chaplain at Charité Hospital, Berlin's main hospital, where he plunged into the Prussian capital's social swirl of salons and intellectual conversation. Berlin was becoming the vanguard of Romanticism. Goethe's *Wilhelm Meister's Apprenticeship* (1795), a prototypical coming-of-age novel about a young man's emotional, intellectual, and artistic development, made a huge impression on aspiring intellectuals and artists of Schleiermacher's generation. Schleiermacher's new friends vowed to find unity in their lives by devoting themselves full-heartedly to something worthy of devotion. One important friend was Marcus Herz, a prominent physician and former student of Kant's, who hosted gatherings of intellectuals in his home. Another was the rising poet and writer Friedrich Schlegel, who moved to Berlin in 1797. Schleiermacher's closest friends were women, especially Herz's multilingual, cultured, beautiful wife Henriette Herz, who was less than half the age of her husband.[11]

Schleiermacher and Henriette had an intimate friendship for many years, meeting every day whenever they were not separated, usually spending entire afternoons together, traveling abroad together, and writing to each other whenever separated. For Schleiermacher, the essential prerequisite for friendship was a highly developed mutual capacity to describe one's feelings. He and Henriette constantly poured out their similar feelings to each other. Both stressed that they connected emotionally, not sexually. Henriette noted that they made a "somewhat comical" pair when traveling abroad, as Schleiermacher was "small, spare, and not very well-built," while she was very tall and full-figured. He said the same thing more dramatically: "Her appearance possesses no charms in my eyes, although her face is undeniably beautiful, and her colossal, queenlike figure is so very much the opposite of mine, that even supposing that we were both free, and that we loved each other and wished to marry, the match would seem to me from this point of view alone so ridiculous and absurd, that only very weighty reasons could induce me to waive the objection." Henriette explained her Platonic soulmate: "He had an irresistible inward craving to commune with friends, to open before them every fold and crevice in his heart and mind, and an equal craving for signs of life and love from his friends."[12]

Schleiermacher's life turned a corner upon meeting Henriette and her husband, who introduced him to Schlegel. A brilliant, mercurial personality, Schlegel was fond of saying that three great events determined what his generation was to be about: the French Revolution, Fichte's *Wissenschaftslehre*, and Goethe's *Wilhelm Meister's Apprenticeship*. Schlegel aspired to write "progressive, universal poetry" that strove infinitely for an unattainable ideal and was "free of all real and ideal self-interest." He coined the term "Romanticism" and urged that the essence of poetry is in its romantic element – the feelings of the human spirit. In Berlin he fell in love with a married woman, Dorothea Mendelssohn Veit, the daughter of philosopher Moses Mendelssohn, which led to a scandalous affair leading to her divorce. Schlegel's barely disguised fictional account of his passionate relationship with Dorothea, *Lucinde* (1799), made him famous, though also reviled; Schleiermacher and Henriette stoutly defended them long after Schlegel and Dorothea moved to Jena in 1799.[13]

Schlegel enthralled Schleiermacher and inspired him. From the beginning of their friendship he urged Schleiermacher to start writing books. At first Schleiermacher protested that he lacked any ambition or desire to be an author; it didn't help that he considered himself vastly inferior to Schlegel intellectually. To his sister Charlotte, Schleiermacher rejoiced at finding an intellectual companion and inspiration: "I always felt the want of a companion to whom I could freely impart my philosophical ideas, and who would enter with me into the deepest abstractions. This great void he has filled up most gloriously. To him I can not only pour out what is already in me, but by means of the exhaustless stream of new views and new ideas which is ever flowing into him, much that has been lying dormant in me, is likewise set in motion."[14]

The key Romantic tropes were already there in Schleiermacher's friendship with Schlegel – the prizing of inward feeling, vision, idealism, and the growth of individuality, although Schlegel proved to be too volatile and unreliable for Schleiermacher not to feel conflicted about him. From the beginning Schleiermacher had an inkling of what might go wrong, telling his sister that Schlegel, though "infinitely superior to me," lacked "tenderness of feeling" and any appreciation of the "pleasing trifles of life." To Schleiermacher these were major faults, lamenting of Schlegel: "That which is merely gentle and beautiful has no great attraction for him, because, judging too much by analogy to his own character, he holds everything for weak that is not fiery and strong … He will always be my superior; but I shall know and understand him more thoroughly than he will ever know and understand me." Schleiermacher prized tender feeling and intimate friendship above everything else. He knew that he needed both in large amounts. To Henriette he observed that he was so dependent on intimacy and affection that he sometimes doubted if he was an individual: "I am the least independent and least self-sufficing of mortals … I stretch out all my roots and leaves in search of affection; it is necessary for me to feel myself in immediate contact with it, and when I am unable to drink in full draughts of it, I at once dry up and wither. Such is my nature; there is no remedy for it; and, if there were, I should not wish to employ it."[15]

Very unhappily, Schleiermacher fell in love with Eleonore Grunow, the wife of a Berlin pastor, with whom he pleaded to dissolve her unhappy marriage in order to marry him. In the meantime he brooded over the book that Schlegel and Henriette Merz urged him to write. Schleiermacher winced at the hostility of their cultured friends to religion; moreover, Schlegel's faith was mere nature-religion. Schleiermacher told Henriette, "My religion is so through and through heart-religion, that I have not room for any other." Some of his friends were old-style rationalist debunkers of supernatural religion; others adopted Kantian ethics with God left out; others treated religion as a backward form of something precious, romantic striving. Schleiermacher was partly sympathetic with these views and convinced that none grasped the unique content and importance of religion. Just as Kant employed a critical analytical method to understand pure theoretical and pure practical reason, Schleiermacher sought to distinguish the essential spirit or "idea" of pure religion from its various historical forms. Though he complained of being a slow reader, slow to grasp ideas, and slower yet in writing, in 1799 Schleiermacher produced an epochal work of ruminating genius in a few months, *Über die Religion: Reden an die Gebildeten unter ihren Verächtern* (*On Religion: Speeches to Its Cultured Despisers*), passing the chapters to Schlegel and Henriette Merz as he wrote them.[16]

Spiritual True Religion

Schleiermacher's opening sentence highlighted his novel apologetic task: "The subject I propose to discuss has been massively denigrated by the very people from whom I especially claim a hearing." At first blush, he allowed, this was not a very promising project. His friends were taken with "suavity and sociability" and "art and learning," giving no thought to religion, which belonged to a past age and which they believed they saw through: "I am quite aware of all this." And yet, he felt compelled to tell them that they understood very little about religion: "To me, what seems a divine impulsion makes it impossible to withdraw my overture inviting precisely you, the cultured detractors of religion, to hear me out."[17]

Schleiermacher knew that his friends were wrong about religion because the thing they spurned had nothing to do with the thing he knew best, his own spiritual wellspring, piety. In his experience, piety was "as it were, the maternal womb in whose sacred obscurity my young life was nourished and prepared for a world still closed to it." Long before he had become a thinker or an adult, his spirit had "found its vital breath in piety." Piety – religious feeling – had sustained him through years of loneliness, religious doubt, and intellectual confusion, making him capable of friendship and love: "As I began to sift out the faith of my fathers and to clear the rubbish of former ages from my thoughts and feelings, piety supported me. As the childhood images of God and immortality vanished before my doubting eyes, piety remained."[18]

Viewed from the outside, Schleiermacher observed, religion appeared to turn on two things, providence and immortality. The cultured despisers were not to be blamed for thinking, like others taking the outside view, that religion is fundamentally about fearing or revering the providential rule of an eternal being and expecting an afterlife. But these are mere "external factors" belonging to other dogmas, opinions, and practices by which religions take form socially and historically, he cautioned. Religion is about the *source* of the external factors, which can only be known from the inside. Schleiermacher didn't blame his friends for despising organized religion; he despised most of it too: "These doctrines and systems very often move forward without having anything at all in common with religion. Personally, I cannot even speak of this without feeling revulsion." Most religious systems, he stressed, are loaded with superstitions, sacrifices, and coarse moral schemes. Even rationalistic forms of modern religion fixated on externals, replacing crude doctrines with "ill-assembled fragments of metaphysics and morals." Schleiermacher shuddered that "rationalistic Christianity" was very short on actual religion, though in a later edition he changed the reference to "purified Christianity," because his younger readers had no memory of dry deism.[19]

To pay attention only to religious externals is to miss religion itself, he admonished: "You do not yet know religion itself at all, and religion is not what you are objecting to." Schleiermacher chided his friends to stop being so superficial: "How easygoing your mode of inquiry has suddenly turned out to be! I am astonished at this voluntary ignorance of yours! Why don't you look at the religious life itself?" He implored them to look especially at experiences of sublime mystical feeling, "moments in which one's feeling is wholly absorbed in an immediate sense of the infinite and eternal and of its fellowship with the soul." To understand religion is to grasp the inspirations of pious soul, "that effusion of insight and ardor which issues from a spirit truly surrendered to the universe. Without this you will experience nothing of religion."[20]

"Surrendered to the universe" smacked of pantheism to many readers, which Schleiermacher denied in the supplementary notes of the book's subsequent editions. *On Religion* was studiously vague in its references to God or the Divine, using *Gottheit* (Deity) most often and *Universum* next most often, plus *Ganz* (whole), *geistige Welt* (spiritual World), *Sein* (being), and *Urwesen* (original being), plus longer phrases meaning the same thing, such as "the object of piety," "the supreme being in this world," "the Spirit of the Whole," "the source of spiritual life," "the supreme Spirit of the world," "the unity of the whole," "being in its totality," "the eternal fountainhead," and "the World Spirit." Schleiermacher used "God" only in specifically Christian contexts or when describing how his acquaintances normally referred to the Divine. He reasoned that he could not change the preconceptions of his readers about divine reality if he relied on the word "God," because it conjured the very connotations he was trying to dispel. Schleiermacher worried less, to his subsequent regret, about the pantheistic connotations of his favored monikers, an impression he compounded by singling out Spinoza, "that saintly outcast," as his role model. "The supreme Spirit of the world permeated his being," Schleiermacher wrote of Spinoza. "The infinite was his beginning and end; the universe was his sole and everlasting love. In sacred innocence and deep humility he saw himself mirrored in the world of the eternal and perceived how he himself was its most worthy image. He was full of religion, of the Holy Spirit." For Schleiermacher, Spinoza's sublime spiritual witness, if not his identification of God with Nature, was the gold standard of piety.[21]

This passage was cited against Schleiermacher for the rest of his life as proof that he was a pantheist, despite his repeated denials. Thirty years later he was still defending the Spinoza passage and denying the motive usually attributed to it, that he tried to replace the Christian God with a pantheistic God of nature that was functionally equivalent to atheism. In Schleiermacher's telling, the point of the Spinoza passage was that piety, being everywhere, existed even where the cultured despisers of piety "sought it least." Spinoza, at the end of the eighteenth century, was wrongly idolized by disbelievers and wrongly condemned by guardians of orthodoxy: "Yet almost no one had noticed his genuinely human, inwardly gentle, and most attractive personality and his deep devotion to the supreme being. If I had been a more cautious person, who always anticipated the worst from his readers, then I would have left a little space to mention that my words provide very little occasion for considering me a Spinozist. But given what I am, that thought did not even occur to me."[22]

Instead Schleiermacher pressed on with a Kantian argument that moved significantly beyond Kant's moralism. Kant uncoupled religion from science while treating consciousness of the moral law as a fact of pure reason; the sheer givenness of the moral law as a demand was the presupposition of his theory about the moral basis of religion. Schleiermacher took for granted Kant's dichotomy between religion and science, but added that religion has no special expertise in morality either. Religious feeling, he urged, not the moral law, is the crucial given that cannot be derived from something else: "At the very outset, religion waives all claims to anything belonging to the two domains of science and morality. It would now return all that has been either loaned or pressed upon it from those sources." Religion is not about explaining or ordering the world, because spiritual feeling is a deeper aspect of human experience than theoretical reason, practical reason, or even sensation.[23]

In formal terms, Schleiermacher fashioned a third way between Continental rationalism and Kant's critical idealism. Leibniz and the rationalist tradition described feeling as a confused and primitive form of knowledge. The rationalists judged that feeling is self-transcending and intentional; thus it counted as a form of knowledge, but a poor one. Kant put feeling in its place by an opposite tack, denying that feeling is self-transcending or intentional, which disqualified it from being a form of knowledge. In Kant's account, feeling was an autonomous faculty consisting of an emotive, noncognitive mode of consciousness that "knew" no truth beyond psychological experience.[24]

Schleiermacher contended that both approaches underestimate feeling. With the rationalists, he conceived feeling as a direct, self-transcending apprehension of reality, something not reducible to a mere psychological state. Feeling, Schleiermacher argued, is the general organ of the subject's receptivity and the pre-conceptual organ that makes possible all thought and experience. It is the immediate presence of undivided being that unites the self to her world, bringing the self into apprehension of the world as a whole. It is not a lowly form of cognition, for it is not a mode of knowing or doing at all; it is not even a third faculty alongside the theoretical and practical faculties. Knowing and doing are determinate, mediated modes of consciousness; moreover, Schleiermacher rejected Kant's faculty psychology of the self, which obscured the fundamental *unity* of the self as a whole agent.[25]

For Schleiermacher, feeling was self-consciousness as such, the autonomous, unifying dimension of the self that pre-reflectively apprehends the world as a whole. "Feeling" (*Gefühl*) was his term for the pre-rational apprehension of reality affected by the self in its immediate self-consciousness. By emphasizing the intentionality and concreteness of consciousness, Schleiermacher anticipated Husserlian phenomenology; by arguing that experience comes into being by feeling the feelings of one's world, he anticipated Whiteheadian panexperientialism. For Schleiermacher, true religion was essentially contemplative, "the immediate consciousness of the universal being of all finite things in and through the infinite, of all temporal things in and through the eternal." It was rooted in an awareness of "the infinite nature of the whole, in the one and all, in God."[26]

Since religion was about relating to everything, Schleiermacher believed that his strategy did not commit the Kantian mistake of confining religion to a box. Religion had to be liberated from science and morality, but not divorced from them: "For what else is science than the existence of things within you, within your reason? What else is art and culture than your existence in things on which you bestow measure, form, and order? And how can either science or art and culture spring to life for you except insofar as the eternal unity of reason and nature, the universal being of all finite things in the infinite, thrives within you?"[27]

Religion is the unifying ground of science and culture, he urged. It flows out of spiritual experience and inspires all intellectual, cultural and moral activity: "True science is perspective fully achieved; true praxis is art and culture created of oneself; true religion is sense and taste for the infinite." The irreducible ground of religion is the self's pre-reflective awareness of its absolute dependence on the eternal ground of being: "To seek and to find this infinite and eternal factor in all that lives and moves, in all growth and change, in all action and passion, and to have and to know life itself only in immediate feeling – that is religion."[28]

True religion does not consist of believing or knowing something about the nature of reality, Schleiermacher stressed. As soon as one identifies particular factors with the divine, one moves out of the religious sphere. *On Religion* implored against the mythical impulse of hypostatizing God as a being outside the world of human experience and natural causality. In a later edition he expanded on the problem of myth, defining mythology as "a purely ideal object explicated in the form of history." Schleiermacher argued that myth reduces God to an object of thought by separating God from the world. Any perspective that conceives God as an outside being that interferes in history or natural events reduces religion to "vain mythology." Enlightenment rationalists were not wrong to take a harsh view of mythical consciousness, though Schleiermacher did not advocate expunging Christianity of its mythical aspects. As long as one recognizes that Christian myth is mythical, he reasoned, and as long as one bears in mind that the Spirit of the Whole is not a being outside the world, it does no harm to retain mythical language in theology and the life of faith.[29]

True religion finds the eternal factor at work in all that lives and has being. We feel our dependence on the unity that underlies "the coinherence of the world," including our relationship to every part of the world. Schleiermacher cautioned that no feeling should be regarded as a "genuine stirring of piety" on the basis of anything particular in the world. Feeling is genuinely religious only as revelatory experience of the Spirit of the Whole. It is God, the sole and highest unity, being felt. One cannot conceive the world as a universal whole apart from a divine ground, and the only way to experience God is through the stirrings of genuine religious feeling that the world in its unity brings forth. The aim of spiritual living is to become one with the universe, which was Schleiermacher's idea of immortality. Since religious feeling is always related to the Divine, he reasoned, never attaching to any mere particular, the content of religious feeling is eternal, like the Divine. Instead of longing to live forever as a separate being, which Schleiermacher considered the very opposite of true religion, religious feeling longs for union with the Divine Spirit of the Whole.[30]

On Religion did not rest with Romantic religious individualism. Schleiermacher admonished that religion is either social or non-existent, because "it is man's nature to be social." One cannot be vitally religious alone, for the more that one is vitally stirred by something, "the more strongly his drive toward sociality comes into play." Thus Schleiermacher risked alienating the cultured friends that he might have convinced thus far to give religion a second chance. To be religious, he insisted, one has to deal with other people, including religious organizations like the Christian church. In his telling, the true church was a spiritual fellowship having "nothing directly to do with the profane world." It was the social form of his idea of true religion. But social religion does not spring into existence straight out of religious feeling, Schleiermacher cautioned. It has to develop out of institutions that cope with the profane world and variously address "the illnesses of humanity." The true church can only emerge out of compromised, backward, and easily denigrated churches in the real world – institutions that provide enough of the "atmosphere" of true religion to inspire new forms of social religion.[31]

On Religion had perfect pitch for the post-Kantian Romantic generation that wanted to be, in the idiom of a later time, spiritual but not religious. Many readers shared Goethe's reaction, that Schleiermacher's rendering of the essence of religion was wonderful and his rearguard attempt to support church Christianity was disappointing. Others celebrated that he mixed the best of Enlightenment rationalism, Pietism, Kantian critical idealism, and Romanticism without giving up on church Christianity. Many chewed over Schleiermacher's cheeky remarks about his intended audience, reading themselves in or out of it. Schleiermacher stressed that he wrote only for liberal, educated, aesthetically sensitive types, namely "the cultured sons and daughters of Germany." It was sad that he had to aim at such a small group, but what else could he do? "It is not blind partiality for my native soil or for my fellow citizens or for those who use the same language that makes me speak as I do. It is the deep conviction that you alone are prepared – and in this respect deserving – of having the sense for sacred and divine things awakened in you."[32]

Only the privileged children of Germany seemed capable of attaining true religion. The English and other British Islanders were too greedy and power seeking to be religious, he opined. They cared only about things that enhanced their wealth and position, their zeal for science was merely "a sham maneuver," and their vaunted prudence was "a bauble." Too many Germans unduly honored the British, Schleier-macher admonished. The Brits prattled a lot about freedom, but usually to justify their insatiable greed: "These people are never in earnest about anything that goes beyond ostensible utility." For example, they stripped the life out of science, "using it only as deadwood to fashion masts and helms for sailing in pursuit of gain." They did the same thing with religion, only worse, since British religion had nothing to do with true religion. England's corrupt state religion was religiously antiquated and morally bankrupt, yet somehow prized by the English: "They know nothing of religion, except that everyone preaches attachment to antiquated practices and defends its precepts."[33]

The French were even worse, by his lights, unspeakably worse: "One who honors religion can scarcely bear to look their way. In their every action, their every word almost, they trample its holiest ordinances under foot." Only ten years removed from the fall of the Bastille, Schleiermacher felt no need to indulge anybody's lingering sympathy for the French Revolution; Napoleon took power eight months after Schleiermacher completed *On Religion*. In Schleiermacher's telling, the French population as a whole was unspeakably rude and lacking any capacity for true religious feeling: "What does religion abhor more than that unbridled arrogance by which the leaders of the French people defy the eternal laws of our world? What does religion more keenly instill than that humble, considerate moderation for which they do not seem to have even the faintest feeling?" The "dazzling beguilement of revolution" turned normal French rudeness and impiety to sheer madness, Schleiermacher believed. An entire nation turned against God, no pious voice had any chance of being heard, and France was paying a terrible price for it, albeit without realizing it.[34]

Twenty-two years later, in the book's third edition, Schleiermacher allowed that he might have exaggerated slightly about the British, though not beyond the boundaries of normal rhetorical "stress." Germans admired British civilization far more than it deserved at the turn of the century, he recalled, and the English had not yet developed their enthusiasm for mission work and Bible distribution. Still, a great deal of this subsequent mission work was bound up with England's undiminished zeal for territorial expansion and enrichment, he observed. Even when the English bothered to promote Christianity, they did so as a secondary business that propped up what they really cared about. Nothing had changed concerning English greed, English science, and English religion; Schleiermacher had no second thoughts about the French; and he noted that he spoke only of England and France because Germans at the turn of the century were not interested in anybody else, "it seemed superfluous to direct similar attention elsewhere."[35]

On Religion found an audience far beyond Schleiermacher's Romantic circle and lifted him to local renown equaling anyone in his circle besides Schlegel, with whom he carried on a difficult friendship. Schlegel's stormy sensuality and impetuousness were alien to him. Increasingly Schleiermacher adopted a private/public strategy, confiding to friends his misgivings about Schlegel while defending him publicly. To Eleanore Grunow, with whom Schleiermacher was virtually betrothed for several years, he explained that Schlegel, despite constantly saying repugnant things, nonetheless stood above most male intellectuals as a moral being. For example, Schleiermacher greatly admired Goethe and Schelling as thinkers, but he could never love them, because they were just thinkers: "Schlegel, on the contrary, has a high moral nature; he is a man who bears the whole world in his heart with love; his sensuousness is not offensively disproportionate to the rest of his powers; and, according to the spirit, he is by no means wanting in uprightness, though, according to the letter, he may sometimes be so."[36]

Schleiermacher had his own reasons to distinguish between the ethical spirit and letter, as he spent six years trying to persuade Grunow to divorce her husband and marry him. The couple met in 1799; soon he was urging her that every woman had a right to her own individuality; and in 1802 Schleiermacher left Berlin for a poorly endowed position as a court chaplain at Stolpe in Pomerania to give Grunow sufficient freedom to choose him. His friends were mystified that she captivated Schleiermacher, since she lacked most of the qualities that he usually prized: sentimentality, sensitivity, beauty, broad culture, and intellectual playfulness. Schleiermacher told them that he admired the strength and richness of her feeling and her ability to express it. At Stolpe he ministered for two years to several tiny Reformed congregations, worked on a translation project of Plato's works that he shared with Schlegel, wrote a book on ethical theory, and pleaded for a positive verdict from Grunow. Schleiermacher surprised himself by adopting the disciplined habits of a scholar, though his book on ethical theory was not very good, as he wrote it in the process of learning the material.[37]

In 1804 he accepted a teaching position in ethics and pastoral theology at the University of Würzburg. This was a breakthrough, but the Prussian throne intervened, countering with a marginal position at its flagship, Halle. Schleiermacher's

Prussian loyalty prevailed, taking the lesser position and its lower pay. For a year he taught as an adjunct Reformed professor at all-Lutheran Halle, after which he was admitted to the full faculty in the fall of 1805, just as Grunow renounced him, which devastated Schleiermacher. He told his friends Ehrenfried and Henriette von Willich that he was crushed with sorrow and pain "that will never leave me ... but whatever can be made of the ruins, I will make of them." Heartbroken, he began his academic career, making Halle's theology faculty the first integrated one in Prussia.[38]

At Halle Schleiermacher got a cool reception at first, but flourished. A mildly rationalist Lutheran pietism was still strong there; Schleiermacher's former teacher, Eberhard, spurned him, sniffing that Halle legitimized an outright atheist as a theologian and preacher. For many of Schleiermacher's new colleagues, his supposed pantheism was a disingenuous form of atheism. Halle had rationalists, Pietists, and conservatives on its faculty, plus mixtures of these types. On the whole Schleiermacher's colleagues were open to historical criticism and demythologizing, but not to his rejection of a hypostatized God of being who intervenes in history. At the same time, classical philologist Friedrich August Wolf, a Goethe disciple and leading myth critic, put down Schleiermacher for clinging to theology. It took Schleiermacher's scholarly work on Plato to change Wolf's mind about his worth as an academic and colleague. Schleiermacher lectured on philosophy, systematic theology, ethics, New Testament, and a field he invented: hermeneutics, the study of interpretation. He told his students that one cannot understand a text without comprehending how understanding itself occurs and that one must be able, in interpreting any text, to enter the frame of mind of the author. For the rest of his career, Schleiermacher elaborated his hermeneutical theory in classroom lectures that he never composed in definitive form or published. He taught that the interplay of whole and part is essential to all understanding; to comprehend a text, one must understand the cultural and linguistic whole in which it is embedded and its individual parts. In 1806, however, Schleiermacher feared that his teaching career was already over, after Napoleon destroyed the university.[39]

In August 1806 the Prussian throne, learning that Napoleon had offered Hanover to England, issued an ultimatum to Napoleon, who responded by smashing the Prussian forces at Auerstadt, Jena, and Halle. Schleiermacher witnessed the fall of Halle to the French invaders and bewailed the incompetence of the Prussian army. His house was plundered and occupied by French troops, students were expelled from the city, the university was dissolved, and Schleiermacher's university church was turned into a grain store. His patriotism soared in response. Unlike Goethe and Hegel, who admired the French conqueror, Schleiermacher seethed with rage at the crushing of old Prussia. He vowed to remain in Halle as long as he had potatoes and salt, working to build a new, reformed, militant Prussian state that expelled the French imperialists and unified the German principalities. In November 1806 he told Henriette Herz, "We are living here in a most feverish state ... The rod of wrath must fall upon every German land; only on this condition can a strong and happy future bloom forth. Happy they who live to see it; but those who die, let them die in faith."[40]

In that mood he fixed on the hope of a united German nation that leaped beyond its feudal mosaic of city-states, princedoms, and mini-states. Prussia was a glorious cultural entity yet to be realized politically; letting go of it was not an option.

Schleiermacher's Romantic aestheticism faded, including his fixation with the individuality of the self; now he stressed that individuality is pointless if it does not serve the common good of the nation. To live under foreign domination was no life at all; history itself is a life of struggle, resistance, sacrifice, and waiting upon the will of God. Schleiermacher vowed to join the struggle for the fulfillment of God's purpose, which surely entailed expelling the French conquerors.

But the French dismembered Prussia and abolished its western universities, granting Halle to Westphalia, which forced Schleiermacher to rethink his pledge to Halle. If he was to help Prussia recover, he had to return to Berlin, the Prussian capital, which he did in 1807. There Schleiermacher plunged into social activism and grieved over the death of his friend Ehrenfried von Willich, an Army chaplain who died in a typhoid epidemic during the siege of Stralsund. Von Willich's widow, Henriette von Kathen Willich, was nineteen years old and a mother of two children. Schleiermacher had an explicitly fatherly relationship with her; she called him "beloved father" and he called her "my dearly beloved daughter" and "my dear child." In May 1809 Schleiermacher married her, in the same month that he became minister of Trinity Church in Berlin. Each became devoted to the other, though Henriette rarely attended Schleiermacher's sermons, because she found his reflective preaching incomprehensible and short on Pietistic orthodoxy.[41]

For the rest of his life Schleiermacher was an every-week preacher at Trinity Church and a professor at the University of Berlin, of which he was a major co-founder. He served on the organizing commission of the new university, headed by Wilhelm von Humbolt, which took seriously King Friedrich Wilhelm III's reported vow to make up for Prussia's physical loss through intellectual gain. For Schleiermacher, the founding of the University of Berlin in 1810 was a major building block in the renewal of Prussian life. He served as university rector in 1815 and as dean of the theological faculty four times, teaching all fields of theology except Old Testament (dogmatics, encyclopedia, exegesis, church history, practical theology, and New Testament) in addition to teaching widely in philosophy (aesthetics, dialectics, ethics, hermeneutics, pedagogy, and psychology). His pulpit at Trinity Church became the focal point of his academic, political, and ecclesiastical efforts to renew Prussian life and culture, where Schleiermacher tested the limits of what could be said against Prussian conservatives and the French conquerors. In 1813, as Napoleon's forces retreated from Russia in defeat, Schleiermacher exhorted his students on to Breslau to join the rout of the vanquished invaders. The following year he called for the creation of a constitutional monarchy and parliament.[42]

As a theologian, a co-founder of a university, and an academic administrator, Schleiermacher faced the question of how theology should be taught at a post-Enlightenment university. This was the question of theological encyclopedia. Fichte, joining the faculty at Berlin, strongly suggested that debates over theological encyclopedia had no place in a modern university because theology didn't deserve its own department. Schleiermacher's response, *Brief Outline of the Study of Theology* (1811), made a case for teaching theology as a unified, integral discipline. Theology, in his conception, divided into three distinct but related fields, which he called philosophical theology, historical theology, and practical theology. Theology is a positive science because it flows from the given of God-consciousness, he argued. The three parts of theology form a cohesive whole through their common relation to a particular mode of faith, "a particular way of being conscious of God." The given of God-consciousness is positive because it takes historical forms. Philosophical theology utilizes the framework and methods of philosophy of religion. Historical theology includes exegetical theology, church history, dogmatic theology, and the study of the church as an organization (which Schleiermacher called "church statistics"). Practical theology is the crown of theological study, covering principles of church service and church government.[43]

Schleiermacher's emphasis on the organic unity of the theological disciplines was novel. His emphasis that theology obtains this unity as a discipline of the church was equally novel for liberal theology. It was so novel that Schleiermacher and his followers did not call themselves liberals, since Kantians owned liberal theology. Confessional theologies before Schleiermacher were organized by biblical or creedal *loci* lacking internal connections. Rationalist theologies rested on philosophical first principles. Kantians prized moral religion and their own scientific rationality. Schleiermacher's approach rested on the unifying religious self-consciousness shared by Christians in the church. Theology, he proposed, is critical reflection on the corporate experience of the Christian community. This approach, despite its novelty, became the dominant one in Germany, establishing how religion should be taught in the modern academy. It helped that Schleiermacher's model was friendly to Pietist appropriation.

From the beginning of Schleiermacher's academic career there were disputes about the weight of his Romanticism, idealism, and purported pantheism over his theology. He parried with and deflected these arguments for his entire career. In his telling, he had a clear position; he pleaded to be understood in the way that he understood himself. But that rarely happened. Routinely he was described, even by allies, as having brought theology into line with a dominant pantheism, idealism, liberalism, or Gnosticism. This outcome had something to do with Schleiermacher's prolonged wavering over the question of philosophical influence, which cast a longer shadow over his work than he admitted. More importantly, it had something to do with his lengthy introduction to his dogmatic system, *The Christian Faith* (1821, 1830), which ranged over the nature of theological knowledge and the nature, history, and types of religion before taking up doctrinal topics that were themselves prolegomena to Christian revelation. By the time that Schleiermacher got to the God-consciousness of Jesus and Christianity, on page 259, he had given an ample impression of doing theology philosophically.[44]

Christian Theology of Religious Feeling

In his early academic career Schleiermacher sought to mediate between Jacobi's fideism and Schelling's transcendental idealism, proposing to conjoin religious feeling and speculative reason as two sides of the human spirit that correspond to each other. Schleiermacher's dialogue, *Christmas Eve* (1806), contained idealist speeches by Eduard taking this line; more directly, in his lectures of 1811 on dialectic, Schleiermacher argued that the immediate consciousness of God in human beings is expressed through both sides of the human spirit. If feeling and reason do not belong together, he argued, the consciousness of God must be split – which would not *be* consciousness of God. Theology and philosophy must go together. Schleiermacher reached for the maximally idealist way of saying it. Since knowing is the totality of all personal existence and never merely a personal consciousness, he argued, "knowing is the pure coinciding of reason with being." The congruence of reason and being is unequivocally necessary, since "nothing can proceed from being as such than what also has its subjective grounding in reason as such." If it were even conceivable that there might be something different in reason than in being, the very reality belonging to reason would be lost along with the necessity of being: "What we find instead is a reciprocal action in which both endure."[45]

That was post-Kantian idealism, construing the absolute in transcendental terms as the condition of the possibility of experience, though Schleiermacher invoked the usual post-Kantian equivocations about "identity" not meaning pure coinciding or mere congruence. For Schleiermacher, identity referred to two distinguishable but mutually presupposing categories or two interlocking domains that are distinguishable but inconceivable apart from each other. Unlike Kant, who posited a Moral Guarantor solely as a postulate of practical reason, Schleiermacher posited that God is a necessary postulate of theoretical reason as well. Against Schelling and other absolute idealists, he contended that the divine cannot be known as such but must be *presupposed* as the identity of thought and being. We cannot know God as we know objects of thought, nor can we understand the identity between knowing and the known. We can only presuppose God *as* this identity: "Except to assert that the deity as transcendent being is the principle of all being and as transcendent idea is the formal principle of all knowing, nothing more is to be said of it in the domain of knowing. All else is simply bombast or an admixing of the religious, which is out of bounds here and can actually have only a corruptive effect if placed within the bounds."[46]

Schleiermacher had all of that going against him after he claimed to exclude philosophy from his dogmatic system. He continued to say that there is no conflict between theology and philosophy, because both are in accord with immediate self-consciousness. But he strenuously denied importing any philosophy into his dogmatics, because philosophy cannot provide the basis for religious faith. Theology needs no basis or content other than that which is given to it by the religious self-consciousness of the Christian community, he insisted. This was all that Schleiermacher claimed to do in *The Christian Faith,* once he got past the cumbersome necessity of locating Christian piety descriptively within the context of world religious history. Constantly he was accused of doing no such thing, which he found exasperating. Instead of achieving real disagreements, he had to protest that he really believed what he said he was doing, which was often ignored or dismissed.

Ten years of hostile reviews and replies came to a head in Schleiermacher's preface to the second edition of *The Christian Faith,* where he denied "most emphatically" that he was the "head of a new theological school" or had founded anything: "I have invented nothing, so far as I remember, except my order of topics and here or there a descriptive phrase." That was too modest and immodest at the same time and for the same reason. Schleiermacher believed that he disclosed the religious truth of Christianity that is common to all Christians and ultimately all genuinely religious people. He did not want it to be categorized as a distinctly modern theology or as peculiar to him because he had greater ambitions for it. In his conception, Christianity did not rest on certain ideas derived from reason or revelation, and neither should theology. If either rested on ideas, intellectuals were sure to own it. His alternative rested on Christian religious self-consciousness, which he argued has two elements. There is a consciousness of God derived from a feeling of absolute dependence that is constitutive of human nature. And there is a modification of this God-consciousness that is caused by every person's inability to give complete reign to God-consciousness in one's heart. The remedy to this problem is the saving influence of Jesus Christ.[47]

Schleiermacher titled his dogmatics *Glaubenslehre*, doctrine of faith, but he gave central place to piety (*Frömmigkeit*), not faith, defying the bad connotations that a century of rationalist battles against Pietism had given to piety. Quickly he plunged readers into a theory about the fundamental openness of the self to an other in self-consciousness. In any moment of consciousness we are aware of our unchanging identity *and* its changing, variable character, he argued. This twofold experience discloses the essential constitutive elements of self-consciousness, a self-caused element (*ein Sichselbstsetzen*) and a non-self-caused element (*ein Sichselbstnichtsogesetzthaben*), which Schleiermacher called the Ego and the Other. The Ego expresses the subject for itself, while the Other expresses the co-existence of the ego with an other. The double constitution of self-consciousness makes it possible for the self, which is constituted only in *relation* to an other, to feel its absolute dependence.[48]

We exist as affective, active, self-conscious creatures only in coexistence with an other. Every self experiences a feeling of dependence, which is common to all determinations of self-consciousness expressing an affective condition of receptivity, and a feeling of freedom, which is common to all determinations expressing movement and change. These feelings are one, Schleiermacher argued, for the subject and the corresponding Other are the same for both.[49]

The totality of all moments of the feelings of dependence and freedom comprise a single reality corresponding in reciprocal relation to an other that makes self-consciousness possible. Since every moment is determined by what is given, which includes objects towards which we experience feelings of freedom, the feeling of absolute dependence cannot be captured or realized in any single moment. But self-consciousness is always awareness of absolute dependence, "for it is the consciousness that the whole of our spontaneous activity comes from a source outside of us in just the same sense in which anything towards which we should have a feeling of absolute freedom must have proceeded entirely from ourselves."[50]

Pre-modern theologies appealed to some notion of God's actuality derived from scripture, tradition, or rationalistic proof. Schleiermacher's dialectic of freedom and dependence pointed to God's possibility and the limits of the human spiritual relation. Theology, he argued, rightly approached, is human reflection inspired by the feeling of utter dependence on God and the experience of Christ as redeemer. Theology begins with and reads off piety, presupposing the affective condition of persons in their innermost self-consciousness. Just as religion is immediate self-consciousness, the dependency and actualization of a self grounded in feeling and involved in thinking and willing, Christian theology is a positive and self-conscious use of language by a subject of religious feeling. There are two levels of self-consciousness – sensible and immediate. At the level of sensible self-consciousness, the self deals with perceptions, ideas, and other objects of awareness. Immediate self-consciousness grounds and unifies all acts of thinking and willing. Feeling, Schleiermacher argued, is related to immediate self-consciousness, the irreducible essence of the self and presence of undivided existence. Religion, a product of feeling, stands for a person's position as the being on which God and world converge. God is not a being, but rather, that which holds all being together, giving integrity to all things.

The essence of any faith is the affective element distinctive to it constant within its various expressions. Schleiermacher allowed that the essence of Christianity is hard to discern among Christianity's profusion of traditions and misguided doctrines, yet it does shine through: The redeeming influence of Christ. Every form of Christianity is rooted in some experience and understanding of Christ's redemptive influence. Every form of Christianity speaks in some way of Christ aiding or making possible the passage from sin or captivity to righteousness.[51]

To be sure, Schleiermacher acknowledged, most theologies are dreadful in this area; he shuddered at juridical atonement theories in which Christ suffered on the cross to satisfy God's wrath or honor: "The forgiveness of sins is made to depend upon the punishment which Christ suffered, and the blessedness of men itself is presented as a reward which God offers to Christ for the suffering of that punishment." Schleiermacher stressed that atonement theories of this type, besides being morally repugnant, utilize magical thinking. It was ridiculous to imagine "something so inward as blessedness" as being brought about "externally, without any inner basis." Schleiermacher countered that sin is anything that arrests or impedes God-consciousness. Evil is a state of God-forgetfulness, not a state of disobedience to God. To be saved is to be transformed from a state of arrested God-consciousness to a state of potent God-consciousness through the redeeming example of Jesus.[52]

For Schleiermacher, that was the key to the distinctiveness of Christianity. Religions are like animal life and grades of consciousness in holding developmental histories. Some are more developed than others, and Christianity is more developed than all. The appropriate rule in this area is that only the true can be the basis for grasping the higher truth of Christianity. Schleiermacher reasoned that some religions are too similar to Christianity to be entirely false. Moreover, if primitive religions contained nothing but error, how was it possible for human communities to move from these religions to Christianity? All religions are true insofar as they are rooted in piety, which is the consciousness of absolute dependence.[53]

But in other religions, Schleiermacher argued, redemption always appears as a derivative aspect of a controlling doctrine or institution. In Christianity the redeeming influence of Jesus is the key to everything else. Schleiermacher's pivotal section on the essence of Christianity put it in the form of a definition: "Christianity is a monotheistic faith, belonging to the teleological type of religion, and is essentially distinguished from other such faiths by the fact that in it everything is related to the redemption accomplished by Jesus of Nazareth." As the unique embodiment of constantly potent God-consciousness, Jesus creates and embodies the possibility of salvation. The redeeming influence of Jesus is the "primary element" in Christianity, which exists only on the basis of this faith and its proclamation. Christianity exalts the redeeming work of Christ and the corresponding experience of redemption in piety. This two-sided concept was the heart of Schleiermacher's theology. In Christianity, he stressed, two central things always go together: "Within Christianity these two tendencies always rise and fall together, the tendency to give pre-eminence to the redeeming work of Christ, and the tendency to ascribe great value to the distinctive and peculiar element in Christian piety."[54]

Schleiermacher, despite having Jewish friends and a Jewish soulmate – Henriette Herz – insisted that Christianity has no special relationship on the level of religious feeling with Judaism, notwithstanding that Jesus and original Christianity were Jewish. Christianity and Judaism are different religions, he stressed. The early Christians that converted from heathenism to Christianity did not have to make a greater leap than those who converted from Judaism to Christianity. If anything, the heathens had less to overcome, which helped to explain why more of them became Christians. To be sure, Schleiermacher allowed, Jews had a monotheistic tradition on their side, but the Greek and Roman worlds were "in many ways prepared for Monotheism." More importantly, Jews that converted to Christianity had to forsake their reliance on the law and their understanding of the Abrahamic promises. The chasm between the Jewish religion of law and the Christian religion of gracious redemption through Jesus was greater than anything that heathens had to cross to become Christians, Schleiermacher contended. The "inward separation" between Christianity and Judaism was immense, yielding Schleiermacher's hermeneutical rule for Christian interpretation of the Old Testament: "Whatever is most definitely Jewish has least value."[55]

Christianity is not, and never was, a renewal movement within Judaism. It is about all things being made new through a Godly example, Jesus Christ. In his sermons Schleiermacher put it plainly. The first desire of every uncorrupted heart, he preached, is to become good, "but to become good, we need an example we can always rely on." Schleiermacher reasoned that only a perfect example of the good adequately guides our feeling and inspires our reason in the direction of the good: "And it is Christ who gives us this sublime example ... He spent the best years of his life going around among the fallen, though for the most part they were ungrateful, to preach the truth to them and to practice virtue among them. Never discouraged by mockery, disdain, persecution, or misinterpretation of his purest motives, his virtue remained ever constant. Everywhere he sought out misery to alleviate it with his gentle healing hand, as he alone always could."[56]

Christ the redeemer was for Schleiermacher the image of perfected humanity, "the image of a soul constantly at one with God." Christ gave himself for and to human beings so that through his indwelling presence all people might become one with him, making his righteousness their own. The love that Christ bears for humankind is divine, Schleiermacher stressed, and through his perfectly God-conscious influence Christ ignites love divine in human hearts. Thus Christ is rightly exalted above all others.[57]

Schleiermacher was emphatic that everyone needs Christ, not merely God-consciousness, because all human beings need fellowship with God, which God-consciousness does not assure. It is possible to be truly religious through the experience of dependence alone, but to have true fellowship with God, one must experience the redeemer: "The distinctive feature of Christian piety lies in the fact that whatever alienation from God there is in the phases of our experience, we are conscious of it as an action originating in ourselves, which we call Sin; but whatever fellowship with God there is, we are conscious of it as resting upon a communication from the Redeemer, which we call Grace."[58]

For Schleiermacher, as for Calvin, sin-consciousness came into existence only through God-consciousness. Human beings become aware of their sin only after their God-consciousness is awakened. But in Christian experience there is no relation to God (and therefore no awareness of sin) that is not bound up with Christ's redeeming influence: "In the actual life of the Christian, therefore, the two are always found in combination: there is no general God-consciousness which has not bound up with it a relation to Christ, and no relationship with the Redeemer which has no bearing on the general God-consciousness." Human subjects owe to Christ the salvation from sin that his redeeming influence brings to their awareness. Because Christians experience Christ as love, they know that God is love. Because they experience Christ as redeemer, they know they are sinners under God's judgment and grace.[59]

To many readers who knew Schleiermacher only as the author of the Romantic *On Religion,* his dogmatics seemed surprisingly churchy and traditional. For many more, especially theologians and clerics, his emphasis on piety wrongly stripped Christianity of its cognitive content. Repeatedly he was accused of Christianizing pantheism or atheism, while some protested that Schleiermacher projected a god out of human subjectivity. A long tradition of critics from the Ritschlian Wilhelm Bender to the Barthian Felix Flückiger charged that his philosophical idealism fatally infected his theology. Several critics from the Tübingen School claimed that Schleiermacher's Christology replaced the historical Jesus with an ideal Christ fashioned out of idealism. Later critics such as Ernst Troeltsch and Karl Albrecht Bernoulli judged that the early critics of his churchy confessionalism were right; Schleiermacher's theology was not sufficiently critical.[60]

Though some of these critiques fueled ample traditions of their own long after Schleiermacher was gone, all were variations on charges that he heard in his later career. Breslau philosopher Christlieb Julius Braniss admonished that Schleiermacher needed to choose between claiming that God does not intervene in history and claiming that Jesus was without sin. Bonn theologian Johann Friedrich F. Delbrück contended that the "innermost essence" of Schleiermacher's system was "irreconcilable with the basic principles of apostolic Christianity." Leipzig theologian Heinrich Gottlieb Tzschirner, a neo-supernaturalist Kantian, charged that Schleiermacher made Christian faith depend on fantasy. Erlangen theologian Isaaco Rust, a conservative-leaning mediationist, accused Schleiermacher of paganizing Christianity with his corrupting appeal to feeling. Gotha General Superintendent Karl Gottlieb Bretschneider, a rationalist-leaning supernaturalist, charged that Schleiermacher's philosophically driven system had a stronger affinity with Roman papalism than with Protestant theology. The crowning insult belonged to Hegel, who objected that Schleiermacher's emphasis on the feeling of absolute dependence reduced religion to something immature and lacking autonomy; Hegel deadpanned that if Schleiermacher was right, "a dog would be the best Christian, since a dog is most strongly characterized by this feeling and lives primarily in this feeling."[61]

Schleiermacher replied that he had no opponents, since he was not interested in founding a school, contrary to his critics. If his critics could prove that he had actually cut his system to fit an idealist or pantheist worldview, or ignored the historical Jesus, or contradicted himself, or paganized Christianity, or proffered a Vatican-like theology, or worst of all, negated Christian freedom, he would have renounced *The Christian Faith* and not bothered with a second edition. As it was, he believed that proof was lacking, which tempted him to settle for the reply, "I am not what they take me to be."[62]

But that would never stem the tide of accusation. Tübingen School ringleader Ferdinand Christian Baur, overlooking his own idealizing tendency, claimed that Schleiermacher's idealistic Christology was Gnostic. Heidelberg theologian Heinrich J. T. Schmid took the opposite tack, likening Schleiermacher's use of philosophy to the Alexandrian school. Baur, Bretschneider, and Tzschirner contended that Schleiermacher's conceptions of divine reality and Christology smacked of Schelling-style idealism. Rust said no, Schleiermacher was really a fideist like Jacobi, forsaking the intellectual defense of Christianity. Schleiermacher replied, "To these persons I could only say that they should first come to agree among themselves." The Tübingen School's constant polemic against Schleiermacher's Gnosticism, in particular, blasted "a Schleiermacher whom I in no way recognize as myself." He paid attention to historical critical scholarship about Jesus, even from the Tübingen School. Since Schleiermacher made everything dependent on the life of Christ in Christians, he found it ridiculous that anyone could accuse him of ignoring the historical person or death of Jesus. Similarly, the idea that absolute dependence is incompatible with freedom struck him as laughably simplistic, especially coming from the theorist of Hegelian dialectic. Schleiermacher pointed to his dialectic of freedom and dependence, and expanded his discussion of it in the second edition of his dogmatics.[63]

Some critiques he took more seriously. Bretschneider denied that feeling and self-consciousness are identical, because some feelings are unconscious or semi-conscious, while self-consciousness requires the awareness of one's "I." Schleiermacher replied that he had a right to conceive feeling more narrowly. Bretschneider argued that feeling can refer only to what is already an object of thought; what matters is the object that produces the feeling, which gives Christianity its specific content. One must have an idea of God before any knowledge of God's determination of one's being is possible. This was exactly what Schleiermacher refused to accept, although he admitted that he had no argument to convince Bretschneider and others like him. He could only repeat that any prior conception of the idea of God is not piety because it is not read off from the mode of determination of one's being. Schleiermacher noted that it was not unusual for intellectuals to have sophisticated ideas about God while lacking any feeling for these ideas. If it was possible to have an idea of God without any feeling for it, it followed that no particular idea of God, considered in and of itself, is necessarily constitutive in piety.[64]

Schleiermacher wearied of denying that he was a pantheist. But he was accused of it so often that he resigned himself to making routine denials. Ever since the Spinoza passage, he reflected, this disagreeable task had been part of his life. His only consolation was that he was tagged an idealist (*Ichheitler*) at least as often as he was tagged a pantheist (*All-Einheitler*). Schleiermacher took back nothing from *On Religion:* "Even the sophisticated tone that predominated in it should not be eliminated because it has successfully countered the false sophistication of frivolous negativism." As for his treatment of divine reality in *The Christian Faith,* it had nothing smacking of pantheism, because he did not traffic in worldview isms. *The Christian Faith* explicated the God-consciousness developed in Christianity and shared by Christians and nothing else: "Whoever thereby thinks of some philosophy must inevitably become confused, and I have detected such confusion in nearly all of the more extensive reviews of my work."[65]

Schleiermacher lamented that even some of his staunchest allies, such as Bonn theologian Karl Immanuel Nitzsch, recycled confusions on this matter. Nitsch was a leading figure in the mediating theology movement and the editor of one of its journals, *Theologische Studien und Kritiken*. He defended Schleiermacher as a theologian of faith and a critic of dogmatic and speculative doctrines, but he contended that *The Christian Faith* incorporated its distinctively Christian content into a concept of universal religious knowledge. Having converted to mediation theology under Schleiermacher's influence, Nitsch made a Schleiermacherian argument against his version of Schleiermacher, criticizing *The Christian Faith* for crossing the line into religious philosophy. Schleiermacher repeated his stock reply, that Christianity and speculative reason are harmonious *and* that they do not belong together. Any notion that Christianity and speculative reason determined each other was toxic for both: "I have been most careful not to deviate even a hair's breadth from this rule." More importantly, "I have never needed a rational theology for my piety, either to nourish it or to understand it. And I have had just as little need of the sensuous theocracy of the Old Testament."[66]

Since virtually every reviewer of *The Christian Faith* misconstrued it, always attributing a religious philosophy to his rendering of the church's faith, Schleiermacher allowed that he must have done something wrong. He was tempted to reverse the book's two parts, beginning with the Christian consciousness and ending with the introductory parts about religion and method. But that would make for a long anticlimax, he noted. Also, one needed to set the table before eating, not afterward. In the second edition he made it clearer that the opening section was mere prolegomena to the real thing, although critics continued to say that his rendering of Christianity was liberal, idealist, experiential, and pantheistic, or surprisingly churchy and traditional. Schleiermacher held out for his view of his project, that he retrieved and expressed the actual redemptive experience of the Christian community: "I am firmly convinced, however, that my position is an inspired orthodoxy that in due time will eventually become orthodox, although certainly not just because of my book and perhaps not until long after my death." He had no need of rational theology and very little need of the Old Testament because he truly believed that "in Christ the old has passed away and everything has become new." The right approach was not to begin with a pre-Christian God or a God of the philosophers and then Christianize it. The right approach was to explicate the Christian consciousness.[67]

Schleiermacher found it sad that so many children of the Enlightenment scorned the pinnacle of their heritage and culture, the spirit of Jesus. He admonished them not to mock something they did not understand. The cultured despisers of Christianity, in their "proud delusions," ignored that even their weaker lights were borrowed from Christ: "The truths which they attribute to reason's own speculations have been spread abroad only through Christianity." If liberal culture wanted to move forward, it needed to hold onto its spiritual center.[68]

These were the keynotes of the first full-orbed liberal theology, which surpassed in influence all the liberal theologies that followed it, and which eventually was recognized as the quintessential liberal theology, long after Schleiermacher was gone. It was an idealistic metaphysic of religious feeling and a bourgeois culture religion, though of course Schleiermacher called it neither of these things, just as he never called it liberal theology. He took idealism so much for granted that he could deny doing so; idealism was the air that Schleiermacher breathed and the language he spoke. His theology was also a type of romantic individualism, although here his objection was warranted, as he never wrote off the church. Schleiermacher insisted that the personal aspect of Christian existence is necessarily bound up with communal and social aspects. To follow Christ includes being in communion with others on the same path; the church is the Christ-following community in which God-consciousness is the determining power. Many who never read his books heard the gospel through Schleiermacher's eloquent, convictional preaching of it.

His prestige as a preacher, Prussian patriot, and eminent thinker built a huge following for Schleiermacher's understanding of Christianity and legitimized it. At home he sustained a loving marriage with a much younger spouse who shared none of his intellectualism and who became enamored of occult visions and prophecies. In the church Schleiermacher watched many of his protégés become important clerical leaders. In the academy his approach to theology became something of a new orthodoxy, just as he predicted. For many Prussians who knew little or nothing of his theology he was a national hero. The so-called "Restoration" of 1815 launched a new political order, state absolutism, under the guise of the old order. Schleiermacher, for many, exemplified the right blend of realism and idealism in dealing with the new order, advocating liberal reforms, working within the system, and standing up for Germany. At his funeral in 1834 thirty thousand Berliners poured into the streets in a display of public mourning unparalleled for a German academic. The long funeral procession took several hours. Schleiermacher's friend Heinrich Steffens later recalled: "It was not something arranged but a completely unconscious, natural outpouring of mourning love, an inner boundless feeling which gripped the entire city and gathered about his grave; these were hours of inward unity such as have never been seen in a metropolis of modern times."[69]

Though Schleiermacher claimed that he founded no school, he was keenly mindful of the one that formed around him led by Nitzsch, J. K. L. Gieseler, Gottfried Christian Friedrich Lücke, Carl Ullmann, August Twesten, and F. W. C. Umbreit. This industrious group was highly effective in winning academic positions and a place in the church. It pressed for a reconciliation between Christian faith and modern science, pressed equally for a union between the Lutheran and Reformed churches in Germany, and was extremely prolific, especially about biblical criticism, where Schleiermacher was a model to emulate and to surpass.

Schleiermacher was well acquainted with rationalist biblical criticism, which he often opposed as holding a simplistic view of its subject, and the historical critical approach of his time, which he respected. Rationalist critics exposed discrepant accounts, or harmonized them; rejected miracle stories, or provided naturalistic explanations for them; stressed that the Bible contains myths, or deduced a rational system from the Bible; and generally approached interpretation as taxonomy. The pre-Kantian "neologians," led by J. S. Semler, dismantled this approach by exploring the history of the text itself. Later, historical critics such as Johann G. Eichhorn, Johann Jakob Griesbach, Johann David Michaelis, and Johann Georg Rosenmüller pioneered forms of textual and source criticism in which reconstructing a text's historical development was held to be crucial to understanding it. Schleiermacher's friend and colleague at Berlin, Wilhelm Martin L. De Wette, was a major contributor to this enterprise.[70]

Schleiermacher's theology was calibrated to avoid refutation from the old rationalist and the new historical critical approaches. If piety was the essence of religion, religion was safe from historical refutation. If Christianity rested on the experience of redemption through Christ, the heart of gospel faith was not in jeopardy. But he also made judgments, both clear and obscure, about specific issues. On the resurrection of Jesus, Schleiermacher was so obscure that Albert Schweitzer took him to say it was a case of "reanimation after apparent death." That was mistaken, as Schleiermacher believed that Jesus died on the cross. But Schleiermacher *was* carefully vague on the resurrection, except to say that it does not matter what really happened. What matters is to know Christ as redeemer, not believing something about Easter appearances. Christianity needs no foundation besides the experience of Christ's redeeming influence and example.[71]

Schleiermacher urged his readers to choose Christianity, because they needed redemption, but his theology worked better as a defense of religion than as an argument for choosing Christianity. His strongest argument was about the integrity of religious experience, not his case for Christianity, although he tried to have it both ways, defending a theory of religion and a claim about the distinct superiority of Christianity. Mid-nineteenth-century theologians debated whether that was the best option.[72]

Some argued that he got the relationship between Christianity and religion exactly right. Others judged that he over-relied on individual subjectivism and a general theory of religion, making his argument for Christianity secondary to his defense of religion. Some neo-Pietists, taking Schleiermacher's Christocentrism more literally than he did, wished that *The Christian Faith* consisted only of volume two. Many others, influenced by Hegel or Schelling, contended that Schleiermacher's religion of consciousness needed a stronger metaphysical basis. Some theologians in the latter group reasoned that the problem was merely that Schleiermacher played down his metaphysical basis; others concluded that going halfway with metaphysical idealism was not credible.

Schleiermacher had a system of knowledge, which showed up in his lectures on dialectics and philosophical ethics. But he placed knowledge and being into opposition, uniting them objectively only in the idea of God. On the subjective level, Schleiermacher held together thought and being only by the *feeling* that correlated to the idea of God, which accompanied all knowledge and action. To the extent that Schleiermacher posited a synthesis of God and feeling, he was a typical post-Kantian idealist. Karl Barth shrewdly noted that this synthetic exception represented, in Schleiermacher's thought, a kind of bracket beyond the antithesis of knowledge and being. Schleiermacher had a Schelling-like philosophy of identity, conceiving the ideal and the real as one, but he fought hard against turning Christianity into a speculative theology, like Schelling, or a philosophy of religion, like Hegel. Even Barth acknowledged Schleiermacher's determined sincerity on this point. For all that Schleiermacher got wrong, Barth judged, he was a valiant proponent of doing Christian theology on its own terms – at least in theory.[73]

That was how most of Schleiermacher's disciples viewed him, even among those who wished that he had not fought so hard to separate theology and philosophy.

The mediating theologians of the 1830s and 1840s lifted Schleiermacher above all others. Nitsch, Ullmann, Twesten, Willibald Beyschlag, Johannes von Hofmann, Johann Peter Lange, and August Neander were prominent in that cause. Others combined Schleiermacher and Hegel, notably Isaac Dorner and Richard Rothe. All were church-friendly synthesizers soaked in German idealism. All played a role in establishing Schleiermacher as the founder and preeminent representative of modern theology.[74]

In 1830 it was commonplace, if one was not a disciple, to put Schleiermacher on the same level with Hegelian theologians Karl Daub and Philipp Marheineke. He had written only one large work, after all; it was hard to foresee how its influence would grow. One reader in Schleiermacher's time, Joachim Christian Gass, got it right. He told Schleiermacher that his dogmatic system heralded "a new era, not only in this one discipline, but in the whole study of theology in general." A decade later, on the day of Schleiermacher's death, church historian August Neander went further, also accurately: "From him a new period in the history of the Church will one day take its origin."[75]

By 1850 Schleiermacher clearly stood above all modern theologians. By 1875 he had nothing like a rival, even as some theologians consigned him to a bygone time. By 1900 his stature was higher still, to the point that he appeared as the founder of an era, not merely a school or movement. By 1920 the era was over, at least in Germany. The whole thing had been a liberal mistake, Barth declared. Modern theology had to start over by saying no to Schleiermacher.

John Locke, British Empiricism, and the Anglican Threefold Cord

In Britain the Kantian revolution played out differently. Schleiermacher never won much of a following in Britain, there was no liberal movement in British theology until the end of the nineteenth century, and when it came, it spoke the language of Hegelian idealism. No British theologian compares to Schleiermacher or Barth in historic significance. The only British religious thinkers of comparable significance, John Locke and Samuel Taylor Coleridge, were not theologians, and did not compare to Kant and Hegel as shapers of modern religious thought. Locke was born in the wrong century to play such a role, and his empiricism was a foil for the Kantian revolution. The English and Scottish Enlightenments produced important philosophical movements, but neither produced a major religious thinker aside from Locke. The star of British empiricism, David Hume, was someone that theologians had to overcome, and Scottish commonsense realism was too complacent to break the mold in theology.

English Anglicanism, for most of its history, was too hampered and corrupted by state power, too insular, and too fixated on its doctrinal continuity with the patristic tradition to make much of an impact on modern theology. The British non-Conforming Protestant traditions had similar problems with parochialism, while English Catholic Modernism had only a brief run at the turn of the twentieth century before the Vatican crushed it. Not until the mid-nineteenth century did a liberal party emerge in English Anglicanism to seriously challenge the church's dominant High Church and evangelical parties, and it was severely put down. Not until the late nineteenth century did British theology absorb biblical criticism and develop viable liberal organizations and periodicals.

Yet the British tradition, for all its hesitancy, patristic fixations, ecclesiastical and political conservatism, absorbing cultural ethos, and lack of major theologians and influence, developed important theological trends featuring a liberalizing impulse. English Anglicanism, from its beginning in the sixteenth century, was the most ecumenical of the Reformation traditions and the only one to lift reason to the status of an authority. Thus it was distinctly open to liberalizing revision, at least in theory.

By historical necessity and spiritual inclination, early Anglican theology was always about ecclesiology. Richard Hooker (1554–1600), the chief architect of the Anglican theological tradition, fixated exclusively on defending an ecclesiastical third way between Roman Catholicism and dissenting Protestantism, as did Anglican theologians John Jewel (1522–1571) and John Whitgift (1530–1604). Hooker's six-volume *Laws of Ecclesiastical Polity*, the first major work of theology and political philosophy to be written in English, was published in the 1590s. It established the distinct Anglican approach to religious authority and provided a theoretical justification of the Elizabethan settlement, attacking dissenting Protestantism.[76]

On religious authority, Hooker taught that theological claims should be based on a threefold conflation of scripture, reason, and tradition in which tradition was subordinate to reason and both deferred to the supreme authority of scripture. On church and state, he contended that the first duty of a Christian commonwealth was to uphold true religion; the church and state were inseparable components of one commonwealth in which the sovereign was the supreme governor of both. On Puritan criticism he was relentless, devoting every book of the *Laws of Ecclesiastical Polity* to refuting Puritan arguments. Drawing on Aristotle and Thomas Aquinas, Hooker made a natural law argument for the divine authority of the state's laws, condemning Puritans for disobeying God's laws; at the same time he charged that the Roman church degraded the catholic tradition by sealing the legitimate authority of scripture and tradition with illegitimate "Popish" religion.

Hooker's fundamental aim, to defend the Elizabethan settlement, was deeply conservative, as was his theology. He took for granted the fundamental doctrines of Christian orthodoxy, cherished the catholic tradition, and defended the Protestant doctrines of the supreme authority of scripture and justification by faith. Yet his commitment to the authority of reason and his ecumenical ecclesiology planted the seeds of Anglican Latitudinarianism and Broad Church liberalism. For Hooker, reason was a formal principle of theology and the means by which a synthesis of scripture, tradition, and philosophy was fashioned. Good theology, as represented by Athanasius, Augustine, Thomas Aquinas, and, with caveats, Calvin, had always used reason as a formal principle and method; Hooker, in his view, merely formalized what good theology had always been. As the divine Logos, reason was even constitutive in the very subject matter of theology. Hooker stressed that the Lutheran and Calvinist Reformers identified the church with doctrinally precise accounts of the correct ministry of Word and sacrament, while Roman Catholic ecclesiology stressed the antiquity, unity, and universality of the church. The true church, Hooker countered, was something simpler and more inclusive – a visible divine society marked by its outward profession of faith. The church existed wherever the essence of Christianity was preached: "The visible church of Jesus Christ is therefore one in outward profession of those things which supernaturally appertain to the very essence of Christianity and are necessarily required in every particular Christian man."[77]

Every Anglican theologian of the seventeenth century subscribed to Hooker's threefold cord, even as Anglicans fought over high church versus low church, and orthodox doctrine versus interpretive latitude. British theologians disputed whether reason took second place behind scripture or third place behind tradition, but Hooker's cord held together until John Locke unraveled it, while claiming otherwise, with an assault on transcendental reason. Locke, an epochal figure in Western thought, vastly transcended the important contribution that he made to religious thought. In some ways he has no equal as a contributor to modern liberal thought. But the crucial thinker for modern Anglican theology was Coleridge, who launched a liberal trend by reclaiming the importance of transcendental reason in theology. German transcendentalism, in Coleridge's usage, restored the threefold cord of classic Anglican theology, all in the name of moving forward by overcoming Locke.[78]

Locke was born in 1632 and raised in strict Calvinism. During the English Civil War he watched his father, an attorney, ride off with the Parliamentary cavalry to destroy the images in Wells cathedral. His father's military commander secured a place for him in England's top boarding school, the Westminster School, where flogging was common, the sermons were Puritan, and Locke excelled in Latin and Greek; he also developed Monarchist sympathies. Subsequently he studied at Christ's Church, Oxford, following the standard Arts curriculum of classical studies, grammar, rhetoric, logic, geometry, and moral philosophy. On the side Locke read Descartes and was influenced by his rationalistic/mathematical method of doubt, which led Locke to physical science and, subsequently, a career in medicine. In 1667 he became personal physician to a prominent politician, Lord Anthony Ashley Cooper, at the time Chancellor of the Exchequer under Charles II, later the first Earl of Shaftesbury.[79]

Locke's entry into Shaftesbury's world of dignitaries, wealth, high culture, and political maneuvering was the turning point of his life. Shaftesbury was an anti-Catholic Evangelical, a founder of the Whig party, a founder of the Carolina colonies, and an important player in Whig resistance to the Catholic king, Charles II. Locke absorbed the ethos and causes of Shaftesbury's inner circle while retaining the status of a senior student at Oxford for thirty years. At Shaftsbury's behest, Locke served as secretary to the Lords Proprietors of the Carolinas and collected information for the English government about the American colonies and trade. In 1671 Locke had a momentous series of discussions with Shaftesbury and others about morality and revealed religion; he later recalled: "After we had a while puzzled ourselves, without coming any nearer a Resolution of those Doubts which perplexed us, it came into my Thoughts, that we took a wrong course; and that, before we set ourselves upon Enquiries of that Nature, it was necessary to examine our own Abilities, and see, what Objects our Understanding were, or were not fitted to deal with."[80]

For a thousand years European thinkers had sought to resolve moral and religious quandaries by poring over authoritative texts. That approach no longer worked, Locke judged; in his time it fueled wars over religion, as Europe fought and divided over the right meaning of its authorities. Locke resolved to start anew, taking no tradition on faith. Instead of making judgments about things by consulting a tradition of opinions about them, he would study the things themselves and the capacity of human reason to understand them, tracing the empirical origins of ideas. For almost twenty years he puzzled over this problem, writing scraps of thoughts and digressions, assembling *An Essay Concerning Human Understanding*, while taking two exiles for safety's sake.

For six years Locke lived in Holland, where Shaftesbury died in 1683, and where Locke completed the *Essay Concerning Human Understanding*. In 1685 James II, a Catholic son of Charles I, succeeded Charles II to the throne, just as the Whigs had feared. Openly professing his Roman allegiance, the king initially supported the Church of England, but swung vigorously pro-Catholic after he put down the Monmouth Rebellion of 1685, colorfully remembered as "the Pitchfork Rebellion." For three years the king fought with Whigs and Church of England hierarchy, setting the stage for the "Glorious Revolution" of 1688. Whig Parliamentarians backed an invading army led by the Dutch Protestant William of Orange, which deposed James II, put William of Orange and his wife on the throne as William III and Mary II, and enabled Locke to return to England in 1689.[81]

Locke was 57 years old at the time and had not published anything of significance. Upon returning to England he was offered an ambassadorial post to the Elector of Brandenburg, the future King Frederick I of Prussia. Locke declined the post; his books had finally started flowing and he was anxious to write more. For nearly thirty years he had labored on a short one titled *A Letter Concerning Toleration;* in the spring of 1689 it was finally published. For twenty years he worked on the *Essay on Human Understanding,* which he published in November 1689. For ten years he wrote *Two Treatises of Government,* which he published in December 1689. The *Essay on Human Understanding* bore his name, while the books on tolerance and liberal governance remained anonymous until his death; Locke acknowledged his authorship in his will. Disciplined, cautious, mild-mannered, and a bachelor who kept extremely detailed records of his financial affairs, Locke probably sought to shield himself from personal attacks by publishing his most controversial books anonymously. That did not prevent him from becoming the most famous intellectual in Europe of his time, and more famous afterward.[82]

At the time, modern science was pushing Aristotle aside. Isaac Newton (1642–1727), a mathematics professor at Trinity College, Cambridge, and subsequently Master of the Mint in London, taught that the world consists of material bodies that interact according to three laws of motion concerning the uniformity of motion, change of motion, and mutuality of action. The universe is a closed system with universal physical laws. Newton's masterwork, *Philosophiae Naturalis Principia Mathematica* (1687), modeled on Euclidean geometry, demonstrated its propositions mathematically from definitions and mathematical axioms. He described the ultimate conditions of his system – absolute time, space, place, and motion – as independent quantities constituting an absolute framework for measure. His belief in God rested chiefly on his admiration for the mathematical order of creation. The *Principia* was hailed immediately as a revolutionary leap forward in understanding, making Newton famous. "The new natural philosophy," as it was called, was Newton's picture of nature as a universal system of mathematical order.[83]

Newton was named to the Royal Society in London in 1672 and was its president from 1703 until his death, where he and Locke were colleagues and friends. Locke's

Essay Concerning Human Understanding, appearing two years after the *Principia Mathematica,* was hailed as a Newton-like contribution to understanding, an epochal text in the history of philosophy that pioneered the modern epistemological project of identifying the empirical origins of ideas. In Book I he rejected the Platonist concept of innate ideas, arguing that that the mind has no innate ideas. In Book II he argued that all ideas are products of sensory experience or reflection on experience. In Book III he discussed how language gets in the way of the attempt to lay hold of reality. In Book IV he described the empirical method of analyzing and making judgments about evidence.

Locke contended that the mind works on its ideas of sensation and reflection through the operations of combination, division, generalization, and abstraction. On ideas he was an empiricist, seeming to argue that ideas are mental objects, although he inspired rival schools of interpretation on this point. On knowledge he was a rationalist, arguing that knowledge is a product of reason working out the connections between ideas, not something produced directly by our senses. On substance he seemed to believe that things possess a substratum that support their properties, although interpretations varied here as well.

Everything that exists or occurs in a mind is an idea, or includes one, Locke taught. All human knowledge is founded on ideas, all of which are acquired by natural faculties – innate powers of mind. Even the idea of God is not innate in the mind, but is acquired by any mind that seriously reflects on the created order. An idea is the immediate object of a mind in the act of thinking. It exists in the mind's intellectual faculty (the understanding), as distinguished from the mind's volitional faculty, and it is always an object of thought or perception.[84]

This theory of knowledge had a vast influence in Western philosophy; following Locke, philosophers conceived epistemology as theorizing about the elements, combinations, and associations of experience, or differently, how perceptions are filtered through the mind's innate capacities that arrange them into ideas. Hume, Kant, Frances Hutcheson, and James Mill philosophized in the Lockean mode, as did George Berkeley, the next great British philosopher after Locke, who set his extreme idealism against the ostensibly skeptical and atheistic implications of Locke's thought.

In political philosophy Locke's intellectual legacy was equally immense. He made the early Enlightenment's signature case for religious toleration as well as historic arguments for the natural freedom and equality of human beings, government by consent, majority rule, the right of revolution, separation of legislative and executive powers, and the rights to life, liberty, and property. In *A Letter Concerning Toleration,* Locke offered religious and philosophical arguments for religious tolerance. True faith cannot be forced, he contended. The Bible contains no command to magistrates to bring people to faith; Jesus and the New Testament never indicate that coercing a faithful response is acceptable. Locke admonished that defenders of religious persecution had a hypocritical tendency to persecute disbelievers for trivial infractions while ignoring larger evils.

Moreover, human understanding is too limited to justify the imposition of any ruler's or church's specific religious beliefs on others, and saving souls is not the business of government. To allow wide berth to religious freedom, Locke argued, the state needed to draw a clear line between itself and the church. The state, or commonwealth, was a society of individuals constituted to protect the life, liberty and property of individuals and the public order. Churches, on the other hand, were voluntary societies of individuals devoted to worshipping God. Since the church posed no threat to the state, the state had no business interfering in the affairs of the church, such as prescribing specific religious beliefs. Religious toleration should be extended to all people who did not pledge civil allegiance to a foreign power, excluding atheists and Roman Catholics, whom Locke deemed a danger to the state and its liberties. Atheists and Catholics could not be trusted to be loyal subjects.[85]

A Letter Concerning Toleration contended that the conditions of communion should be the conditions of salvation and nothing more. Belief in Jesus was essential to salvation; belief in bishops or a specific atonement theory was not. If the churches could agree to that, reunion would be possible, and killing over religion would stop. Locke deeply admired Hooker, but he relinquished Hooker's idea of a church that was coextensive with the state or commonwealth. The divisions within non-Roman Christianity were too deep and impassioned to redeem Hooker's vision of a single, liberalized, unifying national church. *A Letter on Toleration* and the *Two Treatises of Government* called for as much religious tolerance as Locke dared to imagine in a modern republic. In the first treatise, he demolished Robert Filmer's theory of absolute monarchy and the divine right of kings, denying that God made all people naturally subject to a monarch. In the second treatise he offered a natural law alternative to Filmer's theory of Adamic authority, one requiring no special pleading about the authority or meaning of Genesis.[86]

The second treatise famously defended the natural freedom and equality of "men," asking readers to imagine a group of human beings living in a state of nature lacking any government authority or private property. In such a state, Locke reasoned, all persons would have a duty to God not to harm any persons in their life, liberty, or goods, and they would know by virtue of possessing reason that they had such duties. But knowing that they possessed such rights and duties would not guarantee that they exercised them rightly. Some would go too far in defending their rights; others would lack sufficient power to defend their rights. In Locke's telling, this accounted for the emergence of political obligation. Human beings came together to develop governing authorities to resolve certain defects in the state of nature. Leaving the state of nature, they set up governments to correct the sinful tendency of human beings to violate the rights of others to their personhood, labor, and goods. Since governments rested on the relinquishment, to some degree, of natural freedoms, consent was crucial to the process. Governments existed by the consent of the people to protect their rights and to promote the public good. When a government failed to protect these rights, the people had a right to replace it, even by revolution.[87]

Locke had a labor theory of property rights, that persons became the rightful owners of something by mixing their labor with it. The things of the world belonged to God, he allowed, but persons own their own labor by virtue of their God-given powers. When they mixed these powers of labor with unowned things, they became the rightful owners of the things, unless they freely contracted their labor to someone else. In the state of nature, money did not exist, since no one needed it. Each person had a right to as much of the good things that nature provided in common as one could use, which became their property when they "affected" it with their labor. If one gathered a hundred bushels of apples, one had a property in them; they were one's goods as soon as one gathered them. It was wrong, Locke noted, to take more apples than one could consume before they spoiled; hoarding was a form of stealing. But trading for one's advantage was not wrong; if one traded apples for nuts, or nuts for a piece of metal, no harm was done. In the state of nature, accumulating property was fine as long as one used it before it spoiled, left enough for others (the sufficiency condition), and appropriated property only through one's labor.[88]

Locke was rarely quotable, but one of his rare quotable sentences pictured colonial America as something close to Eden: "In the beginning all the world was *America,* and more so than it is now." In the state of nature, he imagined, as in America, the most valuable things were generally of short duration; the sturdy Puritans that fled to America did not pine after gold or diamonds. Locke observed that the invention and growth of money always went hand in hand with the enlargement of possessions, which was generally a good thing, but which necessitated the invention of govern-ments: "For in Governments the Laws regulate the right of property, and the possession of land is determined by positive constitutions."[89]

Until the twentieth century, most interpreters thought that Locke's *Two Treatises of Civil Government* were written in 1688 to justify the Glorious Revolution. In fact, they were written during the Exclusion crisis and were probably intended to justify the revolutionary uprising against the Stuart monarchy – an issue that colors the vexing question of how Locke's theory of "legitimate slavery" should be understood. Locke taught that slavery was legitimate only for unjust aggressors defeated in war. Legitimate slavery is the continuation of a state of war between a lawful conqueror and an unjustly aggressive captive, he reasoned. The conqueror, faced with a choice between killing the aggressor or enslaving him, may legitimately take the latter course, making use of a captive as a slave. No other form or cause of slavery is legitimate, least of all, forms of chattel slavery holding despotic power over others without just cause.[90]

That seemed to rule out any justification for the trans-Atlantic slave trade or chattel slavery, but "just war" is a concept notoriously amenable to interest and will to power, and Locke was intimately connected to the English slave trade. He was involved in it as a government official; he acquired expertise on the slave trade in this capacity; and he bought shares in England's chief slave trading company, the Royal Africa Company. Some scholars have argued that Locke developed his theory of slavery to delegitimize the House of Stuart's enslavement of the English people. Others argue that he was too deeply involved in the slave trade to be as critical of it as he seemed in the *Two Treatises,* and/or that he took for granted that England's national power rested to some degree on the slave trade, which had to be justified. Others doubt that Locke intended to apply his theory of natural rights to black Africans, while others press for the opposite verdict, that Locke was consistently anti-tyrannical, condemning chattel slavery and royal autocracy for the same reason.

Virtually every aspect of Locke's political thought is rife with similar disputes, especially over his concept of the state of nature and his defense of private property. Interpreters clash over whether Locke meant to say that a state of nature existed wherever no legitimate political authority existed, whether he conceived the state of nature as a factual description, whether this concept was compatible with biblical teaching, how literally the "mixing" metaphor should be taken, whether he was a "possessive individualist" defender of unrestricted capitalist accumulation, and whether his sufficiency condition could handle scarcity conditions. Debates on these issues are especially charged in the US American context, where Locke is long-established as a distinctly paradigmatic figure. Colonial and postcolonial Americans revered him as the champion of government by consent, private property, and the "nightwatchman state." At Harvard, America's only university in the seventeenth century, Locke's writings on empiricism and political philosophy were canonical texts. Outside the academy it helped that he was a public intellectual, not a university professor.[91]

Locke was also an Anglican Enlightenment defender of the reasonableness of Christianity and the divine commands of God. We know our own existence by intuition, he argued. We know that God exists by demonstration. And we know all other things by sensation.

Though Locke famously shredded the idea of innate ideas, he regarded the self's intuition of its own existence as being so obvious that it required little comment. One's existence cannot be less evident than one's feeling of pleasure or pain, he asserted. If I doubt the reality of any other thing, "that very doubt makes me perceive my own *Existence,* and will not suffer me to doubt of that." To feel pain or to know that one doubts something is to experience an infallible internal perception of one's existence: "In every act of Sensation, Reasoning, or Thinking, we are conscious to our selves of our own Being; and, in this matter, come not short of the highest degree of *Certainty*."[92]

Locke moved directly from self-certainty to the "certain and evident Truth" that an "eternal, most powerful, and most knowing Being" exists. One cannot really doubt one's existence, he argued. By the same intuitive certainty everyone knows that nothing cannot produce any real being. If we know that there is some real being, and that non-entity cannot produce it, it is evident beyond any doubt that something has existed from eternity, "since what was not from Eternity, had a Beginning, and what had a Beginning, must be produced by something else." Something must be from eternity. In addition, since that which has its being and beginning from another owes its power to the something from eternity, this source must be the origin of all power. Lastly, there would be no knowledge if there had ever been a time when no being had any knowledge. Things that wholly lack knowledge and perception, operating blindly, cannot produce a knowing being, Locke argued. One cannot get self-conscious, perceiving, and knowing beings out of "senseless Matter" any more than a triangle can make itself three angles greater than two right ones. The existence of an eternal, most powerful, and most knowing God is more certain than the knowledge of anything apprehended by the senses, and it is the basis on which other attributes of God's being are derived.[93]

Because we lack innate ideas, Locke argued, we are of necessity ignorant, and hungry for knowledge of any kind. Lacking rational knowledge in particular, we yearn for proofs. In search of certainty, we want clear and determined ideas, which elude us. Where we lack knowledge of our own or even strong testimony from others, we want probability to be on our side. In matters of religion, Locke contended, every sect uses reason as much as it can to defend its doctrines, up to the point where reason no longer works, whereupon it appeals to faith.[94]

Locke realized that he was not describing how Protestants usually described how they did theology. He was describing what really happened, not what Protestants said about beginning with revelation. Beginning with revelation is impossible, he admonished, for there is no such thing as a revealed idea. Any idea that is communicated in revelatory experience must exist in sensation or reflection before it is heard as a revelatory Word. The problem of subjectivity must not be shucked off. Even Paul, transported to the Third Heaven, would not have been able to express any new idea that he received there. Similarly, any truths that come to us by way of revelation must also be discoverable by reason; otherwise we would not understand them. Nothing that we receive in revelation can be clearer or utterly different from our own mental objects, our ideas.[95]

Locke distinguished between knowledge and belief, arguing that no one possesses enough knowledge to actually live by it. Since knowledge is lacking in most areas of life, we form beliefs and depend on them. Something can be rationally believed as true, though not counted as knowledge, if it is established without direct observation or reasoned deduction. To Locke, God's existence was knowable, because it was a condition of human existence; this was the basis of natural theology. But matters of revelation, the basis of revealed theology, belonged to the category of belief, where some beliefs had stronger evidentiary support than others.

Theology deals mostly with beliefs, not knowledge, Locke argued. Natural theology is too limited to support faithful living, and the best revealed theologies conform their beliefs to the strongest evidence. Deistic rationalists, often claiming a kinship with Locke, denied that religion is mysterious and denied that God revealed certain things to human beings. On both counts they had Locke against them. Locke did not claim that religion should spurn anything smacking of transcendent mystery or revelation. Revealed theology has an important role to play, he urged, as long as it does not contradict reason, which is not the same thing as claiming that reason grasps everything worth claiming. The point is to attain as much rational certainty as possible in an area where knowledge is usually lacking: "Whatever GOD hath revealed, is certainly true; no Doubt can be made of it. This is the proper Object of *Faith*. But whether it be a divine Revelation, or no, *Reason* must judge."[96]

Locke was serious about not doubting whatever God revealed; thus the major work of his later life, *The Reasonableness of Christianity as Delivered in the Scriptures* (1695), consisted almost entirely of painstaking exegetical discussions of scriptural passages. For him the divine authority of the Bible was not in question; only the rational meaning of scriptural teaching and narrative was in question. Though Locke displayed his typical penchant for rambling diversions and tedious exegesis, he made a straightforward case for the reasonable essence of Christianity as he understood it. To anyone who reads the New Testament, he argued, it is "obvious" that the biblical doctrine of redemption, and thus the core of the gospel, is founded on the supposition of Adam's fall. Christianity is about the restoration by Christ of something lost by Adam. Locke contended that there were two predominant ways of construing this essential Christian claim, and both were wrong. One party turned Christianity into something unbelievable and repulsive by fixing the guilt of Adam on all human beings. The other party overreacted to orthodox depravity doctrine by denying that the need of personal redemption is the heart of the gospel. The latter strategy "made Jesus Christ nothing but the restorer and preacher of pure natural religion," Locke observed. This was the kind of thing he had heard for years in elite society parlors. What was needed was an "unbiased" account of what the Bible actually said, especially the gospels, which were always about the need of redemption.[97]

But redemption from what? In the Bible, Locke observed, Adam fell from the state of perfect obedience, which the New Testament calls "justice" or, in an alternative translation that Locke allowed, "righteousness." Adam was expelled from paradise, a state of immortal living, for disobeying God. Death was unknown before Adam sinned; afterward all human beings were mortal and bound for death. In Locke's telling, this situation was obviously what the gospel is about; nobody that reads the New Testament honestly could deny that the gospel fixates on the death that came to all human beings by Adam's sin. Unfortunately, a great deal of Christianity took this death to be a state of imputed moral guilt, such that all descendants of Adam supposedly deserve "endless torment in hellfire." This idea is strange and unbelievable in every way, Locke countered. It makes a mockery of the justice and goodness of God. It loads a perversely inflated idea of death onto the simple and literal idea expounded in the Bible. And it is nonsense as morality or law. What sort of law would condemn a felon not merely to lose his life, but to "be kept alive in perpetual exquisite torments?" How could anyone construe that as moral or legal decency?[98]

Locke implored that a great deal of unreasonable and morally repugnant doctrine usually associated with Christianity falls away as soon as one grasps that death in the Bible is about ceasing to be, "the losing of all actions of life and sense." It is not an imputed guilt leading to eternal hellfire. He piled up scriptural passages supporting his view: God will render to each according to his deeds (Romans 2:6). Just as all die in Adam, all will be made alive in Christ (1 Cor. 15:22). All Jews will come forth from their graves; those that did good will be raised to the resurrection of life, and those that did evil will be consigned to the resurrection of condemnation (John 5:29). In Locke's rendering, the New Testament teaches that Christ, the second Adam, restores all human beings to life from the estate of death. The life to which all people are restored is the one they receive at the resurrection. There they recover from the death brought into the world by Adam, but the Bible never says that those consigned to the resurrection of condemnation are condemned because Adam sinned. People are condemned only for their own sins of doing evil and rejecting the grace offered to them.[99]

Locke accepted the New Testament's portrayal of Jesus as a miracle-working Savior who called himself the Messiah and was raised from the dead. In his telling, Jesus was an original and spiritually compelling ethical teacher and exemplar, the first teacher to build up a moral doctrine upon self-evident principles of reason, which he deduced in all its parts by demonstration. Locke allowed that before Jesus, there was a natural law and previous teachers of it, but no one before Jesus "made out all the parts of it, put them together, and showed the world their obligation." This moral doctrine consti-tuted a revelation because it came from the Savior sent by God, whose miracles con-firmed his status as the Messiah. The moral teaching of Jesus bore the unquestionable authority of God. Here as elsewhere, Locke argued, the revelation is the primary thing, but not to the exclusion of reason. Philosophy did not save the world, despite centuries of Greek philosophizing. By the time of Jesus, "philosophy seemed to have spent its strength and done its utmost." Even if the philosophers had been better teachers of ethical living, it wouldn't have made much difference, because people need more than a "train of proofs." They need a demonstration. Philosophy operates by reasoning and proofs, always seeking to dispel doubt by drawing "a thread of coherent deductions from the first principles." Jesus understood, Locke observed, that a plain command has greater spiritual power than any proof. Jesus changed everything by teaching and demonstrating the way to God.[100]

Locke stressed that everyone needs to believe certain things to be saved. Jesus is the Savior and ruler of the world, he was raised from the dead, and he will return to judge the world: "Those are fundamentals which it is not enough not to disbelieve; everyone is required actually to assent to them." He added that this is a very short list, one containing nothing that conflicts with reason: "It is no diminishing to revelation, that reason gives its suffrage too to the truths revelation has discovered."[101]

For generations of sympathetic readers, Locke epitomized the possibility that one could hold fast to Christianity, tolerance, and rationality without contradiction. Despite his Unitarian tendencies and his attack on transcendental reason, Locke insisted that he did not break the Anglican consensus on how theology should be done. Scripture was the paramount authority on all matters of faith and order, and the only source of doctrines necessary for salvation. Church tradition, especially the councils of the fourth and fifth centuries, guided the interpretation of scripture. Reason shaped by scripture, tradition, and sound learning arbitrated the interpretive process.

Every Anglican theologian took this framework for granted. There were differences of emphasis among high church conservatives like Archbishop William Laud who lifted church tradition above reason, liberal catholics like Jeremy Taylor who revered the church's catholic tradition while nonetheless making reason the judge of tradition, and liberal-leaning Anglican Protestants like William Chillingworth and Locke who were cooler to patristic authority. The Cambridge Platonists, a liberal-leaning seventeenth-century group led by Benjamin Whichcote and Henry More, played up the light of reason that linked Anglican liberality to neo-Platonism, Johannine theology, and the early church. But all made a plausible claim to Hooker's legacy, forging an Anglican consensus around the threefold cord of scripture, tradition, and reason. Chillingworth charged that the Roman church, by giving disproportionate authority to church tradition, compelled believers to believe in things contrary to reason. That was morally and intellectually repugnant, he admonished. Chillingworth was prepared to believe "many mysteries, but no impossibilities; many things above reason, but nothing against it." Moreover, "I shall believe nothing which reason will not convince that I ought to believe it."[102]

That was in Locke's spirit, who justly placed himself in the Anglican tradition of holding together revelation and reason. But Locke's empirical concept of reason took Anglican theology in a different direction. The pre-Lockean Anglican idea of reason was either critical, not constructive, as in Chillingworth's hermeneutical concept of it; or robustly neo-Platonist or neo-Aristotelian when constructive, as with the Cambridge Platonists; or a combination of hermeneutical and Hellenistic specula-tive impulses, as with Hooker. Locke's empiricism was more stringent and grounded, tracking the flow of the experience of things of sense. He assaulted the neo-Platonist theory of innate ideas and the neo-Platonist concept of transcendental reason that early Anglican theologians held in common with their favorite patristic theologians. On the same grounds he undermined the authority of patristic Trinitarianism and Christology, playing down Trinitarian and Christological doctrine, which led to theologies that broke explicitly with Nicene Trinitarianism. Though Locke praised the Anglican cord of scripture, tradition, and reason, he diminished the authority of reason within it by reducing rationality to empirical demonstration. That was fine with many evangelicals, who praised Locke for putting reason in its place; speculative reason had an undeniable tendency to undercut the authority of scripture. On the other hand, a vast assortment of free-thinking deists and rationalists were quite sure that Locke belonged to them. Lockean empiricism paved the way to eighteenth-century deism, rationalism, Unitarianism, and atheism, just as Locke's opponents charged, though his bitter critic John Edwards hyperbolically overreached in claiming that Locke himself was an atheist.[103]

For rationalists like John Toland (1670–1722) and Matthew Tindal (1657–1722), Locke was the grandfather of rationalistic deism, his pious protests notwithstanding. For Anglican divines Joseph Butler (1692–1752) and Samuel Clarke (1675–1729), Locke was a great exemplar of rational Christianity, though he went too far in reducing reason to the sense plane and stripping religion of mystery. Butler's *Analogy of Religion* (1736), the greatest English theological work of the eighteenth century, epitomized the early Enlightenment religious attempt to go most of the way with Locke, while holding out for a bit more mystery against a skeptical tide. Butler and other Anglican apologists, notably William Paley, got as much as they could out of scientific, probabilistic, empirical reason, defending Christian beliefs on rational grounds that more or less accepted Locke's strictures on transcendental reason – until Coleridge seized on Kantian transcendentalism.[104]

Samuel Taylor Coleridge and English Romanticism

The Romantic turn in English theology was launched by one of the creative geniuses of English poetry and literary criticism, Samuel Taylor Coleridge, a figure of over-flowing pathos and irony. Coleridge deeply absorbed post-Kantian idealism, and sometimes plagiarized it. He spent most of his emotionally turbulent life battling opium addiction and other personal demons. He had the wrong politics for his Romantic following and the wrong religion for his American Unitarian following. More to his liking, at the end of his life, he was lifted up by English Anglican followers who made him an icon of Broad Church liberalism and was subsequently lauded by Anglo-Catholics who prized him for recovering transcendental reason.

Born in October 1772 in Ottery St. Mary, Devon, England, Coleridge was the tenth child of Ann Coleridge, the thirteenth of John Coleridge, and the last for both. John Coleridge, a parish priest who doubled as schoolmaster, instilled his devotion to moral duty and excellence in what he fondly called his "tribe" of children. Most of his sons became scholars or soldiers, and all except Samuel were launched in their careers when John suffered a fatal heart attack in 1781. Samuel, not quite nine years old when his father died, was sent to Christ's Hospital, a charity school in Greyfriars, London resembling Charles Dickens' severe portrait of English orphanages. Half the boys were orphans and all were poor and neglected. Coleridge loathed the place, spent the rest of his childhood in it, and was scarred by it. Introverted, bookish, intensely lonely, and inclined to reverie, he later described his adolescence as "depressed, moping, friendless, poor orphan, and half starved." In his last year at Christ's Hospital he caught rheumatic fever, for which he was dosed with opium for the first time, and began writing Coleridgean poems about loneliness, feverish illness, and the saving touch of love. For the rest of his life Coleridge wrote affectionate recollections of his nurturing father and bitter remembrances of a mother who allowed him to come home only three or four times in nine years. He also recalled that his reveries featured a mystical yearning for the infinite ground of all things.[105]

In 1791 Coleridge's assiduous reading helped him get into Jesus College, Cambridge. Excitable and self-dramatizing, he partied hard at Cambridge, won a prize for a poem opposing slavery, was inflamed by the idealism of the early French Revolution, and took up the cause of William Frend, a radical Unitarian tutor at Cambridge. Frend was Cambridge's leading prototype of English Jacobinism. A deist and republican, he urged students to take up the egalitarian ideals of the French Revolution. In a pamphlet titled *Peace and Union* he blasted Anglican doctrine, England's declaration of war against France, and oppressive war taxes, setting off a sensational trial that drew a line against religious and political radicalism. Frend was expelled from Cambridge in 1793; shortly afterward, Coleridge, one of Frend's chief supporters, failed to win a coveted scholarship. These twin events disabused Coleridge of expecting a career in the Establishment's universities, courtrooms, or churches, or of wanting one. Opting for debauchery, he ran up a large debt on prostitutes and drinking, joined the army in remorse, was bailed out by his brothers and returned to Cambridge (the army judged that Coleridge was insane anyway), and told his brother George: "I have been a fool even to madness. What shall I dare promise? My mind is illegible to myself – I am lost in the labyrinth, the trackless wilderness of my own bosom."[106]

Coleridge's brothers tried to give him a second chance at Cambridge and an Establishment career, preferably as a lawyer. Instead Coleridge threw himself into "Pantisocracy," his name for a radical democratic communalism blending Unitarian rationalism, French revolutionary radicalism, feminism, nature romanticism, and the American emigration movement. England was hopelessly corrupt, Coleridge believed. It relied on the slave trade, waged a ridiculous war with France, and, fueled by war hysteria and anti-French prejudice, drove one of its best scientists and preachers, Unitarian rationalist Joseph Priestley, into exile in America. Coleridge dreamed of establishing a utopian community that followed Priestley to Pennsylvania. Forging an alliance with another lonely and alienated dreamer, Robert Southey, he envisioned an experimental community that shared property, labor, and self-government equally among its male and female adult members and lived harmoniously with nature, making friends with animals. Coleridge especially favored jackasses, writing verse about the Pantisocratic ideal of a radically inclusive "brotherhood in nature."[107]

Every English city had a Dissenting society that opposed the Test Act of 1673, which prohibited non-Anglicans from holding public offices. These societies usually advocated freedom of the press and opposed slavery; their ranks included deists, atheists, radical evangelicals, and Unitarians; and Unitarians were usually the core group. Birmingham had the strongest Dissenting community until its leader, Priestley, was driven out of England in 1794. Bristol, the center of England's slave trade, had a strong Dissenting community, which attracted Coleridge and Southey to it. In Bristol, Coleridge acquired two of his longtime patrons, Joseph Cottle and John Prior Estlin. He gave lectures condemning the slave trade and Prime Minister

William Pitt's warmongering, and tried to organize a Pantisocratic community with Southey, which failed. The following year, 1795, Coleridge and Southey married, respectively, the sisters Sarah Fricker and Edith Fricker, disastrously in the former case. The same year Coleridge met William Wordsworth, the turning point of his life. Meanwhile he dropped out of Cambridge and resolved to make his living by writing and lecturing.

Coleridge started his career by founding a radical Christian journal, *The Watchman*. The exhausting tedium and difficulty of the work distressed him, as did his wife.

He complained to his publisher, Cottle: "So I am forced to write for bread – write the high flights of poetic enthusiasm, when every minute I am hearing a groan of pain from my Wife – groans, and complaints & sickness! – The present hour, I am in a quickset hedge of embarrassments, and whichever way I turn, a thorn runs into me." Sara Coleridge's complaints and illnesses were nothing compared to her husband's ailments, anxiety, insomnia, and complaining, especially about his wife, all of which he dosed with opium and brandy; English medicine had no concept of addiction. The "hedge of embarrassments," on the other hand, was a professional breakthrough – the final version of his apocalyptic stew of religion and politics, "Religious Musings," which Coleridge published in *The Watchman* and made the closing entry of his first book, *Poems on Various Subjects*. Nearly half the book's 51 pieces were sonnets; a few were long and formal in Milton's style; most were direct, personal, and spontaneous, vividly describing Coleridge's travel adventures and enthusiasms. The book was showered with reviews, mostly appreciative, focusing on the formal poems. His ode to a jackass got the most attention, which was strongly divided. *Poems on Various Subjects* gave notice that a new kind of English poetry was coming, earning unusual attention for a twenty-three year old poet.[108]

The Watchman survived for only ten issues, leaving Coleridge deeply in debt and chastised. In 1796 he shut down the journal and contemplated two options: study German transcendentalism and Romanticism in Germany, or stay in Bristol, make a living as a Unitarian pastor, and eschew radical politics. Both plans replaced his radical activism with a deeper intellectualism. Thus he dropped his fixation with France, replacing it with Germany, especially Kant and J. C. F. Schiller. In both options Coleridge planned to launch a school featuring a threefold curriculum on "man as animal" (the natural sciences), "man as an intellectual being" (ancient metaphysics, Locke, Kant, Schiller, Scottish moral philosophy, and philosopher David Hartley), and "man as a religious being" (history of religions, culminating in Unitarian Christianity).[109]

Coleridge realized that both plans had practicality problems; moreover, he underestimated how difficult it would be for him to drop his political activism in Bristol, the thing for which he was best known. British politics swung sharply to the right during the Napoleonic Wars, cooling Coleridge's ardor for politics. He spent the rest of his life playing down his early radicalism and denying that "English Jacobin" had ever applied to him. In most respects that was disingenuous, but not in the way that mattered most to Coleridge: He had always been religious, yearning for the infinite spiritual source and power of all things. He had never been attracted to the atheistic rationalism of the Jacobins, and when the French Revolution turned out badly, he denied that he had ever made it an object of faith.

Contemplating his two plans, Coleridge scratched out a living as a writer and formed a transformative friendship with Wordsworth. They had met in Bristol in 1795; the following year they began to exchange manuscripts, each praising the other as a genius; in 1797, still pondering the ministry versus Germany, Coleridge moved to a thatched cottage in a remote country village, Stowey, to live a simple life in oneness with nature. There Wordsworth and his sister Dorothy spent the summer of 1797, in a country mansion four miles from Stowey, taking expeditions with Coleridge through the hills and streams of Quantock, all composing and talking poetry. The Wordsworths exhilarated Coleridge, though he was prone to manic upswings in any case; his wife Sara, left to care for the newborn David Hartley Coleridge, was unhappy. The tramping and talking continued in the fall, when Coleridge conceived *The Rime of the Ancient Mariner* and plotted with Wordsworth to revive the ballad form. *Ancient Mariner* began in the popular gothic style of G. A. Bürger, but morphed into a stunning naturalistic tale of an outcast sailor enduring drifting, bad weather, hallucinations, guilt, and spiritual anxiety, all fashioned out of Coleridge's psyche and memories.[110]

Reviews and poems, however, failed to pay Coleridge's bills, and he didn't want to be a journalist or teacher. In January 1798 he opted for the ministry, accepting the Unitarian pastorate at Shrewsbury – where he delivered one sermon. Coleridge was saved from the ministry by playing one of his major patrons, Thomas Wedgwood, into a no-strings-attached annual annuity of 150 pounds for life. Flush with gratitude and excitement, Coleridge resigned from the ministry and vowed to friends that he would use his financial security to defend religion and devote himself to poetry and philosophy. The book that launched English Romanticism, *Lyrical Ballads* (1798), was the first fruit of Wedgwood's generosity.

The idea of a joint volume of ballads and poems was hatched in March 1798 as a way for Coleridge and Wordsworth to finance a trip to Germany. Good poetry was supposed to be rational, moderate, high-minded, formal, and elitist, like the Enlightenment. Coleridge and Wordsworth dared to write about things considered inappropriate for poetry: everyday commonplaces, rural life, seascapes, fantasy, madness. Coleridge later explained that they believed in two cardinal principles: Poetry should be naturalistic, inspiring readers by its "faithful adherence to the truth of nature," and it should be highly imaginative. In his telling, he and Wordsworth accepted a division of labor, aiming toward balance: Wordsworth provided naturalistic pieces about ordinary life and Coleridge contributed imaginative pieces with a supernatural element.[111]

That was slightly misleading, as Coleridge's poetry shimmered with naturalistic imagery and Wordsworth sought to awake powers of imaginative awareness, appreciation, and criticism in his descriptions of everyday life. In any case, two things wrecked the plan of a balanced collection: Wordsworth poured out poems quickly and he regarded himself as the stronger figure. *Lyrical Ballads* contained 23 poems, only one was a ballad, and all but four were by Wordsworth. Seventeen years later, in his rollicking tour-de-force of memoir, philosophy, and literary criticism, *Biographia Literaria*, Coleridge recalled of *Lyrical Ballads:* "My compositions, instead of forming a balance, appeared rather an interpolation of heterogeneous matter." It was a bitter memory for Coleridge, though he still struggled not to show it. The first blow to their friendship occurred in 1800, when Wordsworth denigrated Coleridge's contributions to *Lyrical Ballads* and reduced his role in the book's second edition. Later Wordsworth tired of Coleridge's chaotic lifestyle and his obsession with Sara Hutchinson. By the time that Coleridge wrote *Biographia Literaria*, he was deeply wounded by Wordsworth's rejection; recalling *Lyrical Ballads* called up painful memories of how a treasured friendship had unraveled.[112]

Coleridge and Wordsworth were close friends, however, for a decade, launching English Romanticism together and, for a time, living together. Coleridge's four contributions to the first edition of *Lyrical Ballads* were works of unsurpassed brilliance: *Ancient Mariner,* a sublime medieval ballad of breathtaking force; the symbolic poem *Kubla Khan,* about the Asian emperor Kublai Khan; part one of the narrative poem *Christabel,* an abduction story of protean ambiguity, with Gothic motifs, later favored by vampire novelists; and *The Nightingale,* a conversation poem celebrating the instinctive joy of nightingale songs, which confuted Milton's notion of the nightingale as a melancholy bird. These were Coleridge's greatest poems, along with the second part of *Christabel,* which he completed in 1800, and *Dejection: An Ode,* published in 1802.[113]

Coleridge was one of the great talkers, dominating conversations with everyone in his circle, including the cooler Wordsworth. Voluble, opinionated, conversant on many subjects, and always bursting with grand proposals about multiple projects, Coleridge fascinated Wordsworth, and inspired him, until Wordsworth (in his view) grew past Coleridge. The reviews for *Lyrical Ballads* were just beginning to appear when Coleridge and the Wordsworths sailed for Germany, leaving Sara Coleridge and two children behind. Coleridge rationalized that he would spend only three months in Germany, though he stayed for ten, permanently damaging his marriage.

Just before departing he left a quarto of poems at a London publisher, one of which, "France: An Ode," sought to set the record straight about his supposed Jacobinism. The first stanza invoked the clouds and ocean waves that first inspired the poet to love liberty. The second described the fall of the Bastille. The third recounted the Terror and the declaration of war. The fourth condemned France's recent invasion of Switzerland. Coleridge recalled knowingly that English radicals watched this tragedy with mounting horror. They tried to defend revolutionary republicanism and the Revolution's supposed devotion to it, but the second part became impossible after the Revolution descended into madness. English lovers of liberty tried to believe that France might still, somehow, lead the way to liberty, but then France invaded neutral Switzerland:

> O France, that mockest Heaven, adulterous, blind,
>   And patriot only in pernicious toils!
> Are these thy boasts, Champion of human kind?
>   To mix with Kings in the low lust of sway,
> Yell in the hunt, and share the murderous prey;
> To insult the shrine of Liberty with spoils
>   From freemen torn; to tempt and to betray?[114]

Liberty was still the great prize, Coleridge insisted in the fifth stanza, but the hope of realizing it lay in the mighty force and beauty of nature, not in any current political struggle. He had caught a glimpse of it in the wildness of the ocean and wind:

> And there I felt thee! – on that seal-cliff's verge,
>   Whose pines, scarce travelled by the breeze above,
> Had made one murmur with the distant surge!
> Yes, while I stood and gazed, my temples bare,
> And shot my being through earth, sea, and air,
>   Possessing all things with intensest love,
>   O Liberty! my spirit felt thee there.[115]

Then he sailed to Germany to complete his formal education with deeper philosophic learning.

In Germany Coleridge and the Wordsworths soon parted, as Coleridge wanted to immerse himself in German high culture and Wordsworth wanted seclusion with his sister muse, Dorothy, to write poems. Coleridge learned German, studied at Göttingen under biblical scholar J. G. Eichhorn and natural historian J. F. Blumenbach, resolved to write a biography of G. E. Lessing, switched to a translation of Schiller's *Wallenstein,* and, plotting a major work on metaphysics, ran up a huge debt with Wedgwood buying books on Kantian philosophy. Tragically, his baby son Berkeley died of smallpox, but Coleridge did not return home to console Sara, despite receiving a heartbreaking letter from her. He savored his German sojourn and dragged out his return to England and a grieving wife. Upon returning to Stowey in 1799 he took a newspaper job to pay off his debt, lamented the tedious labor of translating Schiller, and planned new projects in philosophy, poetry, and criticism, some of which he completed. In 1800 he moved to Keswick to be near Wordsworth, telling his friend William Godwin, a radical philosopher, that the landscape of the Lake District would transform him into a god. That was not quite what happened.[116]

By then Coleridge was already on the downward path, at age 27. Depression, anxiety, overwork, rheumatism, a bad marriage, financial insecurity, and his dependence on laudanum wore him down. He fell in love with Dorothy Wordsworth's best friend, Sara Hutchinson, plus Sara's entire family, which was uplifting for a while, but also desperately frustrating, as he could not marry his true love. He had huge ambitions for multiple intellectual projects, but had trouble focusing on any of them. He worked hard on the second edition of *Lyrical Ballads,* now grown to two volumes, only to be pushed aside by Wordsworth, who excluded *Christabel* as inferior, relegated *Ancient Mariner* to the end of volume one, wrote a self-centered preface that ignored Coleridge, and listed only himself as the author.[117]

Coleridge's dream-like medieval ballad of a nature-goddess/sorceress/damsel in distress didn't belong in Wordsworth's collection of modern naturalistic poems, so *Christabel* was thrown out. Wordsworth looked down on *Ancient Mariner* too, because the Mariner had no distinct character, he did nothing but was merely acted upon, the events were disconnected, and the imagery was overwrought. Coleridge read this opinion for the first time when the second edition was published, which crushed him. Humiliated at being pushed aside, and then battered by Wordsworth's criticism, he withstood both by accepting Wordsworth's verdicts. Coleridge needed

Wordsworth's friendship, so he swallowed domineering treatment, even as he told Southey that Wordsworth's preface was "half a child of my own Brain." In other respects Wordsworth remained a devoted friend to Coleridge and appeared oblivious to the hurt that he caused, even as Coleridge's self-confidence crumbled. Coleridge told friends that Wordsworth was the poetic genius and he was merely "a kind of Metaphysician." He did not compare to Wordsworth and he had no business trying to do so; instead, he planned to read his trunk of books on philosophy and try to write one. Coleridge explained to John Thelwall that he aimed to write a book on how feelings formed affinities with each other and with ideas: "As to Poetry, I have altogether abandoned it, being convinced that I never had the essentials of poetic Genius, & that I mistook a strong desire for original power."[118]

Then he plunged into a fateful illness featuring rheumatic fevers, boils, and swollen joints, for which he took a battery of remedies featuring leeches, poultices, bark infusions, brimstone, and opium laced with brandy. The damp of the Lake District was bad for Coleridge's rheumatism; more importantly, emotional factors were always paramount for him. Coleridge was not addicted to opium before his health collapsed in January 1801. Afterward he struggled with addiction for the rest of his life, which eroded his poetic genius. Before and after, he was lazy, neurotic, self-indulgent, and restless, but also capable of extraordinary productive achievements during bursts of concentration. He could be hyperbolically boastful and hyperbolically self-deprecating almost in the same breath. All his friends puzzled over these contradictory impulses. After Coleridge returned from Germany, he puzzled too. Increasingly he turned inward, interrogating the mystery of his psyche, as did a cottage industry of biographers and critics after he was gone.

Molly Lefebure stressed Coleridge's opium addiction and fecklessness in marriage. Norman Fruman and Thomas MacFarland pored over his plagiarism as a clue to his moral character. Oswald Doughty pressed for a verdict of near-insanity. Lefebure and Geoffrey Yarlott dwelt on Coleridge's sexual fantasies. Nicolas Roe contended that Coleridge was consumed by guilt and defensiveness over his early Jacobinism. Many critics contended that religious anxiety was obviously the key to his emotional turmoil. Coleridge himself, for many years, laid the primary blame for his troubles on his purportedly snarling, harping, simple-minded, unappreciative wife. Sara Coleridge admired Wordsworth and her brother-in-law and caretaker, Southey, more than Coleridge, which tortured him. Richard Holmes, defending Coleridge from a chorus of hostile biographers, contended that his greatness far outstripped his numerous faults. But even Holmes buried readers in copious descriptions of pathological behavior, acknowledging that Coleridge badly degenerated after returning from Germany. Declining health, deepening addiction, disappointment, and an obsessive fascination with his own contradictions – an "inward spiraling of his imagination" – diminished his brilliance and achievements.[119]

At the top of a long list of torments for Coleridge, from 1799 to 1812, was the romantic pain that he suffered from his obsession with Sara Hutchinson, whom he called Asra. His first love letter to her was the magnificent "Dejection: An Ode," which he wrote in a mood of decline and regret in 1802. The public version scaled back Coleridge's torrent of lament at being deprived of his true love, but not enough to fool Sara Coleridge.

> A grief without a pang, void, dark, and drear,
> A stifled, drowsy, unimpassioned grief,
> Which finds no natural outlet, no relief,
> In word, or sigh, or tear –
> O Lady! In this wan and heartless mood,
> To other thoughts by yonder throstle woo'd,
> All this long eve, so balmy and serene,
> Have I been gazing on the western sky,
> And its peculiar tint of yellow green.[120]

Coleridge realized that his powers were eroding, even as he pored out reviews, journalism, poems on other topics, and literary criticism, and pondered his religious philosophy. By 1801 he had read a great deal of Kant and post-Kantian idealism, both of which he savored for the idea of a transcendental ground of freedom and spirituality. He told Thomas Poole that he was finished with "all the irreligious metaphysics of modern Infidels – especially, the doctrine of Necessity." In that mood Coleridge returned to Anglicanism, seeking a religion with a stronger sense of God's presence in Jesus, the world, and the soul. But this religious turn did not break his degenerative spiral. In 1804 Coleridge took a nearly three-year sabbatical in the Mediterranean, drifting from Malta to Sicily to Rome, seeking to clear his head, forget Asra, and restart his career. On all counts he failed. By then he was hopelessly chained to a cycle of quitting opium and failing to do so, which damaged his faith in his powers with each failing.[121]

Coleridge half-expected to die during his Mediterranean sojourn. Near its end, he found himself writing about his return to Trinitarian Christianity. He wrote about it as though it were a long settled matter, something centered on his ravaged health and romantic heartbreak, though in fact he had only recently begun to make sense of the Trinity as a tri-unity of unity and distinction bound together by Will, not being. In a letter to Sara Coleridge's wayward younger brother George Fricker, Coleridge took a pastoral tack: "I was for many years a Socinian; and at times almost a Naturalist, but sorrow, and ill health, and disappointment in the only deep wish I had ever cherished, forced me to look into myself; I read the New Testament again, and I became fully convinced, that Socinianism was not only not the doctrine of the New Testament, but that it scarcely deserved the name of a religion in any sense." Rationalistic religion shortchanged Jesus and his redemption, Coleridge urged. It lost the tri-union of God as Will, the idea of Jesus as Logos, and the focus of Christian salvation on the redemption of corrupted will. Even the Anglican rationalism of Locke, Butler, and Paley conceded too much to the mechanistic culture of atheism, producing more infidels. Coleridge, knowing that he desperately needed saving, gently advised Fricker that modern people needed to look "into their own souls, instead of always looking out."[122]

A few weeks later Coleridge dragged himself back to Keswick and a marital confrontation. His friends gasped at his puffy, pitiful appearance. Dorothy Wordsworth found him distracted and ill at ease. Not for the last time, Coleridge rallied himself with a new project. In 1808 he made a splash as a public lecturer in London, giving bravura performances on Shakespeare, Milton, education reform, and other topics. Quickly he discovered that his audiences responded best when he didn't prepare; Coleridge's talkative extroversion and improvised riffs on whatever crossed his mind made him a fascinating speaker, holding his audiences by effusive spontaneity.

But Coleridge's opium addiction made him unreliable for showing up, and he winced at Wordsworth's disapproval; Wordsworth said it was undignified to lecture for a living. In addition, Coleridge still fantasized about marrying Asra, who had become Wordsworth's secretary. To do better at rallying himself, he needed a different project. Coleridge separated from his wife, moved in with the Wordworths in Grasmere, and launched an ambitious, intellectual weekly newspaper, *The Friend,* borrowing Asra as his secretary.

From the beginning Wordsworth pleaded with Coleridge that founding a newspaper in his condition was crazy and so was his obsession with Asra, who was not romantically attracted to Coleridge. Coleridge pressed on, pouring out his wayward brilliance for ten months of weekly issues, dictating articles to Asra on literature, politics, philosophy, art, psychology, religion, education, travel, and current affairs, telling readers that he was offering them the history of his mind. In politics he blasted the violence and fanaticism of the French Revolution and supported Spain's battle against Napoleon; Coleridge obscured his youthful enthusiasm for the early Revolution. In religion he stumped for a liberalized Anglicanism featuring interpretive latitude and blasted Catholicism, especially in Ireland. Admiringly, with a cautionary edge, Coleridge described Martin Luther as an archetype of the visionary revolutionist that projected a private vision onto society. In politics and religion Coleridge argued for a moderate liberalism that eschewed factionalism and extremism. Readers got a strong dose of post-Kantian transcendentalism, which evoked complaints that Coleridge's subjects were too high-flying and his sentences too twisting and obscure. Coleridge tired of the complaints, replying that the point of his paper was to provide a forum that didn't insult the intelligence of intelligent readers. He felt a moral duty to raise the level of civic discourse and to increase the number of intelligent readers.[123]

Coleridge fantasized that the paper would succeed, he would beat his addiction to opium, and Asra would be sufficiently impressed to marry him. Instead Asra spurned him, the paper folded, and Wordsworth wearied of Coleridge's chaotic, sullen, slovenly, opium-fueled, demanding, half-crazed behavior in his home. Coleridge, feeling the need to exit, accepted an invitation to spend the winter with an admirer, Basil Montagu. Wordsworth, feeling duty bound to warn Montagu about Coleridge's terrible behavior and condition, did so. Montagu promptly told Coleridge what Wordsworth said, setting off an ugly fight between Coleridge and Wordsworth that embittered both of them for years.

The break with Wordsworth was devastating for Coleridge, who crashed spectacularly. From 1811 to 1814, Coleridge disintegrated, just as the narrative verse-romance that he and Wordsworth had pioneered soared as a popular genre. Young poets that cut their teeth on *Lyrical Ballads* achieved enormous commercial success. Walter Scott's *Lady of the Lake* was a bestseller in 1810; three years later George Gordon Byron's *The Bride of Abydos* was a runaway bestseller. Coleridge wanted to write a popular work, but he was barely able to produce things that came easily to him, journalism and lectures. If not for the saintly intervention of a retired lawyer, John Morgan, and Morgan's family, who took Coleridge into their home and nursed him through numerous illnesses and overdoses, he probably would not have survived. As it was, in 1813 he hit bottom, nearly dying of a massive opium overdose. Placed in the care of a physician specializing in addiction and suicidal depression, Coleridge realized that he had to face his inner demons or die; he could not keep them at bay any longer through writing and lecturing. To many friends (though not to any family members) he wrote letters confessing his addiction to opium and apologizing for various episodes caused by it. In his telling he averaged a pint of opium per day, "besides great quantities of liquor"; Joseph Cottle judged that the true average was two pints per day, which would have put Coleridge at risk of lethal overdose every day.[124]

Coleridge wrote his most revealing letter to John Morgan, assuring that he was "perfectly sane and vigorous" in his reason, understanding, moral feeling, and sense. However, Coleridge confessed, in a fundamental way, he was clearly insane. For many years he had lived with a "completely deranged" volition, the faculty instrumental to his will. His volition was perverted to the point of being dissevered from his will: "I was perpetually in the state, in which you have seen paralytic persons, who attempting to push a step forward in one direction are violently forced round to the opposite." He had not wanted to abandon his family, mistreat his friends, and destroy his career, but he had done so anyway. If his problem was a corrupted will, nothing less than a spiritual transformation of it would be redemptive for him. Coleridge observed that he previously disagreed with James 2:10 – whoever violates one point of the Law violates all of it – "but my own sad experience has taught me its awful, dreadful Truth." Now he confessed his need of redemption in Christ, having been "crucified, dead, and buried, descended into Hell, and am now, I humbly trust, rising again, tho' slowly and gradually."[125]

Coleridge told Cottle that he was ready to put himself in a sanitarium under the care of a physician. Cottle advised him to go one step farther, confessing that he was possessed by the Devil, not merely opium. Coleridge opted for moderated usage and a demythologized understanding of evil. Friends and critics opined that this time he was beyond any hope of recovery, but in 1814 Coleridge began writing and lecturing again, helping Bristol to celebrate the defeat of Napoleon. He approached John Murray, a prominent publisher who had made a fortune off Scott and Byron. Would Murray be willing to publish Coleridge's translation of Goethe's *Faust*? Murray was interested in Goethe, but not in dealing with Coleridge. Coleridge, bruised but undaunted, resolved that he was overdue to write his masterwork anyway. If Words-worth and Southey could find sizable audiences, so could he. His major work would be about the divine unity of the world, entitled *Logosophia*. It would be a very large book, or perhaps several volumes, beginning with logic, proceeding to Kantian metaphysics and natural theology, and ending with a commentary on the fourth gospel.[126]

Coleridge pored over Kant, Fichte, and Schelling in anticipation of finally writing his masterwork, then had a thought about how to begin: If he began with a literary auto-biography, that would make it easier for him to get rolling *and* easier for his audience to absorb the philosophical sections. Securing a Bristol publisher, Coleridge timorously introduced himself to Byron, asking if he would help secure a London publisher for such a work. Byron agreed, and Coleridge started dictating the ostensible preface to his philosophical system. From April to August 1815 he dictated to John Morgan, delivering a winding, rambling, brilliant rendering of his literary career followed by several chapters of equally rambling but sparkling literary criticism, especially of Wordsworth. By August, Coleridge thought that he was finished, but he had second thoughts; the "preface" had morphed into something too large to exclude metaphysics. The metaphysical/theological section could not wait because it was foundational to everything that Coleridge believed. Hurriedly, pressed by the publisher's deadline, Coleridge dictated eight new chapters of philosophical argument, which he placed in the middle, which necessitated extensive rewriting of the first section (memoir) and third section (literary criticism). More complications and publisher demands ensued, requiring rewriting and delays, all of which yielded a massive, sprawling, profuse two-volume stemwinder defying categorization, *Biographia Literaria*.[127]

The opening paragraph struck a mixed note of defensiveness and bravado, declaring that although Coleridge's writings were few, unimportant, and little read he had things to say about large religious and philosophical questions and the application of his views to poetry and criticism. The idea of beginning with memoir worked for Coleridge, though not as a confession. He said almost nothing about his addiction or marriage, and nothing about Asra. His model for the memoir section was Wordsworth's *Prelude,* except as prose. Vast stretches of *Biographia Literaria* took up a dialogue with Wordsworth, always respectfully, stressing the distinction between fancy and imagination that Wordsworth borrowed from Coleridge, and praising Wordsworth as the preeminent poetic genius of the age.[128]

There are two kinds of imagination, Coleridge proposed, in a paragraph immortalized by citation, defining the English Romantic concept of creativity. The *primary* imagination is the living power of all perception, "a repetition in the finite mind of the eternal act of creation in the infinite I AM." The *secondary* imagination is an echo of the primary imagination that differs from it only in the degree and mode of its operation: "It dissolves, diffuses, dissipates, in order to re-create; or where this process is rendered impossible, yet still at all events it struggles to idealize and to unify." In both cases, imagination is essentially vital and transformative, inspiring all creativity. Coleridge argued that fancy, on the other hand, is merely passive and mechanical, a mode of memory "emancipated from the order of time and space" and modified by willful choice that "has no other counters to play with, but fixities and definites." Fancy imitates and distorts, but does not create, as it is bound up with mechanical operations of the mind.[129]

In Coleridge's telling, Wordsworth owed his unrivalled greatness to the power of his imagination, "that willing suspension of disbelief for the moment which constitutes poetic faith." On the other hand, despite epitomizing the poetic revolution that Wordsworth and Coleridge inaugurated, Wordsworth was less reliable as a guide to what it meant. Coleridge set the record straight about the preface to the second edition of *Lyrical Ballads:* "With many parts of this preface in the sense attributed to them and which the words undoubtedly seem to authorize, I never concurred; but on the contrary objected to them as erroneous in principle, and as contradictory (in appearance at least) both to other parts of the same preface, and to the author's own practice in the greater number of the poems themselves." *Lyrical Ballads* was more expansive and imaginative than Wordsworth's account of it, Coleridge contended. Explicitly, that meant that Wordsworth was a better poet than a critic; implicitly, it meant that Wordsworth should not have marginalized Coleridge on the basis of a faulty theory. To his friends Coleridge ruefully observed that he spent most of his career exalting Wordsworth over himself to the detriment of his reputation; his friends, tending to agree, often judged that Wordsworth was insufferably arrogant.[130]

But Coleridge aimed higher in his masterwork than merely setting the record straight about Coleridge, Wordsworth, and things literary. His subject was the unifying transcendent meaning of human experience from rational perception (which he called Understanding) to artistic vision (which he called Imagination) to transcendent intuition (which he called Reason). In his youth he was drawn to Plato and Plotinus because of the spiritual feeling they conveyed. At Cambridge he absorbed the empiricism of Locke, Hume, and Thomas Hobbes, which traced its lineage to William of Occam and Francis Bacon. British empiricism disapproved of Platonic and German transcendentalism, it had a strong tendency toward materialism, and in the eighteenth century it favored David Hartley's associationist theory in psychology.

Hartley, a British physician and philosopher (1705–1757), taught that neural events and mental events operate on parallel tracks. Like Hume, he relied on a strong distinction between impressions (or sensations) and ideas, although Hartley denied that Hume influenced him. In Hartley's picture, "vibrations" caused sensations by carrying impressions through the nerves to the brain. Neural vibrations peripheral to the brain correspond to the sensations they cause, and vibrations in the brain correspond to ideas. In effect, and quite literally, ideas are vibrations within neural events, or at least, ideas are produced by neural vibrations.[131]

Coleridge was fascinated by the origins of things. In his rationalist days he was especially taken with Hartley, thus his eldest son was named David Hartley Coleridge. But Coleridge always had a mystical streak, which he fed by reading Spinoza, Jacob Boehme, and Goethe. During his German sojourn he leaned toward pantheism, conceiving divine reality as universal Spirit lacking an opposite. Upon returning to Anglicanism he adopted a Trinitarian panentheistic idea of God as essentially Unity and Distinction, anticipating Schelling and Hegel on the Trinitarian nature and unfolding of Spirit. For the rest of his life Coleridge was unabashed in proclaiming that Germany was intellectually superior, "the only Country in which a man dare exercise his *reason* without being thought to have lost his Wits & be out of *his Senses.*" In Coleridge's telling, Locke construed the mind out of the senses, but the German transcendentalists, daring to use their powers of metaphysical reason, construed the senses out of the mind. British thought barely lifted its sights beyond things and mechanics, but the Kantian idealists dealt with everything, and thus brought religion and philosophy together.[132]

Biographia Literaria put it strongly, lamenting that in England parochial positivists like Hartley and Sir James Mackintosh were considered important philosophers. Had modern British philosophy begun with Descartes instead of Hobbes, Coleridge argued, it might have overcome the parochialism to which it was predisposed, though even Descartes played a role in modern philosophy's assault on ideas. As it was, the British tradition was content to follow Hobbes in explaining the association of ideas on mechanical grounds. Coleridge claimed, unfairly, that Hobbes' system was "exclusively material and mechanical," seeming not to notice that Hobbes had a theory of compounded imagination that attributed powers of invention to the mind. On stronger ground, Coleridge drew a straight line from Hobbes to Hume. Hume's

Treatise of Human Nature (1740) described impressions as forceful resolutions of the mind's perceptions, comprising all sensations, passions, and emotions, while ideas were mere "faint images" of perceptions in thought. To Coleridge, that was a sorry fall from Platonist transcendentalism, one that began with Descartes and Locke and which led, inevitably, to the vibrating materialism of Hartley.[133]

Coleridge doubted that anyone, even Hartley, actually believed that ideas are nothing more than given configurative vibrations. The modern downgrading of ideas was a case of reductionism running to absurdity. Taken seriously, Coleridge argued, it negated taking any idea seriously, including the theory of reductionist vibration: "According to this system the idea or vibration *a* from the external object A becomes associable with the idea or vibration *m* from the external object M, because the oscillation *a* propagated itself so as to re-produce the oscillation *m*." But M begins with an essentially different impression than A, Coleridge noted. Assuming that different causes cannot produce the same effect, vibration *a* can never produce vibration *m*, and Hartley's scheme did not explain how *a* and *m* were associated: "It is a mere delusion of the fancy to conceive the pre-existence of the ideas, in any chain of association, as so many differently colored billiard-balls in contact, so that when an object, the billiard-stick, strikes the first or white ball, the same motion propagates itself through the red, green, blue, black, &c. and sets the whole in motion." That is ridiculous, Coleridge implored; more precisely, it is *impossible* to suppose that the same force that constitutes the white ball also constitutes the red or black. It is like saying that the idea of a circle also constitutes the idea of a triangle.[134]

Coleridge allowed that Hartley, to his credit, was not an atheist. On the other hand, when Hartley talked about God, he had to ignore his own philosophy, which claimed that ideas exist only in the vibrations of an ethereal medium common to the nerves and the atmosphere. Coleridge countered that the air that one breathes is the condition of one's life, not its cause: "We could never have learnt that we had eyes but by the process of seeing; yet having seen we know that the eyes must have pre-existed in order to render the process of sight possible."[135]

This was a neo-Platonist argument, one favored by Augustine, but Coleridge made most of his case through Kant, Schelling, and lesser German transcendentalists. Coleridge prized Kant for cutting a path between Locke and Hume. Locke was too confident of the capabilities of reason and Hume was too skeptical. Locke's empiricism ruled out any appeal to *a priori* concepts, deducing his concepts of the understanding from experience, but Locke used them to obtain knowledge transcending the limits of experience. Hume, on the other hand, realized that a pure concept such as "pure mathematics" had to have an *a priori* origin. But Hume failed to explain the unification of synthetic judgments in the understanding. Coleridge accepted Kant's account of this failure. It never occurred to Hume that the understanding itself, through its transcendental concepts, might be "the author of the experience in which its concepts are found." Thus, Hume relied entirely on experience as the basis of knowledge.[136]

This was the way forward in philosophy, Coleridge urged. The German Kantians and post-Kantians were miles ahead of anything happening in England; in fact, the "illustrious sage of Königsberg" was the greatest modern philosopher by far. In British philosophy it was standard fare to dismiss Kant as impossibly turgid, obscure, ridiculous, and overrated. Coleridge, by contrast, was defiantly admiring, insisting that Kant towered above everyone in originality, depth, subtlety, sophistication, and importance. Contrary to British reviewers, Kant was even clear-minded and lucid. In Coleridge's experience, reading Kant was like being grasped by "a giant's hand." After fifteen years of poring over Kant's three *Critiques* and his book on religion, "I still read these and all his other productions with undiminished delight and increasing admiration."[137]

Still, there were problems with Kant, Coleridge allowed – the very problems noted by Schelling. There was the question of what Kant really thought about religion, which was related to the question of what he really thought about the thing-in-itself. Even under a tolerant king, Kant had to be careful what he said about religion; then under Friedrich Wilhelm II he was silenced about religion. Coleridge stressed that Kant did not want to be exiled like Wolff, since Kant would not have done well in exile. He surmised that Kant's fear of persecution probably influenced his decision to exclude religious questions from the *Critique of Pure Reason*. On the other hand, Coleridge admired that Kant pushed hard enough on this question to get into trouble with Friedrich Wilhelm II.[138]

Schelling doubted that Kant ever published what he really thought about religion. If the autonomy of the will, and thus Kant's ground for a moral system, and thus his ground for religion, was as central to Kant's theory of human nature and understanding as he claimed, why did he relegate it to practical reason? Though Kant rested everything religiously on the moral law, Schelling thought that his system was driven by an unacknowledged divine will. The spirit of Kant's system was better than its letter, Schelling judged. Coleridge agreed, pointing to Kant's handling of religion, which to some degree violated the spirit of his system. Coleridge sympathized that Kant had to negotiate a minefield of threats under Friedrich Wilhelm II, "that strange compound of lawless debauchery and priest-ridden superstition." Later, after the bad king was gone, Kant had to deal with Fichte's atheism controversy, which threatened to tar Kant's legacy. To many critics, the meaning of the Fichte controversy was that Kantian idealism led to atheism. Coleridge noted that for Kant, this unpleasant episode supplied "experimental proof" that his longtime caution about religion was amply grounded.[139]

Coleridge agreed with Schelling that Kant's evasiveness about religion had something to do with his evasiveness about the thing-in-itself. Somehow the *noumenon* was crucial to Kant's system, yet he had almost nothing to say about it. Coleridge protested that in Kant's telling, nothing could be said about "the *materiale* of our sensations," the very thing responsible for the sensory element of knowledge. Coleridge, besides rejecting this opinion, couldn't believe that Kant really believed it either. Post-Kantian idealists, beginning with Fichte, had been right to begin here. Fichte protested that according to Kant, the thing-in-itself was inconceivable, existing independent of the categories of understanding. That was absurd, Fichte argued. If the thing-in-itself is inconceivable, how did it play such a large role in Kant's philosophy? To conceptualize the existence of something that is inconceivable is to negate its existence as something inconceivable. Fichte launched the post-Kantian tradition by charging that Kant, for all the importance that he vested in his concept of the thing-in-itself, did not have one.[140]

Coleridge respected Fichte for identifying the key problem with Kant and for trying to correct it. But Coleridge had cut his teeth philosophically during the very period that post-Kantian idealism began to leave Fichte behind, morphing into varieties of absolute idealism. From 1795 to 1802, when Fichte had his glory years at Jena and then crashed, three intersecting groups of German idealists conceived variously named objective idealist or absolute idealist alternatives to Kant and Fichte. One was the Romantic group in Jena and Berlin led by Friedrich Schlegel, Friedrich W. J. Schelling, Friedrich von Hardenberg (better known as Novalis), and Friedrich Schleiermacher. Another was the *Bund der Geister* group in Frankfurt and Homburg, consisting of Friedrich Hölderlin, G. W. F. Hegel, Isaak von Sinclair, and Jakob Zwilling. The third group, the *Bund der freien Männer* in Jena, was closer to Fichte personally and intellectually; it included August Ludwig Hülsen, Johann Erich von Berger, Johann Smidt, Johann Georg Rist, and Johann Friedrich Herbart.[141]

All were products of the Romantic generation, influenced by Goethe, and anxious to advance the Kantian revolution beyond Kant's dualistic impasse of subject and object. Most were monists, believing that the universe consists of a single substance. Most were vitalists, believing that the single universal substance is a constantly developing organism. Coleridge was an assiduous reader of post-Kantian philosophy during the birth of absolute idealism. He had devoured Schelling's early writings and followed Fichte's bitter break with Schelling, which occurred in 1801. Schelling developed an idealist philosophy of nature that rejected Fichte's subjectivism. By 1801 he was finished with being identified as a disciple of Fichte; the breakpoint had occurred for him when Fichte publicly referred to him as a disciple. Coleridge's thinking in this area reflected the excitement that he had felt at catching absolute idealism on its way up. For the rest of his life he called it transcendental idealism, not absolute idealism, which accentuated its basis in Kant, but which, in his case, granted only a minor and mostly misguided role to Fichte.[142]

Full-orbed transcendental idealism began with Fichte, Coleridge acknowledged. Fichte replaced Kant's thing-in-itself with an unconsciously self-limiting I that constructed the world through its dialectical experience of its posited and negated self. But Fichte took a brilliant insight to a subjective extreme, Coleridge argued. Fichte's system of knowledge built up a "heavy mass of mere *notions*" that made transcendental idealism look laughably solipsistic: "His theory degenerated into a crude egoismus, a boastful and hyperstoic hostility to NATURE, as lifeless, godless, and altogether unholy; while his *religion* consisted in the assumption of a mere ORDO ORDINANS, which we were permitted *exoterice* to call GOD."[143]

Good idealism is not about the expansion of a grotesquely self-absorbed ego, Coleridge contended. Warming to ridicule, he threw in a bit of poetic burlesque:

> Here on this market-cross I cry:
> I, I, I! I itself I!
> The form and the substance, the what and the why,
> The when and the where, and the low and the high,
> The inside and outside, the earth and the sky,
> I, you, and he, and he, you and I,
> All souls and all bodies are I itself I!
> > All I itself I!
> > (Fools! A truce with this starting!)
> > All my I! all my I![144]

Fichte, in Coleridge's telling, lost his way in dialectical word-spinning, building one subjective concept out of another. Coleridge took no interest in the later Fichte's attempts to pull back on the subjectivism, since Fichte could not be salvaged on his own terms, and because Coleridge had found a superior thinker anyway, Schelling. Or as Coleridge insisted, knowing that he had an unfolding textual problem with Schelling, he found the transcendentalist who expounded Coleridge's own emerging thoughts.

Schelling was at the height of his creative power when Coleridge plunged into this area. Books poured out of him; he soared to the top of the field just as Fichte imploded; his major works, *Ideas for a Philosophy of Nature* (1797) and *System of Transcendental Idealism* (1800) were formative for Coleridge. In 1809 Schelling took a religious turn that shaped his later thought, but Coleridge's English audience had no concept of early versus later Schelling, for in 1815 Schelling had no English audience, until Coleridge created one for him. More importantly, Coleridge's attraction to post-Kantian idealism had always been religious anyway, fitting his spiritual predisposition. Schelling's religious turn merely caught up to the way that Coleridge interpreted Schelling in the first place.[145]

The latter factor complicated Coleridge's already complex relationship to Schelling. He was obviously dependent on Schelling, but he warned readers that he was less dependent than it might seem. Coleridge worried what "future readers" would think of his reliance on Schelling. Many pages of his book's philosophical mid-section were straight out of Schelling and Johann Gebhard Ehrenreich Maass, a historian of philosophy and follower of the Leibniz-Wolff school. Thus Coleridge cautioned readers that "an identity of thought, or even similarity of phrase will not be at all times a certain proof that the passage has been borrowed from Schelling, or that the conceptions were originally learnt from him." In fact, whole sections of *Biographia Literaria* were close paraphrases or verbatim mosaics of Schelling and Maas, but Coleridge, anticipating "the charge of plagiarism," contended that "many of the most striking resemblances, indeed all the main and fundamental ideas, were born and matured in my mind before I had ever seen a single page of the German Philosopher."[146]

In Coleridge's telling, it was a mere coincidence that he began to formulate a metaphysical position that was virtually identical to Schelling's during the period that Schelling wrote his major works. This coincidence was not "at all to be wondered at," as he and Schelling were both students in the school of Kant and had read some of the same mystics and metaphysical theologians. To be sure, Schelling was prolific in this area while Coleridge had written mostly for his notebooks – Coleridge overlooked that Schelling's flow of books had stopped in 1810. But by 1815, Coleridge regarded himself as a longtime post-Kantian idealist thinker, a product of the same intellectual matrix that produced Schelling and Hegel.[147]

In his notebooks he had worked out an understanding of divine reality as panentheistic distinction-in-unity. Coleridge was attracted to thinkers that conceived reality as a dynamic relationship of opposite poles. Giordano Bruno, Nicholas of Cusa, and Jacob Boehme were exemplary thinkers for him. All were theorists of dynamic polarity, describing the life process as a constant generation of polar opposites that are not mere contrasts. Bruno emphasized the unfolding of polarities. Nicholas had a similar theory of the coincidence of opposites, which he fashioned into a Logos theology. Boehme had a dipolar Logos theology of a decidedly mystical bent, although Coleridge spurned Boehme's alchemical speculations. To Coleridge, Kant was the greatest theorist of dynamic polarity, in his dialectic of sensibility and understanding. Kant led him to other theorists in this line, including Schelling, but as early as 1804, Coleridge stewed over his right to claim intellectual authorship. In 1804 he wrote in his notebook, "(I am proud perhaps but) I seem to know, that much of the matter remains my own, and that the Soul is *mine.*"[148]

Biographia Literaria zigged and zagged on Coleridge's intellectual pride. On the one hand, he had worked this position out for himself; on the other hand, it was fine with him if all the overlaps and resemblances were "wholly attributed to *him.*" A bit defensively, Coleridge claimed that he hadn't read much of Schelling's work, and came late even to the things he read; still, "I regard truth as a divine ventriloquist; I care not from whose mouth the sounds are supposed to proceed, if only the words are audible and intelligible."[149]

Coleridge had an explicitly Christian understanding of transcendentalism before Schelling came to it, and even in Schelling's religious phase, he lacked Coleridge's passionate spiritual feeling. Philosophically, however, Coleridge spoke pure Schelling absolute idealism, conceiving nature as the sum of all objective things and intelligence (or, the self) as the sum of all that is subjective. Nature, they both argued, is exclusively represented and lacking in consciousness, while intelligence is exclusively representative and conscious. The objective and subjective mutually exclude each other, yet all positive knowledge requires a reciprocal concurrence of these two factors. Coleridge urged that there are only two fundamental possibilities about how this happened. Since the objective and subjective mutually exclude each other, one must be primary. Coleridge opted for the idealist school and its problems, while contending that so-called idealism is in fact "the true and original realism" because idealists do not deny the reality of objects of consciousness. Idealism, in his telling, lived in the real world, which included real objects and real subjectivity. With an echo of Micah 6:8, Coleridge implored materialists: "Oh, ye that reverence yourselves, and walk humbly with the divinity in your own hearts, ye are worthy of a better philosophy!"[150]

Coleridge conceived transcendental philosophy as a mind-centered version of idealism deriving everything from an act of free self-positing. For Kant and, especially, Fichte, nature was an organic product of consciousness tending toward the realization of reason. Philosophy theorized the movement from the pure subjectivity of self-consciousness to objectivity or nature. Schelling had started there, aiming to refine Fichte's system, but in the late 1790s he began to say that a deeper course correction was needed, one that took nature more seriously and holistically. Nature is not merely the mind in the process of becoming, or, more precisely, the positing of the not-I. Rather, mind derives from nature and nature derives from mind.

This was Schelling's signature thesis during his glory years of rising fame and prolific production. The highest realization of reason occurs in aesthetic experience, he taught, where the identity between the subjective and objective becomes an object to the experiencing I. In his third phase, however, Schelling changed his mind about exalting art over religion. In 1809 he announced a religious turn in his book *Philosophische Untersuchungen über das Wesen der menschlichen Freiheit* (*Philosophical Investigations Concerning the Nature of Human Freedom*). Schelling argued that reality is ultimately self-directed will, which has its primordial ground in God, and reason develops as the self-revelation of God. Lutheran mystic Jacob Boehme was a formative influence on Schelling and Coleridge in this area, although Coleridge noted that Schelling was chary about admitting it; Schelling waited until the 1830s to do so.[151]

Coleridge, poring over Schelling's *System of Transcendental Idealism* and a later collection of Schelling's thought, *Philosophische Schriften* (1809), shook his head at Schelling's failure to acknowledge his dependence on Boehme. At least he admitted that he depended on Boehme and Schelling. Then Coleridge made a case for God-centered absolute idealism that was straight out of Schelling. For Schelling, as for Coleridge, the absolute identity of subject and object originated in an ideal "I am," which the later Schelling identified with God. For Coleridge, there was no early or later on this matter, since his subject was God from the beginning of his transcendentalist turn. Had Coleridge distinguished between the early and later Schelling, he might have made a better defense of his intellectual independence or at least explained that his panentheistic Trinitarian emphasis on unity-in-difference put him closer to the Christian mainstream than Schelling, who leaned toward pantheism. As it was he defended himself by exaggerating the lateness of his dependence on Schelling.[152]

On the level of Spirit, Coleridge argued, subject and object are identical, each involving the other: "It is a subject which becomes a subject by the act of constructing itself objectively to itself; but which never is an object except for itself, and only so far as by the very same act it becomes a subject." Spirit realizes itself as a "perpetual self-duplication" of one power of life as subject and object, each presupposing the other despite existing only as antithetical realities. For Coleridge, the high point of scriptural narrative was Exodus 3:14, the mastertext of absolute idealism, God telling Moses, "I AM WHO I AM . . . tell the Israelites, 'I AM' has sent me to you." I know myself, and everything else, through myself, and only there. As Coleridge put it, "I am, because I affirm myself to be; I affirm myself to be, because I am."[153]

In that case, Coleridge argued, it is pointless to require any other predicate of the self than that of self-consciousness, for only in the self-consciousness of spirit does the identity of object and representation occur. The very essence of spirit is that it is self-representative: "If therefore this be the one only immediate truth, in the certainty of which the reality of our collective knowledge is grounded, it must follow that the spirit in all the objects which it views, views only itself." Spirit is its own subject, not an object; but spirit is an absolute subject "for which all, itself included, may become an object." Thus spirit is necessarily an act, for spirit, the identity of subject and object, must dissolve this identity to some degree to be conscious of it.[154]

Self-consciousness is possible only by and through the movement of will. Since spirit exists originally as subject over against an object, it is originally infinite, but since it cannot be a subject without becoming an object, it must be both subject and object – the original union of infinite and finite. Just as Schelling argued that transcendental idealist philosophy passes into religion, Coleridge argued that philosophy absorbs religion as philosophy passes into religion: "We begin with the I KNOW MYSELF, in order to end with the absolute I AM. We proceed from the SELF, in order to lose and find all self in GOD."[155]

Biographia Literaria rambled, but also sparkled, to its concluding vision of divine creative power communicated through imagination. Coleridge did not claim that reason establishes or proves Christian faith. It was enough to show that reason is in accord with faith. Head and heart belong together, very much like philosophy and religion, as Enlightenment theologians had said, or like poetry and religion, as Enlightenment theologians had not said. Enlightenment religion rightly held together reason and faith, but it worked with an engineering concept of reason. Coleridge's spiritualized post-Kantian transcendentalism proposed that religion passes "out of the ken of Reason only where the eye of Reason has reached its own Horizon." Faith is but the continuation of reason into the twilight, stealing into darkness: "It is Night, sacred Night! The upraised Eye views only the starry Heaven which manifests itself alone: and the outward Beholding is fixed on the sparks twinkling in the aweful depth, though Suns of other Worlds, only to preserve the Soul steady and collected in the pure *Act* of inward Adoration to the great I AM, and to the filial WORD that re-affirmeth it from Eternity to Eternity, whose choral echo is the Universe."[156]

The reviews were generally bad, ranging from tepid to savage, and Coleridge had to wait two years to get them, finding a medical savior in the meantime. But the savage reviews set off a backlash from Coleridge's lecture-audience admirers and a rising generation of Romantics that claimed him as their inspiration.

Most reviewers protested that organizationally, the book was an out-of-control mess. Some made the connection between the book's organizational problems and the author's personal problems. Most reviewers that took a pass at Coleridge's philosophical sections settled for baleful remarks about the obscurity of German metaphysics. The *New Annual Register* complained that Coleridge's German borrowings were totally unintelligible. The *British Critic,* misspelling Fichte and Schelling, assured that both were inscrutable, as was Kant. John Wilson, in an often-cited review for *Blackwood's Magazine,* derided the "miserable arrogance" of the original Lake School (Coleridge and Wordsworth) and ridiculed Coleridge's "pretended account of the Metaphysical System of Kant, of which he knows less than nothing." William Hazlitt, blasting his former hero in *Edinburgh Review,* pronounced that Coleridge was afflicted with "metaphysic bathos ... fancy-bred from the maggots of his brain."[157]

Hazlitt was a special case. The most eminent critic of his generation next to Coleridge, he had admired Coleridge intensely during their early careers, celebrating that *Lyrical Ballads* enfranchised a new class of poetical subjects that made the new poetry an ally of political radicalism. But Coleridge's political backsliding and immersion in German metaphysics repelled Hazlitt, who had hoped for so much more. A lifelong admirer of Napoleon, Hazlitt was infuriated by Coleridge's patriotic attacks on Napoleon and his pious odes to political moderation and compromise, which Hazlitt considered an unforgivable betrayal of radical republicanism. By the time that *Biographia Literaria* was published in 1817, Hazlitt was known for blasting Coleridge vengefully as a pathetic, conservative, opportunistic charlatan.[158]

In 1816 Hazlitt pioneered a new genre of review by attacking Coleridge's book, *A Lay Sermon,* before it existed. Responding to a pre-publication advertisement, Hazlitt ripped the book ferociously, not knowing that it was not yet published, and in fact, not yet written. In Hazlitt's telling, *A Lay Sermon* was another Coleridge peon to "despotism, superstition, and oppression," even if Coleridge didn't know it: "His mind is in a constant state of flux and reflux: he is like the Sea-horse in the Ocean; he is the man in the Moon, the Wandering Jew ... He belongs to all parties and is of service to none." Then *Biographia Literaria* lumbered from the press, and Hazlitt let loose a fire hydrant of insults, including "maudlin egotism" and "mawkish spleen in fulsome eulogies of his own virtues." As for the German transcendentalists to whom Coleridge had given his heart and mind, Hazlitt was equally certain: Kant's system was "the most willful and monstrous absurdity that ever was invented."[159]

All of that was predictable; Coleridge knew it was coming, telling Southey that Hazlitt was "no man but a monster." But *Biographia Literaria* turned out to be perfectly timed to boost Coleridge's reputation. Many listeners that thronged to Coleridge's lectures understood that he was a genius, however troubled; the savage reviews offended their sense of fairness. More importantly, the ridicule backfired for young Romantics, even though they preferred Hazlitt's politics. Coleridge's first sign that he might be making a comeback was that Byron appreciated and befriended him. Byron told Coleridge that he greatly admired *Christabel* and *Ancient Mariner;* he was so taken with *Christabel* that he unconsciously plagiarized it in his poem *The Maid of Corinth;* and he believed that Coleridge was far greater than Wordsworth, contrary to convention. Coleridge erupted in gratitude and repressed frustration. He told Byron that he had felt wrongly put down for his entire career. His poetic influence on Wordsworth, Scott, and the entire Romantic movement was unrecognized, and it thrilled him that Byron recycled him. Though Byron disliked the philosophical sections of *Biographia Literaria,* he persuaded John Murray to become Coleridge's general publisher, and he smoothed the way for others to claim Coleridge as their inspiration.[160]

Percy Bysshe Shelley, Mary Wollstonecraft Shelley, and John Keats played leading roles in the Coleridge renaissance. The Shelleys lionized Coleridge's poetry, embraced *Biographia Literaria,* and praised him to their circle of friends and followers, always distinguishing between Coleridge's Romanticism and his desultory politics, where they agreed with Hazlitt. In 1821 Percy Shelley's influential essay, *A Defense of Poetry,* bore the strong imprint of *Biographia Literaria;* the year before, in his poem *Letter to Maria Gisborne,* Shelley described Coleridge as "a hooded eagle among blinking owls." To Romanticists of the 1820s, that got it exactly right; Coleridge's immense inner power was constrained by external weaknesses, yet he towered above his contemporaries. Keats took a bit longer to separate Coleridge the poetic and critical genius from Coleridge the political retrograde justly attacked by Hazlitt. But *Biographia Literaria* enthralled Keats, which helped him appreciate Coleridge's poetry, which had a strong influence on Keats' later poetry. To a subsequent generation of academics, *Biographia Literaria* was the gold standard of literary criticism.[161]

Coleridge ascended with a rising Romantic movement, which was still reviled in England in 1820, except by radicals and a handful of academics; Shelley had less than a hundred readers when he died in 1822. Byron's early support was a breakthrough for Coleridge, who enjoyed the irony, years later, of having been lifted up by radical feminists like the Shelleys. At first the Coleridge renaissance mostly set up Coleridge for louder ridicule. *Biographia Literaria* was mocked as a travesty that had to plagiarize its worst parts; Coleridge's expanded, never-finished version of *Christabel* was ripped apart as unhinged raving and absurdity; Hazlitt stayed on the attack, which encouraged others to pile on.[162]

Coleridge responded, uncharacteristically, by attending to his sanity. In April 1816 he put himself under the care of Highgate physician James Gillman, who put him on a detoxification program and weaned him, more or less, from severe opium addiction.

Coleridge was never cured of his addiction. There were many relapses and a few overdose emergencies between 1816 and 1834, when he died as a member of Gillman's household. But under Gillman's care he got his life back, more or less controlled his addiction, lived to see the Coleridge renaissance, and became the sage later idolized by the Victorian generations.

In 1818 he and Hazlitt gave dueling lecture series in London. Coleridge offered a comparative history of literature, the first English attempt of its kind, ranging over European literature from the "Dark Ages" to the eighteenth century. He made an original argument about the influence of Italian Romance writers on English poetry and lingered over certain favorites – Dante, Boccaccio, Chaucer, Cervantes, Shake-speare, Milton, and John Donne. Rambling and emoting gregariously, without notes, Coleridge lifted the intellectual horizon of his audiences beyond wartime insularity, contributing to his own renaissance.[163]

Hazlitt, lecturing a few blocks away, held his audiences equally in thrall, blasting Byron and Wordsworth along with Coleridge. In his telling, Coleridge's journalism was completely worthless, he had no talent for drama, his *Biographia Literaria* was not worth a second round of insults, and only two or three of his poems had any merit. His best poem was *Ancient Mariner,* but even that was too Germanic and heedless to be great, conceiving poetry as a drunken dream. In sum, Coleridge was a total failure not deserving any consideration, except for one thing. Hazlitt reversed course dramatically, telling a tale of genius wasted: "He is the only person I ever knew who answered to the idea of a man of genius. He is the only person from whom I ever learnt anything. There is only one thing he could learn from me in return, but *that* he has not. He was the first poet I ever knew. His genius at that time had angelic wings, and fed on manna. He talked on forever; and you wished him to talk on forever. His thoughts did not come with labor and effort; but as if borne on the gusts of genius, and as if the wings of his imagination lifted him from off his feet. His voice rolled on the ear like the pealing organ, and its sound alone was the music of thought. His mind was clothed with wings; and raised on them, he lifted philosophy to heaven."[164]

Hazlitt wished that Coleridge had learned from him how to remain loyal to republican idealism. Had he done so, the anointed angel of a grubby time might have led England out of darkness. As it was, Hazlitt told his story of genius wasted in order to bury the betrayer. In an earlier time, Coleridge would have returned fire; by 1818 he was finished with political scorekeeping and polemics. Gradually he grew into his gathering legend, mentoring disciples, hearing himself lionized at banquets, and receiving a stream of visitors, all the while concentrating on religious issues.

In Coleridge's last years he labored on a strange, prolix commentary on a commentary, originally titled *The Beauties of Archbishop Leighton*. Robert Leighton was a seventeenth-century Anglican divine of refined sensibility whose scriptural commentaries made a great impression on Coleridge in 1813, the year of his nearly fatal overdose and meltdown. Coleridge admired Leighton's combination of spiritual depth, serenity, and imagination, wishing for some serenity of his own. To friends he described Leighton as "that true *Divine*" and the author of "jeweled pages" of spiritual insight. In 1822 Coleridge pitched a book proposal to Murray on "that wonderful man" Leighton, proposing to reprint some of Leighton's best passages, mostly on 1 Peter, accompanied by comments of his own. A year later the book had a new format, publisher, and title, *Aids to Reflection;* it had also grown much longer than Coleridge intended.[165]

Aids to Reflection was divided into three sections of prudential, moral and religious, and spiritual aphorisms. Most of the aphorisms in the first and second sections were drawn from Leighton, though Coleridge wrote the book's most famous one, in section two. Of the thirty aphorisms in section three, eight were by Leighton and the rest were by Coleridge and his other favorite divines. By relying on aphorisms, Coleridge played up his opposition to rationalistic apologetics. The point was to lead the reader further into religion, he explained, not out of it. His celebrated aphorism in section two showed the difference: "He, who begins by loving Christianity better than Truth, will proceed by loving his own Sect or Church better than Christianity, and end in loving himself better than all." For Coleridge, this admonition was about the necessity of doubt and intellectual openness. God is not a Christian, and if God is the author of Truth, there is no reason to fear any truth: "Never be afraid to doubt, if only you have the disposition to believe, and doubt in order that you may end in believing the Truth."[166]

For twenty years Coleridge pondered a revision of Kant's distinction between *Sinnlichkeit* (sensibility, the power to receive representations) and *Verstand* (understanding, the power of reasoning by means of representations). In 1806, adopting a post-Kantian convention, he called it the distinction between Reason and Understanding, which correlated Reason with *noumena* and Understanding with *phaenonena*. In essence, Coleridge spiritualized Kant's transcendentalism by conceiving Reason as constitutive, the revelation of an immortal soul, not merely regulative. The Understanding apprehends contingent things of experience, he argued, while Reason works in the realm of necessity and universality, containing within itself the revelatory law of its conceptions. In *Biographia Literaria* Coleridge invoked the distinction between Reason and Understanding as a parallel to the distinction between imagination and fancy, describing Reason as transcendent intuition; in *Aids to Reflection* he finally worked out a theory of Reason and Understanding.[167]

Like Kant, Coleridge reasoned that the ultimate ground of morality (and therefore, religion) must be intuitive if the very notion of moral truth is to be secured. Just as Kant distinguished between the sense-bound knowledge of pure reason and the intuitive, constitutively human knowledge of practical reason, Coleridge described the Understanding as sense-bound and Reason as sense-transcendent. In his rendering, the Understanding processes knowledge derived wholly from experience, while Reason gives birth to thought and all life-enhancing action. The Understanding is discursive, but Reason is fixed. The Understanding is a reflective faculty that abstracts, names and compares; it brings no immediate truths; and because it depends on sense experience, it always refers to another faculty as the authority behind its judgments.[168]

Coleridge conceived Reason, by contrast, as essentially spiritual, the realm of conscience, contemplation, and insight – the transcendent power of intuition. The truths of Reason are immediate, he argued, for Reason is self-referential in all its judgments concerning the ground and substance of its truth claims. Religion is about powers of will and being, not understanding. The wellspring of religion is the revelatory power of being, Reason, "the Source and Substance of Truths above Sense," not the sense-bound knowledge of the Understanding. The Understanding produces theologies, but it has no knowledge of religious experience. Coleridge pressed this claim into a defense of Christianity, his most famous religious saying: "Christianity is not a theory, or a speculation, but a life. Not a philosophy of life, but a life and a living process." So how can the truth of Christianity be proved? Coleridge had a two-word answer: "Try it." And what kind of life *is* Christianity? Coleridge started with a six-word answer: "Christianity and REDEMPTION are equivalent terms."[169]

For twenty years he had struggled to clarify his understanding of redemption. Coleridge disliked Calvinism and believed in free will, but he was chastened by his failure to follow Christ by an act of will. He disliked juridical models of atonement but worried that they had too much scriptural support, especially in Pauline theology, to be dismissed. *Aids to Reflection* registered Leighton's influence on Coleridge in the former area and developed a doctrine of redemption as salvation from sin. Following Leighton, Coleridge opted for free will *and* a strong concept of sin, reasoning that human beings possess a free will that is enslaved by sin. This was the "great theme" of Luther and Calvin, Coleridge contended, who were not well served by Lutheran and Calvinist dogmatists that took too literally the Reformers' polemics against proud assertions of free will. Luther and Calvin, rightly understood, were preachers of the redemption of the will from slavery and its restoration to perfect freedom in Christ. To deny free will is to make a mockery of morality, Coleridge implored. Good theology affirms the freedom of the will, its bondage to sin, and the moral necessity of struggling against sin, breaking redemption into four questions: Who or what is the acting cause of redemption, the causative act, the effect caused, and the consequences from the effect?[170]

Coleridge answered that the agent and personal cause of humankind's redemption is Jesus Christ, the incarnate, co-eternal Word of God. The causative act is a spiritual and transcendent mystery passing all understanding. The effect caused is the experience of rebirth into the spirit of Christ. The consequences from the effect are liberation from sin and its penal consequences, which are the same for the sinner relative to God and the sinner's soul. Here Coleridge made room for the biblical language of debt and sacrifice. Redemption is salvation from sin, not from penalty or divine wrath. But the consequences of being saved from sin include the benefits of satisfaction and recon-ciliation alluded to in the Bible's figurative language of debt, sacrifice, and ransom, which Coleridge called "figures of speech for the purpose of illustrating the nature and extent of the consequences and effects of the redemptive Act." Paul employed juridical metaphors to awaken a "due sense of the magnitude" of Christ's saving action and to inspire "love and gratitude due to the Redeemer." Coleridge admonished against reducing redemption to a notion of justice, which was what happened whenever the Bible's juridical atonement language was taken literally as a doctrine. Moreover, substitutionary atonement theory rested on a strange notion of justice, one that failed elementary tests of moral feeling.[171]

Aids to Reflection was slow to find an audience or sympathetic reviews. In 1825, there were precious few readers in England who combined skepticism of orthodox and rationalist apologetics and a willingness to struggle with post-Kantian metaphysics. The book's first edition had to build up such an audience before a second round of reviews praised it as a turning point. Coleridge braced for hostile reviews from *Quarterly Review* and *Edinburgh Review,* only to be ignored by both journals, summarily dismissed in

British Review, and hammered in the *British Critic,* which charged that Coleridge was unorthodox, unclear, and unintelligible.[172]

Coleridge found his breakthrough group at Trinity College, Cambridge, where two faculty members, Julius Hare and Connop Thirlwall, and two students, John Sterling and Frederick Denison Maurice, launched a pro-Romanticist literary society called the "Apostles' Club." The Apostles admired Byron, Wordsworth, Southey, Keats, Shelley, and, above all, Coleridge, although some drew the line at radical Romanticism, spurning Shelley. Maurice found an intellectual lodestar in Coleridge and began his pilgrimage to the Anglican Church under Coleridge's influence; later he became a prominent theologian. All the Cambridge Apostles embraced *Aids to Reflection.* Charles Merivale, Maurice's classmate, later recalled: "Coleridge and Wordsworth were our principal divinities, and Hare and Thirlwall were regarded as their prophets."[173]

American Transcendentalists and evangelicals discovered the book by way of its American edition of 1829, which contained an influential 58-page introduction by James Marsh, president of the University of Vermont. Marsh was an evangelical Calvinist and education reformer who urged students to think for themselves. He was repelled by the rising prestige of materialistic determinism in the academy, which, Marsh reflected, owed much to the reign of Lockean empiricism in the academy. There had to be an alternative to Locke, Marsh believed, even in commonsense America, where Calvinists and Unitarians agreed that Locke was the last word in philosophy. Reading *Biographia Literaria,* Marsh had been intrigued by Coleridge's emphasis on religious experience and his contention that knowing and being are inseparably linked. Reading *Aids to Reflection,* Marsh concluded that Coleridge's religiously vibrant post-Kantian idealism was the needed alternative; otherwise, atheistic determinism was sure to prevail.[174]

Young Unitarian minister Ralph Waldo Emerson, upon reading the American edition of *Aids to Reflection* in 1829, copied into his journal Coleridge's maxim, "Quantum scimus sumus" (we are what we know). Coleridge's next sentence was equally important to him: "That which we find within ourselves, which is more than ourselves, and yet the ground of whatever is good and permanent therein, is the substance and life of all other knowledge." Emerson, having struggled with Hume's naturalistic skepticism, embraced Coleridge's claim that the self possesses an active power of self-determination. In Coleridge's distinction between Reason and Understanding, Emerson found the theory of truth that contained, for him, the convincing ring of truth.[175]

That was the wellspring of American Transcendentalism, as a host of aspiring Unitarian intellectuals and recent Harvard graduates shared Emerson's excitement at making a new religious beginning. They included Amos Bronson Alcott, William Henry Channing, James Freeman Clarke, Margaret Fuller, Frederic Henry Hedge, George Ripley, Sophia Ripley, and Theodore Parker. Some were influenced as much by English idealist Thomas Carlyle, French transcendentalist Victor Cousin, and Swedish mystic Emanuel Swedenborg as by Coleridge. In a variation of Coleridge's scheme, Cousin distinguished between "spontaneous reason," which he described as intuitive, involuntary, and nonreflective, and "reflective reason," which he conceived as deliberative and dependent upon the antecedent action of spontaneous reason. The American transcendentalists were attracted to Cousin's emphasis on the direct immediacy of intuitive truths known by spontaneous reason. Many of them took this to be a

Kantian argument and thus regarded themselves as Kantians, looking past Coleridge's cautionary remarks on the limitations of Kantian reason.[176]

The American enthusiasm for Coleridge was ironic. It began with Marsh, who urged religious conservatives to give up their attachment to Locke. American Calvinist orthodoxy, he lamented, was peculiarly unfortunate in having received the gospel and Lockean empiricism so intimately bound together "that by most persons they are considered as necessary parts of the same system." Marsh criticized the orthodox tendency to exalt a received philosophical system over spiritual experience. He proposed that the "deep-toned and sublime eloquence of Coleridge" deserved to be heard as a credible and, perhaps, more compelling philosophical support system for religious orthodoxy.[177]

This case for Coleridge's option had an ample future in the Broad Church stream of Anglican theology, exactly as Coleridge desired. It was not what inspired American Transcendentalists to call themselves Coleridgeans, for they were radical individualists who disregarded Coleridge's insistence that the will is essentially corrupt. To the Romantic sensibility of Emerson and most American Transcendentalists, Coleridge was the prophet of liberated self-authenticating Spirit. Margaret Fuller declared that "to the unprepared he is nothing, to the prepared, everything." Frederic Henry Hedge proclaimed that in America the genuine Kantians and Coleridgeans were younger-generation liberals. The Lockean establishment at Harvard was too simplistic and unimaginative to comprehend transcendental thinking, Hedge declared. It was time to stop apologizing for the supposed obscurity of Coleridge and the German transcendentalists and time to leave behind a stodgy Old School Unitarianism that venerated John Locke.[178]

Unlike most American Transcendentalists, Hedge had studied in Germany and understood the differences between Kant and Schelling. These differences were washed away in the Emersonian manifestos of American Transcendentalism. Hedge's bold proclamation of the superiority of transcendental thinking exhilarated a vanguard of youthful Unitarian pastors and independent intellectuals; Emerson called him "an unfolding man" who showed the way. James Freeman Clarke, describing the convicting influence of Coleridge upon him, explained that something deep inside him was repulsed by attempts to reduce the soul to sensory things: "So I concluded I had no taste for metaphysics and gave it up, until Coleridge showed me from Kant that though knowledge begins *with* experience it does not come *from* experience. Then I discovered that I was born a transcendentalist." Emerson, a few months after the "unfolding" tribute, told his brother Edward to pay heed to the Coleridgean differences between Reason and Understanding: "Reason is the highest faculty of the soul – what we mean often by the soul itself . . . It never *reasons*, never proves, it simply perceives, it is vision. The Understanding toils all the time, compares, contrives, adds, argues, near sighted but strong-sighted, dwelling in the present the expedient the customary."[179]

The Emersonian Transcendentalists agreed that religion, poetry, and honor belong to Reason. Soon they took up arguing whether they needed to retain the Christian name if they believed in their universal intuitions.[180]

This question was far from Coleridge's spirit, who spent his last years defending his place in the mainstream of Anglican thought. By 1831, when Coleridge published a second edition of *Aids to Reflection*, the book had rave reviews and a significant English following led by Hare's protégés. In fifty years the book went through twelve editions. Frederick Denison Maurice, stressing the distinction between Reason and Understanding, praised *Aids to Reflection* as the most important and delightful work of English theology in many years.[181]

Coleridge had a strong sense of being saved from without and an equally strong conviction that words are living powers of Spirit and transformation, not merely things. All his major writings conveyed the latter belief; in later life he stressed the former experience. In a compilation of occasional writings published after his death, *Confessions of an Inquiring Spirit* (1840), he put both things memorably: "In the Bible there is more that FINDS me than I have experienced in all other books put together." The words of the Bible found him at the greatest depths of his being, "and whatever finds me brings with it an irresistible evidence of having proceeded from the Holy Spirit." This was a banner text for generations of Romantic liberals that reclaimed the Spirit of the Bible while casting aside centuries of dogma about the Bible. Coleridge treaded more carefully in this area. He argued that German biblical criticism was a legitimate enterprise, but he made little use of it. He implored against a mechanical understanding of biblical inspiration, but he was vague about how the authority of scripture should be conceived in the refashioned cord of scripture, tradition, and reason.[182]

His last book during his lifetime, *On the Constitution of the Church and State* (1829), strengthened his mainstream standing by updating Hooker's idea of a National Church as the safeguard of English civilization. Coleridge's proposal retained the National Church by making it more ecumenical and less clerical. He urged that the historic purpose of the National Church, which had to be preserved, was to defend and improve English society. The National Church held in balance things of permanence and progress. It supported liberal latitude in learning, as English Anglicanism had always done, more or less. In Coleridge's proposal, the National Church was distinct from the Church of England and from the church as the universal body of Christ. In essence it was an ecumenical third estate led by a "National Clerisy" consisting of "the learned of all denominations – the sages and professors of the law and jurisprudence; of medicine and physiology; of music, of military and civil architecture; of the physical sciences."[183]

Coleridge reasoned that just as the Church of England and other participating denominations should be differentiated from the National Church, the clergy of various denominations should be differentiated from the liberal arts and scientific intelligentsia that made up the National Clerisy. Ministers were loyal to their particular religious communions; the intelligentsia served the entire people of the state. Roman Catholics, on the other hand, had to be excluded from the National Church – Coleridge opposed the Catholic Emancipation Act of 1829 – because Catholics pledged obedience to the pope. The Reformation was necessary for one reason, he claimed: To oppose the papal Antichrist, a power in the Christian church that subverted Christ's purpose and authority in the name of Christ. Nothing else would have justified the Reformation. As it was, the church raised up a heroic figure, Luther, to save the church from itself, and the English church raised up a wise figure, Hooker, to make sense of the consequences.

Coleridge reveled in Luther's defiant "Here I Stand" appearances before Roman assemblies. He loved to quote Luther's unguarded, boisterous, name-calling table talk, and he urged scholarly acquaintances that English literature grievously lacked a worthy biography of Luther. Repeatedly his letters admonished friends that the thunderously German Luther had more in common with Paul than did England's compromised, bishop-centered, established church. Nearly always Coleridge described Luther as "dear Luther," "heroic Luther," or both. *Aids to Reflection,* declaring that Coleridge would not defend Calvin's "sundry harsh and inconvenient Expressions," allowed that equally rash opinions were "no rarities" in Luther's work.[184]

But Luther and even Calvin fastened on the essential thing, Coleridge urged: The redemption of the will from slavery and its restoration to perfect freedom and union with Christ. This was what mattered; plus Luther did it with great style. Coleridge's contemporaries tended to chalk up his attraction to Luther as a fixation with heroic rebellious types. After he was gone, his followers, confronting the aggressive anti-Protestantism of the Oxford Movement, took instruction from Coleridge's Broad Church pro-Lutheranism, and some regarded him as their Luther.

For sixty years after Coleridge was gone, there was little place in the Church of England for religious liberals. The forerunners of Broad Church liberalism were few and scattered in the 1830s and 1840s – a handful of Coleridgeans at Cambridge led by Hare, an equally tiny group at Oxford led by mathematician/scientist Baden Powell and Oxford Fellow Henry Bristow Wilson – while evangelicals and Anglo-Catholics battled for control of the church. Maurice, the key mediator of Coleridge's legacy, advocated a muddled orthodoxy that opposed theological parties, though he mustered greater clarity in espousing Christian Socialism. A growing "Broad Church" movement acquired its name in the 1850s and quietly won perches in the academy, but never formed anything like an organized third party.[185]

The strongest attempt to create a liberal movement, a book venture organized by Wilson titled *Essays and Reviews* (1860), failed spectacularly, triggering a national uproar. Six of the seven contributors to *Essays and Reviews* – Wilson, Powell, Frederick Temple, Rowland Williams, Charles W. Goodwin, and Benjamin Jowett – were ferociously condemned for espousing Darwinism, Kantianism, German biblical criticism, and other assaults on traditional Christianity. The seventh contributor, Mark Pattison, was usually upbraided for associating with infidels. The fall-out was so severe that it killed the possibility of a liberal theology movement in England for another three decades, although Temple weathered the storm sufficiently to make Archbishop of Canterbury in 1896. By then *Essays and Reviews* was widely viewed as a necessary course correction, surprisingly mild when actually read. And Coleridge, the Luther of Broad Church Anglicanism, had become an icon, a century removed from his conversion to Kantian idealism.[186]

Notes

1. Friedrich D. E. Schleiermacher, *Aus Schleiermachers Leben in Briefen,* 4 vols., ed. Wilhelm Dilthey (Berlin: Reimer, 1858–1863), I: 1; English edition of volumes 1 and 2, Schleiermacher, *The Life of Schleiermacher as Unfolded in His Autobiography and Letters,* 2 vols., trans. Frederica Rowan (London: Smith, Elder and Company, 1860).
2. *The Life of Schleiermacher as Unfolded in His Autobiography and Letters,* quote I: 2; see Martin Redeker, *Schleiermacher: Life and Thought,* trans. J. Wallhauser (Philadelphia: Fortress Press, 1973), 6–9.

3.   *The Life of Schleiermacher as Unfolded in His Autobiography and Letters,* I: 5–6.
4.   Ibid., I: 6–10, "every discourse," 6; Friedrich Schleiermacher to Georg Reimer, April 30, 1802, "here it was," ibid., I: 283–284.
5.   Ibid., "the investigations," I: 11; Friedrich Schleiermacher to Gottlieb Schleiermacher, January 21, 1787, ibid., I: 46–49.
6.   Friedrich Schleiermacher to Gottlieb Schleiermacher, January 21, 1787, ibid., 46–47, 49.
7.   Gottlieb Schleiermacher to Friedrich Schleiermacher, February 6, 1787, ibid., I: 50–53, quotes 50, 52.
8.   Friedrich Schleiermacher to Gottlieb Schleiermacher, undated, ibid., I: 56–58, quotes 56, 57.
9.   Gottlieb Schleiermacher to Friedrich Schleiermacher, March 19, 1787, ibid., I: 62–63, quote 63; Schleiermacher quote, ibid., I: 14; see Keith W. Clements, "Introduction," in *Friedrich Schleiermacher: Pioneer of Modern Theology,* ed. Keith W. Clements (Minneapolis: Fortress Press, 1991), 17–18.
10. *The Life of Schleiermacher as Unfolded in His Autobiography and Letters,* I: 78–125; Friedrich Schleiermacher, *Schleiermacher's Soliloquies: An English Translation of the Monologen,* trans. Horace Leland Friess (Chicago: Open Court, 1957), "beauty of," 74.
11. *The Life of Schleiermacher as Unfolded in His Autoiography and Letters,* I: 133–142; Johann Wolfgang Goethe, *Collected Works,* 12 vols., ed. Victor Lange, Eric Blackall, and Cyrus Hamlin, vol. 9: *Wilhelm Meister's Apprenticeship* (Princeton: Princeton University Press, 1994).
12. *The Life of Schleiermacher as Unfolded in His Autoiography and Letters,* "somewhat" and "He had" quotes, I: 140–141; Friedrich Schleiermacher to Charlotte Schleiermacher, February 12, 1801, ibid., "Her appearance," I: 249.
13. Friedrich Schlegel, *Philosophical Fragments,* trans. Peter Firchow (Minneapolis: University of Minnesota Press, 1991), quotes 31–32; Schlegel, *Dialogue on Poetry and Literary Aphorisms,* trans. Ernst Behler (University Park: Pennsylvania State University Press, 1968); Theodore Ziolkowski, *German Romanticism and Its Institutions* (Princeton: Princeton University Press, 1990), 260–261.
14. Friedrich Schleiermacher to Charlotte Schleiermacher, October 22, 1797, *The Life of Schleiermacher as Unfolded in His Autoiography and Letters,* I: 58–162, quote 159; see Friedrich Schleiermacher to Charlotte Schleiermacher, November 21, 1707, ibid., 162–164.
15. Friedrich Schleiermacher to Charlotte Schleiermacher, December 31, 1797, *The Life of Schleiermacher as Unfolded in His Autoiography and Letters,* I: 188165–169, quotes 167–168; Friedrich Schleiermacher to Henriette Herz, February 15, 1799, ibid., I: 188.
16. Friedrich Schleiermacher to Henriette Herz, March 3, 1799, ibid., I: 193–194, quote 194; Schleiermacher, *Über die Religion: Reden an die Gebildeten unter ihren Verächtern* (Hamburg: Felix Meiner, 1958); English editions, Schleiermacher, *On Religion: Speeches to Its Cultured Despisers,* trans. Richard Crouter (Cambridge: Cambridge University Press, 1988); Schleiermacher, *On Religion: Addresses in Response to Its Cultured Critics,* trans. Terrence N. Tice (1799; Richmond: John Knox Press, 1969).
17. Schleiermacher, *On Religion: Addresses in Response to Its Cultured Critics,* quotes 39, 40.
18. Ibid., 48.
19. Ibid., 52–55, quotes 53, 54, 55.
20. Ibid., quotes 55–56, 58.
21. Ibid., quotes 84; see 68, note 4; Benedict de Spinoza, *On the Improvement of the Understanding; The Ethics; Correspondence,* trans. R. H. M. Elwes (New York: Dover Publications, n.d.)

22. Friedrich Schleiermacher, "Über sein *Glaubenslehre* an Herrn Dr. Lücke, zwei Sendschreiben," *Theologische Studien und Kritiken* 2 (1829), 255–284 and 481–532; English edition, Schleiermacher, *On the Glaubenslehre: Two Letters to Dr. Lücke,* trans. James Duke and Francis Fiorenza (Atlanta: Scholars Press, 1979), quotes 50–51.

23. Schleiermacher, *On Religion: Addresses in Response to Its Cultured Critics,* 48.

24. See Robert R. Williams, *Schleiermacher the Theologian: The Construction of the Doctrine of God* (Philadelphia: Fortress Press, 1978), 25; this section adapts material from Gary Dorrien, *The Word as True Myth: Interpreting Modern Theology* (Louisville: Westminster John Knox, 1997), 13–22.

25. See Immanuel Kant, *Anthropology from a Pragmatic Point of View,* trans. Victor Lyle Dowdell, revd. and ed. Hans H. Rudnick (Carbondale: Southern Illinois University Press, 1978), 9–129; Kant, *Critique of Judgement,* trans. James Creed Meredith (Oxford: Clarendon Press, 1973), 204–227; Karl Ameriks, *Kant's Theory of Mind: An Analysis of the Paralogisms of Pure Reason* (Oxford: Clarendon Press, 1982), 84–123.

26. Schleiermacher, *On Religion: Addresses in Response to Its Cultured Critics,* quotes 79; see Schleiermacher, *Soliloquies,* 10–25; Richard R. Brandt, *The Philosophy of Schleiermacher: The Development of His Theory of Scientific and Religious Knowledge* (New York: Harper & Brothers, 1941), 105–144; Williams, *Schleiermacher the Theologian,* 4–7; Edmund Husserl, *Ideas: General Introduction to Pure Phenomenology,* trans. W. R. Boyce Gibson (New York: Humanities Press, 1976), 41–47.

27. Schleiermacher, *On Religion: Addresses in Response to Its Cultured Critics,* 82.

28. Ibid., 82, 79.

29. Ibid., 162–163.

30. Ibid., 146–147, 154–162, quotes 162, 146.

31. Ibid., 207–271, quotes 208, 209, 233.

32. Ibid., 48.

33. Ibid., 48, 49.

34. Ibid., 49.

35. Ibid., 63–64.

36. Friedrich Schleiermacher to Eleanore Grunow, June 8, 1802, *The Life of Schleiermacher as Unfolded in His Autoiography and Letters,* I: 293–295, quote 295.

37. Friedrich Schleiermacher, *Grundlinien einer Kritik der bisherigen Sittenlehre* (Berlin: Realschulbuchhandlung, 1803); Friedrich Schleiermacher to Eleanore Grunow, August 12, 1802; August 19, 1802; August 26, 1802; September 10, 1802, ibid., *The Life of Schleiermacher as Unfolded in His Autoiography and Letters,* I: 302–303; 303–308; 311–314, 319–324; Redeker, *Schleiermacher: Life and Thought,* 70–71.

38. Friedrich Schleiermacher to Ehrenfried and Henriette von Willich, October 11, 1805, *The Life of Schleiermacher as Unfolded in His Autoiography and Letters,* II: 22.

39. Friedrich D. E. Schleiermacher, *Hermeneutics: The Handwritten Manuscripts,* ed. Heinz Kimmerle, trans. James Duke and Jack Forstman (Atlanta: Scholars Press, 1986), 41–65; Friedrich Schleiermacher to Charlotte von Kathen, June 20, 1806; Friedrich Schleiermacher to Ehrenfried von Willich, *The Life of Schleiermacher as Unfolded in His Autoiography and Letters,* II; Redeker, *Schleiermacher: Life and Thought,* 77–78.

40. Friedrich Schleiermacher to Henriette Herz, November 21, 1806, *The Life of Schleiermacher as Unfolded in His Autoiography and Letters,* II: 40.

41. Henriette von Willich to Friedrich Schleiermacher, March 1807, April 28, 1807, no date; Friedrich Schleiermacher to Henriette von Willich, March 20, 1807, April 1807, May 8, 1807, no date, *The Life of Schleiermacher as Unfolded in His Autoiography and Letters,* II: 44–54.

42. Franz Kade, *Schleiermachers Anteil an der Entwicklung des preussischen Bildungswesen von 1808–1818* (Leipzig: Quelle & Meyer, 1925); Friedrich Schleiermacher, *Gelegentliche Gedanken über deutsche Universitäten im deutschen Sinne* (Berlin: In der Realschulbuch-handlung, 1808); Redeker, *Schleiermacher: Life and Thought*, 91–96.

43. Friedrich Schleiermacher, *Brief Outline on the Study of Theology*, trans. Terrence N. Tice (Atlanta: John Knox Press, 1977), 19–114, quote 19.

44. Friedrich Schleiermacher, *Der christliche Glaube nach den Grundsätzen der evangelischen Kirche im Zusammenhange dargestellt*, 2 vols. (Berlin: G. Reimer, 1821; 2nd edn., 1830); English edition, Schleiermacher, *The Christian Faith*, ed. H. R. Mackintosh and J. S. Stewart (Edinburgh: T. & T. Clark, 1968).

45. Friedrich Schleiermacher, *Die Weihnachtsfeier: ein Gespräch* (Halle: Schimmelpfennig und Kompagnie, 1806); Schleiermacher, *Dialektik, Auftrag der preussichen Akademie der Wissenschaften auf Grund bisher unveröffentlichen Materials*, ed. Rudolf Odebrecht (Leipzig: J. C. Hinrichs, 1942), 260–287; Schleiermacher, *Dialectic, or, The Art of Doing Philosophy*, trans. Terrence N. Tice (Atlanta: Scholars Press, 1996), quotes 17. This text is based on lecture notes by one of Schleiermacher's students, August Twesten; the English edition contains excerpts only.

46. Schleiermacher, *Dialectic, or, The Art of Doing Philosophy*, quote 38.

47. Schleiermacher, *The Christian Faith*, quote viii.

48. Ibid., 12–13.

49. Ibid., 14, 31–34.

50. Ibid., 16.

51. Ibid., 374–389.

52. Ibid., 259–268, 425–438, quote 435.

53. Ibid., 31–38.

54. Ibid., quotes 52, 57.

55. Ibid., 60–62, quotes 60, 62.

56. Friedrich Schleiermacher, "Christ Our Only Savior," in *Servant of the Word: Selected Sermons of Friedrich Schleiermacher*, trans. Dawn De Vries (Philadelphia: Fortress Press, 1987), 29–30; Schleiermacher, *Introduction to Christian Ethics*, trans. John C. Shelley (Nashville: Abingdon Press, 1989).

57. Schleiermacher, "Christ the Liberator," in *Servant of the Word*, 55–56.

58. Schleiermacher, *The Christian Faith*, 262. This emphasis on the double character of Christian experience is slighted in Richard R. Niebuhr's otherwise discerning study of Schleiermacher, *Schleiermacher on Christ and Religion* (London: SCM Press, 1965). Niebuhr invents the term "Christo-morphic" to suggest that Schleiermacher's system as a whole is shaped by Christology.

59. Schleiermacher, *The Christian Faith*, 261.

60. Wilhelm Bender, *Schleiermachers Theologie nach ihren philosophischen Grundlagen dar-gestellt* (Nördlingen: C. H. Bech'sche Buchhandlung, 1876); Felix Flückiger, *Philosophie und Theologie bei Schleiermacher* (Zurich: Evangelischer Verlag, 1947); Carl Albrecht Bernoulli, *Die wissenschaftliche und die kirchliche Methode in der Theologie: Ein enzyklo-padischer Versuch* (Freiburg: J. C. B. Mohr, 1897); Ernst Troeltsch, "Rückblick auf ein halbes Jahrhundert der theologischen Wissenschaft," *Zeitschrift für wissenschaftliche Theologie* 51 (1908), 193–226; see James Duke and Francis Fiorenza, translators' introduction to Schleiermacher, *On the Glaubenslehre: Two Letters to Dr. Lücke*, 10–28.

61. Christlieb Julius Braniss, *Über Schleiermachers Glaubenslehre: Ein kritischer Versuch* (Berlin: Duncker und Humblot, 1821), 197; Johann Friedrich Ferdinand Delbrück, *Erörterungen einiger Hauptstücke in Dr. Friedrich Schleiermachers christliche*

Glaubenslehre (Bonn: Adolf Marcus, 1827), quote 190; Heinrich Gottlieb Tzschirner, *Briefe eines Deutschen an die Herren Chateaubriand, de la Mannais und Montlosier über Gegenstände der Religion und Politik* (Leipzig: Johann Ambrosius Barth, 1828), 28, 33; Isaaco Rust, *De nonnullis, quae in theologia nostrae aetatis dogmatica desiderantur* (Erlangen: Kunstmann, 1828), 65–69; Karl Gottlieb Bretschneider, *Grundansichten* (Leipzig: Johann Ambrosius Barth, 1828), 65–69; Georg Friedrich Wilhelm Hegel, "Vorwort zur Hinrichs' *Religionsphilosophie*," in *Berliner Schriften, 1818–1831*, ed. Johannes Hoffmeister (Hamburg: Felix Meiner, 1956); see James Duke and Francis Fiorenza, translators' introduction to Schleiermacher, *On the Glaubenslehre: Two Letters to Dr. Lücke*, 10–28.

62. Schleiermacher, *On the Glaubenslehre: Two Letters to Dr. Lücke*, 36.

63. Ferdinand Christian Baur, *Primae rationalismi et supranaturalismi historiae capita potiora* (Tübingen: Hopferi de l'Orme, 1827); Heinrich Johann Theodor Schmid, "Über das Verhältnis der Theologie zur Philosophie," *Für Theologie und Philosophie* 1 (1828), 16–73. Schleiermacher, *On the Glaubenslehre: Two Letters to Dr. Lücke*, 37–38, 43–47, quotes 36, 37.

64. Bretschneider, *Grundansichten*, 15; Schleiermacher, *On the Glaubenslehre: Two Letters to Dr. Lücke*, 38–39. Tzschirner made essentially the same argument as Bretschneider in *Briefe eines Deutschen*. 32, 37; see Duke and Fiorenza, translators' Notes to the First Letter, ibid., 105–106.

65. Schleiermacher, *On the Glaubenslehre: Two Letters to Dr. Lücke*, 47–51, quotes 51.

66. Ibid., quotes 52, 53.

67. Ibid., 53–60, quotes 53.

68. Schleiermacher, "Christ Our Only Savior," 34.

69. Redeker, *Schleiermacher: Life and Thought*, quote 213.

70. See Johann Gottfried Eichhorn, *Einleitung in das Neue Testament*, 2nd edn., 3 vols. (Leipzig: Weidmannischen Buchhandlung, 1810–1820); Johann Jacob Griesbach, *Vorlesungen über Hermeneutik des Neuen Testaments, mit Anwendung auf die Leidens und Auferstehungsgeschichte Christi*, ed. J. C. S. Steiner (Nuremberg: In der Zeh'schen Buchhandlung,1815); Johann David Michaelis, *Einleitung in die göttlichen Schriften des Neuen Bundes*, 2 vols. (Göttingen: Jandenhoeck, 1777); Johann Georg Rosenmüller, *Scholia in Novum Testamentum*, 6th edn., 5 vols. (Nuremberg: in officina Felseckeriana, 1815–1831); Wilhelm Martin L. De Wette, *A Critical and Historical Introduction to the Canonical Scriptures of the Old Testament from the German of Wilhelm Martin Leberecht De Wette*, 2 vols., trans. Theodore Parker (Boston: Charles C. Little & James Brown, 1843); Samuel Clarke, *The Scripture Doctrine of the Trinity, in Three Parts* (London: James Knapton, 1712); David Friedrich Strauss, *The Life of Jesus Critically Examined*, trans. George Eliot (1835; reprint, Ramsey: Sigler Press, 1994), 39–92; Christian Hartlich and Walter Sachs, *Der Ursprung des Mythosbegriffes in der modernen Bibelwissenschaft* (Tubingen: J. C. B. Mohr, 1952).

71. Friedrich Schleiermacher, *The Life of Jesus*, trans. S. Maclean Gilmour, ed. Jack C. Verheyden (Philadelphia: Fortress Press, 1975), 36–42. Against rationalist proponents of the resuscitation theory, he admonished: "We cannot represent him as those do who maintain the hypothesis of an apparent death. We cannot think of him as spending this time with his life force at a low ebb," Schleiermacher, *The Life of Jesus*, 455.

72. See B. A. Gerrish, *A Prince of the Church: Schleiermacher and the Beginnings of Modern Theology* (Philadelphia: Fortress Press, 1984), 52–54; Gerrish, *Continuing the Reformation: Essays on Modern Religious Thought* (Chicago: University of Chicago Press, 1993), 176–177; David Friedrich Strauss, *The Christ of Faith and the Jesus of History: A Critique*

of Schleiermacher's Life of Jesus, trans. Leander E. Keck (Philadelphia: Fortress Press, 1977).

73. Karl Barth, *Protestant Theology in the Nineteenth Century: Its Background and History* (London: SCM Press, 1972), 447–452.

74. Carl Immanuel Nitsch, *System der christlichen Lehre* (Bonn: Adolph Marcus, 1829; 6th ed., 1851); Willibald Beyschlag, *Neutestamentliche Theologie,* 2 vols. (Halle: E. Strien, 1891; 2nd edn., 1895); Isaak August Dorner, *A System of Christian Doctrine,* 5 vols., trans. Alfred Cave and J. S. Banks (Edinburgh: T. & T. Clark, 1888); Johannes von Hofmann, *Theologische Ethik* (Nördlingen: C. H. Beck, 1878); Johann Peter Lange, *Christliche Dogmatik,* 3 vols. (Heidelberg: K. Winter, 1849–1852); Carl Ullmann, *Historisch oder Mythisch? Beiträge zur Beantwortung der gegenwärtigen Lebensfrage der Theologie* (Hamburg: Perthes, 1838); Richard Rothe, *Thelogische Ethik,* 3 vols. (Wittenberg: Zimmermann, 1845–1848); Rothe, *Dogmatik. Aus dessen handschriftlichen Nachlasse herausgegeben von Dr. D. Schenkel,* 2 vols. (Heidelberg: J. C. B. Mohr, 1870); Christian Hermann Weisse, *Die evangelische Geschichte kritisch und philosophisch bearbeitet,* 2 vols. (Leipzig: Breitkopf und Härtel, 1838).

75. *Friedrich Schleiermachers Briefwechsel mit J. Chr. Gass,* ed. Wilhelm Gass (Berlin: G. Reimer, 1852), 195; Barth, *Protestant Theology in the Nineteenth Century,* 425.

76. Richard Hooker, *Of the Laws of Ecclesiastical Polity,* abridged edition, eds. A. S. McGrade and Brian Vickers (New York: St. Martin's Press, 1975); Hooker, *Works: Of the Laws of Ecclesiastical Polity,* 6 vols., ed. John Keble (Oxford: Clarendon Press, 1836); John Jewel, *Apologia Pro Ecclesia Anglicana* (1562); new edn., *An Apology of the Church of England* (Ithaca: Cornell University Press, 1963; John E. Booty, *John Jewel as Apologist of the Church of England* (London: S.P.C.K., 1963).

77. Hooker, *Works: Of the Laws of Ecclesiastical Polity,* quote, I: 339; see Izaak Walton, *The Lives of John Donne, Sir Henry Wotton, Richard Hooker, George Herbert, and Robert Sanderson* (London: Oxford University Press, 1973), 176–178; John E. Booty, "Richard Hooker," in *The Spirit of Anglicanism,* ed. William J. Wolf (Harrisburg: Morehouse Publishing, 1979), 4–5; Hooker, *Works: Of the Laws of Ecclesiastical Polity,* III: 586; I: 403–404; Paul Avis, *Anglicanism and the Christian Church: Theological Resources in Historical Perspective* (Minneapolis: Fortress Press, 1989), 54–55.

78. See John S. Marshall, *Hooker and the Anglican Tradition* (London: A. & C. Black, 1963), 66–68; Richard Field, *Of the Church: Five Bookes* (Oxford: William Turner, 1628); Henry Chadwick, "Tradition, Fathers, and Councils," in *The Study of Anglicanism,* ed. Stephen Sykes and John Booty (London: S.P.C.K., 1988), 100–104; *Anglicanism: The Thought and Practice of the Church of England, Illustrated from the Religious Literature of the Seventeenth Century,* ed. Paul Elmer More and Frank L. Cross (London: S.P.C.K., 1962); P. Collinson, *The Religion of Protestants: The Church in English Society, 1559–1625* (Oxford: Clarendon Press, 1982).

79. See Maurice Cranston, *John Locke, A Biography* (New York: Macmillan, 1957); Peter H. Nidditch, Foreword to John Locke, *An Essay concerning Human Understanding,* ed. Peter H. Nidditch (1689; reprint, Oxford: Clarendon Press, 1975), vii–xxv.

80. Locke, *An Essay concerning Human Understanding,* quote 7.

81. See H. D. Traill, *Shaftesbury (The First Earl)* (London: Longmans, Green, 1888); K. H. D. Haley, *The First Earl of Shaftesbury* (Oxford: Oxford University Press, 1968); Peter Laslett, "Introduction: Locke the Man and Locke the Writer," in John Locke, *Two Treatises of Government,* ed. Peter Laslett (1689; reprint, Cambridge: Cambridge University Press, 1988), 16–37; Richard Ashcraft, *Locke's Two Treatises of Government* (London: Allen & Unwin, 1987), 138–141; Ashcraft, *Revolutionary*

Politics and Locke's Two Treatises of Government (Princeton: Princeton University Press, 1986).

82. See John Locke, *Epistola de Tolerantia, A Letter Concerning Toleration* (1689), in Locke, *Works,* 10th edn., 10 vols. (London: J. Johnson, 1801), VI: 1–65; Locke, *Two Treatises of Government*; Laslett, "Introduction: Locke the Man and Locke the Writer," 37–66; Laslett, "Introduction: The Book," in Locke, *Two Treatises of Government,* 3–15.

83. Isaac Newton, *Philosophiae Naturalis Principia Mathematica* (1689); *Sir Isaac Newton's Mathematical Principles of Natural Philosophy and His System of the World*, trans. Florian Cajori (Berkeley: University of California Press, 1934); H. S. Thayer, "Sir Isaac Newton," *Cambridge Dictionary of Philosophy* (Cambridge: Cambridge University Press, 1995), 529–530.

84. Locke, *An Essay concerning Human Understanding;* see J. W. Yolton, *Locke and the Compass of the Human Understanding* (Cambridge: Cambridge University Press, 1970); R. S. Woolhouse, "John Locke," *Oxford Companion to Philosophy*, ed. Ted Honderich (Oxford: Oxford University Press, 1995), 493–496; Woolhouse, *Locke* (Minneapolis: University of Minnesota Press, 1983); Vere Chappell, "Locke's Theory of Ideas," *The Cambridge Companion to Locke,* ed. Vere Chappell (Cambridge: Cambridge University Press, 1994), 26–55.

85. Locke, *A Letter Concerning Toleration,* VI: 3–17.

86. The title page of Locke's *Two Treatises of Government* contained this subtitle: *In the Former, the False Principles and Foundation of Sir Robert Filmer, and His Followers, Are Detected and Overthrown. The Latter Is an Essay Concerning the True Original, Extent, and End of Civil Government.* See *Two Principles of Government,* 135; see Peter Laslett, "Two Treatises of Government and the Revolution of 1688," in Locke, *Two Treatises of Government,* 56–57; Robert Filmer, *Patriarcha and Other Writings*, ed. Johann Sommerville (Cambridge: Cambridge University Press, 1991); *John Locke: A Letter Concerning Toleration in Focus*, ed. John Horton and Susan Mendus (New York: Routledge, 1991); Richard Vernon, *The Career of Toleration: John Locke, Jonas Proast, and After* (Montreal: McGill-Queens University Press, 1997).

87. Locke, *Two Treatises of Government,* 267–282.

88. Ibid., 285–302.

89. Ibid, quotes, 301, 302.

90. Ibid., 283–285, 384–397.

91. See A. John Simmons, *The Lockean Theory of Rights* (Princeton: Princeton University Press, 1992); John Dunn, *The Political Thought of John Locke* (Cambridge: Cambridge University Press, 1969); Leo Strauss, *Natural Right and History* (Chicago: University of Chicago Press, 1953); C. B. Macpherson, *The Political Theory of Possessive Individualism: Hobbes to Locke* (Oxford: Clarendon Press, 1962); James Tully, *A Discourse on Property, John Locke and His Adversaries* (Cambridge: Cambridge University Press, 1980); Tully, *An Approach to Political Philosophy: Locke in Contexts* (Cambridge: Cambridge University Press, 1993); Richard H. Popkin, *The High Road to Pyrrhonism* (San Diego: Austin Hill, 1980); Neal Wood, *The Politics of Locke's Philosophy* (Berkeley: University of California Press, 1983).

92. See Locke, *An Essay Concerning Human Understanding,* quotes 618, 619.

93. Ibid., 620–621.

94. Ibid., 688–696.

95. Ibid., 689–691.

96. Ibid., 693–696, quote 695.

97. John Locke, *The Reasonableness of Christianity As Delivered in the Scriptures* (1695; reprint, Washington, DC: Regnery Gateway, 1965), quotes 1, 2.

98. Ibid., 2, 3.

99. Ibid., 4–17, quote 4.

100. Ibid., 172–185, quotes 174, 178, 179.

101. Ibid., 176–195, quotes 178, 192.

102. William Chillingworth, *The Religion of Protestants a Safe Way to Salvation* (London: E. Cotes, 1664); excerpt reprinted in More and Cross, eds., *Anglicanism*, 103–113, quote 105–106; Jeremy Taylor, *Treatise of 1. The liberty of prophesying, 2. Episcopacie, 3. The history of the life and death of the ever blessed Jesus Christ. 4. An Apology for Authorized and set-forms of Liturgy*, 2 vols. (London: R. Royston, 1650); *Jeremy Taylor: Selected Works* ed. Thomas K. Carroll (New York: Paulist Press, 1990); Benjamin Whichcote, *The Works of the Learned Benjamin Whichcote* (Aberdeen: Alexander Thomson, 1751); *The Cambridge Platonists: Selections from the Writings of Benjamin Whichcote, John Smith and Nathanael Culverwel*, ed. Ernest T. Campagnac (Oxford: Clarendon Press, 1901); Henry More, *Philosophical Writings of Henry More*, ed. Flora I. MacKinnon (New York: AMS Press, 1969); see Falkland, Lucius Cary, *Of the Infallibility of the Church of Rome* (Oxford: H. Hall, 1645); Henry Hammond and Falkland, Lucius Cary, *A View of Some Exceptions Which Have been made by a Romanist to the Ld Viscount Falkland's discourse Of the Infallibility of the Church of Rome* (London: R. Royston, 1650); John Hales, *The Works of John Hales* (Glasgow, 1765; reprint, New York: AMS Press, 1971); John Bramhall, *The Works of the Most Reverend Father in God, John Bramhall* (Oxford: J. H. Parker, 1845); H. R. Trevor-Roper, *Archbishop Laud, 1573–1645* (London: Macmillan, 1940); J. Davies, *The Caroline Captivity of the Church* (Oxford: Oxford University Press, 1992); Henry R. McAdoo, *The Spirit of Anglicanism: A Survey of Anglican Theological Method in the Seventeenth Century* (New York: Charles Scribner's Sons, 1965), 74–75. McAdoo's book is a classic text on the essential continuity of seventeenth-century Anglican theology.

103. See John Edwards, *Some Thoughts Concerning the Several Causes and Occasions of Atheism, Especially in the Present Age. With Some Brief Reflections on Socinianism: and on a Late Book Entitled The Reasonableness of Christianity as Delivered in the Scriptures* (London: J. Robinson, 1695); John McLachlan, *Socinianism in Seventeenth Century England* (Oxford: Oxford University Press, 1951), 326–328.

104. John Toland, *Christianity not Mysterious* (1696; reprint, New York: Garland Publishing, 1978); Matthew Tindal, *Christianity as old as the creation* (London: Thomas Astley, 1730); Samuel Clarke, *The Scripture Doctrine of the Trinity* (London: James Knapton, 1712); Joseph Butler, *The Analogy of Religion to the Constitution and Course of Nature* (1736; reprint, London: London Tract Society, 1855); see William Paley, *The Principles of Moral and Political Philosophy* (1785; reprint, Boston: John West and Co., 1810); Paley, *A View of the Evidences of Christianity* (1794; reprint, New York: Griffin & Rudd, 1814); Paley, *Natural Theology, or, evidence of the existence and attributes of the deity, collected from the appearances of nature* (1802; reprint, New York: Oxford University Press, 2006).

105. James Gillman, *The Life of Samuel Taylor Coleridge* (London: W. Pickering, 1838), quote 12; see James D. Campbell, *Samuel Taylor Coleridge: A Narrative of the Events of His Life* (London: Macmillan, 1894); E. K. Chambers, *Samuel Taylor Coleridge: A Biographical Study* (Oxford: Oxford University Press, 1938); Lawrence Hanson, *The Life of S. T. Coleridge, the Early Years* (New York: Russell & Russell, 1962); Rosemary Ashton, *The Life of Samuel Taylor Coleridge: A Critical Biography* (Oxford: Blackwell,

1996); Richard Holmes, *Coleridge: Early Visions, 1772–1804* (New York: Pantheon Books, 1999).

106. Samuel Taylor Coleridge to George Coleridge, February 8, 1794, *Collected Letters of Samuel Taylor Coleridge*, 6 vols., ed. Earl L. Griggs (Oxford: Oxford University Press, 1956–1971), quote I: 63; cited in Holmes, *Coleridge: Early Visions, 1772–1804*, 55.

107. See *Collected Letters of Samuel Taylor Coleridge*, I: 97–150; Joseph Priestley, *An History of the Corruptions of Christianity*, 2 vols. (Birmingham: J. Johnson, 1782); Priestley, *The Theological and Miscellaneous Works*, 23 vols., ed. John Towill Rutt (London: G. Smallfield, 1818); *New Letters of Robert Southey*, 2 vols., ed. Kenneth Curry (New York: Columbia University Press, 1965).

108. Samuel Taylor Coleridge, *Poems on Various Subjects* (London: C. G. and J. Robinsons; Bristol: J. Cottle, 1796); Coleridge to Joseph Cottle, February 1796, *Collected Letters of Samuel Taylor Coleridge*, I: 185; Holmes, *Coleridge: Early Visions, 1772–1804*, 112–115.

109. Samuel Taylor Coleridge to Thomas Poole, May 1796, *Collected Letters of Samuel Taylor Coleridge*, I: 209–210; see *The Watchman*, ed. Lewis Patton (Princeton: Princeton University Press, 1970).

110. See *Collected Letters of Samuel Taylor Coleridge*, I: 301–355; Holmes, Coleridge: *Early Visions, 1772–1804*, 135–168.

111. Samuel Taylor Coleridge, *The Collected Works of Samuel Taylor Coleridge, Volume Seven: Biographia Literaria, or, Biographical Sketches of My Literary Life and Opinions*, 2 vols., one-volume edition, ed. James Engell and W. Jackson Bate (Princeton: Princeton University Press, 1983), II: 5–12, quote 5.

112. Ibid., quote, II: 8; see *The Letters of William and Dorothy Wordsworth: The Middle Years, 1806–11,* ed. Ernest de Selincourt; 2nd edn., revd. Chester Shaver (Oxford Clarendon Press, 1967).

113. William Wordsworth and Samuel Taylor Coleridge, *Lyrical Ballads, 1798* (London: Oxford University Press, 1969); see Coleridge, *Poetical Works*, ed. Ernest Hartley Coleridge (Oxford: Oxford University Press, 1969); Wordsworth, *Poetical Works*, ed. Thomas Hutchinson (Oxford: Oxford University Press, 1936).

114. Samuel Taylor Coleridge, "France: An Ode," (1798), in Coleridge, *Poetical Works*, ed. Ernest Hartley Coleridge (Oxford: Oxford University Press, 1969), 243–247, quote 246.

115. Ibid., quote 247.

116. See *Collected Letters of Samuel Taylor Coleridge*, I: 415–525; Holmes, *Coleridge: Early Visions, 1772–1804*, 205–275; Molly Lefebure, *The Bondage of Love: A Life of Mrs. Samuel Taylor Coleridge* (New York: Norton, 1987), 113–118.

117. See William Wordsworth and Samuel Taylor Coleridge, *Lyrical Ballads, with Other Poems*, 2 vols. (London: T. N. Longman, 1800); *Wordsworth's Preface to Lyrical Ballads,* ed. J. W. B. Owen (Westport: Greenwood Press, 1979); *William Wordsworth and Samuel T. Coleridge: Selected Critical Essays,* ed. Thomas M. Raysor (New York: Appleton-Century, Crofts, 1958).

118. Samuel Taylor Coleridge to Robert Southey, July 29, 1802, *Collected Letters of Samuel Taylor Coleridge,* "half a child," II: 830; remaining quotes ibid, I: 656, 658; Holmes, *Coleridge: Early Visions, 1772–1804*, 285–296.

119. Lefebure, *The Bondage of Love: A Life of Mrs. Samuel Taylor Coleridge*; Molly Lefebure, *Samuel Taylor Coleridge: A Bondage of Opium* (New York: Stein and Day, 1974); Norman Fruman, *Coleridge, the Damaged Archangel* (New York: G. Braziller, 1971); Thomas MacFarland, *Coleridge and the Pantheist Tradition* (Oxford: Oxford University Press, 1969); Oswald Doughty, *Perturbed Spirit: The Life and Personality of Samuel*

Taylor Coleridge (Rutherford: Fairleigh Dickinson University Press, 1981); Geoffrey Yarlott, *Coleridge and the Abyssinian Mind* (London: Methuen, 1967); Nicolas Roe, *Wordsworth and Coleridge: The Radical Years* (Oxford: Oxford University Press, 1988); Holmes, *Coleridge: Early Visions,* 1772–1804, quote 275.

120. Coleridge, "Dejection: An Ode," *Poetical Works,* 362–368, quote 364.
121. Samuel Taylor Coleridge to Thomas Poole, February 1801, *Collected Letters of Samuel Taylor Coleridge,* II: 706; see Richard Holmes, *Coleridge: Darker Reflections, 1804–1834* (New York: Pantheon Books, 1998), 1–106; J. D. Boulger, *Coleridge as Religious Thinker* (New Haven: Yale University Press, 1961), 219–220.
122. Samuel Taylor Coleridge to George Fricker, October 4, 1806, *Collected Letters of Samuel Taylor Coleridge,* II: 1189.
123. See Samuel Taylor Coleridge, *The Friend,* 2 vols., ed. Barbara E. Rooke (Princeton: Princeton University Press, 1969), I: 277; II: 116–121; 141–147; *Collected Letters of Samuel Taylor Coleridge,* III: 120–280; Holmes, *Coleridge: Darker Reflections, 1804–1834,* 145–196.
124. *Collected Letters of Samuel Taylor Coleridge,* III: 460–490, quote 490; see Joseph Cottle, *Early Recollections, Chiefly Relating to the Late Samuel Taylor Coleridge,* 2 vols. (Bristol: Joseph Cottle, 1837), II: 169; Holmes, *Coleridge: Darker Reflections, 1804–1834,* 354–358; Lefebure, *Coleridge: A Bondage of Opium;* Thomas De Quincey, *Confessions of an English Opium Eater* (1822; reprint, London: J. M. Dent, 1907); Walter Scott, *The Lady of the Lake* (1810; reprint, Cambridge: Riverside Press, 1883); George Gordon Byron, *The Bride of Abydos: A Turkish Tale* (London: J. Murray, 1813).
125. Coleridge to John Morgan, May 14, 1813, *Collected Letters of Samuel Taylor Coleridge,* III: 489–480; see Holmes, *Coleridge: Darker Reflections, 1804–1834,* 356–358; Cottle, *Early Recollections, Chiefly Relating to the Late Samuel Taylor Coleridge,* II: 169–170.
126. See *Collected Letters of Samuel Taylor Coleridge,* III: 465–510, 532–533; Holmes, *Coleridge: Darker Reflections, 1804–1834,* 359–372.
127. See Editor's Introduction to Coleridge, *Biographia Literaria, or, Biographical Sketches of My Literary Life and Opinions,* xli–lxv; Catherine Wallace, *The Design of the Biographia Literaria* (London: Allen and Unwin, 1983); Kathleen Wheeler, *Sources, Processes and Methods in Coleridge's Biographia Literaria* (Cambridge: Cambridge University Press, 1980).
128. Coleridge, *Biographia Literaria,* I: 5; see William Wordsworth, *The Prelude: The Four Texts (1798, 1799, 1805, 1850),* ed. Jonathan Wordsworth (Harmondsworth: Penguin, 1995).
129. Coleridge, *Biographia Literaria,* I: 304–305.
130. Ibid., II: 6, 9–10.
131. David Hartley, *Observations on Man, his frame, his duty, and his expectations* (London: Printed by S. Richardson for James Leake and Wm. Frederick, 1749); see David Hume, *A Treatise of Human Nature,* ed. L. A. Selby-Bigge (Oxford: Clarendon Press, 1978), 1–4.
132. Samuel Taylor Coleridge to C. A. Tulk, September 1817, *Collected Letters of Samuel Taylor Coleridge,* IV: 775; see Jacob Boehme, *The Way to Christ,* trans. Peter Erb (New York: Paulist Press, 1978.
133. Coleridge, *Biographia Literaria,* I: 89–105, quote 93; Thomas Hobbes, *Leviathan,* ed. Richard Tuck (Cambridge: Cambridge University Press, 1991), 15–24; Hume, *A Treatise of Human Nature,* quote 1.
134. Coleridge, *Biographia Literaria,* I: 106–115, quotes 108.
135. Ibid., quote I: 123.

136. Immanuel Kant, *Critique of Pure Reason,* trans. Norman Kemp Smith (New York: Macmillan, 1973), 127.

137. Coleridge, *Biographia Literaria,* quotes I: 153.

138. Ibid., I: 154–155; see Christian Wolff, *Gesammelte Werke* (Hildesheim: G. Olms, 1962); Manfred Kuehn, *Kant: A Biography* (Cambridge: Cambridge University Press, 2001), 361–385.

139. Coleridge, *Biographia Literaria,* I: 154–155, quotes 154, 155; Friedrich W. J. Schelling, *Sämtliche Werke,* 14 vols., ed. K. F. A. Schelling (Stuttgart, 1856–61), I: 285–290, cited in ibid., I: 154–155; J. G. Fichte, "On the Ground of Our Belief in a Divine World-Governance," in *J. G. Fichte and the Atheism Dispute (1798–1800),* ed. Yolanda Estes and Curtis Bowman (Aldershot: Ashgate, 2010), 17–30.

140. Coleridge, *Biographia Literaria,* I: 155; J. G. Fichte, *Science of Knowledge,* trans. Peter Heath and John Lachs (Cambridge: Cambridge University Press, 1982).

141. See Frederick C. Beiser, *German Idealism: The Struggle Against Subjectivism, 1781–1801* (Cambridge: Harvard University Press, 2002), 349–355; Rudolf Haym, *Die romantische Schule* (Berlin: Gaertner, 1870), 655–658; Ernst Behler, *Frühromantik* (Berlin: de Gruyter, 1992), 151–157.

142. See Friedrich W. J. Schelling to J. G. Fichte, November 19, 1800, in *J. G. Fichte: Gesamtausgabe der Bayerischen Akademie der Wissenschaften,* ed. R. Lauth, H. Jacob, and H. Gliwitsky (Stuttgart-Bad Cannstaatt: Friedrich Fromann, 1964), III/4, 362–369; Schelling to Fichte, May 15, 1801, ibid., III/5, 35–36; Beiser, *German Idealism: The Struggle Against Subjectivism, 1781–1801,* 491–505.

143. Coleridge, *Biographia Literaria,* I: 158–160.

144. Ibid., I: 159.

145. F. W. J. Schelling, *Ideas for a Philosophy of Nature,* trans. Errol E. Harris and Peter Heath (1st edn., 1797; 2nd edn., 1803; reprint, Cambridge: Cambridge University Press, 1988); Schelling, *System of Transcendental Idealism,* trans. Peter Heath (1800; reprint, Charlottesville: University of Virginia Press, 1978).

146. Coleridge, *Biographia Literaria,* 161.

147. Coleridge, *Biographia Literaria,* "at all to be," I: 161;

148. *The Notebooks of Samuel Taylor Coleridge,* ed. Kathleen Coburn (Princeton: Princeton University Press, 1957), "I am," 2: 2375, cited in ibid., 160; see Giordano Bruno, *De la causa, principio e uno in Dialoghi italiani,* 3rd edn., ed. G. Aquilecchia (Florence: Sansoni, 1958); Nicholas of Cusa, *Philosophisch-Theologische Schriften,* 3 vols., ed. Leo Gabriel (Vienna: Herder, 1967).

149. Coleridge, *Biographia Literaria,* I: 164.

150. Ibid., quotes, I: 162, 263.

151. F. W. J. Schelling, *Philosophische Untersuchungen über das Wesen der menschlichen Freiheit und die damit zusammenh angenden Gegenst ande* (1809), English editions, Of *Human Freedom,* trans. James Gutmann (Leipzig: Kroner, 1925); *Schelling: Of Human Freedom,* trans. James Gutmann (Chicago: University of Chicago Press, 1937), see xlv–xlvii; Coleridge, *Biographia Literaria,* 161.

152. See F. W. J. Schelling, *Philosophische Schriften: erster Band* (Landshut: Philipp Krüll, 1809).

153. Coleridge, *Biographia Literaria,* I: 275.

154. Ibid., I: 278–279.

155. Ibid., I: 283.

156. Ibid., II: 247–248.

157. Reviews of *Biographia Literaria,* by Samuel Taylor Coleridge, *New Annual Register* 38 (1817), 145; *British Critic* 8 (1817), 460–461; John Wilson, *Blackwood's Magazine* 2

(1817), 3–18; William Hazlitt, *Edinburgh Review* 38 (1817), 488–515; reprinted in *Coleridge: The Critical Heritage,* ed. J. R. de J. Jackson (London: Routledge, 1970), 294–387, Wilson quotes 330, 348; Hazlitt quote 320.

158. See William Hazlitt, *Complete Works,* 21 vols., ed. P. P. Howe (London: J. M. Dent and Sons, 1930–1934).

159. 159 William Hazlitt, review of *A Lay Sermon,* by Samuel Taylor Coleridge, *Examiner* (September 8, 1816), reprinted in *Coleridge: The Critical Heritage,* quotes 249–250; Hazlitt, review of *Biographia Literaria, Edinburgh Review,* quotes 490–491, 497; *Coleridge: The Critical Heritage,* 298–322.

160. Holmes, *Coleridge: Early Visions, 1772–1804,* 414–415, quote 448; see Samuel Taylor Coleridge, *Church and state; A Lay Sermon; Table talk* (New York: Harper, 1884).

161. Holmes, *Coleridge: Darker Reflections, 1804–1834,* 454–456, quote 455; see Percy B. Shelley, *A Defense of Poetry* (1821; reprint, Boston: Ginn and Company, 1890); Shelley, *The Poetical Works of Shelley* (Boston: Houghton Mifflin, 1975); John Keats, *The Poems of John Keats* (Cambridge: Harvard University Press, 1978).

162. See *Coleridge: The Critical Heritage,* 233–265.

163. See Samuel Taylor Coleridge, *Literary Lectures, Lectures 1808–1819: On Literature,* 2 vols., ed. R. A. Foakes (Princeton: Princeton University Press, 1987), II: 815–845; Holmes, *Coleridge: Darker Reflections, 1804–1834,* 465–468.

164. See William Hazlitt, *Lectures on the English Poets* (Oxford: Oxford University Press, 1818); Holmes, *Coleridge: Darker Reflections, 1804–1834,* 468–471.

165. Samuel Taylor Coleridge to Joseph Cottle, April 26, 1814, *Letters of Samuel Taylor Coleridge,* "that true," III: 478; *Coleridge the Talker,* ed. R. W. Armour and R. F. Howes (Ithaca: Cornell University Press, 1949), "jeweled," 310; Coleridge to John Murray, January 18, 1822, *Letters of Samuel Taylor Coleridge,* IV: 197–200, "wonderful," 197; Editor's Introduction to Samuel Taylor Coleridge, *The Collected Works of Samuel Taylor Coleridge: Aids to Reflection,* ed. John Beer (Princeton: Princeton University Press, 1993), xli-lv.

166. Coleridge, *Aids to Reflection,* quotes 107.

167. Samuel Taylor Coleridge to Thomas Clarkson, 1806, *Collected Letters of Samuel Taylor Coleridge,* II: 1198.

168. Coleridge, *Aids to Reflection,* 216–236.

169. Ibid., quotes 216, 202, 307.

170. Ibid., 157–160, 316–334, quote 160.

171. Ibid., quotes 327.

172. Reviews of *Aids to Reflection,* by Samuel Taylor Coleridge, *British Review* (October 1826); *British Critic* (October 1826), reprinted in *Coleridge: The Critical Heritage,* 485–513.

173. Editor's Introduction to Coleridge, *Aids to Reflection,* cx–cxv; Charles Merivale, *Autobiography and Letters,* ed. J. A. Merivale (Oxford: Oxford University Press, 1898), quote 98; see Peter Allen, *The Cambridge Apostles: The Early Years* (Cambridge: Cambridge University Press, 1978).

174. See James Marsh, "Preliminary Essay," in Samuel Taylor Coleridge, *Aids to Reflection,* ed. James Marsh (Burlington: Chauncy Goodrich, 1829), 12–52; P. Carafiol, "James Marsh's American *Aids to Reflection:* Influence Through Ambiguity," *New England Quarterly* 49 (1976), 27–45; Anthony J. Harding, "James Marsh as Editor of Coleridge," in *Reading Coleridge,* ed. W. B. Crawford (Ithaca: Cornell University Press, 1979), 223–251; Editor's Introduction to Coleridge, *Aids to Reflection,* Princeton University Press edition, cxvi–

cxxii; *Coleridge's American Disciples: The Selected Correspondence of James Marsh,* ed. John J. Duffy (Amherst: University of Massachusetts Press, 1973), 75–154.

175. Ralph Waldo Emerson, Blotting Book Y, October 9, 1829, *The Journals and Miscellaneous Notebooks of Ralph Waldo Emerson,* 16 vols. (Cambridge: Harvard University Press, 1961–1982), vol. 3, 1963, ed. William H. Gilman and Alfred R. Ferguson, quote 3:164; Coleridge, *Aids to Reflection,* 1929 edn., quote 257. This section on American Transcendentalism adapts material from Gary Dorrien, *The Making of American Liberal Theology: Imagining Progressive Religion, 1805–1900* (Louisville: Westminster John Knox Press, 2001), 60–67.

176. See Victor Cousin, *Introduction a l'histoire de la philosophie,* 4th edn. (Paris: Didier et cie., 1861), 166–171; Cousin, *Lecons sur la philosophie de Kant* (Paris: Librairie Philosophique de Ladrange, 1844); *The Transcendentalists: An Anthology,* ed. Perry Miller (Cambridge: Harvard University Press, 1950).

177. Marsh, "Preliminary Essay," 12–52; excerpts reprinted in *The Transcendentalists: An Anthology,* 34–39, quotes 38–39; see Noah Porter, "Coleridge and His American Disciples," *Bibliotheca Sacra* 4 (1847), 117–171; Peter Carafiol, *Transcendent Reason: James Marsh and the Forms of Romantic Thought* (Gainesville: University Presses of Florida, 1982).

178. Margaret Fuller, quoted in editor's introduction to Marsh, "Preliminary Essay," *The Transcendentalists: An Anthology,* 35; Frederick Henry Hedge, "Coleridge," *The Christian Examiner* 14 (March 1833), 109–129; reprinted in *The Transcendentalists: An Anthology,* 66–72; see Stephen Prickett, *Romanticism and Religion: The Tradition of Coleridge and Wordsworth in the Victorian Church* (Cambridge: Cambridge University Press, 1976).

179. Ralph Waldo Emerson to Edward Bliss Emerson, December 22, 1833, *The Letters of Ralph Waldo Emerson,* 6 vols., ed. Ralph L. Rusk (New York: Columbia University Press, 1939), "unfolding," 1: 401–402; James Freeman Clarke, *Autobiography, Diary and Correspondence,* ed. E. E. Hale (Boston: Houghton Mifflin, 1891), 39; Emerson to Edward Bliss Emerson, May 31, 1834, ibid., "Reason is," 1: 412–413; see Robert D. Richardson, *Emerson: The Mind on Fire* (Berkeley: University of California Press, 1995), 165–166.

180. See Frederick Henry Hedge, *Reason in Religion* (Boston: Walker, Fuller & Co., 1865); Octavius Brooks Frothingham, *Recollections and Impressions, 1822–1890* (New York: G. P. Putnam's Sons, 1891); Frothingham, *The Religion of Humanity* (New York: David G. Francis, 1873).

181. Frederick Denison Maurice, editorial comments, *Athenaeum* (March 8, 1828), 289–290; (July 30, 1828), 623; (August 6, 1828), 641–642; cited in Editor's Introduction to Coleridge, *Aids to Reflection,* Princeton edition, cxxxiv; see R. Modiano, *Coleridge and the Concept of Nature* (London: Macmillan, 1975), 138–142; John Beer, "Coleridge's Religious Thought: The Search for a Medium," *The Interpretation of Belief: Coleridge, Schleiermacher and Romanticism,* ed. D. Jasper (London: Macmillan, 1986), 47–50.

182. Samuel Taylor Coleridge, *Confessions of an Inquiring Spirit* (London: W. Pickering, 1840; Stanford: Stanford University Press, 1967), quotes 43; see David Pym, *The Religious Thought of Samuel Taylor Coleridge* (Gerrards Cross, Buckinghamshire: Colin Smythe, 1978), 81–93.

183. Samuel Taylor Coleridge, *On the Constitution of Church and State according to the idea of each* (1829; London: Hurst, Chance and Co., 1830; London: Everyman, 1972), quote 46.

184. Coleridge, *Aids to Reflection,* Princeton edition, quotes 159, 160; see Samuel Taylor Coleridge, *Notes: Theological, Political and Miscellaneous* (London: Edward Moxon, 1853), 9–10; Coleridge, *The Friend,* I: 75–76; Avis, *Anglicanism and the Christian Church,* 239–243; Martin Luther, *The Table Talk of Martin Luther,* trans. And ed., William Hazlitt (London: G. Bell and Sons, 1902).

185. See Frederick Denison Maurice, *The Kingdom of Christ, or, Hints to a Quaker Respecting the Principles, Constitution, and Ordinances of the Catholic Church,* 2 vols. (2nd edn., 1842; reprint, London: SCM Press, 1958); Maurice, *Theological Essays* (1853; reprint: New York: Harper & Row, 1957); W. J. Conybeare, "Church Parties, Past and Present," *Edinburgh Review* (October 1853), 272–342.

186. See *Essays and Reviews: The 1860 Text and Its Reading,* ed. Victor Shea and William Whitla (Charlottesville: University Press of Virginia, 2000); Ieuan Ellis, *Seven Against Christ: A Study of "Essays and Reviews"* (Leiden: E. J. Brill, 1980).

4

Dialectics of Spirit

F. W. J. Schelling, G. W. F. Hegel, and Absolute Idealism

The greatest philosopher of the modern experience, G. W. F. Hegel, was deeply rooted in Plato, Aristotle, and Spinoza, and he synthesized the riches of Kantian and post-Kantian idealism. Hegel put dynamic panentheism into play in modern theology, and in some way he inspired nearly every great philosophical idea and movement of the past two centuries. Yet no thinker is as routinely misconstrued as Hegel, partly because his greatest work, the *Phenomenology of Spirit,* defies categorization and is notoriously hard to understand.

In the mid-1790s, post-Kantian idealism became a doctrine about the absolute. The geniuses of absolute idealism, it later turned out, were Hegel and F. W. J. Schelling, in that order. But in the early going, Schelling's genius was obvious, there were many other contenders for genius status among the post-Kantian idealists, and Hegel was not one of them.

The post-Kantian Romantics and objective idealists who invoked the absolute sometimes called it "the unconditioned" or "the infinite." Schelling and Hegel, playing on Spinoza's doctrine of substance, usually called the absolute the "in-itself," or as Schelling put it in 1804, something that is "from itself and through itself" *(von sich selbst und durch sich selbst)*. Spinoza had defined substance as "that which is in itself, and is conceived through itself: in other words, that of which a conception can be formed independently of any other conception." For Spinoza, the key to substance was its independent or self-sufficient essence, something that does not depend on anything else. Thus, substance had to be infinite, because anything less than the whole of all things would depend on something outside itself.[1]

This idea from Spinoza defined the post-Kantian idea of the absolute. To the young idealists that overthrew Kantian idealism in the 1790s, Kantian and Fichtean subjectivism failed to explain the reality of the external world; more importantly to some of them, it turned nature into a mere instrument or medium of moral action. Nature, instead of being an end in itself worthy of spiritual appreciation, was subordinated to

Kantian Reason and Hegelian Spirit: The Idealistic Logic of Modern Theology, First Edition. Gary Dorrien.
© 2012 John Wiley & Sons, Ltd. Published 2015 by John Wiley & Sons, Ltd.

the striving of a moral subject, deriving its value from ethical ends imposed upon it. In the late 1790s, the Romantic and objective idealists who looked to Spinoza (and usually, Goethe) for what was missing in Kantian idealism included Schelling, Schleiermacher, Friedrich Schlegel, and Friedrich von Hardenberg (Novalis) in Jena and Berlin; Hegel, Friedrich Hölderlin, Isaak von Sinclair, and Jakob Zwilling in Frankfurt and Homburg; and a whole fraternity of Fichteans in Jena led by August Ludwig Hülsen. Schelling, a boy genius and Romantic, was the most brilliant of this group and the most productive, until he flamed out. Hegel, a slow starter and only briefly a Romantic, made the strongest bid that any thinker has ever made to be the Protestant Thomas Aquinas, in the process of overtaking Schelling.[2]

Schelling and Hegel argued that Kant wrongly dichotomized between form and content, which yielded a strangely abstract philosophy that knew only appearances, not reality. Kant described a real problem, but he fixated on a relatively primitive mode of self-consciousness in which form and content were separate, which led to a dualistic theory of knowledge predicated on the dichotomy between a knowing subject and its objects of consciousness. Schelling, at the time that Hegel wrote his *Phenomenology of Spirit* (1807), conceived an ultimate identity of thought and being in which only forms were different, and even the forms were only quantitatively, not qualitatively, different. Hegel, up to the *Phenomenology,* deeply absorbed Schelling's absolute idealism; then he objected that Schelling painted with only two colors, tracking the unfolding of the absolute in nature and history. Schelling had the right project, Hegel judged, describing the dialectical development of consciousness in which the universal and the particular came together. But even Schelling was constrained by Kantian modesty, confining himself to what is revealed in nature and history. Hegel pressed on to the logical Idea, pure thought itself, which is not the idea of something.

Spirit empties itself into the world of sensuous particularity in its creation of the world as an experience of itself. Reality is precisely and nothing less than the self-thinking of Spirit. This proposal, which Hegel conceived as a rationale for a modern universal religion of Spirit, did not take over Western Christianity as he hoped. But it became a major school of thought in Western theology and philosophy. It unified the ambitions of eighteenth- and nineteenth-century thought like no other philosophy. It had a critical principle that subverted its own pretensions to systemic completion. It offered a panentheistic conception of the divine as the unification of nature and freedom, finite and infinite, and universal and particular. And most of the great philosophical ideas since Hegel – the philosophies of Marx, Kierkegaard, Nietzsche, Freud, Bradley, Troeltsch, Bergson, Whitehead, Heidegger, Sartre, Derrida, and Žižek, plus the schools of existentialism, psychoanalysis, absolute idealism, historicism, phenomenology, process, structuralism, and deconstruction – are rooted in his thought.

Imagining Hegelian Idealism: Schelling, Hölderlin, and Hegel

Georg Wilhelm Frederick Hegel was born in Stuttgart, in the southern German duchy of Württemberg, in 1770, near the end of the pre-modern reign of kings. His Lutheran family had been in Swabia for nearly a century and a half, inhabiting a Protestant enclave surrounded by Catholic territories. In the year of Hegel's birth the emperor of the Holy Roman Empire, a Catholic absolutist, pressured the prince of Württemberg, Duke Karl Eugen, another Catholic absolutist, to reach a constitutional settlement with his Protestant minority. Thus Hegel grew up in a time of odd concessions to a coming new order. His father, Georg Ludwig Hegel, a lawyer, was a financial official in the court of the Duchy of Württemberg. Both of Hegel's parents stressed the importance of education and culture to their six children (three died before becoming adults); at the age of five, when Hegel enrolled at the Latin School, he already knew the first declension and its nouns, having been schooled in Latin by his mother. Hegel was a voracious reader throughout his life, self-conscious of his status in society, and touchy about affronts to it. As an adolescent he had mixed feelings of entitlement and resentment as a consequence of belonging to the "non-noble notables," the *Ehrbarkeit*. Georg Ludwig Hegel, though successful as a civil servant, was excluded from the higher reaches of government by not being a noble; Hegel, resenting the difference, used it as motivation to stay at the top of his class.[3]

When Hegel was eleven, his mother, to whom he was deeply attached, died of a fever. Hegel mourned the loss of his protector and source of affection. He developed a stutter, never warmed to his father, and rarely mentioned him in later recollections. At fourteen Hegel enrolled at the Stuttgarter *Gymnasium Ilustre,* which was probably a compromise between his father's desire (train for a modern career) and his departed mother's (become a theologian). He kept a foot in both options and flourished at the *Gymnasium,* reading widely on an independent basis, and writing commentaries on his vast reading, though he rarely commented on his feelings. G. E. Lessing, the pioneer of German literary culture, was young Hegel's hero. In Lessing's play, *Nathan the Wise* (1779), Nathan, a Jew, exemplified Lessing's pluralistic version of Enlightenment religion: All religions are essentially one, and all are signs of a common humanity, but the differences between religions should not be denigrated or eradicated. Lessing's real-life model of Enlightenment religion was his friend Moses Mendelssohn. Hegel embraced Lessing's vision of religious commonality appreciated through religious diversity, which allowed him to hold together his mother's pious orthodoxy with Enlightenment ideals.[4]

In that frame of mind Hegel enrolled at Tübingen in 1788, where virtually all Württemberg notables had studied since the fifteenth century. Officially he planned to become a minister or theologian modeled on Lessing's cultured example, enlightening the public with his learning. This was not a far-fetched ambition. Germans were assiduous readers, and one-fourth of all books published in Germany were theological works. On the other hand, Hegel would not have received state funding had he not aimed for the ministry, and numerous scholars have agreed with H. S. Harris that Hegel "never seriously intended to enter the ministry."[5]

Certainly he lost whatever ministerial inclinations he may have felt after beginning his studies at Tübingen. Enlightenment types derided German universities in general as relics of an outmoded semi-feudal order and scholasticism; Tübingen was an extreme case. Despite a rich past, Tübingen had declined drastically by the time of Hegel's arrival, a year before the French Revolution. Nepotism was rampant; professors still came from a small number of privileged intermarried families; they regarded Enlightenment ideals as a threat to their privileges; and not much was left of the university besides the Protestant Seminary – the *Stift* – to which its Catholic duke Karl Eugen had a natural aversion. The university was merely an appendage to the seminary, and both were devoted to the *ancien régime* against the plague of French Revolutionism.

To Hegel, the school was a slightly ridiculous throwback. Like most German universities, Tübingen's student culture was long on drinking, duels, and anti-intellectualism; in addition, seminarians had to wear long black coats vaguely resembling cassocks, which heightened adolescent rebelliousness. Hegel cut classes, lost his top-of-the-class standing, drank lots of wine at many parties, and kept reading, but usually not for class. For two years he studied philosophy and general studies as a seminarian under the philosophy faculty. Hegel studied philology under *Stift* ephor Christian F. Schnurrer, who questioned whether Hegel had enough self-discipline to become a decent tutor, much less a minister. He studied philosophy under philosophical theologian Johann F. Flatt, an expert on Kant, but Flatt was a protégé of Tübingen's leading theologian, Gottlob C. Storr, and Hegel took little interest in Kant at the time. After completing his training in philosophy for a theological degree, Hegel asked his father to allow him to switch to law, but Georg Ludwig Hegel refused. Probably he believed that his son was ethically obliged to keep his word to the seminary and that a political career would lead straight to radical French nonsense. Undoubtedly he worried about the pledge on his property that he had signed to secure Hegel's scholarship at the seminary. So Hegel was compelled to complete his theological training, constantly anxious that the Württemberg authorities might force him to take a ministerial position. The pedestrian dogmatic fare that he was forced to study galled him.[6]

Fortunately he had sympathetic company. At the university Hegel became close friends with Friedrich Hölderlin, a precocious thinker who was not quite aware, as yet, of his poetic gift. Upon moving to the seminary they formed a triumvirate with a new student, Friedrich W. J. Schelling, who was five years younger than Hegel and Hölderlin, and who had known Hölderlin at a Latin school in Nürtingen. Schelling was the son of a chaplain and Orientalist professor at a monastery school in Bebenhausen, near Tübingen. By the age of fourteen he was fluent in six languages and had read Plato's *Timaeus* in Greek and Leibniz's *Monadology* in Latin. The three friends, sharing a room together, influenced and challenged each other, sneered at their teachers, and vowed not to become ministers. Reluctantly they slogged through the seminary curriculum: dogmatics, exegesis, and moral theology in the first year; the same subjects plus polemics in the second year; and polemics and exegesis in the third year. All took instruction from Storr, unavoidably. Storr assumed the verbal inspiration of the Bible, treated the Bible as a storehouse of revealed propositions, and reasoned that Kant's dichotomy between phenomena and noumena relieved theologians of having to explain how Christ could have two natures, since this was a problem only on the level of appearances. For the rest of his life Hegel fixed Storr in mind when he blasted the pathetic backwardness of orthodox theology.[7]

Hegel still had Lessing's model in his head, to become a "man of letters" who helped the German people move forward in their education. But the French Revolution suggested to Hegel and his friends that more was at stake in modernity than merely becoming enlightened. Society itself had to be transformed. Many of their classmates were equally dismissive of their teachers and infatuated with the French Revolution. Years later they invented a fabled story about Hegel, Hölderlin, and Schelling that symbolized the spirit of the time. According to the story, in July 1793 – a year into the

Terror, when the guillotines were operating full time – the three friends erected a "freedom tree" modeled on the revolutionary Maypole and danced around it singing the *Marseillaise* in German. The story is undoubtedly legendary, except for the part about Schelling translating the *Marseillaise* into German, but it gave a true picture. The French revolutionary rhetoric of liberty, equality, and fraternity was intoxicating to the three seminarians. Hölderlin and Schelling believed that philosophy needed to overtake theology as the leading force in society and the academy; together they urged Hegel to imagine himself as a philosopher.

The three friends studied Jacobi intently and debated his critiques of Lessing and Kant, though Hegel lagged behind the other two in mastering Kant's philosophy. Schelling and Hölderlin joined a "Kant Club" at the seminary and were aided by a young radical Kantian on the faculty, Carl Immanuel Diez, who owed his faculty status to being the son of a medical faculty professor. Schelling and Hölderlin, absorbed by Kant's critiques, became intellectual partners to each other, while failing to persuade Hegel to keep up with them. The difference played out for over twenty years. Though Hegel and Hölderlin had a closer personal relationship than either had with Schelling, Schelling's genius bloomed at Tübingen. Hegel, after graduating from the seminary in 1793, floundered as a private tutor in Berne and later moved to an only slightly less depressing tutorial position in Frankfurt in 1797, where he stayed until Schelling secured a minor job for him in Jena in 1801. Meanwhile Schelling introduced himself to Fichte in 1794, absorbed Fichte's critique of Kant, and wrote an impressive work, *Vom Ich als Princip der Philosophie*, the following year. For Schelling, twenty years old, the key thinkers were Spinoza, Kant, and Fichte. Spinoza's system was "infinitely more worthy of respect" than any recent system; Kant's idealism led to Fichte; and Fichte's emphasis on freedom was the key to the idealism that was needed, which would replace Spinoza's determinism with something equally majestic and far more radical. In that spirit Schelling published a breakout work in 1797 – *Ideas for a Philosophy of Nature*, soared to the top of the field, won a position at Jena in 1798 at the age of twenty-three, and succeeded Fichte there a year later.[8]

Hegel, writing to Schelling from Berne, complained of spoiled aristocratic families and having no time to himself; wistfully he dreamed of a post where he could "bring to fruition what I formerly let slip by." Schelling's replies were filled with news of his intellectual adventures: "I live and move at present in philosophy. Philosophy is not yet at an end. Kant has provided the results. The premises are still missing. And who can understand results without premises?" A month later, in February 1795, he told Hegel that the essential difference between Kantian idealism and all dogmatic systems rested in their starting points. Kantian idealism began with an absolute "I" not conditioned by an object; the dogmatic systems began with an absolute object or a not-I; the answer was to reconcile these approaches in a way that preserved Kant's emphasis on human spontaneity and autonomy. That was pure Fichte, but Schelling credited Spinoza: "I have in the interim become a Spinozist! Do not be astonished. You will soon hear how. For Spinoza the world, the object by itself in opposition to the subject, was *everything*. For me it is the *self*." Schelling was taken with the idea of overhauling Spinozist substance with idealist Spirit. He told Hegel, "The alpha and omega of all philosophy is freedom." He also admonished Hegel not to backslide into classical theism; to think with Spinoza and Lessing was to advance beyond the idea of a personal Being: "For you the question has surely long since been decided. For us as well [as for Lessing] the orthodox concepts of God are no more."[9]

Hölderlin had exactly the same vision, although he told Hegel where to find it – in Fichte's *Wissenschaftslehre*: "His Absolute Self, which equals Spinoza's Substance, contains all reality; it is everything, and outside it, is nothing. There is thus no object for this Absolute Self, since otherwise all reality would not be in it." Hölderlin admitted that he could not conceive of consciousness without an object, but that was the point. If *he* was the object, then he was necessarily limited, "if only in time," and thus he was not absolute. In the Absolute Self, he explained, no consciousness is conceivable, and as Absolute Self, one has no consciousness. To the extent that one has no consciousness, one is, for one's self, *nothing,* just as the Absolute Self is, for one's self, *nothing*. Hölderlin urged Hegel to join him and Schelling at the crossroads of Kantian and pre-Kantian philosophy, where Fichte stood. There had to be a way "to get beyond the fact of consciousness in *theory,*" and Fichte was doing it.[10]

Hölderlin better appreciated than Schelling, however, that Hegel wanted to be a public intellectual in Lessing's mode, not an academic philosopher. Hegel still lacked the requisite mastery of Kant's and Fichte's concepts to argue with them, and to the extent that he acquired it in Berne, he tried to use his learning to write critiques of Christianity aimed at the educated public. He assured Schelling, "From the Kantian system and its highest completion I expect a revolution in Germany." There was plenty of work for them to do, in their own ways, to advance the Kantian revolution: "It will proceed from principles that are present and that only need to be elaborated generally and applied to all hitherto existing knowledge." In that mood he studied Kant and Fichte, wrote an essay on the life of Jesus, and began writing a Kantian attack on historic Christianity, though he shielded himself from comparisons to Schelling or even from being expected to comment constructively on Schelling's work: "You cannot expect observations from me on your writing. In this matter I am but an apprentice." As for his writings, Hegel put his guard way up: "My works are not worth speaking of."[11]

Schelling and Hölderlin, catching the note of despondency in their friend's letters, told him to buck up. Shelling wrote to Hegel, "You seem currently to be in a state of indecision and, according to your last letter to me, even depression – which is entirely unworthy of you. Fie! A man of your powers must never permit such indecision to come upon him." Hölderlin, upon moving to a tutorial post in Frankfurt, found one for Hegel too, so they could be together; there Hegel completed his Kantian attack on historic Christianity, "The Positivity of the Christian Religion."[12]

Hegel was a Greacophile who dreamed of reviving Hellenic folk religion in modern garb, a free expression of subjectivity that expresses a people's consciousness of itself as a people. When he compared Socrates and Jesus, Socrates came out better. At Tübingen he wrote an essay about the necessity of replacing "objective" religion with "subjective" religion that prized religious individuality. At Berne he wrote a short piece that lifted Socrates and Jesus above all others, in that order, explaining: "Socrates left behind no Masonic signs, no mandate to proclaim his name . . . He did not, in order to bring people to perfect goodness, outline some detour by way of *him.*" Hegel got this idea of the religious ideal during his seminary days, mainly by reading Rousseau. In Rousseau's *Emile,* the Savoyard vicar expressed it perfectly in his speech about why he did not pray for the power to do good: "Why ask him for what he has already given me?

Has he not given me conscience for loving the good, reason for knowing it, and freedom for choosing it? If I do evil, I have no excuse; I do it because I want to. Asking him to change my will is to ask of him what he asks of me." Rousseau, explaining his religion, put it epigrammatically: "True Christianity is nothing but natural religion explained better."[13]

But Hegel realized that the objective religion of Christianity was not going to disappear, so he had to make the best case that he could for Jesus. All his early writings were devoted to this task. In his "Life of Jesus," Hegel portrayed Jesus as an apostle of reason and virtue. The Jews, Hegel claimed, taking his account straight from Edward Gibbon's *Decline and Fall of the Roman Empire,* debased their religion to the point of base servility to law. Jewish religion, by the time of Jesus, had been stripped of its elements of ethical and intellectual freedom. This was what Jesus was up against. Hegel's mastertext for true Christianity was John 1:1, which he rendered as the deification of reason: "Pure reason, transcending all limits, is divinity itself – whereby and in accordance with which the very plan of the world is ordered. Through reason man learns of his destiny, the unconditional purpose of his life. And although at times reason is obscured, it continues to glimmer faintly even in the darkest age, for it is never totally extinguished." In Hegel's telling, Jesus stood out as a bearer of the light of reason, for which he was killed, like Socrates. His death was a "victory for the Jews," with no hint of the Roman Empire's wrath, as Hegel settled for a spare ethical retelling of the gospel story.[14]

"The Positivity of the Christian Religion" was longer on commentary about the supposedly corrupt legalism of Jesus' religious background, which persecuted him: "Jesus himself was sacrificed to the rising hatred of the priesthood and the mortified national vanity of the Jews." According to Hegel, Jesus was like Socrates and Kant, wanting people to be free to develop their own powers of ethical reflection and virtue. But Jesus fought against a degraded religion only to inspire another one, as Christianity corrupted his enlightened ethical religion into a new legalism. Hegel did not say that the church betrayed the teaching of Jesus; he attributed the corruption to the socio/religious context in which the teaching of Jesus was transmitted. In Hegel's account, Jesus did not issue "positive" teachings (doctrines) pertaining to his person or set up a positive religion; his teachings were based on free reason, not authority. But to get a hearing in a corrupt religious environment, Jesus had to confer some authority upon his person, which set into motion a movement toward positivity, which led to a corrupt religion.[15]

Hegel admired the Greeks and Romans for obeying laws that they laid down. But Greek and Roman religion disintegrated with the collapse of the Greek and Roman republics, which left a void that Christianity filled by promising eternal life to anyone that slavishly obeyed Christian teaching. Hegel urged that European enlightenment was a second chance to recover the spirit of Jesus: "The soul of Jesus was free from dependence on accidental trivialities; the one essential was love of God and one's neighbor and being holy as God is holy." It was "extremely remarkable" that a religion as corrupt as Judaism gave rise to someone as religiously pure as Jesus, Hegel concluded. This was a hopeful portent for the corrupt religion that Jesus inspired: "We do see his successors renouncing Jewish trivialities, but they are not altogether purified of the spirit of dependence on such things. Out of what Jesus said, out of what he suffered in his person, they soon fashioned rules and moral commands, and free emulation of their teacher soon passed over into slavish service of their Lord."[16]

Hegel was isolated and depressed in Berne, but in Frankfurt, reunited with Hölderlin and turned loose in a bustling, cosmopolitan, capital city, he came to life. It helped that he replaced a smug, reactionary aristocratic family with an urbane aristocratic one. For a while he was so enthused about the differences that he tried to adopt Hölderlin's Romantic spirit. Hölderlin had Schleiermacher's feeling for the spiritual meaning of the idealist revolution. Why should Romantic idealists settle for anything less than sense and taste for the infinite? Hölderlin's poetic novel, *Hyperion,* was published shortly after Hegel arrived in Frankfurt, and he worked on his hauntingly beautiful poem *Empedocles* during Hegel's stay there. Hegel, anticipating his move to Frankfurt, wrote a long Romantic poem to Hölderlin, "Eleusis" (a reference to the Eleusinian mysteries connected with Demeter, the Olympian fertility goddess), which overflowed with mystical nature pantheism and his tender affection for Hölderlin:

> Your image, My Beloved, passes before me with the joy of days gone by;
> yet soon it yields to sweeter hopes of our reunion.
> The scene of our long-sought and ardent embrace depicts itself even now
> before my eyes.[17]

In Frankfurt Hegel took a brief Romantic turn that caused him to refashion his fixation with what had gone wrong in Christianity. Now he contended that Christianity is essentially about love divine, the principle of ultimate unity, overcoming human estrangement from God and neighbor. In "The Spirit of Christianity and Its Fate," Hegel lifted Jesus above all others, because Jesus brought love divine into the world and thus changed the God that humans worship. The pure love of Jesus should have been enough to reconcile the world, Hegel argued, refashioning his positivity critique, but the original Christian community could only recognize itself through the factual death and resurrection of Jesus: "The veil stripped off in the grave, the real human form, has risen again out of the grave and attached itself to the one who is risen as God. This sad need which the Christian group felt for a mundane reality is deeply connected with its spirit and its spirit's fate. The love of its members, which made every form of life into consciousness of its object and therefore despised all such forms, did recognize itself as given shape in the risen one; but in their eyes he was not love pure and simple. Since their love, cut off from the world, did not manifest itself either in the development of life or in its beautiful ties and the formation of natural relationships, since their love was to remain love and not become life, they had to have some criterion for the recognition of love before their mutual faith in love could become possible. Love itself did not create a thoroughgoing union between them, and therefore they needed another bond which would link the group together and in which also the group would find the certainty of the love of all."[18]

The pure ideal of love, which Jesus embodied, had to become positive for Christianity to arise. Hegel explained that the love which shunned all positivity was caught in the fate of a too-human group, "and this fate was all the more developed the more the group expanded and, owing to this expansion, continually coincided more and more with the world's fate by unconsciously adopting many of that fate's aspects and also by continually becoming sullied itself in the course of its struggle against that fate." So Hegel stopped going to church, yet he also felt, more deeply than ever, that he had the spirit of Jesus in his mind and heart. The power of love divine at work is that of Spirit working on spirit, he urged: "The outgoing of the divine is only a development, so that, in annulling what stands over against it, it manifests itself in a union with that opposite."[19]

This was the Christian germ of Hegelian dialectic, a mode of argument that Hegel shared with his Romantic idealist friends, though Hegel had the wrong personality for Romanticism, and Hölderlin weaned him from believing that he had to work up more enthusiasm for Fichte's subjectivism. In Frankfurt Hegel and Hölderlin pored over post-Kantian philosophy, pursued romantic interests with women (especially Hölderlin), and debated their intellectual kinship with Spinoza. Both revered the Greeks, Spinoza, Rousseau, and Kant, and both celebrated Schelling's success. Hölderlin and Schelling assumed Fichte's mind-centered derivation of everything from an act of free subjective self-positing. For Fichte (and arguably, for Kant) nature was an organic product of consciousness tending toward the realization of reason. Philosophy theorized the movement from the pure subjectivity of self-consciousness to objectivity or nature.

Schelling had started there, aiming to refine Fichte's system, writing two books at the age of twenty. The first made him a player in philosophy circles, to Fichte's delight; the second made a Fichtean argument with a dramatically Fichtean title: *Of the I as the Principle of Philosophy, or On the Unconditional in Human Knowledge* (1795). Schelling began with Fichte's absolutely self-identical I, an infinite sphere including all reality, which led to the positing of a not-I, which yielded a synthesis through mutual determination and negation of a finite I as limited by a finite not-I: "The absolute sphere of the not-I, if it were simply posited absolutely, would have to cancel the I altogether, because one infinite sphere does not tolerate another. On the other hand, the sphere of the I would cancel the sphere of the not-I, insofar as the latter is posited as infinite." Schelling assured that there is "no remedy" to the striving of the I to remain absolute by drawing into itself the not-I, which is posited only in contrast to the I. Synthesis is achieved only through the restriction of the I through negation, where a finite I is limited by a finite not-I through mutual determination, and "the infinite sphere of negation turns into a finite sphere of reality." The early Schelling, like Hölderlin, followed Fichte in resting everything on Spinoza's principle *determinatio negatio est* ("determination is negation"). They identified Fichte's Absolute Self with Spinoza's cosmic substance, more or less dragging Hegel along: The Absolute Self, being absolute, lacks consciousness, exactly like Spinoza's substance of nature.[20]

But Schelling was also like Fichte in being a protean thinker who changed his mind repeatedly, and in the late 1790s he and Hölderlin made major course corrections, both of which influenced Hegel. Hölderlin worried that going back to Spinoza smacked of pre-Kantian dogmatism. Instead of justifying what he and Schelling wanted to say about the Absolute Self on the basis of a pre-Kantian metaphysics or as a postulate of practical reason, Hölderlin pointed to Kant's *Critique of Judgment*. Aesthetic reason, he argued, not the theoretical fixation with knowing the truth or the practical concern with willing the good, is the wellspring of mystical pantheism. Love of the beautiful is primary and unifying. Hölderlin was a good neo-Platonist, accepting that the true, the good, and the beautiful are different Platonic designations of Being. But he reasoned that the beautiful is a sensory anticipation of Being, not something purely intellectual. Beauty apprehends the One that theoretical and practical reason would fully behold if only they had the capacity to do so. In pure reason the knower is ruled by the object known; in pure willing the object is ruled by the willful subject; both are forms of domination, which Hegel later theorized in the *Phenomenology of Spirit* as "lordship." Hölderlin urged Hegel that love unifies subject and object and that Kant's uniting of nature with teleology in the third *Critique* contained "the entire spirit of his system." Hegel, though playing down his friend's neo-Platonism, took seriously his Kantian theme that beauty is freedom in sensory form. Subject and object are united in the recognition of beauty.[21]

But Hegel was also influenced by Schelling's alternative, to the point where he later struggled to be recognized as a thinker independent of Schelling. Hölderlin's poetic greatness was not heralded until the twentieth century; Schelling skyrocketed to fame at the age of twenty-two with his book *Ideas for a Philosophy of Nature* (1797), which argued that Fichte did not take nature seriously enough. Nature is not merely the mind in the process of becoming, or more precisely, the positing of the not-I, Schelling argued. Rather, mind derives from nature and nature derives from mind. *Ideas for a Philosophy of Nature* launched Schelling's bid for independence from Fichte, though it was still written within Fichte's framework. Schelling's next book, *On the World Soul* (1798) took a further step, announcing that the "first principle" of his philosophy of nature was "to go in search of polarity and dualism throughout all nature." Schelling's next book, *System of Transcendental Idealism* (1800), derived mind and nature from each other by breaking his system into two parallel sciences, philosophy of nature (*Naturphilosophie*) and science of knowledge (*Wissenschaftslehre*).[22]

Schelling was taking his own path, making four arguments that directly challenged Fichte's system. Ego is the highest potency of the powers of nature. Nature is the source of creative intelligence. Reason is able to abstract from the subjectivity of the ego to reach the point of pure subject-object identity. *Wissenschaftslehre* is actually the philosophy of philosophy, not the science of all knowing. Fichte, however, was slow to grasp that Schelling was developing a rival system. Fichte had trouble keeping up with Schelling's books, and getting fired from Jena distracted him. So on November 19, 1800, Schelling spelled out his counter-theses in a letter to Fichte. Schelling hoped to persuade Fichte to come along with him. This was better than a bid for independence; Schelling wanted Fichte to follow him. Fichte, on the other hand, desperately wanted not to lose his prize disciple in the wake of losing his professorship.

But in January 1801, announcing a new version of his *Wissenschaftslehre*, Fichte complained that his system was not sufficiently understood or appreciated, and he expressly declined to comment on the recent works of his "talented co-worker" (*geistvollen Mitarbeiter*), implying that Schelling was merely his disciple. That did it for Schelling; the title of his next book announced his divorce from Fichte: *Darstellung meines Systems der Philosophie*. Schelling had his own system, which was about the pure self-identity of absolute reason. The absolute excludes all differences between subject and object; nothing in itself is finite. Schelling had moved to a severely monistic, Parmenidian concept of original unity in which the only law that expressed the absolute was the law of identity, A=A. The revised edition of *Ideas for a Philosophy of Nature*

(1803) incorporated this shift away from Fichtean transcendentalism, which turned out to be a brief, though fateful phase for Schelling and his relation to Hegel.[23]

From the beginning of his move toward *Naturphilosophie* Schelling struggled with Hölderlin's misgivings about their shared dependence on Spinoza and Fichte. He took seriously Hölderlin's aesthetic option, gradually working a stronger aesthetic component into his thought. Formally Schelling took the conventional Kantian option, treating his pantheist view of nature as a postulate of practical reason. As long as one's justification is practical, he argued, not theoretical, it is not pre-critical to say that the self is self-actualized in relation to nature and that nature is the self in disguise. But that was a very expansive understanding of practical reason, one that clearly invaded transcendental territory when Schelling theorized about the dynamic polarities in nature. *Ideas for a Philosophy of Nature* tried to have it both ways. In the preface to the first edition, Schelling claimed to accept the Kantian restriction that "only a *regulative* use can be made" of metaphysical principles extending over all experience. Pure reason investigates knowledge as such, he explained; the moral nature of human beings singularly rises above the phenomenal world; and philosophy of nature is a species of practical reason that derives from applied principles a determinate system of knowledge.[24]

The essential Kantian problem, Schelling judged, the question of how the mind intuits objects of sense data, cannot be solved if only the mind is thought to be mysterious. The nature of matter is equally mysterious. To solve the problem of the Transcendental Deduction about how synthetic *a priori* concepts apply to the manifold of intuitions given in sensibility, one has to work with a broader metaphysical theory about the relation of subject and object, or noumenal and phenomenal, than the truncated models produced by Kant and Fichte. So Schelling offered theories of matter, chemical process, heat, light, gravitation, electricity, and magnetism, while claiming not to violate Kant's rules. The point was not merely to apply philosophy to natural science – "I can think of no more pitiful, workaday occupation than such an application of abstract principles to an already existing empirical science." Schelling's project, stretching a Kantian theme, was to raise natural science to the level of philosophy.[25]

Kant, in *Metaphysical Foundations of Natural Science* (1786), sketched a dynamic theory of matter as an alternative to the Cartesian doctrine that extension is the fundamental characteristic of matter. The essence of matter, Kant argued, consists of moving force (*bewegende Kraft*), not extension, because the occupation of space must be explained by something more basic, the moving force to repel another motion impinging on a space. Matter, although appearing to be solid and impenetrable, in fact derives from the opposition between an attractive force and a repulsive force. Kant argued that there are only two forces, which express themselves in motion, which can be represented as a line between two points. Attractive force strives to diminish its space and repulsive force strives to expand its space. If matter consisted only of an attractive force, Kant reasoned, it would shrink to a mere point; if it expanded only, it would disperse to infinity. Kant held that material bodies arise from the union of these forces and they exist only as a balance between attractive and repulsive forces: "That property upon which as a condition even the inner possibility of a thing rests is an essential element of its inner possibility. Therefore, repulsive force belongs just as much to the essence of matter as attractive force; and one cannot be separated from the other in the concept of matter."[26]

Schelling seized on this theory of matter, as did others in the late 1790s who applied
Kant's concept to chemistry: A. C. A. Eschenmayer, C. F. Kielmeyer, H. F. Link, and
A. N. Scherer. All favored Kant's dynamic metaphysical concept over the Newtonian,
atomistic, mathematical approach that treated matter as something independent of
force. Contending on *philosophical* grounds that matter consists essentially of attractive
and repulsive forces, Schelling made arguments against mechanistic explanations of the
gravitational attraction of matter, the qualitative chemical determination of matter,
and chemical process. He allowed that some qualities of matter arise when the
equilibrium between attraction and repulsion is upset and one force predominates;
otherwise the two forces would cancel each other out. But always there is a push and pull
of basic forces, he argued; all quality of matter rests "wholly and solely" on the intensity
of these opposing interactions. Schelling's theory of heat rejected mechanical and
kinetic explanations; his theory of light allowed for a special "light-stuff" or substance,
but insisted that light is "the highest degree known to us of the expansive force." Like
all Romantics he was especially taken with electricity, describing positive electricity
as resulting from the elasticity of matter and negative electricity as resulting from its
cohesion. Above all, he stressed that the polarity of basic forces in nature could not
be explained by empirical science; to explain the essential construction of matter, one
was obliged "to ascend to philosophical axioms."[27]

Schelling got as much out of Kant as he could, without resorting to Romantic
variations on Kant's third *Critique*. His fully orbed philosophy of nature, however,
rested on transcendental claims about the basic polarities of nature. Three-fourths
of the way into *Ideas for a Philosophy of Nature,* he finally said it explicitly. Since the
principles of attraction and repulsion precede anything that one might claim about
things of experience, he wrote, "we must surmise from the outset that their origin is to
be sought among the conditions of human knowledge as such, and to that extent our
inquiry will be a *transcendental discussion* of the concept of a matter in general."
Having admitted that much, he had two choices. One was to restrict himself to scientific
analysis, showing that matter occupies space within certain bounds, that force might
be a condition for the possibility of matter, which also occupies space, and that another
force opposed to the first one sets spatial limits to the interactions of forces. But that
approach, Schelling objected, erased the necessity of the concept of matter by resolving
it into its component parts: "It is safer, therefore, to allow the concept to arise, as it
were, before our eyes, and thus to find the ground of its necessity in its own origins.
This is the synthetic procedure."[28]

This was the Fichtean procedure, even if Fichte dealt inadequately with nature and
did not think through the status of the unconditioned in the act of self-positing.
Schelling called this unconditioned totality the "Absolute I"; later he called it simply,
"Being." He made no apology for employing the Kantian/Fichtean transcendental
deduction beyond Kant's boundaries, for he believed that Kant's distinction between
form and matter and the dogmatic postulate it engendered – the thing in itself – were
hopelessly mistaken. The idea of a thing in itself, being excluded from space and time,
floats between something and nothing, Schelling observed; it lacks even "the virtue of
being absolutely nothing." Schelling shook his head that Kant labored to such a
ridiculous solution: "It is, in fact, scarcely credible that such a nonsensical conglom-
eration of things, which, bereft of all sensible characteristics, are nevertheless supposed

to function as sensible things, should ever have come into anybody's head." In the second edition Schelling added that the idea of things-in-themselves came down to Kant through the philosophical tradition "and had lost all meaning in the course of inheritance." The postulated things in themselves do not cause representations in us, so what good are they?[29]

Schelling's alternative posited a mind containing empty *a priori* forms. The only thing left for me to understand, if everything belonging to the presentation of an objective world is eliminated before we begin, is myself. All ideas of an external world must develop out of me, each of us. When we represent things, we represent them in the empty *a priori* forms. The formless objects acquire structure and the forms acquire content. We cannot know how these things come to be represented, Schelling cautioned, but at least the forms are truly empty in the representation, allowing us to represent things as being external to us. Only in the representation do we carry over the concepts of space and time, plus those of substance, being, causality, and the like. Our ideas arise in a necessary succession, "and this self-made succession, first brought forth in consciousness, is called the course of Nature."[30]

Nature begins in a primordial unity containing a primordial opposition (*Ur-Gegensatz*) within itself, Schelling argued. It divides into three potencies (*Potenzen*), a term that he borrowed from the theory of powers in mathematics. The primordial point of union is the Absolute, the Parmenidean One. Duality arises within the Absolute as a "self-division of the undivided absoluteness into subject and object," polarities that must be unified while preserving their difference. Matter, Schelling stressed, is like everything else that exists. Streaming out from the eternal essence, it "represents in appearance an effect, albeit indirect and mediate only, of the eternal dichotomizing into subject and object, and of the fashioning of its infinite unity into finitude and multiplicity." As such, matter is nothing less than the real aspect of absolute knowing, at one with Nature, "wherein the mind of God, in eternal fashion, works infinitude into finitude." Schelling's doctrine of potencies pictured a hierarchy of necessary structures that facilitate this process of unification with difference. The first potency, relative identity, powers the transition of unity into difference; the second potency, relative difference, powers the opposing and complementary movement of difference into unity; the third potency, absolute identity, achieves the identity of identity and difference by encompassing the first two potencies. The third potency, however, is the primary one, Schelling contended. The other potencies emerge from the potency of absolute identity only after the primordial Absolute has self-divided into subject and object.[31]

Schelling's favorite example of polar unity was the magnet, which has positive and negative poles that are not self-subsistent. The poles exist only by being united within the whole magnet, and each can exist only by being united with its opposite. He shook his head that so many critics actually believed in dead matter atomism: "In the *dead object* everything is *at rest* – there is in it no conflict, but eternal equilibrium." Conflict, division, and powers of mind are essential to life, he urged: "In the *mental being* there is an *original* conflict of opposed activities, and from this conflict there first proceeds – (a creation out of nothing) – a real world." *Ideas for a Philosophy of Nature* was a prolegomenon to a system, with a cheeky attitude, pushing Fichte's theme that philosophy was the most important discipline. Chemistry teaches us to read letters, physics teaches us to read syllables, and mathematics teaches us to read Nature, Schelling explained; philosophy teaches us how to interpret what is read.[32]

That was the ambitious goal of his system, which conceived two parallel sciences, philosohy of nature (*Naturphilosophie*) and science of knowledge (*Wissenschaftslehre*), as complementary subdivisions of a "System of Identity" or absolute idealism. In the *System of Transcendental Idealism* Schelling proposed to "enlarge transcendental idealism into what it really should be, namely a system of all knowledge." *Naturphilosophie* tracked the determination of the conscious by the unconscious, deriving mind from nature; *Wissenschaftslehre* tracked the determination of the unconscious by the conscious, deriving nature from mind. Both series are endless, Schelling reasoned, for thought and being form a unity. Reason is realized only at infinity. The highest realization of reason occurs in art, because in aesthetic experience the identity between the subjective and objective becomes an object to the experiencing I. Schelling explained that the work of art reflects "to me what is otherwise not reflected by anything, namely that absolutely identical which has already divided itself even in the self. Hence, that which the philosopher allows to be divided even in the primary act of consciousness, and which would otherwise be inaccessible to any intuition, comes, through the miracle of art, to be radiated back from the products thereof."[33]

Schelling's general proof of the ideality of knowledge – the immediate inference from "I am" – was still straight out of Fichte, though he stressed that the point of a system of transcendental idealism was to show that there is also a factual proof – the very process of deducing the entire system of knowledge from its ideality. To that end he developed a dialectic of idealism and realism. Idealism is the claim that the self's boundary is posited solely by the self, he reasoned, and realism is the claim that the boundary is independent of the self. This polarity is like the others, something mutually determined by negation that leads to a synthesis, which is suggested by the very name, transcendental idealism. Theoretical philosophy explains the ideality of the boundary, in which the limitations on pure reason yield knowledge; practical philosophy explains the reality of the boundary, in which the limitations on practical reason yield objectivity. Transcendental idealism is not some purest form of idealism that screens out the material world, Schelling insisted; to the contrary, it is the type in which idealism and realism mutually presuppose each other, as do theoretical and practical philosophy. There are no given definite sensory inputs, yet the world puts rational constraints on our creativity. Reaching for a meaning-of-it-all statement, Schelling enthused that the highest goal of Nature is to become "wholly an object to herself." This goal is achieved only through human reason, where nature returns to itself and by which "it becomes apparent that nature is identical from the first with what we recognize in ourselves as the intelligent and the conscious."[34]

Despite its systematic form, *System of Transcendental Idealism* turned out to be another transitionary work for Schelling. Gradually he let go of Fichte's dialectical positing by a one-sided moment of its opposite; increasingly he conceived duality as a division within a fundamental neo-Platonic unity. Books kept pouring out of him, always announcing some key change of position. Many scientists scorned Schelling's philosophy of their field, which spurred him to keep writing. By 1805 only Fichte rivaled him as a living force in German philosophy. During these years of fame and influence, Schelling had one defender who understood him better than anyone else and who impressed on the public that Schelling was not merely an exponent of Fichte's system; Schelling had his own standpoint, a better form of idealism. That defender was Hegel. In October 1801, bidding farewell to Fichte, Schelling warned that his defender was about to strike: "Today a book appeared by a very superior head, which has as its title *The Difference between the Fichtean and Schellingian Systems of Philosophy.* I had no part in it, but I also could not prevent it." For a while, Schelling got to crow that one of the smartest post-Kantians was his disciple.[35]

Concept and Intuition: Hegel, Schelling, Kant, and Jena

In November 1800 Hegel wrote a painfully awkward letter to Schelling begging for his help without quite asking for what he wanted. Hegel was virtually unpublished. His father had died the previous year, leaving Hegel just enough inheritance to break from tutoring for a while. It gnawed at Hegel that he might have little talent for poetry or public intellectualism. Hölderlin's love life and his precarious emotional health were unraveling, which had caused him to leave Frankfurt, leaving Hegel stranded. Hegel couldn't help contrasting this situation to that of his friend in Jena. He told Schelling: "I have watched your great public career with admiration and joy; you leave me the choice of either speaking humbly of it or wanting to display myself before you as well. I avail myself of the middle term: I hope we rediscover each other as friends." Hegel wanted to move to Jena to devote himself "to works and studies already begun." In the meantime, "before daring to entrust myself to the literary revel of Jena," he thought that he might work up to it by spending some time in Bamberg. Did Schelling know where he might live there? Hegel ended with a vulnerable flattery pitch: "Of all the men I see around me, only in you do I see someone whom I should like to find as my friend with respect to both expression and impact on the world; for I see that you have grasped man purely, i.e., with all your heart and without vanity." He hoped that Schelling would "find merit" in his own "lower" attempts to accomplish something.[36]

Schelling replied exactly as Hegel hoped, telling him to forget Bamberg and come live with him in Jena, which Hegel did the following January. In Jena he had a chance to become an academic and to join the literary revelers that made German Romanticism famous: Schelling, Friedrich and Dorothea Schlegel, August and Caroline Schlegel, J. C. Friedrich Schiller, Novalis, and Ludwig Tieck, plus lesser luminaries that had followed Fichte to Jena. Schiller had his own magazine, *Die Horen,* as did the Schlegel brothers, *Athenäum.*[37]

Moving to Jena was the turning point of Hegel's life, despite the fact Jena's heyday ended just as he got there, in the wake of Fichte's departure, and nearly all German universities were in a state of crisis, which exacerbated Hegel's prolonged struggle to win a regular academic position. By the turn of the nineteenth century the universities were widely viewed as antiquated institutions teaching useless knowledge. Goethe, in *Faust,* mocked the princes for keeping alive too many useless universities. Afterwards, the Napoleonic shock put more than half of them (twenty-two) out of business, just as Hegel pined for a professorship. Göttingen, founded by Hannover princes in 1737, was a rare exception to the crisis. It flourished by attracting students from the nobility and by demoting theology to subordinate status, which diminished the sectarianism that usually plagued German universities. Ironically, this policy turned out to be good for Göttingen's contribution to theology, as it became the leading force in biblical criticism. At Jena, once his inheritance ran out, Hegel had to scratch out a living by competing for student fees as an unpaid lecturer, and he had to write something before he had any chance of winning students. In the early going, he was saved by his association with Schelling, who made him a co-editor of Schelling's journal, *Critical Journal of Philosophy,* and who was the principal subject of Hegel's first philosophical work, *The Difference between Fichte's and Schelling's Systems of Philosophy.*[38]

At the time Schelling's books were pouring out too fast for readers to keep up, and he was widely viewed, even at Jena, as a disciple of Fichte. Hegel observed, "In those few public utterances in which a feeling for the difference between Fichte's and Schelling's systems of philosophy can be recognized, the aim seems to be more to hide their distinctness or to get around it than to gain a clear awareness of it." Hegel surprised readers by informing them that there were fundamental differences between Fichte and Schelling as to what post-Kantian idealism should be about. In Hegel's telling, Reinhold interpreted Kant principally as a theorist of consciousness, and Fichte took this approach a step further. Both remained deeply Kantian by retaining Kant's dichotomy between conceptual forms and intuited nonconceptual content. For Reinhold and Fichte, Hegel explained, the goal of post-Kantian idealism was to get clearer about the transcendental condition for the experience of objects, and neither philosopher made much of Kant's suggestions about intuitive intellection in the third *Critique.* Fichte, searching for the transcendental first principle, found it in the "I," which posited everything that was not-I. His subjective idealism was simply the flip side of realism, positing the subjective as the "real ground of the objective."[39]

Hegel argued that Kant's discussion of the conflicted nature of consciousness pointed to a better answer than subjective anti-realism. When we see ourselves objectively, Hegel observed, we view ourselves from the outside as bodies in space and time. When we see ourselves subjectively, we view ourselves as free subjects holding a point of view *on* the world around us. The battle between realism and idealism "is in consciousness, and the reality of the objective, just as much as that of the subjective is founded in consciousness." Instead of searching for a first principle that resolves the debate over realism versus idealism, Hegel argued, it is better to show, as Schelling did, that both perspectives are implicated in something that precedes and fuels the terms of each perspective. Schelling called it the absolute; Hegel called it reason: "Reason comes to know itself and deals only with itself so that its whole work and activity are grounded in itself."[40]

Contrasting the faculties of reason and understanding, Hegel described the understanding as a faculty *conditioned* by the world, whereas reason weaves the conditioned findings of the understanding into an unconditioned blend of subjectivity and objectivity. The understanding is finite, it is bounded by things outside itself, and it works on things given to it. Reason, by contrast, is infinite and self-bounding, it works on materials that it gives itself, and it aims at a grasp of the unconditioned whole that resolves the conflicts within the understanding. Hegel rattled off a list of dualisms: "Spirit and matter, soul and body, faith and intellect, freedom and necessity." These dualisms did not plague the modern consciousness, he claimed, but they were supplanted in modern philosophy by the subjectivity versus objectivity debate. Idealist anti-materialism was not the solution to this problem; Reinhold and Fichte embarrassed good idealists by rejecting materialism. Schelling, in Hegel's construal, took the better option by contending that idealist and realist accounts are both necessary in accounting for conscious life. As for how the opposition between subjectivity and objectivity in one consciousness should be understood, Hegel pointed to the shared intuitive awareness in subjective and objective activity. The dipolar structure of Schelling's system was founded on the unity of the intuition of the absolute, Hegel observed. Fichte and Schelling had the same Absolute, but for Fichte, the Absolute was subjective "in the form of cognition," whereas for Schelling, the Absolute was "objective in the form of being." On the things that mattered most in modern philosophy, Schelling showed the way.[41]

This robust defense of Schelling's system and importance put Schelling in a somewhat awkward position, as Hegel defended him in Hegelian fashion, not in Schelling's concepts. It was Hegel, not Schelling, who believed that Kant's concept of intuitive intellection contained the key to resolving the dualisms that Kant bequeathed to philosophy. Hegel's *Difference* book, however, sealed a professional bond between the two friends, boosting Schelling's reputation and enhancing that of the journal they co-edited. It introduced Hegel as a thinker who was dependent on Schelling, an identity that Schelling continued to assume long after it was true. And it showed off Hegel's new writing style, which resembled Kant's in formality and abstraction. Hegel's early writings had a free-flowing breeziness, reflecting his desire to communicate with broad educated audiences. But he was unknown and virtually unpublished when he opted for the academy, technical philosophy, and a forbidding style.

In an article on faith and knowledge in Kantian and post-Kantian idealism, which he wrote for Schelling's journal, Hegel escalated his formality and obscure vocabulary to full Hegelian mode, lining up Kant, Jacobi, and Fichte on the wrong side of the Enlightenment divide over faith and reason, and only Schelling and himself on the right side. Instead of contrasting Kant and Fichte as in the *Difference* book, Hegel contended that on the relation of faith and knowledge, Kant, Jacobi, and Fichte espoused variations on the same Enlightenment "culture (*Kultur*) of reflection," which was merely "the culture of the ordinary human understanding." Kant subjected faith to the criteria of autonomous reason, Jacobi held out for the immediate certainty of religious knowledge through faith, and Fichte completed the reconciliation of finite reason with religious faith that was implicit in Kant's idealism. These thinkers made a lot of noise battling over their differences, Hegel observed. But the differences were minor compared to the defective cultural predisposition that they shared. All three set Enlightenment rationality against faith before attempting to save a role or home for religious faith. Thus, all of them lost reason's ground in the self-manifestation of the absolute.[42]

The Enlightenment culture of reflection went back to Locke and Hume, who tried to explain the world "from the standpoint of the subject," Hegel argued. Modern philosophy was always a battle about the relation of subject and object, theorizing about how the mind operates on bits of data to produce an experienced world. Kant pictured the mind intuiting unknown things-in-themselves; Fichte widened the chasm between subject and object; and Jacobi took the chasm for granted in urging readers that they knew things immediately if they had faith in God. Hegel warned that all three options led straight to psychological idealism. If the transcendental self puts the relations of causality onto givens, it is a short step to the view that human subjects project the categories onto experience, constructing the world. Hegel amplified his argument from the *Difference* book, however, that the later Kant glimpsed the way beyond his dualism of concept and intuition in judging that there are no unsynthesized intuitions of which human subjects can be conscious. Nothing in experience is immediately given to consciousness. Concepts and intuitions are both moments within consciousness, not independent elements that must be synthesized somehow to produce consciousness. In the third *Critique* Kant argued that the synthetic unity of consciousness is underived from anything else and forms the basis of everything within consciousness. Hegel asserted, "The original synthetic unity must be conceived, not as produced out of opposites, but as a truly necessary, absolute, original identity of opposites." Concepts and intuitions have an absolute and original identity in self-consciousness.[43]

This Kantian basis of Hegel's position was hard to see in Kant, Hegel acknowledged, because Kant's first *Critique* made an elaborate case for dualism. Instead of conceiving the mind as having moments within an organic unity, playing up the unity of experience, Kant developed an intricate schema of rules in which the productive imagination applied categories to objects of sense. Hegel would have spared Kant and his readers Kant's torturous attempts to apply the pure concepts of the scheme to empirical intuitions, as even Kant admitted that the mind's application of the rules "is an art concealed in the depths of the human soul, whose real modes of activity nature is hardly likely ever to allow us to discover, and to have open to our gaze." In the first *Critique* Kant conceived the productive imagination as an intermediary mechanism. Hegel countered that if one got rid of Kant's idea that concept and intuition are separate faculties, the productive imagination could be better conceived as the original unity itself of concept and intuition: "This power of imagination is the original two-sided identity. The identity becomes subject in general on one side and object on the other; but originally it is both." In that case, imagination is best understood as reason itself, Hegel argued. Creativity is at work from the beginning of experience, because we take up experience in imaginative spontaneity; we do not merely receive it as given.[44]

Kant's regulative idea in the third *Critique* of an intuitive intellect, "a cognitive power different from and wholly independent of sensibility," provided Hegel's basis to go beyond Kant. Intuitive intellection is the point of identity between nature and freedom. One could say that much on Kant's authority, more or less, Hegel argued, but Kant was wrong about this being a merely regulative idea. Even Kant didn't carry through on this claim when he described experiences of the beautiful as being intrinsically normative. When Kant described the experience of beauty, Hegel observed, "the opposition between intuition and concept falls away," and so did his claim that he merely applied a formal norm to this experience in a regulative fashion.[45]

The Kantian line (Kant and Fichte) and the reaction against it (Jacobi) both recast "the dogmatism of being into the dogmatism of thinking," Hegel declared. Modern philosophy, thinking itself clever, had merely replaced the old metaphysic of objectivity with a metaphysic of subjectivity. The language of inwardness was undeniably popular, Hegel allowed; in fact it was "the latest cultural fashion." But Hegel believed that post-Kantian idealism had led to Romantic excesses, and he was increasingly confident that the best form of absolute idealism spurned Romanticism. Thus he lost some of his enthusiasm for *Bildung*, cultivation into the higher culture of Hegel's literary company. If he and Schelling were on the right path, mere cultivation could not be the ideal, even as Schelling held fast to Romanticism. Kantian idealism and Romanticism, Hegel protested, were about transforming the soul as thing into the ego. From Kant to Jacobi to Fichte, the point of the metaphysic of subjectivity was to transform the soul as practical reason "into the absoluteness of the personality and singularity of the subject." Subjective idealism turned the world of things into a system of "affectations of the subject, and actualities believed in." It rendered the absolute Object of reason as something absolutely beyond rational comprehension.[46]

Hegel judged that Fichtean idealism was the logical culmination of Kantian idealism, which brought the cultural process that it rationalized to an end. He could see it happening in the post-Fichte aftermath of Jena. Kant, Fichte, and even Jacobi had something to contribute to the true philosophy that was coming, Hegel assured: "They have their positive, genuine though subordinate, position within true philosophy." For example, they recognized that thinking is infinity, "the negative side of the absolute." Subjective idealists understood that infinity is the negation of finitude *and* "the spring of eternal movement, the spring of that finitude which is infinite because it eternally nullifies itself." The truth, Hegel wrote, warming up to a stunning metaphorical finish, arises out of this nothing, this "pure night of infinity."[47]

True philosophy conceives infinity as the "negative significance of the absolute," qualified by the positive idea that being is nothing apart from thought, the ego, and the infinite. In other words, Hegel contended, it begins with the identity of thought and being. Subjective idealism, by fixing on the infinity of thought, came closer to the truth than the old metaphysics of objectivity, but true philosophy takes the path of absolute idealism. In the past, the idea of an infinite grief existed only as a historical referent in the development of modern culture; it was expressed in the feeling, "God himself is dead." Hegel argued that philosophy needed to reestablish "the idea of absolute freedom and along with it the absolute passion, the speculative Good Friday in place of the historical Good Friday." Twenty years later, as Hegel lectured on religion and a school of theologians gathered around him, he wished he had not spoken of *replacing* the historical Good Friday. The point, however, was in his next sentence: "Good Friday must be speculatively re-established in the whole truth and harshness of its God-forsakenness." Any idealism that fixed on ideals extricated from tragedy, suffering, brokenness, and Godforsakenness was not saving. For Hegel, absolute idealism was the one philosophy that dealt with everything.[48]

Hegel employed Schelling's theory of potencies to account for the development of self-consciousness, moving from lower to higher levels, and he used Schelling's example of the magnet to illustrate dialectical relationality. From the beginning of his teaching career his industry and gregarious personality helped him attract students; throughout his life Hegel struck some acquaintances as dour, arrogant, and self-absorbed and others as lively, sparkling, sociable, and generous. He switched on and off, depending on the company and situation, though students consistently attested that he was eager to help them whenever asked. Hegel's lecture fees and his editorial work on Schelling's journal helped him get by until his inheritance ran out and Schelling traded Jena for Würzburg in 1803, fleeing a marital scandal.

Schelling's scandal occurred as a consequence of falling in love with Caroline Schlegel, an adventurous woman twelve years older than Schelling, who was married at the time to the esteemed Romantic critic and poet August Schlegel. Caroline, the intellectually brilliant daughter of a Göttingen theologian, widowed in her twenties, had joined the Mainz Jacobins when Mainz was part of revolutionary France. An affair with a French officer led to a pregnancy, after which she was jailed when the Germans recaptured Mainz; she married August Schlegel more or less for protection. Schelling's original involvement was with Caroline's daughter by her first marriage, but the daughter died following an illness, and he began an affair with Caroline, which roiled their Romantic friends, the town, and the university. Some of their friends, never having liked Caroline's independence and intellect, claimed that she killed off her daughter to have Schelling for herself. August Schlegel took it well, trying to sustain various friendships. He granted Carolyn's request for a divorce, defended Schelling, and put down the rumors, but Jena became intolerable for Schelling and Caroline after they married. They moved to Würzburg, a newly organized university currently under Bavarian control, where Catholic bishops and rationalist Protestant theologians attacked Schelling furiously, which heightened his fame. In 1806, after Würzburg was ceded to Austria, Schelling (being a Protestant) had to leave the university, but the Bavarian government compensated him handsomely with a position at the Academy of Sciences, which relieved Schelling of having to teach.[49]

Schelling's departure was eventually liberating for Hegel, but in the early going Hegel barely survived it. He was known only as Schelling's disciple, the former roommate who had come from nowhere to advance Schelling's thought. Now Schelling was gone, the journal was terminated, Hegel's inheritance was nearly spent, and he failed to publish anything significant after the journal shut down. In addition, Hölderlin was descending into severe schizophrenia; Schelling, after visiting Hölderlin in 1803, sadly told Hegel that their friend had deteriorated nearly to the point of insanity, neglecting his exterior "to the point of disgust." Hegel replied that Hölderlin was evidently beyond the point "where Jena can have a positive effect on a person." He hoped that Hölderlin still trusted him, but he could not volunteer for caretaking; Hegel was barely able to provide for himself. He desperately needed a salaried position, but had no hope of getting one without publishing a major work. For several years he kept announcing to students, to Goethe, and to potential supporters that his system was forthcoming, except that it wasn't; Hegel wrote long drafts on logic and the philosophy of nature and kept deciding to start over.[50]

Finally in 1806 he started writing a different kind of book, whatever it was. Was it a theory of knowledge? A philosophy of history? A psychology of worldviews? An Odyssey of the world spirit? A coming of age novel? A romantic masquerade? A modern *Divine Comedy*? A religious philosophy? An account of God's death? Was it the introduction to Hegel's system, as he said, or the first part of his system, as he also said? Was it a patchwork lacking any principal of order, as many scholars said, or did it have a systemic coherence on its own and in relation to his subsequent system, as many scholars said? From the beginning readers debated what Hegel's *Phenomenology of Spirit* was about. According to Karl Michelet, Hegel told his students it was "a voyage of discovery." Writing to Schelling, Hegel launched a dramatizing end-of-an-age legend about the book – that he completed it "in the middle of the night before the Battle of Jena." He had two titles for it: *Science of the Experience of Consciousness* and *System of Science, First Part: The Phenomenology of Spirit;* a confused publisher ran both in the book's first edition. Fortunately it came to be known by Hegel's slightly metaphorical sub-title for his astonishing, experimental, hastily written work of genius.[51]

Phenomenology of Spirit: Conception, Consciousness, Self-Consciousness

The Phenomenology of Spirit (1807) contained chapters devoted to philosophical method (the preface), Hegel's method (the introduction), Consciousness, Self-Consciousness, Reason, Spirit, Religion, and Absolute Knowing. But it was structured on the triad of consciousness, self-consciousness, and reason, which required Hegel to organize most of the book under the third category, rendering reason as the culmination of a triad ("C") and as the heading ("AA") for all that followed. The book overflowed with analyses of methodological debates, epistemology, religious beliefs, ethical theory, Greek tragedy, medieval court culture, modern science and pseudo-science, Romanticism, and much more. Hegel declared that prefaces are pointless, even inappropriate, in works of philosophy, which expound universal truth. Then he took off on a 45-page prefatory tour of philosophical method, by far the book's best chapter, which he followed with 10 pages of introduction, the book's original introduction.[52]

The preface was better than the introduction because Hegel had taken his voyage of discovery by the time that he wrote it. The introduction, having been written first, introduced only the book's first three moments – consciousness, self-consciousness, and reason. Hegel pitched his chapters on consciousness and self-consciousness at the same abstract level as Kant's first *Critique,* after which he took a sharp historical turn, giving rise to scholarly debates that are still brewing over how the book as a whole should be understood. Its two very different introductions, and its wobbly structure, have long been clues that somewhere in the Reason chapter, Hegel started writing a different book.

Some scholars, bewildered by the book's sprawling heterogeneity, disjointed transitions, and smartaleck anecdotes tucked into obscure arguments, judged that there is no book as a whole; Hegel's *Phenomenology* is at least two books patched together, or a patchwork of many things lacking any governing idea. Rudolf Haym, in *Hegel und seine Zeit* (1857), offered the classic version of the two-books argument, contending that the *Phenomenology* was a "palimpsest" of two manuscripts overlaying each other without any internal principle of order. According to Haym, the *Phenomenology* was "a romantic masquerade ... a romantic-fantastic confusion of what is the poet's business and what is the philosopher's business," topped off with "absolutely arbitrary" allusions to Sophocles' *Antigone* and other favorites of Hegel's schoolboy years: "To say everything: the *Phenomenology* is psychology reduced to confusion and disorder by history, and history brought to ruin by psychology." Even worse for Hegel's reputation, Haym portrayed Hegel as the official philosopher of the Prussian restoration. In 1934, Theodor Haering added an influential twist to Haym's reading of the *Phenomenology,* arguing that Hegel would have done better to end the book as he originally planned, with the chapter on Reason; as it was, he ruined it with a clumsy second book on the development of historical spirit toward Absolute Knowing.[53]

Otto Pöggeler, in the 1960s, despite rejecting Haering's philological evidence, gave new life to the two-books argument. Pöggeler contended that when Hegel got to the chapter on Reason, he realized that he was no longer talking about mere consciousness, the relation of a self to an object. His subject had become a self-relation in relation to an object – a social, temporal, historical, self-transforming subject of experience and action. He had begun with a book that replied to Kant and others about how consciousness relates to objects, but found himself writing about the social relation of spirit to itself. By the time that he got to the Reason chapter, Pöggeler explained, Hegel's "science of the experience of consciousness" was over, because his subject had become Spirit, something that determines collectively *for itself* its relation to others and objects. He found his true subject in mid-stream. So instead of moving from Reason to Logic, as he had planned, Hegel relegated logic to a separate work, developed a philosophy of Spirit, kept the parts he had already written, and covered up with a second-thoughts preface and title.[54]

This ingenious interpretation explained for many, and still does to some, why the *Phenomenology* felt like two books. In the 1970s Walter Kaufmann revived an older impression more prosaically – that the book was a mere patchwork lacking any organizing principle. Haym got a lot of things right, Kaufmann judged, but the *Phenomenology* was not two books stitched together. It was more like a grab-bag of charades, "now a tableau, now a skit, now a brief oration." Kaufmann distinguished between the book's conception and its execution. Conceptually, he judged, the book had few rivals for brilliance, ambition, and originality; Plato's *Republic* and Dante's *Divine Comedy* are comparable. Kaufmann had not come to bury Hegel; in fact, he tore apart Karl Popper's influential portrait of Hegel as an enemy of the "open society," showing that Popper's attack on Hegel in *The Open Society and Its Enemies* was a sophomoric travesty of Hegel's thought. But Hegel's *Phenomenology,* for all its genius, had sophomoric tendencies too: "One really has to put on blinders and immerse oneself in carefully selected microscopic details to avoid the discovery that the *Phenomenology* is in fact an utterly unscientific and unrigorous work." In execution, the book was a brilliantly self-indulgent mess; Kaufmann found it incredible that so many Hegelians and others considered it a masterpiece, as it was really "a loose series of imaginative and suggestive reflections on the life of the spirit."[55]

For much of the twentieth century the patchwork interpretation was reinforced, inadvertently, by the biggest names in the field of Hegel interpretation, who fastened on one aspect of the book, its dialectic of lordship and bondage. Alexander Kojève, in the 1930s, launched the French neo-Marxist interpretation of Hegel in his lectures at the *Ecole des Hautes Etudes.* Kojève taught a generation of scholars to read the entire *Phenomenology* as a proto-Marxist critique of oppression – a philosophical anthropology demonstrating that human beings are self-made and historical without remainder. Like most of his protégés, Kojève took no interest in Hegel's other works. For two generations the neo-Marxist readings of Hegel's *Phenomenology* by Kojève, Georg Lukács, Herbert Marcuse, and others dominated the field, competing with Popper's diatribe after World War II. Jean Hyppolite's detailed commentary, *Genesis and Structure of Hegel's Phenomenology of Spirit,* provided a scholarly foundation for this reading, which pressed hard on the parts of Hegel's analysis that were congenial to Marxism and dropped the others.[56]

The trend in recent Hegel scholarship is decidedly against the no-coherence view, although scholars understand Hegel so differently that it stays in play by default. Moreover, it is possible to judge that Hegel changed course in the Reason chapter without failing to deliver a coherent argument. Terry Pinkard treats the book's first part as the propaedeutic to the historical section. Michael N. Forster, amplifying Lukács' historicist reading, contends that the *Phenomenology* is thoroughly historicist without exception, even in its Kantian-like chapters on consciousness and self-consciousness. Tom Rockmore, Robert Stern, and Robert D. Winfield maintain that the book is thoroughly epistemological, using historical descriptions merely to illustrate its logical arguments. Klaus Hartmann, another advocate of the epistemological view, contends that Hegel eschewed metaphysics, developing a hermeneutic of categories. Quentin Lauer holds that Hegel sought to affirm, on modern philosophical terms, the Christian God as the Supreme Being, infinite Spirit, and absolute Reality. Cyril J. O'Regan contends that Hegel's driving concern was religious and heterodox, while Alan M. Olson, steering between claims about orthodoxy and heterodoxy, argues that Hegel developed a speculative pneumatology of Absolute and Free Spirit. Dieter Henrich contends that the *Phenomenology* is integrally founded on Hegel's correlation between the development of mind and the development of conceptions of the world. Merold Westphal argues that the *Phenomenology* successfully integrates transcendental and socio-historical themes, demonstrating the social history of transcendental subjectivity. Mark C. Taylor argues that the key to the book is the key to Hegel's entire system, the attempt to overcome the unhappy consciousness. Jon Stewart contends that the book is exactly what Hegel said it was, a systematic enterprise with equally necessary chapters that build on each other to defend idealistic monism. Robert Pippin, while stressing that Hegel had problems with transitions and structure, argues that the *Phenomenology* is held together by its driving concern with the collective self-transformations of Spirit. Robert C. Solomon, while holding that the *Phenomenology* is organizationally a mess and that "Hegel was a *horrible* writer," contends that Hegel mixed non-methodological philosophy and historical description in a way that served his purpose, to make a ringing non-Romantic, non-Christian, non-religious affirmation that life is worth living and the world is ultimately meaningful.[57]

Hegel himself, puzzling over what to call his gathering torso, was struck by a remark in Kant's *Metaphysical Foundations of Natural Science*. Kant said that his transcendental inquiry into the *a priori* presuppositions of physics was a "phenomenology" of the transformation of appearances into experience. Hegel judged that his account of the movement of spirit in history was much like Kant's phenomenology of the movement in nature. Thus he dubbed the book a "phenomenology" of the true movement of Spirit in history, not its apparent movement.[58]

Phenomenology of Spirit was an analysis of the development and shapes of Spirit, with a systematic part leading to a historical part that blended both kinds of interpretation of the movement of Spirit's thinking itself. Hegel had an obvious debt to Plato, who constructed the world out of pure abstract universals, and a deeper debt to Aristotle, who taught that the knower and the known have a transparent relationship; in a crucial sense, the thinker and the thinker's thoughts are one. But the *Phenomenology* was brilliantly original in theorizing the emergence of social subjectivity. Hegel rejected empirical, naturalistic, and transcendental understandings of subjectivity.

He named the book perfectly, as it was a philosophical account of the emergence of social subjectivity and the prolegomena to a religious philosophy of Spirit. To some extent he ended up with a different book than the one he had planned – dispensing with the chapter(s) on logic, and emphasizing the collective self-determination of Spirit toward Absolute Knowing.

But that *was* his enterprise throughout the book; the no-unity theories are exaggerated. Always, through all of Hegel's prolix theorizing, story-telling, and seeming digressions, he tried to penetrate behind the views and stories on display to the human reality that they reflected. The book was a theory of knowledge *and* a philosophy of history *and* an introduction to Hegel's system. It asked what kind of spirit was behind and within the subjects that Hegel analyzed. It tracked the yearning of the "unhappy consciousness," trapped in a world of despair and death, for which the real was always somewhere else, for eternity. It was a *phenomenology* of Spirit because Hegel's method was descriptive, allowing the immanent development of the subject matter to disclose itself. Thus he used a notoriously Hegelian phrase to describe it, *die Anstrengung des Begriffs,* the effort of the Concept.

The *Phenomenology* had a long section revolving around Sophocles' *Antigone* and scattered quotations from or allusions to Aristophanes, Democritus, Diderot, Goethe, Lessing, Schiller, Shakespeare, and Socrates. It named only six philosophers directly – Plato, Aristotle, Diogenes, Anaxagoras, Descartes, and Kant – and was sparing even in its references to the two modern philosophers that it named. It was loaded with highbrow literary dazzle and biting put-downs of unnamed philosophers, yet Hegel claimed the mantle of science for it. His project was a science of unfolding self-related Spirit, a self-transforming subject. "The true shape in which truth exists can only be the scientific system of such truth," he declared. Instead of settling for the love of learning, Hegel wanted to *know.* He had Romantic friends, but they would have to swallow his rationalism. Science, on the other hand, tended to settle too easily for empiricist reductionism. Hegel admonished against peering at acorns to the exclusion of oak trees with massive trunks and spreading branches: "So too, Science, the crown of a world of Spirit, is not complete in its beginnings. The onset of the new spirit is the product of a widespread upheaval in various forms of culture, the prize at the end of a complicated, torturous path and of just as variegated and strenuous an effort."[59]

Barely a few pages into the preface, Hegel dissociated himself from Schelling's Parmenidian vision of the absolute as pure self-identity. The currently fashionable idealism rested on a single insight, Hegel observed – "that in the Absolute everything is the same." Against the "full body" of scientific research, this philosophy palmed off its Absolute "as the night in which, as the saying goes, all cows are black." Hegel charged that the new idealism, having begun as a critique of formalism, produced a vacuous formalism of its own. Like Spinoza, it expressed the true totally as substance, presupposing the absolute through an intellectual intuition in which subject and object coincided. Hegel asserted that philosophy needed a better method, one founded on the path of science that grasped the true "not only as *Substance,* but equally as *Subject.*" The living substance is being as subject, he proposed; it is actual "only in so far as it is the movement of positing itself, or is the mediation of its self-othering with itself." Hegel took for granted that philosophy is about the Absolute: "The True is the whole." But the whole, the Absolute, realizes itself only through its development;

its very nature is to be a *result*, "the spontaneous becoming of itself." The Absolute is the "I"s' self-reflection and self-determining activity, a transforming *process*, not a special kind of substance.[60]

Hegel realized that it seemed counter-intuitive to describe the Absolute as a result, a spontaneous becoming toward an end. Words like "the Absolute" and "the Divine," he reasoned, do not express their content, any more than the word "zoology" expresses all animals. All such terms and their use in propositions contain a "becoming-other" that is either mediated or has to be taken back. Hegel's famous definition of mediation was a gloss on the Absolute as self-determining activity: "Mediation is nothing beyond self-moving selfsameness, or is reflection into self, the moment of the 'I' which is for itself pure negativity or, when reduced to its pure abstraction, *simple becoming*." There is no truth without reflection, which is a moment of the Absolute: "It is reflection that makes the True a result, but it is equally reflection that overcomes the antithesis between the process of its becoming and the result, for this becoming is also simple, and therefore not different from the form of the True which shows itself as *simple* in its result."[61]

The process of becoming is a return to simplicity. Hegel observed that the embryo is a human being in itself, but not for itself; it becomes a human being for itself only through the cultivation of reason, which makes itself what it is in itself. Just as Aristotle defined nature as purposive activity, Hegel defined reason as purposive activity, "the unmoved which is also *self-moving,* and as such is Subject." Viewed abstractly, the power of reason to move is "*being-for-self* or pure negativity," which ends at the same place as the beginning because the beginning *is* the purpose. Hegel did not shrink from teleology, though he allowed that externalist forms of it had brought teleological reasoning into disfavor. The actual is the same as its idea in only one sense, he argued: "The immediate, as purpose, contains the self or pure actuality within itself." Existent actualities are unfolded movements of realized purpose; the self *is* the restless unfolded becoming that relates to itself and returns to itself.[62]

Hegel spoiled the book's ending before getting out of the preface. The most sublime notion on earth is that of the Absolute as *Spirit,* he declared. If truth is actual only as system and if substance is essentially subject, "the spiritual alone is the *actual*." Spirit is that which has being in itself, that which relates itself to itself, that which has "other-being" and being-for-self, and that which, in its self-externality, abides within itself. In other words, Hegel explained, Spirit is that which is "*in and for itself*." It is an object to itself and it reflects into itself. At first, he cautioned, the being of Spirit in and for itself is only for human subjects, as spiritual substance: "It is *for itself* only for *us,* insofar as its spiritual content is generated by itself." But insofar as Spirit is its own self for itself, this self-generation is the "objective element" of its existence. Hegel urged that this supremely sublime idea of the Absolute as unfolding Spirit belongs "to the modern age and its religion." It is what modern religion should be about, and modern science, for science is precisely Spirit developed to the point of knowing itself as Spirit.[63]

"It is this coming-to-be of *Science as such* or of *knowledge*, that is described in this *Phenomenology* of Spirit," he announced. Knowledge in its first phase, which Hegel called "immediate Spirit," is non-spiritual; it is mere sense-consciousness, the early stage of awareness at which Kant's theorizing got stuck. Hegel cautioned that single individuals are incomplete Spirits. Even a robustly autonomous rational will is no substitute for social subjectivity. Genuine knowledge is earned only at higher stages of the coming-to-be of Spirit, which are social and spiritual. Hegel scorned short-cuts, notably those that began "straight away with absolute knowledge," ascending to the Absolute with a presupposition or an intuition. There is no substitute for tracing the emergence of Spirit through history, culture, and social process, he admonished: "Since the Substance of the individual, the World-Spirit itself, has had the patience to pass through these shapes over the long passage of time, and to take upon itself the enormous labor of world-history, in which it embodied in each shape as much of its entire content as that shape was capable of holding, and since it could not have attained consciousness of itself by any lesser effort, the individual certainly cannot by the nature of the case comprehend his own substance more easily."[64]

It was a terrible irony of modern philosophy that idealists quickly succumbed to formalisms of their own, Hegel judged. Kant had no answer to the Kantian problem of how pure concepts relate to anything real; he had only "a lifeless schema, a mere shadow" that comprehended almost nothing. Kant imagined that his formalism, which endowed forms with some determination of the schema as a predicate, grasped as much as could be known. Hegel replied caustically that on Kantian grounds predicates such as objectivity, magnetism, contraction or the like could be multiplied to infinity, each could be used as a form for another, and each could "gratefully perform the same service for an other," all without learning much of anything: "In this sort of circle of reciprocity one never learns what the thing itself is, nor what the one or the other is."[65]

Fichte was even worse, "pigeon-holing" everything in heaven and earth from a few determinations of a general schema. Hegel's allusion to Fichte lampooned his *Crystal Clear Report to the General Public Concerning the Actual Essence of the Newest Philosophy: An Attempt to Force the Reader to Understand*, chiding that this "report clear as noonday" should not have been necessary, as its thoughts were terribly simple. Hegel chided that Fichte's universe was "like a skeleton with scraps of paper stuck all over it." All flesh and blood were stripped away, but the scraps were easy to read, so people liked them. It was no coincidence that Fichte's popularity coincided with that of monochromatic painting, Hegel judged. All was submerged into the void of the Absolute, "from which pure identity, formless whiteness, is produced," yielding more monochromatic schemas and lifeless transitions.[66]

The purely epistemological sections of the *Phenomenology* had two crucial moments, the first moment of consciousness, which Hegel called "sense-certainty," and the transitional moment from consciousness to self-consciousness, which he discussed in his section on force and understanding. Sense-certainty, the beginning of the experience of consciousness, lacks any preceding form except for negation. It begins by accepting the bare sensuous content of knowledge by consciousness. Hegel warned against getting in the way; sense-certainty is about apprehension, not comprehension: "In apprehending it, we must refrain from trying to *com*prehend it." Then he proposed to explain it. The entire content of sense-knowledge is the pure fact of immediate being – pure immediacy. But pure immediacy breaks into two "thises," Hegel observed, the "I" and an object. The "I" is a pure individual ego; the object is the immediate content to which the "I" stands in relation. Consciousness, by distinguishing two forms standing in relation to each other, compels them into a mediated relation: "I have this certainty *through* something else, viz., the thing; and it, similarly, is in sense-certainty *through* something else, viz., through the 'I.'"[67]

But only an observer understands that, Hegel cautioned. The sensuous conscious-ness merely apprehends; it moves to a view of the mediated relation only through perception. At first, the sensuous consciousness takes the object to be the essential immediate reality, while the ego seems to be a mediated non-essential reality. Sense-certainty apprehends the object as a "This" with two parts, the Now and the Here, though it cannot identify these forms of the object's existence. The Now apparently exists, but no specific Now of day or night is grasped; it is an entity of negation, a universal. The Now is a not-this in itself, applying to all objects, not something that *is* as an object. Hegel explained, "A simple thing of this kind which *is* through negation, which is neither This nor That, a *not-This*, and is with equal indifference This as well as That – such a thing we call a *universal*." The true content of sense-certainty is the universal. Hegel took two runs at saying that the same thing is true of the Here, though both times he overlooked that the second type is logically not an identical movement. When we write down a truth, he observed, it cannot lose anything by being written down, yet it will become stale over time; as for the Here, it may be a tree, but if I look elsewhere, the truth has vanished, turning into a house. Both times he overlooked that the logic of temporal duration differs from extension. In any case, he stressed that Here, like Now, is universal, being equally applicable to everything. The "this" is a mediated simplicity.[68]

The pure being that consciousness apprehends is the essence of sense-certainty. But it is not immediate, Hegel argued, for negation and mediation are essential to it. Thus it is being as a pure universal, an abstraction. Now the relation of knowing and the object is reversed. For mediated being, the object is no longer the essential element in sense-certainty, for the universal that the object has become is no longer what the object was supposed to be. Now, knowing is the essential element for sense-certainty. Hegel's assumption of certainty by the individual subject smacked of Descartes: "Its truth is in the object as *my* object, or in its being *mine;* it is, because *I* know it." Sense-certainty is driven back into the "I." "Here" is a tree because I see it. Yet the same dialectic acts upon itself in this relationship as in the previous one, Hegel reasoned: "I, *this* 'I,' see the tree and assert that 'Here' is a tree; but another 'I' sees the house and maintains that 'Here' is not a tree but a house instead." Both truths have the same certainty and ground of validation, "but the one truth vanishes in the other."[69]

What remains is the universality of the 'I,' which sees, not a tree or a house, but simply sees, mediated by the negation of this tree or house, and indifferent to whatever happens to it, the tree, or the house. The "I" is universal exactly in the sense that Now, Here, and This in general are universal, Hegel contended: "When I say 'this Here,' 'this Now,' or a 'single term,' I am saying all Thises, Heres, Nows, all single items." Oddly, that still overlooked that the composite nature of Now is based on the movement of time, whereas the Here is not logically transitory in the same way. The demonstration of the Here is not a process; only the analysis of a Here is. Pressing on, Hegel stressed that the "I" is universal and that one cannot deduce or find *a priori* "something called 'this thing' or 'this one man.'" Knowing and the object are both *meant* by conscious-ness. Sense-certainty apprehends through experience that its essence is not in the "I" or the object, and its immediacy is not of one or the other, for in both cases "what I *mean* is rather something unessential, and the object and the 'I' are universals in which that 'Now' and 'Here' and 'I' which I *mean* do not have a continuing being, or *are* not." The upshot was the nub of Hegel's thesis that the truth is the whole: "We have to posit the *whole* of sense-certainty itself as its *essence*, and no longer only one of its moments." Only sense-certainty as a whole holds together as immediacy. The Here and the Now are universals that come to be understood as such by consciousness in the process of trying to demonstrate the particular Here and Now.[70]

The critical moment for Hegel's analysis was the transition from consciousness to self-consciousness. He worked up to it by blasting Kant's thing-in-itself doctrine as superficial. For consciousness, Hegel acknowledged, the inner world is empty, "a pure beyond," because consciousness does not (yet) find itself in it. Kant was right that we have no knowledge of this inner world in its immediacy. But that is not because reason is so limited, Hegel argued; it is because in the void *nothing* is known, or, considered from the other side, it is because the inner world is the *beyond* of consciousness: "We have not yet gone deep enough." Hegel analogized that a blind man placed amid the wealth of the supersensible world and a seeing man placed in pure darkness or pure light see the same nothing. If nothing further happens to our inner world in our connection to the world of appearances, we can only stop at the world of appearances, perceiving something as true even as we know it is not true. In that case, Hegel admonished, we are better off with fanciful imagination than with Kant's emptiness, for even reveries are better than emptiness.[71]

But the inner world comes into being from the world of appearances that mediates its coming to self-consciousness. Appearance is the very essence and content of the inner world, Hegel argued, for inward being is essentially the *truth* of appearance: "The supersensible is the sensuous and the perceived posited as it is *in truth;* but the *truth* of the sensuous and the perceived is to be *appearance*." Kant's supersensible realm, cut off from anything known, is in fact, appearance qua appearance. Hegel did not mean that the supersensible world *is* the sensuous world or even the world as it exists for immediate sense-certainty. In Hegel's conception, the world of appearance is the world of sense-knowledge and perception *posited* as an *inner* world, not as something that positively *is*. The inner world comes into being in-itself, as a universal lacking content, for the understanding. The inner essential is the truth of appearance, which stands in a negative, but not merely negative, relation to appearances. Self-consciousness ultimately arises from what Hegel called the "play of forces" that are immediate for the understanding. Force and its expression are dialectical, involving solicited force (a passive medium) and soliciting force (an active, negative unity). In itself, Hegel reasoned, the play of forces is nothing. It exists positively only as a mediating agency. The inner world becomes connected to the understanding through the mediating play of forces, which is the movement of the understanding through which the inner world fills itself out for the understanding. In other words, the understanding is driven to the principle in all things. The play of forces is immediate for the understanding, but "the True" is the simple inner world.[72]

Consciousness already involves self-consciousness, and self-consciousness is thoroughly mediated and dependent upon structures of reduplicated relation. Self-consciousness is essentially a return from otherness, Hegel argued. In conscious self-certainty, what is true for consciousness is something other than itself, which vanishes in its experience. But in self-consciousness we enter "the native realm of truth." The breakthrough to self-consciousness is a reflective movement in which self-consciousness distinguishes from itself "only itself as itself." Here, otherness appears in the form of a being, as a distinct moment, and in the unity of self-consciousness with itself, which is essential to self-consciousness. For Hegel, self-consciousness *is* desire. The sensuous object of desire is only a means; what self-consciousness ultimately desires is unity of the "I" with itself. Self-consciousness, without yet realizing it fully, desires its own desire. Consciousness becomes aware of itself as self-consciousness by realizing that the other that it contemplates is an internal self-distinction repulsed from its "I." Consciousness of the other, in its first stage, is simply a consciousness of the otherness of self-consciousness. It is consciousness of distinction, the moment of self-consciousness. Hegel argued that for self-consciousness to realize itself completely, becoming self-consciousness in itself, it must realize its universality. It must become Reason, grasping the world as a moment of self-consciousness driven by desire. Until then, only observers know it. Self-consciousness in its early development does not understand its own appearance as the realization of Reason.[73]

Kant taught that in making judgments, we follow the rules spontaneously prescribed for us by the Understanding, which are produced by the requirements of every self-conscious subject's reasoning. Hegel questioned on what authority the Understanding issued its purported rules for a universal self-consciousness. What if our desires are like sensory impressions, acquiring normative significance only because we confer significance on them? To Hegel, Kant's Enlightened ethic of issuing laws to himself was indefensible on its own terms, lacking a credible warrant. In its place Hegel socialized the problem, analyzing the relationship of slave and master as an example of independence and dependence in self-consciousness.

Self-consciousness exists only in being acknowledged, Hegel reasoned; it exists only for another. When self-consciousness encounters another self-consciousness, it comes out of itself, finding itself in an *other* being; moreover, it supersedes the other in doing so. This experience teaches self-consciousness that sociality – which Hegel called simply, life – is as essential to its being as pure self-consciousness. The "I" of immediate self-consciousness exists for itself; its dissolution leads to a consciousness that exists for another; in the beginning these two shapes of consciousness coexist in an unequal union of opposition and dependency. One is the master (*Herr*), whose essential nature is to be for itself; the other is the slave or vassal (*Knecht*), whose essential nature is to live for another. Each is the "negative" of the other, Hegel reasoned, each demands recognition from the other, and each has a need for the other to affirm that the law that one enacts is right. Hegel told an idealized story about the struggle between them. In this story, a struggle to the death ensues between the master and slave. The master prevails because he does not fear death as much as the slave; the slave consents to bondage out of this fear. There are no laws; each experiences the other as making brute demands in a predatory struggle for survival. When the master attains dominance, he becomes the author of the law.[74]

This seems to be a resolution of some kind, though a terrible one for the slave, who trembles "in every fiber of its being." But the master's dominance does not work even for the master, because the slave, as a slave, cannot provide a warrant for the master's authority, and the master's self-consciousness depends on the mere things that he consumes, which he owes to the slave's labor. The master's autonomy depends on the mediation of the slave; he is not a master if the slave does not recognize his authority.

But the master has no reason to believe that the slave has any authority to confer authority on him. In Hegel's telling, the master simply imposes his lawless will on the slave. The slave, on the other hand, by obeying the master's rule, internalizes the idea of a moral right. Through his labor he becomes a reflective agent, learning that there is such a thing as subjecting oneself to an external law. Previously he simply feared for his life; now he masters himself, relying on his self-chosen obedience to the law, and he begins to notice that the world is created by his labor. Seeing himself reflected in the products that he makes, and thus no longer alienated from his labor, the slave achieves self-consciousness, rising above the trivialized, possession-oriented consciousness of the master: "Through this rediscovery of himself by himself, the bondsman realizes that it is precisely in his work wherein he seemed to have only an alienated existence that he acquires a mind of his own."[75]

This brief depiction of the recognition and legitimization of self-consciousness is the most famous section of the *Phenomenology*. It has a rich legacy in Marxist and Socialist conceptions of the class struggle, owing partly to Karl Marx's acknowledgment that Hegel grasped the social determination of the self and the importance of alienated labor in history: "Hegel conceives of the self-creation of man as a process, objectification as loss of the object, as externalization and transcendence of this externalization. This means, therefore, that he grasps the nature of labor and understands objective man, true, because real, man as the result of his own labor." The master-slave trope influenced Friedrich Nietzsche's critique of master-slave morality, Martin Buber's analysis of relationality and the struggle for recognition, Simone de Beauvoir's account of the dynamics of gender relations, and Frantz Fanon's critique of colonial racism. It is a key to Hegel's influence in psychoanalytic, political, structuralist, poststructuralist, postcolonial, critical race, and feminist theory, where Hegel's grounding of right in intersubjective purpose and his insights into psychological and sociological conflict are foundational.[76]

The major theorist of the master-slave trope, Alexandre Kojève, viewed it as the cornerstone of the *Phenomenology* and of Hegel's enduring importance, a reading that was taken over by Jean-Paul Sartre, Hyppolite's canonical commentary on the *Phenomenology,* and two generations of neo-Hegelian Marxists searching for a thicker account of human sociality than Marx's. In Kojève's reading, Hegel taught that human beings are begotten "only in and by the fight that ends in the relation between Master and Slave." In "man's" nascent state, Kojève taught, he is "never simply man," but is always and essentially either master or slave. Human reality comes into being only as a social reality; society is human on the basis of being rooted in the struggle between master and slave; the dialectic of history is fundamentally the dialectic of this relation; and history is realized by fully overcoming it. Kojève contended that Hegel's story is not about the struggle for mutual recognition, for the slave recognizes the master's authority; the master is recognized by someone that he does not recognize. Hegel's story is about the rising of slaves to remake the world. Kojève explained, "The Master is fixed in his Mastery. He cannot go beyond himself, change, progress. He must conquer – and become Master or preserve himself as such – or die. He can be killed; he cannot be transformed, educated." The slave, on the other hand, has no fixed condition. He did not want to be a slave; he became one only because he was afraid of being killed. In his terror he understands, without quite noticing it, that the fixed condition of his Master is not the only possibility: "He is ready for change; in his very being, he is change, transcendence, transformation, 'education'; he is historical becoming at his origin, in his essence, in his very existence."[77]

The Slave alone is able to create a new world of his own making where freedom reigns. Kojève read the rest of the *Phenomenology* as a take-off on this theme, noting parenthetically that he took leave of whatever metaphysical meaning that Hegel had in mind. His reading was anthropological. In this telling, the Slave's first resort, ideologically, was Stoicism, through which he tried to persuade himself that he was actually free by virtue of possessing an abstract idea of freedom. But that didn't work and the Slave opted for Christianity after it came along, becoming a Christian Slave. Here, Kojève allowed, the Slave freed himself, at least in theory, from the human Master; Christianity is obsessed with freedom, of a sort: "But although he no longer has a Master, he does not cease to be a Slave. He is a Slave without a Master, he is a Slave in *himself,* he is the pure essence of Slavery." In Christianity, Kojève explained, the Slave is the equal of the Master only before God: "Thus the Christian frees himself from the human Master only to be enslaved to the divine Master." According to Kojève, Hegel taught that the Christian God reduces the Slave to the most absolute slavery imaginable in exchange for being told that he deserves to be treated as a child of God no less than the old masters. The motive for accepting abasement is the same as before, except this is worse. The storied Slave accepted slavery out of fear of losing his biological life. The Christian Slave accepts slavery as the price of his eternal life: "The fundamental motive of the ideology of the 'two worlds' and the duality of human existence is the slavish desire for life at any price, sublimated in the desire for an *eternal* life. In the final analysis, Christianity is born from the Slave's terror in the face of Nothingness."[78]

Hegelianism, in this telling, is about something antithetical to Christianity – the triumph of freedom. It runs through Christianity in order to abolish it. Kojève put it plainly: "To overcome the insufficiency of the Christian ideology, to become free from the absolute Master and the Beyond, to *realize* Freedom and to *live* in the World as a human being, autonomous and free – all this is possible only on the condition that one accept the idea of death and, consequently, atheism." Everything that Hegel said about the cunning of Reason in history drives toward this conclusion, Kojève assured. By 1806, Hegel accepted that it would be a long process; the French Revolution had disabused him of fast transformations. Thus his historical sections on the development of Spirit in law, morality, culture, and society were essential to his analysis, not mere illustrations. But the goal was to overcome Christianity and realize the French Revolution universally, Kojève claimed: "The whole evolution of the Christian World is nothing but a progress toward the atheistic awareness of the essential finiteness of human existence. Only thus, only by 'overcoming' Christian *theology,* will Man definitively cease to be a Slave and *realize* this idea of Freedom which, while it remained an abstract idea – i.e., an ideal, engendered Christianity."[79]

That may be what Hegel actually thought. Kojève, the most influential Hegel interpreter of the twentieth century, built on a substantial nineteenth-century inter-pretive tradition, left-Hegelianism. More recently, many specialists on Hegel, anxious to legitimize their subject to analytic philosophers and other anti-metaphysical types, have tried to separate Hegel's rational ideas from his religious and metaphysical notions. Usually the rational core consists of his system of categories and post-Kantian transcendentalism, while the embarrassing things to be dispensed with include his Spinozist metaphysics, dialectical logic, *Naturphilosophie,* and religious philosophy. Klaus Hartmann launched a school of interpretation in this vein; other leading theorists of a non-metaphysical Hegel include Terry Pinkard, Alan White, and Robert Pippin. This tradition of interpretation rightly emphasizes Hegel's Kantian basis and his idea of social subjectivity (masterfully by Pippin). Like Kojève, it usually stresses Hegel's fixation with the French Revolution, restoring Hegel's relevance to political thought. The *Phenomenology* had a brief chapter on "Absolute Freedom and Terror," in which Hegel blamed the failure of the Revolution on its claim to realize the principle of freedom immediately, which turned it into an abstraction. Self-consciousness cannot be realized immediately, Hegel urged. It occurs only by alienating itself and developing through opposing itself: "The self-alienated Spirit, driven to the extreme of its antithesis in which pure willing and the agent of that pure willing are still distinct, reduces the antithesis to a transparent form and therein finds itself. Just as the realm of the real world passes over into the realm of faith and insight, so does absolute freedom leave its self-destroying reality and pass over into another land of self-conscious Spirit where, in this unreal world, freedom has the value of truth." Spirit, refreshing itself in the thought of this truth, gives rise to a new shape of Spirit, Hegel reasoned – one to which, he implied, the French Revolution lacked the time and patience to realize. This is the moral Spirit.[80]

But one has to dispense with a great deal of Hegel to get a Hegelianism that holds up to analytic tests of real philosophy and postmodern prohibitions against onto-theology. Hegel without Spinoza, dialectic, the philosophy of nature, and Christianity is not Hegel. The left-Hegelian tradition that launched the non-metaphysical reading had the considerable twofold problem, from its beginning, that Hegel unfailingly called himself a Christian philosopher whose entire philosophical scheme was devoted to explicating the truth of Christianity. Then the Kòjeve school read radical liberationist meanings into Hegel that he never came close to saying. British political philosopher John Plamenatz offered a typically Kojève-Hyppolite version of the master-slave trope: "The future is with the slave. It is his destiny to create the community in which everyone accords recognition to everyone else, the community in which spirit attains its end and achieves satisfaction." Hegel, however, never said that. One can get from Hegel a theory about the necessity of reciprocal relationships for the establishment of healthy self-consciousness, social authority, and decent law, and a remarkably proto-Marxist insight into the dynamics and importance of alienated labor. Beyond that, one has to spin hard to make Hegel sound like Marx, a fact that Marx noted sharply. Many nineteenth-century Hegelians took Hegel's uplift-through-service theme as an apologetic for colonialism; a century later, Hegel's best English translator, A. V. Miller, was still pressing that reading. George Armstrong Kelly aptly argues that Hegel's master-slave trope is best viewed from three angles: The neo-Marxist social view, scaling back on exaggerations; the shifting pattern of individual psychological domination and servitude that Hegel addressed more fully; and the fusion of these two processes, especially the interior consequences of the struggle for recognition.[81]

Kojève, tellingly, described Hegel's transition to self-consciousness as resting on four premises: speech, desire (negating action), the existence of several desires, and a possible differentiation among the desires yielding a winner and a loser. But calling these factors *premises* gave them a necessity for the appearance of desire in consciousness that is not Hegelian. A premise or axiom has an empty necessity. Kojève, fixated on making the master-slave dialectic the linchpin of the *Phenomenology*, overlooked that Hegel's point was to describe the transition from understanding to self-consciousness.[82]

Self-consciousness is the overcoming of an object of perception, which Hegel called the process of desire. We negate the apple that we perceive by consuming it, distinguishing an object that exists for itself, which breaks us into self-consciousness. Self-consciousness depends on negating something on which it depends, and it finds satisfaction only in relating to another self-consciousness. The undifferentiated "I" begins as its immediate object. The "I"s' immediacy is broken by desire and satisfied by the reflection of self-consciousness into itself. The satisfaction is real only as a "double reflection," the duplication of self-consciousness. Hegel remarked, "Consciousness has for its object one which, of its own self, posits its otherness or difference as a nothingness, and in so doing is independent." A self-consciousness is as much "I" as object, he stressed. Every self-consciousness exists only for another self-consciousness, for self-consciousness *is* desire, the desire for unity of the "I" with itself.[83]

Structurally, with the emergence of reason, Hegel began the final third of the *Phenomenology*. But reason becoming Spirit took him through the history of the world and of worldviews – a larger topic needing a vaster canvass in which natural religion, art-religion, and revealed religion played crucial mediating roles in the self-realization of Spirit.

Spirit, Absolute Religion, Absolute Knowing

"Reason is Spirit when its certainty of being all reality has been raised to truth, and it is conscious of itself as its own world, and of the world as itself." That is, Hegel argued, reason becomes Spirit when it realizes itself as being all reality. Spirit is the substance and universal, self-identical essence of all that is, "the in-itself of every self-consciousness expressed in thought." Hegel heightened the ethical note, assuring that as substance, Spirit is "unshaken righteous self-identity." In its early stages of development, Spirit shows its ethical character in the laws and customs of society – Spirit *having* reason. When Spirit sees itself and its world *becoming* reason, it becomes ethical substance actualized. As being-for-itself, Spirit is "a fragmented being, self-sacrificing and benevolent," in which all beings have a role. The ethical world, a world "rent asunder into this world and a beyond," is Spirit in its truth. On the one hand, Spirit insinuates itself into the "harsh reality" of cultural process; on the other hand, it is present in the inner reality of faith and insight. The conflict between these two modes of experience is resolved in Spirit coming into its truth – morality.[84]

But Hegel shared Schleiermacher's minimal regard for moral faith, a poor substitute for the Spirit of the Whole that knows itself in consciousness, self-consciousness, reason, and spirit. Science, in pursuing the supersensible inner essence of consciousness, pursues the Absolute, but far short of knowing it as Spirit. The "unhappy consciousness" of self-consciousness shows the pain of the Spirit wrestling in a world of sorrows to know itself, but the unity of the individual self-consciousness and its changeless essence remain "a beyond" for self-consciousness. Reason, struggling with the pain, still lacks religion, exhausting itself in the immediate struggle; thus it misses the Absolute. The ethical conscience, Spirit coming into its truth, finally yields religion, which breaks in two directions. One is the belief in a terrible, unknown night of fate, which is pure negativity in the form of universality. The other believes in a realm of departed spirits, which is the same negativity in the form of individuality. This religious negativity – its belief in the nothingness of necessity – combined with the underworld, becomes belief in heaven, Hegel explained. Even the Enlightenment, by reinstating the supersensible beyond of the understanding, still had a religious belief in heaven. But Enlightenment religion was wholly content with this world; thus it did not mind that its Absolute was empty.[85]

In religion, Hegel taught, Spirit becomes self-conscious. First it becomes self-conscious as immediate Spirit. The moments of the whole – consciousness, self-consciousness, reason, and immediate Spirit – though never existing in separation from one another, are realized only in succession. The Spirit of religion – the totality of Spirit – moves away from its immediacy toward the realization of what it is in itself. Thus it assumes specific *shapes* constituting the different moments of this movement. Each religion, selecting from the shapes that belong to each of its moments, picks out the one that fits its actual Spirit.[86]

Hegel took a brisk tour of the "natural religions" of Persia, India, and Egypt. Persian religion worships the God of light, Spirit knowing itself in the form of a concept, a dark night of essence opposed to its daylight forms. The shape of Persian religion is actually shapeless, Hegel judged, the all-pervading light of sunrise. In Indian religion, self-conscious Spirit withdraws from the shapeless essence into independent forms, from the innocent pantheism of flower religion to the predatory religion of animal spirits. The Spirit becomes an artificer in Indian religion, mediating the battle of spirits, as it does in Egyptian religion, which Hegel found more interesting than Indian religion. In Egypt, he explained, the Spirit pours itself into its products instinctively, like bees building a honeycomb. The first works of the Spirit, the pyramids and obelisks, are products of the abstract understanding – straight lines with plane surfaces and equal proportions, eschewing the incommensurability of roundness. Later the Spirit takes up better representations of itself, picturing the soul as clothed by bodies, or as dwelling in organic nature. Still later the Spirit becomes an artist, creating products in which its self-consciousness shows through: "In this unity of self-conscious Spirit with itself, in so far as it is the shape and the object of its consciousness, its blendings with the unconscious shapes are purged of the immediate shapes of Nature. These monsters in shape, word, and deed are dissolved into spiritual shape; into an outer that has retreated into itself, and an inner that utters or expresses itself out of itself and in its own self; into thought which begets itself, which preserves its shape in harmony with itself and is a lucid, intelligible existence."[87]

That led to a religion of art, in which the Greeks specialized. Hegel dwelt lovingly, as always, on the Greek story, where Spirit no longer mixed thought and the natural incongruously. In the religion of art, he explained, Spirit puts itself into shapes of ethical self-conscious Spirit. It wants only to express itself, eschewing color, custom, and the substantial. Typically it produces an idealized human form, cut from black stone and pervaded by "the light of consciousness," in which only the surface of the form retains its animal covering: "The human form strips off the animal shape with which it was blended; the animal is for the god merely an accidental guise; it steps down alongside its true shape and no longer has any worth on its own account, but is reduced to signifying something else and has sunk to the level of a mere symbol." The artist's own struggling individuality is missing – "He could impart perfection to his work only by emptying himself of his particularity," which leads to disappointment. These artists were emphatically male, as Hegel never had an intellectual relationship with a woman. Even if others admired the artist's work, the artist realized that something in *him* was superior to what he had made.[88]

The work of art demands a higher mode of expression, which it finds in language – self-conscious existence in its immediacy. Hegel contrasted hymnody, especially, with the thing-like character of the statue, which stands outside the artist. The hymn enters the inner life of the self and vanishes. It is present in the moment of its being present and is shared as Spirit meeting Spirit, expressing a common, communal, social, yet inward reality. Art-religion and the national spirit go together, Hegel emphasized. Art-religion lacks the abstract simplicity and depth of the religion of light; thus it does not subordinate the national spirit to the self-consciousness of the individual. National spirits, as they become conscious of their essence, coalesce into a single Spirit. Similarly, Hegel reasoned, language unites various national spirits into a single pantheon, expressing humanity's pure intuition of itself as a universal essence: "The national Spirit combines with the others with which it constitutes through Nature a single nation, in a common undertaking, and for this task forms a collective nation and therewith a collective Heaven." The gods, representing various powers of self-consciousness, preside over nature and society, but they fall into conflict and cancel each other. In tragedy, heroes emerge as exemplars of individual universality. In comedy, actors reduce everything to mockery, encouraging ordinary people to disrespect everything. Hegel, finishing his tour of art-religion, interpreted the debate between Socrates and the Sophists as a closing riff on the irony of comedy. With the loss of conventions, which Hegel called "determinateness," the language of the Good and the Beautiful became empty, "a comic spectacle." Reason, for the Sophists, was reduced to "the sport of mere opinion," the caprice of an individual. Fate is united with self-consciousness in the comic's insight that all determinations are products of self-consciousness and at the mercy of self-consciousness.[89]

In art-religion the Spirit advances from knowing itself as substance to knowing itself as a Subject that creates its own outer shape. On the threshold of revealed religion, Hegel observed that Spirit can be viewed as substance moving out of itself to become self-conscious or as self-consciousness moving out of itself to become substance. The former view begins with the implicit father; the latter view begins with the actual mother. Hegel judged that in the cults closest to Christianity (presumably Isis and Mithras), Spirit is one-sidedly conscious of itself as self-consciousness making itself substance. Here, Spirit is only imagined into existence, meriting "neither belief nor reverence." In revealed religion, he argued, the two standpoints are held together with equal strength. Substance alienates itself from itself to become self-consciousness, while self-consciousness alienates itself from itself to give itself the nature of a thing. Self-knowing Spirit arises through the dialectical realization and necessary movement of consciousness in its immediacy: "The immediate in-itself of Spirit that gives itself the shape of self-consciousness means nothing else than that the actual World-Spirit has attained to this knowledge of itself; it is then, too, that this knowledge also first enters its consciousness."[90]

Hegel stressed that it didn't just "happen" and that God is not a projection of the yearning human mind. The incarnation of the Spirit as a self-conscious Being had to happen in a favorable moment of history and it had to be *believed;* believers had to see, feel, and hear the divinity in God's incarnation for the self-consciousness of the Spirit to be actual in them. (Hegel, though describing Christ at length, refrained from naming him following Kant's example.) Moreover, this experience did not begin with an inner thought that became united with a thought about God; it began with the recognition of God's existence as an individual self-consciousness. The Self of existent Spirit takes the form of "complete immediacy," Hegel affirmed. It is not something produced, as in natural religion or art-religion, nor is it thought or imagined. The God of revealed religion is "sensuously and directly beheld as a Self, as an actual individual man; only so *is* this God self-consciousness."[91]

The "simple" content of absolute religion is this incarnation of the divine being. Spirit is the knowledge of oneself in self-abandonment. In absolute religion, Hegel cautioned, God is not merely "the Good, the Righteous, the Holy, Creator of Heaven and Earth, and so on," which are predicates of a Subject. As long as only the predicates are known, the divine Subject is not yet revealed: "Spirit is known as self-consciousness and to this self-consciousness it is immediately revealed, for Spirit is this self-consciousness itself. The divine nature is the same as the human, and it is this unity that is beheld." Absolute religion is about God knowing God in humanity.[92]

So what is the relationship between Christianity and that? And what is the difference between the knowledge sought in revealed religion and speculative reason? On the latter question, Hegel was unequivocal: There is no difference. Religion is crucially different from philosophy in preferring pictures to concepts, he judged, but both seek the same thing. Throughout the ages, human beings everywhere have searched for the knowledge that the highest forms of religion and philosophy have attained. The yearning of the "unhappy consciousness," trapped in a world of despair and death, for eternity, is universal. Hegel explained that speculative reason knows God as Thought, it knows this Thought as Being and existence, and it knows existence as the negativity of itself. It knows the negativity of existence, the Self, as simultaneously individual and universal. This is exactly what is revealed in revealed religion, he argued. All of world history presses toward this revelation, to behold absolute Being and to find itself in it: "The joy of beholding itself in absolute Being enters self-consciousness and seizes the whole world; for it is Spirit, it is the simple movement of those pure moments, which expresses just this: that only when absolute Being is beheld as an *immediate* self-consciousness is it known as Spirit."[93]

But this notion, Hegel observed, that the absolute essence is individuated in humanity, has yet to be universalized. All of history presses toward it, and Christianity has it in an immediate, partial form, that Spirit knows itself in "an exclusive One or unit." Absolute religion, however, is about an individual Self becoming "equally the universal Self, the Self of everyone." In revealed religion the Notion of Spirit knowing itself as Spirit is revealed in the immediacy of individual self-consciousness, as distinguished from universal self-consciousness. This shape "has not as yet the form of the Notion, i.e., of the universal Self." In absolute religion the Self of immediate actuality is universalized without losing its actuality: "But the proximate form of this universality, the form that is itself immediate, is not yet the form *of thought* itself, *of the Notion as Notion*, but the universality of reality, the 'allness' or totality of the selves, and the raising of existence into an ideational form." The goal of Spirit is to be universalized in the understanding, not merely in religion.[94]

Hegel interpreted the life, death, resurrection, and ascension of Christ, and the sending of the Holy Spirit, as movements in this dialectical process. Christ was the individual man that absolute Being revealed itself to be. In Christ, absolute Being accomplished in itself the movement of sensuous Being, which had to pass over into "having been" in order to become something that all human beings could share. Consciousness no longer saw or heard the One that made God sensually present, Hegel emphasized, yet "it *has* seen and heard Him," which transformed consciousness into spiritual consciousness. In Christ, absolute Being rose up for consciousness as a sensuous existence; in Christ's departure, absolute Being rose up in the Spirit. The consciousness that saw and heard Christ was merely immediate; it knew this objective individual as Spirit, but not itself. When Christ vanished, the immediacy was broken. In the sending of the Holy Spirit, Spirit remained the "immediate Self of actuality," but now as "the *universal self-consciousness* of the community." The original Christian community reposed in its own substance, a universal Subject, which was not merely Christ, but also the consciousness of the community and what Christ was for this community, "the complete whole of the individual as Spirit."[95]

All of this is picture-thinking, the mode of religious thought, Hegel cautioned. The religious consciousness operates in the realm of imagination, thinking the truth in pictures, which give a false independence to given sides of absolute Substance. Absolute religion and speculative reason have the same content, but before the "true content" can receive its "true form" for consciousness, it must be reinterpreted in notational form: "It must raise its intuition of absolute Substance into the Notion, and equate its consciousness with its self-consciousness *for itself*, just as this has happened for us, or *in itself*." The Christian community betrays its own rich spiritual existence when it clings to pictures, or defines itself by the ideas of an imperfect original community, or fixates on the sayings "of the actual man himself." Hegel allowed that this tendency to obsess over things of the past was rooted in the admirable desire to get to the Notion: "But it confuses the *origin* of the Notion as the immediate existence of its first manifestation with the *simplicity* of the Notion." That is the way of impoverishment and suffocation, he admonished. The Christian community betrays its own revelation, community, and future when it settles for "bare externality and singularity," fossilizing a "non-spiritual recollection of a supposed individual figure."[96]

Spirit is essentially a process of three moments, Hegel reasoned. It begins in pure thought (logic); it moves into otherness and pictorial presentation (nature); and it returns from nature into realized self-consciousness (Spirit knowing Spirit). To put it differently, the first distinct moment of Spirit is Essence, God the Father. The second moment is Being-for-self for which the Essence is, God the Word. The third moment is Being-for-self in which the Spirit knows itself in the other, God as Spirit. The existence of the Word is nothing more, nor less, than the Spirit's hearing of its own self: "The distinctions made are immediately resolved as soon as they are made, and are made as soon as they are resolved, and what is true and actual is precisely the immanent circular movement."[97]

Hegel allowed that accounting for evil is hard to do without resorting to picture-thinking. Evil is consciousness turned inward, the withdrawal of consciousness into self-centeredness (*Insichgehen*). Religion offers the Garden of Eden story, and behind that, the fall of the first-born Son of Light (Lucifer), to account for it. The good angels enter the scene to put down Lucifer, helpfully pluralizing the Word's being-for-self; Hegel sympathized that Christianity had to struggle to keep them out of the Godhead, which would have led to a Quaternity at least. Adding the fallen angels to the Godhead would have been even worse. But evil is a terrible problem that, perversely, deepens in some ways with the growth of self-consciousness, Hegel acknowledged. Religious picture-thinking tends to relieve God of any complicity in evil, except to the extent that it attributes a wrathful side to God. Picture-thinking construes evil as something alien to God that happens to God.[98]

Hegel urged that that doesn't work. The world is split apart and nothing exists outside the Absolute Being. Self-centeredness, he argued, the root of evil, is an essential moment in the life of God. Otherwise God could not redeem the world by reconciling self-centered beings: "Absolute Being would be but an empty name if in truth there were for it an 'other,' if there were a 'fall' from it." Instead of rendering evil as something alien from God, which makes God somehow less than reality, Hegel contended that evil Being-for-self is split off from the same Being-for-self that redeems the world. Evil existence is not *in itself* something alien to God. The two forms of Being-for-self are the same, yet they are also different. Hegel remarked, "The whole is only complete when the two propositions are made together, and when the first is asserted and maintained, it must be countered by clinging to the other with invincible stubbornness. Since both are equally right, they are both equally wrong."[99]

The problem of evil cannot be solved if one clings to fixed designations of sameness and non-sameness, or of identity and non-identity, he argued. The dialectical movement of Spirit transforms all such fixations. God *is* selfsame with nature and God *is* not selfsame with nature. Both statements are true and false. Nature is nothing apart from its divine essence, "but this same 'nothing' just as much *is*." It is an abstraction; a pure thought. Being-for-self, in the moment of its antithesis to the spiritual unity sought by being-for-self, is evil. Hegel urged, "The difficulty that is found in these Notions stems solely from clinging to the 'is' and forgetting the thinking of the Notions in which the moments just as much *are* as they *are not*." God becomes fully God only by departing from God's Self in Nature and returning to God's Self in Spirit. The divine good, Hegel assured, prevails in this dialectical realization. Spirit coming to know itself drives out evil selfishness.[100]

It also dispenses with picture-thoughts, which are necessary to a point. Hegel asserted that Christianity rightly construes the death and resurrection of Christ as bringing about the redemption of the world, the inauguration of a universal life of Spirit in a religious community for which Christ dies everyday "and is daily resurrected." But this very affirmation, he contended, negates the picture-thinking in which it is made. For the death of the Mediator, a particular being-for-self, gives rise to a universal self-consciousness. The universal becomes self-consciousness *and* the pure

Spirit of thought becomes actual. The death of Christ marks not only the death of a particular being-for-self, but that of a pictured deity. The picture-God dies in the death of Christ so that God as self-knowing Spirit may live. Christianity is a picture-story about the movement of self-certain Spirit abandoning its unity nature and unchangeableness to embrace the suffering of the world and return to itself. Christianity apprehends in pictorial form the universal process by which Spirit redeems the world by coming to know itself. Hegel ended his discussion of revealed religion with a poetic flourish: "Just as the *individual* divine Man has a father *in principle* and only an *actual* mother, so too the universal divine Man, the community, has for its father its own doing and knowing, but for its mother, eternal love which it only *feels*, but does not behold in its consciousness as an actual, immediate *object*." The religious consciousness holds fast to its faith, not yet grasped in immediacy, of being united with God in love divine.[101]

The final chapter, on Absolute Knowing, was mercifully brief, though not from modesty. In absolute knowing, Hegel argued, self-consciousness surmounts the consciousness of revealed religion as such and becomes aware of itself in all the forms of its history. The intuition of the Divine achieved in religion at its highest, which Hegel called the "beautiful soul," gives way to the Divine intuiting itself. Time is abolished, for time is the Notion itself "that *is there*," the destiny and necessity of not-yet-perfected Spirit, presenting itself to consciousness as an empty intuition. Spirit appears to itself in time only for as long as it does not grasp its pure Notion. When Spirit realizes itself, overcoming the externality of objective substance, time is annulled. Everything that is outward must be transmuted into Spirit realizing itself, the subjective. Time is merely the form of this process.[102]

The Struggle for Recognition

Hegel hoped that his ambitious, creative work would launch a real academic career for him. But his life unraveled as he wrote it, Prussia was smashed as he finished it, and the book, though making him an intellectual player, won him no position. At Jena his neo-Kantian rival, J. F. Fries, was appointed over him to "extraordinary" professor status, infuriating Hegel, who protested to Goethe that he deserved at least the same status as Fries. This was granted, though Hegel's change in status did not change his salary: nothing. Desperate for income, he found a publisher who agreed to make a first payment when his "system" was half-finished, which was hard to verify in this case, as the system veered off to something else in its third chapter. Finding his manuscript sprawling almost out of control, Hegel could not claim to be half-done with whatever the book was, and the publisher refused all payment until he delivered a completed manuscript. Meanwhile Hegel's housekeeper and landlady, Christiana C. J. Burkhardt, became pregnant, by him; Hegel, uncertain of his legal obligations to this married, but recently abandoned friend, felt his moral obligation to provide support for their child, and his shame. Advocates of the patchwork view, notably Kaufmann, were prone to suggest that Hegel's domestic anxieties showed up in the book's unwieldy structure. Though Hegel's preface, in my view, made a convincing case that the book had an integrative argument, he must have paused, while writing it, at blasting his only academic ally, Schelling. But he plunged ahead, bidding to be understood on his own terms. Then he asked Schelling to ignore the insult.[103]

On October 13, 1806, one day before Napoleon routed Prussian troops in a single afternoon on a plateau outside of Jena, Hegel enthused to his friend Immanuel Niethammer: "I saw the Emperor – this world-soul – riding out of the city on reconnaissance. It is indeed a wonderful sensation to see such an individual, who, concentrated here at a single point, astride a horse, reaches out over the world and masters it . . . Such advances as occurred from Thursday to Monday are only possible for this extraordinary man, whom it is impossible not to admire." Even if the revolution of modernity had already passed to Germany, as Hegel had just written in his manuscript, he could not help being thrilled at the sight of Napoleon. Afterward he refrained from complaining when the world-soul devastated his city and disrupted his chance for an academic career. French troops plundered on a house-to-house basis, sparing only the houses that quartered them; Hegel fled his residence, clutching his manuscript; the university was damaged, though Napoleon decided against shutting it down. A month later the university was down to 130 students. Hegel, desperate for income, pleaded with friends, including Schelling, for handouts or a job. Niethammer came through with both, finding a job for Hegel as a newspaper editor in Bamberg in February 1807 – the same month that Hegel's son Ludwig was born. If not for Niethammer, Hegel would not have survived his years of want and waiting, which included the shame of needing to support an illegitimate son.[104]

In March he moved to Bamberg, putting a good face on the only job he could find; in April the *Phenomenology* was published; the following month Hegel wrote to Schelling again, telling him, "My manuscript is finally completed." There were problems with it, Hegel reported; that was why Schelling still did not have a copy. The publisher was being difficult, and Hegel was anxious about how Schelling would react to the book, especially the preface. Working up to the preface, he acknowledged that the manuscript got away from him: "Working into the detail has, I feel, damaged the overview of the whole." He lacked sufficient time to smoothen out the book's interlaced cross-references, and some sections needed further "groundwork" (*Unter-arbeitung*) to be brought into "subjugation" (*unterkriegen*). The ending could have been better, Hegel allowed, but it suffered from the excitement of watching Napoleon march into Jena. Then there was the preface: "In the Preface you will not find that I have been too hard on the shallowness that makes so much mischief with your forms in particular and degrades your science into a bare formalism." Surely, Schelling would see that Hegel was attacking unnamed disciples of Schelling, not Schelling. In addition, Hegel asked Schelling to support him: "I need not tell you, by the way, that your approval of a few pages would be worth more to me than the satisfaction or dissatisfaction of others with the whole. Likewise, I would not know anybody else by whom I would rather have this writing introduced to the public, and from whom I could prefer a judgment on it."[105]

Hegel took for granted that he needed Schelling's support to get favorably noticed. Schelling's reply, six months later, was frosty, with a hint of feeling betrayed, but superficially agreeable. He had read only the preface, which, as far as he could tell, had nothing to do with him: "Insofar as you yourself mention the polemical part of the Preface, given my own justly measured opinion of myself I would have to think too little of myself to apply this polemic to my own person. It must therefore, as you have expressed in your letter, apply only to further bad use of my ideas and to those who parrot them without understanding, although in this writing itself the distinction is not made." Aside from Hegel's confusing preference for science over intuition, it wasn't clear to Schelling that there was much difference between them. Hegel could have construed this response as an invitation. If he wanted Schelling's help, he could tell the public what he told Schelling, that he respected Schelling above all others and did not attack him in the preface. But Hegel was undoubtedly annoyed that Schelling didn't bother to read the book, which meant that he would not be doing anything for it. No more letters passed between them, even though Schelling had asked, "keep me in mind as your true friend."[106]

For eighteen months Hegel ran a newspaper, for which he wrote plain journalistic sentences; in 1808 Niethammer was appointed central commissioner of education and consistory in Munich, which lifted Hegel to a position as rector of the *Gymnasium* in Nuremberg. Meanwhile the *Phenomenology* attracted ample attention, but none that delivered a university position. The early reviews, mostly hostile, had trouble distinguishing between Hegel and Schelling. Others, grasping that Hegel was more rationalistic than Schelling, stressed that at least Schelling was not hostile to Pietism, unlike Hegel. In some cases Hegel was ripe for payback, as he was known for writing slashing reviews; one of Hegel's recent victims, Catholic Bavarian theologian Jacob Salat, surprised Hegel by pulling his punches, asserting blandly that Hegel's book was a rationalistic spin on the idealistic attribution of perfection to humanity. Friedrich Köppen, a Jacobi protégé, judged that Hegel reversed Schelling's mistake; instead of deriving his speculative philosophy from his logical formalism, like Schelling, Hegel tried to derive a logic from his speculative philosophy. Both projects mistakenly refused to develop their ideas out of the experience of particular things, Köppen argued. Jacobi, now president of the Munich Academy of Sciences, and thus a powerful figure in Bavarian intellectual circles, asked J. F. Fries if Hegel was someone to be taken seriously. Fries assured him not, for Hegel, despite claiming that knowledge is in flux and relative, also claimed to have absolute knowledge.[107]

Virtually all reviewers complained that Hegel's extremely turgid, dense, and abstract style was impossibly difficult to comprehend; Hegel, acknowledging the difficulty, defended it as a necessity for rigorous thought. On that count he was thoroughly Kantian. He found it hard to take criticism from Salat and Köppen, as they had secured university positions that he desperately wanted. To be passed over by second-rate thinkers was almost unbearable to him. It helped, however, that these reviewers explained to readers that Hegel stood on his own. Increasingly Hegel's originality and intellectual power were recognized. K. F. Bachmann, a former student of Hegel's at Jena, declared that if Schelling was the Plato of modern philosophy (a plaudit that he often received), Hegel was the "German Aristotle." Bachmann asserted that Hegel deserved to have a school; in fact, he already had one among the former students who admired his system. The next stage of German idealism needed to have Hegel's Aristotelian spirit.[108]

It wasn't clear where post-Kantian idealism was going, especially because Schelling changed again. The *Phenomenology*, though failing to win a university position for Hegel, made him someone to talk about in intellectual circles. By then Schelling had changed his mind about exalting art over religion, and surprisingly, he had only one more book in him, at least for publication.

In 1809 Schelling announced a religious turn in what turned out to be his last important published work, *Philosophical Investigations On the Essence of Human Freedom*. To secure his absolute idealism, and to give a better answer to Kant's question of how enlightened selves can give the law to themselves and still choose evil, Schelling needed an ultimate divine ground. Here the influence of Lutheran mystic Jacob Boehme was pronounced, though Schelling did not fully acknowledge it until the 1830s. As for Kant's question of how evil is possible for self-determining creatures, Schelling judged that Kant merely described the problem without giving much of a solution. His answer was too dualistic and it had no account of whatever motivated moral choices. Schelling's answer focused on the role of the divine in human life.[109]

There is an original unity of reality that shows the longing of the Eternal One to give birth to itself, Schelling postulated. This original One is a striving will, and the oneness is best represented as the principle of chaos, or darkness. God, the principle of light, emerges out of chaos and orders it, uniting the principles of order and disorder within God's being. Human beings are the consequence of this divine ordering, uniting chaotic darkness and ordering light, like God: "The human will is the seed – hidden in eternal yearning – of the God who is present still in the ground only; it is the divine panorama of life, locked up within the depths, which God beheld as he fashioned the will to nature." In human beings alone God loved the world, "and precisely this likeness of God was possessed by yearning in the *centrum* as it came into opposition with the light."[110]

Because human beings emerge from the primordial Oneness, the "ground," Schelling reasoned, they have in relation to God a relatively independent principle within themselves. This principle, without ceasing to be dark in accordance with its ground, is transfigured in light, giving rise to something higher in human being, spirit. The principles of light and darkness are in all things, but human beings, unlike God, are not immediately at one with these principles. The divine consonance *(Konsonanz)* is lacking in human beings, "due to the deficiency of that which has been raised out of the ground." In human agency, light and darkness can be torn apart, which creates the possibility of evil: "The same unity that is inseverable in God must therefore be severable in man – and this is the possibility of good and evil."[111]

Schelling did not conceive the principles of light and darkness as opposing forces, for the rational, ordering principle of light grows out of chaotic, unreasonable darkness. There is no good that does not express the unity of these principles, for there is no personal existence that does not unite them. God, the principle of pure light, is the "center" of existence, the ideal balance of things, which, as love, brings all things to the integrative center out of which personality and individuality emerge: "Selfhood *as* such is spirit; or man is spirit as a selfish [*selbstisch*], particular being (separated from God) – precisely this connection constitutes personality." Selfhood, Schelling explained, because it is spirit, arises from the creaturely into something above it – personality or will beholding itself in freedom. It is no longer an instrument of the productive universal will in nature, for it is raised in freedom above nature: "Spirit is above the light as in nature it raises itself above the unity of the light and the dark principle."[112]

The temptation to choose evil shows the lure of the chaotic disordering impulse in human beings. Schelling's favorite analogy for it was disease, something that emerges "when the irritable principle, which is supposed to rule as the innermost bond of forces in the quiet of the depths, activates itself." Disease is the breaking out of the hidden forces of the ground, a disorder arising in nature through the misuse of freedom, he argued. The transition from disease to health occurs by restoring individual life into "the being's inner glimpse of light," and so does the transition from evil to good. Evil is perversion, an "un-essence" or "un-being" (*Unwesen*). Thus, the Enlightenment attempt to find a rational ground for the choice of evil was mistaken, for evil does not arise from natural deficiency and it is never rationally chosen. Schelling urged that mythology understood evil better than any Enlightenment thinker; the beginning of evil is that "man transgresses from authentic Being into non-Being, from truth into lies, from the light into darkness, in order to become a self-creating ground and, with the power of the *centrum* which he has within himself, to rule over all things." Every sinner holds the faint remembrance, in feeling, "that he was all things, namely, in and with God." The sinner strives hard to return there, "but for himself, and not where he might be all things, namely, in God."[113]

As for the future of evil, Schelling did not claim to know. Does creation have a final purpose? If so, why is it not reached immediately? Schelling's only answer was that God is a life, not merely a Being, and all life has a destiny, "subject to suffering and becoming." From the moment that God separated light from darkness in order to become personal, God subjected God's self to the life process: "Being becomes aware of itself only in becoming." There is no becoming in Being, Schelling acknowledged, but God, by subjecting God's self to the becoming of life, brought Being into awareness of itself through becoming. This is the sacred mystery of religion; Schelling argued that every religion is about the divine becoming temporal and human: "Without the concept of a humanly suffering God, one which is common to all mysteries and spiritual religions of earliest time, all of history would be incomprehensible."[114]

This was the template for Schelling's subsequent work, which ranged over mythology, revelation, and the history of religions. *Philosophical Investigations into the Essence of Human Freedom* sustained Schelling's standing in the top tier of German philosophy long after he stopped adding to it. The book fueled debates over Schelling's rendering of divine necessity that Martin Heidegger and Slavoj Žižek revived in subsequent generations. Orthodox theism taught that if God is as God must be, God could not have been in any other way than God is. Schelling stayed in line with this tradition while making a case for God's emergence and freedom. God always *is* within the ground from which God emerges, Schelling argued. God's emergence is the revelation of a being that was always there, not a transition from nothingness to being. Heidegger judged that Schelling made the most creative attempt of any thinker to combine divine necessity and freedom, a problem that bedeviled Western philosophy from its inception, from which Heidegger took leave.[115]

Schelling promised, at the end of *Philosophical Investigations*, to expound his new system in a multi-volume series. Had Schelling produced it, Hegel would have had stiff competition in determining the direction and character of absolute idealism. Schelling's religious turn took him deeply into the study of myth and mysticism. He argued that God develops in the ideas that thinkers and adherents of all religions hold about God. Having begun as a celebrant of Enlightenment freedom, he brooded in later life over the dark side of freedom, finding his early thought lacking in spiritual depth. At the same time he stressed that philosophy is always a creative work of freedom, a notion that he found lacking in Leibniz's, and now Hegel's, devotion to developing a logical system. In a lecture at Stuttgart in 1810, Schelling put it sharply, objecting that it was "most illiberal," if not downright scholastic, to claim universal validity for a philosophy of one's making. Years later he took to calling Hegel's system a fiction, because Hegel believed that the method and truth of his system were universally valid by themselves.[116]

For twenty-seven years Schelling struggled with struggle itself, laboring periodically on a book, *The Ages of the World,* that described struggle as the wellspring of life and end of creation. He wanted to fashion a more deeply conflicted version of identity philosophy, conceiving free willing as primal being. The 'ground' is groundless, in the sense of being uncaused, he argued: "All life must pass through the fire of contradiction. Contradiction is the engine of life and its innermost essence." But Schelling never finished the book, or anything else. In a way he remained prolific, writing new manuscripts, which he consigned to the drawer for further refinement.[117]

The creative spark was gone. Schelling's beloved Carolyn had been gravely ill when he wrote his book on the origin of good and evil. She died shortly after he finished the book, and he was never the same afterward. Schelling's intense grief lingered for years. The ebullience of feeling that fired his sensational early career was snuffed out, turning him into a wounded type that, for all his continued fame, could not publish his subsequent thoughts. He married a close friend of Carolyn's, with whom he had several children and a fulfilling home life. He converted to Catholicism and taught in Bavaria until 1841, witnessing Hegel's ascendancy with disapproving amazement. For many years Schelling complained to anyone who would listen that Hegel stole his ideas. In the 1820s, after Hegel developed his system and became the dominant figure in European philosophy, Schelling developed a penetrating critique of Hegel's approach to the absolute – one that reverberates in twenty-first-century debates about the legitimization of rationality.[118]

The coming of Hegel, though late to begin, was perfectly timed, and overwhelming. For seven years he taught high schoolers, fretting that his call to the university would never come, even as the *Phenomenology* and the first two volumes of his *Science of Logic* made him a figure of note. In 1811 Hegel announced to Niethammer that he was engaged to a woman, Marie von Tucher, from a patrician family – though he claimed that Marie's father made the engagement contingent on Hegel's success at obtaining a professorship at Erlangen, which was newly reorganized. Niethammer, apparently doubting the condition, told Hegel to marry Marie promptly, stop counting on Erlangen, and above all, stop feeling sorry for himself. Being the rector of a distinguished *Gymnasium* was nothing to denigrate. Did he actually feel insufficiently respected to marry into Marie's family?[119]

Hegel took the scolding penitently and married Marie, who was twenty-one years younger, that year. In 1812 and 1813 he published the first two volumes of his logic, on being and essence; in 1816 he published volume three, on concepts. That year, after Hegel made the short list at Heidelberg, some questioned whether he would be able to teach at a university level after so many years of teaching high schoolers. Others, better informed, realized that Hegel was on a level by himself. In the summer he finally won his coveted chair at Heidelberg. By then Napoleon had crashed spectacularly and

German monarchs were seeking to restore their authority. Hegel, well known for his liberal republican politics, resolved to play a careful hand politically.

Logic, Encyclopedia, Right

Hegel divided his logic into three books because, for him, everything divided into triads, except when his hurried writing of the *Phenomenology* didn't turn out that way. Teaching high school students had taught him how to summarize his thoughts in capsule form, a discipline that paid off as he composed the summary version of his system, *Encyclopedia of the Philosophical Sciences* (1817). There, Hegel explained that thinking has three operations or moments: Thought (the understanding), which is abstract; dialectic, which is negative; and the speculative, which is positive. The understanding fixes the meaning of concepts so that they can be correctly used. Dialectic is the movement of thought in which the formulae of the understanding "supersede themselves, and pass into their opposites." Speculative reason synthesizes the two contraries in a way that both preserves and dissolves them into a new reality. Hegel admonished his students against disparaging dialectic as "nothing more than a subjective see-saw of arguments *pro* and *con*," though he allowed that it often degenerated to the playground. Plato and Socrates were masters of dialectic, he stressed, and in modern times, Kant had revived it. Dialectic, used rightly, countered the "one-sidedness and limitation" of the understanding.[120]

This was more explicit than Hegel's references to dialectic in the *Phenomenology*. There, Hegel used the term "dialectic" only a few times, he did not describe it as a thesis generating an antithesis that leads to a synthesis, and he was not even stringent about using triads. The *Phenomenology* was based on the triad of consciousness, self-consciousness, and reason, and it subdivided consciousness into sensuous certainty, perception and understanding. But the book had only two headings under self-consciousness, and Hegel's lengthy account of reason (almost three-fourths of the whole) had a complex fourfold division. The *Phenomenology* was free-flowing in applying its more-or-less triadic scheme to a surging waterfall of concepts, figures, events, rhetorical forms, and philosophical moves. It paired skepticism against stoicism, which led to the unhappy consciousness, but Hegel did not claim to logically deduce one from the other in dialectical fashion. Skepticism, after all, is not the logical anti-thesis of stoicism, and historical messiness defies logical precision.[121]

Science of Logic, however, was a philosophy of formal logic, an argument about the types and limitations of judgment and inference. Here the dialectic was named repeatedly, featured, and stringently applied, with deductive zeal, for the point of Hegel's logic was to show that the concept is a *movement* that determines itself to be. There is a logical movement from subjectivity to objectivity to idea, a movement that overcomes the impasse of Kantian dualism and restores metaphysical reasoning on modern, post-Kantian terms. If the concepts of mind are universals, Hegel argued, they bridge the Kantian divide between knowing subjects and objects of consciousness. There is no rational basis for dichotomizing between subject and object, or form and content. Rather, the world exists as the externalization of self-consciousness, and self-consciousness exists as a recognized shape of this world as Spirit.

Hegel divided logic into being, essence, and concept (or notion), each of which had its own normative structures that depended on the kinds of judgmental relations at issue. Dramatically, in his opening paragraph, Hegel declared that the Kantian revolution utterly transformed philosophy, except in logic. Modern philosophers no longer taught or wrote about ontology, cosmology, rational psychology, or natural theology – all had "vanished" from the field, obliterated by Kant. But the "higher standpoint" of modern philosophy, which tracked the movement of spirit's awareness of itself, had not encroached on the structure of logic – until now. Hegel believed that logic is not immune to movement, the life process of self-determination into being. The unity that precedes all acts of judgment, he argued, is pure knowing. Thus, he began his logic with the category of pure being, a "thought" lacking any determination.[122]

Hegel showed that the simple act of trying to conceive pure being – the primordial unity of thought and being – immediately generates paradoxes. These ruptures, he argued, are implicit in the very nature of the unity and are brought out by the act of judgment. Logic must think about thinking. It must not rest content with rules about the forms of logical judgment and inference. Rather, logic must deal with the process of reasoning that generates the forms. Hegel put it sharply: "What logic is cannot be stated beforehand." Instead of beginning as formal logic always did, with symbols and rules of thought, logic had to begin "with the subject matter itself."[123]

So his logic began with pure being – pure indeterminateness and emptiness, the most elementary feature of thought. Pure being, as a thought, does not restrict the context in which it is used, and, despite being completely indeterminate, it is something that can be thought. But this thought immediately generates a paradox, Hegel observed – that being and nothing are identical. When we focus on pure being, we realize that we are thinking nothing; when we think nothing, we are led straight back to being. In both cases, lacking any determination, there is nothing to think. But there is something that we think about in both cases, the two thoughts seem to be identical, and yet they are radically different. We cannot predicate being as a category of existence without predicating nothing as a category of existence. Thinking about being takes us straight to nothing and vice versa. The antithesis, nothing, is not the mere logical contradiction of pure being, for it is related to being as a contrary. Hegel allowed that nothing *(Nichts)* might as well be called "not-being" (*Nichtsein*), as long as one keeps in mind that it stands for the absence of all determination, not the denial of being. In the dialectic of being and nothing we confront a fundamental contradiction between identity and opposition: Being is a pure positive (reality without unreality) and nothing is a pure negative (unreality without reality).[124]

This contradiction yields the third category, becoming – the passage of being into nothing, or of nothing into being. When we try to think about being or nothing, Hegel observed, our thought passes from one to another, erasing the thought with which we began. Becoming is this movement in which being and nothing are distinguished by a difference which immediately resolves itself. It is not a unity that abstracts from being and nothing; rather, becoming is the "unseparatedness" of being and nothing. As the unity of being and nothing "it is this *determinate* unity in which there *is* both being and nothing." Being and nothing are both in the unity, but only as vanishing moments. They do not self-subsist, for both sink to the status of distinct, but "sublated" moments of simultaneous preservation and dissolution. Hegel distinguished between two moments of becoming, which he called "ceasing-to-be" and "coming-to-be." Ceasing to be is being passing into nothing, where nothing is equally the opposite of itself, coming to be. Coming to be is nothing passing into being, where being transitions into nothing, ceasing to be. Hegel reasoned that these moments do not reciprocally cancel each other externally, for "each sublates itself in itself and is in its own self the opposite of itself." *Everything* is an intermediate state between being and nothing.[125]

The next round of the dialectic began with the synthesis of the first and second kinds of becoming as one thought – being becoming out of nothing which came out of being. This is not pure being; Hegel called it *Dasein*, "a being," usually translated as "determinate being." Determinate being is the first moment of a dialectic which becomes something by being "qualified," which involves a change of determination going beyond a limit, which sets off the dialectic of finitude and infinitude, and so on. Hegel famously declared: "We call dialectic the higher movement of reason in which such seemingly utterly separate terms pass over into each other spontaneously, through that which they are, a movement in which the presupposition sublates itself."[126]

"Sublate," not really an English term, has to work hard in English versions of Hegel, whose German term *aufgehoben* was equally distinctive. There is no dialectic without it, and the *Science of Logic* was a huge waterfall of dialectics. The doctrine of being began with being, nothing, and becoming, which led to determinate being, finitude, and infinity, which led to being for self as such, the one and the many, and repulsion and attraction. All had dialectics of their own, creating simultaneous cases of reduplicated relation. For example, the dialectic of determinate being, under determinate being as such, contained the dialectics of determinate being in general, quality, and something; under finitude, it contained the dialectics of something and other, determination, constitution, and limit, and finitude; under infinity, it contained the dialectics of the infinite in general, alternating determination of the finite and infinite, and affirmative affinity. Hegel's logic of essence had similar dialectics, which began with essence as reflection within itself, moved to appearance, and culminated in actuality, all with three logical moments divided into triads of their own. His system culminated in his "subjective logic," the doctrine of the notion, which moved from subjectivity (the notion, the judgment, the syllogism) to objectivity (mechanism, "chemism," teleology) to the Idea (life, the idea of cognition, the Absolute Idea).

The conventional account, a staple of philosophy textbooks for centuries, is that Hegel used a three-step method of thesis-antithesis-synthesis. This formula is not wrong, but it is not right either. As a shorthand formula it describes the general structure of Hegel's method in *Science of Logic* and his subsequent major writings. But Hegel *never* employed this formula, it misses his multi-dimensional complexity, and in many renderings it simply ignores the pragmatic commitments that motivated all of Hegel's work not excluding *Science of Logic*.[127]

In the *Science of Logic*, the *Encyclopedia of the Philosophical Sciences*, and Hegel's last published book, *Philosophy of Right* (1821), dialectic expounded the fundamental categories of understanding, including concepts, forms of judgment, and forms of syllogism. He began by describing a category, A. Then he showed that A contains a contrary category, B. Then he showed that category B contains category A; thus, both categories are self-contradictory. This mutually contradictory outcome, though negative, yields a positive outcome, category C, which Hegel called the "negation of the negation" or the "determinate negation." Category C contains A and B, uniting them, but in a way that both preserves and abolishes them – Hegelian *aufgehoben*. Sublation is the process in which A and B are rendered no longer contradictory and not a source of contradiction in C. By rendering A and B to be no longer self-contradictory, Category C is able to preserve and abolish A and B as a new, reciprocal reality. Hegel explained, "It is a fundamental determination which repeatedly occurs throughout the whole of philosophy, the meaning of which is to be clearly grasped and especially distinguished from *nothing*. What is sublated is not thereby reduced to nothing. Nothing is *immediate;* what is sublated, on the other hand, is the result of *mediation;* it is a non-being but as a *result* which had its origin in a being. It still has, therefore, *in itself* the *determinateness from which it originates."* At this point, the next round of the dialectic begins anew, with C playing the "thesis" role that was previously played by A.[128]

Kant revolutionized modern philosophy by asking how one should explain the possibility of knowledge and account for the reality of the external world. His answer, that the mind is active in producing experience through its transcendental categories and the forms of sensibility, contended that there are exactly twelve concepts of pure thought. Hegel demonstrated that there are at least eighty-one pure concepts. Patiently, with tremendous concentration on how thinking actually works in logical reasoning, he made a case for taking seriously the Heraclitan world of becoming, the unity of thought and being, and the logical connection between these notions as a movement from subjectivity to objectivity to idea. His triads were not uniform, as J. N. Findlay noted. Sometimes the second member of the triad was an obvious contrary of the first, as in the relation of essence and appearance. Sometimes the contrast was much weaker, as in the relation of whole and parts to force and its manifestations. The same thing was true of the third members. Some, like measure synthesizing quality and quantity, worked very well. Sometimes Hegel's third member was merely one thing in which two concepts could be united (as in the mediation of identity and difference by the Ground). In other cases, as in the reconciliation of the mechanical and the chemical by teleology, Hegel stretched.[129]

His vast scheme of logical categorizing and dialecticism overwhelmed the pragmatic aspect of his thought, but it was there. Hegel sought to demonstrate that it is in the very nature of thought, and thus of life, to generate complexity from simplicity. The other, by turning upon itself, transforms the opposite into its immediate. Otherness becomes immediacy, otherness reduplicated. What was at stake for Hegel, normatively, in the dialectic of being and nothing, was at stake for him everywhere else: The realization that the world is always coming to be and ceasing to be. Hegel contended that what we are really doing when we distinguish being from nothing is to work out the kinds of inferences that are credible within a world that is always coming and ceasing to be. The *Science of Logic* sustained logic-chopping abstract rigor for 844 pages, but that did not, for Hegel, contradict the socio-historicized account of reason that he expounded in the *Phenomenology.* He was still reasoning about a world in flux that is heading somewhere significant: the realization of Spirit. To say that we know something, Hegel argued, is not to make an objective comparison. It is to make a normative ascription about the entitlement of the person making the claim. Pinkard explains: "Our ascriptions of knowledge are not comparisons of any kind of subjective state with something non-subjective but instead are *moves within* a social space structured by responsibilities, entitlements, attributions, and the undertakings of commitments."[130]

Science of Logic put an end to the question whether Hegel had a position independent of Schelling's. The *Phenomenology* was too puzzling to settle the question for many readers, but Hegel clearly stood on his own by the time that he started teaching at Heidelberg, where he taught for two years, and published the *Encyclopedia*. At Heidelberg he acquired a following, though nothing like his subsequent cult following at Berlin. Two of his best friends on the Heidelberg faculty were theologians, Karl Daub and Friedrich H. C. Schwarz, an augur of his Berlin career; Hegel also befriended Georg Friedrich Creuzer, the founder of the scientific study of mythology. Upon moving to Heidelberg, Hegel exorcised a nine-year psychic torment by rescuing his son Ludwig from an orphanage, apparently against the wishes of Marie Hegel. The *Encyclopedia*, though essentially a summary-manual of Hegel's system, coined the term "objective spirit" for his concept of the social and political embodiments of spirit. Part one was a short version of Hegel's logic; part two dealt with philosophy of nature; part three covered the philosophy of mind. Part two, not for the first time, made some unfortunate choices on scientific debates of the time. In the *Phenomenology*, Hegel took phrenology seriously enough to rattle on for 25 pages about it. In the *Encyclopedia*, he opposed Lamarckian evolution, defended the fixity of natural kinds, and opposed Newtonian light theory, which rendered this part of Hegel's system to early obsolescence. He had scientific colleagues at Heidelberg who tried to warn him. But mostly he grew accustomed to hearing himself called the German Aristotle, a title that he took to the University of Berlin in 1818.[131]

Marie Hegel did not want to live in Berlin with her two children plus Ludwig, a verdict that Hegel accepted until Berlin came through with an offer that he virtually dictated. Despite having scorned Prussia for decades, he was anxious to move to it after the University of Berlin became a powerhouse. In 1818, the burning debate in German philosophy was Hegel versus Fries, though Schelling still had the most adherents. Fries, recently appointed at Jena, combined neo-Kantianism, psychology, conspiratorial anti-Semitism, and liberal activism. He and Hegel despised each other, which earned Fries a disparaging and fateful reference in Hegel's last book, *Philosophy of Right* (1821).

Hegel began to write the *Philosophy of Right* as soon as he moved to Berlin. His aim was to justify the Prussian reform movement to which he and Schleiermacher belonged, establishing what counted as a "right" in general and what was necessary for the realization of freedom. Hegel argued that the goal of free mind is "to make freedom its object, i.e., to make freedom objective as much in the sense that freedom shall be the rational system of mind, as in the sense that this system shall be the world of immediate actuality." The course of history, Hegel argued, could be deduced from absolutely free will, a logical concept. *Philosophy of Right* was not quite a self-contained system, as Hegel derived historically messy ideas about property, the family, civil society, and the like from his master concept. But the book had a strong logical cast, featuring a dialectic of being, essence, and notion, which led to a dialectic of natural will, arbitrary will, and universal free will, which led to a dialectic of abstract right, morality, and ethical life.[132]

Hegel made arguments for two-house parliamentary government, constitutional monarchy, freedom of the press, freedom of public opinion, trial by jury, individual rights based on property, and universal standards by which a person could claim to own property. He supported representing the estates of civil society in legislative bodies, which presented legislative content to a constitutional monarch, who added the royal "I will" to legislation to legitimize it as an expression of the general will. Hegel's idealism was central to his political philosophy. The general will must be *willed*, he argued; it cannot be merely the outcome of a mechanical clash of interests. He tried to stoke a public argument about the right kind of social contract theory. But the early reviews ignored the body of Hegel's argument, aiming solely at his snarky, pithy, aggressive preface, which engulfed him in unwelcome controversy for years and permanently damaged his reputation.

The back-story was a tale of misgivings and suspicions. Hegel was sincere about defending the reform movement; otherwise he wouldn't have plunged immediately into this arena. But he was averse to liberal agitators like Fries and Kantian theologian Wilhelm Martin L. de Wette, whom he considered unbearable demagogues. In addition, Hegel and Schleiermacher were wary of each other, as Hegel had low regard for religious feeling, and Schleiermacher had low regard for speculative philosophy. In 1811 Schleiermacher told the Academy of Sciences in Berlin that speculative philosophy was not really a discipline and it didn't belong in the university. Largely on Schleiermacher's influence, Hegel was never admitted to the Academy of Sciences. Moreover, during the crucial years of post-Napoleonic reordering in Prussia, Hegel did not incur trouble from the conservative government, as did Schleiermacher, and by the time that Hegel completed his book in 1820, many reform activists viewed him with suspicion. His defense of constitutional monarchy was beyond the pale for some, and he seemed too comfortable with his privileges to be trusted, especially after he defended the king's firing of de Wette from his professorship at Berlin. Even conservatives on the faculty senate protested de Wette's summary dismissal, but to Hegel, de Wette had become an out-of-control demagogue, a badly mannered embarrassment to the university.[133]

In that mode, Hegel wrote a nasty put-down of Fries (by name) and de Wette (unnamed) in the preface to *Philosophy of Right*. Fries, Hegel pronounced, was the "ringleader of these hosts of superficiality." Fries poured flattery on impressionable students, always appealing to "heart, emotion, and inspiration," assuring them that their dreams of a liberated society were more important than science. He called himself a philosopher, yet he prattled about the hopeful, communal rise of the people, united by "the holy chain of friendship," which would change society by pursuing "every single project of popular education and popular service." Hegel snorted: "This is the quintessence of shallow thinking, to base philosophic science not on the development of thought and the concept but on immediate sense-perception and the play of fancy."[134]

Philosophy of Right, by contrast, was long on moral duty, law, dutifulness, rational rigor, and rational order. It replaced Hegel's previous enthusiasm for the people with sober descriptions of civil society and the state, which he summarized in a fateful phrase fashioned from one of his favorite sayings. Usually Hegel said, "What is actual is what is efficacious." This time, intending to say the same thing, he declared: "What is rational is actual and what is actual is rational." To many readers and nearly every reviewer, including conservatives, that smacked of an apology for the status quo – Prussian royalist autocracy. The rest of the book, whatever it said, didn't matter. The reviews focused exclusively on Hegel's attack on Fries and Hegel's ostensible defense of the existing order.[135]

Adding to the drama, Fries had been fired recently from Jena on trumped-up accusations. Hegel, it turned out, was a bully who kicked a rival after he was down. Fries supplied a quotable explanation for what happened: "Hegel's metaphysical mushroom has grown not in the gardens of science but on the dunghill of servility." Hegel fought back by insulting his critics. In his telling, all were stupid and insipid, carried away by a few sentences that they didn't understand, judging a book that they hadn't read, which would have been over their heads anyway. That made it worse. Hegel's penchant for scathing sarcasm served him poorly, causing a former friend, Paulus, to lament that according to Hegel, nearly all German philosophers were "insipid." Hegel was the one lacking a certain requisite intelligence, Paulus suggested. How could he think, when the old powers were being restored, that his first order of business should be to put down persecuted liberals?[136]

Hegel never came up with a good answer to that question. His early years at Berlin went poorly on that account, as colleagues and onlookers shunned his superiority complex. He told an inquirer that his book "greatly offended the demagogical populace" because most people wallowed in "superficial self-conceit." But Hegel weathered the storm by giving free reign to the gregarious side of his personality. He served the university energetically in a variety of capacities and won a large and devoted student following. He damaged his health by overworking, though not on books. Becoming a great figure placed demands on his time that precluded new books. Hegel's growing fame brought a stream of visitors to Berlin, a responsibility that he took seriously, just as he had always been a dutiful teacher. The visiting traffic, and his growing student following, crowded into his lectures on logic and metaphysics, philosophical encyclopedia, the history of philosophy, natural law and political science, and the philosophies of art, nature, and world history. In 1821 he lectured for the first time on the philosophy of religion.[137]

Hegelian Philosophy of Religion

Philosophy of religion was beginning to emerge as a discipline in the wake of the downfall of rational theology, a branch of metaphysics. Hegel was anxious to make a contribution to it; more pertinently, in 1821 he heard from students that Schleiermacher's dogmatic system would be published imminently. Quickly Hegel resolved to lecture on religion, telling Karl Daub: "I hear Schleiermacher is also in process of having a work printed on dogmatics. The epigram occurs to me, 'One can go on paying for a long time with chips, but in the end one has to pull out one's purse all the same.' We'll have to wait and see whether this purse too will yield nothing more than chips." After volume one of Schleiermacher's system appeared, Hegel wrote to his protégé H. W. F. Hinrichs: "From Daub I look for an open declaration whether this really is the dogmatics of the United Evangelical Church that one has had the brazen effrontery to offer as such – admittedly only in a preliminary first part." Hegel, too, belonged to the Evangelical Church of the Prussian Union, and he was quite certain that Schleiermacher did not speak for him. How did Schleiermacher summon the audacity to speak for the church as a whole?[138]

In that frame of mind Hegel lectured on religion for the first time, for four hours per week for seventeen weeks, drawing 49 official auditors. In 1824 he returned to religion, drawing 63 auditors. In 1827 the official tally rose to 119 students, one of the largest crowds that he attracted in his career. In 1831 he lectured on religion for the last time, though no enrollment data exists. Always he attracted guests and lecture-grazers. His lectures began with a long discussion of the concept of religion, followed with a longer section on determinate religion, and ended with the consummate religion, Christianity. Never an eloquent podium performer, Hegel spoke deliberately, often pausing to clear his throat, gasp, stare into space, or fumble with his manuscript. He began most sentences with the word "thus," and sometimes he stuttered. As his fame ascended in the 1820s, his deficiencies as a lecturer were converted to endearing local lore; listeners prized his mannerisms as part of the Hegel experience. Hegel was sufficiently ponderous and slow-speaking that creating a verbatim transcript was never difficult for his students, who made money by selling the transcripts. He made use of these transcripts when he repeated a lecture cycle.[139]

Hegel worked hard at revising his lectures, especially on religion, partly from necessity, as he felt obliged to defend his position from critics. His lectures in 1821 were rough and improvised, though exuding unusual directness for him. His lectures in 1824 were the best of the series – lively, fluid, and engaging – which reflected his hard work on a fresh subject, plus his determination to discredit Schleiermacher's subjectivism. By the time that Hegel returned to religion in 1827 and 1831, he had a systematic command of his subject, and he was back to writing more formally; also, he cut back somewhat on the polemics against Schleiermacher. Having launched the series to counter Schleiermacher, Hegel heightened his polemic after Schleiermacher gave him additional fodder. Later he featured his command of something new, Hegelian philosophy of religion. At the end he was most interested in the history of religions.

Hegel shuddered to think that modern theology might content itself with Schleiermacher's subjectivism. By 1821, the liberal movement was overdue for a philosophy of religion that unified the Western understandings of religion and God under a single, modern, rational rubric. Hegel began: "Gentlemen! The object of these lectures is the philosophy of religion, which in general has the same purpose as the earlier type of metaphysical science, which was called *theologia naturalis.*" Hegel's prototype was Leibnizian-Wolffian rational theology, a division of metaphysics that usually followed rational psychology and cosmology. He did not play up the differences between his project and Wolff's, except to observe that the Kantian revolution had occurred between them, changing everything. Hegel explained, "The doctrine that we can know nothing of God, that we cannot cognitively apprehend him, has become in our time a universally acknowledged truth, a settled thing, a kind of prejudice." Before Kant, all science was a science of God; after Kant, educated people took pride in knowing nothing of God. Hegel put it sharply: "It is the distinction of our age, by contrast, to know each and every thing, indeed to know an infinite mass of objects, but only of God we know nothing." In the past, Hegel noted, people desired, above all other things, to know God: "Our age has renounced this need and the efforts to satisfy it; we are done with it." Modern post-Kantians were like the ancient Germans that Tacitus described as being "indifferent to the gods."[140]

The so-called "wisdom" of Kantian modernity turned God into "an infinite phantom, far removed from our consciousness," Hegel lamented; likewise it reduced human cognition to "a vain phantom of finitude, to schemas [that are] the fulfillment of appearance." This theme was a staple of Hegel's lectures in every series. He protested that on Kantian terms, it is impossible to make any sense of Christ's command to "be ye perfect as your Father in heaven is perfect." These words cannot be a command for us if we know nothing of God and of God's perfection, Hegel admonished. Modern people, thinking themselves wise, had reached "the last step in the degradation of humanity," where the profoundly simple words of Jesus became incomprehensible. Hegel set himself squarely against this pathetic outcome, and on the side of Christianity, "according to which we should *know* God *cognitively*, God's nature and essence, and should esteem this cognition above all else."[141]

All human beings have some knowledge of God, Hegel insisted; otherwise they wouldn't be human beings: "No one is so utterly depraved, so lost, so bad, and so wretched as to have no religion at all or to have [no] knowledge or awareness of it." Even people who loathe or deny the spirit within them still have it: "Since we are human beings and not animals, [religion] is not an alien sensation or intuition for us. But what matters is the relationship of *religion* in human beings to *everything else* in their world view, consciousness, cognition, purposes, and interests; this is the relationship that philosophical cognition is concerned with and upon which it essentially works."[142]

The Spirit is the subject and object of religion, Hegel urged. There are not two kinds of spirit, any more than there are two kinds of reason. The spirit of God and the spirit of humanity – divine reason – have the same essence: "Human reason, human spiritual consciousness or consciousness of its own essence, *is* reason generally, is the divine within humanity." Spirit divine is not something hypostatized before or beyond the world, "for God is present, is omnipresent, and strictly *as spirit* is God present in spirit." Hegel declared that religion is "a begetting of the divine spirit, not an invention of human beings but an effect of the divine at work, of the divine productive process within humanity." It is a product of Spirit divine, spirit realizing itself in consciousness. Religion emerges first as faith; it is faith precisely in the mind of God being revealed in nature and history; and it saves the world: "So we must have faith that what has emerged in the world is precisely reason, and that the generation of reason is a begetting of the spirit and a product of the divine spirit itself."[143]

Modern theology, Hegel judged, whether Kantian, historicist, or Schleiermacherian, fell short of knowing much of anything about what really matters in religion. The fact that modern theologians played down the Trinity was terribly instructive; Hegel shook his head that Schleiermacher relegated the Trinity to the appendix, giving it four paragraphs. Hegel countered that the Trinity is the key to how Spirit is explicated; it is precisely God grasping at what God is for God's self within God's self. God the Father makes God's self an object for God's self (the Son), remaining the undivided essence within this differentiation of God's self within God's self; in this differentiation, God loves God's self while remaining identical with God's self – the Holy Spirit.[144]

Hegel realized that Kant and Schleiermacher were not the only poor options for liberal theology, just the most prominent ones. Historicism was increasingly an option in its own right. Most historicists were Kantians like Paulus or Kantian-Romantic types like De Wette, but regardless of their philosophical orientation, they had a pronounced tendency to let the logic of historicism take over, which yielded a historicized idea of religion. Hegel respected what historical critics did with ancient texts. He did not respect, however, what they did with religious truth. Historical knowledge, he explained with edgy scorn, is of a pitifully low order: "This cognition is no concern of ours, for if the cognition of religion were merely historical, we would have to compare such theologians with countinghouse clerks, who keep the ledgers and accounts of other people's wealth, a wealth that passes through their hands without their retaining any of it, clerks who act only for others without acquiring assets of their own." To be sure, Hegel allowed, clerks receive a salary, "but their merit lies only in keeping records of the assets of other people. In philosophy and religion, however, the essential thing is that one's own spirit itself should recognize a possession and content, deem itself worthy of cognition, and not keep itself humbly outside."[145]

Historical theology is second-hand, a mere ledger entry lacking any spiritual content of its own. Hegel took the theology of feeling more seriously, if only because Jacobi and Schleiermacher had turned it into "an established preconception." Hegel blasted Schleiermacher in every lecture cycle, sometimes noting that Jacobi paved the way for the academy to take Schleiermacher's mere feelings with such seriousness. Always, Hegel countered that feelings are subjective, ephemeral, indiscriminate, and very low on cognition. In 1822, writing the preface to Hinrichs' book on the philosophy of religion, Hegel defended the compatibility of reason and religion, forgot to say much of anything about his protégé's turgid book, and allowed that religious faith has a place for spiritual feeling. However, if Hegel was going to say something nice about religious feeling, he couldn't resist a swipe at Schleiermacher. This was the occasion on which Hegel, reprising Schleiermacher on absolute dependence, observed that on Schleiermacher's terms, a dog makes the best Christian, for a dog carries the feeling of dependence "most intensely within itself and lives principally in this feeling. A dog even has feelings of salvation when its hunger is satisfied by a bone."[146]

Schleiermacher, though bruised by this insult, did not respond publicly. He told friends that at least he didn't incorporate Satan into God, like Hegel; later he responded constructively by playing up the freedom part of his dialectic of dependence and freedom. Hegel, meanwhile, having offended Schleiermacher with the dog bit, decided there was no reason to hold back in his next round of religion lectures. Now he took the moral high ground, suggesting that Schleiermacher was the one who stood in danger of sacralizing bad things. Hopes and wishes are feelings, Hegel observed, and people hope for bad things all the time. Merely feeling something doesn't make anything good or true. One can feel that one is courageous, noble, compassionate, or truthful, but what matters is whether one is actually courageous, noble, or the like. It doesn't matter that feelings contain admirable things, "for the very worst things are there too." Conversely, the existence of the content doesn't depend on feeling either, for all sorts of nonexistent imaginary things exist there: "Hence feeling is a form for every possible content, and by being felt the content gains no determinate status." If feeling is the justifying element of religion, the distinction between good and evil is nullified, for evil is every bit as present in feeling as the good: "Everything vile is the expression of [some] feeling."[147]

Feelings and dependency go together, Hegel cautioned: "In feeling I am at my most dependent; the content is completely contingent for me." Moreover, people have a decided tendency to appeal to their feelings when they cannot defend what they are saying, which breaks the commonality between people. Hegel urged that God is essentially in thought, not in feeling; religion is like law, freedom, and ethics in being chiefly intellectual: "We do indeed have feelings of right, freedom, ethics, and we have religious feelings, but feeling is the worst form in which content of this kind is posited." Hegel sympathized when people said that God must be felt in one's heart. He knew what they meant, he assured: "But the fact that the content is located in feeling does not make it true, or self-sufficing, or good or inwardly excellent; it does not make it true in the sense of *actuality.*" Feeling, Hegel admonished, is the locus of subjective being, it is always contingent, and it is usually passive. What matters is to provide good content, not to have nice feelings: "If individuals are going to be good, the content itself must be good; feeling, in and for itself, does not make it good."[148]

Once he warmed to this theme, Hegel had trouble letting it go. Feeling has a place, he allowed, but at the bottom. Dependency has a place too, but at the bottom of any progressive scale of values. Hegel stressed that people of virtue and accomplishment do not spend a lot of time talking about their feelings: "Those who live in the real world, be it practical affairs or scientific inquiry, and who act according to right and justice, law and righteousness, forget themselves in what they are doing and have no feelings in regard to it." Admirable people do not fuss over their particularity. They find their being in doing, and do not indulge in self-reminiscence: "Those who are vain and self-indulgent, on the other hand, willingly invoke their own feelings, their particularity, they want to enjoy it; and this direction of self-indulgence does not issue in true dealings and objective thought." This yielded a vintage Hegel verdict against his Berlin colleague, the age's greatest theologian: Any person, Hegel warned, that is greatly concerned with his or her feelings is not to be trusted and is not yet mature.[149]

Hegel understood the subtle differences between "sensibility" (*Empfindung*) and "feeling" (*Gefühl*). He knew that for Schleiermacher, sensibility was a product of sensations, which are *received* in a mode of immediacy as they are found. Feeling, on the other hand, is the activity of a self, an act of consciousness integrating sensations in a reflected totality. For Schleiermacher, as for Hegel in other contexts, feeling reflected a higher and more active form of self-consciousness than sensibility. But to Hegel, there were higher things at stake than fine distinctions or his reputation for being fair to Schleiermacher; thus he resorted to polemical blasting. It was disastrous for religious thinkers to retreat to subjectivity and/or the faith of the church, he pleaded. If Christian theologians were unwilling to defend the rationality of Christian belief, somebody had to do it.[150]

Hegel urged that thought is the ground upon which God *is*: "The universal is in thought, *only* in thought, and for thought." Thinking is spirit in its freedom. It supplies the content of truth, "the concrete deity," and it delivers this content to sensibility, creating religion. Empirical understanding, to be sure, is mere observing, the external vantage point of the onlooker. When one views consciousness from a higher, spiritual standpoint, one moves far beyond mere observing. Hegel explained: "I forget myself in plunging into the object. I immerse myself in it as I seek to cognize and to conceive God. I surrender my particularity in it, and if I do this I am no longer in the relationship which, as an empirical consciousness, I wanted to maintain." Now one perceives the relationship of consciousness; in the higher understanding, one takes upon oneself a relationship to whatever one perceives. God becomes "no longer a beyond for me," and one becomes interwoven with the object, spirit thinking itself. Hegel loved Meister Eckhart on this theme, helpfully informing students that Eckhart was a fourteenth-century Dominican monk. Eckhart sermonized, "The eye with which God sees me is the eye with which I see him; my eye and his eye are one and the same. In righteousness I am weighed in God and he in me." To Hegel, that was deeper and truer than the Kantian, Schleiermacherian, and historicist theologies of modern Protestantism.[151]

Kant and Fichte didn't understand religion, Hegel lamented. Religion is about making oneself such that the spirit dwells in one's being; it is practice of the presence of Spirit divine. Kant and Fichte, by contrast, reduced religion to a "merely moral standpoint," contending that the good must be brought out and realized within oneself as a religious duty. That assumed, Hegel observed, that the good is not already there "in and for itself." In the Kantian picture, the world stands waiting for rational moral agents to introduce the good from without. In the Hegelian picture, God is good and prevalent in the world; thus, the rational moral agent's role is to "rid myself of my subjectivity, do my share and play my part in this good, in this work, which is accomplished eternally and divinely." Hegel urged that the highest good is no mere ethical prescription; it is willing what God wills, "on which account it is the business of the singular subject to realize itself through the negation of its singularity."[152]

That raised the question of pantheism, which Hegel wearied of answering, but did so anyway. He was not a pantheist, he assured. But more importantly, nobody was a pantheist; Hegel had never met one: "It has never occurred to anyone to say that everything, all individual things collectively, in their individuality and contingency, are God – for example, that paper or this table is God. No one has ever held that." Spinoza and "Oriental pantheism" made "all is one" statements that smacked of pantheism, but neither taught that God is everything. They taught that the divine in all things is the universal aspect of their content, "the *essence* of things." Hegel observed that when Krishna or Vishnu said, "I am the luster or brilliance in metals," they superseded the idea of *everything* being God. Krishna is the luster in metals, not all metal and everything else. As for Spinoza, Hegel contended, he was not a pantheist, and he was certainly no atheist. Spinoza's accusers said that, because he was a pantheist, he was really an atheist. But that was only because they could not liberate themselves from the finite; for the people who screamed "atheist," God stood on the other side of the finite realm. Hegel believed that Spinoza espoused acosmism, the view that finite things are absorbed into the infinite. For Spinoza, there was no aggregate of finitudes, otherwise called the world; thus, the ostensible pantheist formula, "all is one," did not apply to him, as the "all" vanished without a trace.[153]

As for the charge that "pantheists" like him and Spinoza, taking all to be one, made good to be one with evil, and thus abolished religion, Hegel replied that this accusation blended two kinds of misunderstanding. If God were actually everything, God *would* be sublated. But nobody said that. In the Hegel/Spinoza view, Hegel explained, it is the finite that is sublated and the distinction between good and evil is sublated implicitly – in God as the true actuality. Hegel assured that there is no evil in God, quashing rumors about his theodicy. But the distinction between good and evil is valid only if God is evil. Hegel did not believe that evil has any ontological status, much less that such an affirmative element exists in God. "God is good and good alone," Hegel affirmed. The distinction between good and evil does not exist in the divine One, for it arises only with distinction in general. There is no distinction between good and evil until God is distinct from the world, especially human beings. The distinction between good and evil does not apply to God as such. Evil becomes an issue only with the rise of distinction, and the goal of human life is to be one with God, eliminating distinction. Hegel urged: "This is the most sublime morality, that evil is what is null, and human beings ought not to let this distinction, this nullity, be valid within themselves nor make it valid at all. We can will to persist in this distinction, can push it to the point of opposition to God, the universal in and for itself. In so doing we are evil. But we can also deem our distinction to be null and void, and can posit our essential being solely in God and in our orientation toward God. In so doing we are good."[154]

In every lecture cycle Hegel's longest section was the middle one, which he called *Die bestimmte Religion,* best translated as "determinate religion." He offered an extraordinary feast of interpretation, unmatched by any thinker of his time, though much of what he said was wrong. Systematic Western research on Buddhism and Hinduism was just beginning in Hegel's time, his sources of information on Chinese religion and so-called "primitive" religion were equally thin, and Hegel's low view of Islam deterred him from reading much about it. On Buddhism he relied heavily on travel literature and focused on the doctrine of nirvana; on Hinduism he made extensive use of reports by officials of the East India Company, though he also cited translations of the Code of Manu, the Mahabharata, and the Bhagavad-Gita. For Persian religion (Zoroastrianism) Hegel relied on a German translation of a French translation of the Zend-Avesta; for Egyptian religion he leaned on Herodotus and Plutarch, though he also cited current secondary scholarship; on Roman religion he featured two secondary sources, Karl Philipp Moritz and an old favorite, Gibbon's *Decline and Fall of the Roman Empire;* on Judaism he relied on his reading of Hebrew scripture, emphasizing the Pentateuch, Job, and the Psalms. As usual, Hegel showed that he knew the Greeks best of all, though he changed his mind about the standing of Greek religion. By far his chief contemporary source was Creuzer's four-volume myth criticism, though Hegel did not let friendship stand in the way of occasionally disagreeing with Creuzer.[155]

Very few scholars of Hegel's time knew as much as he did about world religions, and no philosopher came close to him. As in the *Phenomenology,* his treatment of determinate religion was a phenomenology of the forms of consciousness assumed by Spirit as it advanced through the history of religion. Though Hegel conveyed a vast amount of historical information (more than in the *Phenomenology,* where it was not always clear which religion he was talking about), his account in the religion lectures was phenomenological (describing concrete states of consciousness) and speculative (privileging the absolute idea as an interpretive construct). On the model of his logical triad of being, essence, and concept, Hegel conceived religions in the mode of determinateness and finitude, interpreting "Oriental nature religions" as religions of pre-reflective immediacy or undifferentiated substance, Jewish religion as differentiation in the form of particularity, Greek religion as differentiation in the form of necessity, Roman religion as differentiation in the form of external purposiveness, and

Christianity as the true, infinite, consummate religion. Roman religion had a special role in Hegel's account, as it showed the limitations of determinate religion. Roman religion was universal, transcending ethnic or national religions, yet it was too prosaic to have much depth or transcendence.[156]

Hegel worked hard at getting right his account of determinate religions. He reached his definitive conception of Christianity as the consummate religion in 1824 and pretty much recycled it afterwards. He reached his definitive conception of the concept of religion in 1827. He never reached a definitive conception on determinate religion, still revising and amplifying substantially in 1831. His most significant change of mind centered on Jewish religion. In 1821 he repeated the standard tropes of his long time anti-Jewish prejudice. In 1824 he revised this view significantly, and in 1827 he reversed his old position, lifting Jewish religion above the Greeks, all the while claiming that Schleiermacher got this issue disastrously wrong.

When Hegel began lecturing on religion, he routinely dismissed Judaism as a servile, legalistic, ingrown religion that should have expired. This was a prejudice straight from his earliest writings; the *Phenomenology* had barely granted Judaism a mention in its account of the history of humanity's self-consciousness. By 1824, however, Hegel had spent three years intently studying religion, and his friend Eduard Gans had convinced him that it was wrong to write off Judaism. Hegel did not give up believing that Judaism reeked of servile consciousness and the master-slave relationship. Like Islam, he argued, only with less fanaticism, Judaism had no concept of a dialectically self-mediated deity. Judaism, like Islam, had only the severe, forbidding One, who was not relational and did not sanction human freedom. Parenthetically Hegel added that Schleiermacher's concept of religious dependence was in this mode; Schleiermacher's mode of piety was Jewish, not Christian. Hegel emphatically disliked the Jewish conviction that Jews alone are God's people and that God alone is their God.[157]

But this time he also saw the sublimity, wisdom, and true spirituality in Jewish faith. The sublime manifests itself in ways that transcend appearance and reality, so that the reality "is simultaneously posited as negated," Hegel asserted. The idea associated with the sublime is exalted above that in which it appears, making its appearance "an inappropriate expression." Hegel admired the sublimity of the prophets and Psalms, and the Genesis creation myth, especially "Let there be light." Sublimity in religion is nature represented as wholly negated, subordinate, and transitory, Hegel argued; Jewish religion is strong on sublimity. Moreover, the Jewish God is more spiritual than previous deities. Jewish religion conceives the finite spirit as essentially consciousness and God as the object of consciousness as God's own essence. In consciousness, Hegel explained, the Jewish God *is* God's own purpose; God is to be recognized and venerated by all people (Ps. 117:1–2). Hegel commended the universality of God's purpose in the opening chapters of Genesis, though he judged that Jewish religion fell woefully short of it. The universal wisdom of Jewish faith "did not become truth for the people of Israel," stuck, as they were, in provincialism and determinacy. Nonetheless, it was wisdom of a high order.[158]

Hegel explained that Jewish religion, unlike Persian religion, had a problem with evil, and a compelling answer as to how evil came into the world. Persian religion, being dualistic, conceived evil as existing in the same way that good exists. Good and evil issued forth from the wholly indeterminate. In Jewish religion, however, God is power, the

One is subject, and God is the creator of all that is. The reality of evil is perplexing, for the God that created all things is absolutely good. Hegel pointed to the myth of Adam and Eve eating from the forbidden tree, the tree of the knowledge of good and evil. The difficult point for Hegel, as for Adam, was that God forbade humanity to acquire knowledge from this tree: "For this knowledge is precisely what constitutes the character of spirit. Spirit is spirit only through consciousness, and the highest consciousness lies precisely in such knowledge. How then can this have been forbidden?"[159]

Hegel, answering his own question through the myth, reasoned that knowledge is a two-sided gift, rife with danger. Human freedom is free to embrace good and evil, including the capacity to do evil. Hegel noted that Jewish religion never did very much with the myth of the Fall. Only in Christianity was this myth seized upon as an explanation for the reality and universality of evil. Christianity grasped the truth in the myth – that evil derives from human nature, it exists as the counterpart of human freedom, and the knowledge of good and evil constitutes likeness to God. But this is fundamentally Jewish wisdom, Hegel stressed.[160]

Previously Hegel had claimed that the Jewish emphasis on the "fear of the Lord" valorized servility, making Jewish religion the antithesis of freedom. Now he claimed that the religion of Israel was actually the first religion of freedom because it commanded fear of the Lord, which delegitimized earthly rulers, abolished idols and dependency, negated human negativity, and yielded absolute trust in the Creator of all things. Jewish religion, Hegel argued, was grounded in something affirmative, the divine-human relationship, even though the people of Israel did not grasp the radical implications of their covenant with God or actualize their universality. In both cases Hegel set his view against Schleiermacher's purported one. In 1821 he claimed that Schleiermacher was wrong for preaching fear of the Lord, a religion of passive dependence and servitude. In 1824 Hegel said that fear of the Lord is actually something affirmative and creative – except when Schleiermacher said it, for Schleiermacher preached a religion of passivity and dependence. Hegel declared: "So absolute fear is not a feeling of dependence, but casting off all dependence and purely abandoning oneself in the absolute self, vis-à-vis which and in which one's own self evaporates and dissolves."[161]

But that was virtually identical with Schleiermacher's concept of absolute *(schlechthinig)* dependence. For Schleiermacher, to be absolutely dependent was to be freed from dependence on all finite things, exactly in the sense of Hegel's "casting off all dependence and abandoning oneself in the absolute self." Schleiermacher and Hegel had the same panentheist concept of how the world process operates and how God saves the world. Both were influenced by Spinoza and forced to live it down. In content, though not in style, there was no difference between Hegel and Schleiermacher in this area. Hegel misconstrued Schleiermacher's concept of absolute dependence. Had Hegel read the second edition of Schleiermacher's *Glaubenslehre*, which stressed that religious feeling is redemptive by liberating the self from worldly dependence, it might have helped, but not likely. Hegel hated that Schleiermacher elevated piety over reason, the real source of his animus against him. Plus, Schleiermacher blocked him from the Academy of Sciences. Had Hegel focused his attack on their real differences, he could have issued a substantive critique, but not one that cut so deeply. As it was, Schleiermacher puzzled over Hegel's fixation with putting him down.[162]

For his highest category, Hegel alternated between *Die vollendete Religion* ("The Consummate Religion") and *Die offenbare Religion* ("The Revealed Religion"). The former predominated, expressing Hegel's conviction that Christianity is religion in its quintessential expression, or as he put it, "the religion in which religion has become objective to itself." Spirit is revelatory, he argued, the essence of God as spirit is "to be for an other," and true religion is revelatory as spirit for spirit: "God is this process of positing the other and then sublating it in his eternal movement. Thus the essence of spirit is to appear to itself, to manifest itself."[163]

The very idea of absolute spirit is to be the unity of divine and human nature, Hegel argued. The reality of God is implicit in the definition of God as absolute Spirit. That is, if God is defined as absolute Spirit, God necessarily exists. Though Hegel admired Anselm's ontological proof of God's existence, he had his own version of it based on his logic. According to Hegel, Anselm's proof rested on an "entirely correct" presupposition underlying all philosophy, the reality of perfection. Anselm described God as that which is most perfect. But if God is merely a concept, Anselm argued, God is not what is most perfect, for the perfect is that which has being, not merely something that is represented. Being is necessarily contained in the concept of what is most perfect, assuming that that which is merely imagined is less perfect than that which is real. Hegel put it concisely, restating Descartes' restatement of Anselm's proof: "God contains all reality; being is a reality; therefore he also contains this reality, being."[164]

But Kant demolished the presupposition that we can pluck being from the concept of God. Hegel accepted Kant's verdict that a fact cannot be derived from a concept. "Existence" and "being" are not concepts of things that can be added to the concept of a thing, for existence and being are not predicates. The content of a quart of milk is the same whether I imagine one or hold one in my hand. If being is not a predicate, it is not a reality, and thus it is not a determination of content or something contained in the concept of God. To the extent that Hegel accepted Kant's terms, he was chastened by Kant's disproof. Anselm's proof was circular; its conclusion was already contained in the presupposition of metaphysical perfection – the unity of thought and reality. Hegel accepted that modern philosophy, after Kant, had to start with the difference between concept and being, thought and reality, ideal and real, from the standpoint of the knowing subject.[165]

But Hegel told his students that the modern presupposition that sense experience contains reality is no more credible than the classical presupposition that it replaced. Post-Kantian philosophy, beginning with the difference between concept and being, had to show that concept and being are unified by the negation of their antithesis. This was the point of Hegel's logic – to *demonstrate,* not merely presuppose, that being is contained in the concept. The concept, as Hegel put it in the *Encyclopedia of the Philosophical Sciences,* is a movement that determines itself *to be;* it realizes itself in the process of determining itself into being, objectifying itself for itself: "The Idea is truth in itself and for itself – the absolute unity of the notion and objectivity. Its 'ideal' content is nothing but the notion in its detailed terms: its 'real' content is only the exhibition which the notion gives itself in the form of external existence, while yet, by enclosing this shape in its ideality, it keeps it in its power, and so keeps itself in it." This definition, Hegel argued, that the Idea *is* the absolute, is itself absolute. Everything comes back to it: "The Idea is the Truth: for Truth is the correspondence of objectivity with the notion."[166]

The concept progresses from subjectivity to objectivity to idea. On that basis Hegel refashioned the ontological proof, stressing that Anselm, Descartes, Spinoza, and Leibniz had presuppositions, so did Kant, and so did Hegel. Kant made some shrewd arguments, but the others had better presuppositions. Anselm presupposed perfection; Descartes, Spinoza, and Leibniz presupposed that God is the first reality; Kant countered that a concept is merely a concept, not something that corresponds to the concrete. The old metaphysical view was based on absolute thought, the unity of concept and reality, while Kant's view was based on the concrete. Hegel contended that the metaphysical view is superior in taking thoughts to be the concrete, not empirical human beings and actuality. The Kantian view is contradictory because it accepts the one-sided subjective concept *and* the concrete as equally valid. One cannot treat empirical actuality as real without bypassing the subjective concept, Hegel warned. The part that Kant got right was in holding up the subjective concept as the starting point; this was an advance on the metaphysical tradition of beginning with an abstract concept of perfection. Hegel summarized: "The older view is at a great advantage in that it is founded on the idea; in one respect the modern view is more advanced, in that it posits the concrete as unity of the concept and reality." But Kantian and post-Kantian thought had a tendency to lapse into mere empiricism, owing to Kant's contradictions and dualism. The way forward, Hegel urged, was to attend to the movement of the Idea in its realization of itself.[167]

The divine Idea explicates itself in three forms: eternal being, the form of universality; being for others, the form of appearance and particularization; and absolute presence-to-self, the form of return from appearance into itself. Whenever Hegel explained why Christianity is the consummate religion, he began with the Trinity and featured the Trinity. The three modes of divine being correspond to three modes of subjective consciousness, he argued. God in God's eternal essence is in pure thought, present to God's self yet manifest. God as being for others is represented, shaping consciousness in its relation to the other. God as absolute presence-to-self is subjectivity as such, partly as immediate subjectivity (disposition, thought, representation, sensation) but also as concept (reason, the thinking of free spirit). Hegel affirmed that the divine Trinity, besides being the fundamental truth of Hegelian philosophy, has the same status in Christianity. Essentially it is the idea of God differentiating God's self while remaining identical with God's self in the process.[168]

Hegel played down the usual talk about the Trinity being mysterious. The doctrine of the Trinity is usually said to be mysterious because it is mystical and speculative, he observed. The assumption is that only sense experience yields certainty, which is lacking in this case. Hegel was defiantly of another mind: "What is for reason is not a secret. In the Christian religion one *knows*, and this is a secret only for the finite understanding, and for the thought that is based on sense experience." In the mode of sense experience, the distinctions in God's being are immediate and natural things are treated as reality. "This is the mode of externality," Hegel cautioned. "But as soon as God is defined as spirit, externality is sublated, and for sense this *is* a mystery; for sense everything is external to everything else – objects change, and the senses are aware of them in different ways."[169]

The change perceived by sense is itself a sensible process occurring in time and space. The sun comes into being, making life possible, but some day it will pass out of existence. Hegel urged his students to think beyond the everyday actuality of temporal existence: "The being of a thing is *now,* and its nonbeing is separated from now; for time is what keeps the determinations apart from another, external to one another." Even the understanding, like sense experience, separates being from non-being, holding fast to abstractions that are apprehended or conceived as existing on their own account. Hegel noted that people routinely scoffed at the Trinity at this level of comprehension, deriding a literalistic understanding of three equals one. Reason, making sense of the Trinity, employs the relationships of the understanding, "but only insofar as it destroys the *forms* of the understanding." Everything concrete contains contradictions, Hegel cautioned. These contradictions are resolved only in the idea, "and the resolution is spiritual unity." Hegel's favorite example was the statement, "God is love." This expression makes God present to sensation; as "love," God is construed as a person; and God is conceived as inherently relational. God is conscious of God's self only in the other, Hegel urged, citing Goethe for support, and there is no consciousness of God apart from consciousness of the other.[170]

Obviously, Hegel acknowledged, the Trinitarian form of Father, Son, and Spirit is childlike, and it conveys a merely figurative relationship. "Love" would be a more suitable term than "Spirit" in this triad, for the Spirit does not enter into this relationship. The Father and the Son are Spirit no less than the third mode, and the Spirit of love is what is truthful. But at the level of spiritual expression, Hegel judged, the childlike form of Trinitarian theology is indispensable. In Christ, God appears in sensible presence: "He has no other figure or shape [*Gestalt*] than that of the sensible mode of the spirit that is spirit in itself – the shape of the *singular human being.*" God must generate the Son to distinguish God's self from God's self in a way that what is distinguished remains wholly God in God's self, "and their union is love and the Spirit." The witness of love/Spirit is the "infinite anguish" of being conjoined as conflicting elements of infinite and finite, objective and subjective.[171]

By the time that he got to the life of Christ, Hegel rushed to Good Friday. His long discussions of the Trinity predisposed him to move straight to the death of God on the cross. Hegel reasoned that he didn't need to separate his treatment of Christ incarnate from his explication of the Trinity; plus, for Hegel, not much was at sake in the gospel stories about Christ's teaching, miracles, and travels. Turning to Good Friday, Hegel cited Johannes Rist's Lutheran passion hymn of 1641, "O Traurigkeit, O Herzeleid":

> O great woe!
> God himself lies dead.
> On the cross he has died.
> And thus he has gained for us
> By love the kingdom of heaven.[172]

The suffering and death of Christ on the cross disclose the very nature of God as loving, self-sacrificial, and affirmative, Hegel asserted. It also posits God's negation – "in death the moment of negation is envisaged." Hegel admonished against making Calvary merely about the sacrificial death of Jesus, an individual: "Heretics have interpreted it like that, but what it means is rather that *God* has died, that *God himself is dead.* God has died: this is negation, which is accordingly a moment of the divine nature, of God himself." God could not be satisfied by anything else than the negation of God's own immediacy, Hegel reasoned: "Only then does God come to be at peace with himself, only then is he spiritually posited." As Father, God is closed up within God's self; as Son, God becomes the other and negates the other for the sake of love. This negation reconciles all who are separated from God to union with God. Humanity is posited in God's death as a moment of God's being. Hegel explained: "Death is love itself; in it absolute love is envisaged. The identity of the divine and the human means that God is at home with himself in humanity, in the finite, and in [its] death this finitude is itself a determination of God." The death of Christ is a death in God. Through God's self-sacrifice in Christ, God reconciles the world to God's self and reconciles God's self eternally with God's self.[173]

The crucial point of the story is the next part, Hegel taught. God raises Christ from the dead to the right hand of God. The nature of God is accomplished: Spirit pouring itself out for the other and returning to itself. A spiritual community takes up this story that this is God's story, revealing who God is. Hegel stressed that the Christian community recognized Christ as a determination of the nature of God raised to the right hand of God. The revelation is not what Jesus said, what he looked like, his miracles, or anything else on the level of sense experience. What mattered is the nature of God as spirit, the witness of Spirit to spirit, the negation of Calvary as an essential moment in the life of God, and the consummated self-realization of Spirit. The spiritual community adopts this story and sustains it, Hegel stressed; there is no life of faith without the community.[174]

But only philosophy can justify the content of the consummate religion, not bishops or history. Hegel put it aggressively: "The story may be full of the passionate disputes of bishops at church councils and so on – this is of no account." The content in and for itself is what matters, not the transmission of church doctrine. Only philosophy, which deals with concepts, can adequately handle the content of true religion, not religion, which deals with pictures. Mixing two concepts of history, Hegel unleashed one of his most famous statements: "Only by philosophy can this simply present content be justified, not by history [*Geschichte*]. What spirit does is no history *(Historie)*. Spirit is concerned only with what is in and for itself, not something past, but simply what is present. This is the origin of the community."[175]

Hegelian theologians fiercely debated what that meant, especially after Hegel was gone. Had Hegel used the term *Historie* in both sentences, he could have been construed as saying that history as bare literal fact justifies nothing and is not the point. Many of his more orthodox disciples took him that way. As it was, Hegel used the term *Geschichte* – interpreted history, or the meaning of history – in the first reference, which raised unsettling questions about the extent to which he regarded *any* historical basis as being intrinsic to Christian truth.

Hegel did not teach that philosophy should replace religion or that the historical core of Christianity was entirely dispensable. He taught his students that philosophy was dependent upon and continued to be fed by religious experience. But he was careful not to say how much of the gospel narrative needed to be historically credible if Christianity was to be accepted as the true religion. The logic of his argument pressed in the direction of minimizing historicity. He could be sloppy with his terms, as in the example from his 1824 lectures noted here. In his subsequent lectures, Hegel used the terms "divine history" and "eternal history" more frequently, emphasizing that God *is* the eternal history. The process by which God self-distinguishes and self-reintegrates is historical (*geschichtlich*). But Hegel left open, for Hegelian theologians, the question of how much one needed to believe about past historical (*historisch*) events or the historical (*geschichtlich*) process in which Spirit comes to self-realization.[176]

Hegel's emphasis on the Trinity raised a similar question differently. Repeatedly he was accused of puffing up the Trinity to cover up his pantheism. Most critics of this sort came from the theological right, which Hegel ignored. But there were liberals and Pietists in Schleiermacher's orbit who said the same thing, and in 1826 young Pietist theologian Friedrich August Gottreu Tholuck, recently transferred from the University of Berlin to the University of Halle, offered a novel version of the anti-Hegel argument that Hegel did not ignore. Tholuck was fervently pious, learned, not yet prominent, and worried that people with dubious Christian credentials were being treated as leading Christian thinkers. Hegel was example A. Hegel's robust Trinitarianism did not impress Tholuck, as Tholuck regarded the Trinity as an unfortunate Nicene pick-up from Aristotelian and neo-Platonist philosophy. Pietists of Tholuck's type were comfortable with rationalist criticism on this topic and with Schleiermacher's consignment of the Trinity to the appendix. Tholuck suggested that Hegel covered his lack of pious feeling with a doctrine of dubiously Christian merit. Hegel replied that he would never "put off such a basic doctrine" on the basis of a merely historical argument, as Tholuck did. Hegel declared: "I am a Lutheran, and through philosophy have been at once completely confirmed in Lutheranism. I detest seeing such things explained in the same manner as perhaps the descent and dissemination of silk culture, cherries, smallpox, and the like."[177]

Hegel shook his head at the thought of a non-metaphysical Christianity. He believed that theologians who spurned metaphysical ideas stood in danger of trivializing the great Christian truths. To friends he groused that pious sincerity provided no immunity from degrading Christianity. To Tholuck he put it more plaintively: "Does not the sublime Christian knowledge of God as Triune merit respect of a wholly different order than comes from ascribing it merely to such an extremely historical course?" Hegel could see a new anti-intellectualism coming in theology that dressed up its backwardness with supportive quotes from Schleiermacher; Tholuck epitomized the type. However, Hegel struggled to keep his sarcasm in check when he warmed to this theme. Pietism had a vast following in Hegel's denomination. Hegel sustained a respectful tone with Tholuck; even writing to him was a sign of respect.[178]

With Catholic critics, however, Hegel was less circumspect. Routinely he blasted the Catholic Church for opposing intellectual freedom. In class he mocked the doctrine of transubstantiation, worrying what it meant if a mouse ate a host. A Catholic priest, responding to complaints from Catholic students, filed a protest to the Ministry of Religious and Educational Affairs about Hegel's anti-Catholicism. Hegel's official reply was scathing: "As Professor of Philosophy at a Royal Prussian university in Berlin, and as a Lutheran Christian, it is only to be expected that I should express myself in such terms on the teachings and spirit of Catholicism. That this should be found remarkable is novel. I would have to consider any other expectation as a personal offense, indeed as an offense perpetrated by the High Government." As a Lutheran, Hegel explained, he expounded the teaching of Martin Luther as true, "and as recognized by philosophy as true." As for the accusations of anti-Catholic animus filed against him, some were based on "misunderstandings," others were "errors and misunderstandings born of feeblemindedness," some were obvious "falsehoods," and others displayed "malicious disparagement." Summing up, Hegel declared: "Should suit be filed because of remarks I have made from the podium before Catholic students causing them annoyance, they would have to blame only themselves for attending philosophical lectures at a Protestant university under a professor who prides himself on having been baptized and raised a Lutheran, which he still is and shall remain. Or else they would have to blame their superiors for failing to warn them or – as happened elsewhere to Catholic theology students – for failing to prohibit their attendance."[179]

In his last years Hegel defended his Christian basis, attended to his followers, took notice that nearly all of them were theologians or religious philosophers, and admonished some that his philosophy was not a closed rational system. He did not claim to understand the content of an unknowable thing-in-itself; even to claim to know that it exists would be too much. The Absolute, Hegel urged, if it is absolute, is not something beyond our knowledge of it. The Absolute holds such knowledge within itself – its very self-knowledge. To attain knowledge in the finite sphere, "a procedure other than that of those [Kantian] categories must be established – a standpoint which the Kantian critique fails to attain."[180]

Religion, Hegel urged, is one of the three basic practices by which people become aware of humanity's highest purposes. Art and philosophy are the other two, but religion is distinct and indispensable. In religion, one joins a community dedicated to experiencing unity with the divine. One cannot be religious on one's own, for the idea of religion is to transcend one's individuality to achieve union with the divine through cultic practices and symbolic representation. In his 1827 lectures on religion he told students that whenever they philosophized about religion, they engaged in religious thinking, which leads beyond mere thinking: "Religion is for everyone. It is not philosophy, which is not for everyone. Religion is the manner or mode by which all human beings become conscious of truth for themselves."[181]

Hegelianism

Thus he wanted theological followers, and he got them. The breakthrough for Hegel occurred in the early 1820s, when Karl Daub and Phillipp Marheineke, both distinguished speculative theologians, converted to Hegelianism. Daub, a struggling type of deep moral integrity, authored a massive two-volume work on the nature of evil in 1816 and 1818. Marheineke, a serene, self-confident type and Hegel's colleague at Berlin, finished a dogmatic system in 1819. Both were followers of Schelling, espousing Schelling's concept of the absolute as an undifferentiated ground of being revealed through intuition. But both were uneasy with Schelling's emphasis on revelatory intuition. Hegel convinced them that his system retained the best parts of Schelling's idealism without Schelling's subjectivism. Daub and Marheineke, upon becoming Hegelians, drew their students to Hegel's circle, which expanded rapidly.[182]

By 1830 there were many Hegelians, most of them theologians or religious philosophers, notably Hermann Hinrichs, Christian Kapp, Isaak Rust, Georg Andreas Gabler, Johann Karl Friedrich Rosenkranz, Karl Friedrich Göschel, Kasimir Conradi,

Friedrich C. Förster, Eduard Gans, Karl Ludwig Michelet, Johann F. G. Eiselen, Friedrich W. Carové, Heinrich T. Rötscher, Leopold Henning, Heinrich Leo, Karl Friedrich Werder, Agathon Benary, and Heinrich G. Hotho.[183]

From the beginning there were debates about the Hegelian line on religion and politics. After Hegel died in 1831, these debates famously intensified, as the Hegelian movement, a burgeoning force in German intellectual life, split into factions. Most of the literature on Hegelianism contents itself with a facile distinction between establishment "right-Hegelians" and the generally younger, politically radical, and un-friendly-to-religion group of left-Hegelians that emerged in the 1830s. The so-called "right-Hegelians," in this telling, were politically accommodationist and theologically conservative, and were led by Marheineke, Förster, Hinrichs, and Göschel. The left-Hegelian ringleaders were David Friedrich Strauss, Ludwig Feuerbach, Bruno Bauer, and Friedrich Theodor Vischer.

But this simple right-left scheme does not work even with these leading examples, as Strauss was a monarchist and only Göschel in the "right" group was theologically conservative. Most Hegelians were not conservative in either theology or politics, despite going down in history as "right-Hegelians," and some of the leading Hegelian opponents of the youthful left insurgency – Rosenkranz, Julius Schaller, and Johann Eduard Erdmann – were equally youthful. The simplest possible rendering of the Hegelian movement has to distinguish among its right, centrist, and left factions, plus distinguish between theology and politics, plus account for the connections between theology and politics, plus leave room for individual cases in a movement that quickly grew beyond its university base to include pastors, Gymnasium teachers, public officials, and independent intellectuals. These fissures did not come from nowhere; all had roots in the Hegelian school over which Hegel personally presided.

In 1827 the Hegelians acquired the essential infrastructure of a movement by founding a journal, *Jahrbücher für wissenschaftliche Kritik (Yearbooks for Scientific Criticism)*, directed by Gans. Hegel spent his last years monitoring in-house back-and-forth, complaining that most of it was not worth his time, and doing it anyway; his school mattered to him. On religion and politics, most Hegelians were in the middle with Hegel, though Hegel drifted rightward politically in his later years. Christianity and Hegelian philosophy, Hegel argued, had the same content, though Christianity, being a religion, trafficked in picture-thinking. All Hegelian theologians played up Hegel's assertion about the identity of content, which raised the question whether one had to espouse Hegel's panentheism to be a Hegelian.

From the beginning there were Hegelian theologians that did not – notably Göschel, Conradi, and Rust. Hegel was gentle with them. He liked having traditional Christian theists on his side; Göschel was a superior court judge in Naumburg and the lay leader of a pietist congregation. Göschel praised Hegel's thought, defended Hegel's orthodoxy, and made clear that he – Göschel – hypostatized divine reality as self-conscious apart from the world. Hegel, in reply, reaffirmed his panentheist concept of Spirit, but lauded Göschel for the "rare excellence" of his thought, calculating that Göschel could be his link to a sizable audience out of reach to most Hegelians, which he turned out to be.[184]

On politics the main issue in Hegel's time was accommodation versus liberal reformism. Here, too, there were ambiguities in Hegel's position that yielded different Hegelianisms. Though Hegelians tried to debate politics, they had to be careful, as the censorship of a repressive restorationist government made it perilous to be anything besides an accommodationist; it was much easier to debate religion. In Hegel's time most prominent Hegelians were accommodationists, especially Marheineke, Hinrichs, Förster, Göschel, Gabler, Henning, and Conradi. There was a liberal reform faction led by Gans and Carové that, by 1835, had grown into the dominant Hegelian party, attracting Michelet, Hotho, Agathon Benary, Ferdinand Benary, Arnold Ruge, Karl Friedrich Werder, Wilhelm Vatke, and many others. Both groups had cause to claim Hegel for their side. Liberals pointed to Hegel's longtime enthusiasm for the French Revolution and his defense of republican principles. Accommodationists pointed to his defense of constitutional monarchy and his increasingly grumpy conservatism. In his last years Hegel told his liberal followers not to get worked up over politics. France's "July Revolution" of 1830 excited many Hegelians, but Hegel told his student Michelet to stop blathering nonsense about the "spirit of the people." One negotiated with individuals, not the spirit of a people, Hegel admonished.[185]

Politically, Göschel bonded with the establishment Hegelians over the politics of accommodation, though he had a populist streak; religiously he was a special case by virtue of reaching a larger audience than any Hegelian. Göschel's *Aphorisms on Ignorance and Absolute Knowing* (1829) defended Hegel's absolute knowing against the "ignorance" of Jacobi and the theology of feeling espoused by Schleiermacher, Fries, de Wette, and Tholuck. In Göschel's telling, the theology of ignorant feeling fell short of Christianity by denying God's objective revelation. Göschel added that Kantian rationalist theologians such as Paulus and Heinrich F. W. Gesenius wrongly divorced reason from faith, and thus philosophy from religion. Hegel's speculative philosophy, by contrast, preserved faith by raising it to the level of knowledge. Göschel emphasized the distinction between reason and the understanding. The rationalist theologies were based on the abstract understanding, which is the source of individual opposition to God's will, while Hegel's approach was a theology of reason, the light of the divine in every person. Reason, Göschel explained, the divine logos, is not a mere human faculty, unlike the understanding. Reason is revelatory, as demonstrated by Hegel's thoroughly Christian philosophy. Göschel declared that the philosopher, to think out of reason, must be enlightened by "his day of Pentecost": "Without a second birth no one can rise from the sphere of natural understanding to the speculative heights of the living concept. That famous bridge that leads in one sudden leap from the limited horizons of the psychological sphere to the philosophical circle of light must be crossed by everyone."[186]

This rendering of the relevant options in theology delighted Hegel, though he issued a caution. Reviewing Göschel's book, Hegel enthused that the book was "thoroughly imbued" with Hegel's belief that Christian truth and rational truth were fundamentally unified. That raised a cautionary point, however, because Hegel did not begin by assuming the truth of Christianity, in the manner of medieval theology. If his philosophy was Christian, as he believed it to be, it was only such by virtue of being led there by the self-determination of reason. His system moved toward the Christian principle, and ultimately affirmed Christianity as the consummate religion, but it did not begin with the principle of any religious tradition – a crucial point that Göschel did not convey. Elsewhere Hegel reluctantly advised his favorite Pietist that believing in a God hypostatized apart from the world was not Hegelian; Göschel needed to give up the idea of a separate supernatural realm. In correspondence Hegel accented the positive, enthusing that Göschel's book "powerfully contributed to a possible lessening of apprehensiveness over philosophy." On the other hand, grumpy Hegel was doleful about the utility of philosophy, as it seemed to have so little impact on the "ignorance, violence and evil passions" of the masses, notably the idiots who were excited about the new government in France. He told Göschel that philosophy might have to realize "that it is destined only for a few." Göschel, fired with movement enthusiasm, admonished his hero to remember who he was supposed to be; he was not supposed to end up with Cicero, sneering at ordinary people.[187]

Being a celebrity wore on Hegel, but he worked hard at building up his following and legacy. In the 1820s he was told repeatedly that Schelling trashed him as a "cuckoo" who planted himself in Schelling's nest and stole his ideas. Schelling deeply resented Hegel's fame and eminence, which by the 1820s overshadowed his own. It was hard for Schelling to accept, having shot into preeminence as a youth, that staying there was not something to which he was entitled, even if he had stopped publishing. He pleaded with audiences large, small, and individual to stop rewarding Hegel for stealing his ideas. Schelling knew what had happened; at least, he believed that he knew. He knew that Hegel was far from brilliant, because he and Hegel had come up together, when Hegel couldn't hold his own in a philosophical discussion. Hölderlin was the smart one, next to Schelling. Then Schelling rescued Hegel from tutoring adolescents, after which Hegel built a career by helping himself to Schelling's ideas. Schelling explained that Hegel was gifted at stealing and transposition, nothing more. He took Schelling's violin concerto and transposed it for piano, refashioning Schelling's ideas in the form of Hegel's misguided rationalism. He trashed Schelling in his first real book, then denied doing it, and then broke off communication with Schelling. Afterwards he ratcheted up the logical cast of his system, all the while failing to acknowledge what he owed to Schelling.[188]

This was a fight that Hegel could not win, except by prevailing. Nothing he could say in reply to Schelling would make him look better. Had Schelling published on this theme, Hegel probably would have defended himself; as it was, he kept his head down. Aside from the scathing put-down in the *Phenomenology,* Hegel did not attack Schelling in his books, nor criticize Schelling personally in public. In the classroom he pointed out his differences with Schelling, but his lectures on the history of philosophy respectfully summarized Schelling's thought, albeit too briefly for Schelling's taste. From the outset of his rift with Schelling, Hegel appears to have settled on the view that it was inevitable. In 1826, lecturing on aesthetics at Berlin, he said as much, reflecting on the cooling of youthful friendships as males moved up in the world: "Every man has to make his way through life for himself and to gain and maintain an actual position for himself. Now when individuals still live in actual relationships which are indefinite on both sides, this is the period, i.e., youth, in which individuals become intimate and are so closely bound into one disposition, will, and activity that, as a result, every undertaking of the one becomes the undertaking of the other. In the friendship of adults this is no longer the case. A man's affairs go their own way independently and cannot be carried into effect in that firm community of mutual effort in which one man cannot achieve anything without someone else." Perhaps Hegel regretted not having written back to Schelling; in any case, he realized that when it mattered, he chose to head off on his own.[189]

Except that he could not leave it there; reconciling with Schelling was important to Hegel. In 1829, shortly after he was elected rector at Berlin for the upcoming academic year, Hegel took a celebrative vacation at Karlsbad, where he learned that Schelling was vacationing somewhere nearby. Hegel found Schelling at a nearby spa and took him for a walk. In Hegel's account, which he told many times, he and Schelling had a warm, friendly time together; Hegel told Marie, "We are both pleased about meeting again, and find ourselves together as cordial friends of old." Schelling's account was decidedly cooler. He told his wife that, sitting in a bath, he heard "a somewhat unpleasant, half-forgotten voice asking for me." It turned out to be Hegel, who acted "as if nothing were standing between us." Hegel tried to induce "scholarly conversation," but Schelling refused, which did not stop them from having "two agreeable hours" talking about non-intellectual things.[190]

The one who felt betrayed felt the gulf standing between them, a source of too much pain to talk about. Schelling belongs to history as the objective idealist link between Fichte and Hegel. If not for Hegel, he would have been remembered on his own. As it is, he is usually viewed as a stepping-stone to Hegel, exactly as he feared. In 1831 Hegel died suddenly, probably of a gastrointestinal disease, though he was pronounced dead from cholera, of which he lacked most of the symptoms. His death was an enormous shock in Berlin, and a deflating one; even Hegel's enemies acknowledged that he was a historic figure. His funeral featured a massive procession through the streets of Berlin, not quite on Schleiermacher's scale, but huge for an academic; Hegel was buried next to Fichte at Dorothea Cemetery.

Förster and Marheineke gave the funeral orations; Marheineke's status as the university's new rector added weight to his pronouncement. Förster, at Hegel's graveside, declared: "Let the dead bury the dead; to us belongs the living; he who, having thrown off his earthly chains, celebrates his transfiguration." In case anybody missed the analogy, Marheineke said it explicitly at the Great Hall of the university: "In a fashion similar to our savior, whose name he always honored in his thought and activity, and in whose divine teaching he recognized the most profound essence of the human spirit, and who as the son of God gave himself over to suffering and death in order to return to his community eternally as spirit, he also has now returned to his true home and through death has penetrated through to resurrection and glory."[191]

That was a portent; Hegelianism was no longer merely an academic theory. It was a modern religious movement led by an academic spiritual community. To comprehend the infinite through Hegel's dialectic was to attain infinity. Marheineke said it pointedly, telling the mourners that Hegel's comprehension of the Spirit's self-realization in nature and history enabled him and others to be elevated to a state of spiritual being. Immediately the Hegelians formed a society to publish a complete edition of Hegel's works, beginning with his lectures on the philosophy of religion. The ringleaders were Marheineke, Förster, Michelet, Gans, Hotho, Henning, Ludwig

Boumann, and Johannes Schulze. They were prolific and industrious, armed with movement zeal, intellectual self-confidence, and religious fervor. The fact that most Hegelians were religious types had consequences for theology and philosophy faculties for decades. Factions developed quickly. So-called "right-Hegelians" defended the doctrine of immortality, treated gospel history as constitutive to Christian truth, and sometimes balked at Hegel's panentheism. Centrist Hegelians stuck closer to Hegel's formulations on religion and built up a dominant liberal Hegelian party on matters political and cultural. Left-Hegelians adopted political radicalism and turned against religion. In philosophy, Hegel's death was like the crash of a supernova, leaving a black hole that no one could fill.[192]

Georg Andreas Gabler, one of Hegel's closest disciples, was named to his chair at Berlin, but that was a stopgap; Gabler was the least creative of the Hegelians. Then the Hegelian School erupted into factions and no obvious successor to Hegel emerged. In 1841 Hegel's chair reopened and King Wilhelm IV, who cared about philosophy, shared the university's anxiety to restore its faded glory. The king had two problems. He despised Hegel's radical "pantheism" and he needed to appoint somebody who remotely approached Hegel's stature. His ambassador to Munich, C. J. Bunsen, quotably expressed the crown's opinion of the Hegelian school and its penchant for radicalism, declaring that somebody had to put an end to the "dragonseed of Hegelian Pantheism," especially its "facile omniscience."[193]

There was only one conceivable candidate for that mission, even if he was 65 years old and had not published a significant work in over thirty years. Schelling was reluctant to leave Munich, where he had ended up, or Bavaria in general. But he yielded to the king's offer of the highest salary ever offered to a professor and guaranteed freedom from the royal censors. For many years he had sought to create a new mythology, struggling to make up his mind whether such a project exceeded the limits and function of reason. Belatedly he decided that it did. He made a similar judgment about his other main ambition, a philosophical mythology, which left him bereft of projects, except his original one – putting post-Kantian idealism on the right path.[194]

Schelling had never stopped believing in the absolute that transcends subjective and objective standpoints. In his prolific early career the absolute held together his transcendental idealism. In his struggling middle career it was the lure and goal of a philosophical mythology that he never quite pulled off. In his last phase, moving to Hegel's chair at Berlin, Schelling resolved that good idealism had to be positive, revelatory, and grounded in reality, in opposition to Hegel's concept of the absolute as the result of the self-cancellation of the finite. Thus he called his inaugural lectures in Berlin *The Grounding of Positive Philosophy.*

Coping with hyperbolic expectations, but also reveling in them, Schelling was ambitious, personal, a bit nostalgic, admiring of Kant, contemptuous of Hegel, and imbued with a self-confident sense of the moment. He assured his vast audience – which included Søren Kierkegaard, Friedrich Engels, Ludwig Feuerbach, and Michail Bakunin – that nothing gained for philosophy by Kant would be lost through Schelling. He declared that the fragmented modern world needed, more than ever, what it had needed in the aftermath of Kant, a philosophy that "takes its vitality from reality itself . . . healing the fragmentation of our time." He promised to speak more personally than philosophers usually spoke, because he was serious about healing the modern world; plus, "my tenure here is decided." He shared Hegel's ambition to provide a new philosophical religion. He acknowledged that Hegel alone "saved" and even "completed" some essential elements of Schelling's philosophy. And he charged that Hegel took post-Kantian idealism in a wholly misguided direction. Schelling had come to rescue German idealism from its Hegelian mistake.[195]

In 1833 the Hegelian School had published Hegel's lectures on the history of philosophy, so Schelling had read what Hegel said about him. Schelling acknowledged that Hegel mostly got him right, better than anyone else. But Hegel's departure from Schelling completely misdiagnosed what was lacking in post-Kantian idealism, Schelling contended. Hegel refashioned Schelling's thinking into a system of thought itself, not a system about reality. Schelling cautioned that Hegel versus Schelling did not come down to the difference between a negative and a positive philosophy, for Schelling had a negative philosophy, too, and Hegel had pretensions to positive philosophy. Hegel's fundamental mistake was to fashion his negation of the negation into a positive philosophy. Schelling put it sharply: "The philosophy that Hegel presented is the negative driven beyond its limits: it does not exclude the positive, but thinks it has subdued it within itself."[196]

Schelling recognized the provenance of Hegel's thesis that the identity of thought and being discloses the capacity of reason to ground itself. Hegel extended Kant's analysis of predication, a move that he learned from Fichte, Schelling, and Hölderlin. Hegel taught that thinking and difference are reflections, respectively, of what they are not – being and identity. The absolute is the result of the self-cancellation of the finite, the negation of the negation – a successive overcoming of finite determinations. This progression culminates in the appearance of the Absolute Idea, in which reason realizes its absolute other as itself and releases itself into nature – the other of the idea. To Schelling, this account of the reflexive unfolding of reason was justified and familiar on the level of the experience of thought; Hegel got it from him. The problem was that Hegel derived the actual world of existence from his logic of the concept. Schelling chided that one could not read more than a few pages of the *Encyclopedia* without stumbling over the problem, as Hegel constantly claimed that reason concerns itself with the "in itself" (*An sich*) of things. This "in itself" is not the fact that things exist, nor even their being, Schelling observed. For Hegel it was the concept, the essence (*Wesen*). The nature of human beings, or of plants, remained the same for Hegel even if there were no people or plants on earth. Schelling declared: "The fundamental thought of Hegel is that reason relates to the in itself, the essence of things, from which [it] immediately follows that philosophy, to the extent that it is a science of reason, occupies itself only with the whatness [*Was*], or the essence, of things."[197]

Schelling assured that he had never believed that. He, too, was an absolute idealist who loved Spinoza, but he had never taught that philosophy cares only about the in-itself of things. Schelling admonished that even Hegel should have realized that he was on the wrong path when he moved from the first book of the *Encyclopedia* to the second book, although, tellingly, Schelling mentioned no specific howlers in Hegel's philosophy of nature. Schelling had a history of howlers of his own in this area that were better off forgotten. Instead he switched to the point that Hegel's logic overwhelmed everything, including subjectivity, not merely nature. Schelling cautioned that he was not a Romanticist; Romanticism had passed, and he did not regard feeling as the exclusive source of philosophy. But philosophy was like poetry and art in needing the "voice" of feeling: "Many a path that leads to error will be spared those who listen to it for the very reason that this sensibility shuns that which is artificial." If Hegel had given his feelings any outlet whatsoever, he might have spared himself and the world a great deal of "laborious and unclear" philosophy.[198]

Post-Kantian idealism was about thought reflecting what it is not – being – as itself, even as thought appears not to be itself. Hegelian reason sought to know itself in being to the point where contradictions cease and Spirit is self-realized. Schelling agreed that knowledge depends on movement; it is not read off from any particular thing. But logic can only deliver a reflection of thought, he contended. The virtual world of the concept and the actual world of existence are inseparable, but they cannot be demonstrated to reflect each other. Thus, philosophy must not claim to comprehend the world process. There must be a slight asymmetry in the identity of thought and being in which the expansive force of thought – the ideal – is slightly stronger than the contractive force of being. Identity is the *condition* of divine revelation through creation, the divine lure of desire that thrives in the interplay of contrary forces. Schelling put it pugnaciously. If people longed for nothing beyond rationalistic certainty, they were free to stick with it: "Only he must give up the desire to possess within the rational philosophy that which it by no means can possess, namely, the real God, the actual chain of events, and a free relationship of God to the world. The confusion that now reigns over this matter must cease."[199]

Hegel's system had a place for movement; it even featured movement, Schelling allowed. But the Hegelian system had no real *other* to the necessity of reason. Thus it had no real God, no actual chain of events, no real opposition, no real freedom, and no God that freely related to the world. In fact, Schelling continued, it was not even correct to speak of real history or development in Hegel's system, because Hegel had no room for a future that was not already contained in the concept. Post-Kantian idealism was supposed to be about the freedom of reason, but Hegel nullified it. Schelling realized that Hegelian theologians were hard at work on this problem, and that Hegel himself tried to make adjustments in his lectures on religion: "In later addendums he allowed this absolute spirit to freely decide to create a world, to externalize itself with freedom into a world." But Hegel did not say that at the creation of the world, Hegelianism was an impossible thought. Hegel never worked his way up to the Christian God, although he took a pass at doing so, which produced Hegelian clerics and theologians. Schelling was embarrassed for Hegel that there existed Hegelian clerics who preached out of the *Phenomenology*. Knowing Hegel as he did, Schelling was sure that the "sentimental, pietistic phrases" of the Hegelian School would have aroused "only disgust in that powerful thinker."[200]

Schelling admonished Hegelian theologians and his audience that it is better to start with Christianity than to work up to it. Certainly, to judge from the catalogue of failed modern alternatives, there was no better place to start: "Christianity is one of the greatest and most significant phenomena of the world. It is in its own way just as good a reality as nature and has the right, just as every other phenomenon, to be left in its singularity and not to be misrepresented only in order to be capable of the next best thing, that is, of applying to it an explanation accessible to everyone." Instead of adapting Christianity to a logical scheme that privileges itself and exploits Christian concepts, it is better to wrestle with the Christian God, the only reality that explains thought and freedom. Reason cannot explain its own existence, Schelling urged. We must begin with the contingency of being and try to make sense of it with our God-given, but limited reason. Before creation, God is the ability-to-be. God's being is creativity, the putting into play of open possibilities. In representative language, which philosophy should not denigrate, God is "he who is the creator, who can begin something, who thus exists before everything, and who is not just an idea of reason."[201]

Schelling's Berlin Lectures overflowed with irony. His audience dwindled steadily from week to week, he never published the manuscript, and he was widely panned for being too obscure, colloquial, old, cozy with the monarchy, and religious. Often he was accused of delivering old stuff or of being stuck in a moment, approximately 1800. Yet these lectures electrified some who heard them. Schelling spoke directly to the longing for reality and a creative future that heralded his arrival in Berlin. He spoke directly to the suspicion that Hegelianism replaced the Christian God with an overreaching concept. He offered an intuitive, existential, open-ended idealism to the reigning idealism that seemed to be none of these things. For fifteen years, transcriptions of his lectures circulated until Schelling's son published them in a collected works. Michail Bakunin, the father of Russian anarchism, told his family in 1841, "You cannot imagine with what impatience I have been waiting for Schelling's lectures. In the course of the summer I have read much of his works and found therein such an immeasurable profundity of life and creative thinking that I am convinced he will now reveal to us a treasure of meaning."[202]

Søren Kierkegaard, on the verge of pouring out books, viewed Schelling as a singular beacon of hope: "I am so happy to have heard Schelling's second lecture – indescribably. Long enough have I sighed and thoughts sighed in me; when he mentioned the word 'reality' concerning the relation of philosophy to reality then the fetus of thought leaped with joy in me as in Elizabeth. I remember almost every word he said from that moment on. Here perhaps clarity can occur. Maybe here clarity can occur … Now I have placed all my hope in Schelling."[203]

Kierkegaard caught Schelling's urgency that philosophy should privilege real life struggles about meaning and meaninglessness. He absorbed Schelling's description of Hegel as the theorist of a closed rational system of pure imageless concepts. He took copious notes on Schelling's lectures, especially his critique of Hegel. A few weeks later, however, Kierkegaard was finished with Schelling, telling his friend Emil Boesen that Schelling "twaddles boundlessly both in the extensive and the intensive sense." He had become too old to attend lectures, Kierkegaard explained, and Schelling had become too old to give them. When the tide turned against Hegel and liberal theology after World War I, the dialectical theologians discovered Kierkegaard, not Schelling. Paul Tillich was an exception in prizing Schelling, but even Tillich made sense of Schelling by correcting him with Kierkegaard's concepts.[204]

Schelling achieved his greatest impact by portraying Hegel as the king of essentialism. This was not the legacy that he wanted, but he had ceded the field to Hegel, who convinced religious thinkers, more than any thinker since Plato, that reason rules the world. Hegelian philosophy, always a religious phenomenon, became more so after Hegel was gone.

Notes

1. F. W. J. Schelling, *System der gesammten Philosophie* (1804), in Schelling, *Sämtliche Werke*, 14 vols., ed. K. F. A. Schelling (Stuttgart: Cotta, 1856–1861), quote VI: 148; Benedict de Spinoza, *The Ethics,* in *Works of Spinoza,* 2 vols., trans. R. H. M. Elwes (London: George Bell and Sons, Bohn Library Edition, 1883), II: 45–271, quote 45; Frederick C. Beiser, *German Idealism: The Struggle Against Subjectivism, 1781–1801* (Cambridge: Harvard University Press, 2002), 349–364.

2. See Theodore Ziolkowski, *Das Wunderjahr in Jena* (Stuttgart: Klett-Cotta, 1998); *Evolution des Geistes: Jena um 1800,* ed. Friedrich Strack (Stuttgart: Klett-Cotta, 1994); Karl Obenauer, *August Ludwig Hülsen* (Erlangen: Junge and Sohn, 1910); Ernst Behler, *Frühromantik* (Berlin: de Gruyter, 1992); Rudolf Haym, *Die romantische Schule* (Berlin: Gaertner, 1870); Beiser, *German Idealism: The Struggle Against Subjectivism, 1781–1801.*

3. See H. S. Harris, *Hegel's Development: Toward the Sunlight, 1770–1801* (Oxford: Oxford University Press, 1972), 1–3; Terry Pinkard, *Hegel: A Biography* (Cambridge: Cambridge University Press, 2000), 1–12; Karl Rosenkranz, *Georg Wilhelm Friedrich Hegels Leben* (Darmstadt: Wissenschaftliche Buchgesellschaft, 1963), 3–7.

4. Gotthold Ephraim Lessing, *Nathan the Wise: A Philosophical Drama,* trans. Rudolf E. Raspe (London: J. Fielding, 1781); Harris, *Hegel's Development: Toward the Sunlight, 1770–1801,* 3–14; Pinkard, *Hegel: A Biography,* 19–20.

5. Harris, *Hegel's Development: Toward the Sunlight, 1770–1801,* 57–72, quote 58; Pinkard, *Hegel: A Biography,* 15–17.

6. Harris, *Hegel's Development: Toward the Sunlight, 1770–1801,* 68–96; Rosenkranz, *Georg Wilhelm Friedrich Hegels Leben,* 32–45; Pinkard, *Hegel: A Biography,* 19–23.

7. Harris, *Hegel's Development: Toward the Sunlight, 1770–1801,* 88–91; Rosenkranz, *Georg Wilhelm Friedrich Hegels Leben,* 42–47; Otto Pfleiderer, *The Development of Theology in Germany since Kant,* trans. J. F. Smith (London: Sonnenschein, 1893), 84-88.

8. F. W. J. Schelling to J. G. Fichte, September 1794, in *F. W. J. Schelling: Briefe und Dokumente,* ed. Horst Fuhrmanns (Bonn: Bouvier, 1962–1975), II: 51–52; Schelling, *The Unconditional in Human Knowledge: Four Early Essays (1794–1796),* trans. Fritz Marti (Lewisburg: Bucknell University Press, 1980); Schelling, *Vom Ich als Princip der Philosophie* (1795), in Schelling, *Sämtliche Werke,* "infinitely," I: 151; Schelling, *Ideas for a Philosophy of Nature as Introduction to the Study of this Science* (1797; 2nd edn., 1803), trans. Errol E. Harris and Peter Heath (Cambridge: Cambridge University Press, 1988); Rosenkranz, *Georg Wilhelm Friedrich Hegels Leben,* 34–40; Beiser, *German Idealism: The Struggle Against Subjectivism, 1781–1801,* 469–470; Pinkard, *Hegel: A Biography,* 33–52; Terry Pinkard, *German Philosophy, 1760–1860: The Legacy of Idealism* (Cambridge: Cambridge University Press, 2002), 139–144.

9. G. W. F. Hegel to Friedrich W. J. Schelling, December 24, 1794, *Hegel: The Letters,* trans. Clark Butler and Christiane Seiler (Bloomington: Indiana University Press, 1984), 28–29, "bring to," 28; Schelling to Hegel, January 5, 1795, ibid., "philosophy," 29; Schelling to Hegel, February 4, 1795, ibid., 32–33, "I have," "the alpha," 32; see *Briefe von und an Hegel,* ed. J. Hoffmeister and J. Nicolin, 3rd edn., 4 vols. (Hamburg: Felix Meiner, 1969-1981), I: 22.

10. Friedrich Hölderlin to G. W. F. Hegel, January 26, 1795, *Hegel: The Letters,* quotes 33. For an interpretation that makes a strong, if slightly exaggerated, case for Hölderlin's importance to the development of absolute idealism, see Dieter Henrich, *Der Grund im BewuBtsein: Untersuchungen zu Hölderlins Denken (1794–1795)* (Stuttgart: Klett-Cotta, 1992), 123–128.

11. G. W. F. Hegel to Friedrich W. J. Schelling, April 6, 1795, ibid., 35–36, "from the" and "it will," 35; Hegel to Schelling, August 30, 1795, ibid., 41–43, "you cannot" 42, "my works," 43; see Hegel, *Three Essays, 1793–1795: The Tübingen Essay, Berne Fragments, The Life of Jesus,* ed. and trans. Peter Fuss and John Dobbins (Notre Dame: University of Notre Dame Press, 1984).

12. Friedrich W. J. Schelling to G. W. F. Hegel, June 20, 1796, ibid., 44.

13. G. W. F. Hegel, "The Tübingen Essay" (1793, in Hegel, *Three Essays, 1793–1795: The Tübingen Essay, Berne Fragments, The Life of Jesus,* 30–58; Hegel, "Berne Fragments," (1793–94), ibid., 59–103, quotes 64; Jean Jacques Rousseau, *Emile* (Paris: Garnier Fréres, 1964), quotes 358, 625, trans. Peter Fuss and John Dobbins in introduction to Hegel, *Three Essays, 1793–1795: The Tübingen Essay, Berne Fragments, The Life of Jesus,* 15–16.

14. Hegel, "The Life of Jesus," (1795), in Hegel, *Three Essays, 1793–1795: The Tübingen Essay, Berne Fragments, The Life of Jesus,* quotes 104, 163; see Edward Gibbon, *The Decline and Fall of the Roman Empire* (New York: Harcourt, Brace, 1960).

15. G. W. F. Hegel, "The Positivity of the Christian Religion," (1795, 1800), in Hegel, *Early Theological Writings,* trans. T. M. Knox (Chicago: University of Chicago Press, 1948), 67–181.

16. Ibid., quotes 181.

17. G. W. F. Hegel to Friedrich Hölderlin, "Eleusis, " August 1796, in *Hegel: The Letters,* 46–47.

18. G. W. F. Hegel, "The Spirit of Christianity and its Fate" (1798), in Hegel, *Early Theological Writings,* 182–301, quotes 293–4.

19. Ibid., quotes 295, 296.

20. Schelling, *The Unconditional in Human Knowledge: Four Early Essays* (1794–1796), quotes 92.

21. Hölderlin to Hegel, January 26, 1795, 33–34; Clark Butler, Commentary in *Hegel: The Letters,* 51–52; Otto Pöggeler, "Philosophy in the Wake of Hölderlin," *Man and World* 7 (1974), 158–176; Pinkard, *Hegel: A Biography,* 79–81.

22. F. W. J. Schelling, *On the World Soul* (1898), in Schelling *Sämmtliche Werke,* quote II: 459; the first edition of Schelling's *Ideas for a Philosophy of Nature* bore this title; the second edition expanded to the title given above, *Ideas for a Philosophy of Nature as Introduction to the Study of This Science.*

23. F. W. J. Schelling to J. G. Fichte, November 19, 1800, *F. W. J. Schelling: Briefe und Dokumente,* II: 294–300; Beiser, *German Idealism: The Struggle Against Subjectivism,* 1781–1801, "talented," 499; Schelling, *Darstellung meines Systems der Philosophie* (1801; reprint, Stuttgart: Fromman-Holzboog, 2009).

24. Schelling, *Ideas for a Philosophy of Nature,* 3–5, quote 3.

25. Ibid., 3–5, Ibid., quote 5.

26. Immanuel Kant, *Metaphysical Foundations of Natural Science,* trans. J. Ellington (Indianapolis: Bobbs-Merrill, 1970), quote 60.

27. Schelling, *Ideas for a Philosophy of Nature,* quotes 216, 73, 224, 172; see A. C. A. Eschenmayer, *Säze aus Natur-Metaphysik auf chemische und medicinische Gegenstände angewandt* (Tübingen: Heerbrandt, 1797); H. F. Linke, *Über einige Grundlehren der Physik und Chemie* (Rostock: Stiller, 1795); Beiser, *German Idealism: The Struggle Against Subjectivism,* 1781–1801, 514; Robert Stern, introduction to Schelling, *Ideas for a Philosophy of Nature,* x–xvi.

28. Schelling, *Ideas for a Philosophy of Nature,* quotes 171, 172.

29. Ibid., quotes 25–26.

30. Ibid., 26.

31. Ibid., quotes 47, 179, 180; see Stern, introduction to ibid., xxi.
32. Schelling, *Ideas for a Philosophy of Nature,* quotes 177.
33. F. W. J. Schelling, *System of Transcendental Idealism* (1800), trans. Peter Heath (Charlottesville: University of Virginia Press, 1978), quotes 1, 230.
34. Ibid., 40–41, 6–7, quote 6.
35. F. W. J. Schelling to J. G. Fichte, October 3, 1801, *Briefe und Dokumente,* II: 348–356, quote 356.
36. G. W. F. Hegel to F. W. J. Schelling, November 2, 1800, *Hegel: The Letters,* 63–64.
37. See Friedrich Schiller, *On the Aesthetic Education of Man,* ed. and trans. Elizabeth M. Wilkinson and L. A. Wolloughby (Oxford: Oxford University Press, 1967); Friedrich von Hardenberg, *Novalis: Philosophical Writings,* ed. and trans. Margaret M. Stoljar (Albany: State University of New York Press, 1997); *Dorothea von Schlegel geb. Mendelssohn und deren Söhne Johannes und Philip Veit, Briefwechsel,* ed. J. M. Raich (Mainz: Franz Kirchheim, 1881).
38. Pinkard, *Hegel: A Biography,* 88–102; Theodore Ziolkowski, *German Romanticism and Its Institutions* (Princeton: Princeton University Press, 1990), 225–230.
39. G. W. F. Hegel, *The Difference Between Fichte's and Schelling's Systems of Philosophy,* trans. H. S. Harris and Walter Cerf (Albany: State University of New York Press, 1977), quotes 79, 127.
40. Ibid., quotes 127, 87; see Pinkard, *Hegel: A Biography,* 153–160.
41. Hegel, *The Difference Between Fichte's and Schelling's Systems of Philosophy,* quotes 90, 169.
42. G. W. F. Hegel, *Faith and Knowledge or the Reflective Philosophy of Subjectivity in the Complete Range of Its Forms as Kantian, Jacobian, and Fichtean Philosophy,* trans. Walter Cerf and H. S. Harris (Albany: State University of New York Press, 1977), quote 64.
43. Ibid., quote 70.
44. Immanuel Kant, *Critique of Pure Reason,* trans. Norman Kemp Smith (New York: Macmillan, 1950), quote A141/B181, 183; Hegel, *Faith and Knowledge or the Reflective Philosophy of Subjectivity in the Complete Range of Its Forms as Kantian, Jacobian, and Fichtean Philosophy,* quote 73.
45. Immanuel Kant, *Critique of Judgment,* trans. Werner S. Pluhar (Indianapolis: Hackett Publishing Company, 1987), quote 290; Hegel, *Faith and Knowledge or the Reflective Philosophy of Subjectivity in the Complete Range of Its Forms as Kantian, Jacobian, and Fichtean Philosophy,* quote 87.
46. Hegel, *Faith and Knowledge or the Reflective Philosophy of Subjectivity in the Complete Range of Its Forms as Kantian, Jacobian, and Fichtean Philosophy,* 189.
47. Ibid., 189–90.
48. Ibid., 191.
49. Pinkard, *German Philosophy, 1760–1860: The Legacy of Idealism,* 192–3; *Hegel: The Letters,* 65.
50. F. W. J. Schelling to G. W. F. Hegel, July 11, 1803, *Hegel: The Letters,* 65–66; Hegel to Schelling, August 16, 1803, 66–67.
51. Pinkard, *German Philosophy, 1760–1860: The Legacy of Idealism,* 221–222, Michelet quote, 221; G. W. F. Hegel to F. W. J. Schelling, May 1, 1807, *Hegel: The Letters,* 79–81, quote 80; Robert Pippin, "You Can't Get There from Here: Transition Problems in Hegel's *Phenomenology of Spirit,*" in *The Cambridge Companion to Hegel,* ed. Frederick C. Beiser (Cambridge: Cambridge University Press, 1993), 52–3.
52. G. W. F. Hegel, *Phenomenology of Spirit,* trans. A. V. Miller (Oxford: Oxford University Press, 1977).

53. Rudolf Haym, *Hegel und seine Zeit: Vorlesungen über Entstehung und Entwicklung, Wesen und Wert der Hegelschen Philosophie* (Berlin: R. Gaertner, 1857), quotes 243–244; Theodor Haering, "Die Entstehungsgeschichte der Phänomenologie des Geistes," in *Verhandlungen des dritten Hegelkongresses,* ed. B. Wigersma (Tübingen: J. C. B. Mohr, 1934), 118–138.

54. Otto Pöggeler, "Zur Deutung der *Phänomenologue des Geistes,*" *Hegel-Studien* 1 (1961), 255–294; Pöggeler, "Die Komposition der *Phänomenologie des Geistes,*" in *Materialien zu Hegels Phänomenologie des Geistes,* ed. Hans Friedrich Fulda und Dieter Henrich (Frankfurt: Suhrkamp, 1973), 329–390; Pöggeler, *Hegels Idee einer Phänomenologie des Geistes* (Freiburg: Karl Alber, 1973), 231–298.

55. Walter Kaufmann, "Hegel's Conception of Phenomenology," in *Phenomenology and Philosophical Understanding,* ed. Edo Pivcevic (Cambridge: Cambridge University Press, 1975), "one really," and "a loose," 229, 220; Kaufmann, *Hegel: Reinterpretation, Texts, and Commentary* (Garden City, NY: Doubleday, 1965), 133–158, "now a tableau," 144; Kaufmann, "The Hegel Myth and Its Method," in MacIntyre, *Hegel: A Collection of Critical Essays,* ed. Alasdair MacIntyre (Notre Dame, IN: University of Notre Dame Press, 1976), 21–60; Karl Popper, *The Open Society and Its Enemies,* 2 vols. (London: Routledge, Kegan & Paul, 1945).

56. Alexander Kojève, *Introduction to the Reading of Hegel: Lectures on the Phenomenology of Spirit,* ed. Allan Bloom, trans. James H. Nichols, Jr. (New York: Basic Books, 1969); Georg Lukács, *The Young Hegel,* trans. R. Livingstone (Cambridge: MIT Press, 1976); Herbert Marcuse, *Reason and Revolution* (London: Routledge, Kegan & Paul, 1941); Jean Hyppolite, *Genesis and Structure of Hegel's Phenomenology of Spirit,* trans. Samuel Cherniak and John Heckman (Evanston: Northwestern University Press, 1974); see George Armstrong Kelly, "Notes on Hegel's 'Lordship and Bondage,'" in MacIntyre, *Hegel: A Collection of Critical Essays,* 189–217.

57. Terry Pinkard, *Hegel's Phenomenology: The Sociality of Reason* (Cambridge: Cambridge University Press, 1994); Michael N. Forster, *Hegel's Idea of a Phenomenology of Spirit* (Chicago: University of Chicago Press, 1998); Tom Rockmore, *Cognition: An Introduction to Hegel's Phenomenology of Spirit* (Berkeley: University of California Press, 1997); Robert Stern, *Hegel's Phenomenology* (London: Routledge, 2001); Robert Dien Winfield, *Overcoming Foundations: Studies in Systematic Philosophy* (New York: Columbia University Press, 1989); Klaus Hartmann, "Hegel: A Non-Metaphysical View," in MacIntyre, *Hegel: A Collection of Critical Essays,* 101–124; Quentin Lauer, S. J., *Hegel's Concept of God* (Albany: State University of New York Press, 1982); Cyril O'Regan, *The Heterodox Hegel* (Albany: State University of New York Press, 1994); Alan M. Olson, *Hegel and the Spirit: Philosophy as Pneumatology* (Princeton: Princeton University Press, 1992); Dieter Henrich, *Between Kant and Hegel: Lectures on German Idealism,* ed. David Pacini (Cambridge: Harvard University Press, 2003), 19–20; Merold Westphal, *History and Truth in Hegel's Phenomenology,* 3rd edn. (Bloomington: Indiana University Press, 1998); Mark C. Taylor, *After God* (Chicago: University of Chicago Press, 2007); Jon Stewart, "The Architectonic of Hegel's *Phenomenology of Spirit,*" in *The Phenomenology of Spirit Reader: Critical and Interpretive Essays,* ed. Jon Stewart (Albany: State University of New York Press, 1998), 441–477; Robert Pippin, *Hegel's Idealism: The Satisfactions of Self-Consciousness* (Cambridge: Cambridge University Press, 1989); Pippin, "You Can't Get There from Here: Transition Problems in Hegel's *Phenomenology of Spirit,*" 52–85; Robert C. Solomon, *In the Spirit of Hegel: A Study of G. W. F. Hegel's Phenomenology of Spirit* (New York: Oxford University Press, 1983), quote xi.

58. Kant, *Metaphysical Foundations of Natural Science,* 119; Pinkard, *Hegel: A Biography,* 203–204.
59. Hegel, *Phenomenology of Spirit,* quotes #5, 3; #12, 7.
60. Ibid., quotes #16, 9; #17, 10; #18, 10; #20, 11.
61. Ibid., quotes #20, 11; #21, 11, 12.
62. Ibid., #22, 12.
63. Ibid., #25, 14.
64. Ibid., quotes #27, 15; #29, 17.
65. Ibid., #50, 29.
66. Ibid., #51, 31.
67. Ibid., #90, 58; #92, 59.
68. Ibid., quote #96, 60.
69. Ibid., #99–101, 61.
70. Ibid., #102–107, 62–64.
71. Ibid., #146, 88–9.
72. Ibid., #147–148, 89–90.
73. Ibid., #166–177, 104–111, quotes #167, 104–105.
74. Ibid., #178–196, 111–119.
75. Ibid., quotes #194, 117; #196, 118–119.
76. Karl Marx, "Economic and Philosophic Manuscripts," (1844), in Marx, *Karl Marx: Selected Writings,* ed. and trans. David McLellan (Oxford: Oxford University Press, 1977), quote 101; Friedrich Nietzsche, *On the Genealogy of Morals,* in *Basic Writings of Nietzsche,* trans. Walter Kaufmann (New York: Modern Library, 1968), 460–492; Martin Buber, *I and Thou,* trans. Walter Kaufmann (New York: Scribner's, 1970); Simone de Beauvoir, *The Second Sex,* trans. H. M. Parshley (New York: Vintage Books, 1989), 64–65; Frantz Fanon, *Black Skin, White Masks* (New York: Grove Press, 1967).
77. Kojéve, *Introduction to the Reading of Hegel,* quotes, 8, 22; see Jean-Paul Sartre, *Critique of Dialectical Reason,* trans. Alan Sheridan-Smith (London: NLB, 1976); Hyppolite, *Genesis and Structure of Hegel's Phenomenology of Spirit,* 172–177.
78. Kojève, *Introduction to the Reading of Hegel,* 56.
79. Ibid., 57.
80. Hegel, *Phenomenology of Spirit,* #582–595, 355–363, quotes #595, 363; see Hartman, "Hegel: A Non-Metaphysical View," 101–124; Pinkard, *German Philosophy, 1760–1860: The Legacy of Idealism,* 236–242; *Rediscovering Hegel,* ed. Terry Pinkard (The Hague: Dordrecht, 1995); Alan White, *Absolute Knowledge: Hegel and the Problem of Metaphysics* (Athens: University of Ohio Press, 1983); Pippin, *Hegel's Idealism: The Satisfactions of Self-Consciousness,* 16–41, 175–260.
81. John Plamenatz, *Man and Society,* 2 vols. (London: Longmans, 1963), II: 155; A. V. Miller, "Analysis of the Text," in Hegel, *Phenomenology of Spirit,* 523; George Armstrong Kelly, "Notes on Hegel's 'Lordship and Bondage,'" in *The Phenomenology of Spirit Reader,* 172–191.
82. Kojève, *Introduction to the Reading of Hegel,* 43.
83. Hegel, *Phenomenology of Spirit,* #176–177, 110.
84. Ibid., #438–443, 263–265.
85. Ibid., #672–675, 410–411.
86. Ibid., #676–683, 411–416.
87. Ibid., #684–698, 416–424, quote #698, 424.
88. Ibid., #699–708, 424–429, quotes #707, 428; #708, 429.
89. Ibid., #709–747, 429–453, quotes #727, 439–440; #746, 452.

90. Ibid., #748–757, 453–458, quotes #756, 458; #757, 458.
91. Ibid., #758, 458–459.
92. Ibid., #759, 459–460.
93. Ibid., #761, 460–461.
94. Ibid., #762, 461–462.
95. Ibid, #763, 462.
96. Ibid., #765–766; 463.
97. Ibid., #770, 465.
98. Ibid., #775–776, 468–469.
99. Ibid., #780, 471–473.
100. Ibid., 473.
101. Ibid., #781–787, 473–478, quotes #784, 475; #787, 478.
102. Ibid., #788–808, 479–493, quotes #795, 483; #801, 487.
103. Pinkard, *Hegel: A Biography,* 221–228; Rosenkranz, *Georg Wilhelm Friedrich Hegels Leben,* 230–232; Kaufmann, "Hegel's Conception of Phenomenology," 221; G. W. F. Hegel to F. W. J. Schelling, May 1, 1807, *Hegel: The Letters,* 79–80.
104. G. W. F. Hegel to Immanuel Niethammer, October 13, 1806, *Hegel: The Letters,* 114; Pinkard, *Hegel: A Biography,* 230–240.
105. Hegel to Schelling, May 1, 1807, 79–80.
106. F. W. J. Schelling to G. W. F. Hegel, November 2, 1807, *Hegel: The Letters,* 80.
107. Pinkard, *Hegel: A Biography,* 258–261; Wolfgang Bonsiepen, "Erste Zeitgenössische Rezensionen der Phänomenologie des Geistes," *Hegel-Studien* 14 (1979), 9–16.
108. Pinkard, *Hegel: A Biography,* 261–265; Bonsiepen, "Erste Zeitgenössische Rezensionen der Phänomenologie des Geistes," 17–30; for the text of the Bachmann review, see Oscar Fambach, *Der Romantische Rückfall in der Kritik der Zeit* (Berlin: Akadmic Verlag, 1963), 428–452.
109. F. W. J. Schelling, *Philosophische Untersuchungen über das Wesen der menschlichen Freiheit und die damit zusammenhangenden Gegenstande* (1809), English editions, *Of Human Freedom,* trans. James Gutmann (Leipzig: Kroner, 1925); *Schelling: Of Human Freedom,* trans. James Gutmann (Chicago: University of Chicago Press, 1937); Schelling, *Philosophical Investigations into the Essence of Human Freedom,* trans. Jeff Love and Johannes Schmidt (Albany: State University of New York Press, 2006).
110. Schelling, *Philosophical Investigations into the Essence of Human Freedom,* 9–32, quotes 32.
111. Ibid., 32, 33.
112. Ibid., 33.
113. Ibid., quotes 34, 55.
114. Ibid., 66.
115. See Martin Heidegger, *Schelling's Treatise on the Essence of Human Freedom,* trans. Joan Stambaugh (Athens: University of Ohio Press, 1985), 35–37; Slavoj Žižek, *The Indivisible Remainder: An Essay on Schelling and Related Matters* (London: Verso, 1996); Jeff Love and Johannes Schmidt, introduction to Schelling, *Philosophical Investigations into the Essence of Human Freedom,* xx–xxvi.
116. F. W. J. Schelling, "Stuttgart Lectures," 1810, cited in Bruce Matthews, introduction to F. W. J. Schelling, *The Grounding of Positive Philosophy: The Berlin Lectures,* trans. Bruce Matthews (Albany: State University of New York Press, 2007), 4; see A. Bowie, *Schelling and Modern European Philosophy: An Introduction* (London: Routledge, 1993); Manfred Frank, *Eine Einführung in Schellings Philosophie* (Frankfurt: Suhrkamp, 1985).

117. F. W. J. Schelling, *The Ages of the World,* trans. Jason Wirth (Albany: State University of New York Press, 2000), 90; see Christian Iber, *Subjektivität, Vernunft und ihre Kritik: Prager Vorlesungen über den Deutschen Idealismus* (Frankfurt am Main: Suhrkamp, 1999).

118. Manfred Frank, *Der unendliche Mangel an Sein* (Frankfurt: Suhrkamp, 1975); Pinkard, *German Philosophy, 1760–1860: The Legacy of Idealism,* 197.

119. G. W. F. Hegel to Immanuel Niethammer, April 18, 1811; Niethammer to Hegel, undated; Hegel to Niethammer, May 30, 1811, in *Hegel: The Letters,* 238–242. Hegel, *Science of Logic,* trans. A. V. Miller (London: George Allen & Unwin, 1969).

120. G. W. F. Hegel, *Encyclopedia of the Philosophical Sciences,* 3 vols., Part I: *Logic,* trans. William Wallace (Oxford: Oxford University Press, 1975), 113–122, quotes 116.

121. For discussions of Hegel's structure and method in the *Phenomenology,* see Pippin, "You Can't Get There from Here: Transition Problems in Hegel's *Phenomenology of Spirit,*" 52–85; Kenley R. Dove, "Hegel's Phenomenological Method," in *The Phenomenology of Spirit Reader,* 52–75; Kaufman, *Hegel: Reinterpretation, Texts, and Commentary,* 167–175; J. Loewenberg, *Hegel's Phenomenology: Dialogues on the Life of Mind* (La Salle: Open Court, 1965), 1–22; Forster, *Hegel's Idea of a Phenomenology of Spirit,* 11–16.

122. Hegel, *Science of Logic,* quotes 25.

123. Ibid., quote, 43.

124. Ibid., 82–105.

125. Ibid., 105–106.

126. Ibid., 105–156, quote 105; see Dieter Henrich, "Formen der Negation in Hegels Logik," in *Seminar: Dialektik in der Philosophie Hegels,* ed. Rolf-Peter Horstmann (Frankfurt: Suhrkamp, 1978), 213–229; John M. E. McTaggart, *A Commentary on Hegel's Logic* (Cambridge: Cambridge University Press, 1910), 13–21; John Burbidge, "Hegel's Conception of Logic," in *The Cambridge Companion to Hegel,* 86–101; Burbidge, *On Hegel's Logic: Fragments of a Commentary* (Atlantic Highlands: Humanities, 1981).

127. J. M. E. McTaggart, the authority beyond numerous textbook renderings of Hegel's ostensible thesis-antithesis-synthesis, described it as "the one absolutely essential element in Hegel's system." Everything in Hegel's system "depends entirely" upon it, he taught. Robert C. Solomon, avenging decades of textbook renderings, leaps to the antithesis, that "Hegel *has no method* as such – at least, not in the *Phenomenology.*" McTaggart, *A Commentary on Hegel's Logic,* 1; Solomon, *In the Spirit of Hegel,* 21.

128. Hegel, *Science of Logic,* quote, 107.

129. See J. N. Findlay, *Hegel: A Re-Examination* (London: George Allen & Unwin, 1958), 72–73.

130. Pinkard, *German Philosophy, 1760–1860: The Legacy of Idealism,* 252; see Henrich, "Formen der Negation in Hegels Logik," 213–229; Robert Brandon, "Some Pragmatist Themes in Hegel's Idealism: Negotiation and Administration in Hegel's Account of the Structure and Content of Conceptual Norms," *European Journal of Philosophy* 7 (August 1999), 164–189.

131. G. W. F. Hegel, *Encyclopedia of the Philosophical Sciences,* Part II: *Philosophy of Nature,* trans. A. V. Miller (Oxford: Oxford University Press, 1970); Hegel, *Encyclopedia of the Philosophical Sciences,* Part III: *Philosophy of Mind,* trans. William Wallace (Oxford: Oxford University Press, 1971); Hegel, *Phenomenology of Spirit,* #309–346, 185–210.

132. G. W. F. Hegel, *Philosophy of Right,* trans. T. M. Knox (Oxford: Oxford University Press, 1952), quote 32.

133. See J. F. Fries, *Wissen, Glaube und Ahndung* (Jena: J. C. G. Göpferdt, 1805); Pinkard, *Hegel: A Biography,* 431–456; Hegel, *Berliner Schriften: 1818–1831,* ed. Johannes Hoffmeister (Hamburg: Felix Meiner Verlag, 1956), 575–602.

134. Hegel, *Philosophy of Right,* 5–6.

135. Ibid., quote 10.

136. Gunther Nicolin, *Hegel in Berichten seiner Zeitgenossen* (Hamburg: Felix Meiner, 1970), Fries quote, 221; Pinkard, *Hegel: A Biography,* 457–463; see Shlomo Avineri, *Hegel's Theory of the Modern State* (Cambridge: Cambridge University Press, 1972); *Hegel's Political Philosophy: Problems and Perspectives,* ed. Z. A. Pelczynski (Cambridge: Cambridge University Press, 1971).

137. G. W. F. Hegel to Edouard-Casimir Duboc, July 30, 1822, *Hegel: The Letters,* quote 493–494; see Hegel, *Lectures on the History of Philosophy,* 3 vols., trans. E. S. Haldane and Frances H. Simson (London: Kegan Paul, Trench, Trübner, & Co., 1892, 1894, 1896); Hegel, *Philosophy of Nature,* 3 vols., trans. M. J. Petry (London: George Allen and Unwin, 1970); Hegel, *Aesthetics: Lectures on Fine Art,* 2 vols., trans. T. M. Knox (Oxford: Oxford University Press, 1975); Hegel, *The Philosophy of History,* trans. J. Sibree (Buffalo: Prometheus Books, 1991).

138. G. W. F. Hegel, *Lectures on the Philosophy of Religion,* 3 vols., ed. Peter C. Hodgson, trans. and ed. R. F. Brown, Peter C. Hodgson, and J. M. Stewart (Berkeley: University of California Press, 1984, 1987, 1985); G. W. F. Hegel to Carl Daub, May 9, 1821, *Briefe von und an Hegel,* II: 262; Hegel to H. W. F. Hinrichs, April 4, 1822, ibid., II: 303, cited in editorial introduction to Hegel, *Lectures on the Philosophy of Religion,* I: 3.

139. Hodgson, editorial introduction to Hegel, *Lectures on the Philosophy of Religion,* I: 2; see Philip M. Merklinger, *Philosophy, Theology, and Hegel's Berlin Philosophy of Religion, 1821-1827* (Albany: State University of New York Press, 1993), 1–16.

140. Hegel, *Lectures on the Philosophy of Religion,* I: 83, 86–87.

141. I: 88.

142. Ibid., I: 91.

143. Ibid., I: 130.

144. Ibid., I: 126–127.

145. Ibid., I: 128.

146. Ibid., "an established," I: 160; G. W. F. Hegel, Foreword to H. F. W. Hinrichs, *Die Religion im inneren Verhältnisse zur Wissenschaft* (Heidelberg, 1822), i–xxviii; reprinted in *Beyond Epistemology: New Studies in the Philosophy of Hegel,* ed. Fredrick G. Weiss, trans. A. V. Miller (The Hague: Martinus Nijhoff, 1974), 227–244, quote 242.

147. Hegel, *Lectures on the Philosophy of Religion,* I: 271–272, 395.

148. Ibid., I: 272, 273, 274.

149. Ibid., I: 275–276.

150. See Richard Crouter, "Hegel and Schleiermacher at Berlin: A Many-sided Debate," *Journal of the American Academy of Religion* 48 (March 1980), 19–43; Crouter, "Rhetoric and Substance in Schleiermacher's Revision of *The Christian Faith* (1821–1822)," *Journal of Religion* 60 (July 1980), 285–306; editor's note, Hegel, *Lectures on the Philosophy of Religion,* I: 269.

151. Hegel, *Lectures on the Philosophy of Religion,* quotes I: 312, 283, 347; Meister Eckhart, *Meister Eckhart: Die deutschen und lateinischen Werke,* ed. J. Quint (Stuttgart: W. Kohlhammer, 1936), I: 201, 2: 252; *Meister Eckhart: Teacher and Preacher,* ed. Bernard McGinn (New York: Paulist Press, 1986), 270.

152. Hegel, *Lectures on the Philosophy of Religion,* I: 349–350.

153. Ibid., I: 375–377.

154. Ibid., I: 378–379.

155. See Karl Philipp Moritz, *Anthousa; order, Roms Alterthümer* (1791; reprint, Tübingen: Niemeyet, 2005); Georg Friedrich Cruezer, *Symbolik und Mythologie der alten Völker,*

besonders der Griechen, 4 vols (Leipzig: Heyer und Leske, 1819–1823); editorial introduction to Hegel, *Lectures on the Philosophy of Religion*, II: 4–12.

156. This description summarizes Peter Hodgson's detailed account in the editorial introduction to Hegel, *Lectures on the Philosophy of Religion*, II: 13–15. Walter Jaeschke contends that Hegel had Jewish religion in mind in his discussion of "light religion" in the *Phenomenology*, not Persian religion. See Walter Jaeschke, *Die Vernunft in der Religion: Studien zur Grundlegung der spekulativen Religionsphilosophie* (Inaugural dissertation, Ruhr-Universitätm 1985), 288–295; cited in Hodgson, editorial introduction, 15, 21.

157. Hegel, *Lectures on the Philosophy of Religion*, II: 423–454.

158. Ibid., II: 432, 434, 436.

159. Ibid., II: 438–439.

160. Ibid., II: 439–440.

161. Ibid., II: 443–445, quote 445.

162. See Crouter, "Hegel and Schleiermacher at Berlin: A Many-sided Debate," 19–43; Crouter, "Rhetoric and Substance in Schleiermacher's Revision of *The Christian Faith* (1821–1822)," 285–306; editor's note, Hegel, *Lectures on the Philosophy of Religion*, II: 444.

163. Hegel, *Lectures on the Philosophy of Religion*, III: 163, 170.

164. Ibid., III: 178–180, quote 178.

165. Ibid., III: 178–181; III: 351–354; Hegel, *Science of Logic*, 575–622.

166. Hegel, *Encyclopedia of the Philosophical Sciences*, Book 1: *Logic*, 274–275.

167. Hegel, *Lectures on the Philosophy of Religion*, III: 183–184.

168. Ibid., III: 186–188.

169. Ibid., III: 192.

170. Ibid., III: 192–193.

171. Ibid., III: 194, 214–215.

172. Ibid., III: 125; see III: 326.

173. Ibid., III: 219–220.

174. Ibid., III: 220–222.

175. Ibid., III: 232–233.

176. See John Edward Toews, *Hegelianism: The Path Toward Dialectical Humanism, 1805-1841* (Cambridge: Cambridge University Press, 1985), 71–94; editor's note, Hegel, *Lectures on the Philosophy of Religion*, III: 232.

177. G. W. F. Hegel to Friedrich August Gottreu Tholuck, July 3, 1826, *Hegel: The Letters*, 519–520, quote 520; see Tholuck, *Die speculative Trinitätlehre des späteren Orients: Eine religionsphilosophische Monographie aus Handschriftlichen Quellen der Leydener, Oxforder und Berliner Bibliothek* (Berlin: F. Dümmler, 1826); Tholuck, *Die Lehre von der Sünde und vom Versöhner, oder, Die wahre Weihe des Zweiflers* (1823; reprint, Hamburg: Friedrich Perthes, 1839).

178. Hegel to Tholuck, July 3, 1826, "does not," 520.

179. G. W. F. Hegel to Karl Sigmund von Altenstein, April 3, 1826, *Hegel: The Letters*, 531–532.

180. G. W. F. Hegel to Edouard-Casimir Duboc, April 29, 1823, 489–500 "a procedure," 498; Hegel, *Encyclopedia of the Philosophical Sciences*, Book 1, *Logic*, 72; Editor's note, *Hegel: The Letters*, 497.

181. Hegel, *Lectures on the Philosophy of Religion*, I: 178–180, quote 180.

182. Karl Daub, *Judas Ischariot, oder das Böse im Verhältnis zum Guten*, 2 vols. (Heidelberg: Mohr & Winter, 1816, 1818); Daub, *Theologumena: sive doctrinae de religione Christiana, ex nautra Dei perspecta, repetendae, capita potiora* (Heidelberg: Mohr & Zimmer,

1806); Daub, Lehrbuch der Katechetik (Frankfurt: August Hermann, 1801); Philipp K. Marheineke, *Die Grundlehren der christlichen Dogmatik* (Berlin: Duncker & Humblot, 1819); Marheineke, *Christliche Symbolik, oder historischkritische und dogmatischkomparative Darstellung des Katholischen, Luterischen, Reformirten und Socianischen Lehrbegriffs* (Heidelberg: Mohr & Zimmer, 1810).

183. See Carl Friedrich Göschel, *Von den Bewwisen für die Unsterblichkeit der menschlichen Selle im Lichte der spekulativen Philosophic* (Berlin: Verlag von Duncker und Humblot, 1835); Kasimir Conradi, *Unsterblichkeit und Ewiges Leben: Versuch einer Entwicklung des Unsterblichkeitsbegriffs der menschlichen Seele* (Mainz: F. Kupferberg, 1837); Philipp K. Marheineke, *Die Grundlinien der christlichen Dogmatik als Wissenschaft* (Berlin: Duncker und Homblot, 1827); Karl Rosenkranz, *Encyklopadie der theologschen Wissenschaften* (Halle: C. A. Schwetschke und Sohn, 1831); Karl Daub, *Die dogmatische Theologie jetziger Zeit oder die Selbstucht in der Wissenschaft des Glaubens und ihrer Artikel* (Heidelberg: J. C. B. Mohr, 1833).

184. G. W. F. Hegel, review of Carl Friedrich Göschel, *Aphorismen über Nichtwissen und absolutes Wissen im Verhältnisse zur christlichen GlaubenserKenntnis* (Berlin: Verlag von Dunker und Humblot, 1829), reprinted in Hegel, *Sämtliche Werke*, vol. 20, ed. Herman Glockner (Stuttgart: Frommon, 1968), 276–313, quote 276; for Hegel's critique of Göschel's hypostatization of divine reality, see Hegel, *Berliner Schriften*, 1818–1831, ed. J. Hoffmeister (Hamburg: Verlag von Felix Meiner, 1956), 324–329.

185. Günther Nicolin, *Hegel in Berichten seiner Zeitgenossen* (Hamburg: Felix Meiner, 1970), 638–682, quote 638; *Hegel: The Letters*, 668–677; *Hegel: A Biography*, 634.

186. Göschel, *Aphorismen über Nichtwissen und absolutes Wissen im Verhältnisse zur christlichen GlaubenserKenntnis*, 160; Toews, *Hegelianism: The Path Toward Dialectical Humanism*, 1805–1841, 90; editor's note, *Hegel: The Letters*, 537.

187. Hegel, review of Carl Friedrich Göschel, *Aphorismen über Nichtwissen und absolutes Wissen im Verhältnisse zur christlichen GlaubenserKenntnis*, quote 276; Hegel, *Berliner Schriften, 1818–1831*, 324–329; G. W. F. Hegel to Carl Friedrich Göschel, December 13, 1830, *Hegel: The Letters*, 543–544; Göschel to Hegel, December 31, 1830, ibid., 545.

188. Nicolin, *Hegel in Berichten seiner Zeitgenossen*, 372, 404–412; Pinkard, *Hegel: A Biography*, 611.

189. Hegel, *Aesthetics: Lectures on Fine Art*, 568–569; see Hegel, *Lectures on the History of Philosophy*, III: 512–545.

190. G. W. F. Hegel to Marie Hegel, September 4, 1829, *Hegel: The Letters*, 398; Pinkard, *Hegel: A Biography*, 620–624, Schelling quotes 623.

191. Nicolin, *Hegel in Berichten seiner Zeitgenossen*, quotes 474, 476; Toews, *Hegelianism: The Path Toward Dialectical Humanism*, 1805–1841, 89; Pinkard, *Hegel: A Biography*, 660.

192. See Toews, *Hegelianism: The Path Toward Dialectical Humanism, 1805–1841*, 71–94, 203–207.

193. Christian Carl J. F. von Bunsen, *Aus seiner Briefen und nach eigener Erinnerung geschildert von seiner Witwe* (Leipzig: F. A. Brodhaus, 1868), quote 133; Friedrich W. J. Schelling, *Philosophie der Offenbarung 1841/42*, ed. Manfred Frank (Frankfurt am Main: Suhrkamp, 1977), 408.

194. Schelling, *Philosophie der Offenbarung 1841/42*, 12–15; Iber, *Subjektivität, Vernunft und ihre Kritik: Prager Vorlesungen über den Deutschen Idealismus*; Translator's Introduction to F. W. J. Schelling, *The Grounding of Positive Philosophy*, trans. Bruce Matthews (Albany: State University of New York Press, 2007), 6.

195. Schelling, *The Grounding of Positive Philosophy*, quotes 96, 108.

196. Ibid., quote 145; see Hegel, *Lectures on the History of Philosophy*, III: 512–545.

197. Schelling, *The Grounding of Positive Philosophy*, quotes 129, 130.

198. Ibid., 150.

199. Ibid., 182; see editor's introduction to ibid., 56; Paul Tillich, *Die religionsgeschichtliche Konstruktion in Schellings positiver Philosophie, ihre Voraussetzungen und Prinzipien* (Breslau: Fleischmann, 1910).

200. Schelling, *The Grounding of Positive Philosophy*, quotes 153.

201. Ibid., quotes 186, 210–211; see Pinkard, *German Philosophy, 1760–1860: The Legacy of Idealism*, 328–329.

202. Bakunin cited by ed. in Schelling, *Philosophie der Offenbarung 1841/42*, 461, 452, and editor in Schelling, *The Grounding of Positive Philosophy*, 13.

203. Søren Kierkegaard, *Søren Kierkegaard's Journals and Papers*, 7 vols., ed. and trans. Howard V. Hong and Edna H. Hong (Bloomington: Indiana University Press, 1967-1978), 5: 5535, journal entry III A 179, November 22, 1841.

204. Søren Kierkegaard to Emil Boesen, February 27, 1842, and Kierkegaard to Peter Kierkegaard, February 28, 1842, Søren Kierkegaard, *Letters and Documents*, trans. Henrik Rosenmeier, *Kierkegaard's Writings*, 25 vols. (Princeton: Princeton University Press, 1978), 25: Letters 69 and 70.

5

Hegelian Spirit in Question
David Friedrich Strauss, Søren Kierkegaard, and Mediating Theology

In the mid-nineteenth century the disciples of Schleiermacher and Hegel built a new theological establishment in Germany, despite failing to produce a historic thinker, and despite evoking withering critiques from debunkers that cast a larger shadow than anything produced by the establishment generations. The greatest of the debunkers, Søren Kierkegaard, was arguably the greatest religious thinker of the nineteenth century, although he had no influence in the nineteenth century. David Friedrich Strauss, another important debunker, agreed with Kierkegaard that liberal theology was a bad idea, although he had different reasons that ruined his academic career before it started. For Strauss and Kierkegaard, it was pathetic how easily the Mediating theologians and Hegelians built a new establishment. But even Strauss and Kierkegaard took for granted that getting the right kind of idealism was imperative for modern religious thought.

Mediating theology (*Vermittlungstheologie*) and Hegelian theology ruled the field together, each with their own journals, and from the beginning there were thinkers who were comfortable in both groups. The leading disciples of Schleiermacher were Carl Ullmann, C. I. Nitzsch, August Twesten, and Willibald Beyschlag. The leading Hegelians, after Philipp Konrad Marheineke died in 1846, were Karl Rosenkranz, Karl Michelet, and A. E. Biedermann. The leading blenders of Schleiermacher and Hegel were Richard Rothe and Isaak August Dorner; usually the blenders favored Hegel. Kantian liberals still claimed to own the liberal badge of honor, but to the children of Schleiermacher and Hegel, that smacked of throwback provincialism. To them it was enough to say that Schleiermacher, or Hegel, or both had fashioned a credible and compelling third way between orthodox overbelief and atheistic disbelief.[1]

Mediating Schleiermacher's Legacy

In 1865 David Friedrich Strauss, looking back on a theological career that he had abandoned and the liberal movement he had attacked, observed ruefully that Mediating

---

Kantian Reason and Hegelian Spirit: The Idealistic Logic of Modern Theology, First Edition. Gary Dorrien.
© 2012 John Wiley & Sons, Ltd. Published 2015 by John Wiley & Sons, Ltd.

Theology had become so successful that even bishops preached it. Strauss was galled at having lost to mushy temporizers like Carl Ullmann, who had a distinguished career at Heidelberg, Halle, and Heidelberg again. Ullmann's success epitomized the main-stream legitimization and success of mediating theology. His book, *The Sinlessness of Jesus* (1828), attracted a vast audience in seven editions for ninety years, teaching that Christianity stands or falls with the person of Jesus, "the only true Mediator between God and man." In Jesus, Ullmann argued, God turned to humanity in grace and human beings beheld the "unveiled glory of Divine Love." Ullmann's ruling idea of redemption was that human sinners, upon apprehending and appropriating the love of God revealed through Christ, are changed into the divine likeness: "If you admit the fact of His holiness, you must go still farther; for you must recognize in Him a personal revelation of God, you must own him as the Reconciler, you must tender Him your homage as the King of the kingdom of God and the Prince of Life."[2]

With Schleiermacher, Ullmann taught that redemption in Christ is the key to Christianity and redemption is a matter of religious feeling. Like many mediating theologians, however, Ullmann wrung more objectivity out of moral influence theory than did Schleiermacher, lamenting that Schleiermacher played down the objective aspects of atonement by locating redemption solely in the individual consciousness. Ullmann wanted the modernizing movement not to lose its capacity to speak of the justification of the sinner before God and of God's forgiveness of sins. He never quite took a position on whether this meant that penal satisfaction should be in play for modern Christians. Salvation had to be more than subjective, Ullmann asserted, but he settled for halfway vagueness about how much more.[3]

In 1835 Strauss made a splash by charging that the gospels are pervaded by myth and that mediating theologians like Ullmann and Schleiermacher settled for halfway mush as a matter of policy. Ullmann rose to defend the gospels and modern theology. The gospels might contain myths, he allowed, but Strauss absurdly exaggerated the amount. Contrary to Strauss, it is easier to explain the church in the light of Christ than the other way around, and there is no reason not to regard the resurrection of Christ as historical and true. Moreover, although Christ is rightly called the archetype (*Urbild*) of true life in God, as Schleiermacher did, or the idea become real, as Hegelians did, he should not be called the idea of God's oneness with humanity, as Strauss did. The locus of the idea become real, Ullmann insisted, is the person of Christ, the sole mediator of the reconciliation and union between God and humanity. At the time Ullmann spoke for most of the Schleiermacher school and even most of the Hegel school on these issues. But with one book, Strauss changed what theologians argued about, which ended his chance of having an academic career.[4]

David Friedrich Strauss and Left-Hegelianism

Strauss came to the Hegelian school from a middle-class Swabian background, a family crisis, and a mediocre seminary education redeemed by one teacher, Ferdinand Christian Baur. His father was a merchant and retailer in Ludwigsburg who, berated by his spouse after suffering a calamitous business failure, responded by taking comfort in evangelical Pietism. Strauss, like his mother, found this reaction embarrassing. In

1821, at the age of fourteen, Strauss enrolled at Tübingen's preparatory school at Blaubeuren, where his teachers were mostly old-style rational supernaturalists, evoking more embarrassment.

Romanticism had seeped into northern Germany; the repressive political atmosphere at Tübingen took politics off the table as something to talk about; and at Blaubeuren Strauss bonded with three classmates, Christian Märklin, Friedrich T. Vischer, and Gustav Binder. All had clerical fathers who were rational supernaturalists. Quickly all four of the friends became Romantics. Writing off their teachers, they made an exception for Baur, a young historical theologian. Baur introduced them to Fichte and Jacob Boehme, and passed on to them his admiration for Schelling and Schleiermacher, although Baur already had misgivings that his favorite philosopher (Schelling) and favorite theologian (Schleiermacher) were too subjective. In 1825 the foursome moved on to Tübingen Seminary, where they dabbled in mysticism and occult phenomena under the influence of Schelling disciple C. A. Eschenmayer, and where they celebrated Baur's promotion to Tübingen; Strauss was again his prize student.[5]

Strauss' occult phase was brief. Absorbing Baur's radical historicism, he adopted Baur's critical approach to mythical consciousness and accepted Baur's insistence that philosophy is indispensable to theology. Any theology is only as strong and compelling as the philosophy supporting it. But if that was true, Strauss reflected, it was imperative to find the best philosophy. He had heard just enough about Hegel to be curious about the differences between Schelling and Hegel. In the summer of 1829 Strauss, Märklin, and Binder plunged into the *Phenomenology of Spirit* on their own, lacking any guidance, tackling one chapter per week. By the end of the summer they were Hegelians.

This conversion threw Strauss and his friends into uncharted territory. Did they know what they were doing? What did it mean for their theological and clerical careers? Nobody on the Tübingen faculty knew Hegel's philosophy. Was it a substitute faith? Could it be preached in Christian pulpits? Strauss' friends struggled with these questions for years, especially after they became pastors; in the early going, Strauss told them not to worry. He was serving a church in Kleiningersheim and his sermons were going well. He tried to keep traditional language to a minimum, but he realized that his congregation wasn't ready for Hegel. Thus he used as much of the traditional picture language as seemed to be necessary, while injecting as much of its Hegelian meaning as possible under the circumstances. Strauss told Märklin, "When I considered how far even in intellectual preaching the expression is inadequate to the true essence of the concept, it does not seem to me to matter much if one goes even a step further. I at least go about the matter without the least scruple, and cannot ascribe this to a mere want of sincerity in myself." Albert Schweitzer, in his send-up of nineteenth-century liberal theology, treated this statement as a showcase example of Hegelian logic.[6]

Märklin, however, worried about the sincerity issue, which helped Strauss to acknowledge that he worried about it too. The following year, while writing a doctoral dissertation on the doctrine of immortality, Strauss told Märklin that they needed to fight the battle for the superiority of the concept with as much integrity as possible; Märklin's troubled conscience over "this whole game with images instead of concepts" might be justified.[7]

Strauss made a similar point differently in his dissertation, stressing that the differences between representative and conceptual reasoning are substantive, not merely formal. Strauss argued that the problem of religious intolerance cannot be solved at the representational level, because religions invest ultimate significance in their pictures, especially about evil. Describing himself as a radical Hegelian, Strauss made a case for a monistic identity between God and the world, not quite grasping that his argument was closer to Schelling and Spinoza than to Hegel. It was not much of a dissertation anyway, running only 30 pages in a slipshod fashion, although Strauss won a faculty prize for defending the doctrine of immortality. Later he claimed that he stopped believing it at the moment that he finished the last sentence.[8]

Strauss had been a pastor for only a few months when he won a prize for a sloppy dissertation that he didn't believe. Now he was determined to hear Hegel lecture in Berlin. He told Märklin that they had to get clear about what kind of idealists they were before they advanced any further in their careers or their lives. Taking a sabbatical in September 1831, Strauss heard Hegel lecture a few times and enjoyed a single, tale-swapping conversation with him. Hegel delighted at meeting such a bright young Hegelian from Tübingen; he pumped Strauss for gossip about Hegelians and Tübingen. But on November 15th Strauss arrived for a second meeting with Hegel only to be told, by Schleiermacher, that Hegel had died of cholera the previous night. Strauss was devastated; in the story usually told about this scene, which could be true, Strauss cried out to Schleiermacher that he had come to Berlin only to study with Hegel. Schweitzer thought this showed a certain want of tact on Strauss' part, considering Schleiermacher's fame. But the outcry part renders a true picture, whether or not it happened: Strauss had come to Berlin to become a Hegelian theologian.[9]

In his disappointment Strauss made contacts with Marheineke and Leopold Henning, established friendships with younger Hegelians Karl Michelet, Agathon Benary, and Wilhelm Vatke, and attended Schleiermacher's lectures and sermons through the spring term. He worked his way into Hegel's cult following, at the height of its cultic fervor. From the beginning Strauss was double-minded about it. In a way, he had found a home, yet it was not what he thought it should be. Strauss worried that the Hegelians conflated Hegelian concepts and traditional Christian doctrine too easily. Hegelianism, to be true to itself, had to be more radical than that. Thus Strauss conceived the idea of a radical Hegelian theology.

Baur's work on symbolism and myth was foundational for Strauss, as was Baur's maxim that history without philosophy is "eternally dead and mute." If history meant nothing lacking a philosophical undergirding, historicists had to have a philosophy. Strauss had gone to Berlin to learn the best one, but Hegel's death threw him on his own prematurely. He had to devise his perspective sooner than he expected, using the sources that he already possessed. Through Baur, Strauss had absorbed Schelling's concept of history as a gradually self-disclosing revelation of the absolute. The idea that philosophy might absorb and improve Christian doctrine had appealed to Strauss initially through his teacher's advocacy of Schelling's idealism. If history is the processive revelation of the divine will or absolute ideal, the subject matter of religion belongs as much to philosophy as to religion. Baur's two-volume *Symbolik und Mythologie* (1824–25) said it plainly, proclaiming that religion and philosophy share the same content and absolute. Strauss had started there, which led him to Hegel – a rationalist alternative to Schelling. Now he found himself among Hegelians who balked at seeing the matter through.[10]

The heart of the matter was Hegel's distinction between the religious image (*Vorstellung*) and the philosophical concept (*Begrif*). Strauss reasoned that if religious thinking is lower and less sophisticated than philosophical thinking, theology must yield to the superrogatory mission of philosophical reason. The Hegelian theologians treaded carefully on this point. Marheinecke, Rosenkranz, and Göschel conceived Hegelianism as a philosophical interpretation of the Christian teaching that a Trinitarian God, by entering history in the crucified Christ, took on the suffering of the world in order to redeem it. The death of Christ was the pivotal point of God's self-unfolding. This divine self-unfolding began with God's being in God's self before the creation of the world, it moved through God's being in nature and history, and culminates in God's return to God's self in Spirit. In the death of Christ, God reconciled God's self to God's self, returned to God's self, and thus abrogated finitude. Strauss agreed that Hegel's idealistic rendering of Christian tropes contained the key to the future and credibility of Christian theology. But the Hegelian evasiveness about picture language had to be faced; Strauss had preached enough evasive sermons to be sure of it.[11]

Strauss believed that Hegel's distinction between representational and conceptual thinking had revolutionary implications. It was the key to making theology modern, even if the Hegelian school and Hegel himself stopped short of saying so. Hegel did not say that his philosophy required religious thinkers to leave behind the myths and doctrines of Christian theology. That, however, was exactly what Strauss believed. To Strauss, the mythic imagination of Christianity had nothing to contribute to any modern theology worthy of the name. Modern theology needed to absorb and transcend the truths of Christianity. Mediating theologians and Hegelians, claiming to be modern, developed hermeneutical theories of myth and symbol. Strauss took no interest in that; he had seen Baur waste too much intellectual energy trying to make sense of unbelievable things. Strauss set out to destroy Christian myth, to clear the way for something better.

Modern theology, Strauss believed, at its best, began with myth criticism. The old-style rationalists introduced the problem, but didn't get very far. The historical critics of Johann Gottfried Eichhorn's generation got further into the problem, but they were too rationalistic to get far enough. Schelling's mid-career work on mythography had drawn upon Eichhorn and other rationalist scholars, though Schelling was vague about his scholarly debts. Schelling conceived myths as ideas presented in pictorial form that are meant to persuade observers of some higher truth. Baur's work in this area was an extension of Schelling's. Baur taught that myth is "the most perfect form in which the ideas of the absolute make themselves palpable" (*Versinnlichen*). The difference between symbols and myths, Baur argued, is that symbols are static images, while myths are visual presentations of ideas "by means of an action."[12]

Baur taught Strauss to interpret myths critically, with a Schelling-like appreciation for myth as a distinctive vehicle of religious truth. To Strauss, the Hegelian distinction between image and concept suggested a better approach to the myth problem than Schelling's too-friendly one, if only the Hegelians would take it. Instead, Hegelians mystified myth much like Schelling. Hegelian theologians taught that the historical data pertaining to Jesus was inherent in the content of Christianity, meaning the idea of divine-human unity. In this area they followed Hegel, who, though careful to avoid quantitative thresholds, denied that the historical data pertaining to Jesus is reducible entirely to imagination (*Vorstellung*). Hegelian theologians reaffirmed Hegel's claim that *Vorstellung* and *Begriff* are interrelated in the development of religious truth. The truth of the divine-human unity, they argued, is necessarily rooted in the historical Christian source of this ideal, which is the basis on which the ideal is known to the religious consciousness.[13]

To Strauss, that was the way of mystification and religious orthodoxy. Hegelian theology obscured the negative aspects of the relation of the concept to history. Writing to Märklin, Hegel put it in the form of a question: "Does the historical character adhere to the content, thus demanding recognition from the concept as well as the imagination, since the content is the same for both, or is it reduced to the mere form [of imagination], to which conceptual thinking is not bound?"[14]

Writing in the Hegelian *Jahrbücker* in 1832, Strauss put it contentiously. The best of the young Hegelians, Rosenkranz, had published a major work, *Encyclopedia of the Theological Sciences*, the previous year. Like Karl Michelet and Heinrich Hotho, Rosenkranz had grown up in a Prussian community of French-speaking Calvinists and converted to Hegelianism during his student years. Strauss took him on, protesting that Rosenkranz was just like the older generation of Hegelian theologians. Instead of interrogating the actual development of Christianity, Rosenkranz deduced the historical truth of Christianity from the concept. That is not legitimate, Strauss objected: "Speculative theology is not related to the historical simply in the fashion of essence to appearance, but as the concept to being (*Sein*) and appearance, and therefore essentially presupposes being and appearance." The only historical representations that deserve to be harmonized with philosophical truth are those that survive vigorous historical deconstruction, he contended. But Hegelian theology, even at its best, was not known for that.[15]

The Hegelian school overstated the affirmative relationship between the Concept and Christian history; thus it produced theological systems that bolstered or even embraced traditional Christian orthodoxy. Rosenkranz, Daub, and Marheineke offered sophisticated forms of Hegelian revisionist Christianity more or less along Hegel's line; to their right, Karl Friedrich Göschel, Kasimir Conradi and Isaak Rust used Hegelian philosophy to bolster traditional Christian supernaturalism. Strauss judged that the former group's greater sophistication was not enough of a difference. Hegelian theology as a whole was too facile in reconciling the Absolute Idea to historical Christianity. The relationship between philosophical reason and historical Christianity was not simply one of essence to appearance, for historical truths could not be established or validated on systematic grounds.[16]

This was the intellectual background to Strauss' controversial two-volume work, *The Life of Jesus Critically Examined* (1835). Strauss conceived it as a three-part work that would establish the negative relation between historical Christianity and the Concept. He believed that Christianity is true as a religion that affirms the immanent relation of divine reality to the world, and that God is incarnate in humanity as a whole, not only in Jesus or any other figure. He proposed to write a constructive theology defending this position. To clear the field for his constructive perspective, however, Strauss had to show why traditional Christianity was not historically credible. He planned an opening section that described orthodox Christian teaching and spirituality, a second section that destroyed the historical basis of traditional Christianity, and a third section that contained his constructive theology.[17]

But his sprawling research soon overwhelmed the entire project; Strauss dropped the first section entirely; his "second" section swelled to 1,500 pages, requiring two volumes, which he ended with a brief appendix on the "dogmatic import" of the historical Jesus. Strauss was 27 years old when his tour de force appeared, seemingly from nowhere. Relentlessly it exposed the mythical elements of the New Testament gospels. Nothing like it had ever been published. Rationalist and early historical critical scholarship had wrestled with aspects of the myth problem, but no one before Strauss had marched straight through the gospel narratives armed with a command of the critical scholarship on scripture and a persistent focus on the myth issue. Strauss noted that the church fathers took for granted "that the gospels contained a history, and secondly, that this history was a supernatural one." On the other hand, critics like Eichhorn and Heinrich Eberhard Paulus rejected the latter presupposition, but they were too rationalistic not to cling "the more tenaciously to the former, maintaining that these books present unadulterated, though only natural, history."[18]

So-called "historical criticism" was not historical enough, because it perpetuated rationalist apologetics, providing naturalistic explanations for biblical events. Paulus described the transfiguration as an autumnal sunrise that transfixed the three disciples in their early-morning drowsiness. He described the raising of Lazarus as a deliverance from a coma and the resurrection of Jesus as a resuscitation.[19] Rationalistic historical criticism, despite assuming that God does not intervene in history, and despite deconstructing the biblical text, still assumed that biblical history is basically historical. Strauss was more rational than that: "The other presupposition also must be relinquished, and the inquiry must first be made whether in fact, and to what extent, the ground on which we stand in the Gospels is historical. This is the natural course of things, and thus far the appearance of a work like the present is not only justifiable, but even necessary."[20]

Strauss deconstructed the historical pretenses of the sacred narrative by playing off the supernaturalist and rationalist methods against each other. He moved straight through the gospels to show that orthodox literalist and rational naturalist interpretations of gospel stories refuted each other. Rationalist criticism, Strauss noted, was strong on things that no modern educated reader accepted, such as angel appearances, Mary's virginal conception, miracle stories, and many other places (especially the genealogical tables and passion narratives) where the gospel narratives were unbelievable and contradictory. Rationalist criticism rightly belabored many of these problems.

But Strauss repeatedly turned the tables on rationalist critics, who offered naturalistic explanations for unbelievable accounts and sometimes suggested that faulty reporting by witnesses was the problem. Strauss ridiculed the "unnaturalism" of rationalist naturalism. Sometimes he preferred the straightforward exegesis of supernaturalists, who at least remained in contact with the biblical texts. Rationalist critics, by contrast, offered tortured conflations of contradictory texts and imaginative yarns on what must have happened. On the whole Strauss regretted that modern biblical criticism was pervaded by rationalist assumptions. The critics that he admired most – Baur, Wilhelm Martin Leberecht de Wette, and Gottlieb Philipp Christian Kaiser – did not shy away from the myth issue, but even the best critics overused naturalistic explanations.[21] Baur explained the angelic appearance at the birth of Jesus as a meteoric phenomenon; he suggested that the baptism of Jesus was accompanied by thunder and lightening and the accidental descent of a dove; he thought that the transfiguration was caused by a storm; and he identified the angels at the tomb of the risen Jesus as gatekeepers wearing white graveclothes.[22]

Strauss did not always reject naturalistic explanations and he did not always find biblical history to be in error. He relied on psychological explanations for some of Jesus' healing miracles and the resurrection appearances, and he judged that the gospels contain a sizable core of reliable historical material. In Strauss' reading, Jesus was a follower of John the Baptist who launched his own messianic ministry in Galilee after John was imprisoned. Jesus remained John's disciple through most of his messianic career, he called disciples of his own, and he proclaimed that the appearance of the messianic Son of Man was immanent. His teachings were preserved in generally reliable form in the synoptic gospels, including the predictions of the apocalypse. Strauss believed that Jesus identified himself with the Son of Man in his later career and was subsequently arrested, tried, and crucified.[23]

This was a stronger core of historical material than neo-orthodoxy, the reigning theology of a century later, bothered to defend. Strauss took little interest in the teaching of Jesus; thus, from his standpoint, it didn't really matter if the synoptic gospels got Jesus more or less correctly, though he judged that they did. Liberal theologians afterward invested considerably more importance in this judgment. Strauss left more biblical history in place than did subsequent critics lacking anything like his reputation for negativity.

He acquired his reputation as a smasher by featuring myth criticism. Strauss argued that the inadequacies of orthodox and rationalist interpretation showed the necessity of emphasizing the myth issue. Orthodoxy made unbelievable historical claims and thus negated genuine history, while rationalism distorted the historical texts by removing the miraculous from them. If theology wanted to be taken seriously in the modern age, it had to face up to the mythical character and origins of Christianity. Stressing the distinction between *Vorstellung* and *Begriff,* Strauss assured that the "eternal truth" of Christianity was not affected by his deconstruction of the gospel narrative: "The supernatural birth of Christ, his miracles, his resurrection and ascension, remain eternal truths whatever doubts may be cast on their reality as historical facts."[24]

Rationalist criticism subverted the religious truth of Christianity by distorting the biblical accounts and by failing to address the mythical character of Christian faith. Strauss argued that myth criticism liberated the truths of Christianity from their mythical origins and forms. The true meaning of the Incarnation is not tied to any putative historical event. Rather, Hegelian philosophy maintained and refined the essence of Christianity, its defining eternal truth – but this essence could only be recognized as such after one left behind the mythical thought forms of traditional Christianity.

So what, exactly, was myth criticism? Strauss gave an unwieldy answer in his first edition, which he improved in the second edition by adding criteria for detecting unhistorical material.[25] His conception of myth emphasized its representational, unconscious, and collective character. Myths are not fables concocted by individuals, he stressed; rather, myths are narrative descriptions of events or ideas that express a community's partly unconscious self-understanding and experience. According to Strauss, the infancy narratives in Matthew and Luke were almost entirely mythical, as were the gospel accounts of relations between Jesus and John the Baptist, most of the miracle stories, the transfiguration, most of the passion narrative accounts, and virtually all of the resurrection and ascension accounts.

On the resurrection narratives, Strauss conceded that "something extraordinarily encouraging" must have happened to the disciples after the death of Jesus that transformed their "deep depression and utter hopelessness" into religious enthusiasm. He judged that the encouraging "something" must have begun after the disciples returned to Galilee "where they gradually began to breath freely, and where their faith in Jesus, which had been temporarily depressed, might once more expand with its former vigor." It was in this place and mood, far from the grave of Jesus, that the disciples first formed the idea of his resurrection. Within several weeks, their intense desire to see Jesus raised to life produced visions in which he appeared and spoke to them. Some of these visions occurred even "before whole assemblies in moments of highly wrought enthusiasm," in which the disciples believed they heard Jesus "in every impressive sound, or saw him in every striking appearance."[26]

Once the idea of a resurrection of Jesus was established in the hearts and minds of his followers, Strauss explained, the great event was quickly "surrounded and embellished with all the pomp which the Jewish imagination furnished."[27] The angels became the "chief ornaments" of the primitive church's Easter myth; they opened the grave of Jesus, kept watch over it, and delivered the tidings of Jesus' resurrection to the women. Baur's maxim applied strongly to the resurrection narratives, that whenever you see reports of angel activities, you're dealing with myth.[28]

Strauss followed Baur in defining myth as "the representation of an event or of an idea in a form which is historical, but, at the same time characterized by the rich pictorial and imaginative mode of thought and expression of the primitive ages." Myths typically present historical accounts of events that "are either absolutely or relatively beyond the reach of experience," such as events pertaining to the spiritual realm, or events which by their particular nature preclude historical witnesses. Myths also typically depict fantastic or marvelous events in the form of highly symbolic language, Strauss observed. He followed Baur in distinguishing among historical myths ("narratives of real events colored by the light of antiquity" in which the natural and supernatural realms are mixed); philosophical myths (in which an idea is clothed "in the garb of historical narrative"); and poetic myths (in which historical and philosophical myths are partly blended together "and partly embellished by the creations of the imagination.") [29]

Some myths are equally historical and symbolic, Strauss conceded; assigning a category is sometimes a judgment call. He accepted Baur's rule that the essential difference between historical and philosophical myths is that the latter seek to advance, symbolize or otherwise support some particular truth claim; in philosophical myths, a legend is invented to serve a dogmatic or persuasive purpose, whereas no such purpose is apparent in historical myths. Strauss observed that biblical myths often piece together the elements of both kinds of myth, but the kind of blend that constitutes the third type of myth obscures the original fact or idea of the narrative "by the veil which the fancy of the poet has woven around it." Poetic myths are too strong on fantasy or marvel to be historical and too lacking in ideas to be philosophical. Schelling, Strauss noted, was struck by the "unartificial and spontaneous origin" of myths in general. The biblical writers and other mythicists of antiquity expressed their ideas in historical narratives to accommodate these ideas to popular consciousness and because their philosophical self-understanding was too undeveloped not to resort to religious imagery.[30]

Strauss allowed that biblical mythology is more restrained and historical than the myths of Greek, Roman and other cultures. Though he placed the Bible's angel narratives, theophanies, and miracle stories in the same mythical category as the fables of Jupiter, Hercules, and Bacchus, Strauss noted that biblical myths are generally less incredible than their pagan counterparts: "Vishnu appearing in his three first avatars as a fish, a tortoise, and a boar; Saturn devouring his children; Jupiter turning himself into a bull, a swan, etc. – these are incredibilities of quite another kind from Jehovah appearing to Abraham in a human form under the terebinth tree, or to Moses in the burning bush." Some biblical stories approach pagan levels of fancy, such as the tales of Balaam, Joshua, and Samson, "but still it is here less glaring, and does not form as in the Indian religion and in certain parts of the Grecian, the prevailing character."[31]

Moreover, in pagan mythologies the gods have a history; they are subjected to time, change, opposition, and suffering. In Hebrew religion, Strauss observed, God is the absolute I Am. Thus, Hebrew religion is not mythological in the narrow sense of the term. It contains no history of the gods, for in Hebrew Scripture, only God's people have a history, not God. To Strauss, this was the taproot of the superiority of Jewish/Christian myth over pagan mythologies. Its ultimate fruit was the Christian/Hegelian Absolute Spirit. Biblical myth is closer to reality than the pagan fables, Strauss emphasized, yet the difference is in degree, not in kind, for biblical myth is still mythical.

Strauss counseled that this is what we should expect. Because Christianity is a religion, it apprehends reality in the form of mythic imagery: "If religion be defined as the perception of truth, not in the form of an idea, which is the philosophic perception, but invested with imagery; it is easy to see that the mythical element can be wanting only when religion either falls short of, or goes beyond, its peculiar province, and that in the proper religious sphere it must necessarily exist." The biblical writers should not be demeaned for expressing their ideas in pre-philosophical images, for myth is necessarily constitutive of religion. The peculiar province of religion is the mythical imagination, which is less rational and self-conscious than the scientific mind.[32]

Ottfried Müller, an expert on Greek mythology, taught that myths are necessary, partly unconscious, and never intentionally deceptive. The notion of myth as a deliberate fabrication is entirely false, he argued. In the strict sense of the term it is wrong even to speak of myths as being "invented," because the mythic imagination lacks the requisite self-awareness to "create" a self-consciously true or false narrative: "It is this notion of a certain necessity and unconsciousness in the formation of the ancient mythi, on which we insist." According to Müller, the inventor of myth is not a rational or individuated interpreter of the world, but merely "the mouth through which all speak, the skilful interpreter who has the address first to give form and expression to the thoughts of all."[33]

Strauss learned this view from Baur, who accepted it. Strauss accepted the parts about necessity, unconsciousness, and communal ownership, but conditionally. As usual, he began with a mild objection, then worked up to a strong one. The distinguishing line between intentional and unintentional fiction is not as readily drawn as Müller and Baur contended, Strauss argued. For example, the gospel narratives often portray Jesus as saying or doing something to fulfill the details of a messianic prophecy. These accounts are clearly contrived, Strauss judged. But does that mean that the gospel writers perceived them as inventions? Strauss reasoned that the gospel writers might well have believed that these recent inventions were historically true and not recently invented; after all, they believed that Jesus was the Messiah. If Jesus was the Messiah, they may have thought, he must have said and done the Messianic things that the church's oral tradition attributed to him. Strauss argued that the Messianic-fulfillment texts are too ambiguous to make a judgment upon; the gospel writers may have realized that these accounts were unhistorical, but perhaps they did not.

But Baur's claim that myth is never intentionally contrived was itself a pious fiction, Strauss insisted. The authors of the Homeric songs surely did not believe that every event in their accounts of the history of the gods actually happened. The writer of Chronicles must have recognized that his account contradicted Samuel and Kings, partly by introjecting later material into the narrative. The author of Daniel must have realized that his account was modeled on the Joseph story and that it made "prophecies" of events already past. To recognize that the ancient authors must have been conscious at times of inventing myths is not necessarily to charge them with "evil design," Strauss allowed; the ancient writers had little concept of the difference between history and fiction and no concept of the rights or morality of authorship. That their fictions were entirely undesigned, however, is not credible. Scripture mixes history and fiction in ways that even the biblical writers must have recognized, Strauss argued. These inventions became myth as they were received in faith by religious communities, thus confirming that they were the fruit "not of any individual conception, but of an accordance with the sentiments of a multitude."[34]

Having gone as far as he did with Baur and Müller on unconsciousness and communal ownership, Strauss knew that he had a problem with the rapid development of Christian myth. How was one to explain that Christianity acquired a rich body of sustainable myth almost from its birth? Strauss replied that it would have been impossible, lacking several centuries of Jewish messianic myth. New Testament Christianity was too complex and developed to have sprung from nothing, he acknowledged. At the same time, early Christianity was too deeply mythical to be categorized as a merely historical religion. The historical explanation for the rapid development of Christian myth is not that early Christianity was not mythical, but that it was based on the long-developing Jewish myth of messianic deliverance. With this structure of religious teaching in place, early church leaders needed only to transfer the messianic legends, "almost all ready formed, to Jesus, with some alterations to adapt them to Christian opinions." Very little of early Christianity's mythical core was newly created.[35]

In the book's third and fourth editions Strauss delineated three kinds of gospel myth – evangelical, pure, and historical. Evangelical myths are products of an idea (*religiose Vorstellung*) about Jesus promulgated by his followers. An idea such as Jesus the Messiah, Strauss explained, may have some relation (often unrecoverable) to something that Jesus said or did, but in either case the idea is determinative, not a factual occurrence. Pure myths have no direct historical basis, flowing directly from the religious imagination. Strauss classified the rending of the Temple veil after Jesus' death and the Transfiguration stories as pure myths, because neither story appears to have any historical basis in the life of Jesus. The Transfiguration story is a slightly reworked messianic redeemer myth and the temple veil account reflects the hostile relationship between first-century Judaism and the early Christian church. Historical myths fuse a definite historical event with a mythical concept culled from the Christ idea; here Strauss placed the calls to the disciples, the barren fig-tree story, and some of the healing stories – mythical embellishments of events probably holding some historical basis.[36]

Though Strauss judged that the gospels are loaded with all three kinds of gospel myth, he found little evidence of the legendary in the New Testament. Here the compressed time factor was crucial, plus the focused power of the Christ idea. Legends are products of oral tradition in which the originating mythical idea (presuming it ever existed) has been lost. Mythical accounts are unhistorical and fictional, but legends are merely unhistorical. Strauss noted that legends are characterized by "indefiniteness and want of connexion." Often they are strange, confused, and pointless, "the natural results of a long course of oral transmission." The New Testament is too urgent and determined to have legends, he reasoned. The idea of Christ as Lord and redeemer fills the gospel narratives, just as it shaped the early church's recollections and interpretations of Jesus.[37]

Strauss admonished that modern people cannot share the mythical consciousness of the biblical writers, even if they try. The authors of the Bible viewed all history "down to the minutest details" in mythical terms. They took for granted that God gives the rain, sends the storm, dispenses war and pestilence, hardens hearts, and suggests thoughts. This is precisely the view of reality that modern science has torn apart, Strauss urged. Modern educated people, "after many centuries of tedious research," no longer attribute everything that happens to the immediate agency of a divine ruler. Science shows "that all things are linked together by a chain of causes and effects, which suffers no interruption." Strauss took for granted that modern theology as a whole was modern precisely as a response to this fact; to him, the strength of the Hegelian approach was that it reclaimed on speculative grounds "that which has been destroyed critically."[38]

History, Myth, and Hermeneutics

The Life of Jesus Critically Examined set off an explosion of outrage, especially for its aggressive assertion that the New Testament is pervaded with myths. The book had no original arguments, but no one before Strauss had so vigorously presented the evidence for the mythical nature of Christianity; the vigor alone was startling. Strauss never developed a coherent theory of myth, and he failed even to relate his two typologies of myth to each other, yet his work outstripped everything remotely resembling it. In 1835, having no real precedent made him vulnerable. Strauss begged his friends to support him after the protests began, to no avail; privately they told him that his sledgehammer tactics were indefensible. Even Baur told him that the book was too relentlessly negative to be good scholarship. Strauss was reduced to rebutting book reviewers himself; in one case, addressing Hegelians, he summarized his situation by describing himself as the only left-Hegelian.[39]

If there was only one left-Hegelian, and he was known for a slashing deconstruction of the gospels, he had no chance of winning an academic position. Strauss was surprised and appalled by this situation; for all his shrewdness in other areas, he had been naive about what he was doing to his career. After two years of hostility and shunning he began to reconsider his approach. Baur's reaction cut him deeply, the second edition got similar reviews, and Strauss admitted to friends that he was terrified at the prospect of never landing a teaching post. In December 1837 he told his friend Adolf Rapp that he was no longer determined to fight for principle; the world could believe what it wanted. If exile was his only alternative, he would agree to "believe" unbelievable things.[40]

In that mood Strauss wrote a third edition that toned down the book's sarcasm and made nearly 100 substantive changes, virtually all of the accommodating sort. His original edition denied apostolic authorship of the gospel of John, denied that John's long discourses were authentic, and did not give special treatment to the fourth gospel, notwithstanding that liberal theologians of Schleiermacher's type loved the fourth gospel for its eloquent discourses and its deemphasis on miracles. In the third edition Strauss appeased Mediating theologians on all these points, offering that it wasn't certain if the discourses were authentic. In his original edition, Strauss portrayed Jesus as a misguided apocalyptic prophet; in the third edition, he emphasized the God-consciousness of Jesus and described Jesus theologically as the embodiment of the divine-human idea. That placed the third edition within the orbit of Schleiermacher's churchly disciples, though Strauss reaffirmed that his Christology was Hegelian. In the preface he remarked that while the book's argument had lost much of its unity in the course of being revised, he hoped that it had gained in truth.[41]

The third edition was Strauss' last bid for an academic career. But soon he was embarrassed at having ruined his book for an unattainable prize. He didn't believe in the book's revisions enough to defend them, and Baur sharply questioned his defense of the possible authenticity of the Johannine discourses. For a brief moment it appeared that Strauss' third edition might save his reputation and career. In 1839, he was appointed to a theology position at the University of Zurich, partly on the strength of his concessions. But the news of his appointment sparked outrage in local churches; the Zurich city council, bowing to popular pressure, pensioned Strauss off at half salary before he taught a single course; and his academic career was over before it began. Strauss' forced "retirement" from Zurich ended his yearning for academic respectability; he no longer cared what professors and ecclesiastics thought of him. He admitted to friends that he had never believed in the third edition's revisions. Mythologizing the spiritual consciousness of Jesus was a Schleiermacher-style evasion that he opposed. Strauss told Märklin that he regretted his attempt to salvage anything from historical Christianity. The religion that was needed had no need of an outside savior.[42]

At last he was free to speak the truth as he knew it. In 1840 Strauss completed a two-volume historical theology, *The Christian Faith* (1840), and a new edition of his book on Jesus. *The Christian Faith* examined the history of Christian doctrine from its biblical origins to its current conflicts with modern science, declaring famously that "the true criticism of dogma is its history."[43] Strauss' fourth edition *Life of Jesus Critically Examined* had the same spirit, restoring the book's original tone and arguments. He explained in the preface that the "intermingling voices of opponents, critics, and fellow laborers, to which I held it a duty attentively to listen, had confused the idea of the work in my mind; in the diligent comparison of divergent opinions I had lost sight of the subject itself." He was finished with everyone who couldn't face up to the mythical nature of Christianity or who failed to do so because they wanted to keep some grubby job in the academy or church or government.[44]

This included most Hegelians, several of whom, during the furor over Strauss' first edition, corrected him with quotes from Hegel. Strauss admitted that they had Hegel on their side. Hegel was "no friend of historical criticism," Strauss acknowledged, and if Hegel had lived to read *The Life of Jesus Critically Examined*, he would not have liked it. Part of the problem was Hegel's "undeniable vagueness" regarding Christology, Strauss reasoned. Since Hegel made a policy of being vague theologically, outright super-naturalists were granted the right to call themselves Hegelians. There was also the fact that in his later years, Hegel tended to emphasize the positive, reconciling function of the dialectic instead of its negative function. His lectures on religion made it clear that he regarded Jesus' life and death as part of the content of religious truth, and Hegel was delicate with those who believed too much in this area, just as he indulged super-naturalists. Strauss singled out Göschel, Gabler, and Bruno Bauer as purveyors of really bad (right-Hegelian) theology; he put Rosenkranz in the center; and only himself on the left, where Hegelian theology did not go by the letter of Hegel. The best Hegelian theology ran with the spirit of Hegel's revolutionary dialectic.[45]

This argument gained an impressive following over the succeeding decade. It was embraced by a new generation of left-Hegelians, led by Bruno Bauer (who converted from right-Hegelianism) and Ludwig Feuerbach, who soon surpassed Strauss in their radical rejection of Christianity.[46] But Strauss did not persist in his claim to being the true Hegelian. Merely five years after his first edition *Life of Jesus* sought to clear the way for a philosophical appropriation of Christianity, his two-volume *The Christian Faith* relinquished the dream of the Hegelian synthesis. The Hegelian promise of a new order of peace in which reason and faith lived together was a pretentious illusion, Strauss declared. No philosophy could hold together Christianity and the modern consciousness, because modernity is a revolution – a transformation of consciousness that renders previous systems of thought irrelevant. The polemics and crushing disappointments of recent years had devoured Strauss' faith that any philosophy could bridge the chasm created by modern reason.[47]

In the end his rationalism devoured any sympathy that he may have felt for Baur-style hermeneutics or Hegelian synthesis. Strauss put it bluntly in his negative criterion for identifying unhistorical material. An account is not historical, he asserted, "when the narration is irreconcilable with the known and universal laws which govern the course of events." The law of cause and effect and other universal laws ruled out all supernatural interventions, prophecies, apparitions, and unexplainable miracles, plus all "intermingling of the spiritual world with the human," a superstition found "only in unauthentic records," which is "irreconcilable with all just conceptions."[48]

Strauss never grasped that his flat-footed rationalism was crude compared to the hermeneutics of understanding that Schleiermacher and Hegel developed. Schleiermacher's hermeneutic theory was reconstructionist, teaching that the meaning of a text is grasped by identifying with the author in such a way that one relives the experience out of which the author wrote.[49] Hegel's theory was integrationist in spirit and execution; for him, the work of interpretation was ultimately carried out by the self-penetration of spirit. As Hans-Georg Gadamer remarks, Hegel conceived the work of historical understanding as a "thoughtful mediation with contemporary life," not as a destruction or restoration of the past. Hegel taught that the work of philosophical mediation is on the same level, dialectically, as the truth it explicates. It is not an external operation conducted after the fact. [50]

Hegel's approach to history, myth, and understanding anticipated key aspects of postmodern hermeneutics, but Strauss' literalistic rationalism ran too deep for him to go there. Strauss took no interest in a hermeneutics of religious myth or symbolism because for him the purpose of historical understanding was to destroy religion. Any judgment about the credibility of biblical history, he insisted, "must be founded on the nature of its particular narratives," not upon any consideration of its literary history or character. Thus he disregarded the teaching of Jesus, the literary character of the gospels, and even the religious purposes of the gospels. Baur lamented that his protégé gave no attention to the gospels as integral literary works; Strauss cared only about destroying the credibility of gospel stories.[51]

To his credit, Strauss anticipated form criticism by breaking each gospel into independent literary units, then comparing these pericopes with parallel stories in other gospels. Form criticism, a valuable tool for detecting oral transmission, can be an aid to comprehending the gospels as literature. Strauss, however, pioneered the kind of form criticism for which context is irrelevant and so is literary character. Abstracting his data from its literary, historical, and religious contexts, he was consumed with exposing how the gospel stories contradict each other, violate universal laws of history, and mythologize the life and meaning of Jesus. Strauss epitomized one-sided hammering, obtaining negative results by a method that predetermined them. Most of his negative historical conclusions were validated by succeeding generations of biblical scholarship. But that did not "mean" what he assumed. Strauss' historical conclusions did not lead necessarily to his philosophical position, for most of his conclusions were taken for granted by generations of liberal and neo-orthodox theologians.[52]

Schweitzer remarked that "in order to understand Strauss one must love him," to which Karl Barth aptly replied that while we should feel sympathy for Strauss, he was not a tragic figure. Strauss was too moody, vain, undisciplined, and self-absorbed to be a great scholar, Barth observed; the subject of his scholarship was never the historical material as such, but merely "the dream-image of his own existence." Strauss put it more factually: "I am not a historian; with me everything has proceeded from dogmatic (or rather anti-dogmatic) concerns." Barth suggested that if Strauss was judged, nonetheless, on the basis of his historical scholarship, he had only himself to blame.[53]

But Strauss was not merely the wild, half-scholarly, destructive historicist that Barth felt free to dismiss. He cast a larger shadow over modern theology than Barth let on, defining the issues over which theologians were forced to make choices and define themselves. Parts of Strauss' monistic idealism, notably his Christology, were retrieved repeatedly for two centuries, usually without attribution. Since religion is the form in which truth presents itself to popular consciousness, Strauss argued, the truth of the divine-human unity was first disclosed to the senses: "In other words, there must appear a human individual who is recognized as the visible God." The death of Christ on Calvary proved the reality of the incarnation by revealing that the God-man knew "how to find a way of return into himself." Strauss reasoned that the unity of the divine and human in Christ subsequently became "a part of the general consciousness; and the church must repeat spiritually, in the souls of its members, those events of his life which he experienced externally."[54]

Unfortunately, the church restricted the incarnation to Jesus. Strauss criticized Christianity for making Jesus the sole bearer of the incarnation, confining the great truth of divine-human unity to the blinkered consciousness of the religious imagination: "Is not the idea of the unity of the divine and human natures a real one in a far higher sense, when I regard the whole race of mankind as its realization, than when I single out one man as such a realization? Is not an incarnation of God from eternity, a truer one than an incarnation limited to a particular point of time?" Pressing this issue was always the point for Strauss. To liberate the truth in Christian myth, the myth had to be broken open: "This is the key to the whole of Christology, that, as subject of the predicate which the church assigns to Christ, we place, instead of an individual, an idea; but an idea which has an existence in reality, not in the mind only, like that of Kant."[55]

Traditional Christianity left the church with impossible contradictions. How could a single historical person have a fully human nature and a fully divine nature? Did Christ possess one will or two? Strauss judged that either answer to the latter question undermines the church's doctrine of incarnation. In the idea of humanity, however, these contradictions disappear: "Humanity is the union of the two natures – God become man, the infinite manifesting itself in the finite, and the finite spirit remembering its infinitude; it is the child of the visible Mother and the invisible Father, Nature and Spirit." Humanity is the worker of miracles in the course of the spirit's mastery of nature; it is the redeemer of sin, which afflicts individuals but "does not touch the race or its history." Strauss urged that humanity realizes its spiritual nature through its triumph over nature and individual evil: "It is Humanity that dies, rises, and ascends to heaven, for from the negation of its phenomenal life there ever proceeds a higher spiritual life; from the suppression of its mortality as a personal, national, and terrestrial spirit, arises its union with the infinite spirit of the heavens."[56]

To Strauss, the miracle of humanity's spiritual transformation was infinitely more important than the historicity of the biblical miracle stories. Most liberals agreed, but rarely said it plainly. Strauss called for a theology of the "infinitely repeated pulsation of the divine life." Instead of confining the incarnation to Jesus, the church needed to recognize that this idea "only attains existence in the totality of individuals." Instead of treating the gospel narratives as history, good theology treated them "for the most part as mere myth." What matters is not any single fact or part of the process, but the process that gives meaning to facts. Strauss urged, "Our age demands to be led in Christology to the idea in the fact, to the race in the individual."[57]

Strauss wanted to spend his career challenging theologians to choose his rationalistic monism over Schleiermacher's mystifying romanticism. Instead he lost his academic career, and abandoned his theological one, after established theologians rejected his rationalist historicism and the Hegelian movement acquired a strident left-faction that ridiculed Strauss for his vanity, political conservatism, and fixation with theology. Two organs of progressive Hegelianism, Arnold Ruge's *Hallische Jahrbücker* and Eduard Meyen's *Literarische Zeitung* were founded in 1838. By 1841, barely six years after Strauss burst upon the scene as a religious radical ahead of his time, he found himself outflanked and often derided by a Hegelian Left that regarded all religion as wish projection. Bruno Bauer, Ludwig Feuerbach, and other recent converts to left-Hegelianism skewered Strauss as a phony left-Hegelian. These attacks got so personal that Strauss broke off all relations with left-Hegelians, which cost him at the very moment that left-Hegelianism took off as an intellectual option. *Hallische Jahrbücker*, though ostensibly identified with progressive Hegelian Christianity, supported Bauer and Feuerbach against Strauss, boosting the journal's reputation and driving Strauss away.[58]

Meanwhile Strauss watched mediating theology grow stronger as the epigones of the 1830s gave way to sophisticated system-builders such as Richard Rothe, Isaak August Dorner, and later, A. E. Biedermann. Rothe developed a creative metaphysical system drawing upon Hegel and Schleiermacher, emphasizing Hegel's concept of revelation, and featuring a strong ethical conscience. Dorner wrote massive works of constructive and historical theology. Biedermann wrote in the center-Hegelian mold of Rosenkranz, holding that the essence of Christianity consists in the incarnational principle revealed in Christ, not in the church's mythological accounts or doctrines about Jesus.[59]

For twenty years Strauss left theology behind. Though successful as a popular writer, he could not bear to read theology, much less write it. In the early 1860s he tried to make a comeback, publishing a popular version of his book on Jesus that restored the Schleiermacherian compromises of the third edition; this edition was titled *The Life of Jesus for the German People* (1864). The popular success of Ernst Renan's *Life of Jesus* (1863) caused Strauss to hope that an attractive version of his own book might find a large audience. But reviewers roasted Strauss' book and he returned to attack-mode, deriding liberal theology as *Speck* (fat) and mediating theology as *Wurst* (sausage). Reclaiming his posture of the late 1830s as an advocate of modern, rationalist, radical Christianity, Strauss took aim at Schleiermacher's lectures on the life of Jesus, which were published in 1865 – 33 years after he had delivered them at Tübingen.[60]

It seemed to Strauss that very little had changed during his twenty year vacation from theology. The mildly liberalizing approach to theology had flourished, in a way, by adopting Schleiermacher's approach, Strauss acknowledged. This approach was the last great attempt "to make the churchly Christ acceptable to the modern world," and it managed to avert the assaults of historical criticism. For Schleiermacher, Christ was a soul constantly in communion with God – the image of perfected humanity. But Strauss charged that Schleiermacher's Christ was derived from Plato, Spinoza, and Kant, not the Bible. Schleiermacher succeeded by substituting a liberal neo-Platonic Christ for the Christ of the Bible shredded by modern criticism. Though Schleiermacher understood that Christianity was mostly myth, he yearned "for a personal Christ who existed historically." According to Strauss, this yearning kept Schleiermacher perpetually conflicted. Schleiermacher knew that modern criticism was right, and he wrote with feeling about spiritual freedom, yet he clung to a fantasized redeemer: "He senses the danger which, coming from the power of the modern ideas which he permitted to permeate himself, threatens the fragment of faith which he has carried over from the past and does not want to give up for anything."[61]

Schleiermacher's Christ was a memory from a forgotten time, like the light of a burned-out star that still appears to the eye. Strauss boasted that stronger souls did not try to save a mythical Christ after the historical Jesus was demythologized: "We may no longer, like Schleiermacher, speak of a redeemer after we have given up the God-man who offered himself as a sacrifice for the sins of the world." It was not credible to substitute a modern "Christ principle" or experience of redemption for the church's historic doctrine of vicarious atonement. Schleiermacher's theology of Christian experience was true only as a reflection of his personal experience, Strauss argued: "It changed nothing in substance." Christian theology could progress beyond its present impasse only by letting go of historical Christianity, "for the ideal of the dogmatic Christ on the one hand and the historical Jesus of Nazareth on the other are separated forever."[62]

For ten years Strauss went back to saying that a truly rational Christianity was the prize and that the epigones of Schleiermacher and Hegel failed to face up to it. The great task of modern theology was to construct the ideal Christ figure apart from the mythical-dogmatic Christ of Christian history. But in 1872 Strauss changed again, saying farewell to Christianity. In *The Old Faith and the New* (1872), he declared that he had ended up where Lessing ended up. The real choice was between orthodox Christianity and rational science; liberal Christianity was a contradiction in terms. We do not know enough about Jesus to make him an object of faith, Strauss argued. Moreover, what we do know is that he was an apocalyptic prophet who cannot be our model. The important questions for modern people dealt with science, technology, the fine arts and practical politics; Jesus was no help with any of that. Thus, liberal Christianity was incoherent. The old faith was absurd, but at least it did not contradict itself; liberal Christianity was doubly absurd because it contradicted both reason and itself. Christianity is not true and is not worth saving.[63]

As Strauss expected, modern theology went on to struggle mightily with the Straussian problem of the historical Jesus versus the Christ of faith, and it echoed his insistence that theology must overcome its mythical elements. What Strauss did not expect, but witnessed with astonishment at the end of his life, was the emergence of a dominant theological liberalism that took his criticism seriously while contradicting his conclusions about what it meant. By the time that he dropped Christianity, Strauss thought he had seen every conceivable modernizing strategy. But the next phase of modern theology was just beginning – Ritschlian historicism, which accepted the Straussian split between the Jesus of history and the Christ of faith and overcame the mythical inheritance of Christianity by claiming fidelity to Jesus.

Strauss suffered for his demolition of biblical history; given the bitter disappointments that he suffered for deconstructing the sacred narrative, it is surprising only that he took so long to reject Christianity. It took him so long because he believed, even to the end, that he had the right project from the beginning. Strauss knew that his best works were inspired by his conviction that the meaning of history is philosophical or religious, never historical. Ironically, he paved the way to theologies that let go of philosophy in the name of sacred history.

Becoming a Self: Søren Kierkegaard

Ritschlian historicism, which took off just as Strauss took leave of Christianity, was the next big thing in theology. But something greater had occurred that almost nobody noticed, unless one read Danish. Søren Kierkegaard rejected liberal theology and Hegelianism for completely different reasons than Strauss. To Strauss, if a biblical story could be shown to be mythical, it was discredited; to Kierkegaard, that was pitifully superficial. It was so pitiful that Kierkegaard never bothered to read *The Life of Jesus Critically Examined,* though he read about it in theology journals.

The biblical story of the fall, Kierkegaard believed, is the best account that we have of sin coming into the world, because it depicts the coming as a leap. To call this account a myth is to trivialize it. Kierkegaard skewered the modernist project, epitomized by Strauss, of replacing biblical truths with a myth of modern progress. Yet he was fully modern to the point of anticipating postmodernism. Kierkegaard blasted epistemic foundations and other shelters from the absurd. Like Hamann and Jacobi, he was an anti-rationalist fideist who wielded reason as a weapon. His emphasis on individual subjectivity made him as idealistic as any post-Kantian. And he anticipated almost every trope of postmodern criticism and consciousness.[64]

In Kierkegaard's case the personal drama looms over and within everything. He was steeped in family tragedy; his intense emotional torment equaled that of his father; he had a bitter rivalry with his only surviving sibling; as an adult he had only one friend; and he chose romantic heartbreak over his one chance at normal happiness. Aptly he noted of himself, while recalling one of his earlier statements about Socrates, "His whole life was a personal preoccupation with himself, and then guidance comes along and adds something world-historical to it." The first part, about self-preoccupation, was obvious. Guidance, in his meaning, was divine; Kierkegaard believed that his life had a religious purpose. The last part, about world-historical significance, was an astounding conviction, considering his circumstances; Kierkegaard believed, rightly, that he was too brilliant not to be discovered eventually as a major thinker.[65]

He spent his entire life in and around Copenhagen, except for four trips to Berlin and a pilgrimage to his father's roots in Jutland. Kierkegaard was unknown outside Denmark when he died in 1855, and he remained unknown for decades afterward. In the early twentieth century he entered the canon as the first existentialist and as an influence on the dialectical theology generation. In the late twentieth century he survived the canon-busting of deconstructionists, who hailed him as a forerunner of postmodernism, not that he would have cared about postmodernism. Kierkegaard's postmodern credentials are real; he subverted authorial authority, specialized in indirect communication, ridiculed the pretensions of theoretical systems, and urged that truth is subjectivity. But what he cared about was the radical possibility of becoming a Christian.

He was born in 1813 as the youngest of seven children to a wealthy merchant, Michael Pedersen Kierkegaard, who retired before Kierkegaard was born, and a mother, Ane Sørensdatter Lund, whom he never mentioned a single time in his vast outpouring of books and diaries. Michael Pedersen had grown up poor in the sheepherding heaths of west Jutland. At the age of eleven he accompanied a sheep dealer to Copenhagen to work for his mother's brother, who had a dry goods shop. As a young man he branched out on his own, selling woven caps and leather gloves, plus goods from Iceland, which led to trading in finer items from France, China, and West India that brought him into conflict with the local guild, in which Michael Pedersen prevailed in a Supreme Court decision. He was also shrewd and lucky as an investor, riding Copenhagen's expanding economy. He married a business partner's sister, but she died of pneumonia less than two years later. Shortly after becoming a widower he impregnated his maid, a distant cousin from a Jutland peasant farming background similar to his own, and married her, eventually parenting seven children with her.[66]

Michael Pedersen Kierkegaard treated his second wife as a low-level employee, communicating to his children that she did not matter. Having retired from work at the age of forty, he was a constant presence in the lives of his children and spouse, and a dominating one. Relentlessly serious and plagued by religious guilt, though not over how he treated his spouse, he attended to everything; Kierkegaard's mother lacked even the status of housekeeper. Søren Kierkegaard later painted a grim picture of his youth, stressing his father's melancholia and his own, though he wrongly claimed that his had no development; he always had it. For many years Michael Pedersen feared that God was mocking him through his success at business and investments. Later he was certain of it as he buried his children.

In 1807 the British fleet bombarded Copenhagen, setting off an economic decline that led to state bankruptcy. Michael Pedersen, however, ended up richer than ever, having bought guaranteed gold-convertible bonds just before the crash. In 1819 the plague of deaths began. Michael Pedersen lost his son Søren Michael, who died of a brain hemorrhage after a playground accident. He lost his eldest and favorite child in 1822, Maren Kirstine, who died of nephritis. Between 1832 and 1834 tragedy stuck four times, taking two daughters, a son, and Ane Sørensdatter Lund Kierkegaard, all while Søren Kierkegaard lived at home as a college student.

Michael Pedersen wanted one of his sons to follow him into the business world, but his oldest son, Peter, was an academic star, and he indulged his youngest son, Søren, as the baby of the family. That left Niels Andreas, who was told to make something of himself in business, despite his desire to go to college. In September 1832, just before Niels was exiled to New Jersey, his sister Nicolene died following childbirth. The following September Niels died of galloping consumption in a hotel room in Paterson, New Jersey. On his deathbed Niels asked to be remembered to his dear mother and did not mention his father, a report that cut Michael Pedersen deeply, adding to the home's gloomy atmosphere. In 1834 Ane Sørensdatter Lund Kierkegaard died of a fever; Søren Kierkegaard, despite never mentioning his mother, was reported by the mother of his university tutor, H. L. Martensen, to be crushed by her loss. A few months later Søren lost another sister, Petrea, to complications following childbirth. By then the remaining Kierkegaards – the patriarch, the oldest son, and the youngest son, were consumed with grief.[67]

Religion was the story of their life, including intellectualizing about it. Michael Pedersen Kierkegaard was intellectually gifted, an earnest reader of rationalist philosophy, especially Christian Wolff, and sufficiently religious to need more than one kind of religion. His peasant Pietist background showed up on weekdays, as he worshiped with the *Herrnhuters,* the Congregation of Moravian Brothers. On Sundays, however, he was a respectable Lutheran, absorbing the liberal-leaning rationalism of the state church. In 1812 an eloquent, Pietist-leaning Lutheran pastor, Jakob Peter Mynster, moved to Copenhagen's Church of Our Lady. Michael Pedersen became a staunch follower of Mynster, identifying with his urbane churchmanship, which heightened in urbanity as Mynster acquired a following. Mynster's chief rival for influence was theologian and politician Nicolai Frederik Severin Grundtvig, a dramatic personality and the leader of Danish Pietism, who built a following by threatening to leave the state church. Grundtvig loosened Pietist orthodoxy on the infallibility of the Bible, but compensated by playing up the authority of the church.

Kierkegaard scholars have wrangled over Michael Pedersen's Moravian weekdays and his seemingly inconsistent opposition to Grundtvig. Did he hedge his bets in the religious politics of his time? Did he give mixed messages to his eldest and youngest sons? Both answers are surely yes; Joakim Garff, Kierkegaard's best biographer, stresses that Michael Pedersen showed "extraordinary reverence for everything connected with rank and distinction" and that we know little about him aside from the outpourings of his youngest son. But another motive was surely in play: Michael Pedersen, though devoted to Mynster and his own respectability, needed both kinds of religion to get through a week.[68]

His sons, grappling with the contradiction, made contrasting choices. Peter Christian Kierkegaard was a hard-working, earnest, gloomy, top-of-the-class type, plagued by indecisiveness. He was also prone to self-righteousness, a tendency that grated on his baby brother. During his college years Peter became friends with leaders of Grundtvig's awakening movement and eventually joined them, more or less. Peter needed a new father figure as relief from the one that he inherited, but he was always ambivalent about Grundtvig, a temporizing trait that eventually helped him to make bishop. In 1848, when Denmark was suddenly transformed into a constitutional monarchy with a representative government, Peter Kierkegaard was a key player in helping the Danish church adjust to modern democracy. Søren Kierkegaard, a livelier youth than he later recalled of himself, took a more complicated religious path that took his entire short lifetime to play out. Until his father died in 1838, Søren Kierkegaard adopted his father's admiration for Mynster, an occasional visitor to the Kierkegaard home. Afterwards he nursed a decidedly different feeling about his father's idol.

As a youth Kierkegaard leveled the playing field with older siblings by teasing them sharply, often sarcastically. Once he declared, "I am a fork, and I will stick you," after which his siblings called him, "The Fork." In one account, he explained that he liked to be able to spear anything on the dinner table, and if his siblings came after him, he would spear them too. At school he struck classmates as strange, with a wild streak. None of his classmates remembered having expected anything of him. All described him as a loner and smart aleck; some reported that he cheated in class. One classmate recalled, "He knew how to make his opponent appear ridiculous." Another classmate added, "His most remarkable talent was the ability to make his target appear ridiculous, and it was especially the big, tall, and powerfully built boys whom he chose as the objects of his derision." A teacher remembered being annoyed that Kierkegaard always had an answer ready before getting the question. It didn't help that his oldest brother was a legendary student and that his father compelled him to wear heavy woolen stockings and a coat ending with a skirt, inviting ridicule. Throughout his life Kierkegaard was afflicted with frail health and a curved spine. In later life he summarized his youth: "Slight, thin and delicate, denied practically all the physical conditions which, compared with others, could qualify me, too, as a whole human being; melancholy, sick in my mind, profoundly and inwardly a failure in many ways, I was given one thing: an eminently astute mind, presumably to keep me from being completely defenseless. Already as a young boy I was aware of my mental dexterity and that in it lay my strength in the face of these far stronger comrades."[69]

The key events of Kierkegaard's life are shrouded in mystery, notwithstanding his extensive journals and papers. In his early twenties, reeling from the deaths of loved ones and the shock of learning his father's terrible secret, Kierkegaard went through a prodigal son phase, running up enormous debts through partying and carrying on. What was the "great earthquake" of his life – the secret that his father confided to him, which triggered his rebellion? How did Kierkegaard eventually reconcile with his father? What happened in his conversion experience? Kierkegaard scholars have pored over his journals and letters for clues to these questions, stymied by Kierkegaard's reticence. In addition, the first editor of Kierkegaard's papers, H. P. Barfod, discarded many items and censoriously cut-and-pasted others, adding to the confusion. Some scholars maintain that the "great earthquake" must have been Michael Pedersen's confession about how he came to marry a second time, a sin that implicated the entire family in illegitimacy and shame. But that explanation is too prosaic for the dramatic impact that occurred.[70]

On his 22nd birthday, in May 1835, Kierkegaard's father apparently told him the terrible secret of his life, which was that as a youth he had cursed God for allowing him to suffer from hunger and cold while tending sheep on the Jutland heath. Kierkegaard later recounted in a journal entry of 1846: "How dreadful, the thought of that man who as a small boy tending sheep on the Hutland heath, in much suffering, starving and exhausted, once stood up on a hill and cursed God! – and that man was unable to forget it when he was eighty-two years old." In 1865 Barfod, working on Kierkegaard's journals in the residence of Bishop Peter Kierkegaard, showed the 1846 entry to the bishop, who burst into tears: "That is my father's story – and *ours,* too." Peter Kierkegaard provided details, which Barfod considered too personal for history, frustrating all Kierkegaard scholars to follow.[71]

Michael Pedersen was unable to forget the heath episode because he believed that he had committed the unforgiveable sin, which cursed him to outlive his children. The story of the family's tragic and guilt-soaked life was that he had condemned the entire family to early death by offending God. For Søren Kierkegaard, this revelation was crushing and liberating at the same time. Its impact was more existential than a story about his sister's illegitimacy would have been. The father's story battered Kierkegaard emotionally, put his past in a morbid light, and made him fearful of his future. It put an end to his childish dependence on his father and awoke his intellectual ambitions.

He later recalled that a feeling of exuberance accompanied the unleashing of his mind, although it took him only so far. Kierkegaard never doubted his intellectual power to do anything that he willed, except to be delivered from melancholia, over which he had no power: "What I am saying will seem to others a vain conceit, but so it was with me in truth, as truly as what I tell next, which to others again will seem a conceit. I say that it never occurred to me that in my generation there lived or was to be born a man who had the upper hand of me – and in my inmost self I was the most wretched of all men. It never remotely occurred to me that, even if I were to attempt the most foolhardy enterprise, I should not be victorious – only one thing excepted, all else absolutely, but one thing not, to throw off the melancholy from which and from its attendant sufferings I was never entirely free even for a day." In his telling, contrary to acquaintances who did not experience him as depressed, Kierkegaard lived in "lonesome inward torment" and depression for his entire life. He could have gone either way with his torment, either hating human beings and cursing God, or loving human beings and praising God. The later Kierkegaard stressed that he never rejected Christianity, even during the rebellious, despairing, alienated self-indulgence of his early twenties. But despair took hold of him; Kierkegaard needed to be rebellious and alienated just to find his own thoughts.[72]

For three years he played the decadent rich kid who neglected his studies, though out of view, Kierkegaard read voraciously. In public he vamped and sneered, wore foppishly tailored costumes, and spent huge sums on books, liquor, La Paloma cigars, Venezuelan pipe tobacco, chic coats (including a favorite lemon-yellow one), walking sticks, silk scarves, tailoring, theater, and cafés, all while living at home. Often he got drunk; generally he made a spectacle of himself in the streets. Kierkegaard may have paid for prostitutes, although that would have been a cash expense. For the expenses of which we have record, in 1836 alone he ran up a debt of 1,262 rixdollars, a figure exceeding the annual salary of a university professor, which made his father tremble upon paying the bill.[73]

Though released, in a way, even euphorically, from his childhood, Kierkegaard fell into despair without realizing it, taking for granted that his absurd life had only a few years remaining at most. After realizing that he was in despair he found no relief; mere recognition of his condition was not saving. A decade later his pseudonym Vigilius Haufniensis reflected in *The Concept of Dread:* "Dread discovers fate, but when the individual would put his confidence in fate, dread turns about and takes fate away; for fate is like dread, and dread is like possibility . . . a witch's letter." For Kierkegaard, despair felt like the invasion of an alien power that he wanted and didn't want at the same time; in any case, he felt powerless over it. He wrote numerous journal entries about feeling insane and entering a lunatic asylum, asserting that he preferred talking with "lunatics" than with sensible types. His father stopped speaking to him, but paid the bills. In 1836 the gloom lifted briefly in the Kierkegaard household as Peter married a vibrant young woman, Maria, remaining at home with her, but she died the following July, bringing the household to a new low.[74]

Kierkegaard's prodigal phase ended with events that we know little about. In 1837 he met Regine Olsen and fell in love with her at first sight. On or shortly after his 25th birthday the following year he reconciled with his earthly father, barely in time. A few days later he reconciled with his heavenly father, experiencing a religious conversion of "indescribable joy" that changed his life unalterably, though he soon returned to writing about the terrible distress and depression that filled his soul: "It's all inexplicable, myself most of all. For me all existence is contaminated, myself most of all. Great is my distress, unlimited. No one knows it but God in heaven and he will not comfort me."[75]

Kierkegaard struggled hard to keep his father's "earthquake" secret, even as he wrote about it allusively. He was more successful in veiling whatever happened between him and Michael Pedersen at the reconciliation, where the initiating act of contrition probably began with the father. Michael Pedersen was in failing health, at age 82, and probably anticipated that he had little time left. Soon afterward, Kierkegaard began to rationalize that Michael Pedersen had raised him in a religiously crazed fashion out of love, to protect his children from the sensuality that had ruined his life. Kierkegaard's account of his religious conversion consisted of a single journal entry. No previous entry indicates that he was contemplating a religious decision, nor did he reflect on the experience afterward, although everything that he wrote bore some relation to it: "There is such a thing as an *indescribable joy* which glows through us as unaccountably as the Apostle's outburst is unexpected: 'Rejoice, and again I say, Rejoice!' – Not a joy over this or that, but full jubilation, 'with hearts, and souls, and voices': 'I rejoice over my joy, of, in by, at, on, through, with my joy' – a heavenly refrain, which cuts short, as it were, our ordinary song; a joy which cools and refreshes like a breeze, a gust of the tradewind which blows from the Grove of Mamre to the eternal mansions."[76]

The fact that he never reflected again on this experience or tried to describe it more precisely had something to do with his denial that he was a mystic; plus, melancholia returned with a vengeance anyway. Kierkegaard considered himself to be too dialectical for mystical visions. But his conversion experience was unmistakably mystical, as his two analogies about it reflected. Like Paul, he was caught up into paradise and heard unspeakable things. Like Abraham at the grove of Mamre, he saw the Lord while sitting in the tent door in the bright daylight; a door opened to him. The following month Michael Pedersen Kierkegaard died, leaving approximately one million dollars and his home to his two sons, who lived together under one roof, very uneasily.

On the day of his father's death, Kierkegaard conveyed the news personally to Mynster, who reportedly had trouble remembering a Michael Pedersen Kierkegaard. Kierkegaard burned with humiliation and revulsion. His father had adored, quoted, supported, and hosted Mynster. He had suffered from his Christian conscience and imposed it on his family. Now his idol couldn't even remember him? Kierkegaard stewed over this alleged incident for seventeen years before recording it in his journal; by then he had made himself notorious on the subject of Mynster and official Christianity.[77]

Though Kierkegaard resumed his clownish public persona after his father died, in private he disciplined his manic intellectual energy. Michael Pedersen had desperately wanted to see him complete his university exams and make something of himself. Now Kierkegaard was motivated to do so, feeling guilty that he deprived his father of a satisfaction that he deserved. He completed his exams in 1840, plotted large books in his head, wrote a dissertation for the *Magister* degree in philosophy (the equivalent of the doctorate in other Copenhagen faculties), *The Concept of Irony,* and plotted his courtship of Regine Olsen. She was fourteen years old when he met her. Kierkegaard waited two years for her to come of age, then courted her as he wrote the dissertation.[78]

For a year they were formally engaged, which Kierkegaard later described as a period of unspeakable psychic agony. He fretted that his melancholy would destroy her; plus, Kierkegaard was just beginning to imagine a career as an author. Fearing that his gloom and intellectualism would overwhelm her, and that marriage would get in his way, Kierkegaard began to hedge. Regine, determined to cure Kierkegaard of melancholy, refused to accept it as a reason to break the engagement. Her family supported her; Regine's father begged Kierkegaard that she was willing to put up with all his problems. Finally Kierkegaard insisted that a cure was impossible and so was marriage, a judgment that enraged her family, caused a scandal in Copenhagen, and inspired Kierkegaard's early pseudonymous books.

Reeling from heartbreak, Kierkegaard defended his decision in *Repetition* and *Fear and Trembling;* still reeling, he went on for hundreds of pages in *Stages on Life's Way* and numerous journal entries: "I do not marry to have another person slave under my depression. It is my pride, my honor, my inspiration to keep in inclosing reserve what must be locked up, to reduce it to the scantiest rations possible . . . Her, or I shall never marry . . . She loved only me, and yet she didn't understand me . . . I had placed in her my last hope in life, and I must deprive myself of it . . . Suppose I had married her. Let us assume it. What then? In the course of half a year or less she would have gone to pieces. There is – and this both the good and the bad in me – something spectral about me, something that makes it impossible for people to put up with me every day and have a real relationship with me . . . At home it will be evident that basically I live in a spirit world. I had been engaged to her for one year and yet she really did not know me. Consequently she would have been shattered. She probably would have spoiled my life too, for I would always be overstraining myself with her because her reality was in a sense too light. I was too heavy for her, she too light for me." [79]

Books poured out of his spirit-existence; in the early going, all had something to do with Regine. *Either/Or* (1843), two volumes "edited" by Victor Eremita, contained the writings of a young man representing the aesthetic view of life and an older friend's defense of the ethical way of life. *Repetition* (1843), by Constantin Constantius, told the story of a young poet who had to break his engagement for ethical reasons and who despaired of mere repetition in the ethical sphere. *Fear and Trembling* (1843), by Johannes de Silentio, explored the idea of faith transcending the ethical, centering on the biblical story of Abraham's willingness to sacrifice his son Isaac at God's command. *Prefaces* (1844), by Nicolaus Notabene, consisted entirely of comical prefaces. *The Concept of Dread* (1844), by Vigilius Haufniensis, offered a critique of philosophical system-building within a psychological reflection on the doctrine of original sin. *Philosophical Fragments* (1844), by Johannes Climacus, contrasted the paradox of "the God in time" to philosophical idealism, epitomized in Socratic recollection. *Stages on Life's Way* (1845), a bundle of documents discovered by Hilarious Bookbinder, was a sequel to *Either/Or*. Kierkegaard wrote in pseudonyms to get himself out of the picture, reasoning that the ideas mattered, not him. More importantly, by using pseudonyms he could be different people, and say whatever he wanted, without having to defend himself, although he also published volumes of edifying discourses on biblical texts under his name.[80]

Hegelianism was ascendant among Denmark's intellectual elite when Kierkegaard sought to enter it in the mid-1830s. Denmark's first Hegelian, Johan Ludvig Heiberg, was the doyen of Danish intellectual culture. Kierkegaard took for granted that breaking into Heiberg's circle was the key to becoming a respected intellectual. Kierkegaard's favorite teacher, Poul Møller, taught Hegel's system, although he poked fun at Hegel's grandiosity. More importantly, Hans Lassen Martensen converted to Hegelianism in 1836, setting an instructive example. Kierkegaard had chosen Martensen as a tutor over Peter Kierkegaard, even though Peter was reputed to be the university's best tutor. At the time Martensen was a follower of Schleiermacher. He lectured on Schleiermacher to Kierkegaard, who proved to be a trying student; in Martensen's telling, Kierkegaard specialized in sophistical repartee, not rigorous study or thought: "I recognized immediately that his was not an ordinary intellect but that he also had an irresistible urge to sophistry, to hairsplitting games, which showed itself at every opportunity and was often tiresome." Kierkegaard never liked Martensen, who may have reminded him of Peter. After Martensen became a Hegelian, Kierkegaard's ill feeling grew, although he respected Hegel's genius and admonished himself not to antagonize Danish Hegelians unnecessarily.[81]

From the beginning Kierkegaard was averse to Hegel's low regard for subjectivity and the individual, a reaction that he shared with Møller. As early as August 1835 Kierkegaard wrote in his journal, "What I really need is to be clear about *what I am to do*, not what I must know, except in the way knowledge must precede all action. It is a question of understanding my destiny, of seeing what the Deity really wants *me* to do; the thing is to find a truth which is truth *for me*, to find *the idea for which I will live and die*. And what use here would it be if I were to discover a so-called objective truth, or if I worked my way through the philosophers' systems and were able to call them all to account on request, point out inconsistencies in every single circle? And what use here would it be to be able to work out a theory of the state, and put all the pieces from so many places into one whole, construct a world which, again, I myself did not inhabit but merely held up for others to see? What use would it be to be able to propound the meaning of Christianity, to explain many separate facts, if it had no deeper meaning for myself and for *my life?*"[82]

In Kierkegaard's telling, he shucked off his father's orthodoxy shortly after entering college: "I grew up so to speak in orthodoxy, but as soon as I began to think for myself the huge colossus gradually began to totter." It was pointless to exchange one colossus, such as orthodox Christianity, for another, such as Hegelianism. The point was to find a truth that really mattered and give oneself to it. In October 1835 he put it stridently, declaring that philosophy and Christianity "can never be united." If one ties Christianity to a philosophy, Kierkegaard judged, one cannot hold to Christian redemption, which extends to the whole person. On second thought, he reflected that Christian philosophy is all right, as long as one begins with Christianity; philosophical theology, however, should not exist. Already he was sounding like Kierkegaard, including his complaint about not being understood: "People understand me so little that they fail even to understand my complaints that they do not understand me."[83]

The Concept of Irony invited misunderstanding by parading and denying Kierkegaard's Hegelianism. It was loaded with Hegelian elements, especially, triadic structures and a Hegelian critique of romantic irony. Kierkegaard's dissertation lauded Socrates for a world-historical achievement that would not have been possible had he been disposed to go along with society. The book's elaborate first part, "The Position of Socrates Viewed as Irony," employed the Hegelian dialectic of possibility, actuality, and necessity, interpreting Socrates as an ironist of absolute negativity. In a lengthy, winding first chapter, Kierkegaard proposed that Socrates might have been an ironist, although Xenophon's Socrates had no trace of irony; chapter 2 showed that Socrates was certainly an ironist; chapter 3 argued that this interpretation had no serious rivals. The irony of Plato's Socrates was world-historical – "He is suspended in ironic satisfaction above all the qualifications of substantial life." In part two, Kierkegaard rated romantic irony much lower, judging that it did not serve the World Spirit. On the primacy of negation, Kierkegaard remained a Hegelian for the rest of his life, though he construed it as Socratic: "Irony as the negative is the way; it is not the truth but the way. Anyone who has a result as such does not possess it, since he does not have the way."[84]

The Concept of Irony was recognizably Kierkegaardian and strangely not. Against Hegel, it argued that existence as an actuality combines the opposing concepts of possibility and negation; existence is always paradoxical. With Hegel, it played up irony as negation. These vintage Kierkegaardian themes redeemed the dissertation for Kierkegaard after he outgrew it. But who was this person that went on about the World Spirit and the dialectic of history?

Kierkegaard later confessed, with chagrin and typical exaggeration, that he was an immature student overly impressed by Hegel, Hegel's importance, and all things modern. His understanding of Hegel when he wrote the *Concept of Irony* was based on Hegel's posthumously published lectures on the philosophy of history, fine art, and the history of philosophy, plus the admiring things that distinguished people said about Hegel. The only non-lecture, non-posthumous work of Hegel's that he cited was the *Philosophy of Right*. Kierkegaard was keen to join the intellectual elite, which was the point of writing a dissertation, in his case one delayed by years of foolishness. Since Hegelianism was, as far as he knew, a philosophy of history, he cast his theory of irony as a semi-Hegelian philosophy of history. Years later he put it ruefully: "Influenced as I was by Hegel and whatever was modern, without the maturity really to comprehend greatness, I could not resist pointing out somewhere in my dissertation that it was a defect on the part of Socrates to disregard the whole and only consider numerically the individuals. What a Hegelian fool I was! It is precisely this that powerfully demonstrates what a great ethicist Socrates was."[85]

Kierkegaard got special permission from the king to write his dissertation in Danish, which he defended in Latin, on September 16, 1841, for seven and a half hours. It was his first and last official academic event at the University of Copenhagen. Faculty dean F. C. Sibbern strongly supported Kierkegaard; nine opponents rose to debate Kierkegaard; Peter Kierkegaard and J. L. Heiberg were two of them. The chief complaint was that Kierkegaard was too verbose and undisciplined. Two weeks later Kierkegaard made his final break with Regine and set out to write books. *The Concept of Irony* got only two reviews in fourteen years, which Kierkegaard took in stride. He was too busy writing new ones to look back, and not interested in defending his dissertation's semi-Hegelian structure and motifs. Moreover, he despised reviewers anyway: "I repudiate all reviews. To me a reviewer is just as loathsome as a streetwalking assistant barber who comes running with the shaving water which is used for all customers and fumbles about my face with his clammy fingers." For the rest of his life Kierkegaard lamented that most people relied on reviewers instead of reading the books that the reviews were ostensibly about.[86]

One review stood out in Kierkegaard's career, helping him to find his way, albeit negatively. Heiberg, reviewing *Either/Or*, observed that the book was much too long, but he took reviewing seriously, so he plunged into it. Before long it was obvious that the author was brilliant and sophisticated. However, *Either/Or*, besides being "a monster of a book," was "dreamlike, amorphous, and ephemeral." Its depiction of the aesthetic way of life desperately needed some gritty reality. A section titled "The Seducer's Diary" promised a break from dreaminess, only to deliver a spectacle of perversity: "One is disgusted, one is nauseated, one is revolted." What sort of human being took pleasure in imagining such a despicably promiscuous and manipulative character? Heiberg, asking himself this question, vowed not to read *Or*, then did so anyway, which surprised him. *Or* made a beautiful case for the ethical way of life, Heiberg reported. It was laced with wit and humor, it had "bolts of intellectual lightning," and it was well-organized. In short, *Or* redeemed the work as a whole, rewarding the effort of reading it.[87]

Either/Or was Kierkegaard's only early work that made a critical splash or sold many copies. Of his first nineteen books, all of which Kierkegaard financed, only *Either/Or* sold out its first printing. Had Heiberg not reviewed it, Kierkegaard might have enjoyed the book's success, including its many positive reviews. As it was, he raged against reviewers for the rest of his life and rued that he had ever sought to be included in Heiberg's salon society. The fact that Heiberg's review was ultimately positive, even glowing, was completely lost on Kierkegaard. Heiberg rarely deemed that anyone beside himself was brilliant; Kierkegaard, seething at the negative parts, turned a corner. Denmark's small literary society had little trouble identifying the author of Kierkegaard's highbrow eruptions. Signe Laessøe (Margrethe Juliane Abrahamson) wrote to her friend Hans Christian Andersen that a "new literary comet," Søren Kierkegaard, had caused a Rousseau-like stir in Denmark with his brilliant, disgusting, demonic work, *Either/Or.* The book's first part, she explained, was aesthetic, "that is, evil," and the second part was ethical, "that is, a little less evil." Part two was widely praised as Kierkegaard's alter ego, "the better half," but she begged to differ, because the supposedly ethical part condemned women to subservience: "We women have to be especially angry with him: Like the Mohammedans, he assigns us to the realm of finitude, and he values us only because we give birth to, amuse, and *save* menfolk." Kierkegaard, realizing that Denmark's intellectual elite was onto him, vowed to turn against the age. He would not waste any more energy or self-respect currying favor with polite society intellectuals impressed by their own learning, liberalism, Hegelianism, feminism, or world-historical pretensions.[88]

If he was going to attack Hegelianism, however, Kierkegaard needed to learn more about it. The *Concept of Irony* was vulnerable on this point, as he realized; moreover, there was too much Hegelianism in it anyway. In the fall of 1841 he attended Marheineke's lectures in Berlin, who struck him as a more learned version of Martensen. Kierkegaard took brief excitement at Schelling's anti-Hegelian lectures before losing patience with Schelling, who was too much like Hegel. He kept up with German debates by following two periodicals, H. N. Clausen's and M. H. Hohlenberg's *Tidsskrift for udenlandsktheologisk Litteratur,* a distinguished, wide-ranging journal, and I. H. Fichte's *Zeitschrift für Philosophie und speculative Theologie,* a mainstay of the speculative, non-Hegelian mainstream of the mediating theology movement featuring Lücke, Nitzsch, Rothe, Neander, and Twesten. Above all, Kierkegaard studied Aristotle, Descartes, and Leibniz for the first time, read Adolf Trendelenburg's Aristotelian critiques of Hegelian logic, and studied Hegelian texts that Hegel actually wrote – all in preparation for the great existential polemics of Johannes Climacus, *Philosophical Fragments* (1844) and *Concluding Unscientific Postscript to Philosophical Fragments* (1846).[89]

Here the postmodernized interpreter must pause. The standard English-language tradition of interpreting Kierkegaard plays down the significance of the pseudonyms, including the ironic subtleties of Kierkegaard's indirect communication. It assumes that Kierkegaard took positions about issues that refer to something, and thus that he wrote to state truths and to clarify issues. On the first issue, the dominant scholarly tradition has routinely misread Kierkegaard, who created authors that did not always agree with each other, and who used pseudonyms in part to prevent readers from reading a system or essential structure into his thought. Kierkegaard insisted that his spiritual vision was higher than all his pseudonymous authors except the last one, Anti-Climacus, who was higher than him. At the end of *Concluding Unscientific Postscript,* having announced his authorship of the pseudonymous works, he declared: "My wish, my prayer, is that, if it might occur to anyone to quote a particular saying from the books, he would do me the favor to cite the name of the respective pseudonymous author."[90]

Much of the scholarship on Kierkegaard, refusing the favor, portrays an essentialist Kierkegaard driven by an essential religious perspective, philosophy, or aesthetic that unifies the Kierkegaardian corpus. Walter Lowrie, Kierkegaard's chief English biographer and translator, treated the pseudonyms as distractions from Kierkegaard's essential religious purpose as expressed in the edifying discourses under his name. Paul Sponheim's *Kierkegaard on Christ and Christian Coherence* (1968) contends that Kierkegaard's works are unified by their focus on the figure and reality of Christ. Stephen Dunning, in *Kierkegaard's Dialectic of Inwardness* (1985), offers a structural analysis of Kierkegaard's theory of stages, brushing aside the plural perspectives among Kierkegaard's pseudonyms. John Elrod, in *Being and Existence in Kierkegaard's Pseudonymous Works* (1975), emphasizes the pseudonyms only to quash them, contending that Kierkegaard used them as vehicles of a single determining aim, a unified self no longer alienated from itself. Sylvia Walsh's *Living Poetically, Kierkegaard's Existential Aesthetics* (1994), reads the pseudonyms as "moments" of a Hegelian-like process of aesthetic consciousness coming to awareness of itself. Louis P. Pojman contends that Kierkegaard's work as a whole, including the pseudonymous literature, is unified by his thoroughgoing rationalism.[91]

This tradition of reducing Kierkegaard's polyphony to one voice was ripe for deconstructionist pushback emphasizing the instability of meaning. Louis Mackey, in *Points of View: Readings of Kierkegaard* (1986), applies Derrida-style deconstruction to "Kierkegaard," declaring that it is not enough to construe Kierkegaard as a literary type or a poet who used philosophy to get his points across. Kierkegaard was not a philosopher or a theologian of any kind, Mackey declares: "By virtue of his authorial self-restraint, his texts exhibit an almost complete abstention from determinate meaning and an almost perfect recalcitrance to interpretation." Roger Poole, upping the deconstructionist ante, stigmatizes as "theological" any interpretation of Kierkegaard that understands his pseudonymous works as advancing philosophical claims. In Poole's telling, "Kierkegaard writes text after text whose aim is not to state a truth, not to clarify an issue, not to propose a definite doctrine, not to offer some meaning that could be directly appropriated." Kierkegaard, Poole claims, was a forerunner of Jacques Derrida and Jacques Lacan, anticipating the deconstructionist view of language as a spiral of words chasing words lacking any referent: "The texts demonstrate to a nicety the Lacanian perception that all we are ever offered in a text is an endless succession of signifiers." Poole cautions, however, that it is possible to play too fast and loose with Kierkegaard's texts, making them say anything that one wants them to say; his showcase example is Mark C. Taylor, who, in Poole's telling, interprets Kierkegaard and all philosophical writing as a free play of subjective fantasy.[92]

The latter judgment is an unfair gloss on Taylor's deconstructionism, since Taylor takes Kierkegaard's philosophical reasoning very seriously, dialectically pairing Kierkegaard's account of absolute difference with Hegel's idea of constitutive relationality. In any case, I take postmodern criticism seriously but not to the point of denying that Kierkegaard wrote to state truths and to take positions about issues that refer to something. Instability, difference, ironic spinning, and polyphony are splashed across the pages of Kierkegaard and his authorial creations. So are philosophical and theological commitments, plus entire works of exceedingly direct communication featuring religious beliefs. *Philosophical Fragments,* a work thick with irony, also conveyed Kierkegaard's deadly earnest commitment, through Climacus, to liberate modern Christianity from philosophical idealism and modernist presumption. Kierkegaard wrote it in his own name, then switched to Climacus the day before it was published. *Concluding Unscientific Postscript,* a work that screamed irony in its title, blared its anti-Hegelianism in the same title.[93]

The End as the Middle: The Fragments and the Postscript

Johannes Climacus claimed that he was not a Christian or a philosopher, and he lacked even an opinion. He was "an idler from love of ease" and an opponent of systems, although even this opposition did not count as an opinion, as holding one was both "too much and too little" in such matters. He came only to dance "in the service of Thought." He hoped to give honor to God and to find some pleasure in dancing, but he would not risk anyone else's life in playing the game, which was what system-builders did: "I have only my life, and the instant a difficulty offers I put in play." But even that was misleading, as he had no intention of dancing with philosophers or with anyone wielding an opinion. His dance partner was the thought of death; the dance itself was with death, in opposition to opinion. Others could bring their history of philosophy baggage to the dance, but he would not dance with them.[94]

Philosophical Fragments had five acts, in the manner of classical drama, and two main characters, Socrates and Christ, whom Climacus called "the God in time." An interlude between the last two acts, questioning whether the past is more necessary than the future, suggested the passage of time; otherwise the context was timeless, featuring dialogue carried by the two main characters, which was interrupted at the end of each chapter by the reader's remarks, to which Climacus replied. The book's subtitle featured Lessing's question: "Is an historical point of departure possible for an eternal consciousness; how can such a point of departure have any other than a merely historical interest; [and] is it possible to base an eternal happiness upon historical knowledge?" The book's dramatic narrative featured Climacus' question: How does Christian paradox differ from Socratic recollection? A different question, never posed by Climacus, loomed over *Philosophical Fragments* and virtually shouted in *Concluding Unscientific Postscript:* Was despair the motivating force of Kierkegaard's dialectic? Did he merely replace Hegel's abstract negation with the despair of subjective spirit?

For Climacus, Socrates was the great alternative to Christ, the shining exemplar of idealistic recollection. Socrates, pondering that a knower cannot seek what one already knows or does not know, formulated the theory of recollection, that all learning and inquiry is a kind of remembering. The learner dispels one's ignorance by coming to oneself in the consciousness of what one already knows. The truth comes from within an individual, not without; the teacher is merely a prod to recollection. Climacus prized Socrates for awakening minds in the streets and marketplace, spurning "false and vain fellowship with clever heads." In Socratic idealism each individual is one's own center, Climacus explained, "and the entire world centers in him, because his self-knowledge is a knowledge of God." Socrates had the courage and self-respect "to be sufficient unto himself, but also in his relations to his fellowmen to be merely an occasion, even when dealing with the meanest capacity." Climacus vastly preferred the magnanimity and brilliance of Socrates to organized Christianity, which gave titles and rank to all manner of mediocre pastors, professors, and church officials mediated "in a common madness."[95]

He took for granted the Socratic model of recollection, especially the primacy of the moment of recognition, while laying a heavy burden on it: "The Moment in time must have a decisive significance, so that I will never be able to forget it either in time or eternity; because the Eternal, which hitherto did not exist, came into existence in this moment." This was the crucial presupposition for the dance. Climacus reasoned that if the moment is to have decisive import, the seeker must be "destitute of the Truth" up to the moment of recognizing it. If the seeker possesses the truth as ignorance, the moment is not decisive; it is merely occasional. Moreover, Climacus argued, even to describe the seeker as a seeker is problematic, for one cannot seek the answer unless one recalls it. Taken seriously, the doctrine of recognition recognizes that so-called "seekers" are in error, devoid of the truth, not seeking it like a proselyte. There is no movement until it is given that the subject bears the condition of being in error in relation to truth. One recognizes that one doesn't want the truth. But how does it help to be reminded of something that one has not known and does not recall?[96]

Climacus allowed that the Socratic teacher helps learners to recognize that they are in error. But that merely drives the learner further from the truth; ignorance is bliss compared to learning that one is devoid of the truth. So the teacher, being merely accidental, drives the learner away; there is no moment between teacher and learner. The Socratic teacher is merely an occasion, "even if he is a God." No one can be taught to see one's error or one's responsibility for it, even if everyone else sees it: "For my own Error is something I can discover only by myself, since it is only when I have discovered it that it is discovered." Climacus explained that this being in error by reason of one's own guilt is called *sin*. There is an apparent freedom in learning that one is in error and is morally responsible for it, for to be free is to be what one is by one's act. But there is no real freedom in being free from the Truth, Climacus admonished; to be exiled by one's own self is to be in bondage, a slave to sin.[97]

Socrates was no help with that, for the Socratic view has no moment. Hegelian idealism was no help either, because for Hegel *every* moment is necessary and the fullness of time. The moment that makes a real difference has a distinct character, Climacus urged. It is brief, temporal, and transient, like all moments, and also past, like every moment in the next moment. But it is also decisive and filled with the eternal, something deserving the name, "the Fullness of Time."[98]

Climacus got that far without appealing to the authority of Christianity or the Holy Spirit; *Philosophical Fragments* was a thought project about thought self-produced. It taught that love is the cause of all suffering, because God is love and God desires in love to share the condition of the lowest and most vulnerable. God is like the seed of an oak planted in earthen vessels, bursting them apart, which is what happens when God implants God's self in human weakness: "This becoming, what labors will attend the change, how convulsed with birth-pangs!" Climacus made a point of his lack of originality, confessing that he plagiarized Christian ideas. He didn't have to be a Christian to grasp the Christian truism that love needs nothing to satisfy its own desire. The movement that satisfies itself completely *is* love; love is the condition of its own need, the only need that is not a privation. Love creates and satisfies its own need, for love and its movement are the same thing. Climacus declared: "We stand here before the *Miracle.* And as we both now stand before this miracle, whose solemn silence cannot be perturbed by human wrangling over mine and thine, whose awe-inspiring speech infinitely subdues all human strife about mine and thine, forgive me, I pray, the strange delusion that I was the author of this poem."[99]

Philosophical Fragments, abounding in paradox, cautioned against slighting paradoxes, "for the paradox is the source of the thinker's passion, and the thinker without a paradox is like a lover without feeling: a paltry mediocrity." Every passion, Climacus observed, at highest pitch, wills its downfall, and reason is not satisfied until it collides with something resulting in its undoing. The "supreme paradox" of thought is that reason constantly tries to discover something that thought cannot think. Proofs of God's existence fall into that category; Climacus waved them off, rehearsing Kant's argument that existence is not a predicate, without mentioning Kant. Reason, like paradox, when played out, ends in frustration, for reason and paradox are linked by passion, and both will their downfall by passion. For Climacus, everything depended on the Moment, the discovery of something that makes a difference: "If we posit the Moment the Paradox is there; for the Moment is the Paradox in its most abbreviated form."[100]

The presence of "the God" is not accidental in relation to the God's teaching, Climacus urged; it is the essential thing. The incarnation *is* the teaching that makes a difference: "If the God had not come himself, all the relations would have remained on the Socratic level; we would not have had the Moment, and we would have lost the Paradox." The God's appearance as a servant is actual, not a disguise, and faith in God incarnate is not a form of knowledge, for "no knowledge can have for its object the absurdity that the Eternal is the historical." Climacus stressed that the object of faith is a contradiction, the paradoxical Moment. Faith is not seeing, for God incarnate is not immediately knowable. Neither is faith an act of will, for human volition operates within the condition of sin and error. Faith is a miracle, the recognition of the eternal given in time, a gift of grace: "Only one who receives the condition from the God is a believer."[101]

Climacus refused all entreaties to make faith less paradoxical, offensive, or risky. He did not believe that the twelve apostles had any advantage over modern inquirers, since history does not change the question of whether God appeared in human form. He did not believe that the past ever becomes necessary, because necessity is wholly a matter of essence; Climacus was more essentialist than Hegel on that point. Nothing is necessary when it comes into existence; the essence of the necessary is to exclude coming into existence. Anything that becomes actual retains the possibility with which it emerged. Climacus admonished that faith cannot be distilled from even the most precisely detailed account. The "historical fact" of the incarnation is the essential thing, not any ostensible details about it. Climacus wanted to leave it there, but he realized that he could not call the incarnation a historical fact without saying something about its historicity. So he obliged: "If the contemporary generation had left nothing behind them but these words: 'We have believed in such and such a year the God appeared among us in the humble figure of a servant, that he lived and taught in our community, and finally died,' it would be more than enough." All that is necessary is to say that the God shared our life and died. This mere note on a page of universal history was enough to spread the faith, and still is; a voluminous account could not do more.[102]

That was the answer to Lessing's question, to the extent that Climacus had an answer; he could not help those lacking a high threshold for paradox. There *can* be a historical departure for an eternal consciousness and it *can* be of more than merely historical interest *if* it is the unique historical fact of the eternal incarnated in the Moment. But basing one's eternal happiness on historical knowledge of it was out of play, for the Moment is recognized only in faith. Climacus did not claim that his hypothesis was truer than the Socratic doctrine. The truth claims were hard to compare, because his thought project assumed "a new organ, Faith; a new presupposition, the consciousness of Sin; a new decision, the Moment; and a new Teacher, the God in Time." He did claim to make an advance on Socrates, despite saying "essentially the same things" as Socrates and not saying them nearly as well. What mattered was to recognize the Moment in faith.[103]

The irony of Climacus was that he waxed urgently and insistently on the Moment without giving himself to it. He was more of a Christian than the many who turned Christ into a theory or a historical conclusion, yet he was still an outsider. He had one question – how he might become a Christian. It didn't matter that he had been born in Copenhagen and raised in an ostensibly Christian culture. Of Kierkegaard's early pseudonyms, Climacus was the one closest to Kierkegaard – a representation of Kierkegaard before his conversion, though he said that he was thirty years old, which was Kierkegaard's age when he started to publish books. Climacus lived on the great questions, he read book after book about Christianity and philosophy, he was skilled at dialectic, and he had a theology emphasizing the leap into faith. Yet he wavered over taking one.

Climacus was also the most strenuous of Kierkegaard's pseudonyms in insisting that a point of view should speak for itself without calling attention to an author and without solving problems that readers needed to solve for themselves. In the more-or-less "promised" sequel to *Philosophical Fragments, Concluding Unscientific Postscript to Philosophical Fragments* (1846), Climacus lauded *Fragments* for not rationally solving the problem that it posed. He praised *Either/Or* for letting readers decide whether they favored the aesthetic or ethical ways of life. He commended *Repetition* for refraining from dogma, as the modern age already had "too much knowledge" and not enough inwardness. He lauded the authors of *Repetition* and *Fear and Trembling* for refusing to write for "paragraph-eaters," information-hungry types lacking any clue of inwardness. He praised *Stages on Life's Way* for refusing to reach a conclusion, which denied readers a feeling of safety, throwing them on their own. He understood that nineteenth-century sophisticates, being "entirely immersed in the great problems of universal history," looked down on his "egotistical vanity" in laying so much stress on his "own petty self." But Climacus was unbowed: "It is not I who have become so presumptuous of my own accord, but it is Christianity itself which compels me to ask the question in this manner. It puts quite an extraordinary emphasis upon my own petty self, and upon every other self however petty, in that it proposes to endow each self with an eternal happiness, provided a proper relationship is established."[104]

Martin Luther got this right; in the end everybody does their own dying. So Climacus would not apologize for spurning the Hegelian spirit of the age, though he borrowed more from Hegel than he let on. He was slightly daunted that *Fragments* was ignored, noting gamely that "it has created no sensation, absolutely none." *Philosophical Fragments* sold 229 copies in three years, its only reviews were brief and dismissive, and Kierkegaard had trouble finding anyone who had read it, although a few acquaintances, offering polite conversation, asked about a sequel. Having burdened the tiny Danish public with fifteen books in two years (counting the separate volumes of edifying discourses), Kierkegaard knew better than to let Climacus complain about the public's reading habits. Pressing on, Kierkegaard decided to write one more book, fully intending it to be his last; Climacus cheekily said of it, "The one thing I am afraid of is a sensation, particularly if it registers approval."[105]

Concluding Unscientific Postscript developed an extensive case for things that Climacus merely asserted in *Fragments*, filling out what he called the "historical costume" of Christianity, and it set the stage for Kierkegaard's coming out, offering a stage theory of religious consciousness. Climacus assured that he respected scholarship. He admired the vast fortress of knowledge erected by philologists and historical critics. He even respected the pious belief of scholars that they were getting more and more objective. What he disputed was that any of it had any bearing for or against faith. Anyone who believed in biblical inspiration had to regard historical criticism of the Bible as a violation of its spirit, and anyone who pursued historical criticism without believing in biblical inspiration could not expect to have inspiration emerge as a result of pursuing critical study. No claim about the reasonableness of faith makes faith more possible, Climacus urged: "Has anyone who previously did not have faith been brought a single step nearer to its acquisition? No, not a single step. Faith does not result simply from a scientific inquiry; it does not come directly at all." The condition of faith is passion, "infinite personal interestedness," which objectivity eliminates. Objectivity is about acquiring certainty, but certainty and passion do not go together.[106]

Modern theology had a "beautiful dream" of fusing objective scholarship with faith. Climacus called this dream an impossibility, because even its most perfect imaginable realization would remain an approximation, the only kind of certainty available to historical reason. The point was not that historical criticism shredded Christianity, for it did no such thing. Some critics defended Christianity, others claimed to discredit Christianity, and others waited for more studies before they ventured an opinion. But even the most radical critics did not prove that Christ did not exist, share his life with others, and die, and they were no different from other scholars in debating mere probabilities. Climacus urged that decisiveness is rooted in subjectivity: "Christianity is spirit, spirit is inwardness, inwardness is subjectivity, subjectivity is essentially passion, and in its maximum an infinite, personal, passionate interest in one's eternal happiness." None of this was affected by scholarly debates over the historicity of biblical narratives that could never be settled anyway.[107]

Turning to the speculative alternative, Climacus imagined a slightly quirky Danish civil servant who didn't assume that he was a Christian. The man's acquaintances found him irritating on this point, as he made a fuss about something that didn't really matter which they held in common. His wife tried to talk him out of it by appealing to geography. How could he doubt that he was a Christian? He was a Dane, and Danes were Christians. He was certainly not a Jew or a Muslim, and paganism had been driven out of Denmark long ago. He was a good citizen of a Lutheran state, so of course he was a Christian. Climacus observed, "We have become so objective, it seems, that even the wife of a civil servant argues to the particular individual from the totality, from the state, from the community-idea, from the scientific standpoint of geography." Individuality counted for so little in modern society that even Danish wives didn't regard their husbands as individuals. Something as insignificant as religion, being shared by every-one, was not to be talked about in polite society. That was in bad taste.[108]

Climacus allowed that this was a homely way to set up a high-flying critique of speculative philosophy; still, the civil servant's wife had a crucial assumption in common with Hegel. Both took for granted that Christianity is essentially something objective. Speculative philosophy, like the wife, viewed Christianity as a historical phenomenon. Climacus countered that Christianity is no more historical than the romantic love of a married couple. Granted, in both cases there is a record of historical facts, but the phenomenal part of Christianity, like the phenomenal part of the couple's relationship, is insignificant compared to what Christianity is really about. For the wedded lovers, Climacus contended, the phenomenal part acquires significance only through their love. Christianity is exactly like that. Treating it as primarily phenomenal, as the Hegelians did, was a total distortion: "Christianity does not lend itself to objective observation, precisely because it proposes to intensify subjectivity to the utmost; and when the subject has thus put himself in the right attitude, he cannot attach his eternal happiness to speculative philosophy."[109]

Climacus had a fixation with Lessing that he had to explain at some point. It was not just Lessing's question about eternal happiness and historical relativity, though Climacus always kept that question in view. It was not Lessing's reputation as an encyclopedic scholar that grabbed Climacus, or the fact that he wrote sage-like wisdom that was admired by scholars and general readers alike. It was Lessing's self-contained individuality that fascinated him: "I refer to the fact that he religiously shut himself up within the isolation of his own subjectivity; that he did not permit himself to be deceived into becoming world-historic and systematic with respect to the religious, but understood and knew how to hold fast to the understanding that the religious concerned Lessing, and Lessing alone, just as it concerns every other human being in the same manner." Lessing understood "that he had infinitely to do with God, and nothing, nothing to do with any man directly."[110]

This was exactly what Climacus believed, so it thrilled him to have a forerunner, much less an eminent one. On the other hand, he admitted that he might have projected his own belief onto Lessing, who was sufficiently slippery that it was hard to be sure who Lessing was or what he believed: "Ah, if I could only be sure! In vain would I try to break through Lessing's defenses with the assaults and with the persuasiveness of my admiration; in vain would I beg, threaten, bluster . . . Ah, if I could only be sure!" As it was, Climacus pressed hard on the theme that he seemed to share with Lessing, that the modern pursuit of objectivity was fatal for subjectivity, religion, and passion of any kind. Climacus was pretty sure that Lessing agreed with him about the necessity of speaking subjectively and indirectly in matters religious; direct communication was for objective types. He wasn't sure what to think about Lessing's dying words to Jacobi, which had caused such a ruckus, except that Climacus admired "the noble Jacobi" for keeping alive the religion of faith. Jacobi had no reason to make up a story about Lessing's pantheism; blaming him was out of play.[111]

Except that Jacobi did not really understand the leap of faith, and he made a clumsy intervention with Lessing, which led to the ruckus. Climacus was anxious to explain how the leap of faith actually works. Jacobi had asked the dying Lessing how things stood with his soul. Lessing replied that, surprise, he was a Spinozist, and had long been one. Jacobi, horrified, tried to evangelize Lessing, then wrote about it after Lessing was gone. But Jacobi, Climacus admonished, did not understand that the leap of faith cannot be taught or communicated directly. Jacobi tried to persuade Lessing to make the leap, but Lessing understood better than Jacobi that doing so is an act of isolation. Only an individual, in an act of private interiority, can make the leap, which concerns something that cannot be thought, and which must be accepted *by virtue* of its absurdity. Climacus admitted that he had not fully understand this uncompromising point until he read a book by Johannes de Silentio titled *Fear and Trembling*. There, he learned that Christianity is rooted in the paradoxical; the "desperate categories" of Christianity are fear and trembling, while logic, historical evidence, and even gospel-based exhortation count for nothing.[112]

Still, it was possible, even desirable, to put it philosophically, which Climacus proceeded to do. He had two theses: (1) A logical system is possible; (2) An existential system is impossible. A logical system cannot include anything that exists or has existed, he asserted. Movement is "unthinkable" in logic, notwithstanding Hegel's ridiculous and overly celebrated claim to introduce movement into logic. Climacus advised readers to consult Trendelenburg's *Logische Untersuchungen* on this point, on which he relied. Trendelenburg argued that movement is an inexplicable presupposition of thinking and being, a common factor between them, and a factor in the continued reciprocity between them. On Trendelenburg's authority, Climacus returned to the formal understanding of logic as defining a realm of pure being in which any relation to actuality is hypothetical. Real logic is indifferent to existence in the sense of actuality. Kant's dichotomy between the analytic and the synthetic held firm for Climacus, though Climacus was like other Kierkegaardian pseudonyms in almost never mentioning Kant.[113]

Hegel taught that logic coincides with metaphysics as the science of grasping the essence of things in *thought*. The whole knows itself by virtue of the process of reflection, and negation – the only principle of thought – negates the prior, hence itself. The beginning *is* and *is not* because it is the beginning – the negation of the negation. Climacus replied that this was to make no beginning at all – at least, not one that made any sense on Hegel's terms. Hegel talked nonsense about his starting point; he didn't actually begin the way that he claimed, which was impossible; but he turned this defect into a strength by playing a sleight-of-hand game.

Hegel, denying that philosophy had to settle for a hypothetical starting point, claimed to begin with pure being – an absolute, abstract starting point lacking any presupposition. In other words, the *Science of Logic* began with pure immediacy, immediacy itself. Climacus was incredulous. How does one begin with the immediate? Did Hegel begin with immediacy immediately, something not mediated? That was absurd, Climacus objected. Everything that Hegel said about immediacy was a product of reflection, since it is impossible to begin immediately with the immediate. Climacus overlooked that Hegel agreed, having written a rather large work of mediated reflection, the *Phenomenology of Spirit*, to make this point. Hegel did not claim that the *Science of Logic* began with no reflection behind it; he did claim, however, very problematically, that the reflection of the *Phenomenology* led to the realm of pure thought. Climacus did not pick up on the difference; thus he missed Hegel's weakest point. Climacus, hammering on the impossibility of an immediate beginning, admonished that a beginning is possible only when reflection comes to a halt, which occurs only by an act of will, a leap: "But when the breach is effected by breaking off the process of reflection arbitrarily, so as to make a beginning possible, then the beginning so made cannot be absolute." The beginning comes into being only through a turning into another being.[114]

When Climacus denied that a system of existence is possible, he did not mean that it does not exist. Reality is surely a system for God, he allowed; however, reality cannot be a system for any existing spirit, for systems are final, and "existence is precisely the opposite of finality." Existence holds things apart, while the system brings things together with finality. Philosophical idealism, Climacus believed, despite its prestige, had the real world against it; there, the dichotomy between thought and being is terribly real. Climacus did not mean that existence is thoughtless, but he pressed the distinctions between thought and being, subject and object, and God and creation. He stressed that thought is abstract, static, and expressing necessity, while being is temporal, having resulted from becoming. Abstract categories are not involved in becoming; therefore Climacus rejected objectivity, founding the individual on the dialectical opposition of thought and being and its existential expression.[115]

Christianity, in his telling, was perfectly in line with this analysis; in fact, Christianity cares only about subjectivity. Climacus put it emphatically: "Christianity protests every form of objectivity; it desires that the subject should be infinitely concerned about himself. It is subjectivity that Christianity is concerned with, and it is only in subjectivity that its truth exists, if it exists at all; objectively, Christianity has absolutely no existence." The highest task of every human being is to become subjective, which always involves the awakening of an ethical impulse. Hegelians, when they tried to wring an ethical impulse out of Hegelianism, claimed that the more one grows in ethical seriousness, the more one sees the ethical in the world process. Climacus rejected that outright, countering that the more one develops in ethical subjectivity, the less one cares about the world-historical process. When individuals devote themselves to becoming subjective, he enthused, "everything is beautifully arranged." Climacus counseled that world history is for God, kings, and eternity to worry about. When people work on becoming subjective, no human life is wasted, for no matter how many individuals may exist, "the task of becoming subjective is given to each."[116]

When Hegelians went on about universal history, Climacus had to stifle rude questions. One had to do with the fact that the Hegelian process had room for all

German academics, but only one Chinese thinker. Was there, perhaps, an imbalance here? Closer to home, the question that he most wanted to ask was: What does it mean to die? If Hegelianism had any wisdom about *that,* he was interested: "I would thus have to ask whether it is in general possible to have an idea of death, whether death can be apprehended and experienced in an anticipatory conception, or whether its only being is its actual being. And since the actual being of death is a non-being, I should have to ask whether it follows as a consequence that death is only when it is not; or whether, in other words, the ideality of thought can overcome death by thinking it, or whether the material is victor in death, so that a human being dies like a dog, death being capable of being conquered only by the dying individual's apprehension of it in the very moment of death." But Hegelian idealism, fixating on a bigger picture, offered no help where one really needed it, the meaning of one's death.[117]

Hegel took a spectacularly wrong turn at some point, but where was it? Climacus, with his emphasis on truth as subjectivity, clearly had some relationship to the post-Kantian idealism that spawned Hegel, but what was it? The crucial section of *Concluding Unscientific Postscript* addressed these questions without posing them explicitly. Climacus urged that everything depends on never forgetting that the subject is an existing individual and that existence is a process of becoming. Human existence (*eksistens*) is a special type of becoming, not merely the existence actualized in rocks and plants. To forget this point, at any point, is to be plunged into the fantastic "chimera of abstraction" of modern philosophy. From the standpoint of the existential individual, the identity of thought and being is an *expectation* of the creature. It cannot be a truth as long as the creature lives in time. This is where modern philosophy went wrong, wherever it was; Climacus did not go back to Descartes, Berkeley or Kant to make a case. It was enough to point to the post-Kantian outcome, "the fantastic realism of the I-am-I," where philosophers bantered about a fantasy world rooted in their own selves while forgetting themselves.[118]

If an existing individual could actually transcend one's self, the truth for that person would be final, and it might even look like idealism. But nobody transcends one's existence, Climacus implored. The I-am-I is a mathematical point, not something that exists. Everybody could occupy it at once; one does not get in the way of another. Climacus did not deny that it *is* possible for an individual to realize existentially the unity of finite and infinite that transcends existence. But this realization occurs only momentarily, in the moment of passion. All of Climacus' dialectical reasoning about subjectivity, passion, existing, the moment, and truth as subjectivity drove to this point. Speculative philosophy held passion in contempt, he observed: "Yet passion is the culmination of existence for an existing individual – and we are all of us existing individuals. In passion the existing subject is rendered infinite in the eternity of the imaginative representation, and yet he is at the same time most definitely himself."[119]

Historians of philosophy were sure to call this a variant of subjective idealism. Climacus didn't care what they called it, although he cared very much about distinguishing himself from post-Kantian subjective and absolute idealists. "Modern philosophy has tried anything and everything in the effort to help the individual to transcend himself objectively," he observed. But modern philosophy was wholly misguided. Existence is persistent and unyielding. To escape it, modern philosophers had become "mere scribblers in the service of a fantastic thinking and its preoccupation." If they really believed themselves, they would advocate suicide as a shortcut to salvation: "The fantastic I-am-I is not an identity of the infinite and the finite, since neither the one nor the other is real; it is a fantastic rendezvous in the clouds, an unfruitful embrace, and the relationship of the individual self to this mirage is never indicated."[120]

There is a crucial difference between essential knowledge and accidental knowledge, Climacus reasoned. Essential knowledge inwardly relates itself to existence, having an essential relationship to existence; accidental knowledge does not. Climacus denied that his idea of essential knowledge smuggled the idealist identity of thought and being into his thought by another name, for he did not proceed by deriving one abstraction from another. Neither did he claim that knowledge, objectively, corresponds to something existent as its object. But he featured the same point that Hegel took from Aristotle, that there is a real linkage between the knower and the known. The difference was Climacus' existentialism, which stressed that the knower is "essentially an existing individual" and which posited that only "ethical and ethico-religious knowledge" qualify as essential knowledge, bearing an essential relationship to the knower's existence.[121]

"Mediation is a mirage, like the I-am-I," Climacus cautioned. From an abstract standpoint, nothing comes into being; everything simply is. There is no mediation without movement; thus, mediation has no place in abstract thought. Climacus allowed that a knowing subject can be an object of objective knowledge, and he assumed by this point that he had disposed of Hegel. However, he argued, because the knowing subject is immersed in the existential process of becoming as an individual, the first task of philosophy must be to explain how a particular knower is related to mediated knowledge. What is the knower in such a moment? Climacus warned, "By forgetting that one is an existing subject, passion goes by the board and the truth is no longer a paradox; the knowing subject becomes a fantastic entity rather than a human being, and the truth becomes a fantastic object for the knowledge of this fantastic entity."[122]

In essential knowing, subjectivity is the truth. Climacus offered a definition: "An objective uncertainty held fast in an appropriation-process of the most passionate inwardness is the truth, the highest truth attainable for an existing individual." We cannot say, objectively, at what point the fork in the road arrives for us, "where the way swings off," because wherever it happens, it is subjective. We do not know what God is doing, where history is going, or what anything means, but these objective uncertainties intensify the infinite passion of our inwardness, where truth is known. Truth is a form of daring, the willingness to accept objective uncertainty "with the passion of the infinite." Climacus put it plainly, that truth and faith are equivalent. If God could be known objectively, there would be no need for the risk of faith; but because God cannot be known objectively, we must believe: "If I wish to preserve myself in faith I must constantly be intent upon holding fast the objective uncertainty, so as to remain out upon the deep, over seventy thousand fathoms of water, still preserving my faith."[123]

If subjectivity is the truth, the truth is, objectively, paradoxical. Hegelians talked about everything working itself out in the truth as a whole. Climacus replied that they didn't even know about tomorrow, or the intentions of another person, much less what God is going to do. Hegelianism was ultimately the conceit that Hegelians could think God. Climacus countered that no existing individual can think God, which is why "God became flesh" is the absolute paradox. The incarnation is the ultimate absurdity – the eternal truth coming into being in time as an existing individual. Climacus observed that it is also religiously offensive, the rankest idolatry from a Jewish perspective. The absurd cannot be rationalized or defended, he cautioned. It can only be believed in fear and trembling: "It behooves us to get rid of introductory guarantees of security, proofs from consequences, and the whole mob of public pawnbrokers and guarantors, so as to permit the absurd to stand out in all its clarity."[124]

On this subject he had a word about Hegelian *aufheben*. The closest Danish approximation (*ophaeve*) does not permit the ambiguities of *aufheben*, he observed, so Danish Hegelians adopted the German term as their own, delighted to have a word that means opposite things. *Aufheben* means to abolish, but also to preserve, and because it means both things at once, it does not really mean either of them. Climacus remarked, "Speculative philosophy removes every difficulty, and then leaves me the difficulty of trying to determine what it really accomplishes by this so-called removal [*aufheben*]." Climacus knew the usual Hegelian reply, that negation is primary in sublation. But in that case, he objected, Hegelianism eliminated paradox and decision, reducing both to something relative. Hegelian theology had the paradox, and a strategy to abrogate it. Thus it lifted itself above Christianity. Hegelian theologians did not say that Christianity is the truth; they said that their understanding of Christianity constituted the truth of Christianity. To Climacus, the difference was qualitative and infinite.[125]

Christianity is like love, Climacus urged. It is either a life-giving passion or it is nothing. The "most stupid thing ever said" about Christianity is that it is true "to a certain degree." Climacus found this idiotic sentiment to be prevalent in modern Christianity. He recalled that he spent many years dawdling aimlessly, watching others get ahead while he frittered away his life, until he realized that modern people had forgotten what it means to exist. Finding his calling, it occurred to him that he should communicate indirectly, "for if inwardness is the truth, results are only rubbish with which we should not trouble each other." God communicates indirectly, Climacus noted pointedly. God is in creation, but God is not there directly. Paganism is about relating to God directly. In Christianity, God is hidden, holy, invisible, mysterious, and transcendently other; "God has absolutely nothing obvious about him." The sheer elusiveness of God triggers an "irruption of inwardness," an infinite desire for the divine that cannot be grasped.[126]

Climacus acknowledged that a couple of others helped him give witness to Christian truths, even as he struggled with the risk of leaping. Hamann was his favorite religious writer, especially for his succinct sentences about faith, although Climacus lamented that Hamann's thought lacked balance. Jacobi was his next favorite theological type, valiantly defending the way of faith over speculation, although Jacobi's skill at dialectic fell short of his deep inwardness. But Hamann wrote very little and was forgotten in the triumph of Hegelianism, and Jacobi was forgotten except as someone to be scorned for outing Lessing and opposing Kant and Hegel. Much like his outlook, Climacus was pretty much on his own.[127]

Climacus struggled to comprehend how absolute idealists could believe that only mind is real, yet he had a similar belief: "The ethical reality of the individual is the only reality." The only thing-in-itself that cannot be thought is individual existence, he explained, making a very rare allusion to Kant, though Climacus was not serious about appropriating Kant's conceptuality. Climacus argued that Kant set modern philosophy down a fateful path by posing the problem of the thing-in-itself eluding thought. Hegel, taking the problem much too seriously, took the "fantastic" option of vanquishing idealistic skepticism by means of pure thought. But Hegel did not break with Kantian skepticism; he tried to overcome it by thinking it through on Kant's terms. Climacus would have saved the entire post-Kantian tradition the problem of rethinking Kant's dualism. Jacobi got it right, in his view; the best response to Kant was to reject Kant's skeptical account of what cannot be known. Climacus explained, "To answer Kant within the fantastic shadow-play of pure thought is precisely not to answer him." Pure thought abstracts from existence – from that which it purports to explain. Instead of trying to climb a ladder of being, or thought, or their identity, to heaven, it is better to have faith in the transcendent God who created a real world and human minds. That is, human beings think and exist as creatures in the divine image, and existence separates thought and being, but God does not think or exist. God creates and is eternal. One becomes a spirit in the transparent grounding of the divine creative power that posits the self.[128]

What really matters, Climacus argued, is to become a Christian, not to understand Christianity. If Christianity were a doctrine, it would not be appropriate to put the difference so starkly. But Christianity is "an existential communication expressing an existential contradiction," not a doctrine. It is about the act of existing. It is centered on the opposite of mediation – the absolute paradox of God taking flesh. And existing is the opposite of speculation. Climacus somehow knew that there was "a tremendous difference between knowing what Christianity is and being a Christian," although he could not speak from experience. The decision to become a Christian is purely an inner one, he assured, although its quality deepens when the decision is also an external act.[129]

It helped that Climacus had read all the books of Kierkegaard's pseudonyms, plus Kierkegaard's discourses, which he reviewed in a long chapter in the middle of the *Postscript*. Thus he was well suited to amplify *Stages on Life's Way* with a stage theory of religion. He distinguished between religiousness A, which was genuinely religious and dialectical, but not specifically Christian, and religiousness B, which was paradoxically dialectical and definitely Christian. Religiousness A, like the ethical stage, retained the idealistic assumption that truth is something to be recollected. In religiousness A, Climacus explained, God is conceived as immanent, eternal truth is believed to be rationally accessible, and one seeks to transform one's pathetic existence through religion. Nobody skips straight to religiousness B; first, one has to deal religiously with the pathos of the absurd. Religiousness A is the first stage of religious existence, it exists in paganism and the world religions, and Climacus judged that Religiousness A, or something less religious, prevailed in the churches.[130]

In his rendering, the transition from the ethical way of life to religiousness A was marked by resignation, suffering, guilt, repentance, and humor. People make this move because the religious impulse brings them into a richer engagement with the whole of existence than does the ethical way of life, even though religion is also more bruising. Medieval Catholicism, being extravagantly religious, offered a rich tableau of Religiousness A at the level of theology and communal religious practice, teaching people to seek atonement with a divine inner principle. According to Climacus, religiousness A was a remedy for guilt and meaninglessness, but not for despair, because despair is totalizing and infinite, relating to the eternal. From the perspective of religiousness A, "all despair is a kind of bad temper." The recollection of Religiousness A is about avoiding despair and finding eternal happiness; on the other hand, nobody can be saved by the absurdity of grace without first being thrust into the pathos of the absurd by religiousness A.[131]

In religiousness A, paradox and offense are smoothed out, eternal happiness is simple, and one believes that one is capable through virtue or some religious practice of awakening to one's kinship with the eternal. Religiousness A is about finding God within one's self. In religiousness B, Climacus taught, paradox and offense are central, despair is a howling reality, and one gives up the illusion of awakening to the eternal within. Religiousness B is about relating to a transcendent God to find salvation.

Climacus did not expect most readers to find B more attractive than A. He only asked them to stop calling the A-type Christianity. In his view, a great deal of Christianity was not even at the A or the ethical stages; it was merely aesthetic, treating religion as a source of gratification and the incomprehensible as something comprehended. Orthodoxy was especially prone to reduce Christianity to aesthetic norms, because orthodoxy idolizes itself. Climacus explained that the aesthetic floats along in immediacy, finding no contradiction in existence. The ethical discovers the contradiction, that human beings are bonded to absurdity and evil, "but within self-assertion." Religiousness A suffers the contradiction religiously, but merely at the level of immanence. Religiousness B, embracing the absolute paradox, "makes the fact of existing the absolute contradiction, not within immanence, but against immanence."[132]

Climacus spared no harshness or offense in describing religiousness B: "Religiousness B is discriminative, selective, and polemical; only upon a definite condition do I become blessed, and as I absolutely bind myself to this condition, so do I exclude every other man who does not thus bind himself." The Christian's eternal happiness is based on a historical fact, which is absurd. This historical fact concerns the embodiment of the eternal God in a human being, a total absurdity. It is characterized by suffering, another absurdity. In Religiousness A, Climacus argued, guilt-consciousness is the medium of existence. To exist is to come into a world of becoming, where existence asserts itself as strongly as possible within immanence. The subject's identity with one's self is preserved, and one seeks to make an adjustment within one's self to remedy guilt. In Religiousness B, sin is the medium of existence; to come into being is to know one's self as a sinner. Sin-consciousness is precisely the breaking of self-identity and immanence. It comes from without; Climacus stressed that nobody had sin-consciousness before God became incarnate in Christ, and Christianity is inherently offensive in its particularity, exclusiveness, and absurdity: "For the believer, the offense is at the beginning, and the possibility of it is the perpetual fear and trembling in his existence."[133]

By the end of the *Postscript*, Climacus had answered the question that he never asked – yes, despair was the motivating force of his dialectic, if not of Kierkegaard's. Climacus replaced Hegel's abstract negation with the despair of subjective spirit, sin-consciousness. In a concluding note he pleaded that it was pointless, and always badly done, to "cram Christianity into a child." Children have no use for Christianity, he explained; sin-consciousness is decidedly something for adults. When people try to raise their children in Christianity, sometimes they opt for violence, forcing "the little exister" into a wholly inappropriate consciousness, which is repugnant. Otherwise they opt for "idyllic mythology," turning Christianity into a ridiculous sentimental tale about being loving and kind and having Jesus for a companion. Climacus, recalling his upbringing in a home where he was smothered in sin-consciousness, offered a twinge of sympathy for parents that forced the issue. They did it out of love for their children, and they deserved credit at least for that. Sentimental Christianity, however, had nothing in its favor. It was a lie that deceived children and adults that they were Christians. Climacus was all for obliterating "a childish orthodoxy, a pusillanimous Bible interpretation, a foolish and unchristian defense of Christianity, [and] a bad conscience on the part of the defenders with respect to their own relation to it."[134]

Very late in the argument, after 530 pages, Climacus clarified that all his talk about truth as subjectivity and Christianity not being a doctrine had nothing to do with downgrading doctrine. If one does not accept Christian doctrine, one is not a Christian, he insisted. His twisting and turning about subjectivity had never been about that. Kierkegaard was unsettled, at the time, by the case of Adolph Adler, a Danish pastor and former Hegelian who claimed to have experienced a direct revelation in which Christ issued a new doctrine. Adler, though genial out of the pulpit, made crazed statements in the pulpit that led to his dismissal from the ministry. For eight years Kierkegaard labored on a book on the problem of Adler, which focused on the problem of authority and the necessity of a doctrinal tradition. He never published the book, being dissatisfied with it, and Climacus' statement in the *Postscript* about doctrine was very terse. Kierkegaard realized that he never worked out a theory of doctrine; almost anything that he might have said would have undercut the force of what he said about truth as subjectivity. In the *Postscript*, Climacus registered the necessary caveat as briefly as possible and moved on. His concern was solely about *how* one becomes a Christian, a matter resting on one thing, the absolute paradox.[135]

One did not have to be an insider to figure out, while reading the *Postscript*, that Kierkegaard wrote it, since the book's middle chapter reviewed all his books, plus the pseudonyms that wrote remarkably like Kierkegaard; plus, the title page of the *Fragments* listed "S. Kierkegaard" as "responsible for publication." In an appendix, Climacus took a last shot at asserting his identity. He was not a Christian, but he was interested in how to become one. He was a humorous type, adept at zingers, and content with his situation, although he hoped for something better. As a comical, polemical, dialectical type he made no presumption to authority; in fact he relished his lack of authority in speaking of matters usually owned by professors and clerics. He was a straightforward monarchist, believing it was better to let one man rule, and leave everyone else free, than to let everybody rule. Climacus shuddered at democracy, which was "the most tyrannical form of government," the triumph of the mob. Feminism appalled him too; the *Postscript* was strewn with deprecating asides about feminine inferiority, although the appendix stayed off this subject. Kierkegaard had no concept of a woman as an intellectual or civic peer.[136]

To the appendix Kierkegaard added an appendix, "A First and Last Declaration," getting something off his chest. He was the author, he acknowledged, "as people would call it," of the pseudonymous works. The pseudonymous authors were not him, he insisted; "there is not a single word which is mine." He was just as far from being the author of *Fear and Trembling*, Johannes de Silentio, as he was from being the knight of faith described in that book. This was a shrewd example, as Kierkegaard identified in that book with Isaac – only a conscious Isaac. He had created pseudonymous authors to be free to dance with the public. If anyone "made a fool of himself" by getting angry with Kierkegaard instead of dancing with the "light ideality" of the actual authors, he could not help that. He pleaded with readers to cite the pseudonyms, not him, when quoting from their works, using a telling example. When the pseudonyms made stray remarks about the rights of women, the saying belonged to the pseudonym. On the other hand, Kierkegaard acknowledged that in a civil sense, he was responsible for what the pseudonyms said; he noted pointedly that the government censor, as a public functionary, had known from the beginning that Kierkegaard wrote the pseudonymous works. *Concluding Unscientific Postscript*, the title, was supposed to be literal. Having delivered his masterwork through Climacus, Kierkegaard was determined to stop writing and take up a country pastorate. He had said all that he had to say.[137]

Provoking Ridicule

Instead he became a lightning rod of controversy and embattlement, and a theologian of Christian spirituality, in his own name. *Concluding Unscientific Postscript* was too sprawling, profuse, and confusing to make even a tiny splash on Kierkegaard's public. In five years it sold sixty copies and was ignored by reviewers, even as Kierkegaard became notorious for other things.

In December 1845, while Kierkegaard waited for the *Postscript* to be published, he ran afoul of a liberal tabloid newspaper, *The Corsair*, which specialized in exposés of the peccadilloes of high-society types. *The Corsair* had favorably reviewed *Either/Or* and *Stages on Life's Way*, and the paper's founder, Aaron Goldschmidt, admired Kierkegaard's genius. In fact, he appreciated that Kierkegaard was the only local dignitary to treat him respectfully. Kierkegaard, however, got into a spat with Peder Ludvig Møller, a literary critic with academic ambitions, which spilled into the *Corsair*.

Møller was naturally fascinated with the promiscuous Seducer in *Either/Or*, having been the model for it. He had a mean streak and a sharp writing style in addition to the arsenal of lures that *Either/Or* depicted. Reviewing *Stages on Life's Way*, Møller opined knowingly that the author was a good writer, but cynical, with too much ironic spinning, and who wrote too much, perhaps out of some physical compulsion, or else as therapy. That was meaner than it looked; Møller was taunting Kierkegaard's lack of sexual experience or attractiveness. Kierkegaard struck back, publishing a facetious letter by Frater Taciturnus that exposed Møller's secret editorial connection to the *Corsair* while stirring up some free advertising for the pseudonymous works. Taciturnus complained that the *Corsair* had praised Victor Eremita and Hilarius Bookbinder. As a poor unknown writer, he demanded the right to be attacked there, which was better than being ignored. Back and forth ensued. Møller cried foul at being tied to the *Corsair*, which cost him his chance at a university career. Taciturnus suggested that Møller lacked the elementary decency to walk past prostitutes and the whorish *Corsair*.

On the other hand, since the *Corsair* was widely read, Taciturnus beseeched it to attack him, since being praised by the vulgar *Corsair* would be unbearable. Goldschmidt obliged with a vengeance, outing Kierkegaard as the strange, pathetic, freakish author of the pseudonymous works who had an unseemly obsession with bringing down Møller.[138]

Quickly it got worse than Kierkegaard had sought. He maintained the pretense that he had nothing to do with the pseudonyms, which insulted the intelligence of every insider and made it impossible to have a real conversation with Goldschmidt. Goldschmidt stayed on the attack, hoping that Kierkegaard would ask him to stop, which didn't happen. A frank word from either of them might have broken the cycle; as it was, Kierkegaard was furious with Goldschmidt by the time that the *Postscript* arrived in bookstores in February 1846. Kierkegaard, encountering Goldschmidt in the street, gave him a mean look and passed by. Goldschmidt, crushed by Kierkegaard's reaction – "I felt accused and oppressed" – resolved to show who was the better person: "I was not the sort of person to be looked down upon, and I could prove it." Goldschmidt sold the paper at a financial loss, although it took six months for the sale to go through; meanwhile the attacks went on. The *Corsair* ripped Kierkegaard for his looks, his strange clothes, and his odd mannerisms. It portrayed him as a rich snob who disdained ordinary people, which was mostly wrong. Kierkegaard's books and indulgent lifestyle had consumed most of his wealth, and he was known for bantering with ordinary people in the streets. The "snob" part was true only in the sense that his sense of superiority prevented him from negotiating a truce or laughing off the caricatures; he resented being spoofed by his inferiors. Kierkegaard could have extinguished the controversy by leaving Copenhagen for a few months, but he kept showing up in the streets and cafés every week, refusing to be cowed, which fed the media circus.[139]

People gaped and leered at Kierkegaard in the streets, ruining one of his chief pleasures; sometimes he took carriage rides into the country for relief. For a while he told himself that he had played it exactly right: "Everything is in order; all I have to do now is to keep calm and say nothing, relying on the *Corsair* to support the whole enterprise negatively just as I want it." To be attacked by a vulgar tabloid reflected on its editor, not him; meanwhile the paper would make him famous, which sold books. Kierkegaard allowed that it was sad that nobody understood him, and that journalism stoked "the loutishness of the mob," reducing individuals to a mass that fed on sensationalism: "Every journeyman butcher feels he can insult me on the *Corsair's* orders; the young students simper and giggle and are happy to see a prominent person trampled upon; the professors are jealous and secretly sympathize with the attacks, and spread them, of course with the proviso that it is a shame." By mid-March he was having second thoughts about his clever idea, admitting to himself that the paper's "endless nonsense" exerted a real influence; he regretted having provoked it. Kierkegaard wished that Goldschmidt would summon his manhood instead of, incredibly, acting morally superior: "Listen, now, little *Corsair!* Be a man for once! It is womanish to pester a man with one's infatuation, it is womanish to keep running after someone with expressions of spurned love just to abuse him; be a man, hold your peace."[140]

The battering took on a life of it's own. Kierkegaard rued that outwardly he had lost his freedom: "When I was a young man and a nobody, I enjoyed my freedom. I could live as I please, driving in my carriage alone, with the windows down in public places – it never occurred to anyone to take any notice of that. But now envy watches my every step to say: it's haughtiness, pride, vanity." He told himself that the battering was sure to die out; meanwhile he fell back on his spiritual resources: "Solitary I have always been; now I have a real chance to practice again." He changed his public persona; Kierkegaard's party-boy days were over. Instead of taking a country pastorate, which Mynster advised him to do, and which Kierkegaard still wanted in his idealistic moments, and instead of ending his authorship with the *Postscript*, he found that he had a great deal more to say, speaking directly.[141]

Training in Christianity, Attack Upon Christendom

On the verge of another gusher of books, Kierkegaard wrote in his journal in 1847, "My existence as an author is the meanest and vilest imaginable." Pondering metaphors for the hellish misery of depression, he reasoned that his suffering was spiritually redemptive, because one cannot love one's neighbor if one has not suffered greatly. Modern Christianity blabbered constantly about the beauty, virtue, and life-giving wonder of love, Kierkegaard observed. But "love is self-denial, rooted in the relationship to God." In this conviction he poured out books about Christian existence. What mattered was to live "Christianly," or at least, to be a witness to it: "I commit myself to making every person I can bring under this category 'the single individual' into a Christian, or, since this is not something one person can do for another, I vouch for him that he will become one. As 'the single individual' he is alone, in the whole world alone, alone face to face with God – surely then he will respond."[142]

Kierkegaard fulfilled this evangelical vow in his second great torrent of books: *Upbuilding Discourses in Various Spirits* (1847), *Works of Love* (1847), *Christian Discourses* (1848), *The Lily in the Field and the Bird of the Air* (1849), *Two Ethical-Religious Essays* (1849), *Three Discourses at the Communion on Fridays* (1849), *The Sickness Unto Death* (1849, by Anti-Climacus), *Practice in Christianity* (1850, by Anti-Climacus), *An Upbuilding Discourse* (1850), *For Self-Examination* (1851), *Judge for Yourself!* (1851), *On My Work as an Author* (1851), *Two Discourses at the Communion on Fridays* (1851), and the unpublished (by him) *Book on Adler, Point of View for My Work as an Author*, and *Armed Neutrality*.[143]

All were intensely spiritual and direct. To many readers these books reeked of judgment and self-righteousness, an impression that Kierkegaard denied vehemently. Nothing galled him more than this misunderstanding. He wrote poetically, without authority, he urged. He did not claim to be the kind of Christian that he described; he was still trying to become a Christian. On the other hand, the real thing had to be described, because modern Christianity had forgotten what it was. Writing *The Sickness Unto Death* and *Practice in Christianity* in 1848, Kierkegaard planned to publish them as one book and retire from writing again. But the world changed in 1848, and on second thought, trying to manage the presumption problem, Kierkegaard decided to publish the two works separately under a pseudonym, Anti-Climacus. These books were pitched at a higher level of ideality than the others, he reasoned; thus, he needed a pseudonym for an author that was higher than him. To confront readers with the pure idealism of gospel Christianity, Kierkegaard had to get himself out of the picture, if only by pretending. He was no apostle, although he prized apostles: "I am a poetic-dialectical genius, personally and religiously a penitent."[144]

Anti-Climacus was a penitent too, but one who's self rested transparently in the power that established his self. Living "Christianly" has nothing to do carrying on about world history, he admonished. It is about venturing in faith to become oneself, a specific individual human being, alone before God. A human being is spirit, which is the self, which is a relation that relates itself to itself. The relation is a third thing between God and the self, both of which relate *to* the relation and *in* the relation to the relation. There is no self without a relation relating itself to itself. The self is not a relation; it is "the relation's relating itself to itself in the relation." Anti-Climacus explained that a human being is a synthesis of the temporal and the eternal, the finite and the infinite, which requires a relation. This is what is at issue in Christianity, the sickness unto death that negates the relation between God and the self, rendering the human being as something less than a self.[145]

Despair is a sickness of the spirit not lacking virtuous qualities, Anti-Climacus argued. To be able to despair is an infinite advantage for human beings over animals and a necessity for salvation. Yet to be in despair is utter ruination. Anti-Climacus started with a definition: "Despair is the misrelation in the relation of a synthesis that relates itself to itself." The synthesis is merely a possibility; it is not the faulty relation. If the synthesis were the problem, despair would not exist. Despair would be something constitutive in human nature; thus it would not be despair. Anti-Climacus cautioned that despair is not like leprosy, a disease to which one succumbs, or even like death, which is unavoidable. Despair lies *within* the spirit of an existing individual, who is a synthesis. In its original state, the synthetic self rests transparently in the power that established it; otherwise the self would not experience despair. Despair is the sign that something has gone terribly wrong. It comes from the relation in which the synthesis relates itself to itself apart from the source of its being.[146]

The sickness unto death is spiritual, Anti-Climacus stressed. Nobody dies, physically, from it, for despair is the inability to die. To be sick *unto* death is like being mortally ill and wanting to die, but not dying. As long as death looms as our greatest danger, we fight for life, but when a greater danger emerges, we hope for death. Despair is a mortal illness, "the hopelessness of not even being able to die." Everybody has it to some degree: "No human being ever lived and no one lives outside of Christendom who has not despaired, and no one in Christendom if he is not a true Christian, and insofar as he is not wholly that, he still is to some extent in despair."[147]

The Sickness Unto Death grappled with varieties of denial. Anti-Climacus noted that many people do not recognize their despair; some don't even know that they have a self. The "secular mentality" of the modern age is a species of self-annihilation, the meaningless absurdity of shrunken spirits that mortgage themselves to the world: "They use their capacities, amass money, carry on secular enterprises, calculate shrewdly, etc., perhaps make a name in history, but themselves they are not; spiritually speaking, they have no self, no self for whose sake they could venture everything, no self before God – however self-seeking they are otherwise." Fatalists believe in determinism; philistine-bourgeois types believe in triviality; Anti-Climacus urged that both are pointless dead-ends. A self needs possibility in the same way that breathing needs oxygen; one cannot breath necessity alone. Fatalists suffocate themselves, leaving room for, at most, a mute God to whom one does not pray. Anti-Climacus warned that anyone who lacks a living God lacks a living self too. Bourgeois philistines, thinking much smaller, take a different path to the same end, confining possibility to "a certain trivial compendium of experiences as to how things go." Lacking imagination, and thus lacking spirit, they cannot imagine a living God who delivers the self from despair. Fatalists at least have enough imagination to despair of possibility, but the whole point of the philistine-bourgeois mentality is to fixate on the "trite and obvious."[148]

Denial is prevalent, Anti-Climacus stressed. The most common forms of despair are forms of denial, and modernity is all about covering up the meaningless despair of ordinary life. As for those who recognize the sickness unto death within themselves, he urged that narrow is the way; only faith can root out despair. It does no good merely to have a true conception of one's illness. People with high levels of consciousness suffer the most despair, not necessarily to a good end. Many people despair over something earthly, which does no good. Others despair over the eternal or oneself, which Anti-Climacus put in the same category, because God and the self go together: "The greater the conception of God, the more self there is; the more self, the greater the conception of God." To be in despair is to lose the eternal and oneself; it is to be in sin, which becomes *sin* only before God. People do not seek relief from the guilt of their sin if they are not in some kind of crisis relationship with God. To trust in God's deliverance is to be delivered from the bondage of sin: "For this very person's sake, God comes into the world, allows himself to be born, to suffer, to die, and this suffering God – he almost implores and beseeches this person to accept the help that is offered to him!"[149]

And yet most people reject it. Why is that? Anti-Climacus replied that most people lack the "humble courage" to dare to believe that God suffered and died for them. The gospel faith is too much – to the extent of being offensive. It is offensive, Anti-Climacus explained, "because it is too high for him, because his mind cannot grasp it, because he cannot attain bold confidence in the face of it and therefore must get rid of it, pass it off as a bagatelle, nonsense, and folly, for it seems as if it would choke him." The ordinary self lacks the charity and imagination to allow God to do anything remotely as extraordinary as Christianity claims that God has done for each person; thus the gospel message is offensive.[150]

The book was starting to sound like preaching, apologetics or both; Anti-Climacus assured that it had nothing to do with apologetics. Nothing is more "extraordinarily stupid" than trying to defend Christianity, he insisted. Defenders of Christianity are like Judas, betraying Christ with a kiss, except that their treason is born of stupidity: "To defend something is always to disparage it." If one gives one's treasure to the poor, one does not begin with a speech defending charity. That would be stupid, diminishing the value of the benevolent action. But Anti-Climacus could not rest with accusing apologists of stupidity. People who defend Christianity with arguments and evidence have a deeper problem, he charged. They only pretend to be Christians: "He who defends it has never believed it." Faith is not the end of an argument, and the gospel is offensive to reason all the way down.[151]

The Sickness Unto Death worked hard at being relevant without getting too personal or topical. It was pervaded by Kierkegaard's struggle with despair, but kept the focus off him, which made it easy to switch to a pseudonym after he finished writing it. The book criticized modern society's addiction to the world while playing down the revolutions of 1848. Anti-Climacus flashed his monarchical bias only briefly, asserting that modern society needed Socrates more than it needed a republic or a new social order. He was for the state church too, although aggrieved at the one that existed, which "pantheistically abolished" the infinite qualitative difference between God and the exiting individual, "first in a highbrow way through speculation, then in a lowbrow way in the highways and byways." After Denmark became a democracy and Kierkegaard decided again that he couldn't stop writing, he featured his critique of Christendom, where middlebrow leveling was gaining.[152]

Practice in Christianity took the first step toward Kierkegaard's attack on Christendom, though he paused upon completing it. He wrote the book in 1848, but did not publish it until August 1850, when Kierkegaard personally delivered a copy to Mynster. Ominously he told Mynster why he had held back on publishing it: He had hoped that one of them would be dead before the book went to press. That seemed to come from nowhere, as Kierkegaard had always supported Mynster in public and had never missed a sermon. Mynster may have had an inkling, as he was perceptive, and Kierkegaard had been pouring ill feelings about him into his journal. In any case, Mynster read the book promptly, and, according to royal chaplain Just Henrik V. Paulli, hated it. In Paulli's telling, Mynster complained, "It makes profane sport of the holy."[153]

In fact, *Practice in Christianity* was barely a warm-up for the polemics to come after Mynster was gone and Martensen succeeded him as primate of Denmark. The book contained little outright attacking, being closer to the mold of Kierkegaard's edifying discourses than to his philosophical polemics. It never mentioned Mynster by name, and it defended the privileges of the state church. Kierkegaard had no interest in democratic reforms that muddled between the established order and the single individual. The reform movements stood for parties, sects, indecision, and endless debate; for Kierkegaard, that was sheer barbarism, liberal style. But Anti-Climacus had a critique of the state church that gave heartburn to Mynster. He contrasted the gospel of Jesus and a church religion that was sort of about Jesus. He bluntly claimed that Christendom was not acquainted with Christianity. He urged that the way of Christ is opposed to the ways of the world. To love God is to hate the world, Anti-Climcaus implored. A church that dwells comfortably in the world cannot follow Christ to the cross; it isn't even disposed to try: "The day when Christianity and the world become friends – yes, then Christianity is abolished."[154]

Did that mean that all Christians should be martyrs? Was this a fantasy about an impossible church? Anti-Climacus replied that it was the gospel for every individual Christian. The question was not, "Must every Christian do it?" The right question was, "What must I do to follow Christ?" The church, a self-respecting conservative institution, is supposed to challenge individual Christians with this question. Anti-Climacus admonished that if the church fails to do that, it betrays Christ, who came into the world to be our prototype, seeking to inspire disciples, not to attract admirers. The modern church settled for admiring Christ and making its own peace with the modern world. Abdicating its spiritual authority, it abolished Christianity in Christendom through leniency and accommodation: "Without authority, Christianity creeps around in Christendom in worn-out, decrepit clothes, and we do not know whether we should take our hats off to it or whether it should bow to us, whether we need its compassion, or it needs our compassion."[155]

According to Paulii, who told Kierkegaard, Mynster was offended by this account of his ministry and legacy. Kierkegaard came to his next meeting with Mynster expecting to hear about it. For months he had railed against Mynster in his journal, protesting that his pastor/bishop/spiritual mentor was bathed in adulation, honor, abundance, and distinction. Mynster was adept at keeping the church rolling, even in the crisis of 1848, but that had nothing to do with following Christ. Mynster pretended that most Danes were Christians, who rewarded him for pretending with eloquence. Kierkegaard wailed: "In Christian terms, Bishop Mynster's life is a lie . . . Is this 'Christian wisdom' which is so worldly wise? Is this Christianity which is so worldly? Is this truth which is so untrue? Is this serving God which is so self-serving?"[156]

But even Kierkegaard expected Mynster to erupt with indignation, defensiveness or *something* after being attacked in *Practice in Christianity.* Instead, Mynster let it roll off with a genial, "whatever." Greeting Kierkegaard, he declared that he had no business or right to give a reprimand. He reminded Kierkegaard that they had had this conversation before, and Mynster had always said the same thing: "I have nothing at all against each bird singing its own song." For that matter, "Indeed, people can say what they like about me." He judged that half of *Practice in Christianity* was an attack on him and the other half attacked Martensen. In a "friendly and personal" way, according to Kierkegaard, Mynster told him that he doubted the book would do any good, but he had no grievance against Kierkegaard for publishing it. Then the two religious thinkers and longtime acquaintances resumed their normal shoptalk.[157]

At first Kierkegaard didn't know what to think. Had Paulii deceived him? But that seemed unlikely, and as Kierkegaard stewed over the meeting, he decided that Mynster was even slicker than he had thought. He had always respected Mynster's piety and eloquent preaching, while repressing his misgivings about Mynster's smooth geniality. A bishop had to be a political operator. But now it seemed that Mynster had no moral character. If he played even an attack on his spiritual leadership as a diplomatic issue, he stood for nothing except power and privilege. Worse yet, Mynster used his power to smooth the way for his worst possible successor, Martensen.

Mynster was a disappointment, but not someone to hate; at least, Kierkegaard gave no sign of despising Mynster until very near the end of Kierkegaard's life. However, Kierkegaard loathed Martensen. Mynster appointed Martensen as an extraordinary professor of theology, nominated him to the Scientific Society, made him a Knight of the Dannebrog, and appointed him as court chaplain at Castle Church, where he preached liberal sermons to gatherings of the semi-Christian upper class. Martensen's glittering career grated on Kierkegaard, who peppered his journal with potshots at Martensen's "velvet cummerbund," knighthood, liberalism, and prestige.[158]

Martensen's major work, *Christian Dogmatics,* offered a personal theism version of Hegelian theology, emphasizing the trinity as the central doctrine of Christianity and as the organizing principle of his system. He expounded the doctrines of creation, fall, and divine providence within the doctrine of the Father; the incarnation and mediation of Christ within the doctrine of the Son; and the procession of the Spirit and life of the church within the doctrine of the Spirit. Though Martensen kept Hegel's name out of his dogmatics, rarely mentioning any modern thinker, he cited Mynster and Schleiermacher several times. His system was strong on systematic coherence, a point that he featured in a snarky blast at unnamed polemical types "who do not feel the tendency toward coherent thought, but are able to satisfy themselves by thinking in random thoughts and aphorisms, sudden discoveries and hints."[159]

Christian Dogmatics appeared at approximately the same time as *The Sickness Unto Death*. It was hailed as a work of epochal significance that put Denmark on the map of modern theology, and it was soon published in Swedish, English, German, and French editions, all to acclaim. Meanwhile *The Sickness Unto Death,* one of Kierkegaard's greatest works, received no reviews and sold hardly any copies. There is no evidence that Kierkegaard plowed through Martensen's 500-page textbook, but he certainly skimmed it and read the preface, where he saw himself derided as a purveyor of random thoughts and aphorisms. He was appalled: "Martensen's *Dogmatics.* Really, it's ridiculous! There has been talk here now about system, scholarship, scholarliness, etc. – then finally the system arrives. Gentle Father of Jesus! My own most popular work is more rigorous in its conceptual definitions, and my pseudonym Johannes Climacus is seven times more rigorous."[160]

Martensen was good at buttering up people who boosted his career, Kierkegaard noticed, which explained his citations of Mynster in a work of dogmatics. Mynster, the devotional preacher who made his name by opposing systems! Skimming to Martensen's section on the order of salvation, Kierkegaard gagged over a sentence that seemed to be aimed at him: "[The individual] cannot fulfill his sanctification by living in egoistic and sickly fashion as an individual." Now Martensen was calling him sickly too, in contrast to Martensen's robust health and healthy-mindedness. Kierkegaard seethed that Martensen knew nothing of suffering for Christ; Martensen actually believed that his pampered lifestyle and adulation had something to do with being a virtuous Christian. A real Christian does not make an idol of "health," Kierkegaard told himself; Jesus had no gospel of health. Martensen was "a web of untruth and triviality who can cause only harm." Kierkegaard recalled that when Martensen came home from his German sabbatical, bringing Hegelian theology to Denmark, he "aroused such a tremendous sensation with this novelty." That was his real claim to having accomplished something. Martensen was a reporter and a religious celebrity, not a thinker or a Christ-following Christian. He was good at captivating audiences with rhetorical categories borrowed from Hegelians, but it was pitiful that he got so far by doing so: "He is enjoying a huge success, and young students are in the meantime taking the opportunity to inform the public in print that with Martensen a new era, epoch and era, etc. is beginning. The perniciousness of allowing young people to do such a thing, turning everything on its head."[161]

Meanwhile Kierkegaard withdrew increasingly into himself, cutting back on socializing, and writing mostly to himself. His most creative period had ended with the *Postscript,* though he produced the sublime *Sickness Unto Death* in his later mode of edifying reflection on traditional Christian themes. *Practice in Christianity,* his last substantial work, pleasantly surprised him by attracting favorable attention; the title alone made it more inviting than most of Kierkegaard's books. But he plotted no major works, retreating to his journal, with an eye on history. He believed that any one of his best works – *Fear and Trembling, The Concept of Dread, Philosophical Fragments, Concluding Unscientific Postscript, The Sickness Unto Death* – would be enough to make him an important thinker, once he was gone. In the meantime he had to suffer misunderstanding and dismissal on things that mattered and ridicule about things that didn't matter.

His journal grew into his major work. Sometimes Kierkegaard reflected on the *Corsair* controversy: "Not one single cleric risked preaching against such demoralization, backbiting, lies, etc. And they all had the excuse that it was beneath their dignity." With an eye on history he described the underwhelming response to the *Postscript*: "What an achievement, after all, is *Concluding Postscript*, in fact more than enough for three professors." But since he was not important, readers assumed that the book was not important: "Nowhere was it mentioned. It sold perhaps fifty copies, so that its publication cost me, including the fee for proof-reading (100 rigsdaler), about 400 to 500 rigsdaler, besides the time and trouble. Meanwhile I was portrayed in a rabble-rag which in the same little land had 3,000 subscribers." The moral of the story: "Geniuses are like thunderstorms: they go against the wind, terrify people, clear the air."[162]

Repeatedly he returned to the subject of Regine, recounting the story, justifying his decision, assessing her marriage to Fritz Schlegel, and fantasizing about reconciling with her. Near the end of his life Kierkegaard was still fantasizing about reconciling with her "on the grandest scale." Regine would dump Schlegel for him, they would announce their love to the world, he would transform her "into a triumphant figure" to whom he apologized before the world for breaking their engagement, and – presumably privately – he would scold her for resisting so vehemently his decision to break the engagement. Meanwhile, in the real world, Schlegel nixed Kierkegaard's proposal to start a new relationship with Regine and Kierkegaard had to settle for fantasy. Kierkegaard, in his will, left everything to Regine, including author's rights, which Fritz Schlegel refused; shortly before Kierkegaard's death Schlegel took Regine to the Danish West Indies, where he was governor.[163]

In his last years Kierkegaard gave himself to his obsessions with Regine, Mynster, Martensen, and what he called "the idea," New Testament Christianity. Outwardly, his life in the early 1850s was uneventful. The reform movements of the time struck him as boring, secularizing, leveling, and spiritually corrupting. He stayed out of the fray and wrote little for publication aside from a brief work titled *For Self-Examination*. Inwardly he seethed and fixated, caught in an emotional frenzy that he traced to a moment of illumination in 1848 in which he gave himself to "the idea." In 1849 Kierkegaard put it vividly: "My life now is in rapport with ideality; I feel personally under a religious obligation; half measures and chatter I cannot abide, my life is in all respects either-or ... If wantonness and crudeness and envy are allowed to treat an authorial endeavor that is in every way respectable as I have been treated, well now, one must put up with the fact that I form a suspicion concerning the right of such a country to call itself purely Christian; one must put up with the fact that I force up the price of being Christian. I may well suffer as a result, but I will not let go of the idea. If people press harder on me, well, I shall suffer more, but I cannot let go of the idea, and so the counter-pressure which I exert will become even stronger."[164]

That is exactly what happened in the six years that remained to him, except that people did not press harder on him aside from occasional gibes in the tabloid press. Kierkegaard turned against Danish Christianity as a whole, denying that Denmark had any Christians. He reserved special condemnation for professors, especially professors of theology, and clergy, especially clergy who were professors. Mynster, the symbol of the lie that Danes were Christians, provoked Kierkegaard every Sunday. The more beautifully and movingly that he preached, the more unbearable he became to Kierkegaard: "Just when Mynster is most admired, at his most brilliant moments, he is also most untrue from a Christian point of view." It didn't help that Peter Kierkegaard became a force in polite society as a reform politician and Grundtvigian; according to Kierkegaard, Peter took the path of "dribbling oneself way in trifles . . . in the name of cordiality and conviviality, but in our age of envy and leveling it is how to make a hit."[165]

In 1851 Mynster referred to Kierkegaard and Goldschmidt as "talents of a kind," an unbearable insult for Kierkegaard, who had waited, when it mattered, for Mynster to condemn the tabloid attacks on him. Kierkegaard reflected that he finally had a "hard fact" on his side if he chose to attack Mynster, although Mynster had in mind Goldschmidt's post-*Corsair* journalistic career. Back and forth Kierkegaard debated whether the time for a "collision" had come. Unfortunately, he was personally devoted to Mynster, and soon he would need to take a country pastorate, as his inheritance was nearly spent. On the other hand, it killed him to watch the church take the path of liberalizing secular accommodation without at least putting up a fight. Mynster would never fight for Christianity; he was a pure managerial liberal with a pious streak. Kierkegaard put it bluntly: "I have a passion for the truth and ideas that is utterly foreign to him. It is in this that I am opposed to him."[166]

Increasingly he generalized his contempt for Martensen to all professors, calling them "ridiculous" and "the most repellent of inhumans." Though Kierkegaard reminded himself to love ordinary people and to some extent managed to do so, he despised professors, especially up-and-coming assistant professors like the ones who lauded Martensen's genius and reminded Kierkegaard of young Martensen: "The *docents* are an abomination to me." Professors, in his telling, "demoralized the race" by reaping worldly rewards in the name of wisdom: "The infamy of it is that these scoundrels, this brigand band, squeezes itself between the one and the other as though, under cover of serving the idea as well, to betray the true servants and confuse the people, all for the sake of a measly earthly advantage." All deserved to burn in hell, Kierkegaard wrote; if there were no hell, God would need to invent one to punish them. He shuddered at leaving his fate in their hands: "Once I'm dead, how busily the *docents* will go about butchering and dressing me and mine for the market, what competition there will be to say the same, in finer language if possible – as if that is what mattered."[167]

Theology professors were the worst: "They write books and then more books about those books, and books to keep it all under review – periodicals in turn are kept going simply through people writing about these, printers flourish, and many, many thousands have jobs – and the life of not a single one of these hired hands even remotely resembles a Christian existence – yes, it occurs to not a single one of them to take up the New Testament and read it directly and simply, and before God to ask himself the question: Does my life remotely resemble the life of Christ, so that I might dare call myself a follower – I, Professor of Theology, Knight of Dannebrog, honored and esteemed, with a fixed salary and free professorial housing, and author of several learned books about Paul's three journeys?" The concept of a "theology professor" is an outrageous absurdity, Kierkegaard believed, "the greatest satire on 'the apostle.'"[168]

But there was something even worse, a professor who doubled as a cleric: "There is nothing, nothing, nothing, not the most despairing liberal, not a mighty persecutor of religion, nothing so dangerous in Christianity as an official priest and professor." No enemy of Christianity inflicted remotely the harm on Christianity as the church did by allowing professors to double as clergy, he insisted. New Testament Christianity rested wholly on the "life-and-death struggle between man and God." The church, by ordaining professors, or by allowing clergy to become professors, proved that "man has tricked God out of Christianity." Kierkegaard urged that Christianity needed to be what it was in its original idea. If the church followed Christ, it would have no reason to worry about outside criticism. The gospel cannot be ruined or defeated by outside disbelievers. The deadly enemy for Christianity was internal perversion, which is what happened when worldly types became clergy and professors opted for a double helping of worldly honor.[169]

Kierkegaard expanded on this theme in *For Self-Examination,* offering a vintage riff on reasons giving birth to doubt. In the usual telling, he noted, disbelievers made rational objections to believing in Christ, so Christians felt obligated to refute the objections. But that is not what really happened, he claimed. First the intellectual types within Christianity perverted it by proving the truth of Christianity with reasons or by advancing reasons that supported Christian faith. These reasons fostered doubt, "and doubt became the stronger." Christianity is about *imitating Christ,* making Christ the prototype of one's life. That was abolished, Kierkegaard explained. Now the need for reasons was felt more keenly than ever, but these reasons were already a form of doubt, "and thus doubt arose and lived on reasons." The church did not grasp that the more it depends on reasons, the more it nourishes doubt. So doubt grew stronger. Kierkegaard likened it to pacifying a monster with food, which merely whets the monster's appetite. To kill the monster of doubt, one has to starve it of reasons, exactly as Luther did. In the modern world, Kierkegaard reflected elsewhere, some professors said that Christianity was mythology, and others made a nice living by defending Christian concepts or the historicity of biblical events. He countered that the so-called Christian professors kidded themselves about doing a good deed; being a Christian has everything to do with living as Christ lived and nothing to do with anything else.[170]

In Kierkegaard's telling, he kept waiting for Mynster to say that Christianity did not exist in Denmark, but every Sunday Mynster pretended otherwise, deepening Kierkegaard's misery. Then the most respected figure in Denmark died, in January 1854. Martensen, preaching at Mynster's memorial service in the Royal Chapel, referred to the late bishop as a "witness to the truth," which sent Kierkegaard over the edge. He could not bear such a lie, especially from Martensen. Immediately he wrote a response, "Was Bishop Mynster a 'Truth-Witness,' one of 'the Authentic Truth-Witnesses' – Is *This the Truth?*" A witness to the truth, Christianly defined, is someone who suffers for Christ and is "unfamiliar with everything called enjoyment," Kierkegaard declared: "A truth-witness is a person who in poverty witnesses for the truth, in poverty, in lowliness and abasement, is so unappreciated, hated, detested, so mocked, insulted, laughed to scorn – so poor that he perhaps has not always had daily bread, but he received the daily bread of persecution in abundance every day." No authentic witness to the truth is admired or moves forward in life, he added: "A truth-witness, one of the authentic truth-witnesses, is a person who is flogged, mistreated, dragged from one prison to another," and then, inevitably, dragged to a cross, "or beheaded or burned or broiled on a grill." Truth-witnesses are not exalted at state funerals; executioners throw their bodies away. Did that describe Bishop Mynster?[171]

Kierkegaard finished this article in February, but withheld publishing it until December, to avoid playing a role in the jockeying over Mynster's successor during an election year. Martensen had been the royal court chaplain since 1845 and was supported by conservatives in the ruling government to succeed Mynster as Bishop of Sjaelland. In April 1854 he was named to the see, narrowly prevailing over H. N. Clausen, who was supported by the opposition National-Liberal Party and by the king; later that year the National-Liberals gained power. Kierkegaard, waiting for the politics to play out, wrote in his journal that the situation had changed "regarding my melancholic devotion to my dead father's priest." He was ready to attack Mynster, Martensen, and Danish Christianity as a whole. It was just a question of waiting for a seemly moment, as he didn't want to give aid to political liberals. Politically he was a tragic conservative: "The state is human egoism writ large, on a grand scale ... The state is less of a good than an evil, a necessary evil, in a way a useful, expedient evil." On himself he was conflicted differently: "Alas, I have been granted the eminent intellectuality of a genius. On the other hand, I am not by any manner of means what might be called a holy person, by no means one of those deep religious originals."[172]

In December Kierkegaard finally published his attack on Martensen for lying about Mynster. The initial public reaction was stunned and perplexed, since Kierkegaard had always supported Mynster publicly. Where did this indignation come from? If it was genuine, why did he wait to express it until Mynster was gone? The perplexity soon gave way to outrage that Kierkegaard smeared a recently departed spiritual leader. Kierkegaard's former teachers called it "sickly" and "unjust"; others called it an outrageous desecration; Joanne Heiberg, wife of the doyen and formerly sympathetic to Kierkegaard, called him an "unfaithful beast." Ten days after Kierkegaard's attack was published the new primate of Denmark added that Kierkegaard's underlying argument was "arbitrary" and "crude." Martensen noted that if one had to be a martyr to be a truth-witness, the apostle John failed the test. Martensen believed in the one holy universal Church, so the unity of the church was important to him. But Kierkegaard's Christianity was "without Church and without history," Martensen observed. Kierkegaard had nothing to say about the church as the historical body of Christians, besides condemning it; the unity of the church meant nothing to him; he cared only about "extraordinary trials" and people with "extraordinary powers and gifts," notably himself.[173]

Martensen puzzled over Kierkegaard's idealization of one kind of suffering, since there were many kinds, and many of the worst fanatics suffered too. Had Kierkegaard become "so obsessed by a *fixed* idea" that he lost "the simplest presence of mind?" Or was he merely using a narrow idea of Christianity to create a sensation? Martensen could not tell, but he was surprised in either case that "such a practiced sophist" as Kierkegaard settled for something so arbitrary and crude that it was "almost banal to refute it." As for Kierkegaard's contention that Mynster lacked the elementary moral character of a Christian, Martensen replied that Mynster's moral character was not in question, but Kierkegaard, by defaming a revered Christian leader in the wake of his death, one that he had claimed to support for decades, raised plenty of questions about his. In a glancing shot aimed at Kierkegaard's heart, Martensen compared him to Thersites, the freakish, hunch-backed wretch of Homer's *Iliad*. Years later Martensen recalled that Kierkegaard's attack "was intended to be a mortal blow, to destroy me utterly, and to make it impossible for me to hold the high position that had recently been entrusted to me." As far as he could tell, Kierkegaard was motivated by "fanatical" sectarian zeal and "simple, personal animosity, not to mention hatred."[174]

Kierkegaard responded to none of Martensen's points. There was only one point at issue, he replied: Did Martensen speak truthfully in calling Mynster a witness to the truth? For Kierkegaard, the answer was plainly negative. There was such a thing as New Testament Christianity, it alone deserved to be called Christianity, it did not exist in Denmark, Mynster had never tried to witness to it, and Martensen had no idea of it. This was what mattered. Originally, Kierkegaard observed, Christianity was called the Way, but "the Way has now become something else, not the one in the New Testament – in abasement, hated, abandoned, persecuted, and cursed to suffer in this world – no, the Way is: admired, applauded, honored, and knighted to make a brilliant career!" In the New Testament, Christianity was about sacrificing everything for Christ and retaining the "cheerful boldness of faith" in the face of possible martyrdom. In Martensen's sermonizing, it was about realizing one's success dreams in a way that people admired.[175]

Kierkegaard realized that he would lose a debate about small points. He was not aiming for a debate anyway, although he complained afterwards that Martensen never replied to him again. Kierkegaard was aiming for the biggest disruption he could cause. In his journal he wrote a piece about how to bring about a cultural catastrophe: "One omits some intermediary steps, adduces a conclusion without giving the premises, draws a consequence without first indicating what it is a consequence of, and the like." This leads to a clash between the agent of disruption and all others, which leads to "a catastrophe." Kierkegaard observed that clashes between a genius and his age are fairly commonplace, but these are immediate affairs that nobody sets up deliberately. He had something bigger in mind, which had to be planned. To cause the greatest possible shock to Danish society, he had to be ruthless, strategic, aggressive, and not worry about treating others harshly.[176]

Kierkegaard gave his last months to that cause. He ended his journal and took up cultural warfare, although he still occasionally scrawled notes to himself on loose sheets; one was about fighting off priests and professors, "these greedy and virulently self-reproductive parasites." He wrote twenty-two blistering articles for the *Faedre-landet,* the same tabloid in which Frater Taciturnus had launched the *Corsair* debacle. Most were laced with sarcasm and ridicule; one was titled, "That Bishop Martensen's Silence is (1) Christianly Indefensible; (2) Ludicrous; (3) Obtuse-Sagacious; (4) in More Than One Regard Contemptible." Martensen, in Kierkegaard's telling, "threw a garbage can of insults and abusive remarks over me – and then took off."[177]

But the *Faedrelandet* was a limited vehicle, constrained by page limits and other voices, so Kierkegaard launched a pamphlet series titled *The Moment*. One summarized its thesis in the title, "That the Pastors are Cannibals, and in the Most Abominable Way." Kierkegaard explained that pastors, being university educated, had no interest in living "the suffering truth" of New Testament Christianity; they preferred to live off Christianity by consuming it. Another pamphlet described the church-talk of pastors as "formula, rigmarole, something official, from a handbook or a music box." Repeatedly he charged that Christendom was founded on hypocrisy. New Testament Christianity was the truth, "but people sagaciously and knavishly invented a new kind of Christianity, one that builds the tombs of the prophets and adorns the graves of the righteous and says: If we had lived in the days of our fathers."[178]

One pamphlet took aim at Martensen's decision to enter the clerical business. Martensen was already a big success as a professor before he felt the need to preach sermons, Kierkegaard recalled. If he had satisfied his need by spreading himself around at area pulpits, Mynster, "with his sensitive nose," would have smelled something odious. Officially, preaching is not supposed to be done for ego gratification, and ministry is supposed to involve ministering on weekdays. But installing Martensen as royal court chaplain took care of both problems. There, Martensen's itch to sermonize was construed as something admirable, there was no congregation to worry about, and he put himself in position to become bishop. "Yet the good-natured population notices nothing, is touched by this religious need," Kierkegaard observed. Mynster and Martensen had the same religion: Both were Epicurean hedonists living high off Christianity and clueless admiration.[179]

Both were virtuosos at equivocation, too – the calling card of the church leader. Kierkegaard pounded on this theme, that Mynster and Martensen were good at relativizing everything pertaining to real Christianity in the service of their comfort and the privileges of the church. Grundtvig was no different, he claimed. For a moment Martensen worried that Kierkegaard was preparing to join the Grundtvigian insurgency, but Grundtvig dismissed Kierkegaard as an over-intellectual "scoffer," and Kierkegaard replied that Grundtvig was no less worldly than Martensen. Grundtvig simply played to a different faction of the population, riding on the backs of poor folks; all he cared about was attaining freedom for himself and his group. The church was corrupt because it had corrupt leaders who competed for status in a corrupt society: "The entire age has sunk into the deepest indifferentism, has no religion at all, and is not even in the condition of being able to have religion."[180]

Repeatedly Kierkegaard disclaimed the mantle of superiority, except for genius. He did not look down on the semi-Christianity of others, since he was not a Christian, either. He was trying to become a Christian and wished that others would do the same. He took extreme measures because he saw nothing worth reforming; the entire house had to come down. He stopped going to church, showing up at the reading room of the Athenaeum every Sunday just as services began. When Michael Andersen Kierkegaard lost his wife in May 1855, Kierkegaard refused to attend the funeral, because it was in a church; Kierkegaard asked his "dear uncle," who was actually a cousin, to excuse him. His tabloid articles and pamphlets were widely read, setting off a storm of reaction, some of which gave him pause. Sibbern was stunned that Kierkegaard resorted to tabloid journalism, the very thing he had derided for years. Political liberals crowed at Kierkegaard's attacks on church leaders. Many observers puzzled over Kierkegaard's decision to besmirch his reputation for intellectual seriousness. Kierkegaard, stewing over the contradictions, allowed that he was contentious by nature: "By nature I am so polemical that I really feel in my element only when surrounded by human mediocrity and scurviness." But he really was surrounded by it, he contended, and his true seriousness showed in his decision to do something radical that was otherwise against his will: "True earnestness does not actually emerge until a person of competence is compelled against his desire by something higher to undertake the work, that is, a person of competence against his desire."[181]

Near the end, struggling with declining health – probably tuberculosis of the spine marrow – at the age of 42, Kierkegaard penned a verdict that Nietzsche would have appreciated had he read enough Kierkegaard, and that twentieth-century existentialists embraced: "The basic depravity of our times is that personality has been abolished. No one in our time dares to be a personality, everyone shrinks in cowardly anthrophobia from being *I* over against, perhaps in opposition to, others." Kierkegaard tried to identify analogies for his situation – Luther? Paul? But nobody qualified: "I quite literally have no analogy to cite, nothing corresponding in eighteen hundred years of Christianity. In this way, too – facing eighteen hundred years – I stand quite literally alone." In his last issue of *The Moment*, September 1855, which he did not live to publish, Kierkegaard judged that only Socrates was a comparable figure. Moreover, "there is not one single contemporary who is qualified to review my work." The only competent reviews ever written of his work had been written by – him. In conclusion, his authorial career, and what it cost him, could be expressed in a single line: "I was never like the others."[182]

But that was not quite his last word. At the end of his last composition, Kierkegaard added a postscript to "the common man." He had not segregated himself from common people, he noted. He had lived on the street and dealt with everybody. Neither did he belong "to any class-egotism," having spurned the option of becoming somebody: "So if I belong to anyone, I must belong to you, you common man," despite the fact that common people, enticed by money-grubbing tabloid operators, "have been willing enough to consider me and my life ludicrous." Kierkegaard's final word to his fellow common people was to steer clear of pastors: "One thing I beseech you for God in heaven's sake and by all that is holy: Avoid the pastors, avoid them, those abominations whose job is to hinder you in even becoming aware of what true Christianity is and thereby to turn you, muddled by gibberish and illusion, into what they understand by a true Christian, a contributing member of the state Church, the national Church, and the like."[183]

Peter Kierkegaard, skilled at the religious politics that his brother despised, was in a tricky spot for years. He tried to be a decent brother, while serving in political offices and keeping one foot in the Gruntvigian movement, though Søren resented that Peter never defended him from tabloid lampooning. In July 1855 Peter was egged on at a Gruntvigian conference to talk about his brother's theology. Speaking off the cuff, he explained that Søren was a mystical-ascetic type who wanted everyone to have a living faith; however, Søren prescribed a "swimming exercise without safety belts over seventy thousand fathoms of water." In fact, he told people to leap into the water headfirst. Peter allowed, in a concession to his brother, that Christianity was not "what the sniveling pastors say it is." But neither was Christianity "what jesting or damning prophets seek to make it into."[184]

That crossed an unforgiveable line as far as Søren Kierkegaard was concerned; his brother had publicly taken sides against him, while playing it for laughs to a Grundt-vigian audience. The next time that Peter tried to visit him at home, Søren refused to speak to him. On his hospital deathbed in October he refused again. Kierkegaard explained to his friend Emil Boesen that Peter could be defeated only by action, not by debate; he was finished with his brother. Boesen, trying to be a pastor and friend at the same time, gently asked Kierkegaard whether there was anything that he still wanted to say. Kierkegaard opted for reminiscence, recalling that his "thorn in the flesh" prevented him from marrying or having a normal life. Boesen tried again; did he want to qualify any of his recent statements? Kierkegaard replied: "Do you think I should tone it down, by speaking first to awaken people, and then to calm them down? Why do you want to bother me with this?" He had not overreacted to Mynster; somebody had to expose Mynster's true character and legacy: "You have no idea what sort of a poisonous plant Mynster was. You have no idea of it; it is staggering how it has spread its corruption. He was a colossus. Great strength was required to topple him, and the person who did it had to pay for it."[185]

Kierkegaard's funeral in November at the Church of Our Lady attracted a large crowd of common people and no dignitaries. Martensen commented bitterly that it was tactless for the family to bury him on a Sunday, between two services, let alone in "the nation's most important church." But he could not prevent the family from embarrassing the nation one last time. Peter Kierkegaard's eulogy was quiet and sad, with no polemics, but he apologized for his brother's emotional struggle, which many took as code that Søren had become unhinged: "The vision of the deceased had become partially darkened and distorted from exertions and suffering in the heat of battle, causing his blows to fall wildly and blindly." Afterward Peter made bishop of Aalborg and was haunted by the memory of his brother. He had never been able to criticize his father, despite getting rougher treatment than Søren; later he was consumed with guilt over Søren's fate. In 1875 Peter resigned his bishopric, explaining that he did not deserve to be a bishop; four years later he returned his royal decorations; in the 1880s he descended into helpless depression.[186]

He played a key role, however, in allowing his brother not to be forgotten. In 1859 Peter published Kierkegaard's *The Point of View for My Work as an Author;* in 1876 he published *Judge for Yourself!* More importantly, in the 1860s Peter commissioned H. P. Barfod to assemble three volumes of Kierkegaard's journals and unpublished papers, which aroused bitter memories for some when the first volume was published in 1869. Martensen protested that publishing such material showed a tactless lack of consideration for Kierkegaard, since much of it displayed "the sickly nature of his profound sensibility, which increasingly got the upper hand as the years progressed." Many others found the journal to be Kierkegaard's most fascinating and illuminating work, which stirred new interest in his books.[187]

Martensen did his best to keep Kierkegaard down – in all three volumes of his memoirs. Kierkegaard was not a great thinker, Martensen kept assuring. Kierkegaard was a flashy "humorist" with a clever mind and a staggering ego. In a pensive moment, Martensen allowed that perhaps things would have gone better between them had he shown some enthusiasm for Kierkegaard's dissertation. He had disliked Kierkegaard's repetitiveness, his winding sentences, his "affected and mannered expressions," and his incredible belief that he was a genius. In fact, he disliked the same things in all of Kierkegaard's subsequent works. But perhaps he could have been spared Kierkegaard's wrath had he mustered some enthusiasm for *The Concept of Irony.* As it was, Martensen tried to get along with Kierkegaard afterwards, but that never worked out either: "I was so opposed to his essential being – experimenting and self-enclosed as it was, and which seemed to me to be unavoidably linked to the danger of some inner falsity in his character – that I was unable to feel any desire for a closer relationship."[188]

It disturbed Martensen, moving into the 1880s, that Kierkegaard was never quite forgotten. Despite his unhealthy view of things and the "moral vileness" of his attack on Mynster, or perhaps because of them, Kierkegaard had a real following at the end of his life, Martensen acknowledged. Mostly it was among sectarians, atheists, women, and youth, contributing "in no small measure to the growth and strengthening of unbelief in this country." Equally disturbing, highbrow types had a tendency to indulge his rhetorical fireworks and conceits. When surveys of Danish literature were conducted, Martensen observed, it was not unusual for Kierkegaard to be praised as an important thinker, even a reformer. This had to be corrected before it became a national myth: "If we consider the whole of his activity and ask, What, in the end, has been accomplished with these rich gifts, with these remarkable talents? – then the answer must certainly be, Not very much! It is certainly true that he has awakened a profound and fervent sort of unrest in many souls. But the many half-truths, the many false paradoxes and false witticisms can hardly have assisted any soul in finding serenity and peace." Kierkegaard bequeathed no great truth to religion or philosophy, wrote nothing that deserved to last, and did immense harm, Martensen insisted. He was a "noble instrument with a cracked sounding board," and the crack became larger and larger.[189]

Martensen had reason to believe that the Kierkegaard phenomenon would not get worse. Though Kierkegaard's religious writings were objects of ambivalent local pride in Denmark, he never acquired a philosophical following. The few monographs on his philosophy before 1900 were negative. In Germany, nineteenth-century theology carried on as though Kierkegaard had never lived. For a while it stuck with Hegel and/ or Schleiermacher in Germany, before England and the United States had significant liberal theology movements. Then it opted for Ritschlian historicism, which yielded social Christianity and the History of Religions school, all of which Kierkegaard would have considered at least as ridiculous as Hegelianism.

Kierkegaard had to wait for a generation that did not believe in the progress of modern culture and which shared at least some of his radical rejection of history. For him, history had no answers and it did not clarify ideas. History muddled ideas and corrupted them, distorting whatever it touched. Kierkegaard had one historical norm, "New Testament Christianity," but he never bothered to defend it historically, realizing where that would take him. To be discovered, he had to be read in German by youthful thinkers who were disillusioned with history, such as Karl Jaspers and Karl Barth.[190]

Kierkegaard stood out from his time by not belonging to it. Liberal theology, believing in reason, historical criticism, and modern cultural progress, was about the wrong things. It let go of any real connection to New Testament Christianity and sought to replace muddled state church orthodoxies that were already hopelessly compromised. Kierkegaard spurned Schleiermacher-style liberalism as a boring and enervated waste of time. He repudiated Hegelianism and his debts to it, except for the parts that he called something else. Had he lived to see the Social Gospel, he would have blasted that too.

All got in the way of the one important thing that he shared with the modernizing age that he rejected, its idealistic impulse, which he absolutized. Historicism undermined his pure contemporaneousness with Jesus. Rational objectivity and metaphysics opposed truth as subjectivity. Dogmatism distorted Jesus and Christian subjectivity. Liberalism was about perfecting modern culture, not following Jesus. Kierkegaard was keenly aware that he offered a dubious advertisement for the pure ideality that he sought. Thus he tried to deflect objections by creating a last pseudonym, Anti-Climacus. His lesser pseudonyms pointed to the ideal, using their imaginations, while pondering the leap. Kierkegaard put his name to reflections reflecting post-leap Christian consciousness, yet he was still the same melancholic genius absorbed with himself and his need to ridicule. Anti-Climacus knew what the ideal was, because he lived it. But who was that, and how did he know?

In every age Kierkegaard catches readers who thrill to his negative dialectics without buying his religious concept of the point of it all. In Berlin, on the threshold of his authorial explosion, Kierkegaard amused himself by interrogating a dinner companion, young theologian Peter Conrad Rothe. Rothe had just returned from a grand tour of lecture grazing. His mind was filled, to his delight, with Hegelian and Schleiermacherian theology. Kierkegaard needled him mercilessly, exposing Rothe's inability to explain the great things he had learned. Kierkegaard would lure a proposition out of Rothe, pretend not to understand it, turn it over dialectically, and press Rothe to explain it in different words, reducing him to babbling confusion. Suddenly remembering an appointment, Kierkegaard would dash out of the restaurant, leaving Rothe to explain himself to chortling companions. This happened several times; *Either/Or* had variations on the scene. Many readers read Kierkegaard for the sheer unparalleled intellectual sport.[191]

The readers who introduced Kierkegaard to the English-speaking world were of a very different mind. Walter Lowrie, by far the leading example, translated most of Kierkegaard's works into English and authored the two biographies on which generations of English-reading students of Kierkegaard depended. Near the end of his second biography Lowrie acknowledged that he loved Kierkegaard, but not the cheeky brat, the prodigal son, or the unhappy lover, nor even "the genius who created the pseudonyms." The Kierkegaard that he loved was the frail individual who wrote shimmering religious philosophy and spiritual theology despite being thrown into a world in which he was "utterly unfitted to cope." This Kierkegaard, Lowrie wrote, "in fear and trembling, fighting with fabulous monsters, ventured as a lone swimmer far out upon the deep, where no human hand could be stretched out to save him, and there, with 70,000 fathoms of water under him, for three years held out, waiting for his orders, and then said distinctly that definite thing he was bidden to say, and died with a hallelujah on his lips."[192]

To love Kierkegaard, Lowrie explained, he had to be able to venerate him, "and I learned to venerate him only when I saw that he had the courage to die as a witness for the truth." Much of the literature on Kierkegaard pits venerating Lowrie-types against deconstructionist advocates of Kierkegaardian sport. But Kierkegaard is better viewed whole than as an object of religious admiration or as a prophet of the death of presence. His one-sided rage for subjectivity radiates in every direction as critique and witness, yielding existentialisms, anti-historicisms, postmodernisms, and other isms that he would not have cared about, and speaking to uncountable individualities, about which he cared passionately.[193]

Notes

1. See C. I. Nitzsch, *System der christlichen Lehre* (Bonn: Adolph Marcus, 1829); August Twesten, *Vorlesungen über die Dogmatik* (Hamburg: Perthes, 1838); Willibald Beyschlag, *Die Christologie des Neuen Testaments* (Berlin: Rauh, 1866); Beyschlag, *Leben Jesu*, 2 vols. (Halle: Strien, 1885); A. E. Biedermann, *Christliche Dogmatik* (1869); Richard Rothe, *Theologische Ethik*, 3 vols. (Wittenberg: Zimmermann, 1845–1848); Rothe, *Zur Dogmatik* (Gotha: Perthes, 1863).

2. David Friedrich Strauss, *The Christ of Faith and the Jesus of History: A Critique of Schleiermacher's Life of Jesus*, trans. Leander E. Keck (Philadelphia: Fortress Press, 1977), 4; Carl Ullmann, *Die Sündlosigkeit Jesu: Eine apologetische Betrachtung* (Hamburg: Perthes, 1828), English version of sixth German edition, Ullmann, *The Sinlessness of Jesus: An Evidence for Christianity*, trans. R. C. L. Brown (Edinburgh: T. & T. Clark, 1858), quotes 266, 288. Sophia Taylor's 1901 English translation of Ullmann's seventh German edition extended the book's English popularity for twenty years.

3. Carl Ullmann, *Das Wesen des Christentums* (Hamburg: Perthes, 1845), 45–47.

4. Carl Ullmann, review of David Friedrich Strauss, *The Life of Jesus Critically Examined*, in *Theologische Studien und Kritiken*, 9 (1836), reprinted in Ullmann, *Historisch oder Mythisch? Beiträge zur Beantwortung der gegenwärtgen Lebensfrage der Theologie* (Hamburg: Perthes, 1838), 770–816.

5. David Friedrich Strauss, "Zum Andenken an meine Mutter," in Strauss, *Gesammelte Schriften*, 12 vols., ed. E. Zeller (Bonn: E. Strauss, 1876–1878), I: 90–99; Strauss, "Literarische Denkwürdigkeiten," in *Gesammelte Schriften*, I: 8–9; Theobald Ziegler, *David Friedrich Strauss*, 2 vols. (Strassburg: K. J. Trubner, 1908), I: 56–60; John Edward Toews, *Hegelianism: The Path toward Dialectical Humanism, 1805–1841* (Cambridge: Cambridge University Press, 1985), 166–169; Peter C. Hodgson, "Editor's Introduction: Strauss's Theological Development from 1825 to 1850," in David Friedrich Strauss, *The Life of Jesus Critically Examined*, trans. George Eliot, ed. Peter C. Hodgson (Ramsey: Sigler Press, 1994), xx.

6. David Friedrich Strauss to Christian Märklin, December 26, 1830, in Strauss, *Ausgewählte Briefe von David Friedrich Strauss*, ed. E. Zeller (Bonn: E. Strauss, 1895), 4–6; Ziegler, *David Friedrich Strauss*, I: 63–69; Albert Schweitzer, *The Quest of the Historical Jesus: A Critical Study of its Progress from Reimarus to Wrede*, trans. James M. Robinson (1906; reprint, New York: Macmillan, 1968), 68–69.

7. David Friedrich Strauss to Christian Märklin, June 27, 1831, MSS in the Schiller National-Museum, Marbach, Germany, cited in Hodgson, "Editor's Introduction: Strauss's Theological Development," xxi, and Toews, *Hegelianism: The Path Toward Dialectical Humanism, 1805–1841*, 172. This section on Strauss adapts material from Gary Dorrien, *The Word as True Myth: Interpreting Modern Theology* (Louisville: Westminster John Knox Press, 1997), 25–45.

8. David Friedrich Strauss, "Die Lehre von der Wiederbringung aller Dinge in ihrer religionsgeschtlichen Entwicklung," in Gotthold Müller, *Indentität und Immanenz: Zur Genese der Theologie von David Friedrich Strauss* (Zürich: EVZ-Verlag, 1968), 50–82; stopped believing citation in Leander E. Keck, "Editor's Introduction," in Strauss, *The Christ of Faith and the Jesus of History*, xxii.

9. David Friedrich Strauss to Christian Märklin, May 31, 1831, *Ausgewählte Briefe von David Friedrich Strauss*, 7; Ziegler, *David Friedrich Strauss*, I: 94; William J. Brazill, *The Young Hegelians* (New Haven: Yale University Press, 1970), 96–101; Toews, *Hegeli-*

anism: The Path Toward Dialectical Humanism, 1805–1841, 174–175; Schweitzer, *The Quest of the Historical Jesus,* 70.

10. Ferdinand Christian Baur, *Symbolik und Mythologie, oder die Naturreligion des Alterthums,* 2 vols. (Stuttgart: J. B. Metzler, 1824–1825), quote, I: xi; Müller, *Identität und Immanenz: Zur Genese der Theologie von David Friedrich Strauss,* 72–95; F. W. J. Schelling, *Vorlesungen uber die Methode des academischen Studium* (Stuttgart: J. G. Cotta, 1830); see Peter C. Hodgson, *The Formation of Historical Theology: A Study of Ferdinand Christian Baur* (New York: Harper & Row, 1966), 9–12.

11. See Philipp K. Marheineke, *Die Grundlinien der christlichen Dogmatik als Wissenschaft* (Berlin: Duncker und Homblot, 1827); Karl Rosenkranz, *Encyklopädie der theologschen Wissenschaften* (Halle: C. A. Schwetschke und Sohn, 1831); Carl Friedrich Goschel, *Von den Bewwisen für die Unsterblichkeit der menschlichen Selle* (Berlin: Verlag von Duncker und Humblot, 1835); Karl Ludwig Michelet, *Vorlesungen über die Persöhnlichkeit Gottes und Unsterblichkeit der Seele oder die ewige Persohnlichkeit des Geistes* (Berlin: Verlag von Ferdinand Dummler, 1841); Kasimir Conradi, *Unsterblichkeit und Weiges Leben: Versuch einer Entwicklung des Unsterblichkeitsbegriffs der menschlichen Seele* (Mainz 1837); G. W. F. Hegel, *Berliner Schriften, 1818–1831,* ed. J. Hoffmeister (Hamburg: Verlag von Felix Meiner, 1956), 324–329.

12. Keck, "Editor's Introduction," Baur quote, lv; see Hodgson, *The Formation of Historical Theology,* 14–15.

13. On Hegel's understanding of the relation of religious and philosophical truth, see Quentin Laur, S.J., *Hegel's Concept of God* (Albany: State University of New York Press, 1982), 21–56; and John Burbidge, *Hegel on Logic and Religion* (Albany, NY: State University of New York Press, 1992), 141–153.

14. David Friedrich Strauss to Christian Märklin, February 1832, cited in Hodgson, "Editor's Introduction: Strauss's Theological Development," p. xxiii.

15. David Friedrich Strauss, "Rosenkranz: Encyklopädie der theologischen Wissenschaften," in Strauss, *Charakteristiken und Kritiken: Eine Sammlung zerstreuter Aufsätze aus den Gebieten der Theologie, Anthropolgie, und Aesthetik* (Leipzig: O. Wigand, 1839), quote 224; originally published in the Hegelian *Jahrbücher für wissenschaftliche Kritik,* 1832; see Towes, *Hegelianism: The Path Toward Dialectical Humanism, 1805–1841,* 163–164; Rosenkranz, *Encyklopädie der theologschen Wissenschaften.*

16. See Karl Daub, *Die dogmatische Theologie jetziger Zeit oder die Selbstsucht in der Wissenschaft des Glaubens und ihrer Artikel* (Heidelberg: J. C. B. Mohr, 1833); Göschel, *Von den Beweisen für die Unsterblichkeit der menschlichen Seele;* Göschel, *Der Mensch nach Leib, Seele und Geist diesseits und jenseits* (Leipzig: Dorffling und Franke, 1856); Kasimir Conradi, *Selbstbewusstseyn und Offenbarung, oder die Entwickelung des religiösen Bewusstseyns* (Mainz: Kupferberg, 1831); Strauss, "Rosenkranz: Encyklopädie der theologischen Wissenschaften," 224–225.

17. Hodgson, "Editor's Introduction: Strauss's Theological Development," xxiii.

18. Strauss, *The Life of Jesus Critically Examined,* li.

19. Heinrich Eberhard Gottlob Paulus, *Das Leben Jesu, als Grundlage einer reinen Geschichte des Urchristenthums* (Heidelberg: Winter, 1828); Paulus, *Philologisch-kritischer Commentar uber das Neue Testament,* 4 vols. (Lübeck: Bohn, 1804–1805); Schweitzer, *The Quest of the Historical Jesus,* 48–57.

20. Strauss, *The Life of Jesus Critically Examined,* li.

21. See Wilhelm Martin Leberecht de Wette, *Lehrbuch der historisch kritischen Einleitung in die Bibel Alten und Neuen Testaments,* 4th edn., 2 parts (Berlin: G. Reimer, 1833–1834); de Wette, *Ueber Religion und Theologie: Erlauterung zu seinem Lehrbuche*

der Dogmatik (Berlin: G. Reimer, 1821); F. C. Baur, *Die christliche Gnosis, oder die christliche Religions-Philosophie in ihrer geschichtlichen Entwiklung* (Tubingen: C. F. Osiander, 1835).

22. Strauss, *The Life of Jesus Critically Examined*, 60.
23. Ibid., 275–471.
24. Ibid., lii.
25. Ibid., 87–92.
26. Ibid., 739–743.
27. Ibid., 744.
28. Ibid., 57.
29. Ibid., 52–53.
30. Ibid., 53–54.
31. Ibid., 76.
32. Ibid., 80.
33. Ibid., 81.
34. Ibid., 86.
35. Ibid., 86.
36. Ibid., 87.
37. Ibid., 87.
38. Ibid., 78, 757.
39. David Friedrich Strauss, *Streitschriften zur Verteidigung Meiner Schrift uber das Leben Jesu und zur Charakteristik der gegenwartigen Theologie*, III (Tubingen: C. F. Osiander, 1841), 95.
40. Strauss, *Ausgewählte Briefe von David Friedrich Strauss*, 48; see Toews, *Hegelianism: The Path Toward Dialectical Humanism, 1805–1841*, 276.
41. Strauss, *The Life of Jesus Critically Examined*, "Preface to the Fourth German Edition," lviii.
42. David Friedrich Strauss to Christian Märklin, November 3, 1839, MSS in Schiller National-Museum, Marbach, cited in Toews, *Hegelianism: The Path Toward Dialectical Humanism, 1805–1841*, 281.
43. David Friedrich Strauss, *Die christliche Glaubenslehre in ihrer geschichtlichen Entwicklung und im Kampfe mit der modernen Wissenschaft dargestellt*, 2 vols. (Tubingen: C. F. Osiander, 1840–1841), I, 71.
44. Strauss, "Preface to the Fourth German Edition," p. lviii.
45. Strauss, *Streitschriften*, III, 60–94. See Göschel, *Von den Bewwisen fur die Unsterblichkeit der menschlichen Seele* (Berlin: Verlag von Duncker und Humblot, 1835); Goschel, *Der Mensch nach Leib, Seele und Geist diesseits und jenseits* (Leipzig: Dorffling und Franke, 1856); and Georg Andreas Gabler, *Die Hegelsche Philosophie* (Berlin: Verlag von Alexander Duncker, 1843). Strauss placed Rosenkranz in the center of the Hegelian right/center/left continuum, because, though he sought to uphold the idea of an individual historical incarnation through speculative philosophy, Rosenkranz gave up any claim to grounding speculative theology in the gospel history. See Strauss, *Streitschriften*, III, 94–126.
46. See Bruno Bauer, *Die Posaune des jungsten Gerichts uber Hegel den Atheisten und Antichristen: Ein Ultimatum* (Leipzig 1841); Ludwig Feuerbach, *The Essence of Christianity*, trans. George Eliot (New York: Harper & Row, 1957).
47. Strauss, *Die christliche Glaubenslehre*, I, 1–2.
48. Strauss, *The Life of Jesus Critically Examined*, 88.
49. See Friedrich Schleiermacher, *Hermeneutics: The Handwritten Manuscripts*, trans. James Duke and J. Forstman, ed. H. Kimmerle (Missoula, Montana: Scholars Press, 1977).

50. Hans-Georg Gadamer, *Truth and Method,* 2nd revd. edn., trans. Joel Weinsheimer and Donald G. Marshall (New York: Crossroad, 1989), quote 168–169; see Gadamer, *Hegel's Dialectic: Five Hermeneutical Studies,* trans. P. Christopher Smith (New Haven: Yale University Press, 1976).

51. Strauss, *The Life of Jesus Critically Examined,* 461; F. C. Baur, *Kritische Untersuchungen über die kanonischen Evangelien* (Tubingen: L. F. Fues, 1847), 41–46, 71–74.

52. See Hodgson, "Editor's Introduction: Strauss's Theological Development," pp. xxix–xx-xi, xxx; Klaus Koch, *The Growth of the Biblical Tradition: The Form-Critical Method* (London: Adam & Charles Black, 1969); Rudolf Bultmann, *The History of the Synoptic Tradition,* trans. John Marsh (New York: Harper & Row, 1963), 2–7, 39–54.

53. Schweitzer, *The Quest of the Historical Jesus,* 69; Karl Barth, *Protestant Theology in the Nineteenth Century: Its Background & History* (1959; reprint, Valley Forge: Judson Press, 1976), 542–543.

54. Strauss, *The Life of Jesus Critically Examined,* 778.

55. Ibid., 780.

56. Ibid., 780–782.

57. For a right-Hegelian interpretation of divine reality as hypostatized being (fully self-conscious independently of the world) and a critique of Strauss's non-hypostatized panentheism, see Gabler, *Die Hegelsche Philosophie,* 89–215.

58. David Friedrich Strauss, *Briefe von David Friedrich Strauss an L. Georgii,* ed. H. Maier (Tübingen: J. C. B. Mohr, 1912), 39; Strauss, *Briefwechsel zwischen Strauss und Vischer,* 2 vols., ed. A. Rapp (Stuttgart: E. Klett, 1952–53), I: 95, 105; Bruno Bauer, *Die Posaune des jüngsten Gerichts über Hegel den Atheisten und Antichristen: Ein Ultamatum* (Leipzig: O. Wigand, 1841); Toews, *Hegelianism: The Path Toward Dialectical Humanism, 1805–1841,* 282–287; Brazill, *The Young Hegelians,* 73–79.

59. See Isaak August Dorner, *Entwicklungsgeschichte der Lehre von der Person Christi,* 2nd edn., 4 vols. (Stuttgart: S. G. Liesching, 1846–1856); Biedermann, *Christliche Dogmatik* (1869); Rothe, *Zur Dogmatik.*

60. David Friedrich Strauss, *Das Leben Jesu, für das deutsche Volk bearbeitet,* 2 vols. (Leipzig: Brockhaus, 1864); see Ziegler, *David Friedrich Strauss,* II: 589–592; Ernst Renan, *The Life of Jesus,* trans. Charles Wilbour (New York: Carleton, 1864); Strauss, *The Christ of Faith and the Jesus of History: A Critique of Schleiermacher's Life of Jesus,* trans. Leander Keck (Philadelphia: Fortress Press, 1977), 168–169; Friedrich Schleiermacher, *The Life of Jesus,* trans. S. Maclean Gilmour (Philadelphia: Fortress Press, 1975).

61. Strauss, *The Christ of Faith and the Jesus of History,* 4, 162, 166.

62. Ibid., 166–167, 169.

63. David Friedrich Strauss, *The Old Faith and the New,* trans. Mathilde Blind (New York: Henry Holt, 1873), 13–107; G. E. Lessing, *Lessing's Theological Writings,* ed. Henry Chadwick (Stanford: Stanford University Press, 1957), 12–13.

64. Søren Kierkegaard, *The Concept of Dread,* trans. Walter Lowrie (Princeton: Princeton University Press, 1957), 29.

65. Søren Kierkegaard, *Papers and Journals: A Selection,* trans. Alastair Hannay (Harmonds-worth: Penguin, 1996), quote 382.

66. Walter Lowrie, *Kierkegaard* (New York: Oxford University Press, 1938), 8–15; Alastair Hannay, *Kierkegaard: A Biography* (Cambridge: Cambridge University Press, 2001), 30–39; Joakim Garff, *Søren Kierkegaard: A Biography,* trans. Bruce H. Kirmmse (Princeton: Princeton University Press, 2005), 3–9.

67. Hannay, *Kierkegaard: A Biography,* 31–34; Garff, *Søren Kierkegaard: A Biography,* 9–10; Hans Lasson Martensen, *Af mit Levnet,* 3 vols. (Copenhagen: Gyldendal, 1882–83), I:

78–79, reprinted in *Encounters with Kierkegaard: A Life as Seen by His Contemporaries,* ed. Bruce H. Hirmmse, trans. Bruce H. Kirmmse and Virginia R. Laursen (Princeton: Princeton University Press, 1996), 196.

68. See Bruce H. Kirmmse, *Kierkegaard in Golden Age Denmark* (Bloomington: Indiana University Press, 1990); Kirmmse, "'Out with it!': The Modern Breakthrough, Kierkegaard, and Denmark," *The Cambridge Companion to Kierkegaard,* ed. Alastair Hannay and Gordon D. Marino (Cambridge: Cambridge University Press, 1998), 15–39; Walter Lowrie, *A Short Life of Kierkegaard* (Princeton: Princeton University Press, 1942), 22–26; Garff, *Søren Kierkegaard: A Biography,* 10–17, quote 13; Hannay, *Kierkegaard: A Biography,* 36–39.

69. P. E. Lind to H. P. Barfod, September 16, 1869, and Frederik Welding to H. P. Barfod, September 3, 1869, in *Encounters with Kierkegaard: A Life as Seen by His Contemporaries,* "he knew," 11, "his most," 8; Kierkegaard, *Papers and Journals: A Selection,* entry of 1854, "slight," 593–594; see Lowrie, *A Short Life of Kierkegaard,* 42–43; Hannay, *Kierkegaard: A Biography,* 42–44; Garff, *Søren Kierkegaard: A Biography,* 17–22; *Encounters with Kierkegaard: A Life as Seen by His Contemporaries,* 3–18.

70. Hannay, *Kierkegaard: A Biography,* 121–125; Garff, *Søren Kierkegaard: A Biography,* 131–138. George Brandes, the originator of the psycho-biographical tradition in Kierkegaard biography, favored the infidelity explanation; see Brandes, *Den unge Søren Kierkegaard* (Copenhagen: Levin & Munksgaard, 1929).

71. Kierkegaard, entry of 1846, *Papers and Journals: A Selection,* 204; Peter Kierkegaard quote in Garff, *Søren Kierkegaard: A Biography,* 136; see Garff, *Søren Kierkegaard: A Biography,* 132–137.

72. Søren Kierkegaard, *The Point of View for My Work as an Author: A Report to History,* trans. Walter Lowrie (New York: Oxford University Press, 1939), 78.

73. Garff, *Søren Kierkegaard: A Biography,* 102.

74. Kierkegaard, *The Concept of Dread,* 143; Kierkegaard, *Journals and Papers: A Selection,* "lunatic," 1837, 72; see Lowrie, *A Short Life of Kierkegaard,* 92–127; Hannay, *Kierkegaard: A Biography,* 89–90.

75. Søren Kierkegaard, entry of May 19, 1838, in Kierkegaard, *Journals and Papers,* 7 vols., ed. and trans. Howard V. Hong and Edna H. Hong (Bloomington: Indiana University Press, 1967–78), "indescribable joy," 5: 5324; Kierkegaard, entry of May 12, 1839, "it's all inexplicable," in Kierkegaard, *Journals and Papers: A Selection,* 102.

76. Kierkegaard, entry of May 19, 1838, *Journals and Papers,* 5: 5324.

77. Søren Kierkegaard, entry of June 29, 1855, in Kierkegaard, *Papers and Journals: A Selection,* 642; Kirmmse, "'Out With It!': The Modern Breakthrough, Kierkegaard, and Denmark," 27.

78. Søren Kierkegaard, *The Concept of Irony, with Continual Reference to Socrates,* trans. Howard V. Hong and Edna H. Hong (Princeton: Princeton University Press, 1989); see Hannay, *Kierkegaard: A Biography,* 131–132; "Søren and Regine: The Engagement and Afterwards," *Encounters with Kierkegaard: A Life as Seen by His Contemporaries,* 33–54.

79. Søren Kierkegaard, *Stages on Life's Way,* trans. Howard V. Hong and Edna H. Hong (Princeton: Princeton University Press, 1988), "I do" and "her," 197; Kierkegaard, *Papers and Journals: A Selection,* entry of 1841, "she loved," 141; entry of 1841, "I had placed," 143; entry of September 7, 1849, "suppose" and "'at home," 421–422; see Kierkegaard, *Fear and Trembling* and *Repetition,* ed. and trans. Howard V. Hong and Edna H. Hong (Princeton: Princeton University Press, 1983).

80. See Søren Kierkegaard, *Either/Or,* 2 vols., ed. and trans. Howard V. Hong and Edna H. Hong (Princeton: Princeton University Press, 1987); Kierkegaard, *Prefaces: Light Read-*

ing for Certain Classes as the Occasion May Require, by Nicolaus Notabene, trans. William McDonald (Tallahassee: Florida State University Press, 1989); Kierkegaard, *Eighteen Upbuilding Discourses,* ed. and trans. Howard V. Hong and Edna H. Hong (Princeton: Princeton University Press, 1990).

81. Martensen, *Af mit Levnet,* I: 78–79, reprinted in *Encounters with Kierkegaard: A Life as Seen by His Contemporaries,* 196; see *Between Hegel and Kierkegaard: Hans L. Martensen's Philosophy of Religion,* ed. Curtis L. Thompson and David J. Kangas (Atlanta: Scholars Press, 1997).

82. Søren Kierkegaard, journal entry of August 1, 1835, Kierkegaard, *Papers and Journals: A Selection, 32; see The Journals of Kierkegaard,* trans. Alexander Dru (New York: Harper Torchbooks, 1959), 44–48; Niels Thulstrup, *Kierkegaard's Relation to Hegel,* trans. George L. Stengren (Princeton: Princeton University Press, 1980), 14–38.

83. Kierkegaard, *Papers and Journals: A Selection,* "I grew up," June 1, 1835, 30; "can never," October 17, 1835, 40–41; "people understand," February 1836, 49.

84. Kierkegaard, *The Concept of Irony,* 272–329, quotes 217, 327.

85. Kierkegaard, entry of 1850, *Journals and Papers,* 4: 4281.

86. Kierkegaard, entry of 1843, *Journals and Papers: A Selection,* 162; see Garff, *Søren Kierkegaard: A Biography,* 195–199.

87. Garff, *Søren Kierkegaard: A Biography,* 218–222, quotes 219.

88. Signe Laessøe to Hans Christian Andersen, April 7, 1843, in *Encounters with Kierkegaard: A Life as Seen by His Contemporaries,* 57.

89. Howard V. Hong and Edna H. Hong, "Historical Introduction" to Kierkegaard, *The Concept of Irony,* x–xiv; Thulstrup, *Kierkegaard's Relation to Hegel,* 262–281; Friedrich A. Trendelenburg, *Logische Untersuchungen* (Berlin: G. Bethge, 1840); Trendelenburg, *Die logische Frage in Hegel's System* (Leipzig: F. A. Brockhaus, 1843); Trendelenburg, *Elementa logices Aristoteleae* (Berlin: G. Bethge, 1844).

90. Søren Kierkegaard, *Concluding Unscientific Postscript to Philosophical Fragments,* trans. David Swenson and Walter Lowrie (Princeton: Princeton University Press, 1941), quote 552.

91. Paul Sponheim, *Kierkegaard on Christ and Christian Coherence* (New York: Harper & Row, 1968); Stephen N. Dunning, *Kierkegaard's Dialectic of Inwardness* (Princeton: Princeton University Press, 1985); John Elrod, *Being and Existence in Kierkegaard's Pseudonymous Works* (Princeton: Princeton University Press, 1975); Sylvia Walsh, *Living Poetically, Kierkegaard's Existential Aesthetics* (University Park: Pennsylvania State University Press, 1994); Louis P. Pojman *The Logic of Subjectivity: Kierkegaard's Philosophy of Religion* (Birmingham: University of Alabama, 1984); see Roger Poole, "The Unknown Kierkegaard: Twentieth-Century Receptions," in *The Cambridge Companion to Kierkegaard,* 61–64.

92. Louis Mackey, *Points of View: Readings of Kierkegaard* (Tallahassee: Florida State University Press, 1986), quote xxii–xxiii; Roger Poole, *Kierkegaard: The Indirect Communication* (Charlottesville: University of Virginia Press, 1993), quotes 7, 9; Poole, "The Unknown Kierkegaard: Twentieth-Century Receptions," 66–72; see Mark C. Taylor, *Altarity* (Chicago: University of Chicago Press, 1987); Taylor, *Journeys to Selfhood: Hegel and Kierkegaard* (Berkeley: University of California Press, 1980); Taylor, *After God* (Chicago: University of Chicago Press, 2007); Sylviane Agacinski, *Aparté: Conceptions and Deaths of Søren Kierkegaard,* trans. Kevin Newmark (Tallahassee: Florida State University Press, 1988).

93. For interpretations of Kierkegaard that aim for a similar balance, see Merold Westphal, *Becoming a Self: A Reading of Kierkegaard's Concluding Scientific Postscript* (West

Lafayette: Purdue University Press, 1996); and H. A. Nielsen, *Where the Passion Is: A Reading of Kierkegaard's Philosophical Fragments* (Tallahassee: Florida State University Press, 1983).

94. Søren Kierkegaard, *Philosophical Fragments, or, A Fragment of Philosophy, by Johannes Climacus,* trans. David F. Swenson and Howard V. Hong (Princeton: Princeton University Press, 1962), quotes 3, 6, 7.

95. Ibid., quotes 13, 14.

96. Ibid., 16.

97. Ibid., 17.

98. Ibid., 22.

99. Ibid., 43, 45.

100. Ibid., quotes 46, 64.

101. Ibid., quotes 68, 76, 129.

102. Ibid., quote 130.

103. Ibid., 139; see M. Jamie Ferreira, "Faith and the Kierkegaardian Leap," *The Cambridge Companion to Kierkegaard,* 207–234.

104. Kierkegaard, *Concluding Unscientific Postscript,* quotes 235, 236, 19.

105. Ibid., quotes 3, 4; see Niels Thulstrup, "Commentator's Introduction" to Kierkegaard, *Philosophical Fragments,* xciv.

106. Kierkegaard, *Concluding Unscientific Postscript,* quotes 18, 30.

107. Ibid., quotes 31, 33.

108. Ibid., quote 50.

109. Ibid., quote 55.

110. Ibid., quote 61.

111. Ibid., quotes 61, 65.

112. Ibid., quote 96.

113. Ibid., 99–100; see Trendelenburg, *Logische Untersuchungen*; Trendelenburg, *Die logische Frage in Hegel's System*; Westphal, *Becoming a Self: A Reading of Kierkegaard's Concluding Unscientific Postscript,* 87–89.

114. Kierkegaard, *Concluding Unscientific Postscript,* quote 103; G. W. F. Hegel, *Science of Logic,* trans. A. V. Miller (London: George Allen & Unwin, 1969), 25–29, 43–64.

115. Kierkegaard, *Concluding Unscientific Postscript,* quote 107.

116. Ibid., quotes 116, 142.

117. Ibid., quote 150.

118. Ibid., quotes 176; see C. Stephen Evans, *Kierkegaard's "Fragments" and "Postscript": The Religious Philosophy of Johannes Climacus* (Atlantic Highlands, NJ: Humanities Press, 1983); Evans, *Passionate Reason: Making Sense of Kierkegaard's Philosophical Fragments* (Bloomington: Indiana University Press, 1992).

119. Kierkegaard, *Concluding Unscientific Postscript,* 176.

120. Ibid., 176.

121. Ibid., 177.

122. Ibid., 177–178.

123. Ibid., 182.

124. Ibid., 190.

125. Ibid., 199–200.

126. Ibid., quotes 205, 216, 219.

127. Ibid., 223–224; see J. G. Hamann, *Sämtliche Werke,* 2 vols., ed. J. Nadler (Vienna: Herder), 1957; Friedrich Heinrich Jacobi, *wider Mendelssohns Beschuldigungen betreffend die Briefe über die Lehre des Spinoza* (Leipzig: Bey Georg Joachim Goeschen, 1786);

Jacobi, *F. H. Jacobi: The Main Philosophical Writings and the Novel "Allwill,"* ed. and trans. George di Giovanni (Montreal: McGill-Queen's University Press, 1994); Jacobi, *David Hume über den Glauben, oder, Idealismus und Realismus* (1787; reprint, New York: Garland, 1983).

128. Kierkegaard, *Concluding Unscientific Postscript*, 292–293, 296, quote 292. Ronald Green, in *Kant and Kierkegaard: The Hidden Debt* (Albany: State University of New York Press, 1992), argues that Kierkegaard was essentially a Kantian who concealed his debt to Kant. This thesis fastens on Kantian differences with Hegel that are certainly there in Kierkegaard. However, the point of Climacus' polemic was to buttress his case for the very anti-Kantian religion of Religiousness B.

129. Kierkegaard, *Concluding Unscientific Postscript*, 339.

130. Ibid., 386–493; see George Pattison, *Kierkegaard: The Aesthetic and the Religious* (London: Macmillan, 1992); Sylvia Walsh, *Living Christianly: Kierkegaard's Dialectic of Christian Existence* (University Park: Pennsylvania State University Press, 2005).

131. Kierkegaard, *Concluding Unscientific Postscript*, quote 492.

132. Ibid., 493–508, quote 507.

133. Ibid., quotes 517, 519.

134. Ibid., quotes 523, 535.

135. Ibid., 537–544; see Søren Kierkegaard, *The Book on Adler*, trans. Howard V. Hong and Edna H. Hong (Princeton: Princeton University Press, 1998).

136. Kierkegaard, *Concluding Unscientific Postscript*, quote 548; see Wanda Warren Berry, "The Heterosexual Imagination and Aesthetic Experience in Kierkegaard's *Either/Or, Part One,*" *International Kierkegaard Commentary: Either/Or, Part One*, vol. 3 (Macon: Mercer University Press, 1995); Berry, "Kierkegaard and Feminism: Apologetic, Repetition, and Dialogue," in *Kierkegaard in Post/Modernity*, eds. Martin J. Matustik and Merold Westphal (Bloomington: Indiana University Press, 1995), 110–124.

137. Kierkegaard, *Concluding Unscientific Postscript*, quotes 551, 553.

138. "Goldschmidt and the Corsair Affair," *Encounters with Kierkegaard: A Life as Seen by His Contemporaries*, 65–88; Garff, *Søren Kierkegaard: A Biography*, 375–402; Lowrie, *A Short Life of Kierkegaard*, 92–127; Hannay, *Kierkegaard: A Biography*, 317–324.

139. Meïr Aron Goldschmidt, *Livs Erindringer og Resultater* I (Copenhagen: Gyldendal, 1877), 214–216, reprinted in *Encounters with Kierkegaard: A Life as Seen by His Contemporaries*, 65–77, quotes 75.

140. Kierkegaard, *Papers and Journals: A Selection*, "everything is" and "every journeyman," March 1846, 213, 216; March 16, 1846, "endless nonsense," 220; 1846, "listen, now," 219.

141. Ibid., 1846, "when I," 228; March 1846, "solitary," 215.

142. Ibid., 1847, "my existence," 266; 1847, "love is," 268; 1847, "I commit," 278.

143. Søren Kierkegaard, *Upbuilding Discourses in Various Spirits*, trans. Howard V. Hong and Edna H. Hong (Princeton: Princeton University Press, 2005); Kierkegaard, *Works of Love*, trans. Howard V. Hong (New York: Harper and Row, 1962); Kierkegaard, *Christian Discourses*, trans. Walter Lowrie (London: Oxford University Press, 1940); Kierkegaard, *Without Authority: The Lily in the Field and the Bird of the Air/Two Ethical-Religious Essays/Three Discourses at the Communion on Fridays, An Upbuilding Discourse/ Two Discourses at the Communion on Fridays*, trans. Howard V. Hong and Edna H. Hong (Princeton: Princeton University Press, 1997); Kierkegaard, *For Self-Examination/Judge for Yourself!*, trans. Howard V. Hong and Edna H. Hong (Princeton: Princeton University Press, 1990).

144. Kierkegaard, *Journals and Papers*, "I am," VI: 6317.

145. Søren Kierkegaard, *The Sickness Unto Death: A Christian Psychological Exposition for Upbuilding and Awakening,* trans. Howard V. Hong and Edna H. Hong (Princeton: Princeton University Press, 1980), quote 13.

146. Ibid., quote 15.

147. Ibid., quotes 18, 22.

148. Ibid., quotes 35, 41.

149. Ibid., quotes 80, 85.

150. Ibid., 85–86.

151. Ibid., 87.

152. Ibid., quote 117.

153. Kierkegaard, *Papers and Journals: A Selection,* entry of 1850, 508–510, quote 508; Hannay, *Kierkegaard: A Biography,* 390–391.

154. Søren Kierkegaard, *Practice in Christianity,* trans. Howard V. Hong and Edna H. Hong (Princeton: Princeton University Press, 1991), quote 224; see Kierkegaard, *Papers and Journals: A Selection,* entry of 1850, 510.

155. Kierkegaard, *Practice in Christianity,* 227.

156. Kierkegaard, *Papers and Journals: A Selection,* entry of 1849, 447.

157. Ibid., entry of 1850, quote 485.

158. Ibid., entry of 1850, 508–510, quotes 509.

159. Hans Lassen Martensen, *Den christelige Dogmatik* (Copenhagen: C. A. Reitzel, 1850), quote iv; English edition, Martensen, *Christian Dogmatics: Compendium of the Doctrines of Christianity,* trans. William Urwick (Edinburgh: T. & T. Clark, 1895); Garff, *Søren Kierkegaard: A Biography,* 576–580, preface citation 580. The preface was cut from the English edition.

160. Kierkegaard, *Papers and Journals: A Selection,* entry of 1849, quote 447.

161. Martensen, *Den christelige Dogmatik,* 407; Kierkegaard, *Papers and Journals: A Selection,* entry of 1850, "a web," 476; entry of 1849, "aroused," and "he is," 439; ibid, entry of 1849, 401; ibid., entry of 1849, 411; entry of 1850, 484–485. The English edition of Martensen's text reads, "He cannot accomplish his sanctification by leading an egotistic, morbid, and isolated life," Martensen, *Christian Dogmatics,* 396. See Garff, *Søren Kierkegaard: A Biography,* 579.

162. Kierkegaard, *Papers and Journals: A Selection,* entry of 1849, "not one," 410; entry of 1849, "what an," 404; entry of 1849, "geniuses," 405.

163. Ibid., entry of August 24, 1849, 412–419; entry of September 7, 1849, 421–422; entry of 1849, 432–432; entry of 1849, 446; entry of May 1852, 538–541, "grandest" and "triumphant," 541.

164. Ibid., entry of 1849, 435.

165. Ibid., entry of 1850, "just when," 494; entry of 1850, "dribbling," 511.

166. Ibid., entry of 1852, 535–537, quotes 536.

167. Ibid., entry of 1854, "ridiculous," "most repellent," "once I'm," 605; entry of 1854, "the *docents,*" "demoralized," and "the infamy," 608.

168. Ibid., entry of 1850, 491.

169. Ibid., entry of 1854, 575.

170. Søren Kierkegaard, *For Self-Examination/Judge for Yourself!,* trans. Howard V. Hong and Edna H. Hong, quotes 68; Kierkegaard, *Papers and Journals: A Selection,* entry of 1852, 550.

171. Søren Kierkegaard, "Was Bishop Mynster a 'Truth-Witness,' one of 'the Authentic Truth-Witnesses' – Is *This the Truth?*" in Kierkegaard, *The Moment and Late Writings,* trans. Howard V. Hong and Edna H. Hong (Princeton: Princeton University Press, 1998), 3–6, quotes 5, 6.

172. Kierkegaard, *Papers and Journals: A Selection,* entry of March 1, 1854, "melancholic," 568; entry of 1854, "the state," 621; entry of 1854, "alas," 607.

173. Hans Lassen Martensen, "On the Occasion of Dr. S. Kierkegaard's Article in *Faedre-landet, no. 295,"* in Kierkegaard, *The Moment and Late Writings,* 360–367, quotes 362; see Garff, *Søren Kierkegaard: A Biography,* 734–736; Kirmmse, *Kierkegaard in Golden Age Denmark,* "sickly" and "unfaithful," 482–483.

174. Martensen, "On the Occasion of Dr. S. Kierkegaard's Article in *Faedrelandet, no. 295,"* quotes 362; Martensen, *Af mit Levnet,* III: 12–23, reprinted in *Encounters with Kierkegaard: A Life as Seen by His Contemporaries,* 201–205, quotes 201.

175. Søren Kierkegaard, "The Point at Issue with Bishop Martensen, as Christianly Decisive for the, Christianly Viewed, Dubious Previously Ecclesiastical Order," in Kierkegaard, *The Moment and Late Writings,* 19–24, quotes 22, 23.

176. Kierkegaard, *Papers and Journals: A Selection,* entry of December 1854, 637–638.

177. Ibid., entry of 1855, "these greedy," 640; Søren Kierkegaard, "That Bishop Martensen's Silence is (1) Christianly Indefensible; (2) Ludicrous; (3) Obtuse-Sagacious; (4) in More Than One Regard Contemptible," in Kierkegaard, *The Moment and Late Writings,* 79–85, quote 79.

178. Søren Kierkegaard, "That the Pastors Are Cannibals, and in the Most Abominable Way," in Kierkegaard, *The Moment and Late Writings,* 321–323; quote 321; Kierkegaard, "The Official/the Personal," ibid., "formula," 172; Kierkegaard, "What Christ Judges of Official Christianity," ibid., 129–137, "but people," 135;

179. Kierkegaard, ibid., "What I Call an Optical Illusion," ibid., 329–331, "with his," 329; "yet the," 330.

180. Søren Kierkegaard, "The Measure of Difference and Thereby in Turn the Actual Difficulty with Which I Have to Contend," ibid., 206–210, "the entire," 208; see Garff, *Søren Kierkegaard: A Biography,* 766–768.

181. Søren Kierkegaard to Michael Andersen Kierkegaard, May 2, 1855, in Kierkegaard, *Letters and Documents,* trans. Henrik Rosenmeier (Princeton: Princeton University Press, 1978), 418–419; Kierkegaard, "Exordium," in Kierkegaard, *The Moment and Late Writings,* "by nature," 92, "true earnestness," 91.

182. Kierkegaard, *Papers and Journals: A Selection,* entry of August 30, 1855, "the basic," 645; Kierkegaard, "My Task," *The Moment and Late Writings,* 340–347, "I quite," 340–341; "there is not," 343; "I was never," 344. Nietzsche resolved to read Kierkegaard, but fell into insanity shortly afterward.

183. Kierkegaard, "My Task," quotes 346, 347.

184. Garff, *Søren Kierkegaard: A Biography,* 770.

185. "Boesen's Account of His Hospital Conversations with Kierkegaard," in *Encounters with Kierkegaard: A Life as Seen by His Contemporaries,* 121–128, quotes 125; see Garff, *Søren Kierkegaard: A Biography,* 787; Hannay, *Kierkegaard: A Biography,* 412–415.

186. Hans Lassen Martensen to L. Gude, November 18, 1855, in *Encounters with Kierke-gaard: A Life as Seen by His Contemporaries,* "the nation's," 135; Hannay, *Kierkegaard: A Biography,* "the vision," 422.

187. Martensen, *Af mit Levnet,* I: 78–79, reprinted in *Encounters with Kierkegaard: A Life as Seen by His Contemporaries,* "the sickly," 196.

188. Martensen, *Af mit Levnet,* II: 140–148, reprinted in *Encounters with Kierkegaard: A Life as Seen by His Contemporaries,* 196–201, quotes 199, 200.

189. Martensen, *Af mit Levnet,* III: 12–23, reprinted in *Encounters with Kierkegaard: A Life as Seen by His Contemporaries,* 201–205, quotes 202, 203, 204, 205.

190. See Kierkegaard's *International Reception: Southern, Central, and Eastern Europe,* ed. Jon Stewart (London: Ashgate, 2009).

191. "Hans Brøchner on Kierkegaard," *Encounters with Kierkegaard: A Life as Seen by His Contemporaries,* 230–231.

192. Lowrie, *A Short Life of Kierkegaard,* 208, 209.

193. Ibid., 209.

6

Neo-Kantian Historicism
Albrecht Ritschl, Adolf von Harnack,
Wilhelm Herrmann, Ernst Troeltsch,
and the Ritschlian School

In the 1850s Albrecht Ritschl, a young theologian trained in Tübingen School historicism, judged that German theology had made bad bargains by shortchanging the social and historical aspects of Christianity and subordinating scriptural idioms to the concepts of Schleiermacher and Hegel. In the 1860s he began to do something about it. In the 1870s he put theology on a different track by playing up historical criticism, stressing the social character of the gospel, and reclaiming Kantian modesty. Modern theology, in Ritschl's view, despite accepting historical criticism, usually tried to get around it. Modern theologians were too defensive in dealing with history. Instead of relying on metaphysics and immunization strategies, theology needed to reclaim the kingdom-oriented religion of Jesus and embrace historical consciousness. The school that he launched swept the field by doing so.

The Ritschlian School took control of theology in late nineteenth-century Germany, not without significant opposition. Guardians of conservative orthodoxies defended them in every locale and tradition. Epigones of Schleiermacher and Hegel retained important positions in the field. Kantian liberals, averse to church and devoted to freethinking culture, continued to regard themselves as the only real liberals. But from 1880 to 1920 nearly all the major theological thinkers were Ritschlians, and budding theologians flocked to Germany to hear them.[1]

One was the major theological figure of his generation, Adolf von Harnack. Another was the founder of the Ritschlian School, Wilhelm Herrmann. Another was the leader of the history of religions school, Ernst Troeltsch. Other leading Ritschlians within Germany alone included Johannes Gottschick, Theodore Häring, Julius Kaftan, Ferdinand Kattenbusch, Friedrich Loofs, Martin Rade, Max Reischle, Friedrich Traub, and Georg Wobbermin. All grappled with Ritschl's historicism, judging that he got it approximately right (Harnack), or took it too far (Herrmann), or did not take it far enough (Troeltsch). Liberal theology at its high tide projected a sunny, confident, outward-reaching progressivism even as it debated whether it had a secure historical

Kantian Reason and Hegelian Spirit: The Idealistic Logic of Modern Theology, First Edition. Gary Dorrien.
© 2012 John Wiley & Sons, Ltd. Published 2015 by John Wiley & Sons, Ltd.

basis, though Troeltsch cautioned that all modern progress could be reversed. Every liberal tradition before the Ritschlian ascendancy was tempted to say, even when it resisted doing so, that theology needed no historical basis but had one anyway. The Ritschlian School was supposed to be an exception, but after it was accused of not being sufficiently historicist, even the Ritschlian School produced a theology claiming that Christianity didn't really need whatever historical basis it possessed. On this defining issue there were different Ritschlian theologies in Germany. On German nationalism and culture-Protestantism, there was more agreement, which proved to be fatal for German liberal theology. In every case, Ritschlian theology was as idealistic as the Mediating and Hegelian traditions that it spurned.[2]

Ritschlian Theology

Albrecht Ritschl was born to theology and the Prussian Union Church, the state church that united the Lutheran and Calvinist communions despite intense opposition from Lutherans. His father, George Karl Ritschl, was a formidable, Lutheran, conservative bishop of the state church. In seminary Albrecht dropped his father's theological conservatism but retained his Lutheran piety, ecumenism, and moralism, including his upper-class sense of social responsibility. Albrecht began his theological studies at Bonn, where he studied under conservative mediationist Immanuel Nitzsch; he liberalized a bit at Halle, where he earned a doctorate in 1843 under mediationist Julius Müller and neo-pietist F. A. Tholuck; he liberalized a bit more under mediationist Richard Rothe at Heidelberg; and in 1845 he finally won his father's reluctant permission to study with Ferdinand Christian Baur at Tübingen, where Ritschl promptly converted to Baur's historicism.[3]

Ritschl's relationship with Baur was stormy, competitive, brief, and crucial to his theological development. By then Baur had lived down his influence on David Friedrich Strauss and built the Tübingen School into a powerhouse. He taught Ritschl to interpret Christianity as a total historical reality and to look for Hegelian triads in whatever he undertook. Following Strauss, Baur had adopted Hegel's concept of the self-disclosure of Spirit in and through historical process, employing the conventional rendering of Hegel's dialectic as thesis-antithesis-synthesis. In Baur's telling, early Christianity featured a struggle between the "Judaizing" and "Hellenizing" factions of the early church, represented respectively by the Jerusalem-based apostles (especially Peter) and the Hellenistic Gentile converts to Christianity, whose perspective was championed by Paul. According to this scheme, the Johannine literature was a synthesis of the Jewish-Hellenistic conflict, which led to Catholicism.[4]

This rendering of early Christian history was very influential. Baur developed it in the late 1840s and early 1850s, when Ritschl wrote his first two books, *The Gospel of Marcion and the Gospel of Luke* (1846) and *The Emergence of the Old Catholic Church* (1850). For the most part, Ritschl cast his early work in Baur's mold, but he declared in the second book that historical criticism should be a "pure art" unto itself without depending on a dogmatic or philosophical system.[5]

The Tübingen School was prolific and cutting-edge, contending that Hegelian idealism and historical criticism belonged together. It stood for a scholarly version of

Strauss' ideal, without Strauss' exaggerations and drama. Ritschl's call for a "pure" historicism contradicted Baur's principle that history is empty apart from philosophy, which set off years of tense, contentious, name-calling exchanges among Baur, Ritschl, Eduard Zeller, Albert Schwegler, and other insiders. Baur wanted Ritschl to be his protégé, but bristled at his independence. Ritschl prized his connection to Baur, but also criticized him. Accusations of impudence and bad faith abounded. Finally in 1853 Baur published his major work, *Das Christenthum und die christliche Kirche der drei ersten Jahrhunderte*, provoking a fateful round of position taking. Ritschl contended that the early church was too complex to be explained by Baur's simplistic three-part scheme. In 1856 he wrote to his father, "What a superstition this old Hegelian has in the objective nature of his views ... It is a pity that he has become so obstinate." The following year Ritschl issued a revised edition of his second book, blasting Baur for distorting Christian history. Baur described Catholicism as a synthetic product of the early church's conflict between Judaizers and Hellenizers. Ritschl replied that Catholicism was no synthesis, but rather a negation of Judaism by a triumphant Hellenistic faction that redefined Christianity in its own image. Catholicism stood for corruption and deracination, erasing the Jewish character of Christianity.[6]

Unfortunately, Ritschl attacked one kind of prejudice, anti-Semitism, with another, anti-Catholicism. But anti-Semitism was the greater evil in this context, and harder to oppose. Theologians routinely denigrated the Jewish aspects of Christianity as being more primitive and legalistic than its non-Jewish aspects. Schleiermacher claimed that the "higher elements" in Christianity derived from its non-Jewish sources. Leading biblical scholars such as Julius Wellhausen littered their writings with similar assurances. Ritschl replied that Christianity's worst problem was its historic anti-Jewish bias. Claiming the spirit of Martin Luther for his view, Ritschl played up Luther's polemic against the "Babylonian captivity" of the church and played down Luther's diatribes against Jews. Years later, as the Ritschlian School took over German theology, many Ritschlians casually dropped Ritschl's pro-Jewish view in the name of a bourgeois "simple gospel" that needed very little from its Jewish heritage.[7]

Ritschl sometimes exaggerated Baur's reliance on Hegelian philosophy, which misled generations of scholars after Ritschl became famous and Baur was forgotten. Baur's historical theology was usually grounded in historical research, some of which had a lasting impact on the field. But the break between Baur and Ritschl occurred over a serious disagreement, not a misinterpretation. Baur believed that every theology needs a philosophical basis, Hegel provided the best philosophy, and historical criticism is not a substitute for metaphysical reasoning. Any worthwhile theology must combine historicism and a metaphysical ground. To Ritschl, however, historicism was a golden key that made metaphysical speculation unnecessary. From 1846 to 1864 he taught at Bonn. In 1857 he left church history to become a theologian. In 1864 he moved to Göttingen and changed the field of theology by contending that the essence of Christianity is discovered through historical interpretation.[8]

If Christianity is essentially a movement, Ritschl reasoned, one's context always matters in figuring the meaning of Christian faith. His theology was driven by two principal concerns of his age, the challenge of Darwinian evolution and the bitter disputes between conservative confessionalists and pietists in the Prussian church. As a modern theologian Ritschl was anxious to avoid religious conflicts with science; as a pro-Bismarck defender of the Prussian state, including the state union church, he was appalled at the erosion of the church's moral and social authority. Ritschl's social vision was conservative, but with a reformist tinge; his interpretation of the kingdom of God was strongly ethical, but grounded in his concern to preserve social order and authority; he was frightened by the radicalism of Christian Socialists, even though many of them became Ritschlians.

His solution to the religion and science problem came straight from Kant, with a social twist. Essentially it refashioned Kant's moral interpretation of Christianity and adopted his proposal to expunge metaphysics from theology. Science describes the way things are or appear to be, Ritschl argued, while theology is about the way things should be. Religious knowledge is never disinterested; it consists of value judgments about reality, especially judgments contributing to personal and social good. Ritschl explained in *The Christian Doctrine of Justification and Reconciliation*: (1874): "Religious knowledge moves in independent value-judgments, which relate to man's attitude to the world, and call forth feelings of pleasure and pain, in which man either enjoys the dominion over the world vouchsafed him by God, or feels grievously the lack of God's help to that end."[9]

The goal of true religion is to attain the highest possible good. In Christianity, Ritschl argued, the content of this good is found in the central ideas of the apostolic tradition, a job for historical criticism. The point is not to uncover what Jesus really said. Quests of the historical Jesus kept getting this wrong, feeding the impression that authentic Christianity should be based on whatever historical critics discovered about the Jesus of history. Ritschl urged that Christianity is fundamentally a social-historical movement with a particular religious ethical character. What matters is to uncover the collective Christian experience of value inspired by Jesus: "It would be a mistaken purism were anyone, in this respect, to prefer the less developed statements of Jesus to the forms of apostolic thought."[10]

Ritschl took for granted that Christians should believe that Christianity is the highest form of good religion. What makes a religion good is its concern with value; Christianity is the best religion because it is concerned above all with the realization of social and ethical value. Historical research showed that the essence of Christianity was and is the kingdom of God as valued by the Christian community. But the kingdom is valued as absolute only by those who follow Jesus, Ritschl noted. To others it is a matter of indifference what Jesus taught about sin, redemption, or the kingdom. It follows that Christian truth cannot be grasped outside the Christian community; it can be comprehended only within the inner history of the church's life and practices. The value of the kingdom becomes a matter of knowledge only within the inner history of the church's life. From this perspective, Ritschl taught, Jesus is knowable as the embodiment of humanity's highest ideal; he is the redeemer of humankind who incarnates and inaugurates the realization of the kingdom.[11]

Schleiermacher defined Christianity as a monotheistic faith belonging to the teleological (moral) type of religion, and distinct from other religions "by the fact that in it everything is related to the redemption accomplished by Jesus of Nazareth." To Ritschl this definition was a breakthrough in Christian thought, because it defined Christianity, for the first time, by its relation to the history of religion. But there was a serious problem with Schleiermacher's system, he contended. The correct procedure is to explicate the Christian idea, then compare it with "other species and stages of religion." This approach puts the gospel at the center and confirms the distinct nature of Christianity "by calling the general history of religion to our aid." On first impression Schleiermacher seemed to take this approach, but he failed to explicate the relation between Christianity's generic religious qualities and its distinctive characteristic, because he shortchanged the very thing that he described as Christianity's distinct nature – its teleological character. Ritschl observed, "If the Divine final end is embodied in the Kingdom of God, it is to be expected that the redemption which has come through Jesus should also be related, as a means, to this final end." No topic, however, received "less justice" in Schleiermacher's dogmatics than the end-oriented moral character of Christianity.[12]

Sometimes Schleiermacher construed Christian God-consciousness in relation to redemption, and sometimes by reference to the kingdom. But he never explained the relation between the redeeming work of Christ and the kingdom. This alone yielded a skewed account of Christianity, Ritschl judged. Plus, the whole system operated with a neutral idea of religion and Schleiermacher's abstract monotheism. Even the fact that he referred everything ultimately to redemption through Jesus militated against getting Christianity right. Schleiermacher gave the appearance of working outward from the history of religion, but he did not really take instruction from it. Otherwise he would not have settled on a neutral, unreal definition of religion. Ritschl proved his point by pointing to Schleiermacher's prejudice against Hebrew religion. Schleiermacher got Christianity wrong because he was blind to the deep bonds between Judaism and Christianity. This was a very serious fault, Ritschl concluded, for in Hebrew religion "the concrete conception of the one, supernatural, omnipotent God is bound up with the final end of the Kingdom of God, and with the idea of a redemption."[13]

Christianity, Ritschl stressed, purged the kingdom idea of its nationalism: "In Christianity, the Kingdom of God is represented as the common end of God and the elect community, in such a way that it rises above the natural limits of nationality and becomes the moral society of nations." As the religion of perfect moral value, Christianity presents the possibility of justification and renewal through relation to Christ: "We have in Christianity a culmination of the monotheistic, spiritual, and teleological religion of the Bible in the idea of the perfected spiritual and moral religion." In Christianity, the spiritual realities of redemption and the final end are essential and mutually related. Christ's redemption and kingdom condition each other in the historical experience of the church. At least, this is what Christianity is supposed to be; Ritschl acknowledged that Protestantism often exaggerated personal redemption and ignored the social ethical part. The church needed to learn what it means to pray "thy kingdom come," for the coming of God's reign "is the very purpose of God in the world, as Jesus himself recognized."[14]

Ritschl's image for this double character of the gospel became synonymous with the Ritschlian School: an ellipse determined by two foci, personal redemption and the kingdom of God. Christians know Jesus as their redeemer, but they are also supposed to follow Jesus, who was devoted to the kingdom of God. Ritschl stressed that theology and ethics go together; the mark of true Christianity is its mutually relational double character in which the religious and ethical dimensions perpetually interact and advance through history: "Christianity, then, is the monotheistic, completely spiritual, and ethical religion, which, based on the life of its Author as Redeemer and as Founder of the Kingdom of God, consists in the freedom of the children of God, involves the impulse to conduct from the motive of love, which aims at the moral organization of mankind, and grounds blessedness on the relationship of sonship to God, as well as on the Kingdom of God."[15]

Before Ritschl stormed the field, modernizing theologians were fond of saying that Christianity is a life, not a doctrine. Coleridge-quoters turned this saying into a cliché. In Ritschlian theology Christianity became a movement, not a doctrine. Ritschl's emphasis on the practical and ethical mission of Christianity inspired liberals to change the world with the gospel at the very time that the church had to cope with new challenges to belief from science and secular culture. He urged that Christian faith is outward-moving, public, historical, and socially engaged. Theology, rightly approached, does not concern itself with questions studied by science, it takes a pass on metaphysical questions, and it refuses to retreat to an inward spirituality walled off from public criticism. Metaphysical reason cannot justify its distinctions between physical and spiritual realities, Ritschl contended. Thus it has nothing to contribute to the Christian interpretation of God's relation to the world. Ritschl was emphatic that theologians do not understand the nature of the soul or the interrelations of God's being: "We know nothing of a self-existence of the soul, of a self-enclosed life of the spirit above or behind those functions in which it is active, living, and present to itself as a being of special worth." Christian theology, rightly approached, is about God's redemptive and ethical *effects* in history, things that people can see and act on.[16]

This strategy was enormously influential in theology. It claimed to recover the religion of Jesus for modern Christianity, especially the kingdom of God. It created a dominant theological school in Germany, made Ritschl a historic figure in modern theology, and provided a theological basis for the Social Gospel movement in North America. It was also ironic, as Ritschl's star fell after his followers took over the field in the late nineteenth century. The Ritschlian movement offers the rare example of a school outshining its founder. Ritschl was short on personal magnetism, his writing style was clumsy and verbose, his politics were stodgy and conservative compared to the North American social gospelers that he influenced, and some of his followers surpassed him in scholarly depth, creativity, and lasting influence.

Chief among them in Germany were Adolf von Harnack, Ernst Troeltsch, and Wilhelm Herrmann. Harnack made historic contributions to the field of church history and popularized a bourgeois kernel-and-husk version of Ritschlian theology. Troeltsch developed the history of religions approach to religion by de-Christianizing Ritschl's historicism. Herrmann founded the Ritschlian School as a movement and subsequently fashioned an existential Schleiermacherian version of Ritschlian theology that influenced Karl Barth. Even in courses on dogmatics, Ritschl's writings faded from memory, as Julius Kaftan and Theodor Häring updated Ritschlian theology.

Afterward Ritschl fell further from memory. When the dialectical theologians turned against liberal theology in the 1920s, they attacked Schleiermacher, Harnack, Herrmann, and Troeltsch, but ignored Ritschl, who no longer mattered. Barth delivered a brutal coup de grace, summarily dismissing Ritschl as a cultural Protestant accommodationist – in Barth's words, "the very epitome of the national-liberal German bourgeois of the age of Bismarck." But the Ritschlian idea of a gospel-centered and socially oriented liberal historicism far outlasted Ritschl's provincial version of it.[17]

Adolf von Harnack and the Spirit of Liberal Protestant Theology

The greatest Ritschlian, Harnack, never doubted that Ritschl put theology on the right track by viewing Christianity as essentially historical and social-ethical. Like Ritschl, Harnack came to the church, academy, and German establishment by family tradition, though in his case the German part had to be struggled for, in Russian territory. Born in 1851 in Dorpat (today Tartu), a Russian majority town in Livonia (then a province of Russia, today in Estonia), Harnack belonged to the German-speaking, Prussian nationalist elite that ruled his hometown. He also belonged to the German generation that witnessed the transformation of the North German Federation into the German Empire in 1871, which turned the Prussian King Wilhelm I into the German Emperor, which was not quite the same thing (to the relief of Austrians, federated monarchs, and Swiss) as being Emperor of Germany. Both of these identity markers cast a long shadow over Harnack's life and thought.

At the time of Adolf's birth his father, Theodosius Harnack, was a professor of church history and homiletics at Dorpat. A pastoral theologian for most of his career at Lutheran universities, Theodosius was relentlessly serious in disposition, and devoted to Martin Luther. In 1853 he moved his family to Erlangen, a Lutheran university town in Bavaria, but in 1865 he brought them back to Dorpat, which Adolf Harnack considered home for the rest of his life.[18]

There Adolf belonged to a German aristocracy that fought off all encroachments on the superiority of German culture, politics, and religion. A brilliant student – his four siblings, including a twin brother, were also gifted – he was deeply influenced by his father's scholarly discipline and his fervor for things German, especially Lutheranism. German historical criticism reached him early, despite his father's theological conservatism. At the age of eighteen, just before he began his university studies at Dorpat, Harnack told a friend: "I am an enthusiastic theologian; I hope to find in this scholarly discipline the *way* towards solving the major problems of our life ... I do not desire to be given the fullness of ready-made statements of faith, rather, I want to produce every statement in that web by myself and then make it my own."[19]

That was very close to how Harnack went on to do theology. At Dorpat he studied under his father and Moritz von Engelhardt, learning the methods of historical scholarship. In 1872 he enrolled at the University of Leipzig for his doctoral dissertation and habilitation-dissertation, finished each in one year, and joined the Leipzig faculty in 1875. From the beginning he argued that rigorous historical criticism was the key to renewing theology as an academic discipline, and he was staggeringly productive. In 1876 Harnack founded (with his friend Emil Schürer) a theological journal, *Theologische Literaturzeitung,* which soon became a major player in the field. The following year he met Ritschl for the first time and bonded with him, writing shortly afterward: "The future of Protestantism as a religion and a spiritual power lies in the direction which Ritschl has indicated."[20]

Ritschl provided the theology for the liberal historicist option; Harnack provided a grand scale historical foundation for it. Essentially he interpreted the history of Christian thought and practice as an integral part of the world's intellectual history. In 1879 Harnack moved to the University of Giessen in Hesse, where he began his *History of Dogma* (an enormous three-volume work published in English in seven volumes) and took over as sole editor of *Theologische Literaturzeitung*. Subsequently he taught at Marburg from 1886 to 1888, where he forged a close friendship with Herrmann. At both career stops his scholarly reputation soared, as did his reputation for provoking church conservatives.[21]

Harnack used *Theologische Literaturzeitung* as a forum for his views, battling for liberal theology and writing hundreds of punchy book reviews that sorted out who was worth reading and who was not. His commanding stewardship of the journal would have been enough to make him a controversial figure; as it was, for Harnack the journal was a sideline enterprise, an augur of his remarkable capacity for scholarly and administrative productivity. In 1885 the first volume of his *History of Dogma* appeared, stoking a field-wide debate over his liberalism. Conservatives protested that Harnack treated Christian scripture and doctrine as source material, not as norms for personal faith; he exaggerated the corrupting influence of Hellenization on Christian doctrine; and he sprinkled his writings with harmful denials, such as that Jesus did not institute baptism in the name of the Trinity, Ephesians and the gospel of John were not apostolic, and the Virgin Birth was not historical. Theodosius Harnack was one of the protesting conservatives, grieving publicly that the author of *History of Dogma* evidently did not believe in Christ's resurrection and other fundamental Christian doctrines. Thus, his son was not really a Christian theologian.[22]

This verdict wounded Harnack, as did its opposite, pressed by academic critics, that he was too churchy and insistently Christian to be a real academic. In the latter telling, Harnack allowed his loyalty to liberal Protestantism to override his academic objectivity; thus his scholarship yielded liberal Protestant readings of Jesus and the early church. Harnack replied that there had to be a third way between the conservative orthodoxy of the churches and the increasingly secular disbelief of the academy. Schleiermacher made a good start, but Ritschl made the essential course correction by going historical. Mere exegesis would never move theology forward, and neither would dogmatics; only rigorous historical understanding would unveil what was original and valuable in Christianity. To that end he wrote institutional history as the history of ideas, carefully tracking the development of codes, rules, doctrines, customs, and practices in the history of Christianity, as well as the groups, societies, and states in which these cultural forms and institutions developed, always to show to what extent Christianity carried out the purpose for which it was founded. Always he found that the pure religious purpose of Jesus was corrupted by Hellenization.[23]

The second volume of *History of Dogma* appeared in 1887; the following year Harnack was invited to a church history chair at the nation's most prestigious university, Berlin. He was 37 years old, and already a legendary figure in the field. Volume two stressed that church history was a degenerative story of paganization and authoritarian corruption in which the church replaced its original gospel spirit with a regime of authoritarian Hellenistic doctrines and ecclesiastical structures. Protestant Christianity,

Harnack urged, needed to renew the Reformation by ridding itself of its accumulated pagan superstructure.

The Supreme Council of the Evangelical Church, the highest office of the Prussian state church, replied by vetoing Harnack's appointment to Berlin, warning that rewarding his heretical opinions would be disastrous for German Christianity. The church had to take a stand against allowing a semi-Christian theologian to join the leading theological faculty supported by the state. Harnack and his defenders replied that his *academic* worthiness was not in question (two years later he was elected to the prestigious Academy of Sciences). The question was whether theology was a real academic discipline, free from church dogmatism and control. A bitter, heated, and very public controversy ensued; at its height, in the "year of three Emperors," Emperor Frederick died, leaving it to Emperor Wilhelm II and Chancellor Bismarck to decide whether church conservatives should prevail over the authority and prestige of the academy. In September 1888 Wilhelm II overruled the church office, formally approving Harnack's appointment, adding tartly that he wanted no bigots in his university.[24]

Harnack thrived in Berlin. Students and lecture-grazers from many countries flocked to hear him, especially North Americans; Walter Rauschenbusch and William Adams Brown were among them. At the podium Harnack was a riveting performer with a knack for cutting through tangled webs of doctrine and historical detail. Cordial, eloquent, and gifted with charm, he was skilled at making his historical subjects come alive, which made him adept with lay audiences. Visitors were constantly surprised that his fame and formal manners did not make him unapproachable. Harnack was unmistakably a product of the Prussian aristocracy, but he tempered his presumed superiority with a kindly disposition and a sincere evangelical piety, telling his audiences that Jesus Christ is the central fact of human history. All that came before Jesus and all that came after him must be interpreted in light of his creative personality. Harnack's career was laced with irony, though irony itself was a minor trope for him. To his regret, he was never able to patch his relations with Prussian Church officials, which disqualified him from examining candidates for ordination. He became a towering church leader despite lacking any standing in his own church.

His disciplined clarity was a central feature of his work and a central factor in his vast influence and productivity. Harnack had a clear, plainly liberal theology that attracted people who were mystified by Schleiermacher and even Ritschl. Often he urged that the ancient, evangelical faith of Christianity had to be expressed in a new, simple, and compelling way. In addition, he had a sympathetic imagination that enabled him to explicate vividly the ideas, social contexts, and personalities of figures such as Marcion and Augustine, two of his favorites. William Adams Brown recalled, "I have heard many great lecturers, but Harnack was the only man I could hear for two hours a day for six days in the week, for two years, and at the end, look forward as eagerly to the last lecture as to the first. There was a freshness about his mind, an ability to see things in proportion, that I have never found equaled in any other teacher." To Brown, Harnack was the quintessential theological scholar – "a man of conviction, disciplined by knowledge and tempered with sympathy."[25]

In Berlin Harnack's books kept flowing: four books of speeches and essays, six volumes of New Testament studies, a four-volume history of the Prussian Academy, an introductory survey of the Greek Church Fathers running over 1,000 pages, the final volume of his *History of Dogma,* and a massive two-volume work, *The Mission and Expansion of Christianity in the First Three Centuries,* which contained his own maps and revealed little known sources of early Christianity. In addition to the Prussian Academy of Science he was named to the academies of Amsterdam, Gotenburg, Naples, Oslo, Rome, Stockholm, and Uppsala, and he lectured at universities across Europe and North America. In 1899, students from non-theological faculties at Berlin asked Harnack if he would give them an introductory version of his teaching about the essence of Christianity. That winter he delivered sixteen lectures to a packed house of 600 students from all faculties of the university, plus admirers and church critics. The book version, published under the title, *What Is Christianity?* (1900), instantly rivaled Schleiermacher's *On Religion* as a classic expression of liberal theology, lifting Harnack to another level of international renown.[26]

The abiding exception to this litany of acclaim was the Prussian Church. In 1892 a Prussian Church pastor in Württemberg was deposed for refusing to require sponsors of baptismal candidates to recite the Apostles' Creed as a demonstration of their faith. Harnack avoided an ensuing controversy over the creed, got drawn into it by his students, and plunged in with a typical Harnack opinion. The creed was tolerably acceptable for worship services, he advised, but it was not a good test for ordination candidates. He preferred a shorter statement of faith, in modern language, lacking a Virgin Birth, which set off another conservative church furor against him. Harnack got the blaze going with an article in *Christliche Welt;* his book version went through 27 editions. Any chance that he had of repairing his relations with church leaders died with the first edition.[27]

But Harnack was not content with books, lectures, running a journal, becoming famous, and offending religious conservatives. He seemed never to find enough to do, and the rise of Socialist movements got his attention, mostly by frightening him. Harnack could see radical Christian Socialism coming on the wing of the proletarian movement, which would not be good for Germany or modern Christianity. In 1890 the Kaiser issued several decrees on social questions, encouraging church leaders to defend the Reich's conservative welfare state. Later that year Harnack, Adolf Stöcker, Friedrich Naumann and other Protestant leaders founded the Evangelical Social Congress as a forum for shaping and promulgating German social Christianity.

Stöcker had a conservative, church-centered following that responded to emotional populist rhetoric; Naumann was more political than religious, and got more so while trying to work with church people; Harnack spoke for the group's academic and liberal evangelical mainstream. Stöcker, a court chaplain to Kaiser Wilhelm, espoused an anti-Semitic brand of Christian Socialism aimed at luring the working class away from Social Democracy. In his early career he aimed most of his polemical fire at capitalism and the anti-Christian animus of Social Democracy, restricting his anti-Semitic insults to occasional asides, but in the 1890s he ramped up his popular following by featuring anti-Semitic rants and broadsides. In 1896 Stöcker led his followers out of the Congress to found a rival, culturally conservative group, the Church Social Conference. Naumann, Stöcker's chief rival in the early years of the Congress, was a middle class, intellectually formidable, strongly nationalistic, liberal imperialist and Christian Socialist who supported Wilhelm II, sustained a close friendship with Max Weber, and tried to believe that the church could be an agent for raising the condition of the working class. In the mid-1890s he gave up on the church and entered politics, joining the Reichstag in 1907; in 1919 Naumann became a cofounder of the German Democratic Party. Harnack tried to hold together the Congress, while speaking for a German social gospel mainstream that was more academic than church-centered, yet stressed its connection to the church, and prized its civil manners.[28]

Though Harnack shuddered at the radical politics and anti-clericalism of Social Democracy, he perceived its moral power. Many Congress participants identified with Christian Socialism, blasting the "Godless" ideology of laissez-faire capitalism. Harnack agreed with the latter judgment, calling capitalist ideology "Manchesterism." Any gospel centered civilization had to curb the worst abuses of its economic order, he acknowledged; the abuses of modern industrial society were no exception. But the gospel of Jesus was above politics, focusing on the moral and spiritual character of individuals, and there had to be a third way between radical Socialism and its opposite, British and American capitalism. These were the twin concerns of German social Christianity as Harnack conceived it. It had a social conscience, but focused on individual morality. It left policy questions to experts and denied that the church had any business trying to transform the social order.

Harnack's address to the 1894 Evangelical Social Congress was a milestone in the group's history and collective identity. He argued that the social mission of the church had changed in modern times, but the gospel had not changed, including the limits that it placed on social action. Some Congress conservatives disputed that anything had changed or should have changed; Harnack tried to assure them he was mostly on their side. The church's first and primary obligation was still to preach the gospel of personal faith, he declared. Its second obligation was to strengthen and renew Christian congregations as formative spiritual communities. Harnack lamented that the Social Democratic movement was doing better in this area than the churches: "It has succeeded in creating and maintaining, among a migratory population, and in face of obstacles of every kind, an organization closely knit, operative alike in the cities and the provinces, both national and international. Why could we not do the like?"[29]

He warned that if the churches did not renew themselves as mission-oriented spiritual communities, it was pointless even to speak of the church's social mission; the preconditions for carrying out a social gospel would not exist. Ritschl and the new movements for social Christianity were both right: the church had a mission to do something about the social order. This was especially the case, Harnack observed, in nations like Germany, where "our Church still holds a great and influential place in the State, and in the life of the nation." If the church neglected the social ideals of the gospel, it would be condemned as "an accommodating tool in the hands of an 'Aristocratic Government.'" That was the situation already, Harnack acknowledged; the church had to change it by advancing "evangelical social ideals."[30]

But what did that mean? It did not mean, Harnack admonished, that the church should advocate economic justice, for the gospel has nothing to do with questions of economic policy: "It has nothing to do with such practical questions of social-economics as the nationalization of private property and enterprise, land-tenure reforms, restriction of the legal hours of work, price-regulations, taxation, and insurance." The church was not competent to make pronouncements on economic policy, and even if it acquired the competence, it had no business doing so, since meddling in such matters led straight to secularization. Harnack did not want Christian thinkers to compromise the church's spiritual standing or integrity by taking a position on tax fairness. The gospel was above anything having to do with economic justice or policy.[31]

But "serious moral evils" belonged to a different category, he judged. The church had to oppose prostitution, even if that required meddling in politics. It had to oppose dueling and anything that undermined the sanctity of marriage and family life. It had to support welfare provisions that lent a helping hand to people in distress. It had to speak against class prejudice of every kind. And it had to be an advocate of peace. Harnack was a "peace through strength" type who squared the gospel command to peacemaking with German militarism by claiming that a strong German nation was indispensable to the peace and unity of Europe. He believed that the greatness of Germany rested on two pillars: the German armed forces and German scholarship. From 1908 to the summer of 1914, Harnack spoke up for peace through strength, urging his audiences to step away from the path to war. In 1909 he told a group of British clergy, "On the soil of science and Christianity the cry 'war' is as madness, a cry out of an abyss from which we have long ago emerged."[32]

In Harnack's case, one act of loyalty to Fatherland, Emperor, and culture Protestantism led to another. In 1903 he assumed the presidency of the Evangelical Social Congress. Two years later he added a major commitment to his portfolio, becoming Director General of the Royal Library (renamed the Prussian State Library after World War I). Harnack held these two positions concurrently for six years, greatly expanding the library on Berlin's main avenue, Unter den Linden. In 1911 he gave up the Social Congress presidency because the Emperor had a new job for him, running the Kaiser Wilhelm Gesellschaft, which founded scientific research institutes. Harnack's twin directorships for the Emperor overlapped by ten years. Upon retiring from teaching in 1921 he left the Royal Library, but presided over the research foundation through years of postwar political crisis, monetary deflation, economic depression, and demands to change the foundation's name, which he resisted, until his death in 1930; afterwards it was renamed the Max Planck Gesellschaft.

Harnack never doubted that his social prominence and devotion to highbrow German culture were good for liberal theology, although he lived to see both ridiculed by a postwar generation. He was a personal favorite of Wilhelm II, who prized Harnack as the epitome of Prussian diligence, competence, patriotism, objectivity, and German cosmopolitanism, and who rewarded him with a knighthood in 1914; Harnack was the last scholar in royal Prussia to be honored with hereditary nobility.

At the turn of the twentieth century, in a very different world than the one that he lived to see, Harnack delivered his celebrated lecture series on the essence of Christianity. At the time he was rector of the university, another administrative sideline for him. He spoke extemporaneously without notes, but a student made a stenographic record, which delighted Harnack. A year later *What Is Christianity?* was an international bestseller.

Harnack's operative theology took very little material from the history of Christian doctrine. True Christianity "is something simple and sublime," he told the Berlin students: "It means one thing and one thing only: Eternal life in the midst of time, by the strength and under the eyes of God." Christianity is a religion, he reasoned, and religion was always essentially about the existing human self, not doctrines, ethics, or social order. He loved Goethe's statement that although humanity is always advancing, human beings remain the same. This insight illuminated Harnack's concept of Christianity as the true religion. Religion pertains to the life and condition of the human self that never changes while living in the midst of change, he argued. True religion is always concerned with the fundamental human problems of living, suffering, meaning, and death. And what is the basis of the highest form of religion known to human history? Harnack replied that the answer is both simple and exhaustive; it is "Jesus Christ and his Gospel."[33]

In the spirit of Ritschl, F. C. Baur, and the Tübingen School, Harnack cautioned that this answer is exhaustive because it includes the history of Christianity as a whole. Christianity is not fundamentally a doctrine, but a life, "again and again kindled afresh, and now burning with a flame of its own." To grasp the nature of this dynamic object, one must pay attention to its history: "Just as we cannot obtain a complete knowledge of a tree without regarding not only its root and its stem but also the bark, its branches, and the way in which it blooms, so we cannot form any right estimate of the Christian religion unless we take our stand upon a comprehensive induction that shall cover all the facts of its history." This conviction animated his massive historical scholarship. Cardinal Manning famously quipped that the church overcomes history by dogma. Harnack replied that the very opposite is true: It is only through historical criticism that dogma can be purified. The vocation of the historical theologian is to break the power of the traditions that fossilize Christianity into something alien to the gospel of Jesus.[34]

Harnack's scholarship and his bruising conflicts with the Prussian Church drove him to a free church perspective, though he never actually joined one. His detailed scholarly works and his popular writings both stressed that genuine Christianity was incompatible with the bureaucratic ecclesiastical systems of the Roman Catholic, Orthodox, and Protestant state churches. During the controversy over his appointment to Berlin in 1888 he implored that historical criticism was an indispensable ally of true Christianity. Its purpose was not to destroy biblical faith and church tradition, but to build up the Christian faith on its most credible and compelling basis, which happened to be its original basis.[35]

What Is Christianity? said it eloquently, that the gospel core of Christianity is simple, sublime, and historically relevant. Replying to Strauss on the prevalence of myth and legend in the gospels, Harnack observed that Strauss was a prisoner of his own rationalistic narrowness, lacking a literary or historical understanding of his subject. Thus he failed to comprehend the kind of literature that he attacked. Strauss dismissed as mythical every gospel account that could be questioned on historical grounds, but the gospel writers made no pretense of presenting disinterested historical accounts. Harnack explained that the gospels are not works of history in the modern sense of the term, but testimonies of faith "composed for the work of evangelization." Their purpose is to inspire faith in the person and mission of Jesus.[36]

All four of the gospels are products of Jewish didacticism composed under the short-lived conditions of first-century Jewish Christianity, Harnack explained. They were written by representatives of a diminishing religious community that was in the last stages of its absorption by the Hellenistic church. To treat the gospels as primarily history or myth is to miss their unique character as the faith literature of a disappearing community of memory: "This species of literary art, which took shape partly by analogy with the didactic narratives of the Jews, and partly from catechetical necessities – this simple and impressive form of exposition was, even a few decades later, no longer capable of exact reproduction." That is, with the triumph of Hellenistic Christianity, the peculiar gospel blend of history recounted from the perspective of Jewish Christian faith and tradition became alien to the church. It was no longer a living possession, and the style of gospel expression "was then felt to be something strange but sublime." The question of how to interpret these alien texts became problematic for the early church, and it remained so.[37]

Though Harnack emphasized the distinctive literary character of the gospels, he did not dismiss them as historical sources: "They are not altogether useless as sources of history, more especially as the object with which they were written is not supplied from without, but coincides in part with what Jesus intended." The gospel picture of Jesus' life and teaching is basically reliable, he judged. Strauss was wrong to say that the gospels are riddled with myth, "even if the very indefinite and defective conception of what 'mythical' means in Strauss' application of the word, be allowed to pass." In Harnack's reading, only the infancy and childhood narratives were truly mythical. Strauss treated every miracle story as a mythical invention, but Harnack noted that the modern concept of "miracle" as a violation of the laws of nature was unknown in the ancient world. The gospel writers lived at a time in which marvelous events seemed to happen nearly every day. They lived in a world filled with the sights and sounds of wonder, in which they held little concept of the difference between what is naturally possible and impossible. At this level of awareness, Harnack observed, miracles do not exist, for no one "can feel anything to be an interruption of the order of Nature who does not yet know what the order of Nature is."[38]

It followed that the gospel writers surely did not attribute as much significance to their miracle stories as did modern supernaturalists and rationalists. Moreover, Harnack cautioned, even in the hyperrationalistic age of modernity, our understanding of nature is incomplete and our knowledge of psychic forces is very poor. The discerning gospel reader must keep in view the gulf separating the modern and ancient worlds *and* the limitations of modern understanding. He explained, "Miracles, it is true, do not happen; but of the marvelous and the inexplicable there is plenty. In our present state of knowledge we have become more careful, more hesitating in our judgment, in regard to the stories of the miraculous which we have received from antiquity. That the earth in its course stood still; that a she-ass spoke; that a storm was quieted by a word, we do not believe, and we shall never again believe; but that the lame walked, the blind saw, and the deaf heard, will not be so summarily dismissed as an illusion."[39]

Strauss reduced Christianity to myth, in his case because he wanted to clear the ground for a philosophical substitute for Christianity. Harnack countered that neither the Bible's genuinely mythical elements nor its miracle stories are central to Christianity. "It is not miracles that matter; the question on which everything turns is whether we are helplessly yoked to an inexorable necessity, or whether a God exists who rules and governs, and whose power to compel Nature we can move by prayer and make a part of our experience." Just as Ritschl said very little about the nature of divine reality apart from God's effects upon people in their formation of value judgments,

Harnack eschewed all metaphysical speculation about God, Jesus, and the nature of reality. It was enough to say that Christianity, at its heart, has a threefold message, which Harnack called the Gospel. In his rendering it was the very gospel of Jesus: the kingdom of God, the infinite value of the human soul under the rule and love of God the Father, and the promise of righteousness and eternal life.[40]

This core of Christian teaching and identity is summarized in the Lord's Prayer, he observed. Jesus pointed not to himself, but to the providential care of the Father. His teaching was centered on the reality of the coming kingdom, which Harnack defined as a cooperative social order in which human beings live under the rule of love and conquer their enemies by gentleness. The kingdom begins in the heart of an individual, he explained, "by entering into his soul and laying hold of it." It is "the rule of the holy God in the hearts of individuals." Ultimately, to Harnack, there was no distinction between the God of Jesus Christ and the kingdom proclaimed by him, for "God" and "kingdom" were signifiers for the same spiritual reality: The question of the kingdom "is not a question of angels and devils, thrones and principalities, but of God and the soul, the soul and its God." The business of theology is to faithfully separate this unchanging "kernel," the gospel of Jesus, from the "husk" of its various cultural and doctrinal forms as expressed in the New Testament, ante-Nicene Christianity, and subsequent church history.[41]

Harnack's renown as a preeminent historical theologian lent considerable authority to his constructive proposals. He took a different attitude to Hebrew Scripture than to the New Testament, allowing for greater deconstructive myth criticism in the former case, because he found very little of the gospel in Hebrew Scripture. Harnack acknowledged that the gospel infancy narratives are purely mythical and that mythical elements exist in any biblical story featuring angels, devils, absolute miracles, and predictions of the apocalypse; he told his classes that any story with an angel visitation was obviously shot through with myth. But the core of the gospel is not mythical, he insisted. None of the early church's mythical trappings impinge on its gospel core. The gospel of Jesus is about the soul and its God, not devils or virgin births. In Harnack's telling, a sentence such as "I am the Son of God" was not a gospel statement, but an addition to the gospel. The early church should not be censured for adding to the gospel, he cautioned; understandably, it remembered Jesus in the light of its faith in him. But for modern Christianity, everything depends on keeping the essential distinction clear. Christian faith must not be identified with the church's mythical or doctrinal expressions of its faith in Jesus.

This category included all doctrinal statements about the historicity of the resurrection of Jesus. Harnack distinguished between "the Easter faith" that belongs to the gospel and "the Easter message" that, despite its presence in the earliest forms of Christian preaching, does not belong to the gospel kernel: "The Easter *faith* is the conviction that the crucified one gained a victory over death; that God is just and powerful; that he who is the firstborn among many brethren still lives." This faith is not the end of an argument or a conclusion drawn from historical evidence, he stressed. It is faith in God's sustaining power over death. The gospel story of doubting Thomas, though often misconstrued as a proof-story, is a testimony to gospel faith, in which those who have not seen are exhorted to believe. Harnack observed that this faith is assumed when the disciples on the road to Emmaus are chastised for not believing in the resurrection, "even though the Easter message had not yet reached them." The Easter message, on the other hand, is the church's effort to substantiate and codify its faith in the risen Christ. It contains vivid accounts of Jesus' resurrection appearances and lists of witnesses to them. Harnack placed 1 Corinthians 15 and most of the resurrection accounts in Luke, Matthew and John into this category, as well as any apologetic argument for the resurrection that draws on this evidence.[42]

The problem with the Easter message is the problem of all attempts to rationalize or prove Christian faith claims, he argued. To believe in God on the basis of evidence is to believe in the evidence, not God. In the case of the Easter message, it is to base Easter faith on some reconstruction of the evidence. But the New Testament accounts are too fragmented and inconsistent to bear the weight of this colossal question of faith. How can we base Easter faith on the Easter message when it isn't clear which account or conflation of accounts is the right one? Harnack advised, "Either we must decide to rest our belief on a foundation unstable and always exposed to fresh doubts, or else we must abandon this foundation altogether, and with it the miraculous appeal to our senses." Certainly, the Easter faith arose from historical experiences, Harnack allowed, but only one thing about the nature of these experiences is certain to us – that the grave of Jesus "was the birthplace of the indestructible belief that death is vanquished, that there is a life eternal."[43]

This is gospel kernel; the rest is mythical, apologetic or doctrinal husk. Harnack cautioned that all forms of gospel husk inevitably become antiquated over time; every attempt to rationalize, codify or prove Christianity eventually becomes an obstacle to Christian faith. The same thing was true of many aspects of the "religion of Jesus," which nineteenth-century liberals contrasted to Christian orthodoxy. Harnack cautioned that Jesus believed in devils and may have believed in an imminent apocalypse, all of which belonged to the category of dispensable husk. But the gospel itself is timeless, he argued. It is never falsified or rendered irrelevant by an "advanced" age, for its constitutive elements are eternal. Though variable in form and expression, the truth of the gospel is unchanging; it is a message of spiritual truth to human beings who are themselves unchanging in the midst of historical change.

More than any other figure during the heyday of liberal Protestant theology, and more than any figure period except Schleiermacher, Harnack defined the liberal approach to theology. He did it so commandingly that for decades, sympathizers and critics merely cited Harnack to establish what liberalism stood for, overlooking that his version was highly particular to time and place, and in key respects already outdated during his time. Even the memory that Kantians had long claimed to own liberal theology was forgotten after Harnack made liberalism synonymous with the Ritschlian School. Along with his friends Herrmann and Troeltsch, Harnack dominated liberal theology at the turn of the century. Thousands of his students became pastors and several became important theologians. Harnack's authority as a critical scholar bolstered the self-confidence of liberal Christians that the mediating approach was the right one. He taught liberal theologians to judge Christian history by its relationship to the gospel core and by its results. With Baur, he insisted that the Hellenization of Christianity beginning with Paul is the central problem of Christian history; with Ritschl and against Baur, he maintained that the heart of Christianity is not an idea but a spiritually and socially redemptive way of life.

Harnack's insistence on the necessity of continuing the Reformation was a favorite liberal battle-cry; when other liberals made it, they usually cited Harnack, leaning on his scholarship. He did not deny that the church requires an institutional structure, and his many volumes on the development of Catholicism expressed a grudging respect for the institutional and religious genius of the Catholic system. But Harnack went to extremes in throwing things out. He set Paulinism and early Catholicism against Jesus and the gospel. He shook his head at Trinitarian speculation and disputed the authority of the ecumenical councils. He contended that the Apostles Creed should not be a test of Christian belief. And he took a dim view of orthodox Christology. It should be enough to follow Martin Luther in describing Jesus as the "mirror of God's paternal heart," Harnack argued. If the church wrote a new confession saying this and nothing more about Christ's divinity, it would "get free from the entire ancient dogma and, at the same time, hold fast to the root of faith."[44]

At the end of his career in 1921, returning to the subject of his doctoral dissertation – Marcion – Harnack took a fateful further step, one that fascist "German Christianity" made hay from a decade later, by urging Christians to expunge the Old Testament from the Christian Bible. He allowed that it would have been disastrous for Christianity had the early church taken the Gnostic option of excluding Hebrew Scripture from the Christian Bible (in Marcion's case, everything except Luke and Paul was excluded). That would have reduced Christianity to otherworldly sectarianism. By the sixteenth century the church was long overdue to stand on its own (New Testament) basis, Harnack believed. The Reformers, however, were too weighed down by "the power of a fateful heritage" to fully recover the gospel faith.[45]

Harnack implored that all of that was long past. In the twentieth century it was only a "paralysis of religion and the church" that kept the church from getting rid of the Old Testament. He told his friend Karl Holl that he had raised his children not to regard Hebrew Scripture as part of Christian Scripture, because it was "antiquated and only in certain parts still appealing and valuable. It is the law and history of the Jews; *our* book is the New Testament." Modern theology, to move forward, had to extend the Reformation by eliminating all traditions and structures that obscured the face and word of Jesus.[46]

Harnack's timing for this proposal was less apt than he supposed. He thought that reopening the canon issue might be possible in a moment of postwar trauma and defeat. Perhaps something constructive could be wrung out of the smashing of the old order and the ravages of a lost war. In 1921 he was only beginning to grasp that a very different kind of postwar crisis theology was emerging – one that got its bearings by repudiating Harnack and Schleiermacher.

During World War I Harnack found little time or inspiration for major scholarly work. The war began for him on August 1, 1914, when the Emperor asked him to compose a call to war. When Harnack started to write it, the enemy nations were France and Russia. Before he had finished, he was told to add Great Britain, which stunned him; Harnack prized his British friends. Within a month he had lost most of them. Some British scholars tried to distinguish between Prussian militarism (bad) and German scholarship (good, but cowardly in dealing with the militarism problem). Harnack trembled with rage at reading such things. He would not accept moral criticism from acolytes of the British Empire. He believed that all Germans had an obligation to support and maintain the glorious legacy of German civilization, which rested on superior armed forces and a tradition of scholarly and artistic excellence. He believed that the war had been forced upon Germany and that Western Christian civilization was at stake in Germany's fate. He signed numerous public declarations that said it defiantly.[47]

One was a declaration by German intellectuals to Protestant Christians outside Germany, announcing that Germany accepted no blame for the war: "We are deeply convinced that we have to lay the blame on those who for a long time have woven the net of conspiracy against Germany and who have now thrown it on us in order to suffocate us." Another took aim at the culture versus militarism issue, declaring that German militarism was perfectly compatible with German culture, having grown out of German culture for its protection: "Without German militarism German culture would long ago have vanished from the earth." Another blasted Germany's enemies for perpetuating the militarism versus culture canard, declaring that all lands of the German Reich – not only Prussia – were united in fighting to save Germany and Western Christian civilization: "Our belief is that salvation for the very culture of Europe depends on the victory that German 'militarism' will gain: manly virtue, faithfulness, the will to sacrifice found in the united free German people." The most famous one, issued on October 3, 1914 as the "Manifesto of Ninety-Three German Intellectuals to the Civilized World," denied that Germany caused the war, denied that Belgium was neutral when Germany invaded it, dismissed the militarism versus culture argument, and fervently concluded: "Believe us! Believe, that we shall carry on this war to the end as a people of culture to whom the legacy of a Goethe, a Beethoven, and a Kant is as holy as its own hearths and homes."[48]

The latter declaration repulsed Karl Barth when he read it in October 1914, finding that nearly all his theological teachers had signed it, notably Harnack and Herrmann. Liberal theology had folded into nationalistic militarism. Reading recent issues of *Die Christliche Welt,* a Ritschlian journal, Barth was disgusted by its appeal to a "religious war experience." Harnack could be florid on this topic, enthusing that "this highspirited disposition, ready to embrace life and death equally, is very closely akin to religion." He exulted that many people who had no religious feeling before the war now had it fervently: "People who had neglected their inner life, now feel themselves borne up high on the wings of religion and, as if by magic, sense themselves freed from the weight which clung to their feet, gaining a new relation to their brothers and an awareness of the transcendent meaning of their lives."[49]

Harnack never took back his statements about the meaning of the war and its necessity. During the war, long after religious war enthusiasm had faded, he organized efforts to care for displaced and orphaned children, expand educational opportunities, promote early marriage, and provide treatment for tuberculosis and venereal disease. He also criticized war profiteers. After the war he admitted to friends that he and the government overestimated Germany's military power and that people like him had to face up to living in a different world. Politically he remained a respected player in Germany, encouraging people of his generation to give up their nostalgia for monarchy and the Reich. Harnack did not really agree with the new constitution, but he supported it anyway, contending that Germany had to become a modern democracy. He refrained from joining a political party, though many parties tried to recruit him; in 1921 he was asked to be the Wiemar government's ambassador to the United States, which he declined. Harnack wanted to finish his career by reclaiming his place as a theological and scholarly leader.[50]

That did not happen, as the Barthian revolt overturned Germany's theological establishment. Harnack, for all his iconic status, had never led the way in theological rethinking anyway. He was the symbol and leading scholar of liberal theology, but never its leading theorist. One would not have guessed from his writings that the Ritschlian School was deeply conflicted by the turn of the century. At the very moment when Harnack spoke with clear and commanding assurance to an international audience and William Newton Clarke's *An Outline of Christian Theology* (1898) played a similar role in a rising American movement, the Ritschlian theologians sharply debated whether they had any ground of certainty or should want one. Wilhelm Herrmann, the Ritschlian School's leading theologian, never really believed that historicism was the key to Ritschl's achievement. When a Ritschlian spin-off calling itself the *Religionsgeschichtliche Schule* charged that Ritschlian theology was too Christian and provincial to be good historicism, Herrmann had to decide what he did believe. His debates with Ernst Troeltsch cast a long shadow over the Barthian revolution to come and the liberal tradition that survived it.[51]

Wilhelm Herrmann, Ernst Troeltsch, and the Scope of Historical Criticism

Johann Wilhelm Herrmann, born in Melkow, Prussia in 1846, had two role models of the kind of luminous piety for which he became known. The first was his father, a neo-Pietist Lutheran pastor who served humble congregations of poor and working class people and was well versed in Schleiermacher. The second was his graduate mentor at Halle, neo-Pietist Lutheran theologian Friedrich August Tholuck, with whom Herrmann lived for over two years as his personal secretary, and where Herrmann also studied under Julius Müller and Martin Kähler. Tholuck combined Schleiermacher and Hegel with apologetic arguments they eschewed. He befriended his students, taught them not to fear historical criticism, and radiated a child-like sincerity that made him a magnet for nineteenth-century students eager to combine modern learning and personal faith. Herrmann epitomized the type, which took him into a theological career after he graduated from Halle in 1870 and served an infantry stint in the Franco-Prussian War.[52]

Herrmann first met Ritschl in Tholuck's home, during his student days. In 1875 he began his teaching career at Halle, where he became the first theologian to call himself a Ritschlian. After four years at Halle he moved to Marburg, where he taught until his retirement in 1916. From the beginning he attracted students and friends in Tholuck's manner, for similar reasons. Herrmann radiated joy and conviction. He told his students that the living Christ can be known personally and that theology needs no other basis. Karl Barth, otherwise a critical source, later recalled that both assurances were utterly convincing in Herrmann's classroom, exposed to his vibrant spirit. "Herrmann was *the* theological teacher of my student years," Barth wrote, adding elsewhere that he thoroughly absorbed Hermann's theology.[53]

To a significant degree this was a defensive resort, for by 1907, when Barth studied under Herrmann at Marburg, the Ritschlian establishment was reeling from attacks by a mostly younger generation of Ritschlians, the *Religionsgeschichtliche Schule,* which identified more with the skeptical academy than the church. Ernst Troeltsch was their leading theorist. The history of religionists charged that Ritschl and his church-centered disciples compromised the critical spirit of historical criticism with dogmatic Christian assumptions. Ritschlian theology, for all its vaunted liberalism, was firmly controlled by its belief in the superiority of Christianity.

This objection challenged Ritschlian theology at its core. Disputing the Ritschlian claim to a critical historical foundation, the *Religionsgeschichtliche* scholars contended that true historicism is not compatible with any religious claim to dogmatic absoluteness or finality. To understand Christianity historically is to locate its emergence within the widest possible context of religious history, they argued. Instead of playing up factors that make Christianity distinctive, a truly critical method must pay attention to aspects of Christian myth and ritual that are common to other religious traditions. The first *Religionsgeschichtliche* critics were insurgent Ritschlians at Göttingen in the late 1880s: Troeltsch, Wilhelm Bousset, Hermann Gunkel, William Wrede, Alfred Rahlfs, and Johannes Weiss. Soon their group expanded to include Rudolf Otto, Ulrich von Wilamowitz-Moellendorff, and Albrecht Dieterich.[54] By 1897 the church-oriented Ritschlians and the insurgent *Religionsgeschichtliche* group were factional rivals, as Gustav Ecke documented in his book of that year, *Die Theologische Schule Albrecht Ritschls.*[55]

The same year, Troeltsch observed with a tinge of boasting, "The rise of a comparative history of religion has shaken the Christian faith more deeply than anything else." The Troeltschian historicists argued that cult and liturgy (not theology) form the experiential center of every religious tradition. They taught that religions can be understood scientifically only if they are examined by historical critical criteria not deriving from or belonging to any particular religious tradition. They contended that most religions are syncretistic blends of various sources and traditions. They shook the field of theology by picturing Jesus as a failed apocalypticist. And like earlier generations of mythical-school critics, but with the authority of a more comprehensive and ostensibly scientific approach to religion, they argued that Christian scripture is pervaded with mythical teaching and narrative.[56]

The *Religionsgeschichtliche* scholars claimed to carry out the logical implications of the Tübingen School criticism in which Ritschl was trained. In the late 1890s they gained effective control over the flagship journal of German theological liberalism, *Die Christliche Welt,* which had been a stronghold of the Ritschlian School. For many liberals this was a troubling development that threatened to undermine liberal conviction, take away the social gospel Jesus, and relativize everything. For many of them Herrmann was the theologian of the hour – the one who saw it coming and who fought the Troeltschian upsurge.[57]

Though Herrmann was, in effect, the founder of the Ritschlian School, he had a conflicted relationship with Ritschl nearly from the beginning, and he significantly influenced Ritschl's mature thinking.[58] His early writings focused on the role of metaphysics in theology. In *Die Metaphysik in der Theologie* (1876) and *Die Religion im Verhältnis zum Welterkennen und zur Sittlichkeit* (1879), Herrmann argued that

Catholicism, Protestant orthodoxy, and liberal theology shared a serious mistake, making theology dependent on metaphysical arguments. Sometimes theologians put it plainly, asserting that all religious statements must be grounded in a metaphysical system. Herrmann countered that metaphysical reasoning is not a way into true religion but rather a way of evading or losing the life of faith that constitutes true religion.[59]

This argument became a touchstone of the Ritschlian School, though it was Herrmann, not Ritschl, who first made a sustained neo-Kantian case for it. By the early 1870s Ritschl's blend of Tübingen-school historicism and neo-Kantian moralism made him the dominant figure in Continental Protestant theology, a stature he secured in 1874 by completing his three volume magnum opus, *Die christliche Lehre von der Rechtfertigung und Versöhnung.* Along neo-Kantian lines he argued that religious knowledge belongs to the realm of value judgments, the heart and goal of true religion is to attain the highest possible good, and true knowledge of this good as defined by Christianity is attainable through historical critical research.[60]

None of these arguments prevailed without a fight; Pietist conservatives and confessional Lutherans blasted Ritschl for selling out Christian orthodoxy. Lutherans Christoph Ernst Luthardt (of Leipzig) and Franz Hermann Frank (of Erlangen) attacked Ritschl's liberalism, as did Pietist theologian Hermann Weiss (of Tübingen). Ritschl, like many liberals of his social class and temperament, wanted to win without having to fight. He could be short-tempered and imperious with his followers – Herrmann later recalled that he demanded deference from them – but he tried to avoid controversies with critics. Liberalism would not win if it had to battle constantly with conservatives, Ritschl believed. In the early 1880s, however, Herrmann and others persuaded Ritschl that he had to defend their position from outright attacks. A polemical salvo against Hermann Schultz, one of Ritschl's closest disciples, drove Ritschl to enter the lists against his critics.[61]

He took his polemical touchstone from Herrmann, who claimed that Ritschl's critics compromised the gospel by identifying Christianity with a metaphysical position. Every guardian of orthodoxy foisted assumptions about the nature of reality or the propositional nature of religion onto the gospel faith, Herrmann explained. The same thing was true of the liberal theologies that preceded Ritschl, he added. Herrmann charged that all were grievously mistaken, as did Ritschl following him. In Ritschl's telling, all his critics put forth an "unseemly mingling of metaphysics with revealed religion," which corrupted their exegesis: "When they allege that they surpass me in their concern for Christianity, it is only a deception which mirrors their unexamined faith in a false epistemology."[62]

This polemic obscured Ritschl's reliance on Kant's account of the limitations of pure reason and the qualitative distinction between pure and practical reason. Ritschl and Herrmann used Kantian arguments to secure an independent ground for religious claims, reasoning that science describes the way things are, or appear to be, while theology (as a function of moral reason) is properly about the way things should be. Thus religious knowledge is never disinterested, consisting always of value judgments about reality, which makes theology independent.[63]

Herrmann was clearer than Ritschl about what this did not mean. Aided by conversations with neo-Kantian philosophers Hermann Cohen and Paul Natorp, his colleagues at Marburg, Herrmann acknowledged that theologians had to address epistemological problems and delineate the boundaries of philosophical theorizing for theology, which he took from Kant's division of knowledge into science (logic), ethics, and aesthetic judgment.[64] This scheme, applied to the interpretation of religion, raised the question of the place of religion itself. Kant reduced religion to the sphere of moral reason; Natorp reformulated Schleiermacher's alternative, that religious feeling is a deeper aspect of human experience than any kind of reason or even sensation; Cohen followed Kant in relegating religion to morality.[65]

Insofar as Kantian philosophy accounted for the kinds of knowledge attained in natural science, ethics, and aesthetic judgment, Herrmann was a straightforward neo-Kantian, acknowledging his debt to Kant more explicitly than did Ritschl. But he was also less Kantian than Ritschl in a crucial respect. Ritschl polemicized against mingling metaphysics with theology without clarifying the boundaries of his dependence on Kantian theory. Herrmann adopted a Kantian account of the kinds of knowledge that are knowable to philosophy while insisting that the reality known to true religion is another kind of knowledge. Kantian philosophy saved a place for religion by reducing faith to a postulate of morality, but this strategy rendered the reality known to religious faith as an object of human creation.[66]

This is exactly what theology must never do, Herrmann contended. To incorporate religion into a general theory of knowledge is to treat being as a function of thinking. In biblical terms, it is to commit idolatry. Kant viewed religion as a postulate of moral reason; Herrmann countered that true religion is an independent power through which God saves a lost human being. He did not deny that morality has an important role to play in the inner drama of salvation. In his *Ethik,* Herrmann argued that it is through morality that a lost soul comes to discover that he or she is lost. The experience of inner moral conflict is a necessary precondition for every saving encounter with Christ. But moral experience itself is not saving, he cautioned. We are saved by faith, as Martin Luther taught, not by moral achievement. Through faith we learn that God is unique, mysterious, and transcendent. Because the reality known to true faith is knowable only to faith, and not to any other kind of cognition, the religious way and kind of knowing is fundamentally different from all other forms of knowledge. Metaphysics must be eliminated from theology because the kind of knowing that occurs in science and logic "absolutely does not reach to the reality of our God." Since philosophy and science have no access to divine reality, theology must not seek any support from these disciplines or any other discipline.[67]

This conviction, that Christian truth is based on itself, had a long run in theology after Barthian dialecticism overthrew the liberal establishment. Barth's desire to become a theologian was confirmed by Herrmann's warm-hearted devotion to Christ and his insistence that Christian truth requires no basis outside itself. Herrmann was not ashamed of the gospel and not impressed with outside criticisms of its truth. Barth sustained that attitude long after he left Herrmann's theology behind.[68]

For liberals, however, Herrmann's insistence on the self-authenticating character of revelatory experience and its independent basis for theology were more problematic. It smacked of Schleiermacher and immunization strategy at the very time that liberal theology was at the height of its prestige. Herrmann's fideism conflicted with the liberal impulse to address other disciplines, modern culture, and challenges to belief. Why would a self-confident liberal movement retreat to an immunization strategy?

Herrmann's bottom-line answer was that fideism is true: Revelation cannot be established by something else. Later he stressed his connection to Schleiermacher and got more stringent about theological independence, largely as a consequence of his debates with Troeltsch. Troeltsch was fond of saying that as soon as one concedes an inch to historical criticism, it takes a mile. Sometimes he added that for conservatives, historical criticism was very much like the devil. Herrmann cautioned that this was a huge problem for liberals too. Because Ritschl and Harnack conceded much more than an inch to historical criticism, their theologies were vulnerable to being devoured by it.[69]

In a broad sense of the term, Herrmann's revision of Ritschlian theology remained a Ritschlian strategy. Like Ritschl, he never doubted that Christianity is founded historically in what he called "the fact of Jesus." Like Ritschl, he never took much interest in the quest of the historical Jesus, because the historical Jesus was not the point religiously. For Ritschl and Herrmann, what mattered was the historicity of Christ's redeeming and reconciling work in the life of the Christian community, not the historicity of any particular details in the gospel narratives. Jesus called people to saving faith by calling them to himself as Lord and Savior. The deep historical core of Christian faith is securely established, whatever the truth may be about the sayings or miracles of Jesus recorded in the gospels. Ritschlian theologians explained that Christian truth is historical by virtue of its relation to "the man Jesus," who inspired the kingdom-bearing community of value that constitutes the historical body of Christ.

Herrmann took all of this for granted, but in the late 1880s, with a wary eye on the *Religionsgeschichtliche* upsurge, he began to back away from Ritschl's claim that Christian faith is grounded in historical facts that are open to historical criticism and confirmed by it. In 1886 Herrmann published a major work, *Der Verkehr des Christen mit Gott* (hereafter, *The Communion of the Christian with God*), which introduced a variation on the Ritschlian strategy. Herrmann argued that what matters is the inner life of Jesus known to faith, not the history-making life and teaching of Jesus. To call Christianity "historical" is not to claim that Christian faith is founded on historical facts confirmed by historical criticism. Rather, it is to claim that Christianity is grounded in an experience of communion with God, mediated by Christ, which occurs in history. Christianity is historical in the sense that it bears the spiritual reality and power that makes history. As historical reality, it is comprehensible only to those who participate in its effects, not to Troeltschian onlookers.[70]

Another Kind of Ritschlianism

Many of Ritschl's critics mistakenly understood him to base his theology on a picture of the historical Jesus constructed by historical criticism. Some noted that strategies of this kind were vulnerable to being falsified by historical criticism. Troeltsch's group protested that Ritschl's judgments about Christian history were controlled by dogmatic presuppositions. Herrmann wrote *The Communion of the Christian with God* partly to defend the Ritschlian School from these lines of criticism. His first edition made a strong appeal to the inspiring personality of Jesus as the basis of Christian faith, while assuring that the gospel picture of Jesus is historically reliable. His later editions cut back on the historical assurances while continuing to describe Jesus as "the historical fact" through which God's love is revealed to people of faith. In both cases he tried to provide a stronger basis for an essentially Ritschlian theology by shifting from the life and teaching of Jesus to the inner life of Jesus.

Ritschl grasped from the beginning, however, that Herrmann was actually breaking ranks. He told Herrmann that he could scarcely find himself in the book. He had to read it several times before he could convince himself that it contained anything of value.[71] Gradually, over several years, Herrmann acknowledged that his position owed as much to Schleiermacher as to Ritschl. He told his students that Schleiermacher marked a new stage in the history of religion and it was Schleiermacher who freed him from authoritarian faith. Ritschl's core was the historical, kingdom-bringing effect of Christ's life and teaching, but Herrmann moved away from the very notion of a critically established historical core. The history of religions movement spurred him to clarify his alternative to it. In his telling, the Troeltschians were restricted to spectator-knowledge about Christianity. Most of them took a pass on real theology, and even the one who tried to write history of religions theology – Troeltsch – had only flat, onlooker things to say. Troeltsch never got beneath the surface of things because his method bracketed out the life of faith by which Christian truth is known.[72]

But there was something about Ritschl's appeal to historical science that created obstacles to proclaiming and hearing the gospel, Herrmann judged. The problem was deeper than the usual misunderstanding about Ritschl's appeal to the historical Jesus. It was that Ritschl's reliance on history took on the character of an apologetic device, diminishing the power of the gospel claim to truth. Ritschl used historical science as an apologetic crutch, bringing readers to Christianity by convincing them that his historical arguments about it were correct. Herrmann countered that apologies for Christianity nearly always obscured or detracted from the gospel faith. Mystical approaches made Jesus peripheral to a quest for unmediated communion with God. Orthodoxies overloaded Christian teaching with legalistic doctrines. Metaphysical theologies distorted the gospel by turning it into an abstraction.[73]

Herrmann recognized that history is a special case, because Christianity is historical. He believed that his approach affirmed the historical character of Christianity in a way that saved (by reformulating) the Ritschlian approach to history. He held fast to the historical "happenedness" of the "fact" of Jesus and refrained from attacking Ritschl directly.[74] But even the first edition of *The Communion of the Christian with God* saved Herrmann's harshest words for unnamed thinkers who understood Christianity as "historical facts that require faith." In later editions, he heightened his polemic against historical apologetics. Many defenders of Christianity supposed that the power that saves lies in the gospel narratives about Jesus, he observed. In this understanding, the Christian message was an invitation to believe in a list of facts about Jesus narrated in the gospels and systematized in church dogma.[75]

Herrmann replied than no one has ever been saved by information. What saves is the person of Jesus as we encounter and experience him as a fact. Put differently, we do not meet, in faith, the historical Jesus sought by historians, but rather the living presence of the personality of Jesus. Christian faith is founded on the inner life of Jesus, which is known by faith. It has no basis outside itself. Pietism at its best got this right, Herrmann noted. Like Tholuck, he believed that Christianity is founded on a specific experience of sin and regeneration. Like Tholuck, he insisted that regeneration is the necessary precondition of all theological knowledge. But Pietism was mostly a disaster for Protestantism, Herrmann cautioned. It usually degenerated into doctrinal conservatism, abounding in crude systematic schemes, explaining the basis of faith and how faith comes about. This doctrinal tendency obscured the pure individuality of faith and betrayed the gospel.[76]

That is, historic Pietism usually degenerated into a form of the apologetic mistake. Herrmann ripped it mercilessly and repeatedly for that reason. His alternative blended Schleiermacher and Tholuck in a revised Ritschlian framework. Like Tholuck he played up his Lutheranism, claiming Luther for his side, professing no interest in a liberal Protestantism cut off from its Reformation roots. Herrmann proposed to recover the deepest religious truths of the Reformation in forms of understanding appropriate to modern times. The key was Luther's doctrine of justification by faith, which, in Herrmann's hands, rejected all religious creedalism and legalism.

Rightly understood, he argued, justification by faith stands against all attempts to make any other doctrine essential to Christianity or to establish support for Christianity on any basis outside the experience of faithful communion with God. Herrmann explained, "The basis of faith can only be what produces faith as the inward experience of pure trust." The gospel does not invite people to decide whether certain biblical narratives or doctrines are true. Those who treat faith as cognitive assent, Herrmann charged, make themselves "faith's executioners." Ostensibly defending biblical truth, "they do not notice that they themselves are profaning it when they lay upon others as a ceremonial law what is in truth a gift of God's grace." By God's grace and through the mediation of Christ, Christians are brought into a saving communion of the soul with the living God. That is the gospel faith, Herrmann urged: "True religion, the blessed life of the spirit, is given to us only when we are willing to obey the simplest demand of the moral law, namely, to know ourselves."[77]

He acknowledged that Luther was not entirely true to this understanding of salvation by faith alone. Luther lived at a time when biblical infallibility was taken for granted by Christians, and he fervently accepted "these mental possessions of his time." Herrmann distinguished between Luther's Christianity and Luther's theology. The latter was built on the dogmatic assumptions of medieval Catholicism; the former broke through these assumptions to the possibility of living by faith alone through God's unmerited love and grace. Though Luther wedded the gospel faith to Catholic dogmatism, "in reality they had nothing to do with each other." To take Luther seriously is not to perpetuate the outmoded mental possessions of his time, Herrmann urged. It is to hold fast without conditions or apologetic weapons to the new life in Christ.[78]

The same lesson applied to the New Testament. The idea that one should accept all doctrines expounded in the New Testament is "to put it plainly, a monstrous fiction," Herrmann wrote. In his rendering, the New Testament had authority solely by virtue of its capacity to bring Christians into communion with God: "If, however, we have learned to fix our eyes on that which God's revelation produces in the inner life of a Christian, then, in our reading of Scripture, we shall constantly meet with an authority by which we shall be safely led and wonderfully uplifted."[79]

Herrmann stressed that Christian truth is "a secret in the soul" that cannot be handed from one person to another. It is impossible to prove to an unbeliever that

Christianity is true, because Christian knowledge "is grasped in its truth only by those who occupy already the standpoint of faith." Actual communion with God is the only nourishment on which faith can be fed. One does not become a Christian by accepting doctrines about God or Christ, for doctrines are expressions of a life of faith. They cannot be true for someone who is not in a faith-relation to God: "The thoughts of others who are redeemed cannot redeem me. If I am to be saved, everything depends on my being transplanted into that inner condition of mind in which such thoughts begin to be generated in myself, and this happens only when God lifts me into communion with Himself."[80]

Herrmann had only a slight acquaintance with Kierkegaard, who had little influence in theology before 1920. Like Kierkegaard he affirmed that his approach to Christianity was obviously subjective and yet not merely subjective in the sense that really mattered, because in faith we lay hold of an objective reality, divine revelation. To push aside the knowledge that is obtainable only through faith, Herrmann warned, is to be cut off from objective reality, that which makes reality possible: "The objective reality of which we are thinking is something quite different from the thoughts of faith which are formulated in the common doctrine. These thoughts have no power to generate the communion of the Christian with God; they are only the expression of that sense of new life which comes with such communion. But everything depends on being able clearly to grasp the objective reality which, by its sheer bulk, produces in the Christian the certainty that he is not without God in the world."[81]

Herrmann's idea of revelation was cribbed from Schleiermacher and Hegel, though he felt no need to trace the genealogy, after two generations of German mediating theology. Revelation is that which brings human beings into actual communion with God, he argued. It is not propositional, but occurs as event. It is not to be identified with thoughts of faith, although faith produces true thoughts. Revelation occurs as events of grace that produce true thoughts of faith. Put differently, "we can regard as the thoughts of our own faith only what comes home to us as truth within the sphere of our actual communion with God." Revelation is revelatory experience of the divine, not lumps of propositional information.[82]

Ludwig Feuerbach, outflanking Strauss on the Hegelian left, contended that "God" is merely the wish-being of religious desire. Herrmann replied that we know in faith that God is real because we know the man Jesus whom God sent. When a critic protested that liberal Protestantism was subjective, he advised, "We can only suppose that for him Jesus is not objective." Herrmann took his stand on the experience of Jesus as God's Word to us: "We are Christians because, in the human Jesus, we have met with a fact whose content is incomparably richer than that of any feelings which arise within ourselves."[83]

And how is Jesus mediated to us? Herrmann cautioned that "the mere historian" is of little help: "It is a fatal error to attempt to establish the basis of faith by means of historical investigation." The basis of a true faith must be something fixed, he explained, but the verdicts of historical research are constantly changing. Lessing posed the right question, Herrmann believed: How can a merely probable truth serve as the basis for eternal happiness? Herrmann gave a Kierkegaardian answer: Because historical reason renders merely probable verdicts, "it is impossible to attach religious conviction to a mere historical decision." The person who knows Christ does not fret over fads and trends in historical scholarship: "We have no such anxiety; on the contrary, we declare that the historical appearance of Jesus, in so far as it is drawn into the sphere of this attempt to establish the probable truth, cannot be a basis of faith. It is only a part of that world with which faith has to wrestle."[84]

Herrmann allowed that every reader inevitably asks to what extent the gospels convey accurate historical information, and that historical criticism rightly does its best to address such questions. But the crucial religious question lies beyond the scope of historical reason, he argued. It is not what we make of the gospel story, but what the content of the story makes of us. Through faith and the fellowship of the Christian community we are led into Christ's presence and receive a picture of his inner life. The inner life of Jesus becomes part of our reality in the same way that any historical personality meaningfully enters our lives.

This was still a type of Ritschlian theology, but one that overthrew Ritschl's use of scripture and historical reason to establish the content of faith that Christians should believe. Herrmann judged that Ritschl's historical foundationalism made him the "last great representative of orthodox dogmatics."[85] Ritschl never quite relinquished the concept of scripture as a source of prescriptive ideas about the content of faith. Herrmann urged Christian thinkers to break free of Ritschl's vestigial dogmatism: "Only he who yearns after an honest fullness for his own inner life can perceive the strength and fullness of that soul of Jesus, and whenever we come to see the Person of Jesus, then, under the impress of that inner life that breaks through all the veils of the story, we ask no more questions as to the trustworthiness of the Evangelists. The question whether the portrait of Jesus belongs to history or fiction is silenced in every one who learns to see it at all, for by its help he first learns to see what is the true reality of personal life."[86]

Revelation as Freedom from History

The fact that Ritschl disliked Herrmann's first edition of *Communion* helped Herrmann throw off Ritschl in the book's successive editions. *Communion* sounded more like Schleiermacher with each edition, and in 1906 Herrmann's *Christlich-protestantische Dogmatik* gave an almost purely Schleiermacherian account of Christian faith while barely mentioning Ritschl. There were still a few equivocations about doing theology wholly without weapons. Herrmann appealed to the "historical facts" of Christianity and he left a bit of room for three kinds of apologetic arguments, allowing that theologians had to defend the integrity of religion against atheist debunkers, establish the relationship between religion and ethics, and defend religion as the only possible ground of a unifying concept of reality.[87]

But these caveats cut against the spirit of Herrmann's position and left him vulnerable to Troeltschian objections. Thus he gradually relinquished the notion of a critically established historical core of Christian faith. Herrmann's later editions of *Communion* heightened its polemic against historical apologetics. He continued to speak of the "historical fact" of Jesus, but dropped his Ritschlian assurance that historical criticism always yields the Christ of faith. By the time that Barth studied at Marburg, Herrmann was almost free of crutches and defenses. A few years later, responding to Troeltsch's attacks on him, he dropped his last apologetic equivocations.[88]

Herrmann completed his prolonged process of relinquishment in the years just before World War I, embracing what Troeltsch, not unfairly, called "the agnostic theory about the nature of religious knowledge." Troeltsch cautioned that Herrmann's deepening anti-historicism was an instructive example of "subjective mysticism," the upshot of abandoning "firm and adequate knowledge."[89] Less charitably he declared in 1911 that Herrmann's religious claims were "obscure and mystical," if not "violently" willful, and that Herrmann's refusal to ground his religious claims in historical criticism was "almost incomprehensible to people who think historically and critically." Herrmann managed to preserve the orthodox claim to a religious absolute, Troeltsch remarked, but he completely failed the test of historical credibility.[90]

The part about clinging to orthodoxy offended Herrmann, who replied that Troeltsch was the one clinging to a security blanket, a supposedly scientific historicism presuming its own certainty *and* its right to serve as the test of religious faith. Herrmann admonished that faith is not a form of scientific knowledge. By confusing religion and science, Troeltsch distorted the experiential character of religious truth. The history of religions approach reduced the truth of Christianity, the experience of Christ, to a mere idea.[91] Herrmann made a clean break with all such confusions and his earlier concessions to them. Without giving up his belief that Christianity possesses a factual grounding in history, he denied that theology should establish a historical critical ground for its religious claims. With no apologetic asides he insisted that all religious statements about God, creation, morality, and everything else are lifeless and groundless apart from their source in religion itself.[92]

Herrmann urged Christian thinkers to see the Kantian revolution all the way through. Kant liberated religion from its distorting connection to scientific reason, but he failed to recognize that religion possesses an independent and underivable essence. The early Schleiermacher corrected Kant's identification of religion with the ethical will, but Schleiermacher's later system lost the Kantian recognition that religion belongs only to a particular kind of individual experience. Schleiermacher's dogmatic system deduced religious reality from the unity of human self-consciousness. This strategy may have described the condition of the possibility of religion, Herrmann allowed, but it obscured through its ostensible universality that which constitutes true religion itself. True religion is a historical phenomenon existing only in the life of individuals.[93]

True religion is comprehensible only to those who live in it. Herrmann did not deny that people of good will can be shown the *way* to religion. Because religion belongs to history and not to nature, inevitably it bears an historical character. But true religion is never created or experienced as a product of moral will, historical reason, or any human initiative. We are saved only by that which is given to us in revelation.

What we need, we must be given. A person can become a truly live self *[das etwas für sich selbst sein will]* only by experiencing a reality that one cannot produce from within oneself. "We seek God when we long for such a reality," Herrmann wrote. "When we encounter such a reality, God reveals himself to us."[94] True religion is the simultaneously liberating and submissive response to revelation, and revelation is the experience of a spiritual Power "which acts on us as the manifestation of pure goodness." To experience the working of this Power is to settle, or have settled for us, the question whether God is a reality: "It simply depends on whether we remain loyal to the truth, that is, whether we are prepared to treat the fact of such a Power as what it really is for us. The moment we desire dependence upon it, and submit ourselves to it in reverence and trust, this spiritual Power is really our soul's Lord." Only the Spirit gives life. The Spirit often works through the moral will, but it is never merely a product or function of morality. True religion is an awakening to the revelation of God's Spirit in all the life-giving movements of one's inner life.[95]

Herrmann and Harnack had the same politics and the same answer to the history of religionists' picture of Jesus as a failed apocalypticist: Jesus' worldview doesn't really matter, because it is irrelevant to the question of faith and true religion. It belongs to the same category as his belief in devils. But Herrmann and Harnack also described the character and presence of Jesus' kingdom faith in a way that fit their account of true religion.[96] Herrmann taught that the kingdom of God is, above all, the rule of God in the hearts of Christ-following individuals, which comes only by God's initiative and is knowable only through revelatory experience: "The Kingdom of God comes from the other world. It is not the result of human activity, but a gift of God." It does not matter that Jesus and the early church believed many things that we do not believe, for what links us to Jesus is the revelatory experience of God as righteous, providential, and loving.[97]

Through such experiences we come to know the inner life of Jesus. Herrmann insisted that religion finds its true origin without remainder "in revelation understood as a unique personal experience," *[als ein eigenes Erlbenis erfasster Offenbaung].* In 1909, at the height of his debates with Troeltsch, Natorp, and Cohen that clarified his position, Herrmann remarked that his entire career was devoted to showing that the only true ground of religious teaching is "that experience which is its revelation."[98] Understood correctly, he explained elsewhere, theology is rightly pursued only as explication of a revealed Word of God: "If a Christian has come to recognize the constraining power which comes upon him from the Person of Jesus as a revelation of God, he can take as a word of God only that which is in some way recognizable as an expression of this fact." Revelatory experience discloses the life-giving presence and Power of the Revealer: "Christian faith is that renewal of the inner life which men experience in contact with Jesus as he becomes for them that revelation of God which is the foundation of God's rule in their hearts." The church, accordingly, is the community of those who know Christ as the revealed spiritual Power of their lives. The true unity of the Christian community, the only unity worth having, derives from sharing this experience in common.[99]

Faith is a spiritual gift of God's Spirit. Herrmann told his students that one would have to be secretly ashamed of the Spirit's gift to defend it with reasons. Barth later recalled that there was a ring in Herrmann's voice, "the ring of prophetic utterance." He was the prophet of religious experience expressed wholly without weapons. To Herrmann, Roman Catholicism was a tragic mutilation of Christianity because it equated revelation with doctrine. He condemned this error ferociously, calling it "dishonest," "immoral," and "seductive evil" – and his students cheered when he reminded them that he wasn't speaking only of Catholicism. Barth recalled that "we listened gladly when traditionalism on the right, rationalism on the left, mysticism in the rear were thrown to the refuse dump, and when finally 'positive and liberal dogmatics' were together hurled into the same pit." All of the early twentieth-century

Ritschlian theologians contended that Troeltsch went too far, taking Ritschlian historicism to an extreme that relativized everything. Herrmann stood out by offering the purest alternative to Troeltsch. Theology had its own basis, the Troeltschians were wrong, and they were not destined to inherit the academy.[100]

A great deal of what came to be called "neo-orthodoxy" refashioned themes from Herrmann in orthodox dress, usually without attribution: revelation is divine self-revealing, theology is the explication of a self-authenticating revelation, faith is not assent to doctrine or the outcome of an argument, history is not a basis or subject of faith, apologetics is not a legitimate theological enterprise, and Christian faith is not a worldview. Herrmann's liberal successors were left with the perplexing question of how the "inner life" of Jesus could be ascertainable if the biblical testimony about it belongs to the period of second generation Christian reflection. His Barthian and Bultmannian successors waved off that problem, replacing Herrmann's appeals to the inner life of Jesus with a doctrine of biblical authority. In the triumph of Barthian neo-Reformation theology, Herrmann was forgotten, but appropriated, while Troeltsch was scorned as a purveyor of historical relativism. After neo-orthodoxy was toppled in the 1960s, and the problems of historical relativism and cultural pluralism gained high priority in theology, much of the field gave Troeltsch a second hearing.

Ernst Troeltsch: The Relativity of Christianity and the History of Religion

Troeltsch had a cooler religious temperament. He was born in 1865 in Haunstetten near Augsburg, the city of the Augsburg Confession, where a Protestant minority and Catholic majority had a long history of trying to get along. Troeltsch's father, also named Ernst, was a studious medical doctor, politically conservative and conventionally Lutheran, who favored the monarchy and a single German state and was consumed with his work. The elder Ernst Troeltsch passed these dispositions to his son Ernst, pushing him, as Troeltsch later recalled, into scientific studies: "There were skeletons, anatomical compendia, electrical machines, books of plants, books about crystals, etc." At an early age Troeltsch adopted his father's scientific bent, but as a student at Erlangen he opted for theology, because it combined his two chief interests, metaphysics and history.[101]

Quickly he judged that Erlangen was too stuffy and theologically conservative for him. Plotting a transfer, Troeltsch forged a lifelong friendship with his classmate Wilhelm Bousset, later remarking on their teachers: "We had a cool respect for these gentlemen and regarded them as antiques from the time of the German Federation, as relics of the fight between neo-pietism and the Enlightenment." On other occasions he allowed that at least they really knew their Lutheranism, which he absorbed. At the age of twenty Troeltsch aptly described his synthetic cast of mind in a letter to Bousset, observing that he strove for balance between thought and feeling, realism and idealism, mechanism and supranaturalism, and knowledge and disposition: "I suffer the fate of all those who want to do justice to two masters: they do not do justice to either. But I cannot do other than serve the two masters I know. I can only guess at the point which unites them."[102]

Troeltsch was never an either/or type that thought in alternatives; to him, either/or thinking was simplistic, always geared to fix something or to take a stand. From his early career onward he sought to comprehend the historical character of knowledge and culture, especially religion, from a unitary standpoint grounded in science, and he admonished his students not to demean compromises. Any theology, to be credible, must make recognizable contact with the real world of empirical and historical experience described by science, and life itself is a constant process of finding compromises between and among complex possibilities.

In search of a theological model, he transferred to Berlin, where Julius Kaftan taught a scholastic brand of Ritschlian theology. Troeltsch loved the museums in the capital city of the Reich, he admired Bismarck intensely, his nationalist feelings soared, and Kaftan proved an able teacher. But Troeltsch disliked the class resentments and crude speechmaking of the social Christian movement in Berlin; after a few months, the city's noise and largeness also wore on him. Instead of listening to a Ritschlian dogmatist in Berlin, why not study under Ritschl himself in Göttingen? He told Bousset: "Ritschl is in the air everywhere there, and with every breath one person supports him and another opposes him. I grant you, this movement has also had a powerful effect on me and I plan to go there."[103]

From 1886 to 1888 Troeltsch studied under Ritschl and persuaded Bousset to join him. Later he recalled that it was Ritschl "who really first won us over to theology." Ritschl made theology real to him by conceiving it as social and historical. He urged his students to acquire a detailed knowledge of early Christianity and the Reformation, and Troeltsch never forgot his debt to him: "It is difficult nowadays to get an idea of the authority, dignity, and power with which this significant but completely unromantic, indeed unpoetic man, attracted us by virtue of his intellectual acumen, the grand yet strict structure of his systematic theology, his purity and superior character. Today's generation of students is less inclined to such dedication and there is no longer his like." At Göttingen Troeltsch and his classmates – Bousset, Alfred Rahlfs, Hermann Gunkel, and William Wrede – compared the rival historicisms of Ritschl and Göttingen Orientalist and Septuagint scholar Paul de Lagarde, who pioneered the history of religions approach. All of them tacked in Lagarde's direction, though Troeltsch moved slower. At the same time he puzzled over his metaphysical basis, or need of one, writing a half-prize winning paper on philosopher Rudolf Hermann Lotze, Ritschl's colleague and friend at Göttingen who had recently moved to Berlin.[104]

Lotze, a post-Kantian idealist, espoused a theory of the organic unity of nature in spirit that influenced Troeltsch deeply. Troeltsch wanted to believe in a spiritual ground of unity within and behind historical particularities. At Göttingen he struggled to make up his mind whether metaphysics should be expunged from theology and whether Ritschl would be better off adopting Lotze's idealism. In 1888 he returned to Erlangen for his theological exams, subsequently returned to Göttingen for his Habilitation thesis, and decided that living without an idealistic philosophical theology was not really an option for him. Philosophically Troeltsch began as a Lotze-type idealist, then blended Wilhelm Dilthey's hermeneutical philosophy with it, until just after the turn of the century, when he shifted to a neo-Kantian philosophy of value.[105]

He began his teaching career in 1890 as a Privatdozent at Göttingen, where Troeltsch adopted Lagarde's history of religions approach. Lagarde, an eminent scholar, wrote extensively in German and Latin on biblical criticism and philology, reconstructed manuscripts for almost half the Hebrew Bible, and edited texts in Greek, Hebrew, Persian, Coptic, and Aramaic, including an Aramaic translation (*Targum*) of the Prophets. A strong personality who exhorted his students to get involved in social causes, he and Ritschl were personal and intellectual rivals. Lagarde was deeply pious, nationalistic, and convinced that his approach to religion helped to purify German Christianity. He charged that Ritschl was too theological to understand religion and too Pauline to be the theologian that Germany needed. Troeltsch and his friends embraced Lagarde's claim that theology should compare religions on an objective basis, eschewing Ritschl's Pauline provincialism. In Lagarde's case, however, this claim to objectivity was savagely ridiculous, as he was a violent anti-Semite who played a leading role in the revival of anti-Semitism in late nineteenth-century Germany. Lagarde heightened the "Jesus versus Judaism" tradition in German criticism, advocating a national Christianity purged of Jewish and Pauline elements. An active player in the Prussian Conservative Party, he supplemented his scholarly tomes with vile screeds describing Jews as vermin needing to be exterminated as soon as possible; his *Schriften für das deutsche Volk* was a classic of anti-Semitic bigotry that the Nazis, notably Alfred Rosenberg, subsequently canonized.[106]

Troeltsch's group played a careful hand with Lagarde's anti-Semitism. In public Troeltsch avoided the topic; in private he attributed Germany's growing anti-Semitism, with a wry tone, to political opportunism and religious rivalry. For the post-Ritschlians, one historic failure led to another. They failed to credit their teacher, Ritschl, for his admirable opposition to anti-Jewish interpretations of Christianity, which were at the heart of his bitter conflicts with Lagarde. They demurred on the increasing anti-Semitism of the academy in which they sought position and tenure. Sometimes they sanitized Lagarde-style "Jesus versus Judaism" arguments, as in Bousset's book *Jesu Predigt in ihrem Gegensatz zum Judentum* (*Jesus' Preaching in Contrast to Judaism*, 1892), though Troeltsch held out for a more balanced approach, viewing Jesus as a product of Hebrew faith and also transcending it. For the most part the post-Ritschlians, while founding a "universal" approach to religion, failed to say that inter-faith decency and anti-Semitism were antithetical.[107]

For them the methodological issue was consuming. By the time of Ritschl's death in 1889, his last group of followers believed that the history of religions method marked an advance on Ritschl just as Ritschl marked an advance on the Tübingen School. In 1892 Troeltsch moved to Bonn to become a junior professor; two years later he was called to a chair at Heidelberg, where he taught until moving to Berlin in 1915, where he dedicated the second volume of his collected works to Lagarde. At Heidelberg he became the major theologian of the history of religions school.

The Heidelberg faculty was in a low period when he got there. For years Troeltsch complained to friends that he had no conversation partners in Heidelberg, much less anyone to look up to: "It's a pity that this is such a dead and lifeless faculty." His actual community consisted of thinkers across the country that he studied and met at conferences, notably neo-Kantian philosopher Wilhelm Dilthey, and his former Göttingen classmates. Dilthey, a pioneering advocate of hermeneutics, championed the relevance of historical consciousness for the human sciences (*Geisteswissenschaften*) as distinct from the natural sciences. He taught that the value of each historical event arises from its historical particularity, its "individuality," and that each event should be evaluated only as its own intention and content demand. One should not apply norms to an event that are historically inappropriate to it, which demeans its value; rather, the "hermeneutic circle" of the interpreter is a recurring movement between the implicit and the explicit, the particular and the whole. Troeltsch drew on Dilthey in his early work, and on Bousset, Gunkel, and Wrede, who were quicker to make a scholarly mark. In 1895 Bousset published a book on the Anti-Christ legend in Jewish and Christian folklore; Troeltsch lauded it with a movement spirit, calling it something "common to the young Göttingen school, an unrestricted history-of-religions method which investigates in purely historical and philological terms the varied material of the religious movements which supported and surrounded Christianity."[108]

This was the way forward, Troeltsch believed. The Ritschlians started with Christianity, an independent entity grounded in faith; the post-Ritschlian historicists started with religion, of which Christianity is one among others. In 1897 he put it aggressively, asserting that "a grand new discipline, the history of religion" dismantled the claims of Christianity to superiority and universal truth. Moreover, even the idea of religion as an independent sphere of life disappears when one takes seriously "this maelstrom of historical diversity." This does not mean that historical relativism is the final truth, he argued; it is terribly important to take historical relativism seriously *and* not to treat it as the final word. Troeltsch proposed to do that by holding fast to three fundamental truths supported by historical consciousness: Mind has an independent potency not derived from nature, all religions are identical at their core, and some forms of religious consciousness are more advanced than others in advancing beyond nature and historical provincialism.[109]

On powers of mind, Troeltsch took his German idealism mostly from Lotze and Hegel, conceiving self-consciousness as the necessary presupposition of all thinking and the world of objects. Lotze stressed that the natural sciences, being mechanistic, do not explain the reality or unity of consciousness. Only spirit, a transcendent and unifying reality, accounts for the experience of freedom and other powers of mind. Troeltsch argued that it also accounts for the essential unity of religions: "Everywhere the basic reality of religion is the same: an underivable, purely positive, again and again experienced contact with the Deity." The basic reality of religion is the same everywhere because the human spirit is the same everywhere. Humanity has a common dynamism of spirit that advances in different ways through the mysterious movement of divine Spirit in and through the human spirit. The more that religions advance toward their ultimate goal, the more they strive for the truth "in its totality and fullness," moving beyond the spell of nature and local mythology.[110]

Troeltsch judged that most religions remained nature religions firmly bound to their respective mythologies. Buddhism was a partial exception by virtue of its universalistic aspects, but it remained the religion of a monastic order, catering to a spiritual elite. In Buddhism, Troeltsch explained, most of humanity was condemned to a cycle of reincarnations in an endlessly repetitive world-historical process going nowhere. The Deity was replaced by "a merely impersonal order of redemption" lacking any inner necessity to gather all humanity for a redemptive purpose. Islam was another partial exception, albeit a slight one. On the one hand, Troeltsch argued, Islam inherited a unified deity and a few universal moral maxims from its Jewish and Christian background. On the other hand, it marked a regression from the religions it succeeded, because it had an arbitrary and severe God, its "few paltry moral commandments" did not derive from the essential inner nature of the divine, and its continuing ties to the Arab world and war were obvious and predominant.[111]

Only one religion thus far, Christianity, was truly universal, Troeltsch argued. Christianity inherited a huge advantage, the response of the religion of Israel to the demise of the state of Israel. Judaism survived by transcending its origins as a provincial nature religion, lifting purity of heart above priestly ritual and dogma, and looking forward to a universal consummation of history. Christianity, a religion founded on the person of Jesus, built on the prophetic universal religion of Jesus. Because Christianity was based on personal faith in Jesus and a universal expectation for history, it did not relapse into a religion of nature, degenerating into pantheism or mysticism. In Christianity, God was experienced in the individual heart and the outward social world, and all people were included in God's plan. Troeltsch concluded that Buddhism was too pessimistic and otherworldly to be a universal religion of redemption, and neo-Platonism was too mystical, notwithstanding the Christian debt to neo-Platonism. Only Christianity got all the way to universal redemption, by breaking completely with nature religion: "It is because of its empirical uniqueness and the inner coincidence of what it is with what it demands that we recognize in the Prophetic-Christian religion the high-point, or rather a new point of departure, in the history of religion; not a conclusion or end calling for rest but the beginning of a new day for the world, with new work and new struggles."[112]

Troeltsch acknowledged that this argument carried forward the German Enlightenment and idealist traditions. Lessing had an early version of it, Schleiermacher offered a classic version, and Hegel's version was the dominant one in modern theology. But Lessing virtually equated his "eternal gospel" with Enlightenment rationality. Schleiermacher made religion conform to his metaphysical monism, nearly dissolving the particularity and diversity of religions into a "romantic Spinozism" that treated all religions as merely different ways of conceiving one's immanence in God. Hegel had an extreme case of metaphysical monism, explaining everything as the logical unfolding of the idea in its dialectical necessity. In Hegelian idealism the contingent, particular, and unruly aspects of actual religion did not show through. Troeltsch urged that the best strategy was to discipline German idealism with scientifically validated research. It was hard to give up the illusion of control, he allowed; the fear of being drowned by historical relativism drove modern people to become fervent patriots, social justice enthusiasts, or advocates of non-religious altruism. But these were bad bargains: "The recognition will come that religion is the true home of all such ideals, and that, above all, an assured and joyous faith in an absolute goal must be found again in it."[113]

Repeatedly Troeltsch was accused of dissolving Christian revelation into historical relativism; he jousted with the Ritschlian ringleaders Ferdinand Kattenbusch and Julius Kaftan over this issue. Kattenbusch told *Christliche Welt* editor Martin Rade that he could "take the rustic fellow" well enough personally – references to Troeltsch's boisterous Bavarian temperament abounded in this circle – but he was appalled at Troeltsch's relativizing approach to theology. Kaftan told Rade that he had "a formal horror of this history-of-religions method which ends up treasuring and stressing most what is alien to us, as children do." The only dogmatics it was capable of producing was a "stupid" one, he judged. If Christianity is not absolute, theology is pointless, but the claim of absoluteness rests on a judgment of faith, which the Troeltschian upstarts ruled out.[114]

In 1896 the *Christliche Welt* circle gathered in Eisenach for a conference, where Kaftan gave a learned, ponderous, somewhat scholastic lecture on the Logos doctrine. Ernest discussion ensued, and Troeltsch erupted, rushing to the podium to declare: "Gentlemen, everything is tottering!" He held the floor for several minutes, giving examples, painting in broad strokes, making his points vigorously. Most of the audience stared at him with disgust, notably Kattenbusch, who chided Troeltsch for his "shabby theology." Troeltsch stormed out of the room, slamming the door behind him. Troeltsch's student Walther Köhler later recalled that the older Ritschlians were shocked by Troeltsch's behavior and position, "but we younger ones pricked up our ears."[115]

Kaftan responded with a sharp attack on Troeltsch titled, "The Independence of Christianity," which made its central point in the title. One either begins with faith in the Christian revelation or one does not, Kaftan argued. If one begins there, the Christian claim to absoluteness is justified; if one does not begin with a judgment of faith, working up to absoluteness is impossible and historical relativism devours anything that one might offer in its place. Privately Troeltsch seethed at Kaftan's condescending treatment, telling Bousset that he would have no more personal dealings with Kaftan. In public he kept his feelings a bit more leashed, retorting that he would not be corrected by Kaftan's rules for correct theology, which relegated theology to a ghetto of special pleading. The pertinent either/or, Troeltsch argued, was whether theology had to claim a special exception from the usual methods of the sciences. Put differently, it was the question whether theology had to begin with a supernaturalist revelation. Troeltsch urged that on his approach, theology broke out of its ghetto, it plainly rejected supernaturalism, and it did not separate Christianity from its context in the history of religions. Kaftan-style Ritschlian theology used historical criticism in the manner of an "apologetic hunter" venturing into the wilderness only to shoot down evidence for a dogmatic certainty assumed from the outset. Troeltsch countered that real historical reason gets its truths by finding them, not by gathering historical evidence for dogmas it assumes.[116]

It is certainly true, he allowed, that critical historical consciousness combined with atheism leads straight to historical relativism, which leads to nihilism. Troeltsch wanted nothing to do with that; for him the point of creating a thoroughly historicist approach to theology was to prevent atheistic academics from owning historical criticism. He was a gatekeeper on both sides of this prescription, upholding stringent standards of what counted as historical criticism while conceiving history as the disclosure of divine reason. Historical reason lives by probability, he stressed; all it can do is measure degrees of probability, noting analogies between similar events of the past and present, and holding fast to the similarity of all historical events. Hindu and Christian miracle stories must get the same treatment; Troeltsch despaired of the Ritschlian School distinction between *Heilsgeschichte* (salvation history) and *Historie* (secular ordinary history), which blended historical criticism with saving facts known only to believers: "Today all kinds of things are labeled as 'historical' and as 'facts' which are nothing of the kind, and which ought not to be so labeled, since they are miraculous in nature and can only be apprehended by faith." Theology had no future in the academy if theologians had to have their own kind of history.[117]

At the same time, sometimes within the same paragraph, Troeltsch urged religious thinkers not to let go of the big picture. The human spirit is the same everywhere; it has a single divine source that radiates in many directions; and in the religion of the Hebrew prophets and Jesus, "a God distinct from nature produced a personality superior to nature with eternally transcendent goals and the willpower to change the world."[118]

By the turn of the twentieth century Troeltsch was known for his biting, analytical, and programmatic articles and reviews on these themes, his willingness to fight with Ritschlians and religious conservatives, and no books. Then the books poured forth, beginning with a classic, *The Absoluteness of Christianity and the History of Religions* (1902), which began as a lecture to the *Christliche Welt* circle. By then he had begun to relinquish what remained of his neo-Hegelian idealism in favor of a neo-Kantian philosophy of value, which required him to refashion his alternative to atheistic relativism and his claim that Kaftan was wrong about the impossibility of working up to a claim of absoluteness for Christianity.

Characteristically he began with a grand generalization about the modern world, that it represented "a unique type of culture" by taking an "unreservedly historical view" of all things human. In antiquity, Troeltsch observed, history was the history of single states. In Catholic culture it became the history of humankind, but everything was interpreted through church dogma. Modern culture took the next step by affirming the universal ambitions of the Catholic idea while dissolving its dogmas in the flow of events. For modern historical consciousness all things were in play as subjects of interpretation, "first measuring them by their own criteria and then combining them into an overall picture of the continuous and mutually conditioning factors in all individual phenomena that shape the unfolding development of mankind."[119]

From its beginning, Troeltsch noted, Christianity struggled with the problem of its relationship to other religions. Paul was the first to construe Christianity as a new, independent, universal religious power, but he relied "disproportionately on Judaism" and his unrepeatable inner experiences in theorizing what Christianity is about. Later generations had no recourse to Paul's vision of Christ, his inner struggle with the limits and demands of Jewish law, or his ecstatic experiences of the Spirit. To make Christianity intelligible to Christians and outsiders, the church forged a coat of armor, the doctrines of supernatural revelation and the incarnation, which led to the Logos theory: All moments of truth contained in the world's various religions and philosophies are expressions of the mind of God at work in the world, and Christ is the perfect revelation of the divine mind, the incarnation of divine Reason.[120]

Troeltsch judged that these two approaches to the problem served the church remarkably well, until the modern period. The Pauline tradition relied on the miracle of an inner renewal transcending all natural powers and a structure of dogma about it, while the Logos tradition treated non-Christian religions as blinkered anticipations or reflections of the absolute truth revealed in Christianity. In the latter case, Christianity represented the perfect realization of the essence of religion. For modern theology, however, the first approach was not really an option, since it was too subjective, authoritarian, and dependent on miracle claims to pass modern tests of credible belief.

In Troeltsch's view, the Logos tradition was the only serious contender in this field, specifically the modern, idealistic, evolutionary version of it espoused in liberal theology. First, history was subordinated to the concept of a uniform, homogeneous, self-actuating power or universal principle; second, this concept was raised to the status of a universal norm or ideal constituting that which is of value in all events; lastly, the two concepts were bound together by a concept of evolutionary development.

But the modern spirit is very tough on even the most liberal Logos theology, Troeltsch cautioned. Modern history knows nothing of an all-inclusive principle that regulates the emergence of everything individual, constitutes the essence and fulfill-ment of all value, and is the norm of all things: "The modern idea of history knows no universal principle on the basis of which the content and sequence of events might be deduced. It knows only concrete, individual phenomena, always conditioned by their context and yet, at bottom, underivable and simply existent phenomena." Troeltsch allowed that modern historical consciousness may grasp universally valid ideas, or at least, ideas said to be universally valid, but it knows no values that coincide with actual universals. Rather, it knows only ideas that appear in individual form and make their claim for universal validity by resisting other ideas.[121]

Idealistic theories of graded progression miss what actually happens, he contended. Real history offers no evidence of gradual progression to higher orientations: "Only at special points do higher orientations burst forth, and then in a great, soaring devel-opment of their uniquely individual content." Harnackian kernel and husk strategies had similar problems. Here, the aim was the same as the theory of graded progression, to dispense with centuries of outdated dogma. But Harnackian liberals failed to notice that the absolute and the relative are not so easily separated. Absolutizing the kernel, instead of preserving a credible absolute, absolutizes the husk as well; meanwhile, the relativity of the husk relativizes the kernel. Troeltsch urged that searching for a transhistorical absolute within history is counter-productive, for the most important religious ideas are always closely bound up with the leading ideas of a given age. The truest parts of Christianity are not things that can be lifted above history, for Christianity is a historical movement. Even the retrograde aspects of Christian tradition have a place in it: "What was once lightly set aside as husk is now receiving proper recognition in authentic historical studies, not because it is of primary importance but because what is primarily important is not an ahistorical, eternal, and ever unfolding principle but a living, individual complex of concrete reality, a whole that has become what it is under very specific circumstances."[122]

This was the post-Ritschlian *Religionsgeschichtliche* approach, focusing on the particularities of historical periods and the interrelationships of cultural structures. No historical period is a mere rung on a ladder, Troeltsch stressed; each has its own ethos and meanings. The Tübingen School was a breakthrough for its time, but it operated in scale-oriented theories about early Christianity and Catholicism. Real history does not unfold in schemes about logically related members of ascending series. Troeltsch noted that Lagarde was the first religious scholar to get this right. Divorcing the actual, particular, historical development of religion from all theological and philosophical schemes about it, Lagarde called for "impartial, dedicated study of the history of religion that would make use of ever available means for conscientious research." Admittedly, Lagarde had an agenda – to demonstrate the greatness of

Christianity when stripped of its dogmatic and apologetic dross. But what mattered was his model of impartial research, not his motivation for it. Lagarde-style historical objectivity "has won the day" in historical scholarship, Troeltsch contended; it needed to win the day in theology while theology still had a place in the academy.[123]

The Ritschlian School resisted this verdict by insisting on the necessity of a Christian epistemology. Conceiving Christianity as the historical kingdom movement of Jesus, it claimed that one must be in the movement to understand it. Troeltsch replied, "It is obvious, however, that this is only toying with the concept of what it means for something to be historical and individual." He allowed that Ritschl, unlike some Ritschlians, was sufficiently historical to spurn all appeals to miracles. But it was telling that Ritschl left the concept of miracle "in an odd state of suspense" *and* that some Ritschlians appealed to a special understanding of miracles wrought by faith. In both cases, Ritschlian theology sought a credible way to set Christianity apart from everything else. Troeltsch observed, "Everything non-Christian is instantly brought into conformity with that way of thinking which sees other religions in terms of natural revelations and postulates of universal scope, while Christianity is understood in terms of supernatural absolute revelation."[124]

To be sure, the Ritschlian School found a liberal way to claim absoluteness, placing its revelation in the same "curious state of suspense" that it lumped miracles. The upshot, Troeltsch argued, was a theology of absoluteness lacking any form of absoluteness. On the one hand, Jesus and the early Christian movement were absolute; on the other hand, they were historical, and Ritschlian theology had nothing else to fall back on – no miracles, no infallible church or Bible, and no Logos theory of Christ as the fulfillment of religion. The Ritschlian School was already fading, Troeltsch believed, because it was based on a contradiction. It wanted to be historical without accepting "the consequences of what it means to be historical."[125]

Troeltsch countered that in every moment of its history, Christianity is "a purely historical phenomenon, subject to all the limitations to which any individual historical phenomenon is exposed, just like the other great religions." To make it special by appealing to a special understanding derived from faith was to fail the essential requirement of modern critical consciousness. But Troeltsch no longer had a neo-Hegelian notion of the Absolute working itself out through the permutations of history. In its place he espoused a neo-Kantian theory of value orientation, which he took from the southwest German Kantians Wilhelm Windelband and especially Heinrich Rickert. Critical consciousness does not exclude norms, Troeltsch argued; rather, the most important task of critical history is to discern the value orientations that occur within history and to construe them as a unified whole. These norms, and whatever ways they are unified, are always individual, particular, socially conditioned forms of striving toward a goal. History consists of relative, situated tendencies toward an absolute goal that is never completely realized in history. Religion is about cultivating and realizing value orientations, and some religions do it better than others, Troeltsch contended. What matters, above all, is to bring about "the victory of the highest values and the incorporation of all reality into their frame of reference."[126]

He stressed that historicism does not rule out making comparative judgments. To the contrary, making critical comparisons is fundamental to historical reason. A historicist project that refused to discern value orientations in history and make value-laden judgments about them would be an absurdity, a capitulation to nihilism. Troeltsch argued that the best judgments emerge from the critical comparison of value orientations. Historical criticism, rightly conceived, begins with descriptions of historical phenomena, which lead to the taking of a position about the value orientations occurring in history, which requires philosophical reflection. The very fact that certain things – such as, religions – can be compared shows that they are related "to something common and universally valid within them." Historical reason does not yield Hegelian universal principles, but it does identify orienting goals and ideals.[127]

On this slightly refigured basis Troeltsch made his usual argument that Christianity comes out on top. Religions of law are inferior to redemption religions, he contended, which disposed of Judaism and Islam. Judaism never broke free from the bonds of blood and cult, and thus never got to ethical universalism, while Islam had an arbitrary deity and "immortalizes all kinds of Arabic idiosyncrasies." Historical science, in Troeltsch's telling, narrows the field to two redemption strategies, but it cannot make the decision between them, which must be made on the basis of religious conviction. In the final analysis one must choose between meditating on Transcendent Being or non-Being (Brahmanic acosmism or Buddhist quietism), or holding fast to a history-transforming personalism rooted in the Christian God, "the ground of all life and of all genuine value." Troeltsch urged that Christian personalism is more profound religiously and has a higher ethical goal than the Indian redemption religions: "It alone, by virtue of a higher world deriving from its own reality and inner necessity, takes empirical reality as actually given and experienced, builds upon it, transforms it, and at length raises it up to a new level." Christianity alone makes a complete break from nature religion, he asserted. Only in Christianity is the higher world conceived as "infinitely valuable personal life" that creates and shapes all things.[128]

Is that enough to sustain a personal Christian faith? Troeltsch implored that it should be enough to know that one is on the right path. It should be enough for a Christian to know that Christianity is the "high point" and "convergence point" of world religious development (still smacking of Hegel, denials notwithstanding). Put differently, he wrote, it should be enough to know that one has "the best and most profound truth that exists" without believing that non-Christians are completely cut off from the truth. In this case, Christianity is still the normative religion, but not the absolute religion; it is normative for Christians and for all history up to the present time, while the future belongs to God: "What Jesus brings is simply the highest and definitive truth, the truth that is bound to endure, the truth that receives from him a power which grasps a man inwardly and totally. Yet it is this same Jesus who relegated the absolute religion to the world to come." In the preaching of Jesus, and in Christianity rightly understood, the coming kingdom is the only absolute.[129]

Already known as a battler, Troeltsch plunged deeper into battle. Ludwig Ihmels led a chorus of conservative protests that Troeltsch abandoned any claim to supernatural certainty. Carl F. G. Heinrici, with a sharper polemical edge, lumped Troeltsch with Strauss and other naturalistic anti-Christians. Max Reischle contended that Troeltsch's personalism opened gaps for supernatural influence. Many critics charged that Troeltsch's historicism devoured any real basis for theology. Troeltsch replied that doing without supernatural certainty was axiomatic for modern theology; his pertinent predecessor was Lagarde, not Strauss; he gave no role to supernatural influence; and saving theology from utter historical relativism was the whole point of his work. He did not believe that the history of religions approach ruled out theological reflection; everything that he cared about was at stake in preventing this outcome: "To build up a theological faculty that had no official knowledge of normative religious truth, that had to hunt for it like an explorer for the North Pole or a water witcher for water, would be a manifest absurdity. In religious matters he who would teach others must already have a position of his own and must be convinced that maintaining a position is a meaningful possibility."[130]

Thus he achieved prominence chiefly as the leading theologian of the history of religions approach, and as a battler, though Troeltsch found himself battling more than he liked. "I'm always being hounded," he told Bousset. Troeltsch was willing to do a certain amount of fighting for intellectual freedom and a modern approach to theology, but he wanted to be known as a balanced, scholarly, conciliatory type. He was slow to take up social issues, as he was basically conservative politically, bourgeois in temperament and style, and averse even to the mild social Christianity of the Evangelical Social Congress. But in 1897 he became friends with his new economics colleague at Heidelberg, Max Weber, who admonished Troeltsch that sitting out the age of the Social Question was not really commendable; meanwhile Harnack prodded Troeltsch to participate in the Congress. Weber's wife, Marianne Weber, encouraged Troeltsch to adopt a more positive view of democracy and feminism, though she later recalled making little progress with him.[131]

Political Ethics and Social Christianity

In 1904 Troeltsch unveiled his social philosophy in a speech to the Evangelical Social Congress in Breslau, taking for granted the triumph of realism in German thought about state and society. The generations that venerated Kantian and Hegelian cultural goals of the state had passed, he observed. For his generation, schooled in the ascendancy of Germany under Bismarck, politics was obviously about power, power was the essence of the state, and a strong army was the backbone of the state. Troeltsch added that Marxism, in its own way, taught a similar lesson: All political, philosophical, and ethical theories were byproducts of given configurations of power, which they rationalized. But even from a hardcore realist perspective, he reasoned, there were crucial matters to sort out concerning the relation of Christianity to modern society. Assuming that some kind of political ethic was needed, what were the spiritual and political forces in modern life that might produce the best one?[132]

Troeltsch identified liberalism, nationalism, democracy, and conservatism as the four key forces. All had an important role to play, though democracy and conservatism were more important than liberalism and nationalism. Liberalism, the ethic of a constitutional state (*Rechtsstaat*) serving a free culture, limited the role of the state to maintaining order and protecting high culture. Troeltsch acknowledged that Lockean-style liberalism made historic gains for individual freedom, which were precious to modern consciousness and definitive of it. Nonetheless, the merely negative liberty of a limited state was no place to rest, and Germany had not done so. Nationalism was a stronger and more creative force in German life, he contended. No state becomes a nation until the individuals in it identify with the state, and if one identifies with the state, "one no longer needs to fear any superior power, except possibly God." Troeltsch took for granted that any state with growing power is aggressive and devoted to conquest, but when expansion is no longer possible, governments aim for stability and preserving the status quo. In his view, Friedrich Naumann was the model nationalist, his socialism notwithstanding, because Naumann was smart and prudential and his motivating concern was always to serve Germany's national interest.[133]

But patriotism cannot be the "last word" in a political ethic, Troeltsch cautioned. The ethical value of a state rests on the spirit of its political institutions, the richness and depth of its culture, and the ethical ideas permeating its society, plus nationalistic feeling. From a political ethical standpoint, Switzerland had great value, despite being tiny and low on nationalistic fervor, while Turkey, though large and nationalistic, "has none at all." Troeltsch argued that a strong, ethically valuable state must have ethical principles that penetrate the inner structures of its institutions and define the social good. Democracy and conservatism had this capacity to ascribe an intrinsic ethical value to the state; liberalism and nationalism did not.[134]

Unfortunately, Troeltsch lamented, democracy was identified in German society with the proletarian movement. This had to change if the true importance of democracy and its deep connection to Christianity were to be realized. Troeltsch implored that the Socialists did not own democracy; far from it, because the democratic principle stood for transcending the class struggle, "its ideal is social peace." At its root, he argued, democracy is an ethical idea, "the great idea of human rights," which holds that every person has a moral right to independent value. The democratic idea of human rights stood against "exploitative colonialism" and "absolute male domination," although the qualifiers were important to Troeltsch; outright anti-imperialists and feminists made him nervous. Taken seriously, he advised, "the human rights of alien races would be protected in a program of peaceful colonization." Troeltsch stressed that modern democracy differed from that of antiquity because it was Protestant, springing from the Reformed ideal of popular sovereignty, not aristocratic or revolutionary. Even in an age of Socialist movements, the strongest ally of democracy was "the Christian feeling that the poor and humble must be supported in their aspirations."[135]

But democracy had to be chastened by the aristocratic impulse; otherwise it was stupid and self-devouring. Troeltsch described modern conservatism as essentially aristocratic, understood in the political sense as the power of privileged individuals and groups to pass on the power to rule. Conservatism, so understood, rested on a profound truism, "the presupposition of the inequality of human nature, which is fundamental and can never be eliminated." Without this vast inequality in "native endowment," he argued, it would not be possible for human beings to form communities and societies, sort out divisions of labor, and instill habits of loyalty, modesty, piety, trust, and responsibility. Even the existence of the modern state depended on inequality, for it would not have arisen on liberal terms as a contract among atomistic individuals. Aristocratic conservatism, Troeltsch declared, resting on the wisdom of the ages and confirmed by everyday experience, held to a "genuine and legitimate" fundamental ethical principle: "Authority, not majority!" Because human beings are unavoidably and vastly unequal in intelligence, competence, goodness, and power, they need authority desperately. To recognize this "indisputable fact" and its moral wisdom is to "appreciate the moral values that are destined to grow from these inequalities and power-based relations."[136]

Democracy and conservatism needed each other, nationalism had an important role too, and liberal liberties were to be safeguarded. Troeltsch denied that the United States, lacking an aristocracy, did not need a conservative tradition. The United States was too young and liberal to have an aristocratic tradition, he allowed, but that would change as it got older: "For everything historical is aristocratic, and all aristocracy entails conservatism." In foreign policy he admired modern conservatism for its nationalistic realism, but only to a point, admiring also Kant's liberal democratic dream of a cooperative federation of nations. Troeltsch noted that conservatism was nearly always nationalistic, not shy about going to war, and always concerned with preserving its privileges: "It will sanction the domination of small states by large ones and the subjection of inferior races by those more capable of rule and richer in culture; it will regard the idea of rule by the white race as the natural consequence of the place the white race has won for itself in history." This observation, begging for a word of judgment at the Congress, did not get one; Troeltsch let his audience decide whether white supremacism was a bad thing.[137]

In any case, he concluded, Christianity was part of the mix, but it didn't really settle anything. Christianity had no political ideas at its birth; after it got into politics it had to borrow from Aristotle and Roman law; and its significance in modern politics was indirect. Its chief contribution to political ethics was its religious and ethical personalism, which challenged individuals to fulfill their God-given capacities for love, creativity, and faithfulness. Christianity idealized Adam, the primordial man of paradise free from sin and all structures of dominion, but it also lived in the real world of sin, guilt, proprietary distinctions, and violence. It commanded moral feeling and works of mercy for the dispossessed, but it had no politics: "Today we know with certainty that the gospel contains no direct political and social instructions; it is fundamentally non-political. It deals only with the highest goals of personal life and of personal community, and anticipates the realization of this ideal in its expectation of the imminent end of the world and in the coming kingdom of God."[138]

The heart of Christian ethics was the love ethic of Jesus, which had no place in a political ethic. Troeltsch urged that the best Christian contribution to political ethics lay elsewhere, in its secondary ideas of personhood and submission to natural orders. The former idea was a bulwark of democracy; the latter idea went with conservatism; Christianity needed to help fuse the two ideas politically. He cautioned that these ideas would never be enough for any state, which had a moral idea of its own, nationalism, that it needed for its identity and self-preservation, and which it did not get from Christianity. This idea was purely political; Troeltsch claimed that Christianity had never been able to do "anything directly" with it, seeming to forget centuries of Christian nationalisms. In any case, the political role of Christianity was to press its ideas of personality and obedience on the state: "Christianity introduces something new and vital into political ethics, namely, an unconditional appreciation of the person and a respectful modesty." To the question of which idea – democracy or conservatism – was more important in 1904, Troeltsch answered, neither, because the crucial thing was to bring them together. Democrats and conservatives inveighed against each other with spiteful polemics. Perhaps the Evangelical Social Congress could help: "The two ideas must find each other and reach an accommodation."[139]

Like Weber, Troeltsch was restless, skeptical, prone to nervousness and melancholy, and fretted about losing his capacity for scholarly productivity. He was a loner, but leaned on his friends and craved discussion. To some observers he seemed extroverted; to others he seemed passive and resigned; in reality he zigged and zagged as a mixture of both, except at the lecture podium, where the extrovert prevailed. He could write a punchy sentence, but favored long, winding sentences that piled up clauses, abstractions, and many-sided descriptions. He did not have clear positions before he embarked on his research or even started writing; he found his answers along the way. Like Weber he was tremendously productive and gifted with rare analytical power, writing vast works on broad themes that were crammed with detail. His friend Friedrich Meinecke compared him to a thundering mountain stream that briskly whisked huge loads downriver as though at play. Harnack, with customary vividness, captured Troeltsch at the lecture podium: "His manner was unique and at the same time captivating. He did not aim to formulate his ideas sharply and concisely but with repeated efforts and with an overflowing eloquence which was amply, even overabundantly at his command, he tossed an observation to and fro, assailing it from all sides and putting it in different contexts until it appeared purified and clear. His mind acted like a powerful centrifugal machine or like a rotating drum which shook and tossed about the subject until it was cleansed from all foreign parts and loomed up in its own individuality."[140]

In 1904 Troeltsch was asked to review a new edition of Greifswald theologian Martin von Nathusius' book on the church and the social question. The book was terrible, he judged; it showed that modern theologians had a pathetic understanding of social Christianity, despite talking about it constantly. Nathusius confused two understandings of the "social" in social Christianity, failing to distinguish between the social character of the gospel and its sociological effects, and he made a mess of the relationships between State and society. Instead of a review, Troeltsch began to think about a major work that paralleled Harnack's *History of Dogma*. Like Harnack, it would feature the notion of a self-unfolding of the religious idea, surveying the development of Christian social thought to the modern age (though Harnack stopped at the Reformation).[141]

But Troeltsch believed that Harnack's understanding of his subject and discipline was insufficiently sociological; thus, Harnack treated ideas as continuous realities and he underemphasized the social factors that shaped Christian doctrine. Troeltsch rejected the idea of a dogmatic subject that stays identical with itself through the permutations of history, for "Christianity" is as various as the many historical groups and traditions claiming the name. A new model was needed, one built on historical sociology and the history of religions. In that spirit Troeltsch labored for many years on *The Social Teaching of the Christian Churches* (1912), later recalling, "This time I dispensed with any programmatic preliminary work and instead of all the mere spitting I devoted myself with indescribable toil to piping." On occasion he boasted that his magnum opus created a new discipline.[142]

For several years he played down the notion that his research was leading to a big book. Characteristically, Troeltsch claimed that he had no underlying or overarching argument. The massive articles that he published between 1908 and 1910 did not defend a thesis; he merely sought to uncover what happened. But his studies of Christian social teaching elicited favorable comparisons to Harnack and Weber, which Troeltsch monitored closely. He cared intensely about his academic reputation, intending all along to produce a massive book.[143]

Meanwhile his thinking found a wider audience by accident, after Weber begged off from speaking at the Ninth Congress of German Historians in 1906 and sent Troeltsch in his place. Weber was asked to speak on the significance of Protestantism in the rise of the modern world, a topic pegged to his new book, *The Protestant Ethic and the Spirit of Capitalism* (1905), which argued that Calvinist salvation anxiety was a major cause of the rise of capitalism. Troeltsch filled in with a typical excursus, "The Significance of Protestantism for the Rise of the Modern World," taking aim at the cult of Martin Luther. On the one hand, he argued, Protestantism unarguably contributed to modern progress in law, government, economics, and high culture, and it accommodated the modern world very well. On the other hand, liberal Protestants needed to stop kidding themselves about their proximity to Luther. There was a chasm between the pre-modern and modern worlds, and the Reformers belonged to the other side.[144]

Troeltsch did not actually relegate Luther and Calvin to the Middle Ages, although for decades afterward, offended critics charged him with doing so. In his reading the Reformation of Luther and Calvin was a momentous phase of transition from the old world of feudal authoritarianism to the new world of freedom and modernity. It broke the Catholic monopoly on religious authority and set the stage for new possibilities. But Luther and Calvin, Troeltsch insisted, did not cross into the new world, not even with one foot. They gave a Protestant twist to Catholic problems, modifying medieval religion. Politically, socially, and religiously, Calvinism was more progressive than Lutheranism, and some elements of the Anabaptist and mystical movements were more progressive than Calvinism. But all of that merely put into play developments that, in the eighteenth century, were transformed by modernity. Modernity, Troeltsch argued, began with Enlightenment criticism and the rise of capitalism and the modern state. Protestantism contributed the ideas of freedom and personality to it, but Protestantism itself became modern by being transformed by modernity, not by fulfilling something in its nature.

Troeltsch ended with a cautionary Weberian flourish, refashioning Weber's dread of the iron cage of modernity. In Troeltsch's telling, Protestantism made one important contribution to modern Western civilization, "an extraordinarily strong religious and metaphysical foundation, which, moreover, exists independently of it." Liberal Prot-estantism helped to inspire and hold together a civilization that prized individual freedom, created vast new wealth, broke the power of disease, supported scholarship and high culture, and fostered a culture of material and spiritual progress. However, Troeltsch warned, there was a destructive underside to all this enlightenment and progress – powerful social trends that threatened to stop progress cold, if not destroy it: "Our economic development is rather tending in the direction of a new bondage, and the great military and bureaucratic States, in spite of all their parliaments, are not wholly favorable to the spirit of liberty. Whether our science, which is falling entirely into the hands of specialists, our philosophy, exhausted by a feverish attempt to test all standpoints, and our art, with its tendency to foster over-sensibility, are more favorable to it, there is good reason to doubt."[145]

The cause of freedom was increasingly battered and suffocated, Troeltsch admonished. Progressive optimism notwithstanding, the West seemed to be heading toward an era of oppression by giant corporate, governmental, and unionist entities. If he was right, it was more important than ever for liberal Protestants to uphold their distinct contribution to modern civilization, their freedom-loving metaphysic of religious personalism. This religious worldview established freedom on "a foundation which an all-too-human humanism cannot destroy," he claimed. The best hope of Western civilization rested on "faith in God as the power whence freedom and personality come to us; namely, Protestantism." Troeltsch urged the German historians, and his readers, to hold fast to it: "Otherwise the cause of freedom and personality may well be lost in the very moment when we are boasting most loudly of our allegiance to it, and of our progress in this direction."[146]

This was the burning social and religious concern underlying Troeltsch's painstaking research for *The Social Teaching of the Christian Churches,* which he undertook while pouring out lecture monographs and pamphlets with characteristically Troeltschian titles: "Religion and the Science of Religion" (1906), "The Separation of Church and State and the Teaching of Religion" (1907), "Luther and the Modern World" (1908), and "The Significance of the Historical Existence of Jesus for Faith" (1911). Always he sought to interpret human history as a flow of events operating within complex webs of interacting social, historical and natural factors. Nearly always he registered his animating conviction that everything was tottering.[147]

The Social Teaching of the Christian Churches, when it finally appeared in 1912 as the 1,000 page first volume of Troeltsch's collected works, registered a strong sense of tottering. Troeltsch recalled that when he began his career as a Ritschlian theologian he held Ritschl's twofold concept of how theology should proceed, relating a distinct concept of traditional doctrine to a critical understanding of the modern intellectual and religious situation. But then he came to doubt that Ritschl got either of them right. The Ritschlian strategy assimilated a dubious rendering of the Christian story to an equally questionable interpretation of the modern situation, covering up the actual contrasts between them. Troeltsch explained, "Thus I found myself confronted by a double task: to make clear to myself both the ecclesiastical dogmatic tradition of Protestantism in its own historical sense, and the intellectual and practical situation of the present day in its true fundamental tendencies."[148]

That explained his twofold fixation with the history of Protestantism and the emergence of the modern world. Troeltsch told himself that he was laying the historical groundwork for his systematic theology and philosophy of religion. But the more that he studied modern problems, the more he found himself pulled into social ethics. If Christianity was "first and foremost a matter of practice," its chief problems belonged to the sphere of practical life, the very area where the thinking of modern churches was most confused and out of date. Theology in the modern age had to grapple, above all, with the social problem.[149]

Troeltsch offered long, thick, penetrating descriptions of social teaching in the early Christian movement, early Catholicism, medieval Catholicism, and numerous varieties of European Protestantism. Adopting Weber's concept of ideal types, he argued that the Christian community, from its very beginning as an independent movement, developed three types of Christianity rooted in three distinct models of social organization. In Troeltsch's telling the gospel of Jesus was a religion of free piety, strong on spiritual intimacy and lacking any concern with organizing a cult or creating a religious community, much less prescribing a political ideology. These sociological deficits gave rise to three coping strategies; in effect, three kinds of Christianity: An institutional church model dispensing objective means of grace and redemption, a sectarian model of true believers living apart from the world, and a mystical Christianity stressing inward spiritual experience and playing down external forms of worship, doctrine, and organization.

Each of these ideal types produced a distinct theology, he argued. The church type, epitomized by medieval Catholicism, played down the need for subjective holiness, conceiving Christ as the Redeemer whose saving work is mediated to believers through the sacraments of the church. The sect type was a voluntary society of born-again believers, lower class and strongly eschatological, which conceived Christ as a lawgiving Lord of history destined to complete his work of redemption in the Second Coming. Troeltsch noted that the "very varied sect-movement" originated as a complement to Catholicism and was "almost entirely vanquished in the Catholic sphere" until it exploded in the Anabaptist and other radical movements of the sixteenth century. The mystical type, being intensely inward and individual, was even more various in Christian history; here Troeltsch had to settle for capsule descriptions of prominent individuals and their communities, notably George Fox and the Society of Friends. The Christ of mystical Christianity was an inward spiritual principle, "the Divine Spark which lies hidden in every mind and soul, stifled by sin and by the finite, yet capable of being quickened into vitality by the touch of the Divine Spirit working on and in our souls."[150]

Troeltsch acknowledged that ideal types are ideal constructs – useful tools – not anything that actually exists. Medieval Catholicism housed and sanctioned mystical theologies; Magisterial Calvinism, though belonging to the institutional church category, had strong sectarian elements; the Quakers would have been forgotten had they not adopted an Anabaptist ecclesiology and struggled to accommodate the real world. Personally, Troeltsch favored the mystical type, noting its later history in German idealism and liberal theology, and he respected the sectarian type for standing for something. But neither of these types produced a major social philosophy. Neither of them had a solution to the historic problem of how to relate a gospel of "infinite sublimity and childlike intimacy" to the larger world of culture, politics, nationalism and other religions. The sectarian movements took a stab at the Sermon on the Mount as counter-cultural communities cut off from the world, sometimes flipping to apocalyptic vengeance. The mystics took refuge in spiritual religion, which was too private to change anything. These approaches, besides having no answer to the original problem, were even more deficient in addressing the modern problem of out-of-control capitalism, labor unrest, urbanization, nationalism, militarism, and technology; Troeltsch described the modern social problem as "all this distress which weighs on our hearts and minds like a perpetual menace."[151]

Only the church type had the capacity to be creative and expansive, he argued. In its entire history up to the nineteenth century, Christianity (discounting Orthodoxy, which was out of view) produced only two major social philosophies: medieval Catholicism and Calvinism. The first was built on the spiritual unity of a feudal, patriarchal civilization featuring a supreme church. The second created a covenantal Protestant Christendom by combining aspects of asceticism, pietism, Free Church ecclesiology, state church governance, democracy, liberalism, vocational diligence, and the "glorification of work for its own sake." Both models, Troeltsch stressed, had an impressive history, having applied the "inner impulse of Christian thought" to the worlds of their time. And both were spent forces by the nineteenth century. The Catholic doctrine of the Catholic State was as laughable as the Vatican's opposition to evolution and historical criticism, and Calvinism fared little better under modern criticism. There was no serious contending Christian social philosophy in modern times. There was only the glimmer of one in the Christian Socialist movement.[152]

Troeltsch's treatment of Christian Socialism was odd, surprisingly appreciative, and truncated. Formally his study ended with the eighteenth century, but he peeked ahead on occasion, as in his long section on varieties of sectarianism, and he ended the book with an excursus on the current situation, which required some understanding of the century just passed. Christian Socialism got a brief mention near the end of his discussion of Protestant sectarianism. Obviously it was a form of sectarianism, he asserted; it recycled "the familiar characteristics of the primitive Christian tendency, the characteristics of the aggressive sect which believes in an actual transformation of conditions in this world." Troeltsch explained that modern Christian Socialists got to be Socialists by listening to Social Democratic speeches, which helped them to see things in the Bible that they hadn't noticed previously. Once they did so, they joined the sectarian tradition, usually without putting it that way, and modernized its usual tropes: "The Kingdom of God and reason, the Kingdom of God realized *on earth,* the invincible faith in the victory of goodness and in the possibility of overcoming every human institution which is based upon the mere struggle for existence, the Christian Revolution: this is the primitive, splendid ideal of the sect."[153]

It was surprising to Troeltsch, in a patronizing way, that Christian Socialists educated in modern universities actually believed they had laid hold of the original gospel faith. But the Christian Socialists had something that no other modern group possessed, he allowed: an understanding of Christianity that harmonized traditional Christian norms with modern social views. Moreover, they did it by becoming the first movement to reject centuries of authoritarianism and conformism in ethics: "Christian Socialism alone has broken through these theories, and forced men to think out afresh the social ethic of Christianity and its relation to the actual changes in the social order. It has laid bare the worm-eaten condition of the previous conventional Christian ethic, which, at its best, offered something for the ethics of the family and the individual, but which, on the other hand, had no message for social ethics save that of acceptance of all existing institutions and conditions, much to the satisfaction of all in authority. Christian Socialism has regained for the Christian ethic its Utopian and revolutionary character; once more it has brought upon its heralds the reproach of Christ, which officials of Church and State are always ready to hurl at all who indulge humanitarian sentiment or in idealistic dreams."[154]

Troeltsch cheered the Christian Socialists for breaking through, even as he judged them doubly naïve. Theologically they were innocents, invoking words of Jesus as though they blazed through the centuries; politically they were innocent and dangerous, fantasizing about an international proletariat that refused all calls to war except perhaps class war. Even if Christian Socialism became the church's third great social philosophy, the church needed something else. A truly modern, critical, effective, and inspiring way of engaging the world through Christianity was needed. But Troeltsch admitted that he didn't know what it was: "If the present social situation is to be controlled by Christian principles, thoughts will be necessary which have not yet been thought."[155]

His only constructive thoughts toward that end were his usual ones about upholding a Christian personalist worldview. Only Christianity provided a strong basis for personality and individuality, he urged. Through its concept of Divine Love, only Christianity embraced and united all human souls. Ethically, only Christianity solved the problem of inequality, by viewing all people as children of God loved by God, without denying the "patent fact" that people varied greatly in intelligence and competence. Lastly, Christianity, being the consummate religion of love and personality, promoted charity as the fruit of the Christian Spirit, though Troeltsch held off from claiming that only Christianity promoted charity.[156]

Beyond that he was chastened about the relevance of modern Christianity: "Every idea is still faced by brutal facts, and all upward movement is checked and hindered by interior and exterior difficulties." Once the church lost its doctrinal certainties and social power, there was no answer; there was only the search for a new one: "Nowhere does there exist an absolute Christian ethic, which only awaits discovery; all that we can do is to learn to control the world-situation in its successive phases just as the earlier Christian ethic did in its own way."[157]

The Social Teaching of the Christian Churches made Troeltsch famous, dominated its field for decades, and eased his transition to philosophy. Generations of theologians and social ethicists that rejected his theology taught his historical account as definitive. His typology of church, sect, and mysticism was canonical for decades, inspiring H. Richard Niebuhr's equally famous typology of religion and culture models in *Christ and Culture*. In 1915 Troeltsch accepted a chair in philosophy at Berlin, claiming for the rest of his life not to have left religion behind, despite what theologians said. For decades afterward his reputation in theology was based on *Social Teaching*, his writings on the absoluteness of Christianity, and the fact that he quit theology, not that he taught systematic theology eleven times, for two semesters each time, during his 31 years at Heidelberg, and thus must have had a system of some sort. Troeltsch contributed to this skewed impression by declining to publish his lectures in systematic theology, which he called *Glaubenslehre* ("teaching of faith"), following Schleiermacher, rejecting the term "dogmatics" for smacking of timeless, nonhistorical dogma. To the end of his theological career and beyond it, he told his students that he was closer to Schleiermacher in method, approach, and inner feeling than any theologian of his time.[158]

This boast was important to Troeltsch personally, even as it annoyed fellow theologians. He had essentially the same doctrinal positions as Schleiermacher, but so did many liberals that he claimed to surpass in affinity with Schleiermacher. Claiming a deep affinity with Schleiermacher helped Troeltsch cope with his anxiety and frustration with theology as a field, and his doubts about his contribution to it. From the beginning of his academic career he questioned whether he had chosen the right field. He told Bousset that he doubted whether anyone would be able to make a real advance in theology. Troeltsch seized on the history of religions approach as soon as it arose, and he believed fervently that it marked a huge advance in the study of religion. But every time that he taught systematic theology, he realized that history of religions scholarship was a very limited resource for theology. On doctrine after doctrine, he found himself refashioning Schleiermacher and criticizing the mediating and Ritschlian schools for presuming to have improved on Schleiermacher; Troeltsch called them "hodgepodge" theologies.[159]

In 1913 he professed to disagree with Schleiermacher on only one important point, explaining that Schleiermacher tried not to be a monist, but failed: "Schleiermacher's dogmatics is everywhere saturated with pantheistic thinking, shot through and through with an atmosphere that breathes heavily of Spinoza and Goethe – an atmosphere to which our own present day also stands very close, albeit more as a caricature." For Troeltsch, moving from neo-Hegelian idealism to neo-Kantian idealism had been an important adjustment, but no more than an adjustment. He was still a German idealist who held fast to the personalizing impulse in life. Neo-Kantian idealism was a definite advance on Schleiermacher's monism, Troeltsch believed, because it gave free reign to personality, ethics, and will, and the reality of a pluralistic external world.[160]

At times Troeltsch also allowed that the later Schleiermacher emphasized Jesus' impression of divinity in a one-sided way that led to Herrmann's disastrous mistake of setting faith against knowledge. Schleiermacher taught that to feel the spiritual power of Jesus' personality as mediated by the church and the gospel picture of Jesus is to be convinced of his divinity; doubt is an outsiders' problem. Troeltsch, appalled that Herrmann took this argument all the way to a fideistic blind alley, urged liberals to keep their heads, avoiding blind alleys. It matters, for knowledge and faith, whether Jesus really existed, Troeltsch admonished. It matters whether the gospel picture of Jesus is more or less reliable. No particular detail, or even hundreds of them together, are crucial for Christian faith, but the "general results of the research" do matter for faith. In this area Troeltsch pleaded with liberals to stick with history and make the case for a more-or-less reliable gospel picture: "We do not need to know everything. The main points, the person of Jesus and the worship of Christ, stand firm; and they must be grasped in their inner continuity." Troeltsch liked to think that Schleiermacher was on his side, and would have said so, had he read Herrmann. In any case, otherwise Schleiermacher got the main things right. The right strategy is to begin with religious feeling and uphold Christianity "as the highest living power."[161]

When he taught theology, Troeltsch asked his students to view him as one who updated Schleiermacher's theology with a stronger historical consciousness. To his friend Friedrich von Hügel, a Catholic mystical theologian, Troeltsch wrote letters revealing a more tender piety than he showed elsewhere. Something in his friendship with von Hügel allowed Troeltsch to disclose a deeper wellspring of spiritual yearning than he otherwise wrote about, with the partial exception of occasional letters to Bousset. But he was remembered for the things he battled about, portrayed as the last lion of the old German liberalism and a symbol of its futility who dissolved any possible ground for theology by embracing historical relativism. Troeltsch's move to a philosophy chair was chastening to his theological followers, giving the impression of a secular turn, which he reinforced by becoming deeply involved in politics.[162]

Troeltsch's initial reaction to the war was Augustinian, grieving at the terrible "antitithesis of the wicked earthly world and the blessed heavenly world." On various occasions during the war he lamented its savage destruction and hatred, even as he gave patriotic speeches urging Germans to vanquish their enemies. His willingness to fire up crowds at rallies and conferences brought him public renown far beyond his academic base. On one occasion he emoted, "Oh! If only the speaker this hour could turn every word into a bayonet, if only he could transform them into rifles, into cannon!" Like his French and English counterparts in the early years of the war, Troeltsch enlisted God and history in support of his nation, lauding the German army as an instrument of salvation. He exhorted his audiences, *"Be German, remain German, become German!"* Sometimes he stooped to racist appeals. In Troeltsch's telling, the German boys on the western front fought for the lofty values expressed in the song, *Deutschland, Deutschland, über Alles,* while fighting against a motley horde of "Asiatic Indians, Negroes, Frenchmen, Englishmen, and Belgians" united by nothing but "slanders and lies about German barbarians." Toeltsch extolled the German virtues of bravery, duty, and seriousness, and called for a federation of central European powers. After the war he gamely urged Germans not to despair, argued that the new Germany had to be a democracy, and won election to the Prussian State Assembly in 1919 as a member of the German Democratic Party, a centrist party co-founded by Weber. He also served for two years as parliamentary Under-Secretary of State in the Prussian Ministry of Culture.[163]

To the end of his life Troeltsch insisted that philosophy of religion remained his first love and that he intended to cap his career by writing a major work in that field. But his life was cut short by heart failure in 1923, leaving a major two-volume work on historicism only half completed, and no philosophy of religion. In the eight years that remained to him at Berlin, Troeltsch sealed his somewhat skewed reputation in theology by letting go of his anchor, the idea of personality as a universal principle. The major work of his last years, *Der Historismus und seine Probleme* (1922), still had a metaphysical substructure, a monadology drawn from Leibniz in which every partic-ular, conditioned, individual finite spirit "participates intuitively" in the divine Spirit. Troeltsch theorized that history consists fundamentally of individual totalities – *wholes* that synthesize psychical processes and natural conditions. Historical wholes such as families, social classes, states, cultural epochs, revolutions, and schools of thought are original, partly unconscious, integral unities of meaning and value. A universal history, he proposed, should focus on them. Troeltsch wanted very much to write one, but in his last years he concluded that a universal history was not possible, or was possible only in a qualified way – he could be quoted either way, being conflicted.[164]

Sometimes he argued for a universal history leading to a modern cultural synthesis resting on four pillars: the ancient Hebraic tradition, classical Greece, the Hellenistic-Roman period, and the Occidental Middle Ages. Non-Western history had little to contribute to universal history, and Troeltsch barely glanced at non-Occidental philosophies of history. But elsewhere in *Der Historismus und seine Probleme,* and emphatically in his last book, *Der Historismus und seine Überwindung* (1924), published after his death, he argued that the dream of a universal history had to be given up. On occasion, in the former mode, Troeltsch still argued that historical wholes possess a common spirit or mind that is properly the object of historical reason, theology, and especially the philosophy of history. In his last book he argued, with seeming finality, that we know nothing of "humanity" or a Common Spirit. All that we know are particular groups, families, races, classes, schools, sects, and the like from the past six thousand years, a tiny fraction of the human experience, and in his case, all that he really cared about was the background to the European story.[165]

In the latter mode, Troeltsch gave up his idea of personality as a universal principle, on the ground that the idea of personality is too Christian to be universal. In place of his vision of historical development as the shaping of community life in accordance with a universal norm epitomized in Christianity, he settled for what he called "Europeanism." In place of claiming that Christianity is the best religion, he settled for saying it was the best religion for Europe. Troeltsch still made a strained appeal to universality: "For us there is only the universal history of European culture" (*Universalgeschichte der europäischen Kultur*), or, stressing Europeanism as an idea, "For us there is only a universal history of Europeanism" (*Weltgeschichte des Europäertums*). In both cases he accepted that any idea claiming universality is as thoroughly particular and historical as any other idea. No historically conscious European had an idea of universality or a concept of values that was not decidedly European.[166]

This was not something to regret in the case of Europeanism, Troeltsch urged, for Europeanism was an idea worth defending and renewing on its own terms. It deserved "ism" status alongside capitalism, liberalism, Expressionism, and the like, if not above them. Europeanism had a vital, scientific, and emancipatory historical individuality. It valorized individuality and critical rationality more than any other culture, and its carryover into the United States was a major point in its favor. Troeltsch took pride that Americans looked to Europe for high culture and intellectual leadership, filling their museums with European art. America's ascendancy as a world power had a chance of being good for Europeanism, he noted. As American economic, political, and military power expanded, it carried European culture with it. The danger in this area, he cautioned, was that America was highly unpredictable and it lacked much of a historical sense; thus it made a questionable repository for European culture. If America turned out to be a "vacant possession" for Europeanism, something precious would be lost – the full blooming of European individuality.[167]

Troeltsch lived just long enough to see the rise of a postwar theological generation for which "cultural theology" was a sneer term, let alone "Europeanism," despite the fact that dialectical theology was every bit as Eurocentric in its own way. He tried to empathize with the younger generation, recognizing that its critique of cultural optimism was at least half-right. But Troeltsch was repelled by the Barthian leap into irrationalism and its recycling of Christian dogmas from an authoritarian past. He shook his head that "logical and historical reasons" meant nothing to a youthful generation determined to repudiate its teachers: "Anti-historicism, irrationalism, intuitionism – things with which we older people have concerned ourselves passionately and scrupulously – have already become comfortable and pleasant dogmas for many of the young."[168]

That was a sad spectacle to Troeltsch, one that pushed aside his questions after Barthian neo-Reformationists took over the field of theology. The stubborn liberals who kept liberal theology alive during the decades of neo-orthodox domination, however, kept asking Troeltschian questions. They insisted that Troeltschian questions must not be brushed away, even as many liberals gave short shrift to some of Troeltsch's answers and blanched at his legitimizing of racial, gender, class, and imperial privileges. In the long run, liberal theology was better off for keeping Troeltschian questions in play while rejecting his prejudices.[169]

Harnack, speaking at Troeltsch's funeral, put the former point sharply, albeit with a caveat about Troeltsch's personality. Troeltsch was not a "comfortable" person, Harnack observed. He made it difficult for people to know him, and "he could wound by his arrogance and offend by his impetuosity." Yet these characteristics were contradicted by the expansive, dialogical, outward reaching way that he lived and worked. Troeltsch had an enormous power of spiritual "consumption," Harnack remarked. He was always eager to learn from others, to face challenges to his position, and to refashion his position by assimilating the learning and criticism of others. This example of liberal engagement was Troeltsch's most important contribution to theology; he was sufficiently free to be open to critical challenges and to give himself as he was.[170]

Even that did not quite place Troeltsch where he belonged, something that Harnack naturally had trouble doing. The three most important and influential figures in the making of modern theology are Kant, Hegel, and Schleiermacher. The next most important figure on this list belonged to Harnack's generation, but was not Harnack.

Notes

1. See Otto Pfleiderer, *Philosophy and Development of Religion*, 2 vols. (Edinburgh: William Blackwood and Sons, 1895); Auguste Sabatier, *Religions of Authority and the Religion of the Spirit*, trans. Louise Seymour Houghton (New York: McClure, Phillips & Company, 1904).

2. See Julius Kaftan, *Dogmatik* (Freiburg: J. C. B. Mohr, 1897); Theodor Häring, *Zur Versöhnungslehre, eine dogmatische Untersuchung* (Göttingen: Vandenhoeck und Ruprecht, 1893); Martin Rade, *Die Wahrheit der christlichen Religion* (Tübingen: J. C. B. Mohr, 1900); Ferdinand Kattenbusch, *Von Schleiermacher zu Ritschl. Zur Orientierung über den gegenwärtigen Stand der Dogmatik* (Giessen: Ricker, 1892); Friedrich Loofs, *Leitfaden zum Studium der Dogmengeschichte* (Halle: M. Niemeyer, 1889); Max Wilhelm T. Reischle, *Christliche Glaubenslehre in Leitsätzen für eine akademische Vorlesung*, 2nd edn. (Halle: Max Niemeyer, 1902); Reischle, *Die Frage nach dem Wesen der Religion Grunglegung zu einer Methodologie der Religionsphilosophie* (Freiburg: J. C. B. Mohr, 1889).

3. See Horton Harris, *The Tübingen School: A Historical and Theological Investigation of the School of F. C. Baur* (Grand Rapids: Baker Book House, 1990), 101–112; Otto Ritschl, *Albrecht Ritschls Leben*, 2 vols. (Freiburg: J. C. B. Mohr, 1892, 1896); Albert Temple Swing, *The Theology of Albrecht Ritschl*, trans. Alice Mead Swing (New York: Longmans, Green and Company, 1901), 10–22; Rolf Schafer, *Ritschl* (Tubingen: J. C. B. Mohr, 1968); Philip Hefner, "Albrecht Ritschl: An Introduction," in Albrecht Ritschl, *Three Essays*, trans. and ed. Philip Hefner (Philadelphia: Fortress Press, 1972), 1–50.

4. See Hefner, "Albrecht Ritschl: An Introduction," 7–10; Peter C. Hodgson, *The Formation of Historical Theology* (New York: Harper & Row, 1966), 62, 67, 277; and Philip Hefner, *Faith and the Vitalities of History: A Theological Study Based on the Work of Albrecht Ritschl* (New York: Harper & Row, 1966), 70–90; F. C. Baur, *Das Christenthum und die christliche Kirche der drei ersten Jahrhunderte* (Tubingen: L. F. Fues, 1853); 133.

On Baur's Hegelianism, see Barth, *Protestant Theology in the Nineteenth Century,* pp. 499–507; George Rupp, *Christologies and Cultures* (The Hague: Mouton, 1974), 146–147; Hodgson, *The Formation of Historical Theology,* 25–27. On the tridimensional structure of Hegel's dialectic, which, playing out the simultaneous meanings of the concept of *Aufhebung,* always involves three simultaneous cases of reduplicated relation, see Dieter Henrich, "Formen der Negation in Hegels Logik," in Rolf-Peter Horstmann, ed., *Seminar: Dialektik in der Philosophie Hegels* (Frankfurt: Suhrkamp Taschenbuch Verlag, 1978), 213–229; and Jean Hyppolite, *Genesis and Structure of Hegel's Phenomenology of Spirit,* trans. by Samuel Cherniak and John Heckman (Evanston: Northwestern University Press, 1974), 3–26, 51–74.

5. See Hodgson, *The Formation of Historical Theology,* 214–217; Albrecht Ritschl, *Die Entstehung der altkatholischen Kirche* (Bonn: Adolph Marcus, 1850).

6. Harris, *The Tübingen School: A Historical and Theological Investigation of the School of F. C. Baur,* quote 108; Baur, *Das Christenthum und die christliche Kirche der drei ersten Jahrhunderte.*

7. For example: "Hence the rule may be set up that almost everything else in the Old Testament is, for our Christian usage, but the husk or wrapping of its prophecy, and that whatever is most definitely Jewish has least value," Schleiermacher, *The Christian Faith,* 62. For text and discussion of Harnack's proposal to "make a clean sweep here" and remove the Old Testament from the Christian scriptures, see Hans-Joachim Kraus, *Geschichte der historisch-kritischen Erforschung des Alten Testaments* (Neukirchen-Vluyn: Neukirchener Verlag, 1969), 384–390. On Wellhausen's anti-Judaism, see Rolf Rendtorff, "Die jüdische Bibel und ihre antijüdische Auslegung," *Auschwitz – Krise der christlichen Theologie: Eine Vortragsreihe,* ed. Rolf Rendtorff and Ekkehard Stegemann (Munich: Christian Kaiser, 1980), 99–116; Lou H. Silberman, "Wellhausen and Judaism," *Semeia* 25 (1982), 75–82; see Martin Luther, "The Babylonian Captivity of the Church," in *Martin Luther's Basic Theological Writings,* ed. Timothy F. Lull (Minneapolis: Fortress Press, 1989), 267–313.

8. For his denial that he was a strict Hegelian in any sense, see F. C. Baur, *Ausgewählte Werke in Einzelausgaben,* 5 vols., ed. Klaus Scholder (Stuttgart: Friedrich Fromann Verlag, 1963–1975), 1:313. See Baur, *Die christliche Gnosis, oder die christliche Religions-Philosophie in ihrer geschichtlichen Entwicklung* (Tübingen: C. F. Osiander, 1835).

9. Albrecht Ritschl, *The Christian Doctrine of Justification and Reconciliation* ed. H. R. Mackintosh and A. B. Macaulay (Edinburgh: T. & T. Clark, 1902), 205.

10. Ibid., 3.

11. Ibid., 1–2.

12. Schleiermacher, *The Christian Faith,* 52; Ritschl, *The Christian Doctrine of Justification and Reconciliation,* 8–9.

13. Ibid., 9.

14. Ibid., 10; closing quote from Albrecht Ritschl, "Instruction in the Christian Religion," reprinted in Ritschl, *Three Essays,* 229.

15. Ritschl, *The Christian Doctrine of Justification and Reconciliation,* 11–13; see Ritschl, "Instruction in the Christian Religion," 232–240.

16. Ritschl, *The Christian Doctrine of Justification and Reconciliation,* ibid., quote 20–21; Albrecht Ritschl, "Theology and Metaphysics," reprinted in Ritschl, *Three Essays,* 149–217.

17. In Barth's words, "the very epitome of the national-liberal German bourgeois of the age of Bismarck." Karl Barth, *Protestant Theology in the Nineteenth Century* (Valley Forge: Judson Press, 1973), 656.

18. See Agnes von Zahn-Harnack, *Adolf von Harnack* (Berlin: Walter de Gruyter & Company, 1936, 2nd edn. 1951); Martin Rumscheidt, "Harnack's Liberalism in Theology: A Struggle for the Freedom of Theology," in *Adolf von Harnack: Liberal Theology at Its Height,* ed. Martin Rumscheidt (Minneapolis: Fortress Press, 1991), 9–41; Wilhelm Pauck, "Adolf von Harnack," in *A Handbook of Christian Theologians,* ed. Dean G. Peerman and Martin E. Marty (Cleveland: World Publishing Co., 1965), 86–111; *Adolf von Harnack: Christentum, Wissenschaft und Gesellschaft,* eds. Kurt Nowak, et al. (Göttingen: Vandenboeck & Ruprecht, 2003).

19. Zahn-Harnack, *Adolf von Harnack,* quote 23; see Rumscheidt, "Harnack's Liberalism in Theology: A Struggle for the Freedom of Theology," 10–11.

20. Zahn-Harnack, *Adolf von Harnack,* quote 64.

21. See Adolf von Harnack, *History of Dogma* (1st German edn., 3 vols., 1885, 1887, 1889; 3rd German edn., English trans., 7 vols., trans. Neil Buchanan (Eugene: Wipf and Stock Publishers, 1997).

22. Zahn-Harnack, *Adolf von Harnack,* 104–105.

23. Ibid., 128–131; Adolf von Harnack, "Was hat die Historie an fester Erkenntnis zur Deutung des Weltgeschehens zu bieten?," in Harnack, *Ausgewählte Reden und Aufsätze,* eds. Agnes von Zahn-Harnack and Axel von Harnack (Berlin: Walter de Gruyter & Co., 1951), 191–192; see Rumscheidt, "Harnack's Liberalism in Theology: A Struggle for the Freedom of Theology," 16; Wilhelm Pauck, "The Significance of Adolf von Harnack among Church Historians," *Union Theological Seminary Quarterly Review,* Special Issue (January 1954), 13–24; G. Wayne Glick, *The Reality of Christianity: A Study of Adolf von Harnack as Historian and Theologian* (New York: Harper & Row, 1967).

24. Zahn-Harnack, *Adolf von Harnack,* 127; Rumscheidt, "Harnack's Liberalism in Theology: A Struggle for the Freedom of Theology," 15–16; Pauck, "Adolf von Harnack," 87.

25. William Adams Brown, *A Teacher and His Times: A Story of Two Worlds* (New York: Charles Scribner's Sons, 1940), quotes 87, 84; see Adolf von Harnack, *Marcion, das Evangelium vom fremden Gott* (Leipzig: J. C. Hinrichs Verlag, 1921); Harnack, *Die Entstehung der christlichen Theologie und des kirchlichen Dogmas* (Gotha: Klotz Verlag, 1927).

26. Adolf von Harnack, *Reden und Aufsätze,* 2 vols. (Giessen: Alfred Töpelmann, 1906); Harnack, *Aus Wissenschaft und Leben,* 2 vols. (Giessen: Alfred Töpelmann, 1911); Harnack, *New Testament Studies,* 6 vols., trans. J. R. Wilkinson (New York: G. P. Putnam's Sons, 1908–1925); Harnack, *The Apostles' Creed,* trans. Thomas Bailey Saunders (London: A. & C. Black, 1901); Harnack, *The Constitution and Law of the Church in the First Two Centuries,* trans. F. L. Pogson (New York: G. P. Putnam's Sons, 1910); Harnack, *Thoughts on the Present Position of Protestantism,* trans. Thomas Bailey Saunders (London: A. & C. Black, 1899); Harnack, *The Mission and Expansion of Christianity in the First Three Centuries,* 2 vols., trans. James Moffatt (New York: Harper & Row, 1962); Harnack, *What Is Christianity?,* trans. Thomas Bailey Saunders (1900; reprint, Philadelphia: Fortress Press, 1986);

27. Adolf Harnack, "In Sachen des Apostolikums," *Christliche Welt* (1892), 768–770; Harnack, *The Apostles' Creed,* trans. Thomas Bailey Saunders (London: A. & C. Black, 1901); Johannes Rathje, *Die Welt des freien Protestantismus: Ein Beitrag zur deutsch-evangelischen Geistesgeschichte, dargestellt an Leben und Werk von Martin Rade* (Stuttgart: Ehrenfried Klotz Verlag, 1952), 64–74.

28. See Adolf Stöcker, *Sozialdemokratie und Sozialmonarchie* (Leipzig: Verlag von Fr. Wilh. Grunow, 1891); Stöcker, *Predigten von Stöcker* (Berlin: Buchhandlung der Berliner

Stadmission, 1890); Stöcker, *Das moderne Judenthum in Deutschland, besonders in Berlin: zwei Reden in der christlich-sozialen Arbeiterpartei* (Berlin: Weigandt und Grieben, 1880); Friedrich Naumann, *Jesus als Volkmann* (Göttingen: Vandenhoeck und Ruprecht, 1894); Naumann, *Briefe über Religion* (Berlin: Buchverlag *Die Hilfe*, 1903), 41–48; James Bentley, *Between Marx and Christ: The Dialogue in German-Speaking Europe, 1870–1970* (London: New Left Books, 1982), 18–22.

29. Adolf Harnack, "The Evangelical Social Mission in the Light of the History of the Church," paper delivered at the Evangelical Social Congress, Frankfurt, May 17, 1894, published in Harnack and Wilhelm Herrmann, *Essays on the Social Gospel,* trans. G. M. Craik (New York: G. P. Putnam's Sons, 1907), 3–91, quotes 77–78.

30. Ibid., 80–81, 81.

31. Ibid., 83.

32. Ibid., "serious," 83; Zahn-Harnack, *Adolf von Harnack,* "on the soil," 301; see Rumscheidt, "Harnack's Liberalism in Theology: A Struggle for the Freedom of Theology," 23.

33. Harnack, *What Is Christianity?,* 8, 10.

34. Ibid., quotes 11; see Zahn-Harnack, *Adolf von Harnack,* 130–133.

35. Zahn-Harnack, *Adolf von Harnack,* 130–131; see Wilhelm Pauck, *Harnack and Troeltsch: Two Historical Theologians* (New York: Oxford University Press, 1968), 33–34; Harnack, "The Present State of Research in Early Church History," in Rumscheidt, ed., *Adolf von Harnack: Liberal Theology at Its Height,* 182–193.

36. Harnack, *What Is Christianity?,* 20; David Friedrich Strauss, *The Life of Jesus Critically Examined,* 4th German edn., trans. George Eliot (Philadelphia: Fortress Press, 1972).

37. Harnack, *What Is Christianity?,* 20–21.

38. Ibid., 23–25.

39. Ibid., 27–28.

40. Ibid., 30, 51–52; see Harnack, "The Two-Fold Gospel in the New Testament," in Rumscheldt, ed., *Adolf von Harnack: Liberal Theology at its Height,* 146–154.

41. Harnack, *What Is Christianity?,* 56.

42. Ibid., 160–161; see Harnack, "Christianity and History," in Rumscheldt, ed., *Adolf von Harnack: Liberal Theology at its Height,* pp. 63–77.

43. Harnack, *What Is Christianity?,* 162.

44. Harnack, *History of Dogma,* vol. 1, trans. Neil Buchanan (Boston: Little, Brown, and Company, 1905), 41–136; Harnack, *What Is Christianity?,* 190–245; Zahn-Harnack, *Adolf von Harnack,* "get free" quote, 161; Pauck, "Adolf von Harnack," 109.

45. Harnack, *Marcion, das Evangelium vom fremden Gott,* 217–220, "power of," 217.

46. Ibid., "paralysis," 217; Zahn-Harnack, *Adolf von Harnack,* "antiquated," 244–245; Pauck, "Adolf von Harnack," 108–109.

47. Zahn-Harnack, *Adolf von Harnack,* 348–349.

48. *An die evangelischen Christen im Auslande* (September 4, 1914), "we are," and *An die Kulturwelt* (October 4, 1914), "without German culture," cited in Rumscheidt, "Introduction: Harnack's Liberalism in Theology," 25; "Declaration of Professors in the German Reich," (October 23, 1914), "our belief," Humanities Web Documents, www.humanitiesweb.org, accessed August 18, 2009; "Manifesto of Ninety-Three German Intellectuals to the Civilized World," (October 3, 1914), Humanities Web Documents, www.humanitiesweb.org, accessed August 18, 2009. The latter document is often misdated, as on this site.

49. Zahn-Harnack, *Adolf von Harnack,* quote 350; see Rumscheidt, "Introduction: Harnack's Liberalism in Theology," 25–26.

50. Zahn-Harnack, *Adolf von Harnack,* 374–384; Rumscheidt, "Introduction: Harnack's Liberalism in Theology," 27–28.

51. See William Newton Clarke, *An Outline of Christian Theology* (New York: Charles Scribner's Sons, 1898).

52. See Wilhelm Herrmann, *Faith and Morals,* trans. Donald Matheson and Robert W. Stewart (New York: G. P. Putnam's Sons, 1904); Robert T. Volkel, *The Shape of the Theological Task* (Philadelphia: Westminster Press, 1968); Daniel Deegan, "Wilhelm Herrmann: A Reassessment," *Scottish Journal of Theology* 19 (1966), 188–203; Claude Welch, *Protestant Thought in the Nineteenth Century,* 2 vols. (New Haven: Yale University Press, 1972, 1985), II: 44–45; Friedrich August Gottreu Tholuck, "Theological Encyclopedia and Methodology," *Bibliotheca Sacra* 1 (1844), 194–195, 565–566.

53. Welch, *Protestant Thought in the Nineteenth Century,* II: 44; Karl Barth, "The Principles of Dogmatics According to Wilhelm Herrmann," in Barth, *Theology and Church: Shorter Writings 1920–1928,* trans. Louise Pettibone Smith (New York: Harper & Row, 1962), "teacher," 238; Barth, appendix to *Karl Barth-Rudolf Bultmann Letters, 1922–1966,* trans. Geoffrey W. Bromiley (1971; reprint, Grand Rapids: Wm. B. Eerdmans Co., 1981), "absorbed," 153.

54. See Ernst Troeltsch, "Historical and Dogmatic Method in Theology," trans. Ephraim Fischoff (1898), and "The Dogmatics of the History-of-Religions School," trans. Walter E. Wyman, Jr. (1913), both reprinted in Troeltsch, *Religion in History,* ed. James Luther Adams (Minneapolis: Fortress Press, 1991), 11–32, 87–108; Troeltsch, *Die Absolutheit der Christentums und die Religionsgeschichte* (Tübingen: J. C. B. Mohr-Paul Siebeck, 1902, reprint 1912); Hans-Georg Drescher, *Ernst Troeltsch: His Life and Work,* trans. John Bowden (Minneapolis: Fortress Press, 1992), 70–97; Joachim Wach, "Introduction: The Meaning and Task of the History of Religions (Religionswissenschaft)," in *The History of Religions: Essays on the Problem of Understanding,* ed. Joseph M. Kitagawa (Chicago: University of Chicago Press, 1967); Helmut Koester, "Early Christianity from the Perspective of the History of Religions: Rudolf Bultmann's Contribution," in *Bultmann: Retrospect and Prospect,* ed. Edward. C. Hobbs (Philadelphia: Fortress Press, 1985), 63–67.

55. Gustav Ecke, *Die theologische Schule Albrecht Ritschls und die Evangelische Kirche der Gegenwart* (Berlin: Reuther & Reichard, 1897). See Johannes Rathje, *Die Welt des freien Protestantismus: Ein Beitrag zur deutsch-evangelischen Geistesgeschichte, dargestellt an Leben und Werk von Martin Rade* (Stuttgart: Ehrenfried Klotz Verlag, 1952), 102–103; and Bruce L. McCormack, *Karl Barth's Critically Realistic Dialectical Theology: Its Genesis and Development 1909–1936* (New York: Oxford University Press, 1995), 40-41.

56. Ernst Troeltsch, "Christentum und Religionsgeschichte," *Preussische Jahrbücher* 87 (1897), 415–447; reprinted in Troeltsch, "Christianity and the History of Religion," *Religion in History,* trans. James Luther Adams, 77–86, quote 77; on the early mythical school tradition, see Christian Hartlich and Walter Sachs, *Der Ursprung des Mythosbegriffes in der modernen Bibelwissenschaft* (Tübingen: J. C. B. Mohr, 1952); and David Friedrich Strauss, *The Life of Jesus Critically Examined,* trans. George Eliot (1892; reprint, Ramsey: Sigler Press, 1994, English edn.), 39–92.

57. See Rathje, *Die Welt des freien Protestantismus,* 103; Peter C. Hodgson, *The Formation of Historical Theology: A Study of Ferdinand Christian Baur* (New York: Harper & Row, 1966).

58. Wilhelm Herrmann, "Der evangelische Glaube und die Theologie Albr. Ritschls," in Herrmann, *Gesammelte Aufsätze,* ed. F. W. Schmidt (Tübingen: J. C. B. Mohr, 1923), 1–25. On Herrmann's influence over Ritschl regarding the relationship between theology and metaphysics, see Hermann Timm, *Theorie und Praxis in der Theologie Albrecht Ritschls und Wilhelm Herrmanns* (Gütersloh: Gerd Mohn, 1967), 98.

59. Wilhelm Herrmann, *Die Metaphysik in der Theologie* (Halle: Max Niemeyer, 1876); Herrmann, *Die Religion im Verhältnis zum Welterkennen und zur Sittlichkeit* (Halle: Max Niemeyer, 1879).

60. See Albrecht Ritschl, *Die christliche Lehre von der Rechtfertigung und Versöhnung,* 3 vols. (Bonn: Adolph Marcus, 1870–1874); Rolf Schafer, *Ritschl* (Tübingen: J. C. B. Mohr, 1968); Otto Ritschl, *Albrecht Ritschls Leben,* 2 vols. (Freiburg: J. C. B. Hohr, 1892, 1896).

61. See Wilhelm Herrmann, "Albrecht Ritschl, seine Größe und seine Schranke," *Festgabe von Fachgenossen und Freunden A. von Harnack zum seibzigsten Geburtstag dargebracht,* ed. Karl Holl (Tübingen: J. C. B. Mohr, 1921), 405–406.

62. Albrecht Ritschl, "Theology and Metaphysics," (1881), trans. Philip Hefner, reprinted in Ritschl, *Three Essays* (Philadelphia: Fortress Press, 1972), 164, 179.

63. See Wilhelm Herrmann, "Kants Bedeutung für das Christentum" (1884), in Herrmann, *Schriften zur Grundlegung der Theologie* I, ed. Peter Fischer-Appelt (Munich: Chr. Kaiser Verlag, 1966), 104–122; Theodor Mahlmann, "Das Axiom des Erlebnisses bei Wilhelm Herrmann," *Neue Zeitschrift für systematische Theologie* 4 (1962), 11–18; Peter Fischer-Appelt, *Metaphysik im Horizont der Theologie Wilhelm Herrmanns* (Munich: Chr. Kaiser, 1965); Immanuel Kant, *Religion Within the Limits of Reason Alone,* trans. Theodore M. Greene and Hoyt H. Hudson (Chicago: Open Court Publishing Company, 1934).

64. See Wilhelm Herrmann, "Hermann Cohens Ethik" (1907), Herrmann, "Die Auffassung der Religion in Cohens und Natorps Ethik" (1909) and Herrmann, "Der Begriff der Religion nach Hermann Cohen" (1916) in Herrmann, *Schriften zur Grundlegung der Theologie* II (1967), 88–113, 206–232, 318–323. On Marburg neo-Kantianism, see Simon Fisher, *Revelatory Positivism?: Barth's Earliest Theology and the Marburg School* (Oxford: Oxford University Press, 1988), 7–71; and McCormack, *Karl Barth's Critically Realistic Dialectical Theology,* 42–49.

65. See Wilhelm Herrmann, "Die Auffassung der Religion in Cohens and Natorps Ethik," in Herrmann, *Gesammelte Schriften,* ed. Friedrich Wilhelm Schmidt (Tübingen: J. C. B. Mohr, 1923), 377–405; Paul Natorp, *Religion innerhalb der Grenzen der Humanität,* 2nd edn. (Tübingen: J. C. B. Mohr, 1908); Hermann Cohen, *Reason and Hope: Selections from the Jewish Writings of Hermann Cohen,* trans. E. Jospe (New York: W. W. Norton, 1971); Friedrich Schleiermacher, *On Religion: Addresses in Response to its Cultured Critics,* trans. Terrence N. Tice (Richmond: John Knox Press, 1969), 69–157; Schleiermacher, *The Christian Faith,* ed. H. R. Mackintosh and J. S. Stewart (Edinburgh: T. & T. Clark, 1989), 5–31. For a thorough discussion of Herrmann's relation to Natorp and Cohen, see Fisher, *Revelatory Positivism?,* 72–169.

66. See Herrmann, "Kants Bedeutung für das Christentum," 104–123; Herrmann, "Die religiöse Frage in der Gegenwart," and "Die Auffassung der Religion in Cohens and Natorps Ethik," in Herrmann, *Schriften zur Grundlegung der Theologie* II, 114–149, 206–232.

67. This theme pervaded Herrmann's lectures on dogmatics for many years, including the period in which Barth studied under Herrmann. The final edition of these lectures (1916) was published in 1925 as *Dogmatik* (Stuttgart: Verlag Friedrich Andres Perthes, 1925).

The English edition was titled *Systematic Theology*, trans. Nathaniel Micklem and Kenneth A. Saunders (New York: Macmillan Company, 1927). Herrmann would not have objected to the change in title by his English translators, since he viewed "dogmatics" as a relic of Catholicism and Protestant Scholasticism. "For with us there cannot be a systematic but only a historical science of dogma, since Evangelical Christianity cannot have any dogmas in the old sense of the term," he explained. He used the word only because "there is no point in unnecessarily abandoning a familiar term" (16). On religion as an independent saving power, see Herrmann, "Kants Bedeutung für das Christentum," 119–122, and Herrmann, "Religion," in ibid., 282–297. On the experience of moral conflict as a precondition for saving faith, see Wilhelm Herrmann, *Ethik* (Tübingen: J. C. B. Mohr, 5th edn., 1913; reprint 1921), 90–96. Closing quote in Wilhelm Herrmann, "Zur theologischen Darstellung der christlichen Erfahrung," in Herrmann, *Gesammelte Aufsätze*, 245, quoted in McCormack, *Karl Barth's Critically Realistic Dialectical Theology*, 55–56; see Herrmann, *Systematic Theology*, 18, 26–27, 33–35.

68. Barth, "The Principles of Dogmatics According to Wilhelm Herrmann," 258.

69. Troeltsch, "Historical and Dogmatic Method in Theology," 10.

70. Wilhelm Herrmann, *The Communion of the Christian with God: Described on the Basis of Luther's Statements*, trans. J. Sandys Stanyon (Philadelphia: Fortress Press, 1971, 2nd English edn. 1906, revd. in accordance with the 4th German edn. of 1903), 36–37, 59–60. See Herrmann, "Der evangelische Glaube und die Theologie Albrecht Ritschls," 11–25; Herrmann, "Der geschichtliche Christus der Grund unseres Glaubens," (1892) in Herrmann, *Schriften zur Grundlegung der Theologie* I, 149–185.

71. See Herrmann, "Albrecht Ritschl, seine Größe und seine Schranke," 405–406; discussion in McCormack, *Karl Barth's Critically Realistic Dialectical Theology*, 53.

72. Wilhelm Herrmann, "Die Absolutheit des Christentums und die Religionsgeschichte," (1902) in Herrmann, *Schriften zur Grundlegung der Theologie* I, 193–199; citations from Ferdinand Kattenbusch concerning Herrmann's regard for Schleiermacher quoted in Barth, "The Principles of Dogmatics According to Wilhelm Herrmann," 246.

73. Herrmann, *The Communion of the Christian with God*, 19–49.

74. On the theme that Christian faith requires the historical fact of Jesus, see Wilhelm Herrmann, "Warum bedarf unser Glaube geschichtlicher Tatsachen?" (1884), in Herrmann, *Schriften zur Grundlegung der Theologie* I, 81–103.

75. Herrmann, *The Communion of the Christian with God*, lxv–lxvi, 5, 37–48.

76. On Pietist accounts of faith, see Herrmann, *Systematic Theology*, 34–36, 43–47.

77. Herrmann, *The Communion of the Christian with God*, lxvii, 7.

78. Ibid., 49–51.

79. Ibid., 14–15.

80. Ibid., 17, 42.

81. Ibid., 45.

82. Ibid., 46.

83. Ibid., 36–37, 48; see Ludwig Feuerbach, *The Essence of Christianity*, trans. George Eliot (New York: Harper & Row, 1957, lst German edn. 1841).

84. G. E. Lessing, *Lessing's Theological Writings*, ed. Henry Chadwick (Stanford: Stanford University Press, 1957), 12–13; Herrmann, *The Communion of the Christian with God*, 69–70, 71–72.

85. Herrmann, "Die Lage und Aufgabe der evangelischen Dogmatik in der Gegenwart," in Herrmann, *Gesammelte Aufsätze*, 118–119; see Herrmann, *The Communion of the Christian with God*, 74–75; Herrmann, "Warum bedarf unser Glaube geschichtlicher Tatsachen?," 94–101.

86. Herrmann, *The Communion of the Christian with God*, 75.

87. Wilhelm Herrmann, *Christlich-protestantische Dogmatik* (1906), in Paul Hinneberg, ed., *Die Kultur der Gegenwart: Ihre Entwicklung und ihre Ziele* I: IV, 2 (Druck und Verlag von B. G. Teubner: Berlin und Leipzig, 1909), 129–180; reprinted in Herrmann, *Schriften zur Grundlegung der Theologie* I, ed. Peter Fischer-Appelt (Munich: Chr. Kaiser Verlag, 1966), 298–358; see Herrmann, "Der evangelische Glaube und die Theologie Albr. Ritschls," (1890) in Herrmann, *Gesammelte Aufsätze*, ed. F. W. Schmidt (Tübingen: J. C. B. Mohr, 1923), 1–25; Herrmann, "Die religiöse Frage in der Gegenwart," (1908), in Herrmann, *Schriften zur Grundlegung der Theologie* II (1967), 114–149; Karl Barth, "The Principles of Dogmatics According to Wilhelm Herrmann" (1925), reprinted in Barth, *Theology and Church: Shorter Writings 1920–1928,* trans. Louise Pettibone Smith (New York: Harper & Row, 1962), 247–248. Herrmann's first edition *Der Verkehr des Christen mit Gott* was published in 1886; revised editions were published in 1892, 1896, 1903, 1908 (5th and 6th edns.), and 1921. The J. Sandys Stanyon-R. W. Stewart second English edition was based on the fourth German edition.

88. Wilhelm Herrmann, "Die Absolutheit des Christentums und die Religionsgeschichte: Eine Besprechung des gleichnamigen Vortrags von Ernst Troeltsch" (1902), in *Schriften zur Grundlegung der Theologie* I, 193–199; Herrmann, *Christlich-protestantische Dogmatik* (1906), in Hinneberg, *Kultur der Gegenwart* I: IV, 2, 604–624; Herrmann, "Der Widerspruch im religiösen Denken und seine Bedeutung für das Leben der Religion," (1911), in Herrmann *Schriften zur Grundlegung der Theologie* II, 233–246; James M. Robinson, *Das Problem des Heiligen Geistes bei Wilhelm Herrmann* (Marburg: K. Gleiser, 1952), 16–22.

89. Ernst Troeltsch, "Half a Century of Theology: A Review" (1908), in Troeltsch, *Ernst Troeltsch: Writings on Theology and Religion,* ed. and trans. Robert Morgan and Michael Pye (Louisville: Westminster John Knox Press, 1990), 58, 66, 75.

90. Ernst Troeltsch, "The Significance of the Historical Existence of Jesus for Faith" (1911), in ibid., 191–192.

91. Wilhelm Herrmann, "Die Bedeutung Der Geschichtlichkeit Jesu Für Den Glauben: Eine Besprechung des gleichnamigen Vortrags von Ernst Troeltsch," (1912), in Herrmann, *Schriften zur Grundlegung der Theologie* II, 282–289. See Herrmann, "Die Lage und Aufgabe der evangelischen Dogmatik in der Gegenwart" (1907) in Herrmann, *Gesammelte Aufsätze,* 95–96, 126–138; reprinted in Herrmann, *Schriften zur Grundlegung der Theologie* I, 1–89.

92. Wilhelm Herrmann, *Dogmatik* (Stuttgart: Verlag Friedrich Andres Perthes, 1925); English edition, *Systematic Theology (Dogmatik),* trans. Nathaniel Micklem and Kenneth A. Saunders (New York: Macmillan Company, 1927), 21. These lectures were published shortly after Herrmann's death by Martin Rade in the form in which Herrmann last presented them, which was during the winter semester of 1915/1916.

93. Herrmann, *Systematic Theology,* 26–29. See Friedrich Schleiermacher, *The Christian Faith,* ed. H. R. Mackintosh and J. S. Stewart (Edinburgh: T. & T. Clark, 1989), 142–256; Herrmann, "Die Lage und Aufgabe der evangelischen Dogmatik in der Gegenwart," *Gesammelte Aufsätze,* 106–122.

94. Wilhelm Herrmann, "Hermann Cohens Ethik," (1907) in Herrmann, *Schriften zur Grundlegung der Theologie* II, 108–109.

95. Herrmann, *Systematic Theology,* 35–37.

96. Wilhelm Herrmann, "The Moral Teachings of Jesus," in Adolf Harnack and Wilhelm Herrmann, *Essays on the Social Gospel,* trans. G. M. Craik, ed. Maurice A. Canney (New York: G. P. Putnam's Sons, 1907), 175–185.

97. Herrmann, *Systematic Theology*, 44; Herrmann, "The Moral Teachings of Jesus," 206–225.

98. Wilhelm Herrmann, "Die Auffassung der Religion in Cohens und Natorps Ethik," (1909), Herrmann, *Schriften zur Grundlegung der Theologie* II, 208.

99. Herrmann, *Systematic Theology*, 58–59, 62, 84. There is little direct evidence of a Kierkegaardian influence upon him, but Herrmann knew enough about Kierkegaard to at least mention him on occasion in this connection; see Herrmann, "Die Lage und Aufgabe der evangelischen Dogmatik in der Gegenwart," *Gesammelte Aufsätze*, 96.

100. Barth, "The Principles of Dogmatics According to Wilhelm Herrmann," 248, 267.

101. Ernst Troeltsch, *Gesammelte Schriften*, 4 vols: l. Bd. Die Soziallehren der christlichen kirchen und gruppen.-2. Bd. Zur religiösen lage, religionsphilosophie und ethik.- 3. Bd. Der historismus und seine probleme. l.Buch: Das logische problem der geschichtsphilosophie.-4. Bd. Aufsätze zur geistesgeschichte und religionssoziologie (Tübingen: J. C. B. Mohr, 1912–1925); Troeltsch, *Meine Bücher* (1922), in ibid., 4: 3–18, quote 4; excerpt, "My Books," in Troeltsch, *Religion in History*, 365–378, quote 365.

102. Ernst Troeltsch, "Die 'kleine Göttinger Fakultät' von 1890," in Drescher, *Ernst Troeltsch: His Life and Work*, "we had," 8; Troeltsch to Wilhelm Bousset, July 30, 1885, in Drescher, ibid., "I suffer," 11–12.

103. Ernst Troeltsch to Wilhelm Bousset, December 23, 1885, in Drescher, *Ernst Troeltsch: His Life and Work*, 19.

104. Troeltsch, "Die 'kleine Göttinger Fakultät' von 1890," "who really" and "it is," 282; Drescher, *Ernst Troeltsch: His Life and Work*, 20–27.

105. See Hermann Lotze, *Metaphysik* (Leipzig: F. Meiner, 1912); Lotze, *Logik* (Leipzig: Weidmann'sche Buchhandlung, 1843); Lotze, *Grundzüge der Äesthetik* (Leipzig: S. Hirzel, 1884).

106. See Paul A. de Lagarde, *Gesammelte abhandlungen* (Leipzig: F. A. Brockhaus, 1866); Lagarde, *Librorum Veteris Testamenti canonicorum* (Göttingen: Prostat in aedibus Dieterichianus Arnoldi Hoyer, 1883); Lagarde, *Onomastica sacra* (Hildesheim: G. Olms, 1887); Lagarde, *Schriften für das deutsche Volk* (1878; reprint, Munich: J. F. Lehmann, 1934); Fritz Stern, *The Politics of Cultural Despair: A Study in the Rise of the Germanic Ideology* (Berkeley: University of California Press, 1961), ch 1.

107. Wilhelm Bousset, *Jesu Predigt in ihrem Gegensatz zum Judentum: ein religionsgeschichtlicher Vergleich* (Göttingen: Vandenhoeck & Ruprecht, 1892); see Bousset, *Kyrios Christos* (Göttingen: Vandenhoeck & Ruprecht, 1913).

108. Ernst Troeltsch to Wilhelm Bousset, July 23, 1895, "it's a pity," and "common to," Drescher, *Ernst Troeltsch: His Life and Work*, 62; Wilhelm Bousset, *Der Antichrist in der Uberlieferung des Judentums, des Neuen Testaments und der alten Kirche* (Göttingen: Vandenhoeck und Ruprecht, 1895); see Wilhelm Dilthey, *Selected Works*, ed. Rudolf A. Makkreel (Princeton: Princeton University Press, 1985).

109. Troeltsch, "Christianity and the History of Religion," *Religion in History*, quotes 78.

110. Hermann Lotze, *Microcosmos: An Essay Concerning Man and His Relation to the World*, 2 vols., trans. Elizabeth Hamilton and Emily E. C. Jones (Edinburgh: T. & T. Clark, 1888); Lotze, *Grundzüge der Religionsphilosophie* (Leipzig: G. Hirzel, 1884); Troeltsch, "Christianity and the History of Religion," quotes 79.

111. Troeltsch, "Christianity and the History of Religion," quotes 83.

112. Ibid., quote 84.

113. Ibid., quotes 84, 86.

114. Ferdinand Kattenbusch to Martin Rade, January 17, 1898, in Rathje, *Die Welt des freien Protestantismus*, 94; Julius Kaftan to Martin Rade, March 29, 1901, in Rathje, *Die Welt des*

freien Protestantismus, 95; both cited in Drescher, *Ernst Troeltsch: His Life and Work,* 86, 362.

115. Walther Köhler, *Ernst Troeltsch* (Tübingen: J. C. B. Mohr, 1941), 1; see Köhler, "Ernst Troeltsch," *Zeitschrift für deutsche Kulturphilosophie* 9 (1943), 1–21.

116. Julius Kaftan, "Die Selbständigkeit des Christentums," *Zeitschrift für Theologie und Kirche* 6 (1896), 373–394; Troeltsch to Bousset, January 27, 1897, in Drescher, *Ernst Troeltsch: His Life and Work,* 364; Ernst Troeltsch, "Geschichte und Metaphysik," *Zeitschrift für Theologie und Kirche* 8 (1898), 1–69, quote 9.

117. Troeltsch, "Historical and Dogmatic Method in Theology," quote 21.

118. Ibid., quote 27.

119. Ernst Troeltsch, *Die Absolutheit des Christentums und die Religionsgeschichte* (Tübingen, 1902), English edn., *The Absoluteness of Christianity and the History of Religions,* trans. David Reid (Louisville: Westminster John Knox Press, 2005), quotes 45, 47.

120. Ibid., 57.

121. Ibid., quote 67.

122. Ibid., quotes 69, 72.

123. Ibid., quotes 78, 79.

124. Ibid., quotes 80, 82.

125. Ibid., quotes 82, 83.

126. Ibid., quotes 85, 94; see Heinrich Rickert, *Die Grenzen der naturwissenschaftlichen Begriffsbildung. Eine logische Einleitung in die historischen Wissenschaften* (Tübingen, Leipzig: J. C. B. Mohr, 1902); Rickert, *Kulturwissenschaft und Naturwissenschaft* (Tübingen: Mohr, 1921); Rickert, *Zur Lehre von der Definition* (Tübingen: Mohr, 1915).

127. Troeltsch, *The Absoluteness of Christianity and the History of Religions,* quote 98.

128. Ibid., quotes 112, 144.

129. Ibid., quotes, 121, 123.

130. Ludwig Ihmels, *Die Selbständigkeit der Dogmatik gegenüber der Religionsphilosophie* (Erlangen: Deichert, 1901); Carl Friedrich Georg Heinrici, *Dürfen wir noch Christen bleiben? Kritische Betrachtungen zur Theologie der Gegenwart* (Leipzig: Dürr, 1901); Max Reischle, "Historische und dogmatische Methode der Theologie," *Theologische Rundschau 4* (Jahrgang 1901), 261–275, 305–324; Troeltsch, *The Absoluteness of Christianity and the History of Religions,* Foreword to the first edition, 25–41, quote 26.

131. Ernst Troeltsch to Wilhelm Bousset, August 5, 1898, in Drescher, *Ernst Troeltsch: His Life and Work,* 98; Marianne Weber, *Max Weber, ein lebensbild* (Tübingen, Mohr, 1925), 240–241.

132. Ernst Troeltsch, "Political Ethics and Christianity," 1904 Address to the Evangelical Social Congress, trans. James Luther Adams, reprinted in Troeltsch, *Religion in History,* 173–209.

133. Ibid., quote 179.

134. Ibid., quotes 179, 180.

135. Ibid., quotes 181, 182, 184.

136. Ibid., quotes 185.

137. Ibid., quotes 187, 188.

138. Ibid., quote 198–199.

139. Ibid, quotes 203, 208.

140. James Luther Adams, Foreword to Ernst Troeltsch, *The Social Teaching of the Christian Churches,* 2 vols., trans. Olive Wyon (1st English edn., New York: Macmillan, 1931; 1st German edn., Troeltsch, *Die Soziallehren der christlichen Kirchen und Gruppen,*

Gesammelte Schriften I (Tübingen: J.C. B. Mohr, 1912); Louisville: Westminster John Knox Press, 1992), Meinecke and Harnack quotes, I: x.

141. Martin von Nathusius, *Die Mitarbeit der Kirche an der Lösung der sozialen Frage* (Leipzig: Hinrichs, 1893, 1894, 1904).

142. Drescher, *Ernst Troeltsch: His Life and Work,* 222–224, "this time," 222.

143. See Troeltsch, *The Social Teaching of the Christian Churches,* I: ix–xx.

144. Max Weber, *The Protestant Ethic and the Spirit of Capitalism,* trans. Peter Baehr and Gordon C. Wells (German edn., 1905; New York: Penguin, 2002); Ernst Troeltsch, "Die Bedeutung des Protestantismus für die Enstehung der modernen Welt," April 1906 address to the Ninth Congress of German Historians, Stuttgart; amplified edition published under the same title in *Historische Zeitschrift 97* (1906), 1–66; English edition, Troeltsch, *Protestantism and Progress: The Significance of Protestantism for the Rise of the Modern World,* trans. J. Montgomery (1912; reprint, Philadelphia: Fortress Press, 1986).

145. Ibid., 100–101.

146. Ibid., 101.

147. See Ernst Troeltsch, *Wesen der Religion und der Religionswissenschaft* (1906), in Troeltsch, *Gesammelte Schriften II,* 452–499; Troeltsch, *Die Trennung von Staat und Kirche, ders Staatliche Religionsunterricht und die theologischen Fakultät* (Tübingen, 1907); Troeltsch, "Luther und die moderne Welt," in Das Christentum, ed. P. Herre, Leipzig, 69–101, and Troeltsch, *Gesammelte Schriften IV,* 202–254; Troeltsch, *Die Bedeutung der Geschichtliichkeit Jesu für den Glauben* (Tübingen, 1911).

148. Troeltsch, *The Social Teaching of the Christian Churches,* I: ix.

149. Ibid., I: xx.

150. Ibid., II: 688–784, quotes 700, 738.

151. Ibid., quotes II: 999, 1011.

152. Ibid., II: 1011, 1012.

153. Ibid., II: 726–727.

154. Ibid., II: 727–728.

155. Ibid., II: 1012.

156. Ibid., II: 1005.

157. Ibid., II: 1013.

158. Ernst Troeltsch, *Glaubenslehre,* ed. Gertrud von le Fort (Berlin: Duncker und Humblot, 1925; English edn., *The Christian Faith,* trans. Garrett E. Paul (Minneapolis: Fortress Press, 1991), 113; see H. Richard Niebuhr, *Christ and Culture* (New York: Harper & Row, 1951).

159. Ernst Troeltsch to Wilhelm Bousset, May 27, 1896, in Drescher, *Ernst Troeltsch: His Life and Work,* 57; Troeltsch, *The Christian Faith,* "hodgepodge," 16.

160. Troeltsch, *The Christian Faith,* quote 113.

161. Troeltsch, "The Significance of the Historical Jesus for Faith," 187–188; Troeltsch, *The Christian Faith,* quotes 92, 97, 17; see Sarah Coakley, *Christ Without Absolutes: A Study of the Christology of Ernst Troeltsch* (Oxford: Oxford University Press, 1988); Walter E. Wyman, Jr., *The Concept of Glaubensehre: Ernst Troeltsch and the Theological Heritage of Schleiermacher* (Chico: Scholars Press, 1983); *Ernst Troeltsch and the Future of Theology,* ed. John Powell Clayton (London: Cambridge University Press, 1976).

162. See *Ernst Troeltsch: Briefe an Friedrich von Hügel, 1901–1923,* ed. Karl-Ernst Apfelbacher and P. Neuner (Munich: Paderhorn, 1974); Friedrich von Hügel, *The Mystical Element of Religion* (London: J. M. Dent & Sons, 1923).

163. Ernst Troeltsch, "Friede auf Erden, *Die Hilfe* 51 (Dez. 17, 1914), "antithesis," 833; Troeltsch, *Nach Erklürung der Mobilmachung* (Heidelberg: Carl Winters

Universitätsbuchhandlung, 1914), "Oh!," 6; Troeltsch, *Das Wesen des Deutschen* (Heidelberg: Carl Winters Universitätsbuchhandlung, 1915," "Be German," 32; Troeltsch, *Unser Volksheer* (Heidelberg: Carl Winters Universitätsbuchhandlung, 1914), "Asiatic," 5; all cited in Robert J. Rubanowice, *Crisis in Consciousness: The Thought of Ernst Troeltsch* (Tallahassee: University Presses of Florida, 1982), 99–130, quotes on 101, 102, 103, 104; see Gustav Schmidt, *Deutscher Historismus und der Uebergang zur parlamentarischen Demokratie* (Lübeck and Hamburg: Matthiesen, 1964).

164. Troeltsch, "Friede auf Erden, "antithesis," 833; Ernst Troeltsch, *Der Historismus und seine Probleme* (Berlin: R. Heise, 1924, and Troeltsch, *Gesammelte Schriften,* III), quote III: 677.

165. Troeltsch, *Der Historismus und seine Probleme,* 765–767; Ernst Troeltsch, *Der Historismus und seine Überwindung* (Berlin: 1924); English edn., Troeltsch, *Christian Thought: Its History and Application,* ed. F. von Hügel (London: University of London Press, 1923; reprint, New York: Meridian Books, 1957), 123–136, 218–222; see Rubanowice, *Crisis in Consciousness: The Thought of Ernst Troeltsch,* 62–98.

166. Troeltsch, *Der Historismus und seine Probleme, Gesammelte Schriften,* III: 702–720, quotes 708, 710; see Troeltsch, *Christian Thought: Its History and Application,* 121–144.

167. Troeltsch, *Der Historismus und seine Probleme, Gesammelte Schriften,* III: 728–729.

168. Ernst Troeltsch, "Ein Apfel von Baume Kierkegaards," *Christliche Welt* 35 (1921), 186–189; English edn., "An Apple from the Tree of Kierkegaard," trans. Louis De Grazia and Keith R. Crim, in *The Beginnings of Dialectic Theology,* ed. James M. Robinson (Richmond: John Knox Press, 1968), 311–316, quote 314.

169. See Gary Dorrien, *The Making of American Liberal Theology: Idealism, Realism, and Modernity, 1900–1950* (Louisville: Westminster John Knox, 2003); Dorrien, *The Making of American Liberal Theology: Crisis, Irony, and Postmodernity, 1950–2005* (Louisville: Westminster John Knox, 2006).

170. Harnack's funeral address was published in *Christliche Welt* 37 (1923), 101–105; cited in Drescher, *Ernst Troeltsch: His Life and Work,* 316. On Troeltsch's legitimizing of cultural and imperial privilege, see Constance Benson, *God and Caesar: Troeltsch's Social Teaching as Legitimation* (New York: Transaction Publishers, 1999).

7

Idealistic Ordering
Lux Mundi, *Andrew Seth Pringle-Pattison, Hastings Rashdall, Alfred E. Garvie, Alfred North Whitehead, William Temple, and British Idealism*

In Britain post-Kantian idealism and liberal theology arose at the same time, a century after Samuel Taylor Coleridge encountered both in Germany. By then the modern crisis of belief was far advanced. In the Anglican churches transcendental idealists led the way in building up a liberal movement, riding a powerful wave of Hegelian philosophy. In the non-conforming denominations the liberal founders were usually Ritschlians or minimally churched Kantians who took a more skeptical view of transcendental reflection. In both cases the prolonged British resistance to modern theology and the Kantian revolution were called off.

From the beginning of the liberal upsurge in Britain, liberal theology was a wider phenomenon than the group that built a party organization in the Church of England. Some important liberal thinkers were independent religious philosophers, such as Andrew Seth Pringle-Pattison, who distinguished Christian personal idealism from Absolute idealisms prominent in English philosophy. Some belonged to Non-conforming traditions, such as Alfred E. Garvie, a liberal evangelical Congregationalist. Some were Broad Church types who regretted that liberalism became a distinct party, notably William Temple, the major Anglican figure of the twentieth century and an early adapter of Whiteheadian organicism.

But the main vehicle of British liberal theology was a party organization, the Churchmen's Union for the Advancement of Liberal Religious Thought. Despite its name, this group usually preferred the term "Modernist" to "liberal." It had an energetic organizational leader, Henry D. A. Major, and a preeminent thinker, Hastings Rashdall. It boasted many leading scholars including J. F. Bethune-Baker, F. C. Burkitt, F. J. Foakes-Jackson, Percy Gardner, W. R. Inge, Ian Ramsey, and Charles E. Raven. It flourished well into the 1940s, it still exists, and its longevity owes something to Anglican peculiarities that caused its late start. Ironically, the liberal upsurge did not begin with liberals; it began in the Church of England's Anglo-Catholic party, the Tractarians.

Kantian Reason and Hegelian Spirit: The Idealistic Logic of Modern Theology, First Edition. Gary Dorrien.
© 2012 John Wiley & Sons, Ltd. Published 2015 by John Wiley & Sons, Ltd.

The Tractarian Movement was named after its trademark publication series, *Tracts for the Times,* published from 1833 to 1841. Led by John Keble, John Henry Newman, Edward Bouverie Pusey, and Richard H. Froude, it was an aggressive version of High Church Catholicism, centered at Oxford, which was later called Anglo-Catholicism. The Tractarians blasted Protestantism as a modern individualistic perversion of the Catholic faith and liberal theology as a modern species of apostasy. Repeatedly they charged that "Germanism" was the worst of both. There is only one Catholic Church, they argued, which has three branches: Roman Catholicism, Orthodoxy, and Anglicanism. Until 1845, when Newman gave up on the branch theory and converted to Roman Catholicism, the Tractarians were often called "Newmanites." After 1845 they were often called "Puseyites." By 1889 the heyday of the Tractarian movement had long past, but it remained the dominant theological party in the Church of England.

Lux Mundi and Liberal Catholicism

In 1860, a group of Broad Church Anglicans led by Henry Bristow Wilson and Benjamin Jowett tried to spark a liberal movement in English theology by publishing a reader titled *Essays and Reviews*. The reaction was so spectacularly negative that the book killed liberal theology in England for another generation. In 1889 the generation of Oxford theologians that cut its teeth on the reaction to *Essays and Reviews* was ready to say a word on behalf of modernizing reinterpretation. It helped that Hegelian idealism was taking over British philosophy and that a handful of English Congregationalists and Presbyterians had gravitated to Ritschlian historicism. More important was that late-Victorian intellectuals were publishing rueful poems and memoirs about losing their faith. Still more important was that English Anglicanism was overdue to legitimize biblical criticism and Darwinian evolution. Most important was that the young Oxford theologians had conflicted feelings about their own party, Anglo-Catholicism. The Broad Church party was too battered and defeated to spark a liberal renewal; the spark had to come from an unlikely place, which was led by figures that disliked much of what arose with them.

E. B. Pusey's last protégés at Oxford exemplified the truism that generational experience cannot be replicated. In 1875 Charles Gore, a new fellow at Trinity College and a formidable personality, sought a supportive group of colleagues. The group that Gore assembled consisted originally of himself, Henry Scott Holland, Edward S. Talbot, and J. R. Illingworth; later it added seven others; all were Tractarians who worried that English Anglicanism was suffocating of Tractarian rigidity and Evangelical anti-intellectualism. The group studied, socialized, and worshipped together, and by 1886 it had largely dispersed through career moves. Three years later it published a movement collection that launched a new era of Anglican theology, *Lux Mundi: A Series of Studies in the Religion of the Incarnation*.[1]

Lux Mundi had a tinge of nostalgia for college memories and a strong dose of modernizing admonition. Despite being products of Tractarian ritualism and polemics, the eleven *Lux Mundi* theologians felt modernity pressing upon them. The crisis of belief had become unavoidable; all of Gore's friends had friends that had dropped Christianity. In the 1850s Oxford and Cambridge had begun to grant degrees to non-Anglicans; in 1871 both institutions adopted open admissions policies for undergraduates and fellows, breaking the control of the Church of England. Gore's group judged that their teachers were fixated on reactionary fantasies. Anglo-Catholicism had the right idea, but doctrinally it was too rigid, ecclesiastically it was too coercive, and politically it was reflexively right wing. It was nice that some Anglo-Catholic priests ministered to the urban poor, but that would never break the identity of Tractarianism with religious and political reaction. If the church as a whole was to restore its credibility in a modernizing world, it had to stand for the right of free inquiry. Newman, struggling with the problem of historical consciousness in the 1840s, had solved it by taking shelter in Roman Catholicism. Afterword, Pusey and Henry P. Liddon slammed the door on historical consciousness, clinging to an Anglo-Catholic orthodoxy that conceded nothing to biblical criticism. Gore and his friends struggled with that legacy during their years at Oxford. Holland dubbed the group "the Holy Party," which grew to include Francis Paget, Aubrey Moore, R. L. Ottley, W. Lock, Arthur Lyttleton, R. C. Moberly, and W. J. H. Champion.[2]

Gore was the first Principal of Pusey House, a memorial to the Tractarian leader. He owed his appointment to Liddon, who viewed Gore as a likely movement successor. Talbott was the first Warden of Keble College, named after John Keble; Moberly was the son of a Tractarian bishop; Holland was a colleague of Liddon's at St. Paul's Cathedral, London. Liddon judged, correctly, that Gore had the requisite autocratic temperament to be a major Tractarian leader; Gore spent much of his subsequent career as a bishop condemning the rise of a liberal party. But in 1889 Gore opened the door to a liberal upsurge, declaring in the preface to *Lux Mundi:* "The epoch in which we live is one of profound transformation, intellectual and social, abounding in new needs, new points of view, new questions."[3]

The next generation of Anglican leaders had to be persuasive and relevant without falling back on coercion, Gore urged. He was against innovation in theology, which abandoned the church's founding truths. But theology needed to "take a new development," one representing more than a mere intensification or unfolding of an existing tendency. Gore offered a banner statement that shocked and sickened Tractarian leaders. Instead of subordinating modern intellectual and moral problems to an assumed orthodoxy, he declared, the church was overdue to "put the Catholic faith in its right relation to modern intellectual and moral problems."[4]

In other words, the church had to stop treating modern thought as an enemy of Christian faith. Darwinian evolution and biblical criticism had to be accommodated, and British theology had much to gain from idealistic philosophy. All the *Lux Mundi* authors were influenced by the rising prestige of idealism in British philosophy, which traced to one person, Oxford neo-Hegelian T. H. Green. Green had studied under Benjamin Jowett at Balliol College in the late 1850s, was elected a fellow of Queens College in 1860, and taught at Oxford until 1882, when he died of blood poisoning at the age of forty-five. Deeply involved in activist liberal politics, he had a huge impact on English philosophy, swinging the field toward a spiritual interpretation of the world. Against Hume's skeptical empiricism and John Stuart Mill's utilitarianism, Green argued that the very existence of art, morality, religion, and science shows that reality does not reduce to the things of sense. Empirical psychologies wrongly reduced self-consciousness to a series of events, failing to explain its unity. Green taught his students that the self-generating spiritual consciousness of human beings is the place to look for God, not some ostensible beginning or end of nature. God, to exist as anything except an unrealized potential, must be actualized in the world.[5]

That was too pantheistic for Gore, whose commitment to biblical and Nicene supernaturalism kept him from vesting much importance in a modern philosophical trend, and who spurned Green's low Christology too. But Gore absorbed the ethical aspect of Green's idealism. Most of the *Lux Mundi* authors owed a larger debt to Green, prizing his spiritualizing impact on British philosophy. And Holland and Illingworth were deeply influenced by Green, as were the metaphysical idealists that took over British philosophy in the 1880s and 1890s: Edward Caird, John Caird, Bernard Bosanquet, F. H. Bradley, R. B. Haldane, James Ward, Andrew Seth Pringle-Pattison, and Hastings Rashdall. Holland, for the rest of his career, praised Green for rescuing Oxford students and British philosophy "from the sway of individualistic sensationalism."[6]

Lux Mundi, unlike *Essays and Reviews,* was a real book, carefully fashioned into a coherent whole with a consistent message about the importance of the Incarnation, evolutionary theory, and the legitimacy of biblical criticism. It stressed that the Logos doctrine envisages the Word at work in nature, humanity, art, science, culture and everything else. Illingworth, rector of Longworth Church and sometime Fellow of Jesus College, Oxford, exemplified the idealistic turn in British theology. Conservative on doctrine and biblical criticism, he went on to write influential works on the sacredness of personality human and divine, blending Anglo-Catholic Platonism and Coleridge-style idealism. For ten years *Lux Mundi* had germinated at Illingworth's Rectory, where Gore's group met to worship together and discuss theology. *Lux Mundi* was Illingworth's breakout work as a theologian; afterwards the books flowed until his death in 1915. In *Lux Mundi's* signature chapter on evolution and the Incarnation, he contended that evolutionary theory helped the church recover its magnificent, neglected, cosmic vision of the re-consecration of the universe to God: "Evolution is in the air. It is the category of the age ... We cannot place ourselves outside it, or limit the scope of its operation."[7]

In Illingworth's telling, the Reformation fixated on justification, which reduced atonement to a selfish concern and widened the gap between things sacred and profane. It was "far otherwise" with the Church Fathers and the Scholastics, he argued. The Greek Fathers, Augustine, Aquinas, and Bonaventure were "substantially unanimous" in upholding the Pauline and Johannine concept of Christ as the eternally pre-existent reason and Word of God. To them, creation embodied divine ideas and thus revealed the divine character. Every creature was a theophany, a divine word telling something of God. The whole world was a kind of gospel of the Word by which the world was created. Illingworth favored the Scotist variation of Logos theology, viewing the Incarnation as the predestined climax of creation not contingent on the existence of sin, but he allowed that speculation on this question was "beyond that which is written." What mattered was that the Catholic tradition kept a place for reason and matter instead of falling into a one-sided Gnosticism, Arianism, pantheism, materialism, or rationalism. Aquinas, despite favoring Aristotle over Plato, did not lose the grand cosmic vision that the Church Fathers built out of Platonism and the Bible. The Protestant Reformers, unfortunately, did lose it: "In the countries most influenced by the Reformation it has dropped too much out of sight."[8]

Illingworth enthused that Darwinian evolution helped the church remember its true subject, the meaning and redemption of everything. Resisting Darwinian theory, some theologians held out for the essential difference between organized and inorganic matter; others drew a sharp line between human rationality and animal instinct. Illingworth cautioned against bottom-line dualisms. Science had already broken down seemingly impassable barriers between different kinds of things. Moreover, science was sure to break down more of them. It was not good strategy, Illingworth advised, to invest doctrinal significance in a scientific gap. God's method of working behind and within every phase of matter and its beginning did not need to be a matter of "controversial importance." What mattered was to be open to learning however God did it, which was likely to be "more magnificent" than the church imagined.[9]

Illingworth worried more about debunkers of early Christian Platonism than about the destructive force of Darwinian theory. As early as the second century, he noted, critics of Christianity charged that it was merely a malign outgrowth of a dying neo-Platonism. Anti-Christian polemics in every age repeated the charge, and certain forms of modern historical criticism specialized in it. Illingworth countered that these critiques had "no force whatever" if one believed that the divine Logos works universally in the world in cooperation with human reason. Christianity was not contaminated by its contact with a declining Platonism. Rather, the decay of Greek philosophy allowed it to be incorporated into a larger, spiritually vital life. The true successors of Plato and Aristotle were the Church Fathers and Scholastics, not Celsus, Lucian, and Porphyry. Illingworth wanted modern theologians to approach other religions in much the same way that Justin Martyr and other Fathers approached Greek wisdom, looking for signs of Eternal Reason while contending that only Christianity is a truly universal religion by virtue of proclaiming God's ultimate revelation in Jesus Christ: "The Incarnation opened heaven, for it was the revelation of the Word; but it also re-consecrated earth, for the Word was made flesh and dwelt among us. And it is impossible to read history without feeling how profoundly the religion of the Incarnation has been a religion of humanity."[10]

This was Anglo-Catholic music in a decidedly modernist mode. Critics and admirers of *Lux Mundi* devoted more attention to Illingworth than to any contributor except, predictably, Gore, an outsized personality who assigned himself the most explosive topic, biblical inspiration. Gore expressed great force of conviction and certainty in everything that he did. A powerful thinker, always pressing to persuade, he brushed aside rival views throughout his career. His overflowing self-confidence flowed from being born to wealth and the Whig aristocracy in 1853, growing up in a Victorian mansion in Wimbledon, and winning highest academic honors at Harrow and Oxford. At the age of eight or nine Gore turned against his parents' Low Church religion, deciding that he belonged in the High Church party. As an adolescent he attended Anglo-Catholic churches in London and identified with the Tractarian Movement, while retaining his parents' liberal Whig politics. At Harrow, Gore was influenced by biblical scholar B. F. Westcott, who taught him to prize rigorous scholarship and to care about the poor; at Oxford he moved straight from Balliol scholarship student to Trinity Fellow, creating the "Holy Party" with his customary blend of conviction and industry.[11]

"I am profoundly convinced" was a favorite Gore phrase. At the age of twenty-five, in his first publication, Gore announced that he was profoundly convinced that faith and reason go together, faith has a primarily moral basis, and faith is "natural and rational to a man" because it points to the divine ground of rationality and truth. Gore stuck to these core convictions for the rest of his life, always stressing, with existential urgency, that they possess a biblical basis. In his late career, after he had resigned from years of bitter wrangling as a bishop and taken up writing large books that defended his theological position, Gore offered a rare word of personal reflection, recalling his college days: "I have, ever since I was an undergraduate, been certain that I must be in the true sense a free thinker, and that either not to think freely about a disturbing subject, or to accept ecclesiastical authority in place of the best judgment of my own reason, would be for me an impossible treason against the light. I must go remorselessly where the argument leads me."[12]

This freethinking aspect of Gore's personality came through in *Lux Mundi*, although the conflict between his liberal rationalism and Anglo-Catholic conservatism was already on display, plus his remorseless tendency. He had read enough of Heinrich G. A. Ewald's seven-volume *Geschichte des Volkes Israel* to be dissuaded from opposing the German historical critical picture of how the Old Testament was constructed. Samuel R. Driver, Pusey's successor at Oxford, was another important influence on Gore, pioneering a British tradition of higher critical scholarship. On the other hand, Gore conceded very little to New Testament criticism, which helped him to win hearts and minds in 1889. In his telling, the Old Testament had "a most unspiritual appearance," as it abounded in "worldliness," "material sacrifices," and a "low standard of morals." Historical criticism, he argued, offered a convincing account – "the force of which is very great" – of the Pentateuch's composition and redaction, and it explained why Chronicles was exaggerated in comparison to parallel accounts in Samuel and Kings. Describing the distinction between Deuteronomic and Priestly Code history, Gore remarked: "What we are asked to admit is not conscious perversion, but unconscious idealizing of history, the reading back into past records of a ritual development which was really later." Inspiration ruled out deliberate deception or pious fraud, he assured, "but it appears to be quite consistent with this sort of idealizing – always supposing that the result read back into the earlier history does represent the real purpose of God, and only anticipates its realization."[13]

Gore cushioned the shock to his chief audience by assuring that the New Testament has none of the Old Testament's religious and moral problems, and few of its historical problems: "It is of the essence of the New Testament, as the religion of the Incarnation, to be final and catholic: on the other hand, it is of the essence of the Old Testament to be imperfect, because it represents a gradual process of education by which man was lifted out of depths of sin and ignorance." Authority, Gore explained, rightly under-stood, is the process of education described by Plato in *The Republic*. Authority implants right instincts and antipathies in the growing mind of a child, at a time when the child does not understand the reasons of things, which enable the child to grow into a "certain inner kinship" with the right reasons of things, making truth a friend. That is how God's Spirit operates in the Bible, gradually lifting believers from lower to higher ground: "He lifts man by little and little, He condescends to man's infirmity; He puts up with him as he is, of only He can at the last bring him back to God."[14]

By the time that we reach the high ground of the New Testament, Gore reasoned, "a whole set of presuppositions about God, about the slavery of sin, about the reasonableness of redemption, must be present with us." Otherwise we could not understand the New Testament, something that requires the guiding hand of the Church. Gore suggested that under the fragmenting and corrosive pressures of modernity, an appropriate respect for the Church's teaching authority was needed more than ever: "It is, we may say, becoming more and more difficult to believe in the Bible without believing in the Church." No doctrine of biblical inspiration takes the place of the Church as an authoritative community of witness and interpretation, for without the Church, there is no reason to believe that Hebrews belongs in the New Testament while Clement does not. Neither can a mere individual Bible-reader make sense of the problems pertaining to Christ's divinity and humanity, such as, what Christians should believe about the self-emptying aspect of Christ's Incarnation.[15]

Gore ended with provocative comments on these topics, *kenosis*, and biblical inspiration. Philippians 2: 5–7 was his keystone Christological text: Christ "did not regard equality with God as something to be exploited, but emptied himself *(kenosis)*, taking the form of a slave" (NRSV). The Incarnation, Gore declared, was "a self-emptying of God to reveal Himself under conditions of human nature and from the human point of view." To make sense of how Christ could be divine and yet self-limited in some way, the Church needed to distinguish between that which Christ revealed and that which he used. Gore explained that Christ revealed God, God's mind and character, and within certain limits, God's threefold being. Christ also revealed "man's" sinfulness and spiritual capacities, God's purpose of redemption, and God's purpose in founding the Church. But Christ revealed these things under the conditions of a true human nature, Gore reasoned. Christ used human nature – including its conditions of experience, growth in knowledge, and limitations of knowledge – in order to feel and see as human beings ought to feel and see. These two things, revelation and use, were distinct; Christ revealed divine truth by using human nature. Thus his divinity was not at risk if Christ made statements about science, history, or the future that turned out not to be accurate, for Christ restrained "the beams of Deity as to observe the limits of the science of His age, and He puts Himself in the same relation to its historical knowledge."[16]

As for biblical inspiration, Gore stressed that it is an indispensable article of faith and that the church had never defined what it is. The latter fact is something for which every modern Christian should feel grateful, he urged. The historic Creeds say very particular things about the Virgin Birth, the two natures and resurrection of Christ, and the Trinity. Thus, all Christians are required to believe very particular things about these matters. But this is not true of biblical inspiration: "We cannot make any exact claim upon any one's belief in regard to inspiration, simply because we have no authoritative definition to bring to bear upon him. Those of us who believe most in the inspiration of the Church will see a Divine Providence in this absence of dogma, because we shall perceive that only now is the state of knowledge such as admits of the question being legitimately raised."[17]

Only with the rise of modern critical knowledge did the Church sufficiently understand the development of the scriptural text to make sound judgments about the nature of its inspiration. There is such a thing as taking historical criticism too far, Gore cautioned. German scholarship often favored novelty for its own sake, lacking a proper spirit of reverence for its subject. What was needed was to allow free inquiry within the walls of a faithful, confident Church that found the right balance between criticism and reverence.[18]

Lux Mundi was an earthquake in English Christianity. It went through ten editions in its first year and inspired predictable reactions from every quarter. Opponents of biblical criticism, evolution, philosophical idealism, the modern world, and everything else that *Lux Mundi* sought to accommodate condemned the book ferociously. Evangelicals objected that *Lux Mundi* perpetuated the usual Anglo-Catholic slurs against the Reformation and betrayed the usual Anglo-Catholic reverence for Scripture. High Church conservatives were mortified that the book came from their party; Liddon, in particular, was deeply distraught and enraged by the book, especially Gore's contribution to it.

In Liddon's telling, *Lux Mundi* as a whole was rationalistic and Pelagian; it demeaned the divine infallibility of the Bible; and most grievously, Gore caused immense harm by claiming that Jesus had mistaken ideas. To Liddon it was an essential gospel truism that the knowledge "infused into the human soul of Jesus was ordinarily and practically equivalent to omniscience." Reviewers debated Gore versus Liddon on the latter point long after it became clear that *Lux Mundi* had changed Anglican theology. Fourteen years after *Lux Mundi* was published, a twelve-member group of Anglican leaders declared: "Since the human mind of our Lord was inseparably united to the eternal word, and was perfectly illuminated by the Holy Spirit in the discharge of his office as teacher, he could not be deceived, nor be the source of deception, nor intend to teach, even incidentally, for fact what was not fact." Twenty-one years after that, William Temple opined that conservatives were wrong about biblical criticism but right about kenosis theology: "The difficulties are intolerable ... To say that the Creative Word was so self-emptied as to have no being except in the Infant Jesus is to assert that for a certain period the world was let loose from the control of the creative Word." Gore stood his ground on kenosis doctrine, wrote a major work in defense of it – *The Incarnation of the Son of God* (1891) – and helped to make the idea respectable in Anglican theology. At the same time, he responded to the controversy over *Lux Mundi* by defending the absolute authority of the Christian creeds on all matters on which the creeds made statements. If the infant Jesus did not exercise providential government over all things, Gore contended, some version of kenotic doctrine had to be consistent with the Nicene, Apostles, and Athanasian creeds.[19]

The meaning of *Lux Mundi* is indicated by what happened to its contributors. Moberly won a Regius chair at Oxford; Ottley succeeded Moberly in 1903; Paget became Bishop of Oxford; Talbot became bishop, successively, of Rochester, Southwark, and Winchester. Holland became a major social reform leader while teaching for a total of thirty-two years at Christ Church, Oxford, interrupted near the middle by twenty-six years at St. Paul's Cathedral, London. Gore moved on to Westminster Abbey, served bishoprics at Worcester, Birmingham, and Oxford from 1902 to 1919, wrote prolifically on theological and social problems, and became the dominant church leader of his time, although he bruised too many feelings to make Archbishop of Canterbury. Far from damaging their careers by producing a notorious book, the *Lux Mundi* authors swept to leadership positions in a new establishment that accepted biblical criticism, evolution, and especially, philosophical idealism. Gore, tellingly, called his perspective "liberal Catholicism." This was not merely his position or that of his group, he argued; it was the best name for Anglicanism as a whole, a communion that blended Catholic substance and a liberal spirit. But that idea was compatible with theologies that Gore did not recognize as legitimate in the Church of England, which made him an embattled figure in a church that he dominated but never controlled.[20]

Lux Mundi was a sign, not the necessary cause of anything. England had stymied modern theology for as long as possible, which would have broken through without *Lux Mundi*. The time for Coleridge-style idealism and Broad Church liberalism had come, sixty years after Coleridge was gone. As it was, *Lux Mundi* legitimized the Broad Church party, aiding its resurgence, but also impeded it by showing that Broad Church types had no corner on free inquiry, biblical criticism, and evolution. If Anglicanism as a whole was rightly understood to be a form of liberal Catholicism, or liberal Protestantism, or both, the need for a liberal Modernist party was debatable. Liberal Modernist leaders had to debate that proposition from the beginning of their resurgence in the 1890s.

Getting Hegel and Personality Right: Andrew Seth Pringle-Pattison

Idealistic theologians and religious philosophers led the way – Andrew Seth Pringle-Pattison, Hastings Rashdall, John Caird, Edward Caird, James Ward, and, a bit later, C. C. J. Webb and William Temple. All were influenced by Green and determined to strengthen the Christian basis of his undeveloped system. All rode and contributed to the Hegel vogue that swept British philosophy, though religious idealists were determined to correct the religious deficiencies of absolute idealism, which amplified Green's. It was not clear to what extent Green identified the human spirit with the Absolute, but the school of British absolute idealism that he inspired played down or denied the individual personality of selves, or the personality of the Absolute, or both. F. H. Bradley, Bernard Bosanquet and Richard B. Haldane were major figures in this school. To them, all relations were internal; everything was logically connected to everything else; "individual personality" had meaning, at best, only in relation to its total context. To absolute idealists the whole was individual and universal, a *concrete* universal containing all things. Divine Spirit and human spirit were unified, though sometimes, absolute idealists cautioned that even putting it that way was potentially misleading, as it reinforced the old dualism. J. M. E. McTaggart, another prominent absolute idealist, denied the existence of God; for McTaggart, ultimate reality consisted of a system of eternal selves forming an unconscious unity.[21]

To the religious idealists, the ascendance of British absolute idealism was a mixed blessing. It was exciting to ride the vogue of Hegelianism after decades of fighting off skeptical empiricism and atheistic rationalism. Idealism was unquestionably the key to making theology modern. But absolute idealists made claims about divine and human personality that were problematic for Christian theology. Pringle-Pattison, a Scottish Anglican religious philosopher, and Rashdall, an English Anglican religious philosopher, led the way in wedding British theology to the right kind of idealism.

Pringle-Pattison was born Andrew Seth in Edinburgh in 1856; in 1898 he added the name Pringle-Pattison to fulfill the terms of a bequest granting him an estate. Educated at Edinburgh University in the mid-1870s and influenced by his lifelong friendship with Haldane, he undertook two years of graduate study in Berlin, Jena, and Göttingen, hearing Rudolf Hermann Lotze at Göttingen, although he resisted Lotze's anti-Hegelian blend of idealism and realism. Pringle-Pattison was a Hegelian when he returned to Edinburgh University in 1880 to begin his academic career. In *The Development from Kant to Hegel* (1882), he straightforwardly presented Hegelian idealism as the answer to Kantian problems: Kant wrongly blocked any possible access to noumenal reality by separating powers of mind from phenomenal objects; Kant's arbitrary dualism yielded an unacceptable agnosticism about almost everything worth knowing; Hegel showed the way forward by overcoming the dualism of subject and object.[22]

Pringle-Pattison tried to believe, with Hegel, that self-consciousness rests in an abstract Absolute for which Hegel claimed ultimate concreteness. Had Pringle-Pattison stayed on that track, he would have joined a burgeoning school in its heyday. But something gnawed at him – his feeling that Kant was right to locate self-consciousness in individual selves, and that Hegel obliterated individuality in the name of lifting it to something higher. It surprised Pringle-Pattison that German Hegelians brushed past this issue, concentrating on refuting materialism. Somehow Pringle-Pattison had to overcome Kant's dualism without violating his own intuition that individuality is real and important.

In Britain, Illingworth and Edward Caird grappled with this problem, but Illingworth was rooted in the neo-Platonism of the Greek Fathers, which rested on a static a-temporal theory of forms, and Caird claimed that Hegel offered the best rendering of the essential unity of God and humanity exemplified in Christ. The law of the life of spirit is "self-realization through self-abnegation," Caird argued. This law holds for God and human beings alike; in fact, "the Spirit that works in man to 'die to live' is the Spirit of God." Caird contended that Hegel did not merely accommodate his philosophy to Christianity; Hegel unfolded the "essential meaning" of Christ's incarnation and teaching.[23]

That was no longer believable to Pringle-Pattison, because he doubted that Hegel theorized a personal God or personal individuals. In 1887, in a book titled *Hegelianism and Personality,* Pringle-Pattison cleared a path for a soon thriving school of personal idealism. British philosophy, he acknowledged, owed a singular debt to Green for changing the field. But Green merely criticized and pointed to something better; his thought was not a place to rest. He was a Hegelian of sorts, although the best part of his thought – his ethical idealism – owed more to Kant and Fichte. Green adopted, more or less, Hegel's theory of a universal or divine Self, but he was vague about how this spiritual principle operated in individuals. Moreover, Pringle-Pattison argued, it was probably just as well that Green was vague on the latter point, for his thought leaned toward absolute idealism. Being clear about it would not have helped religious thinkers find their way. The real problem for religious idealism was not Green's vagueness or even the denial of individuality by British Hegelians. It was that British Hegelians got Hegel right. Hegelian philosophy was about the identification of human and divine self-consciousness. In Pringle-Pattison's view, Hegel wrongly took an identity of type for a unity of existence, conceiving all of consciousness as something unified in a single divine Self.[24]

To be sure, Pringle-Pattison allowed, Hegel was the greatest modern philosopher, expounding "what is profoundest and best in modern philosophy." Fichte's system was essentially ethical, consumed with duty; Schelling was basically a philosopher of nature; Hegel's vastly more ambitious and impressive system was anchored by logic. Hegel expanded Kant's table of the categories, and no modern philosopher compared to Hegel for sheer brilliance. In Pringle-Pattison's view, Hegel was right to designate self-consciousness as the ultimate category of thought, although he mystified this notion, which referred to knowledge as such, by employing grandiose concepts for it such as the "Absolute Idea" and the "pure Ego." Pringle-Pattison noted that Hegel's absolute idea was nothing more than Aristotle's principle that the knower and the known have a transparent relationship; in a crucial sense, the thinker and the thinker's thoughts are one. The key to Hegel was the problematic thing that he did with this Aristotelian principle.

Hegel's concept of the Absolute Idea was a logical notion belonging to the category of logical abstraction; it was the scheme or form of self-consciousness. On the other hand, Pringle-Pattison observed, Hegel's idea of Absolute Spirit was metaphysical, dealing with facts of existence, not logical. But Hegel did not acknowledge that his philosophy of nature and philosophy of Spirit were metaphysical, offering a theory of existence. Had Hegel admitted the obvious on this point, Pringle-Pattison judged, his system would have been more believable. Instead, Hegel fused the two categories, presenting his logic as a metaphysic. Hegelian logic was supposedly absolute, not a logic of subjective thought; thus it was the only possible metaphysic.[25]

Hegel claimed to deduce nature from the logical Idea, describing nature as the Idea in the form of otherness. To be sure, Pringle-Pattison allowed, Hegel never claimed to describe anything that actually occurred, just as he did not claim that the Idea was factually antecedent to nature and Spirit. Hegel's system was an abstraction, not a description of a factual process. Nature, like the thought-determinations comprising the Absolute Idea, was an abstraction lacking any independent factual existence; both existed only within the life of Spirit. Thus, logically speaking, Spirit was the only factual reality. Pringle-Pattison replied that in that case, Schelling was right to judge that deduction had nothing to do with it. Dialectic was powerless to bridge the chasm between thought and nature, so Hegel simply leaped across it. His sparkling metaphors of deduction were just that – metaphors conveying no factual meaning. Pringle-Pattison remarked that the whole point and design of Hegel's system was "to elude the necessity of resting anywhere on mere fact." Hegel excited religious thinkers by showing logically that spirit exists by a necessity of thought. Pringle-Pattison argued that this attempt to construct the world out of pure abstract universals was, like Plato's, fascinating, but unconvincing.[26]

"We must touch reality somewhere," Pringle-Pattison urged. "Otherwise our whole construction is in the air." Here, Kant's critique of the ontological proof of God's existence was to the point. Kant powerfully demonstrated the impossibility of deriving a fact from a concept. "Existence" and "being" are not concepts of things that can be added to the concept of a thing, Kant argued, for existence and being are not predicates. To say that something exists does not add any value to it. Pringle-Pattison argued that to speak meaningfully of God's existence, one must show that God's existence is an immediate certainty or that it is bound up with facts of experience.[27]

Hegelian idealism magnificently refashioned the Platonic idea that reason rules the world, or at least, that there is reason in the world. In Pringle-Pattison's view, all modern religious thinkers were in Hegel's debt for that. But Hegel went much further, describing nature as a reflection of the thought-determinations of the Idea, or more poetically, as spirit in alienation from itself. Pringle-Pattison replied that factual reality is not a mere abstraction and it deserves at least as much attention as the logic of the notion. Nature is not rational in the manner of Hegelian logic. Things exist side by side in space, or successively in time, with utter indifference to logical passage. The size and number of planets have no logic, and it is not very helpful to sweep all such matters under the category of contingency, as Hegel did. Above all, Pringle-Pattison argued, Hegel's version of idealism, despite its unmatched brilliance, was not the one to adopt on the ultimate question of the nature of divine reality.[28]

Even putting it that way seemed to require a position about what Hegel said about God, but Pringle-Pattison stressed that Hegel was slippery on this subject, which inspired rival schools of thought. Hegelian theologians and atheistic left-Hegelians based their antithetical interpretations on the same texts, which spoke of Self-consciousness in general, not of divine self-consciousness or human self-consciousness. This was the key to the riddle of Hegel's religion, Pringle-Pattison argued. Hegel's subject was Spirit, not divine Spirit or human spirits; in Hegel's vision, the world process was always about the realization of Spirit as self-conscious reason. But Spirit and reason are abstractions, Pringle-Pattison cautioned; only spirits and self-conscious selves are real. Though Hegel referred to God as the Absolute Spirit, even this concept did not establish that Hegel conceived God as a singular intelligence, a Subjective Spirit. Here the idiomatic peculiarities of German *Geist* abetted Hegel's evasiveness. In German, the article goes with the noun, so Hegel's references to *der absolute Geist* did not necessarily refer to a concrete Subject, as English translations implied. Hegel persistently described the realization of Absolute Spirit in art, religion, and philosophy while carefully avoiding any discussion of the real Spirit or spirits for which all such realizations ostensibly took place.

The point was not that Hegel tried to trick anybody; Pringle-Pattison admired Hegel enormously and took no interest in attacking his motives. The point was that Hegel's ambiguity about divine reality was inherent in his absolute idealism, which treated notions as ultimate reality and real things as exemplifications of notions. Hegel began with an abstract concept of Self-consciousness in general, theorizing the entire world process of existence as the evolution and realization of this abstraction. Thus, his entire theory was purely abstract from start to finish. Pringle-Pattison took seriously Hegel's claim that his idea of Spirit, or the concrete Idea, improved on previous Christian understandings of the divine-human unity. But Hegel's rendering of this idea was concrete only with reference to the logical Idea preceding it, not in the sense of designating anything that existed. Absolute Spirit – a product of the self-creative projection of the Idea into existence – was "real" only as a real duplicate of the Idea; Pringle-Pattison called it "the notion of knowledge hypostatized." This idea united God and human selves by stripping both of all real contents except the notion of intelligence as such. In Hegelian theory, God and selves were sublimated into a logical concept.[29]

To Pringle-Pattison, this scheme surpassed all modern attempts to rehabilitate neo-Platonist Logos theology and Nicene Trinitarianism. Moreover, there was a wonderful irony in Hegel's relentlessly abstract theorizing. Because he was so fiercely determined to trace the work of reason through the chaotic flow of mere stuff, Hegel grappled with historical experience more profoundly and extensively than all other philosophers. Pringle-Pattison marveled at the vast knowledge of world history that Hegel paraded in his lectures on art, religion, history, and philosophy. But this display of learning, he objected, always served Hegel's system. It yielded "not an actual history but a philosophized history." It was history conceived and interpreted as the development of Hegelian Spirit in time. In Pringle-Pattison's telling, Hegel had one subject, and two lines of thought about it, which he never fused together. Hegel's subject was the realization of self-consciousness, Spirit achieving insight into its own nature. Nothing else was important, or, even, real. In pursuit of this subject, he moved in two directions, from above and below.[30]

The first approach began with God, specifically the neo-Platonist Christian God of Trinity in unity, which in Hegel's scheme was the idea of knowledge as such. The second approach traced the process in which the Absolute came to itself through the historical development of humanity. Since these approaches had different starting points, Pringle-Pattison argued, one was bound to prevail over the other, and since the second approach at least took a pass at actual existence, it prevailed in Hegel's usage. Though Hegel had a mystical Platonist streak, he was averse to seeking the Divine in an ideal separate from the world; thus he insisted that God had to be found in the world or not at all. Pringle-Pattison loved Hegel's saying that God is "Spirit in all spirits," not a Spirit beyond the stars. Unfortunately, this golden truism of religious idealism was marred by Hegel's absolute idealism, which identified the Absolute with the subject of development. Pringle-Pattison cautioned that if the universe lacks any self-conscious existence beyond that which is realized in the self-consciousness of individuals, there is no real deity or divine transcendence in the world; there is only a deified humanity. At most, God exists only in the consciousness of individuals and worshipping communities.[31]

Pringle-Pattison acknowledged that Hegel could be read differently, as an advocate of personal idealism. Many Hegelian theologians denied that Hegel denied that God might have a separate personality or self-consciousness, and Hegel made numerous statements that sounded like personal theism. It was impossible to be certain what Hegel really believed. But Pringle-Pattison advised theologians to make their case for personal idealism without insisting that Hegel agreed with them, because the "drift of Hegel's mind" was toward absolute idealism. If Hegelian idealism was about an impersonal system of abstract thoughts – the Absolute – coming to consciousness of itself, it was hard to say no to atheistic left-Hegelians like Feuerbach, Strauss, and Bauer, who took literally Hegel's statements about the iron necessity of his logic and dispensed with the supreme Spirit. If Hegel's project was to construct reality wholly out of a logical Idea, the atheistic Hegelians had cause to claim that they brought the Hegelian project to its logical conclusion. Pringle-Pattison put it dramatically, warning that if the Idea is all in all, human beings and God are stripped of personality, cynical realism is bound to prevail, and Hegel's chauvinistic Prussian conservatism was a plausible position: "If we take away from Idealism personality, and the ideals that belong to personality, it ceases to be Idealism in the historic sense of the word. To call it so is merely confusing the issues, for it has joined hands with the enemy, and fights for the other side of the field."[32]

Good idealism is progressive, hopeful, and life-giving, Pringle-Pattison urged. It sticks with the commonsense truism that there is no thought without a thinker, spurning Hegel's strange concept of the self-existence of thoughts. It accepts that human beings lack any capacity to trace the development of God; all that we can do is trace the development of human thoughts about God. Religion is about the subjective spirit of human selves, Pringle-Pattison contended. It has a ground to stand upon even as it reaches for the stars. It was sheer "effrontery" on Hegel's part "to narrow down the Spirit of the universe to a series of events on this planet." Worse yet, in Hegel's account the spiritual development of the Absolute was confined pretty much to the shores of the Mediterranean, an attitude that yielded his laughable claim in the *Philosophy of Right* about the Prussian state's world-historical superiority: "This is the absolute turning point; mind rises out of this situation and grasps the infinite positivity of this its inward character, i.e. it grasps the principle of the unity of the divine nature and the human, the reconciliation of objective truth and freedom as the truth and freedom appearing within self-consciousness and subjectivity, a reconciliation with the fulfill-ment of which the principle of the north, the principle of the Germanic peoples, has been entrusted."[33]

Pringle-Pattison countered that real idealism is allergic to Hegel's arrogant nation-alism and false universalism. It accentuates ethical subjectivity and the struggle for unrealized ideals. The real thing has a buoyant zeal for moral progress, prizing ethical feelings that fuel struggles for social justice. The *Philosophy of Right* abounded in pedestrian admonitions to do one's duty, keep to one's station, and not make trouble; Pringle-Pattison remarked that it reeked of a "satisfied acquiescence in things as they are, which the years bring to the man of the world – a mood as far removed as possible from the atmosphere of moral endeavor." Idealistic ethical feeling, by contrast, is contentious, energetic, generous, and visionary. It flows naturally from being enlivened as an ethical and spiritual being by the Spirit of a personal God: "I have a centre of my own – a will of my own – which no one shares with me or can share – a centre which I maintain even in my dealings with God Himself." My self, and every self, is the apex of the principle of individuation by which the world exists. As such, Pringle-Pattison insisted, each self is "impervious" to other selves, "impervious in a fashion of which the impenetrability of matter is a faint analogue."[34]

That put it too strongly, conveying exclusivist connotations that clashed with Pringle-Pattison's meaning. His point in rejecting the fusion of selves in a logical universal was to play up the uniqueness of each self. To Pringle-Pattison, the idea that selves literally merged in a Universal Self or Absolute was an impossible contradiction, worse even than the idea of bodies occupying the same space. *Hegelianism and Personality* launched a British school of thought on this theme, after which Prin-gle-Pattison regretted having reached for the term "impervious." He spent the rest of his career pleading that getting personality right – human and divine – is the key to creating a genuinely progressive and ethical theology. We must describe God as personal, he told his lecture audiences, because personality is and reveals the highest that human beings know. There is such a thing as intrinsic value, which yields an intelligible world, because personality is the central clue to the ultimate nature of reality and the one thing that cannot be explained by something else.[35]

Pringle-Pattison denied that idealists should be pan-psychists, rendering all bits of external nature as mind-stuff or tiny minds. Here he was closer to Bosanquet than to Bradley; it was enough for idealists to say that nature as a whole is complementary to mind and it possesses no existence of its own apart from mind, just as mind would be spiritually and ethically void if it lacked a world. Bosanquet, however, like Bradley, was a sharp critic of personal idealism, which he equated with the idea of a substantial self or unitary self, which he condemned as "irrational." Pringle-Pattison replied in his Gifford Lectures of 1912 and 1913, *The Idea of God in the Light of Recent Philosophy*, that one did not have to believe in the old doctrine of a substantial self or a soul to be a personal idealist. In fact, it was important not to believe it.[36]

There is no such thing as a mere individual, he explained. Modern thought is relational and dynamic all the way down. A self can exist only in relationship with a system of reason and an objective world from which the self receives its content. Bosanquet contended that something deeper and more real than the subjects of experience underlies them; Pringle-Pattison agreed, but countered that this does not render the finite self as a vanishing distinction, for finite centers do not overlap in existence. The very *raison d'etre* of a self is to be a distinct focalization of a common universe. Bosanquet allowed that personalities possess an aspect of "distinct unshareable immediacy," but he insisted that this aspect is unimportant; it is, at most, a condition of finiteness, which "lies in powerlessness." Pringle-Pattison urged that good idealism, instead of falling into Bosanquet's monism, kept its balance between individualism and organicism, nominalism and realism, and pluralism and monism: "The universal is no less an abstraction, if it is taken as real, or as possessing substantive existence, independently of the individuals whose living tissue it is. They realize themselves through it; it realizes itself in them. Thus a social whole is the sustaining life of its individual members, but it melts into thin air if we try to treat it as an entity apart from them."[37]

Absolute idealists had a one-sided dread of pluralism, Pringle-Pattison judged; pluralists, in reaction, displayed a one-sided dread of monism. Thus Bosanquet dissolved the world into a collection of qualities that were ultimately housed in the Absolute. Bradley described the individual subjects of experience as mere "adjectives" of the one Reality, which his philosophy "merged" into the Absolute. American pragmatist William James, overreacting to Bosanquet, Bradley, and Josiah Royce, lapsed into a pragmatic pluralism that left the world ripped into incoherent shards. James protested that philosophers preferred elegant logical solutions to the real world. He contended that religious and social ideals were better defended by an open-minded radical empiricism that tracked the flow of experience, which was relational and fluid. Radical empiricism approached the only reality that had any meaning, he urged; it respected the human experience of plurality and different kinds of unity in a world of flux and sensation. Non-empirical philosophies were simply unreal, parading mere suppositions about reality, "notes taken by ourselves." In James' striking images, speculative philosophy held reality no better than a net holds water, fashioning abstract "cut out and fix" concepts.[38]

Pringle-Pattison admired the "stirring quality" of James' philosophy and the "appeal it makes to our active nature." He appreciated that James was still an idealist of sorts and an advocate of moral religion. He even admired that James faced up to the implications of his radical pluralism by arguing for a finite God and an "unfinished world." But James' "struggling deity" was a high price to pay for avoiding monism, Pringle-Pattison urged. Moreover, Jamesian moral religion was too secular and utilitarian to be much of a religion: "The deeper expressions of religious faith and emotion – the utterances of the saints, the religious experts – appear quite irreconcilable with the pluralistic conception of a finite God, an unfinished world and a dubious fight."[39]

The victory for which morality fights has already been won on the religious plane through Christ and the promise of the kingdom of God, Pringle-Pattison asserted. It is the "assurance of this victory" that inspires individuals to be courageous and hopeful in fighting for the good. Just as the absolute idealists overreacted to something they were right to avoid, the myth of a substantial self, James overreacted against the absolute idealist concept of finite beings as mere objects of the Absolute. Pringle-Pattison, saying no to both, held out for a personal panentheistic idealism that conceived God as suffering in, with, and for the world: "The Absolute is conceived by James from the beginning to end of his polemic as purely cognitive, not the doer and sufferer in the world's life, but an eternally perfect spectator of the play." Modern Christianity, Pringle-Pattison urged, has a better option: "No God, or Absolute, existing in solitary bliss and perfection, but a God who lives in the perpetual giving of himself, who shares the life of his finite creatures, bearing in and with them the whole burden of their finitude, their sinful wanderings and sorrows, and the suffering without which they cannot be made perfect."[40]

Pringle-Pattison made a winsome case for holding the most attractive idealism. Living until 1931, he influenced British theology and was cited repeatedly at conferences of the Churchmen's Union. He influenced a stream of religious philosophers that sought to wring as much personality as possible out of absolute idealism, notably Edward Caird, Josiah Royce, Henry Jones, A. E. Taylor, and W. E. Hocking. He lived to see his work cited with admiration by Edgar S. Brightman, Albert C. Knudson, and other stalwarts of American personal idealism. His intellectual affinity with Borden Parker Bowne, the founder of Boston Personalism, was so strong that Knudson sometimes cited the two thinkers interchangeably. However, Pringle-Pattison did not see the analytic tradition coming, nor did his allies. *The Idea of God in the Light of Recent Philosophy,* a work of 435 pages ranging widely over recent philosophical trends, never mentioned G.E. Moore or Bertrand Russell. Pringle-Pattison could not imagine that the kind of small-bore arguments favored by Moore and Russell might topple idealism as an option in philosophy. To him, analytic philosophy was mere tool sharpening at best, not philosophy; it took a pass on the big questions that real philosophy was about.[41]

British theologians stuck with idealism long after the tide turned against it in Anglo-American philosophy. Philosophical idealism at its best and worst possessed a religious character that appealed to theologians. Thus they were not inclined to give it up merely because Moore and James poked a few holes in it, or later, merely because World War I savagely destroyed the hope of a better and better progressing world.

Though British liberal theology was a wider phenomenon than its Anglican party, the party was central to it and definitive of it. Liberals started to build the infrastructure of a movement in 1898, beginning with a weekly magazine, *The Church Gazette: A Review of Liberal Religious Thought,* which gave birth later that year to an organization, the Churchmen's Union for the Advancement of Liberal Religious Thought. The weekly lasted two years; in 1904 it was replaced with a quarterly, *The Liberal Churchman,* which lasted four years; in 1911 Churchmen's Union activist Henry D. A. Major founded a monthly, *The Modern Churchman,* which became the movement's (unofficial) flagship under Major's 46 years of editorship. In 1919 Major opened a theological college at Oxford, Ripon College, which became the intellectual center of the Modernist movement. Today the Modern Church Union still publishes the journal under the name *Modern Believing.* Many of the most distinguished Anglican scholars of the early twentieth century were affiliated with the Churchmen's Union, notably J. F. Bethune-Baker, F. C. Burkitt, F. J. Foakes-Jackson, Percy Gardner, Percival Gardner-Smith, William Ralph Inge, Kirsopp Lake, William Sanday, and B. H. Streeter. But the major thinker of the Churchmen's Union in its first generation was religious philosopher Hastings Rashdall, in whose work the best and worst aspects of post-Victorian liberal idealism were amply displayed.[42]

Idealistic Elitism: Hastings Rashdall

In Rashdall the liberal movement found an advocate of high intellectual power, conviction, and immense erudition. It also found an effective apologist whose success owed something to his assurance that liberal idealism was compatible with preserving the social privileges and white supremacism of British polite society. The son of an Eaton Square, London rector, Rashdall was educated at Harrow and New College, Oxford. In 1889 he was elected a fellow of Hertford College, Oxford; the following year he joined the reformist Christian Social Union at its founding; in 1895 he returned to New College as a fellow and dean of divinity, and started writing books. In 1897 he got his first splash of public renown by debating his former teacher, moral philosopher Henry Sidgwick, on the right of liberal clergy to be clerics. Sidgwick, a former Broad Church liberal turned agnostic, contended that no cleric had a right to disbelieve in the New Testament miracles, especially the virginal conception of Jesus. Rashdall replied that it was quite possible to give a valid ministerial witness to Christ without believing in the New Testament's miracles. As long as one did not deny the divinity of Christ or teach that Christ's resurrection was a mere case of subjective delusion, it was not only possible, but desirable for modern clergy to take a skeptical view of miracle stories.[43]

Two years later, preaching at the annual conference of the newly founded Churchmen's Union for the Advancement of Liberal Religious Thought, Rashdall returned to the subject of what was essential and what was not. In his view there were "three great essentials" of the Christian faith: belief in a personal God, personal immortality, and a "unique and paramount revelation of God in the historic Christ." Rashdall urged his fellow liberals to hold firmly to this threefold foundation and to critically interrogate everything else: "Of the vast superstructure of doctrinal and ritual and ethical tradition which has been built upon and around the essential Christianity which we find in the moral and religious consciousness of Jesus the Son of God, not all is of equal value. There is a great deal of hay and stubble that has simply got to be cleared away."[44]

Many Churchmen's Union conferences afterward took exactly that tone, where a dominant mainstream of liberal Protestants melded somewhat uneasily with a smaller group of Catholic-leaning Modernists. Major, the group's indomitable organizational leader, insisted from the beginning that liberal Protestants, liberal Catholics, independent radicals, and Broad Church temporizers were equally welcome as long as they cleared away unbelievable things and upheld the essential things with a reverent spirit. Often described as the Pope of Anglican Modernism, both in affection and derision, Major was an assiduous gatekeeper of the dispensable/essential distinction. Anglican Modernism, though often accused by conservatives of fixating on its disbeliefs, in fact accentuated its positive beliefs as expounded by Major and Rashdall: Trinitarian panentheism, degree Christology, Abelardian atonement doctrine, universal salvation, a minimalist view on miracles, and the right of clergy to believe such things in the Church of England. From 1910 to 1917 Rashdall served as canon of Hereford Cathedral in addition to his professorial position at New College, and from 1917 until his death in 1924 he served as Dean of Carlisle.

As a theologian Rashdall's chief legacy was to clear a space for liberal Modernism in British theology and ecclesiastical life. As a philosopher his chief legacy was his theory of ideal utilitarianism. To him there were tensions between theology and philosophy, but no clear distinction between them. Rashdall's aim was to keep philosophy religious, to keep religion philosophical, and to keep both in step with modern thought. The best and worst parts of his thought were products of his attempt to hold together Christian ideals and his concept of rational order. Though Rashdall had trouble deciding whether he was primarily a theologian or a moral philosopher, he stressed the difficulty of being both at the same time, because there were rival authorities to negotiate. Christian ethics is about following Christ; moral philosophy is about following the dictates of a rationally informed moral conscience; sometimes these things conflict. In the modern age, Rashdall believed, good theology had to be liberal, modernist, critical, philosophical, personal, idealistic, and unabashedly Christian, and it had to reconcile, as far as possible, the conflicts between these things.[45]

Had it been up to him, Rashdall would have saved British philosophy from much of its torturous grappling with post-Kantian German idealism. The best form of idealism is a British tradition, he argued; it was Berkeley's subjectivism, though Berkeley made a few mistakes about sensation that Kant corrected. Basically, Rashdall explained, Berkeley extended Platonist idealism by extending Locke's analysis of the secondary qualities of matter to the primary qualities of matter. Locke taught that the material universe is essentially a system of material bodies mechanically interacting in space, and that its operation depends on certain primary qualities of matter – solidity, figure, extension, motion, and number. Ideas arise in the mind through a process of mechanical stimulation in the sense organs. Some ideas represent to the mind real things, while others such as sound and color have no real counterpart in physical reality.[46]

Berkeley charged that this picture is absurd, defying common sense. If color is merely an apparent feature of physical reality, how did Locke know that *any* of his ideas correctly represent reality? If blue and sound depend on the existence of mind in the universe, how did Locke know that big or small, round or square, or solid or fluid would still exist even if mind disappeared? If we are aware only of our own ideas, as Locke admitted, how could Locke know that the universe is a vast machine? Berkeley contended that Locke did not know it because matter is not real; only mind is real. Knowledge is a succession of feelings, or more precisely, the apprehension of a succession of ideas, not something governed by actual self-existing matter, which is merely an idea. To Rashdall, this was the key breakthrough for modern idealism; Berkeley grasped the ideational character of knowledge as a succession of feelings. Moreover, Berkeley did not ignore the relational aspect of knowing, that knowledge requires sensations *and* mental relations. He only failed to stress the distinction and to think it through, and thus he had to be corrected by Kant.[47]

For Locke, as for most empiricists, the rock bottom sense of matter as reality was keyed to its space-occupying quality. Rashdall, applying Kant's transcendental idealism, countered that the essence of spatiality is that objects are perceived as existing side by side with other things. Space is made up of relations, a notion that lacks any meaning apart from a mind that relates one thing to another *and* for which things are related. Relatedness means nothing without a mind that holds together both terms of a relation. Rashdall explained that the relation between two points is not *in* either point by themselves; the relation is in the "between," which does not exist in any one or several isolated points of space: "It must exist only in some one existent which holds together and connects those points." There is no relatedness without mind, there is no space without relatedness, there is no matter without space, and thus, Rashdall argued, following Berkeley, there is no matter without mind.[48]

Berkeley was ridiculed in his time for pressing an absurd argument denying the existence of matter, and Rashdall allowed that Berkeley went too far, reducing space and substance to mere feelings. Kant's transcendentalism was the necessary corrective, for the apprehension of one feeling by another feeling is not itself a feeling and cannot be explained by mere feeling. But Rashdall stressed that Berkeley put Kant on the right track by showing that relations and sensations require powers of mind, and Kant showed that even to call things "bundles of sensations," as Berkeley did, implied that the bundles are as constitutive in thinghood as the sensations. Thus Kant put great store in his bundled "categories" of Substance, Quantity, Quality, and the rest.

Rashdall pressed for a post-Kantian subjective idealist verdict: There is no object without a subject. There is nothing in matter that does not imply mind. A thing exists for "another," but a consciousness exists for itself; the very being of a mind consists in being itself conscious. A mind, unlike a thing, is not made what it is by being experienced by another mind; it is what it is for itself. Since matter is unintelligible without mind, it must never have existed without mind. Ultimately nothing exists except minds and their experiences. But since matter as a whole does not exist merely for our minds, which know only a tiny bit of the universe, there must a divine Mind that knows the whole.[49]

Rashdall sympathized with people who took idealism halfway, combining mind and matter. For religious purposes, he allowed, it doesn't really matter if one cannot handle the idealist view that nature exists in the mind of God. One can do just as well, religiously, by thinking of nature as something real that was created and sustained in existence by the mind of God. But Rashdall urged his readers and lecture audiences to go all the way if they could, which was more coherent and which fully thought through what it means to believe in God. Some kind of unity must underlie the diversity of things, he argued. The world does not arise by the coming together of two realities governed by no law. All things come together as parts of a single intelligible whole. The idea that nothing exists, ultimately, except minds and their experiences does not come readily to most people, Rashdall acknowledged. Usually it requires years of mental and spiritual effort and a "considerable course of habituation." Like Pringle-Pattison, Rashdall urged his readers and lecture audiences not to settle for impersonal or atheistic versions of idealism, which subverted everything that was precious to the real thing.[50]

For Rashdall the other idealisms were allies to a point, because one had to make a case for idealism before working up to the apex of the metaphysical pyramid. First one establishes that things exist for mind, not for themselves; things are real only when taken in connection with mind, not as self-subsistent realities. This position carries with it the idea that a soul, or mind, or self experiences the things. Here the influence of Hegel and Bradley was much too great in British thought, Rashdall believed, because there is no reason to sell short the full personality of human beings and the divine. Human and divine personality both imply a feeling, thinking, and willing consciousness, a "certain permanence" that enables a person to distinguish oneself from the objects of one's thought (even as idealism construes the ultimate essence of these objects as experiences of consciousness) and powers of action. Almost nobody denies that persons feel and think, Rashdall observed. Moreover, there is no thought without attention, which is an act of will. Thought is an act, which is performed with a motive, which implies feeling, and willing is essentially connected with feeling, thought, and the capacity of a self to distinguish one's self from its successive experiences and from other consciousness. Thus the idea of a person is the idea of a consciousness that feels, thinks and wills through powers of self-distinguishing, individual, active being.[51]

Rashdall was much clearer about what personality requires than about where to draw the line on the personhood of animals and children. Personality is a matter of degree, he acknowledged; some animals grow into a good deal of it, and a newly born infant "is no more of a person than a worm." There is no moment in a child's development when one can say, "Today thou art a person." Rashdall took for granted that the capacity for moral choice, which requires a rational negotiation of conflicting impulses, is a key test of personality, but he advised against looking for a magic moment. Experience suggests a continuum, not an ontological duality, even though Rashdall and Pringle-Pattison, by insisting on the reality of individual personalities, had a dualistic epistemology, attributing causation to divine and human minds. Rashdall urged that it is better to admit that non-divine personality cannot be fully understood than to deny it exists, just as theologians said the same thing about divine personality. The very point of espousing a strong idealism is to avoid metaphysical dualism. The whole world exists in a single mind, the omniscient and eternal mind of God, which is *sui generis;* the world existed before any human minds existed; and the world exists for its singular, divine creator. Personal idealism, rightly conceived, walks the tightrope between metaphysical pluralism, which conceives souls as independent of God, and metaphysical monism, which renders the human soul as merely an aspect or channel of the divine.[52]

Rashdall detected the monist fallacy "in almost every line of almost every Hegelian thinker (if I may say so with all respect) whom I have read." This was the fallacy that the essence of anyone's experience is exactly the same for all others. Rashdall countered that the essence of personality is to know oneself, to be for oneself, to feel and think for oneself, to act on one's knowledge, and to know that one acts. Personal idealism recognizes the gulf between knowledge and reality, he stressed. No knowledge that one person has of another person, no matter how intimate, erases the distinction between a mind as it is for itself and as it is for another. The essence of a person is what one is for oneself. Rashdall put it sharply, aiming at Bradley and Royce: "All the fallacies of our anti-individualist thinkers come from talking as though the essence of a person lay in what can be known about him, and not in his own knowledge, his own experience of himself." Not all Hegelians made that mistake, Rashdall allowed; McTaggart made the opposite mistake of affirming individuality by denying God's existence. But most Hegelians that spurned Christian theism pressed hard on the Hegelian assumption that knowledge is the whole of Reality. Personal Christian idealism, a perspective open to thinkers like Caird, who read Hegel differently, or Pringle-Pattison and Rashdall, who differently refashioned post-Kantian dialectics, countered that feeling and willing are as crucially constitutive of Reality as knowledge. God is the feeling, thinking, and willing Mind that gives rise to many minds. God is limited by the existence and freedom of other selves, but God is not limited by anything that does not ultimately proceed from God's nature or will.[53]

Rashdall's supreme self-confidence in defending personal theism gave ballast to a rising Modernist movement in theology. He was fond of saying that he stood in the left wing of the church and the right wing of the philosophy guild. For him, debates over the credibility of biblical criticism belonged to another century, and British biblical scholars had almost a century of catching up to do, which was happening by the 1890s. With an icy edge, Rashdall observed that British theology was slow to give up its pre-modern idea "that pieces of information have been supernaturally and without any employment of their own intellectual faculties communicated at various times to particular persons." But by the early twentieth century, he noted, even conservative theologians played down the doctrine of biblical infallibility and recalibrated their appeals to biblical miracles. Instead of defending revelation on the evidence of miracles, they invited readers to believe in miracles on the evidence of a revelation, which was a step into the modern world.[54]

As an idealist, Rashdall spoke confidently of revelation as revelatory experience. All truth is revealed truth, a partial communication of the divine Mind to human souls. In sorting out revelatory claims, he argued, two principles apply: (1) Revelation is always a matter of degree, and (2) nothing should be accepted as revelatory merely because it came to a particular person or was recorded in a particular place; everything must be tested by rationality and critically interpreted experience. Rashdall stressed that theologians needed to study the major world religions, not merely their own, for revelatory clues. It was a professional disgrace, he wrote, the "besetting sin" of Western religious philosophy, that religious thinkers somehow considered it legitimate to ignore all religions besides Christianity and Judaism. Routinely religious philosophers theorized about religious truth and meaning while displaying "great ignorance as to the real facts of religious history." Rashdall wanted Christian thinkers to look for truth in world religions without stooping to the illusion that all religions possess an equal amount of truth. For example, "the real student of comparative Religion knows that it is only at a rather advanced stage in the development of Religion that Religion becomes in any important degree an ethical teacher at all." Even the "highest" religions had conflicting theologies and ethical systems, he noted, and most religions were low on both.[55]

To Rashdall, Buddhism was the most serious alternative to Christianity, because it was highly developed, while Judaism was too close to Christianity to count as a real alternative. Buddhism had a sophisticated worldview, an ethic of humanity and charity, and a discipline of spiritual practices. Christians had things to learn from Buddhists on these counts, Rashdall observed. But on some things Buddhism and Christianity were very different, and on the most important things they were utter opposites. Buddhism was ascetic, its idea of futurity was pessimistic, and it fixated on avoiding suffering. Most important, Buddhism was the very opposite of Christianity in its atheism and its denigration of personal consciousness. There was no bridge from Christianity to Buddhism concerning the flourishing of personality and the worship of a personal God, Rashdall cautioned; the two most developed world religions were antithetical on the things they cherished most.[56]

In Rashdall's telling, Christianity alone taught the great truths to which one was led by a religious philosophy based on reason and conscience. Christianity taught a religion of feeling, thinking, and willing divine Consciousness understood in the light of the highest moral idealism. It taught the doctrine of personal immortality and a humanistic ethic of care for the world. It conceived universal love as the essence of divine reality and the essence of ethical religious life. Above all, it had a historical Redeemer who taught these very things. Rashdall remarked, "Amid all aberrations and amid all contamination by heterogeneous elements, the society or societies which look back to Christ as their Founder have never in the worst times ceased altogether to teach these truths; and now they more and more tend to constitute the essence of Christianity as it is today." The modern liberal approach to Christianity reclaimed the life-giving essence of Christianity, exactly as liberal theologians claimed, and the Church of England, though late in allowing liberal theology, was being lifted and renewed by it.[57]

Rashdall admired the Germans for inventing liberal theology, but he had mixed feelings about the capacity of the Ritschlian School to keep it going. The Ritschlians got the main thing exactly right, Rashdall judged – the essence of Christianity is the picture of the life, teaching, character, and personality of Christ. Ritschlian theology rightly described Christianity as a historical movement making a specifically Christ-centered appeal to the moral and religious consciousness of humankind. But Rashdall argued that the Ritschlians exaggerated the distorting impact of Christian doctrine in church history, and they lost their balance on philosophy too, spurning philosophical arguments and support. On the former issue, they exaggerated the problem of Hellenization; on the latter, they simply assumed God's existence, which was not credible. Rashdall admonished: "We must first believe that there is a God to be revealed before we can be led to believe in Christ as the supreme Revealer." Any theology that proposed to speak persuasively to the modern world had to commend itself to modern reason. It was not enough to say that religion is about value and that the truth of religion rests on value judgments. Rashdall allowed that this approach worked quite well in expounding the supreme value of Christ's character and in making a case for Jesus as the representative of God to humanity – once one believed in God. But no value judgment establishes God's existence, for value and existence are different kinds of things.[58]

Rashdall preferred the second-century apologetics of Justin Martyr to the question-begging of Ritschlian theology. Instead of privileging Christian claims about Jesus that lifted Christianity above other religions and philosophy, it was better to show "the essential reasonableness of Christ's teaching about God and its essential harmony with the highest philosophic teaching about duty, about the divine nature, about the soul and its eternal destiny." The Ritschlian School was too contemptuous of neo-Platonism and all philosophy, and it gave short shrift even to Judaism by beginning with the Jesus movement. Thus it wrongly treated Christ as the only Revealer, instead of as the supreme Revealer. Rashdall urged that one does not have to arrogate Christianity above other religions in order to uphold the superiority of Christianity; in fact, the most credible way of defending Christianity is the rational one.[59]

Rashdall worked hard at exemplifying liberal Christian rationalism. High-minded, earnest, erudite, and deeply pious, he was dedicated to making theology modern, but he distrusted the appeal to religious experience that fueled liberal theology in the schools of Schleiermacher and Ritschl. Next to Rashdall, the leading figure in the Churchmen's Union was W. R. Inge, a prolific, sharp-tongued Cambridge University theologian who served from 1910 to 1935 as Dean of St. Paul's. Inge espoused, with polemic flare, a theologically liberal and politically conservative version of neo-Platonist mysticism. Rashdall countered that it was not really possible to be a neo-Platonist in the modern age, and mysticism wasn't the answer either. If one breathed the atmosphere of "modern Science and modern Culture," Rashdall admonished, one was compelled to show it in one's theology. Trying to think like Plato or Athanasius was akin to pretending; moreover, Christianity would not be taken seriously if its theologians retreated to claims about their spiritual experiences.[60]

The point was to make Logos theology make sense within modern consciousness, not to drop Logos theology. Like most Anglican theologians, Rashdall prized the Logos idea of the revelation of the divine Mind in consciousness, nature, and especially Jesus Christ. There was a wing of the Churchmen's Union that stripped away the Logos idea as an unfortunate addition to the gospel of Jesus, but Rashdall preferred to modernize and universalize it, stripping the Logos idea of the ancient idea of a Being separate from God: "We cannot say intelligibly that God dwells in Christ, unless we have already recognized that in a sense God dwells and reveals Himself in Humanity at large, and in each particular human soul." For Rashdall, liberal Logos theology and elitism folded together, as he explained straightforwardly: "The more developed intellect reveals God more completely than that of the child or the savage, and (far more important from a religious point of view), the higher and more developed moral consciousness reveals Him more than the lower, and above all the actually better man reveals God more than the worse man."[61]

Occasionally, on the lecture circuit, usually while expounding on the progress of the human race or the fitness of a body to a soul, Rashdall casually clinched his point with a racist aside or illustration. Speaking to Cambridge students in 1909, he did it with typically brutal arrogance: "We never find the intellect of a Shakespeare in connection with the facial angle of a Negro; bodies which resemble the bodies of their parents are connected with souls between which a similar resemblance can be traced." Rashdall took for granted that virtually everyone in his audiences shared his assumptions about the inferiority of black persons and other ethnic communities that the British Empire colonized. Thus he rarely bothered to defend his prejudice. The inferior humanity of blacks was obvious to him, not something to argue about; it was merely a point of reference or example. If bodies were fitted exactly to the souls that souls inhabited, it was not even necessary to distinguish cultural white supremacism from the more deeply pernicious idea of ontological difference. Race was biological as well as cultural; black persons were truly inferior beings.[62]

In his major work, however, *The Theory of Good and Evil* (1907), Rashdall went beyond casual asides; the first volume of his defense of ideal utilitarianism built up to the obliteration of inferior races. Rashdall ruined a compelling and sophisticated work of moral theory in the process, all in the name of the triumph of the good, a savage irony to which he was oblivious.

His analysis of alternative moral theories was acute. Psychological hedonism, though ably espoused by Jeremy Bentham and increasingly influential in moral philosophy, wrongly claimed that the desire for pleasure is the only rational motive of human conduct. Rashdall argued that very few pleasures can be explained without admitting the role of disinterested desires, and if a particular kind of pleasure is really the point, as Bentham argued, that showed that human beings desire something besides mere pleasure. In addition, hedonistic theories wrongly contended that the rightness of a moral act is determined by its motive. Rejecting intuitive and deontological theories, Rashdall argued that intuitionism reduces morality to mere caprice and that deontological theories, by identifying moral rightness with given formal rules of conduct, opt out from the real work of moral theory, which is to struggle with moral problems. Rationalistic utilitarians like Kant and Henry Sidgwick did better at struggling with the problems, but Kant's moral criterion of universalizing the situation lacked any specific content as to the kind of good that moral actors should strive to attain, and Rashdall judged that Sidgwick never resolved the contradictions between his rationalistic concept of duty and his hedonistic concept of the ultimate good.[63]

Rashdall's alternative, ideal utilitarianism, determined the goodness of an act by whether it promotes universal well-being or the general good of society. It was ideal because it espoused a non-hedonistic concept of the ethical end; it was utilitarian because of its teleological emphasis on consequences. The idea of moral rightness has no content or meaning without a prior idea of what is morally good, Rashdall argued. An action is morally right if it promotes what is morally good, and it cannot be right if it does not. Rashdall had a place for moral feeling, but it was subordinate to the rational capacity to make moral judgments; he allowed that pleasure is part of the ideal end to be sought, but it is far from the whole thing. In his telling, "ideal utilitarianism" was merely a new name for the great tradition of Western ethical theory deriving from Plato, Aristotle, and Christianity. In ethical theory, modernity was something of a curse, not a blessing. Hedonistic utilitarians like Bentham ruined the term "utilitarian," perhaps irreparably, and only in the modern age had anyone propounded the "crude and absurd theory" that the morality of an act can be determined apart from its consequences. Rashdall, seeking to restore and refine an ancient tradition amid modern confusions, cautioned that no ethical question can be answered without making a judgment about whose good is to be promoted. In deciding that question, two principles of justice apply: equality and just reward.[64]

The equality principle is essential to the Christian worldview and intrinsic to Christian ethics, Rashdall affirmed. It is the principle that "every human being is of equal intrinsic value, and is therefore entitled to equal respect." This was the keystone, which was qualified by the second principle of justice, "that the good ought to be preferred to the bad, that men ought to be rewarded according to their goodness or according to their work." Rashdall affirmed that every individual is entitled to equal consideration. That is, in judging whether an action serves the general good of all individuals, the principles of justice require that equal consideration be given to the well-being of every individual that is to be affected by the action. An individual does not lose one's right to equality of consideration "even when the equal rights of others demand that in practice he should receive no good at all." There is no justice if ninety people out of a hundred are given consideration and the other ten are ignored, for the ninety and the ten "are entitled to consideration precisely in the ratio of ninety to ten." Considering possible exceptions, Rashdall gave first place to battlefield situations where ten soldiers died to save ninety. But this was not really an exception if full consideration is given to the rights of the minority before action is taken, he judged; the principle of equal consideration does not prescribe any actual equality of outcome or well-being, and in this case, the general good is served by the sacrifices of the ten.[65]

The moral end to be sought is equal well-being, or more precisely, as much equality as is consistent with creating a maximal amount of good to distribute. The ideal is not equality of condition, Rashdall urged, because that does not produce equal amounts of actual well-being to persons of different capacities. Neither is equality of opportunity the true idea of social justice, because that is impossible and undesirable for the same reasons. Rashdall quipped that if the State took seriously the duty to ensure equality of opportunity, it would have to supply every child with an equally good mother. Moreover, even modest conceptions of the equal opportunity standard were bound to produce strange results. That opened the door through which Rashdall charged headlong, notwithstanding his left-leaning politics and ostensible commitment to equal consideration. He warned, "The distinction between men of different race, between the sexes, between the sick and the whole, will have to be equally ignored." Any conceivable rendering of equal opportunity justice led to "absurd and unjust" consequences. Socialists who prated about equal opportunity were either stupid or pretending, he charged. Were they prepared to compensate Laplanders for not living in the Riviera? Were they willing to put Johannesburg and London on the same level?[66]

Rashdall acknowledged that England needed more equality of opportunity, and that striving for it made sense as an ethical and political goal to the extent that such efforts led to greater good and a more equal distribution of good. But it was terribly important not to confuse actual well-being with social movements for equal condition or opportunity, he urged. These movements sometimes made gains toward equality, which was usually good, but if taken too seriously they were destructive and redistributionist, degrading English society. Rashdall counseled that some inequality was a condition of well-being, because freedom and the unequal distribution of abilities unavoidably yielded unequal results. Moreover, only one type of equality was always practicable and right – equality of consideration. The principle of equal consideration supported efforts to achieve greater equality of well-being, but only on the condition that the greater equality to be achieved did not infringe the equal right of each person to enjoy as much good as was maximally possible.[67]

When, specifically, did social justice movements go too far? Rashdall started with his least important example and moved upward. "The number of persons capable of the highest intellectual cultivation and of enjoying the good incidental to such high cultivation is unquestionably a small minority," he observed. Only a few would ever enjoy such goods, and it was undeniably very expensive to keep England's most privileged classes in operation. But if the Socialists succeeded in abolishing the upper class, he warned, the harm caused to English society and culture would be immense. It was terribly important to prevent Socialism from going that far. Even worse was the specter of a Socialist Europe. If an "omnipotent Social Democracy" were established throughout Europe, universities would be savaged, German professors would be treated like commoners, research and scholarship would plunge to low levels, and Greek and Latin would be forgotten. Rashdall shuddered to imagine the University of Berlin reduced to the level of "a South American University." Of course, that was a fantasy, he allowed; moreover, if an omnipotent Social Democracy managed to transform Europe into something like a giant Moravian mission settlement, one could make a case that that would be a moral advance. Rashdall mused that if he possessed the power to turn Europe into a dull Moravian mission or leave it as it was, he would have a hard time deciding. Perhaps the principle of equal consideration would favor dull, earnest, religious, uncultured equality.[68]

Meanwhile the real world was still there, and Rashdall reached for a trump case that clarified what really mattered. Even if some readers had doubts about the previous examples, he had one more on which "probably no one will hesitate," meaning, no one who mattered. In essence, it was that superior white people needed to sustain the progress of the human race by repelling the inferior races. In Rashdall's telling, it was increasingly obvious "that all improvement in the social condition of the higher races of mankind postulates the exclusion of competition with the lower races." It was pointless to hope that the world's inferior races might sufficiently overcome their backwardness to contribute things of value to the new world order, he declared. The advanced parts of the world needed to keep their moral sentimentality in check. It was more important to build up civilization by pushing ahead than to serve a principle of justice by trying to lift up the weak and backward. The inferior races were backward because they were inferior; they were so far behind that not even Socialism could save them. To build up civilization, the superior races had to prevent the inferior ones from pulling them downward. Rashdall spelled it out: "That means that, sooner or later, the lower Well-being – it may be ultimately the very existence – of countless Chinamen or negroes must be sacrificed that a higher life may be possible for a much smaller number of white men."[69]

The good that higher races enjoyed was more important than whatever good that the lower races may have enjoyed, Rashdall insisted: "We distinctly adopt the principle that higher life is intrinsically, in and for itself, more valuable than lower life, though it may only be attainable by fewer persons, and may not contribute to the greater good of those who do not share it." He did not say how it was that the love ethic of Christianity, the teaching and spirit of Jesus, the principles of equality and just reward, and the principle of equal consideration meant nothing when the issue was the maintenance of white supremacism. Rashdall's assumed answer was that this was what it meant to be guided ethically by the consequences of one's actions. What mattered, ethically, was to preserve and build up an advanced civilization. He took for granted that his readers cared little or nothing about non-white peoples; Rashdall referred casually, with only a slight hint of apology, to "our comparative indifference to the welfare of the black races." To the extent that he felt obliged to say something on behalf of downtrodden people, he offered that "if the higher life is ever to become possible on any large scale for black men it can only be through the maintenance and progress of a higher race." The ethical imperative for educated white people was to keep advancing. For the sake of human progress, privileged white Christians had to defend their advantages in wealth, property, legal access, and social privilege. Racism on a personal level needed to be restrained by good manners, but racism on an institutional level was an utter necessity for the advancement of the human race.[70]

None of this disqualified Rashdall from playing a leadership role in the most liberal wing of the Church of England. To the contrary, he was lionized by liberals for his enlightenment, tolerance, kindness, and opposition to bigotry. Rashdall's prejudices and imperial ambitions were so commonly shared that he was not challenged to defend their dissonance with his rhetoric of liberal enlightenment. To liberals he was the late-arriving warrior against dogmatic backwardness that stood up for the integrity and necessity of liberal theology. His biographer, P. E. Matheson, made no mention of Rashdall's racism, but stressed that Rashdall was widely admired for his humility, piety, graciousness, and hospitality, and his "most generous and genial benevolence." Rashdall could be fierce in controversy, Matheson acknowledged, but he was never mean. Whenever liberal clerics got in trouble for their liberalism, Rashdall defended them forcefully, making it possible for the liberal movement to survive and expand.[71]

Like most of his fellow British citizens, Rashdall was surprised when Europe erupted into war. He told friends that he had long worried about German militarism, but he had not really feared for England's safety, feeling secure behind the British fleet. For two or three days before the British government declared war he struggled with his conscience, until the government called the nation to war. In 1916 Rashdall recalled, "I had no doubts at all, and have preached warlike sermons ever since." Rashdall counseled clerics and his sermon audiences against torturing themselves over the horrors of war. The Great War was forced upon England, he reasoned; nothing could be done about it; the war was not a judgment on British culture or religion; and it was pointless for British Christians to consider the war some kind of spiritual failure on their part: "Christianity is not calculated to put an end to horrors unless people really accept it, and it is evident that the Germans have not accepted the Christian ideal at all."[72]

Meanwhile Rashdall labored on a major work, *The Idea of Atonement in Christian Theology*, taking aim at a subject on which British theologians had proceeded cautiously thus far, until Rashdall laid waste to a vast doctrinal heritage. The idea of atonement had a paradoxical role in Christian life and thought, he observed. The idea of being saved through Christ's death on the cross was much dearer to most Christians than the idea of Christ's incarnation, even though the incarnation was better defined, beautiful, and, for Anglicans, central to worship, while the doctrine of atonement was loaded with ideas that were "definitely irrational, repellant, and immoral." Rashdall took for granted that most of his readers already shuddered at the repellant aspects of ransom and substitutionary theory. Two centuries of rationalist, Unitarian, liberal, and Broad Church criticism had taken a toll: "The revolt against these theories is, indeed, already pretty general."[73]

But it was one thing to be embarrassed by bad atonement doctrines and something else to be freed from them. Rashdall noted that there was a long, biblically rooted tradition of atonement doctrine that was not morally or intellectually repugnant. It was the moral influence tradition of Origen and Abelard. The atonement idea that the modern church needed was not something that the church had to invent from scratch. It was already there in the theology of Origen, Abelard, Schleiermacher, and Coleridge. The doctrine of moral influence redemption, however, would not win broad acceptance in the church until the "surviving debris of shattered systems" was thoroughly cleared away. To that end Rashdall offered a work of massive scholarly erudition.[74]

Rashdall ranged over the teaching of Jesus concerning forgiveness, Pauline doctrine, the teaching of primitive Christianity, the Patristic theories of Clement of Alexandria, Irenaeus, Tertullian, and Origen, the later Greek Fathers, Latin theology (especially Augustine, Anselm, and Abelard), Scholastic theology, and the Lutheran Reformation. He traced the development of various subjective, ransom, and substitutionary theories, arguing that, leaving aside a few problematic statements of Paul featuring metaphors of the Jewish altar, the ways of thinking about the atonement that prevailed in the early church lacked any concept of objective expiation or substitution. Rashdall contended that the kingdom of God was the center of Jesus' teaching and that the ransom passage in Matthew 20:26–28 and Mark 10:45 ("to give his life as a ransom for many") was probably not a genuine saying of Jesus. If the saying was genuine, it reflected Jesus' sense that he would die a sacrificial death that spared his followers from a similar fate: "As His life had been a life of service for others, so would His death be." Jesus had no atonement doctrine aside from this suggestion, Rashdall argued, and no Christian thinker (with the debatable exception of Paul) had an objective understanding of atonement until the late second century.[75]

Objective atonement theory began with Irenaeus, who took up the Pauline idea of a parallelism between the "First Adam" through whom sin came into the world and the "Second Adam" – Christ – through whom the powers of death were defeated. Irenaeus' theory of the "recapitulation" of all things in Christ set into motion the juridical picture of the cross as a ransom paid to Satan. The human race, having fallen into sin, was lawfully the servant of Satan; thus, God owed the Devil a debt that God could not lawfully or justly repudiate. The debt could be paid and the power of Satan broken only by the sacrifice of God's Son, which tricked the Devil into giving up the lawful authority that he held over humankind. Rashdall acknowledged that a few Greek Fathers questioned the ransom theory, preferring to speak of atonement as deification or moral transformation, but the ransom theory dominated the Eastern church, sometimes in combination with subjective motifs, and in Western Christianity ransom theory was utterly dominant until the twelfth century. Anselm, rejecting the strange notion that Satan held any rights or authority over God, conceived the cross as a sacrifice that appeased God's wrath over sin; Christ bore the punishment for sin as a substitutionary sacrifice that satisfied God's wrathful righteousness. Abelard, in Rashdall's telling, had a much better idea, though one that resounded with much less influence through the Middle Ages and Reformation.[76]

Instead of turning God into the problem, as Anselm did by focusing on the satisfaction of God's wrath, Abelard insisted that human sin was the problem, which could be cured only by God's ever-gracious love. The cross is a revelation of love divine, inspiring loving and ethical imitation, not a ransom or sacrifice paid to Satan or God. Rashdall observed, "We get rid altogether of the notion of a mysterious guilt which, by an abstract necessity of things, required to be extinguished by death or suffering, no matter whose, and of all pseudo-Platonic hypostasizing of the universal 'Humanity.'" In Abelard's idea, the efficacy of Christ's death had nothing to do with tricking Satan or appeasing a wrathful God; it was explicitly a moral and spiritual influence on the mind of the sinner, and nothing more. It was the view of redemption that went with the biblical faith that God is love. The death of Christ was redemptive by moving the sinner "to gratitude and answering love – and so to consciousness of sin, repentance, amendment." Rashdall stressed that this was not really Abelard's idea, as there was nothing in it that was original to him. The Pauline and Johannine writings were filled with this idea of salvation, as was early Christian testimony. The best Greek theology retained this idea in its statements about deification, teaching, with Athanasius, that God became human so that humans could become divine. But Greek theology overshadowed deification with cosmic courtroom imagery, and Rashdall judged that even Abelard focused too much on the cross, detaching it from Christ's saving life and teaching. With twelfth-century Abelard, however, "At last we have found a theory of the atonement which thoroughly appeals to reason and to conscience."[77]

Rashdall wanted modern theologians to say it that plainly, without hedging about discredited atonement theories or trying to dress them up. Modern Christianity needed to ruthlessly expunge bad atonement theologies from its worship and theology, trusting that the love of God revealed in Christ is more than enough to inspire Christian commitment. "Love is essentially contagious," he implored. The cross is a perfect and inspiring revelation of love divine. Even if Jesus were only a great teacher who exemplified the way of love divine, that would be enough for Christianity. But Rashdall believed more than that. He explained, "If we can say that in humanity generally there is *some* revelation of God – a growing, developing, progressive revelation, and a higher degree of such a revelation in the heroes, the saints, the prophets, the founders and reformers of great religions, then the idea of an incarnation becomes possible." If it is plausible to think of God as being revealed to some degree in all people, "then it becomes possible to think of Him as making a supreme, culmi-nating, unique revelation of Himself in one human character and life."[78]

Rashdall was an idealist as long as he got to keep his privileges. In his books idealism got the first word and the last word as philosophy and theology, and he inclined to mild reformism in politics, as long as it didn't cost him. In religion he contended that the "great spiritual dividing line" was between "those who really accept Christ's ideal of life and those who do not." He counted himself among the former, notwithstanding his convictions about letting go of justice and repressing inferior races. Speaking from experience, he urged that one kind of idealism leads to another. If one believed in Christ's ideal of life, it was usually possible to believe also that the universe is guided by a conscious Will that is best understood in the light of Christ's ideal: "Those who believe that love is the thing of highest value in human life will generally believe also that 'God is love indeed, and love Creation's highest law.'"[79]

That was, indeed, a nearly perfect summary of the liberal gospel in his time. In the last year of his life, 1923–1924, Rashdall served as the fifth president of the Churchmen's Union, an outfit usually remembered as something more liberal than it was. For many years conservatives referred to the Union's monthly, the yellow-covered *Modern Churchmen,* as "the Yellow Peril." Scholarly references to the Union liberals usually follow suit, describing them as near-Unitarians who believed in the perfectibility of humankind and the building of the kingdom on earth. Yet every leading figure in the group believed in Christ's divinity, confessing this faith in reverential terms, and most of the Union's leading figures were not ardent social gospelers. The Churchmen's Union gave fewer clerics to social justice causes than did the Anglo-Catholic party. It had an outspoken Socialist and pacifist, Charles Raven, but he was an exception. Mostly it was very tame theologically and politically, with room for political conservatives. It enforced reverent norms about Jesus and early Christianity. And nearly all its trademark theological claims were absorbed into mainstream British Christianity by the 1950s.[80]

The Girton Conference of 1921, the most controversial episode in the Union's long history, exemplified the group's tameness, controversy notwithstanding. In several noted works two prominent members of the Union, F. J. Foakes-Jackson and Kirsopp Lake, seemed to violate the group's reverent norms about Jesus and early Christianity, which got them into trouble. Foakes-Jackson and Lake took seriously the German critical picture of Jesus as a mistaken apocalypticist, which offended British liberals; in addition, they argued that Christianity became a mystery religion after it passed from Palestine into the Graeco-Roman world. For Foakes-Jackson and Lake, the latter argument was a set-up for their thesis that the early church was best understood as a form of "sacramental Catholicism." On the first day of the Girton conference in 1921, the Churchmen's Union liberals lined up against Foakes-Jackson and Lake, especially Lake. Major, subsequently summarizing the problem with perfect pitch, observed that although liberalism was often accused of stripping "our Lord of His miraculous characteristics," it never stripped Jesus of "His moral and spiritual supremacy." Major and the Union liberals agreed that Lake took that fateful step, something that Modernist theology could not abide.[81]

On the second day of the conference, Rashdall reiterated what liberals should believe about Jesus: Jesus did not claim divinity for himself; he was in the fullest sense man; his human soul did not pre-exist; he was divine; his divinity did not necessarily imply the Virgin Birth or any other miracle; his divinity did not imply omniscience either; God is like Christ; and the Logos was not a separate consciousness of Deity. These were staple convictions; Rashdall had said and published all of them many times. J. F. Bethune-Baker, following Rashdall to the podium, gave a similar talk, although he ended on a more radical note, declaring that human beings are as necessary to God as God is necessary to human beings.[82]

These speeches set off a raging public reaction against Rashdall and other liberals that carried on for two years. Press coverage, beginning with a single misrepresentation, and Gore, reacting to the press coverage, blasted the Union liberals mercilessly. Max Pemberton, writing in the *Sunday Pictorial,* launched the mistaken idea that Rashdall denied Christ's divinity: "There are some of us still left who believe in the divinity of Christ, and who totally fail to understand how men who believe the contrary can honestly occupy the pulpits of our State churches and take money for teaching people to deride the ancient faith." Gore piled on, warning of further heresies: "I feel sure that the denial of miracles and the abandonment of belief in Christ's Godhead will be found to carry with them an abandonment of Divine Revelation altogether, and those who abandon the specific Christian Creed will find themselves not in the Unitarianism of Dr. Martineau, but much lower down."[83]

Rashdall replied immediately that he had spent his entire career defending the divinity of Christ and personality of God, he believed in the Trinity, he opposed Foakes-Jackson and Lake forthrightly, and his speech had said so. It didn't matter. Gore retreated slightly, allowing that the Modernists were devoted to Christ, but he insisted that they had been allowed to go too far in denying essential Christian doctrines, which stoked a media blaze against Rashdall. Repeatedly Rashdall defended himself in sermons and articles, compiling a book of three self-defending sermons and an article, *Jesus Human and Divine* (1922). It was a sad end to a mostly distinguished career, tormenting Rashdall nearly to the end of his days, for which Gore never apologized, though Rashdall was consoled by public and private testimonials from allies to his deep piety, sincerity, and theological leadership. Writing to a clerical friend, A. H. Cruickshank, Canon of Durham, Rashdall appealed for one: "Stupid (or malicious) people don't see the difference between asserting that Jesus did not claim Divinity and asserting that He was not divine. Please contradict the lying reports as you have opportunity."[84]

Rashdall was by far England's leading theological liberal of his generation, though not its best. Pringle-Pattison, though less renowned, was generally a better exponent, though Rashdall was better than Pringle-Pattison on the logic of incarnation. Both were tempted to say that a Christian Logos theology could work without Jesus, but Rashdall worked harder at not saying it. Pringle-Pattison, citing Chrysostom's dictum that "man is the true Shekinah," settled for a caution against making too much of Jesus. The incarnation was surely the center of Christianity, he assured, but it was hard to say how much history that required: "Whatever else it may mean, it means at least this – that in the conditions of the highest human life we have access, as nowhere else, to the inmost nature of the divine." Pringle-Pattison and Rashdall took for granted that their treasured Victorian language of ideals, progress, the higher things, and reaching for the "highest life" was essential to making Christianity modern. Rashdall, however, lived long enough to see it become embattled in the face of wartime and postwar disillusions, and Pringle-Pattison lived to see it become quaint.[85]

Liberal Evangelicalism: Alfred E. Garvey

Rashdall and Pringle-Pattison typified the liberal British Anglican take on the Ritschlian School: It winsomely recovered the essential thing, the kingdom-oriented Spirit of Jesus, but its anti-metaphysical bias was impossible. The rationalist strain of the Anglican tradition and its commitment to classical Logos theology prevented most Anglican liberals from adopting the dominant liberal theology of their time. A religion lacking a metaphysic of the soul and of reality itself was sadly lacking. There were liberals in the Churchmen's Union that were closer to Ritschl and Harnack on this issue than to Rashdall, but the leading Ritschlian liberals in Britain were Non-conformists.

A. M. Fairbairn, a Congregational theologian and principal of Mansfield College, Oxford in the 1890s, was an important advocate of liberal evangelicalism and a forerunner of British Ritschlian theology. In his major work, *The Place of Christ in Modern Theology* (1893), he contended that the old theology was "primarily doctrinal and secondarily historical," while the new theology that was needed would be "primarily historical and secondarily doctrinal." Fairbairn stressed that moving to a historically oriented theology would be a major challenge for Evangelicals and Anglicans, for both groups had authoritarian theologies. Evangelicals appealed to an infallible Bible; Anglicans treated Patristic theology as authoritative; both approaches failed the tests of modern critical consciousness. But Fairbairn had a neo-Hegelian cast of mind, which impeded his historicist aspirations, and he ignored the Ritschlian School, resting on his knowledge of Tübingen School criticism. In 1898, anticipating a sabbatical leave in India, Fairbairn asked young Congregational pastor Alfred E. Garvie to lecture in his place at Oxford. Garvie proposed several topics, including Ritschlian theology; Fairbairn, judging that British theology was overdue to deal with the Ritschlian School, told Garvie to lecture on it.[86]

Garvie was born in 1861 in Zyrardow, a Polish town under Russian rule. His parents were Scottish, he chafed at growing up under Russian tyranny, and he suffered from poor health throughout his bookish childhood. Mastering three languages during long periods of convalescence, he later reflected that his Scottish Reformed upbringing helped to explain "why my Scottish and British patriotism has always been qualified by internationalism, and my congregational loyalty by ecumenicity." Garvie was educated at Glasgow University and felt called to Presbyterian ministry, but he could not subscribe to the Westminster Confession. Upon learning that Congregationalists had no creeds, he converted to Congregationalism and took graduate training at Mansfield College, Oxford, where he studied under Fairbairn. Garvie was a pastor in Montrose when Fairbairn asked him to lecture in his place; later he served for thirty years as a theology professor at New College, Hampstead and its successor institution, New College, London.[87]

In 1899 British readers had little idea of the Ritschlian School. The first volume of Ritschl's three-volume magnum opus, *The Christian Doctrine of Justification and Reconciliation,* was published in an English edition in 1872, but it was ignored for over thirty years. An English translation of Leonhard Stählin's book *Kant, Lotze, and Ritschl* introduced Ritschlian theology to a British audience in 1889, but Stählin ridiculed Ritschl and taunted English readers: "What Germany thinks today, Britain will begin to think tomorrow." In the 1890s a few Ritschlian works were translated into English: Julius Kaftan's *The Truth of the Christian Religion* (1894); Herrmann's *The Communion of the Christian with God* (1895); Hans H. Wendt's *The Teaching of Jesus* (1896), and several volumes of Harnack's *History of Dogma*. But the only British scholars to write substantial assessments of these works wrote to refute them. The two leading British evangelicals of the time, Scottish Reformed theologians James Denney and James Orr, led the attack on the Ritschlian School. Denny's critique in *Studies in Theology* (1895) was severe; Orr's critique in *The Ritschlian Theology and the Evangelical Faith* (1898) was more detailed and respectful, but strongly rejectionist. Cambridge theologian P. T. Forsyth, a leading liberal evangelical, appreciated Herrmann's Christocentrism, but rejected other Ritschlians. When Garvie took up his subject in 1898 and published *The Ritschlian Theology* the following year, the only explicitly pro-Ritschlian work in the English language was American theologian A. C. McGiffert's *History of Christianity in the Apostolic Age* (1897) – which did not discuss Ritschl.[88]

Garvie was not a Ritschlian, either, as he made clear. But he was attracted to certain substantive aspects of Ritschlian theology and he was indebted to Ritschl's method. He felt keenly that British and American theologians should better understand why the Ritschlian School dominated their field. Describing Ritschlian theology as a calibrated response to the crisis of modern Christianity, he introduced English readers to Ritschl, Herrmann, Harnack, and Kaftan, and analyzed Ritschl's basic concepts and method.

The crisis of theology was severe to the point of having "fallen on evil days," Garvie announced. Not only was theology no longer highly esteemed; for many modern thinkers it did not even count as a form of knowledge. The founder of sociology, Auguste Comte, relegated theology to the superstitious childhood of the human race. The founder of Social Darwinism, Herbert Spencer, was more generous in a condescending way, assigning to science the entire realm of knowledge and to religion "the vast region of the Unknowable." At the same time, Garvie observed, late-Victorian intellectuals could usually be counted on to say that society needed religion to provide morality. Comte's positivism yielded a pathetic religion of humanity as a replacement for real religion, and evolutionary publicist T. H. Huxley admitted that science provided no basis for morals. In Garvie's telling, the Ritschlian School was shrewd in proposing that theology still had a job to do, as an intellectual interpreter of religion, though this bargain was problematic.[89]

The modern mind distrusted philosophy, Garvie observed, it took great confidence in science, it respected historical criticism, and it was concerned with the social problem. Ritschlian theology was geared to these predispositions. Just as Kant carved a path between Hume's skepticism and Christian Wolff's Enlightenment rationalism, the Ritschlian School followed Kant in affirming the objective validity of scientific knowledge and its subjective limitations. Garvie suggested that German theology, and more recently English theology, would have done better to stay with Kant's modest idealism than to fly in the air with Hegel. The Ritschlians were attuned to the modern distrust of philosophy. They appreciated the tremendous explanatory power of science. They made Christianity relevant to the modern struggle for a good society. And they rightly privileged historical consciousness. Though Garvie was anxious to defend his evangelical credentials, he admonished evangelicals to stop shielding themselves with biblical inspiration: "Any theologian who imagines that his doctrine of the inspiration of the Scriptures secures him against any dangerous assaults from historical criticism is simply deceiving himself; for of all the Christian doctrines it is just this doctrine which is most seriously affected by the methods and results of historical criticism. Only by a man who has a marvelous capacity for *intellectual insulation* can the theories of verbal inspiration and the absolute inerrancy of the Scriptures be maintained."[90]

A model of fairness and courtesy, Garvie was distressed by Ritschl's lack of both. He stressed that Ritschl had no empathy for anyone not sharing his viewpoint, and he routinely skewered his opponents, often after misrepresenting them. But Garvie grasped that Ritschl's self-involved aggressiveness sparked his creativity, combining dependence and originality. Ritschl's mind "always moved in opposition to the opinions of others," Garvie explained. "His critical antagonism was the impulse to his constructive advance." Though Ritschl had a vast storehouse of historical knowledge, history itself never particularly interested him; his work was fueled by "an aggressive practical purpose to keep theology always as a servant of the moral and the religious life," at which he succeeded.[91]

In Garvie's telling, Ritschl's practical tendency was the key to his intellectual individuality, followed by his historical positivism and philosophical skepticism. On occasion Ritschl lapsed into speculative indulgences, such as his deduction of the idea of the kingdom of God from the love of God, or his idea of divine eternity as God's consistency in the realization of God's eschatological purpose in time. But for the most part Ritschl's practical tendency took control, subordinating thought and feeling to will. He hated mysticism and sentimental Pietism, favoring a muscular Protestant piety "of a thoroughly manly sort, reverent, reticent, candid, practical, energetic, and assertive." He forced this sensibility on his disciples, though Garvie noted that none of the major Ritschlians was as harshly estranged from Pietism as Ritschl, and all were "in closer touch with the practical piety of the Church than he was." In Garvie's judgment, Ritschl made a creative contribution to theology by playing up the historical character of revelation, finding the divinity of Christ in Christ's activity. On the other hand, Ritschl took this idea too far, claiming that every predicate that applied to Christ applied to Christians by virtue of their relation to him. To Garvie, that smacked of the pantheist idea of humankind as the Son of God, even though Ritschl was otherwise far from a pantheist.[92]

Garvie admired the Ritschlians for swinging liberal theology away from speculative rationalism to an emphasis on revelation realized in history. He prized the Ritschlian emphasis on the Christian community as the continuation of Christ's revelatory action. He praised the Ritschlian School for rejecting the wholesale rationalist attack on miracles; rightly, the Ritschlians tended to weigh historical evidence about biblical miracles on a case-by-case basis. He judged that Ritschl's views on sin and atonement were, unfortunately, conventionally liberal, rejecting the doctrines of original sin, divine wrath, and vicarious atonement. However, Herrmann and Kaftan retained the full wealth of evangelical conviction on these points, which showed that the Ritschlian approach did not have to substitute bourgeois conventions for gospel truths. Garvie noted that Herrmann and Kaftan stressed the reality of evil, the curse of sin, and the idea that Christ's suffering for the salvation of the human race involved an aspect of vicarious satisfaction.[93]

But the greatest strength of the Ritschlian theology, Garvie argued, was its method, not its various renderings of doctrinal content. The Ritschlian approach conceived the formal principle of dogmatics as the early Christian community's confession of faith, not the Bible in its entirety. It conceived the regulative principle of dogmatics as the person and kingdom-centered work of Christ and the material principle as the experience of salvation through Christ. On the formal principle, Garvie stressed, Ritschl was a better Ritschlian than Harnack, as Harnack privileged the teaching of Jesus over its development by early Christianity. To some degree the Ritschlian approach restrained the destructive animus of historical criticism, though Garvie wished that Ritschl had been more restrained, and Harnack much more. In Garvie's view, the Ritschlian School lacked an adequate doctrine of scriptural authority, contenting itself with the assertion that the Bible contained literary sources of an historical revelation. That was not enough; the church needed to say that the relationship between its literary sources and historical revelation was essential and organic. But this was a difficult problem for modern theology as a whole, Garvie allowed. No theological perspective had solved it, historical criticism constantly piled up new problems, and there was no reason why the solution could not come from the Ritschlian School.[94]

Modern theology needed to refashion the old idea of biblical inspiration, conceiving the biblical writers as agents of a revelatory process, in order to bring together the truths of historical revelation and its literary records. Garvie put it plaintively, with a critical jab at liberal subjectivism: "When this necessary and essential relation between the Holy Scriptures and divine Revelation is recognized, then the ritual, prophetical and historical preparation for Christ, the evangelical testimony regarding Christ, and the apostolic interpretation of Christ will be accorded an authority over Christian faith and life which will deliver us from the individual limitations, and the subjective impressions, which mark so much modern theological thinking." The point was to re-establish *spiritual* authority, he explained, "not an arbitrary and external restrain imposed on the mind." It was authority *within* Christian experience that liberated the mind "from error by submission to self-evidencing truth." In Garvie's telling, apostolic Christianity was inspired by this liberating experience of self-authenticating revelation. Modern theologians needed to "relive" that experience in order to rethink the doctrinal part. The Ritschlian School, by conceiving theology as the discourse of a normative community of faith, helped to show how theology might focus on Christian experience without falling into subjectivism.[95]

The Ritschlian Theology opened a door in British theology to the dominant liberal theology of its time, especially in the Non-conforming traditions. James Orr tried to close the door, but failed; Garvie became a leading advocate of liberal evangelicalism; and the tiny left liberal flanks of the Congregational and Presbyterian traditions became more aggressive. The Ritschian critique of Hellenistic substance philosophy had already made inroads in British theology, because British scholars consumed Harnack's scholarship and relied on it even as they opposed some of his critical verdicts. Garvie's intervention further injected Ritschlian arguments about historicism, neo-Kantianism, and the Jesus of history into the mainstream of Anglican and non-Conforming theology. Orr, defending evangelical orthodoxy, contended against Garvie that the Ritschlian School already had all the sympathy it deserved, and that "sympathy may require to give way to a sense of its very serious defects, and it may become a duty to speak very plainly respecting them." Garvie, in reply, cited Forsyth's verdict that Orr's critique of Ritschlianism was "perfectly fair, but it is little in tune." Garvie added that many reviewers did not find Orr to be strong on fairness, either. In Garvie's view, British theology was overdue for a fair, tuneful, and critical account of the Ritschlian School that reduced the insular atmosphere and conservatism of British theology.[96]

Garvie's success at this endeavor gave ballast to Non-conforming theologians to his left such as Congregationalists K. C. Anderson and R. J. Campbell and Presbyterian John Oman. Anderson observed: "It is an open secret that some of the leaders of the Churches of Great Britain who in their youth broke with the traditional theology have been saved to Evangelicalism, if not to orthodoxy, through the medium of Ritschlian theology." Anderson took no interest in dressing up the old evangelicalism.

He doubted that the Ritschlian School deserved its liberal image, since it gave so much encouragement to liberal evangelicals like Garvie. In particular, Anderson argued, Ritschl and Garvie appeared to maintain that contemporary spiritual experience provided some kind of evidence for the truth of past historical events. That was not credible, he urged. The Ritschlian approach rested on an impossible correlation between past outward events and present inner experiences, basing its claim for the divinity of Christ on a personal experience of Christ's moral worth. In Anderson's view, the credible alternative was to separate evidentiary claims about the Jesus of history from moral or spiritual claims about the Christ of faith.[97]

This objection applied with some force to Herrmann and Garvie, a bit less to Ritschl, and not at all to Harnack, as subsequent debates brought out. British debates about the merits and varieties of Ritschlian theology reduced the insular ethos of British theology and spurred a shift toward the work of Christ, exactly as Garvie intended. It also boosted emerging left-liberal wings in the Non-conforming churches, less to his liking. Anderson's historicism was a representative option in the latter circles, as was John Oman's neo-Kantian personalism, which emphasized the centrality of freedom in morality and the centrality of dependence in religion. R. J. Campbell, minister at London's most prominent Non-conformist church, City Temple, made the biggest splash, preaching a gospel of pantheistic monist idealism. Campbell taught that Jesus was divine only because his life was governed by love and there was no metaphysical distinction between God and humanity: "Humanity is Divinity viewed from below, Divinity is humanity viewed from above." For several years Campbell was controversial as the leader of a radical "New Theology," although he later recanted and became an Anglican priest.[98]

The question whether Garvie made Ritschlianism too attractive was debated for twenty years in British theology; often Garvie had to remind new players that he was too evangelical to be a full-fledged Ritschlian and that his book, if one actually read it, was clear about why. But even this admonition showed the problem, because on Garvie's terms, the Ritschlian approach was fully compatible with a stronger evangelical theology. Orr made the original complaint that Garvie gilded the lily; in Orr's telling, Garvie covered up the destructive aspects of Ritschlian theology by focusing on its evangelical aspects wherever he could find them. Scottish Free Church theologian H. R. Mackintosh similarly charged that Garvie gave an unduly favorable portrait of Ritschlian theology by representing as characteristic of the school the best parts of its various members. Garvie replied that he never credited the entire Ritschlian School with merits that were peculiar to any of its individual exponents; moreover, British reviewers had a tendency to condemn the entire school on the basis of one or two bad parts by one or two members, so he was determined not to do so. He explained the distinctive principles of the school, sorted out comparative defects and merits, and struggled to imagine how his critics thought he should have done it differently, presuming that they favored fairness.[99]

Garvie succeeded admirably in his task, and he had a long and prolific career, writing books on religious education, preaching, apologetics, discipleship, peacemaking, missions, theology, and biblical studies. A buoyant personality and ardent peace activist, he opposed the Anglo-Boer War of 1899–1902, vigorously defended the rights of conscientious objectors during World War I, and played a major role in the ecumenical peace movement of the 1920s, although he judged that the peace movement was impaired by fractious debates over absolute pacifism. He was devoted to the Congregational Church, but more to ecumenism. He identified proudly with liberal evangelicalism, but stressed evangelical; Garvie would not have been comfortable at Churchmen's Union conferences at which Modernism was treated as an object of faith.[100]

His most important work had a Herrmannian title, *Studies in the Inner Life of Jesus* (1908). Stoutly Garvie upheld the Ritschlian method of dealing with the person of Christ by beginning with Christ's work, in his case by featuring long quotes from Herrmann. The mission of Jesus was to establish the kingdom of God on earth and to invite human beings to a filial relationship with God, Garvie affirmed, citing Ritschl. Christ's rule was primarily kingly, but he ruled his kingdom as God's prophet to humanity and as humanity's priest to God. Garvie argued that Ritschl was right to subordinate the prophetic and priestly functions of Christ to the divine kingdom, but Ritschl went too far, mainly because he had an inadequate conception of sin, guilt, and judgment. Thus Ritschl shortchanged Christ's priestly function of redemption. As priest, Garvie contended, Christ was entirely sufficient to bring human beings unto God. God's chief purpose in creation and providence was to make himself known in truth and grace so that all might be brought into the fellowship of love with God. But if that was so, Garvie argued, "the supremacy of Christ in revelation and redemption must have a cosmical as well as historical significance and value."[101]

Christ did not merely teach or show that all things work together for good, nor was his faith merely faith in God's providence to make things come out right. Garvie explained, "If the Kingdom of God is the essential purpose of God in the world, then He who establishes and maintains and extends this kingdom, not only is mediatorially supreme in it; but the supremacy, not necessarily as a physical omnipotence, but as a moral and spiritual sovereignty, directive of the cosmic evolution, extends to the whole universe." That was a beyond-Ritschl buildup to the Herrmannian title theme, on which Garvie made no attempt to say it better or differently than Herrmann. Nearly four pages of quotations from Herrmann made Garvie's case that the gospel possesses a self-authenticating revelatory core commanding its acceptance. Christ effected salvation by bringing God and human selves together in loving fellowship. Christ's religious consciousness (the prophetic function) and his perfect moral character (priestly) constituted his saving efficacy whereby the kingdom of God was established.[102]

In the book that made Garvie a player in English theology, *The Ritschlian Theology,* he argued that Christian thinkers needed to create their own metaphysics out of Christian ideas, not borrow one from non-Christian or dubiously Christian philosophers. In *Studies in the Inner Life of Jesus,* he sketched what it would look like. It was an incarnational metaphysic of personal idealism. Christ is the "creative act of God" in which the perfect Word entered the world by an act of loving kenosis, Garvie taught. Personality is the highest stage of cosmic evolution, through which the cosmos apprehends the meaning of things and applies itself to its aims. Created personality is dependent and progressive, needing the world for its self-development; through it the creature returns to the Creator, "for the created personality conceives and cannot but conceive as *personal* the ultimate cause, final purpose, and essential nature of all that is."[103]

Was that anthropomorphic projection, constructing a God out of the self? Garvey replied that it was suprapersonal theism, a theomorphic perspective pointing to that which is in and beyond the highest possible experience: "Man conceives and aspires to absolute ideal personality as well as perceives and experiences limited actual personality in himself. Beyond truth, holiness, blessedness, love, it is impossible to go in thought; above these it is impossible to soar in desire. To conceive God as suprapersonal is to refuse to think of God in the highest terms of thought possible."[104]

Averse to labels, Garvie did not call his position idealism or progressivism or anything of the sort. In an age when all liberals spoke the language of idealism, one didn't have to call it anything. But Garvie's summary of his perspective invoked, in italics, the three master categories of the age: "We must first of all consider the relation of God to the world, which is the scene of the Incarnation; that relation for the thinking of today is expressed in the category of *immanence;* we must next ask ourselves how we can describe the process of this Divine activity in and through the world, and at once the term *evolution* suggest itself as an answer; and lastly we must seek to get an adequate category for the highest stage of that evolution, in which we may assume there is disclosed to us the ultimate cause, the final purpose, and the essential nature of that process, and who can doubt that *personality* is the clue which we seek?"[105]

Idealistic Ordering: William Temple

The major Anglican leader and thinker of the twentieth century, William Temple, agreed with Garvie about the centrality of immanence, evolution, and personality, having come of age just after the liberal surge began. He was of the liberal ascension, and contributed to it, but he was not really in it, regretting that the movement settled for party status. In Temple's thought English liberal idealism acquired an organic realistic cast and took a tragic-necessity view of England's wars against Germany. But what mattered most about Temple was the model of intellectual Christian leadership that he offered to a world audience during the crisis of World War II. Obese for his entire life, and afflicted with painful gout, he struck most acquaintances as being happy all the time, though averse to displays of emotion. He was also a figure of immense spiritual depth, serenity, intellectual distinction, joviality, humility, affection, and passion for social justice, as noted by a clerical colleague: "Here was a man in a class and on a level by himself, by far the greatest Englishman of his day."[106]

He was born in 1881 in the Palace at Exeter, the second son of Frederick Temple, then bishop of Exeter. Frederick Temple was one of the notorious "Seven against Christ" liberals who contributed to *Essays and Reviews* in 1860, and the one whose subsequent success at church politics legitimized Broad Church liberalism. He was a quintessential Victorian whose lifespan matched Queen Victoria's almost exactly and who presided at her Diamond Jubilee in 1897, having been enthroned Archbishop of Canterbury the year before. He came late to marriage, having been a bishop for five years before marrying an aristocratic woman, Beatrice Lascelles, who grew up in two castles; Frederick was nearly sixty years old when William, his second son, was born. William Temple adored his parents and grew up wanting to be like them. He mused that his mother got most of her education by soaking up conversations with family guests such as William Gladstone and Matthew Arnold. From an early age Temple wanted to be a cleric like his father, though he grew up to be more genial, and he dropped his father's Tory politics and colonial racism. In 1891 Archbishop of Canterbury E. W. Benson wrote in his diary that it was always "very painful" to witness the treatment that Frederick Temple received in the House of Lords. Frederick Temple was the strongest and most ethically principled member of the House, Benson judged, but his style was rough and provincial, and he reeked of independence, and thus he was dismissed with disdain by "the cold, kindly, worldly wise, gallant, landowning powers."[107]

William Temple exemplified the secure and polished difference of being to the manner born. Jolly, kindly, and gifted, he was schooled at Rugby, where his father had formerly served as Headmaster. At Rugby Temple made friendships easily and developed his lifelong devotion to Robert Browning's philosophically religious poetry. On his father's urging he aimed for Balliol College, Oxford, where he enrolled in 1900, studying philosophy under Edward Caird, who succeeded Benjamin Jowett as Master of Balliol in 1893. Temple imbibed Caird's Hegelian logic and social idealism. At Balliol Temple joined the protectionist Tariff Reform League, but annoyed members by arguing that protectionism would make England poorer, in a good way, by forcing England to become more cooperative and communitarian in its economic life. By all accounts, as a college student he was already fully himself. Offered approximately thirty positions upon graduating from Balliol in 1904, Temple accepted a post as philosophy Fellow at Queen's College, Oxford, and, to the discomfort of many colleagues, took up a strong interest in economic justice.[108]

Temple gave six years to an academic career, specializing in classical and English philosophy. He kept reading Hegel, surprised himself by developing an admiration for Spinoza, and took study leaves in Germany with his friend R. H. Tawney, a Socialist economic historian. Temple alarmed faculty colleagues by plunging into Socialist activism and by laughing uproariously in the Oxford Senior Common Room. Some colleagues found his laughter unbearable; Julian Huxley disagreed, later recalling: "It was laughter in the grand manner and on the largest scale, earth-shaking laughter that shook the laugher too. While it infected everybody who heard it with cheerfulness, it was a potent disinfectant against all meanness, prurience, and petty-mindedness. It was the intensely valuable complement of Temple's deep seriousness." In 1908 Temple announced his commitment to democratic socialism at the Pan-Anglican Congress, declaring: "The Christian is called to assent to great steps in the direction of collectivism ... If Christianity is to be applied to the economic system, an organization which rests primarily on the principle of competition must give way to one which rests primarily on cooperation." The following year he assumed the presidency of the Workers' Educational Association, an organization providing courses in humanities and social science for workers, which he served as president until 1924, and he was ordained to the priesthood by Archbishop of Canterbury Randall Davidson, putting him on a clerical track: Headmaster of Repton School from 1910 to 1913, and Rector of St. James, Piccadilly, London from 1914 to 1919.[109]

In 1906 Temple had broached the possibility of ordination with Francis Paget, Bishop of Oxford, who turned him down because Temple admitted to having doubts about the virgin birth and resurrection. Liberals worried that this refusal spelled trouble for their movement; *Lux Mundi* Catholics like Paget and Gore had not let go of creedal fundamentalism. Temple responded by approaching Davidson, his father's successor at Canterbury, who supported Temple's candidacy. It helped that Temple played down his doubts; his distinction between faith (trust and commitment) and belief (propositional assent) helped him get through a three-year ordination process. Modernists tagged Temple as a promising theological leader for their side, but he had close friendships with Gore (who became Bishop of Birmingham in 1905 and Bishop of Oxford in 1911) and Holland, which raised doubts about his theological orientation. From the beginning Temple was elusive about his theological position; later he became more so. He took Modernist criticism for granted without claiming the party label; he was deeply rooted in Johannine theology, which allowed him to skirt historical critical questions; always he claimed as much of the orthodox tradition as he found to be possible, on Johannine grounds. In 1912 he made his first important contribution to theology by contributing to B. H. Streeter's liberal reader, *Foundations: A Statement of Christian Belief in Terms of Modern Thought, by Seven Oxford Men*.[110]

Foundations was the *Essays and Reviews* and *Lux Mundi* of its generation, except modern theology was no longer shocking in 1912. At the time Streeter was a young biblical scholar and a Fellow and Dean at Queen's College, Oxford, having been ordained to the Anglican priesthood in 1899; later he attained renown for the "Streeter hypothesis" identifying four documents as the solution to the synoptic problem (the literary relationships between the gospels of Mark, Matthew, and Luke). Explaining the purpose of *Foundations,* Streeter declared: "The world is calling for religion; but it cannot accept a religion if its theology is out of harmony with science, philosophy, and scholarship. Religion, if it is to dominate life, must satisfy both the head and the heart, a thing which neither obscurantism nor rationalism can do." In the modern context, any attempt to settle an issue by appealing to external authority qualified as obscurantist. One of Streeter's authors, Neville S. Talbot, explained that in the British context, "modern" meant post-Victorian. All seven of Streeter's contributors – the others were Richard Brook, A. E. J. Rawlinson, R. G. Parsons, and W. H. Moberly – had come of age in the age of Darwinism, modern criticism, and liberal theology, Talbot stressed. All took for granted the necessity of making British Christianity modern.[111]

Streeter's chapter on "The Historic Christ" generated the most controversy; Temple tried to avoid controversy, but fell into it anyway. Streeter observed that in 1889 the conservative parties were shocked by Gore's acknowledgement that the human knowledge of Jesus was limited by the mind of his age. Many clerics still opposed kenosis theology, though Streeter insisted that one could not reject it without making the humanity of Jesus unreal. More recently, he noted, it was liberal theology that came in for a shock, as the history of religions school contended that Jesus was an apocalypticist fixated on the imminent end of the world. Streeter offended conservatives and liberals alike by taking the apocalyptic thesis seriously, though he contended for a gospel balance between the kingdom as a present social ethical reality and the kingdom as an eschatological act of God. Even more controversial was his treatment of the synoptic resurrection narratives, which espoused an objective vision theory. Streeter argued that Paul's reference to "a spiritual body," though ambiguous, was hard to improve upon, as it stood against theories of hard-body literalism, naturalistic explanation, and subjective experience: "The appearances to the disciples can only be styled 'visions,' if we mean by vision something directly caused by the Lord Himself veritably alive and personally in communion with them." God's very Spirit held the power to resurrect to new life "where all the nerve of sense is numb," as Spirit to Spirit.[112]

Streeter's scholarly, detailed, closely reasoned chapter set the style and tone for the 538-page volume, though he acknowledged that his resurrection theory was his alone; none of his fellow contributors explicitly endorsed it. The group could not agree what to say about the Virgin Birth, except that it was not a foundation, so they left it aside. *Foundations* was a liberal provocation in a calm, judicious, faithful, churchly academic voice, which Temple adopted after a weak beginning. Swamped by administrative duties at Repton and his crammed calendar of activism and lecture touring, Temple tossed off a chapter on the divinity of Christ with his customary felicity, was told by his collaborators that scholarly exactitude was the standard for every chapter, and rewrote it in good humor. Later he was grateful to have offered his best work for what turned out to be a showcase forum.[113]

Like all contributors to *Foundations,* Temple emphasized religious experience, though he argued that the usual liberal way of affirming Christ's divinity was mistaken. The central doctrine of Christianity, the divinity of Christ, is "really a doctrine about God," not about Jesus, he reasoned. The usual liberal approach began with a concept of divinity, then asked if the Jesus experienced in Christian experience is divine. But Temple observed that the logical attributes of God – omniscience, omnipotence, and the like – do not apply very well to Jesus, and neither do the moral attributes of Christ necessarily apply to the Ruler of the Universe. The crucial question for religious faith is the character of the Divine. Instead of beginning with the question, "Is Jesus divine?" it is better to begin with the question, "What is God like?"[114]

Temple answered this question in the manner of his favorite gospel, John, by beginning with the experience of Jesus as the Logos. The disciples believed in a supreme power that underlies all reality. In the ancient world it was called the Logos; in later ages it was called Natural Law; in both cases, Christians derived their understanding of the *character* of the ultimate principle from the experience that the disciples had of Jesus. The mind and character of God were expressed in Jesus, an impression of love divine. Temple argued that the central thing in Christianity is this experience of the Jesus-character of the Power underlying all things. In early Christianity, this belief led to the problem of how Jesus should be described, where, unfortunately, a materialistic concept of substance prevailed, yielding an unfortunate orthodoxy.[115]

The early Christian theologians were logical realists, conflating Platonism and Aristotelianism, Temple explained. Sameness in things was explained by appealing to a common quality. If two objects were green or two actions were just, it was because an independent substance of greenness or justice was present in these objects or actions. Temple stressed that the church took logical realism for granted for over a thousand years; Anselm condemned Roscellinus at Soissons in 1092 for teaching that a universal such as "green" or "justice" was merely a name given to particular things that alone had real existence. Eventually the church made room for nominalist disbelievers in universals, but even nominalism was merely the flip side of logical realism, a contrasting version of static, abstract universalism. Since Greek philosophy had no doctrine of progress, Temple argued, it was impossible for Hellenized Christianity to conceive humanity as capable of developing into something divine. Early Christian theology conceived humanity and Divinity as substances absolutely distinct from one another, and it had little concept of personal individuality.[116]

Temple observed that the early Christian theologians did not grasp that "because I am I, I cannot be any one else." This lack of a concept of individuality prevented pre-Nicene and Nicene theologians from developing a psychology of will; moreover, they saw no problem with teaching that God and Christ were the same person. Early Greek theology described Christ's humanity as impersonal, reasoning that in Christ, humanity as a whole was united to the Godhead. The Incarnation, it followed, was at least potentially about the deification of all humanity, and redemption was about a change of substance, not a change of will. Redemption is salvation from death, not the bondage of sin. Temple acknowledged that Paul of Samosata, Bishop of Antioch from 260 to 268, challenged this scheme by emphasizing the problem of will, but Paul was condemned as a Monarchianist in 268 and deposed by a synod in Antioch the following year, and even he sharply distinguished between will and substance, giving priority to substance. Every early Christian theologian conceived Christian experience in terms of substance, which made the Arian controversy inevitable.[117]

Johannine theology taught that the personal and moral character of the world-principle was revealed in the person of Jesus. Greek philosophy, however, was preoccupied by a different problem: How to bridge the gulf between the eternal changeless God and God's transitory creation? In Greek philosophy, the Logos became practically a second God; it explained the created world only if it was secondary. Temple noted that Arius had logic on his side in contending that the Son could not be co-eternal with the Father, for Christ could not be the mediator of *creation* if he was "of one substance with the Father." Assuming substantialism, and that Christ was the link between the eternal God and the perishable world, Christ must have been, in his own nature, something between God and the world. So reasoned Arius, fatefully.[118]

The Athanasian party, in Temple's rendering, rightly rebelled against the Arian second God, because redemption is more important religiously than creation, and Christ could not be the mediator of redemption if he was not, in the received language, of one substance with the Father. Logically, Arianism was a better answer than Athanasian orthodoxy to the problem of creation, but if Athanasius had lost to the Arians, the church probably would have lapsed into a neo-Platonist philosophical society. Athanasius, speaking the same language, rescued Christianity as a religion of redemption by insisting that everything was at stake in the difference between "like substance" and "same substance." Temple explained: "The religious value of the Athanasian doctrine lies in the union of the two natures or substances; God united Himself to Humanity (the Incarnation) in order that in and through that act Humanity should be united to Him (the Atonement)." As Athanasius put it, "He was made man that we might be made divine," or literally translated, "He was humanized that we might be deified." The point of Athanasian orthodoxy, Temple stressed, was to fuse the natures of God and humanity so that neither was denigrated. But Athanasian orthodoxy was merely an assertion, not an explanation; thus its triumph led immediately to Christological controversies. The Apollinarian party conceived Christ as a divine Spirit in a human body, which destroyed the unity of human nature with the Divine on which redemption depended; plus it abolished the human, suffering, personal Christ. The Nestorian party proposed that Christ had two personalities, human and divine, which saved the human Christ, but destroyed the unity of God and humanity in Christ's person.[119]

Chalcedon ostensibly resolved the problem of Christology, but in fact, Temple argued, it merely demonstrated "the bankruptcy of Greek Patristic Theology." The formula of Chalcedon taught that Christ was one person in two natures – the divine of the same substance as the Father and the human of the same substance as human beings. That merely stated the problem, Temple noted; it was not an answer. Chalcedon, besides excluding some faulty options, offered no solution and explained nothing, because Greek theology was paralyzed by its materialistic doctrine of substance and Latin theology was too functional to solve problems about substances. Patristic theology stressed that matter is extended and observable while spirit is not. It missed the crucial difference between matter and spirit, that matter is dead while spirit is irreducibly charged with powers of life. Temple explained, "Matter is only an object while spirit is subject as well; matter can only move in space or enter into new combinations while spirit thinks and feels and wills, and exists in these activities." Hellenistic substance smacked of intangible matter, which confused everything that Christianity needed to say about God, Christ, humanity, and the relations between them.[120]

Temple judged that Greek theology had the great merit of expressing the unity of God and nature and the great defect of having little to say about the moral problem of life. In Greek theology, human nature existed as something separate from individual human beings and the adoption of this indivisible human nature by the divine Word deified all that shared in human nature. Redemption was from death, not from sin; the distinction between God and humanity had to do with eternity and transience, not holiness and sin. Redemption was about a change of substance, not the transformation of will. Temple affirmed and implicitly denied that the Greek Fathers did as well as they could with their inherited categories. He said that they did as well as they could, but he also noted that the seeds of a better theology existed in Plato's doctrine of the soul as the self-mover of creation and in Aristotle's doctrine of energy as activity. Origen tried to put Christian theology on a spiritual plane, Temple noted; Origen rightly contended that Christ must have had a human soul because the Logos could be united only with a soul. But Origen got into trouble on other issues and even his thought was dominated by the imagination, which is static and materialistic.[121]

In Temple's telling, Western theology marked a "very real advance" on Greek theology because it struggled with the problem of morality, which had to do with the will, rights, and duties of persons, not substances. Western theology as an independent tradition began with Augustine's response to the Pelagian controversy over the freedom of the will. On the key point, Temple sided with Augustine against Pelagius: The moral problem is not the Pelagian one of opposition between a free moral will and bad desires, for the human will is made up of conflicting impulses that do not deliver the self from its bondage to egotism. Augustine's prayer, "Give me chastity, but not yet," was exactly the point, Temple argued: "He really wanted to be pure, and he also really wanted to indulge a little longer; and it was the same *he* who wanted both." Augustine didn't need a stronger will, for his will was just himself; what he needed was to be saved by a power beyond himself. Temple judged that Augustinian psychology helpfully changed the subject to spiritual deliverance from moral bondage; on the other hand,

Augustine got numerous things wrong, and Western theology opted for juristic models that focused on deliverance from the penalty of sin, not sin itself, which undermined the Western church's attempt to lift theology to a spiritual plane.[122]

Temple's story of Christian doctrine, like Rashdall's after him, led to Abelard's correction of Anselmian atonement theory, which he called "the best of the post-Apostolic theories." Complaints about the subjectivity of this theory were misguided, Temple argued. Christ's atonement was wrought *for* human beings and it takes place *within* human beings; it is not wrought *by* or *outside* human beings. Moreover, in addition to producing a certain effect on human subjectivity, the cross reveals God's loving character, just as Abelard said, though Temple had two caveats. Abelard did not explain *how* Christ's death was a manifestation of love divine; he merely asserted it. And Abelard did not express the antagonism between God and sin, leaving no room for God's hatred of sin.[123]

How should Christology be lifted to its rightful spiritual plane? Temple pointed to R. C. Moberly's book, *Atonement and Personality* (1901), for the first part of his answer. Moberly taught that Christ was God *identically*, not generically, and that Christ was Man *inclusively*, not generically. To Temple this was the right approach, if one interpreted these statements idealistically, identifying spirit with will. The purposive content of Christ's Spirit (his will) was the same as the Father's, though Christ's will as a subjective function was different from the Father's. Christ and the Father were one, though Christ was not the Father. Temple reasoned that Christ and the Father desired the same things because their wills were united: "Christ is identically God; the whole content of His being – His thought, feeling, and purpose – is also that of God." Formally, as pure subjects, God and Christ were distinct; but materially, the content of the consciousnesses of God and Christ were one and the same, as God and Christ had the same affections, love, experiences of suffering, and glory.[124]

Temple's Hegelian training showed through when he warmed to this subject. In essence he held that Christ was identical with God except in the subjective functional sense in which they were distinct. Paradox is unavoidable in this area, Temple advised. Moreover, the limitations of language compound the paradox, and philosophy has no answer to the problem of how universality and particularity are logically related. Christianity presents a particular (Jesus) that is a perfect instance of its own universal (the Divine) – a sublime example of the logical problem of particularity and universality. Similarly, Christology is bound up with the perennial puzzle of the relation of subject and object. Though every experience has a subject and object, ultimately they are never separable. Subject and object are nothing without each other. The activity of thinking, though distinguishable from every given thought, does not exist apart from thoughts. There is no self that possesses thoughts and purposes; there is only a self that exists precisely in thinking its thoughts and willing its purposes. Analogizing to Christology, Temple noted that two people can be of one mind or will by sharing the same thought or purpose. To speak of Christ's distinct subjective function from God is to refer to something that is distinguishable in thought, yet it is not a separate thing from the content of Christ's being, in which Christ and the Father are one.[125]

The same logic applies to the statement that Christ is inclusively human. Modern idealism handles this issue better than classical Christianity, Temple argued. Instead of interpreting Christ's inclusiveness as something substantial, which raises quantitative problems, idealistic Christianity conceives it as something spiritual and qualitative. Christ's inclusiveness is accomplished spiritually, through personal influence; humanity is in Christ just as Christ is in God. Temple explained that human beings do not surrender their freedom when they yield to Christ's Spirit: "We love Him (a little) because He is Himself and we are what we are – and we believe that if we loved Him wholly and took His Purpose for our own, with all the pains that must involve, we should find in that the true consummation of our being." The right question for Christology, "What is God like?" has a one-word answer, Christ. The succeeding question, "What is Humanity?" similarly points to Christ: "We do not know what Humanity really is, or of what achievements it is capable, until Divinity indwells it." Just as human subjects only know what matter is when Spirit dwells in it, "we only know what Man is when God dwells in him."[126]

Foundations delivered the message that a new generation of liberals, confident in their learning and station, had arisen to change British theology. All its authors gave primacy to religious experience, which amplified the book's impact. By 1912 it was not unusual for individual British theologians to show Schleiermacher's influence, but *Foundations* delivered a powerful collective argument for modernizing Christian teaching along experiential and idealistic lines. It sparked a furor of protest for that reason, which lifted its authors to prominence in *Lux Mundi* fashion. Gore was enraged by Streeter's chapter, which he claimed struck destructively at the core of Christian faith. Ronald Knox, a Fellow and chaplain at Trinity College, Oxford and a leading Anglo-Catholic, made a splash with a witty, contentious, book-length attack on the *Foundations* group that became a touchstone for other hostile reviewers.[127]

Knox claimed that the Streeter group, being thoroughly modern, did not ask whether a given doctrine was true, coherent, edifying, scriptural, or orthodox. It cared only about making doctrines palatable to the modern mind. Since the modern mind was skeptical and poorly versed in matters theological, modern theology had to pitch its wares at a low level. Knox introduced "Jones," a banker in a provincial town who was fed too much Hegel at college, retained a taste for serious reading, attended church only occasionally, had no definite religious beliefs, and took pride in his vague skepticism. Jones' bishop and a local vicar somehow thought that Jones was just "the sort of man we want to take orders," and the *Foundations* group evidently agreed. Instead of asking how they might persuade Jones to accept Christian doctrine, they fed him religious liberalism, hoping it might lure him back to church. Knox declared, "Jones is the hero of *Foundations,* all the way through." Since Jones could not swallow miracles, the Atonement, an infallible Bible, or an infallible Church, the Streeter modernists assured him that they didn't either: "The whole book appears to be an attempt to reach, not a fixed deposit of truth, but an irreducible minimum of truth which will just be 'inclusive' of Jones."[128]

That inspired a barrage of similar ridicule, usually with less wit, to which some *Foundations* authors earnestly replied in public forums. Temple took a different tack, writing a lengthy personal letter to "My dear Ronnie." Knox had confessed that whatever interest he had sustained in metaphysical theology came "entirely" from Temple's lectures at Oxford; Temple, keeping defensiveness to a minimum, assured Knox that he took "very great delight" in his response to *Foundations*. Moreover, Temple confided, of all the contributors to *Foundations,* except perhaps Talbot, he was probably the one closest to Knox on doctrinal matters. On the other hand, he and Knox were far apart methodologically. The methodological difference was what mattered, not the question of how to approach Jones. Temple explained: "I am not a spiritual doctor trying to see how much Jones can swallow and keep down; I am more respectable than that; *I am Jones himself asking what there is to eat.*"[129]

Knox observed that modern theologians proceeded inductively, applying to the Bible the same critical tools they took to any other book and interrogating doctrines from the standpoint of modern rationality. Temple acknowledged that his thought process had an inductive component, but he was too Hegelian to be either merely inductive or deductive: "I approach a group of facts, they suggest a theory; in the light of the theory I get a fuller grasp of the facts; the fuller grasp suggests modifications of the theory – and so on – until we reach a systematic apprehension of the facts, where each fits into its place." If that sounded like circular reasoning, Temple felt no need to deny it: "As old Caird used to say, 'there is no harm in arguing in a circle if the circle is large enough.'" Theologically, Temple began with the church's assertion that the church has the promise of the Spirit and is guided by the Spirit. He took for granted that the church is fallible in grasping the Spirit's guidance. His critical thrusts poked into areas where improved understanding might be necessary. He did not disbelieve every miracle story in the Bible; he believed that Christ walked on water; he accepted the Virgin Birth, although he did not find "any real theological significance" in it; and he believed in Christ's bodily resurrection, though the bodily part was not essential to his faith. Temple told Knox that only one thing in *Foundations* disturbed him – the deference that Streeter, Rawlinson, and Parsons paid to the apocalyptic thesis. This was a serious matter; certainly Jesus rejected "the apocalyptic idea of Messiahship," and if Temple thought that Jesus expected an immediate cataclysmic occurrence other than his own death and resurrection, "I *think* I should have to renounce Christianity." As for his improvement on Chalcedon, Temple told Knox that the church should welcome improvements, however small they may be.[130]

Knox contended that Chalcedon and Temple had the same problem: Both invoked distinctions that exist only in thought, not in actuality. Greek theology applied its distinction between the Universal and the Particular to Jesus as if this were a valid distinction in actuality, and Temple did the same thing by distinguishing between the human will and divine will in Jesus. In Temple's formulation, the will of Christ was both human and divine simultaneously. It was human because that which willed was human, and it was divine because that which was willed was the divine will. Knox objected that this distinction exists only in thought, not in actuality. It was a purely intellectual distinction between the content and the form of a single will. Temple avoided heresy by not attributing two wills to Jesus, but in actuality two persons never share one mind or will. Knox admonished that instead of pretending that modern metaphysics solves the mystery of the union of the divine and human natures in Christ, it was better to say that metaphysics cannot even express it adequately, much less explain it.[131]

Temple replied that "in a very real sense" it *is* possible for two persons to share the same mind or will. Form and content are inseparable in mind, they are identical in content, and the identity of content affects the form, "though I confess I cannot say in what way." Even if Hegelian metaphysics didn't solve the problem of Chalcedon, it certainly made an advance, because the concepts of spirit and will are more fluid and spiritual than the category of substance. Temple explained that he got his belief about the superiority of subject over substance from Hegel and various Hegelians, and on the subject as will, he was especially indebted to Josiah Royce. The chief reason that he loved Hegelian philosophy was that it supported his refusal to choose between Antioch and Alexandria. On Hegelian grounds, Temple affirmed that Jesus was a human individual *and* an all-inclusive Personality.[132]

Temple had one foot in the Anglo-Catholic party without belonging to it. He had no feet in the organized Modernist movement, yet many Modernists looked to him as the hope of liberal theology in England. He never shared the Modernist tendency to emphasize its disbeliefs, and, unlike most Modernists, he did not belong to the church's liberal Protestant wing. Sometimes the view that he represented was called modernist orthodoxy. Temple was fond of saying that his ideal of the church had no sharply defined boundaries; the unity of the church was like a ray of light, bright at its center and shooting out in all directions without definite ending points.

In 1914 he became rector of St. James, Piccadilly, London, where for four years of wartime pastoral service he avoided war sermons, except for admonitions against hating Germans. Some of Temple's friends insisted that he had "a natural inability to do anything badly"; however, pastoral care was not his strong suit. Averse to displays of emotion, he was geared for big thoughts, activism, and running things, not small-talk and the pastoral parts of parish ministry. In 1916 his concept of an engagement present for his fiancé, Frances Anson, was a collection of his ten books. Temple's spiritual sincerity and eloquence, however, came through to his congregants; plus, many experienced his joviality as a welcome tonic during the war. Temple urged his parishioners to "keep clear the character of God," refusing to enlist God as a partisan in the Great War or to speak of the war as God's judgment or will: "We can trace the actual causes of the war, and we know quite well that its causes were in human wills, and we are not at liberty to say that God intervened in the history of the world to inflict anguish and pain by means of the war . . . The sin which led immediately to the outbreak of war we may believe to be mainly in one nation, but the root is to be found among all peoples, and not only among those who are fighting, but neutral peoples just as much. The punishment for that sin comes through the moral order which God has set up in the world, an order which reacts upon those who break it."[133]

This religious outlook survived the war perfectly intact. World War I knocked the bourgeois optimism out of English theology, but not its animating idealism. English theologians of Temple's generation did not have to ask why their leaders launched a catastrophic war that destroyed the nation. England was aggressed against, theologians reasoned. Even British pacifists usually held that Germany was the aggressor. For Temple, there was no "English problem" analogous to the problem of German militarism and nationalism, and there was no issue of complicity for English liberalism comparable to the German one. Liberal theology had barely gotten started in England; it could not be guilty even if there was British guilt to be portioned out for the sins of British imperialism. During the war, Temple played down the imperial angle; afterwards he risked public rebuke by insisting that liberal internationalism was the alternative to wars of empire. For him, the war was tragic and terrible, but nothing like a refutation of his idealism. On religious and philosophical matters he said the same things during and after the war as he said before it.

Mens Creatrix (1917), for example, was written in odd moments over ten years. Essentially it was a neo-Hegelian treatise on the incarnation as the alpha and omega of philosophy, featuring a dialectic of Plato-Aristotle. Temple favored Plato's "good man" over Aristotle's "good citizen," but he argued that neither had a concept of ethical sacrifice and progress, which Christianity provided: "The creative mind in man never attains its goal until the creative mind of God, in whose image it was made, reveals its own nature, and completes man's work. Man's search was divinely guided all the time, but its completion is only reached by the act of God Himself, meeting and crowning the effort which He has inspired."[134]

Temple agreed with Pringle-Pattison that idealism should lead to ethical idealism and progressive politics; otherwise it wasn't really idealism. In 1918 he sponsored a resolution at Canterbury Convocation advocating a living wage, unemployment insurance, and collective bargaining. Red-baited as a Socialist by Tory clergy, he replied that he had, indeed, been a Socialist for many years and had recently joined the Labour Party. After the war Temple undertook exhausting speaking tours on behalf of social justice causes and the Life and Liberty Movement, which successively campaigned for ecclesiastical freedom without disestablishment. In 1920 Prime Minister David Lloyd George asked Temple for his permission to appoint him as Bishop of Manchester. Temple, slightly dazed at the offer, hesitated to accept Episcopal responsibility, especially in a notoriously conservative diocese, then said yes. Consecrated the following year, he resigned from the Labour Party, reasoning that bishops should stay out of party politics; his friend Tawney, noting that the church had plenty of Tory bishops, failed to dissuade him.[135]

In 1924 Temple chaired an historic ecumenical gathering in Birmingham, the Conference on Christian Politics, Economics and Citizenship ("COPEC"). Gore pressed for economic democracy; Temple played the role of conference consensus-builder. COPEC was a milestone for the world ecumenical movement. The same year, acting on a suggestion by Gore, Temple expanded a footnote from *Mens Creatrix* into a treatise on the incarnational basis of his thought, activism, and ministry, *Christus Veritas*.[136]

Theologians and ordinary believers, Temple observed, contemplating God's eternal omniscience, usually picture God as knowing all time at a moment of time. But that cannot be right, for the divine Mind that comprehends time as an object is extra-temporal. God must grasp time eternally, Temple argued, not in any moment. God did not have one will for world history apart from the incarnation and then have another will for history with an incarnation. Citing Royce's logical idea of a series perfectly representing a larger series of which it is a part, Temple reasoned that Christianity is the consummate example. Christ's incarnation was a part of history that revealed the principle of the whole. Through the incarnation, history was fashioned into an exposition of the very divine will and principle that history reveals. The life, death, and resurrection of Christ was a series contained within a larger series, the history of the world, yet it was representative of the whole by virtue of the spiritual influence that it exercised upon the whole: "As we must regard history in the light of eternity, so we must conceive eternity in the light of history. History and eternity must be so conceived as to interpret each other."[137]

Christianity, as Temple construed it, was about the fusion of transcendence and immanence. The transcendent aspect was always dominant, and God was "never so transcendent as when He is most immanent." Temple still believed that the unity of God and humanity in Christ was truly expressed as a unity of *will*, the whole being of a person organized for activity. But this notion is potentially misleading, he allowed, because in human beings the will is incomplete, lacking the perfection of personal unity. It is better to say that God and humanity were *personally* united in Christ – the person of the man, Jesus, was God the Son. Temple allowed that this formulation resurrects the patristic debate about whether the humanity of Jesus was impersonal. Adjusting for modern usage, he agreed with Leontius of Byzantium that personhood is best understood as the entirety of a spiritual being, not as an ultimate point of reference. There was no kenosis. The second person of the Trinity, relinquishing nothing in the Incarnation, added to his divine attributes a fully human experience. Jesus was a single living Being with a human personality that was subsumed in his divine personality. Though Temple still believed that Greek patristic theology was bankrupt, he qualified what that meant. Chalcedon marked the definite failure of all attempts to construe the incarnation in the categories of substance, essence, and nature. It was this history that was bankrupt, not the formula. The formula did what it needed to do: It showed the impasse to which the debate had come, it stated the essential facts, it excluded some definite mistakes, and it refused to explain that which it lacked the language to explain.[138]

Pringle-Pattison, at the outset of the Hegelian ascendancy, said that it was a good thing only by half. Forty years later Temple said the same thing, noting that Hegelianism still dominated British philosophy. Hegelianism was spiritual and theistic, a bulwark against atheistic materialism, he acknowledged. But its absolute idealist variation left no room for a specific incarnation, since the God of absolute idealism never did anything in particular in any sense other than that in which he/it does everything in general. Temple believed that Britain's regnant absolute idealism was a chief cause of the church's recent failure to attract high quality ordination candidates; as he put it, "comparatively few men of the highest ability and education are at present offering themselves for ordination." For him, writing religious philosophy was an evangelical imperative: "I believe that a very slight touch to the intellectual balance may make the scales incline the other way." Instead of focusing on arcane problems in dogmatics, which left religious philosophy to non-theologians, Temple wanted theologians to offer a robust Christian worldview to the upcoming generation, or better, a "Christo-centric metaphysics."[139]

That was his strong suit. After Temple became a bishop he played up his orthodoxy, but his method and positions changed little. Many claimed never to see him unhappy; his personality was constantly cheerful, causing Gore to grouse that there was one thing harder to take than his own foul temper. Like Gore, however, Temple had a social conscience that pulled him into bruising social justice struggles. Often he cited, as his own feeling, the banner slogan of striking and unemployed workers: "Damn your charity, we want justice." In 1926, after seven years of ferment in the coal industry, miners struck hard, pulling off a general strike. Temple played a prominent role as a mediator, and was sharply criticized for favoring the miners. A bit defensively, he allowed that perhaps he should not have campaigned in public for a settlement, which prolonged the strike. Addressing the structural issue, he was less apologetic. Temple contended that the existence of large corporate enterprises could be justified morally only if they conducted themselves "in the spirit of public service." Small businesses usually passed this test, he argued, but corporate enterprises failed it constantly. Temple doubted that corporations were compatible with democracy and the long-term needs of communities: "If that is so, the case for a movement in the Collectivist direction seems to be proved, whether or not the whole journey is to be travelled to a complete Socialist State."[140]

Three years later Temple's antagonist in the coal strike, Prime Minister Stanley Baldwin, appointed him Archbishop of York, where Temple became a world figure. To Baldwin, Temple obviously towered above other candidates, his bad politics notwithstanding; eleven years later Winston Churchill made the same judgment in elevating him to Canterbury. Writing and lecturing prolifically, Temple chaired the Council of the British Broadcasting Company, chaired the Lambeth Conference of Anglican Bishops in 1932, was a member of the Privy Council, played a leadership role in every major ecumenical conference of the 1930s, delivered the Gifford Lectures of 1932-'33 and 1933-'34, and strongly supported the League of Nations – in addition to visiting the 457 parishes in his diocese. In 1931 he began to warn that Europe was heading toward another world war. Temple called for a foreign policy based on cooperation and international law, and in 1932, at a disarmament conference in Geneva, he blasted the War Guilt clause of the Versailles Treaty. Historically, he argued, it was factually wrong to blame Germany solely for World War I; morally, it was offensive: "The voice of Christendom must be raised ... We have to ask not only who dropped the match but who strewed the ground with gunpowder." That set off an outcry in Britain against attributing war guilt to England and criticizing England on foreign soil. Temple, brushing off the outcry, urged Archbishop of Canterbury Randall Davidson – who was like a second father to him – to sign a statement confessing that England shared in the guilt for the war, which Davidson refused. Besides supporting the League of Nations, Temple wanted it to be stronger, and he sometimes idealized it. The goal of history is the commonwealth of value, he contended; by that standard, the founding of the League marked "an epoch of significance not only for our historical period but for History itself when viewed in relation to Eternity."[141]

No Anglican archbishop had ever presented the Gifford Lectures. Temple drafted snatches of his Gifford Lectures in trains and hotels, and improvised the rest as he lectured from November 1932 to March 1934. The book version, *Nature, Man and God* (1934), recycled his usual themes: Spirit is a *vera causa,* a real source and cause of process. Spirit is the nature of the Supreme Reality that created all things. The Will of Christ is one with the Will of God and expressive of it, but not identical with it. Will and Personality are ideally interchangeable terms. To believe in God on the basis of experience and reason is to have an apprehension of universal import corresponding to the supreme claim of Truth. Love Divine creates and calls out from created things the Love that all things were created to be and to express.[142]

Fifteen years after the Barthian revolt shook German theology, Temple had no trace of Barth's polemic against philosophical theology. "Crisis theology" did not suit his temperament or mode; always he was an advocate of reasoned faith. But the crisis of capitalist civilization left a mark on Temple, causing him to change his philosophical position. Marxist materialism spoke powerfully to the Depression generation, he noted. It was so relevant to contemporary experience that "only a Dialectic more comprehensive in its range of apprehension and more thorough in its appreciation of the inter-play of factors in the real world, can overthrow it or seriously modify it as a guide to action." Temple judged that the long reign of mind-centered idealism was over in theology and philosophy; a new dialectic was needed, which he called dialectical realism. To make his essentially idealistic perspective make sense to a generation that no longer believed in progress or idealism, he had to find a realistic basis for it, one that claimed to build upon "the inter-play of factors in the real world."[143]

He found it in the school of organic realism founded by University of Manchester philosopher Samuel Alexander, University of Bristol philosopher C. Lloyd Morgan, and especially, Alfred North Whitehead, which had a theological following at Cambridge University led by Christian historian J. F. Bethune-Baker, biblical theologian Alexander Nairne, and theologian Charles E. Raven. Temple did not convert to organic realism as a school of thought, which was later called "neo-classical metaphysics," "process thought," or "Whiteheadian organicism." But he drew deeply upon its theory of emergent evolutionism and significantly boosted its status as an option for theology.[144]

Organic Realism as Theology: Temple and Alfred North Whitehead

Process thought is defined by its metaphysical claim that becoming is more elemental than being because reality is fundamentally temporal and creative. Broadly speaking, it includes all theologies and philosophies that conceptualize becoming, event, and relatedness as fundamental categories of understanding. From a common sense standpoint, the world consists of material things that endure in space and time, while events are occurrences that happen to things or that things experience. In the process view, by contrast, events are the fundamental things, the immanent movement of creativity itself. Heraclitus and Theravada Buddhism belong to the process tradition, as do Hegel, Schelling, Alexander, Lloyd Morgan, Henri Bergson, Charles Sanders Peirce, William James, and Teilhard de Chardin.

But more narrowly and conventionally speaking, process thought is the school of Alfred North Whitehead and Charles Hartshorne that developed out of the British organic realism of the 1920s. Alexander, in the Gifford Lectures of 1916–1918, and Lloyd Morgan, in the Gifford Lectures of 1922–1923, pictured the world as a graded order of successively higher emergent levels containing novel elements. Alexander distinguished between God's body – the entire universe of space and time – and the quality of God's deity. God's body is "always the whole Space-Time," he argued, but it varies in its empirical constitution, deity, and growth of value. Lloyd Morgan, with a religious flourish that appealed more to theologians, declared at the end of his first series of Gifford Lectures: "If we acknowledge God we nowise *supersede* interpretation under emergent evolution; we *supplement* it by accepting something more in a richer attitude of piety." Lloyd Morgan's second series accented the religious theme: "In spiritual regard I am faced by mystery. And in presence of mystery, the spiritual attitude, if monistic, cannot as I think be other than mystic. That is part of its emergent character; to be emergent in some human persons falls within Divine Purpose."[145]

Whitehead, in the second phase of his career, helped to develop this school of thought; in his third phase he constructed the major metaphysical system of the twentieth century. The three phases of his career corresponded with his teaching appointments at Trinity College, Cambridge; University College, London; and Harvard University. From 1885 to 1914 Whitehead explored the logical foundations of mathematics; from 1914 to 1924 he worked on the philosophy of natural science, especially theoretical physics; from 1925 to his death in 1947 he concentrated on metaphysics.

Methodologically Whitehead's later system had strong parallels to Heideggerian phenomenology. Like Heidegger, he took immediate human experience as his point of departure, in his case as a panexperientialist. Whitehead taught that perceiving, valuing, and remembering are structural clues to the interpretation of experience and that feeling is the essential clue to being. Like Alexander and Lloyd Morgan, he was an emergent evolutionist and dynamic organicist in the tradition of Henri Bergson, rejecting the mechanistic view of nature as a machine-like system of pushes and pulls. Things are complexes of motions that possess within themselves their own principle of motion, Whitehead taught. Evolution contains a *nisus* (striving) toward higher levels of novel emergence, and each entity is related to all others in a living organismic universe. Although an avowed atheist for most of his career, in the mid-1920s Whitehead began to argue that God exists as the source of cosmic order. His book *Science and the Modern World* described God as "the ground for concrete actuality"; the following year, in *Religion in the Making* (1926) he described God as "the binding element in the world," contending that human consciousness is universalized in God's being. In 1929 he developed these vague notions in his major work, *Process and Reality.*[146]

Whitehead argued that the fundamental units of reality are "actual entities" or "actual occasions" that realize some value and pass out of existence in the process of being succeeded by similar entities. Actual entities are experiencing subjects, he reasoned; more precisely, the real internal constitution of the fundamental things that make up the universe *is* their experience. Like the monads of Leibnizian philosophy and the energy quanta of post-Newtonian physics, Whitehead conceived actual entities as complex, highly active, and interdependent units. Building on Leibniz's relation of "perception" to "apperception," he coined the term "prehension" to designate the process by which an actual entity grasps another entity as an object of its experience. The coming-into-being of the subject must be accounted for, he argued, and all actual entities are simultaneously the subject that experiences and the "superject" of its experiences. Against the notions that a stable subject has experiences and that matter has no feeling, Whitehead developed the idea of a self-creating subject and a full-scale temporalist panexperiential theory of reality.[147]

Creative process includes the becoming of new subjects as well as the appearance of new patterns among things, he argued. The basic units of nature have experiential features; actual entities are experiencing subjects that realize some value and pass out of existence in the process of being succeeded by similar entities or occasions. The irreducible constitution of the things that make up the universe *is* their experience. Individuals do not have feelings; they become through feeling. The subject emerges by feeling its way into being; or more precisely, one's experience comes into being by feeling the feelings of one's world. Thus, every self is a complex unity of feeling that emerges in response to one's feelings of the world.

Whitehead described the becoming of an actual entity as a "concrescence," the merging of various aspects of experience into a unity, and he distinguished between two kinds of actual entities, which he called "God" and "actual occasions." Every actual occasion originates physically, but God's prehensions are underived, constituting God's primordial nature. The universe itself is "a creative advance into novelty," a temporal, relational, and cumulative advance: "The ancient doctrine that 'no one crosses the same river twice' is extended. No thinker thinks twice; and, to put the matter more generally, no subject experiences twice." Whitehead reasoned that this is what Locke should have meant when he described time as a "perpetual perishing." More importantly, Kant's first analogy of experience was wrong because it assumed the permanence of substance. Whitehead countered that forms are permanent, not substance: "Forms suffer changing relations; actual entities 'perpetually perish' subjectively, but are immortal objectively." That is, in the process of passage, actual entities lose their subjective immediacy, but gain objectivity as forms.[148]

Whitehead was deeply impressed by the mysterious fact that the evolving universe, for all its chaotic randomness, possesses a high degree of order. The universe consists of countless billions of droplets of experience that occur and pass away. By themselves, they possess nothing that stands in the way of chaos and mutual destruction, and yet the universe is also orderly and pervaded by examples of mutual adjustment.

Each event strives toward the realization of some value, and each event is succeeded by similar events. How should one account for the existence of the creative process of life? How should one account for the mutual support that makes the creative process possible?

These questions framed Whitehead's descriptions of creativity and God. He conceived creativity as "the creative advance into novelty" and God as a concrete actual entity that envisages pure potentials; the latter, Whitehead called "eternal objects." The world never reaches completion, he taught, and neither does God, for "both are in the grip of the ultimate metaphysical ground, the creative advance into novelty." God should not be defined as a being hypostatized before creation; rather, divine reality is always in process with creation. God and the world are necessary to each other. In Whitehead's system, God's primordial nature was the total potentiality of all existing entities at all moments of their actualization; the existence and freedom of each self-actualizing entity are made possible by its participation in God's primordial nature. But the reality of freedom also makes it possible for self-actualizing entities to choose evil. Every self-actualizing subject possesses the power to actualize or negate the life-enhancing aim of God's primordial nature. God is the highest exemplification of all metaphysical principles, not an exception to them. As a primordial reality, God is "the unlimited conceptual realization of the absolute wealth of potentiality." God lures God's subjects to make creative, life-enhancing choices, but God does not infringe the freedom of the moral agent to make choices. With a poetic flourish, Whitehead described God as "the lure for feeling, the eternal urge of desire."[149]

God's primordial nature constitutes the universe of creative possibilities, while God's consequent nature consists of the accumulated actualization of the choices of self-actualizing entities. In other words, God's consequent being is shaped through its process of interrelation with moral subjects. Whitehead explained: "By reason of the relativity of all things, there is a reaction of the world on God. The completion of God's nature into a fullness of physical feeling is derived from the objectification of the world in God. He shares with every new creation its actual world; and the concrescent creature is objectified in God as a novel element in God's objectification of that actual world." God's primordial nature is conceptual and does not change, but God's consequent nature is derivative and conscious, and thus changes along with the creative advance of the world. Whitehead reasoned that the two natures interact through the "weaving of God's physical feelings" in God's consequent nature upon the concepts of God's primordial nature. The reality of God is shaped by the interaction of God's originating conceptual experience and God's conscious, physical, consequent experience: "He does not create the world, he saves it; or, more accurately, he is the poet of the world, with tender patience leading it by his vision of truth, beauty, and goodness."[150]

Whitehead was not the kind of philosopher that looked down on theologians; in fact he wanted theological followers. At Harvard he told one of his teaching assistants, Nels Ferré, that he wanted theologians to rethink his cosmological system in the categories of theological and metaphysical universals. His system was basically an extrapolation of his early work in philosophy of science, he explained; he reasoned in terms of physics and biology, and thus his thought was predominantly geocentric. He hoped for Whiteheadian theologians that made it theocentric.[151]

In English theology this project got off to a strong beginning and faded to near-extinction as philosophy turned positivistic and theology turned neo-orthodox. White-headian theology became a movement in the United States, not in England. The first theologians to take Whitehead seriously, however, were English thinkers schooled in the organic realism of Alexander and Lloyd Morgan. J. F. Bethune-Baker, a Cambridge theologian and leading Modernist, was an early advocate, declaring in 1925: "It is human experience that concerns us chiefly, and when we regard it as the highest outcome yet achieved of the whole cosmic process, and that process itself as having Deity as its inherent urge and the emergence of Deity in its fullness as its goal, we know that everything that tends to the highest qualities of which we have experience, in human beings and human society, is an indication of what is ultimate and real."[152]

In 1927, two major works drawing deeply on British organic realism appeared from disparate wings of the Church of England. Lionel Thornton, an Anglo-Catholic, appropriated Whitehead in *The Incarnate Lord,* while Charles Raven, a progressive Modernist, appropriated Whitehead and Lloyd Morgan in *The Creator Spirit.* Raven, citing Lloyd Morgan on Spirit as the emergence of spiritual value and Whitehead on the organism as a unit of emergent value, declared: "We cannot rightly speak of divine intervention at particular points; for the whole process is within the divine purpose; nor can we speak of natural and supernatural spheres if we mean to imply the existence of diverse orders of being; we must reject *au fond* all radical dualism or pluralism." God is All in all, Raven argued, the "Nisus" directive of events expressed in diverse modes and degrees of manifestation. The whole scheme of life is a real and continuous evolution: "Just as the study of embryology has thrown light upon the origin of a species, because every organism recapitulates the chief phases of its ancestral development, so the course of psychic history from bare life to cognition and to purposive planning can be traced in the early phases of growth."[153]

Was this the direction that English theology should go? Temple's attitude toward organic realism was much like the one he had taken toward absolute idealism.

Philosophically it was the best contemporary option, but it had to be more explicitly Christianized, with a real Incarnation and a God that did specific things such as raising the dead. He did not want to believe that Barthian neo-orthodoxy had any real future in England, although that is what happened. Neo-orthodoxy ignored science, while Whiteheadian organicism was consistent with the modern understanding of evolution as a long, slow, gradual process of layered stages in which complex forms of life built upon simple ones. Whitehead's expertise in relativity theory was a major strength of his system, which conceived the universe as dynamic and interconnected.

So Temple gave it two cheers, showing, without saying explicitly, that his neo-Hegelian worldview folded into the Whiteheadian scheme. Both, after all, were temporalized versions of Platonism. It seemed to Temple that a great dialectical movement of thought – Cartesianism – was finally passing away in the world-historical crisis of the 1930s. Modern thought, lured into a tunnel by Descartes, had approached a phase of Hegelian antithesis, which Temple noted is usually a briefer phase than that of thesis or synthesis. Every dominant thesis has inertia and the impression of common sense going for it; the antithesis is a protest against the limitations of the thesis; once the antithesis has been worked out and its shortcomings exposed, it gives way to a synthesis. The thesis, in the case of modern thought, was the Cartesian project of beginning with radical doubt, which Temple called mere "academic doubt," since Descartes did not really doubt that the world was out there or that he was distinct from his kitchen.[154]

Descartes, pretending to doubt everything, set modern philosophy down the path in which Berkeley abolished the material world and Hume claimed that he didn't have a mind, all that he had was a flux of ideas caused by nothing, held by nothing, and merely happening. Temple judged that Hegel and, especially, the English Hegelian tradition came closest to reuniting reason and experience. Hegelianism, however, shared the standard philosophic sin of conceiving cognition as the original form of apprehension. Temple still believed in the real priority of Spirit, but he no longer believed in the metaphysical priority of the Subject in the subject-object relation of knowledge. One does not have to uphold the primacy of Spirit as Subject of knowledge to uphold a spiritual worldview, he contended. In fact, it is important not to say that the mind begins with itself and its ideas before apprehending the external world through construction and inference.[155]

Idealism had to be corrected by organic evolutionary theory. Temple acknowledged that Bosanquet and especially Pringle-Pattison took a step in the right direction, but both were still essentially intellectualistic. The breakthrough corrective came from the organic school, especially Whitehead, which viewed the world as apprehended as something that antedates apprehension. Temple judged that Whitehead, singularly, took on the problem of apprehension, although there were problems with Whitehead. If apprehension occurs within a given physical world, Temple reasoned, and if one assumes with modern science the postulate of continuity, one must conceive apprehension as the action and reaction of electrons or as the action and reaction of embryonic apprehensions. The former option was plainly absurd; the latter option was the key to Whitehead's system.[156]

Temple pointed to Whitehead's principle that consciousness presupposes experience. It was hard to be sure whether Whitehead meant that consciousness presupposes experience as its historical condition, its logical ground, or both. Temple, acknowledging that Whitehead's language was often awkward, judged that historical condition was the point in this case. But in any case, he argued, Whitehead clearly denied that experience presupposes consciousness. For Whitehead, consciousness was a "special element" in the subjective form of certain feelings. Actual entities are sometimes conscious of certain parts of their experience and sometimes not, and the complete formal constitution of an actual entity *is* its experience. Here the awkward language was unavoidable, Temple observed, since, to most readers, the terms "feeling," "subject," and even "experience" usually imply consciousness. Moreover, the doctrine of continuity guarantees awkwardness of expression, as one must find some way of expressing the movement from the inorganic to the organic, or from the organic to the personal. Whitehead did the best that he could; it helped that modern psychology spoke of aspects of experience lying just below or beyond consciousness. Temple took no position on the nature of the physical structure of reality; Whitehead's view that it was rudimentarily organic was a leading possibility. What mattered was that whatever it is, it preceded consciousness. Whether or not all existence is organic, the organic principle is the means by which all apprehensions of the world must be understood and placed.[157]

Experience precedes consciousness even if Whitehead overstretched in describing all actions and reactions of physical entities as experience. Temple took seriously that Whitehead might not have overstretched. Bergson noted that organisms adjust to their environment and to the adjustments of environments to themselves; Temple added that daisies might indeed "feel" the warmth of the sun to which they respond by opening their petals. In any case, Temple agreed with Whitehead that consciousness first arises emotionally, as an organic reaction coming to awareness of its significance through feelings of pleasure and pain. As Whitehead put it, the feeler is "the unity emergent from its own feelings, and feelings are the details of the process, intermediary between this unity and its many data." Consciousness, in its earliest forms, is an awareness of feeling within an environment and a responsive feeling thereby evoked. Temple marveled at the difference between this picture and the idealism in which he was trained, which speculated about how the mind passed from its ideas to an external world. In the Whiteheadian scheme, the mind arose and moved through its apprehension of an actual world through feelings that the world elicited. Temple declared: "Such a view of the growth of mind is necessitated by the picture which modern science gives of its history and of the history of the organism in the development of which it is found to exist."[158]

The mind discovers beauty and extension in the world, which are there in the initial datum. This is not naïve realism, Temple cautioned; an object apart from knowledge is not exactly what it is for knowledge. His view, dialectical realism, conceived the subject-object relation as ultimate in cognition; neither the subject nor the object is reducible to the other. All apprehension is of objects and is interpretive from the beginning: "Thus we are led to the view that thinking is grounded in the process of adjustment between organism and environment and is indeed an extension of that process." Thought expands by adjusting to wider environments: "Intellectual growth is a perpetually fuller responsiveness to the truth of the environment; aesthetic growth to its beauty; moral growth to its goodness; religious growth to its spiritual character expressed in all of these."[159]

The mind *emerges* through the process of apprehensions and adjustments that it apprehends. The fact that the world gives rise to minds that apprehend the world tells us something extremely important about the world, Temple argued – that there is a deep kinship between Mind and the world. The world has a relation of correspondence to Mind, something that every rational being experiences in discovering oneself to be an occurrence within the natural process with which one recognizes kinship. But mind and matter are related dialectically. Matter does not generate thought, nor does thought generate matter. The world of matter, always a relative flux of forms, lacks a self-explanatory principle, while mind has the principle of purpose or rational choice. Since there is no materialist explanation for the emergence of mind, Temple contended, and because mind contains a self-explanatory principle of origination, it is reasonable to believe that Mind contains the explanation of the world process: "The more completely we include Mind within Nature, the more inexplicable must Nature become except by reference to Mind." Put differently, if mind is part of nature, nature must be grounded in mind; otherwise nature could not contain it.[160]

Temple did not worry that materialists would ever prove otherwise. To suppose, he argued, that consciousness was caused by some combination of non-conscious physiological functions is to imagine a fantastic disparity between cause and effect – one that strips the idea of causation of meaning. It is like supposing that a robot parked at a street corner will turn into a police officer if traffic becomes sufficiently congested. Whether or not one adopts Whitehead's thoroughgoing panexperientialism, what matters is whether mind is real. Since mind has an obvious tendency to take control, becoming the principle of unity of anything through which it is active, the case for the reality of mind is very strong. There is no freedom, beauty, or goodness without it, and no explanation of consciousness: "Thus, starting without any of the presuppositions of Idealism, and from an initial view far nearer to Materialism, we are none the less led to an account of the living organism, and specially the human organism, as essentially and fundamentally spiritual, or at least mental."[161]

Defenders of the free activity of mind pointed to its detachment from successiveness. Temple judged that the two leading theories in this area were Kant's and Whitehead's. Kant, conceiving reality as timeless, construed time as a form of perception imposed by the mind upon its experience, a necessary idea. But that turned the objective world into a construct of the experiencing subject, Temple objected. Whitehead's temporal organicism gave time and nature their due, conceiving the experiencing subject as arising out of the world that it feels and constructing its nature as a response to the way that it feels the world. Temple allowed that Whitehead was not always consistent in carrying through this idea; for example, Whitehead described actuality as "incurably atomic," which violated his theory that the primary datum of experience is a continuum. Temple, holding to the continuum principle, argued that Process is real, Mind arises as an episode of the world process, the distinguishing feature of Mind is its capacity to freely survey the process, Mind apprehends the process as an organic unity, it achieves a certain superiority to the process, and the value of past events can change as a consequence of successive events. Either the world process had a Spiritual quality from the beginning, or Mind was superadded to natural objects by a superior Mind. Temple, sticking with the continuum principle, contended for the former.[162]

The world process as such stands in need of explanation, Temple urged. Here he took leave of Whitehead, whose proposed explanation – the primordial nature of God – did not explain anything. Whitehead helpfully maintained that there can be no relevant novelty without God, but he did not explain how, *with* God, there *can* be novelty. The primordial nature of God was merely a name for something desired as essential, an explanation for the initiation of the flux. Temple argued that unless God is something other than the ground of possibility, it does not help to say, as Whitehead did, that God is the ground of possibility. Such a statement has no more explanatory value than to say that the ground of possibility is the ground of possibility. In Whitehead's scheme, Temple judged, "primordial nature of God" was an impersonal stand-in for "Eternal Word," "creativity" was an impersonal stand-in for "Father," and "consequent nature of God" was an impersonal stand-in for "Holy Spirit." Temple acknowledged that Whitehead's description of God's consequent nature said some beautifully poetic things that sounded very much like Christian theology. But it was hard to see how Whitehead could justify his end-of-the-book description of God as "the great companion – the fellow-sufferer who understands" after he excluded personality from his description of Organism in process.[163]

Whitehead appealed to coherence to justify his assurances about the perfection of God's subjective aim and God's ethically attractive consequent nature. Reality makes sense; thus, the philosophy of organism described a union of comprehensiveness with coherence. But this optimistic conclusion defies ordinary experience, Temple objected. It is a species of Leibnizian fudge that contradicts the everyday human experience that power is often divorced from the good. Christian theologians do not describe the world as good because they find the world to be actually good and getting better. Christianity holds that the world is good because it is the creation of a morally perfect Creator. Whitehead, aside from a few phrases smacking of personal theism that he smuggled into his closing pages, stopped at the impersonal category of the organism, conceiving God and the world as completely correlated to each other. God and the world were explained by each other. The upshot of this correlation, Temple argued, was that the complex totality of God plus the world was not explained. Whitehead could not say *why* reality is whatever it is; for him, God was not a Creator and there was nothing beyond the organic picture of inner unification through the coordination and mutual adjustment of functions.

Temple urged that Whitehead would have done better to recognize that "Personality is always transcendent in relation to Process." A personal self, though surely a single organism determined by the behavior of its parts, is also more than an organism because it is purposive, determining itself by reference to an ideal of itself. Freedom of mind implies self-transcendence, and thus a self that transcends; Temple stressed that a person is always in a crucial sense on one's own account above and beyond one's activities. An impersonal principle of organism cannot account for a world process that includes personality. More importantly, personality expresses itself supremely in love and fellowship: "If we take as our ultimate principle Personality, not only as purposive mind, but as mind of which the actual purpose is love, then the occurrence of persons within the World Process is truly explained by the principle to which that process is referred; and there is no other principle known to us whereby human fellowship, which is the culmination of the Process hitherto, is truly explained at all."[164]

Temple conceived the world process as the medium of God's personal action and God's active purpose as the determinant element in every actual cause. It is pointless to only half believe in God, he admonished. The concept of divine personality must be taken "in bitter earnest," conceiving God's purposive Mind as the immanent principle of the world process. Temple took process thought as seriously as one could without giving up God's eternal perfections. God's saving purpose is unchanging, because it is perfectly good and persists through time. But God is neither changing nor unchanging, because God does not persist through time; God eternally is.[165]

In the end, Temple's dialectical realism was an adjustment, not a fundamental break. To his conflation of neo-Hegelian personal idealism and Christian neo-Platonism he added an organic evolutionary realist dimension. The world has an immanent reason, a Logos, he taught. If this principle is impersonal, it is a principle of logical coherence. If it is personal, it is purposive, moral, spiritual, and a principle of variation, for personality, whether human or divine, is immersed in the world process at the level of immanent reason. Beyond the flux of the world process, however, "there is the personality itself, transcendent, and, in proportion to its completeness of integration, unchangeable." God immanent is a principle of adjustment, but God transcendent "is the eternally self-identical – the I AM." This dialectic, Temple urged, not Whitehead's scheme of God and world, is at the heart of things. God transcendent is the eternal I AM, while in God immanent, God is self-expressed and the world is implicit.[166]

Temple's liberal idealism and his insistence on the organic continuity principle suggested that all existence is a medium of revelation. In a later chapter of *Nature, Man and God* he said it explicitly. If there is an ultimate reality that is the ground of everything else, he argued, and this reality is not personal, there can be no special revelation; there can be only the uniform procedure of general revelation. But if there is a personal ultimate reality that is the ground of everything else, all existence is revelation and there is a rational ground for expecting special revelations: "Either all occurrences are in some degree revelation of God, or else there is no such revelation at all; for the conditions of the possibility of any revelation require that there should be nothing which is not revelation. Only if God is revealed in the rising of the sun in the sky can He be revealed in the rising of a son of man from the dead; only if He is revealed in the history of Syrians and Philistines can He be revealed in the history of Israel; only if He chooses all men for His own can He choose any at all; only if nothing is profane can anything be sacred. It is necessary to stress with all possible emphasis this universal quality of revelation in general before going on to discuss the various modes of particular revelation; for the latter, if detached from the former, loses its root in the rational coherence of the world and consequently becomes itself a superstition and a fruitful source of superstitions. But if all existence is a revelation of God, as it must be if He is the ground of its existence, and if the God thus revealed is personal, then there is more ground in reason for expecting particular revelations than for denying them."[167]

Revelation is the "full actuality" of the relationship between nature, humanity, and God. For Temple, everything was revelatory, but not everything was equally revelatory of the divine character. The principle of revelation is the "coincidence of event and appreciation," the apprehension by a mind arising out of the world process of the process for what it is – the self-expression of the divine mind. Temple stressed, against centuries of church doctrine, that revelation is not the communication of doctrine.

The church construed revelation as propositional because the Greek and Scholastic theologians wrongly elevated conceptual thinking above revelatory experience. Temple countered bluntly: "There is no such thing as revealed truth. There are truths of revelation, that is to say, propositions which express the results of correct thinking concerning revelation; but they are not themselves directly revealed." Revelation, though given primarily in objective events, is revelatory only when apprehended by discerning minds. Like beauty, it exists objectively, but it is subjectively conditioned.[168]

This was the voice that stood out, and prevailed, in English theology in the 1930s and early 1940s – rounded, philosophical, self-confident, liberal in a Broad Church sense of the term, orthodox in a broad sense of the term, and quintessentially Anglican. Temple's theology refashioned an Anglican tradition while sailing against a tide of redemption theologies in European Protestantism. It was a theology of manifestation and explanation, preoccupied with reconstructing a Christian worldview. Temple took for granted that his audiences were schooled in the "Greats" course and that philosophy should be employed across the entire range of theological topics.

The idea that revelation is personal and existential, not propositional, was already commonplace in the schools of liberal and dialectical theology influenced by Hegel, Herrmann, Barth, and Brunner, but Temple's version of it had immense influence in British and American theology. Repeatedly he was cited as the pertinent quotable authority on this subject. Reviewers of *Nature, Man and God* expressed astonishment that Temple managed to deliver a work of such magnitude while managing a large diocese, leading the ecumenical movement, immersing himself in social justice causes, and lecturing and writing on other topics. How did he do it? Temple gave the best clue to F. R. Barry, later Bishop of Southwell, who arranged a mission at University Church, Oxford, in 1931 at which Temple spoke eight times: "When I book an engagement I spend a few minutes in thinking what line to take, and then I don't think about it anymore. When I get to the church I find it has done itself."[169]

Nature, Man and God, a work of 520 pages, made only two glancing references to Karl Barth. The first noted the existence of a "school of Barth and Brunner" which emphasized the "indestructible note of authority." The second asserted that Barthian theology was a heresy because, like all other heresies, it exaggerated a Christian truth. In Barth's case, Temple explained, the truth was the priority and transcendent spiritual power of revelation; the heresy was Barth's denial that reason and conscience should be called upon to validate revelatory claims. Temple warned that Barth's option was "fanatical" because it left theology defenseless against the charge that revelation is mere superstition. Otherwise the Barthian ascendancy was not worth mentioning; Temple assumed that Brits were too balanced to fall for it, which turned out not to be true. There was already a band of Scottish Protestant Barthians – John McConnachie, J. H. Morrison, Norman Porteus, H. K. MacKintosh, and A. J. MacDonald – when Temple began his Gifford Lectures; moreover, in 1933 Edwyn Hoskyns offered to English readers a translation of Barth's sixth edition *Epistle to the Romans,* which launched the school of Barth and Brunner in England.[170]

Temple delivered his Gifford Lectures from the confident vantage point of having swung English theology in his direction. In the 1920s the Anglo-Catholic party reached the height of its dominance, but in 1925 Temple took over as chair of the Church of England's Commission on Doctrine. By the 1930s his influence surpassed that of any cleric or theologian, and the two theologians that rivaled him for influence – Oliver Chase Quick and W. R. Matthews – were both orthodox Modernists of Temple's type. The Commission on Doctrine was established in 1922, in the wake of the Girton Conference controversy, to establish essential doctrine for the Church of England. Evangelicals, Anglo-Catholics, and Modernists were represented on it, though not the ultra-conservative wings of the Evangelical and Anglo-Catholic parties. Temple was considered a representative of the liberal school, along with Raven, Matthews, Streeter, and the commission's chair, Bishop Hubert Burge of Oxford, who died in 1925. Rashdall declined to participate on the ground that the commission was a bad idea, and Major was not asked to participate; thus the *Modern Churchman* gave it minimal coverage. After Temple took over as chair he played a strong hand, believing that his combination of Modernism and orthodoxy best united the church's factions.[171]

By the time that Temple gave the Gifford Lectures the commission had been working for over a decade. In 1938 the group finally published its Doctrine Report, which reflected Temple's strong hand. The report espoused Temple's concept of revelation and allowed for symbolic interpretation of the creeds; Modernists hailed it as a victory for their side, and conservatives of the Evangelical and Anglo-Catholic parties organized petition campaigns against it, to no avail. The center of gravity had shifted in English Anglicanism, exactly as Temple claimed. Major, asked by allies to mount a campaign of support for the Doctrine Report, tactfully declined, realizing that the liberal cause had already won. Defending Temple would have been overkill that didn't help Temple or the Churchmen's Union.[172]

Temple undoubtedly agreed. His friendships with numerous Modernists, especially Raven, were important to him. He told Rashdall shortly before Rashdall's death that his work had been of "supreme value" to him. He even tried to get along with Inge, who was caustic and a bitter critic of Temple's politics. But Temple was closer to Gore, personally, than to anyone in the Modernist movement, and he firmly believed that liberals had made a mistake by forming a party. To Temple, most of what Modernists called Modernist theology was not a basis for a distinct theological faction, but simply that which was accepted by "all educated Christians." He protested that when Modernists paraded their acceptance of evolution and biblical criticism as a party, they wrongly implied that others in the church did not hold these views. Moreover, to the extent that the Modernist movement was actually distinct, it stripped Christian faith of its mystery and spiritual depth.[173]

E. W. Barnes, Bishop of Birmingham, was a prominent leader in the Churchmen's Union. Temple told him that Modernists would have a greater "leavening capacity" in the church if they abolished the Union. Barnes declared that the Virgin Birth could not be used to prove the divinity of Christ and that evolution had only recently been accepted in the church. Temple replied that "hardly anybody" in the church still built their faith on miracles – "if miracles are accepted, it is on the basis of a faith already and independently accepted" – and that the Church of England made its peace with evolution in the mid-1880s, thanks partly to his father. Barnes taught that the story of Adam and Eve was "incompatible with modern knowledge, and the serious theologian sets it aside." Temple replied that good theology does not set aside anything without first inquiring about its spiritual value under a better expression. Obviously, Temple observed, both of the creation stories in Genesis are myths. The first story, "as soon as it is taken as a myth, is an overpoweringly good myth." The second story is "a very good myth, curiously congruous with evolution," because the Fall described in it is *upwards*, gaining the knowledge of good and evil.[174]

Regarding Rashdall's book on atonement, a pillar of the Modernist movement, Temple told Barnes that it was "a great achievement, but essentially a bad piece of theology." Temple explained that Rashdall never asked *why* Paul or Augustine wanted to believe the things that Rashdall disliked; he did not ask what spiritual value the "bad" atonement doctrines had for those that propounded these doctrines. But this is "the very thing that matters most," Temple urged. In his view, too much of the Churchmen's Union proceeded in Rashdall's fashion, parading its disbeliefs, which set off offended reactions from conservatives that didn't help the church either.[175]

The rest of the Temple story belongs to world politics, social ethics, and ecclesiastical history, not theology; by the time that Europe fell into war again, Temple's ecclesiastical and ecumenical responsibilities had taken over his life. In the late 1930s he held out for international law and the League of Nations, arguing in 1938 that England could justify rearming only if it prized international justice above the national interest. The following year he watched Hitler's aggression with mounting horror, falling into silence for several weeks and moaning about the moral numbness of the world, which was a self-description. On September 3, 1939 he announced to the congregation at Bishopthorpe Cathedral that England was at war.

The fact that Temple's generation had already lived through a world war and the economic anarchy of the 1920s, when the wartime promise of homes for returning soldiers was betrayed, spurred Temple and others to anticipate the next postwar world after World War II began. In January 1941, during the darkest days of the German air raids, Temple chaired a postwar planning conference at Malvern organized by the Industrial Christian Fellowship. T. S. Eliot, Dorothy Sayers, W. G. Peck, Richard Acland, Kenneth Ingram, and Middleton Murray were prominent participants. Acland and Ingram pushed for democratic socialism; Temple, composing the group's consensus document, declared that private ownership of the major means of production "may be a stumbling block" to building a good society.[176]

The Malvern Conference generated enormous publicity, moving Temple to say what he really thought. *Christianity and the Social Order* (1942), his most widely read work, made a case for economic democracy on natural law grounds. At Malvern he revealed that he had recently studied Catholic neo-Thomist philosopher Jacques Maritain's writings on natural law and been deeply influenced by Maritain. Three years later, addressing the Aquinas Society, Temple admitted that he was not an expert on Aquinas, unlike his father; nonetheless, he had come to believe that Aquinas had much to teach the modern world about the proper relation of means and ends: "In his conception of property and in the principles which underlie the doctrines of the Just Price and the Prohibition of Usury, I am convinced that St. Thomas offers exactly what the world needs." *Christianity and the Social Crisis*, defining natural law as "the proper function of a human activity as apprehended by a consideration of its own nature," applied this Aristotelian/Thomist concept to modern political economy.[177]

The reason why certain goods are produced is that consuming them satisfies certain needs, Temple observed. The natural law of production is that it exists for consumption. An economic system conforms to natural law insofar as the needs of consumers determine and regulate the extent of production. But any system that allows profit or a similar factor to regulate production defies the natural order of things. Unless an economic system is regulated in conformity with its own natural laws, it will not generate just wages and prices. When private profit is lifted above common need as the regulative principle, the economy naturally generates a widening gap between rich and poor.

Temple stressed that there is nothing wrong with profits as such. The Christian natural law tradition recognized the rights of producers and traders to earn a profit, which is deserved if it is earned by one's service to the community. Natural law theory preceded Kant in teaching that a person is never to be treated as a means to an end, but always as the true end or end-in-itself. The consumer is a person whose interest is the true end of the economic system. But Temple argued that capitalism violated the natural order by regarding the person "only as an indispensable condition of success in an essentially profit-seeking enterprise." Modern capitalism reversed the true order of things by making consumption dependent upon production and production dependent upon finance.[178]

Capitalism was good at producing material goods, Temple allowed, but even in its heyday it featured unemployed workers and unmet human needs coexisting side by side, while economic resources were wasted in speculation and corporate mergers. Then the Depression yielded staggering rates of unemployment and unmet need. Temple called for a decentralized democratic socialism that democratized the factors of production, especially the investment process: "It is important to remember that the class-war was not first proclaimed as a crusade by Marx and Engels; it was first announced as a fact by Adam Smith. Nothing can securely end it except the acquisition by Labour of a share in the control of industry. Capital gets its dividends; Labour gets its wages; there is no reason why Capital should also get control and Labour have no share in it."[179]

His program featured a fixed rate on the distribution of profit to private share-holders, a wage-equalization fund to maintain wages in bad times, mutual export trade, a socialized monetary system, social use of land, and above all, an excess-profits tax to retire the capital debts of corporations and build up economic democracy. Temple wanted to gradually eliminate capitalists from existing corporations, though not from the system as a whole. In his book *The Hope of a New World* (1941), he called for an excess profits tax payable in the form of shares to worker funds that gradually gained democratic control over the corporations. This would be a type of guild socialism, Temple acknowledged, though he cautioned against a "blueprint" mentality. In *Christianity and the Social Crisis* he advocated a "withering capital" scheme in which, once the interest paid on an investment was equal to the amount invested, the principal was reduced by a specified amount each year until the claim to interest on dividends was eliminated. To facilitate the conversion to a capital investment policy based on human and economic need, Temple argued that the state should take over existing securities on a redemption basis, and he advocated converting all big private banks into public utility corporations, urging that allowing private financial corporations in a modern democracy was as anachronistic as private currency.[180]

The worst thing about capitalism was that it fueled and legitimized the imperialism of major powers like England, Temple contended. All the major capitalist powers unfairly used their leverage to exploit the resources and vulnerable economic position of poorer nations. Temple believed that aiming for a favorable trade balance was morally indefensible, since it attempted to gain advantage at a loss to others. The natural law of commerce is that commerce should aim for mutual gains among all trading concerns. As far as possible, international commerce should be organized as a negotiated volume of trade, "so planned as to utilize to the utmost the productive capacity of all parties to the transaction."[181]

Temple was incredulous that citizens of modern democracies tolerated private banks. If society had advanced beyond private currency, why should it allow banks to make money by charging interest on credit? Money has three functions, he observed: to facilitate exchange, to measure value, and to facilitate claims to goods and services. In each case money is merely an intermediary, a means to wealth, not wealth itself, since wealth is the true end of economic activity. Following Aquinas, Temple argued that the true goal of enterprise is to create prosperity for the sake of human need. Thus, one should not be able to make a living, much less a fortune, out of lending money. Charging interest on the loan of currency is morally legitimate, Temple allowed, because the lender transfers a real claim, but when credit is created and loaned by a book entry, no charge beyond the cost of administration is justifiable. The answer was to convert all big private banks into public utility corporations, or when necessary, state enterprises.[182]

Lastly, he advocated socializing land. Temple was fond of saying that the primary requisites for life are air, light, land, and water, and that, thankfully, no one claimed to own the first two. In his book *The Church Looks Forward* (1944), he remarked: "I suppose if it were possible to have established property rights in air, somebody would have done it by now, and then he would demand of us that we should pay him if we wanted to breath what he called *his* air. Well, it couldn't be done, so it hasn't been done. But it could be done with land, and it has been done with land; and, it seems to me, we have been far too tender towards the claims that have been made by the owners of land and of water as compared with the interests of the public." Temple saw no reason why anyone should be paid large sums of money "for merely owning the land on which our cities are built." Private ownership of urban land served no public purpose and undermined public planning, while rural land, if used productively, should be privately owned on a leasehold basis.[183]

Meanwhile Temple was enthroned Archbishop of Canterbury at the height of the war, in 1942, just as allied bombing began to turn the Battle of Britain, and just after *Christianity and the Social Order* was published. Archbishop of Canterbury Cosmo Lang told friends that he stepped down to make way for Temple, although Temple thought that his politics would disqualify him from being selected, certainly by Winston Churchill. Inge spoke for many political conservatives in wishing that Churchill had seen it that way, declaring that Temple's appointment to Canterbury was "a disastrous choice" for war-ravaged England. George Bernard Shaw took a different view, later recalling: "To a man of my generation, an Archbishop of Temple's enlightenment was a realized impossibility."[184]

From the beginning of the war Temple was the church's national voice, delivering radio addresses that spoke for and to the conscience of the nation. In August 1939 he declared that although "no positive good" was achievable by force of arms, "evil can be checked and held back by force, and it is precisely for this that we may be called upon to use it." On October 3 he summoned the nation to fight with "deep determination, accompanied by no sort of exhilaration, but by a profound sadness . . . Nazi tyranny and oppression are destroying the traditional excellencies of European civilization and must be eliminated for the good of mankind. Over against the deified nation of the Nazis our people have taken their stand as a dedicated nation." Unfailingly respectful to pacifists, Temple stated repeatedly that war is contrary to the mind of Christ and to the building of God's kingdom. But British Christians faced the necessity of stopping a Nazi enemy bent on oppression and annihilation: "Where the method of redemptive suffering is possible and the people concerned are capable of rising to it, it is no doubt the best of all; but there is no way that I can see in which we could redemptively suffer so as to change the heart of Germany and deliver Poles and Czechs; and if there is, our country is not yet anything like prepared to do it. So once again we have to do the best we can, being what we are, in the circumstances where we are – and then God be merciful to us sinners!"[185]

Thus he spent his last years speaking the language of tragedy, crisis, and lesser evils, all against his nature. Temple and his wife Frances, a justice of the peace, lived a precarious wartime existence in Lambeth, which was badly damaged in the air raids. They stayed in Canterbury through the worst of the raids, and Temple made a point of preaching in churches where the bombing was most severe. Repeatedly he urged the government to accept Jewish refugees and rescue Jewish prisoners in Europe; in numerous broadcasts he admonished that to support the war was to accept moral responsibility for whatever was required to defeat Nazi Germany; and his radio sermons were broadcast to troops in Europe and Africa.

In 1944 Temple died suddenly of pulmonary embolism, setting off a flood of grief-filled eulogies. President Franklin Roosevelt hailed him as "an ardent advocate of international cooperation based on Christian principles [who] exercised profound influence throughout the world." Reinhold Niebuhr wrote that Temple was the most intellectually distinguished churchman of his time and a faithful Christian whose life was "completely and successfully integrated around love for Christ." Niebuhr's colleague John Bennett, one year before Temple died, made an equally perceptive assessment that was cited frequently in eulogies: "William Temple receives publicity for everything except the thing that he is most concerned about – personal religion." Lord William Beveridge, founder of the British welfare state, reflected that as an unfailing opponent of nationalistic hubris, jingoism, greed, cynicism, and injustice, "William Temple seemed to many of us the ideal destined leader. He was greater than his office. His loss to the world in its untimeliness is second only to the loss of Franklin Roosevelt."[186]

Having carried nineteenth-century metaphysical idealism into the 1940s despite the ravages of World War I, economic calamity, and the decline of the British Empire, Temple realized that World War II would play out differently for British theology. When Temple gave the Gifford Lectures, there was no neo-orthodox movement in England; five years later, neo-orthodox condemnations of liberal idealism, rationalism, and naturalism were commonplace in England. In November 1939 Temple observed that "the world of today is one of which no Christian map can be made." His generation of liberalizing theologians, he confessed, had believed "a great deal too light-heartedly" in the sovereignty of the God of love. In Temple's early career he had blanched at Gore's insistence that if not for the miracles of Christ, especially the resurrection, he would have no more reason to believe that God was revealed in Christ than to believe that God was revealed in Nero. More than thirty years later, Temple had more sympathy with Gore's position.[187]

"There is a new task for theologians today," Temple acknowledged. "We cannot come to the men of today saying, 'You will find that all your experience fits together in a harmonious system if you will only look at it in the illumination of the Gospel.'" The generation that cut its teeth on the Great Depression, a collapsing empire, and now, a lonely battle against Nazi tyranny was not interested in a religion of explanation. Even England was due for a theology of crisis. The task of the church in the world of 1939 was to convert the world with a message of redemption: "Its need can be met, not by the discovery of its own immanent principle in signal manifestation through Jesus Christ, but only by the shattering impact upon its self-sufficiency and arrogance of the Son of God, crucified, risen and ascended, pouring forth that explosive and disruptive energy which is the Holy Ghost." Temple anticipated years of postwar battles over social justice and post-colonialism. He assured that Christ was the source of all true fellowship. But to achieve true fellowship, he admonished, Christ had to "break up those fellowships with which we have been deluding ourselves . . . We must expect the movement of His spirit among us to produce sharper divisions as well as deeper unity."[188]

Temple's generation, in his telling, had taken the church for granted. The new generation, he believed, took the church more seriously, both in criticism and as a source of hope in a dark time: "We must dig the foundations deeper than we did in pre-war years, or in the inter-war years when we developed our post-war thoughts." Someday, theologians would have the luxury of reclaiming the "larger and serener task" of explaining the world in a religious philosophy. There would be another "Christian map of life" in another time; Temple even presumed that it would be offered to "a new Christendom," not grasping how that would sound to a post-colonial world: "But that day can barely dawn while any who are now already concerned with theology are still alive."[189]

In that mood British Anglican thinkers lauded Temple as the greatest in their line and the symbol of a time that had passed.

Notes

1. *Lux Mundi: A Series of Studies in the Religion of the Incarnation*, ed. Charles Gore (1889; 5th edn., New York: John W. Lovell Co., n.d.); see Fredrick Temple, Rowland Williams, Baden Powell, Henry Bristow Williams, Charles Wycliffe Goodwin, Mark Pattison, and Benjamin Jowett, *Essays and Reviews: The 1860 Text and Its Reading*, ed. Victor Shea and William Whitla (Charlottesville: University of Virginia Press, 2000).

2. See Henry P. Liddon, *Life of Edward Bouverie Pusey, doctor of divinity, canon of Christ church; regius professor of Hebrew in the University of Oxford*, 4 vols. (London: Longmans, 1894–1898); John Henry Cardinal Newman, *Apologia Pro Vita Sua* (1863; reprint, New York: Doubleday, 1956); G. L. Prestige, *The Life of Charles Gore: A Great Englishman* (London: Heinemann, 1935), 10–13; Charles Gore, Preface to *The Life and Work of John Richardson Illingworth*, ed. A. L. Illingworth (London: John Murray, 1917), xi; V. F. Storr, *The Development of English Theology in the Nineteenth Century*

(London: Longmans, 1913), 429–430; James Carpenter, *Gore: A Study in Liberal Catholic Thought* (London: Faith Press, 1960), 27–29.

3.   "Editor's Preface," *Lux Mundi: A Series of Studies in the Religion of the Incarnation,* quotes vii.

4.   Ibid., ix.

5.   T. H. Green, *Works of T. H. Green,* ed. R. L. Nettleship, 3 vols. (London: Longmans Green, 1885–8); Green, *Prolegomena to Ethics,* ed. A. C. Bradley (Oxford: Clarendon, 1883).

6.   S. C. Carpenter, *Church and People: 1789–1889* (London: S.P.C.K., 1933), Holland quote, 482–483; see C. C. J. Webb, *Religious Thought in England* 100–101.

7.   J. R. Illingworth, "The Incarnation and Development," *Lux Mundi: A Series of Studies in the Religion of the Incarnation,* quotes 151; see Illingworth, *Personality, Human and Divine; the Bampton Lectures, 1894* (London: Macmillan, 1894); Illingworth, *Reason and Revelation: An Essay in Christian Apology* (London: Macmillan, 1906).

8.   Illingworth, "The Incarnation and Development," quotes 153, 155, 156.

9.   Ibid., quotes 162.

10.   Ibid., quotes 167, 176.

11.   Charles Gore, *The Reconstruction of Belief: Belief in God; Belief in Christ; The Holy Spirit and the Church,* one-volume edn. (New York: Scribner's, 1926), vii–viii; Carpenter, *Gore: A Study in Liberal Catholic Thought,* 23–30.

12.   "I am profoundly" and "naturally" quotes, in Charles Gore, "The Nature of Faith and the Conditions of Its Exercise," printed privately by J. Parker, 1878, cited by Carpenter, *Gore: A Study in Liberal Catholic Thought,* 30; Gore, *The Reconstruction of Belief: Belief in God; Belief in Christ; The Holy Spirit and the Church,* "I have," vi.

13.   Charles Gore, "The Holy Spirit and Inspiration," *Lux Mundi: A Series of Studies in the Religion of the Incarnation,* 263–302, quotes 274, 294, 295; see Heinrich Georg August Ewald, *The History of Israel,* 7 vols. (London: Longmans, Green, 1876–1888); Samuel R. Driver, *A Critical and Exegetical Commentary on Deuteronomy* (Edinburgh: T. & T. Clark, 1902); Driver, *Modern Research as Illustrating the Bible* (London: Henry Frowde, 1909).

14.   Gore, "The Holy Spirit and Inspiration," quotes 271, 274.

15.   Ibid., quotes 282, 283.

16.   Ibid., quotes 300, 301.

17.   Ibid., 299.

18.   Ibid., 301–302.

19.   H. P. Liddon, *The Divinity of Our Lord and Savior Jesus Christ* (London: Rivingtons, 1867), 474; William Stubbs, *Ordination Addresses* (London: Longmans, 1901), 173-182); Arthur Michael Ramsey, *From Gore to Temple: The Development of Anglican Theology between Lux Mundi and the Second World War, 1889–1930* (London: Longmans, Green & Co., 1960), 7–8, 30–43, 1903 quote cited, 8; William Temple, *Christus Veritas* (London: Macmillan, 1924), 142; Charles Gore, *The Incarnation of the Son of God* (London: John Murray, 1891); Bernard M. G. Reardon, *Religious Thought in the Victorian Age* (London: Longman, 1995), 330–334.

20.   On Gore's invocation of "liberal Catholicism," see Charles Gore, *The Basis of Anglican Fellowship in Faith and Organization* (London: Mowbray, 1914), 23; Gore, *Catholicism and Roman Catholicism* (London: Mowbray, 1928), 47; Gore, *Dominant Ideals and Corrective Principles* (London: Mowbray, 1918), 93–94; Carpenter, *Gore: A Study in Liberal Catholic Thought,* 42–61.

21.   See John Caird, *The Fundamental Ideas of Christianity* (Glasgow: James MacLehose, 1899); Edward Caird, *The Evolution of Religion,* 2 vols. (Glasgow: James MacLehose,

1894); James Ward, *Naturalism and Agnosticism*, 2 vols. (London: Macmillan, 1909); C.C.J. Webb, *God and Personality* (London: Allen & Unwin, 1919); F. H. Bradley, *Appearance and Reality: A Metaphysical Essay* (Oxford: Oxford University Press, 1893); Bradley, *Essays on Truth and Reality* (Oxford: Oxford University Press, 1914); Bernard Bosanquet, *Psychology of the Moral Self* (New York: Macmillan, 1897); Bosanquet, *The Principle of Individualism and Value* (London: Macmillan, 1912); Bosanquet, *The Value and Destiny of the Individual* (London: Macmillan, 1913); Richard B. Haldane, *The Pathway to Reality*, 2 vols. (London: John Murray, 1903, 1904); J. M. E. McTaggart, *Studies in the Hegelian Dialectic* (1896; 2nd edn., New York: Russell and Russell, 1964).

22. Andrew Seth [Pringle-Pattison], *The Development from Kant to Hegel, with chapters on the philosophy of religion* (London: Williams and Norgate, 1882); Andrew Seth [Pringle-Pattison] and Richard B. Haldane, *Essays in Philosophical Criticism* (London: Longmans, Green, 1883); see "Andrew [Seth] Pringle-Pattison," in "Gifford Lectures," University of Edinburgh, www.giffordlectures.org, accessed February 10, 2010.

23. Edward Caird, *Hegel* (Edinburgh: Wm. Blackwood and Sons, 1883), quotes 218; see Andrew Seth [Pringle-Pattison], *Scottish Philosophy, a comparison of the Scottish and German answers to Hume* (Edinburgh: W. Blackwood and Sons, 1885).

24. Andrew Seth [Pringle-Pattison], *Hegelianism and Personality* (Edinburgh: W. Blackwood and Sons, 1887; reprint, New York: Burt Franklin, 1971); 3–7.

25. Ibid., 79–106, quote 83.

26. Ibid., 101–115, quote 110; see G. W. F. Hegel, *Logic: Part One of the Encyclopedia of the Philosophical Sciences* (1830), trans. William Wallace (Oxford: Clarendon Press, 1975); Hegel, *Philosophy of Nature: Part Two of the Encyclopedia of the Philosophical Sciences* (1830), trans. A. V. Miller (Oxford: Clarendon Press, 1970).

27. Pringle-Pattison, *Hegelianism and Personality*, quote 118; Immanuel Kant, *Critique of Pure Reason*, trans. Norman Kemp Smith (New York: Macmillan, 1933), 500–507.

28. Pringle-Pattison, *Hegelianism and Personality*, 120–148.

29. Ibid., 149–159, quote 155.

30. Ibid., quote 173.

31. Ibid., quote 187.

32. Ibid., quotes 188, 193–194.

33. Ibid., quote 195; G. W. F. Hegel, *Philosophy of Right*, trans. T. M. Knox (Oxford: Clarendon Press, 1952), quote.

34. Pringle-Pattison, *Hegelianism and Personality*, quotes 209, 216, 217.

35. Andrew Seth Pringle-Pattison, *The Idea of God in the Light of Recent Philosophy: Gifford Lectures, 1912 and 1913* (2nd edn., New York: Oxford University Press, 1920), 389–390.

36. Ibid., 243–264; Bosanquet, *The Value and Destiny of the Individual*, 32–33.

37. Bosanquet, *The Value and Destiny of the Individual,* ix–xxi, 53–55, quotes xxi; Pringle-Pattison, *The Idea of God in the Light of Recent Philosophy*, 265–266.

38. Bradley, *Appearance and Reality*, 225–227; Pringle-Pattison, *The Idea of God in the Light of Recent Philosophy*, 270–274; William James, *A Pluralistic Universe* (New York: Longmans, Green & Co., 1909), quotes 253; see James, *Pragmatism: A New Name for Some Old Ways of Thinking* and *The Meaning of Truth* (1907; reprint, Cambridge: Harvard University Press, 1978); James, *Essays in Radical Empiricism* (New York: Longmans, Green, and Co., 1912); Josiah Royce, *Studies of Good and Evil: A Series of Essays upon the Problems of Philosophy and of Life* (New York: D. Appleton, 1898).

39. Pringle-Pattison, *The Idea of God in the Light of Recent Philosophy*, 393–396, quotes 395, 396; see James, *A Pluralistic Universe*, 43–82.

40. Pringle-Pattison, *The Idea of God in the Light of Recent Philosophy*, 396, 411.

41. See Josiah Royce, *The World and the Individual,* 2 vols. (New York: Macmillan, 1899); W. E. Hocking, *The Meaning of God in Human Experience: A Philosophic Study of Religion* (New Haven: Yale University Press, 1912); Edgar S. Brightman, "The Unpopularity of Personalism," *Methodist Review* 104 (January 1921), 9–28; Brightman, "Personalism" in *A History of Philosophical Systems,* ed. Vergilius Ferm (New York: Philosophical Library, 1950), 344; Albert C. Knudson, *The Philosophy of Personalism: A Study in the Metaphysics of Religion* (New York: Abingdon Press, 1927), 62, 66, 172, 187, 312; G. E. Moore, "The Nature of Judgment," *Mind* (April 1899); Moore, "The Refutation of Idealism," *Mind* 12 (October 1903), 433–453; Moore, *Philosophical Studies* (London: K. Paul, Trench, Trubner, 1922); Bertrand Russell, *My Philosophical Development* (London: Allen & Unwin, 1959), 53–62.

42. See J. F. Bethune-Baker, *The Way of Modernism & Other Essays* (Cambridge: Cambridge University Press, 1927); F. C. Burkitt, *"The Failure of Liberal Christianity" and Some Thoughts on the Athanasian Creed* (Cambridge: Bowes and Bowes, 1910); F. J. Foakes-Jackson and Kirsopp Lake, *The Beginnings of Christianity* (London: Macmillan, 1920); Percy Gardner, *Exploratio Evangelica: A Survey of he Foundations of Christianity* (London: Adam and Charles Black, 1907); Gardner, *Modernism in the English Church* (London: Methuen, 1926); Percival Gardner-Smith, *The Christ of the Gospels* (Cambridge: W. Heffer & Sons, 1938); William Ralph Inge, *Faith and Knowledge* (Edinburgh: T. & T. Clark, 1905); Kirsopp Lake, *The Historical Evidence for the Resurrection of Jesus Christ* (London: Williams & Norgate, 1912); William Sanday, *Bishop Gore's Challenge to Criticism. A Reply to the Bishop of Oxford's Open Letter on the Basis of Anglican Fellowship* (London: Longmans, Green, 1914); Sanday, *Divine Overruling* (Edinburgh: T. & T. Clark, 1920); B. H. Streeter, ed., *Foundations: A Statement of Christian Belief in Terms of Modern Thought by Seven Oxford Men* (London: Macmillan, 1912); Alan M. G. Stephenson, *The Rise and Decline of English Modernism* (London: S.P.C.K., 1984), 52–59.

43. Henry Sidgwick, "The Ethics of Religious Controversy," *International Journal of Ethics* 6 (April 1896), 273–290; Hastings Rashdall, "Professor Sidgwick on the Ethics of Religious Controversy: a Reply," *International Journal of Ethics* 6 (January 1897), 137–168; see Percy E. Matheson, *The Life of Hastings Rashdall* (London: Oxford University Press, 1928); Hastings Rashdall, *The Universities of Europe in the Middle Ages,* 2 vols. (Oxford: Clarendon Press, 1895).

44. Hastings Rashdall, "Unity in Diversity," *Church Gazette* (October 14, 1899), quotes 715; see Rashdall, *Doctrine and Development* (London: Methuen, 1898); Rashdall, *Christus in Ecclesia* (Edinburgh: T. & T. Clark, 1904).

45. See Hastings Rashdall, *Conscience and Christ: Six Lectures on Christian Ethics* (London: Duckworth & Co., 1916), vii–viii.

46. George Berkeley, *A Treatise concerning the Principles of Knowledge* (1710), and *Three Dialogues between Hylas and Philonous* (1713), ed. G. J. Warnock (La Salle: Open Court, 1994); John Locke, *An Essay concerning Human Understanding* (Oxford: Clarendon Press, 1975), 104–155; Hastings Rashdall, *Philosophy and Religion: Six Lectures Delivered at Cambridge* (New York: Charles Scribner's Sons, 1910), 11–15, quote 27.

47. Berkeley, *A Treatise concerning the Principles of Knowledge,* 50–75; Rashdall, *Philosophy and Religion: Six Lectures Delivered at Cambridge,* 10–11.

48. Rashdall, *Philosophy and Religion: Six Lectures Delivered at Cambridge,* 10–11, 31–32, quotes 11.

49. Rashdall, *Philosophy and Religion: Six Lectures Delivered at Cambridge,* 15–16.

50. Ibid., 18–19, 120–121, quote 19; see Hastings Rashdall, "Personality: Human and Divine," in *Personal Idealism,* ed. Henry Cecil Sturt (London: Macmillan, 1902), 207–223.

51. Rashdall, "Personality: Human and Divine," 209–210.

52. Ibid., quotes 210, 211.

53. Ibid., quotes 215–216.

54. Rashdall, *Philosophy and Religion: Six Lectures Delivered at Cambridge*, quote 139.

55. Ibid., 127–150, quotes 149, 149–150.

56. Ibid., 149–152.

57. Ibid., quote 154.

58. Ibid., quote 162.

59. Ibid, quote 163.

60. William Ralph Inge, *Personal Idealism and Mysticism* (London: Longmans, Green, & Co., 1907); Inge, *The Philosophy of Plotinus,* 2 vols. (London: Longmans, Green, & Co., 1919); Inge, *Outspoken Essays* (London: Longmans, Green, & Co., 1922); Rashdall, *Philosophy and Religion: Six Lectures Delivered at Cambridge,* quote 176.

61. Rashdall, *Philosophy and Religion: Six Lectures Delivered at Cambridge,* quotes 180.

62. Ibid., quote 95.

63. Hastings Rashdall, *The Theory of Good and Evil: A Treatise on Moral Philosophy,* 3 vols. (Oxford: Clarendon Press, 1907), I: 7–183.

64. Ibid., I: 184–221, quote 216.

65. Ibid, quotes I: 223, 226.

66. Ibid., quote I: 231.

67. Ibid., I: 231–234.

68. Ibid., quotes I: 234, 236.

69. Ibid., quotes I: 238, 238–239.

70. Ibid., quotes I: 239, 241.

71. Matheson, *The Life of Hastings Rashdall,* 234, 254–255, quote v.

72. Hastings Rashdall to P. F. Rowland, January 31, 1916, reprinted in ibid., 159–160.

73. Hastings Rashdall, *The Idea of Atonement in Christian Theology* (London: Macmillan and Co., 1919), quotes ix.

74. Ibid., quote ix.

75. Ibid., quote 32.

76. Ibid., 233–357.

77. Ibid., quotes 358, 360.

78. Ibid., quotes, 447, 448.

79. Ibid., quotes 463.

80. For a typically antagonistic rendering, see Roger Lloyd, *The Church of England, 1900–1965* (London: SCM Press, 1966); for Raven's politics, see Charles Raven, *Christian Socialism: 1848–1854* (London: Macmillan, 1920); Raven, *Is War Obsolete?* (London: G. Allen and Unwin, 1935); Raven, *The Theological Basis of Christian Pacifism* (London: Fellowship of Reconciliation, 1952).

81. Henry D. A. Major, editorial, *Modern Churchman* (September 1921), quote 194, cited in Alan M. G. Stephenson, *The Rise and Decline of English Modernism,* 117; see Major, "Modern Churchmen or Unitarians?" *Hibbert Journal* 20 (1922), 208–219; F. J. Foakes-Jackson and Kirsopp Lake, *The Beginnings of Christianity* (London: Macmillan, 1920); Foakes-Jackson, "Christ in the Church: The Testimony of History," in *Essays on Some Theological Questions of the Day,* ed. Henry Barclay Swete (London: Macmillan, 1905); Foakes-Jackson, "The Cambridge Conference of the Churchmen's Union," *Hibbert*

Journal 20 (January 1922), 193–207; Kirsopp Lake, *The Historical Evidence for the Resurrection of Jesus Christ* (London: Williams & Norgate, 1912); Lake, *The Religion of Yesterday and To-Morrow* (Boston: Houghton Mifflin, 1925).

82. Hastings Rashdall, "Christ as Logos and Son of God," *Modern Churchman* (September 1921), 279–284; Stephenson, *The Rise and Decline of English Modernism,* 117–119.

83. Stephenson, *The Rise and Decline of English Modernism,* quotes 123.

84. Hastings Rashdall to A. H. Cruickshank, August 18, 1921, reprinted in Matheson, *The Life of Hastings Rashdall,* 209–210; Stephenson, *The Rise and Decline of English Modernism,* 123–124; Rashdall, *Jesus Human and Divine* (London: Andrew Melrose, 1922).

85. Pringle-Pattison, *The Idea of God in the Light of Recent Philosophy,* quote 157.

86. A. M. Fairbairn, *The Place of Christ in Modern Theology* (London: Hodder & Stoughton, 1893), quotes 3; Alfred E. Garvie, *The Ritschlian Theology: Critical and Constructive* (1st edn., 1899; 2nd edn., Edinburgh: T. & T. Clark, 1902), v.

87. Alfred E. Garvie, *Memories and Meanings of My Life* (London: George Allen & Unwin, 1938), quote 53.

88. Albrecht Ritschl, *The Doctrine of Justification and Reconciliation,* trans. John S. Black (London: Edmonston & Douglas, 1872); Leonhard Stählin, *Kant, Lotze, Ritschl,* trans. David W. Simon (Edinburgh: T. & T. Clark, 1889), quote vii; Julius Kaftan, *The Truth of the Christian Religion,* trans. George Ferries (Edinburgh: T. & T. Clark, 1894); Wilhelm Herrmann, *The Communion of the Christian with God,* trans. From second edition by J. Sandys Stanyon (London: Williams & Norgate, 1895); Hans H. Wendt, *The Teaching of Jesus* (Edinburgh: T. & T. Clark, 1896); James Denney, *Studies in Theology: Lectures delivered in Chicago Theological Seminary* (London: Hodder & Stoughton, 1895); James Orr, *The Ritschlian Theology and the Evangelical Faith* (London: Hodder and Stoughton, 1898); P. T. Forsyth, *Faith and Criticism* (London: Sampson Low, Marston & Co., 1893); Arthur C. McGiffert, *A History of Christianity in the Apostolic Age* (New York: Charles Scribner's Sons, 1897).

89. Garvie, *The Ritschlian Theology: Critical and Constructive,* 1–5, quotes 1, 2.

90. Ibid., 5–20, quote 15.

91. Ibid., quotes 368.

92. Ibid., quotes 371, 372.

93. 88 Ibid., 383–387.

94. Ibid., 379–382.

95. Ibid., quotes 390, 391.

96. James Orr, "Ritschl and After," review of *The Ritschlian Theology: Critical and Constructive,* by Alfred E. Garvie, *British Weekly* (November 23, 1899); P. T. Forsyth, "A German Theologian," *The Speaker* I (1899), 317–319, quote 318; Garvie, "Additional Notes to the Second Edition," *The Ritschlian Theology: Critical and Constructive,* 397.

97. K. C. Anderson, *The Larger Faith* (London: A. & C. Black, 1903), 45; John W. Oman, *Vision and Authority* (London: Hodder & Stoughton, 1902); see R. Roberts, "Jesus or Christ? An Appeal for Consistency," *Hibbert Journal* (January 1909); Thomas A. Langford, *In Search of Foundations: English Theology, 1900–1920* (New York: Abingdon Press, 1969), 223–227.

98. Oman, *Vision and Authority;* John Oman, *Grace and Personality* (Cambridge: Cambridge University Press, 1917); R. J. Campbell, *The New Theology* (London: Williams & Norgate, 1907), quote 75.

99. Orr, "Ritschl and After"; H. R. Macintosh, "The Ritschlian Theology: Critical and Constructive," review of *The Ritschlian Theology: Critical and Constructive,* by Alfred E. Garvie, ibid., *Critical Review* 10 (1899), 37–42; Garvie, "Additional Notes to the Second Edition," 399–400.

100. See Garvie, *Memories and Meanings of My Life*; Alfred E. Garvie, *The Christian Certainty amid the modern perplexity* (London: Hodder & Stoughton, 1910); Garvie, *Studies of Paul and his gospel* (London: Hodder & Stoughton, 1911); Garvie, *Can Christ Save Society?* (New York: Abingdon Press, 1933); Garvie, *The Christian Doctrine of the Godhead* (London: Hodder and Stoughton, 1925); Garvie, *The Christian Belief in God in Relation to Religion and Philosophy* (London: Harper and Brothers, 1933); Garvie, *The Christian Ideal for Human Society* (New York: Richard R. Smith, 1930); Garvie, *Revelation Through History and Experience* (London: I. Nicholson and Watson, 1934); Garvie, *A Guide to Preachers* (London: Hodder and Stoughton, 1906).

101. Alfred E. Garvie, *Studies in the Inner Life of Jesus* (New York: George H. Doran, 1908), quote 475.

102. Ibid., 474–478, quote 475; see Herrmann, *The Communion of the Christian with God,* 66–81.

103. Garvie, *The Ritschlian Theology: Critical and Constructive,* 393; Garvie, *Studies in the Inner Life of Jesus,* quote 529.

104. Garvie, *Studies in the Inner Life of Jesus,* quote 529.

105. Ibid., 521.

106. A. E. Baker, "William Temple – the Man," in W. R. Matthews, ed., *William Temple: An Estimate and an Appreciation* (London: James Clarke & Co., 1946), 94–112, quote by Canon Tapper on occasion of Temple's enthronement at Canterbury, 100.

107. Arthur C. Benson, *Life of E. W. Benson,* 2 vols. (Macmillan: New York, 1899), II: 394; F. A. Iremonger, *William Temple, Archbishop of Canterbury: His Life and Letters* (London: Oxford University Press, 1948), 1–11; Joseph Fletcher, *William Temple: Twentieth Century Christian* (New York: Seabury Press, 1963), 234–242.

108. William Temple to Godfrey F. Bradby, July 26, 1933, reprinted in Iremonger, *William Temple, Archbishop of Canterbury: His Life and Letters,* 45–46; see Fletcher, *William Temple: Twentieth Century Christian,* 245–246; Iremonger, *William Temple, Archbishop of Canterbury: His Life and Letters,* 12–59.

109. Iremonger, *William Temple, Archbishop of Canterbury: His Life and Letters,* 60–72, "greatest" quote, 71; Huxley quote 65; Pan-Anglican Congress, *General Report,* 2 vols. (London: S.P.C.K., 1908), II: quote 100–101; Fletcher, *William Temple: Twentieth Century Christian,* 246–247.

110. B. H. Streeter, ed., *Foundations: A Statement of Christian Belief in Terms of Modern Thought, by Seven Oxford Men* (London: Macmillan, 1912).

111. B. H. Streeter, "Introduction," and Neville S. Talbot, "The Modern Situation," in ibid., vii–xi, quote vii, and 3–24; see B. H. Streeter, *The Four Gospels: A Study of Origins, Treating of the Manuscript Tradition, Sources, Authorship and Dates* (London: Macmillan, 1924).

112. B. H. Streeter, "The Historic Christ," in *Foundations: A Statement of Christian Belief in Terms of Modern Thought, by Seven Oxford Men,* 75–145, quote 136.

113. Iremonger, *William Temple, Archbishop of Canterbury: His Life and Letters,* 155–158.

114. William Temple, "The Divinity of Christ," *Foundations: A Statement of Christian Belief in Terms of Modern Thought, by Seven Oxford Men,* quote 213.

115. Ibid., 213–221.

116. Ibid., 223–225.

117. Ibid., quote, 225.
118. Ibid., 227.
119. Ibid., quotes 228, 229; see Athanasius, *On the Incarnation of the Word*, trans. Archibald Robertson, in *The Library of Christian Classics*, III: *Christology of the Later Fathers*, ed. Edward R. Hardy (Philadelphia: Westminster Press, 1954), 55–110, quote 107.
120. Temple, "The Divinity of Christ," quotes 230, 231.
121. Ibid., 232–233.
122. Ibid., quotes 233, 236.
123. Ibid., 242.
124. Ibid., 246–249, quote 249; see R. C. Moberly, *Atonement and Personality* (London: John Murray, 1901).
125. Temple, *The Divinity of Christ*, 249–252.
126. Ibid., quotes 253, 259.
127. See Charles Gore, *The Basis of Anglican Fellowship: An Open Letter to the Clergy of the Diocese of Oxford* (London: Mowbray, 1914); William Sanday, *Bishop Gore's Challenge to Criticism* (London: Longmans, Green, 1914); Langford, *In Search of Foundations: English Theology, 1900–1920*, 127–138; Ronald A. Knox, *Some Loose Stones: Being a Consideration of Certain Tendencies in Modern Theology illustrated by reference to the book called "Foundations"* (London: Longmans, Green, 1913).
128. Knox, *Some Loose Stones*, quotes 9, 10.
129. William Temple to Ronald Knox, October 29, 1913, reprinted in Iremonger, *William Temple, Archbishop of Canterbury: His Life and Letters*, quotes 161, 162; Knox, *Some Loose Stones*, 149.
130. Temple to Knox, October 29, 1913, 163, 164.
131. Knox, *Some Loose Stones*, 152–153.
132. Temple to Knox, October 29, 1913, 164.
133. William Temple, "The War and Judgment," sermon of February 1916, reprinted in Iremonger, *William Temple, Archbishop of Canterbury: His Life and Letters*, 173–174; "natural inability" quote in Baker, "William Temple – the Man," 103.
134. William Temple, *Mens Creatrix: An Essay* (London: Macmillan, 1917), quote 354.
135. See Gary Dorrien, *The Democratic Socialist Vision* (Totowa: Rowman & Littlefield, 1986), 24; John C. Cort, *Christian Socialism* (Maryknoll: Orbis Books, 1988), 169; Iremonger, *William Temple, Archbishop of Canterbury: His Life and Letters*, 282–312.
136. See Sidney Dark, *The People's Archbishop: The Man and His Message* (London: James Clarke & Co., 1942), 30–31.
137. Temple, *Mens Creatrix: An Essay*, 318, 360; William Temple, *Christus Veritas: An Essay* (London: Macmillan, 1924), quote, 89–90; see Josiah Royce, *The World and the Individual* (New York: Macmillan, 1900).
138. Temple, *Christus Veritas: An Essay*, 124–153, quotes 285, 134.
139. Temple, ibid., quotes ix.
140. William Temple, *Essays in Christian Politics and Kindred Subjects* (London: Longmans, Green, 1927), 42–57, quote 44; see John Kent, *William Temple: Church, State and Society in Britain, 1880–1950* (Cambridge: Cambridge University Press, 1992), 135–148.
141. Iremonger, *William Temple, Archbishop of Canterbury: His Life and Letters*, 363–386, "the voice," 376; Fletcher, *William Temple: Twentieth Century Christian*, 266–268; William Temple, *Nature, Man and God* (London: Macmillan, 1934), quote, 448–9.
142. Temple, *Nature, Man and God*, 3–56.
143. Ibid., ix–x.

144. See S. Alexander, *Space, Time, and Deity,* 2 vols. (London: Macmillan, 1920); C. Lloyd Morgan, *Emergent Evolution* (London: Williams and Norgate, 1923); Lloyd-Morgan, *Life, Mind and Deity* (London: Williams and Norgate, 1925); J. F. Bethune-Baker, *The Way of Modernism & Other Essays* (Cambridge: Cambridge University Press, 1927), 50–91; Bethune-Baker, *The Old Faith and the New Learning* (London: S.P.C.K., 1907); Alexander Nairne, *Mater scientiarum* (Cambridge: Cambridge University Press, 1922; Nairne, *The Meaning of the Incarnation* (London: S.P.C.K., 1934).

145. Alexander, *Space, Time, and Deity,* II: 341–429, quote 366; Morgan, *Emergent Evolution,* "if we," 300; Lloyd-Morgan, *Life, Mind and Deity,* "in spiritual," 312–313.

146. Alfred North Whitehead, *Science and the Modern World* (New York: Macmillan, 1925); Whitehead, *Religion in the Making* (New York: Macmillan, 1926), quote 158; see Henri Bergson, *Creative Evolution* trans. Arthur Mitchell (New York: Henry Holt, 1911); Bergson, *The Creative Mind: An Introduction to Metaphysics,* trans. Mabelle L. Andison (New York: Philosophical Library, 1946); Lewis S. Ford, *The Emergence of Whitehead's Metaphysics, 1925–1929* (Albany: State University of New York Press, 1986); Martin Heidegger, *Being and Time,* trans. John Macquarrie and Edward Robinson (New York: Harper & Row, 1962); Heidegger, *The Basic Problems of Phenomenology,* trans. Albert Hofstadter (Bloomington: Indiana University Press, 1988); Gene Reeves and Delwin Brown, "The Development of Process Theology," *Process Philosophy and Christian Thought,* eds. Delwin Brown, Ralph E. James, Jr., Gene Reeves (Indianapolis: Bobbs-Merrill, 1971), 22–23. This section adapts material from Gary Dorrien, *The Making of American Liberal Theology: Crisis, Irony, and Postmodernity, 1950–2005* (Louisville: Westminster John Knox, 2005), 62–65.

147. Alfred North Whitehead, *Process and Reality: An Essay in Cosmology* (New York: Macmillan, 1929), 27–54. Since this is the edition of Whitehead's book that was used for decades, it is the one I will cite. This edition contained numerous typographical and editing errors, as did an English edition published by Cambridge. A corrected edition, edited by David Ray Griffin and Donald W. Sherburne, was published in 1978 by Free Press.

148. Ibid., 27–54, quotes, 43–44; see Alfred North Whitehead, *Adventures of Ideas* (New York: Macmillan, 1933; reprint, New York: Free Press, 1967), 175–190; William A. Christian, *An Interpretation of Whitehead's Metaphysics* (New Haven: Yale University Press, 1959), 11–13.

149. Whitehead, *Process and Reality,* quotes, 521, 522. See the Griffin and Sherburne corrected edition, 343–346, although all the quotes remain the same.

150. Ibid., quotes, 523, 524, 526.

151. Nels F. S. Ferré, *The Universal Word: A Theology for a Universal Faith* (Philadelphia: Westminster Press, 1969), 140.

152. J. F. Bethune-Baker, "Evolution and Incarnation," lecture to a clerical society in Birmingham, 1925, published in Bethune-Baker, *The Way of Modernism & Other Essays,* 75–91, quote 90.

153. Lionel Thornton, *The Incarnate Lord* (London: Longmans, Green and Co., 1928); Charles E. Raven, *The Creator Spirit: A Survey of Christian Doctrine in the light of Biology, Psychology and Mysticism* (Cambridge: Harvard University Press, 1927), quotes 83, 85.

154. Temple, *Nature, Man and God,* quote 66.

155. Ibid., 57–81.

156. Ibid., 110–111.

157. Whitehead, *Process and Reality,* "special element," 72; Temple, *Nature, Man and God,* 111–118.

158. Whitehead, *Process and Reality,* quote 122; Temple, *Nature, Man and God,* quote, 124.

159. Temple, *Nature, God and Man,* quotes, 128.

160. Ibid., quote 133.

161. Ibid., quote 201.

162. Whitehead, *Process and Reality,* 84; Temple, *Nature, Man and God,* 201–213.

163. Temple, *Nature, Man and God,* 257–259; Whitehead, *Process and Reality,* 497.

164. Temple, *Nature, Man and God,* quotes 261, 263; see Jack F. Padgett, *The Christian Philosophy of William Temple* (The Hague: Martinus Nijhoff, 1974), 67–79.

165. Temple, *Nature, Man and God,* quote 269.

166. Ibid., quote 295.

167. Ibid., quote 306–307.

168. Ibid., quotes 312, 315, 317.

169. F. R. Barry, Foreword to William Temple, *Christian Faith and Life* (1931; reprint, London: SCM Press, 1963), quote 13.

170. Temple, *Nature, Man and God,* quotes 23, 396; John McConnachie, "The Teaching of Karl Barth: A New Positive Movement in German Theology," *Hibbert Journal* 25 (1926/7), 385–400; McConnachie, *The Significance of Karl Barth* (London: Hodder & Stoughton, 1931); J. H. Morrison, "The Barthian School, I: An Appreciation," *Expository Times* 43 (1931/1932), 314–317, quote 314; Norman W. Porteus, "The Barthian School, II: The Theology of Karl Barth," *Expository Times* 43 (1931/1932), 341–346; A. J. MacDonald, "The Message and Theology of Barth and Brunner," *Theology* 24 (1932), 197–207, 252–258, 324–332; Richard H. Roberts, "The Reception of the Theology of Karl Barth in the Anglo-Saxon World: History, Typology and Prospect," in Roberts, *A Theology on Its Way?: Essays on Karl Barth* (Edinburgh: T. & T. Clark, 1991), 105–109; Karl Barth, *The Epistle to the Romans,* 6th edn., trans. Edwyn C. Hoskyns (London: Oxford University Press, 1933); see Barth and Emil Brunner, *Natural Theology: Comprising "Nature and Grace" by Professor Emil Brunner and the Reply "No!" by Dr. Karl Barth,* trans. Peter Fraenkel (London: Geoffrey Bles, 1946).

171. See Oliver Chase Quick, *The Christian Sacraments* (London: Nisbet, 1927); Quick, *The Testing of Church Principles* (London: John Murray, 1919); W. R. Matthews, *Studies in Christian Philosophy* (London: Macmillan, 1921); Matthews, *The Purpose of God* (London: Nisbet, 1935); Matthews, *God in Christian Thought and Experience* (London: Nisbet, 1939); Stephenson, *The Rise and Decline of English Modernism,* 135–138.

172. 1922 Doctrine Commission, *Doctrine in the Church of England* (1938), excerpts in *The Anglican Tradition: A Handbook of Sources,* ed. G. R. Evans and J. Robert Wright (London: S.P.C.K., 1991), 401–410; Stephenson, *The Rise and Decline of English Modernism,* 155–161.

173. William Temple to Ernest William Barnes, January 1930, reprinted in Iremonger, *William Temple, Archbishop of Canterbury: His Life and Letters,* quote 490; see Barnes, *Should Such a Faith Offend? Sermons and Addresses* (London: Hodder & Stoughton, 1927); Barnes, *The Rise of Christianity* (London: Longmans, Green, 1947).

174. Temple to Barnes, January 1930, quotes 491, 492.

175. Ibid., 491, 492.

176. This section adapts material from Dorrien, *The Democratic Socialist Vision,* 30–42; see Alan M. Suggate, *William Temple and Christian Social Ethics Today* (Edinburgh: T. & T. Clark, 1987), 98–125;

177. William Temple, "Thomism and Modern Needs," *Blackfriars* (March 1944), reprinted in Temple, *Religious Experience and Other Essays and Addresses* (London: James Clarke & Co., 1958), 229–236, "in his," 231; Temple, *Christianity and the Social Order*

(Harmondsworth, Middlesex: Penguin Books, 1942); "the proper," 77; see Kent, *William Temple: Church, State and Society in Britain, 1880–1950* (Cambridge: Cambridge University Press, 1992), 148–167.

178. Temple, *Christianity and the Social Order*, quote 78.

179. Ibid., quote 96.

180. Ibid., 110–114; William Temple, *The Hope of a New World* (New York: Macmillan, 1941), 54–62.

181. Temple, *Christianity and the Social Order*, quote 115.

182. Ibid., 116.

183. Ibid., 117; William Temple, *The Church Looks Forward* (New York: Macmillan, 1944), quote 116.

184. Fletcher, *William Temple: Twentieth Century Christian*, 280; Adam Fox, *Dean Inge* (London: John Murray, 1950), Inge quote 157; Iremonger, *William Temple, Archbishop of Canterbury: His Life and Letters*, Shaw quote, 475.

185. Iremonger, *William Temple, Archbishop of Canterbury: His Life and Letters*, August 1939 excerpt of broadcast address, 540; excerpt of October 3, 1939 address, 540; "where the method," letter of November 1939, 543; see Temple, *William Temple's Teaching*, ed. A. E. Baker (London: James Clarke, 1949), 190–198.

186. Iremonger, *William Temple, Archbishop of Canterbury: His Life and Letters*, Roosevelt quote, 627; Beveridge quote, 631; *William Temple: An Estimate and an Appreciation*, Niebuhr quote, 110; Bennett quote in *Anglican Theological Review* 25 (July 1943), 3, cited in Fletcher, *William Temple: Twentieth Century Christian*, 269.

187. Text reprinted in Ramsey, *From Gore to Temple: The Development of Anglican Theology between Lux Mundi and the Second World War, 1889–1930*, 160–161, quote 160.

188. Ibid., 160–161.

189. Ibid., 161.

8

The Barthian Revolt
Karl Barth, Paul Tillich, and the Legacy of Liberal Theology

The major event of twentieth-century theology was a postwar explosion, the Barthian overthrow of the liberal establishment. No theological movement in Christian history effected a more dramatic transformation of its inherited landscape than the one led by Karl Barth in the 1920s and 1930s. For two centuries the pressure of modern science and historical criticism made the liberal strategy in theology seem imperative. That presumption was overturned with astonishing swiftness in the early 1920s, as Barthian "crisis theology" displaced liberalism in much of the Western Protestant world with a neo-Reformation perspective that, in Barth's case, combined dialectical brilliance, spiritual power, a prophetic edge, and a great and strange narrowness.

Every aspect of the Barthian revolt is loaded with irony. It blasted liberal theology for baptizing the zeitgeist, even as it did the same thing with the disillusioned spirit of its own age. It condemned liberal theology for abandoning the doctrine of revelation, even as it featured a liberal doctrine of revelation. It proclaimed that liberal theology was dead, even as Rudolf Bultmann and Paul Tillich created new forms of liberal theology. It led to a school called "neo-orthodoxy," a term that Barth hated for reasons that distinguished him from most Barthians. It changed the field profoundly, yet none of the major crisis theologians carried out Barth's approach to theology, and Tillich developed the twentieth century's major theological alternative – a system grounded in German idealism. After Barth was gone, and the age turned postmodern, the field of theology prized interreligious and postcolonial causes that were alien to Barth, except for the ways in which his thought brilliantly prefigured postmodern consciousness.

Karl Barth was born in Basel, Switzerland, in 1886, where he spent most of his life, though not as a youth. His mother, Anna Barth, was a hard-edged personality who made Barth allergic to strong-willed women for the rest of his life. His father Fritz Barth, a former pastor, taught at the College of Preachers in Basel, a new institution dedicated to opposing liberal theology and training preachers in biblical theology. In 1888 a group of theological conservatives, called "positives," at the University of

Kantian Reason and Hegelian Spirit: The Idealistic Logic of Modern Theology, First Edition. Gary Dorrien.
© 2012 John Wiley & Sons, Ltd. Published 2015 by John Wiley & Sons, Ltd.

Berne in the Swiss capital, called Fritz Barth to succeed Adolf Schlatter as a biblical theologian; thus, Karl Barth grew up in a conservative Reformed household near the university.

Fritz Barth, although reliably orthodox, had an independent streak. He prized scholarship, had friendly relations with Adolf Harnack, and tried on various occasions to mediate between his orthodox base and an ascending liberal opposition. In 1904 Karl Barth began his studies in theology, at Berne, where, despite his father's opposition, he embraced biblical criticism. Aching for the real thing, Barth moved to Berlin for a semester in 1906 and hung on Harnack's every word, admiring his lectures on Christian doctrine. At Fritz's behest, Barth moved to Tübingen to study under Schlatter, where he sneered at Schlatter's conservatism. After that he studied at Marburg under Wilhelm Herrmann, where he embraced Herrmann's Christocentric blend of Kant, Ritschl, and Schleiermacher. In 1908 he was ordained in a service conducted by his father in the Berne cathedral. Years later Barth recalled that he entered the ministry as a pure Marburg liberal who had "absorbed Herrmann through every pore."[1]

Herrmann's warm-hearted devotion to Christ assured Barth that liberal theology retained the essential gospel faith. Rationalistic forms of liberalism had no appeal to Barth, and Ernst Troeltsch's de-Christianized historicism left him cold, but Herrmann had the evangelical spirit. Barth later reflected: "One of the best remedies against liberal theology and other kinds of bad theology is to take them in bucketsful. On the other hand, all attempts to withhold them by strategem or force only causes people to fall for them even more strongly, with a kind of persecution complex." The moral of the story: Fritz Barth saved his son from a lifelong fascination with liberal theology by allowing him to study bad theology at prestigious schools. But when Barth turned away from his acquired liberalism, his father's conservative orthodoxy was not an option.[2]

For two years Barth preached liberal sermons at a German-speaking Reformed church in Geneva where Calvin had preached, and where his tiny audience found him strange. Afterwards, moving to Safenwil, Switzerland, he preached to a tiny congregation of farmers and shopkeepers that also shook their heads in perplexity. In both places only women attended church; Barth urged them to "think seriously about yourselves," to strive for the highest ideals, and to "try to become valuable." After services he puzzled that no one found his interpretations as inspiring or edifying as he had when he heard them from Herrmann.[3]

Ministry proved unsettling at best, but Barth's early ministry coincided with the emergence of the Religious Socialist movement in Switzerland, led by Zurich pastor Hermann Kutter and University of Zurich theology professor Leonard Ragaz. The Religious Socialists, especially Kutter, were religiously serious in a way that was new to Barth. They spoke and behaved as though it made all the difference in the world whether one believed in God. Barth later recalled, "From Kutter I simply learnt to speak the great word 'God' seriously, responsibly, and with a sense of its importance."[4]

Kutter was not ashamed of the gospel and not impressed with the achievements of capitalist civilization. Barth's exposure to Religious Socialism shook loose some of his acquired bourgeois culture-religion. He told his congregation that without a commitment to a kingdom-bringing social justice, their religion was a pack of lies. Having been touched, as he later recounted, "for the first time by the real problems of real life," he immersed himself in trade union issues and socialist theory, blending liberal theology with socialist politics. Barth still assumed, with Schleiermacher and Herrmann, that religious experience must be the generative ground of theology. At the same time he resisted the disturbing suspicion that he had been corrupted by the cultural chauvinism and nationalism of his German teachers.[5]

That suspicion helped to motivate Barth's railing against German and English militarism, which he kept up nearly every week from the pulpit for a year before Europe descended into war. He urged his tiny congregation that the teaching of Jesus was irreconcilable with the murderous violence of war and that modern Christians had to be anti-war. For a while Barth imagined that at least some of his teachers must have agreed. But on August 1, 1914 the Kaiser called the German nation to war, in an address written by Harnack. Two months later, 93 prominent German intellectuals issued a ringing manifesto of support for the Kaiser's war policy. Barth read the manifesto with revulsion, finding the names of nearly all his German theological teachers, including Harnack and Herrmann. He later compared the experience to the twilight of the gods.[6]

The spectacle of seeing his mentors promote the Kaiser's militarism was deeply alienating to Barth. Their appeal to a religiously normative "war experience" and their failure even to raise the question of national idolatry made him doubt the integrity of their theology. If liberal theology was so easily pushed aside by political expediency or so readily turned into an instrument of patriotic hubris, what good was it? In Barth's telling, the question answered itself: "A whole world of exegesis, ethics, dogmatics and preaching, which I had hitherto held to be essentially trustworthy, was shaken to the foundations, and with it, all the other writings of the German theologians." Liberal theology was obviously bankrupt, and he had to find an alternative to it.[7]

Actually it was not that simple. The story of how Barth rebelled against his liberal teachers and changed the direction of modern theology is the founding narrative of twentieth-century theology, notwithstanding that a good deal of it is wrong or exaggerated. Contrary to the story that Barth told, his career did not consist of a series of dramatic conversions, it took him six years to break from liberal theology, his development of an analogical method was an elongated affair too, and he never stopped being a dialectical theologian. His path to Barthian theology was more winding and complex than the usual rendering of it, partly because Barth told the story from the perspective of his later theology. I dissected this extremely tangled story in *The Barthian Revolt in Modern Theology*. Here it is enough to summarize, pausing briefly over his involvement in Religious Socialism.

The Religious Socialists were divided between an idealistic faction that wanted to Christianize the social democratic movement and a more quietist faction that wanted Christian Socialists to stay out of party politics. The first group, led by Ragaz, urged that Christians had a social mission to transform society into the kingdom of God. The second group, led by Kutter, warned that Christian Socialists would lose their Christian character if they entered the political struggle for power. The Ragaz activists blasted German militarism, they condemned the war unequivocally, and they had a coherent strategy of social and political transformation. The Kutter group sympathized with Germany and kept quiet about the war, yet it was also more radical in its Socialist identity. Most of the Ragaz-idealists lined up with Eduard Bernstein's social democratic revisionism, while Kutter sided with the radical Marxism of Karl Kautsky.[8]

Barth was torn between them. Politically he tended to side with the social democratic idealists. What was the point of calling for Socialism if you refused to work with actual unions and Socialist parties? Plus, the Ragaz-activists were right about the war. Unlike most of the European Socialist movement, which surprised and appalled Barth by marching off to war, the Ragaz social democrats held fast to the Socialist opposition to war. Barth was inclined to write off Kutter as a pro-German quietest, but his closest friend, pastor Eduard Thurneysen, cautioned him against that dismissal. Thurneysen suggested that Kutter's emphasis on "waiting for God" contained a deeper spiritual wisdom than Ragaz's eagerness to see signs of the kingdom in the anti-war opposition and the Socialist movement. Kutter understood that every hearing of the Word of God is problematic. While Ragaz stressed ethical idealism and the politics of social democracy, Kutter and Christoph Blumhardt stressed that people are enslaved without God. By the fall of 1915 Barth agreed that the religious part of Religious Socialism needed its own language, sphere, and basis. It needed to wait upon a God that does not submit to human plans. Instead of an activist agenda for building the kingdom, Christian Socialism needed formative spiritual communities that waited upon the movement of God's Spirit in the world.[9]

That was the crucial turn in Barth's twisting and turning path to a neo-Reformation theology. The first name by which the Barthian revolt came to be known was "crisis theology." Barth wrote that before the kingdom of God can become real to modern Christians "there must come a crisis that denies all human thought." Crisis theology was a reaction against the slaughter and destruction of World War I and the complicity of Barth's teachers in sacralizing the German war effort. More broadly, it was a response to the ferocious judgment of the war on European cultural pretension. Liberal theologians gave the impression of being comfortable with God and proud of their sophistication. Crisis theology was about shattered illusions, the experience of emptiness before a hidden God, and what Barth called the unexpected surge of spiritual meaning that he found in "the strange new world within the Bible."[10]

In January 1916 Barth told Thurneysen that he was becoming "frighteningly indifferent" to historical questions. To be sure, he allowed, he was prone to anti-historicism, which showed in his attraction to Herrmann. For years Barth debated Paul Wernle, a Troeltschian theologian at Basel, on this point. Wernle contended that historical consciousness was enriching and that the future of theology belonged to the history of religions school. To Barth this was a very dismal prospect; historicism made theology weak and shallow, and he doubted that any theologian could embrace Troeltschian historicism without being devoured by it. In a lecture in November 1915 titled "Wartime and the Kingdom of God," Barth argued that God was absent from modern life; Wernle cautioned that Barth was falling into apocalypticism. Two months later Barth told Thurneysen that soon they would have to "strike a great blow against the theologians."[11]

The following July he mentioned to Thurneysen that he was assembling a "copy-book" of comments on Paul's letter to the Romans that summarized Paul's message in modern language. Barth noted that he had discovered a "gold mine" for this project, a collection of biblical commentaries authored by his father's favorite teacher and spiritual exemplar, Württemberg biblical scholar Johann Tobias Beck. "As a biblical expositor he simply towers far above the rest of the company, also above Schlatter,"

Barth enthused. Beck had taught biblical interpretation to Barth's father and grand-father. His respect for the divine inspiration and canonical integrity of scripture gave his scholarship a spiritual depth that Barth missed in liberal criticism. It also brought Barth closer in feeling to the memory of his recently deceased father. He told Thurneysen that Beck's old-fashioned approach was "in part directly accessible and exemplary for us." It disclosed a world of religious meaning – the spiritual world of the Bible – that liberal scholarship never managed to find. Barth remarked, "The older generation may once more have some pleasure in us, but a bit differently from what it intended."[12]

Barth didn't know where he was going, but he was clear that he needed something stronger than his acquired liberalism. He fastened on the problem of the sermon, partly from practical necessity. He gave talks to pastors facing the same problem, where Barth admonished that the gospel message was too strong for modern ears because modern theologians and ministers reduced the gospel to their own "pitiably weak tones." Biblical criticism deconstructed the Bible's literary and religious history to get at its meaning, which obscured the spiritual truth of scripture, negating the driving spiritual force that makes the Bible holy scripture. Barth declared, "If we wish to come to grips with the contents of the Bible, we must dare to reach far beyond ourselves. The Book admits of nothing less." The answer that scripture gives is its own strange new world, "the world of God." There is a rushing stream in the Bible that carries us away if we allow ourselves to be taken by it: "We need only dare to follow this drive, this spirit, this river, to grow out beyond ourselves toward the highest answer."[13]

Faith opens the strange new world of the Bible to us, Barth urged. We cannot enter the world of scriptural truth by reading the Bible with false modesty or academic restraint, for these are passive qualities. Faith is a form of spiritual daring; more importantly, scripture offers an invitation to dare, an expression of divine grace. A new world enters and suffuses our ordinary world by the grace of God's Spirit, through faithful openness to the Word that scripture contains: "We may not deny nor prevent our being led by Bible 'history' far out beyond what is elsewhere called history – into a new world, into the world of God."[14]

Barth reasoned that the kingdom of God is not a second world standing apart from the existing "real" world. It is this existing world made new through the inbreaking power of the Spirit. At the same time, the Bible is not about how to find one's way to God and it is not terribly helpful with moral and practical questions. The Bible is about God's glory and sovereignty, and how God has found the way to estranged human beings. Barth praised the old conservatives for holding to this truism against Schleier-macher and the biblical critics; everything was at stake in taking revelation seriously: "Our fathers were right when they guarded warily against being drawn out upon the shaky scaffolding of religious self-expression."[15]

That raised the slippery issue of Pietism, since the "fathers" that Barth had in mind were conservative-leaning Pietists such as Beck, Friedrich August G. Tholuck, and C. H. Rieger. These were Barth's guides as he worked through Romans, in addition to commentaries by Calvin and Johannes Bengel. He also drew on his father's lecture notes and on Kutter's articles on Romans. Barth was wary of Pietist enthusiasm. At its worst it yielded gruesome revival preaching and fear-mongering threats of hellfire that Barth found repugnant. Even at its best it turned into a stopgap for the evangelical liberalism that Barth was trying to overcome. He told Thurneysen that when the moment came to strike a blow against the theologians, they would have to untangle the web of Pietist and historicist influences that they imbibed from their teachers.

Barth fretted that his conversion to biblical revelation came too late; he told Thurneysen, "If only we had been converted to the Bible *earlier* so that we would now have solid ground under our feet!" In fact, his turn against his teachers was perfectly timed. The colossal carnage of the war refuted, in Germany, the enthusiastic pro-war sermons of the early war. In Switzerland Barth preached to congregants who feared that the war would never end or that it would spill into their country. After February 1917 many of them feared that the Bolshevik revolution would spill into their country. By then all were pressed hard by commodity shortages and inflated living costs. Barth was never one to flatter his congregation with easy religion; even during wartime, he gave a blistering sermon against the kind of congregation that yearned for a pastor "who pleases the people." But he also preached sermons resembling the exuberant, hopeful, sometimes lyrical tone of his forthcoming book on Paul's letter to the Romans.[16]

Barth's *Römerbrief* was published in December 1918 with no thought of acclaim or a wide audience; he later recalled, "I had no inkling of the repercussions which would follow." With its appearance twentieth-century theology began. His first edition proclaimed that Paul taught that true history is made only through the inbreaking power of the Spirit. This spiritual truth could not be grasped by historical criticism or by cutting Paul's theology to fit the worldview of modern academic culture. Liberal theology contrasted the Christ myth of Paul to the social gospel of Jesus. It criticized Paul's Christology, his idea of blood redemption, his typology of Christ and Adam, his disregard of the historical Jesus, his devotion to scriptural authority, and his nonhistorical use of scripture. Barth's early sermons had recycled Harnack, Herrmann, and Marburg New Testament scholar Adolf Jülicher on these points. He had entered the ministry believing that Luther was superior to Paul and that Schleiermacher was superior to everyone. From the pulpit he had grappled candidly with the problem of how he should preach about contrived or mythological Pauline texts.[17]

Now he proclaimed that Paul's mythical gospel of redemption and resurrection was the true gospel of Christ. This was the source of the book's exuberant spirit, Barth's joyful discovery that Paul was greater than Luther, Calvin, and even Schleiermacher. In Barth's telling, Paul's religious message was a history-changing and history-transcending theology of salvation, grace, and glory. The core of this message was that Christ, through his redeeming death and resurrection, inaugurated a new world-embracing aeon of the Spirit that is the world's true salvation. The gospel is the proclamation of a new creation. As the redeeming "hinge of history," Jesus has inaugurated a new aeon of real history that is different from the old unreal aeon of sin and death. In the old aeon, Barth explained, God was hidden to the "old Adam" because of humankind's bondage to sin. In the new aeon of Christ's triumph over sin, God's sovereign grace works upon all unbelief and sin, as well as upon all faith and righteousness, to bring about God's purpose.[18]

Paul was an apostle of the kingdom of God who speaks to people of every age. The differences between his age and the modern age were unimportant. Modern biblical criticism had a rightful place as a preparatory discipline, Barth allowed, but beyond that, it did very little to help readers apprehend the Bible's meaning. Barth declared that if he were compelled to choose between biblical criticism and the old doctrine of biblical inspiration, "I should without hesitation adopt the later, which has a broader, deeper, more important justification." Biblical criticism, by itself, had little value, whereas the doctrine of inspiration was concerned with apprehending scriptural meaning. Liberal theology was weak because it historicized and psychologized the gospel. Barth preferred "to see through and beyond history into the spirit of the Bible, which is the Eternal Spirit."[19]

That was an echo of Plato's theory of forms and Kant's thing-in-itself. For Barth, as for Plato and Paul, salvation was about the restoration of a broken ideal and the hunger for a new age. For Barth, as for Plato and Kant, there was a "real reality" that lies beyond the world of appearance. In the new aeon of Christ's triumph over sin, God's grace worked upon faith *and* unbelief and sin to bring about God's purpose. Like the expressionist writers and painters that Barth admired at the time, he distinguished between the surface appearances of the so-called "real world" and the "real reality" that lies beneath the world of appearances. He embraced the expressionist thesis that true reality can be glimpsed only by disrupting or breaking up the world of appearances that empirical disciplines treat as "real." In Barth's telling, this was precisely what Paul's message of salvation accomplished. Paul's letter to the Romans offered an idol-breaking critique of every merely human strategy of salvation.[20]

To Barth, "so-called history" – the empirical subject of historical research – was the phenomenal world history in which people find themselves living under the judgment of sin and death. Paul did not believe, Barth cautioned, that ordinary history contains no sign of God's better world. Paul believed that the presence of the Law contains the promise of a world in which sin and death do not prevail. For Paul, the existence of the Law was "the highpoint of *so-called* history." But this Law can only judge and point, Barth explained; it cannot save, since it cannot generate a human capacity to fulfill its demands. Salvation comes only from the better world that the Law promises but cannot deliver. It comes only through the world of God, where no complete repudiation has ever taken place. God's concern is always the entire world. God works through belief and unbelief alike to bring about God's purpose of saving the entire world.[21]

But that was still a version of liberal theology, replacing historicist liberalisms with spiritual idealism. It emphasized experiences of value and treated the gospel message as a progress report, placing Moses, Plato, Kant, and Fichte in the same kingdom-bringing line as prophets of God's righteousness. On redemption, Barth was closer to Andreas Osiander than to Luther or Calvin. Osiander, a mid-sixteenth-century Lutheran theologian, opposed Luther's doctrine of imputed righteousness, contending that salvation triggers a substantial transference of Christ's righteousness to the believer. Barth's idea of salvation as the disclosure of a transforming "true world" of God, to the extent that it had a Reformation basis, was a page from Osiander. His first edition *Römerbrief* lumped religious socialism with liberal theology, Pietism, and conventional church religion as faulty vehicles of salvation, but he still spoke of the kingdom in Christian Socialist terms as the hidden "motor" that drives "so-called history" through its own "real history." In essence, Barth's first edition registered his joyful discovery of the supernatural nature of the kingdom, which breaks into human life as a world-transforming divine Word. The Word breaks into the world to create a new age of the Spirit.[22]

The book got a smattering of mixed reviews, all of which commented on its spiritual passion and torrential flow of metaphor, and it found a small group of appreciative readers, whom Barth had to caution against enthusiasm. He conceived the book as an exercise in theological scholarship, not a source of religious enthusiasm. Philipp Bachmann, stressing the "burning zeal" of Barth's work, described it favorably as a type of "'pneumatic-prophetic exegesis' redolent with an inexhaustible vividness." Young Emil Brunner, in a generally enthusiastic review, noted that the book's apparent naiveté produced a first impression of astonishment and surprise. Adolf Jülicher, decidedly unfavorable, allowed that Barth "knows how to speak penetratingly, at times charmingly, and always with colorful vividness."[23]

But did Barth's "pneumatic-prophetic exegesis" make sense? Did it offer a compelling expression of the gospel? The first stirrings of what became the "crisis theology" movement took place in the postwar debates over these questions. Jülicher played a leading role in this discussion, albeit as a liberal foil. It appalled him that Barth, a graduate of Marburg, explicitly lifted biblical inspiration over historical criticism. Jülicher admonished that denigrating "scientific exegesis" was not the way forward in theology. With sadness he noted that for young theologians like Barth and Friedrich Gogarten, nothing was more certain "than that there is no more progress in history, that development is forever at an end, and that no optimism in the interest of culture moves us anymore." Gogarten did not even try to make sense of history, and Barth was only slightly less extreme. Jülicher noted that Barth dressed up his book with often-mistaken scholarly glosses on textual and exegetical problems, which showed, at least, that he recognized that interpreting a difficult text from ancient times in a foreign language requires some critical expertise. But critical knowledge was a source of conflict for Barth, Jülicher explained, because Barth believed that the true meaning of scripture is spiritual, not historical. Barth tried to pass through historical understanding to the spiritual world of the Bible.[24]

There is a name for this kind of theology, Jülicher lectured. In the mid-second century, Marcion developed the very theological position that Barth now advanced as original to himself via Paul's letter to the Romans. The Marcionite Gnostics were explicit advocates of the anti-historical spiritualism that Barth read into Paul. They believed that those who came before themselves attained merely a historical understanding, not a spiritual understanding. Theologically, Jülicher observed, Marcion proceeded "with the same sovereign arbitrariness and assurance of victory, with the same one-sided dualistic approach of enmity to all that comes from the world, culture, or tradition, and never tired of tossing a few pet ideas in front of us." Marcion was not a pure Gnostic and neither was Barth, Jülicher allowed; so far, only Gogarten had taken a pure Gnostic flight from history. If Gogarten was a new Valentinus, stretching out his arms in writhing pain "toward the blessed pleroma above," Barth was a new Marcion, half-Gnostic, "with his radical dualism of all or nothing and his wrath against those who take only half."[25]

The first edition of *Romans* took a similar pounding from lesser-known scholars such as Karl Ludwig Schmidt (who also compared Barth to Marcion) and young Rudolf Bultmann, who dismissed the book as "enthusiastic revivalism" that reinterpreted history as myth. Bultmann welcomed Barth's critique of culture-religion, but judged that otherwise it offered "little else than an arbitrary adaptation of the Pauline Christ myth." Barth, absorbing these reviews, tried at first to take them in stride. He told Thurneysen that Jülicher's critique felt more like a "gentle evening rain" than a "fearful thunderstorm." He found it fascinating that biblical scholars and other liberals were so eager to pin a heretic's hat on him. In the face of such criticism, he judged, it was best to avoid the spectacle of a youthful rebellion against an aging establishment: "In the presence of these scholars who know twenty-five times as much as we do we shall in the future lift our hats more respectfully, even though it seems to us quite idolatrous."[26]

At least the liberal establishment was taking the trouble to refute him; to Barth, that showed that "the idol totters." In a sensational address at the 1919 Tambach Conference on Religion and Social Relations, Barth gave notice that he sought to knock the idol off its pedestal. At Tambach he met Gogarten – a prolific, aggressive, brilliant young pastor, never lacking in cheek – for the first time, and made several new friends, notably Günther Dehn and Hans Ehrenberg. Barth declared, "We must win again the mighty sense of reality in which Paul is one with Plato and the prophets. Christ is the absolutely *new from above;* the way, the truth, and the life of *God* among men; the Son of Man, in whom humanity becomes aware of its *immediacy* to God." He gave a rousing farewell to politicized religion, including religious socialism. The last thing that theology needed was to secularize Christ "for the sake of social democracy, or pacifism, or the youth movement, or something of the sort – as yesterday it would have been for the sake of liberal culture or our countries, Switzerland or Germany."[27]

This display of otherworldly bravado appealed to many pastors and academics in the aftermath of the war. They were finished with Christian arguments for supporting or renewing German society, at least for a while. Some were embarrassed at having preached pro-war sermons. Many felt that even the more respectable proponents of politicized culture religion – Harnack, Troeltsch, Friedrich Naumann – had brought Christianity to a point of religious bankruptcy. Naumann had started as a Christian Socialist, trying to dissuade workers from the anticlericalism of the Social Democrats, while resisting his group's anti-Semitic wing. He had drifted to a politically moderate nationalism that pulled back on his Christian and Socialist commitments, eventually founding the German Democratic Party, a left-liberal party to the right of the Social Democrats. His lodestar was national power, always in the name of building a healthy social order. During the war Barth had argued with Naumann about their diverging trajectories, as Naumann defended Germany's war aims. After the war Barth recalled that Naumann kept up with church affairs "with a certain mild superiority, as one who has looked behind the scenes and no longer lets himself be taken in." Naumann remembered his Christian Socialist days with a sad smile, having moved beyond his youthful idealism. In 1918 he was sufficiently prominent to be considered for the presidency of the new government. Barth's reaction was, "All these things will I give thee, if thou wilt fall down and worship me."[28]

By 1920 many of the academics and pastors who came to conferences were looking for a new kind of modern Christianity. Barth's show-stopping appearance at Tambach made him a figure to be reckoned with in German theology. The doors of German universities and church groups opened to him. Gogarten became Barth's most important ally next to Thurneysen, emphasizing the non-religious worldliness of biblical piety. Prone to sharp replies, Gogarten gave many on behalf of himself and Barth, insisting that time and history made no difference to faith. Liberal scholars like

Jülicher derided Barth's spiritual exegesis with "superior mockery," Gogarten observed. But the joke was on them for believing that their historical tools took hold of the content of Christian faith. The age of liberal theology was over: "It is the destiny of our generation to stand between the times." Gogarten admonished that Christian theology was supposed to be about God's Word, but liberal theologians were not open to any word that could not be subjected to scientific control: "Your concepts were strange to us, always strange ... You do not know how it tormented us that we could hear nothing more ... You left us empty ... We received much that was scholarly, much that was interesting, but nothing that would have been worthy of this word."[29]

Liberal theology relativized everything that it touched, and its value was relative to the world of its time. With self-absolving drama, Gogarten declared that the guilt for German de-Christianization and national catastrophe rested on the old liberals: "We never belonged to your period." He observed that to his teachers, he and Barth seemed to be, somehow, radical and reactionary at the same time. Though fed a diet of Schleiermacher, Ritschl, Harnack, and Jülicher, they turned to Nietzsche and Kierkegaard: "Today we are witnessing the demise of your world. We can be calm about all that concerns this decline as if we were seeing the extinction of something with which we had no connection at all." In the crisis of European civilization, Gogarten urged, the only response that sufficed was to become open to God's creative activity and endure the divine judgment.[30]

"Here is a dreadnought on our side and against our opponents," Barth enthused to Thurseysen. "I have great expectations concerning him." Barth admired Gogarten's intellectual energy and his zeal for battle against the theological establishment. He took great satisfaction, for a while, in having such a tenacious ally, ignoring that both of them relied on arguments about faith, history, and Luther that they got from Herrmann, a pillar of the discredited passing establishment. By 1920 Barth could see the idol tottering. At a student conference at Aarau he ridiculed the idea of an outside or objective approach to theology, adding that biblical piety is against religion too. In Barth's telling, biblical piety held fast to a peculiar kind of worldliness that refused to regard anything as sacred. Only God is sacred, and in the scriptural witness God is holy, incomparable, and unattainable. God cannot be grasped or put to use; God is only to be served and can only be served in obedience: "He is not a thing among other things, but the *Wholly Other,* the infinite aggregate of all merely relative others. He is not the form of religious history but is the Lord of our life, the eternal Lord of the world." Though Barth still described the Easter message in Herrmannian liberal terms, he ascribed an importance to it that was foreign to most liberal preaching: "The Easter message becomes truth, movement, reality, as it is expressed – or it is not the Easter message which is expressed. Let us be satisfied that all Biblical questions, insights, and vistas focus upon this common theme."[31]

One bewildered listener, Harnack, was appalled. He told a friend, "The effect of Barth's lecture was just staggering. Not one word, not one sentence could I have said or thought. I saw the sincerity of Barth's speech, but its theology frightened me." Harnack compared Barth's thinking to a meteor "rushing toward its disintegration," judging that "this sort of religion is incapable of being translated into real life." To Barth directly he allowed that perhaps the church needed to be shaken up "a bit," but he advised Barth to keep his religious worldview to himself and not make an "export article" of it. In Barth's telling of their encounter, "Finally I was branded a Calvinist and intellectualist and let go with the prophecy that according to all the experiences of church history I will found a sect and receive inspirations."[32]

To Harnack, Barth's approach to theology was apocalyptic and self-negating. If Barth was the future, modern theology was finished as a critical, rational enterprise worthy of academic respect. From Harnack's perspective, the worst aspect of Barth's theology was its eschatological character, but Barth decided the opposite – that to really break from liberalism, he had to heighten his eschatological alternative. By then he had decided not to re-issue his book on Romans; it was already alien to him. Barth had written it in the fresh excitement of a conversion experience, but on reflection, he realized that his rendering of Paul was still a form of liberalism. He was put off by some of the book's positive reviews, which praised Barth's "enthusiasm." He had begun to study Kierkegaard, Fyodor Dostoyevsky, and Swiss anti-theologian Franz Overbeck, absorbing something from each that made him dissatisfied with his book. The second edition had to be a different book.[33]

Fire Alarm of a Coming New World

The exuberant mood of the first edition gave way to the angry, sharp-edged, and prophetic spirit of the book's immediately famous second edition of 1921. The first edition was long on repetition, exaggeration, hyperbole, dashes, exclamation points, and other expressionist techniques, but the second edition was loaded with them. Both editions showed Barth's affection for the two Blumhardts, Johann Christoph Blumhardt (1805–1880), a renowned Lutheran preacher and healer, and his son Christoph Blumhardt, the first Lutheran pastor in Germany to join the Social Democratic Party. The vibrantly eschatological faith of the Blumhardts gave Barth compelling examples of living in the reality of the resurrected Jesus. Barth owed more to his friendship with the younger Blumhardt than he owed to Kierkegaard, Dostoyevsky, or Overbeck; on the other hand, Blumhardt was a Christian witness, not a theorist. To overhaul his book, Barth needed some different concepts, which he got from Kierkegaard, Dostoyevsky, and Overbeck.[34]

The immediate problem was the governing schema. Barth's first edition *Romans* featured a sacred history (*Heilsgeschichte*) scheme in which the stream of God's "real history" made episodic appearances in the history of Israel (especially the prophets) and in figures such as Socrates and Plato before it broke fully into the world in the fullness of time (the new age) in Jesus Christ. Brunner interpreted this scheme as an endorsement of liberal divine indwelling, a "divine reservoir in us." Barth shuddered at Brunner's review; at Aarou he put it stridently. God is not an object or a process within or among other subjects. God is the "wholly other" Spirit of sovereign glory and grace, "the infinite aggregate of all merely relative others." Harnack was right about Barth's purpose at Aarou; his speech was a declaration of independence from the liberal tradition. Thus Barth had to rewrite his entire book. Under the influence of Kierkegaard's and Overbeck's attacks on Christendom, he eliminated his organic metaphors of the kingdom and overhauled the age-of-Adam/age-of-Christ scheme that supported his concept of sacred history.[35]

Overbeck was a strange figure whose theological legacy got weirder after Barth appropriated him. An atheist, he taught New Testament and early church history from 1870 to 1897 at Basel, and his best friend was Friedrich Nietzsche. Overbeck had no animosity for Christianity; he simply believed that the Christian religion was untrue and that it was fated to become extinct by "a gentle fading away." Employing an early form of form criticism, he taught that genuine Christianity ended with the apostolic age. The earliest Christian communities were intensely eschatological and apocalyptic, expecting an imminent apocalyptic intervention from above. Overbeck invented the term *Urgeschichte* (primal history) to describe early Christianity's relationship to historical process. The early Christians lived in history but were not part of it, he explained; their world was a counter-world to ordinary history. They had no concept of "Christianity" as a new religion that would produce its own historical tradition. They hoped and expected to be delivered from history very soon by a history-ending act of God.[36]

Overbeck acknowledged that it was necessary and inevitable that the postapostolic church relinquished the apocalyptic consciousness of original Christianity. He believed that Paul was a transition figure who belonged already to a second stage of adjusted Christian awareness while retaining some marks of apocalyptic super-history. Overbeck found signs of the church's early adjustment in the book of Acts. But institutional Christianity, he insisted, is not Christian at all. Genuine Christianity thrived on the super-historical expectation of Christ's imminent second coming. Christianity, when it lost this expectation, lost its vitality and itself. Patristic Christianity adopted the literary forms of the dominant profane culture, the unique consciousness and literature of early Christianity were lost altogether, and an oxymoron, "historical Christianity," replaced the gospel faith. The only kind of "Christianity" that could make its peace with history was the kind that turned a super-historical faith into a religion.[37]

Overbeck believed that he was witnessing the final stage of this degenerative process in the bourgeois culture-Protestantism of his time. Modern Christianity was totally corrupt. It perpetuated the illusion of remaining within Christianity in order to keep its place at the cultural table. Bismarck, the perfect symbol of this degeneration, cared nothing for Christianity, but he valued the social benefits of culture Protestantism. Overbeck warned that those who defended modern Christianity were kidding themselves about their relation to Christianity and the viability of their apologetics. In actuality they were twice removed from genuine Christianity, first by their historical religiosity and second by their modernism. Their actual religion was modernism, but rather than face up to their novel situation within the so-called "Christian tradition," they pathetically linked themselves with Luther, Augustine, Paul, and Jesus. Overbeck's later work sought to free modern people from this regressive attachment by playing up the contradictions between modern culture and genuine Christianity.[38]

In 1919 Overbeck's lecture notes and papers were published, fourteen years after his death, by one of his former students. The book was badly edited, but its blast against the very idea of "Christian religion" was intoxicating to Barth, who prized Kierkegaard for similar reasons. Just as Kierkegaard emphasized the qualitative break between time and eternity, and claimed that Christianity did not exist in modern Christendom, Overbeck contended that one must choose between Christianity and history. "Historical" means "subject to time," Overbeck explained, but only a thoroughly distorted "Christianity" could be subject to time. History is precisely the basis on which genuine Christianity cannot be established, for the religion of Christ himself never had any historical existence whatsoever under the name of Christianity. Overbeck and Kierkegaard gave ballast to Barth's animus against all forms of Christian religiosity and historicism. Both were allies in his struggle to "kick against the pricks" of Christendom. "We rejoice at this book," Barth declared. "We greet it gladly in the hope that it will raise up comrades for us in our loneliness."[39]

History was a dead end. In 1910, Barth had listened to Troeltsch lecture at Aarau about the coming end of Christendom and the advent of a cultural ice age. This depressing experience gave him a forbidding picture of where the historical approach led. Overbeck and Kierkegaard helped Barth move beyond Herrmann's compromised anti-historicism, which was sufficiently compromised that Herrmann felt comfortable in liberal Protestantism. With Overbeck, Barth affirmed that Christian history is an unavoidably degenerative process; in Overbeck's words, history is "an abyss into which Christianity has been thrown wholly against its will." With Kierkegaard, Barth affirmed that Christianity is about the invasion of the eternal into time in the moment. With Dostoyevsky he judged that the church prefers to give people what they want – mystery, authority, miracle – rather than preach freedom through Christ. With Christoph Blumhardt, Barth conceived Christianity as a kingdom faith that proclaims the transformation of the present from beyond.[40]

His appropriation of Overbeck was strange at best. Barth played up Overbeck's remark that "theology can no longer be established through anything but audacity," brushing past Overbeck's next sentence, that even audacity would be useless to anyone who had "already lost faith in theology as a result of studying early church history." Barth's acquaintance with Blumhardt shielded him from Overbeck's destructive edge, giving him a picture of a vibrant modern Christianity that was thoroughly eschatological. Both Blumhardts founded their ministries on the anticipation of a new outpouring of the Spirit of the risen Jesus. Overbeck and the younger Blumhardt stood together in Barth's mind, but faced in opposite directions: "Blumhardt stood as a forward-looking and hopeful Overbeck; Overbeck as a backward-looking, critical Blumhardt. Each was the witness to the mission of the other."[41]

Together these witnesses helped Barth declare his break from liberal theology. His second edition *Romans* retained the Pauline dialectic of Adam and Christ, but stopped describing the new creation under Christ as a new world that becomes a "life process" in human history. The new world cannot be born until the old world has died, he judged. All human history stands under the sign of sin, death, and judgment, including Christian history. Liberal theology taught that history has an inner capacity for renewal because God is an aspect of the temporal order. Barth's reply was a version of Kierkegaardian Religiousness B and the sickness unto death: History is not a life process brought to fulfillment by a divine indwelling. History is the life of the old world that exists under the judgment of death. History lives "between the times" – between the primal divine history that Overbeck called *Urgeschichte* and the Parousia that will bring history to an end.

Moreover, the "object" of theology is not an object at all, or a process within or among other objects. Writing theology is like trying to draw a bird in flight, Barth analogized. Apart from the movement, theology has no standpoint or ground. That is, apart from the movement of the Spirit that transcends and penetrates human history, theology is "absolutely meaningless, incomprehensible, and impossible." Barth warned that theologians were tempted to make an objectified thing of the movement. Apart from God's history-shaking movement in history, "a movement which has neither its origin nor its aim in space, in time, or in the contingency of things," theology is nothing but idolatry.[42]

Barth realized that his negative dialecticism stood in danger of losing any basis for making positive affirmations. With Blumhardt's witness in mind he declared, "There *must still* be a way from there to here." Theology, Barth reasoned, is possible only as "inner waiting" for and openness to God's revelation: "However much the holy may frighten us back from its unattainable elevation, no less are we impelled to venture our lives upon it immediately and completely." To be a faithful Christian is to live, like Blumhardt, in "the fullness of what is" while waiting inwardly "for that which seeks to be through the power from on high."[43]

For Barth, both aspects of "hurrying and waiting" were crucial. Blumhardt lived in the fullness of the present historical crisis. He had no use for compromised Socialism, compromised Christianity, or compromised fusions of them. He did not try to lure workers away from Social Democratic socialism. Neither did he accommodate the gospel faith to modern cultural sensibilities, like liberal theology. He joined the Social Democratic party outright and refused to trim either his Socialism or his Christianity. Barth observed, "No world war and no revolution could make him a liar." Though Blumhardt lost his pastorate and most of his German followers in the process, he was joyful in anticipating God's kingdom. Barth remarked: "The unique element, and I say it quite deliberately, the prophetic, in Blumhardt's message and mission consists in the way in which the hurrying and the waiting, the worldly and the divine, the present and the coming, again and again meet, were united, supplemented one another, sought and found one another."[44]

That was the ideal, something that Barth had to have if he was going to dance so perilously with Overbeck and Kierkegaard. Blumhardt's radical Socialism was sustained by his Christian hope, which he never reduced to his politics. He saw the idol in most forms of Christianity, Socialism, and Christian Socialism. Barth, dedicating himself to the critique of idolatry, described all religions as monuments to the "no-God." The only basis for a non-idolatrous affirmation of God and the world, he contended, is "the possibility of a new order absolutely beyond human thought." Only a kingdom-oriented eschatological Christianity bears any true relation to Christ. But for the kingdom to become an actual possibility for theology, "there must come a crisis that denies all human thought."[45]

Barth's second edition *Romans* announced that the death rattle of Christendom presented such a possibility. The gospel message is "the fire alarm of a coming new world," he declared. Leaning on Kierkegaard's notion of the "moment" and his dialectic of time and eternity, Barth presented the apparent crisis of the moment as a permanent, universal condition that negates all human strategies of salvation. Human history stands under the crisis of judgment, he warned. This crisis was the presupposition of Paul's message. Barth explained: "In this world men find themselves to be imprisoned. In fact the more profoundly we become aware of the limited character of the possibilities which are open to us here and now, the more clear it is that we are farther from God, that our desertion of Him is more complete, and the consequences of that desertion more vast than we had ever dreamed."[46]

Barth insisted that God's power to save us from this imprisonment cannot be detected in the world of nature or in our souls. God is unknown, "and precisely because He is unknown, He bestows life and breath and all things." God's power is completely different from the powers of observable forces: "It is the KRISIS of all power, that by which power is measured, and by which it is pronounced to be something and – nothing, nothing and – something." God is neither a power alongside other powers nor a supernatural power standing above other powers. God's power, Barth reasoned, is "that which sets all these powers in motion and fashions their eternal rest. It is the Primal Origin by which they all are dissolved, the consummation by which they all are established." God's power is "pure and preeminent" and beyond all other powers.[47]

Luther taught that faith directs itself toward invisible realities. Only that which is hidden can provide an opportunity for faith. Barth emphasized that this is a Pauline theme: "The Gospel of salvation can only be believed in; it is a matter for faith only. It demands choice. This is its seriousness." The gospel is a scandal to those who cannot accept its inner contradiction, but to those who cannot escape the necessity of the contradiction, the gospel becomes a matter of faith: "Faith is awe in the presence of the divine incognito; it is the love of God that is aware of the qualitative distinction between God and man and God and the world; and therefore it is the affirmation of the divine 'No' in Christ, of the shattering halt in the presence of God." The righteousness of God is manifested wherever God's faithfulness encounters human faithfulness. Barth contended that this is the theme of the Pauline gospel message.[48]

All of Kierkegaard's major theological concepts were there: the dialectic of infinite qualitative distinction, the "divine incognito" of the incarnation, the scandal of faith, the sickness unto death, the dialectic of revelatory unveiling, the leap, the paradoxical character of the gospel, and the "Moment," the transhistorical divine act through which God breaks into history from beyond. The only Kierkegaardian trope that Barth left behind was his preoccupation with how one becomes a Christian, which was too self-absorbed for Barth's purpose. Like Kierkegaard, Barth insisted that faith is "always a leap into the darkness of the unknown, a flight into empty air." Faith cannot be communicated to oneself or to one from another; it must be revealed. Because the revelation in Christ is that of God's righteousness, it is necessarily "the most compete veiling of His incomprehensibility." Through Christ, God is revealed "as the Unknown, speaking in eternal silence." Just as Kierkegaard argued that true Christianity is destroyed when it becomes a form of direct communication, losing its capacity to shock, Barth asserted that in Jesus "the communication of God begins with a rebuff, with the exposure of a vast chasm, with the clear revelation of a great stumbling block." To have faith in Jesus is to call upon God in God's utter incomprehensibility and hiddenness. To live faithfully is not to seek rational stability or religious comfort, but to embrace "the absolute scandal of His death upon the cross."[49]

Luther taught that Romans 3:22–24 is the kernel of Christian scripture: "For there is no distinction, since all have sinned and fall short of the glory of God; they are now justified by his grace as a gift, through the redemption that is in Christ Jesus." With Luther and Kierkegaard, Barth proclaimed that the righteousness of God is displayed by the absolute separation between God and humanity. Nothing can be known about God apart from this recognition. The paradoxical nature of Christianity must be maintained absolutely; otherwise the scandal is obscured. Overbeck got it right, Barth contended; Christianity is a problem "which is itself essentially a riddle," which hangs a question mark on every human achievement. Barth admonished: "Nothing must be allowed to disturb this paradox; nothing must be retained of that illusion which permits a supposed religious or moral or intellectual experience to remove the only sure ground of salvation, which is the mercy of God." Religion never saved anyone, but because God is merciful and God has laid upon all people without distinction the command to have faith, the possibility exists "that all flesh may see His salvation."[50]

Barth stressed that this message of salvation pays no respect to circumstance. Appropriating Kierkegaard's concept of the Moment, Barth heightened his claim that Paul speaks to all people of every age. Salvation, he declared, is about the invasion of the eternal into time in the Moment, which is not a "moment" *in* time, but the eschatological Moment in which redeemed sinners are clothed with the righteousness of God: "We remove from the 'Moment' when the last trump sounds all likeness to the past and the future, and thereby proclaim the likeness of all times, of all past and future." In God there is no past or future. The fact that Paul lived long ago is irrelevant to the truth of his message. If Paul was right, Barth contended, we lack any ground for boasting except hope: "We are deprived of the possibility of projecting a temporal thing into infinity or of confining eternity within the sphere of time."[51]

The dialectic of time and eternity made paradox the essential language of faith. Barth's text abounded with metaphors of disruption, cleavage, and faith. For him, as for Kierkegaard, God was an impossibility whose possibility cannot be avoided. "God is pure negation," Barth declared. "He is both 'here' and 'there.' He is the negation of the negation in which the other world contradicts this world and this world the other world. He is the death of our death and the non-existence of our non-existence." Barth likened the grace of God to an explosion that blasts everything away without leaving a trace. Divine grace is not a religious possibility standing alongside sin, he cautioned. It is a "shattering disturbance, an assault which brings everything into question." Then how does the new world of the Spirit make contact with the existing world of Adam? In a striking image, often quoted, Barth replied that it touches the old world "as a tangent touches a circle, that is, without touching it." Because the new creation does not touch the old world, "it touches it as its frontier – as the new world." Christianity is true only as eschatology.[52]

This eliminated the possibility of systematic theology, among other things. Barth was fine with that, until he became a theology professor: "If I have a system, it is limited to a recognition of what Kierkegaard called the 'infinite qualitative distinction' between time and eternity, and to my regarding this as possessing negative as well as positive significance: 'God is in heaven, and thou on earth.'" Within time, the receiver of grace experiences eternity in the absolute moment of revelation and anticipates the complete overcoming of time by eternity.[53]

Did that mean that God is part of the dialectic of finite and infinite existence? Did the prohibition on projecting temporal things into infinity apply to the dialectic itself? Kierkegaard interpreted the divine-human relation from the standpoint of the reflective self. He tried to explain how an existing individual could appropriate revelation and become a Christian. Against Hegel's absorption of the individual into the dialectic of Spirit, Kierkegaard held out for the reality of the reflective individual self who finds unique, unsubstitutable truth in the process of seeking self-knowledge. His existentialism was straightforward and consuming, emphasizing the existential nature of Christian truth. For Kierkegaard, the necessary precondition for becoming a Christian was to become unconditionally turned inward. Did Barth go that far with Kierkegaard? Did crisis theology rest on the Kierkegaardian dialectic of existence and its theory of religious truth as existential encounter?

Many Barthians assumed that both answers were "yes." In the early going, Gogarten and Brunner were prominent among them. For decades, most interpreters of Barth said the same thing, interpreting early Barthian theology as a Kierkegaardian analysis of the human predicament that appealed to revelation as the solution to a fallen human existence. Gogarten, Brunner, Bultmann, and many other theologians associated with the Barthian movement conceived the divine-human relation on the basis of Kierkegaard's dialectical understanding of the structure of human existence.[54]

This reading of Barth's crisis theology is a foundation of the conventional interpretation of Barth's theological development, classically formulated by Hans Urs von Balthasar, according to which Barth shifted, in the early 1930s, from a predominantly dialectical mode of argument to a predominantly analogical mode. Balthasar explained that Barth, under the pressure of his need to find a constructive ground for dogmatic statements, and under the influence of his study of Anselm's approach to theology as faith seeking understanding, developed a method that mediated between the theologies of exaggerated immanence (liberalism) and transcendence (crisis theology). Barth's analogy of faith, in this telling, was carefully constructed as an alternative to the Roman Catholic analogy of being. His development of the analogy of faith and his repudiation of existential dialecticism made it possible for him to construct his massive dogmatic system, *Church Dogmatics*. On various occasions in his later career Barth endorsed the main outline of this reading. Those who dissent from von Balthasar's enormously influential account find themselves in the awkward position of claiming that they understand Barth better than he understood himself.[55]

But Barth's recollections of his early career were often faulty and he had a lifelong tendency to exaggerate the degree of his various shifts of position. Contrary to the claim that he dropped dialectical reasoning in his later theology, and despite his lament that he was "the originator of this unfortunate term" (dialectical theology), his later theology contained key dialectical elements, especially the dialectic of veiling and unveiling. These factors and others related to them fuel the revisionist account of Barth's development formulated by Michael Beintker, Ingrid Spieckermann, Bruce McCormack and others, which corrects the exaggerated claim that Barth fundamentally changed his position in the early 1930s. Barth was never a thoroughgoing Kierkegaardian, because he did not adopt Kierkegaard's anthropocentric starting point. He never dropped his dialecticism, although his thinking became increasingly analogical in the 1920s and 1930s. And even his crisis theology writings already made "Barthian" arguments against yoking the gospel faith to any philosophical analysis or worldview.[56]

Though Barth's second edition *Romans* leaned on Kierkegaard's concepts, the point of his theological turn was to focus on God as the subject of revelation. This was the eschatological turn in the Arau speech that horrified Harnack, that "the Bible has only *one* theological interest ... interest in God Himself." The Bible takes no interest in religious experience or the sacred whatsoever, Barth insisted; it cares only about God's holy presence and rule. Thus, in the ordinary sense of the term, the Bible has no interest in "history." Barth's second edition *Romans* hammered on this point, brushing aside Kierkegaard's preoccupation with the integrity of individual human existence: "There is only life under His judgment and under His promise; there is only life characterized by death but qualified, through the death of Christ, as the hope of life eternal. The Lord alone is the assurance of promise."[57]

The crucial difference between Barth and most of his allies in the crisis theology movement was there from its beginning. He was not always clear or consistent in expressing it. The contrasts between Barth and Tillich were too obvious not to acknowledge, but Barth declined, in the early going, to accentuate his differences with Gogarten and Bultmann. He had movement reasons for holding back; in addition, he wasn't sure that he could defend his position from their objections. In 1921 Barth began his academic career as Honorary Professor of Reformed Theology at Göttingen, a position for which he felt grossly unqualified. He had no doctorate, he did not own a copy of the Reformed confessions nor had he ever read them, and he had, as he confessed, "other horrendous gaps in my knowledge." For years he struggled to fill the gaps, immersing himself in the history of Christian dogmatics, whereby he became a dogmatic theologian himself.[58]

Barth's second edition *Romans* shot him into prominence as the prophet of a new age of theology. His soaring, dramatic, volcanic prose and his torrential flow of metaphor made the reigning liberalism seem sterile by comparison. If history stands under the crisis of divine judgment and death, a different fundamental dialectic was needed. The dialectic of the first edition was too optimistic, like liberalism. The later Barth turned to Luther and Calvin to get his bearings, but in 1921 Barth didn't know either of them very well. His second edition *Romans,* leaning on Kierkegaard, stressed the infinite qualitative difference between God and humankind. In the Hegelian and Marxist traditions, dialectic is a critical process, the dynamic of history that makes history move. Barth, explicating Paul's theology via Kierkegaard, affirmed the movement, but also its dissolution. Paul did not think of God as an aspect of the historical or evolutionary process, Barth stressed. To Paul, God was a personal supracosmic reality, absolute in power, and free for us precisely because he was sovereign.

Crisis theology was an explosion of culture-sundering dialectics that played up the Kierkegaardian cleavages between God and world, existence and essence, and faith and reason. Against liberal theology, Barth asserted the priority of the Word of God for theology; but against Protestant orthodoxy, he rejected any identification of the divine Word with the biblical text. Barth took his doctrine of revelation from Herrmann, who got it from Hegel: revelation is divine *self*-revealing, not the disclosure of propositional truths about God or anything else. Barth did not acknowledge, however, that the linchpin of his theology was a liberal idea; he never managed to say it. He did say that any human apprehension of revelation is limited by the incomprehensible otherness of God and the impossibility of extricating oneself from the revelatory act. Theology made progress only as a dialectical process of question and answer, answer and question, in faithful anticipation of the Spirit's movement, through which an always-fallible discernment of the ineffable divine mystery takes place.

For as long as Barth believed that the crisis theologians held in common Barth's Pauline rendering of faith, he held back on his disagreements with most of them. Faith is the miraculous possibility of constantly new beginning. There is no way to faith, for faith is its own presupposition. Faith is a form of daring, a leap into the unknown, not a possession or the end of an argument. The early Barth put it in self-dramatizing, Kierkegaardian fashion, boasting about leaping into the dark. The later Barth dropped his wild Expressionist tropes and his reliance on Kierkegaard, settling for traditional doctrines that he interpreted as analogies of faith; otherwise he could not have written twelve volumes of *Church Dogmatics*. But in both cases Barth pressed the Pauline theme that faith is a spiritual gift of the Holy Spirit, and he did it dialectically, stressing that God remains hidden even when disclosed in revelation. Faith is not a matter of grasping a revelation that cannot be held, but a matter of being open to being held in God's ever-gracious hands.

Dialectic in the Service of Dogmatics

When Barth put it negatively, he charged that liberal theology turned faith into a human achievement, it consigned Paul's religious claims to the worldview of mythical consciousness, and it evaded the true subject matter of scripture, the Spirit of Christ. His teachers were appalled by these arguments and their electrifying impact on theology. How could Barth think he could move directly from Paul's epistle to the crisis of modern civilization? How could he expound Paul's skewed interpretation of Hebrew scripture, his deprecation of the historical Jesus, his theory of blood redemption, and his doctrine of predestination as though Paul were above criticism? How could he ignore the chasm between Paul's mythological worldview and modern consciousness? Barth waved off the guardians of liberalism, noting that their books on Paul were tame and boring. Paul was never boring, and he always stood on the edge of heresy. If Barth was some kind of heretic, that made him something like Paul. Barth countered that at least he tried to understand what the Bible said before he dismissed it.[59]

But Rudolf Bultmann was a different kind of critic. Bultmann was a product of the history of religions school at Marburg, where his *Doktorvater,* Johannes Weiss, taught him to understand early Christianity in its context among the religions of the eastern Mediterranean during the Hellenistic age. His early writings distinguished between the noncultic Jesus of Palestinian Christianity and the mythical Christ of cultic Hellenistic Christianity. Bultmann's theological perspective was similar to Barth's, though more liberal. In 1921 his pioneering work in form criticism, *The History of the Synoptic Tradition,* established the probable community origins of the sayings and narrative units of the synoptic gospels. It also established him as a major figure in biblical scholarship. Bultmann went on to become the leading New Testament scholar of the twentieth century. Three times, over a thirty-year period, Barth and Bultmann debated how theology should be done. The first debate was about biblical interpretation; the second was about theology and philosophy; the third was about theology and myth. But it was always the same argument about the place of worldviews in theology.[60]

Though Bultmann dismissed Barth's first edition *Romans,* he took a mixed view of the second edition, praising Barth's recovery of Paul's existential understanding of faith, while objecting that Barth still interpreted history as myth. Bultmann complained that Barth distorted the heterogeneous character of scripture by treating it exclusively as a witness to the Spirit of Christ. The Spirit of Christ was surely to be found in Paul's letter, Bultmann allowed, but so were Hellenistic sacramental beliefs, strains of Jewish theology, the history of the Pauline Christ myth, and Gnostic redeemer myths. Barth's either/or was unrealistic. One did not have to choose between historical criticism and attending to the Word in the words. No writer speaks only from the subject matter. Even Paul listened to other spirits besides the Spirit of Christ. To Bultmann, good biblical scholarship approached the text as a witness to Christ *and* a heterogeneous construction.[61]

Barth replied that this seemingly reasonable approach had its own distortions. The Spirit of Christ does not compete within scripture alongside other spirits, he argued. To take that approach is to fall back into liberalism, where the critic identifies favorite passages with the Spirit of Christ and writes off the rest as myth or conjecture. To Barth, the point was to perceive "that the whole is placed under the crisis of the Spirit of Christ." Of course the text as a whole contains the voices of other spirits, he acknowledged; heterogeneity was obvious. But how was the whole to be understood in relation to its true subject matter, the Spirit of Christ? That was the question. The answer was not to arrogate oneself above Paul or the gospel writers as their schoolmaster: "We must be content if, despite other spirits, we are not wholly bereft of the Spirit; content if, standing by Paul's side, we are able to teach and learn; content with a readiness to discern in a spiritual fashion what is spiritually intended; and satisfied also to recognize that the voice with which we proclaim what we have received is primarily nothing but the voice of those other spirits."[62]

The closing phrase was crucial for Barth, and characteristic of him; he acknowledged that his apprehension of the Word was fallible, relative, and riddled with cultural blinders. He did not possess God's truth; all he could do was listen for it in the strange medium of the scriptural text. In his view, the liberal establishment subordinated this concern to its concern for respectability, reducing God to a manageable cipher of the whole. Barth countered that the divine Word can be expounded "only in weighty negations [and] preached only in paradoxes." The Word of God, which is never a thing, is the transformation of everything in the world; thus it must be "apprehended as the negation of the starting-point of every system which we are capable of conceiving."[63]

This exchange brought Barth and Bultmann together as friends and collaborators. In the early 1920s the differences between them seemed less important than their commitment to an existential theology of the Word. Bultmann's *History of the Synoptic Tradition* reinforced Barth's anti-historical bias by showing that the synoptic narratives provide little historical information about Jesus. Barth, mortified that he knew barely enough to keep one class session ahead of his classes, worked on his knowledge deficit, telling Thurneysen, "All day long I am reading pell-mell hundreds and hundreds of pages: Heim, Thomas Aquinas, Fr. Strauss, Alex. Schweizer, Herrmann." Barth despaired at finding himself "so to speak without a teacher, all alone in the vast field." He vowed at first not to change his approach to theology, which had lifted him to prominence and a teaching position, but soon he felt the limitations of his negative dialecticism. Dialectical spinning would never support the church as an institution or teach his students what they needed to know. Barth took for granted that the Bible "had to be the master in Protestant dogmatics" and that he had to learn Reformation theology, but how was he to do that "if no one instructs me?" In this state of mind he read Heinrich Heppe's *Reformed Dogmatics,* a collection of texts on the loci of dogmatics by sixteenth- to eighteenth-century Reformed theologians. He also studied Heinrich Schmid's parallel compendium of Lutheran texts. He later recalled that he approached "the old churchmen" with apprehension and soon found, as expected, that they were "out of date, dusty, unattractive, almost like a table of logarithms, dreary to read, stiff and eccentric on almost every page I opened."[64]

But the old dogmatists also impressed Barth. Their seriousness, theological rigor, and devotion to the church were chastening to him. Having assumed responsibility for teaching Reformed theology to the church's next generation of leaders, Barth allowed himself to be taught by the old churchmen. It was a formative experience. Though much that he read brought to mind Herrmann's caustic riffs on orthodox dogmatism, Barth noticed that the old dogmatists did not gerrymander like liberals. They were spiritually disciplined, dealing with all the major themes of the Bible. He told Thurneysen that "after much head shaking and astonishment" he found himself agreeing with the Reformed and Lutheran dogmatists on almost every point and heard himself saying things in class that he could never have dreamed of during his pastoral career.[65]

Gradually Barth's theology and rhetoric became more chastened, realistic and dogmatic as a consequence of becoming a Christian dogmatic theologian – not merely a teacher of Reformed theology. Against his Lutheran colleagues at Göttingen, who disputed his right to teach dogmatics, Barth argued that strictly speaking, there is no *Reformed* dogmatics or *Roman Catholic* dogmatics. There is only a Christian tradition of dogmatic theology that is carried out within different confessional traditions. In the process of self-identifying as a dogmatic theologian, he gradually eliminated the expressivist metaphors and word plays from his work. Barth later recalled that in the mid-1920s he began to learn "along with a great centralization of what was material, to move and express myself again in simple thoughts and words." His language became more representational and mimetic as a function of his resolve to serve the church.[66]

By 1923, crisis theology had passed from being a lecture circuit fad to a theological movement. It founded a journal, *Zwischen den Zeiten* (*Between the Times*), and attracted the most promising theologians of the postwar generation, including Bultmann, Brunner, Günther Dehn, Erik Peterson, Heinrich Schlier, and Georg Merz. For Barth, the journal's name was a compromise. Gogarten wanted to call it *The Word.* Barth, already tiring of Gogarten, replied that it would be better to call it *The Ship of Fools;* they did not possess the Word. They settled on the title of a recent article by Gogarten, which carried its own presumption, which Harnack resented. Harnack disbelieved that the liberal era was over, but even if the Barthians overthrew liberal theology, he warned, they would not rule for long, because Barthian theology was self-negating. It was not academic, so it did not belong in the academy, and it was too intellectual for Pietist and revival movements, so they would never claim it either. If Barthian theology took over, no one would bother to teach it. Harnack spelled out why in a public challenge in 1923, "Fifteen Questions to Those Among the Theologians Who Are Contemptuous of the Scientific Theology."[67]

Harnack's fifteen questions boiled down to eight. Did the despisers of scientific theology really believe that the meaning of scripture could be understood without critical historical knowledge? If the basis of faith is a radical either/or, what is the relation of religious experience to faith? If God and the world are radically dissociated, how can people be nurtured into the life of faith? If God and the world are so radically separate from each other, how should the biblical analogy between love of God and love of one's neighbor be understood? Did the despisers really believe that the tradition of Goethe, Kant, and Beethoven was worthless from a Christian standpoint? What about the scriptural affirmation (Phil. 4:8) that God is knowable through the apprehension of the good, true, and beautiful? If Jesus Christ is the center of the gospel, but we disparage historical science, how can we be sure that we are relating to the true Christ, and not a Christ of our imagination? Even granting that the liberal tradition had problems, was there really a credible alternative to it?[68]

Barth replied that he had nothing against historical criticism and he was not contemptuous toward scientific theology. His objection was that it strayed too far from its Reformation roots. Liberal theology, Barth observed, tried to understand scripture through a combination of inner openness, experience, and critical reflection, but the Reformers trusted none of these things. Luther and Calvin had the crucial corrective to modern theology. The meaning of scripture is knowable only in faith through the power of the Holy Spirit, which is the Spirit of the Bible. The Word of God in the words of scripture is knowable only to believers through the operative power of the Spirit. For this reason, Barth urged, the purpose of theology is identical to the purpose of preaching, which is to take up and pass on the Word of Christ. True theology is concerned with bringing people to Christ, not with validating people's religious experiences. It does not strategize about how to bring people to God, but confesses with Jesus that "no one can come to me unless the Father who sent me draws him" (John 6:44).[69]

Barth acknowledged that there is a connection between the peace of God which passes all understanding and the human experience of the good, true, and beautiful, but this connection is the Wholly Other Spirit of God, "the divine *crisis*, which is the only basis on which it is possible to speak seriously of the good, true, and beautiful." The connection between experience of God and experience of the good is not a human possession or an aspect of religious experience. It followed for Barth that Harnack's concern to make modern Christianity stand with Goethe and Kant had nothing to do with the gospel: "True statements about God can only be made at all where one knows he is placed not on some height of culture or of religion, but before revelation and thereby under judgment." The theologian stands with Goethe and Kant only in the sense that all human beings stand under judgment. Harnack wanted to enlist Christianity in the struggle of modern liberal culture against "barbarism," but the gospel takes no interest in that, Barth declared: "The gospel has as much and as little to do with 'barbarism' as it has to do with culture."[70]

As for how crisis theology, spurning historical criticism, made sure that its Jesus was not a construct of Barth's imagination, Barth replied that historical criticism had a role to play in this area, especially for those who failed to grasp that we no longer know Christ according to the flesh (2 Cor. 5:16). Historical criticism confirms this truism for those who need to hear it from historians, Barth observed. At the same time, historical criticism also confirms that historical knowledge cannot be the basis of faith: "The reliability and common nature of the knowledge of the person of Jesus Christ as the midpoint of the gospel can be no other than that of a *faith* awakened by God." Barth implored theologians to regain the "courage to be objective." If they regained the courage to become witnesses of the revealed Spirit of Christ, they would have less to fear from science and less reason to sanctify whatever scientists currently believed. Barth was only beginning to think with Luther and Calvin, but he stressed that liberal theology was woefully wrong not to regard Luther, Calvin, and Paul as real theologians.[71]

Liberal theology called itself scientific, but in fact it was highly subjective and culturally over-determined. Barth pressed hard on this claim, but Harnack replied that Barth's subjectivism was out of control. Barth's disinterest in history and his emphasis on the absolute otherness of God were perfectly suited for make-it-up theology. Harnack admonished against severing "every link between faith and what is human," which betrayed the spirit of the gospel. Barth's Wholly Other otherness and his contempt for Christian education opened a chasm between faith and humanity. Moreover, his disinterest in historicity was alien to the gospel witness. If Barthian theology prevailed, Harnack warned, theology would dissolve: "It will not be taught any more at all, but exclusively handed over to revival preachers, who freely create their own understanding of the Bible and who set up their own dominance." As theology, Barthianism was self-negating: "I sincerely regret that your answers to my questions only show the size of the chasm that separates us."[72]

Barth replied that the historical reality of the revealed Christ proclaimed by the gospel is not the so-called historical Jesus, but the risen Christ. We do not know the historical Jesus, but through God's revelation we do know the risen Christ of faith. The way to Christ is the same for us as it was for the early Christians; it is the way of revelation and faith alone. Faith is not an experience of dependence or even a will to righteousness; it is the acceptance of God's saving Word in all its offense to human reason, culture, and pride. It followed for Barth that liberal attempts to overcome the mythical aspects of Christianity were misguided. Liberal theology sought to make Christianity credible by separating its mythical forms from a domesticated religious worldview that could be believed. It took the offense out of revelation and sought to gain control over the religious content of Christianity by putting aside those aspects of revelation that were no longer believable.[73]

Barth countered that gutting Christian revelation was far worse than straightforwardly disbelieving it. At least atheists took Christianity seriously. This was the key to Barth's seemingly disingenuous claim that he supported the most radical biblical criticism. He observed that from David Friedrich Strauss onward, biblical critics showed that in the Bible "we are dealing with testimonies and always *only* with testimonies." Radical critics emphasized the evangelical character of the gospel narratives. Barth implored that theology did not need another strategy to salvage a credible piece of history or religion from the gospel. It needed to recover the Reformers' openness to God's world-transforming Word. To his students at Göttingen, Barth put it bluntly: "By the Spirit scripture bears witness that it is God's Word. It needs no other arguments, and there is no possibility of doubting it, because *in* it as the witness of the prophets and apostles, and also *over against* it (and therefore in us), God the Spirit bears witness to himself."[74]

The Barthian revolt, never lacking in irony, transformed the field of theology without persuading many people to approach theology in Barth's fashion. This irony showed up at the beginning of the crisis theology movement, it blared dramatically in the 1930s, and it persisted throughout Barth's career, although he attracted a sizable school of allies and protégés in his later career. Long after he was recognized as the major theologian of the twentieth century, Barth remained oddly isolated in the field. His initial attack on liberal theology set him against all his teachers and most of the theological establishment. He later recalled that during his early career at Göttingen, it took him several years to absorb that he was alienated "from almost the whole of modern theology." He responded by building a theological movement, but his severely neo-Reformation approach to theology and his dogmatic turn caused rifts with his allies. At Göttingen, working on his first lecture cycle of dogmatics, Barth confessed to Thurneysen that he often sighed "under the awareness of the complete isolation of the whole undertaking."[75]

Hermann Kutter offered a telling, if extreme, sign of this isolation. In the early 1920s Kutter barely tolerated Barth's crisis theology writings. After Barth became a dogmatic theologian and crisis theology became an organized movement, Kutter's tolerance ran out. For a time he had considered Barth to be a disciple. In 1925 Kutter sadly informed Thurneysen that he could no longer sustain a spiritual fellowship with Barth: "I can do no other than recognize in the Barthian theology, however interesting and healthy it may be for the rest of theology, a straying away from that which – imperfectly enough! – burns in my heart and soul." For Kutter, the gospel mission was to proclaim the reality and coming of God. Barth, however, turned Kutter's faith into a vain theological movement and controversy – "a ready meal for the theological eagles who are delighted that in disputing about the *concept* of God they may forget the striving after *God himself* and stake everything on the fact that the question of God is a theological uproar from which they can take their profit."[76]

Kutter did not dispute that "the Barthian crisis" was good for theology as a field. Later that year, upon retiring as Zurich city pastor, he still respected Barth enough to recommend him as his successor. But he could no longer speak to Barth directly. Building a movement that battled over concepts did not compare to speaking in God's own Word and Spirit, Kutter admonished: "No theology is of any account when we have to do with God himself. Only God's coming mattered to me, however little I am in a position to give a fitting expression to this great concern."[77]

Thurneysen protested in reply that Barth did theology precisely in Kutter's spirit. The whole point of Barthian theology was to make theology relinquish its concepts in order to bear witness to God: "Our whole intention is no other than to draw forth as clearly as possible from this preparatory witness of theology the actual witness that must follow through in the preaching." Thurneysen told Kutter that it was through Kutter's witness that he and Barth came to realize that bearing witness to God had to be their central concern. Was it really necessary to assume that theology could never bear witness to God truly? More personally, "Are you really going to turn away from us as though we had already failed?" Thurneysen allowed that he and Barth had taken a risky course, one that posed the "frightful danger" of betraying the spiritual concern that they shared with Kutter, but he pleaded that they did not deserve to be treated as though they had already hopelessly betrayed it.[78]

Emil Brunner, many years later, repeated Kutter's charge that Barth betrayed the spirit of his early thinking and preaching. Brunner traced the point of betrayal to Barth's dogmatizing turn in 1924. Kutter claimed that it happened earlier, when Barth conceived a crisis theology movement. In both cases Barth was quick to shake the dust from his feet. He told Thurneysen that he could not have matched Thurneysen's civility if he had been forced to reply to Kutter. He grasped that Kutter was assigning him to "the same pit with Ragaz." That was fine with Barth, as long as Kutter recognized "that he, too, with his GOD is in it." As it was, he had no patience for a debate about who served God or merely a concept of God. To Barth, the difference between Kutter and him was that he was developing an appreciation for theology as a work of the church. The religious socialists saw themselves as advocates of a new church or as prophets within the churches, but Barth's cram sessions with the old churchmen gave him a deeper sense of connection to the church's institutional and doctrinal tradition. He had never been a sectarian, he stressed; even his early crisis theology was inside criticism. His pilgrimage out of liberal theology had led to the Bible, then to dogma, and then to the church as the sign of divine grace and context of Christian speech. This pilgrimage carried him far from Kutter, whose posture now seemed "so reactionary, so irrelevant" to him. Not for the last time, Barth moved on without looking back.[79]

The "masters of the old theological school" deepened Barth's sense of connection to the pre-modern church, including the early church fathers and medieval scholastics. Generally he followed the order of loci of Reformed orthodoxy, beginning with the doctrine of revelation, and he developed a new appreciation for Trinitarian doctrine, which he described as "the problem of the inalienable subjectivity of God in his revelation." But Barth was a creative type, even in dogmatics. Although he regretted having to begin with a prolegomenon, he developed a novel one that breathed new life into dogmatic theology by conceiving preaching as its focal point.[80]

For Barth, preaching was more than Sunday sermonizing or even the general ministerial work of pastors; it included all forms of genuine Christian witness. He distinguished three ways in which the Word of God is disclosed – as revelation, as scripture, and as preaching. Barth was emphatic that scripture is not revelation; rather, scripture comes from revelation. Neither is preaching to be equated with either revelation or scripture, although preaching comes from revelation and scripture: "Revelation is from God alone, scripture is from revelation alone, and preaching is from revelation and scripture." This does not mean that revelation is the Word of God more than scripture, or that scripture is the World of God more than preaching. Barth explained: "There is no first or last, no greater or less. The first, the second, and the third are all God's Word in the same glory, unity in trinity, and trinity in unity."[81]

The old dogmatists identified scripture as revelation and developed their doctrine of scripture before dealing with the Trinity, the incarnation, or the work of the Holy Spirit. In effect, for most of this tradition, the seventeenth-century doctrine of biblical inerrancy became the basis of all other doctrines.[82] Barth's doctrine of the threefold Word broke the equation of scripture with revelation and placed the doctrine of scripture after the Trinity, the incarnation, and the Holy Spirit. He envied Aquinas and Calvin, who plunged straight into real theology; Aquinas and Calvin did not have to explain their concepts or method. Barth, apologizing for beginning with a prolegomenon, conceded: "We are not allowed to imagine that we are at another point in history. We adjust under protest, but we still adjust." It was too late to repeal the scholastic turn of seventeenth-century Protestantism and the liberal religious consciousness of the nineteenth century. Barth believed that these developments distorted the great themes of the Reformation, but he also accepted that he could not simply return to Luther and Calvin. The only worthy option was a new Reformation theology. In the modern age, dogmatics had to be modern: "It must be part of a conversation; it must be open to discussion." Instead of drawing straight from the subject of dogmatics, one had to speak also about the subject.[83]

In addition to getting biblical inerrancy wrong, the Reformed dogmatists got natural revelation wrong, ascribing great importance to it. Barth declared, "for my part, although I am Reformed, I want no part of it." Like Herrmann, he wanted no part of a support system strategy that appealed to apologetic proofs; unlike Herrmann, he threw out appeals to revelatory experience and conscience too. Barth's first edition *Romans* had a role for the revelation of God in conscience; now he took it back: "Either God speaks, or he does not. But he does not speak more or less, or partially, or in pieces, here a bit and there a bit. This is a contradiction in terms, an anthropomorphism, a basic naturalizing of revelation which fits Schleiermacher very well, but which ought not to have found any place among the older Reformed." The old dogmatists built a case for natural revelation from the confession that all truth is God's truth. Barth countered that this confession is rightly understood as referring only to the totality of truth: "Truth that really goes back to God cannot be a particle of truth. It is either the whole truth or it does not go back to God and is not revelation at all."[84]

Zwingli taught that only God can make us certain of God's grace. For Barth, the implication of this principle for the doctrine of scripture was that scripture *is* God's Word because it is *God's* Word. Luther and Zwingli understood that no human proof proves or disproves that scripture is God's Word; however, the guardians of Protestant orthodoxy were unable to uphold this principle. Barth invoked Calvin as a mostly sympathetic witness on this point, although he allowed that Calvin made room for apologetic and natural revelation arguments. At least Calvin played the apologetics game to the glory of God, investing no real importance in his arguments. By the time that the Westminster Divines wrote the Westminster Confession in 1647, most Reformed dogmatists identified orthodoxy with apologetic proofs about the heavenly infallibility and majesty of biblical prose. This was a baleful regression, Barth believed, one that continental scholastics perfected. Instead of trusting in the self-authenticating sufficiency of God's Word, Protestant scholastics put their faith in dubious probabilistic arguments.[85]

Similarly, Barth's case against orthodox propositionalism recycled Herrmann – that the old dogmatists took refuge in the verbal inspiration of scripture because they could not abide the paradox of confessing that scripture is the Word of God in human words. Barth explained, "They could no longer bear to stand on the knife-edge between faith and unbelief in face of this purely historical entity. They could no longer bear to read the Bible as a human word, to read the texts exactly as they are with all that they imply when read historically." Confronted with early biblical criticism, Protestant orthodoxy reduced Christian doctrine to a system of formulas, reduced holy scripture to a book of propositions, and obscured the paradox of the hiddenness of God's revelation in scripture. In effect, Barth contended, the old dogmatists rejected revelation itself by refusing to recognize that the historical character of scripture veils God's presence in scripture.[86]

"They did not have too much faith but too little," Barth urged. "They did not see in the growing seriousness of the historical approach a challenge to balance the scales the other way, to undertake the venture of faith and obedience more boldly." By turning revelation into direct revelation, the old dogmatists set revelation aside. They created a paper pope, "from which we are to get oracles as we get shoes from a shoemaker." Besides the obvious irony of Protestant papal machinery, Barth noted, there was a deeper irony: The old dogmatists inadvertently historicized revelation by reducing it to the words of the Bible. Reformed theologian Francis Turretin and Lutheran theologian Johann Gerhard had a different purpose in mind when they divinized the biblical text. Nonetheless, by refusing to recognize the paradox of God's hiddenness in scripture, they launched the fatal historical process by which revelation was subjected to historicizing human control, a game that liberals were bound to win. Barth declared: "I need not describe the disaster which then followed on the other side. Marching, not without cause, under the banner of truth and credibility, historicism would never have taken on the openly anti-Christian significance that it did had Christianity itself, and especially Christian theology, ventured to insist on its own truth and credibility, and to maintain the *indirect* identity of the Bible with revelation." This was the project that had to be taken up at the end of the liberal era, Barth urged, "and it will be a very painful process."[87]

In both cases the logic was Herrmannian, but where Herrmann appealed to the autonomy of faith as a revelatory experience, Barth appealed to the totalizing efficiency of God's revelation in the Word. Revelation is its own basis, he insisted. It has no need of supporting arguments or proofs and it lacks nothing as the proper basis for theological affirmations. Theology, in Barth's rendering, was "scientific reflection on the Word of God which is spoken by God in revelation, which is recorded in the holy scripture of the prophets and apostles, and which now both is and should be proclaimed and heard in Christian preaching." This formula distinguished three addresses within the single Word of God: in revelation alone God speaks, in scripture the biblical writers speak, and in preaching the number of possible speakers is theoretically unlimited. But in all three cases, for Barth, the Word of God was one; it is always God's speaking.[88]

Barthian theology was a creative new blend of Reformation, orthodox, and liberal theology, one that gave extraordinary new importance to preaching construed in a wide sense of the term. For Barth, it was only as preaching that the Word of God bears an ongoing character. Strictly speaking, the Word of God is not ongoing as revelation, for the Word as revelation "never took place as such." Barth explained: "Revelation is what it is in time, but as the frontier of time remote from us as heaven is from earth. Nor is God's Word ongoing as holy scripture. It is in time as such. It took place as the witness given to revelation. But in itself it is a self-enclosed part of history which is as far from us as everything historical and past."[89]

We do not live in a historical context that is continuous with the experiences of the apostles. Barth's often-misconstrued attempt to see "through and beyond history into the spirit of the Bible" did not presume otherwise. There is no conceivable extension of scripture that could belong to the present, he argued. If one of Paul's missing letters to Corinth were found, it would still belong to the past. This is why the movement of the

Word as preaching was so crucial to Barth's interpretation of the Word as a threefold event. Only as Christian preaching does the Word remain ongoing. The Word becomes present as preaching in the same way that the Holy Spirit makes God present. Just as the Holy Spirit proceeds from the Father and the Son, the Word as preaching proceeds from revelation and scripture.

Harnack, incredulous at Barth's eschatological mentality, was equally incredulous at the role that Barth assigned to preaching. Barth replied that by Harnack's criterion, Luther and Calvin failed to qualify as theologians, as well as the apostle Paul. Harnack replied that, indeed, from the standpoint of critical theology, those who expressed their Christianity as witnesses were objects of theology, not subjects. Paul and Luther were not real theologians, and neither was Barth. The debate ended there, but Barth did not need to reply; he had already said it. For him, Paul, Luther, and Calvin were better models than any liberal theologian. It was liberal theology that obliterated the content of theology, he charged. Harnack's content was the simple gospel that he found beyond the scriptural text and apart from the Holy Spirit by using historical criticism. Liberal theology gave to this meager human concoction the exalted place that the Reformers gave to the correlation of scripture and Spirit. So-called scientific theology replaced the Word of God with a liberal academic impression of it. Barth allowed that theology had to be approached differently in the classroom than in the pulpit; he did not give sermons to his students. But the theme of Christian theology, "scientific" or otherwise, could not be something different from that which is conveyed in the pulpit.[90]

The Word becomes present as speaking. Preaching is the Word made present. The purpose of dogmatic theology, Barth reasoned, is to aid the preacher's reflective understanding of God's Word and the role of preaching in making the Word present. Through studying theology, the witness struggles with the totality of the prophetic and apostolic witness, coming to understand the Bible as holy scripture. Barth exhorted his students never to stop struggling with the text. It is always easier to talk about something that one has experienced non-paradoxically as one's own possession, he cautioned. Theology is a reminder that preaching is supposed to make God's Word present, not to describe the preacher's experiences.[91]

In 1925 Barth accepted a chair in dogmatics and New Testament exegesis in the Protestant faculty of theology at Münster, where he taught for five years. Two years later he published the first volume of a projected dogmatic system, *Christliche Dogmatik*, which took a hard line against theological dependence on philosophy. Barth spent the mid-1920s trying to throw off the existentialist and expressionist influences that lit up his book(s) on Romans. If he believed his own argument about how theology should proceed, he had to listen, as much as possible, to the Word in its own voice, not read existential philosophy or his politics into it. Barth winced as Bultmann, Brunner, Gogarten, and Tillich refused this advice. In *Christliche Dogmatik*, Barth argued that philosophy gets in the way of allowing the Word to express itself, and in really bad cases it becomes a substitute for the Word, negating what theology is supposed to be about. He made a strenuous case for this position while retaining some existential elements. Later Barth decided that the existential retentions ruined the whole thing, so he had to start over, rewriting the book under a new series title, *Die Kirchliche Dogmatik* (*Church Dogmatics*).[92]

To Bultmann, Barth's dogmatic turn and his stricture against philosophy were both disastrous; he emphasized the latter. It was simply wrong and self-defeating to maintain "a sovereign scorn for modern work in philosophy," he told Barth. Eliminating philosophy was not an option for theology, because every theology is guided by implicit or explicit philosophical assumptions about the knower and the known. The choice was between using philosophy intelligently or badly; in Barth's case, it was done badly, because he left himself in the clutches of an outdated ontology. Bultmann urged that instead of allowing an assumed philosophy to control one's thinking, it was better to use philosophy intelligently as an aid to theology. That was how he used Heideggerian phenomenology; at the time Bultmann was Martin Heidegger's col- league at Marburg, during Heidegger's *Being and Time* phase. Barth's scorn for philosophy deprived him of the tools that he needed to break free from the discredited ontology of Protestant scholasticism.[93]

Barth's reply was irenic and somewhat evasive. For over a year he tried to avoid this debate with Bultmann, telling him that they needed to leave each other alone to pursue their separate courses. He was not ready to defend his position or to answer Bultmann's objections. After Bultmann objected anyway, Barth conceded that he had a valid point. Bultmann's description of the pertinent choice made enough sense to Barth that he declined to defend in principle his lack of a philosophical orientation. It was undoubt- edly true that his theology contained philosophical assumptions and concepts, Barth allowed. If he had to defend himself, his point was not really that theology should be purged of philosophy, but that it should not be dependent on a single philosophical perspective. He used philosophical concepts in an eclectic fashion whenever they helped him to explicate his meaning. Theology needed to be free to do its own work, which was not possible if it was chained to a philosophical system. At the same time, he recognized that his haphazard use of philosophy exposed him to the charge of "a terrible dilettantism." In 1928, Barth was willing to live with the charge, stopping short of the judgment that his friends were accommodating the gospel to alien philosophies.[94]

But by 1930 this judgment seemed no longer deniable to him. Bultmann, Brunner, Gogarten, Tillich and many others in Barth's circle of dialectical theologians variously accommodated Christianity to modern philosophy and culture. In many respects, Bultmann and Tillich were liberals theologically, and Barth had strong misgivings about Gogarten and Brunner. He admonished Bultmann that all of them represented "a large scale return to the fleshpots of Egypt." Even dialectical theologians were committing the liberal mistake of understanding faith as a human possibility, and thus surrendering theology to philosophy. The new dialectical theologies were no better than the old liberalism, Barth scorned; in fact, the old Religious Socialism of the pre- war period was better than Bultmann's Heideggerian phenomenology, Brunner's theology of natural revelation, Gogarten's "states of life" theo-philosophy, and Tillich's ontology of ultimate concern. A bit later he put it sharply to Bultmann, scolding him that by conflating the gospel message with a modern worldview, "You have done something that one ought not to do." If Bultmann asked why this was so terrible, Barth could only reply "not with an argument, but with a recitation of the creed."[95]

The faith itself was at stake in the battle of theologies, a conviction that deepened in Barth after Hitler ascended to power in Germany. The spectacle of pro-Nazi "German

Christianity" confirmed Barth's worst fears about the evils of paganized theology. Barth was not surprised when Gogarten did a brief dance with fascism, and Heidegger and theologian Emanuel Hirsch became outright Nazi apologists. He was surprised when Bultmann joined the Confessing Church resistance movement in which Barth played a leadership role. Barth assumed that Bultmann's infatuation with Heideggerian philosophy would lead him straight into German Christianity. In November 1933 he confessed to Bultmann that he had somehow misjudged him. Bultmann, stunned to learn that Barth had expected him to join the German Christians, replied that obviously Barth had never really understood him.[96]

Barth conceded the obvious, while noting that in most cases his suspicions were sadly confirmed. For several years, while Barth wrote the early volumes of *Church Dogmatics*, he and Bultmann resumed their previous debates, though with a strained wariness, especially on Barth's part. Bultmann complained that Barth was too devoted to church dogma to let the text speak for itself; he imposed the lid of dogmatics so tightly over his exegesis that the voice of the Word could not be heard through it: "After a few sentences one knows all that will be said and simply asks occasionally how it will be produced out of the words of the text that follow." Barth countered that Bultmann's sermons were tedious and his theology merely circled around the anxieties of believers, which was not the same thing as proclaiming Christ. He also expressed his discomfort that Bultmann quietly took the Hitler loyalty oath in 1934.[97]

Barth used philosophy eclectically, but that was hard for readers to see in light of his polemics against Bultmann, Brunner, German Christianity, and Roman Catholicism in the 1930s. For decades he was routinely described as a despiser of philosophy. Brunner defended a very limited concept of natural theology, based on the idea of an autonomous knowledge of God or "point of contact" that resides in every person by virtue of having been created in the image of God. Human beings, he argued, despite the ravages of sin, possess a passive capacity to be reached by revelation; otherwise they could not hear the Word when it was spoken. Barth replied furiously that Brunner betrayed the Reformation principles of *sole fide* and *sola gratia*, taking "the downward path." In the same spirit he charged that the Catholic analogy of being was an invention of the anti-Christ and the most serious reason not to be a Roman Catholic. Debates on these issues preoccupied much of the theological field in the 1930s and 1940s, making Barth the giant theological figure of his time, but one lacking disciples who approached theology in his fashion, as he often complained.[98]

This irony was noted in the Barthian house organ, *Zwischen den Zeiten*. In 1928 one of the journal's mainstays, Paul Schempp, observed that Barth, for all his success in transforming the field of theology, stood "just as much alone today as he was ten years ago." By then no one disputed that something called "the Barthian movement" had overthrown the liberal establishment in Germany and spread throughout Protestant Europe. Yet there was something strange about Barth's dominance, as Schempp suggested. Barth changed the field, and towered above it, yet hardly anyone accepted his stringent insistence that theology must be based on the Word of God alone.[99]

There was another isolating factor of a more personal sort. Barth was a gregarious type with a sharp sense of humor who made friends easily. His most intimate relationship, however, created a very awkward situation for his wife Nelly Barth, their four children, and everyone else who got reasonably close to him. In 1913 he had married a member of his congregation, Nelly Hoffmann, pretty much at the insistence of his mother Anna Barth, who saw in Nelly a personality much like her own. The marriage was unhappy from the beginning, causing Barth to lament that he paid a high price for failing to stand up to his mother. In 1925 he met Charlotte von Kirschbaum, a nurse and brilliant student of theology, who became his secretary, research assistant, and constant companion. Many years later Barth told Eberhard Busch that he had been deeply lonely until he met her. Barth and von Kirschbaum worked and traveled together; he clashed with his mother over the relationship; and in 1929 von Kirschbaum moved into Barth's household in Münster. She continued to live with him until 1966, dedicating her life to him and his work. Barth asked Nelly Barth for a divorce in 1933, but she refused. The arrangement for which she settled was a source of tension and heartache in the Barth household for decades. Barth's students divided over the question whether he and von Kirschbaum were lovers, but all agreed that she was sunny, kindly, maternal toward them, and indispensable to his work.[100]

In 1930 the Barth household moved to Bonn, where Barth taught as Professor of Systematic Theology, and where his courses attracted large crowds of students, many from outside Germany. In 1932 he launched the *Church Dogmatics*. The following year, after Hitler and the National Socialists seized power in Berlin, Barth became the chief theological voice of the Confessing Church movement, which resisted the Nazi campaign to blend Christianity with German fascism. In this capacity he authored the historic Barmen Declaration of 1934. The following year he was dismissed from his position at Bonn for refusing to sign the required oath of loyalty to Hitler. He returned to Switzerland in 1935 to become Professor of Systematic Theology at the University of Basel, where he remained until his retirement in 1962. By the time that Barth moved to Basel, even his staunchest critics acknowledged his preeminence in the field. The publication of his massive second half-volume of dogmatics in 1938 confirmed that he was set upon a mind-boggling scale for his definitive theological project.[101]

Yet Barth noted in 1938 that he was still very much alone among the theologians. For all the world-shaking influence of the Barthian school, it seemed to him that there was no Barthian school. In one sense this was fine with Barth; he often claimed that he was not a Barthian either and that he wanted no responsibility for supervising a school. But he wanted theologians to approach theology as he did, and he recognized that he was strangely isolated notwithstanding his eminence: "My lifework seems to be wanting in a certain accumulative power – even more, that a certain explosive, or in any case centrifugal, effect seems to inhere in it."[102]

Barth's renderings of Calvin on natural theology and of Aquinas and Augustine on the analogy of being were subjected to withering criticism. He got awful reviews for his blistering attack on Brunner, even from critics who appreciated that Barth's vehemence had much to do with the politics of anti-fascist resistance. His relationship with von Kirschbaum was a source of constant murmuring against him in the field, smacking of scandal, or at least, something strange and dubious. He broke many friendships but continued to make new friends, who built a Barthian school in the 1940s and 1950s. In the end, Barth did not lack allies and protégés, notably Günther Dehn, Hermann Diem, Oscar Cullmann, Hans Joachim Iwand, Karl Steinbauer, and Ernst Wolf. A generally younger stream of Barthians included Georg Eichholz, Walter Fürst, Helmut

Gollwitzer, Frederick Herzog, Heinz Kloppenburg, Walter Kreck, Eduard Schweizer, Walter Sigrist, Lili Simon, Karl Gerhard Steck, Thomas F. Torrance, Hellmut Traub, and Hans Heinrich Wolf.

Of the crisis theologians, only Thurneysen remained on good terms with Barth, except for the complicated case of Bultmann, with whom Barth had a final round of controversy in the 1940s. For twenty years Barth puzzled over Bultmann's insistence on wedding his theology to a philosophical system. Why did Bultmann refuse to let the Word demonstrate its truth? If he really believed that Barth's dogmatism got in the way of explicating the Word in the scriptural witness, why didn't he offer a better example? Instead of keeping philosophy in its place, Bultmann filled his theology with Heideggerian ruminations on being, preunderstanding, anxiety, and authenticity. Why did he have so little confidence in the power of the biblical Word?

Barth puzzled over this question until 1941, when Bultmann's sensational essay on the problem of New Testament mythology provided the answer, at least to Barth. The article owed some of its electrifying impact to its bluntness. In starkly straightforward language Bultmann asserted that the world picture of the New Testament is thoroughly mythical and completely out of play for modern people. Everywhere the New Testament assumes that the universe has three decks, earth is a theater of supernatural agency, and God, angels, Satan, and demons intervene in natural occurrences. The only way to make sense of biblical religion in a modern context is to thoroughly demythologize the Bible without giving up the saving message of the gospel kerygma.[103]

As a theologian Bultmann sought to demythologize the world picture of early Christianity while reclaiming, through existential interpretation, the gospel message of salvation from the bondage of sin and death. The deepest purpose of myth is not to convey information about history or the world, he argued. To repudiate myth on the basis of its factual claims is to miss the point. The subject of myth is always the human situation in the world. Through myth we recognize that we are dependent on the powers that rule over the world. Myth itself is demythologizing inasmuch as it speaks about a transcendent power that relativizes and subverts the authority of familiar powers. Thus, the objective representations of myth are never the point and should hold little interest for modern Christians.

Bultmann allowed that the Bible features a peculiar mix of history and myth, which posed special problems for demythologizers. The passion narratives fold together the crucifixion and resurrection of Jesus without any acknowledgement that the former is historical and the latter is mythical; moreover, the New Testament repeatedly renders historical events as having cosmic significance. But what mattered in all such cases was to recover the existential truth of the gospel. Modern people cannot accept a mythological interpretation of the cross, Bultmann insisted; the meaning of the cross depends entirely on our experience of being crucified with Jesus. The cross is an eschatological event that, linked with the resurrection, proclaims that Christ has broken the power of death universally. There is no basis for believing in this saving effect of Christ's death and resurrection except that it is proclaimed as such; faith is nothing but simple hearing and accepting of the Word proclaimed. To Bultmann, demythologizing was analogous to the Pauline/Lutheran doctrine of justification by faith alone. Just as the doctrine of justification destroyed the illusion of control and security in the sphere of salvation, demythologization destroyed every false security based on objective knowledge. True security is found only by abandoning every form of security, recognizing that every person before God has empty hands.[104]

By mid-century these arguments about the mythical worldview of scripture and modern meaning of Christianity dominated the field of theology. Conservatives generally regarded Bultmann's position as an outright attack on Christianity and responded accordingly; others questioned whether the human mind can ever dispense with myth; many protested that Bultmann completely subjectivized theology; some argued that Bultmann overestimated the problem of myth as a stumbling block to modern belief; others objected that Bultmann arbitrarily stopped short of demythologizing the kerygma (the original gospel message). In reply, Bultmann usually restated his concept of the kerygmatic center of Christianity, which contained no objective "facts" accessible to knowledge or prior to faith. This irreducible core of the Christian faith, as he usually rendered it, was unabashedly circular; it was "that which gives meaning to an occurrence to whose historicity it testifies."[105]

But Bultmann was not always that clear. He failed to sustain a clear definition of myth; he failed to distinguish adequately between analogy and myth, which raised problems for his God-language; and he could be quoted both ways on whether Easter faith had any factual basis. Sometimes he included the historical Jesus and the Easter appearances in the content of the kerygma. These inconsistencies helped to stoke an enormous literature about him, as interpreters assailed or defended different Bultmanns. Barth complained that Bultmann was not sufficiently intelligible to be understood. But to Barth, Bultmann clearly had two major problems. He reversed the pattern of the New Testament message and he vested far too much importance in demythologizing and worldviews.

The first problem was fundamental and fatal. Bultmann started with an experiencing subject that heard the gospel message, accepted it in faith, experienced a transition from one state of being to another, and experienced one's self as an object of God's redemptive act. But that was the gospel in reverse, Barth protested; every part of the gospel message is distorted by turning it into an existential trope. Instead of presenting Christ as the kerygma, Bultmann presented the Christ event as something that is known in and through the kerygma. Instead of featuring a doctrine of Christ, Bultmann featured a doctrine of existential transformation that drove Christ to the margin. Even in the resurrection, Christ could not break out of his kerygmatic prison, because he was not allowed a life of his own; nothing could be said until the disciples inaugurated the church.[106]

More importantly, from Barth's perspective, Bultmann's project recycled the old liberalism in dialectical dress, trying to adapt Christianity to the best available worldview. Barth countered that theology should not be in the business of endorsing worldviews or any independent theory of existence. Rather than commit itself to any particular worldview, he argued, Christian theology should use or appropriate as many worldviews and forms of language as are necessary to explicate the truth of God's Word. Just as theology should not privilege literal meaning over the language of narrative, paradox, irony, and dialectic, neither should theology commit itself to the enervating task of adopting and then discarding one worldview after another. A healthy pluralism in philosophy and rhetorical forms is needed if theology is to be free to locate the event of correspondence between human word and divine truth.[107]

Barth acknowledged that there are myths and even outright fairy tales in the Bible. Though he preferred to speak of biblical "saga" rather than "myth" in order to distinguish biblical myth from the monist mythologies of other religions and philosophies, he urged that by either name, the mythical aspects of scripture should not be regarded as dispensable for theology. In Barth's view, demythologizers unfairly demeaned the biblical worldview in their attempts to adapt Christianity to a modern worldview: "We ought not to overlook the fact that this particular worldview contained a number of features which the primitive community used cautiously but quite rightly in its witness to Jesus Christ." Moreover, Barth insisted, some of these mythical features remain indispensable to Christian speech: "We have every reason to make use of 'mythical' language in certain connections. And there is no need for us to have a guilty conscience about it, for if we went to extremes in demythologizing, it would be quite impossible to bear witness to Jesus Christ at all."[108]

As usual, Barth agreed with radical critics for conservative reasons; in this case, Bultmann's best critics were radicals like Fritz Buri. If Bultmann was going to make such a fuss about getting rid of a mythological worldview, he needed to stop talking about a personal God, the saving meaning of the cross and resurrection, and the irreducible core of the kerygma.[109]

From the beginning of the Barthian revolt, though Barth never lacked a strong reply, the strange narrowness that he imposed on theology was a stumbling block for theologians, even for Barthian theologians. Barth was rigidly devoted to *Sola Scriptura*. He ignored natural science and the natural world, paid little attention to social science, and claimed not to fathom why a Christian theologian should be interested in other religions. He was famous for his obnoxious performances at conferences, sometimes treating colleagues very rudely. He was more political than is often claimed, but he addressed political issues very selectively and sometimes eccentrically, as in his narrowly calibrated opposition to German Christianity, his non-opposition to Communism, and his quietly supportive but above-it-all relationship to democratic socialism. His later theology stifled the rhetorical dialectics that gave his early work its spiritual power. For all of Barth's warnings about the narrowness and hubris of theological systems, his dogmatics took on the appearance of a massive new Scholasticism. He claimed not to want followers, but he blasted even close followers when they dissented from his positions. Though he claimed to accept the necessity of biblical criticism, he made practically no use of it.

He was also anti-feminist, and only slightly reconstructed on this subject by the time that he wrote about the relation of male and female humanity in *Church Dogmatics*. In 1934 Henriette Visser't Hooft, the wife of Barth's friend, ecumenical leader W. A. Visser 't Hooft, wrote an article objecting to the domination-and-submission motif of 1 Cor. 11:5–9 and related scriptural passages. Against the Pauline implication that women exist for the sake of men, she argued for an egalitarian Christian ethic of mutual interest, trust, and responsibility. Barth replied that she simply misunderstood the spiritual necessity of patriarchy. In a private letter he explained that there were crucial reasons why the New Testament shared the patriarchal outlook of Hebrew scripture. The New Testament assumes everywhere that Christ belongs to the people of Israel, Barth noted; it further assumes that as a man, Christ confirmed Adam's superiority. More importantly, if Paul had assumed an ethic of mutuality between men and women, he would not have been able to express the superiority of God over humanity. This was the heart of the issue for Barth. "It is just so," he lectured, that man is superior to woman just as God is superior to humanity. It was "just so" that the Bible assumes an ethic of father rule, not mutuality.[110]

Fourteen years later, at the founding World Council of Churches assembly in Amsterdam, a handful of women dared to assert that good ecumenical Christianity should recognize the equal rights of women in church and society. American theologian Georgia Harkness, speaking at the conference's section on the Life and World of Women in the Churches, argued for the equality of women and men in the church. Barth took the floor to declare that Harkness was completely wrong, explaining that scripture teaches that man is the head of woman. Harkness cited Galatians 3:28 for support; Barth countered with Ephesians 5. The scene was painfully embarrassing to W. A. Visser 't Hooft, the General Secretary of the World Council, who basically agreed with Barth, but who lived with Henriette Visser 't Hooft. He later recalled that unfortunately, Barth "made fun of such women who, in his eyes, appeared to 'rush to equality.'" Henriette Visser 't Hooft told Barth that she was deeply saddened by his sarcasm and chauvinism. Barth's performance got poor reviews, and the following year, when a friend asked him if he remembered meeting a female theologian from the United States, Barth retorted, "Remember me not of that woman!"[111]

Three years later, *Church Dogmatics* III: 4 offered Barth's definitive discussion of the theology and ethics of gender. Fortunately, Henriette Visser 't Hooft must have given him second thoughts about his male chauvinism. The patronizing rhetoric of "it is just so" gave way to a torturous grappling with the problem of gender relations from a scriptural perspective. Although his English translators mistakenly represented him as denying any "false superiority" of men over women, Barth's German text did not speak of "true" or "false" superiority. He affirmed that men are not superior to women in any way. At the same time, he admonished that the church is obliged to adhere to the biblical doctrine that women are "second in sequence" to men. As sons of Adam, he asserted, men bear a "primacy of service" before God in the divine order revealed by scripture: "We cannot avoid the fact that it is real subordination." Moreover, although women were "entitled to complain" about any disrespectful or discriminatory treatment that they received, Barth opined that they were not entitled to complain about their "second place" spiritual status as daughters of Eve. That much was still just so, according to the Bible, and thus, according to Barth.[112]

Barth's chauvinism hardly stood out among male theologians of his time, but the downside of his devotion to *Sola Scriptura* and its self-authenticating authority was constantly lamented by theologians, exalting and limiting his influence at the same time, as he ruefully noted. Since Barth and Bultmann had important things in common, their clashes over which of them was more narrow and dogmatic were productive. Barth had less in common, however, with Tillich, and thus his exchanges with Tillich were less fruitful.

Yet Tillich was Barth's only rival as a theologian of historic importance from the 1920s to the 1960s. His disagreements with Barth centered on the very issues that made Barth strangely prominent and marginal at the same time. Barth's relationships to German idealism and liberal theology remain to be fully teased out, once we have Tillich in view. In Tillich's case, the affinities between German idealism and the neo-Reformation concepts that he shared with Barth were prominently featured.

Refashioning German Idealism: Paul Tillich

Tillich was born in Starzeddel, Germany, in 1886, where his father was a Lutheran pastor and parish superintendent. He earned his doctorate in philosophy in 1910 at the University of Breslau, where he wrote a dissertation on Schelling's philosophy of nature, and his licentiate in theology in 1912 at the University of Halle, where he studied under postliberal gadfly Martin Kähler. Schelling's nature romanticism spoke to Tillich, as did that of Goethe and Hölderlin. Tillich loved Schelling's sense of nature as the finite expression of the infinite ground of all things. He had begun his career as a pastor in the Evangelical Church of the Prussian Union when Germany went to war. Tillich volunteered to serve as an Army chaplain. At the time he knew little or nothing about politics, the class struggle, women, the working class, or himself, but he was eager to serve king and fatherland.[113]

The war burned a hole in Tillich's psyche that showed for the rest of his life. For four years at the western front he endured bayonet charges, battle fatigue, and nervous waiting, the disfigurement and death of friends, mass graves, and two nervous breakdowns. The battle of Champagne in 1915 marked a personal turning point. Tillich ministered all night to the wounded and dying as they were brought in, "many of them my close friends. All that horrible, long night I walked along the rows of dying men, and much of my German classical philosophy broke down that night." It seemed to him that the world was ending. A friend sent him a picture of herself sitting on a lawn, clothed in a white dress; Tillich wrote to her that it was inconceivable to him that something like that still existed. In the French forest, while reading Nietzsche's *Thus Spoke Zarathustra*, Tillich experienced a rare emotional lift; Nietzsche's ecstatic affirmation of life and his searing assault on Christian morality were intoxicating to the depressed chaplain. Tillich later recalled that he entered the forest a dreaming innocent and emerged from it a wild man.[114]

The only kind of theology that deserved to be written after the war had to address the abyss in human existence that the war revealed. Tillich judged that Schelling perceived the terrible void in life, but Schelling's romantic idealism compelled him to cover it up. Tillich later reflected, "The experience of the four years of war tore this chasm open for me and for my entire generation to such an extent, that it was impossible ever to cover it up." At the Spandau military base in Berlin, he witnessed the final disintegration of the Kaiser's government in 1918. While Germany abolished the monarchy and inaugurated a republic, Tillich developed a keen interest in political theory, stopped going to church, and developed friendships with a wide circle of Berlin intellectuals and bohemians. He began his academic career in 1919 at the University of Berlin, still dressed in his army grays and Iron Cross. In his first lecture Tillich opined that Troeltsch's *Social Teachings of the Christian Church* would become a classic; later that year, in a speech to the Kant Society of Berlin, he developed a signature thesis, that religion is the substance of culture and culture is the form of religion. The following year Tillich joined a band of religious socialists in Berlin, half of whom were Jews, and developed some of the key ideas of his theological system.[115]

These ideas included Tillich's later-famous concepts of kairos, religious socialism, and the demonic, his theory of the mythical essence of religion, and his dialectic of heteronomy and autonomy. Tillich argued that postwar Germany needed a socialist revolution that broke the power of the capitalist class while recovering a pre-modern sense of the sacred. This vision of a socialist transformation of Europe was linked to his belief in Germany's "kairotic" potential. *Kairos,* in Greek, is literally the "right time," distinguished from formal time, *chronos.* In Tillich's appropriation, the term implied a regenerative transformation of consciousness. The *kairos* was the rare historical moment when the eternal breaks into the ambiguous relativity of existence and creates something new. Tillich believed that Germany's humiliation and defeat contained kairotic potential, when bold new directions were suddenly possible. Bourgeois culture was corrupt and discredited, he argued; however, the socialisms of the social democratic and Marxist movements were products of the same spiritually bankrupt culture that these movements opposed. Europe needed an emancipatory religious socialism that synthesized and transcended the "heteronomous" consciousness of the pre-modern, authoritarian, theocratic past and the "autonomous" consciousness of the modern, individualistic, bourgeois present.[116]

This hope of kairotic liberation reflected Tillich's experience of personal transformation. In postwar Berlin he cultivated interests in art, literature, psychoanalysis, and politics; immersed himself in the culture of bohemian cafés and dance clubs; and indulged himself sexually, even after remarrying after a brief first marriage. He thrived on his new friendships and interests, sexual and otherwise, and rationalized that he could not fulfill his intellectual potential if he did not satisfy himself erotically, although he never completely threw off feelings of guilt about his promiscuity. In 1924 Tillich wrote in *Blätter für Religiösen Sozialismus,* "I have come to know the Bohéme; I went through the war; I got involved in politics; I became fascinated by the art of painting, and, in the course of this winter, with greatest passion by music." His second wife, Hannah Gottschow, shared his sexual lifestyle during their years in Germany, though not after they were exiled to the United States. Tillich was sexually promiscuous for the rest of his life, a fact that, after they moved to America, Hannah Tillich bitterly regretted and he assiduously kept secret.[117]

In 1924 he made a career move to Marburg; the following year he moved to the Dresden Institute of Technology. Tillich expounded his idea of a spiritually grounded socialism in *The Religious Situation* (1926), calling for a "faithful realist" revolt against bourgeois civilization. In much of European art, philosophy, and science, it was happening, he argued. The expressionist and postexpressionist movements in painting, the Nietzschean and Bergsonian philosophies of life, the Freudian discovery of the unconscious, and the Einsteinian revolution in physics were characterized by a fundamental openness to "the Unconditioned," Tillich's God term. Theology and the churches, however, lagged behind.[118]

Tillich recognized the prophetic spirit in Barth's dialecticism and acknowledged that it spoke powerfully to many people. Barth had taken the lead in helping the church respond to the postwar crisis of European civilization. But Barthian theology was merely a sophisticated form of otherworldliness, Tillich judged. In essence, Barth offered the God of Pauline supernaturalism as the answer to modern religious needs. This prescription, even in Barth's able rendering of it, was neither credible nor even cognizant of its religious elements. Tillich admonished that Barth's religion of faith was still religion, notwithstanding his polemics against religion.[119]

Barth replied that Tillich's God, the Unconditioned, was a "frosty monster" that smacked of Schleiermacher and Hegel, not Martin Luther. Barth rejected Tillich's "broad, general steamroller of faith and revelation, which, when I read Tillich, I cannot help seeing affecting everything and nothing as it rolls over houses, men and beasts as if it were self-evident that everywhere, everywhere, judgment and grace reigned, that everything, simply everything, is drawn into the strife and peace of the 'positive paradox.'" Tillich countered that Barth's otherworldly appeal to revelation ignored modern challenges to belief. If theologians wanted to say something worth saying, they had to become philosophers of culture as well as theologians: "Revelation is revelation to me in my conscious situation, in my historical reality."[120]

In 1929 Tillich landed his dream job, professor of philosophy at the University of Frankfurt, a the age of forty-three. For four years he exulted in Frankfurt's academic stature, his sophisticated new friends, the large following of students that he attracted, and his swirl of social engagements. In a way, Tillich was politically aware, finding a home among the Hegelianized Marxists later dubbed the "Frankfurt School." His colleagues included Leo Lowenthal, Adolph Löwe, Karl Mannheim, Kurt Riezler, Max Horkheimer, and Karl Mennicke. His first doctoral student was Theodor Adorno. Constantly they debated social theory and politics. But the Frankfurt Schoolers were more inclined to theory than real-world politics, and they noted that Tillich was an extreme case, prone to a childlike optimism and a professorial obliviousness to ordinary life. Tillich dreamed of a religious socialist movement not linked to any party. He spurned electoral politics until 1929, when he reluctantly held his nose and joined the Social Democrats as a concession to political reality; the Nazis were gaining.[121]

But he still refused to believe that cultured Germany might turn to the thuggish National Socialists; thus he never became an active member of the Social Democrats. In June 1932, witnessing a savage attack upon Jewish and leftist students at Frankfurt by Nazi students and storm troopers, Tillich belatedly realized that his beloved nation was on the brink of a catastrophe. That summer he wrote a book, *The Socialist Decision,* which warned against a German stampede toward fascism and a second world war. Tillich called for a union of middle class and proletarian forces to stop fascism. Hitler, however, was appointed chancellor over a coalition government in January 1933, while the book was in production; the March elections gave Hitler a solid majority; on March 21 he was granted dictatorial powers. Tillich's imaginary coalition of proletarians and middle-class Christians chose fascism. His book was printed too late to leave the warehouse, Tillich was declared an enemy of the state, and with great reluctance he accepted an offer of refuge by Union Theological Seminary.[122]

Tillich knew next to nothing about American theology. He dreaded that American culture was provincial and superficial. He told friends that leaving cultured Germany was a kind of death for him. Though he was grateful to the United States and Union Seminary for rescuing him from likely harm, he doubted that he could continue his theological and philosophical work anywhere outside Germany, and he found American academe especially unpromising. American philosophy was pragmatic and empiricist. American theology seemed undeveloped at best. American students bantered with professors practically as equals, a phenomenon that shocked Tillich at first. Yet it was in the United States that he won astounding academic and public renown as a theologian.

In 1936 Tillich tried to introduce himself by explaining that Barth was an authoritarian theologian and that he was a theologian in the liberal tradition. Barthian theology played a prophetic role in the Confessional Church's resistance to fascism, Tillich allowed, "but it created at the same time a new heteronomy, an anti-autonomous and anti-humanistic feeling, which I must regard as an abnegation of the Protestant principle." For Tillich, the "Protestant principle" was the constitutively Protestant commitment to the spirit of criticism. Though Tillich made occasional broadsides against "liberal theology," he always had Ritschlian theology in mind. He took for granted that he belonged to the broader liberal tradition, as did the most authentically Protestant theologians: "It was and is impossible for me to associate myself with the all too-common criticism of 'liberal thinking.' I would rather be accused of being 'liberalistic' myself, than aid in discounting the great and truly human element in the liberal idea."[123]

Tillich's opposition to Ritschlian liberalism centered on two convictions that he took from his doctoral mentor at Halle, Martin Kähler, plus Tillich's rejection of Ritschl's bourgeois conservatism. Kähler taught that the Pauline/Lutheran doctrine of justification is the central doctrine of Christianity and that the foundation of Christian belief is the biblical picture of Christ, not the changing picture of the historical Jesus yielded by historical criticism. These convictions enabled Tillich to play a role in the dialectical theology movement; he shared Barth's neo-Reformation theme that no human belief, claim, or work has any saving value. The doctrine of justification relativized all orthodoxies while affirming that the burden of human sin is overcome by the paradoxical judgment that the sinner is just before God. Like Kähler, Tillich spurned the liberal tendency to dissolve the paradox of justification into moral categories, and he embraced Kähler's thesis that the center of Christianity is the picture of Christ that thrives in human experience and is preached by the church. Tillich overlooked that both of these arguments could be made on Ritschlian grounds. Negatively, what mattered was that the Ritschlian School tended to moralize the gospel, it clung to the shifting tides of historical criticism, and it identified with the bourgeoisie. For Tillich, liberal criticism was the glory of liberal theology, but liberal dogmatics tended to be religiously shallow.[124]

Before World War I, Tillich believed that Schelling's philosophy of existence and his interpretation of history as the history of salvation showed how the disciplines of theology and philosophy should be united. After the war, Tillich still ranked Schelling above other religious philosophers, but he judged that Schelling played down the experience of the void. Tillich's experience of the abyss in existence effected the only intellectual turn that he ever made. "The World War in my own experience was the catastrophe of idealistic thinking in general," he recalled. For philosophy to be true and real, it had to speak to the existential realities of estrangement, despair, the void, the demonic, and death.[125]

His models for philosophical thinking of that sort were Nietzsche and Martin Heidegger. Tillich and Heidegger were colleagues at Marburg in 1924 when Heidegger conceived *Being and Time*. Tillich was fascinated by Heidegger's description of human beings as the unique type of being through whom Being (the primordial ground) presents itself to be known. He absorbed Heidegger's vivid theorizing of the "thrown" character of human "being-there" (*Dasein*) and the perils that attend the self's coming-to-awareness of its arbitrarily given ("thrown") existence. Heidegger's account of the choice between "authentic" and "inauthentic" existence impressed Tillich and Bultmann as a powerful, modern, existential way of expressing the truths of Pauline theology. Like Bultmann, Tillich theologized Heidegger's description of the inauthentic self falling into anxiety, or replacing its first (infantile) totalized form of life with a substitute, or giving up caring ("fallenness"). He took over Heidegger's notion that the authentic self faces up to one's nothingness and becomes a caretaking "being-toward-death" by changing the form of one's totalized givenness. Authentic existence, Heidegger argued, is the way of death-accepting courage and care for the world.[126]

Although Heidegger was an atheist, Tillich emphasized the Christian wellspring of his thinking. Although Heidegger was a Nazi, Tillich stayed off the topic of Heidegger's politics, not knowing the extent of Heidegger's commitment to fascism. Tillich stressed that much of Heidegger's ostensibly original language derived from the sermon literature of German Pietism. Heideggerian philosophy did not include the theological answer to the problem of existence or offer a philosophical version of this answer, since that would be idealism, not existentialism. However, existentialism asked the question in a fresh and radical way. For Tillich, existential analysis clarified and developed the ontological problem to which faith and theology were the answer. It did not replace idealism or theology; it supplemented the philosophical account of reality that undergirded theology. Philosophically, Tillich gave central place to Schelling and Heidegger, while affirming that "the boundary line between philosophy and theology is the center of my thought and work."[127]

For Tillich there was always a dialectic. His central one was the dialectic of sacramental consciousness (mythic and heteronomous) contradicted by rational consciousness (myth-negating and autonomous) leading to his own system, which he called theonomous religion or religious socialism. The central dialectic of his own system paired idealism with Marxism. German idealism was life and bread to Tillich, beginning with Kant's demonstration that the possibility of theoretical knowledge cannot be explained by pointing to the realm of things. Tillich explained, "I grew up in the atmosphere of German idealism, and doubt that I can ever forget what I learned from it." For him, idealism was essentially the principle of identity, not a metaphysical system. It was the point where subject and object came together, "a principle for analyzing the basic character of all knowledge." More precisely, "I am epistemologically an idealist, if idealism means the assertion of the identity of thought and being as the principle of truth."[128]

With Kant and Schelling, Tillich conceived idealism as a philosophy of freedom – the approach that takes most seriously the human penchant for creativity, asking questions, recognizing absolute demands, and perceiving meaningful forms in nature, art, and society. There is a correspondence between reality and the human spirit that is best expressed in the concept of meaning, Tillich argued; he agreed with Hegel about the unity of objective and subjective spirit: "Whenever idealism elaborates the categories that give meaning to the various realms of existence, it seeks to fulfill that task which alone is the justification of philosophy."[129]

But Tillich had no stake in Hegel's system, or even Schelling's. The later Schelling was sensitive to the problem of essentialist systems, Tillich noted. Schelling grasped that reality is the manifestation *and* contradiction of pure essence and that, above all, "human existence itself is an expression of the contradiction of essence." Schelling had an existential impulse, but he kept it on a leash. Tillich reveled in Kierkegaard's one-sided attacks on essentialism, his unleashed polemics on behalf of subjectivity, and his profound reflections on anxiety and despair, which cleared the way for Tillich to appropriate Nietzsche and Heidegger.[130]

Kierkegaard was a corrective within the idealist framework; Marxism offered a critique of the ideological character of all intellectual schemes; Tillich held Kierkegaard and Marx together as a dialectical antithesis. For Kierkegaard and Marx, Tillich noted, truth was bound to the situation of the knower. Kierkegaard emphasized the situation of the individual, while Marx emphasized the social situation. In both cases, knowledge of pure essence had to wait for contradictions within existence to be recognized and overcome. Tillich spurned the utopian, economistic, materialist, and atheist aspects of Marx's thought, but he took seriously Marx's ideology critique, which taught him that every vision and concept of harmony is untrue under the conditions of the class struggle. Tillich had no interest in the kind of idealism that set Hegel or Schelling against Marx as an either/or. For Marx, truth was found in the interest of the exploited class that becomes conscious of itself as the force that overcomes the class struggle. For Tillich, the paradoxical truth of Marxist criticism was intelligible from a Christian standpoint: The greatest possibility of obtaining a truth not tainted by ideology occurs at the point of despair, "in man's greatest estrangement from his own nature."[131]

For years Tillich struggled with the English language, finding it easy to read, but hard to understand and extremely difficult to speak. He taught at Union Theological Seminary from 1933 to 1955, at Harvard University from 1955 to 1962, and at the University of Chicago Divinity School from 1962 until his death in 1965, lecturing across the nation and world after his books made him famous, although he never became more than a passable English speaker. He took little interest in American theology, although he enjoyed personal interactions with American theologians. For many years Tillich missed Germany desperately, while doubting that he would be able to construct his system in a foreign land.

From 1942 to 1944 he delivered weekly radio addresses for the Voice of America that were broadcast in Germany. Beginning at an Allied low point in the war and concluding just before D-Day 1944, Tillich delivered 112 speeches. Each began with the salutation, "My German friends!" Passionately he called for the defeat of fascism and the federation of Europe; repeatedly he condemned the Nazi annihilation of the Jews. His first address declared that "the Jews are the people of history, the people of the prophetic, future-judging spirit" and that the blood of the Jews was "upon us and our children." In December 1942 Tillich began to give detailed descriptions of the death trains and the machine-gun executions of Jews: "Today they are being hauled away to mass death by German hangmen, by those who are trash and the disgrace of the German people, and you are standing by! Can you stand by any longer, German officers, when you still have a sword to use and an honor to lose?...Do you know that the cattle cars that roll through the German cities with this burden of wretchedness are bolted up for days; that no bread and water is let in, no dying or dead are let out; and that at the end of the journey, frequently over half of the deportees are lying dead on the ice-cold floor of the car? And you want to be spectators of that, German clergy, you who are praying for German victory?"[132]

Tillich had been schooled in the hope of a unified Europe led by Germany. Now he declared that this dream had been forfeited by the spectacular evil of the Nazi torturers and executioners: "I believe that National Socialism was the outbreak and the concentration of nearly all that was diseased within the German soul. Long have these poisons accumulated within it." At Advent he warned: "You can't have it both ways. Whoever follows National Socialism must persecute the child in the manger." German life had become "pre-human," he lamented; Germans needed to be reborn into the human race: "Two thousand years of German education out of barbarity into humanity have been taken back. The chivalry of the Middle Ages toward the enemy is forgotten, but the cruelty of the Middle Ages has arisen again and has brutalized the hearts and trampled all nobility underfoot. The humanity of the classical age of Germans is being made contemptuous, but the warlike instincts of the German past have become intensified beyond all boundaries." The Nazi regime was based on "the desire for human degradation, abuse, and elimination of the enemy," Tillich declared: "National Socialism is brutality coupled with lust for revenge and a deep inner weakness." With a hopeful spirit he assured: "Everything that is creative in the German people demands a return to the human race … For all nations – but particularly for Germany, the country of Middle Europe – everything will depend on the fact that the national remains subordinated to the human race as a whole."[133]

In 1948 Tillich returned to Germany, gave numerous lectures, and was warmly received, as long as he stayed off the topic of German guilt. Tillich was disturbed by the self-pity of his German friends and their refusal to think of themselves as guilty for the fate of the Jews; he reasoned that their feeling of guilt was so great that they were forced to repress it. He criticized Barth and the Confessing Church for protesting only against the Nazi perversion of Christianity, but he had an unexpectedly jovial reunion with Barth in Basel. Another reunion with a former friend, Nazi theologian Emanuel Hirsch, was much harder for Tillich, as Hirsch was blind, impoverished, bitter, and unapologetic. Numerous German universities offered teaching positions to Tillich, who carefully considered each one, but returned to the United States. He had become an American, and he no longer worried that he could not write theology outside Germany. A collection of his articles, *The Protestant Era,* was published to great acclaim in 1948, as was a collection of his sermons, *The Shaking of the Foundations.* He had begun to write the first volume of his *Systematic Theology,* one of the major works of twentieth-century theology. To a friend Tillich wrote, "Harvest time is here; indeed I am now gathering in my harvest!"[134]

To much of his audience and even to many of his colleagues at Union Theological Seminary it was puzzling that Tillich was so indebted to Nietzsche and Heidegger. How could a theologian sympathize with Nietzsche's anti-Christian atheism? The answer was that Tillich's idealist wellspring freed him to take daring excursions into the realms of radical doubt and criticism. He did not worry that he would lose his idealist language and inspiration – analytic philosophy had nothing to tempt him. Moreover, Nietzschean disbelief aggressively stated the negative side of what Tillich believed. The God that Nietzsche and Heidegger rejected, Tillich argued, was the God that is bound to the structural dichotomy of subject and object. If God is an object for human subjects, and human beings are objects for God as a subject, God deprives every subject of her subjectivity by reducing her to an object of God's all consuming power. Tillich stressed that the human subject, if merely an object, revolts, trying to make God into an object, "but the revolt fails and becomes desperate." If God is a being among other beings, God inevitably becomes the enemy of freedom and subjectivity: "This is the God Nietzsche said had to be killed because nobody can tolerate being made into a mere object of absolute knowledge and absolute control."[135]

The crowning irony of Tillich's ironically famous American career was that his masterwork, *Systematic Theology,* had to be translated into German. There he unfolded the distinct fund of concepts about religion, God, Christ, and myth that he refashioned from Schelling, Hegel, and German mysticism, employing a method of correlation. Tillich's method began with existential questions raised in the modern cultural situation, which he answered by reinterpreting Christian symbols. Christianity has true answers to the challenges of modern disbelief, he urged, but the agenda for theology must be shaped by the challenges, not by the answers. Claiming to speak out of revelation and faith alone is not credible or real. Tillich explained, "Every theologian is committed and alienated; he is always in faith *and* in doubt; he is inside *and* outside the theological circle. Sometimes the one side prevails, sometimes the other; and he is never certain which side really prevails."[136]

The Christian answer is the theologian's ultimate concern, but no formulation of it is infallibly correct or culturally unconditioned. Religion is ultimate concern, Tillich argued, which is unconditional, "independent of any conditions of character, desire, or circumstance." To absolutize something that is merely relative and conditional is idolatrous. This was the key to the critique of religion that Tillich shared with Barth, except that Tillich did not exempt Christian theology from being religious. He urged that religion is demonic to the extent that it absolutizes an idol of its own making. Good theology gives itself only to the unconditioned; thus, the object and first formal criterion of theology is that which concerns us ultimately: "Only those propositions are theological which deal with their object in so far as it can become a matter of ultimate concern for me."[137]

The second formal criterion of theology was about the appropriate content of ultimate concern. Tillich held that a worthy ultimate concern must determine our being or not-being. Nothing that does not possess the power of threatening or saving one's being deserves to be an ultimate concern. "Being," for Tillich, did not refer to existence in time and space, for existence is constantly threatened and saved by things and events that fall short of ultimacy. Being is the "whole of human reality, the structure, the meaning, and the aim of existence." True religion is about cosmic meaning, the saving of the whole that is threatened. It is unconditionally concerned about that which conditions human existence beyond the conditions that indwell and surround human beings.[138]

Just as Schleiermacher described true religion before making an argument for Christianity as the best example of true religion, Tillich described the twofold criterion of good theology before making an argument for Christianity as the best theological answer. Christian theology is like other theologies, he observed; it is *logos* of *theos,* a rational interpretation of religious rituals, symbols, and myths. But Christian theology is founded on a transcendent claim, that the Logos entered history in and through the life of a human being, Jesus. The essential Christian affirmation is that the divine logos, the mind of God, was uniquely revealed in the event of Jesus as the Christ. Tillich did not aspire to orthodoxy in the manner of William Temple, yet he held fast to the same basis of Christian identity. Christianity is distinctively concrete and universal, Tillich argued. It makes a claim about Jesus that is more concrete than any mystical vision or metaphysical principle, yet no vision or principle is as universal as the logos, "which itself is the principle of universality." Compared to the logos, everything else is particular, including the half-God Arian theology that nearly captured Christianity in the fourth century. Tillich was grateful that the Athanasian party prevailed, because Arian theology sold short the universality and the concreteness of the Johannine confession that the Word became flesh and dwelt among us.[139]

Tillich recognized four sources of theology – the Bible, church history, history of religions, and culture – while dissenting from the liberal convention of conceiving personal experience as a theological source. Schleiermacher derived the entire content of Christianity from the religious consciousness of the Christian; other varieties of liberal theology and pietism treated personal experience as a source of theology; Tillich countered that experience is the medium through which the sources of theology speak to religious thinkers. Theologians experience the power of their sources before analyzing them. Experience is receptive, not productive, for the productive power of experience is limited to the transformation of what is given to it. True reception intends only reception; if it intends something else, such as transformation, it falsifies that which is received. The event of Jesus Christ is infinite in its meaning, Tillich acknowledged, but as the singular, defining event of Christianity, it is the criterion of religious experience. Experience is a vehicle for theology, not a norm or independent source, for the event of Jesus as the Christ is given to experience, not derived from it.[140]

Here the idealist emphasis on the creativity and primacy of experience had to be held in check. Tillich reasoned that if a univocal unity existed between the (regenerated) human spirit and the divine Spirit, it would be appropriate to conceive experience as an independent source of theology. But on this point he remained a good Lutheran. Pietists, Methodists, mystics, sanctificationists, moral perfectionists, and sectarians had a history of making exorbitant claims for regenerated experience, Tillich judged. Liberal idealists, too, had a tendency to obscure the eschatological aspect of the Christian vision of divine-human unity, reading themselves into the incarnation of Christ. Tillich had a strong concept of the experience of new being in Christ; it was the linchpin of his Christology. But he had a firmly Lutheran sense of the not-yet of divine-human unity. Even the saint remains a sinner, Tillich admonished. Revelation may occur through modern saints, just as it occurred through the prophets and apostles, but revelation always comes *to* the saints and *against* their nature, not from them: "Insight into the human situation destroys every theology which makes experience an independent source instead of a dependent medium of systematic theology."[141]

Above all, beyond his immensely influential theories of religion, correlation, ultimacy, new being, and religious socialism, Tillich taught many theologians and non-theological scholars of religion, plus a vast public audience, how to think about myth and symbolism. Here the influence of the later Schelling was pronounced. Like Schelling, Tillich argued that myth is an essential component of human life and thought, and symbols convey the mythical truths of religion. Myths are not merely prescientific explanations of events in the world, Tillich stressed; they are constellations of symbols that express humanity's relation to that which concerns human beings ultimately. Though science is anti-mythical in its study of objects, even science is myth-creative in its conceptual theorizing. Science makes sense of the world by making use of concepts (such as "evolution") that are transcendent to things. By its nature, myth (like science) seeks to unify creation, or at least make it intelligible, under a single conceptuality.

The key to myth is its unifying impulse, yet ironically, myth is true only in its broken form. To the mythical consciousness, Tillich argued, the transcendent realm is perfectly knowable, and the workings of the natural world are readily explainable. Pure unbroken myth is always a history of the gods. With the rise of Hebrew monotheism, the mythical unity of religion and science began to break apart. God was transcendent; his name was not to be spoken; he lived even if his nation died. Human consciousness of the relativity of knowledge in the transcendent realm and the natural world made each realm more independent.[142]

But Tillich urged that the desacralization of the world does not negate the necessity of true myth. Rather, the breaking of mythical consciousness allows the true character of myth to come forth as an aspect of thought. Even in its broken state, the mythical imagination seeks to find the hidden wholeness of reality. In this meaning-seeking drive to reunify the world, broken myth has its primary value for theology. The world of things described by science is related to its unconditioned ground, the unconditioned transcendent is interpreted from the viewpoint of modern knowledge, and the unifying impulse of religion is restored in the broken symbol. In other words, Tillich argued, science becomes myth-creative out of its need to theorize that which transcends the world of things, theology accepts the authority of science regarding knowledge of the natural world, and theology relates all such knowledge to the religious transcendent. Myth, in its drive to unify these fields of experience, participates in and points to the unconditioned: "The thing referred to in the mythical symbol is the unconditioned transcendent, the source of both existence and meaning, which transcends being-in-itself as well as being-for-us."[143]

Because symbolism is the language of faith, myth is intrinsic to every act of faith. Tillich cautioned that this does not make it beyond criticism. All mythical speech must be demythologized by modern knowledge before it can be useful for theology. The religious ultimate transcends space and time, but myth expresses its stories of the divine in the framework of space and time; it even negates the ultimacy of the divine by dividing the divine into multiple figures. Demythologizing, Tillich argued, to the extent that it breaks and deliteralizes religious myth, is an indispensable aspect of theology. On the other hand, any demythologizing strategy that negates myth is terribly wrong, because it silences the experience of the Holy, depriving religion of its language. Anti-mythical rationalism fails to understand that myth and symbol are ever-present forms of human consciousness. One can replace a myth by another myth, but myth itself is constitutive to the spiritual life.[144]

The test of a myth or a symbol, Tillich taught, is whether it expresses the spiritual realities in which it participates and to which it points. Symbols differ from signs inasmuch as symbols participate in the reality to which they point. Symbols and signs both point beyond themselves to something else, but symbols participate in the meaning and power of the reality for which they stand. A symbol opens up the deepest dimension of the human soul and reality, which is the ultimate power of being. It radiates the power of being and meaning of that for which the symbol stands. It is true to the extent that it expresses the inner necessity that it carries for consciousness. That is, a religious symbol is true to the extent that it reaches its Unconditioned referent. Tillich explained, "The only criterion that is at all relevant is this: that the Unconditioned is clearly grasped in its Unconditionedness. A symbol that does not meet this requirement and that elevates a conditioned thing to the dignity of the Unconditioned, even if it should not be false, is demonic." To worship anything less than the Unconditioned transcendent is to commit idolatry.[145]

Interrogating German Liberal Theology and Idealism

In the broad sense of the term that included Kant, Schleiermacher, Schelling, Hegel, and Troeltsch, Tillich was a liberal, and said so. His theology was in the German idealist line of these figures, though mediated by Kierkegaard, Marx, Heidegger, Barthian dialecticism, and the horrors of the twentieth century. For Barth, by contrast, it was imperative to find an alternative to the liberal tradition, not merely its Ritschlian iteration. All of Barth's differences with Tillich cut to this one. Yet Barth had complicated relationships with Kant, Schleiermacher, Hegel, and Herrmann. He shared a great deal with Hegel and Herrmann, though he rarely discussed this fact. He took for granted Kant's dichotomy between pure reason and practical reason, which legitimized his own circumscribed idea of theology as a discipline. He shared almost nothing with Troeltsch, although he discussed Troeltsch often, since Troeltsch represented a plausible and deadly option that had to be kept in mind in order to be avoided. Ritschl, for Barth, was too superficial and corrupted by cultural religiosity to be worth keeping in mind; thus, Barth dismissed Ritschl with contempt. Schleiermacher, for Barth, was the most complicated case of all, the one with which Barth was never quite finished.

Barth respected Kant for standing alone as the epitome of the Enlightenment and as its most important critic – the singular figure through whom the eighteenth century "understood and affirmed itself in its own limitations." Kant did not rely on the authority of anyone else, Barth stressed. Kant lived by the light of his own reason, exactly as he prescribed, and he established that criticism entails being critical "of knowledge itself and of knowledge as such," imposing Kantian modesty on overblown Enlightenment ambitions. Barth, in his admiration mode, reached for his highest compliment, comparing Kant to Mozart: "In Kant's philosophy, as in the music of Mozart, there is something of the calm and majesty of death which seems suddenly to loom up from afar to oppose the eighteenth century."[146]

Barth waved off any responsibility to examine Kant's critiques of reason in detail. For a theologian, he averred, it was enough to grasp the upshot of Kantian criticism for Christianity. On the one hand, Barth admired Kant's willingness to defy the spirit of the age by emphasizing the radical evil of human beings, and he respected Kant for contorting his prose so that he never said the name of Jesus, even as Kant expounded on the "teacher of the Gospel" and the "founder of the Church." Kant had the courage of his convictions, showing how his rules should be carried out. On the other hand, Barth observed, Kant's "vulgar Pelagian doctrine of justification" was a pitiful response to the human predicament, which showed the fateful limitations of Kant's rationalistic and moralistic concept of Christianity. For Kant, a passage of scripture was true only to the extent that it advanced the moral concerns of practical reason. Barth chided that this hermeneutic distorted vast portions of the Bible that are about other things. Kant's entire rendering of religion rested on a single "if, then" proposition. If the reality of religion is limited to that which is subject to the self-critique of reason, it is nothing more than whatever fits the ideally practical nature of reason. The Ritschlian School, Barth observed, took this Kantian option, for better and for worse. Barth, for his part, embraced a different Kantian trope, even if Kant "laughed up his sleeve" when he said it. In *The Dispute of the Faculties,* Kant contended that theologians were scribes of a church faith that expounded whatever God supposedly said in the Bible, while philosophers were bound by the dictates of reason. That division of labor, Barth said, was fine with him.[147]

But that was misleading, because Barth used philosophy eclectically, and the bent of his thought resembled one philosopher in particular – Hegel. Barth admired Hegel above all philosophers, notwithstanding Hegel's hubris, and also because of it. Barth took seriously Hegel's claim that Christian ideas were fundamental to his system, not mere window dressing. Hegel had defining Christian commitments and a theological basis. Moreover, Barth recognized that his theology had key affinities with Hegel's, especially in its revelatory Trinitarian objectivism. Like Hegel, Barth traced the objective unfolding of divine Spirit in threefold form, arguing that God is who God is in God's *action*.

But Hegel epitomized the philosophical colonization of theology, just as Troeltsch epitomized historicism run amuck. Hegel's God was the *event* of reason writ large, the whole of wholes; for Barth, the Christian God was either wholly Other or not really God. Hegel's God self-revealed out of logical necessity; for Barth, that was horribly wrong, since the revealed God of Christian grace is the threefold sovereign *One* who *loves* in *freedom*. Barth took for granted the "system" interpretation of Hegel; thus he missed the primacy of negation in Hegel's dialectic. Yet he appreciated the difficulty of refuting Hegel. With keen admiration of a kind, Barth cautioned his students to think three times before they disagreed with Hegel, "because we might find that everything we are tempted to say in contradiction of it has already been said within it, and provided with the best possible answer."[148]

For Barth, the Hegelian system was a stupendous perfection of the "philosophy of self-confidence," the realization of Western idealism. If one believed in idealizing reason, one could not do better than Hegel. In fact, if the Enlightenment had the right project, using only one's understanding, it was pointless to stick with Kant, because Kant left the mind in a hopeless conflict with the objects of mind and the contingencies of history. Barth argued that Hegel got somewhere by folding objects, history, and human destiny into his theory of mind. Hegel was the "great perfecter and surpasser of the Enlightenment" because he resolved the great conflicts between reason and revelation, subject and object, the God in us and the God in Christ, and thought and being, and he did it "to a highly satisfactory conclusion." Hegel left out nothing and he thought everything through. Barth explained, "It is nothing less than everything which is in question, and everything must continually be in question, the ultimate included, for the ultimate, too, in the self-movement of truth, must ever and again become the first." Knowing – science itself – exists only in the event, like God, the idea or mind of all events.[149]

Barth admired Hegel's audacity in making philosophers and theologians deal with Christian concepts; he especially admired Hegel's emphatic Trinitarianism. The leading theologians of Hegel's time, Barth noted, "had absolutely no desire for a renewal of the doctrine of the Trinity. In propounding it Hegel was theologizing in his own way, alone and acknowledging no master, against the philosophers and the theologians." Hegel, to his immense credit, unlike Schleiermacher, did not shrink from claiming certain knowledge of truth. Hegel was not content to secure a home for Christianity in personal feeling; he reached for the Creator of heaven and earth, the Lord over life and death. Barth explained, "Knowledge of God could be the knowledge of irreconcilable contradictions and their eternal vanquishing in the mind. Knowledge of God could mean the passage through the contradictions of reason to the peace that is higher than all reason, and the emergence into these contradictions in comforted despair." This was Hegel's audacity, to make the modern age see itself through the looking glass of Christian truth. Hegelian philosophy was a "theological invasion," Barth contended. It challenged intellectuals to found their precious modernizing consciousness on a theology, just as Hegel allowed his philosophy to be transformed into a theology.[150]

This invasion, Barth observed, did not succeed, because "this partner, modern cultural awareness, did in fact let Hegel down." Hegel, the greatest modern philosopher, was a great success, but on nothing like the scale that he sought. Modern consciousness did not seek to understand itself in its own depth, and it did not want to be reconciled with Christianity. Non-Hegelian liberal theologians, aping their secular colleagues, judged that Hegel was too demanding. His conditions were too theological, and he claimed too much in claiming to know about God. Barth begged to differ. The problem was that Hegel did not demand enough of modern consciousness. There was not too much Christian theology in Hegel's system, but too little, *if* it was to seem "worthy of belief."[151]

Barth acknowledged that Hegel had a robustly positive and historical understanding of revelation, not mentioning the Barthian dependence on it. Moreover, Hegel "emphatically affirmed" the uniqueness and divinity of Christ; Barth took no interest in questioning whether Hegel was "really" a Christian. Those who questioned it were usually secular types who refused to believe that Hegel meant what he said, since that made Hegel unlike them. But Hegelian idealism conceived God and Christ as elements of a system, Barth argued. For Hegel, Christ was the gift of necessity, not of free grace: "With Hegel, God and man can never confront one another in a relationship which is actual and indissoluble; a word, a new word revelatory in the strict sense, cannot pass between them; it cannot be uttered and cannot be heeded." Hegel had no concept of objective revelation apart from the objectivity of everything that exists for consciousness. Hegelian revelation, like all knowledge of other kinds, must pass through objectivity, since knowledge is bound up with the moment of perception. This objectivity, Barth explained, which includes the objectivity of revelation, "is anything but indissoluble." Hegel granted objective revelation the status of revelation at the level of religious imagination, but he charged philosophy, "the delegated authority of mind," with the task of raising religious imagery to forms of thought suited to mind.[152]

Barth pressed hard on the upshot for Christianity. Even if Hegelians allowed ministers and ordinary folk to go on speaking in pictures, Hegelianism was about reducing that which is revealed to its purely logical content. Reason, in Hegelian theology, is as revelatory as the imagination; plus reason has a higher calling. Barth offered a striking picture to describe it: "When God manifests himself the philosopher of religion has already understood him in the preliminaries of this act, and he already has the lever in his hand which he has only to depress to advance from God's act of revealing to the higher level of God being manifest, in which every given thing, all duality, is annulled, all speaking and listening has lost its object and been transformed again into pure knowing, the knowing of the human subject, as it originally proceeded from him." Hegel had a stronger concept of God's aliveness than most theologians of his time, Barth allowed; however, it was the aliveness of thought being thought by living selves. Hegel's God lived as the life of human thinkers, a "merely thinking and merely thought God" before whom actual human selves either stand as idols or dissolve to nothing.[153]

Barth realized, however, that Hegel could be read differently on the issue of individual personality, and he did not rest there. Even if he was wrong about equating Hegel's God with human acts of life, he knew for sure that Hegel abolished God's sovereignty. Hegel's God was "his own prisoner," Barth judged. Hegel had a concept of divine omniscience as God's comprehension of all things, but Hegel's God had no freedom not to self-reveal. In Hegelian dialectic, a mind that does not manifest itself is not a mind, and Hegel described God as being utterly manifest. Barth remarked: "Hegel, in making the dialectical method of logic the essential nature of God, made impossible the knowledge of the actual dialectic of grace, which has its foundation in the freedom of God." Hegel's God is not free from human beings. To Barth, that was a dreadful non-starter, for God cannot be free for human beings if God is not free from human beings. God is free in God's relationships to all that is not God. Precisely because God is sovereign, Barth contended, God is free to transcend all that is other than God's self and is free to be immanent within all things. That is, God is free to be the God of radical Christian grace poured out on all humanity for the salvation of the world.[154]

Hegel tried to be the Protestant Thomas Aquinas, but he did not bring enough Christianity with him, and his project was impossible anyway within the culture of modernity. For better or worse, Barth contended, Schleiermacher was the theologian of liberal Christianity and the modern era. This was not even a judgment for Barth; it was obvious, a given. To Barth's teachers, especially Herrmann, Schleiermacher towered over modern theology and Christianity. Barth carried that impression with him into his ministry and never wavered from it. The Barthian revolt in theology, at its beginning, was about breaking free of liberal theology without losing Schleiermacher.

For six years Barth struggled with the question whether Schleiermacher had launched modern theology down a sub-Christian path. He was slow to render a verdict because he wanted desperately to be linked to Schleiermacher. As late as 1920, Barth assured himself that Schleiermacher would have approved of the redirection in his thinking. He accepted Herrmann's reading that Schleiermacher's understanding of Christianity did not derive from a general theory of religious consciousness; Schleiermacher was centered on Jesus and redemption. As for the capitulation of German theologians in

1914 to nationalism and militarism, Barth did not believe it was a logical outgrowth of Schleiermacher's nationalism and modernism. For the rest of his life, Barth insisted that Schleiermacher would not have signed "that horrible manifesto."[155]

But he did change his mind about Schleiermacher's fatally compromised Christianity leading logically to something worse. In 1921 Barth told Thurneysen that he had the muzzle of his gun trained upon Schleiermacher and was ready to declare war upon him. Later that year, Barth's second edition *Romans* blasted Schleiermacher for turning the gospel into a religion. Liberal theology treated the gospel of Christ as one human possibility among others, Barth explained: "Since Schleiermacher, this attempt has been undertaken more consciously than ever before in Protestant theology – and it is the betrayal of Christ."[156]

This stunning reproach was the culmination of Barth's half-dozen years of straining not to believe that the problem began with Schleiermacher. He later recalled that he was finally unable to resist the verdict that the corrupted culture-Protestantism of his teachers "was grounded, determined, and influenced decisively" by Schleiermacher. In 1923 he told his students at Göttingen that they needed to study Schleiermacher in order to understand themselves: "If anyone still speaks today in Protestant theology as though he were still among us, it is Schleiermacher. We *study* Paul and the reformers, but we *see* with the eyes of Schleiermacher and think along the same lines as he did." Modern academic theologians simply assumed that the subject of theology is religion, Barth observed. All presumed to understand the meaning of Christianity by studying the phenomenon of religious self-consciousness. That was the liberal project that linked Kant and Schleiermacher to Schelling, Hegel, Ritschl, Harnack, Troeltsch, and modern theology as a whole.[157]

Barth pressed his students to recognize the immensity of Schleiermacher's influence on them. It was from Schleiermacher, usually indirectly, that they took their governing assumptions about the nature of Christianity and how it should be studied. To be sure, Schleiermacher inspired a wide range of liberal theologies – confessional, Pietist, rationalist, mediationist, and so on. Granted, the nineteenth century produced a few dissenters from the liberal juggernaut – Kierkegaard, Beck, Overbeck, Kutter, both Blumhardts, and a few others. In other contexts Barth included his father in this list. But these figures made little impact on their time, he stressed, and all other currents of nineteenth-century religious thought had to accommodate the overwhelming influence of liberal theology. Barth continued: "Theologically the 'genius' of the major part of the church is that of Schleiermacher. All the so-to-speak official impulses and movements of the centuries since the Reformation find a center of unity in him: orthodoxy, pietism, the Enlightenment. All the official tendencies of the Christian present emanate from him like rays: church life, experiential piety, historicism, psychologism, and ethicism."[158]

Barth reprised Joachim Christian Gass' prediction of 1822, that Schleiermacher's dogmatics launched a new era of theological studies, and August Neander's declaration on the day of Schleiermacher's death, that Schleiermacher inaugurated a new period of church history. These prophecies were amply fulfilled, Barth told his students; the proof was that they lived in what was still Schleiermacher's period of church history: "When we learn to know Schleiermacher we learn to know ourselves and the main characteristics of the theological situation today." He recalled that the last significant theological movement to break from Schleiermacher's focus on religious consciousness was quickly absorbed by it. Ritschl tried to place liberal theology on a historical basis, but his school soon produced theologies that depended on Schleiermacher more than Ritschl. The problem of historical relativism that Ritschl unleashed drove Herrmann to set faith against history; locally, Barth observed, it produced the kind of psychologized religious theorizing that Georg Wobbermin dispensed at Göttingen.[159]

Barth implored his students to imagine that Schleiermacher's epoch could be brought to an end. This possibility had to be imagined, because the road taken by Schleiermacher and followed by nearly every theologian afterward led to a dead end. Herrmann and Troeltsch were gone, having died in 1922 and 1923, respectively. Barth judged that the present situation in theology amounted to a standoff between their epigones. He further judged that neither side deserved to call itself a legitimate heir of the Reformers. The experience of teaching Schleiermacher's system stoked Barth's feelings of repugnance and betrayal. He told Thurneysen that often he had to resist the urge to cry out that Schleiermacher's theology was "just one gigantic swindle." In the classroom Barth restrained himself, more or less, until the end of the semester, when he told his students that his course preparations had been "fairly shattering" for him.[160]

"When I embarked with you on this material, which I had not examined closely for many years, I was prepared for something bad," Barth reported. "But I was not prepared to find that the *distortion* of Protestant theology – and we have to speak of such in view of the historical importance of the man – was as deep, extensive, and palpable as it has shown itself to be." Schleiermacher's thinking was worst on the most important issues, Barth contended. It was precisely on the nature of revelation, the Bible as holy scripture, miracles, God, and immortality that Schleiermacher departed the furthest from authentic Christian teaching and thus damaged the cause of Protestant theology.[161]

Barth confessed that as a Protestant he found this verdict to be an "oppressive and almost intolerable thought." He worried that Protestantism would be unable to regain any confidence in the power of its truth. He fretted that the spiritual ravages of liberal theology made it very difficult to affirm the doctrine of the providence of God ruling over the church. He urged, however, that the church had to make an honest appraisal of these ravages. Otherwise, nothing worthy of the name "Protestantism" would emerge from the ashes of the past century of Protestant theology. Modern theology interpreted the doctrine of divine providence in accord with its faith in historical progress, but Barth cautioned that providence is also rendered in history as divine judgment. His second edition *Romans* described history as the footprint of God's wrath.[162]

That was the meaning of the Schleiermacher period in church history, Barth declared: The dead end at which liberal theology had arrived was a sign of the wrathful judgment of God on modern Protestantism itself. In this situation, anything less than revolutionary resistance was insufficient. Faithfully Christian thinking could only take the form of "a *theological revolution*, a basic No to the whole of Schleiermacher's doctrine of religion and Christianity, and an attempted reconstruction at the *very* point which we have constantly seen him hurry past with astonishing stubbornness, skill, and audacity."[163]

Barth did not lack partisan cunning in making it happen; he recognized that the moment was ripe for his attack on the tottering liberal tradition. In the aftermath of the

Great War, no European could believe that the world was getting better. Catholic theologian Karl Adam famously remarked that Barth's second edition *Romans* fell "like a bomb on the playground of the theologians." Tillich, though sharply critical of Barth's supernaturalism, told him that his book was a prime symptom of the dawning of a history changing "kairos." Barth cautioned his students that there was no occasion for triumphant superiority at the tomb of Schleiermacher. It was not clear what would replace the distorted theology by which liberals accommodated German idealism, romanticism, moralism, rationalism, and historicism. Barth concluded: "Schleiermacher undoubtedly did a good job. It is not enough to know that another job has to be done; what is needed is the ability to do it as well as he did his."[164]

This was the sizable project that Barth assigned to himself and his movement. Liberal theology made the human subject the subject of theology and turned Christ into a mere predicate; therefore it had to be replaced. But the Barthian movement never quite became the "theological revolution" that Barth envisioned. Barth lacked the essential qualities of a movement leader and he eventually disavowed the movement labels assigned to him. Moreover, his theology and the offshoots it inspired contained too many liberal elements to become a genuinely third way, notwithstanding the loud claims by Brunner, Gogarten, and a younger generation of "Barthians" to be exactly that. By 1932 Barth was embarrassed at the simplistic anti-liberal rhetoric that prevailed among Barthians. His own broadsides against liberalism were not simplistic, he insisted. He never forgot that liberals invented modern theology, developed the tools of modern scholarship, and built up a vast structure of knowledge. Things had changed so dramatically that now the field was loaded with shallow types who did not bother to learn Schleiermacher's system before they dismissed it as ridiculous.

Barth, teaching Schleiermacher to his students at Bonn in 1932, ran through a list of nineteenth-century tributes (the founder of an era in theology . . . the founder of a new period of church history . . . the church father of the nineteenth century . . . a king in the realm of the mind). Then he admonished his students: "We have to do with a hero, the like of which is but seldom bestowed upon theology. Anyone who has never noticed anything of the splendor this figure radiated and still does – I am almost tempted to say, who has never succumbed to it – may honorably pass on to other and possibly better ways, but let him never raise so much as a finger against Schleiermacher." Now Barth claimed that it was "impossible to consider Schleiermacher thoroughly without being very strongly impressed." The more that he studied Schleiermacher, the more humbled he felt at Schleiermacher's genius. When people criticized Schleiermacher prematurely, he cautioned, they made themselves look ridiculous.[165]

It was not just young Barthians who did so. Barth pointed to Brunner's *Die Mystik und das Wort* (1924) as a prime example of simplistic blasting. Brunner had a declarative, cocksure manner that Barth disliked from the outset. Later, Brunner's lucid accessibility made him the most popular exponent of Barthian theology, which made Barth cringe; and in 1934 they clashed dramatically over natural revelation. Barth, warning his students how not to argue about Schleiermacher, pointed to Brunner, who tagged Schleiermacher as a mystic, urged that mysticism was a bad thing, and countered with revealed Christianity. Barth hated that Brunner used the Reformation doctrine of the Word as a positivist club or "solid quantity," suitable for polemical thrashings. In Barth's view, Brunner was a chief purveyor of slogan-based Barthianism.

The very title of Brunner's book conveyed slogan theology and a distortion of Schleiermacher. To be sure, Barth argued, there was a mystical side to Schleiermacher, which came through in the apologetic side of his work. But Schleiermacher was a bourgeois Prussian churchman who identified fundamentally with the movement of modern civilization, not with individual mysticism. Not to get that about Schleiermacher was not to get him at all.[166]

Schleiermacher was a guardian of modern peace and order, Barth contended; his mystical side served the cause of peace and order; and his theology, fittingly, was a theology of mediation. His devotion to the Prussian state, though more liberal and ethical than Hegel's, was equally fervent, and he was perfectly at home in the movement of his time for a united Protestant church that was independent of the state and devoted to it. On the notoriously tangled question of how Schleiermacher could be a Christian apologist and a speculative philosopher while excluding both from his theology, Barth explained that there were different sides to Schleiermacher's thought. As a moral philosopher and philosopher of religion, Schleiermacher took up apologetic and speculative questions belonging to these fields, suspending his beliefs about Christianity. The neutral academic approach to religion had a place in Schleiermacher's mind and his university. There he analyzed Christianity on the same level as other communities of faith. When Schleiermacher expounded the doctrine of Christian faith in Christian pulpits, theology classes, and his dogmatics, he spoke out of his Christian beliefs, where apologetics and speculation did not belong. Or at least, they belonged only to the prolegomenon; Barth sympathized with Schleiermacher's internal debate about putting the prolegomenon last to convince readers that his theological basis was decidedly Christian.[167]

Barth offered a striking image of Schleiermacher in his apologetic mode – a virtuoso who played Christianity like a violin. Schleiermacher played the notes and airs of Christianity in a way that its cultured critics could tolerate, or even mildly respect. Like a virtuoso, Barth explained, Schleiermacher spoke as a free master of his subject, not its servant. This was the quintessential modern moment in theology, because the rationalist theologians preceding Schleiermacher still took for granted that they had to defend and conserve Christianity. Schleiermacher, citing no authorities for support, proceeded on thoroughly modern terms. One could be a Christian and even a theologian in the same way that one was a philosopher or an artist, approaching the material in a creative way, and illuminating it out of one's own power. Barth explained: "Christianity can be mastered at least in so far as, using the insight we have into its nature and value, we can treat, control and rule the Bible and dogma with unrestricted freedom."[168]

A good deal of nineteenth-century theology debated Schleiermacher's division of labor, questioning whether he should have provided a speculative basis for theology or the principles of Christianity. Barth had a grudging respect for Schleiermacher's disciples, such as Nitzsch and Ullmann, who kept theology separate from apologetics and philosophy of religion. He admired Schleiermacher for insisting that theology had its own work to do. Schleiermacher had a Schelling-like system of knowledge, conceiving the ideal and the real as one, Barth acknowledged. But he united knowledge and being objectively only in the idea of God; otherwise he placed knowledge and being in opposition. On the subjective level, Schleiermacher held together thought and being only by the *feeling* that correlated to the idea of God, which accompanied all knowledge and action. That was Schleiermacher's idealism pushing through – a kind of bracket beyond his antithesis of knowledge and being. But Schleiermacher worked hard at keeping his philosophy out of his theology. Barth admonished his students that Schleiermacher took seriously the centrality of Christian redemption, at least as he conceived it, however much he fiddled upon Christianity in his apologetic and philosophical modes.[169]

That left the problem of Schleiermacher's theology. Barth struggled to be fair. In his speeches on religion, Barth observed, Schleiermacher described religion as the moment of the unity of intuition and feeling, which occurs beyond all thought and action; intuition is the receptive side of the act of awareness, and feeling is the spontaneous side. Religion is the unity of the opposition of receptive intuition and spontaneous feeling. But Schleiermacher dispensed with this dialectic in his dogmatics, Barth observed. In the *Glaubenslehre*, feeling included the moment of intuition. The later Schleiermacher conceived feeling as the wellspring of knowledge and action, the true self-awareness, in contrast to knowledge and action, which are mere functions. Thus, feeling is the (subjective) representation of truth.[170]

Schleiermacher's dogmatic system rested entirely on a theology of pious self-awareness, Barth stressed. More precisely, it rested on the feeling of a peace that passes all understanding. Preaching had a prominent role in this theology, but the Word of God was secondary, because Schleiermacher exalted to first place the experience of spiritual peace. Of the three modes of speech, he rated the poetical highest; the oratorical next; and the didactic last; moreover, he rated music above all three, where feeling sings gloriously to heaven. Theology, being merely a human word, and low level discourse at that, was "relatively non-binding" for Schleiermacher. Barth explained, "That is why Schleiermacher finds it possible to adapt his theology so carefully to the educated awareness of his time, without worrying too much or nearly so much about whether his theology was doing justice to his subject, Christianity. That is why for him, dogmatics is nothing more nor less than the 'representation of the opinion of the Church,' a branch of the church lore of the present, paraphrasing historically and empirically in systematic order the reality of the pronouncements, which are possible and necessary at the time, of the spirit affected by the Christian religion."[171]

Schleiermacher began, Barth noted, with a Romantic "fear of objective and expressible pronouncements." Then he turned this fear into a dogmatic method, "which is typical of Schleiermacher's theology as few other things are." He took it so seriously that there was no difference between his formal principle and his material principle. Schleiermacher's entire rendering of Christianity was about Christian pious self-awareness contemplating and describing itself. Barth observed that in the very places where Luther and Calvin appealed to the gospel, the Word of God, or Christ, Schleiermacher appealed to religion or piety. The Reformers correlated the Word of God with human faith, which had its basis entirely in the Word of God. Schleiermacher reversed the Reformation dialectic; for him, the initiative, center, and point of it all was the reaching out of pious self-awareness to God.[172]

Barth did not deny that one could work up a Christian theology in this fashion. In a remarkable aside that tantalized bridge-building theologians for decades, he noted that one could even interpret Schleiermacher as a theologian of the Holy Spirit. What if everything that Schleiermacher said about religious experience was predicated on a doctrine of the prior action and call of the Holy Spirit? What if the divinity of the Holy Spirit was the actual center of Schleiermacher's theology? Barth acknowledged that one did not have to turn Schleiermacher on his head to make this case. The interesting question, for Barth, was that if one interpreted Schleiermacher as a theologian of the Holy Spirit, what happened to the divinity of the Logos? The Reformers were theologians of the Word *and* the Holy Spirit, Barth reasoned. They had no trouble holding these things together because they were Trinitarians who began with the divinity of the Logos. Emphatically, the Reformation asserted the primacy of the divine Word, which was also a theology of the Holy Spirit to such a degree that it was also a theology of faith, which proved that the divine Word was its true center.[173]

Could anything like that be said of Schleiermacher? Barth was doubtful, and not only because Schleiermacher consigned the Trinity to the appendix. The Lord Jesus, as an objective historical motif, was a "problem child" for Schleiermacher, Barth noted. Schleiermacher struggled hard to offer a Jesus that modern consciousness might accept. He was like a sculptor working a block of marble. The tradition gave Schleiermacher an unpalatable image of Christ, and he worked hard to do something with it, so modern educated types would not leave Christianity behind. Barth allowed that Schleiermacher was more or less successful in this effort, working out "a tolerably modernized Christianity" and showing, "in tolerably convincing fashion," that modern people needed Christianity. But the fact that he had to struggle so hard for this dubious objective was unsettling. Barth noted that Luther's doctrine of faith had no such problem. Luther's teaching of the Word led straight to Christ, the Spirit, and the conviction of faith: "With Luther the divinity of the Logos demands in the most direct way possible the divinity of the Spirit." Instead of twisting and turning to make Christianity somehow appear to be credible, relevant, illuminating, or at least tolerable, Luther proclaimed a gospel in which the divinity of the Logos and the Spirit were "open, self-evident, and alive." Barth wished that modern theologians would give up trying so hard; unfortunately, they had Schleiermacher as a model.[174]

There was also the problem that Schleiermacher understood faith as a human experience, not as revelation. Schleiermacher correlated faith with experience and Christ with history, Barth observed. Faith and Christ were the foci of an ellipse, which rendered the relationship of faith between the human subject and God as a human possibility. Barth contended that this was not a debatable point as a question of how to interpret Schleiermacher. For Schleiermacher, each side of the relationship corresponded to a mode of human cognition, both sides were brought into a mediating relationship, and Schleiermacher could not have been more explicit in saying so. Here again, Schleiermacher reversed the Reformation understanding, for which faith is a revelatory gift of the Holy Spirit, not a human work.[175]

Finally, for Schleiermacher, Christ was the revealer and redeemer as the distinct agent of a higher life. Barth allowed that Schleiermacher probably did the best that he could with this claim on modern terms. To his credit, Schleiermacher fought against the natural religion of the Enlightenment, which had an afterlife in a great deal of rationalist and post-Kantian idealism. He insisted that Christianity is a positive, revelatory religion, not a universal religion of reason. Still, Schleiermacher's modernism compelled him to restrict the positivity of Christianity, its revelatory basis, to the individuality that it received from the manifestation of Christ. He could not say, on modern progressive terms, that Christ was the "incomparable climax" of humanity's composite existence, so he did not. For Schleiermacher, Christ was the archetypal image as the historical beginning of a particular religion. As such, Barth allowed, Schleiermacher was able to say various orthodox sounding things about Christ. He wrung as much absoluteness as he could out of Christianity, rendering it as the highest of religions and so on. But he did not have an answer for those who asked why it was wrong to manage without Christ. He could not tell them why they should not wait for one still to come. All he could do was repeat that everything that we have of a higher life, we have from Christ.[176]

Barth cautioned his students that Schleiermacher did not regard himself as a destroyer of Reformation theology. He thought that he saved as much of Christianity as was possible on modern terms. Barth took pride that Schleiermacher was a forerunner, and, unlike many Barthians, he never regarded Schleiermacher as a heretic, someone not belonging to the Christian community. In later life he told interviewers that no modern theologian compared to Schleiermacher as a systematician and that Schleiermacher understood the beauty of theology more than any succeeding theologian. To theologian Terrence Tice, Barth recounted a conversation that he had with Brunner after Brunner's book on Schleiermacher came out: "After his book, I said to him we should get together and study the matter. He said he couldn't [and deep, flushed emotion crept into Barth's face, halfway between tears of sorrow and rage], that he had burned his papers! He was done with him! [A sweep of the arm, a look of extreme disgust.] Imagine! For me, Schleiermacher is present, within the church, my comrade, the finest of them all!"[177]

Barth wrote about Schleiermacher with particular authority and familiarity, partly because he taught Schleiermacher many times, and also because he never forgot Herrmann's ringing lectures. He never doubted Herrmann's assurance that Schleiermacher was the greatest of modern theologians. In the late 1920s Barth left Herrmann behind, even as a foil, something he could not imagine doing with Schleiermacher. Without Herrmann, however, there would have been no Barthian theology. Barth opposed Schleiermacher, but he fashioned his own position by refashioning arguments of Herrmann's. He was loath to put it that way; thus he never did. But lacking Barth's Herrmannian elements, his theology would have been the suffocating, positivist "neo-orthodoxy" that his critics charged it to be.

In 1925, Herrmann's lectures on dogmatics were published, offering Barth an unnerving reminder. He told Thurneysen, "Yes, I see in it, certainly in a respectable form, as though through a reversed telescope, the place from which we have come. Should we not perhaps have remained there?" That was a typical rhetorical ploy; Barth did not really doubt that he had made the right choice. He envied liberals for their positions, not their theology. But his letter suggested another kind of misgiving. Though Barth now waxed enthusiastically about angelology and the Virgin Birth, he was still his teacher's disciple in crucial respects. He had to be careful about how he criticized Herrmann, in light of his debt to him.[178]

By 1925, Herrmann's piety and assurances were like echoes from a lost world to Barth. His list of Herrmannian themes that seemed hopelessly wrong to him included Herrmann's emphasis on individual experience, his self-contradictory claim to universality, his inadequate account of how people come to faith, his appeal to the "inner life" of Jesus, his monophysite Christology, his strained (if rare) appeals to Scripture, his strained (and too frequent) appeals to Luther, his relegation of the Trinity to three paragraphs at the end of his dogmatics, and his disregard for the authority of Scripture and church tradition. Herrmann eschewed Schleiermacher's universalistic theorizing about the nature of (religious) consciousness, but that did not stop him from claiming universal validity for his account of the "way to religion." He rightly resolved to do theology without weapons, but he substituted individual religious experience for the weaponlessness of the divine Word. He rejected orthodox Christology as mythical and replaced it with the emaciated monophysite assurance that God works upon us through "the Power of the man Jesus."[179]

These were terrible trades, Barth judged. Having stumbled only recently upon the Alexandrian doctrine of the union of the Logos and human nature in Christ, Barth lectured that "orthodox Christology is a glacial torrent rushing straight down from a height of three thousand meters; it makes accomplishment possible." By comparison, Herrmann's Christology was a "hopeless attempt to raise a stagnant pool to that same height by means of a hand pump; nothing can be accomplished with it."[180]

This withering judgment was the key to Barth's dogmatic turn and his polemical dismissal of liberal theology as being literally weak, shriveled, and deflated. Liberal theology replaced the great doctrines of Scripture and Christian tradition with its own domesticated pieties and cultural prejudices, some of which were no longer up-to-date. Herrmann's Christology reduced Christ to an inspiring religious leader. He got nothing more out of the Trinity than the reminder that God is an unsearchable mystery. By 1925, Barth had begun to glimpse the staggering difference that orthodox Christology and the orthodox theme of the inalienable subjectivity of God's triune self-relation would make for his own theology.[181]

Barth admonished: "It is scarcely enlightening to say of the Bible and dogma (in specific relation to the impossible theory of the 'power of the man Jesus') that they are expressions of human faith, 'religious ideas of other men,' and therefore they are not binding upon us." If the Bible and the church's dogma are *nothing but* the religious thoughts of opinionated writers, "then they have *no* authority; neither can they gain it." He countered that Christian theologians cannot establish Scriptural authority or the authority of conciliar dogma as an afterthought. Experience cannot establish genuine authority: "An authority is either there or not there. What is not authority from the beginning cannot become such."[182]

The Bible has no authority at all for faith if it is not treated from the outset as the church's unique authoritative witness to revelation. On every issue, Barth judged, Herrmann's creative and often inspiring spirit needed the corrective discipline of the divine Word. The church fathers and reformers spoke a deeper, richer and ultimately more liberating language of faith because they experienced the freedom that derives from submitting to the sovereignty of the Word.

These bruising judgments were delivered in a tone that said, "good-bye to all that." Though Barth never stopped arguing with Schleiermacher, he never dealt again with Herrmann. Aside from a few scattered references in the later volumes of the *Church Dogmatics* and a dismissive half-paragraph in the first volume, Herrmann disappeared from his theological horizon, even as a cautionary example.[183] Barth's later work took for granted the themes that he took from Herrmann. He did not bother to deal with

Herrmann when he reformulated these themes and he completely lost interest in debating the kind of liberal Protestantism that Herrmann represented. Even his debates with Bultmann largely ignored Herrmann's influence over both of them, despite the fact that Barth's disagreements with Bultmann were explicable as conflicting interpretations of Herrmannian tropes.[184]

Barth took his interpretation of revelation as self-revelation and his insistence that revelation is self-authenticating from Herrmann. Eventually, he appealed to Calvin to support the latter argument, but his doctrine of revelation was too Hegelian to have an orthodox backstop. Like Herrmann, Barth aggressively pressed the implications of conceiving revelation as self-revealing and self-authenticating: Revelation is not doctrine, faith is not assent to doctrine, revelation is not any "thing" at all, faith is not the outcome of an argument, apologetics is not a legitimate theological enterprise, Christian faith is not a worldview, and critically established history is not the basis of faith. Taking over these arguments, Barth reshaped them through his commitment to the priority and authority of the divine Word. Herrmann taught that it was enough for faith to apprehend the inner life of Jesus; Barth countered that it was enough only for faith to live by the inscripturated Word of Christ in its Spirit-illuminated realism and sovereignty.

Just as Herrmann posited the existence of a radically autonomous theological ground and lauded Kant for liberating theology from scientific reason, Barth stood for theological autonomy and accepting the Kantian peace with science. Christian truth, while belonging to history, is independent from the methods and conclusions of historical and scientific criticism.[185] Barth did not dispute the plausibility or integrity of the history of religions approach on its own terms, and he gave it a prolegomenal function in theology, even though he hardly ever used it. Christian theology, he reasoned, in its own sphere, must listen to scripture in a different way, attending to a self-authenticating Word.[186]

This appeal to a self-revealing Word was more powerful, theologically, than Herrmann's resort to the inner life of Jesus. Herrmann stressed biblical passages referring to the messianic consciousness of Jesus that later biblical scholarship, notably Bultmann's *History of the Synoptic Tradition,* attributed to the church.[187] Though Herrmann emphasized that he appealed to the power of Jesus himself, mediated by the gospel records, and not to the factuality of Jesus as attested by the gospels or even historical criticism, he left to others the unpromising question of how the "inner life" of Jesus could be ascertainable if all biblical testimony about it belongs to the period of second generation Christian reflection.[188]

In the 1950s and 1960s, proponents of the "new hermeneutics" movement sought to rehabilitate Herrmann's picture of Jesus as the ground of faith. Ernst Fuchs and Gerhard Ebeling proposed that instead of focusing on the Bultmannian question of how Jesus became the object of faith, it was more fruitful to return to Herrmann's question of how Christ's witness of faith became the basis of Christian faith. The "new hermeneutical" theologians found crucial support for their challenge to Bultmann's existentialism in the later Heidegger's theory of language as the primal speaking voice of being. Bultmann embraced the early Heidegger's phenomenological account of the "throwness" of human existence, adopting Heidegger's view that language is objectivizing and secondary to existence. Heideggerian theory undergirded Bultmann's claim that the aim of good biblical scholarship is to recover the understanding of existence that underlies the language of the Scriptural text. But Heidegger's later work described language as the event in which being is disclosed; language is the phenomenon closest to human being, not something objectivizing and secondary to it. Fuchs and Ebeling adopted this concept of language as the speaking voice of being, contending, against Bultmann, that history is the history of language spoken as a response to the call of being. Following the later Heidegger's emphasis on the creative primal character of language, they construed the significance of Jesus as the "language event" (Fuchs, *Sprachereignis)* or "word event" (Ebeling, *Wortgeschehen)* of faith. They proposed to recover the "language event" behind the formulations of early Christian preaching, a project that required a new quest of the historical Jesus.[189]

Bultmann opposed this historical quest for the same reasons that he opposed its predecessors. Although all the players in this debate cited Herrmann for support, Bultmann suggested that his combination of historical criticism and existential interpretation saved the core of Herrmann's message in its most credible form. He objected that those who invested theological significance in the "inner life" of Jesus or the "language event" behind the early church's kerygma unavoidably based Christian faith on some purported historical fact about Jesus. Thus, the latter-day Herrmannians launched another ill-advised quest of the historical Jesus, notwithstanding Herrmann's categorical rejection of historical questing, which exposed "Christian faith" to the possibility of historical refutation. They tried to rescue Herrmann's "inner life of Jesus" motif by clothing it with a new form of its supposed objective content. Bultmann protested that the "new hermeneutics" theologians thereby lost the Herrmannian insight that faith *is* an existence. That was what came from treating faith as the acceptance of some particular historical fact.[190]

Herrmann's appeal to the saving power of Christ's inner life was fraught with the very historical complications that he tried to avoid. Barth shook his head at the outbreak of a controversy over Herrmann's legacy on this subject. To him it was as though theology had returned to the sandbox. The gains of his return to the revealing Word were swept away even by theologians that he respected, such as Fuchs and Ebeling. From Barth's first-edition *Romans* onward, he sought to listen for the Word of God that disrupts and transcends historical categories. There *is* a Christian self-authenticating alternative to history of religions historicism, he urged, but its basis is the revealed Word that eludes human control. To read the Bible with the presuppositions of *religionsgeschichtliche* criticism is to close off the possibility that the Word will be heard. To interpret the biblical creation stories as myths analogous to the myths of other religions is to understand scripture according to the presuppositions of a colonizing academic discipline. By this procedure the biblical witness is discarded at the outset.

Dialectics of the Open Word

To Barth the crucial point was always the Herrmannian theme that Christ himself is the future and ground of all redemptive possibility. The eschatological Word is enough. It is never an object of perception or cognition, but can only be believed. The Word is different from all other objects because it gives itself. Barth echoed Herrmann's admonition that the crucial choice is between living faithfully by the ever-renewing Spirit of Christ and resorting to sickly substitutes. His list of poor substitutes was considerably longer than Herrmann's, who opposed apologetics but nearly always spoke of religion in positive terms. Barth's list of faith-negating substitutes included every form of natural theology, religious symbolism and ritual practice. It included even the notion that the Word is expressed or made visible through symbols such as the cross or the dove. "We do not believe in symbols," he admonished. Symbolism is a philosophical means of communication, but Christian theology testifies to what God has done. Theology proclaims and repeats the spoken Word offered to the church. Barth explained: "We are *told* to testify by our lives, to live within the community of the Church, to take part in the work of proclamation. But who is told to light candles?" Paul, if he visited modern churches, undoubtedly would find most worship services uninspiring and barren, "but he would not suggest that we light candles!" Barth urged that the church needed an outpouring of the Spirit of Christ. To prescribe pictures and symbols in this situation was like telling an ailing hospital patient to change his bed.[191]

Barth's Protestant severity was oblivious to the Spirit of Christ in the images, music, and practices of sacramental religion. He was passionately devoted to Mozart, but his theology had no room for it as a vehicle of divine expression.[192] When pressed on the point, he allowed that God is free to use any means that God may desire to speak to the church. He even professed to be ready "to be open to God's Word as in fact it may be spoken to me also in nature, history, art, and who knows, even my own heart and conscience." However, he knew of only one means by which God speaks to the church. We meet Christ only through Scripture and Scripturally based preaching.[193]

For Barth the issue of apologetics was like the problem of candles. With Kierkegaardian and Herrmannian conviction he insisted that Christian faith does not need and is not strengthened by any outside evidence that might be cited. Every attempt to defend Christianity takes place on a standpoint outside faith, which subjects the truth of the gospel to a pagan criterion of rationality or meaning. Only the movement of the Word sustains faith, not arguments for God's existence or the resurrection of Jesus. To appeal to an outside apologetic is to impede oneself (or the church) from living a Spirit-filled life of faith. In effect, it is to deny revelation. Barth implored: "We cannot believe and yet at the same time not believe but want to know [on independent grounds]. This is not to believe at all." If one could prove the resurrection of Jesus historically, it would not *be* the resurrection, for revelation is its own basis. History as a category is too poor and overburdened with scientific conditions to contain the transhistorical conquest of death that God accomplished and revealed through Christ.[194]

Barth insisted that his approach was not fideistic or anti-historical in the narrow sense, because he used reason to understand faith. He did most of his own exegesis in the *Church Dogmatics* because, as he complained, most scholars were content to take the text apart and leave the reconstructive work of theology to theologians. Barth was too wary of this enterprise to make use of its findings. In 1948 he remarked, "The time does not yet seem to have arrived when the dogmatician can accept with a good conscience and confidence the findings of his colleagues in Old and New Testament studies." Conventional biblical scholarship conceived its task too narrowly for his taste, refusing to acknowledge its religious assumptions or consequences. As long as this situation obtained, Barth declared, "so long as so many still seem to pride themselves on being utterly unconcerned as to the dogmatic presuppositions and consequences of their notions, while unwittingly reading them into the picture, the dogmatician is forced to run the same risk as the non-expert and work out his own proof from Scripture."[195]

Did that smack of "revelational positivism," the "like it or lump it" (*"Friss Vogel, oder stirb"*) approach that Dietrich Bonhoeffer criticized in 1944? Bonhoeffer was a Barthian theologian and a conspirator against the Nazi regime. He was arrested by the Nazis in 1943, wrote letters to his friend Eberhard Bethge from prison, and was executed at the Flossenbürg concentration camp in 1945. Bethge published the letters in a famous book, *Letters and Papers from Prison* (1953). In one letter Bonhoeffer wrote: "Barth was the first theologian to begin the criticism of religion, and that remains his really great merit. But he put in its place a positivist doctrine of revelation which says, in effect, 'Like it or lump it': virgin birth, Trinity, or anything else; each is an equally significant and necessary part of the whole, which must simply be swallowed as a whole or not at all. That isn't biblical. There are degrees of knowledge and degrees of significance; that means that a secret discipline must be restored whereby the *mysteries* of the Christian faith are protected against profanation."[196]

Bonhoeffer did not dispute that Barth got his themes from scripture. What he disputed was that "like it or lump it" was a biblical way of thinking. Scripture does not identify faith with a particular scheme of doctrines, Bonhoeffer protested: "The positivism of revelation makes it too easy for itself, by setting up, as it does in the last analysis, a law of faith, and so mutilates what is – by Christ's incarnation! – a gift for us." The virgin birth, for example, is a marginal theme in the New Testament, yet Barth blasted theologians who rejected it. For Bonhoeffer, that mutilated the gift in the very name of protecting Christ's incarnation. Barth, having rejected the old orthodoxy on biblical inspiration, presumed that he did not deserve to be called a positivist. Bonhoeffer countered that "positivism of revelation" fit him perfectly, because the logic of "like it or lump it" was no less authoritarian than the old orthodoxy.[197]

For decades, Barth's critics had said the same thing, notably Tillich, Bultmann, and most liberals. But they were not iconic martyrs, as Bonhoeffer became after the war. The publication of Bonhoeffer's criticism wounded Barth personally and his reputation. He protested that Bonhoeffer's statements were "enigmatic," made no sense as a critique of him, and made no sense coming from Bonhoeffer.[198] He questioned whether Bonhoeffer's memory was justly served by publishing the letters.[199] For the rest of his life Barth insisted that "positivity of revelation" did not apply to him, because he never threw doctrines at people in a take it or leave it fashion.[200] The only sense that he could make of Bonhoeffer's criticism, Barth claimed, was that Bonhoeffer was "an impulsive, visionary thinker" who was prone to be seized briefly by a flash of insight until he gave himself to a different one. Barth surmised that in prison, Bonhoeffer's recollection of *Church Dogmatics* must have become rather hazy, which yielded his bizarre aphorisms about Barthian positivism.[201]

"Revelational positivist," however, stuck to Barth for the rest of his life, as he ruefully perceived. In later life he caustically described himself as "the poor neo-orthodox theologian, the supernaturalist, the revelational positivist, as I had to hear from so many quarters on both sides of the Atlantic." Bonhoeffer's iconic stature gave weight to his restatement of a long-running critique of Barth's theology. Barth lamented that this situation degraded Bonhoeffer's reputation and his own. Writing to Bethge, he speculated that Bonhoeffer might have recovered his better judgment had he survived the war: "Might he not later have simply dropped all those catchy phrases? Even when he uttered them, did he himself really know what he meant by them?"[202]

The key phrase in this dispute, however, is not that difficult to piece out. In a broad sense of the phrase, Barth certainly was a positivist of revelation, and in its narrow sense, he was not. Broadly speaking, he was a positivist inasmuch as he made historical claims on dogmatic grounds and defended certain doctrines on holistic dogmatic grounds. For example, Barth began to uphold the historicity and doctrine of the Virgin Birth after he became a dogmatic theologian and committed himself to an Alexandrian-type Christology. The incarnation is not about the indwelling of a human subject by a divine Subject, he contended. It is about the union of Christ's human and divine natures in a single divine Subject, the divine person of the Logos. The unity of Christ's divine and human natures is a unity of divine Subject. Logos theology, so conceived, renders Christ's human nature as having no personhood of its own. Barth explained, "It is *anhypostatos* – the formula in which the description culminates. Or, more positively, it is *enhypostatos*. It has personhood, subsistence, reality, only in its union with the Logos of God."[203]

It followed for Barth, who was grateful to find Reformed and Lutheran support, that Mary is rightly called the Mother of God *(theotokos)* because the one whom she bore was *nothing apart* from being God's Son. Christ's human nature was real only in the person of the Logos, and human nature has subsistence only in and through the Logos. Reformed and Lutheran scholastics agreed that the Logos completely indwells the human, subsisting in the human nature of Christ; Reformed dogmatists added that the Logos also transcends the human Christ; Lutheran dogmatists called that "the Calvinist extra," fearing that it compromised the affirmation that God is wholly present in the incarnation. Barth, taking the Reformed view, reasoned that the Logos in Christ's flesh and the Logos outside Christ's flesh are the same totality.[204]

Barth upheld the truth and necessity of the virginal conception of Jesus on these grounds. The doctrine of the Virgin Birth expresses "the absolutely miraculous character of revelation" better than any doctrine except the resurrection of Christ, he reasoned. The two doctrines are intimately joined: "God is in the flesh, in time, in the world of contradiction, himself human, pilgrim man, a man like any other, yet God, so that the time is fulfilled, and a limit is set for the contradiction." In the gospel narrative Christ is flesh of Adam's flesh and born like all others, yet he is also God born of the Virgin Mary and conceived by the Holy Spirit. It is pointless and spiritually wrong to rationalize any part of this divine mystery, Barth urged. The doctrine of Christ's conception by the Spirit can only be rejected or believed; parthogenesis in animals or plants has no more relevance to the Virgin Birth than occultism has to Christ's resurrection.[205]

Barth acknowledged that the doctrine of Christ's virginal conception is weak on biblical attestation and that the kind of arguments by which he espoused it had become foreign to Protestant theology. The former fact did not faze him and the latter fact, in his view, was the crucial clue to the weakness of modern Protestantism. It does not matter that the earliest traditions in the New Testament do not mention the virgin birth story, he urged; Luke and Matthew perceived that the story is indispensable to

Christianity. Moreover, Barth sought not merely to restore certain doctrines or even to reclaim the authority of the Word for theology. His larger aim was to recreate a theological discourse that Protestants stopped speaking in the eighteenth century. "To take it up again is not so easy," Barth conceded. He began by trying to discern the sense of early Christian doctrine. He was convinced that Christianity could not give up the Trinity and the Virgin Birth without losing its soul. The history of modern Protestantism was his proof. Having sold its soul to modernity, modern Protestantism was reduced to a desiccated intellectualized religiousness. Barth's *Church Dogmatics* began with a blistering denunciation of the spiritual ravages of this loss, assailing the "constantly increasing barbarism, tedium, and insignificance of modern Protestantism." He found an ample following for that view, sharing theological leadership into the 1960s with Tillich, Bultmann, and Reinhold Niebuhr, until his death in 1968.[206]

In the narrow sense of the term positivist, however, Barth was not one. He would not have been the dominant theologian of the twentieth century had he appealed to established dogmas prior to or apart from his exegetical conclusions, and he grasped that subject position and total context are crucially determinative in religious knowledge. Barth rightly protested that theologians routinely took positions about the nature of the Word and the scope of scriptural authority without specifying the context in which the Bible is properly approached and interpreted. He found what he believed by interrogating the scriptural data in a complex process of historical and ecclesial hermeneutics that he described in his threefold doctrine of the Word of God.

The Word of God revealed is Jesus Christ, he reasoned. The Word of God written is the Scriptural witness. The Word of God proclaimed is the preaching of the church. These three forms of God's Word are not separable, yet there is a clear ordering among them. The biblical witness is subordinate to the revealed Word, Jesus Christ, to whom it points, and the church's proclamation is subordinate to the biblical witness. Barth approached the biblical witness as Christian scripture only in this comprehensive context. The three forms are like concentric circles, with Christ at the center, scripture encircling Christ, and the church's proclamation encircling the biblical witness. The flow of authority is from the center (Christ) through the inner circle (Scripture) to the outer circle (church), but the order of knowing moves from the church to Scripture to Christ.[207]

Barth knew nothing of Christ, except in the church through the witness of the church's written Word. More precisely, he argued, the Word discloses itself through the power of the Spirit by means of the church's canonical Scripture and its proclamation. We meet the Word of God only indirectly. The revealed Word underlies the other forms of the Word, but it is never revealed in abstract form. Just as scripture must be proclaimed in the church to become God's Word, the revealed or "direct" Word of God is revealed only in the twofold mediation of Scripture and proclamation.[208]

Though the field, inevitably, spoke of "Barthian theology," Barth conceived his work as exegesis and reflection on a radically open Word of Christ. The priority of the Word precluded a definitive system. Barth changed his mind on numerous issues, notably on baptism, the humanity of God, the analogy of being, and the role of narrative in scripture. What mattered was to keep listening, not to have a system. Rightly approached, he cautioned, the process of authentication does not occur to individuals in Kierkegaardian isolation. The Word is indissolubly unified with the texts, tradition, and present life of the church, and the theologian must distinguish between the Word and the text, the text and the Christian community, and the church's creeds and future possibilities.

No dogmatic system or method can deliver the community's self-understanding from this paradoxical and relative process. The gospel conveys the radically new possibilities of God, which are glimpsed only indirectly and in fragments. The Word of Christ is an eschatological reality that relativizes all historical possibilities and achievements. In this sense above all others, Barth's theology remained a dialectics of the open Word.

Notes

1. Karl Barth, Autobiographical Sketch for the Faculty Album of the Faculty of Evangelical Theology at Münster, 1927, reprinted in *Karl Barth-Rudolf Bultmann Letters, 1922–1966*, trans. and ed. Geoffrey W. Bromiley (Grand Rapids: Eerdmans Company, 1971), 151–157, "absorbed Herrmann," 153; Eberhard Busch, *Karl Barth: His Life from Letters and Autobiographical Texts* (London: SCM Press, 1976), 9–10. This chapter adapts material from Gary Dorrien, *The Barthian Revolt in Modern Theology* (Louisville: Westminster John Knox Press, 2000); and Dorrien, *The Word as True Myth: Interpreting Modern Theology* (Louisville: Westminster John Knox Press, 1997).

2. Busch, *Karl Barth: His Life from Letters and Autobiographical Texts*, 43–44.

3. See Karl Barth, *Predigten 1913*, ed. Nelly Barth and Gerhard Sauter (Zurich: TVZ, 1976), 67–68, 166–168, 213–220; Karl Barth and Eduard Thurneysen, *Suchet Gott, so werdet ihr legen!* (Bern: G. A. Baschlin, 1917); Barth, Autobiographical Sketch for the Faculty Album of the Faculty of Evangelical Theology at Münster, 154–155; Jochen Fahler, *Der Ausbruch des 1. Weltkrieges in Karl Barths Predigten, 1913–1915* (Bern: Peter Lang, 1979); and Bruce L. McCormack, *Karl Barth's Critically Realistic Dialectical Theology: Its Genesis and Development, 1909–1936* (Oxford: Clarendon Press, 1995), 92–107.

4. See Herman Kutter, *Social Democracy: Does it Mean Darkness or Light?* (Letchworth: Garden City Press, 1910); Kutter, *They Must; Or, God and the Social Democracy* (Chicago: Co-operative Printing Company, 1906); Leonhard Ragaz, *Der Kampf um das Reich Gottes in Blumhardt Vater und Sonhund Weiter!* (Erlenbach-Zurich: Rotapfel Verlag, 1922); Ragaz, *Le Message revolutionaire* (Zurich: Neuchatel, 1941); Ragaz, *Israel, Judaism and Christianity* (London: Victor Gollanez, 1947); Busch, *Karl Barth*, 76; Karl Barth and Eduard Thurneysen, *Revolutionary Theology in the Making: Barth-Thurneysen Correspondence, 1914–1925*, trans. James D. Smart (Richmond: John Knox Press, 1964), 27–32.

5. Barth, Autobiographical Sketch for the Faculty Album of the Faculty of Evangelical Theology at Münster, quote 154; see Karl Barth, "Jesus Christ and the Movement for Social Justice" (1911), Friedrich-Wilhelm Marquardt, "Socialism in the Theology of Karl Barth," and George Hunsinger, "Conclusion: Toward a Radical Barth," in George Hunsinger, ed. and trans., *Karl Barth and Radical Politics* (Philadelphia: Westminster Press, 1976, 19–46, 47–76, 181–233.

6. Busch, *Karl Barth*, 81.

7. Barth's October 1, 1914 letter to Martin Rade quoted in McCormack, *Karl Barth's Critically Realistic Dialectical Theology*, 114; Busch, *Karl Barth*, 81–82.

8. See Kutter, *Social Democracy: Does it Mean Darkness or Light?;* Kutter, *They Must; Or, God and the Social Democracy;* Ragaz, *Der Kampf um das Reich Gottes in Blumhardt Vater und Sonhund Weiter!*

9. Barth, *Predigten 1913*, 252; Thurneysen quote in Busch, *Karl Barth*, 97; Barth, Autobiographical Sketch for the Faculty Album of the Faculty of Evangelical Theology at Münster, 154–155.

10. Karl Barth, "Biblical Questions, Insights, and Vistas," in *The Word of God and the Word of Man*, trans. Douglas Horton (Gloucester: Peter Smith, 1978), "there must," 80; Barth, "The Strange New World Within the Bible," in *The Word of God and the Word of Man*, 28–50.

11. Karl Barth to Eduard Thurneysen, January 1, 1916, *Revolutionary Theology in the Making*, quotes 35–36; see Busch, *Karl Barth: His Life from Letters and Autobiographical Texts*, 75, 87; *Karl Barth-Eduard Thurneysen: Briefwechsel, i. 1913–1921* (Zurich: TVZ, 1973), 103.

12. Karl Barth to Eduard Thurneysen, July 27, 1916, *Revolutionary Theology in the Making*, 38. On Beck's relation to Barth's family, see Eberhard Jüngel, *Karl Barth, a Theological Legacy*, trans. Garrett E. Paul (Philadelphia: Westminster Press, 1986), 23.

13. Barth, "The Strange New World Within the Bible," 33–34.

14. Ibid., 34, 37.

15. Ibid., 44–45.

16. Barth's sermon, "The Pastor Who Pleases the People," was published without his consent in *Die christliche Welt* 14 (1916), 262–265. See James D. Smart, *The Divided Mind of Modern Theology: Karl Barth and Rudolf Bultmann, 1908–1933* (Philadelphia: Westminster Press, 1957), 77–78; Arthur C. Cochrane, "The Sermons of 1913 and 1914," in *Karl Barth in Re-View: Posthumous Works Reviewed and Assessed*, ed. H. Martin Rumscheidt (Pittsburgh: Pickwick Press, 1981), 1–5; Karl Barth and William Willimon, *The Early Preaching of Karl Barth: Fourteen Sermons with Commentary by William H. Willimon* (Louisville: Westminster John Knox, 2009).

17. Barth, Autobiographical Sketch for the Faculty Album of the Faculty of Evangelical Theology at Münster, "I had," 155; Karl Barth, *Der Römerbrief* (Bern: G. A. Baschlin, 1919).

18. Barth, *Der Römerbrief*, 1–22, 321–327.

19. Ibid., 1.

20. Ibid., 417–422; on Barth's early expressionism, see Hans Urs von Balthasar, *The Theology of Karl Barth*, trans. John Drury (New York: Holt, Rinehart & Winston, 1871), 70–71; Wilhelm Pauck, *Karl Barth: Prophet of a New Christianity?* (New York: Harper & Brothers, 1931), 19–20; Hans Frei, "An Afterword: Eberhard Busch's Biography of Karl Barth," in *Karl Barth in Re-View*, 98–102; Stephen H. Webb, *Re-Figuring Theology: The Rhetoric of Karl Barth* (Albany: State University of New York Press, 1991), 8–18.

21. Barth, *Der Römerbrief*, 48–49, 64–66, 76–86, 321–328. See Smart, *The Divided Mind of Modern Theology*, 83–84; McCormack, *Karl Barth's Critically Realistic Dialectical Theology*, 142–143.

22. Barth, *Der Römerbrief*, 105, 186, 308. Barth later characterized his shift away from the conceptuality of his first-edition *Romans* as a "shift from Osiander to Luther." See Barth to Thurneysen, December 3, 1920, *Revolutionary Theology in the Making*, 55. On Osiander, see David Steinmetz, *Reformers in the Wings* (Philadelphia: Westminster Press, 1971), 91–99.

23. Philipp Bachmann, "Der Römerbrief verdeutscht und vergegenwärtigt: Ein Wort zu K. Barths Römerbrief," *Neue kirchliche Zeitschrift* 32 (1921), 518; Emil Brunner,

"*The Epistle to the Romans*, by Karl Barth: An Up-to-Date, Unmodern Paraphrase," in *The Beginnings of Dialectic Theology*, ed. James M. Robinson, trans. Louis De Grazia and Keith R. Crim (Richmond: John Knox Press, 1968), 63; Adolf Jülicher, "A Modern Interpreter of Paul," in *The Beginnings of Dialectic Theology*, 72.

24. Jülicher, "A Modern Interpreter of Paul," quote 79.

25. Ibid., 78–79.

26. Rudolf Bultmann, "Ethical and Mystical Religion in Primitive Christianity," in *The Beginnings of Dialectic Theology*, 221–235, quotes 230, 232; Barth to Thurneysen, July 14, 1920, *Revolutionary Theology in the Making*, 52–53.

27. Karl Barth, "The Christian's Place in Society," in *The Word of God and the Word of Man*, 272–327, quotes 277, 286.

28. Karl Barth, "Past and Future: Friedrich Nauman and Christoph Blumhardt," in *The Beginnings of Dialectic Theology*, 38–39; see Naumann, *Briefe über Religion* (Berlin: Buchverlag *Die Hilfe*, 1903); Barth, "*Die Hilfe* 1913," *Die Christliche Welt* 28 (August 15, 1914), 776; Andreas Lindt, *Leonhard Ragaz: Eine Studie zur Geschichte und Theologie des religiösen Sozialismus* (Zollikon: Evangelischer Verlag, 1957), 205–216.

29. Friedrich Gogarten, "The Holy Egoism of the Christian: An Answer to Jülicher's Essay: 'A Modern Interpreter of Paul,'" *The Beginnings of Dialectic Theology*, 82–87, "superior," 87; Gogarten, "Between the Times," *The Beginnings of Dialectic Theology*, 277–282, "it is," and "your concepts," 277.

30. Gogarten, "Between the Times," quotes 278; see Gogarten, "The Crisis of Our Culture," *The Beginnings of Dialectic Theology*, 283–300.

31. Barth to Thurneysen, October 27, 1920, *Revolutionary Theology in the Making*, "here is," 53; Barth, "Biblical Questions, Insights, and Vistas," "he is," 73–74, "the Easter," 86.

32. Agnes zon Zahn-Harnack, *Adolf von Harnack* (Berlin: Walter de Gruyter, 1951), "not one" and "rushing," 415; Barth to Thurneysen, October 27, 1920, *Revolutionary Theology in the Making*, "a bit," "finally," 50.

33. Barth to Thurneysen, October 27, 1920, 53; Karl Barth, "Preface to the Second Edition," Barth, *Epistle to the Romans*, 6th edn., trans Edwyn C. Hoskyns (1933; reprint, Oxford: Oxford University Press, 1975), 2–5.

34. See Eduard Buess and Markus Mattmüller, *Prophetischer Sozialismus: Blumhardt, Ragaz, Barth* (Freiburg: Edition Exodus, 1986); Eduard Thurneysen, *Christoph Blumhardt* (Munich: Chr. Kaiser Verlag, 1926); *Karl Barth-Eduard Thurneysen: Briefwechsel*, I: 29–33.

35. Emil Brunner, "*Der Römerbrief* von Karl Barth," *Kirchenblatt für die Reformierte Schweiz* 34 (1919), 30–31; Barth, "Biblical Questions, Insights, and Vistas," 74.

36. Franz Overbeck, *Christentum und Kultur: Gedanken und Anmerkungen zur modernen Theologie*, ed. Carl Albrecht Bernoulli (Basle: Benno Schwabe & Co., 1919), "gentle," 68; discussion of *Urgeschichte*, 20–28. This posthumously published collection of Overbeck's notes is the volume that Barth read.

37. Overbeck, *Christentum und Kultur: Gedanken und Anmerkungen zur modernen Theologie*, 54–63; see Niklaus Peter, *Im Schatten der Modernität: Franz Overbecks Weg zur "Christlichkeit unserer heutigen Theologie"* (Stuttgart: J. B. Metzler Verlag, 1992).

38. Overbeck, *Christentum und Kultur: Gedanken und Anmerkungen zur modernen Theologie*, 148–149, 274–275; Karl Barth, "Unsettled Questions for Theology Today," in Barth, *Theology and Church: Shorter Writings 1920–1928*, trans. Louise Pettibone Smith (New York: Harper & Row, 1962), 66–68.

39. Barth, "Unsettled Questions for Theology Today," "kick" and "we rejoice," 57–58, Overbeck, *Christentum und Kultur: Gedanken und Anmerkungen zur modernen Theo-

logie, 9–10, 242; see Franz Overbeck, *Über die Christlichkeit unserer heutigen Theologie*, 2nd edn. (Leipzig: C. G. Naumann, 1903), 25–32.

40. Barth, "Unsettled Questions for Theology Today," 60–61, Overbeck, *Christentum und Kultur: Gedanken und Anmerkungen zur modernen Theologie*, "into," 7; see Eduard Thurneysen, *Dostoiewski* (Munich: Chr. Kaiser Verlag, 1921); Thurneysen, *Christoph Blumhardt*. Barth later recalled that it was Thurneysen who first "put me on the trail" of Kutter, Blumhardt, and Dostoevsky; see *Revolutionary Theology in the Making*, 72.

41. Overbeck, *Christentum und Kultur: Gedanken und Anmerkungen zur modernen Theologie*, quotes 16; Barth, "Unsettled Questions for Theology Today," quote 56.

42. Barth, "The Christian's Place in Society," 282–283.

43. Ibid., "there must," "however," 287; Barth, "Past and Future: Friedrich Naumann and Christoph Blumhardt," "fullness," 44.

44. Barth, "Past and Future: Friedrich Naumann and Christoph Blumhardt," 44–45.

45. Barth, "Biblical Questions, Insights, and Vistas," 80.

46. Barth, *The Epistle to the Romans*, quotes 38, 37.

47. Ibid., 36.

48. Ibid., 39, 42.

49. Ibid., 98–99, 105.

50. Ibid., 100.

51. Ibid., 108–109, 116.

52. Ibid., 141–142, 225.

53. Barth, "Preface to the Second Edition," in *The Epistle to the Romans*, 10.

54. See Emil Brunner, *The Theology of Crisis* (New York: Charles Scribner's Sons, 1929); Brunner, *Wahrheit als Begegnung* (Zurich: Zwingli-Verlag, 1938); Eberhard Jüngel, "Von der Dialektik zur Analogie: Die Schule Kierkegtaards und der Einspruch Pertersons," in *Barth-Studien* (Gütersloh: Gütersloher Verlagshaus Gerd Mohn, 1982), 127–179; Thomas F. Torrance, *Karl Barth: An Introduction to His Early Theology, 1910–1931* (London: SCM Press, 1962), 44–45.

55. See Hans Urs von Balthasar, *The Theology of Karl Barth*, trans. John Drury (New York: Holt, Rinehart and Winston, 1971), 48–100; Torrance, *Karl Barth: An Introduction to His Early Theology, 1910–1931*, 48–147.

56. See Michael Beintker, *Die Dialeektik in der dialektischen Theologie Karl Barths* (Munich: Chr. Kaiser Verlag, 1987); Ingrid Spieckermann, *Gotteserkenntnis: Ein Beitrag zur Grundfrage der neuen Theologie Karl Barths* (Munich: Chr. Kaiser Verlag, 1985); McCormack, *Karl Barth's Critically Realistic Dialectical Theology: Its Genesis and Development, 1909–1936*; William Stacy Johnson, *The Mystery of God: Karl Barth and the Postmodern Foundations of Theology* (Louisville: Westminster John Knox Press, 1997).

57. Barth, "Biblical Questions, Insights, and Vistas," "the Bible has," 73–74; Barth, *The Epistle to the Romans*, "there is," 512; see McCormack, *Karl Barth's Critically Realistic Dialectical Theology: Its Genesis and Development, 1909–1936*, 239.

58. "Autobiographical sketch of Karl Barth from the faculty album of the faculty of evangelical theology at Münster," 156. John McConnachie, *The Significance of Karl Barth* (London: Hodder & Stoughton, 1931), Adam quote, 43.

59. Barth to Thurneysen, April 20, 1920, in *Revolutionary Theology in the Making: Barth-Thurneysen Correspondence, 1914–1925*, 49–50; Barth to Thurneysen, July 14, 1920, ibid., 52–53.

60. Rudolf Bultmann, *The History of the Synoptic Tradition*, trans. John Marsh (New York: Harper & Row, 1968).

61. Rudolf Bultmann, "Ethical and Mystical Religion in Primitive Christianity," 1920 essay reprinted in Robinson, *The Beginnings of Dialectic Theology*, 221–235, quote 230; Bultmann, "Karl Barth's *Epistle to the Romans* in its Second Edition," 1922 review article reprinted in Robinson, *The Beginnings of Dialectic Theology*, 117–120.

62. Karl Barth, "Preface to the Third Edition," *Epistle to the Romans*, 19.

63. Barth, *Epistle to the Romans*, 278.

64. Barth to Thurneysen, March 20, 1924, *Revolutionary Theology in the Making*, 176. The original edition of Heppe's *Reformierte Dogmatik* appared in 1861 as the second volume of his collection of writings on reformed theology. Quote from Karl Barth, "Foreword," in Heinrich Heppe, *Reformed Dogmatics*, trans. G. T. Thomson (London: Allen & Unwin, 1950), v.

65. Karl Barth and Eduard Thurneysen, *Briefwechsel Karl Barth-Eduard Thurneysen, II: 1921–1930* (Zurich: Evangelischer Verlag, 1974), 328–329.

66. Karl Barth, *The Göttingen Dogmatics: Instruction in the Christian Religion*, trans. Geoffrey W. Bromiley (Grand Rapids: Wm. B. Eerdmans Publishing Company, 1991), 292–293.

67. *Zwischen den Zeiten* was ed. Georg Merz and coed. Barth, Gogarten, and Thurneysen; see *Revolutionary Theology in the Making*, 113–114.

68. Adolf von Harnack, "Fifteen Questions to Those Among the Theologians Who Are Contemptuous of the Scientific Theology," *Die Christliche Welt* (January 11, 1923), reprinted in *The Beginnings of Dialectic Theology*, 165–166; this debate is also reprinted in H. Martin Rumscheidt, *Revelation and Theology: An Analysis of the Barth-Harnack Correspondence of 1923* (London: Cambridge University Press, 1972), 29–53; and *Adolf von Harnack: Liberal Theology at its Height*, trans. Martin Rumscheidt (Minneapolis: Fortress Press, 1991), 87–106.

69. Karl Barth, "Fifteen Answers to Professor von Harnack," *The Beginnings of Dialectic Theology*, 167–170.

70. Ibid., 168–169.

71. Ibid., 169–170.

72. Adolf von Harnack, "An Open Letter to Professor Karl Barth," *The Beginnings of Dialectic Theology*, 171–174, quotes 173, 174.

73. Karl Barth, "An Answer to Professor von Harnack's Open Letter," *The Beginnings of Dialectic Theology*, 175–185.

74. Ibid., "we are dealing," 180; Barth, *The Göttingen Dogmatics*, "by the," 222–223.

75. Barth, "Foreword," in Heppe, *Reformed Dogmatics*, "from almost," v; *Karl Barth-Eduard Thurneysen Briefwechsel*, "under," II: 238–239.

76. Hermann Kutter to Eduard Thurneysen, February 5, 1925, *Revolutionary Theology in the Making*, 210.

77. Ibid., 211; see Thurneysen to Barth, June 11, 1925, ibid., 226–227.

78. Eduard Thurneysen to Hermann Kutter, February 11, 1925, ibid., 212–215, quotes 214.

79. Barth to Thurneysen, March 4, 1925, ibid., 215–216; Emil Brunner, *Truth as Encounter*, 2nd revd. edn. trans Amadus W. Loos and David Cairns (Philadelphia: Westminster Press, 1964), 41–46. The original edition of this book, *Wahrheit als Begegnung* (1938), did not contain the attack on Barth.

80. Barth, *The Göttingen Dogmatics*, "masters," I: 386; Barth to Thurneysen, May 28, 1924, *Revolutionary Theology in the Making*, "the problem," 185.

81. Barth, *The Göttingen Dogmatics*, I: 15.

82. See Francis Turretin, *Institutes of Elenctic Theology*, 3 vols., trans. George Musgrave Giger (Phillipsburg: Presbyterian and Reformed Publishing Co., 1992), I: 55–167.

83. Barth, *The Göttingen Dogmatics*, I: 18–20.

84. Ibid., I: 91–92.

85. Ibid., I: 219–222; see Karl Barth, *The Theology of John Calvin*, trans. Geoffrey W. Bromiley (Grand Rapids: Wm. B. Eerdmans Publishing Co., 1995), 53–54, 158–164.

86. Barth, *The Göttingen Dogmatics*, I: 217.

87. Ibid., quotes I: 58–59, 216–218.

88. Ibid., I: 3.

89. Ibid., I: 15.

90. Barth, "An Answer to Professor Adolf von Harnack's Open Letter," 176–177; Adolf von Harnack, "A Postscript to My Open Letter to Professor Karl Barth," 186.

91. Barth, *The Göttingen Dogmatics*, I: 63–64.

92. Karl Barth, *Die christliche Dogmatik im Entwurf, I: Die Lehre vom Worte Gottes. Prolegomena zur christlichen Dogmatik* (Munich: Chr. Kaiser Verlag, 1927).

93. Rudolf Bultmann to Karl Barth, June 8, 1928, in *Karl Barth/Rudolf Bultmann Letters, 1922–1966*, trans. Bernd Jaspert, trans. and ed. Geoffrey W. Bromiley (Edinburgh: T. & T. Clark, 1982), 38–39.

94. Karl Barth to Rudolf Bultmann, June 12, 1928, in ibid., 40–42.

95. Karl Barth to Rudolf Bultmann, February 5, 1930, ibid., 49–50, "fleshpots," 49; Barth to Bultmann, June 20, 1931, ibid., "you have done," 65.

96. Rudolf Bultmann to Karl Barth, July 7, 1934, ibid., 75.

97. Rudolf Bultmann to Karl Barth, December 10, 1935, ibid., 82–83; Karl Barth to Rudolf Bultmann, December 22, 1935, ibid., 84.

98. Emil Brunner and Karl Barth, *Natural Theology: Comprising "Nature and Grace' by Professor Dr. Emil Brunner and the Reply "No!" by Dr. Karl Barth*, trans. Peter Fraenkel (London: Geoffrey Bles, 1946), "downward," 89; Barth, *Church Dogmatics: The Doctrine of the Word of God*, I:1, trans. G. T. Thomson (Edinburgh: T. & T. Clark, 1936), analogy of being, x.

99. Paul Schempp, "Marginal Glosses on Barthianism," *Zwischen den Zeiten* 6 (1928), 529–539, reprinted in *The Beginnings of Dialectic Theology*, 192–200, quote 192.

100. Renate Köbler, *In the Shadow of Karl Barth: Charlotte von Kirschbaum*, trans. Keith Crim (Louisville: Westminster John Knox, 1989), 23–45; Suzanne Selinger, *Charlotte von Kirschbaum and Karl Barth: A Study in Biography and the History of Theology* (University Park: Pennsylvania State University Press, 1998), 1–20.

101. See Karl Barth, *The German Church Conflict*, trans. P. T. A. Parker (Richmond: John Knox Pres, 1965). For the text of the Barmen Declaration, see Arthur C. Cochrane, *The Church's Confession Under Hitler* (1962; reprint: Pittsburgh: Pickwick Press, 1976), 237–247.

102. Karl Barth, "How My Mind Has Changed," in Barth, *How I Changed My Mind* (Richmond: John Knox Press, 1966), 41.

103. Rudolf Bultmann, "New Testament and Mythology," in Bultmann, *New Testament and Mythology and Other Basic Writings*, trans. and ed. Schubert M. Ogden (Philadelphia: Fortress Press, 1984), 1–43. This is a cleaner translation than the one by Reginald H. Fuller featured in the noted work ed. Hans Werner Bartsch, *Kerygma and Myth: A Theological Debate* 2 vols. (London: S.P.C.K., 1954, 1962), I: 1–44.

104. Bultmann, "New Testament and Mythology, 28–43.

105. Rudolf Bultmann, "Bultmann Replies to His Critics," in Bartsch, *Kerygma and Myth: A Theological Debate*, I, 191–211; Hans Werner Bartsch, "The Present State of the Debate," *Kerygma and Myth: A Theological Debate*, II, 1–82, quote 74.

106. Karl Barth, "Rudolf Bultmann – An Attempt to Understand Him," *Kerygma and Myth: A Theological Debate*, II, 83–132.

107. See Karl Barth, *Church Dogmatics: The Doctrine of Creation*, III:2, trans. Harold Knight et al. (Edinburgh: T. & T. Clark, 1960), 446–447.

108. Barth, *Church Dogmatics: The Doctrine of Creation*, III:2, quote 446–447; see Karl Barth, *Church Dogmatics: The Doctrine of Creation*, III: 1, trans. J. W. Edwards et al. (Edinburgh: T. & T. Clark, 1958), 79–89.

109. See Fritz Buri, *Theologie der Existenz* (Stuttgart: Paul Haupt, 1954).

110. Henriette Visser 't Hooft, "Is There a Woman's Problem?" *The Student World* 27 (1934), 12–15.

111. Georgia Harkness, "Days of My Years," unpublished autobiographical sketch written for the Pacific Coast Theological Group (1950s), Georgia Harkness Collection, United Library, Garrett-Evangelical Theological Seminary/Seabury-Western Seminary, 28; W. A. Visser 't Hooft, *The Fatherhood of God in an Age of Emancipation* (Geneva: World Council of Churches, 1982), 58–59; Jürgen Moltmann, "Henriette Visser 't Hooft," in *Gotteslehrerinnen*, ed. Luise Schottroff and Johannes Thiele (Stuttgart: Kreuzz Verlag, 1989), 169–179.

112. Karl Barth, *Church Dogmatics: The Doctrine of Creation* III: 4, trans. A. T. Mackay et al. (Edinburgh: T. & T. Clark, 1961), 116–240, quotes 171, 173.

113. Paul Tillich, "Die religionsgeschichtliche Konstruktion in Schellings positiver Philosophie, ihre Voraussetzungen und Prinzipien" (doctoral dissertation, University of Breslau, 1910); Tillich's dissertation for the licentiate of theology was published under the title *Der Begriff des Uebernatürlichen, sein dialektischer Charakter und das Prinzip der Identät, dargestellt an der supranaturalistischen Theologie vor Schleiermacher* (Königsberg: Madrasch, 1915). This section on Tillich adapts material from Gary Dorrien, *The Making of American Liberal Theology: Idealism, Realism, and Modernity* (Louisville: Westminster John Knox Press, 2003), 484–493, 501–503.

114. Paul Tillich, *The New Being* (New York: Charles Scribner's Sons, 1955), 52; [cover story, no byline], "To Be or Not to Be," *Time* 73 (March 16, 1959), "many of them," 47; Pauck and Pauck, *Paul Tillich: His Life and Thought*, 40–41, 51; Tillich, "Autobiographical Reflections of Paul Tillich," in *The Theology of Paul Tillich*, ed. Charles W. Kegley and Robert W. Bretall (New York: Macmillan, 1952), 12; Tillich, *My Search for Absolutes* (New York: Simon & Schuster, 1967), 39; Tillich, *On the Boundary: An Autobiographical Sketch* (New York: Charles Scribner's Sons, 1966), 52.

115. Paul Tillich, *The Interpretation of History*, trans. N. A. Rasetzki and Elsa L. Talmey (New York: Charles Scribner's Sons, 1936), quote 35; for extensive discussions of Tillich's early religious socialism, see Gary Dorrien, *Reconstructing the Common Good* (Maryknoll: Orbis Books, 1990), 48–76; Ronald H. Stone, *Paul Tillich's Radical Social Thought* (Atlanta: John Knox Press, 1980); Eduard Heimann, "Tillich's Doctrine of Religious Socialism," in *The Theology of Paul Tillich*, 312–325.

116. Paul Tillich, "Kairos," *Die Tat* 14 (August 1922), 330–350; Tillich, *Masse und Geist* (Berlin: Verlag der Arbeitsgemeinschaft, 1922); Tillich, *Das System der Wissenschaften nach Gegenständen und Methoden* (Göttingen: Vandenhoeck & Ruprecht, 1923); Tillich, *The Interpretation of History*, 123–175; Tillich, *Political Expectation*, ed. James Luther Adams, trans. James Luther Adams and Victor Nuovo (New York: Harper & Row, 1971), 58–88.

117. Paul Tillich, "Die religiöse und philosophische Weiterbildung des Sozialismus," *Blätter für religiösen Sozialismus* 5 (May 1924), 18; Pauck and Pauck, *Paul Tillich: His Life and Thought*, quote 83; Hannah Tillich, *From Time to Time* (New York: Stein and Day, 1973).

118. Paul Tillich, *Die religiöse Lage der Gegenwart* (Berlin: Ullstein, 1926); English edition, *The Religious Situation*, trans. H. Richard Niebuhr (New York: Henry Holt, 1932).

119. Paul Tillich, "Kritisches und positives Paradox: eine Aufeinandersetzung mit Karl Barth und Friedrich Gogarten," *Theologische Blätter* 2 (November 1923), 263–269; English edition, "Critical and Positive Paradox: A Discussion with Karl Barth and Friedrich Gogarten," in *The Beginnings of Dialectic Theology*, ed. James M. Robinson, trans Louis De Grazia and Keith R. Crim, 133–141.

120. Karl Barth, "The Paradoxical Nature of the 'Positive Paradox': Answers and Questions to Paul Tillich," in *The Beginnings of Dialectic Theology*, 142–154, quotes 147, 149; Tillich, *Religiöse Verwirklichung* (Berlin: Furche Verlag, 1929); chapter, "Realism and Faith," reprinted in Paul Tillich, *The Protestant Era*, trans. James Luther Adams (London: Nisbet & Co., 1951), 74–92, quote 91.

121. See Max Horkheimer and Theodor W. Adorno, *Dialektik der Aufklärung* (New York: Social Studies Association, 1944); *The Essential Frankfurt School Reader*, ed. Andrew Arato and Eike Gebhardt (New York: Continuum, 1982); Martin Jay, *The Dialectical Imagination: A History of the Frankfurt School and the Institute of Social research, 1923–1950* (Boston: Little, Brown & Co., 1973).

122. See Paul Tillich, *Die sozialistische Entscheidung* (Potsdam: Alfred Protte, 1933); English edition, *The Socialist Decision*, trans. Franklin Sherman (New York: Harper & Row, 1977); Wilhelm and Marion Pauck, *Paul Tillich: His Life and Thought* (San Francisco: Harper & Row, 1989), 130–131.

123. Paul Tillich, *The Interpretation of History*, trans. N. A. Rasetzki and Elsa L. Talmey (New York: Charles Scribner's Sons, 1936), 26, 29; see Tillich, "The Protestant Principle and the Proletarian Situation," in Paul Tillich, *The Protestant Era*, trans. James Luther Adams (London: Nisbet & Co., 1951), 237–259; Tillich, *On the Boundary: An Autobiographical Sketch* (New York: Charles Scribner's Sons, 1966). This section on Tillich adapts material from Gary Dorrien, *The Making of American Liberal Theology: Idealism, Realism, and Modernity* (Louisville: Westminster John Knox Press, 2003), 490–493, 501–503.

124. Tillich, *The Interpretation of History*, 31–35; Martin Kähler, *Die Wissenschaft der christlichen Lehre* (Leipzig: A. Beichert, 1893); Kähler, *The So-Called Historical Jesus and the Historic, Biblical Christ*, trans. Carl E. Braaten (Philadelphia: Fortress Press, 1988); Kähler, *Dogmatische Zeitfragen: Angewandte Dogmen* (Leipzig: A. Deichert, 1908).

125. Tillich, *The Interpretation of History*, quote 35.

126. See Martin Heidegger, *Being and Time*, trans. John Macquarrie and Edward Robinson (New York: Harper & Row, 1962); Heidegger, *The Basic Problems of Phenomenology*, trans. Albert Hofstadter (Bloomington: Indiana University Press, 1988); Paul Tillich, *Theology of Culture* (New York: Oxford University Press, 1959); Tillich, *The Courage to Be* (New Haven: Yale University Press, 1952).

127. Tillich, *The Interpretation of History*, 39–40; Tillich, *The Protestant Era*, quote 93; Tillich, *Theology of Culture*, 10–29, 112–126.

128. Tillich, *On the Boundary: An Autobiographical Sketch*, quotes 81–82. This later translation of the first part of Tillich's *Interpretation of History* is clearer in this section.

129. Ibid., 83.

130. Ibid, quote 83.

131. Ibid., quote 86; see Tillich, *Protestantisches Prinzip und proletarische Situation* (Bonn: Friedrich Cohen, 1931); Tillich, *The Protestant Era*, 237–259.

132. Paul Tillich, *Against the Third Reich: Paul Tillich's Wartime Radio Broadcasts into Nazi Germany*, ed. Ronald H. Stone and Matthew Lon Weaver, trans. Matthew Lon Weaver (Louisville: Westminster John Knox Press, 1998); "The Question of the Jewish People,"

March 31, 1942, quotes 14, 16; "Dark Clouds Are Gathering," December 1942, quotes 89.

133. Ibid., "Where Hope Lies This Advent Season," December 8, 1942, quote 93; "The Fourth War Christmas," December 15, 1942, quote 98; "The Tenth Anniversary of Hitler's Regime," February 1943, quote 118; "The Germanic Legacy," March 2, 1943, quote 122; "Germany's Rebirth into the Human Race," March 23, 1943, quotes 134.

134. Pauck and Pauck, *Paul Tillich: His Life and Thought*, 201–219, "harvest time," 219; see Paul Tillich, *The Shaking of the Foundations* (New York: Charles Scribner's Sons, 1948); Tillich, *Systematic Theology*, 3 vols. (Chicago: University of Chicago Press, 1951, 1957, 1963).

135. Paul Tillich, *The Courage to Be* (New Haven: Yale University Press, 1952), quotes 184, 185.

136. Tillich, *Systematic Theology*, I: 10.

137. Ibid., I: 12.

138. Ibid., I: 14–15, quotes 14.

139. Ibid., I: 16–18, quote 16; II: 97–180.

140. Ibid., I: 40–45.

141. Ibid., quote, I: 46; see II: 118–136.

142. Paul Tillich, "Das religiöse symbol," *Blätter für deutsche Philosophie* I (1928); revised version, Tillich, "The Religious Symbol," *Journal of Liberal Religion* 2 (1940), 13–33; further revised version, Tillich, "The Religious Symbol," *Symbolism in Religion and Literature*, ed. Rollo May (New Yorki: George Braziller, 1960), 75–98; Tillich, *Theology of Culture*, 36–38.

143. Tillich, "The Religious Symbol," *Symbolism in Religion and Literature*, 87–89, quote 89.

144. Paul Tillich, *Dynamics of Faith* (New York: Harper & Brothers, 1957), 48–54, quote 50; Tillich, *Systematic Theology* II: 152; Tillich, *Biblical Religion and the Search for Ultimate Reality* (Chicago: University of Chicago Press, 1955), 78–85.

145. Paul Tillich, "The Meaning and Justification of Religious Symbols," in *Religious Experience and Truth*, ed. Sidney Hook (New York: New York University Press, 1961), 4, 10; Tillich, "The Religious Symbol," quote 91; Tillich, *Theology of Culture*, 53–67; Tillich, *Dynamics of Faith*, 53–54; Tillich, *Systematic Theology*, II: 152.

146. Karl Barth, *Protestant Theology in the Nineteenth Century* (London: SCM Press, 1959; reprint, Valley Forge: Judson Press, 1973), quotes 266, 269.

147. Ibid., quotes 303, 287, 312.

148. Karl Barth, *Church Dogmatics: The Doctrine of God*, II: 1, ed. G. W. Bromiley and T. F. Torrance (Edinburgh: T. & T. Clark, 1957), 257–321; Barth, *Protestant Theology in the Nineteenth*, quote 396.

149. Barth, *Protestant Theology in the Nineteenth Century*, 409, 413.

150. Ibid., 414.

151. Ibid., 414–415.

152. Ibid., 419.

153. Ibid., 419.

154. Ibid., 420; see Barth, *Church Dogmatics: The Doctrine of God*, II: 1, 297–321.

155. Terrence Tice, "Interviews with Karl Barth and Reflections on His Interpretations of Schleiermacher," in *Barth and Schleiermacher: Beyond the Impasse?*, ed. James O. Duke and Robert F. Streetman (Philadelphia: Fortress Press, 1988), 47; Karl Barth, "Concluding Unscientific Postscript on Schleiermacher," author's postscript to Barth, *The Theology of Schleiermacher: Lectures at Göttingen, Winter Semester of 1923/24*, ed.

Dietrich Ritschl, trans. Geoffrey W. Bromiley (Grand Rapids: Wm. B. Eerdmans, 1982), 261–279, quote 264.

156.   *Karl Barth-Eduard Thurneysen: Briefwechsel*, I: 489–492; Barth, *Epistle to the Romans*, 225.

157.   Barth, "Concluding Unscientific Postscript on Schleiermacher," "was grounded," 264; Barth, *The Theology of Schleiermacher: Lectures at Göttingen, Winter Semester of 1923/24*, xiii.

158.   Barth, *The Theology of Schleiermacher: Lectures at Göttingen, Winter Semester of 1923/24*, xv.

159.   *Friedrich Schleiermachers Briefwechsel mit J. Chr. Gass*, ed. Wilhelm Gass (Berlin: G. Reimer, 1852), 195; Barth, *The Theology of Schleiermacher: Lectures at Göttingen, Winter Semester of 1923/24*, xiv–xv; see Georg Wobbermin, *Systematische Theologie nach religionspsychologischer Methode*, 3 vols. (Leipzig: J. C. Hinrichs, 1913).

160.   Barth to Thurneysen, February 5, 1924, *Revolutionary Theology in the Making*, 168; Barth, *The Theology of Schleiermacher: Lectures at Göttingen, Winter Semester of 1923/24*, 259.

161.   Barth, *The Theology of Schleiermacher: Lectures at Göttingen, Winter Semester of 1923/24*, 259.

162.   Ibid., "an oppressive," 259; Barth, *The Epistle to the Romans*, 43.

163.   Barth, *The Theology of Schleiermacher: Lectures at Göttingen, Winter Semester of 1923/24*, 259–260.

164.   John McConnachie, *The Significance of Karl Barth* (London: Hodder & Stoughton, 1931), Adam quote, 43; Barth to Thurneysen, April 2, 1922, *Revolutionary Theology in the Making*, 95; Paul Tillich, "Kairos," in Tillich, *The Protestant Era*, trans. and ed. James Luther Adams (London: Nisbet & Co., 1951), 37–58; Barth, *The Theology of Schleiermacher: Lectures at Göttingen, Winter Semester of 1923/24*, "Schleiermacher undoubtedly," 260.

165.   Barth, *Protestant Theology in the Nineteenth Century*, quotes 427, 426.

166.   Ibid., 428, 436–437, quote 428; see Emil Brunner, *Die Mystik und das Wort: der Gegensatz zwischen moderner Religionsauffassung und christlichem Glauben dargestellt an der Theologie Schleiermachers* (Tübingen: n.p., 1921); Brunner, The *Theology of Crisis*; Brunner, *Wahrheit als Begegnung*; Brunner, *Man in Revolt: A Christian Anthropology*, trans. Olive Wyon (Philadelphia: Westminster Press, 1942); Brunner, *Reason and Revelation: The Christian Doctrine of Faith and Knowledge*, trans. Olive Wyon (Philadelphia: Westminster Press, 1946).

167.   Barth, *Protestant Theology in the Nineteenth Century*, 437–445.

168.   Ibid., quote 447.

169.   Ibid., 447–452.

170.   See Friedrich Schleiermacher, *On Religion: Addresses in Response to Its Cultured Critics*, trans. Terrence N. Tice (Richmond: John Knox Press, 1969), 42–44; Schleiermacher, *The Christian Faith*, ed. H. R. Mackintosh and J. S. Stewart (Edinburgh: T. & T. Clark, 1928), 6–12; Barth, *Protestant Theology in the Nineteenth Century*, 453–454.

171.   Barth, *Protestant Theology in the Nineteenth Century*, 454–455.

172.   Ibid., 455–459, quote 455.

173.   Barth, *Protestant Theology in the Nineteenth Century*, 460; see *Barth and Schleiermacher: Beyond the Impasse?* eds. James O. Duke and Robert F. Streetman (Philadelphia: Fortress Press, 1988).

174.   Barth, *Protestant Theology in the Nineteenth Century*, 461–462.

175.   Ibid., 463–464.

176. Ibid., 468–470.

177. Tice, "Interviews with Karl Barth and Reflections on His Interpretations of Schleiermacher," Interview of July 27, 1960, quotes 50.

178. Barth to Thurneysen, February 15, 1925, *Revolutionary Theology in the Making: Barth-hurneysen Correspondence, 1914–1925*, 203–204; Wilhelm Herrmann, *Dogmatik* (Stuttgart: Verlag Friedrich Andres Perthes, 1925); English edition, *Systematic Theology (Dogmatik)*, trans. Nathaniel Micklem and Kenneth A. Saunders (New York: Macmillan Company, 1927), 21. These lectures were published shortly after Herrmann's death by Martin Rade in the form in which Herrmann last presented them, during the winter semester of 1915/1916.

179. Karl Barth, "The Principles of Dogmatics According to Wilhelm Herrmann" (1925), reprinted in Barth, *Theology and Church: Shorter Writings 1920–1928*, trans. Louise Pettibone Smith (New York: Harper & Row, 1962), 256–269; see Wilhelm Herrmann, *Christlich-protestantische Dogmatik* (1906), in Paul Hinneberg, ed., *Die Kultur der Gegenwart: Ihre Entwicklung und ihre Ziele* I: IV, 2 (Druck und Verlag von B. G. Teubner: Berlin und Leipzig, 1909), 129–180; reprinted in Herrmann, *Schriften zur Grundlegung der Theologie* I, Peter Fischer-Appelt, ed. (Munich: Chr. Kaiser Verlag, 1966), 298–358; Herrmann, "Der evangelische Glaube und die Theologie Albr. Ritschls" (1890), in Herrmann, *Gesammelte Aufsätze*, ed. F. W. Schmidt (Tübingen: J.C.B. Mohr,1923), 1–25; Herrmann, "Die religiöse Frage in der Gegenwart," (1908), in Herrmann, *Schriften zur Grundlegung der Theologie* II (1967), 114–149; Herrmann, "Die Absolutheit des Christentums und die Religionsgeschichte: Eine Besprechung des gleichnamigen Vortrags von Ernst Troeltsch" (1902), in *Schriften zur Grundlegung der Theologie* I, 193–199; Herrmann, *Christlich-protestantische Dogmatik* (1906), in Hinneberg, *Kultur der Gegenwart* I: IV, 2, 604–624; Herrmann, "Der Widerspruch im religiösen Denken und seine Bedeutung für das Leben der Religion" (1911), in Herrmann *Schriften zur Grundlegung der Theologie* II, 233–246; James M. Robinson, *Das Problem des Heiligen Geistes bei Wilhelm Herrmann* (Marburg: K. Gleiser, 1952), 16–22.

180. Barth, "The Principles of Dogmatics According to Wilhelm Herrmann," 265.

181. Herrmann, *Systematic Theology*, 152.

182. Barth, "The Principles of Dogmatics According to Wilhelm Herrmann," 269.

183. Karl Barth, *Church Dogmatics: The Doctrine of the Word of God* I: 1, trans. G. T. Thomson (Edinburgh: T. & T. Clark, 1936), 96; Barth, *Church Dogmatics: The Doctrine of Creation* III: 4, trans A. T. Mackay et al. (1961), 307, 326, 457, 516, 526; Barth, *Church Dogmatics: The Doctrine of Reconciliation* IV: 1, trans. G. W. Bromiley (1956), 287, 755, 761.

184. For an interpretation that insightfully and, I believe, rightly emphasizes Herrmann's influence over Barth and Bultmann, see Hendrikus Berkhof, *Two Hundred Years of Theology: Report of a Personal Journey*, trans. John Vriend (Grand Rapids: Wm. B. Eerdmans Publishing Company, 1989), 163–207.

185. See Barth, *Protestant Theology in the Nineteenth Century*, 266–312; John D. Godsey, ed., *Karl Barth's Table Talk* (Edinburgh: Tweeddale Court, *Scottish Journal of Theology*, Occasional Papers, 10, 1963), 61.

186. Barth to Thurneysen, January 1, 1916, *Revolutionary Theology in the Making*, 36; see Joachim Wach, "Introduction: The Meaning and Task of the History of Religions (Religionswissenschaft)," Joseph M. Kitagawa, ed., *The History of Religions: Essays on the Problem of Understanding* (Chicago: University of Chicago Press, 1967), 1–19; Wach, *Types of Religious Experience: Christian and Non-Christian* (Chicago: University of Chicago Press, 1972), 3–29; Ernst Troeltsch, "The Dogmatics of the 'Religionsgeschichtliche Schule,'" *American Journal of Theology* 17 (January 1913), 4;

187. Bultmann, *The History of the Synoptic Tradition*, 150–166.

188. See Wilhelm Herrmann, *The Communion of the Christian With God: Described on the Basis of Luther's Statements*, trans. J. Sandys Stanyon, ed. Robert T. Voelkel (Philadelphia: Fortress Press, 1971), 72–75, 87. See editor's discussion, 361.

189. Ernst Fuchs, *Zum hermeneutischen Problem in der Theologie; Die existentiale Interpretation* (Tübingen: J. C. B. Mohr, 1959); Fuchs, *Studies of the Historical Jesus*, trans. Andrew Scobie (London: SCM Press, 1964); Fuchs, "The New Testament and the Hermeneutical Problem," *New Frontiers in Theology II: The New Hermeneutic*, eds. James M. Robinson and John B. Cobb, Jr., eds. (New York: Harper & Row, 1964), 111–146; Gerhard Ebeling, *The Nature of Faith*, trans. Ronald Gregor Smith (Philadelphia: Muhlenberg Press, 1961), 44–71; Ebeling, *Word and Faith*, trans. James W. Leitch (Philadelphia: Fortress Press, 1963), 201–246, 288–304; Ebeling, *Theology and Proclamation: A Discussion with Rudolf Bultmann*, trans. John Riches (London: Collins, 1966), 32–81; James M. Robinson, "The German Discussion of the Later Heidegger," in Robinson and John B. Cobb, Jr., eds., *The Later Heidegger and Theology I: New Frontiers in Theology* (New York: Harper & Row, 1963), 3–76; 32 Martin Heidegger, *Holzwege* (1936–1946) (Frankfurt: Klostermann, 1950), 61; Heidegger, *Poetry, Language, Thought*, trans. Albert Hofstadter (New York: Harper & Row, 1971), 189.

190. On the Fuchs/Ebeling new hermeneutic, see Rudolf Bultmann, "The Primitive Christian Kerygma and Historical Jesus," *The Historical Jesus and the Kerygmatic Christ*, eds. Carl E. Braaten and Roy A. Harrisville (Nashville: Abingdon Press, 1964), 24; Bultmann, *Des Verhältnis der urchristlichen Christusbotschaft zum historischen Jesus, Sitzungsberichte der Heidelberger Akadamie der Wissenschaften* (Heidelberg: Carl Winter Universitätsverlag, 1960), 17–25. On Herrmann, see Bultmann, "On the Question of Christology," (1927), in Bultmann, *Faith and Understanding*, trans. Louise Pettibone Smith (Philadelphia: Fortress Press, 1987), 132–144.

191. Quoted in Godsey, ed., *Karl Barth's Table Talk*, 23.

192. See Karl Barth, "Wolfgang Amadeus Mozart," trans. Walter M. Mosse, in Walter Leibrecht, ed., *Religion and Culture: Essays in Honor of Paul Tillich* (New York: Harper & Brothers, 1959), 61–78.

193. Karl Barth, *The Göttingen Dogmatics: Instruction in the Christian Religion* I, trans. Geoffrey W. Bromiley, ed. Hannelotte Reiffen (Grand Rapids: Wm. B. Eerdmans Publishing Company, 1991), 33–34.

194. Karl Barth, *Church Dogmatics: The Doctrine of Creation*, III: 3, trans. G. W. Bromiley and R. J. Ehrlich (Edinburgh: T. & T. Clark, 1960), p. 403; see Barth, *Church Dogmatics: The Doctrine of Reconciliation*, IV: 3,1, trans. G. W. Bromiley (Edinburgh: T. & T. Clark, 1961), p. 109.

195. Barth, *Church Dogmatics: The Doctrine of Creation*, III: 2, ix.

196. Dietrich Bonhoeffer to Eberhard Bethge, May 5, 1944, in Bonohoffer, *Letters and Papers from Prison*, ed. Eberhard Bethge, trans. Reginald Fuller, et al. (New York: Macmillan & Co., 1971), 286.

197. Ibid., 286–287; Bonhoeffer to Bethge, June 8, 1944, ibid., 329.

198. Karl Barth to P. Walter Herrenbrück, December 21, 1952, "From a Letter to Superintendent Herrenbrück," in *World Come of Age*, ed. R. G. Smith (Philadelphia: Fortress Press, 1967), "enigmatic," 90; Karl Barth to Eberhard Bethge, May 22, 1967, in Barth, *Letters, 1961–1968*, ed. Jürgen Fangmeier and Hinrich Stoevesandt, trans. Geoffrey W. Bromiley (Edinburgh: T. & T. Clark, 1981), 250–253.

199. Karl Barth to Hanfried Müller, April 7, 1961, quoted in Busch, *Karl Barth: His Life from Letters and Autobiographical Texts*, 381.

200. Barth to J. Glenthoj, September 7, 1956, and conversation with pastors and laypeople from the Pfalz, September 1953, quoted in Busch, *Karl Barth: His Life from Letters and Autobiographical Texts*, 381.

201. Barth to Herrenbrück, December 21, 1952, 90.

202. Barth, "Concluding Unscientific Postscript on Schleiermacher," "the poor," 271; Barth to Bethge, May 22, 1967, 252.

203. Barth, *The Göttingen Dogmatics*, 156–158, quote 157.

204. Ibid., 157–160.

205. Ibid., quote 160.

206. Ibid., "to take," 167; Barth, *Church Dogmatics: The Doctrine of the Word of God*, I: 1, "constantly," xi.

207. Ibid., 98–140; Scott C. Saye, "The Wild and Crooked Tree: Barth, Fish, and Interpretive Communities," *Modern Theology* 12 (October 1996), 443–444.

208. Barth, *Church Dogmatics* I: 1, 121.

9

Idealistic Ironies
From Kant and Hegel to Tillich and Barth

In theory it was always possible, even in the nineteenth century, for a religious thinker to be definitely modern but not liberal. Kierkegaard exemplified the possibility, and many of Frederick Denison Maurice's admirers claimed it of him and themselves. In theory it was likewise possible to be theologically liberal and not be idealistic. But that did not happen. Liberal theology, then and now, even when it claims to be predominantly naturalistic or realistic, ends up privileging idealizing motifs, by virtue of being liberal and religious.

In Germany, philosophical idealism had a long run at the center of the nation's intellectual life before falling from its exalted status in the late nineteenth century. In England, philosophical idealism rose to predominance at the very time that it faded in Germany. In both cases religious thinkers kept it going long after it lost its favored status in philosophy faculties and the general intellectual culture. In both cases, religious thinkers recognized that the Kantian problems of mind and subjectivity do not go away even if one changes the subject. In both places, social idealism was a latecomer, being stifled by repressive political cultures and by the elitist presumptions of liberal movements. In both places, religious thinkers found stray allies in philosophy faculties after idealism fell from fashion. And in both places, even the Barthian revolt against two centuries of liberal theology did not dissolve its idealistic impulse.

The modern revolution in philosophy launched by Descartes was modern for casting aside the authority principle and for conceiving epistemology as the philosophy of mind – the activity of a thinking self. Locke's empiricism paved the way to the modern departure in religious thought by eroding the power of external authority to establish or compel belief in any particular thing, but Locke made a greater impact by putting epistemology at the center of philosophical debate. With Locke, epistemology became a map or theory of the elements, combinations, and associations of experience. Hume, taking up this project, contended that there are no links between facts in the world of

---

Kantian Reason and Hegelian Spirit: The Idealistic Logic of Modern Theology, First Edition. Gary Dorrien.
© 2012 John Wiley & Sons, Ltd. Published 2015 by John Wiley & Sons, Ltd.

experience; facts are only conjoined, not connected, in experience. These developments – the overthrow of external authority, the epistemological concern with subjectivity, and Hume's claim that we know only ideas and impressions – set the table for Kant's revolution.

Kant took Hume seriously, even as he fought off Hume's skepticism. If no one had ever seen causality or experienced necessity, as Hume contended, Kant had to let go of his rationalist attempt to discover the nature of things by logic. Kant realized that he had not solved the perennial problems of metaphysics – necessity, the extension of the universe, the existence of God and the soul, and the indivisible elements in space. Contrary to countless renderings of Kant, however, he did not renounce metaphysics in the *Critique of Pure Reason*, four-fifths of which expounded a theory of metaphysics. Neither did his system rest on the attempt of the first *Critique* to establish the metaphysical foundations of science and the limits of metaphysics in solving this problem. The key to Kant's system was the key to German idealism as a whole, ironies and prejudices notwithstanding – the emancipating and unifying reality of freedom.

Early Enlightenment rationalism and empiricism launched the modern liberation from external authority and mounted a spirited defense of the authority of reason. But the early Enlightenment did not play up the link between reason and freedom, and its advocacy of the authority of reason was novel and fresh. Kant, upon launching the Kantian revolution, was slow to grasp the importance of freedom for his argument, though he recognized that Enlightenment was no longer new or innocent. He took seriously the accusation that the Enlightenment had a legacy of harm to religion, morality, and the social order. Kant had the germ of his freedom argument in his conviction that scholastic and rationalist metaphysics alienated human beings from their freedom by projecting the source of morality into a world transcending human powers. He wanted metaphysics to do something useful, establishing the universal rights of humanity. But he did not fully grasp, in his first *Critique*, where his critical idealism was going. Kant published two editions of the first *Critique* before he took hold of freedom, in the *Critique of Practical Reason*, as the key to rationality and morality. There he declared that reason is the only secure ground of moral truth, and freedom is "the keystone of the whole architecture of the system of pure reason."[1]

Kant called the liberating project of modernity the giving of the law to one's self. Hegel called it the concept's giving itself actuality. In both cases, German idealism was about the realization of truth in free self-determination. The principles of justice that define our rights should not rest on a given concept of virtue, as in Aristotle; rather, a just society respects each individual's freedom to discover the good life. Kant contended in the second *Critique* that freedom is the only idea of speculative reason whose possibility we know *a priori*. Although we do not understand this idea, he allowed, we know it as the condition of the moral law, something that we do know. If we had no freedom, we would not be able to grasp the existence of the moral law within us. For Kant, the concept of mind as a subject of knowledge was impossible lacking the idea of a world governed by laws. No concept of mind as a subject of knowledge is possible lacking the idea of a world governed by laws. In any concept of mind, some concept of the world is implied; otherwise there would be no self-understanding of the mind. Mental activity, as such, implies the existence of a world in which mental activity occurs.[2]

This idea, that the concepts of mind and our images of the world are deeply interconnected, was picked up by the entire post-Kantian idealist tradition. The very term, *Weltanschauung*, which Fichte was the first to employ as a philosophical concept, depends on Kant's idea of the mind-world relationship. Fichte emphasized the role of one's image of the world in understanding anything. Hegel correlated the stages of the development of mind with the development of worldviews, conceptions of the world. Dieter Henrich aptly observes that on Hegelian terms "we cannot talk about either one apart from the other." The development of mind and worldviews go together.[3]

Kant's moral worldview featured three postulates – freedom, God, and immortality. Freedom, however, belonged to a special category for Kant, because only its possibility is knowable *a priori*. The idea of freedom is a condition of the moral law, unlike the ideas of God and immortality, which are conditions of the necessary object of any will that is determined by the moral law. Kant argued that we cannot exercise our pure practical reason to its fullest capacity without holding to a worldview postulating the existence of freedom, God, and immortality. But without freedom, we would not know that there is a moral law.[4]

By limiting causality to a law of the mind, Kant made room for the possibility of freedom. By insisting on the actuality of the moral law, Kant made room for the actuality of freedom, for there is no moral activity if the moral subject is not free. Freedom *is* autonomy, Kant argued: "The autonomy of the will is the sole principle of all moral laws and of duties conforming to them; heteronomy of choice, on the other hand, not only does not establish any obligation but is opposed to the principle of duty and to the morality of the will."[5]

For Kant, morality had one principle – independence from all desired objects and external pressures. This independence he conceived as freedom in the negative sense. Positive freedom is the self-legislation of pure practical reason. There is no moral activity apart from freedom, for moral activity is precisely the regulation of a free self's desires through the universal moral law, the "categorical imperative," which is valid unconditionally because it is valid for the will of every rational human being. A will is free only if it is determined by itself as the author of the law that binds it, and it is good only if its free decisions are wholly determined by the demands of the moral law. Kant allowed that if a person acts out of self-interest, self-preservation, sympathy, compassion, or any other motive besides that of duty to the universal moral law, it is possible to do good things. But these motives do not express a good will, since they are always conditioned by circumstances. An action possesses moral worth only if it expresses one's determination to live by the categorical imperative under any circumstance. We know that we ought to do right; this was Kant's single certainty. The moral law is simple, absolute, sublime, and not that hard to figure out. To actually do the right thing, however, we have to fight off the desires of sense, especially the terribly human tendency to deny or demean the humanity of a fellow human subject.[6]

Kant contended that if one takes seriously that the maxim of one's will should be universalized, one will never act in a way that denies the humanity of another human being. Persons are to be treated as ends in themselves, not as means to an end. He did not mean that one must not use others as a means to exchange goods or to be driven from one place to another or anything of that sort. Kant meant that every person's humanity must be recognized as an end in itself. A person's humanity is the matrix of capacities that directly and indirectly permit rational self-conscious activity, and human dignity is not subject to negotiation or exceptions.

For the various traditions of post-Kantian idealism that Kant launched, his concept of persons as moral ends in themselves was indispensable, even when idealists fell, like Kant, woefully short of actually treating all human beings as moral ends in themselves. Kant was the towering figure who dethroned the things of sense; even Hegel looked up to Kant for this reason. If the mind is the determining factor in the production of experience, the religious bias in favor of spiritual creativity had a philosophical ground.

But the post-Kantians wailed against Kant's thing-in-itself so loudly that Kant's reasons for resorting to it were obscured. Kant started with Descartes: I know that I exist by knowing about myself. The only thing that is given *in* self-consciousness is consciousness of the self itself. Everything else is given *to* self-consciousness. If something were not given *to* self-consciousness, Kant reasoned, there would be no combining activity that makes "I think" a possibility. But if something is given to self-consciousness, it cannot be something that self-consciousness produced. Kant distinguished the way that something is given to self-consciousness from that which is given. Space and time, the forms of sensibility, are distinct from that which is given through these forms. The forms, by themselves, do not contain what is given through them, as there is no matter in space. The point of Kant's distinction between *noumena* and *phenomena* was the difference between that which is given and its being given in spatial and temporal form. There must be a difference between things as they are and things as they are through something else. Henrich explains, "What Kant means by the thing-in-itself is that there are no conditions affecting the essence of the givenness of things *per se.*" All thinking operates through spatial and temporal predicates. The thing-in-itself is a limiting concept that designates that which we cannot think, much less know.[7]

Fichte and Schelling, by discarding or refashioning the unknowable thing-in-itself, seriously considered themselves to be better Kantians than Kant. The thing-in-itself marred Kant's magnificent achievement in dethroning the things of sense. Ironically, it also triggered transcendental idealisms transcending Kant's boundaries, which, for Kant, made it a terrible joke that Fichte and Schelling considered themselves to be better Kantians. From Schelling onward the post-Kantians with a religious bent protested that Kant wrongly disclaimed knowledge of human souls. Kant could not get along without a knowable human soul, so he replaced it with dubious substitutes. In effect, Kant had five egos. One he called the empirical ego, which is bound by causation. Another he called the transcendental unity of apperception, a logical point of reference, whereby a knowing self collects one's self enough to perceive links between one's more-or-less collected self and the world of appearances. His third ego was the ego as a thing-in-itself, which is unknowable. His fourth ego was the goal of knowledge, which he called the ego as a transcendental ideal. His last ego he called the moral ego, which posits its own freedom. Post-Kantians were no less perplexed than anti-Kantians. How could it be rigorous and modest, epistemologically, to have five egos? Eugene Lyman called this outcome "a real bedevilment of the situation."[8]

Many religious idealists preferred to speak of the soul as a knowable first principle, though not as a substance. Modern idealism did not view the soul as a material substance (as in popular piety) or an immaterial substance (as in Plato) or even a thinking substance (as in Descartes' identification of the soul with consciousness). Modern thought conceived activity, not a static notion of substance, as essential to being. Thus Leibniz conceived the soul as the spiritual cause of material phenomena. Berkeley conceived it as the perceiving activity that creates ideas and the world of things. Kant argued that the mind builds up its world for itself through its transcendental categories of thought.

Post-Kantians prized Descartes for conceiving the soul as immediate and certain, and matter as an uncertain inference. But Descartes' absolute dualism of body and soul was impossible, treating the body as an automaton. Post-Kantian idealists, especially the Hegelian and personal idealists, contended that the knowing subject and the subject's activity are one. There is no thought without a thinker, no activity without an agent, no consciousness without a subject, and no reality without self-consciousness. The soul is real precisely as a self's self-consciousness of its unity and self-identity. The Kantian categories of thought are the preconditions of experience that make experience possible; they cannot be imported into the mind from without. But against Kant, if the categories of thought do not apply to things-in-themselves, these things cannot be affirmed at all.[9]

Religious idealists took special interest in the problem of Kant's exclusion of purpose or will from pure reason. Even if one accepted Kant's account of knowledge as an *a priori* synthetic activity of mind and his epistemic dualism of subject and object, it did not follow that one had to accept his restriction of pure reason to knowledge of phenomena. One could grant that reason has no direct access to reality and that science is necessarily restricted to appearances without accepting Kant's denial that experience yields truthful metaphysical clues about reality. Many religious post-Kantians objected that the cosmological argument for God's existence retains immense value as an argument even if Kant was right that it does not qualify as a proof. Even Kant said that, but his arbitrary restriction of pure reason to science had a powerful delegitimizing effect on arguments for God's existence. When Kant described practical reason and aesthetic judgment, he had a role for the power of will; when he described pure reason, he had room only for rules of mind through which the mind intuits objects of sense data.

But these rules of mind through which reason reaches the world of things do not unify the self or the world of appearances. The Kantian categories, by themselves, do not unite the forms of sensibility; neither do space and time. The categories alone place a tenuous subject among isolated things and events. There is no knowing without self-conscious intelligence, and intelligence is nothing without will. There were Romantic, absolute, and personal idealistic versions of this objection, but the personal idealists who were religious pressed it the hardest. Some religious idealists conceived will or purpose as a category of thought on the same plane as causality, negation, existence, or necessity. One could conceive will as a factor in pure reason without claiming that will, as a category, plays a definite role in elementary experience. Every event has a cause and takes place in time, but most events do not require a purpose. What mattered for personal idealists, whether or not one construed will as a fundamental category of understanding, was that will is indispensable to reflection and constitutive of it. The higher forms of thought require will; there is no reflective reason without it.

Even if purpose is hidden to intuition, it is revealed to and in reflection. Mere mechanical causality is lifeless and meaningless, but reflective thought is all about life and meaning.[10]

Kant's thing-in-itself and his compartmentalization of will went together, both problematically. The thing-in-itself had no content and it failed the tests of the categories. It was not in space or time; it was not one or many; it was not a cause or an effect. Therefore it yielded nothing except a brake on knowing. More importantly, the deepest, most direct, and most certain knowledge that reason possesses is the reflective self's knowledge of itself – which Kant excluded by restricting pure reason to knowledge of phenomena. Absolute and personal idealists fashioned more robust ideas of reason than that, often claiming that the logic of Kant's system pressed in their direction.

A certain amount of special pleading was inevitable, given the drama with which this story unfolded. The breakups between Kant and Fichte, and Fichte and Schelling, traced to the problems attending Kant's inability to explain the reality of the external world. Fichte, claiming to overcome Kant's dualistic impasse, ended the first edition of the *Wissenschaftslehre* with an infinitely striving ego stuck in a circle of consciousness against an infinitely resistant non-ego. The Romantic, absolute, and personal idealists, rejecting Fichte's instrumental rendering of nature, claimed to break free of Fichte's subjectivist impasse. Nature could be given its due as an end in itself by objectifying the principle of subject-object identity. There must be a single universal substance that appears equally within the subject and object of experience. This page from Spinoza led Schelling, Hölderlin, Schlegel, Schleiermacher, Coleridge, and Hegel to the Romantic idea of intellectual intuition. Subsequently it led Schelling and Hegel to revive the very kind of metaphysics that Kant condemned: Theoretical reason making knowledge claims about the absolute or unconditioned.[11]

Schelling and Hegel had no problem with Kant's demolition of Leibnizian-Wolffian rationalism, which contended that the concepts of the understanding apply directly to the unconditioned. Kant rightly attacked rationalist dogmatism and its mechanical concept of reason, countering that the concepts of the understanding cannot be extended beyond experience. But Schelling and Hegel argued that Kant never threw off his own mechanical rationalism. Kant's idea of theoretical reason was still ruled by the principle of sufficient reason – that there must be a sufficient reason or cause for every event. In effect, Kant reduced reason to logic, the extension of the concepts of the understanding, which yielded his verdict that there cannot be any knowledge of the unconditioned through reason. Schelling and Hegel based their alternative on the distinction between reason and understanding. Kant's objections to metaphysics were valid for the understanding, which is ruled by the principle of sufficient reason, but they were not valid for reason, which consists essentially of the power to grasp things as parts of the whole.[12]

Negatively, post-Kantian idealism was an argument about the limitations that Kant placed on reason; positively, it took up Kant's monist suggestion in the third *Critique* that intellectual intuition might transcend these limitations. Kant had a role for intuition as a purely immediate representation, and he occasionally said things about it that smacked of absolute idealism. Fichte, building on Kant, put intellectual intuition at the heart of his system, describing it as a form of self-knowing consisting of a subject-object identity. Through intellectual intuition, one attains knowledge of one's noumenal self, which transcends the phenomenal realm of nature. The Romantic idealists seized on this idea, taking it beyond Kant and Fichte. There is a form of rational knowing that is not limited by the principle of sufficient reason and that is not subject to the limitations that Kant placed on reason, they argued. It is the knowledge of my identity with the universe as a whole.

This idea permeated and defined Romantic idealism. Goethe, Schlegel, Hölderlin, Coleridge, and Wordsworth had versions of it; Schleiermacher expounded it in *On Religion: Speeches to its Cultured Despisers.* But Romantic idealism fixated on Romantic feeling, as in Schleiermacher's definition of religion as "sense and taste for the infinite." Though the Romantic idealists claimed to take nature more seriously than Kant and Fichte took it, it was hard to say how they avoided Fichte's vicious circle of subjectivity. This was the key to Schelling and Hegel. Schelling, the ultimate Romantic before taking his objective idealist turn, and Hegel, whose Romantic flirtation was very brief, developed full-orbed systems of metaphysical idealism that made knowledge claims about the absolute.[13]

Intellectual intuition, in their rendering, was the capacity to see the universal in the particular and the infinite in the finite. In intellectual intuition one grasps an individual as a member of a whole, perceiving how its inner identity depends upon the totality of which it is a part. Contrary to Fichte, intellectual intuition is not merely about knowing one's noumenal self as the ground of one's autonomy. It is about knowing one's identity with the universe as a whole. As such, contrary to Fichte and Kant, intellectual intuition is a source of metaphysical knowledge about eternal forms. In intellectual intuition one sees all of nature acting through one's self. Schelling reasoned that intellectual intuition is contemplative, not something by which one explains or deduces something. To explain an object is to show how it is acted upon by other objects and caused to act as it does. To deduce an object is to derive it from a higher principle as an instance of the higher principle. To contemplate an object is to apprehend it in itself apart from its relations with other objects, grasping the universal in the particular. In intellectual intuition, Schelling argued, one grasps the entire universe from the point of view of the thing contemplated, recognizing that all objects in themselves are the same.[14]

Reason is essentially holistic, comprehending things by their place within the whole. There is only one universe, in which every something is organically constitutive of an absolute whole. Through intellectual intuition one grasps the unity of universal and particular, the ideal and the real. Anything that I think or do is ultimately God thinking and acting through me.

Schelling got from Spinoza the idea of God thinking and acting through human subjects. He featured it during the phase of his career that launched absolute idealism and Hegel. Dramatically, Schelling declared that Spinoza was the first thinker to comprehend "with complete clarity" that thought and extension are merely modifications of the same principle, for mind and matter are one: "His system was the first bold outline of a creative imagination, which conceived the finite immediately in the idea of the infinite, purely as such, and recognized the former only in the latter." Spinoza had the right subject, the universal spirit of the world; subsequently and differently, Leibniz had it too. Schelling caustically contrasted this magnificent idea of what philosophy was about with "the speculative chimera of a world of *things-in-themselves*, which, known and intuited by no mind, yet affects us and produces all our ideas."[15]

For a while, echoing his Romantic friends in Jena, Schelling exalted art as the medium and proof of intellectual intuition. Only in aesthetic experience are the subjective and objective poles of the absolute united, he argued. But Schelling's pure Romantic phase was very brief. By 1802 he was already lifting philosophy above art; by the following year he was emphatic about it. For a while his philosophy was a dark Parmenidian vision of the absolute as pure self-identity excluding all opposition between things and any difference between subject and object. The strict monism of *Darstellung meines Systems der Philosophie*, however, turned out to be another phase. Schelling's intellectualistic denial of the finite made no sense of the terribly real suffering and death of his wife Carolyn, and Hegel parodied pure self-identity as the night when "all cows are black." In 1809 Schelling opted for religion and myth, which gave him a better basis to make sense of freedom, evil, and the divine ground of all things.[16]

In chapter 4 I emphasized the ways that Schelling and Hegel diverged after Hegel published the *Phenomenology of Spirit*. Here it is appropriate to emphasize that most of Hegelianism was already in place before the parting. The idea that subject-object identity is the principle of all knowledge was not distinct to Schelling and Hegel. What they did with it, by developing systems of absolute idealism, was distinct to them, which Hegel got mostly from Schelling.

Kantian idealism already had the idea of subject-object identity through Kant's transcendental argument that we know only what we create. Hegel, pressing the same "spirit of Kant" argument that Schelling used in his more generous moments, argued that the identity of subject and object is the fundamental principle of Kantian reason. However, Hegel observed, Kant turned this identity itself, which is reason, into "an object of philosophical reflection," which erased the identity "from its home ground." Reason, instead of ruling the understanding, was subordinated to it. Hegel objected that Kant limited the identity of subject and object to twelve acts of pure thought. On second thought, there were only nine, because Kant's categories of modality (possibility/impossibility, existence/non-existence, and necessity/contingency) determine nothing objectively.[17]

Aside from the few things that are objectively determined by the categories, Hegel noted, Kant left a rather large empirical realm of sensibility and perception on its own, an absolute *a posteriori* realm. For this entire realm, the only *a priori* principle apparently in play was a merely subjective maxim of aesthetic reason – the faculty of reflective judgment. Sometimes Hegel argued that Kant should have been with him, based on the *Critique of Judgment*. Usually he protested that Kant raised non-identity to an absolute principle without saying it quite so bluntly. This was what came from subordinating reason to understanding and pitting thought against being. Hegel and Schelling contended that reason has far greater capacities than Kant allowed, it extends to knowledge of the absolute, and there cannot be any difference between knowing the absolute and the absolute itself.[18]

Ironically, the linchpin of the Schelling/Hegel theory of intellectual intuition was Kant's theory of mathematics. Kant taught that mathematics is a form of intuition that proceeds by constructing concepts. To construct a concept is to express the *a priori* intuition that corresponds to the concept, he argued. All particulars are treated as pure cases of the universal. When I draw a triangle, I do not borrow the pattern from any experience. Geometry is an intuition of space requiring nothing from experience, abstracting from all accidental features. Kant, of course, denied that mathematics could be the model for philosophy; he regretted having lost so many years trying to prove otherwise. Mathematics, he reasoned, is a form of sensible intuition that deals with the universal in the particular, while philosophy is a form of intellectual intuition that must content itself with treating the particular in the universal.[19]

Schelling and Hegel rejected this distinction and admonition, contending that the unity of ideality and reality shows through in mathematics and philosophy alike. Schelling noted that arithmetic treats the particular in the universal, which refuted Kant's generalization that mathematics always deals with the universal in the particular. Mathematics does not exclude intellectual intuition, Schelling argued. The difference between mathematics and philosophy is that the intellectual intuition of mathematics is reflected in sensibility, while the pure intellectual intuition of philosophy is reflected into itself. Kant and Fichte, by conceiving the subject as nothing more than the "I" that accompanies one's representations, left philosophy with a knowing subject that knows nothing besides the products of its activity. Since the Kantian subject could not know objects in themselves, it was stuck in the very dilemma that Jacobi warned about: Either it knew itself or it knew nothing. Schelling and Hegel, endorsing Jacobi's reading of Fichte, judged that Fichte landed in the nihilism of subjective idealism, caught in the endless circle of consciousness, and that Kant avoided a similar fate only by espousing the indefensible idea of something that produces all ideas while being known by no mind – the thing-in-itself.[20]

The only way to ensure the possibility of knowledge is to reconstruct Kant's principle of subject-object identity, Schelling and Hegel argued. This principle is not about the self-knowledge of a finite subject. It is about the self-knowledge of the absolute within a finite subject. Instead of trapping subject-object identity inside the circle of its own representations, Schelling and Hegel lifted subject-object identity outside this circle by equating the self-knowledge of a knowing subject with the self-knowledge of the absolute. Absolute idealism was a reworking of Spinoza in dynamic form, and a renewal of the Platonic doctrine that all knowledge participates in divine self-knowledge. My knowledge is not merely something that I know from my own consciousness. It is knowledge of the absolute through the object itself. Schelling put it vividly: "Not I know, but the all knows in me, if the knowledge that I call mine is an actual and true knowledge."[21]

Frederick Beiser aptly notes that the absolute idealists made a stronger argument about the possibility of knowledge than about how they knew that their knowledge participated in divine self-knowledge. The threats of skepticism and nihilistic subjectivism were terribly real, as Jacobi contended. Schelling and Hegel made a strong case for absolute idealism as an alternative to not knowing much of anything. But Schelling and Hegel, on their terms, could not say how any knowing subject, such as either of them, knew that he had absolute knowledge. For Schelling and Hegel did not know the absolute; on their terms, it was only the absolute that knew itself. Human subjects lack any power to know the absolute, which is not something that exists outside human subjects. As Beiser says, "the only reason that knows the absolute is that of the absolute itself."[22]

Schelling and Hegel got that far together, then parted ways. Hegel blasted Schelling for beginning his system with absolute knowledge, as if it could be shot from a gun. What was needed was a phenomenology of the coming-to-be of knowledge itself. Hegel declared that everything was at stake in the question whether the absolute could be grasped and expressed "not only as *Substance*, but equally as *Subject."* The burden of the *Phenomenology of Spirit* was to show that finite knowledge is bound up with knowledge of the infinite. In that pursuit Hegel surpassed Schelling so resoundingly that Schelling, in his later career, had to change course again just to stand and breathe on his own. His last version of absolute idealism, an anti-climax, portrayed Hegel as the epitome of logic-driven essentialism and himself as the anti-Hegelian champion of freedom and subjectivity.[23]

This rendering, in its time and for decades afterward, damaged Schelling's reputation more than Hegel's, as it reeked of sour grapes and creative decline, though Schelling's version of Hegel had a long life through Kierkegaard and innumerable textbook accounts. In Germany, and later in England, "idealism" usually meant Hegelian idealism. Schleiermacher's prominence in theology helped to keep alive a more existential, Schelling-like concept of idealism, but Schleiermacher insisted that he did not smuggle his idealism or any other philosophical commitment into his theology, a claim that fueled decades of enervating debate among Mediating theologians. Since Schleiermacher played down philosophy when he wrote theology, or at least claimed to do so, the mediating theologians who blended Schleiermacher and Hegel usually fit religious feeling into Hegelian concepts, not the other way around. Schleiermacher's dualistic concept of his enterprise recycled familiar debates about Kantian dualism and the necessity of overcoming both.

For the Hegelians, including the mediating theologians who synthesized Hegel and Schleiermacher, Hegel's rehabilitation of metaphysical reason was an epochal achievement. It synthesized classical Christianity, modern Lutheranism, the Enlightenment, the boon for Greek classicism that preceded Romanticism, and the Romantic movement. It provided assurance for generations of religious thinkers that Kant's strictures on reason were unnecessary and that Kant's truncated moral religion was not something for which religious types had to settle. The school of Kant had only a trickle of theological followers in the mid-nineteenth century, even as it claimed the liberal banner for itself. It did not compare to the theological following for Hegel and Schleiermacher. There were occasional appeals from freethinkers and Kantian rationalists to go "Back to Kant," but nothing came of them until the 1870s, when a major back-to-Kant spinoff took over German theology.

Philosophically, this was the meaning of the Ritschlian episode. Until the rise of the Ritschlian movement, every major attempt to struggle creatively with Kant had something to do with overcoming Kantian dualism. Fichte, Schelling, Schleiermacher, and Hegel stood for different ways of transcending Kant's limitations. Mediating theology sustained the legacies of Schleiermacher and Hegel, often by mediating between them. Ritschlian theology called a halt to the post-Kantian attempt to reach the divine. It settled for Kantian moral religion, albeit with a stronger social consciousness, and the Kantian realm of finitude, albeit with a stronger historical consciousness. To the Ritschlians, it was galling to hear Hegel described as the philosopher of Protestantism, a title that rightly belonged to Kant. Ritschl knew nothing of the soul or absolute knowledge. The only window out of historical human finitude that he knew was Kant's moral faith, which belonged to the realm of value and practical reason. As far as Ritschl was concerned, ontology never saved anyone and it did not belong in Protestant theology. Mysticism was pointless too, although Herrmann, feeling the thinness and instability of Ritschlian historicism, resorted to a mystical feeling of Jesus. Schleiermacher was the default option for backsliding Ritschlians like Herrmann, but most of the Ritschlian School fused the liberal Jesus of liberal historicism with Kant's account of what religion was good for, conceiving Christianity as a kingdom movement of a particular social ethical character.

The Ritschlian movement was stunningly successful in sweeping the field of theology and exalting Kant's place within it. But its very success set up liberal theology for a mighty fall in Germany, and its rendering of Kant featured a stodgy dualism based on the first *Critique* and a simplistic fact versus value dualism based on the second *Critique*. This was not a very imaginative reading of Kant. Kant himself, to the end of his life, kept returning to the question of what his system was about. Each time, he used a different metaphor of reason to describe the actual multi-dimensionality of an apparently dualistic system.

In the first *Critique* he described reason as an organic totality that coordinates the dualistic structural distinctions between sensibility and understanding, reason and understanding, and reason and judgment. Each cognitive faculty exists for the sake of the others and for its own sake, Kant argued. Reason, more broadly than the specific faculty of reason that is distinct from experience and understanding, embraces all cognitive faculties, aiming at a totality that makes experience complete. Kant explained that pure speculative reason is peculiar in two ways. It measures its own capacity by the different ways that it chooses the objects of its thinking and it takes account of the many ways by which problems are put before it. Regarding the first peculiarity, nothing in *a priori* cognition can be ascribed to the objects of thought except that which the thinking subject takes out of itself. Regarding the second, pure speculative reason, considered as a unity of principles of cognition, is a unity that subsists for itself. Every part exists for the sake of all the others and its own sake, "and no principle can safely be taken in *any one* relation, unless it has been investigated in the *entirety* of its relations to the whole employment of pure reason."[24]

For example, Kant's distinction between reason and understanding yielded his distinction between the intellectual world and the sensible world. But reason cannot be a unifying principle if it does not aim for a totality of combination that completes experience. Thus, even Kant used an organic metaphor for reason, even in the first *Critique*. Henrich rightly argues that Kant needed a "feedback loop" between his ontological system and his theory of how the various faculties of mind combined with each other. Though Platonic dualism ran deep in Kant's thought, even Kant needed a basis for defining what his philosophy was about. Fichte, Schelling, and Hegel, perceiving the problem on Kant's terms, devised systems that were strong on this point. Hegelian idealism was nothing if not a system that returned to itself in self-conscious comprehension.[25]

Kant's epistemology was a philosophy of mind, not a science of formal objects. He began with the self and its mental activities, not a formal theory of rules about logical or objective realities. Henrich observes that, reading the first *Critique*, one might expect

Kant to incorporate his cognitive framework into an ontological framework. But that never happens. Kant derived his idea of the two worlds from his theory of an active self, a self that requires something given. The idea of something given yielded the distinction between *noumena* and *phenomena*, two worlds that constituted Kant's operative ontological framework. However, once Kant put into play the theory of two worlds, he could not return to the self, because the self could not be construed as a member of one world or the other, and Kant could not conceive the self as a relation between the two worlds as long as he conceived the self as merely a subject that combines what is given to it.[26]

Kant took three passes at describing what his system was about. In the first *Critique* he explained that he tried to solve the problem of metaphysics. In the *Critique of Judgment*, in a discussion prized by post-Kantians and especially Hegel, Kant contended that his philosophy demonstrated the continuous transition from acts of understanding to reason to practical reason, including the apprehension of beauty. This was a larger boast than claiming to solve the problem of metaphysics; Kantian philosophy was a theory of the achievements of mind. But Kant made a larger claim in his essay, "What Real Progress Has Metaphysics Made in Germany since the Time of Leibniz and Wolff?" Reason has a destination, Kant argued; his philosophy was structured to justify this destination. Philosophy, rightly conceived, swings on two hinges, like a door. One hinge is the ideality of space and time; the other is the reality of the idea of freedom.[27]

The destination of reason is the idea of freedom. In his last attempt to explain what his system was about, Kant took hold of his breakthrough theme in the second *Critique*, that reason is a vault whose keystone is freedom. *Critique of Practical Reason* put it boldly: "The concept of freedom, in so far as its reality is proved by an apodictic law of practical reason, is the keystone of the whole architecture of the system of pure reason and even of speculative reason." All other ideas gain stability and objective reality only by attaching themselves to the idea of freedom. Even the necessary ideas of God and immortality become real only through "the fact that there really is freedom, for this idea is revealed by the moral law." If we do not insert the keystone to the vault of reason, Kant argued, the vault will not work. When we insert the keystone of freedom, the vault becomes self-supporting. Freedom is autonomy, the self-originating of law, as in the categorical imperative – an absolute law that is precisely the law of freedom without remainder.[28]

For Kant, freedom belonged to reason, not to understanding, because freedom makes absolute commands that one act in a certain way and it requires the totality of a subject's volitions. In addition, freedom is practical, extending beyond theoretical reason. Freedom is a type of causality, Kant suggested; it determines laws for the intelligible world and it causes actions with knowable effects in the sensible world. It belongs to the intellectual world, yet it has effects on the sensible world. Kant's philosophy was a theory about the connection between the principles of the intellectual world and the sensible world through practical reason and the subordination of everything to freedom. This idea of freedom as the link between the intellectual and sensible world and the unity of the self was Kant's feedback loop from his ontological framework to the principles of his system, even though Kant never quite put it that way. Henrich explains: "We need understanding in order to get to totality; we need totality in order to get to freedom; and we need freedom in order to get to the significance of the total system."[29]

The idea of freedom made it possible for Kant's system to be developed into a whole, even though one cannot start with this idea. Since the non-existence of freedom cannot be proven, we are entitled to believe in it if it appears to be a necessary belief. But Kant's argument for freedom did not rest merely on whether one wants to believe in it. It included the chastening fact that if we do not believe in our freedom, we cannot trust anything that our reason tells us. Kantian idealism, though more chastened than the idealisms to which it gave birth, was as obsessed as any of them with the problems of subjectivity, the emancipating power of reason, the moral necessity of freedom, the necessity of not being suffocated by subjectivism, and the necessity of freedom for reason.

German idealism had a long run, and it was never refuted. It dominated continental philosophy in the nineteenth century and dramatically ascended in Britain at the end of the nineteenth century. In its Kantian form it always raised the question of settling for metaphysical agnosticism and moralistic religion; thus, theologians preferred Hegel or Schleiermacher, usually up to the point where Hegel's system began to feel over-reaching for attempting to logically explain the divine, or Schleiermacher's system was criticized for resting everything on subjective feeling. Whenever post-Kantian idealism was faulted for replacing the free sovereignty of God with a merely human idea, or for asserting that human history somehow came to its fulfillment with Schelling or Hegel, somebody called for returning to Kantian restraint.

The rise of science was the key to the latter story. It was not a coincidence that Ritschlian theology swept the field during the period that scientific naturalism rose to a place of dominance in the academy and German intellectual culture. Ritschl was deeply concerned to save a place for religion in a society and academy that increasingly exalted science over other ways of knowing. In the 1860s he had to fend off critics who said that science is the only way of knowing and that Darwin refuted the Christian doctrine of creation. Ritschl's Kantianism was carefully calibrated to make peace with the natural sciences. If the newly powerful scientific establishment wrote off the puzzles of subjective self-consciousness and the development of spirit, Ritschl was prepared to say that religion is not about these things anyway. Religion had plenty of work to do by sticking to its home turf and allowing science to explain how things work. This ostensibly Kantian strategy bought a century of peace for theology from scientific refutation; even the Barthian repudiation of Ritschlian theology left this part of Ritschl's legacy intact. On Kantian terms, supposedly, religion and science were incommensurable discourses about different worlds, never mind that Kantian transcendentalism did not really support such a tidy dualism and that Kant denied that scientists know the world in itself.[30]

Idealism as White Supremacist Ordering

Here the ironies are rich, intertwined, and sometimes perverse. The highest-flying forms of idealism faded in Germany, accommodating scientific materialism, during the same period that British philosophy, despite its centuries-long tradition of empiricism, opted for neo-Hegelianism. Darwinian theory came from England, but it achieved prominence faster in Germany, where the soaring prestige of science made Germany more hospitable to evolutionary theory. In Germany, philosophers fell off their Fichtean pedestal as the priests of the truth shortly after Darwin published *The Origin of Species* in 1859. The spirit of the age, still fixed on progress, now sought progress through the spectacular advances in chemistry, physics, biology, and industrialization. The University of Berlin became a powerhouse of scientific research, where the philosophy faculty lost its central unifying status. Philosophy, though still mostly idealist, no longer mattered very much. Back-to-Kant movements arose in German theology and philosophy while German scientists, reflecting the growing prestige of their fields, lectured the world on the Darwinian breakthrough.[31]

But it was not really Darwinism that prevailed in German thought, since the leading German advocate of Darwinian evolution, Ernst Haeckel, had a grab-bag of Lamarckian, recapitulationist, monist, and racist beliefs that "improved" on Darwinian natural selection. A great deal of nineteenth-century science, claiming to transcend philosophical idealism, recycled it in perverse forms, offering pseudo-scientific support for racist ordering.

Eighteenth- and nineteenth-century naturalists generally followed the father of modern taxonomy, Swedish zoologist Carl Linnaeus (1707–1778), in dividing *Homo sapiens* into four categories: American (which Linnaeus described as copper-colored, choleric, and regulated by custom); Asiatic (sooty, melancholic, and governed by opinions); African (black, languid, and governed by caprice); and European (fair, sanguine, and governed by laws). They disagreed about monogenesis versus polygenesis. Georges Cuvier (1769–1832), the leading theorist on this topic in the early nineteenth century, taught that there were three races (white, yellow, and black) within one human species. Until Darwin published *The Origin of Species*, however, the theory of polygenic origins was gaining in social respectability and scientific acceptance.[32]

The leading theorists of polygenic origins – eighteenth-century English physician Charles White, nineteenth-century American physician Samuel George Morton, and nineteenth-century Swiss/American naturalist Louis Agassiz – insisted that the anatomical and intellectual differences between African blacks and European whites were too great for them to belong to the same species. Morton claimed that mulattoes were sterile. Agassiz reported that, upon moving to the United States in 1846, he was overcome with instinctive loathing upon meeting blacks. He took for granted that all white Americans shared his natural repugnance, whether or not they were prejudiced, as he assured he was not, and that his research was purely objective anyway. Polygenic theorists devoted a great deal of energy to determining exactly how many distinct races of human beings existed on the planet. If it was obvious that more than one existed, the question of how many there were was fundamental.[33]

Darwinian theory ostensibly put an end to the monogenist versus polygenist debate. Now the question shifted to the evolution of different racial groups within the human species and the scientific basis for distinguishing between them. Darwin judged in *The Descent of Man* (1874) that changes occurred through sexual selection, where slight differences in strength, attractiveness, and body type yielded advantages in mating and propagation. Though his statements about sexual selection were sketchy, Darwin was a straightforward believer in white superiority and male superiority. He ranked human groups hierarchically from the "savage" to the "civilized," which gave ballast to an already thriving measuring industry. English evolutionist T. H. Huxley and French anthropologist Paul Broca focused on skin color, but that got nowhere in finding or measuring a determinant of race. Phrenology, the study of crania, had a large following before and after Darwin; racial theorists pressed hard on facial angles, jaws, and skull size, to no avail. Broca was a leading researcher in this area too. By the early 1880s, scientists were giving up on phrenology as a method for distinguishing races from each other, as Caucasians alone included every possible head shape. If racial superiority/ inferiority was as real and important as many scientists believed, there had to be a better way of accounting for it.[34]

Ernst Haeckel was a major player in this baleful enterprise. Germany's leading evolutionist, Haeckel taught zoology and comparative anatomy at Jena from 1862 to 1909. He published widely on biology, philosophy, naturalism, and art, blending his own racism, monist-romantic philosophy, and Lamarckian belief in the inheritability of acquired characteristics with Darwin's theory of natural selection. Haeckel coined many terms in biology, including anthropogeny, ecology, phylum, and phylogeny. He accepted Darwinian natural selection, but rejected Darwin's verdict that natural selection is the main mechanism for generating biological diversity. Haeckel taught that the environment acts directly on organisms, yielding new races, and that the survival of a race depends on its interaction with its environment. A major theorist of recapitulation, Haeckel argued that every individual's biological development (ontogeny) recapitulates the entire evolutionary development (phylogeny) of its species, although scholars disagree on whether Haeckel espoused a strong version of recapitulation theory. The strong version – that there is a one-to-one correspondence between phylogeny and ontogeny, such that ontogeny repeats forms of the ancestors – was refuted in early twentieth-century biology. The weak version – that phylogeny and ontogeny are interconnected, such that recapitulation builds upon the ancestral embryonic process of development – is still in play as a theory explaining the similarities between all vertebrate embryos at early stages of development.[35]

Along with Huxley, Broca, Friedrich Müller, and numerous others, Haeckel devoted much effort to studying human hair as a possible determinant of racial difference and basis of racial classification. But that got nowhere. The hierarchical ordering of the races, he believed, was obvious, as was the key distinguishing factor, intelligence. But how should intelligence be calibrated? Haeckel puzzled over that question until his friend, linguist August Schleicher, applied Darwinian theory to the development of language. Schleiescher theorized that language developed after speechless *Urmenschen*, having evolved out of apelike ancestors, split into several species. Languages developed independently within each of these species, aiding the (Lamarckian) evolution of the human race. The use of language molded the brains of different groups to the grammatical and conceptual structures of each language, he argued. Language was the key to the intelligence problem, because its evolution corresponded very closely to the evolution of the brain. Schleiecher judged that the Indo-Germanic and Semitic languages surpassed those of other groups.[36]

Haeckel judged that Schleiecher's account of the development of human language from multiple pre-human ancestral groups rehabilitated polygenic theory: "If one views the origin of the branches of language as the special and principal act of becoming human, and the species of humankind as distinguished according to their language stem, then one can say that the different species of men arose independently of one another." The most subtle and sophisticated languages produced human species with the highest potential, Haeckel reasoned. The Semitic and Indo-Germanic species, in his telling, were the highest evolved, led by the Berber, Jewish, Greco-Roman and German groups. Africans were at the bottom, as everyone that Haeckel respected agreed. Sometimes he got very specific about racial superiority. In his influential two-volume *History of Creation* (1868), Haeckel declared: "The Caucasian, or Mediterranean man (*Homo Mediterraneus*), has from time immemorial been placed at the head of all the races of men, as the most highly developed and perfect. It is generally called the Caucasian race, but as, among all the varieties of the species, the Caucasian branch is the least important, we prefer the much more suitable appellation proposed by Friedrich Müller, namely, that of *Mediterranese*. For the most important varieties of this species, which are moreover the most eminent actors in what is called 'Universal History,' first rose to a flourishing condition on the shores of the Mediterranean ... This species alone (with the exception of the Mongolian) has had an actual history; it alone has attained to that degree of civilization which seems to raise men above the rest of nature."[37]

White Mediterranean types were not merely superior, in Haeckel's telling; almost nobody else was worth mentioning. Hume, Kant, Hegel, and Rashdall had said it equally plainly, but now, white supremacist liberalism had the backing of higher authority. Haeckel stood out, in a crowded field, for conferring the prestige of science on vile prejudices. Although some of the literature about him exaggerates his anti-Semitism – Haeckel respected the intelligence and achievements of Jews, and he did not promote Nazi-like biological theories about them – he provided plenty of material for the Nazi and eugenics movements, which cited him profusely on white supremacy and the wrongness of helping the weak and vulnerable. Haeckel, like Herbert Spencer and Alfred Russel Wallace in England, was a zealous Social Darwinist, imploring against government policies that helped the unfit to survive. In 1906 he co-founded the Monist League at Jena as a platform for Social Darwinian weeding out, imploring that human beings are not qualitatively distinct from nature in any way. Nature is one, he urged, nature rules, and societies are products of natural selection no less than chimpanzees and biology professors. For Haeckel, white supremacism passed beyond the realm of opinion or even value; it was a self-evident fact, a datum of Enlightened learning and self-benefiting human progress.[38]

German idealism, although meriting its name in crucial ways, helped to pave the way to Haeckel's toxic mockery of idealism, partly on the authority of its brightest light, Immanuel Kant. Kant was a keen student of race research and an outspoken opponent of polygenesis. He was one of the first to attempt a scientific definition of race based on a clear distinction between race and species, a project that Darwin subsequently rejected as arbitrary.

Kant realized that the research on race smacked, at least partly, of crackpot science. In 1775, announcing an upcoming course on race, he declared that the research on this topic "will certainly include something for the understanding, but it will be more of a game for it than a deep investigation." Though Kant believed that Linnaeus and others had compiled reliable scientific knowledge about the existence of different races, he doubted that they understood why the human species had divided into races or what end this division served. In Kant's telling, there were four distinct races: "(1) the white race; (2) the Negro race; (3) the Hun race (Mongol or Kalmuck); and (4) the Hindu or Hindustani race." All other racial groups derived from these four races through interbreeding or through living in a specific climate for an insufficient period to have taken on the character of the race peculiar to that climate. The Hun and Hindu races, however, were mediating types, Kant argued; thus he gave them short shrift. In his view, which he described as a "self-evident" truism needing no proof, whites and blacks were "the base races," standing at the opposite ends of the racial continuum: "They do comprise two different races. This is because each of them perpetuate themselves in all regions of the earth and because both, when they interbreed, necessarily produce half-breed children, or blends (Mulattoes)."[39]

Kant reasoned that nature equipped the human species to exist and adapt in pretty much the same way that it equipped all organic life. Both were endowed with natural adaptive capacities that he called "seeds" (*Keime*) – predispositions that were hardwired into the organism as a whole. External factors, especially air quality and sunlight, stimulated the power to activate certain seeds. These seeds became deeply rooted, stifling other seeds, giving birth to a race. Once a race formed, Kant argued, it resisted further transformation, "because the character of the race has become predominate in the productive powers." Kant believed that all four races were prefigured *in potentia* in the first human beings, the stem genus; the original human beings carried the seeds of all four races. This prototype, although lost, must have closely resembled the white race, because the white race was obviously superior to the others. Kant said all this "without any prejudice." Human beings were best fitted for the temperate climate in which the white race flourished, he explained, whites had the best skin color, and no race remotely compared to whites in cultural accomplishment.[40]

But even that did not quite express the extent of white superiority for Kant, because it separated whites from other races only by degree. Whites, to be sure, were a race, Kant allowed; however, they had progressed so far beyond the other races that they were no longer a race in the ordinary sense of the term. The white race, by advancing in the direction of enlightened cosmopolitan perfection, was moving beyond race. It was expanding globally to bring the world to perfection, recreating the world in its image. Kant assured his students that no race on earth stood a chance of thwarting the global dominion of race-transcending white people. The Hindu people were educable in the arts, but not in the sciences. They never changed, they were too calm to change the world, and they had no capacity for abstract concepts. American Indians were even worse off, lacking drive, passion, and romance. They were lazy and apathetic, they had few children, and they didn't even cuddle. The "Negro race," in Kant's telling, had some virtues, but none that helped it advance. Negroes were educable to a degree, Kant allowed; they were sensitive, had some drive, and had a sense of honor. But they were so talkative and vain, filled with affect and passion, that they were fit only to be servants.[41]

Kant did not say, in public, that the non-white races would have to be weeded out for the world to reach its enlightened destiny. He was sensitive enough to realize how that would sound. Plus, Germany had no colonies during the period – the mid-1770s to the mid-1780s – when Kant did most of his waxing about the struggle of the races, and he enjoyed chiding the English for colonizing so much of the world. But in a note to himself, Kant did say it: "All of the races will be stamped out; they will undergo an inner rotting or decay leading to their utter eradication." Native Americans and people of African descent were incapable of ruling themselves, Kant wrote; moreover, he lamented the spectacle of "interbreeding" *(sich vermischen)* in Mexico, where "the Spaniards" had created a new race. That would never work, and it detracted from the benefits of Spanish colonization.[42]

Kant believed that race itself would end when the white race prevailed. The triumph of enlightened civilization went hand-in-hand with the triumph of whiteness. More precisely, the triumph of enlightened civilization was inseparable from the triumph of whiteness, being identical with it, although Kant was guarded about how he said that in public. The business of "stamping out" the other races *("Alle racen werden ausgerottet werden")*, after all, had a brutal side to it; Kant was glad that Germany did not have to get into the colonization business to make history and nature come out right. The lower races lacked sufficient capacity to develop, he judged; thus, their "inner rotting" would lead to their dissolution. In the meantime, England and France, "the two most civilized nations on earth," were keen to bring capitalism (England) and cultured refinement (France) to backward parts of the world.[43]

Kant would have preferred to see the French take the lead in this area, as France was by far the most refined and courteous nation on earth. The French, Kant explained, spoke with feeling, in the language of high society ladies, and they were hospitable to strangers. The "trust-inspiring civility" of French society contrasted sharply with the "haughty rudeness" of the British, who spoke the language of interest and commerce, preferred to dine alone, and, although benevolent with their own kind, treated foreigners like dirt. Kant speculated that the British got their appetite for imperialism through geographical circumstance, not natural character. They had no natural character, as the "old stock of Britons" dissolved from centuries of German and French immigration. Protected by geography from foreign invasions, the British islanders became a nation of aggressors, "a mighty nation of maritime commerce." The "mercantile spirit" pervaded British society and fueled its appetite for conquest. Thus, the British projected a rude and materialistic idea of civilization, Kant judged, but one that helpfully taught the world a vital lesson – that one must make a character for one's self, "that is, see to it that he acquires one." The British were not kind like the French, and they expected nobody to love them. They merely claimed respect for themselves, building a more-or-less liberal order through which they allowed people to live according to their own will.[44]

In all of this, and one thing more, Kant legitimized standard European bigotries about the humanity and cultures of racially alien others, all in the name of Enlightenment. The one thing more was his contempt for Jews, whom he regarded as aliens within, "Palestinians living among us." Kant wrote very little about European Jews, not because he was sensitive about insulting them, but because he took for granted that they were degenerate. European Jews, Kant contended, amounted to a separate nation within the European nations. They were the opposite of pure reason, embodying the grubby impurity of matter. He called them "a nation of deceivers" and "a whole nation of merchants," which meant the same thing – that nearly all Jews were consumed with the spirit of usury. The few exceptions that Kant recognized – notably Moses

Mendelssohn and Markus Herz – proved nothing to the contrary. According to Kant, Jews ignored the moral norms and legal regulations of decent society pertaining to material gain. Honor meant nothing to them, for they turned deception into a way of life, cheating the very people "among whom they find protection."[45]

In Kant's telling, the only moral principle to which Jews subscribed in dealing with their European protectors was "buyer beware." He resented their dishonesty and lack of gratitude, but claimed to put aside moralizing about both, as that was a waste of time, a "futile project." The Jews were not going to be shamed out of being usurious cheaters, Kant assured. Instead of assimilating into decent society, they clung to their religion, "an old superstition that is recognized by the government under which they live." Instead of becoming productive members of the European nations that gave them refuge, they compensated their losses and struggles by cheating their protectors.[46]

Kant reasoned that this strategy made sense if one grasped that Europe's Jews were united by a provincial, materialistic religion that cut them off from larger moral concerns. Skilled at making money, an old story that pre-dated Solomon, they relied on their religion, their clannishness, and their deviousness to make more of it: "Because they had far-reaching commercial relations with people of their own language and religion, these merchants, after the destruction of their city, were able to migrate gradually into far-distant lands (in Europe) taking language and religion with them, maintaining their connection with each other, and finding security in whatever countries they went to because of their profitable bargaining." Kant believed that the very success of the Jews threatened to subvert the European hope of an enlightened civil society devoted to the autonomy of life. Jewish aliens, by sneering at the norms of decent society, represented a kind of contagion that contaminated European societies.[47]

Fortunately, Kant confined most of his exertions on this theme to the classroom, but his opinions about the Jewish presence in modern Europe were of a piece with his assessment of Jewish religion, on which he sought and gained a large influence. The Jewish religion "immediately preceded" Christianity, Kant allowed; it even "provided the physical occasion for the founding" of the Christian church. But on the level that mattered – the conceptual level – "the Jewish faith stands in absolutely no essential connection" to Christianity. Kant explained that the Jewish faith, at its founding, was merely a collection of statutory laws supporting a political state. It had no spiritual or moral character. It had the Ten Commandments, but they were purely external, making no claim on the moral dispositions of believers. Later it added some moral appendages, but they were foreign to Judaism. Kant declared, "Strictly speaking Judaism is not a religion at all but simply the union of a number of individuals who, since they belonged to a particular stock, established themselves into a community under purely political laws, hence not into a church." The essential idea of Judaism was political, a type of religious nationalism, Kant explained. It lived on even if the state or the seemingly religious parts of the religion dissolved, because it stood for political theocracy, not religion. Kant insisted that faith in a future life is essential to every real religion. Any religion that lacked a doctrine of eternal life, such as original Judaism, failed an elementary test of being a religion. Kant was sweeping and categorical in this area, insisting that Christianity rested on "an entirely new principle ... a total revolution in doctrines of faith."[48]

On this theme Kant had a large legacy, legitimizing a de-Judaized Christianity that Schleiermacher, the early Hegel, Harnack, and Herrmann recycled, to mention only major liberal religious thinkers. The only major German liberal theologian to repudiate the Kantian tradition on this subject was Ritschl, who watched his own followers dismiss his emphasis on the Jewish social-ethical and historical character of Christianity as an eccentric confusion.[49]

In theology, the eclipse of Hegelian idealism by science and positivism gave ballast to Ritschl's reassertion of Kantian modesty on what could (not) be known about God and the soul. Ritschlian theology was even better known for emphasizing the social-ethical basis of Christianity and the Kantian distinction between fact and value, which yielded radically democratic, Social Gospel forms of Ritschlian theology that Ritschl loathed. Though the Ritschlian mainstream and its principal offshoots sustained forms of Kantian and post-Kantian idealism philosophically, all cosigned philosophy to a back seat. Harnack stuck close to Kant's boundaries and, more than Ritschl, to Kant's individualism. Herrmann moved steadily toward and then surpassed Schleiermacher's claim to religious autonomy. Troeltsch reclaimed Hegel's world-historical purview and categories, but emphatically on historicist grounds that relativized the purview and the categories.

The Kantian revolution made permanent contributions to modern philosophy and theology. It established that experience is never merely given and that the meaning of experience is always a creative construction. The process by which we achieve self-consciousness about our relation to the world is fundamental to every claim that we make about knowing anything in any field of inquiry. Before Kant, it was possible to conceive nature *per se* as the source of meaning. Even Berkeley assumed that sense experience is produced outside the human mind. After Kant it was no longer plausible to render human experience and human creativity as mere epiphenomena of the things of sense, although that did not stop generations of dogmatic naturalists and positivists from trying.

Kant and post-Kantian idealism unleashed a new self-consciousness about the irreducible role of creative imagination in all knowing and the contestability of all norms. In its Kantian mode it underwrote two centuries of peace for theologies in coping with the tremendous advances of science in explaining how things work. But Kantian philosophy and its offshoots were notoriously abstract and intricate. Schelling and Hegel made bets on scientific topics that did not pan out. The rising prestige of science pulled philosophy away from the big questions that absorbed religious types. G. E. Moore, writing in *Mind* in 1899, gave a preview of British philosophy's small-bore, analytic future, contending that facts are independent of experience and hold a status of their own. Four years later he made a frontal assault on idealism that turned out to be historic, albeit somewhat to his subsequent embarrassment.[50]

Deflating Idealism: G. E. Moore and the Analytic Turn

George Edward Moore turned against philosophical idealism shortly after absorbing it in the late 1890s as a protégé of J. M. E. McTaggart at Trinity College, Cambridge. He explained why in a legendary article of 1903, "The Refutation of Idealism," which

Moore wrote as a Prize Fellow at Trinity College, mixing audacity with modest low-pitched realism.

Moore did not dispute that the universe as a whole might possess intelligent and purposeful consciousness. He even hoped "devoutly" that reality is, indeed, spiritual. Ultimately, idealism might be right, Moore argued. However, lower down, idealism was definitely wrong in contending that *esse est percipi* – whatever is, is experienced; or literally, to be is to be perceived. Modern idealists, in Moore's telling, began with Berkeley's subjective idealism, but they granted the existence of things not experienced by individuals. Thus, they reasoned that these things must form part of some experience. Since an object necessarily implies a subject, and the world as a whole must be an object, we must conceive the world as belonging to one or more subjects. Every object of our experience belongs to us as subjects. Moore noted that some idealists took a further step, reasoning that because thought enters into the essence of all reality, there must be a spirit behind or within all things that enables spirit to encounter spirit in its object.[51]

Moore took a pass on the big picture. Perhaps idealists were right that all objects of our experience belong to us, the world belongs to subjects, and the world process is about the unfolding of spirit. Moreover, he lauded modern idealists for distinguishing between sensation and thought, a point in their favor against sensationalism and empiricism. Thought and sensation are distinct forms of consciousness, or ways of experiencing. But the idealist principle that whatever is, is experienced, is not right, Moore contended. Idealists did not prove any of their big picture claims by relying on it. Moore's idealist teachers – McTaggart and F. H. Bradley – taught him that the object of experience is inconceivable apart from a subject. What makes something real is its presence as an inseparable aspect of an experience. To Moore, there was something terribly unreal about this perspective, even as it rightly distinguished between objects of thought and objects of sense. Idealism, he urged, rests on a failure to perceive the distinct difference between subject and object.

Idealists somehow failed to perceive that there is anything in "yellow" that is not in the sensation of yellow, a mistake that they compounded, with perfect logic, by making a necessity claim: Whatever is, is experienced *necessarily*. Moore explained: "To assert that yellow is necessarily an object of experience is to assert that yellow is necessarily yellow – a purely identical proposition, and therefore proved by the law of contradiction alone." Moore acknowledged that most post-Kantians, having read Kant on the limits of analytic claims, did not base their position on appeals to the law of contradiction. Most idealists combined analytic and synthetic claims, and they strenuously denied that they failed to adequately distinguish between the sensation or the idea of something and its object. Otherwise they had no reason to acknowledge that yellow is a sensation and no basis for combining analytic and synthetic claims. Many idealists even stressed that yellow is distinct from the sensation of yellow; otherwise they had no basis for contending for the necessity of an inseparable unity. Moore realized that he was making a reductionist argument about the logic of idealism that did not represent the ways that idealists usually argued.[52]

A great deal of post-Kantian idealism, especially of the Hegelian sort, featured the logic of reflexive relationality. One began with a distinction; the things distinguished were said to form a unity of some kind; forming a unity, these things were said to be what they are because of their relation to each other. Neither thing, nor the unity, would be what it is apart from the relation. To consider either thing by itself was to misconstrue it by abstracting from it. Moore acknowledged that this was how post-Kantian idealists generally operated. Hegelianism conquered modern philosophy by arguing in this fashion. To Moore, this was a baleful victory: "The principle of organic unities, like that of combined analysis and synthesis, is mainly used to defend the practice of holding *both* of two contradictory propositions, wherever this may seem convenient. In this, as in other matters, Hegel's main service to philosophy has consisted in giving a name to and erecting into a principle, a type of fallacy to which experience had shown philosophers, along with the rest of mankind, to be addicted. No wonder that he has followers and admirers."[53]

It was very hard, if not impossible, to have a fair argument with Hegelians, because they did not play fairly. They refused to be pinned down to straightforward formulations of their doctrines. Moore struggled to imagine how anyone could not see that yellow and the sensation of yellow are very distinct. He was certain that what he meant by asserting the distinction was not what post-Kantian idealists meant. No idealist shared his respect for the self-standing reality of objects. He believed that *esse* and *percepi* are as distinct from each other as are "yellow" and "bitter." Anyone who really believed that would never say that whatever is, is experienced, even if one said it on Hegelian terms. But Moore could not prove the difference, and he vowed not to try. Halfway through his article, he announced "a complete break in my argument," changing the question. *Esse* and *percepi* had taken him only so far, and most idealists didn't press this argument anyway. Moore switched to the question, "What is a sensation or idea?"[54]

The sensation of green is different from the sensation of blue, yet the two sensations have something in common by virtue of being sensations, Moore reasoned. What is it, and how does this common element relate to the differences between the two sensations? Moore agreed with idealists that consciousness is the common element. Every sensation has consciousness, for which all sensations are alike, and something else, the object of sensation, for which sensations differ from each other. The existence of these two factors sets up three possibilities that differ significantly from each other, Moore argued. The sensation of blue comes and goes in one's mind, and whenever it comes, either the consciousness exists, or the blue exists, or both. These are three logically distinct possibilities, Moore stressed; to say, "blue exists" is different from saying that "blue and consciousness exist." Moreover, when the sensation exists, consciousness obviously exists also. In this case, there are only two possibilities: Either consciousness and the sensation both exist or consciousness alone exists. Here again, the existence of blue cannot be the same thing as the existence of the sensation of blue, for that would make blue either the same thing as blue plus consciousness *or* the same thing as consciousness alone. Moore cautioned against identifying any object of sensation with the corresponding sensation; to do that is either to identify a part with the whole of which it is a part *or* to identify it with the other part of the same whole.[55]

Moore held out for the possibility of conceiving the existence of blue even if one has no sensation of it. In his view, no other option made sense, even though he opposed, in his telling, the entire history of Western philosophy in saying so: "I need not conceal my opinion that no philosopher has ever yet succeeded in avoiding this self-contradictory error." Actually, Moore had an ample tradition of logical realists on his side, but they brought too much baggage for him to claim solidarity with them or to disclaim his own originality. Idealists, skeptics, and empiricists stood together in identifying blue with the sensation of blue, he noted. The problem of consciousness is sufficiently perplexing that some people even opted for materialism, refusing to grapple with the problem. The correct view, Moore argued, is to affirm consciousness and its objects and to deny that objects are merely the content of an idea or a sensation.[56]

Blue is not merely the content of the sensation of blue, for the content is *what* we assert to exist when we assert that something exists. To conceive blue as merely part of the content of the sensation of blue is to treat the sensation as though it were a whole constituted exactly like any other thing. In this case, Moore reasoned, a sensation of blue, a blue book, and a blue hat differ in the same way from each other as qualities of a thing. A sensation of blue and a blue book have the same kind of difference as exists between a blue book and a blue hat. That cannot be right, Moore argued, even though most philosophers took for granted that blue relates to the sensation or idea of blue as its content and that blue is therefore part of *what* is said to exist when one experiences the sensation. A skeptic about mental images, Moore refused to get tangled in the problems about them. He doubted that there are such things as mental images, but denied that it matters one way or the other in attaining a correct understanding of ideas and sensations. A sensation is an experiencing of something, an occurrence of knowing, Moore proposed. Consciousness is common to all sensations and ideas, such that, when a sensation of blue exists, we know that there exists an awareness of blue. This awareness is something distinct from blue, it also has a distinct relation to blue, and this relation is not that of substance to content. The relation is always exactly the meaning of "knowing."

To know "blue" is not to hold in one's mind an image of which blue is the content, Moore contended. Neither does anyone's awareness of the sensation of blue depend on one's awareness of a mental image of a blue thing. To have knowledge of blue is to be aware of one's awareness of blue. There is a unique relation between blue and the awareness of it that content theories miss. Moore declared: "And what I contend is that this omission is *not* mere negligence of expression, but is due to the fact that though philosophers have recognized that *something* distinct is meant by conscious-ness, they have never yet had a clear conception of *what* that something is. They have not been able to hold *it* and *blue* before their minds and compare them, in the same way in which they can compare *blue* and *green*." The reason for this failure, he judged, is that consciousness is distinctly slippery, even for idealists. Whenever one tries to catch hold of it sufficiently to determine what it is, it seems to vanish. On the other hand, when we interrogate the sensation of blue, "all we can see is the blue; the other element is as it were diaphanous." Moore did not doubt that there is a consciousness element to pursue and to distinguish. He did not claim to have *shown* the reality of consciousness more clearly than idealists. He only claimed to have given a truer account of the problem.[57]

Blue is probably not part of the content of the sensation of blue, and even if it is, the sensation is not the sensation *of* blue. Moore shook his head at the idea of "blue awareness," the idea of blue as a content of experience. What we know is that we have awareness of blue. Idealists, Moore noted, usually had no trouble admitting that some things exist of which they were not aware. They even admitted that some things of which they were sometimes aware existed even when they were not aware of them, such as other minds. But that meant that they were sometimes aware of something that was not an inseparable aspect of their experience. They *knew* things that were not constitutive of their experience. This was exactly what Moore believed about sensations and ideas: One can be aware of something that is not an inseparable aspect of one's experience. The idealist fixation with getting outside the circle of one's ideas or sensations is a non-problem, for merely to have an idea or a sensation is to be outside the circle. Moore contended, "It is to know something which is as truly and really *not* a part of *my* experience, as anything which I can ever know."[58]

If idealists were right that the object of a sensation is the content of that sensation, they could not be aware of themselves or of real things. Moore admonished that the mere content of awareness is aware *of* nothing at all. On idealist grounds, all that one can say is that one has an awareness with a certain content: "It can never be true that there is in him a consciousness *of* anything." Idealists, despite projecting so much confidence that they existed and that reality is spiritual, conceived both realities as mere contents of an awareness, "which is aware of nothing." Moore lamented that Berkeley and Kant lured philosophy into this blind alley. Berkeley supposed that a knower knows directly only one's sensations and ideas; Kant subjectively relativized the objectivity of things in space. Moore countered that a knower is as directly aware of material things in space as the knower is of one's sensations. Modern philosophy wasted three centuries on the Cartesian problem, trying to prove that something exists corresponding to existing sensations. It was better to turn the question around, Moore urged. Since the evidence for material things is every bit as strong as the evidence of our sensations, what reason is there to suppose that material things do not exist? If one seriously doubts that matter exists, one should doubt that experience exists too. The reasonable option is to operate on the supposition that matter and spirit exist.[59]

"The Refutation of Idealism" struck a rising generation of realists as a blast of brilliant common sense, a deliverance from Kantian and Hegelian obscurity. Moore's willingness to attack idealism with mere common sense inspired others to do likewise, making common sense philosophically respectable again. In the same year that Moore "refuted" idealism, he published an intuitionist theory of ethics, *Principia Ethica*, which described a simple, non-analyzable awareness of "good." Meta-ethically, Moore was a non-naturalist in the tradition of McTaggart, Hastings Rashdall, and Henry Sidgwick; normatively he espoused an ideal consequentialism that echoed Rashdall and McTaggart. But Moore's fresh, incisive style attracted a larger audience than any of these predecessors, showing that what came to be called "analytic" philosophy had a constructive bent for everyday matters. "The Refutation of Idealism" and *Principia Ethica* lifted Moore to prominence in philosophy, helping to launch a two-sided analytic movement of logical positivists and linguistic analysts led by Moore, Bertrand Russell, A. J. Ayer, Ludwig Wittgenstein and Rudolf Carnap that challenged the hegemony of post-Kantian idealism. Teaching at Cambridge from 1911 to 1939, Moore rose to the top of British philosophy, edited the journal *Mind* from 1921 to 1944, and was a member of the famous "Bloomsbury Group" of literary intellectuals that included John Maynard Keynes, Lytton Strachey, Leonard Woolf, Virginia Woolf, and E. M. Forster.[60]

In 1920 he was still refuting his idealistic teachers, contending that Bradley's doctrine of internal relations violated common sense. A dog owner who gives away his dog does not become a different person, Moore chided. The same "I" that might be related to certain things in particular ways might not have been so related. Some relations are internal and some are external, exactly as common sense and ordinary speech suppose. Reality is not One, contrary to idealists of the Absolute sort. In 1922, however, when Moore published a collection of his most influential essays, he would have preferred not to republish his most famous one, because parts of it embarrassed him. The article that launched his career now seemed to him "to be very confused, as well as to embody a good many down-right mistakes." Not including it, however, was out of the question. "The Refutation of Idealism" may not have refuted idealism, but it was historic in changing what philosophers argued about.[61]

Moore's specific arguments against idealism were less important and lasting than the boldly common sense spirit in which he advanced them. He played a major role in turning the tide against idealist theory, although he retained his idealist rejection of empiricism, and he never claimed that metaphysics was nonsense. Moore was not a throwback to a "hard" world. He did not think that he could refute anti-realism by raising his hands, although he was often accused of thinking so. He struck some friends, notably Keynes, as being unworldly, although other friends, notably Leonard Woolf, described him as a paragon of common sense. In either case, Moore challenged metaphysical thinkers to recognize the great difficulties that they faced in making clear claims, a challenge that they were slow to take seriously. Bradley responded at length to William James, but he dismissed Moore as irritatingly small-bore. On stronger ground, idealists pushed back that Moore had clarity problems of his own. What could he mean in claiming that something named "green" could exist lacking any experience of green? What exactly was this "green"?[62]

Some critics refuted Moore by noting that he failed to distinguish between cases in which *esse* is *percipi* and cases in which it is not. Brown University philosopher C. J. Ducasse, employing Samuel Alexander's distinction between the cognate accusative (striking a stroke, waving a farewell) and the objective accusative (striking a man, waving a flag), argued that Moore overlooked that existential independence does not correlate with every form of distinctness. When an accusative, such as stroke, is connately coordinate with an activity – in this case, striking – it does not exist independently of existence. A stroke exists only in the striking, just as a jump exists only in the jumping. The nouns "stroke" and "jump" name a kind of activity that means something independent of an occurrence, while the verbs "striking" and "jumping" name a kind of activity *and* allude to existence, the occurrence of the kind of activity that they name. Contrary to Moore, Ducasse argued, "green" and "bitter" are forms of cognition connate with sense; they are names of species of experience itself, not names of objects of experience. To sense green is to sense "greenly," to sense bitter is to taste "bitterly." Moore, in his later career, conceded that the first part of Ducasse's argument was right. In essence, it was a page from Berkeley, who argued that experience is the *esse* of ideas, but that some existents are not ideas. Moore acknowledged that the *esse* of existents of the latter sort is not experience. A toothache cannot exist without being felt; in this case, *esse* is *percipi*. On the other hand, Moore shuddered at sentences like, "I taste bitter," which invited subjectivist spinning of the idealist sort, and he admonished that the moon does not have to be experienced to exist.[63]

Idealism Fading and Embattled

Up to the Great War, leading idealists such as Pringle-Pattison and Bradley thought that James posed a greater threat to idealist hegemony than did Moore and the analytic upsurge. James had strong idealist-like concepts of relationality and process, he espoused a type of moral idealism, and his critique of idealism applied mostly to its monist versions. Personal idealists like Pringle-Pattison, pointing to James' attack on monism, felt closer to James than to Bradley, while judging that neither had a sufficiently vital religion. Bradley, too, played up his affinities with James. He agreed with James that ideas about God and the Absolute "are true and real just so far as they work." He stressed that he and James shared a denial of transcendence: "Truth indeed must not become transcendent."[64]

But James did not follow through on his "what works" idea of pragmatism, Bradley protested. James identified pragmatism with several doctrines that either didn't work or that he defended on other grounds: a militant commitment to pluralism, a belief in the absolute mutability of the universe, a belief in the "absolute reality of individual disaster and evil," and a doctrine of human freedom that, although Bradley couldn't make out what it was, clearly was not based on pragmatism. James was hopelessly double-minded, Bradley judged. He prescribed an approach to philosophy that he did not practice. In the end, Bradley concluded, it was clear that James worked all along with a transcendent Ideal, an approach that does not work and which James himself criticized. For Bradley, it was doubly unfortunate that when James contradicted himself, he espoused wrong views about pluralism, the mutability of the universe, tragedy, evil, and apparently, human freedom.[65]

On the eve of World War I, Bradley did not feel the tide turning against idealism. Metaphysical idealism was growing stronger in British philosophy, he contended, and the alternatives to it were puny, contradictory, or both. He apologized even for writing so much about Jamesian pragmatism. This subject did not occupy "a corresponding space in my mind," he assured. It was only that James attracted a lot of attention by attacking Bradley and Hegelianism; thus Bradley had to respond. As late as 1914, it was possible for the leading absolute idealist to think that his school had no bigger problem than that.[66]

But Bradley was kidding himself, for Edwardian England was coming to an end, and the analytic revolt against idealism was in full sway. Edwardian England was a brief and hollowed out version of Victorian England. The Victorian expansion of the English empire waned. The Boer War drained the English economy and dominated English international affairs. The clash between corporate capitalism and a growing labor movement made labor strife routine. And the Victorian belief that England had a national mission waned along with the English empire and economy. In 1910 nine kings rode in the funeral procession for Edward VII. By then English society was racked with protest movements over economic oppression, the rights of women, imperial overreach, Irish home rule, and political representation. Virginia Woolf, putting it dramatically, observed: "On or about December 1910 human character changed ... All human relations have shifted – those between masters and servants, husbands and wives, parents and children. And when human relations change there is at the same time a change in religion, conduct, politics and literature."[67]

J. H. Muirhead was a witness to the change in philosophy: "There was much in the temper of the time that favored reaction. Idealism had had a long innings, owing partly to the great ability of the group of thinkers who had initiated the movement on both sides of the Atlantic and the inherent weakness of the form of empiricism which in those days was its chief opponent." It helped, Muirhead observed, that idealism, "amid a general dissolution of traditional beliefs," was so good at vindicating the best and most attractive parts of religion, ethics, politics, and the arts: "But new forces were at work. It was not only that old beliefs were undermined, but men were ceasing to be interested in the background of experience on which they rested. New interests concerned with the science and art of human life filled the horizon." English idealism was ripe for a fall because much of it stood against the modern preoccupation with movement and relativity. The "system" view of Hegel prevailed among English Hegelians, and Bradley-style absolute idealism stripped from it Hegel's stress on movement, relativity, and negation. Muirhead noted that Bradley's idealism had "a certain ghostliness" about it that seemed remote from the new world being created.[68]

The fate of liberal theology in Germany and Britain, so closely related in the late nineteenth and early twentieth centuries, diverged dramatically afterward. For most of the nineteenth century the German tradition was a cautionary spectacle to British church leaders. John J. Conybeare, in his Bampton Lectures of 1824, told his Oxford audience that the world would be better off if all German theology were buried "at the bottom of the German ocean." Five years later Hugh James Rose warned his congregation at Cambridge University that there was "a large party" of German academics and clergy who, "calling themselves Christians," stripped Christianity of its positive doctrines and everything smacking of supernaturalism. By 1915 British theology had its own ascending liberal movement, which did not stop British patriots from linking Germany's poison gas bombs to its "poison gas of Modern Thought." British pamphleteers explained that long before Germans started the Great War, "the German apostles of Kultur launched upon this country (and others) their 'Higher critic' theories, poisoning the minds of men in regard to the divine Inspiration and Authority of Holy Scriptures."[69]

After the war, British liberals and traditionalists alike carried on as though nothing had happened. The war had no effect on how British theologians approached their field or what they said about it, aside from a few German-readers who advised that Barth was worth reading. War-ravaged Britain repressed its grief and resumed its as-we-were arguments over evangelicalism, Anglo Catholicism, and modernism. German theologians, by contrast, had to ask why their leaders and teachers promoted a catastrophic war that destroyed the nation – a devastating question that overthrew the storied liberal tradition in German theology, from which it never recovered. German theology in the 1930s did not lack impressive liberal thinkers. Rudolf Otto made pioneering contributions to History of Religions theology, conceiving the holy as a terrifying *(tremendum)* and fascinating mystery of faith, the numinous. Karl Heim wrote sophisticated works on divine transcendence and divine action that anticipated the creation of a religion-and-science dialogue. Paul Tillich refashioned the idealism of Schelling, Hegel, Troeltsch, and Otto in dialogue with existentialism, Marxism, and psychoanalysis. However, Otto retired from Marburg in 1929. Heim's career was just beginning in the early 1930s. And Tillich had to flee to the United States in 1933 to avoid persecution by the Nazi government.[70]

Most liberal German theologians sneered at the democratic institutions of the Weimar Republic, like the rest of Germany's Protestant cultural elite. Germany had thin traditions of liberal politics and democracy and no tradition of liberal democracy. The dominant strain of German political thought favored a strong state and a collective idea of social order. Ritschl's culture Protestantism was perfectly suited for it; in Germany, even the social gospel was conservative and nationalistic. German liberals, before World War I, shared the dominant predispositions of German political culture. They prized a chauvinist idea of German greatness over individual freedom and democratic politics. They took a low view of civic engagement and a lower one of equality. Some prized Hegelian objective spirit over democracy and individuality. After World War I they still looked down on liberal democracy, with updated rationales, which led straight to rolling over for the Nazis. The nation that produced Kant, Hegel, Schleiermacher, Goethe and Beethoven and an unmatched literature of creative individuality went on to produce a government of satanic ambitions feeding on toxic resentments.[71]

Even Tillich, one of the few heroes of this story among liberal theologians, came late to the realization that his snotty denigration of liberal democracy was a bad idea in Germany. Had the politics played out differently, Tillich might have become the Schleiermacher or Ritschl of his generation in German theology. As it was, he had to settle for exile in the United States, at the age of forty-seven, after his thinking was already fully formed, where he showed that German idealism still had plenty of intellectual and spiritual power, if not in Germany.

Tillich and the Future of Idealism

In his later career Tillich traveled widely and was showered with awards and media praise. Retiring from Union Theological Seminary in 1955, he loved his "postretirement" seven years at Harvard, where he welcomed his liberation from the churchlike atmosphere of seminary life and prided himself on never going to church. Nearly every weekend during his Harvard years Tillich spoke to large audiences for sizable fees across the country, usually speaking on some aspect of his theology of culture, such as depth psychology and the fine arts; in 1959 he made the cover of *Time* magazine. His travels to Greece, Japan, and Egypt gave ballast to his late life interest in the theology of world religions, in which he made a slight, but influential, beginning that showed the relevance of his idealism to a very different religious situation than the one he had known.[72]

Tillich offered four rules for how interreligious dialogue should proceed and three arguments for a Christian theology of religions. The rules were that each participant must respect the value of the other's religious conviction, be able to represent her own religious perspective with conviction, presuppose the existence of a common ground that makes dialogue and conflict possible, and be open to criticism of one's perspective. Tillich did not claim that all religions are fundamentally alike; his own experiments in interreligious dialogue accentuated differences.

He emphasized that Buddhism contains nothing like the social, political, and personalistic symbol of the kingdom of God, and thus there is no analogy in Buddhism for the liberal, democratic, and socialist offshoots of Christianity. Buddhism has a strong sense of compassion, but no will to transform social structures; it is about salvation from reality, not transformation of reality. Tillich cautioned that this does not mean that dialogue between Christianity and Buddhism is pointless; for one thing, history itself compels Buddhists to take history more seriously; for another, many points of commonality exist. But the purpose of dialogue, for him, was not merely to claim or look for commonalities.[73]

The three ideas on which Tillich based his theology of religions were geared to his claims about idolatry, the Unconditioned, ultimate concern, Hegelian dialectic, and the logos: (1) Christianity is rightly conceived as a faith that transcends religion and non-religion, not as one religion among others. (2) The Hegelian principle of dialectical participation (that things and the universe are non-identical but united by participation) is better than the Eastern principle of identity (that things and the universe are one), although Tillich allowed that the Eastern principle (especially in Japanese Buddhism) affords a keener sense of the religious significance of nature. (3) Eastern wisdom, like every form of wisdom, belongs to the self-manifestations of the logos; thus, if Christ is rightly called the incarnation of the logos, all forms of Eastern wisdom must be included in the interpretation of Jesus as the Christ.[74]

This scheme turned on Tillich's identification of Christ with the universal principle of divine self-manifestation. Johannine theology, Tillich believed, saved the early church from turning Christ into the property of a factional party. The church fathers, grasping the universality of the logos idea, taught that the logos is present in all religions and cultures. Tillich contended that Christianity began to think of itself as one (embattled) religion among others only after Islam emerged in the seventh century. Christianity became fanatically exclusive, lost its universalistic self-confidence, and thereby lost its inclusiveness as a religion of Spirit. Tillich's favorite pre-nineteenth-century Christian thinkers – Nicholas of Cusa, Erasmus, Zwingli, Faustus Socinus, Jacob Boehme, Locke, Kant – held in common a rejection of medieval exclusivism. In his telling, they renewed the universalism of early Christianity, which led to the Enlightenment project of judging all religions by the same rational criterion. The Enlightenment faith in reason gave birth to the philosophy of religion, in which Christianity was subsumed under the universal concept of religion.[75]

This story had the appearance of recovery and progress, but Tillich cautioned that Enlightenment religion produced a faulty kind of universality. The type of Christian universalism that informed eighteenth- and nineteenth-century philosophers of religion led to humanist relativism, in which Christianity became merely the exemplar of the species religion. This was a dead end, despite the great names associated with it: Kant, Schleiermacher, Hegel, Schelling, and Troeltsch. The giants of liberal theology subsumed Christianity under the concept of religion, construing Christianity as the best realization of religion, but their concept of religion was itself a Christian-humanist construction of their own making. Troeltsch was sensitive to the problem of the circularity of liberal Christianity, Tillich noted; thus, Troeltsch gave up the claim to universality, settling for "Europeism," the claim that Christianity is the ideal religion for Western civilization. Instead of contesting the religions of the East or ranking

Christianity above them (outside the West), Troeltsch advocated a cross-fertilization strategy of cultural exchange and dialogue.[76]

Tillich did not claim that he had developed a better strategy than the liberal one, but he believed that he made a beginning. The better idea was a nonparochial understanding of religion and a conception of Christianity that transcends religion and non-religion. Liberal theology tried to find a home for religion in moral reason (Kant), religious feeling (Schleiermacher), metaphysical knowledge (Hegel), and the community of faith (Ritschl). Tillich countered that the best home for religion is everywhere. Religion is the dimension of depth in all the functions of humanity's spiritual life; it should not be reduced to one function of the human spirit. The Bible pictures no temples in the kingdom, for in the fulfillment of the kingdom, God shall be all in all. It followed that the way forward in theology is not to relinquish one's religious tradition for the sake of a universal concept that is not universal and is merely a concept: "The way is to penetrate into the depth of one's own religion, in devotion, thought and action. In the depth of every living religion there is a point at which the religion itself loses its importance, and that to which it points breaks through its particularity, elevating it to spiritual freedom and with it to a vision of the spiritual presence in other expressions of the ultimate meaning of man's existence."[77]

Universally, if the Holy is experienced, three movements or elements are present. Tillich employed a familiar dialectic to describe them. The founding element is the experience of the Holy within the finite, which he variously called the sacramental basis of religions or, within Christianity, the "Catholic substance." Universally, in everything that exists, the Holy appears in a special way. The second element is the critical check against idolatry, the "demonization of the sacramental," which can take the form of mysticism or, in modern Christianity, the Protestant principle. Mysticism and the Protestant principle, in Tillich's rendering, were judgments against the absolutization of all concrete expressions of the Ultimate: "The Holy as the Ultimate lies beyond any of its embodiments." The embodiments of the Holy are needed, but they are merely secondary to the Ultimate itself. The third constitutive aspect of the experience of the Holy is the ethical or prophetic element. Justice is a universal principle that transcends every particular religion, Tillich argued, and the denial of justice in the name of the Holy is always demonic. Religion without justice becomes a party to evil, while religion without the sacramental and mystical-critical elements becomes moralistic and eventually secular.[78]

Tillich's idea of a theology of religions thus rephrased his original theology of religious socialism. In 1965, near the end of his life, in his last public appearance, he offered a typically Tillichian name for the unity of the three elements that smacked of Hegel, "the religion of the concrete spirit." The history of religions has an inner aim, he proposed, which is to become the sacramental-mystical-prophetic religion of the concrete spirit. The entire history of religions is a struggle to realize the religion of the concrete spirit, which is the fight of the Unconditioned against religion within religion. Tillich recalled Harnack's statement that Christianity embraces everything within the history of religions, a remark that contained a germ of truth, but which Harnack failed to follow through. Harnack failed to see, Tillich argued, that the truth of his observation called for a more positive relationship between Christianity and the history of religions. Instead, Harnack settled for the bourgeois moralism of the

Ritschlian School, in his case with a high-bourgeois flavor. Tillich's last word was a plea for the universalism of concrete spirit: "The universality of a religious statement does not lie in an all-embracing abstraction which would destroy religion as such but in the depths of every concrete religion. Above all, it lies in the openness to spiritual freedom both from one's own foundation and for one's foundation."[79]

These ideas, and Tillich's charismatic presentation of them, had an unsurpassed legacy among twentieth-century theologies. Barth had a greater impact on twentieth-century theology by virtue of changing the field, but the legacy of Barthian theology was limited by Barth's church-based neo-Reformationism. Rudolf Bultmann's influence overlapped significantly with Tillich's, but Bultmann was primarily a biblical scholar, and his approach to demythologizing was eclipsed by Tillich's. Reinhold Niebuhr took the lead in debunking the optimistic idealism and pacifism of a great deal of liberal theology, but he did so primarily as a social ethicist. Karl Rahner had the Schleiermacher role in twentieth-century Roman Catholic theology, fashioning a "transcendental Thomist" appropriation of post-Kantian idealism and Heideggerian phenomenology, but the twentieth century was nearly two-thirds over before there was such a thing as liberal Catholic theology. Thus, Rahner and liberal Catholic theology stand outside the historical frame of the present work.[80]

Among the theological giants that arose between the two world wars and dealt with the fading force of liberal theology and idealism, Tillich stands out for influencing the entire field of theology *and* for shaping how non-theological scholars of religion viewed religion *and* for reaching a vast public audience. Mid-century Barthians, Ritschlians, confessionalists, Niebuhrians, Roman Catholics, evangelical liberals, conservative evangelicals, mystics, Whiteheadians, religious humanists, Chicago School empiricists, and religious studies scholars often paid little attention to each other, but none ignored Tillich.

The key to his fame was that Tillich made religion make sense to vast audiences that did not belong to a religious community or that were on their way out. Reflecting on his ministry to post-churched people, Tillich recalled his chaplaincy during World War I: "If I used Biblical language to the soldiers, it meant nothing to them – they were about to die, and yet the Bible had nothing to say to them. I preached sermons, therefore, that never used any of the language of the Bible. They were a little mystical, a little poetical, and also had a touch of common sense, and they had an effect." His popular writings used a similar strategy to great effect, especially after he stopped writing about socialist politics and played up his interest in depth psychology.[81]

In his later life he found it impossible to resist the exaggerated praise that was showered on him continually. Tillich's friends described him as peaceable, kindly, gentle, and unpretentious, with a strong sensual magnetism, and secretive about his sexual promiscuity. The same friends admitted that in later years he sometimes fell for his image. Wilhelm Pauck, a close friend of Tillich's, recalled: "At times he was strangely inflexible and omniscient in manner; he sometimes assumed the pose of the 'famous man' glancing Narcissus-like at his own image." Journalist Ved Mehta caught a similar impression near the end of Tillich's life. Tillich assured Mehta that the influence of his thought reverberated throughout the world except for England, where people didn't worry about despair, and he complained about the burdens of his renown: "I have so many pressures on me. If you only knew the pressures! My letters have been growing each year – sometimes there are twenty-five or thirty a day. I reply to all of them. I use this office and my secretary only for writing letters. It's the agape in me. If I had been born in Tibet, I would have retired twenty years ago. It would not have been my role to answer letters."[82]

In 1963 Tillich was the featured speaker at *Time* magazine's fortieth-anniversary party. Addressing a glittering audience of cover-story celebrities like himself, Tillich lectured on the ambiguity of achievement, cautioning that the human condition is an "inseparable mixture of good and evil, of creative and destructive forces, both individual and social." American society, for example, was remarkably free and democratic, but it was also mindlessly commercialized, fixated on material expansion, and lacking in spiritual depth. Tillich exhorted the *Time* achievers to "fight against being absorbed by the culture as another cultural good." Like all his best sermons, this one was addressed to himself.[83]

The impasse between the kind of philosophy that Tillich treasured and the kind that increasingly replaced it is captured in two anecdotes about Tillich, G. E. Moore, and Bertrand Russell. On one occasion Tillich gave a lecture on existential philosophy to the Philosophy Club at Columbia University. Moore rose to complain: "Now really, Mr. Tillich, I don't think I have been able to understand a single sentence of your paper. Won't you please try to state one sentence or even one word, that I can understand?" Moore seemed to take pride that Kierkegaard, Nietzsche, Heidegger, and Tillich were incomprehensible to him. Tillich was publicly gracious in dealing with criticism of this kind, but it grieved him that British and American philosophy departments reduced philosophy to language analysis and logic. How could philosophy write off the great questions that linked it to Plato, Aristotle, Leibniz, and Kant? Years later, Tillich told Mehta that religion is part of life; everyone has an ultimate concern. The question about religion has to do with the kind of religion that a person or community holds. Mehta was skeptical; what about someone like Bertrand Russell, who claimed to have no religious feelings? Tillich replied: "They deceive themselves. There are certain people who just can't see the color green, and one can't argue with them. Russell would be one of them."[84]

Tillich told his audiences that no great philosopher settled for mere analysis and no great philosopher approached his work by saying, "Let me now philosophize a bit between breakfast and lunch time." All philosophy worthy of the name struggles between skepticism and faith, and between demonic and divine forces, he insisted. All creative philosophers struggle with the mystery of existence, caught between the possibilities of affirming and negating life. Schelling and Hegel were his favorite philosophers, in that order, but Tillich allowed that Hegel was long on hubris and Schelling had even more of it. Both of them tried to soar to heaven, Tillich explained. Moreover, Tillich regretted that one side of Hegel's work got carried away with logic, as in the *Encyclopedia*, where Hegel constructed a giant mill that constantly droned the same noise in the same rhythm "so that if a concept goes into the mill you know ahead of time what will come out of it."[85]

Tillich prized the other Hegel – the philosopher of life who wrote the *Phenomenology of Spirit* and delivered his sprawling, profound, opinionated lecture series on religion, art, nature, and the history of philosophy. Unlike modern anthropologists, who studied bones and culture but not the human spirit, Hegel grappled with the "essence of man." Unlike analytic philosophy, which banished everything pertaining to the soul, Hegel was the greatest theorist of the human spirit as the self-manifestation of the divine Spirit. For daring to grasp "the essential structures of all things," Tillich was willing to make allowances for Hegel's shortcomings.[86]

More than anyone of his time, Tillich succeeded in renewing a liberal understanding of religion, in his case by blending German idealism, logos Christology, neo-Reformation theology, mysticism, and existential philosophy. The other theological giant of Tillich's generation, Karl Barth, contended that Tillich betrayed neo-Reformation theology with his idealism, mysticism, and existentialism. But even Barth, contrary to countless renderings of his theology, did not avoid philosophy or oppose using philosophy in theology. Barth acknowledged that theology operates in the same context as philosophy. He accepted that theology cannot avoid coming to terms with the two boundaries of human thought, the problem of realism and idealism. He worked out a dialectical approach to the problem that gave the upper hand to idealism, despite the fact that he was a theological realist. More importantly, his dialecticism and open-ended pluralism played out in ways that prefigured postmodern criticism and fluidity.[87]

The Neo-Kantian/Postmodern Barth: Realism, Idealism, and Dialecticism

Barth acknowledged that every theology has a deep stake in the differences between realism and idealism. Realism is oriented to the question of reality, he reasoned, while idealism is oriented to the question of truth. Theological realists, asserting that the external world is real apart from human awareness of it, contend that God is real apart from human awareness of God. By holding firm to God's objective existence, Barth argued, theological realists rightly resist any suggestion that theological knowledge belongs to a special framework apart from philosophical knowledge. One cannot say, "God is" without affirming, in the language of realism, that God takes part in being. Thomas Aquinas, expounding the classical form of this argument, derived a third proposition from it: Everything that exists as such participates in God. God is being itself, the origin and perfection of all that is. Everything that exists, by virtue of being created, is dissimilar to the Creator, yet there is a similarity between the Creator and everything that exists by virtue of sharing being. In particular, Aquinas argued, there is something in the being of human beings that is analogous to the being of God.[88]

Barth leaned on Jesuit theologian Erich Przywara in this area, wary of overstating the Catholic doctrine of *analogia entis* (analogy of being). Przywara conformed to the language of *similitude Dei* and *major dissimilitudo* decreed by the Fourth Lateran Council (1215), emphasizing the dissimilarity between God and creature; in his formulation, the analogy of being asserted "greater dissimilarity in great likeness." For many Thomists, that was too Augustinian to get the balance right. Barth, brushing aside Thomist versus Augustinian debates, asserted that the Catholic analogy of being affirmed the similarity *and* dissimilarity to God "which I myself have as knower and the thing outside me has as the known." Thomist realism, in Barth's telling, balanced the scale "as skillfully as possible" between inner and outer experience, creaturely similarity and dissimilarity, and God's objective and subjective givenness. But the point of all this balancing was to justify moving from one's knowledge of a directly experienced real world to knowledge of God, Barth objected. The realist "confidently supposes that in what is given he is able to encounter something similar to God, and this confidence gives definition to his teaching." Theological realism, even at its best, was always about reading off knowledge of God from that which is given, not from another source or means.[89]

Barth protested that any God that is read off from the given world is less than the Wholly Other God of grace and glory that holds power over the world. The God of God's Word comes as light into darkness, announcing something new. The God derived from the analogy of being is merely a hidden feature of the world. Theological realism reduces God to fate, Barth contended. At its best, it retains a doctrine of revelation and grace, but operationally, it makes revelation and grace superfluous. Barth asked, "Does revelation really do no more than confirm and reinforce supernaturally a naively presupposed human capacity and necessity apparently somehow given with our existence?" This doctrine of revelation, he judged, and its accompanying notion of grace as the fulfillment of nature, disastrously reinforced the paganizing tendency of Catholic spirituality. Catholic theology, by making God's reality accessible apart from God's revelation in the Word, abstracted God's reality from the event of grace. The upshot was that it lost God's actual presence. Barth explained, "For grace is the event in which God comes to us in his Word, an event over which God has sole control, and which is strictly momentary. Otherwise God could not be distinguished from a hidden feature of reality as such. He could not be distinguished from fate." The possibility of experiencing God is open to us not because it is fated by God's presence, but because God chooses to come to us.[90]

Barth's "no" to idealism was less harsh and more admonitory. Idealism always emphasizes critical reflection, he observed. Plato, Augustine, Calvin, Descartes, Kant, and Hegel were alike in pressing the question of the nature of truth. Barth observed: "Idealism means the self-reflection of the spirit over against nature. It discovers a correlation between thinking and truth." In the idealist tradition, the dualism of subject and object is overcome through the movement of the creative logos. Idealist thinking, by lifting reason or self-reflected spirit over the power of fate, obtains power over the limitations that fate imposes on human life.[91]

For this reason, Barth acknowledged, idealism, in its essential character, has a deeper affinity with theology than realism. Theology is inherently idealistic because it describes the being or movement of spirit as the key to the nature of reality. This was a sizable concession, given Barth's realist insistence on the given reality of God and the necessity of beginning with God's revealed Word. Barth explained, "Even realist theology cannot be theology without drawing heavily on idealism." Even if one begins with the given reality of God, one has to deal with the problem that the truth about God's reality is not given. Thus, even Aquinas developed a negative theology. Barth acknowledged that the great strength of the idealist tradition is that it emphasizes God's non-objectivity. At its best, which, by his lights, meant Augustine and Calvin, idealistic theology insists that all thinking and speaking about God is inadequate. It protects the divine mystery from being identified with other objects. It directs attention to the unknown God of transcendence. Without the corrective antidote of critical idealism, Barth warned, theology inevitably degenerates into "pagan monstrosity."[92]

Idealism is closer to the truth than realism. For precisely this reason, however, Barth warned that it poses a greater danger to theology than realism. The difference between the realist "God is reality" and the idealist "God is truth" makes idealism prone to a destructive pride, Barth explained. The idealist emphasis on the transparency of reality enables idealists to give witness to the divine truth that shines within, behind, and beyond the real, but it also tends to brush aside the chastening realist focus on the accidental and particular truths of history. This is a fatal weakness, Barth warned; a proud theology is always a monstrosity. Idealist theology, no matter how critical, is demonic if it trusts in the power of its rationality. Barth declared: "If theology is to remain grounded in God's revelation, then the idealist is going to have to dampen his ardor for a generally accessible truth, and to join forces with the realist. He is going to have to grant that 'accessibility' here can only mean the possibility of God's access to us, not of our access to God." It is hard for idealists to stick with the single revelatory event of Christ, Barth observed; the idealist tradition has a built-in tendency to treat revelation as a general human possibility. The possibility of distinguishing truth from reality, which idealists treasure, is itself made possible only by revelation, which is a possibility specific to God alone.[93]

Barth was allergic to liberal idealisms that linked the self-transcendence of created spirit to God's transcendent Spirit. The object of theology is neither spirit nor nature, he admonished. Since the divine object of theology cannot be reached with a ladder of consciousness, theology belongs no more to the humanities than to the natural sciences. The object of theology is "the Word dwelling in inapproachable light." All that theology can do is to bear witness to its object; theology cannot produce or express it. Faith is a possibility given by God through the Word, not, in any constitutive sense, a human work. Barth urged, "There can be no question of reciprocity between God's action and our own. It is strictly a matter of the command in which we know our obedience to be grounded." True theology, refusing to make a case that the divine command exists, rests content with bearing witness that God's command is spoken through the Word.[94]

This attempt to navigate between realism and idealism raised more questions than it answered. Barth made no attempt to judge whether Augustine, Calvin, or even Aquinas averted the dangers. He treated the Catholic analogy of being as a product of Thomist realism without acknowledging that this doctrine had deeper roots in Augustine's ontological idealism. He offered a contentious rendering of Przywara's position while relying upon it, evoking criticism on both counts. And he aggressively featured his narrowness, declaring, shortly afterward, that he was finished with all variations of the Augustinian notion that the divine-human relation contains an element of continuity. Przywara said that human beings are "open upwards" to God on the basis of a continuity in being between God and creation; Barth replied that human beings lack any vantage point for surveying their relation to God. The Augustinian attempt to understand the divine-human relation on a model of similarity and dissimilarity in being is a denial of revelation and grace, Barth contended. Human beings lack any inherent capacity or endowment of being for knowing God. The only point of continuity is the miracle of God's love that comes from without as a gift.[95]

This impossible position carried Barth into his blowout with Brunner, where he had no answer for Brunner's question as to how anyone could recognize a revelation.

Barth's renderings of Augustinianism and the entire tradition of natural theology were debated for decades, but not his dead-on contention that idealism is second nature for all theology, especially liberal theology.

Barth's strength was his weakness. He got universalism, radical politics, and radical eschatology out of the gospel, all by insisting on the exclusive witness of a self-authenticating revelation. He was notoriously narrow, and yet this very narrowness opened out to something very much like postmodern diversity and fluidity. Despite the many ways in which he reveled in dogmatism, his vision was pluralistic and discursively open-ended. He insisted that Christian theology is healthy and free only when it remains open to a multiplicity of philosophies, worldviews, and forms of language. By fixing on the truth of grace, he relativized the problems of method and discursive form.

Barth's thought was too sprawling and complex to be reducible to any single theme, but one thing, above all, helped to make him the greatest theologian since Schleiermacher: His persistent refusal to reduce God to an aspect of the temporal order. Liberal theology often took this option implicitly without quite saying it. Whiteheadian theology took it explicitly, conceiving God as an actual entity that competes for space with creativity and is subordinate to it. Barth, by refusing to defend God with arguments that reduced God to the logic of a system, pointed to the ineffable mystery and glory of the divine. He spoke of God as negating and transcending Christian theism, although his early writings were stronger on this theme than the later ones. By insisting on the transcendent holiness of the divine, Barth tried to liberate theology from its subservience to philosophy, bourgeois culture, and church tradition.

His opposition to the colonization of theology prefigured the postmodern critique of totalizing discourse without its nihilist presumption that there is no ground of truth. Poststructuralist theory criticizes the colonizing effect of philosophical systems, which pre-empt the possibility of recognizing true difference. Barth's polemic against theological modernism anticipated the postmodern critique of philosophical foundationalism in this respect. By refusing to render Christianity as an illustration of mythic truth, existential analysis, process metaphysics, or a similar criterion, he broke apart the modern preoccupation with ascertaining the methodological limits of truth.

Barth's project anticipated the critical thesis of Gadamerian hermeneutics, that modern philosophy truncates the limits of truth in its subservience to method. With powerful force Barth protested against the totalizing implications of all claims to methodological neutrality, epistemological foundationalism, and philosophical pre-understanding. The interpreter has no chance of hearing a new word if she brings her preunderstanding to the text as a final norm. The Word does not seek to be mastered by us in order to be understood by us, he urged. It seeks rather to lay hold of us in our openness to its voice. We glean something of God's Word through the mystery of the subject matter, which invites us through human words and the movement of the Spirit to "investigate the humanity of the word by which it is told."[96]

Barth stood for methodological pluralism, not an impossible blank slate. He accepted that theology had to use philosophy and hermeneutical theory; his point was that theology should not sanction or presuppose any fixed canon of truth or importance. His theory of the threefold Word implied simultaneously the indissoluble unity of the Word with the texts, tradition, and present life of the church, but also the necessity of always distinguishing between the Word and the text, the text and the community, and the present creeds and future possibilities. Because human beings are immersed in transience and relativity, he urged, it is perilous to identify the gospel message with the questionable possibilities emerging out of the historical process. The gospel conveys the radically new possibilities of God, which are fallibly understood in the present, which stand on the borderline of human achievements, and which become evident in the negation of these achievements.

The key to Barth's theology was the dialectical Paulinism of his *Romans* commentary, although he misled generations of interpreters by claiming to have left dialecticism behind after he became a dogmatic theologian. His theology remained an affirmation of the dialectical movement of God in self-revelation, that God becomes objective without ceasing to be hidden. True knowledge of God begins with the recognition of God's hiddenness, not with an act of imagination or creativity. God is incomprehensible, for God does not exist in the sphere of human power. No myth or doctrine or scriptural word, by itself, can bring us to God or show God to us. It becomes God's Word by grace through the movement of God's Spirit.

The myth of the dying god becomes divine speech through God's action in Christ. Only there is the hidden God apprehensible, Barth taught, taking Christocentrism for granted, and even there, the hidden source of revelation is apprehended only indirectly. If Kant was right about human knowing, which Barth did not doubt, God must make God's self known as *phenomenal* if God is to be known. God, to be known, must become part of the creaturely realm. In Christ, Barth reasoned, God becomes present to human knowing as the subject of human knowing, not its object. The hidden God is apprehended by faith, not by sight; in sign, not in being. The Word made flesh is the sign of all signs, but it is made known only after the flesh, through the Spirit. For in Christ we see the human face of God in and through the movement of the Spirit.[97]

That is dialectical theology, which Barth expounded in the *Church Dogmatics* long after he left behind the language of crisis, existentialism, and dialectics. In my view, he remained more dialectical than every version of Barthian neo-orthodoxy; on the other hand, the problem with Barth was that he was never dialectical enough. He offered the God of Pauline supernaturalism as an answer to modern religious needs, which spoke powerfully to many in his generation, and he was very good at blasting certain kinds of idolatry. But he failed to bring together the "yes" and "no" of his dialectic. In his early career Barth was relentlessly one-sided, denying that his religion of faith was still a religion. No point of identity between God and humankind was allowed; even Brunner's tiny, passive capacity for receiving revelation was forbidden. In his later theology Barth developed analogical models for the relationship between God and humankind, and he spoke of the humanity of God.[98]

But that didn't lure him any further into the real world of culture, nature, philosophy, other religions, or anything else that wasn't Western Protestant Christianity. He took for granted Kant's dichotomy between science and theology and gave no further thought to science. Barth's dialectic was paradoxical, not relational. It had no inner movement from one state to another by an inner dynamic. It engaged the world only episodically, when his Christian identity was provoked. Mostly it kept modern criticism at bay, defining theology as church-based explication of a self-authenticating revelation.

Theology has to be more real and relational than that, breathing freely in a world where everything is relative because everything is related. The liberal idealist tradition launched by Kant, Schelling, Hegel, and Schleiermacher, despite its shortcomings, was strong on dynamism and relativity. Modern theology operates in the shadow of these thinkers on that account.

Notes

1. Immanuel Kant, *Critique of Practical Reason*, trans. Lewis White Beck (Indianapolis: Bobbs-Merrill, 1956), 3–5, "keystone," 3; see Kant, *Critique of Practical Reason*, in Kant, *Practical Philosophy*, ed. and trans. Mary J. Gregor (Cambridge: Cambridge University Press, 1996), 133–271.

2. Kant, *Critique of Practical Reason*, 4–5, 8–9; see Mark C. Taylor, *After God* (Chicago: University of Chicago Press, 2007), 108–109.

3. Dieter Henrich, *Between Kant and Hegel: Lectures on German Idealism*, ed. David Pacini (Cambridge: Harvard University Press, 2003), 19–20, 46–61, quote 20; see J. G. Fichte, *Attempt at a Critique of All Revelation*, trans. Garrett Green (Cambridge: Cambridge University Press, 1978), 119.

4. Kant, *Critique of Practical Reason*, 4.

5. Ibid., 33–34.

6. See Immanuel Kant, *Foundations of the Metaphysics of Morals*, trans. Lewis White Beck (Indianapolis: Bobbs-Merrill, 1969); Henry E. Allison, *Kant's Theory of Freedom* (Cambridge: Cambridge University Press, 1990); Allison, *Kant's Transcendental Idealism* (New Haven: Yale University Press, 1983).

7. Henrich, *Between Kant and Hegel: Lectures on German Idealism*, 49; Immanuel Kant, *Critique of Pure Reason*, trans. Norman Kemp Smith (New York: Macmillan, 1973), B295/A236–B315/A260, 257–275.

8. Eugene Lyman, "The Place of Intuition in Religious Experience and Its Validity as Knowledge," *Journal of Religion* 9 (March 1924), 113–132, quote 129; see Lyman, *The Meaning and Truth of Religion* (New York: Charles Scribner's Sons, 1933); Albert Knudson, *The Philosophy of Personalism: A Study in the Metaphysics of Religion* (New York: Abingdon Press, 1927), 72–74; Gary Dorrien, *The Making of American Liberal Theology: Idealism, Realism, and Modernity, 1900–1950* (Louisville: Westminster John Knox Press, 2003), 307–310.

9. See Rudolf Hermann Lotze, *Metaphysic in Three Books: Ontology, Cosmology, and Psychology*, trans. T. H. Green, Bernard Bosanquet, et al. (Oxford: Clarendon Press, 1884); Lotze, *Microcosmos: An Essay Concerning Man and His Relation to the World*, 2 vols., trans. Elizabeth Hamilton and E. E. Constance Jones (Edinburgh: T. & T. Clark, 1885); Borden P. Bowne, *Theory of Thought and Knowledge* (New York: American Book Company, 1897); Bowne, *Metaphysics* (New York: Harper & Brothers, 1898); Knudson, *The Philosophy of Personalism*, 72–74; and Dorrien, *The Making of American Liberal Theology: Idealism, Realism, and Modernity, 1900–1950*, 308–310.

10. See Lotze, *Metaphysic in Three Books: Ontology, Cosmology, and Psychology*, 302–314; Lotze, *Microcosmos: An Essay Concerning Man and His Relation to the World*, I: 240–263, 640–681; Andrew Seth Pringle-Pattison, *The Idea of God in the Light of Recent Philosophy* (New York: Oxford University Press, 1920), 20–38; Borden Parker Bowne, *Personalism* (Boston: Houghton, Mifflin & Co., 1908), 257–277; Bowne, *Metaphysics*, 263–271; Bowne, *Theory of Thought and Knowledge*, 302–316.

11. J. G. Fichte, *The Science of Knowledge*, ed. and trans. Peter Heath and John Lachs (Cambridge: Cambridge University Press, 1982), 264–286.

12. F. W. J. Schelling and G. W. F. Hegel, *Fernere Darstellungen*, in Schelling, *Sämtliche Werke*, 14 vols., ed. K. F. A. Schelling (Stuttgart: Cotta, 1856–1861), IV: 390–411; Schelling to Hegel, February 4, 1795, *Briefe und Dokumente*, ed. H. Fuhrmanns, 3 vols. (Bonn: Bouvier, 1962–1975), II: 65; Schelling, *The Unconditional in Human Knowledge: Four Early Essays (1794–1796)*, trans. Fritz Marti (Lewisburg: Bucknell University Press, 1980); Schelling, *Vom Ich als Princip der Philosophie* (1795), in Schelling, *Sämtliche Werke*, I: 150–154; Schelling, *Ideas for a Philosophy of Nature*, Second edition, 1803, trans. Errol E. Harris and Peter Heath (Cambridge: Cambridge University Press, 1988), 13–17; Hegel, *The Difference between Fichte's and Schelling's System of Philosophy*, trans. H. S. Harris and Walter Cerf (Albany: State University of New York Press, 1977), 79–83; Frederick C. Beiser, *German Idealism: The Struggle Against Subjectivism, 1781–1801* (Cambridge: Harvard University Press, 2002), 578–582.

13. Friedrich Schleiermacher, *On Religion: Addresses in Response to its Cultured Critics*, trans. Terrence N. Tice (Richmond: John Knox Press, 1969), quote 82; see Heinrich Heine, *Die romantische Schule* (1836; reprint, Dresden: Verlag der Kunst, 1955); Rudolf Haym, *Die romantische Schule* (Berlin: Gaertner, 1882); E. Behler, *Früromantik* (Berlin: De Gruyter, 1992); W. Silz, *Early German Romanticism* (Cambridge: Harvard University Press, 1929).

14. Schelling and Hegel, *Fernere Darstellungen*, IV: 390–411; F. W. J. Schelling, *Vorlesungen über die Methode des akademischen Studiums* (1803), in Schelling, *Sämtliche Werke*, V: 212–256; Beiser, *German Idealism: The Struggle Against Subjectivism, 1781–1801*, 580–582.

15. Schelling, *Ideas for a Philosophy of Nature*, quotes 15, 16.

16. Schelling, *Vorlesungen über die Methode des akademischen Studiums* (1803), V: 348; F. W. J. Schelling, *Darstellung meines Systems der Philosophie* (1801; reprint, Stuttgart: Fromman-Holzboog, 2009); Schelling, *Philosophical Investigations into the Essence of Human Freedom*, trans. Jeff Love and Johannes Schmidt (Albany: State University of New York Press, 2006); G. W. F. Hegel, *Phenomenology of Spirit*, trans. A. V. Miller (Oxford: Oxford University Press, 1977), quote 9.

17. Hegel, *The Difference Between Fichte's and Schelling's System of Philosophy*, quotes 80.

18. Ibid., 81.

19. Immanuel Kant, *Critique of Pure Reason*, trans. Norman Kemp Smith (London: Macmillan, 1973), A 713/B741–A/719/B747, 576–580.

20. F. W. J. Schelling, "Über die Construktion in der Philosophie," in Schelling, *Sämtliche Werke*, V: 125–134; Friedrich Heinrich Jacobi, *Jacobi to Fichte*, in Jacobi, *The Main Philosophical Writings and the Novel Allwill*, ed. and trans. George di Giovanni (Montreal: McGill-McQueen's University Press, 2009), 497–532; Beiser, *German Idealism: The Struggle Against Subjectivism, 1781–1801*, 587–588.

21. F. W. J. Schelling, *System der gesammten Philosophie*, in Schelling, *Sämtliche Werke*, quote, VI: 140; Beiser, *German Idealism: The Struggle Against Subjectivism, 1781–1801*, 592.

22. Beiser, *German Idealism: The Struggle Against Subjectivism, 1781–1801*, 593.

23. Hegel, *Phenomenology of Spirit*, quote 14.

24. Kant, *Critique of Pure Reason*, B xxiii, 25. This quotation is perhaps clearer in the translation by Paul Guyer and Allen Wood, which reads, "and no principle can be taken with certainty in *one* relation unless it has the same time been investigated in its *thoroughgoing* relation to the entire use of pure reason." Kant, *Critique of Pure Reason*, ed. and

trans. Paul Guyer and Allen Wood (Cambridge: Cambridge University Press, 1998), B xxiii, 113–114.

25. Henrich, *Between Kant and Hegel: Lectures on German Idealism*, "feedback," 51. Henrich taught at Harvard for the first time in 1973, when he was a professor of philosophy at Heidelberg. I studied under him in 1975, and he continued to teach at Harvard and Columbia until 1984. See Dieter Henrich, "The Basic Structure of Modern Philosophy," *Cultural Hermeneutics* 22 (1974), 1–18; Henrich, "Fichte's Original Insight," trans. David Lachterman, in *Contemporary German Philosophy* (University Park: Pennsylvania State University Press, 1982); Henrich, "Self-Consciousness: A Critical Introduction to a Theory," *Man and World* 4 (1971), 2–28.

26. Henrich, *Between Kant and Hegel: Lectures on German Idealism*, 51–52.

27. Immanuel Kant, *The Critique of Judgement*, trans. James Creed Meredith (Oxford: Oxford University Press, 1973), 3–39; Kant, *What Real Progress Has Metaphysics Made in Germany since the Time of Leibniz and Wolff?*, trans. Ted Humphrey (New York: Abaris Books, 1983), 157. See Kant, *Critique of the Power of Judgment*, trans. Paul Guyer and Eric Matthews (Cambridge: Cambridge University Press, 2000); Henrich, *Between Kant and Hegel: Lectures on German Idealism*, 52–53.

28. Kant, *Critique of Practical Reason*, 3–4.

29. Henrich, *Between Kant and Hegel: Lectures on German Idealism*, 59.

30. See Amos Funkenstein, *Theology and the Scientific Imagination from the Middle Ages to the Seventeenth Century* (Princeton: Princeton University Press, 1986), 346–363; Ian G. Barbour, *Issues in Science and Religion* (Englewood Cliffs: Prentice-Hall, 1966), 74–79.

31. See Charles Darwin, *On the Origin of Species* (London: John Murray, 1859); Friedrich Paulsen, *German Universities* (New York: Charles Scribner's Sons, 1906); Charles F. Thwing, *The American and the German University* (New York: Macmillan, 1928); Gertrude Himmelfarb, *Darwin and the Darwinian Revolution* (Garden City: Doubleday, 1959).

32. Carolus Linnaeus, *Systema naturae per regna tria naturae, secundum classes, ordines, genera, species, cum characteribus, differentiis, synonymis, locis*, 3 vols. (Hale: Curt, 1760–1770), I: 20–24; Georges Cuvier, *Le Régne animal*, 5 vols. (Paris: Deterville Libraire, 1829–30), I: 180.

33. William Stanton, *The Leopard's Spots: Scientific Attitudes toward Race in America, 1815–1859* (Chicago: University of Chicago Press, 1960), 15–53; Thomas F. Gossett, *Race: The History of an Idea in America* (New York: Schocken Books, 1965), 54–64; George M. Frederickson, *Racism: A Short History* (Princeton: Princeton University Press, 2002), 51–75.

34. Charles Darwin, *The Descent of Man* (New York: John Murray, 1874), 166–168; Gossett, *Race: The History of an Idea in America*, 63–83; M. Ruse, *The Darwinian Revolution* (Chicago: University of Chicago Press, 1979).

35. M. K. Richardson and G. Keuck, "Haeckel's ABC of evolution and development," *Biological Reviews* 77 (2002), 495–528; "Ernst Heinrich Philipp August Haeckel," *Britannica Concise Encyclopedia, Britannica.com*, 2006, accessed September 120, 2010. Richardson and Keuck show that Haeckel did not argue for recapitulation theory in its strongest possible forms. See Ernst Haeckel, *The Riddle of the Universe at the Close of the Nineteenth Century* (1900; reprint, Cambridge: Cambridge University Press, 2009).

36. August Schleicher, *Über die Bedeutung der Sprache für die Naturgeschichte des Menschen* (Weimar: Hermann Böhlau, 1865), 16–19; Robert J. Richards, *The Tragic Sense of Life: Ernst Haeckel and the Struggle over Evolutionary Thought* (Chicago: University of Chicago Press, 2008), 255–261.

37. Ernst Haeckel, *Natürliche Schöpfungsgeschichte* (Berlin: Georg Reimer, 1868), "if one views," 511; cited in Richards, *The Tragic Sense of Life: Ernst Haeckel and the Struggle over Evolutionary Thought*, 260; Haeckel, *The History of Creation*, 2 vols. (1876; 6th edn., New York, D. Appleton and Co., 1914), "the Caucasian," 2: 429.

38. For the view that Haeckel was a violent anti-Semite and a chief forerunner of the Nazi movement, see Daniel Gasman, *Haeckel's Monism and the Birth of Fascist Ideology* (New York: Peter Lang, 1998). For a similar view, though more moderate about Haeckel's anti-Semitism, see Richard Weikart, *From Darwin to Hitler: Evolutionary Ethics, Eugenics, and Racism in Germany* (New York: Palgrave Macmillan, 2004). For a reading that views Haeckel's anti-Semitism as "behavioral," not racial, and as constitutive of his animus against all orthodox religions, see Richards, *The Tragic Sense of Life: Ernst Haeckel and the Struggle over Evolutionary Thought*, 273–275.

39. Immanuel Kant, Lecture Advertisement, 1775, in *Akademie-Ausgabe of Kant's Gesammelte Schriften* (Berlin: G. Reimer, 1910-), II: 429, cited in J. Kameron Carter, *Race: A Theological Account* (Oxford: Oxford University Press, 2008), 83; Kant, "Of the Different Human Races" (1777), in *The Idea of Race*, eds. Robert Bernasconi and Tommy L. Lott (Indianapolis: Hackett, 2000), "the white," and "Negroes," 12, "they do," 9.

40. Kant, "Of the Different Human Races," quotes 16, 19.

41. Ibid., 20–22; *Menschenkunde, Akademie-Ausgabe of Kant's Gesammelte Schriften*, XXV.II: 1187–1188; cited in Carter, *Race: A Theological Account*, 90–91.

42. Immanuel Kant, *Reflexionen, Akademie-Ausgabe of Kant's Gesammelte Schriften*, quotes, XXV: 878; cited in Carter, *Race: A Theological Account*, 92; see Mark Larrimore, "Sublime Waste: Kant on the Destiny of the 'Races,'" in *Civilization and Oppression*, ed. Cheryl J. Misak (Calgary: University of Calgary Press, 1999), 103–114.

43. Kant, "*Reflexionen*," 878; Immanuel Kant, *Anthropology from a Pragmatic Point of View*, ed. Hans. H. Rudnick, trans. Victor Lyle Dowdell (Carbondale: Southern Illinois University Press, 1978), "two most," 226.

44. Kant, *Anthropology from a Pragmatic Point of View*, quotes 226, 229.

45. Ibid., quotes 101.

46. Ibid., 101.

47. Ibid., 102; see Carter, *Race: A Theological Account*, 105; Sara Eigen and Mark J. Larrimore, eds., *The German Invention of Race* (Albany: SUNY Press, 2006).

48. Immanuel Kant, *Religion Within the Boundaries of Mere Reason and Other Writings*, ed. and trans. Allen Wood and George Di Giovanni (Cambridge: Cambridge University Press, 1998), quotes 130, 132.

49. See Jonathan M. Hess, *Germans, Jews, and the Claims of Modernity* (New Haven: Yale University Press, 2002); Michael Mack, *German Idealism and the Jew: The Inner Anti-Semitism of Philosophy and German Jewish Responses* (Chicago: University of Chicago Press, 2003).

50. G. E. Moore, "The Nature of Judgment," *Mind* 8 (April 1899), 176–193; see Moore, "Mr. McTaggart's 'Studies in Hegelian Cosmology,'" *Proceedings of the Aristotelian Society* 2 (1901–1902), 177–214.

51. G. E. Moore, "The Refutation of Idealism," *Mind* 12 (October 1903), 341–370, reprinted in Moore, *Philosophical Studies* (1922; reprint, London: Routledge & Kegan Paul, 1965), 1–30, quote 3.

52. Ibid., quote 14.

53. Ibid., quote 16.

54. Ibid., quotes 17.

55. Ibid., 17–18.

56. Ibid., quote 19.

57. Ibid., quotes 25.

58. Ibid., quote 27.

59. Ibid, quotes 28.

60. G. E. Moore, *Principia Ethica* (Cambridge: Cambridge University Press, 1903); Henry Sidgwick, *The Methods of Ethics* (1st edn., 1874; 6th edn., London: Macmillan, 1901); Hastings Rashdall, *The Theory of Good and Evil*, 2 vols. (Oxford: Oxford University Press, 1907).

61. G. E. Moore, "External and Internal Relations," in Moore, *Philosophical Studies*, 276–309; Moore, "Preface" to Moore, *Philosophical Studies*, quote viii.

62. John Maynard Keynes, *Two Memoirs* (London: Rupert Hart-Davis, 1949), 92–93; Leonard Woolf, *Sowing: An Autobiography of the Years 1880–1904* (London: Hogarth Press, 1960), 147; F. H. Bradley, *Essays on Truth and Reality* (Oxford: Oxford University Press, 1914), 127–158. See G. E. Moore, "A Defense of Common Sense," in *Contemporary British Philosophy*, ed. J. H. Muirhead (London: Allen & Unwin, 1925), 193–223; Moore, review of *Religion in the Making*, by Alfred North Whitehead, *The Nation and Athenaeum* (February 12, 1927), 664; Thomas A. Langford, *In Search of Foundations: English Theology, 1900–1920* (New York: Abingdon Press, 1969), 80–87. Moore used the hand-raising example in his lecture of November 22, 1939 to the Henriette Hertz Trust, "Proof of an External World," published in *Proceedings of the British Academy* 25 (1939), 273–300; reprinted in *Classics of Analytic Philosophy*, ed. Robert R. Ammerman (Indianapolis: Hackett, 1990), 68–84.

63. C. J. Ducasse, "Moore's Refutation of Idealism," in *The Philosophy of G. E. Moore*, ed. Paul Arthur Schilpp (La Salle: Open Court, 1942; 3rd edn., 1968), 223–252; G. E. Moore, "A Reply to My Critics," ibid., 653–660.

64. Andrew Seth Pringle-Pattison, *The Idea of God in the Light of Recent Philosophy*, Gifford Lectures, 1912–1913 (2nd edn., New York: Oxford University Press, 1920), 393–399; Bradley, *Essays on Truth and Reality*, quotes 128.

65. Bradley, *Essays on Truth and Reality*, 131.

66. Ibid., vi.

67. Virginia Woolf, "Mr. Bennett and Mrs. Brown," *The Hogarth Essays* (London: Hogarth Press, 1924), quote 4–5; Barbara Tuchman, *The Guns of August* (New York: Macmillan, 1962), 1–2; George Dangerfield, *The Strange Death of Liberal England* (London: Constable, 1936); Langford, *In Search of Foundations: English Theology, 1900–1920*, 39–47.

68. John Henry Muirhead, *The Platonic Tradition in Anglo-Saxon Philosophy* (London: Allen & Unwin, 1931), quote 279; see Muirhead, *Reflections by a Journeyman in Philosophy* (London: Allen & Unwin, 1942).

69. John Josias Conybeare, *The Bampton Lectures for the year MDCCCXXIX* (Oxford: Oxford University Press, 1824), cited in Keith Robbins, *Protestant Germany Through British Eyes* (London: German Historical Institute, 1993), 14; Hugh James Rose, *The State of Protestantism in Germany* (London: 1829), xxvii–ix; Mark D. Chapman, "Anglo-German Theological Relations in the First World War," *Zeitschrift für neuere Theologiegeschichte* 6 (1999), "poison," 109; cited in Friedrich Wilhelm Graf, "What Has London (or Oxford or Cambridge) to Do with Augsburg?," in *The Future of Liberal Theology*, ed. Mark D. Chapman (Aldershot, England: Ashgate Publishing, 2002), 18–19.

70. See Rudolf Otto, *The Idea of the Holy*, trans. John W. Harvey (London: Oxford University Press, 1928); Otto, *Naturalism and Religion*, trans. J. Arthur Thomson and Margaret R. Thomson (New York: G. P. Putnam's Sons, n.d.); Karl Heim, *God Transcendent: Foundation for a Christian Metaphysic*, trans. Edgar P. Dickie (London: Nisbet and Co., 1935);

Heim, *Christian Faith and Natural Science* (New York: Harper and Brothers, 1953); Heim, *The Transformation of the Scientific Worldview* (New York: Harper and Brothers, 1953).

71. See Fritz K. Ringer, *The Decline of the German Mandarins: The German Academic Community, 1890–1933* (Cambridge: Harvard University Press, 1972), 435–445; E. V. Hartshorne, *The German Universities and National Socialism* (Cambridge: Harvard University Press, 1937), 87–100; Fritz Stern, *The Politics of Cultural Despair* (Berkeley: University of California Press, 1961).

72. [cover story, no byline], "To Be or Not to Be," *Time* 73 (March 16, 1959), 46–52; Wilhelm Pauck and Marion Pauck, *Paul Tillich: His Life and Thought* (San Francisco: Harper & Row, 1989), 248–249. This section on Tillich adapts material from Gary Dorrien, *The Making of American Liberal Theology: Idealism, Realism, and Modernity* (Louisville: Westminster John Knox Press, 2003), 512–521.

73. Paul Tillich, *Christianity and the Encounter of World Religions* (New York: Columbia University Press, 1963; reprint, Minneapolis: Fortress Press, 1994), 39–47.

74. Paul Tillich, "On the Boundary Line," *Christian Century* 77 (December 7, 1960), 1435–36.

75. Tillich, *Christianity and the Encounter of World Religions*, 25–26.

76. Ibid., 23–32; see Ernst Troeltsch, *Religion in History*, trans. James Luther Adams and Walter F. Bense (Minneapolis: Fortress Press, 1991).

77. Paul Tillich, *Theology of Culture*, ed. Robert C. Kimball (New York: Oxford University Press, 1959), 3–9; Tillich, *Christianity and the Encounter of World Religions*, quote 61–62.

78. Paul Tillich, "The Significance of the History of Religions for the Systematic Theologian," in *The Future of Religions*, ed. Jerald C. Brauer (New York: Harper & Row, 1966), quote 87; see Tillich, *The Protestant Era*, 238–240; Tillich, *Christianity and the Encounter of World Religions*, 20.

79. Tillich, "The Significance of the History of Religions for the Systematic Theologian," 80–94, quotes 88, 94.

80. See Reinhold Niebuhr, *Moral Man and Immoral Society: A Study in Ethics and Politics* (New York: Charles Scribner's Sons, 1932); Niebuhr, *An Interpretation of Christian Ethics* (New York: Harper & Brothers, 1935); Karl Rahner, *Geist in Welt* (Munich: Kösel-Verlag, 1957); English edition, *Spirit in the World*, trans. William V. Dych (New York: Herder and Herder, 1968); Rahner, *Foundations of Christian Faith: An Introduction to the Idea of Christianity*, trans. William V. Dych (New York: Seabury Press, 1978).

81. Ved Mehta, *The New Theologian* (New York: Harper & Row, 1965), quote 51.

82. Pauck and Pauck, *Paul Tillich: His Life and Thought*, 275; Mehta, *The New Theologian*, 45.

83. Paul Tillich, "The Ambiguity of Perfection," *Time* (May 17, 1963), 69, cited in Pauck and Pauck, *Paul Tillich: His Life and Thought*, 273–274.

84. John Herman Randall, "The Philosophical Legacy of Paul Tillich," in *The Intellectual Legacy of Paul Tillich*, ed. James R. Lyons (Detroit: Wayne State University Press, 1969), 21–51, Moore quote 23; Mehta, *The New Theologian*, 50.

85. Paul Tillich, *A History of Christian Thought*, ed. Carl E. Braaten (New York: Simon & Schuster, 1968), 411, 412.

86. Ibid., 415, 417.

87. Karl Barth, "Fate and Idea in Theology," (1929), in *The Way of Theology in Karl Barth: Essays and Comments*, ed. H. Martin Rumscheidt, trans. George Hunsinger (Allison Park: Pickwick Publications, 1986), 25–61. This section on "Fate and Idea in Theology," adapts material from Gary Dorrien, *The Barthian Revolt in Modern Theology* (Louisville: Westminster John Knox Press, 2000), 93–95.

88. See Thomas Aquinas, *Summa Theologica*, 5 vols., trans. Fathers of the English Dominican Province (Westminster: Christian Classics, 1981), Pt. 1, Q. 2, Art. 3, 13–14.

89. Barth, "Fate and Idea in Theology," 33; Erich Przywara, "Gott in uns oder Gott über uns? (Immanenz und Transzendenz im heutigen Geistesleben," *Stimmen der Zeit* 105 (1923); Przywara, "Das katholische Kirchenprinzip," *Zwischen den Zeiten* 7 (1929), 277–302; Przywara, "Metaphysik, Religion, Analogie," in *Analogia entis; Schriften* 3 (Einsiedeln: Johannes Verlag, 1962), quote 334.

90. Barth, "Fate and Idea in Theology," 38–40.

91. Ibid., 43.

92. Ibid., 46–47.

93. Ibid., 47–48.

94. Ibid., 51.

95. Karl Barth, *The Holy Spirit and the Christian Life: The Theological Basis of Ethics*, trans. R. Birch Hoyle (Louisville: Westminster John Knox Press, 1993), 5; Erich Przywara, *Religionsphilosophie katholischer Theologie* (Munich: Druck und Verlag von R. Oldenbourg, 1926), 22; see Przywara, "Das katholische Kirchenprinzip," 277–302; B. Gertz, *Glaubenswelt als Analogue; Die theologische Analogie-Lehre Erich Przywaras und ihr Ort in der Auseinandersetzung um die analogie fidei* (Düsseldorf: Patmos-Verlag, 1969, 251–259; Hans Urs von Balthasar, *The Theology of Karl Barth*, trans. John Drury (New York: Holt, Rinehart & Winston, 1971), 249–250, 269–270; Eberhard Jüngel, *God as the Mystery of the World: On the Foundation of the Theology of the Crucified One in the Dispute between Theism and Atheism*, trans Darrell L. Guder (Grand Rapids: Eerdmans, 1983), 282–283; Michael Beintker, *Die Dialektik in der "dialektischen Theologie" Karl Barths* (Munich: Chr. Kaiser Verlag, 1987), 246–251; Bruce McCormack, *Karl Barth's Critically Realistic Dialectical Theology: Its Genesis and Development, 1909–1936* (Oxford: Clarendon Press, 1995), 388–389.

96. See Hans-Georg Gadamer, *Truth and Method*, 2nd edn., trans. Joel Weinsheimer and Donald G. Marshall (1960; New York: Crossroad, 1989); Karl Barth, *Church Dogmatics: The Doctrine of the Word of God*, I: 2, trans. G. T. Thomson and Harold Knight (Edinburgh: T. & T. Clark, 1956), 470–471. This section on Barth adapts material from Gary Dorrien, *The Word as True Myth: Interpreting Modern Theology* (Louisville: Westminster John Knox Press, 1997), 230–231.

97. Karl Barth, *Church Dogmatics: The Doctrine of God*, II: 2, trans. G. W. Bromiley et al. (Edinburgh: T. & T. Clark, 1957), 179–204.

98. See Karl Barth, *The Humanity of God* (Richmond: John Knox Press, 1960).

Index